CW01033147

SIR JOHN BETJEMAN'S GUIDE TO
ENGLISH PARISH CHURCHES

SIR JOHN BETJEMAN'S GUIDE TO

ENGLISH PARISH CHURCHES

Revised and Updated by
NIGEL KERR

with a Foreword by Henry Thorold

HarperCollins*Publishers*

HarperCollins*Publishers*
77–85 Fulham Palace Road,
Hammersmith, London W6 8JB

Published by HarperCollins*Publishers* 1993

1 3 5 7 9 8 6 4 2

First published in Great Britain by
William Collins Sons & Co. Ltd, 1958

A catalogue record for this book is
available from the British Library

ISBN 0 00 217727 7

Set in Linotron Ehrhardt by
Rowland Phototypesetting Ltd
Bury St Edmunds, Suffolk

Printed in Great Britain by
HarperCollinsManufacturing, Glasgow

To the memory of

ST AGNES, KENNINGTON, 1877
CHRIST CHURCH, SALFORD, 1830

*fine churches of unfashionable date
demolished since the war*

Contents

ENGLAND

WALES

List of Illustrations

Foreword

Collins Guide to English Parish Churches, edited by John Betjeman, was first published in 1958; it soon became a classic. Here, thirty-five years later, is the fifth edition, revised by Nigel Kerr.

John Betjeman was always an enthusiast, always a learned amateur, always great fun. On one occasion he and I and Jack Yates (whose name occurs in the original Acknowledgements) were sitting in Jack's beautiful house in Louth. Jack was reading out the descriptions of the parish churches in *Kelly's Directory of Lincolnshire* (1937): 'the parish church of St Mary is an ancient edifice of stone in the Norman style', or 'the parish church of St Guthlac, standing on an eminence, is an edifice of stone in the Early English style,' or 'the parish church of All Saints, built on rising ground, is an edifice of stone in the Decorated style.' 'Come on, dear boy,' said John, 'let's have a change: can't you find an edifice of tin somewhere?' Jack was master of the situation, and turned up Markby; 'Christ Church', he read 'is an edifice of iron in a plain Gothic style.' All collapsed in laughter. Such was the scholarship that went into the book.

'It had long bothered my friend Mr John Piper and me . . .', wrote John Betjeman in *The Purpose of this Book* – the name of John Piper is for ever closely linked with this book. He regarded John Betjeman's Introduction as 'one of his very best pieces of prose'. 'I remember gratefully', he wrote, 'many happy laughs and animated discussions during its making, about churches which were "winners", or "too dim" for inclusion, and whether illustrations were "musts" or "not quites",' and so on.

Nigel Kerr who has revised it is of their company. A man blessed with an acute brain, infectious enthusiasm and learning lightly worn, he was a native of Lincolnshire, and read Archaeology at Cardiff, narrowly missing a first. He worked as an archaeologist all over England, directing the major excavation of the Anglo-Saxon cemetery on Loveden Hill – which is visible from our garden, here at Marston. It was through archaeology that he met his wife Mary, herself an architect; together they wrote several books, of which the most important are *A Guide to Anglo-Saxon Sites* (1982), *A Guide to Norman Sites* (1984), and *A Guide to Mediaeval Sites* (1988). They made their home at a beautiful small, stone manor house at Spanby in Lincolnshire.

Nigel had for many years been aware of a vocation to the priesthood, and in 1988 went to Westcott House, Cambridge; he was ordained deacon in 1990, and priest in 1991 at Peterborough, becoming curate of Oakham in Rutland, within easy reach of Spanby. All the time work went on there on the revision of the *Guide to Parish Churches*, assisted by Mary. We always hoped that the new edition of this, and my own *Collins Guide to the Ruined Abbeys* might be published together – and thanks to Mr Stuart Proffitt of Collins and to Mary and other friends this has proved possible.

Before his lamented death on 30 January 1993 Nigel had asked me to write a paragraph or two on John Betjeman and John Piper – as he had never known them; and Mary has now asked me to add a paragraph or two about Nigel himself. This is indeed a happy obligation. It is remarkable enough that these two books should both be the work of a Lincolnshire author; it is even more remarkable that both should come in origin from the same small village of Marston, for from childhood I knew Nigel's grandfather farmer, church-warden and lay-reader of Marston. So, with a full heart, I can end

In piam memoriam, J. B., J. P., N. K.

HENRY THOROLD
Marston Hall, Grantham
Passion Sunday, 1993

The Purpose of this Book

It had long bothered my friend Mr John Piper and me that there was no selective list of English parish churches, judging the buildings by their atmosphere and aesthetic merit. For instance, when motoring through a district we had not hitherto explored, we would see a church on some nearby hill or in a valley and wonder whether it was worth diverting our journey to go and see it. If it were an old church, would it be ruined inside by Victorian 'restoration'? If it were a 19th- or early 20th-century church, who was the architect? The answers to these questions can be found, by reading between the lines in Kelly's admirable county directories. But these are bulky things to carry about and do not describe churches in large cities. Other answers can be found in Dr Pevsner's Penguin *Buildings of Britain*, but these are not yet complete and one passes, in a motor car or train, quickly from one county to another, nor does one always need quite so much information as he gives for a cursory visit. Of one thing we could be quite certain and that was that the more old-fashioned guide books and works on church architecture would give no more information about the look of a church from the point of view of artists and Anglicans. They are concerned, primarily, with the search for style or with particular details which interested their authors such as brasses, bells or church plate or woodwork. Very learned and painstaking these books are. We both possess hundreds of them. Then there was no work which listed the better of the many hundreds of 19th- and early 20th-century churches. Because we felt the need for such a book, this work was undertaken.

There are over 16,000 parish churches in England and, as editor, I had to decide the limitations of the work. I therefore excluded all cathedrals except a few which, though they might contain a bishop's throne, were originally built as parish churches and had only recently been ennobled, e.g. Derby and Leicester. I also had to exclude the many fascinating college, almshouse and hospital chapels, often unknown and difficult of access. Even so there was probably no one who had visited every parish church in England and could undertake the task—and the task as first envisaged was this:

1. Churches should be listed under counties.
2. Only Church of England parish churches should be included.
3. No church should be included which does not have one or more of these qualifications:
   a. Wholly un-'restored' by the Victorians with box-pews, clear glass and three-decker pulpit, or

    b. so well-restored as to have preserved the atmosphere of the past.

    c. though heavily restored by Victorians, still magnificent as *architecture*, e.g. the parish churches of Louth and Newark.

    d. containing one object which, regardless of date, was aesthetically worth bicycling twelve miles against the wind to see. This, I thought, ought to rule out objects of 'antiquarian interest' like banner-stave lockers and squints.

    e. not built later than 1930 as it is an invidious task to distinguish between the works of living architects often obliged to use cheap mass-produced materials.

We have been unable to deal with essentially specialist subjects such as bells, organs and brasses in a book of so large a scope.

Discussion with friends put me in touch with Mr E. T. Long, F.S.A., who was the one person qualified to produce such lists because he has visited more old churches in the country than most and made notes. Mr Long's lists when compiled, exactly complied with the conditions. But, after much heartburning, I decided that they needed expansion and extension for the following reasons–they were written as I had originally suggested, in the shortest terms just giving approximate dates of styles and, where necessary, the name of the objects to be seen under (d). But I thought the language might be too technical and unexplanatory for those who were uninitiated in the terms of ecclesiology: they left out some 19th-century churches: they were inevitably one man's judgment and consequently had a certain impersonality when applied to the whole of England. But these lists by Mr Long, together with his brief accounts of the architectural characteristics of the churches of each county, were the basis of this book and without them it could never have been written, for they proved a stimulant and source of information to each of the writers in the next stage of the task.

The next stage was to find, in every county of England, an enthusiast for its churches to whom Mr Long's texts could be sent and who, reading them, would make his own additions and expansions. I had decided that each English county was so different and that there were so many aspects of aesthetic judgment, that variety in style and choice was essential; such variety would anyhow never let slip the most splendid churches in each county.

When the authors had been discovered and persuaded to write, and the lists arrived, I found there were still parts of the book missing. First, architecture does not consist of buildings themselves, but also of their setting. Authors were asked to write 'setting' after a church where the site or village was attractive. I found it necessary to supply brief prefaces to each county and large city, describing its characteristics in scenery and building materials and houses. Some of them I wrote myself, others were supplied by contributors. Both owe much to Mr Long's original notes.

Finally, I had to presume that there were some readers who would want to know about the history of the growth of our churches (never better expressed than by Professor K. Hamilton Thompson in his two short monographs on *The Growth of the English Parish Church*, and *The Ground Plan of the English Parish Church*), and so I wrote two preliminary chapters compiled, I fear, in overpopular terms and dangerously resembling the well-known advertisements of Mr Kirkland Bridge, giving the pre- and post-Reformation stories of parish churches in terms of their buildings, fittings and adjuncts and methods of worship.

So here at last is gathered into one volume an aesthetic and atmospheric assessment of English and Manx parish churches. I do not think that any really outstanding church will have escaped the sieve of the contributors, though there must be many borderline cases which might have been included and are not. Obviously counties like Norfolk, Suffolk and Somerset, where old churches are thick on the ground, had to have a larger quota given them than, let us say, Middlesex or Westmorland. The standards contributors set themselves were influenced by the churches in the county as a whole. Tastes change and personal opinions vary and this volume is the expression of many. It is inevitable that it will have more detractors than friends; some will say the 19th century is overstressed. I would remind these last that the majority of our parish churches are 19th century. Others will be disappointed at some favourite church being omitted. I now ask them to send me the information about the church and the reasons why they think it should be included. Still more may find inaccuracies and omissions in the descriptions. To all who would like this book to be as complete and accurate as it can be within the limited prescribed, I appeal for information to me, c/o the publishers, in case there should ever be another edition.

J. B.

INTRODUCTION
by John Betjeman

Part One
THE OLD CHURCHES

To atheists inadequately developed building sites; and often, alas, to Anglicans but visible symbols of disagreement with the incumbent: 'the man there is "too high", "too low", "too lazy", "too interfering" ' – still they stand, the churches of England, their towers grey above billowy globes of elm trees, the red cross of St George flying over their battlements, the Duplex Envelope System employed for collections, schoolmistress at the organ, incumbent in the chancel, scattered worshippers in the nave, Tortoise stove slowly consuming its ration as the familiar 17th-century phrases come echoing down arcades of ancient stone.

Odi et amo. This sums up the general opinion of the Church of England among the few who are not apathetic. One bright autumn morning I visited the church of the little silver limestone town of Somerton in Somerset. Hanging midway from a rich-timbered roof, on chains from which were suspended branched and brassy-gleaming chandeliers, were oval boards painted black. In gold letters on each these words were inscribed:

TO GOD'S
GLORY
&
THE HONOR OF
THE
CHURCH OF
ENGLAND
1782

They served me as an inspiration towards compiling this book.

The Parish Churches of England are even more varied than the landscape. The tall town church, smelling of furniture polish and hot-water pipes, a shadow of the medieval marvel it once was, so assiduously have Victorian and even later restorers renewed everything old; the little weather-beaten hamlet church standing in a farmyard down a narrow lane, bat-droppings over the pews and one service a month; the church of a once prosperous village, a relic of the 15th-century wool trade, whose soaring splendour of stone and glass subsequent generations have had neither the energy nor the money to destroy; the suburban church with Northamptonshire-style steeple rising unexpectedly above slate roofs of London and calling with mid-Victorian bells to the ghosts on the edge of the industrial estate; the High, the Low, the Central churches, the alive and the dead ones, the churches that are easy to pray in and those that are not, the churches whose architecture brings you to your knees, the churches whose decorations affront the sight – all these come within the wide embrace of our Anglican Church, whose arms extend beyond the seas to many fabrics more.

From the first wooden church put up in a forest clearing or stone cell on windy moor to the newest social hall, with sanctuary and altar partitioned off, built on the latest industrial estate, our churches have existed chiefly for the celebration of what some call the Mass, or the Eucharist and others call Holy Communion or the Lord's Supper.

Between the early paganism of Britain and the present paganism there are nearly twenty thousand churches and well over a thousand years of Christianity. More than half the buildings are medieval. Many of those have been so severely restored in the last century that they could almost be called Victorian – new stone, new walls, new roofs, new pews. If there is anything old about them it is what one can discern through the detective work of the visual imagination.

It may be possible to generalize enough about the parish church of ancient origin to give an impression of how it is the history of its district in stone and wood and glass. Such generalization can give only a superficial impression. Churches vary with their building materials and with the religious, social and economic history of their districts.

The Outside of the Church – Gravestones

See on some village mount, in the mind's eye, the parish church of today. It is in the old part of the place. Near the church will be the few old houses of the parish, and almost for certain there will be an inn very near the church. A lych-gate built as a memorial at the beginning of this century indicates the entrance to the churchyard. Away on the outskirts of the town or village, if it is a place of any size, will be the arid new cemetery consecrated in 1910 when there was no more room in the churchyard.

Nearer to the church and almost always on the south side are to be found the older tombs, the examples of fine craftsmanship in local stone of the Queen Anne and Georgian periods. Wool merchants and big farmers, all those not entitled to an armorial monument on the walls inside the church, generally occupy the grandest graves. Their obelisks, urns and table tombs are surrounded with Georgian ironwork. Parish clerks, smaller farmers and tradesmen lie below plainer stones. All their families are recorded in deep-cut lettering. Here is a flourish of 18th-century calligraphy; there is reproduced the typeface of Baskerville. It is extraordinary how long the tradition of fine lettering continued, especially when it is in a stone easily carved or engraved, whether limestone, ironstone or slate. The tradition lasted until the middle of the 19th century in those country places where stone was used as easily as wood. Some old craftsman was carving away while the young go-aheads in the nearest town were busy inserting machine-made letters into white Italian marble.

The elegance of the local stone carver's craft is not to be seen only in the lettering. In the 18th century it was the convention to carve symbols round the top of the headstone and down the sides. The earlier examples are in bold relief, cherubs with plough-boy faces and thick wings, and scythes, hour glasses and skulls and cross-bones diversify their tops. You will find in one or another country churchyard that there has been a local sculptor of unusual vigour and perhaps genius who has even carved a rural scene above some well-graven name. Towards the end of the 18th century the lettering becomes finer and more prominent, the decoration flatter and more conventional, usually in the Adam manner, as though a son had taken on his father's business and depended on architectural pattern-books. But the tops of all headstones varied in shape. At this time too it became the custom in some districts to paint the stones and to add a little gold leaf to the lettering. Paint and stone by now have acquired a varied pattern produced by weather and fungus, so that the stones are probably more beautiful than they were when they were new, splodged as they are with gold and silver and slightly overgrown with moss. On a sharp frosty day when the sun is in the south and throwing up the carving, or in the west and bringing out all the colour of the lichens, a country churchyard may bring back the lost ages of craftsmanship more effectively than the church which stands behind it. Those unknown carvers are the same race as produced the vigorous inn signs which were such a feature of England before the brewers ruined them with artiness and standardization. They belong to the world of wheelwrights and wagon-makers, and they had their local styles. In Kent the chief effect of variety was created by different-sized stones with elaborately-scalloped heads to them, and by shroud-like mummies of stone on top of the grave itself; in the Cotswolds by carving in strong relief; in slate districts by engraved lettering. In counties like Surrey and Sussex, where stone was rare, there were many wooden graveyard monuments, two posts with a board between them running down the length of the grave and painted in the way an old wagon is painted. But most of these wooden monuments have perished or decayed out of recognition.

'At rest', 'Fell asleep', 'Not dead but gone before' and other equally non-committal legends are on the newer tombs. In Georgian days it was the custom either to put only the name or to apply to the schoolmaster or parson for a rhyme. Many a graveyard contains beautiful stanzas which have not found their way to print and are disappearing under wind and weather. Two of these inscriptions have particularly struck my fancy. One is in Bideford

and commemorates a retired sea-captain Henry Clark, 1836. It summarizes
for me a type of friendly and pathetic Englishman to be found hanging about,
particularly at little seaports.

> For twenty years he scarce slept in a bed;
> Linhays and limekilns lull'd his weary head
> Because he would not to the poor house go,
> For his proud spirit would not let him to.
>
> The black bird's whistling notes at break of day
> Used to wake him from his bed of hay.
> Unto the bridge and quay he then repaired
> To see what shipping up the river stirr'd.
>
> Oft in the week he used to view the bay,
> To see what ships were coming in from sea,
> To captains' wives he brought the welcome news,
> And to the relatives of all the crews.
>
> At last poor Harry Clark was taken ill,
> And carried to the work house 'gainst his will:
> And being of this mortal life quite tired,
> He lived about a month and then expired.

The other is on an outside monument on the north wall of the church at
Harefield, near Uxbridge, one of the last three country villages left in
Middlesex. It is to Robert Mossendew, servant of the Ashby family, who
died in 1744. Had he been a gentleman his monument would at this time
have been inside the church. He was a gamekeeper and is carved in relief
with his gun above this inscription.

> In frost and snow, thro' hail and rain
> He scour'd the woods, and trudg'd the plain;
> The steady pointer leads the way,
> Stands at the scent, then springs the prey;
> The timorous birds from stubble rise,
> With pinions stretch'd divide the skies;
> The scatter'd lead pursues the sight
> And death in thunder stops their flight;
> His spaniel, of true English kind,
> With gratitude inflames his mind;
> This servant in an honest way,
> In all his actions copies Tray.

The churchyard indeed often contains cruder but more lively and loving
verses than the polished tributes inscribed in marble tablets within the church

to squires and peers and divines of the county hierarchy. The Dartmoor parish of Buckland Monachorum displays this popular epitaph to a blacksmith which may be found in other parishes:

> My sledge and hammer both declin'd,
> My bellows too have lost their wind.
> My fire's extinct, my forge decay'd,
> And in the dust my vice is laid,
> My coal is spent, my iron's gone,
> My nails are drove, my work is done.

Though such an epitaph can scarcely be called Christian, it is at least not an attempt to cover up in mawkish sentiment or in crematorial good taste the inevitability of death.

The Outside

The church whose southern side we are approaching is probably little like the building which stood there even two centuries before, although it has not been rebuilt. The outside walls were probably plastered, unless the church is in a district where workable stone has long been used and it is faced with cut stone known as ashlar. Churches which are ashlar-faced all over are rare, but many have an ashlar-faced western tower, or aisle to the north-east or south-east, or a porch or transept built of cut stone in the 1th century by a rich family. Some have a guild chapel or private chantry where Mass was said for the souls of deceased members of the guild or family. This is usually ashlar-faced and has a carved parapet as well, and is in marked contrast with the humble masonry of the rest of the church.

Rubble or uneven flints were not considered beautiful to look at until the 19th century. People were ashamed of them and wished to see their churches smooth on the outside and inside walls, and weather-proof. At Barnack and Earl's Barton the Saxons have even gone so far as to imitate in stone the decorative effects of wooden construction. Plaster made of a mixture of hair or straw and sand and lime was from Saxon times applied as a covering to the walls. Only the cut stone round the windows and doors was left, and even this was lime-washed. The plaster was thin and uneven. It was beautifully coloured a pale yellow or pink or white according to the tradition of the district. And if it has now been stripped off the church, it may still be seen on old cottages of the village if any survive. The earlier the walls of a church are, the less likely they are to be ashlar-faced, for there was no widespread use of cut stone in villages until the late 14th century when transport was better, and attention which had formerly been expended on abbeys was paid to building and enlarging parish churches.

And this is the place to say that most of the old parish churches in England are building rather than architecture. They are gradual growths, as their outside walls will shew; in their construction they partake of the character of cottages and barns and the early manor house, and not of the great abbey churches built for monks or secular canons. Their humble builders were inspired to copy what was to be seen in the nearest great church. The styles of Gothic came from these large buildings, but the village execution of them was later and could rarely rise to more than window tracery and roof timbering. Even these effects have a local flavour, they are a village voluntary compared with the music played on a great instrument by the cathedral organist. Of course here and there, when the abbeys declined, a famous mason from an abbey or cathedral might rebuild the church of his native place, and masons were employed in rich wool districts of East Anglia, the Midlands and parts of Yorkshire and Devon to build large churches which really are architecture and the product of a single brain, not the humble expression of a village community's worship. Much has been discovered about the names and work of medieval architects by Mr John Harvey in his book *Gothic England* and in the researches of Messrs. Salzman, and Knoop and Jones.

These outside walls on which the sun shews up the mottled plaster, the sudden warm red of an 18th-century patching of brick, the gentle contrast with the ashlar, the lime-washed tracery of the windows, the heating chimney-stack in local brick climbing up the chancel wall or the stove pipe projecting from a window, these are more often seen today in old watercolours in the local museum, or in some affectionate and ill-executed painting hanging in the vestry shewing the church 'before restoration in 1883'. Most of our old churches have been stripped of their plaster, some in living memory. The rubble has been exposed and then too often been repointed with grey cement, which is unyielding and instead of protecting the old stones causes them to crack and flake in frosty weather, for cement and stone have different rates of expansion. To make matters worse the cement itself has been snail pointed, that is to say pointed in hard, flat lines, so that the church wall looks like a crazy pavement.

Old paintings sometimes shew the external roofs as they used to be. The church roof and chancel are scarcely distinguishable from the cottage roofs. If the original steep pitch survives, it is seen to be covered with the local tiles, stones or thatch of the old houses of the district. 15th-century and Georgian raisings or lowerings of the roof and alterations to a flatter pitch generally meant a re-covering with lead, and the original pitch may be traced on the eastern face of the tower. Victorian restorers much enjoyed raising roofs to what they considered the original pitch, or putting on an altogether new roof in the cathedral manner. The effect of those re-roofings is generally the most obviously new feature on the outside of an old church. Red tiles and patterned slates from Wales or stone tiles which continually come down because they are set at a pitch too steep for their weight, are the usual materials. Instead of being graded in size, large at the eaves and getting smaller as they reach the ridge, the stone tiles are all of the same size so that the roof is not proportioned to the walls. The ridges are usually crowned with ridge tiles of an ornamental pattern which contrast in colour and texture with the rest. The gable ends are adorned with crosses. The drainage system is prominent and there will be pipes running down the wall to a gutter. On the rain-water heads at the top of these pipes there will probably be the date of the restoration. The old way of draining a roof was generally by leaden or wooden spouts rushing out of the fearsome mouths of gargoyles and carrying the water well beyond the walls of the church into the churchyard. If the water did drip on to the walls the plaster served as a protection from damp. Butterfield, a comparatively conservative and severely practical Victorian restorer, in his report on the restoration of Shottesbrooke church (1845) remarks of the flint walls of that elegant building, 'There are no parapets to any part of the Church, and the water has continued to drip from the eaves for five centuries without any injury to the walls.' On the other hand the water has continued to drip from the eaves of Sir Edwin Lutyens' fine church of St Jude-on-the-Hill, Hampstead Garden Suburb, London, and over its Portland stone cornice with considerable injury to the brick walls in less than half a century. The nature of the wall surface, the pointing, and the means devised for draining the water clear from the wall foundation once it has reached the ground, have much to do with keeping out the damp.

Sometimes we may find on the outside walls a variety of scratches, marks and carvings. The only ones of any beauty will probably be the consecration crosses, where the Bishop anointed the walls with oil when the church was newly built. They are high up so that people would not brush them in going past. Similar crosses may be seen on stone altars inside the church. The small crosses which are cut roughly in the jambs of doorways were, according to the late E. A. Greening Lamborn, an angry antiquarian with a good prose style, probably put there not for consecration but 'to scare away evil spirits and prevent them crossing the threshold'. There is a whole literature devoted to masons' marks on the walls of churches, outside and in, and to the 'scratch dials' or 'mass clocks' which look like sundials lacking a gnomon, to be found on the outside south walls of many churches. The masons' marks are triangles, diamonds, bent arrows, circles, squares and other shapes looking rather like boy scout signs, cut into ashlar in some churches, notably the large ones, and surviving where stone has not been re-tooled by the Victorians. Often they may be only scribbles. But they seem to help some antiquaries to give an exact date to buildings or portions of a building. Scratch dials or mass clocks were used generally to show the time when Mass was to be said (usually 9 a.m. in medieval England). Others are primitive clocks. But they, like the parish registers, belong to the non-visual side of church history and it is with the look of a church that this book is primarily concerned.

Finally there are on the outside of churches the gargoyles spouting water off the roof and the carved heads to be found either side of some windows and the figures in niches on tower or porch. Gargoyles can be fearsome, particularly on the north side of the church, and heads and statues, where they have survived Puritan outrage and Victorian zeal, are sometimes extremely beautiful or fantastic.

The church porch flapping with electoral rolls, notices of local acts, missionary appeals and church services (which will occupy us later) gives us a welcome. Though the powers of the parish vestry have been taken over by parish councils and local government, church doors or the porches which shelter them are often plastered with public announcements. Regularly will the village policeman nail to the church door some notice about Foot-and-Mouth Disease when the British Legion Notice Board has been denied him or the Post Office is shut. Most church porches in England are built on the south side, first as a protection for the door from prevailing south-west gales. Then they were used as places for baptism, bargains were made there, oaths sworn, and burial and marriage services conducted. Above some of them, from the 14th century onward, a room was built, usually for keeping parish chests and records. In these places many a village school was started. At first they may have been inhabited by a watchman, who could look down into the church from an internal window. In counties where stone is rare there are often elaborate wooden porches, notably in Sussex, Surrey and Essex.

Professor E. A. Freeman, the great Victorian ecclesiologist, thought little of a man who went up the churchyard path to the main door, which is more or less what we have done, and did not go round the whole building first. But he was an antiquary who took his churches slowly, speculated on them and did detective work about dates of extensions. On a day when the wind is not too cold and the grass not too long and wet, a walk round the outside of the church is always worth while. On the farther side, which is generally the north, there may well be extensions, a family mausoleum for instance, of which there is no sign inside the church beyond a blocked archway. Mr John Piper and I had a peculiar experience through not going round the outside of the derelict church of Wolfhamcote near Daventry in Warwickshire. The lovely building was locked, the windows smashed, and the sun was setting on its lichened stone. There was only one cottage near and we could make no one hear. So we climbed through a window in the south aisle. Bat-droppings were over rotting floors and damp stains on the ochre-plastered walls, and in the fading light we saw that the altar cloth had been raised and revealed a black tunnel with light at the end, a most peculiar thing to see beyond an altar. We approached and saw there were stairs going down under the table leading to a passage in which brass-studded coffins lay on shelves. When we went round the outside of the church we saw that beyond the east end was a Strawberry Hill Gothick extension, the mausoleum of the Tibbits family. Vestries are more usual on the north side of churches than mausolea, and very ugly most of them are, hard little stone sheds leant against the old walls. There will be almost for certain a north door blocked or bricked-up long ago, with the trace of its arch mouldings still there. There may even be a north porch. But unless the village and manor house are to the north of the church this side of the churchyard will be gloomy and its tombs will be, at the earliest, 19th century, except for a very few near the east end. And so round by the sexton's tool-shed and the anthracite dump and the west door of the tower, we return to the south porch.

Notice the stonework round the outside doors. Often it is round-headed and of Norman date, an elaborate affair of several concentric semi-circles of carved stone. It may even be the only Norman work left in the church and may originally have been the chancel arch before the chancel was enlarged and a screen put across its western end. The later medieval rebuilders respected the Norman craftsmanship and often kept a Norman door inside their elaborate porches.

There is often difficulty in opening the door. This gives the less impatient of us a chance of looking at the door itself. Either because the business of transferring the huge church lock was too difficult, or because here was a good piece of wood older than any of the trees in the parish, church doors have survived from the middle ages while the interiors on to which they open have been repaired out of recognition. The wood of the door may be carved or be decorated with old local ironwork. If it is an old door it will invariably open inwards. So first turn the iron handle and push hard. Then if the door seems to be locked, turn the handle the other way and push hard. Then feel on the wall-plate of the porch for the key. Church keys are usually six or eight inches long and easy to find. If there is no sign of the key and all vestry doors are locked, call at a house. If the path leading through the churchyard to a door in the vicarage wall is overgrown and looks unused, you may be sure the vicarage has been sold to wealthy unbelievers and there is no chance of getting the key from there. The houses to choose are those with pots of flowers in the window. Here will be living traditional villagers who even if they are chapel will probably know who it is who keeps the church key. Men are less likely to know than women, since men in villages are more rarely church-goers. Villagers are all out on Saturday afternoons shopping in the local town. Only an idiot and the dog remain behind.

The Porch and Bells

Down one step – for the churchyard will have risen round an old building – and we are in the church itself.

The practised eye can tell at a glance how severe the restoration has been, and often indeed who has done the damage. For instance almost every other church in Cornwall, beside many farther east, was restored by Mr J. P. St Aubyn late in the last century, and he has left his mark at the church porch in the form of a scraper of his own design, as practical and unattractive as his work. We must remember, however much we deplore it, that the most cumbersome bit of panelling bought from a Birmingham firm without regard for the old church into which it is to go, the sentimental picture for the Art Shop, the banner with the dislocated saint, the Benares ware altar vases, the brass commemorative tablet, the greenish stained-glass window with its sentimental Good Shepherd – often have been saved up for by some devout and penurious communicant. It must be admitted that spirituality and aesthetics rarely go together. 'Carnal delight even in the holiest things,' says Father R. M. Benson, founder of the Cowley Father '(habits of thought and philosophy, acquisition of knowledge, schemes of philanthropy, aesthetic propriety, influence in society) hinders the development of the Christ-life by strengthening the natural will.' So when one is inclined to lament lack of taste and seemingly wilful destruction of beauty in a church, it is wise to remember that the incumbent, even if he be that rarity a man of aesthetic appreciation, is probably not to blame for modern blemishes to the fabric. He is primarily a missioner and he cannot offend his parishioners on so unspiritual a matter. The reader who casts his mind back to his early worship as a child will remember that a hymn board, or a brass cross or a garish window were, from his customary gazing on them Sunday after Sunday, part of his religious life. If as an older and more informed person his taste and knowledge tell him these things are cheap and hideous, he will still regret their passing with a part of him which is neither his intellect nor his learning. How much more will an uninformed villager, whose feeling always runs higher where the church is concerned than a townsman's, cling to these objects he has known as a boy, however cheap they are. When the vicar or rector felt himself entitled to be a dictator, he could with more impunity and less offence than now, 'restore' the old church out of recognition. He could hack down the box-pews, re-erect a screen across the chancel, put the choir into surplices and move it from the west gallery to the chancel, and substitute a pipe organ for the old instruments. Even in those days many a disgruntled villager left the church to try his voice in chapel or to play his instrument in the old village band. It is a tribute to the hold of our church that congregations continued to use their churches after restorations in Victorian times. Perhaps the reason for the continued hold is that the more ritualistic performance of the Church Services made church more interesting. There is no doubt that Evangelicals were worried at the success of Tractarian methods. But picture your own childhood's church whitewashed on the advice of the Diocesan Advisory Committee, your pew gone and a row of chairs in its place, the altar different, and the chancel cleared of choir-stalls and the choir non-existent as a consequence. Were it not your childhood's church, you would consider this an improvement. One part of you may consider it an improvement despite associations, but not the other. Conservatism is innate in ecclesiastical arrangement. It is what saves for us the history of the village or town in wood and glass and metal and stone.

Let us enter the church by the tower door and climb to the ringing chamber where the ropes hang through holes in the roof. Nowhere outside England except for a very few towers in the rest of the British Isles, America and the Dominions, are bells rung so well. The carillons of the Netherlands and of Bourneville and Atkinson's scent shop in London are not bell ringing as understood in England. Carillon ringing is done either by means of a cylinder worked on the barrel-organ and musical box principle, or by keyed notes played by a musician. Carillon bells are sounded by pulling the clapper to the rim of the bell. This is called chiming, and it is not ringing.

Bell ringing in England is known among ringers as 'the exercise', rather as the rearing and training of pigeons is known among the pigeon fraternity as 'the fancy'. It is a class-less folk art which has survived in the church despite all arguments about doctrine and the diminution of congregations. In many a church when the parson opens with the words 'Dearly beloved brethren, the Scripture moveth us in sundry places . . .' one may hear the tramp of the ringers descending the newel stair into the refreshing silence of the graveyard. Though in some churches they may come in later by the main door and sit in the pew marked 'Ringers Only', in others they will not be seen again, the sweet melancholy notes of 'the exercise' floating out over the Sunday chimney-pots having been their contribution to the glory of God. So full of interest and technicality is the exercise that there is a weekly paper devoted to it called *The Ringing World*.

A belfry where ringers are keen has the used and admired look of a social club. There, above the little bit of looking-glass in which the ringers slick their hair and straighten their ties before stepping down into the outside world, you will find blackboards with gilded lettering proclaiming past peals rung for hours at a stretch. In another place will be the rules of the tower written in a clerkly hand. A charming Georgian ringers' rhyme survives at St Endellion, Cornwall, on a board headed with a picture of ringers in knee-breeches:

We ring the Quick to Church and dead to Grave,
Good is our use, such usage let us have
Who here therefore doth Damn, or Curse or Swear,
Or strike in Quarrel thogh no Blood appear,
Who wears a Hatt or Spurr or turns a Bell
Or by unskilful handling spoils a Peal,
Shall Sixpense pay for every single Crime
'Twill make him careful 'gainst another time.
Let all in Love and Friendship hither come,
Whilst the shrill Treble calls to Thundering Tom,
And since bells are our modest Recreation
Let's Rise and Ring and Fall to Admiration.

Many country towers have six bells. Not all these bells are medieval. Most were cast in the 17th, 18th or 19th centuries when change-ringing was becoming a country exercise. And the older bells will have been re-cast during that time, to bring them into tune with the new ones. They are likely to have been again re-cast in modern times, and the most ancient inscription preserved and welded on to the re-cast bell. Most counties have elaborately produced monographs about their church bells. The older bells have beautiful lettering sometimes, as at Somerby, and South Somercotes in Lincolnshire, where they are inscribed with initial letters decorated with figures so that they look like illuminated initials from old manuscripts interpreted in relief on metal. The English love for Our Lady survived in inscriptions on church bells long after the Reformation, as did the use of Latin. Many 18th- and even early 19th-century bells have Latin inscriptions. A rich collection of varied dates may be seen by struggling about on the wooden cage in which the bells hang among the bat-droppings in the tower.

Many local customs survive in the use of bells. In some places a curfew is rung every evening; in others a bell is rung at five in the morning during Lent. Fanciful legends have grown up about why they are rung, but their origins can generally be traced to the divine offices. The passing bell is rung differently from district to district. Sometimes the years of the deceased are tolled, sometimes the ringing is three strokes in succession followed by a pause. There are instances of the survival of prayers for the departed where the bell is tolled as soon as the news of the death of a parishioner reaches the incumbent.

Who has heard a muffled peal and remained unmoved? Leather bags are tied to one side of the clapper and the bells ring alternately loud and soft, the soft being an echo, as though in the next world, of the music we hear on earth.

I make no apology for writing so much about church bells. They ring through our literature, as they do over our meadows and roofs and few remaining elms. Some may hate them for their melancholy, but they dislike them chiefly, I think, because they are reminders of Eternity. In an age of faith they were messengers of consolation.

The bells are rung down, the ting-tang will ring for five minutes, and now is the time to go into Church.

The Interior Today

As we sit in a back pew of the nave with the rest of the congregation – the front pews are reserved for those who never come to church – most objects which catch the eye are Victorian. What we see of the present age is cheap and sparse. The thick wires clamped on to the old outside wall, which make the church look as though the vicar had put it on the telephone, are an indication without that electric light has lately been introduced. The position of the lights destroys the effect of the old mouldings on arches and columns. It is a light too harsh and bright for an old building, and the few remaining delicate textures on stone and walls are destroyed by the dazzling floodlights fixed in reflectors from the roof, and a couple of spotlights behind the chancel arch which throw their full radiance on the brass altar vases and on the vicar when he marches up to give the blessing. At sermon time, in a winter evensong, the lights are switched off, and the strip reading-lamp on the pulpit throws up the vicar's chin and eyebrows so that he looks like Grock. A further disfigurement introduced by electrical engineers is a collection of meters, pipes and fuses on one of the walls.* If a church must be lit with electricity – which is in any case preferable to gas, which streaks the walls – the advice of Sir Ninian Comper might well be taken. This is to have as many bulbs as possible of as low power as possible, so that they do not dazzle the eye when they hang from the roof and walls. Candles are the perfect lighting for an old church, and oil light is also effective. The mystery of an old church, however small the building, is preserved by irregularly placed clusters of low-powered bulbs which light service books but leave the roof in comparative darkness. The chancel should not be strongly lit, for this makes the church look small, and all too rarely are chancel and altar worthy of a brilliant light. I have hardly ever seen an electrically lit church where this method has been employed, and we may assume that the one in which we are sitting is either floodlit or strung with blinding pendants whose bulbs are covered by 'temporary' shades reminiscent of a Government office.

Other modern adornments are best seen in daylight, and it is in daylight that we will imagine the rest of the church. The 'children's corner' in front of the side altar, with its pale reproductions of water-colours by Margaret W. Tarrant, the powder-blue hangings and unstained oak kneelers, the side altar itself, too small in relation to the aisle window above it, the pale stained-glass figure of St George with plenty of clear glass round it (Diocesan Advisory Committees do not like exclusion of daylight) or the anaemic stained-glass soldier in khaki – these are likely to be the only recent additions to the church, excepting a few mural tablets in oak or Hopton Wood stone, much too small in comparison with the 18th-century ones, dotted about on the walls and giving them the appearance of a stamp album; these, thank goodness, are the only damage our age will have felt empowered to do.

---

* I have even seen electric heaters hung at intervals along the gallery of an 18th-century church and half-way up the columns of a medieval nave.

The Interior in 1860

In those richer days when a British passport was respected throughout the world, when 'carriage folk' existed and there was a smell of straw and stable in town streets and bobbing tenants at lodge gates in the country, when it was unusual to boast of disbelief in God and when 'Chapel' was connected with 'trade' and 'Church' with 'gentry', when there were many people in villages who had never seen a train nor left their parish, when old farm-workers still wore smocks, when town slums were newer and even more horrible, when people had orchids in their conservatories and geraniums and lobelias in the trim beds beside their gravel walks, when stained glass was brownish-green and when things that shone were considered beautiful, whether they were pink granite, brass, pitchpine, mahogany or encaustic tiles, when the rector was second only to the squire, when doctors were 'apothecaries' and lawyers 'attorneys', when Parliament was a club, when shops competed for custom, when the servants went to church in the evening, when there were family prayers and basement kitchens – in those days God seemed to have created the universe and to have sent His Son to redeem the world, and there was a church parade to worship Him on those shining Sunday mornings we read of in Charlotte M. Yonge's novels and feel in Trollope and see in the drawings in *Punch*. Then it was that the money pouring in from our empire was spent in restoring old churches and in building bold and handsome new ones in crowded areas and exclusive suburbs, in seaside towns and dockland settlements. They were built by the rich and given to the poor: 'All Seats in this Church are Free.' Let us now see this church we have been describing as it was in the late 1860s, shining after its restoration.

Changed indeed it is, for even the aisles are crowded and the prevailing colours of clothes are black, dark blue and purple. The gentlemen are in frock coats and lean forward into their top hats for a moment's prayer, while the lesser men are in black broad-cloth and sit with folded arms awaiting the rector. He comes in after his curate and they sit at desks facing each other on either side of the chancel steps. Both wear surplices: the Rector's is long and flowing and he has a black scarf round his shoulders: so has the curate, but his surplice is shorter and he wears a cassock underneath, for, if the truth be told, the curate is 'higher' than the rector and would have no objection to wearing a coloured stole and seeing a couple of candles lit on the altar for Holy Communion. But this would cause grave scandal to the parishioners, who fear idolatry. Those who sit in the pews in the aisles where the seats face inward, never think of turning eastwards for the Creed. 'Hymns Ancient and Modern' has been introduced. The book is ritualistic, but several excellent men have composed and written for it, like Sir Frederick Ouseley and Sir Henry Baker, and Bishops and Deans. The surpliced choir precede the clergy and march out of the new vestry built on the north-east corner of the church. Some of the older men, feeling a little ridiculous in surplices, look wistfully towards the west end where the gallery used to be and where they sang as youths to serpent, fiddle and bass recorder in the old-fashioned choir, before the pipe organ was introduced up there in the chancel. The altar has been raised on a series of steps, the shining new tiles becoming more elaborate and brilliant the nearer they approach the altar. The altar frontal has been embroidered by ladies in the parish, a pattern of lilies on a red background. There is still an alms dish on the altar, and behind it a cross has been set in stone on the east wall. In ten years' time brass vases of flowers, a cross and candlesticks will be on a 'gradine' or shelf above the altar. The east window is new, tracery and all. The glass is green and red, shewing the Ascension – the Crucifixion is a little ritualistic – and has been done by a London firm. And a smart London architect designed all these choir stalls in oak and these pews of pitch-pine in the nave and aisles. At his orders the new chancel roof was constructed, the plaster was taken off the walls of the church, and the stone floors were taken up and transformed into a shining stretch of red and black tiles. He also had that pale pink and yellow glass put in all the unstained windows so that a religious light was cast. The brass gas brackets are by Skidmore of Coventry. Some antiquarian remains are carefully preserved. A Norman capital from the old aisle which was pulled down, a pillar piscina, a half of a cusped arch which might have been – no one knows quite what it might have been, but it is obviously ancient. Unfortunately it was not possible to remove the pagan classical memorials of the last century owing to trouble about faculties and fear of offending the descendants of the families commemorated. The church is as good as new, and all the medieval style of the middle-pointed period – the best period because it is in the middle and not 'crude' like Norman and Early English, or 'debased' like Perpendicular and Tudor. Nearly everyone can see the altar. The Jacobean pulpit has survived, lowered and re-erected on a stone base. Marble pulpits are rather expensive, and Jacobean is not wholly unfashionable so far as woodwork is concerned. The prevailing colours of the church are brown and green, with faint tinges of pink and yellow.

Not everyone approved of these 'alterations' in which the old churches of England were almost entirely rebuilt. I quote from Alfred Rimmer's *Pleasant Spots Around Oxford* (*c.* 1865), on the taking down of the body of Woodstock's classical church.

Well, during the month of July I saw this church at Woodstock, but unhappily, left making sketches of it till a future visit. An ominous begging-box, with a lock, stood out in the street asking for funds for the "restoration". One would have though it almost a burlesque, for it wanted no restoration at all, and would have lasted for ever so many centuries; but the box was put up by those "who said in their hearts, Let us make havoc of it altogether". Within a few weeks of the time this interesting monument was perfect, no one beam

was left; and now, as I write, it is a "heap of stones". Through the
debris I could just distinguish a fine old Norman doorway that had
survived ever so many scenes notable in history, but it was nearly
covered up with ruins; and supposing it does escape the general
melèe, and has the luck to be inserted in a new church, with open
benches and modern adornments, it will have lost every claim to
interest and be scraped down by unloving hands to appear like a
new doorway. Happily, though rather late in the day, an end is
approaching to these vandalisms.

The Church in Georgian Times

See now the outside of our church about eighty years before, in, let us say,
1805, when the two-folio volumes on the county were produced by a learned
antiquarian, with aquatint engravings of the churches, careful copper-plates
of fonts and supposedly Roman pieces of stone, and laborious copyings of
entries in parish rolls. How different from the polished, furbished fane we
have just left is this humble, almost cottage-like place of worship. Oak posts
and rails enclose the churchyard in which a horse, maybe the Reverend Dr
Syntax's mare Grizzel, is grazing. The stones are humble and few, and lean
this way and that on the south side. They are painted black and grey and
the lettering on some is picked out in gold. Two altar tombs, one with a
sculptured urn above it, are enclosed in sturdy iron rails such as one sees
above the basements of Georgian terrace houses. Beyond the church below a
thunderous sky we see the elm and oak landscape of an England comparatively
unenclosed. Thatched cottages and stone-tiled farms are collected round the
church, and beyond them on the boundaries of the parish the land is still
open and park-like, while an unfenced road winds on with its freight of huge
bonnetted wagons. Later in the 19th century this land was parcelled into
distant farms with significant names like 'Egypt', 'California', 'Starveall',
which stud the ordnance maps. Windmills mark the hill-tops and water-mills
the stream. Our church to which this agricultural world would come, save
those who in spite of Test Acts and suspicion of treachery meet in their
Dissenting conventicles, is a patched, uneven-looking place.

Sympathetic descriptive accounts of unrestored churches are rarely found
in late Georgian or early Victorian prose or verse. Most of the writers on
churches are antiquarians who see nothing but ancient stones, or whose zeal
for 'restoration' colours their writing. Thus for instance Mr John Noake
describes White Ladies' Aston in Worcestershire in 1851 (*The Rambler in
Worcestershire*, London, Longman and Co., 1851). 'The church is Norman,
with a wooden broach spire; the windows, with two or three square-headed
exceptions, are Norman, including that at the east end, which is somewhat
rare. The west end is disgraced by the insertion of small square windows

and wooden frames, which, containing a great quantity of broken glass, and a stove-pipe issuing therefrom impart to the sacred building the idea of a low-class lodging house.' And writing at about the same time, though not publishing until 1888, the entertaining *Church-Goer* of Bristol thus describes the Somerset church of Brean: 'On the other side of the way stood the church – little and old, and unpicturesquely freshened up with whitewash and yellow ochre; the former on the walls and the latter on the worn stone mullions of the small Gothic windows. The stunted slate-topped tower was white-limed, too – all but a little slate slab on the western side, which bore the inscription:

JOHN GHENKIN
Churchwarden
1729

Anything owing less to taste and trouble than the little structure you would not imagine. Though rude, however, and old, and kept together as it was by repeated whitewashings, which mercifully filled up flaws and cracks, it was not disproportioned or unmemorable in aspect, and might with a trifling outlay be made to look as though someone cared for it.'

Such a church with tracery ochred on the outside may be seen in the background of Millais' painting *The Blind Girl*. It is, I believe, Winchelsea before restoration. Many writers, beside Rimmer, regret the restoration of old churches by London architects in the last century. The despised Reverend J. L. Petit, writing in 1841 in those two volumes called *Remarks on Church Architecture*, illustrated with curious anastatic sketches, was upbraided by critics for writing too much by aesthetic and not enough by antiquarian standards.

He naturally devoted a whole chapter to regretting restoration. But neither he nor many poets who preceded him bothered to describe the outside appearance of unrestored village churches, and seldom did they relate the buildings to their settings. 'Venerable', 'ivy-mantled', 'picturesque' are considered precise enough words for the old village church of Georgian times, with 'neat', 'elegant' or 'decent' for any recent additions. It is left for the Reverend George Crabbe, that accurate and beautiful observer, to recall the texture of weathered stone in *The Borough*, Letter II (1810):

> But 'ere you enter, yon bold tower survey
> Tall and entire, and venerably grey,
> For time has soften'd what was harsh when new,
> And now the stains are all of sober hue;

and to admonish the painters:

> And would'st thou, artist! with thy tints and brush
> Form shades like these? Pretender, where thy brush?
> In three short hours shall thy presuming hand

Th' effect of three slow centuries command?
Thou may'st thy various greens and greys contrive
They are not lichens nor light aught alive.
But yet proceed and when thy tints are lost,
Fled in the shower, or crumbled in the frost
When all thy work is done away as clean
As if thou never spread'st thy grey and green,
Then may'st thou see how Nature's work is done,
How slowly true she lays her colours on . . .

With the precision of the botanist, Crabbe describes the process of decay
which is part of the beauty of the outside of an unrestored church:

Seeds, to our eye invisible, will find
On the rude rock the bed that fits their kind:
There, in the rugged soil, they safely dwell,
Till showers and snows the subtle atoms swell,
And spread th' enduring foliage; then, we trace
The freckled flower upon the flinty base;
These all increase, till in unnoticed years
The stony tower as grey with age appears;
With coats of vegetation thinly spread,
Coat above coat, the living on the dead:
These then dissolve to dust, and make a way
For bolder foliage, nurs'd by their decay:
The long-enduring ferns in time will all
Die and despose their dust upon the wall
Where the wing'd seed may rest, till many a flower
Show Flora's triumph o'er the falling tower.

Yet the artists whom Crabbe admonishes have left us better records than
there are in literature of our churches before the Victorians restored them.
The engravings of Hogarth, the water-colours and etchings of John Sell
Cotman and of Thomas Rowlandson, the careful and less inspired records
of John Buckler, re-create these places for us. They were drawn with affection
for the building as it was and not 'as it ought to be'; they bring out the beauty
of what Mr Piper has called 'pleasing decay'; they also shew the many
churches which were considered 'neat and elegant'.

It is still possible to find an unrestored church. Almost every county has
one or two.

The Georgian Church Inside

There is a whole amusing literature of satire on church interiors. As early
as 1825, an unknown wit and champion of Gothic published a book of
coloured aquatints with accompanying satirical text to each plate, entitled

Hints to Some Churchwardens. And as we are about to enter the church, let me quote this writer's description of a Georgian pulpit: 'How to substitute a new, grand, and commodious pulpit in place of an ancient, mean, and inconvenient one. Raze the old Pulpit and build one on small wooden Corinthian pillars, with a handsome balustrade or flight of steps like a staircase, supported also by wooden pillars of the Corinthian order; let the dimensions of the Pulpit be at least double that of the old one, and covered with crimson velvet, and a deep gold fringe, with a good-sized cushion, with large gold tassels, gilt branches on each side, over which imposing structure let a large sounding-board be suspended by a sky-blue chain with a gilt rose at the top, and small gilt lamps on the side, with a flame painted, issuing from them, such Pulpits as these must please all parties; and as the energy and eloquence of the preacher must be the chief attraction from the ancient Pulpit, in the modern one, such labour is not required, as a moderate congregation will be satisfied with a few short sentences pronounced on each side of the gilt branches, and sometimes from the front of the cushion, when the sense of vision is so amply cared for in the construction of so splendid and appropriate a place from which to teach the duties of Christianity.'

And certainly the pulpit and the high pews crowd the church. The nave is a forest of woodwork. The pews have doors to them. The panelling inside the pews is lined with baize, blue in one pew, red in another, green in another, and the baize is attached to the wood by brass studs such as one may see on the velvet-covered coffins in family vaults. Some very big pews will have fire-places. When one sits down, only the pulpit is visible from the pew, and the tops of the arches of the nave whose stonework will be washed with ochre, while the walls will be white or pale pink, green or blue. A satire on this sort of seating was published by John Noake in 1851 in his book already quoted:

> O my own darling pue, which might serve for a bed,
> With its cushions so soft and its curtains of red;
> Of my half waking visions that pue is the theme,
> And when sleep seals my eyes, of my pue still I dream.
> Foul fall the despoiler, whose ruthless award
> Has condemned me to squat, like the poor, on a board,
> To be crowded and shov'd, as I sit at my prayers,
> As though my devotions could mingle with theirs.
> I have no vulgar pride, oh dear me, not I,
> But still I must say I could never see why
> We give them room to sit, to stand or to kneel,
> As if they, like ourselves, were expected to feel;
> 'Tis a part, I'm afraid, of a deeply laid plan
> To bring back the abuses of Rome if they can.
> And when SHE is triumphant, you'll bitterly rue
> That you gave up that Protestant bulwark – your pew.

The clear glass windows, of uneven crown glass with bottle-glass here and there in the upper lights, will shew the churchyard yews and elms and the flying clouds outside. Shafts of sunlight will fall on hatchments, those triangular-framed canvases hung on the aisle walls and bearing the arms of noble families of the place. Over the chancel arch hang the Royal Arms, painted by some talented inn-sign artist, with a lively lion and unicorn supporting the shield in which we may see quartered the white horse of Hanover. The roofs of the church will be ceiled within for warmth, and our boxed-in pew will save us from draught. Look behind you; blocking the tower arch you will see a wooden gallery in which the choir is tuning its instruments, fiddle, base viol, serpent. And on your left in the north aisle there is a gallery crowded under the roof. On the tiers of wooden benches here sit the charity children in their blue uniforms, within reach of the parish beadle who, in the corner of the west gallery, can admonish them with his painted stave.

The altar is out of sight. This is because the old screen survives across the chancel arch and its doors are locked. If you can look through its carved woodwork, you will see that the chancel is bare except for the memorial floor slabs and brasses of previous incumbents, and the elaborate marble monument upon the wall, by a noted London sculptor, in memory of some lay-rector of the 18th century. Probably this is the only real 'work of art' judged by European standards in the church. The work of 18th-century sculptors has turned many of our old churches into sculpture galleries of great interest, though too often the Victorians huddled the sculptures away in the tower or blocked them up with organs. No choir stalls are in the chancel, no extra rich flooring. The Lord's Table or altar is against the east wall and enclosed on three sides by finely-turned rails such as one sees as stair balusters in a country house. The Table itself is completely covered with a carpet of plum-covered velvet, embroidered on its western face with IHS in golden rays. Only on those rare occasions, once a quarter and at Easter and Christmas and Whit Sunday when there is to be a Communion service, is the Table decked. Then indeed there will be a fair linen cloth over the velvet, and upon the cloth a chalice, paten and two flagons all of silver, and perhaps two lights in silver candlesticks. On Sacrament Sundays those who are to partake of Communion will leave their box-pews either at the Offertory Sentence (when in modern Holy Communion services the collection is taken), or at the words 'Ye that do truly and earnestly repent you of your sins, and are in love and charity with your neighbours', and they will be admitted through the screen doors to the chancel. They will have been preceded by the incumbent. Thereafter the communicants will remain kneeling until the end of the service, as many as can around the Communion rails, the rest in the western side of the chancel.

The only object which will be familiar from the Victorian church is the

font, still near the entrance to the church and symbolical of the entrance of
the Christian to Christ's army. Beside the font is a large pew whose door
opens facing it. This is the christening pew and here the baby, its parents
and the god-parents wait until after the second lesson, when the incumbent
will come forward to baptize the child in the presence of the congregation.
Some churches had Churching pews where mothers sat.

Our churches were, as Canon Addleshaw and Frederick Etchells have
pointed out in *The Architectural Setting of Anglican Worship*, compartmented
buildings. So they remained from 1559 (Act of Uniformity) until 1841 onwards
when Tractarian ideas about the prominence of the altar, the frequent
celebration of Holy Communion and adequate seating for the poor – for the
population had suddenly increased – caused a vital replanning of churches.
What we see in 1805 is a medieval church adapted to Prayer Book worship.
The object of having the Prayer Book in our own language was not so
doctrinal and Protestant, in the Continental sense, as is often supposed, but
was to ensure audible and intelligible services. The compartments of the
building were roughly three. There is the font and christening pew which
form a Baptistry. There is the nave of the church with the pews facing the
pulpit which is generally half-way down the church against one of the pillars,
and the nave is used for Matins, Litany and Ante-Communion. Some of the
larger churches have one end of an aisle or a transept divided off with the
old screens which used to surround a Chantry chapel in this part. This the
parson might use for weekday offices of Matins and Evensong when
the congregation was small and there was no sermon.

The lime-washed walls form a happy contrast with the coloured baize
inside the box-pews, the brown well-turned Stuart and Georgian wood-work
and the old screens, the hatchments which hang lozenge-shaped on the wall
above family pews, and the great Royal Arms in the filled-in tympanum of
the chancel arch. Behind the Royal Arms we may see faintly the remains of
a medieval painting of the Doom, the Archangel Michael holding the balance,
and some souls going to Heaven on one side of him, others to Hell on the
other side. In other parts of the church, too, the pale brick-red lines of the
painting which once covered the church may be faintly discernible in sunlight.
Mostly the walls will be whitewashed, and in bold black and red, with cherubs
as decorative devices, will be painted admonitory texts against idolatry. The
Elizabethan texts will be in black letters; the later and less admonitory
Georgian ones will be in the spacious Roman style which we see on the
gravestones in the churchyard. In the Sanctuary on either side of the altar
are the Lord's Prayer and the Commandments painted in gold letters on
black boards, and perhaps Moses and Aaron flank these, also painted
on boards by a local inn-sign painter. An oil painting of the *Crucifixion* or
The Deposition of our Lord or some other scriptural subject may adorn the
space above the altar table. Far more people could read than is generally
supposed; literacy was nearly as rife as it is today. There was not the need

to teach by pictures in the parish church that there had been in the middle ages.

The lighting of the church is wholly by candles. In the centre of the nave a branched brass candelabrum is suspended by two interlocking rods painted blue, the two serpent heads which curl round and interlock them being gilded. In other parts of the church, in distant box-pews or up the choir gallery, light is from single candles in brass sconces fixed to the woodwork. If the chancel is dark, there may be two fine silver candlesticks on the altar for the purpose of illumination. But candles are not often needed, for services are generally in the hours of daylight, and the usual time for a country evensong is three o'clock in the afternoon, not six or half-past six as is now the custom.

Outside the church on a sunny Sunday morning the congregation gathers. The poorer sort are lolling against the tombstones, while the richer families, also in their best clothes, move towards the porch where the churchwardens stand with staves ready to conduct them to their private pews. The farm-workers do not wear smocks for church, but knee breeches and a long coat and shoes. Women wear wooden shoes, called pattens, when it is wet, and take them off in the porch. All the men wear hats, and they hang them on pegs on the walls when they enter the church.

> How still the morning of the hallowed day!
> Mute is the voice of rural labour, hushed
> The ploughboy's whistle, and the milkmaid's song.
> The scythe lies glittering in the dewy wreath
> Of tedded grass, mingled with fading flowers,
> That yester morn bloomed waving in the breeze.
> Sounds the most faint attract the ear, – the hum
> Of early bee, the trickling of the dew,
> The distant bleating, midway up the hill.
>
> With dove-like wings, Peace o'er yon village broods:
> The dizzying mill-wheel rests; the anvil's din
> Hath ceased; all, all around is quietness.
> Less fearful on this day, the limping hare
> Stops, and looks back, and stops, and looks on man
> Her deadliest foe. The toilworn horse, set free,
> Unheedful of the pasture, roams at large;
> And as his stiff unwieldly bulk rolls on,
> His iron-armed hoofs gleam in the morning ray.

So the Scottish poet James Graham begins his poem *The Sabbath* (1804). All this island over, there was a hush of feudal quiet in the country on a Sunday. We must sink into this quiet to understand and tolerate, with our democratic minds, the graded village hierarchy, graded by birth and occupation, by clothes and by seating in the church. It is an agricultural world as yet little touched by the machines which were starting in the mills of the midlands and the north. The Sabbath as a day of rest and worship touched all classes. Our feeblest poets rose from bathos to sing its praises. I doubt if Felicia Hemens ever wrote better than this, in her last poem (1835), composed less than a week before she died.

> How many blessed groups this hour are bending,
> Through England's primrose meadow paths, their way
> Towards spire and tower, midst shadowy elms ascending,
> Whence the sweet chimes proclaim the hallowed day:
> The halls from old heroic ages grey
> Pour their fair children forth; and hamlets low,
> With whose thick orchard blooms the soft winds play,
> Send out their inmates in a happy flow,
> Like a freed rural stream.
>   I may not tread
> With them those pathways, – to the feverish bed
> Of sickness bound, – yet, O my God, I bless
> Thy mercy, that with Sabbath peace hath filled
> My chastened heart, and all its throbbings stilled
> To one deep calm of lowliest thankfulness.

One is inclined, seeing the pale whites and ochres and greys, relieved here and there with the warm brown red of local bricks, which we associate today with Georgian England, to forget how highly coloured were the clothes of the people. Thomas Hood's early poem *The Two Peacocks at Bedfont* (1827) describes with the colours of an aquatint the worshippers entering that then countrified Middlesex church:

> So speaking, they pursue the pebbly walk
> That leads to the white porch the Sunday throng,
> Hand-coupled urchins in restrained talk,
> And anxious pedagogue that chasten wrong,
> And posied churchwarden with solemn stalk,
> And gold-bedizened beadle flames along,
> And gentle peasant clad in buff and green,
> Like a meek cowslip in the spring serene;
>
> And blushing maiden – modestly array'd
> In spotless white – still conscious of the glass;
> And she, the lonely widow that hath made
> A sable covenant with grief, – alas!
> She veils her tears under the deep, deep shade,
> While the poor kindly-hearted, as they pass,

Bend to unclouded childhood, and caress
Her boy, – so rosy! – and so fatherless!

Thus as good Christians ought, they all draw near
    The fair white temple, to the timely call
Of pleasant bells that tremble in the ear, –
    Now the last frock, and scarlet hood and shawl
Fade into dusk, in the dim atmosphere
    Of the low porch, and heav'n has won them all . . .

The Lord of the manor and his family have entered their private pew, hidden
in a transept and with a separate entrance. Their liveried servants sit on a
bench behind them. All round the church is an array of hats hanging on
pegs on the walls above the pews. The parson, who has entered the church
in his long white surplice and red silk hood of an Oxford Master of Arts,
takes his place in the second desk of the three-decker. The parish clerk is
below him to say 'Amen'. He begins Morning Prayer, facing the congregation.
He then mounts to the pulpit and preaches a sermon, which is usually read.
Extempore preaching was a sign of 'enthusiasm'. The Devon poet N. T.
Carrington well describes a morning service in *My Native Village* (1830):

Ah, let me enter, once again, the pew
Where the child nodded as the sermon grew;
Scene of soft slumbers! I remember now
The chiding finger, and the frowning brow
Of stern reprovers, when the ardent June
Flung through the glowing aisles the drowsy noon;
Ah admonitions vain! a power was there
Which conquer'd e'en the sage, the brave, the fair, –
A sweet oppressive power – a languor deep,
Resistless shedding round delicious sleep!
Till closed the learned harangue, with solemn look
Arose the chaunter of the sacred book, –
The parish clerk (death-silenced) far-famed then
And justly, for his long and loud – Amen!
Rich was his tone, and his exulting eye
Glanced to the reedy choir, enthroned on high,
Nor glanced in vain; the simple-hearted throng
Lifted their voices, and dissolved in song;
Till in one tide, deep welling, full and free
Rung through the echoing pile, old England's psalmody.

The singing is from metrical psalms which are bound with every prayer book.
The versions used were generally those awkward quatrains by Tate and
Brady. They are easily committed to memory. The minister or clerk reads

out the stanzas and then the congregation sings, stanza by stanza, those few who cannot read committing the lines to memory. The custom, still prevailing in some Evangelical churches and many chapels, of the minister's proclaiming the first verse of the hymn, is doubtless a survival of these days. Two of Tate and Brady's metrical psalms, 'Thro' all the changing scenes of life' and 'As pants the hart for cooling streams', survive, cut down, in modern hymn books. An appendix to the Psalms was also printed, consisting of rhyming doxologies and a few hymns for special occasions such as 'While Shepherds watched'. From this appendix grew the separate hymn book, of which the most famous and successful was *Hymns Ancient and Modern* (1861), which consisted first of 273 hymns.

The parson's sermon is the end of the service unless it is 'Sacrament Sunday'. For the sermon has come after the Nicene Creed and not at the end of the office of Morning Prayer. It was the custom to have Morning Prayer, Litany and Ante-Communion. The whole service lasted about two hours. As the time of eating was at three o'clock, this was no great inconvenience. But one can understand where the deep-rooted English idea that church worship is boring had its origin. The layman was asked to take part in the monkish offices of Morning and Evening Prayer (an anglicized and potted version of the daily offices of monks and nuns) as well as in the celebration of Communion, always the central act of worship of the Church. The English habit of attending but not receiving Communion was the origin of the Ante-Communion service alone being read, and 'Sacrament Sundays' being special and rare occasions; for it was ordered in the Prayer Book that two or three people must be willing to partake of the Sacrament before it could be celebrated. This order was made with the intention of encouraging people to communicate. But the habit of abstaining was too strong, hence the diminution of the service to Ante-Communion.

The Church in the Fifteenth Century

There will be no end to books on the Reformation. It is not my intention to add to them. Rather I would go back to the middle of the 15th century, when the church we have been describing was bright with its new additions of tower, porch, aisles and clerestory windows, and to a medieval England not quite so roseate as that of Cardinal Gasquet, nor yet so crime-ridden as that of Dr Coulton.

The village looks different. The church is by far the most prominent building unless there is a manor-house, and even this is probably a smaller building than the church and more like what we now think of as an old farm. The church is so prominent because the equivalents of cottages in the village are at the grandest 'cruck houses' (that is to say tent-like buildings with roofs coming down to the ground), and most are mere hovels. They are grouped round the church and manor-house and look rather like a camp. There is far more forest everywhere, and in all but the Celtic fringes of the island agriculture is strip cultivation, that is to say the tilled land is laid out in long strips with no hedges between and is common to the whole community, as are the grazing rights in various hedged and well-watered fields. There are more sheep than any other animals in these enclosures. The approaches to the village are grassy tracks very muddy in winter. Each village is almost a country to itself. Near the entrance to the churchyard is the church house where the churchwardens store beer or 'church ales' for feasts. This is the origin of so many old inns being beside the churchyard in England. The graveyard has no tombstones in it. The dead are buried there but they are remembered not in stone but in the prayers of the priest at the altar at mass. Everyone goes to mass, people from outlying farms stabling their horses outside the churchyard. The church itself looks much the same. The stone tower gleams with new cut ashlar; the walls of the church when they are not ashlar are plastered.

Not only does everyone go to church on Sunday and in his best clothes; the church is used on weekdays too, for it is impossible to say daily prayers in the little hovels in which most of the villagers live. School is taught in the porch, business is carried out by the cross in the market where the booths are (for there are no shops in the village, only open stalls as in market squares today). In the nave of the church on a weekday there are probably people gossiping in some places, while in others there are people praying. There was no privacy in the middle ages, when even princes dined in public and their subjects watched them eat. The nave of the church belonged to the people, and they used it as today we use a village hall or social club. Our new suburban churches which are used as dance halls during the week with sanctuary partitioned off until Sunday, have something in common with the medieval church. But there is this difference: in the middle ages all sport and pleasure, all plays and dancing were 'under God'. God was near, hanging on his Cross above the chancel arch, and mystically present in the sacrament in the pyx hanging over the altar beyond. His crucifixion was carved on the preaching cross in the churchyard. People were aware of God. They were not priest-ridden in the sense that they bowed meekly to whatever the priest said. They had decided opinions and argued about religion and the clergy, and no doubt some went to church reluctantly. But no one thought of not going to church. They believed men had souls and that their souls must be exercised in worship and customed by sacraments.

Let us go in by its new south porch to our parish church of five-hundred years ago. Many of the features which were there when we last saw it are still present, the screen and the font for instance, but the walls are now painted all over. Medieval builders were not concerned with 'taste'. But they were moved by fashion. If the next village had a new tower, they must have one like it. If the latest style at the nearest big abbey or bishop's seat made their own building seem out of date, then it must be rebuilt. At the time of which we are writing, the style would be Perpendicular. Only the most shewy features of earlier building – a Norman chancel arch removed in a few instances to the south door, a 'decorated' window with rich tracery, and perhaps a column with sculptured foliage capital of Early English times – might be spared if they could be made to look well. The builders were chiefly concerned with making the interior of the church as rich and splendid as possible, something to bring you to your knees. Most parish churches, even the smallest, had three altars, one in the chancel and one on either side of the chancel arch.

Where we go in, there is a stoup made of stone or metal, containing Holy Water. And somewhere near, very prominent, is the font. Over it is a painted wooden cover, rising like a church steeple and securely clasped down to the basin of the font and locked. This is because the font contains Baptismal Water, which is changed only twice a year at Easter and Whitsun when it is solemnly blessed. The cover is raised by means of a weight and pulley. The plaster walls are covered with paintings, mostly of a dull brick-red with occasional blues and greens and blacks. The older painting round any surviving Norman windows is picked out in squares to resemble masonry. Chiefly the paintings are pictures. There will be scenes in the life of Our Lady on the north wall, and opposite us probably a huge painting of St Christopher carrying Our Lord as a child on his shoulders and walking through a stream in which fishes are swimming about and fishermen hooking a few out around St Christopher's feet. It was a pious belief that whoever looked at St Christopher would be safe that day from sudden death. The belief is kept alive today on the dashboards of motor-cars. All the windows will be filled with stained glass, depicting local saints and their legends. Our Lord as a baby and receiving homage as the Saviour will be painted somewhere on the walls. But chiefly there will be pictures and images of Our Lady, who will probably be portrayed more often in the church than her Son. Our Lady was the favourite saint of England, and more old churches are dedicated to her than to anyone else. The Christianity of late medieval England was much concerned with Our Lord as Saviour and Man, and with Our Lady as His mother.

The wooden chancel roofs will all have painted beams, red, green, white and gold and blue. The nave rood may not be painted but over the rood-beam just above the chancel arch it will be more richly carved and painted than elsewhere. The stone floor of the church is often covered with yew boughs or sweet-smelling herbs whose aroma is stronger when crushed underfoot. Strong smells were a feature of medieval life. People did not wash much or change their clothes often, and the stink of middens must have made villages unpleasant places in hot weather. Crushed yew and rosemary must have been a welcome contrast in the cool brightness of the church. Five-hundred years ago, most churches had a few wooden benches in the nave. In some districts,

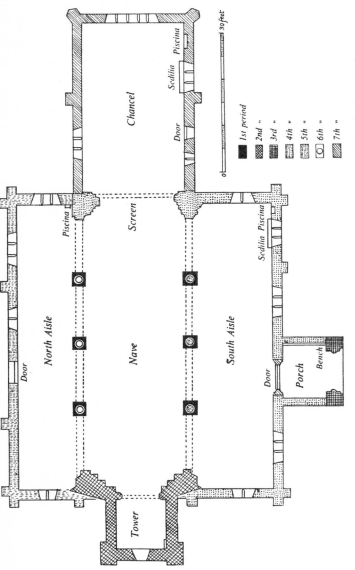

The growth of a medieval church: At Harringworth in Northamptonshire there had been an aisleless church, to which a tower had been added at the end of the 12th century. In about 1300 a new north aisle had been built, with a new altar at the east end. Soon after the whole of the south aisle and arcade were built. The work was done in a very conservative spirit. During the next few years, the north arcade was entirely rebuilt so as nearly to match that on the south. Thus the work, beginning with the north aisle, and extending over some 30 or 40 years, finished on the side on which it began.'

(From 'The Ground Plan of the English Parish Church')

notably Devon, Cornwall and parts of East Anglia, these were elaborately carved. In most places they were plain seats of thick pieces of oak. People often sat along the stone ledges on the wall or on the bases of the pillars. And the pillars of the nave had stone or wooden brackets with statues of saints standing on them. Everywhere in the church there would be images of saints. Though some worshipped these and thought of them as miraculous, such was not the teaching of educated priests of the Church. John Mirk, prior of Lilleshall, who flourished c .1403, wrote thus:

> Men should learn by images whom they should worship and follow. To do God's worship to images is forbidden. Therefore, when thou comest to church, first, behold God's Body under the form of bread upon the altar; and thank Him that He vouchsafe every day to come from the holy heaven above for the health of thy soul. Look upon the Cross, and thereby have mind of the passion he suffered for thee. Then on the images of the holy saints; not believing on them, but that by the sight of them thou mayest have mind on them that be in heaven: and so to follow their life as much as thou mayest.

And here in the nave, the people's part of the church, we have not yet looked eastward to Our Lord upon the Cross. His figure hanging on a wooden cross over the chancel arch, with St Mary and St John weeping on either side of Him at the foot of the cross, looks down from above the screen. This dominates the nave, and behind it or above it, painted on the east wall, is the depiction of the Doom. There, above His Body on the Rood, is a painting of the Resurrected Christ, the severe judge. His wounds are shewn, His hands are raised with the nail prints in them, and His eyes fix you as you stare up. Angels blow trumpets around Him, and there rising from their graves are naked souls, painted as naked bodies but wearing head-dresses, tiaras, crowns and mitres to shew their rank in life. On one side they enter rather joylessly the gates of heaven. On the other, with terrible imagery, are shewn devils with sharks' teeth and rolling eyes, hauling off the helpless souls to the gaping mouth of hell, a yawning cauldron in the bottom corner of the picture. The artists had a far more enjoyable time drawing devils and hell than angels and heaven. For one sweet-faced saint or tender portrait of Our Lady surviving in the wall-painting in our islands, there must be two or three alarming devils.

It is appropriate that here in the nave, with Our Lord looking down sadly from the Cross and sternly from His glory, people should be reminded of how to live while on earth if they wish to escape hell. And while we look at the judgement on the wall, let us listen to John Bromyard, a Dominican Friar of c. 1390, preaching against the rich:

> Their souls shall have, instead of palace and hall and chamber, the deep lake of hell, with those that go down into the depth thereof.

In the place of scented baths, their body shall have a narrow pit of earth; and there they shall have bath more black and foul than any bath of pitch and sulphur. In place of a soft couch, they shall have a bed more grievous and hard than all the nails and spikes in the world; in place of inordinate embraces, they will be able to have there the embraces of the fiery brands of hell . . . Instead of wives, they shall have toads; instead of a great retinue and throng of followers, their body shall have a throng of worms and their soul a throng of demons. Instead of large domain, it shall be an eternal prison house cramped for both.

Heaven is represented in the chancel beyond the richly-painted screen, where the priest murmurs scarcely audible Latin and where the Body of Our Lord under the form of bread, hangs above the altar in a shrouded pyx. Much chatting goes on in the church during sermon and Mass, and we may now approach the screen to examine it and the jewel-like blazing richness beyond, in the holiest part of the church.

Through the screen which runs across the whole width of the church, you may glimpse the richest part of all this teaching imagery. The altars at the end of the aisles are either guild chapels, or family chapels, each with their paid priests. The Shoemakers may have an altar dedicated to Crispin, and will subscribe for its upkeep and to keep its lights burning. Another chapel may be kept up by a guild which pays a priest to say Mass for the Souls of its departed members. The secular descendants of these guilds are the trade unions and burial societies of today. The big town churches such as those at Coventry, Stamford and Bristol had many guild chapels with priests maintained to serve them. And many altars contained a relic of a saint. The walls round the altars were painted, the roofs above them were richer and more elaborately painted than those in the people's part of the church, the altar hangings were of the richest silks and threaded with jewels, the fair linen-cloth laid upon the altar itself a white, plain contrast with the elaborate hangings. The floors of the chancel are of marble or tiles. Brasses of dead priests shone bright among them. You may see what they looked like in illuminated missals. The ornaments on the altar were few, candles perhaps, and if a cross, then a small one to help the priest in his devotions – for here in the chancel we meet the risen Lord. Only in the nave is He dead on the cross, as large as life.

Few people will make their communion at Mass. Indeed it is rare for anyone to make his communion except at Easter. People think of the Mass as something offered for them rather than something of which they partake the sacred elements.

On a hot summer Sunday morning in the country, when I have been reading Chaucer to the sound of bells pouring through the trees, I have been able dimly to imagine this late medieval religion. Life is short for everybody.

It is matter of fact. The pictures on the church walls are not thought of as 'art', but are there to tell a story. Small parish churches were not consciously made beautiful. They were built and decorated for effect, to be better than the church in the next village, to be the best building in the village itself, for it is the House of God, and God become Man – that was the great discovery – offered here upon the altar. All sorts of miraculous stories were invented about Him, and even more about His mother. Because He was Man born of woman, he becomes within the grasp of everyone. Few of the extravagances of German and Spanish late medieval art are found in English representations of the scourging, the crucifixion and the deposition. Jesus is thought of as the baby of poor people who received the tributes of a king. His mother is the most beautiful woman in the world – and how many lovely, loving faces of Our Lady we may see in the old glass, wall-paintings and statues which survive in England. And she bore a Spotless Son who was God and Judge of all. No wonder she was loved by the pious English.

The miracles of Our Lord were not so interesting to these people as the miracles they ascribed to His saints. Here extravagancy knew no bounds. St Petroc sailed in a silver bowl from Cornwall to an isle in the Indian Ocean. St Winifred was beheaded by an angry lover, but her head was reunited to her body and she became an abbess. There were saints like St Quintin who cured dropsy, saints for toothache, and for colds and fever, and for finding things. There were patron saints for every craft and trade. There were miraculous images which winked, or flew to bedsides; there were statues of saints that had never been, like the Maid Uncumber in old St Paul's Cathedral.

Though for the everyday things of life there were friendly saints who helped, life itself must have been terrifying, a continual rush to escape hell. Our Lord and His Mother were the loving and human part of it; hell was the terrifying part. The Devil was seen. His fellow devils yawned as gargoyles with bats' wings on the north walls of the church, black against the evening sky. The white teeth of devils and their red eyes gleamed out of the darkness. Evil spirits lurked behind stones on lonely moors and ranged the deep woods. Good and evil fought together in the roar of the storm. All thought, all sight, every breath of the body, was under God. The leaping sciapod, the man-eating mantichora, the unicorn, might easily be met in the forest by men with imaginations, which as easily would expect to see Our Lady flying through the air, or the local saint, for centuries enshrined in his altar, walking down the street. The witch cast her evil spells, blood and death lay around everywhere, the entrails of a man hung, drawn and quartered, shone black with flies in the sun, silvery lepers tinkled their bells, creating loneliness around them. The fear that men felt is expressed in the grotesque carvings over the north walls of churches, and in the corbels and bosses of roofs, and in bench-ends, screens and miserere stalls. Their humour is shewn there too. Chiefly in the figure of Our Lady do we see the tenderness and sweetness of this late religion.

So when we walk down a green lane like an ancient cart track towards the ringing church-bells, we can see the power of God in the blossom and trees, remember legends of the saints about birds and stones, and recall miracles that happened in the parish at this or that spot. And on a feast day we can see the churchyard set out with tables for the church ale when Mass is over, and as we enter the nave we can see it thronged below the painted roof and walls with people in the village, young and old, and the rest of the parish crowding in with us. Human nature may not have been better. Life was as full, no doubt, of wrong and terror as it is today. How different it was is expressed in the words of Froude:

> For, indeed, a change was coming upon the world, the meaning and direction of which even still is hidden from us, a change from era to era. The paths trodden by the footsteps of ages were broken up; old things were passing away and the faith and the life of ten centuries were dissolving like a dream. Chivalry was dying; the abbey and the castle were soon together to crumble into ruins; and all the forms, desires, beliefs, convictions of the old world were passing away never to return. A new continent had risen up beyond the western sea. The floor of heaven, inlaid with stars, had sunk back into an infinite abyss of immeasurable space; and the firm earth itself, unfixed from its foundations, was seen to be but a small atom in the awful vastness of the universe. In the fabric of habit which they had so laboriously built for themselves, mankind were to remain no longer.
>
> And now it is all gone – like an unsubstantial pageant faded; and between us and the old English there lies a gulf of mystery which the prose of the historian will never adequately bridge. They cannot come to us, and our imagination can but feebly penetrate to them. Only among the sleeping on their tombs, some faint conceptions float before us of what these men were when they were alive; and perhaps in the sound of church bells, that peculiar creation of medieval age, which falls upon the ear like the echo of a vanished world.

The Churches Before The Fifteenth Century

To imagine our church in earliest times of Christian England is, alas, to enter the controversial world of archaeology. There was a Christian Church in the Roman settlement at Silchester, Berkshire, and its remains have been excavated. It had an apse at the west end instead of the east where one would expect it to be, and the altar which is supposed to have been wooden and square, was also in the west. The east end was square. The church is said to be 4th century. Only the foundations remain. The form of worship was probably more like that of the Orthodox church today than the western rite.

But there are enough later pre-Conquest churches remaining to give us an idea of the architecture of those times. They are called Saxon. There are two types. The southern, of which the earliest churches are found in Kent – three in Canterbury, St Mary Lyminge, Reculver, and, most complete, Bradwell, Essex, all of which are 7th century – were the result of the Italian mission of St Augustine, and were reinforced after the coming of St Theodore in 669. In plan and style they resembled certain early Italian churches. The northern group found in Northumberland and Durham are survivals of the Celtic church, and their architecture is said to have come from Gaul, and is more barbaric looking than that of their southern contemporaries. Their three distinctive features were, according to Sir Arthur Clapham, an unusual length of nave, a small chancel, less wide than the nave, and very high side walls. In the northern group, the most complete is Escombe, Durham (7th and early 8th century?), a stern building, nave and chancel only, with squared rubble walls, small windows high up and square or round headed, and a narrow and tall rounded chancel arch. We have a picture of the interiors of these northern churches from near contemporary accounts. The walls and capitals and arch of the sanctuary were adorned 'with designs and images and many sculptured figures in relief on the stone and pictures with a pleasing variety of colours and a wonderful charm'. We learn, too, of purple hangings and gold and silver ornaments with precious stones. Elsewhere in England the most considerable remains of pre-Conquest work are those at Monkwearmouth (Durham), Jarrow (Durham), Brixworth (Northants), Deerhurst (Glos), Bradford-on-Avon (Wilts), the tower of Earls Barton (Northants), Barton-on-Humber (Lincs), Sompting (Sussex), the Crypts at Repton (Derby), Wing (Bucks), and Hexham (Northumberland). From the pre-Conquest sculpture, like the crosses at Bewcastle and Ruthwell, and the carvings at Langford (Oxon), Romsey (Hants), Bexhill (Sussex), St Dunstan's Stepney (London), and the moving relief of the Harrowing of Hell in Bristol Cathedral, and from such enrichment as survives in such objects as St Cuthbert's stole (Durham), the Alfred Jewel in the Ashmolean Museum, Oxford, the beautiful drawing in the Winchester Psalter and Lindisfarne Gospels in the British Museum, we know that these Romanesque masons, sculptors and illuminators were very fine artists, as fine as there have ever been in England.

However, it is safer to try to imagine our parish church as it was in Norman times, as far more of our old churches are known to be Norman in origin than pre-Conquest, even though as in the church of Kilpeck (Herefordshire) the pre-Conquest style of decoration may have continued into Norman times. It is narrow and stone built. Let us suppose it divided into three parts. The small, eastward chancel is either square-ended or apsidal. Then comes the tower supported internally on round arches. The nave, west of the low tower, is longer than the chancel. The windows are small and high up. The church

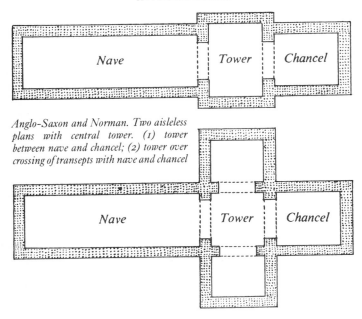

Anglo-Saxon and Norman. Two aisleless plans with central tower. (1) tower between nave and chancel; (2) tower over crossing of transepts with nave and chancel

is almost like a fortress outside. And it is indeed a fortress of Christianity in a community where pagan memories and practices survive, where barons are like warring kings and monasteries are the centres of faith. These small village churches are like mission churches in a jungle clearing.

There are no porches, and we enter the building by any of the three doors to the nave on the north, south or west. Inside, the walls of the nave are painted with red lines to look like blocks of stone. The raftered roof is hidden by a flat wooden ceiling which is painted with lozenges. The floor of the nave is paved with small blocks of stone or with red tiles. There are no pews. We can only see the chancel through a richly moulded round arch, that very arch which is now the South Door of your parish church. Above this chancel arch is a painted Doom, not quite so terrifying as that of the 15th-century church, for all the painting here is in the manner of the mosaics still seen in basilicas of Italy and eastern Europe.

The splays of the windows in the nave have figures of saints painted on them. But it is through the chancel that we see the greatest riches. Stained glass is rare. If there is any it is in the sanctuary and black with much leading and giving the impression of transparent mosaics. The walls are painted everywhere with figures, also recalling mosaic pictures. There are bands of classic style, patterns dividing them. The altar is of stone, small and box-like, recalling the tombs of Christians in the catacombs of Rome in the very earliest

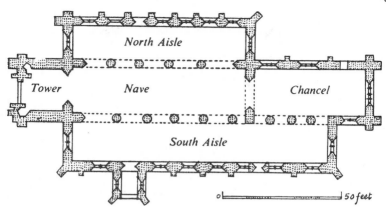

Gothic additions to a Norman plan. Raunds, Northamptonshire. Probably this was a Norman aisleless church consisting of nave and chancel of equal width. A tower and a north aisle to the nave were added in the 13th century. In the 14th century a south aisle was added. The original Norman walls were pierced and turned into arcades.

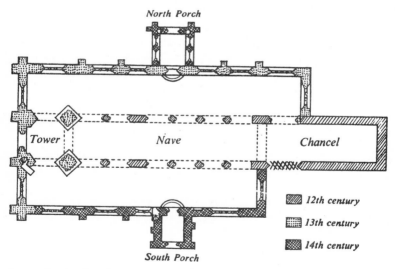

A town church enlarged in the 13th and 14th centuries so as to provide guild chapels. Grantham, Lincolnshire

days of Christianity. The altar stands well away from the eastern, semi-circular end of the apse. It is covered with a cloth hanging over its four sides, decorated with vertical bands.

Our Lord is depicted on the cross as a King and Judge, not as a man in anguish as in later crucifixions. The religion of the time was less concerned with Him and Our Lady as human beings, more concerned with the facts of Judgement, Death and Hell. It was more ascetic and severe.

Part Two

THE NEWER CHURCHES

Of the 16,000 parish churches in England more than half have been built since the 17th century, and the majority of these were erected in the last and present centuries. Guide books, almost wholly antiquarian in outlook, still dismiss even 18th-century churches as 'modern', while Victorian buildings are usually beneath their consideration. Yet some of the noblest churches are post-Reformation, from cathedrals like St Paul's and Truro and Liverpool, to the great town churches designed by such architects as Hawksmoor, Gibbs, Street, Butterfield, Pearson, Brooks, Nicholson and Comper.

The first post-Reformation churches differed little in plan from those of medieval times. Wren in some of his churches for the City of London seems to have tried to build uncompartmented churches, where Baptism, Morning and Evening Prayer and Holy Communion could all be conducted in an undivided space, without the priest and his assistants moving out of sight and earshot.

Usually the plan was the nave with three-decker pulpit dominating for Matins, Litany and Evensong, a screen through which the congregation passed for Communion, and a Bapistry at the west end. The earliest post-Reformation churches usually had west galleries for organ and choir and also side galleries, because by the 17th century the population had begun to increase, especially in the towns where many new churches were built. The churches of the 17th and 18th centuries were mostly built on the English medieval plan. The only noticeable new feature in the more traditional churches was that the chancels were shallower and broader than those surviving from earlier times.

The style of tracery and decoration and wood-carving certainly changed. Windows were square-headed in the 16th century, and thereafter became round-headed. Grapes and cherubs and a cornucopia of fruit cascaded down the sides of altar-pieces, wreathed round the panelling of pulpits, and flattened themselves into patterns on the ceiling. The Renaissance style of Italy became the fashion. But it was an English version. Wren's Portland stone steeples and lead spires, so happily clustering round St Paul's Cathedral, are a recollection of Gothic architecture, though most of them are Renaissance in detail.

The interior of even the most room-like classic church of the 17th and early 18th centuries generally differs from its contemporary Dissenting interior. In the former there is provision for the expounding of the Word, and for the two chief sacraments; in the latter there is provision for the Word, but there is no suggestion of an altar about the table that is set for Communion. There may be some significance in the hour-glasses so often found beside the Anglican pulpits. They were intended as a check on the length of the sermon, and perhaps as a reminder to parson and people that there were other offices of the Church to be performed than preaching. Only for the short period when the Commonwealth ejected ordained priests of the Church, who returned with the Restoration, can these interiors have resembled Dissenting meeting houses.

Some of our finest scuplture is to be found in the monuments erected in all parish churches new or old during the 17th, 18th and early 19th centuries. A whole illustrated literature of this has been developed by the late Mrs Esdaile and Mr Rupert Gunnis. The work of great sculptors ignored or despised by the Victorians, such as Roubiliac, Rysbrack, Stone, Wilton, the Bacons, Hickey and Paty, has received recognition owing to their writings.

From the middle of the 18th century until its end, new churches were Classic, usually in the manner of the Brothers Adam, with chaste decorations in low relief in interior plaster and woodwork, and comparatively plain exteriors. The individuality of architects was beginning to assert itself over traditional plan and local styles. Cross-shaped churches were built with altar at the eastern axis and there were square and octagonal churches as well as proprietary chapels with the pews all arranged for a view of the occupier of the pulpit. These last buildings came as near to a Dissenting chapel as Anglicanism permitted.

Gothic never died. The style was driven by the Renaissance out of churches and houses into barns, farms and cottages. It was revived in a romantic form, suggesting Strawberry Hill (1733), even in the 17th century. And a slender case might be made for its never having died even in ecclesiastical building. There are Stuart churches which are Tudor Gothic, such as Low Ham in Somerset (1624), and Staunton Harald in Leicestershire (1653), which are like late Perpendicular medieval churches, and not a conscious revival but a continuance of the old style. St Martin-in-the-Fields, London, until its rebuilding by Gibbs in 1721, had been continuously rebuilt in the Gothic style since the time of Henry VIII. There are churches like St John's, Leeds (1632), and Compton Wynyates (1663), which are a mixture of Classic and Tudor Gothic. Then there are the first conscious imitations of old forms by architects, such as Sir William Wilson's tower of St Mary's, Warwick (1694), and Wren's tower and steeple to St Dunstan-in-the-East (1698), and his towers of St Mary Aldermary (1711) and St Michael's Cornhill (1721). There is an interesting and well-illustrated chapter on this subject of the earlier revival of Gothic in M. Whiffen's *Stuart and Georgian Churches*. The plan of these buildings was almost always traditional with an emphasized chancel. Now and then a Lutheran element crept in. In the Gothic church of Teigh in Rutland (1783), the small font is fixed by a brass bracket to the Communion rails. But the seats face north and south and the pulpit is at the west end.

In the reign of Queen Anne Parliament passed an act to remedy the insufficiency of accommodation for worship in London and the vicinity. Leading architects of the time like James Gibbs, Archer and Hawksmoor were employed, and several fine churches which challenge those of Wren were the result. Other large towns, for this was a time when the population of the midlands was rapidly expanding, followed London's example.

Throughout the 18th century there was great interest in theology. Anyone looking through the library of a country house can verify this, for he will find rows of superbly bound volumes of sermons and controversial pamphlets and histories of religion. In the spas and the richer parts of London, private chapels were built for favourite clergy. They are well described by T. Francis Bumpus in *London Churches, Ancient and Modern*:

> Well pewed, well warmed, undedicated, unendowed, unconsecrated, here captivating preachers of the Morphine Velvet, lavender-kid-glove school of theology dispensed the most comfortable doctrines. The pews were filled, and the good promoters were amply repaid by the pious tenantry, but accommodation for the poor was never thought of.

Not all proprietary chapels were like this. Some were undoubtedly missions for teaching the Faith to the rich and indifferent or for bringing the Gospel to the poor. When town parishes grew very large in the 18th century, it was sometimes the custom for a chapel to be rented or built, and, if it did not succeed, to be sold again, or in some instances taken over by dissenters. St Martin-in-the-Fields had two such chapels which have now disappeared, and there were three in the parish of St Margaret Westminster and seven in the parish of St Pancras.

Few of these proprietary chapels survive as such today. Sometimes there is, in a large provincial town, one very Evangelical church, in classic style, whose patronage is in the hands of private trustees. This may well once have been an 18th-century proprietary foundation. In 1746 there were nineteen in London, excluding chapels belonging to Royal and Episcopal Palaces, Almshouses, Prisons, Livery Companies and Inns of Court. Those which have not been pulled down or become Dissenting places of worship, have been consecrated and turned into parish churches. I remember one in Bath called Kensington Chapel, which was Calvinistic yet Anglican, but which is now a furniture store. At another in Homerton, London, known as Ram's Episcopal Chapel, I attended worship, and the clergyman wore a black gown and bands for preaching. This charming 18th-century chapel is now, alas, demolished. At Christ Church, North Brixton, London, is an extremely original and impressive episcopal chapel re-erected in 1904 in the Byzantine style from designs by Professor Beresford Pite. It was built privately and in it the black gown was still used in 1952.

Another reason for the erection of new churches in the 18th century was the inadequacy of medieval buildings. They could sometimes hold galleries erected in the aisles and at the west end, but no more. Old prints shew us town churches which have almost the appearance of an opera house, galleries projecting beyond galleries, with the charity children away up in the top lighted by dormers in the roof, pews all over the aisles and in the chancel, and only here and there a pointed arch or a bit of window tracery to shew that this was once a gothic medieval church. Walls began to bulge, stone decayed, structures were unsound and ill-behaved children could not be seen by the beadle and clerk. The only thing to do was to pull down the building. A surviving interior of this sort is the parish church of Whitby. To go into it is like entering the hold of a ship. There are box-pews shoulder high in all directions, galleries, private pews, and even a pew over the chancel screen. Picturesque and beautiful as it is, with the different colours of baize lining the pews, and the splendid joinery of varying dates, such an uneven effect cannot have pleased the 18th-century man of taste. Therefore when they became overloaded with pews, these old churches were taken down and new ones in Classic or Strawberry Hill Gothick style were erected on the sites.

In the country there can have been little need to rebuild the old church on the grounds of lack of accommodation. Here rebuilding was done at the dictates of taste. A landlord might find the church too near his house, or sited wrongly for a landscape improvement he was contemplating in the park, or he might simply dislike the old church on aesthetic grounds as a higgledy-piggledy, barbarous building. Most counties in England have more than one 18th-century church, now a sad relic in a park devastated by timber merchants, still crowning some rise or looking like a bit of Italy or ancient Greece in the pastoral English landscape.

Eighteenth-century churches are beautiful primarily because of their proportions. But they were not without colour. Painted hatchments adorned the walls, gilded tables of the Commandments were over the altar, with Moses and Aaron on either side, the Royal Arms on painted wood or coloured plaster was above the chancel opening, coloured baize lines in the pews, rich velvets of all colours were hanging from the high pulpit and the desks below it, an embroidered velvet covering decked the altar in wide folds, gilded candles and alms dish stood on the altar. The art of stained glass was not dead in the 18th century as is often supposed. East windows were frequently coloured, with pieces of golden-yellow 16th-century foreign glass brought back from a Grand Tour, and gold, blue and dark green glass, partly pot-metal and partly coloured transparency, such as went on being made in York until late in the century. Another popular kind of window was the coloured transparency – a transparent drawing enamelled on to glass, like the Reynolds' window in New College, Oxford, by such artists as Eginton of Birmingham, Peckitt of York, James Pearson and Jervais.

After 1760 country churches were often rebuilt in the Gothick taste. Pointed windows, pinnacled towers and battlemented walls were considered ecclesiastical and picturesque. They went with sham ruins and amateur antiquarianism, then coming into fashion. The details of these Gothick churches were not correct according to ancient examples. Nor do I think they were intended to be. Their designers strove after a picturesque effect, not antiquarian copying. The interiors were embellished with Chippendale Gothick woodwork and plaster-work. Again nothing was 'correct'. Who had ever heard of a medieval box-pew or an ancient ceiling that was plaster moulded? The Gothick taste was but plaster deep, concerned with a decorative effect and not with structure. The supreme example of this sort of church is Shobdon, Herefordshire (1753).

Amid all this concern with taste, industrialism comes upon us. It was all very well for the squire to fritter away his time with matters of taste in his country park, all very well for Boulton and Watt to try to harness taste to their iron-works at Soho, as Darby before them had tried at Ironbridge; the mills of the midlands and the north were rising. Pale mechanics, slave-driven children and pregnant women were working in the new factories. The more intelligent villagers were leaving for the towns where there was more money to be made. From that time until the present day, the country has been steadily drained of its best people. Living in hovels, working in a rattling twilight of machines, the people multiplied. Ebenezer Elliott the Corn Law Rhymer (1781–1849) was their poet:

> The day was fair, the cannon roar'd,
>   Cold blew the bracing north,
> And Preston's mills, by thousands, pour'd
>   Their little captives forth . . .
>
> But from their lips the rose had fled,
>   Like 'death-in-life' they smiled;
> And still, as each pass'd by, I said,
>   Alas! is that a child? . . .
>
> Thousands and thousands – all so white! –
>   With eyes so glazed and dull!
> O God! it was indeed a sight
>   Too sadly beautiful!

A Christian himself, Ebenezer called out above the roar of the young industrial age:

When wilt thou save the People?
  O God of mercy, when?
The people, Lord, the people,
  Not thrones and crowns, but men!
Flowers of thy heart, O God, are they;
Let them not pass, like weeks, away, –
Their heritage a sunless day.
  God save the people!

The composition of this poem was a little later than the Million Act of 1818, by which Parliament voted one million pounds towards the building of churches in new districts. The sentiments of the promoters of the Bill cannot have been so unlike those of Elliott. Less charitable hearts, no doubt, terrified by the atheism consequent on the French Revolution and apprehensive of losses to landed proprietors, regarded the Million Act as a thank-offering to God for defending them from French free-thinking and continental economics. Others saw in these churches bulwarks against the rising tide of Dissent. Nearly three hundred new churches were built in industrial areas between 1819 and 1830. The Lords Commissioner of the Treasury who administered the fund required them to be built in the most economical mode, 'with a view to accommodating the greatest number of persons at the smallest expense within the compass of an ordinary voice, one half of the number to be free seats for the poor'. A limit of £20,000 was fixed for 2,000 persons. Many of these 'Commissioners' or 'Waterloo' churches, as they are now called, were built for £10,000. The most famous church of this date is St Pancras in London, which cost over £70,000. But the money was found by private subscription and a levy on the rates. For other and cheaper churches in what were then poorer districts the Commissioners contributed towards the cost.

The Commissioners themselves approved all designs. When one reads some of the conditions they laid down, it is surprising to think that almost every famous architect in the country designed churches for them – Soane, Nash, Barry, Smirke, the Inwoods, the Hardwicks, Rickman (a Quaker and the inventor of those useful terms for Gothic architecture, 'Early English', 'Decorated' and 'Perpendicular'), Cockerell & Basevi and Dobson, to name a few. 'The site must be central, dry and sufficiently distant from factories and noisy thoroughfares; a paved area is to be made round the church. If vaulted underneath, the crypt is to be made available for the reception of coals or the parish fire engine. Every care must be taken to render chimneys safe from fire; they might be concealed in pinnacles. The windows ought not to resemble modern sashes; but whether Grecian or Gothic, should be in small panes and not costly. The most favourable position for the minister is near an end wall or in a semicircular recess under a half dome. The pulpit should not intercept a view of the altar, but all seats should be placed so as to face the preacher. We should recommend pillars of cast iron for supporting the gallery of a chapel, but in large churches they might want grandeur. Ornament should be neat and simple, yet variable in character.'

In short, what was wanted was a cheap auditorium, and, whether Grecian or Gothic, the solution seems always to have been the same. The architects provided a large rectangle with an altar at the end in a very shallow chancel, a high pulpit on one side of the altar and a reading desk on the other, galleries round the north, west and south walls, an organ in the west gallery, and lighting from two rows of windows on the north and south walls, the lower row to light the aisles and nave, the upper to light the galleries. The font was usually under the west gallery. The only scope for invention which the architect had was in the design of portico and steeple, tower or spire.

Most large towns have at least one example of Commissioners' Churches, particularly in the north of England, where they were usually Gothic. None to my knowledge except Christ Church, Acton Square, Salford (1831) survived exactly as it was when its architect designed it. This is not because they were badly built. But they were extremely unpopular with the Victorians, who regarded them as cheap and full of shams and unworthy of the new-found dignity of the Anglican liturgy. The usual thing to do was to turn Grecian buildings into 'Byzantine' or 'Lombardic' fanes, by filling the windows with stained glass, piercing the gallery fronts with fretwork, introducing iron screens at the east end, adding a deeper chancel and putting mosaics in it, and of course cutting down the box-pews, thus ruining the planned proportions of the building and the relation of woodwork to columns supporting the galleries. The architect, Sir Arthur Blomfield, was a specialist in spoiling Commissioners' Churches in this way. Gothic or Classic churches were 'corrected'. In later days side chapels were tucked away in aisles originally designed for pews. Organs were invariably moved from the west galleries made for them, and were fitted awkwardly alongside the east end.

One can visualize a Commissioners' Church as it was first built, by piecing together the various undisturbed parts of these churches in different towns. The Gothic was a matter of decoration, except in St Luke's new church, Chelsea, London, and not of construction. A Commissioners' Church will be found in that part of a town where streets have names like Nelson Crescent, Adelaide Place, Regent Square, Brunswick Terrace and Hanover Villas. The streets round it will have the spaciousness of Georgian speculative building, low-terraced houses in brick or stucco with fanlights over the doors, and, until the pernicious campaign against Georgian railings during the Nazi war, there were pleasant cast-iron verandahs on the first floor and simple railings round the planted square. Out of a wide paved space, railed in with Greek or Gothic cast iron according to the style of the building, will rise the Commissioners' Church, a brick structure with Bath stone dressings, two rows of windows and a noble entrance portico at the west end. Such churches are generally locked today, for the neighbourhood has often 'gone down';

the genteel late Georgian families who lived there moved into arboured suburbs at the beginning of this century, and their houses have been sub-let in furnished rooms.

But Commissioners' Churches, which provided worship for nearly five million people, had a dignity and coherence which we can appreciate today now that the merits of Georgian Architecture are recognized. They were the last auditory buildings of the Establishment to be erected for about a century. Through the rest of the 19th century, most new churches might be considered inauditory buildings, places where the ritual of the service could best be appreciated, where sight came first and sound second.

By 1850 began a great period of English church building, which is comparable with the 15th century. Much as we regret the Victorian architect's usual 'restoration' of an old building, when he came to design a new one, he could produce work which was often original and awe-inspiring. To name only a few London churches, All Saints, Margaret Street; St Augustine's, Kilburn; St James the Less, Victoria; St Columba's, Haggerston; Holy Trinity, Sloane Street; Holy Redeemer, Clerkenwell; St Michael's, Camden Town; and St Cyprian's, Clarence Gate, are some large examples of the period which have survived Prussian bombing. To understand the inspiration behind these churches, we must leave architecture for a while and turn to the architects and the men who influenced them; architects such as Pugin, Street, Butterfield, Pearson, Gilbert Scott, Bodley and the Seddings, and priests such as Newman, Keble, Pusey, Neale, Wilberforce, and later Lowder, Mackonochie and Wainwright.

The Commissioners' Churches were built to provide more space for the worship of God. But in what way was God to be worshipped? And even, who was God? Those 19th-century liberals who survived the shock of the French Revolution took up a line which we can still find today in the absurd Act inaugurated by R. A. Butler (1944) about the teaching of religion in State Schools. The liberal view was, as Newman described it, 'the doctrine that there is no positive truth in religion, but that one creed is as good as another.' This view commended itself to Dissenters in the beginning of the last century, since they saw in it the liberty to expound their doctrines, and perhaps to win the world to believe them. It commended itself to those whom scientific discovery was driving to unwilling agnosticism. And, of course, it commended itself to materialists who had not yet made a dogma of materialism.

In the late Georgian Church there was little of such liberalism. People were divided into Low Church Evangelicals and old-fashioned 'High and Dry'. By the 1830s the great Evangelical movement was, as W. S. Lilly says, 'perishing of intellectual inanition'. Beginning, in Apostolic wise, with 'the foolishness of preaching, it had ended unapostolically in the preaching of foolishness.' The evangelical tea-parties, revelations, prophecies, jumping, shaking and speaking in strange tongues which went on in England in those days within and without the Church make fascinating reading. But they have left no enduring architectural monument, except for some of the buildings belonging to the Catholic Apostolic Church. The other party in the Church of England, the 'high and dry', was orthodox and uninspiring. Once a quarter, after preparing themselves by means of those Queen Anne and Georgian manuals of devotion which we sometimes find bound up in old prayer books, its members moved through the chancel screen on Sacrament Sunday to partake of the outward and visible signs of inward and spiritual grace. Their parsons wore the surplice and the wig, and abhorred change. They were not quite so negative as they are made out to be. There are several instances in the late 18th and early 19th centuries of screens being erected across chancels to shut off from the nave the place where the Sacrament was partaken.

The Church of England at this time drew its ministers from men who were scholars or gentlemen, usually both. Harriet Martineau's acid biography of Bishop Blomfield (1786–1857) in her *Biographical Sketches*, rather cattily says:

> In those days, a divine rose in the Church in one or two ways, – by his classical reputation, or by aristocratic connection. Mr Blomfield was a fine scholar; ...

Let us try to put ourselves into the frame of mind of somebody living in the reign of King William IV. Let us suppose him just come down from Oxford and still in touch with his University. The grand tour was no longer so fashionable. A squire's son usually went abroad for sport. Few came back with works of art for the adornment of their parks or saloons. Most country house libraries stop at the end of George IV's reign, except for the addition of sporting books and works of reference on husbandry, law and pedigrees of family and livestock. A studious man, such as we have in mind, would have turned his attention to antiquity and history. The novels of Scott would have given him a taste for England's past. The antiquarian publications of Britton would have reinforced it. In Gothic England he would have found much to admire. And the people of his village were still the product of agricultural feudalism. Tenantry bobbed, and even artisans touched their hats. Blasphemy shocked people, for many believed that Christ was the Incarnate Son of God.

Our young man would undoubtedly read *The Christian Year* by the Reverend John Keble (1827). It is hard to see today how this simple and unexciting, oft-reprinted book could have fired so many minds. Perhaps the saintly life of the author, who had thrown up academic honours and comfort to live among simple villagers as their minister, had something to do with it. At any rate, Newman regarded that book as the foundation of the Tractarian movement. The verses of *The Christian Year* were a series composed to fit in with the feasts, fasts and offices of the Book of Common Prayer. They drew people back to the nature of the Established Church. And the *Tracts for the Times* which followed, from Keble's Assize Sermon of 1833 up to Tract XC by Newman on the Thirty-nine Articles in 1841, would certainly influence him greatly. In these he would learn how the Church was finding herself part of the Catholic Church. Although many great men, greatest of all Newman, have left her for the Church of Rome, others remained faithful. Their witness in England in the last century is apparent in the hundreds of churches which were built on Tractarian principles in new suburbs and towns, in the church schools, public and elementary, in the Sisterhood buildings, in the houses of rest erected by good people of the kind one reads about in the novels of Charlotte M. Yonge, who was herself a parishioner and friend of Keble.

English architecture was also beginning a new phase of professionalism in the reign of William IV. Architects had in the past been regarded either as builders or as semi-amateurs who left the details of their designs to masons and plasterers. There had been great architects since the time of Wren. There was also a host of lesser men who in domestic work were pursuing their local styles and imitating the splendid designs of the metropolis, rather as village builders in monastic times had tried to reproduce in village churches the latest styles at the abbeys. But for years now architecture had been becoming a profession. Architects designed buildings and produced their own beautiful, detailed drawings. Less was left to the builder and the gifted amateur. In 1837 the Institute of British Architects was incorporated by Royal Charter. Architects were by now rather more like doctors and lawyers than artists.

The most influential was Augustus Welby Northmore Pugin (1812 – 52), who was said by his doctor to have crammed into his forty years of existence the work of a hundred years. Pugin's life has been entertainingly described by his contemporary Benjamin Ferrey in *Recollections of Augustus Welby Pugin*, 1861, and lately his life has been written by Michael Trappes-Lomax, who stresses his Roman Catholicism. Sir Kenneth Clark in *The Gothic Revival*, the Revd. B. F. L. Clarke in *Nineteenth Century Churchbuilders*, and John Summerson in an essay in *The Architectural Review*, (April 1948), have all written most illuminatingly about him.

In 1841 Pugin published his *Contrasts* and his *True Principles of Christian Architecture*. Herein he caricatured in skilful drawings the false Gothick of the Strawberry Hill type, and lampooned everything that was classical. To contrast with these he had made beautiful shaded drawings of medieval buildings, particularly those of the late 14th century. He did not confine his caricatures to architecture, and peopled the foregrounds with figures. In front of pagan or classical buildings he drew indolent policemen, vulgar tradesmen and miserable beggars; before the medieval buildings he drew vested priests and pious pilgrims. He idealized the middle ages. His drawings were sincere but unfair. The prose accompaniment to them is glowing and witty.

Pugin's own churches, which were almost all Roman Catholic, are attempts to realize his dreams. But for all the sincerity of their architect, the brass coronals, the jewelled glass by Hardman of Birmingham, the correctly moulded arches and the carefully carved woodwork have a spindly effect. St Chad's Roman Catholic Cathedral at Birmingham, St Augustine's Church, Ramsgate, and St Giles's, Cheadle, are exceptions. It is not in his buildings but in his writing that Pugin had so great an influence on the men of his time.

Pugin is sometimes supposed to have joined the Church of Rome for aesthetic reasons only. It is true that he saw in it the survival of the Middle Ages to which he desired the world to return. But the Roman Catholics of his time were not whole-heartedly in favour of the Gothic style he advocated, and to his annoyance continued to build in the classic style of the continent or else in the plaster-thin Gothick he despised. The Church of England, newly awakened to its Catholicism, took more kindly to his doctrines, so that although he came in for some mild criticism from *The Ecclesiologist* (the organ first of the Cambridge Camden Society, and from 1845 of Catholic-minded Anglicans in general), Pugin contemplated writing an essay called: 'An Apology for the separated Church of England since the reign of the Eight Henry. Written with every feeling of Christian charity for her Children, and honour of the glorious men she continued to produce in evil times. By A. Welby Pugin, many years a Catholic-minded son of the Anglican Church, and still an affectionate and loving brother of the true sons of England's church.'

I do not think it was solely for aesthetic reasons, or even for doctrinal reasons, that Pugin joined the Church of Rome. He possessed what we now call, 'social conscience'. He deplored the slums he saw building round him. He abhorred the soullessness of machinery, and revered hand craftsmanship. His drawings of industrial towns contrasted with a dream-like Middle Ages, his satire on the wealthy ostentation of a merchant's house – 'On one side of the house machicolated parapets, embrasures, bastions, and all the show of strong defence, and round the corner of the building a conservatory leading to the principal rooms, through which a whole company of horsemen might penetrate at one smash into the heart of the mansion! – for who would hammer against nailed portals when he could kick his way through the greenhouse?' – are summed up in the two principles of Gothic or Christian architecture which he delivered to the world. These are they. 'First, that there should be no features about a building which are not necessary for convenience, construction, or propriety; second, that all ornament should consist of enrichment of the essential construction of the building.' Pugin's principles, and his conviction that the only style that was Christian was Gothic, are fathered by popular opinion on Ruskin. But Ruskin was not fond of Pugin. He disliked his Popery, and he thought little of his buildings. If one must find a successor to Pugin, it is the atheist William Morris. Both men liked simplicity and good craftsmanship. Both had a 'social conscience'. Pugin dreamed of a Christian world, Morris of a Socialist world, but both their worlds were dreams.

Let us imagine our young man again, now become a Tractarian clergyman. His convictions about how best to honour the God he loves, and how to spread that love among the artisans in the poorer part of his parish, are likely to take form in a new church. And, since he is a Tractarian, it must be a beautiful church. His reading of Pugin, the publications of the Cambridge Camden Society and *The Ecclesiologist*, will have inspired him. He will have no truck with the cheap Gothic or Norman Revival of the Evangelical school. A pamphlet such as that of Revd. W. Carus Wilson's *Helps to the Building of Churches, Parsonage Houses and Schools* (2nd Edition, Kirby Lonsdale, 1842) will have digusted him. Here we find just the sort of thing Pugin satirized: 'A very neat portable font has been given to the new church at Stonyhurst, which answers every purpose; not requiring even the expense of a stand; as it might be placed, when wanted, on the Communion Table from which the ceremony might be performed. The price is fourteen shillings; and it is to be had at Sharper's, Pall Mall East, London.' Such cheese-paring our clergyman would leave to the extreme Protestants who thought ostentation, stained glass, frontals, lecterns and banners smacked of Popery, and who thought with Dean Close of Cheltenham that 'the Restoration of Churches is the Restoration of Popery'. This explains why, to this day, unrestored churches with box-pews are generally Evangelical and locked. But the Evangelical did not wholly reject Gothic. Ullenhall (Warwicks) and Itchen Stoke (Hants) are Victorian Gothic churches designed to have the Table well away from the East wall and the lectern and pulpit dominant. Ullenhall retains its Protestant arrangement, and this arrangement was originally, we must remember, the 'High Church' of the 17th and 18th centuries. The Early English style was regarded as plain and primitive. Very few churches were built in a classic style between 1840 and 1900. The choice before young vicar is no longer Gothic or Classic, but what sort of Gothic?

Architects were turning their attention to churches. And the younger men were all for Gothic. Most architects were God-fearing folk of the new middle class. They felt privileged to build churches to the glory of God. Many of them were instructed in theology; they subscribed to *The Ecclesiologist* and to various learned antiquarian publications. They delighted to discuss the merits of Norman, and Decorated, Early English and Perpendicular, or Early, Middle and Late Pointed, according to which terminology they favoured. In the early 'forties they were still following Pugin. Pugin's chief Anglican equivalents were Benjamin Ferrey, Carpenter and Gilbert Scott. These men, and many others, were capable of making very good imitations of a medieval fabric. With the aid of the numerous books of measured drawings that were appearing, it was possible to erect almost exact copies of such famous monuments of the Middle Ages as the spire at Louth, the tracery of the Angel Choir at Lincoln, and the roof of Westminster Hall. The scale was different it is true, and architects had no compunction about mixing copies of what they considered the 'best' features of old churches in their new ones. They thought that a blend of the best everywhere would make something better still.

The earlier Gothic revival churches, that is to say those of late Georgian times, were in the late 14th-century style. One may see in some prim and spacious Georgian square, brick imitations of King's College Chapel and Bathstone dressings. But in the late 1840s architects were attaching moral properties to Gothic styles. Pugin had started the idea and his successors surpassed him. Since Gothic was the perfect style, what was the perfect style of Gothic? I do not know who it was who started the theory that early Gothic is crude, middle is perfection, and late is debased . But – certainly from the middle of the 1840s – this theory was held by most of the rising young church architects. Promoters of new churches who could afford it were advised to have something in the Middle Pointed or Decorated style. This is the reason why in mid-Victorian suburbs, while speculative builders were still erecting Italianate stucco mansions, in the last stuccoed gasp of the Georgian classic tradition – South Kensington and Pimlico in London are examples – the spire of Ketton or Louth soars above the chimney-pots, and a sudden break in the Palladian plaster terraces shews the irregular stone front, gabled porch and curvilinear tracery of a church in the Decorated style. Church architecture was setting the fashion which the builders followed, and decades later, even employing church architects (such as Ferrey at Bournemouth), they erected Gothic residences in the new winding avenues of housing estates for the upper middle classes. Most of the work of the late 'forties and early 'fifties was in this copying style. When an architect had a sense of proportion, there were often impressive results. Carpenter and his son and their partner Slater were always good. Their Lancing School Chapel must be regarded as one of the finest Gothic buildings of any period in England, and their London church of St Mary Magdalen, Munster Square, so modest outside, is spacious and awe-inspiring within.

The most famous copyist was Gilbert Scott. He and his family have had a great influence on English architecture over the past century. Gilbert Scott was the son of a Buckinghamshire parson, the grandson of the Calvinist clergyman Thomas Scott, whose Commentary on the Bible greatly influenced Newman as a youth. There is no doubt of Scott's passionate affection for Gothic architecture. He pays a handsome tribute to Pugin's influence on his mind: 'Pugin's articles excited me almost to fury, and I suddenly found myself like a person awakened from a long, feverish dream, which had rendered him unconscious of what was going on about him.'

Our young clergyman would almost certainly have applied to Gilbert Scott for his new church. He would have received designs from Scott's office. They would have been a safe, correct essay in the middle pointed style, with tower and spire or with bellcot only, according to the price. Scott himself, except when he first started in private practice, may not have had much to do with the design. He collected an enormous staff, and from his office emerged, it is said, over seven hundred and forty buildings between 1847 and 1878 when he died. When one considers that an architect in private practice today thinks himself busy if he has seven new buildings to do in a decade, it seems probable that Scott eventually became little more than an overseer of all but his most important work. His 'restorations' were numerous and usually disastrous.

Yet Scott, who was eventually knighted for his vast output, had a style of his own – a square abacus to his columns, plate tracery in the windows, much stone foliage mixed up with heads, and for east or west windows, three equal lancets with a round window above them. In five churches of his, St Giles, Camberwell; St George's, Doncaster; Leafield, Oxon; Bradfield, Berks, and St Anne, Alderney, I can trace it clearly. He liked to build something big. He dispensed with a chancel screen. Instead of this, he often interposed between the congregation in the nave and the rich chancel, a tower or transept crossing which was either darker or lighter than the parts it separated. Add to this a sure sense of proportion and a workmanlike use of stone, and the dull mechanical details of his work are forgotten in the mystery and splendour of the interior effect. Scott realized some of Pugin's dreams for him. But he never did more. He was at heart a copyist and not a thinker in Gothic.

Church architecture by the 'fifties was very much an affair of personalities. The big London men and a few in the provinces had their individual styles. As Sir Charles Nicholson remarked in his comments on Henry Woodyer's beautiful building St Michael's College, Tenbury (1856), which was designed as a church choir school: 'It was never, of course, intended that the College should be mistaken for anything other than a 19th-century building: for Gothic revival architects did not attempt such follies, though their enemies accused them of doing so.' What is true of St Michael's College, Tenbury, is true also of most of the churches built in England after 1850. The chief of those architects who 'thought in Gothic' are listed below.

William Butterfield (1814–1900) was the most severe and interesting of them. He first startled the world in 1849 with his design for All Saints, Margaret Street, London, built on the cramped site of an 18th-century proprietary chapel where lights had been used on the altar since 1839, and a sung celebration of the Holy Communion introduced. All Saints embodies architectural theories which Butterfield employed in most of his other churches throughout his long life. It is constructed of the material which builders in the district were accustomed to use, which in London at that time was brick. Since bricks do not lend themselves to the carving which is expected of a Gothic building, Butterfield varied his flat brick surfaces with bands of colour, both within and without. In those days the erroneous impression prevailed that Gothic decoration grew more elaborate the higher it was on a building. The patterns of bricks in Butterfield's buildings grew, therefore, more diversified and frequent towards the tops of walls, towers and steeples. But their arrangement is not usually capricious as it is in the work of some of the rather comic church architects who copied him, like Bassett Keeling. Where walls supported a great weight, they were striped horizontally, where they were mere screen walls, diaper patterns of bricks were introduced. Inside his churches Butterfield delighted to use every coloured stone, marble and other material he could find for the money at his disposal. He was a severely practical man, and a planner and constructor first. His decoration was meant to emphasize his construction.

The plan of All Saints is in the latest Tractarian manner of its time. The high altar is visible from every part of the church. Indeed to this day not even the delicate and marked style of Sir Ninian Comper's side altar in the north aisle takes one's eye from the chancel. Butterfield disapproved of side altars and never made provision for them in his churches. The chancel is the richest part of the building, and the chancel arch, higher than the arcades of the nave, gives it an effect of greater loftiness than it possesses. There is, of course, no screen. The other prominent feature of any Butterfield church is the font. That sentence in the Catechism on the number of Sacraments, 'Two only, as generally necessary to salvation, that is to say Baptism, and the Supper of the Lord', is almost spoken aloud by a Butterfield church; altar and font are the chief things we see. But when we look up at arches and roofs, we see Butterfield the builder with his delight in construction. His roofs are described by that fine writer Sir John Summerson as 'like huge, ingenious toys'. The phrase is as memorable as all Butterfield's roofs, of which the ingenuity and variety seem to have been the only sportiveness he permitted himself.

In person Butterfield was a silent, forbidding man who looked like Mr Gladstone. He was an earnest Tractarian with a horror of everything outside the liturgy of the Book of Common Prayer. Except for one Noncomformist chapel in Bristol, designed when he was a youth, and unlike the rest of his work, he built only for Tractarians. He supplied no attractive drawings to tempt clients. He was a strong disciplinarian in his office, and on the building site, scaffolding and ladders had to be dusted before he ascended to see the work in progress. He was averse to all publicity and show, and had little to do with any other architects. People had to take Butterfield or leave him. And so must we. Yet no one who has an eye for plan, construction and that sense of proportion which is the essential of all good architecture, can see a Butterfield church without being compelled to admire it, even if he cannot like it.

George Edmund Street, R.A. (1824–81), is chiefly remembered now for the Law Courts in London. He was in Gilbert Scott's office before setting up on his own. Early in his career he received the patronage of such distinguished High Churchmen as Prynne, Butler of Wantage, and Bishop Wilberforce of Oxford. Street himself was a Tractarian, singing in the choir at Wantage and disapproving of ritual without doctrine. The churches he built in the late 'fifties and throughout the 'sixties, often with schools and parsonages alongside them, are like his character straightforward and con-vinced. They are shorn of those 'picturesque' details beloved of the usual run of architects of the time. The plan of Street's buildings is immediately apparent from the exterior. Some of his village schools of local stone built early in his career in the Oxford Diocese are so simple and well-proportioned, and fit so naturally into the landscape, that they might be the sophisticated Cotswold work of such 1900 architects as Ernest Gimson and F. L. Griggs. Street's churches are built on the same principles as those of Butterfield, one altar only, and that visible from all parts of the church, a rich east end, and much westward light into the nave. Street had a sure sense of proportion, very much his own; his work, whether it is a lectern or a pulpit or a spire, is massive, and there is nothing mean about it nor over-decorated. This massive quality of his work made Street a bad restorer of old buildings, for he would boldly pull down a chancel and rebuild it in his own style. He was a great enthusiast for the arts and crafts. With his own hands he is said to have made the wooden staircase for West Challow Vicarage in Berkshire. His ironwork was drawn out in section as well as outline, and there were some caustic comments written by him in the margin of his copy of Gilbert Scott's *Personal and Professional Recollections* (in the RIBA Library) where Scott confesses to leaving the detail of his ironwork to Skidmore of Coventry, the manufacturer. Street was an able sketcher of architecture, and clearly a man who could fire his pupils with his own enthusiasm, even though he never allowed those pupils a free hand in design, doing everything down to the smallest details himself. Street's influence on English architecture is properly appreciated in H. S. Goodhart Rendel's *English Architecture Since the Regency*. It comes down to us through his pupils, among whom were Philip Webb and Norman Shaw, whose domestic architecture brought about the small house of today, William Morris, to whom the Arts and Crafts Movement owes so much, and J. D. Sedding, the church architect and craftsman.

The third of the great mid-Victorian church builders was John Lough-borough Pearson (1817–97). His later buildings are of all Victorian churches those we like best today. He was, like Street and Butterfield, a Tractarian. Before designing a building he gave himself to prayer and receiving the Sacrament. He seems to have been a more 'advanced' clergyman than his two comparable contemporaries, for in his later churches he made ample provision for side altars, and even for a tabernacle for the reservation of the Blessed Sacrament. Pearson was articled in Durham to Ignatius Bonomi, the son of an elegant 18th-century architect. His early work in Yorkshire is competent copying of the medieval, and just distinguishable from the work of Gilbert Scott. But somewhere about 1860 he paid a visit to France, and early French Gothic vaulting seems to have transformed him. He built St Peter's, Vauxhall, London, in 1862. Like most of his later work it is a cruciform building with brick vaulting throughout and with a clerestory. St Peter's seems to have been the pattern of which all his subsequent churches were slight variants. Sometimes he threw out side chapels, sometimes he made aisles under buttresses. The Pearson style was an Early English Gothic with deep mouldings and sharply-pointed arches; brick was usually employed for walls and vaulting, stone for ribs, columns, arches and window tracery. Pearson also took great trouble with skyline, and his spires, flèches and roofs form beautiful groups from any angle.

One more individualistic Gothic revivalist was William Burges (1827 – 81), who was as much a domestic architect and a furniture designer as an ecclesiastical man. He delighted in colour and quaintness, but being the son of an engineer, his work had a solidity of structure which saved it from ostentation. His east end of Waltham Abbey and his cathedral of St Finbar, Cork, are his most beautiful church work, though Skelton and Studley Royal, both in Yorkshire, are overpowering in their rich colour and decoration, and very original in an early French Gothic manner.

Neither Butterfield, Street, Pearson nor Burges would have thought of copying old precedents. They had styles of their own which they had devised for themselves, continuing from the medieval Gothic but not copying it.

These big men had their imitators: Bassett Keeling who reproduced the wildest excesses of the polychromatic brick style and mixed it with cast-iron construction; S. S. Teulon who, in his youth, did the same thing; E. Buckton Lamb who invented a style of his own; Henry Woodyer who had a fanciful, spindly Gothic style which is original and marked; William White and Henry Clutton, both of whom produced churches, strong and modern for their times; Ewan Christian, the Evangelical architect, who could imitate the style of Pearson; or that best of the lesser men, James Brooks who built several 'big-boned' churches in East London in a plainer Pearson-esque manner. There was also the scholarly work in Italian Gothic of E. W. Godwin, and Sir Arthur Blomfield could turn out an impressive church in almost any style.

There is no doubt that until about 1870 the impetus of vigorous Victorian architecture went into church building. Churches took the lead in construction and in use of materials. They employed the artists, and many of the best pictures of the time had sacred subjects. The difficulties in which artists found themselves, torn between Anglo-Catholicism, Romanism and Ruskin's Protestantism, is described well in John Steegman's *Consort of Taste*.

After the 'seventies, Norman Shaw, himself a High Churchman, became the leading domestic architect. The younger architects turned their invention to house design and building small houses for people of moderate income. Bedford Park was laid out by Norman Shaw in 1878. It was a revolution – a cluster of picturesque houses for artistic suburbanites. And from this time onwards we have a series of artistic churches, less vulgar and vigorous than the work of the now ageing great men, but in their way distinguished: slender, tapering work, palely enriched within in Burne-Jonesian greens and browns. The Middle Pointed or Decorated style and variants of it were no longer thought the only correct styles. People began to admire what was 'late' and what was 'English', and the neglected glory of Perpendicular, long called 'debased', was revived, and even the Renaissance style was used. For as the Reverend B. F. L. Clarke says in his *Church Builders of the Nineteenth Century*, 'the question of Style was coming to be regarded as being of small importance'.

The last quarter of the 19th century was a time when the Tractarian movement firmly established itself. Of the eight Religious Communities for men of the Anglican Church, six were of the 1890s, and one, the 'Cowley Fathers' (Society of St John the Evangelist), was founded in 1865. Of the forty-five Communities for women, the first two, the Society of the Holy and Undivided Trinity and the Society of the Most Holy Trinity, Ascot, were founded in 1845, and well over half the rest are of Victorian origin. There are now in the Church of England more religious Communities than there were in medieval England, and this does not include Communities in Scotland, Wales, Ireland, America, Asia, Africa and Australia.

This was a time when the church was concerning herself with social problems, and building many new churches in England as well as establishing dioceses abroad. Many, and often ugly, little churches were built of brick in brand new suburbs. Cathedral-like buildings, subscribed for by the pious from wealthy parishes, were built in the slums. At the back of *Crockford's Clerical Directory* there is an index of English parishes with the dates of their formation. If you look up an average industrial town with, say, ten churches, you will find that the majority will have been built during the last half of the 19th century. Oldest will be the parish church, probably medieval. Next there will be a late Georgian church built by the Commissioners. Then there will be three built between 1850 and 1870, three built between 1870 and 1900, and two since then, probably after the 1914 war and in new suburbs.

It is entertaining, and not completely safe, to generalize on the inner story of the Church and its building in Victorian and later times. In, let us say, 1850, the vicar of the parish church had become a little old for active work, and left much to his curates. His churchmanship took the form mainly of support for the Establishment and hostility to Dissent. The word 'Dissenters' applied to Nonconformists always had a faint note of contempt. Methodists and Baptists were building chapels all over the rapidly growing town. Their religion of personal experience of salvation, of hymn-singing, ejaculations of praise; the promise of a golden heaven after death as a reward for a sad life down here in the crowded misery of back streets, disease and gnawing poverty; their weekday socials and clubs which welded the membership of the chapels in a Puritan bond of teetotalism, and non-gambling, non-smoking and well-doing: these had an appeal which today is largely dispersed into the manufactured day-dreams of the cinema and the less useful social life of the dance hall and sports club. Chapels were crowded, gas-lights flamed on popular preachers, and steamy windows resounded to the cries of 'Alleluia, Jesus saves!' A simple ceremony like total immersion or Breaking of Bread was something all the tired and poor could easily understand, after their long hours of misery in gloomy mills. Above all, the Nonconformists turned people's minds and hearts to Jesus as a personal Friend of all, especially the poor. Many a pale mechanic and many a drunkard's wife could remember the very hour of the very day on which, in that street or at that meeting, or by that building, conviction came of the truth of the Gospel, that Jesus was Christ. Then with what flaming heart he or she came to the chapel, and how fervently testified to the message of salvation and cast off the old life of sin.

Beside these simple and genuine experiences of the love of Christ, the old-established Church with its system of pew rents, and set prayers and carefully-guarded sacraments, must have seemed wicked mumbo-jumbo. No wonder the old Vicar was worried about the Dissenters. His parish was increasing by thousands as the factories boomed and the ships took our merchandise across the seas, but his parishioners were not coming to church in proportion. He had no objection therefore when the new Bishop, filled with the zeal for building which seems to have filled all Victorian bishops, decided to form two new parishes out of his own, the original parish of the little village which had become a town in less than a century. The usual method was adopted. Two clergymen were licensed to start the church life of the two new districts. These men were young; one was no doubt a Tractarian; the other was perhaps fired with the Christian Socialism of Charles Kingsley and F. D. Maurice. Neither was much concerned with the establishment of churches as bulwarks against Dissenters, but rather as houses of God among ignorant Pagans, where the Gospel might be heard, the Sacraments administered, want relieved, injustice righted and ignorance dispelled. First came the mission-room, a room licensed for services in the clergyman's lodging, then there was the school, at first a room for Sunday school only, and then came the mission church made of corrugated iron. Then there was an appeal for a church school and for a permanent church. For this church the once young clergyman, now worn after ten years' work, would apply to the Incorporated Church Building Society, and to the Church Building Fund of his own diocese; he would raise money among his poor parishioners, he would give his own money (this was a time when priests were frequently men of means), and pay his own stipend as well. The site for the church would be given by a local landowner, and who knows but that some rich manufacturer whose works were in the parish would subscribe. Whatever their Churchmanship, the new parishes formed in the 'fifties generally had their own church within twenty years.

All this while the Commissioners' Church in the town, that Greek Revival building among the genteel squares where still lived the doctors, attorneys and merchants, had an Evangelical congregation and disapproved of the old 'high and dry' vicar of the parish church. The congregation and incumbent disapproved still more of the goings on of the Tractarian priest in charge of one of the two new districts. He lit two candles on the Table which he called an 'altar', at the service of the Lord's Supper he stood with his back to the congregation instead of at the north end of the Table, he wore a coloured stole over his gown. He was worse than the Pope of Rome or almost as bad. The ignorant artisans were being turned into Roman Catholics. The pure

Gospel of the Reformation must be brought to them. So a rival church was built in the Tractarian parish, financed by the Evangelical church people of the town, and from outside by many loyal Britons who throughout England, like Queen Victoria herself, were deploring the Romish tendency in the Established Church.

Many years have passed since this controversy, and the rival Evangelical fane probably has now a clergyman who always wears a surplice and sometimes a coloured stole, who has lights on the altar and faces east to celebrate Holy Communion, while the priest and congregation of the neighbouring Tractarian church, who now have incense, reservation of the Blessed Sacrament, daily mass, confessions and a High Mass on Sundays, still regard him as 'low church'.

If one may generalize about the ecclesiastical works of the last half of the century, when so many new churches were built, so many new dioceses established at home and abroad, one can say this. From the 'forties to the middle 'sixties, the majority of the new churches were built as missions to the poor in towns; from the middle 'sixties until the end of the century, and increasingly since then, most new churches have been built in the suburbs. This is not to say that the poor became neglected. Rich manufacturers, settled down as squires in country near Birmingham, Manchester, Liverpool, London, the Potteries and the East Riding, also often rebuilt their country parish church as did those established landowners who were pious and still wealthy. Hence the many rebuilt churches in the Home Counties, Cheshire, Shropshire, Warwickshire and Worcestershire. The 'Lux Mundi' group of the 'nineties, the Christian Socialism of such men as Father Adderley, Canon Scott Holland and Bishop Gore whose theology emphasized the Incarnation, laid great stress on the idea that the Catholic faith must play a part in the everyday life of factory and shop and not be a matter of Sunday worship only. Thus we find many slum Tractarian parishes building new mission churches on their smoky, overcrowded outskirts, churches with the names of black letter saints in the Calendar who always seem to be 'high': St Anselm, St Cyprian, St Erkenwald, St Mary Magdalen.

We like to think that the reason for the missions to the suburbs from the middle 'sixties onwards was that there were fewer poor. There may be some truth in this, but the reason lies more in the great growth of the middle classes – clerks, rich wholesalers and retailers, the Pooters, those dear, solid bits of English backbone. Few of them were more than one generation from a country village, and the churchgoing habit was ingrained in them from youth. They are the reason for the tall Perpendicular walls of St Philip's Church, in red brick with stone dressings, rising above the oak paling and evergreens where Victoria Drive intersects Tollemache Avenue. The Tollemaches, deriving an unexpected income in house rents from what had been a sandy warren, gave the site; the merchants in the detached houses at the richer end of Victoria Drive gave the woodwork; the rich brewer whose family have by now been absorbed into the country squirearchy gave the stained glass; and either George Gilbert Scott junior, John Olrid Scott, G. F. Bodley, J. D. Sedding, Norman Shaw, or, if it is in the North Country, Austin and Paley, designed the church. These architects were the young men who emerged from the enormous office of Sir Gilbert Scott, or the gay craftsman's studio of Street. They carried the faith of their masters with them. They were generally Tractarians, of a more advanced sort than their masters. They were musical and artistic. They knew such men as Burne Jones and Rossetti, and, much as they abhorred his atheism, they admired the decorative work of Street's pupil William Morris.

I think that the well-spring of this later church architecture is the work of George Gilbert Scott junior, who was a close friend of G. F. Bodley. This talented man was a scholar who wrote that learned and interesting *History of English Church Architecture until the Reformation*. He was not only a medievalist. He was one of the first Victorians to appreciate again the work of the Renaissance. The few churches he built are a foretaste of the work of Bodley and his followers. In 1877 he dared to build St Agnes, Kennington, London, in the despised Perpendicular style. What is more, he used brick walls, put a screen and rood across the chancel arch, and had a chancel under the same roof as the nave. He designed side chapels for daily services, he had no capitals to the piers in the nave arcades, and he filled the windows with glass by an unknown young artist called Kempe.*

But we can see other churches influenced by the Neo-Perpendicular movement, and many of these are very fine buildings, no more imitations of medieval than were the works of the older Victorians. They are, however, less Victorian than the daring experiments of the 'fifties and 'sixties, and they seem, like the small houses designed by Norman Shaw, to come into our time or at any rate into the 1920s. Because they are near us, we do not appreciate their originality. In our desire to see a new style emerge from new materials, we notice only that the mouldings and fittings are copies of medieval Gothic. We do not realize that the proportions, plan and liturgical arrangement are nothing like our old churches.

See in your mind's eye a church built in the neo-Perpendicular style by G. G. Scott junior, Bodley, W. H. Bidlake of Birmingham, Edgar Wood, Sir Ninian Comper, W. D. Caroe, Sir Charles Nicholson, Temple Moore, J. D. Sedding, Edmund Sedding, Charles Spooner, E. P. Warren, Walter Tapper, Niven and Wigglesworth, Austin and Paley, to name a few of these later Victorian architects. If you cannot see it, I will try to re-create such a church, and you will remember it in some newish suburb of a provincial town where you stayed with an aunt, or on a holiday in the outskirts of a south-coast watering place, and you can read of it in Compton Mackenzie's *Sinister Street*. 'Ting-ting' the single bell calls to Sung Eucharist, because the tower, designed

---

* This church was destroyed by the Southwark Diocese after war damage.

for a full peal of bells, was never completed. Rather gaunt without it, the church rises above the privet and forsythia and prunus of its little garden, for there is no churchyard to these churches; we have reached the era of municipal cemeteries, and it is in their marble acres that the dead of this new parish are to be found. Inside the church, the tall nave is filled with chairs, and the narrow aisles are not used on a Sunday, as they give a view only of side altars where the weekday Celebrations and the very early Sunday masses are said. The floor is of oak blocks, the walls are cream and clean, the woodwork of the thick Devonshire style chancel screen, carved by Harry Hems of Exeter, is unstained. In more recent times a coloured statue of Our Lady under a gilded canopy is seen against one of the eastern-most pillars of the nave. Through the screen we glimpse a huge reredos painted green and red and gold, with folding doors. The high altar has a purple frontal, because just now it is Lent. The floor of the sanctuary is paved with black-and-white marble. Riddel posts with gilt angels on them – the famous 'English altar' introduced by Sir Ninian Comper in the 'eighties – hold curtains round the north, south and east of the side altars. The windows are filled with greenish glass in which are patches of dark blue, red and gold. These are the work of Kempe, and they allow more light into the church than earlier Victorian windows. The chief beauty of the church is its proportion. These architects favoured two kinds of proportion when they were building in the Gothic style – almost all of them designed Byzantine and classic churches as well – and they were either height and narrowness, or breadth and length. Their churches either soar or spread.

The Sung Eucharist is probably from the Prayer Book and with a crowd of acolytes at the altar. Blue incense rises to the golden reredos and the green Kempe window. The English Hymnal is used, and plain-song or more probably, Eyre in E [flat] or Tours in C. Candlelights twinkle in the mist. The purple Lenten chasuble of the priest is worn over amice, alb, stole and maniple, and there is discussion of these things after the service and before among servers and the initiated. We are in a world which feels itself in touch with the Middle Ages and with today. This is English Catholicism. There is much talk of Percy Dearmer, correct furnishings and vestments, the Prayer Book and how far one is justified in departing from it. After church the acolytes in their Sunday suits hang round the porch, and the young curates too, and there is a good deal of backslapping and chaff. For months the Mothers' Union and women's guilds of the church have been working on banners and a frontal to be ready for Easter. From these suburban parishes much of the Church life of modern England has sprung. They have trained their people in faith and the liturgy, they have produced many of the overseas missionaries and parish priests of today.

We are in modern times, out of the older and rich suburbs with their garden city atmosphere of guild craftsman and Sarum Use, and into the big building estates. The large areas of semi-detached houses, built by private speculators or councils, have been eating up our agricultural land since 1920. They have been brought about by the change in transport from steam to motor-bus and electric train. People are moving out of the crowded early Victorian industrial lanes and terraces, into little houses of their own, each with its little patch of garden at the back and front, each isolated from its neighbour by social convention, in districts where miles of pavement enlivened by the squeak of perambulators lead to a far-off bus route and parade of chain stores, and a distant vita-glass school, used as a Community Centre in the evenings. To these places, often lonely for all the people in them, is the new mission Church.

Just as there is today no definite modern style in England, except in what is impermanent – exhibition buildings, prefabs, holiday camps and the like, so there is no definite modern church style. In the period between the two wars church architects were too often concerned with style, and they built places of worship which vied with the local Odeon or with by-pass modern factories in trying to be 'contemporary'. They now look dated, and will, I fear, never look beautiful. But the purpose of the church remains the same as it was at the beginning of this book, to be a place where the Faith is taught and the Sacraments are administered.

Bedfordshire

Introduction

The north-bound train traveller from St Pancras retains a poor impression of Bedfordshire, the verdict generally being one of flat Midland scenery, at its more unrelieved; this is as unfair as it is uninformed. Sadly, many of the villages and small towns within easy reach of the M1 or major stations have been engulfed by large modern housing estates. However, it must be admitted at once that the central clay vale is a wilderness, raped for brick-making, and with a similar fate awaiting still-virgin land. Otherwise the county, for its limited area, is varied to a degree that is unique. In the north the Ouse winds through a landscape of gracious tranquillity, a summer country of stone villages and broad water meadows which rises in the north-east to a continuation of Walpole's 'dumpling hills' of Northamptonshire. This is often surprisingly lonely country and, though the woods are now few and far between, the ghost of the old 'Bruneswald' forest still haunts the land.

In the centre of the county lies the Greensand ridge, a corridor of fifteen miles which Hoskins in his *Midland England* considers 'unsurpassed in sanctity and peculiar purity'; it broadens in the west to the ducal country of Woburn, scenically magnificent with pine-woods and open heaths. In the east, being in part overlaid by clay and dissected by the River Ivel, the scenery is even more varied, and the several estate villages must be the *genius loci* of the 'cottage orne', in particular Old Warden, which retains a delightful Victorian picture-book quality almost unimpaired.

Beyond the Greensand the Gault clay valley is a prelude to the chalk hills, and, save around Toddington where a considerable elevation is reached, is subdued to them; it is largely unspoiled country, much of it formerly marsh of which Flitwick Moor remains as a fragment. There are one or two chalk outliers in the valley, of which Shillington church hill is the most renowned, and Billington the most beautiful.

The chalk reaches its greatest development at Dunstable, but its greatest beauty in the folded coombes and open windswept downs around Barton. At Totternhoe Knolls, a promontory of the lower chalk overlooking the vast Aylesbury Vale and the line of the Chilterns to the west, lies the site of the old quarries that gave to this area a building stone of poor external weathering quality, but one which served as inspiration for a local school of 13th-century carving, little known, but of high artistic merit.

Luton forms an industrial and suburban area 'as unexpected as it is

unprepossessing', and with the dreadful tentacle that links it to Dunstable
has straddled a large area of the foothills to the Downs. Much of the
surrounding countryside is losing the battle against suburbia, and unforgivable
crimes have been committed in the hills, the worst perhaps the cutting of
the skyline at Totternhoe. In spite of all this, however, much charming
country remains, particularly around Studham and Kensworth, where at 700
feet the chalk attains its highest elevation in the county.

The varied geology of Bedfordshire is echoed in the variety of its churches;
in the north of the county the influence of Northamptonshire masons appears
in the number of stone spires, fine ashlar masonry, and the use of the
ferruginous brown stone which has been the scenic ruin of the iron-mining
districts of the neighbour county. Wymington is the finest example, but
Swineshead, Podington, Keysoe, Colmworth and Pertenhall have churches
of very great merit. Two of the grandest buildings in the county, Felmersham
church of the 13th century, and Odell of the 15th, lie in this area. The
sandstone country has contributed a building stone which gives great character
to the churches of the district; Tingrith, Flitton and Northill are the most
perfect examples, and at Husborne Crawley church the stonework in the
tower is from the strata that gave the hills their name, being all shades of
deep green, from a brilliant malachite to an almost navy blue. The churches
of the south of the county are sometimes not very convincing from the outside,
since the Totternhoe stone has often weathered so badly that they have been
encased in 19th-century cement plaster with frightful aesthetic result. Flint
used in chequerboard pattern with clunch is a feature here and there, and
a very attractive one. The showplaces of the area are Dunstable Priory, and
the churches of Leighton Buzzard, Eaton Bray and St Mary's, Luton.

Bedfordshire has until this century lain far enough from London to escape
the overbuilding of, for example, Hertfordshire, and in consequence Victorian
church building is limited to Bedford, Luton and one or two examples
connected with the big estates, of which Clutton's magnificent St Mary's,
Woburn is outstanding. Butterfield did a little work at Milton Ernest church,
doubtless while engaged on his work at the Hall. Scott gave Turvey church
a chancel which it would be a euphemism to call a vigorous example of his
mature style; more suitable to some rich inner London suburb than a village
church, it is saved by impeccable craftsmanship, and a Collyweston roof.
Scott also worked at Eversholt in 1864 but on a more limited scale. There
is one building that must be seen by those who like their Victorian architecture
'neat', and that is the Bury Park Congregational church of 1895, an early
example of art nouveau Gothic which is one of Luton's many architectural
surprises; it is difficult to imagine it ever having been on paper! There is
one interesting 20th-century church, St Andrew's Blenheim Crescent, Luton,
a fine work by Sir Giles Gilbert Scott in his Cambridge University library
manner, with red brick and pantile roofs.

There has been a certain amount of ill-considered church restoration in the county, for example certain palpable falsities at Felmersham, referred to in the lists, but in the main, save for the barbarous rebuilding of Cardington, the county has been well served by its church restorers. Professor Richardson's rebuilding of Eaton Socon after the fire must rank as an achievement of a very high order, and the same may be said of his restoration at Streatley and elsewhere.

B.W.

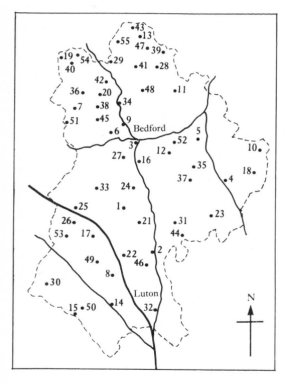

15 Eaton Bray
16 Elstow
17 Eversholt
18 Eyeworth
19 Farndish
20 Felmersham
21 Flitton
22 Harlington
23 Henlow
24 Houghton Conquest
25 Hulcote
26 Husborne Crawley
27 Kempston
28 Keysoe
29 Knotting
30 Leighton Buzzard
31 Lower Gravenhurst
32 Luton
33 Marston Moreteyne
34 Milton Ernest
35 Northill
36 Odell
37 Old Warden
38 Pavenham
39 Pertenhall
40 Podington
41 Riseley
42 Sharnbrook
43 Shelton
44 Shillington
45 Stevington
46 Streatley
47 Swineshead
48 Thurleigh
49 Toddington
50 Totternhoe
51 Turvey
52 Willington
53 Woburn
54 Wymington
55 Yelden

1 Ampthill
2 Barton-le-Cley
3 Bedford
4 Biggleswade
5 Blunham
6 Bromham
7 Carlton

8 Chalgrave
9 Clapham
10 Cockayne Hatley
11 Colmworth
12 Cople
13 Dean
14 Dunstable

Selected List of Churches

AMPTHILL
St Andrew
8m/12km S. of Bedford TL 0338
Close-like setting; small; 14th-century arcades and chancel. Over-restored; fine sandstone exterior. Well-maintained churchyard.

BARTON-LE-CLEY
St Nicholas
6m/10km N. of Luton TL 0832
Oasis in housing estate under chalk hills; Perpendicular tower, 15th- and 17th-century pews with linenfold panelling. 14th-century roof replete with angels, carved bosses and apostles.

BEDFORD
TL 0449
St Mary, St Mary's Square
Saxon/Norman, and 16th-century with 19th-century additions. Norman crossing tower with Perpendicular top. (Bedfordshire County Council.)
St Paul, St Paul's Square
This, the largest church in Bedford, is in its final form mainly a work of the 19th and early 20th centuries, but its magnificent silhouette and striking scale justify the process. The S. aisle with its porch is medieval, the former a fine two-storeyed structure of the 15th century. It is from this side that one first appreciates that the building is a 'hall church', its clerestory windows being directly over those of the aisles. The tower and spire are modern, a somewhat enriched reconstruction of an original 14th-century feature. The modern W. door, a slightly anachronisitc combination of 14th- and 15th-century details, is very fine in effect. F. C. Eden did much to improve the interior, and the chancel is now a model of rubrical correctness.

BIGGLESWADE
St Andrew
9m/15km S.E. of Bedford TL 1844
Large, mainly Perpendicular. Elaborate vaulted two-storey porch; tower of 1720. 15th-century S. aisle roof with bosses.

BLUNHAM
St Edmund and St James
2m/3km N.W. of Sandy TL 1551
Massive yet delicate sandstone and limestone tower in thatch and whitewash village. Norman W. door, otherwise mainly Perpendicular, including the fine stone screen between the chancel and the S. chapel.

BROMHAM
St Owen
3m/4km W. of Bedford TL 0051
Parkland setting above the river; medieval in origin, largely rebuilt by Butterfield, 1868. Two-storey S. porch contains parish library of 1740. Alabaster tomb of 1603 and a recycled triple brass in chancel.

CARLTON
St Mary the Virgin
7m/11km N.W. of Bedford SP 9555
Norman and later with delightful small 15th-century chancel screen; 16th-century pews and 17th-century pulpit.

CHALGRAVE
All Saints
4m/6km N. of Dunstable TL 0027
Isolated site on plateau overlooking the Chiltern hills. A wonderful unspoiled interior, no doubt due to its poverty. The 13th-century carving of the nave arcade capitals is very fine and belongs to the Totternhoe stone group mentioned later. There are 15th-century traceried bench ends in the old pewing. The tower was reduced to its present height in 1889, consequent upon the failure of the Totternhoe stone as at Eaton Bray. Wall-paintings, impressive as an overall scheme, with heraldry, unusually featuring St Martin.

CLAPHAM
St Thomas of Canterbury
2m/3km N.W. of Bedford TL 0352
Important for the enormous Saxon tower with Norman top stage. 13th-century font; 17th-century communion table; chancel by Sir Giles Gilbert Scott, 1861–2.

COCKAYNE HATLEY
St John
2m/3km E. of Potton TL 2549
The church is Gothic, refitted like a college chapel in the 1820s with important baroque woodwork from France and Belgium; the stalls from Aulne Abbey date from 1689. Fine 13th-century and later painted glass, 15th- and 16th-century Cockayne brasses.

COLMWORTH
St Denys
7m/11km N.E. of Bedford TL 1058
Prominent 15th-century building with lofty spire and finely proportioned Perpendicular interior. In the chancel is the Dyer monument of 1641, one of the best in the county.

COPLE
All Saints
4m/6km E. of Bedford TL 1048
Attractive village. Structure mainly Perpendicular, including the delicate screen; 16th-century pews and chapels and a good collection of brasses.

DEAN
All Saints
11m/18km N. of Bedford TL 0467
Scattered and unspoiled village embowered in trees. The church has a perfect country interior; the roofs are wonderful specimens belonging to the 15th-century remodelling, when only the 13th-century chancel arch and the 14th-century tower and spire were retained. Old pewing and fine screens at the W. end of both chapels and across the chancel arch.

DUNSTABLE
St Peter
5m/8km W. of Luton TL 0121
This truncated fragment of Dunstable Priory still has a grandeur, particularly in its fine Norman nave of *c.* 1150, which makes the disappearance of the eastern parts a tragedy. The W. front is a magnificent makeshift, Norman and Early English in combination, of which the most lovely feature is the N.W. door, a sumptuous 13th-century creation loaded with ornament. Restored by Bodley in 1900 and later by Richardson. Scholarly re-creation of the Norman vaulting of the S. aisle, based upon the survival of three bays at the E. end. How much of the original material has been re-used is hard to tell,

but the general effect greatly enhances the monastic character of the building.

EATON BRAY
St Mary the Virgin
3m/4km W. of Dunstable SP 9720
Externally a complete 15th-century reconstruction and W. tower effectively conceal an interior, the core of the original 13th-century building, which has nave arcades of absolute and quite unexpected magnificence. That on the N. is the richer, with deep mouldings and conventional leaf-carving on the capitals, a *tour de force* of craftsmanship. On the S. arcade the decoration is simpler and the mouldings plainer, but the corbels at each end are wonderfully detailed. 13th-century font, a large bowl with four columns at the corners, richly carved to match the N. arcade. The village may well have been the centre of the Totternhoe stone school of carving. Thomas of Leighton may have been responsible for the 13th-century ironwork on the S. door.

ELSTOW
St Mary and St Helen
2m/3km S. of Bedford TL 0546
A church of monastic foundation, this truncated but magnificent remnant of a Norman cruciform church is the central feature of one of the most attractive villages in the county. The W. front was begun in the 13th century, but was never finished; it decayed until sensitive restoration by Professor Richardson. Two coeval 13th-century bays remain at the W. end inside, the rest being massive Norman work. The detached 15th-century bell-tower, witness to the religious doubts of the young John Bunyan, completes a noble composition.

EVERSHOLT
St John the Baptist
3m/4km E. of Woburn SP 9932
Wooded setting; 14th- and 15th-century Perpendicular; heavy Scott restoration of 1864, but details and fittings spared.

EYEWORTH
All Saints
4m/6km E. of Biggleswade TL 2445
Tree-rich setting. Steeple rebuilt after severe storm damage in 1967. Mostly 14th- and 15th-century with good 17th-century Anderson monuments.

FARNDISH
St Michael and All Angels
4m/6km S.E. of Wellingborough SP 9263
Tiny, of Northamptonshire type; 12th-century, except tower. Unusual S. doorway with alternating light and dark voussoirs.
    R.C.F.

FELMERSHAM
St Mary
6m/10km N.W. of Bedford SP 9957
Superb site looking out over the river. Begun in 1220 and finished in 20 years, this is the finest 'Early English' church in the county. The W. front is a noble arcaded composition. The raising of the nave walls in the 15th century to give a low pitched roof and clerestory, with a tower in place of an intended spire, created a fine four-square composition. Competent but inadmissible restoration in the chancel, carried out by J. Brandon in 1850, when he reinstated lancet windows to match the existing. Wonderful interior, particularly the great clustered piers of the crossing contrasting with the delicacy of an excellent 15th-century screen.

FLITTON
St John the Baptist
2m/3km S.E. of Ampthill TL 0535
Mainly late 15th-century Perpendicular. Impressive collection of 16th-century and later monuments, notably in the De Grey mausoleum at E. end.

HARLINGTON
St Mary the Virgin
7m/11km N.W. of Luton TL 0330
Wide view from churchyard. Charming interior with 13th-century arcades, carved nave roof-bosses, a good font and some 15th-century benches.

HENLOW
St Mary the Virgin
2m/3km E. of Shefford TL 1738
Mainly 15th-century with massive tower and early 14th-century arcades. Good range of 17th- and 18th-century mural tablets.

HOUGHTON CONQUEST
All Saints
2m/3km N. of Ampthill TL 0441
Sandstone and ashlar, 14th-century onwards, W. tower of 1393; stalls, glass, 15th-century wall-paintings and Conquest brasses.

HULCOTE
St Nicholas
4m/6km N. of Woburn SP 9438
Approached by a trackway. The initials of the builder, Richard Chernock, d. 1615, are picked out in the door studs. Delightful chaste interior retains coloured Chernock monument.

HUSBORNE CRAWLEY
St Mary Magdalene
2m/3km N. of Woburn SP 9535
Beside a farm in wooded, hilly setting. Tower built of unusual green sandstone. Restored in 19th century; 16th-century and later monuments.

KEMPSTON
All Saints
2m/3km S.W. of Bedford across R. Ouse. TL 0347
Riverside setting; Perpendicular outside, including the tower. 12th-century chancel arch, Early English arcades.

KEYSOE
St Mary the Virgin
8m/12km N. of Bedford TL 0762
Prominent spire; 14th- and 15th-century roofs; 14th-century font with French inscription. On the tower is a tablet recording a miraculous survival of a fall from the spire, and the survivor's comments as he fell.

KNOTTING
St Margaret
4m/6km S.E. of Rushden TL 0063
A delightful unrestored church with Norman nave, 13th-century chancel and transept and W. tower dated 1615. Simple 16th- and 17th-century furnishings and chancel gates dated 1637.

LEIGHTON BUZZARD
All Saints
11m/18km N.W. of Luton SP 9225
Attractive market-town setting; this is the finest parish church in the county. 13th-century, of cruciform plan and with a gigantic spire. The walls were raised in the 15th century and the magnificent timber roofs of typical flattish pitch were then constructed. The complete collegiate late 15th-century chancel, with seating and screens intact, is the great treasure of All Saints. Medieval graffiti on the piers, including a drawing of a Decorated window in the S. chapel. The elaborate ironwork on the W.

door may be by Thomas of Leighton, creator in 1294 of the delicate grille at the tomb of Queen Eleanor in Westminster Abbey. Good Kempe windows, 1887–1905. Excellent restoration after a major fire in 1985.

LOWER GRAVENHURST
Our Lady
2m/3km S.E. of Clophill TL 1135
14th-century Decorated, the work of Robert de Bilhemore whose brass is in the chancel. Unspoiled interior with pulpit, screen and benches.
    R.C.F.

LUTON
TL 0821
St Andrew, Blenheim Crescent
A fine church by Sir Giles Gilbert Scott, 1931–2. In red brick with pantile roofs and a massive W. tower. Effectively lit by grouped clerestory windows.
St Mary, Church Street
This magnificent church resists, by sheer architectural merit, the desolation of its setting. Begun in the 13th century, enlarged in the 14th, it reached its present form in the 15th when Lord Wenlock built his sumptuous chapel. Octagonal 14th-century baptistry, a work of great richness and competence. The W. tower has flint and clunch chequerwork panels, the latter, in part, replaced by harder limestone in modern times. Street's work in the chancel is of a dark richness, but the external refacing of the E. end was heartless. 14th-century font and canopy; Wenlock tombs.

MARSTON MORETEYNE
St Mary the Virgin
6m/10km S.W. of Bedford SP 9941
A magnificent building practically rebuilt in 1445 in the typical and slightly 'pursey' style of the time. A legacy of what Harvey called 'the rich harvest of the 1440s'. Very grand nave inside with slender pillars, the roof resplendent with bosses and angels. Detailing is bold and confident, though lacking the full richness of stained glass and screening. The detached bell-tower is a fine massive building; the whole is reminiscent of neighbouring Elstow.

MILTON ERNEST
All Saints
5m/8km N.W. of Bedford TL 0156
Norman chancel, 15th-century nave roof

and screen with rich, dark Butterfield embellishments. The Rolt family provided a wall monument, a chandelier (1728) and dole shelves in the N. aisle.

NORTHILL
St Mary the Virgin
2m/3km S.W. of Sandy TL 1446
Attractive blend of Totternhoe clunch and ironstone; 14th-century collegiate stalls. Golden glass of 1664 commissioned by the Grocers' Company.

ODELL
All Saints
8m/12km N.W. of Bedford SP 9657
Set on an eminence in a good stone village, an excellent example of a unified 15th-century church. Grand W. tower of Northamptonshire type; the gentle batter up to a pinnacled parapet relieves what might otherwise be an overpowering bulk. Lovely interior with tall arcades, an original rood screen and very satisfying diamond-pattern flooring in nave and aisles. 15th-century stained glass: a group of seraphs in the E. window of the S. aisle of a rare and naive beauty.

OLD WARDEN
St Leonard
4m/6km W. of Biggleswade TL 1343
Norman tower arch, Jacobean panelling and an abundance of other carved woodwork, much of it culled from abroad. Monuments include a lifesize Classical statue of Sir Samuel Ongley, d. 1726.

PAVENHAM
St Peter
5m/8km N.W. of Bedford SP 9855
On the hillside above one of the loveliest of the riverside villages, Pavenham church, like Old Warden, is full of carved panelling and rich woodwork, most of it installed in 1848; Jacobean in the main, consisting of everything from marquetry to high relief. Two-storey 13th-century S. porch, otherwise mostly Perpendicular.

PERTENHALL
St Peter
2m/3km S.W. of Kimbolton TL 0865
Secluded among trees; Norman with Gothic chancel. Delicate 15th-century screen with traces of paint; 17th-century communion rail and benches.

PODINGTON
St Mary the Virgin
5m/8km S.E. of Wellingborough SP 9462
Stone Nene Valley village. Mostly 13th-century, with 14th-century leaning spire. Norman font; monuments and Orlebar wall-plaques.

RISELEY
All Saints
8m/12km N. of Bedford TL 0462
Thatch and timber-framed village. 15th-century tower, roofs and seating; also a squint and fragments of Anglo-Saxon masonry.

SHARNBROOK
St Peter
7m/11km N.W. of Bedford SP 9959
Mostly Perpendicular outside, including the noble spire which surmounts a Decorated tower. Sensitive modern restoration. Massive Magniac mausoleum (19th-century) in the churchyard.

SHELTON
St Mary the Virgin
5m/8km E. of Higham Ferrers TL 0368
Remote and rustic, delightfully chaste inside. Norman and later fabric. Pews, screen and clear glass form a comely assemblage; a few wall-paintings.

SHILLINGTON
All Saints
3m/4km S.W. of Shefford TL 1234
A wonderful hill-top site, typical of many similar church-crowned hills along the line of the Chilterns. Alas, it was rather too long to fit the top comfortably, a factor which doubtless caused the failure of the tower footings in 1701. The present red-brick erection is not really worthy of the church. A clerestoried hall, hardly interrupted in its continuity from W. to E., this building is mainly a work of 1300, only slightly altered subsequently. The rood screen inside forms the only actual division and, save for the loss of its loft, is perfect. A vaulted crypt lies under the chancel; there are brasses, pews and screens to delight the eye.

STEVINGTON
St Mary the Virgin
4m/6km N.W. of Bedford SP 9853
On a terrace above the Ouse. Pre-Conquest tower, complete with long-and-short quoins,

and windows; 14th-century nave roof with shield-bearing supporters; brass to Sir Thomas Salle, d. 1422.

STREATLEY
St Margaret
5m/8km N. of Luton TL 0728
Mainly 14th-century, including the arcade; Victorian brick chancel; pews and pulpit with linenfold panelling. Well restored by Richardson.

SWINESHEAD
St Nicholas
10m/16km N. of Bedford TL 0565
Handsome Decorated church, including the tower, slender recessed spire and arcades. Richly carved Easter Sepulchre, good misericords and a fine W. door.

THURLEIGH
St Peter
6m/10km N. of Bedford TL 0558
By castle motte. Early Norman central tower with S. door, a crude Adam and Eve carved in the tympanum. Otherwise mostly Perpendicular with some early glass and a brass of *c.* 1420.

TODDINGTON
St George of England
5m/8km N. of Dunstable TL 0028
Beside a spacious green on a commanding hill-top site. Grand cruciform 13th–15th century; resplendent nave roof bedecked with angels, the whole suited to the former prosperity of this town. Unique three-storeyed priest's house on N. side.

TOTTERNHOE
St Giles
2m/3km W. of Dunstable SP 9821
This church, built from the quarries in the village, has an unusually fine exterior. In the gable of the nave is flint flushwork in the Chiltern style. Begun in the 14th century and adorned in the 16th by a pinnacled skyline, providing a most satisfactory silhouette. Inside, all is space and light with carved roofs and woodwork, brasses and a good E. window by John Piper.

TURVEY
All Saints
7m/11km W. of Bedford SP 9452
Victorian-Jacobean Ouse Valley village; pre-Conquest church with 14th–15th century

additions, sumptuously 'improved' by Sir Giles Gilbert Scott. Exuberant scrolled iron-work on S. door by the local man, Thomas of Leighton. A fine collection of 15th- and 16th-century brasses and monuments, largely to the Morduant family.

WILLINGTON
St Lawrence

4m/6km E. of Bedford TL 1149
Grand early 16th-century, paid for by Sir John Gostwick, d. 1545, who was in the service of Henry VIII; his tomb is beside the altar. Memorable N. chapel with helmets and monuments.

WOBURN
St Mary

5m/8km N. of Leighton Buzzard SP 9433
St Mary's was erected in 1865–8 by William, eighth Duke of Bedford, to the designs of Henry Clutton, Bath stone being used throughout. It is an absolutely magnificent building; the interior is vaulted in stone and the echoes of the Ile de France are strong. The tall reredos by Caroe, choir-stalls and pulpit are later additions.

WYMINGTON
St Lawrence

2m/3km S. of Rushden SP 9564
Begun in 1350 by John Curteys, who, with his wife, is buried in the chancel. This church must be an example of work carried out by masons based on jobs in the neighbouring county of Northamptonshire, but working here on a slightly tighter budget. All the Nene Valley features are to be seen, though delightfully out of scale, particularly in the tower and spire which are lavishly ornamented. The interior is rich and complex, with a fine nave roof; with the remains of a suitably horrific 'Doom', old pewing and some colour still on capitals and arches, the building provides the county's best instance of the luxuriant spirit of the 14th century.

YELDEN
St Mary

4m/6km E. of Rushden TL 0167
Mostly Decorated, including the handsome ogee tomb recess in the S. aisle. Wall-paintings, brasses, Perpendicular font cover and pulpit from which Bunyan preached on Christmas Day, 1659.

Berkshire

Introduction

Berkshire has four chief types of scenery. In the east of the county, on the London side, is much wild heath and pine-wood, the sort of country which, almost uninhabited until the 19th century, now grows public institutions like schools, prisons and barracks, and small modern villas along the main roads and by electric railways. The Thames forms the northern border, and here is orchard-land extending several miles south until the Downs are reached. The south-west and west of the county are mostly chalk downs, and the scenery is similar to the Wiltshire downland into which it merges. The older houses and farm buildings of these districts are timber, brick and cob, and generally thatched or red-tiled. The towns, except for Faringdon, are all built of brick and are all, except for Reading, comparatively small. The far north-west corner of the county is limestone, and Faringdon, and such villages as Wytham, Coleshill, the Coxwells and Buckland, are like Cotswold places with houses and churches built of golden-grey stone.

Until the end of the last century, when transport from London turned half of the county into a semi-suburb, Berkshire was thinly populated. There the churches were cottage-like with wooden belfries, thatched barns, farms and houses of downland hamlets. A few small flint towers arose from pleasant red-brick towns beside the Thames and Kennet, and there still are a great many commons and heaths, such as are so beautifully described by Miss Mitford in *Our Village*, and in the far north-west, already mentioned, is the limestone district which looks like the Cotswolds. The brickwork in Berkshire was never so impressive as that of Kent and Sussex, nor is its limestone area comparable for beauty with Oxfordshire and Gloucestershire, except for the 13th-century tithe barn at Great Coxwell, one of the great medieval monuments of England. The eastern and London half of the county was transformed first by railways and again by buses, bringing more monied people from London, who have settled down in detached residences wherever the train service is convenient. These people built themselves new churches, and rebuilt old ones.

Berkshire is not a great county for ancient churches. The only grand example is St George's Chapel at Windsor (Perpendicular). Avington and Padworth have complete and small Norman churches. The best old churches will be found not in the Kennet valley, where these two are, but along the north slopes of the Downs, to which stone for building could be brought fairly easily by river and then by trackway. The few big medieval churches of Berkshire, with the exception of Lambourn and Newbury, are in the northern half of the county – Blewbury, East Hagbourne, Wantage, Sparsholt, Uffington, Childrey, Cholsey, North Moreton, Stanford-in-the-Vale, Faringdon, Abingdon, Sutton Courtenay, Cumnor, Shottesbrooke and Warfield. The churches on the downs and commons were nearly all small cottage-like buildings. One may see aquatints of some of them in *Views of Reading Abbey and the Principal Churches Connected Therewith* (1805), and in Buckler's drawings in the British Museum. They had flint and rubble walls, rendered (or plastered) outside (the flint Norman towers of Shefford and Welford were built circular, like many church towers in East Anglia, because of the lack of stone for the corners); the roofs were of tile with dormer windows, and there was usually a wooden belfry at the west end, and a 17th- or 18th-century porch in brick. Such buildings must have seemed very unecclesiastical to rich and pious landowners long or newly settled in Berkshire, which by the 19th century had become a 'home county' influenced by the prosperity of the metropolis. So they were pulled down or else vigorously restored, stripped of their external and internal plaster, retaining perhaps only an arcade or a window of the original building. Some churches of this small cottage type survive, as at Avington, Ashampstead, Catmore, East Shefford, Padworth, Wasing and Wootton.

The great Victorian architects left their mark on Berkshire. But because the county was not much industrialized until the present century, there is less Victorian building than in Middlesex, Surrey or Kent. G. E. Street (1824–81), who lived at Wantage at the beginning of his successful career, designed many charming church schools and vicarages in that district, and a bold new church and adjoining buildings at Boyne Hill, Maidenhead. Butterfield beautifully and conservatively restored Shottesbrooke and published a monograph about it. The best work of Victorian architects, together with that of the 18th and present centuries, is noted in the lists below. On the whole Berkshire has not been well served by those who rebuilt its churches. They had more money at their disposal than sensibility. But at least they built churches.

J.B.

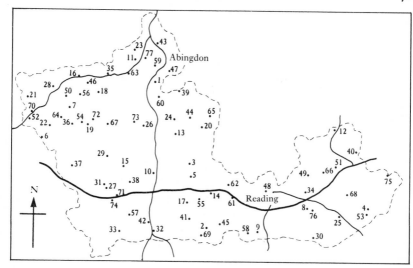

1	Abingdon	27	East Shefford	53	Shrivenham
2	Aldermaston	28	Faringdon	54	South Ascot
3	Aldworth	29	Fawley	55	Sparsholt
4	Ascot Heath	30	Finchampstead	56	Stanford Dingley
5	Ashampstead	31	Great Shefford	57	Stanford-in-the-Vale
6	Ashbury	32	Greenham	58	Stockcross
7	Baulking	33	Hamstead Marshall	59	Stratfield Mortimer
8	Bearwood	34	Hurley	60	Sunningwell
9	Beech Hill	35	Hurst	61	Sutton Courtenay
10	Beedon	36	Kingston Bagpuize	62	Theale
11	Besselsleigh	37	Kingston Lisle	63	Tidmarsh
12	Bisham	38	Lambourn	64	Tubney
13	Blewbury	39	Leckhampstead	65	Uffington
14	Bradfield	40	Long Wittenham	66	Wallingford
15	Brightwalton	41	Maidenhead	67	Waltham St Lawrence
16	Buckland	42	Midgham	68	Wantage
17	Bucklebury	43	Newbury	69	Warfield
18	Charney Bassett	44	New Hinksey	70	Wasing
19	Childrey	45	North Moreton	71	Watchfield
20	Cholsey	46	Padworth	72	Welford
21	Coleshill	47	Pusey	73	West Challow
22	Compton Beauchamp	48	Radley	74	West Hendred
23	Cumnor	49	Reading	75	Wickham
24	East Hagbourne	50	Ruscombe	76	Windsor
25	Easthampstead	51	Shellingford	77	Wokingham
26	East Hendred	52	Shottesbrooke	78	Wootton

Selected List of Churches

ABINGDON
St Helen
6m/10km S. of Oxford SU 4997
Set among 17th- and 18th-century brick almshouses by the Thames. A large town church with a spire and five parallel aisles, so that it is broader than it is long. There are decidedly graceful arcades and the whole building is mostly 14th-, 15th- and 16th-century Perpendicular. Distinguished and unique painted roof of late 14th century. Font cover and pulpit 17th-century; Hawkins monument (1782) by John Hickey. Late Georgian stained and enamelled glass window in N.W. corner; reredos by G. F. Bodley, 1897.

ALDERMASTON
St Mary the Virgin
8m/12km E. of Newbury SU 5965
Norman details. 13th-century painted glass roundels of the Annunciation and the Coronation of the Virgin; 14th- and 15th-century wall-paintings.

ALDWORTH
St Mary the Virgin
3m/4km W. of Streatley SU 5579
Huge stone effigies of the De La Beche family, supposedly 14th-century, set beneath wonderfully carved cusped canopies.

ASCOT HEATH
All Saints
6m/10km S.W. of Windsor SU 9268
T. H. Rushforth, 1864. Good paintings in the aisle and chancel by Heaton, Butler & Bayne.

ASHAMPSTEAD
St Clement
3m/4km S.W. of Streatley SU 5676
Extensive 13th-century wall-paintings including the Annunciation and Christ in Majesty.

ASHBURY
St Mary the Virgin
7m/11km E. of Swindon SU 2685
Of Norman origins, with good 13th-century

work including fine tracery. Excellent two-storey porch with delicate star vault; Perpendicular arcades and king-post roof; chapel in N. transept by Martin Travers.

BAULKING
St Nicholas
4m/6km S.E. of Faringdon SU 3190
Small, rustic; mainly 13th-century; good nave roof, surprisingly dated 1708, and Jacobean pulpit.

BEARWOOD
St Catherine
near Sindlesham SU 4878
1846 by Good; ashlar fabric and glass by Wailes. Angelic monument of 1870 by Matthew Noble.

BEECH HILL
St Mary
6m/10km S. of Reading SU 6964
Lovely rural setting; a delightful church by Butterfield, 1866–7. A large tiled roof covers nave and chancel, with tile-clad bellcote. Colourful interior with good furnishings, tiling, and stained glass by Gibbs.

BEEDON
St Nicholas
7m/11km N. of Newbury SU 4878
Setting; charming early 13th-century with triple lancets at E. end; old roof to nave .

BESSELSLEIGH
St Lawrence
4m/6km N.W. of Abingdon SP 4501
Set in tree-shaded park; Cotswold style and small. Only church in county to retain all its box pews and all original seating and ritual arrangements. Churchyard monument by Eric Gill, 1932.

BISHAM
All Saints
½m/1km S. of Marlow across R. Thames SU 8585
Setting. Heavily restored by Ferrey, 1849. Tower 12th-century. Hoby monuments 16th- and early 17th-century.

BLEWBURY
St Michael and All Angels
3m/4km S. of Didcot SU 5385
A picturesque village of brick and cob and thatch among willows and orchards at foot of Downs; the large cruciform church in various medieval styles is, for Berkshire, large, spacious, light and impressive with pre-Perpendicular work predominating.

BRADFIELD
St Andrew
3m/4km S.W. of Pangbourne SU 6072
Brick and timber village and public school in a high, gravelly district. Church almost wholly rebuilt by Sir George Gilbert Scott, 1847, and turned into something which, inside, is long-drawn, mysterious and vast in his transitional style, known as 'square abacus'.

BRIGHTWALTON
All Saints
8m/12km N. of Newbury SU 4279
The church groups well with the school, also by G. E. Street, 1862; glass attributed to Burne-Jones over font. Reredos with Christ in Majesty by Thomas Earp. The Early Decorated style is explored in a traditional way with superb timber roofs and furnishings.

BUCKLAND
St Mary the Virgin
4m/6km N.E. of Faringdon SU 3498
Large cruciform church, various dates. S. transept rich late-Victorian, with mosaic decorations by Powell's.

BUCKLEBURY
St Mary
6m/10km N.E. of Newbury SU 5570
Village; 15th-century flintwork, early 18th-century interior and windows by Brangwyn, 1912–19.

CHARNEY BASSETT
St Peter
4m/6km N. of Wantage SU 3894
Village; 12th-century, refashioned in late 15th century. Good Norman tympanum over S. door.

CHILDREY
St Mary the Virgin
2m/3km W. of Wantage SU 3687
One of the most interesting churches in Berkshire. Mainly Perpendicular and Decorated, cruciform; 12th-century lead font, screen and chancel stalls 15th-century, brasses 15th-century.

CHOLSEY
St Mary
2m/3km S.W. of Wallingford SU 5886
Setting; cruciform with central tower; 12th-century with 13th–14th century additions.

COLESHILL
All Saints
4m/6km W. of Faringdon SU 2393
Setting; 12th–13th century fabric with 15th-century tower; refashioned in 18th century and restored by Street.

COMPTON BEAUCHAMP
St Swithun
5m/8km S. of Faringdon SU 2887
Small medieval church built of chalk, at the foot of the Downs and beside a moated manor house, a beautiful situation. Uplifting white interior decorated with gilded altar, classic font cover, gilded monuments, rich rood and other furnishings, mostly by Martin Travers (20th century).

CUMNOR
St Michael
4m/6km W. of Oxford SP 4604
12th-century and later; unusual 17th-century spiral tower staircase.

EAST HAGBOURNE
St Andrew
1m/2km S.E. of Didcot SU 5388
Picturesque village of cob, timber framing and thatch. Spacious church, mostly 14th- and 15th-century. Many fine 18th-century tombs. Interior light and full of texture; old wooden roofs, some 14th-century glass.

EASTHAMPSTEAD
St Michael and All Angels, and St Mary Magdalene
S. district of Bracknell SU 8667
J. W. Hugall, 1866; five Burne-Jones windows, 1876. 15th- and 16th-century brasses.

EAST HENDRED
St Augustine of Canterbury
4m/6km E. of Wantage SU 4588
Heavily restored but grouping well. 13th-century arcades, 17th- century pulpit with

canopy and hour-glass, other good wood-work.

EAST SHEFFORD
St Thomas
1m/2km S.E. of Gt Shefford SU 3975
A small, simple church with wooden bell-turret. Wall-paintings discovered by Eve Baker; good 14th- and 15th-century monuments to members of the Fettiplace family; pleasant pewed interior.
R.C.F.

FARINGDON
All Saints
11m/18km N.E. of Swindon SU 2895
Large, cruciform town church, backed by trees of Faringdon House, and looking down towards market-place of this limestone country town. Interior over-pewed, but is mostly 12th- and 13th-century, and has many vistas. Stiff-leaved foliage, Early English carving on capitals; 17th- and 18th-century monuments to Unton and Pye families.

FAWLEY
St Mary
4m/6km S. of Wantage SU 3981
Well set on the Berkshire Downs, a fine church by G. E. Street, 1865–6. Sombre in rock-faced ashlar. Excellent contemporary furnishings. Mosaic by Salviati and windows by Morris and John Piper.

FINCHAMPSTEAD
St James
4m/6km W. of Newbury SU 4165
Various dates with brick tower, 1720. Norman pillar piscina and font.

GREAT SHEFFORD
St Mary
5m/8km N.E. of Hungerford SU 3875
Norman with round tower, rare in Berkshire, and tub-shaped font.

GREENHAM
St Mary
Suburb of Newbury SU 4865
A small church by H. Woodyer, 1875–6, in flint with narrow lancets. Dramatic W. bellcote. Stencilled interior contains baptistry with marble piers.

HAMSTEAD MARSHALL
St Mary
4m/6km W. of Newbury SU 4165
Adjunct of vanished country house, whose large brick-walled garden and sculptured piers remain. Little rustic and medieval church, mostly Jacobean and Georgian inside with some old high pews, three-decker pulpit and brick floors.

HURLEY
St Mary the Virgin
4m/6km N.W. of Maidenhead SU 8283
River-valley setting. Long and narrow nave of former priory; Norman and later; 16th- and 17th-century monuments.

HURST
St Nicholas
5m/8km E. of Reading SU 7973
Set among trees and old brick and timber cottages, the brick having the dark richness of old Middlesex brick. Brick tower, 1612; church Norman and later. Interior full of 17th-century woodwork, and many grand 17th- and 18th-century monuments.

KINGSTON BAGPUIZE
St John the Baptist
6m/10km W. of Abingdon SU 4098
Originally J. Fidel of Faringdon, 1799–1800, apsed and altered in 1882. Tuscan W. doorway and a pretty cupola on wooden columns. Canopied Fettiplace monument, 1710.

KINGSTON LISLE
St John the Baptist
5m/8km W. of Wantage SU 3287
Village; 12th-century, refashioned in 14th century and later; late 14th-century wall-paintings of Saints Peter and Paul and Herod's Feast.

LAMBOURN
St Michael and All Angels
12m/19km N.W. of Newbury SU 4376
Small downland town of racing stables. Grand cruciform medieval church of various dates, starting with late Norman, to which were added the 15th- and 16th-century chapels, the 16th-century work being much more than village masonry. In an arch of the S. transept lively carving of hounds coursing a hare; 16th-century tombs and brasses and remains of glass. The whole interior very white, and pleasantly plastered exterior.

LECKHAMPSTEAD
St James
6m/10km N. of Newbury SU 4376
S. S. Teulon, 1859. Cruciform, flint with red-brick dressings and bands; polychromatic brick interior; well-crafted timber roof with huge cusped trusses.

LONG WITTENHAM
St Mary the Virgin
3m/4km N.E. of Didcot SU 5493
Village; mainly 13th- and 14th-century with earlier and later details; much 17th-century woodwork, some from Exeter College, Oxford.

MAIDENHEAD
All Saints, Boyne Hill
5m/8km W. of Slough SU 8881
A Tractarian group – vicarage, school, church buildings, church, separate tower and spire (1865), all by G. E. Street, 1854–8, in local red brick. The buildings look well from all directions. Interior of church vast, violently coloured, richly dark with, as in all Street buildings, careful detail in ironwork, wood and coloured decoration.

MIDGHAM
St Matthew
5m/8km E. of Newbury SU 5567
Hill-top setting. A flint church of the Decorated style by John Johnson, 1869, with S.W. broach spire. Magnificent interior with showy polished granite piers, excellent carving and tiled chancel floor.

NEWBURY
16m/25km W. of Reading SU 4767
St George, Wash Common
F. C. Eden, 1933; white exterior and tunnel-vaulted in the Italian manner.
St Nicholas
Late town Perpendicular, much restored. Gothic archways in churchyard. Fine carved pulpit of 1607 and 16th-century brasses.

NEW HINKSEY
St John the Evangelist
district of Oxford, in S. of city centre SP 5104
Sir Ninian Comper, 1899, unfinished, having nave and aisles but no chancel. Reredos and banner also by Comper.

NORTH MORETON
All Saints
2m/3km E. of Didcot SU 5689
Attractive brick and cob and timber village.

Fair-sized village church, late 13th-century. Superb 14th-century chantry chapel of Stapleton family, with geometrical tracery and spirited carving outside, its E. window of five lights filled with 14th-century glass, showing the Passion and incidents in the life of Our Lady, St Peter, St Paul and St Nicholas. Remains of 14th-century glass in other windows.

PADWORTH
St John the Baptist
8m/12km S.W. of Reading SU 6166
A large, plain 18th-century house, with the aisleless Norman (12th-century) church beside it. Exterior still plastered, and with charming limewash on the tracery of the five Perpendicular windows. The interior is impressive and seems vaster than Avington, with which it compares for Norman perfection. Semi-domed apse, Norman chancel arch and north and south doors; remains of wall-painting; 18th-century monuments.

PUSEY
All Saints
4m/6km E. of Faringdon SU 3596
1745–50 and early 19th-century in the Greek taste with Venetian windows and screens. Monuments and a fine Entombment relief of *c.* 1500.

RADLEY
St James the Great
2m/3km N.E. of Abingdon SU 5199
Oxfordshire-style limestone, with fine 18th-century headstones in churchyard. Dark, and interior filled with 16th- and 17th-century armorial glass, well repaired and added to by Thomas Willement, 1840. 17th-century stalls in chancel and other old woodwork elsewhere.

READING
36m/58km W. of London SU 7173
Christ Church, Christ Church Road
H. Woodyer, 1861–74. Spirited High Victorian essay with rich reredos by Birnie Philip and Hardman glass. Upper part of the chancel arch is filled with reticulated tracery: the Veil of the Temple. Originally a chapel of ease.
St Bartholomew, London Road
Excellent chancel and transepts by Bodley, 1881, attached to an earlier nave by Waterhouse, 1879; his first large-scale essay in church building. Red and grey brick.

St Giles, Southampton Street
By J. P. St Aubyn, 1873, in the Early English style. Aisle walls 13th-century; genuine Perpendicular tower with added steeple; monuments.

St Laurence, Market Place
Mostly 15th-century with Perpendicular tower. Good inlaid 18th-century pulpit and very fine organ case of 1741; monuments, including that to John Blagrave, d. 1611, author of *The Mathematical Jewell.*

RUSCOMBE
St James the Great
adjoins Twyford to E. SU 7976
Norman chancel with 14th-century heavy wagon roof. Remainder of church and tower is brick with moulded brick window details, 1638–9. Tympanum with 17th-century paintings, recently restored, of the Commandments.

SHELLINGFORD
St Faith
2m/3km S.E. of Faringdon SU 3193
Aisleless, stone-spired limestone church beside remains of an old house. Interior rendered impressive by Frederick Etchells' restoration of 1948. Low, new box pews; plastered walls; tall Norman chancel arch; wide, light chancel with fine 17th- and 18th-century monuments; fragments of 15th-century glass reset in E. window.

SHOTTESBROOKE
St John the Baptist
3m/4km E. of Twyford SU 8477
A park-surrounded church in flat country near Maidenhead. Externally and internally a singularly complete cruciform Decorated design with central tower and lofty, elegant spire, all after 1337. Deeply moulded curvilinear window tracery. The church is clearly the work of one man, and he an architect with an outstanding sense of proportion. The white interior is tall and light and full of delicately carved 14th-century details, particularly Founder's tomb (hard white chalk) in N. transept, and sedilia in chancel. Brasses and pieces of 14th-century glass. This complete church is just the sort of thing the more medievalist Victorians tried to copy and could not quite manage. The Victorian restoration by G. E. Street, 1854, has done little harm.

SHRIVENHAM
St Andrew
6m/10km N.E. of Swindon SU 2489
17th-century rebuilding around a 14th-century central tower; a Tuscan arcade cheek by jowl with Perpendicular windows. Good pulpit, benches and panelling.

SOUTH ASCOT
All Souls
6m/10km S.W. of Windsor SU 9268
J. L. Pearson, 1896–7. S. Chapel by Martin Travers. Green frontal for high altar by Rev. Ernest Geldart. Kempe windows and painted wall-decoration by Heaton, Butler & Bayne.

SPARSHOLT
Holy Cross
3m/4km W. of Wantage SU 3587
Cob and thatched village at foot of N. Downs. Spired church has plastered exterior and several stately Decorated 14th-century traceried windows. Interior spacious and countrified with ancient wooden nave roof, stone floors and, in S. transept, three carved wooden effigies of 14th century, one of a woman being singularly beautiful. Hard chalk sedilia in chancel and Easter Sepulchre (14th-century). Fragments of medieval glass; chancel, unfortunately stripped of plaster, has unlovely E. window.

STANFORD DINGLEY
St Denys
5m/8km S.W. of Pangbourne SU 5771
Flint with weatherboarded bell-turret. Interesting interior from 12th century. Glazed medieval bricks built into the N. respond of the chancel arch. Traces of 13th-century paintings.

STANFORD-IN-THE-VALE
St Denys
5m/8km N.W. of Wantage SU 3493
Village; mainly 13th- and 14th-century. Good piscina and remarkable Jacobean font with carved, panelled wooden casing.

STOCKCROSS
St John
3m/4km W. of Newbury SU 4368
1839. Blue brick. Elegantly refurbished by Sir Ninian Comper in 1905.

STRATFIELD MORTIMER
St Mary
6m/10km S.W. of Reading SU 6664
R. Armstrong, 1869. Rock-faced ashlar with broach spire. Inscribed Anglo-Saxon coffin lid and 15th-century brasses.

SUNNINGWELL
St Leonard
2m/3km N. of Abingdon SP 4900
Delightful heptagonal W. porch of 1562 in which Ionic columns are mixed with Gothic windows; it was supposed to have been given by Bishop Jewel of Salisbury.

SUTTON COURTENAY
All Saints
3m/4km N.W. of Didcot SU 5093
A show Thames-side village with wide, tree-lined street of old houses of various dates. Large church for Berkshire, of various dates, too, from 12th century onwards. 15th-century woodwork, remains of glass, old floors, some box pews. Nothing is outstanding, but the general effect outside and within is of gradual growth through the centuries; full of gentle texture and colours.

THEALE
Holy Trinity
5m/8km W. of Reading SU 6471
E. Garbett, 1822; an early and scholarly essay after the style of Salisbury Cathedral. Tower by J. Buckler. Here also is the chantry chapel of Bishop Waynflete, d. 1486, removed from Magdalen College, Oxford in 1830.

TIDMARSH
St Laurence
1m/2km S. of Pangbourne SU 6374
Fine Norman S. doorway of two Decorated orders; rare 13th-century polygonal apse; intriguing timber bell-turret designed by Victorian rector's wife.

TUBNEY
St Lawrence
4m/6km W. of Abingdon SU 4398
By A. W. N. Pugin, 1844–7. Nave with bellcote and ogee-headed windows, stencilled decoration on chancel roof. Octagonal font given by Queen Adelaide.

UFFINGTON
St Mary
4m/6km S. of Faringdon SU 3089
Large cruciform stone and pebble-dashed church, almost wholly Early English, at a corner of chalk and thatched vale village. 17th-century school-house nearby. Church quite cathedral-like outside, though spire fell in 18th century. Stone porches, transeptal chapels. Interior rather bare after restoration by G. E. Street, 1850. Clear glass; 17th-century monuments.

WALLINGFORD
12m/19km S.E. of Oxford SU 6089
St Leonard
Norman, and Victorian Norman, by Hakewill, 1849, who built the W. tower and S. arcade. Splendid 12th-century arches.
St Peter
Nave and tower 1760–9, the elegant openwork spire designed in 1777 by Sir Robert Taylor.
R.C.F.

WALTHAM ST LAWRENCE
St Lawrence
3m/4km E. of Twyford
Exterior largely Victorian; Norman and Gothic within. Decorated screen. Lych gate by N. Hannen, 1907.

WANTAGE
St Peter and St Paul
13m/21km S.W. of Oxford SU 3988
Large cruciform; 13th-century with Perpendicular additions. Perpendicular stalls with misericords; 14th-century effigies and brasses.

WARFIELD
St Michael the Archangel
2m/3km N. of Bracknell SU 8872
Large and fine for Berkshire, mostly 14th-century Decorated. Light, spacious and stately chancel, E. window with beautiful tracery and much carved chalk. Remains of 14th-century glass, 15th-century wooden screen and loft in N. aisle; also graceful 19th-century stone screen by G. E. Street, who restored the whole church most carefully.

WASING
St Nicholas
1m/2km S.W. of Aldermaston SU 5764
Park setting; small medieval church enlarged in 18th century. Collected 16th- and 17th-century painted glass.

WATCHFIELD
St Thomas
3m/4km E. of Highworth SU 2490
A small church by Street, 1857–8. Steep pitched roofs to church and bellcote. Well-proportioned with late 13th-century flavour. Simple interior and furnishings.

WELFORD
St Gregory
5m/8km N.W. of Newbury SU 4073
T. Talbot Bury, 1852–5, including the rebuilt Norman round tower; setting, brasses and tombs.

WEST CHALLOW
St Laurence
2m/3km W. of Wantage SU 3688
Village; rustic church with 14th-century double bellcote and porch with 15th-century bargeboards.

WEST HENDRED
Holy Trinity
3m/4km E. of Wantage SU 4488
Not such a show village as its neighbour, East Hendred, but stream-side church, mostly 15th-century Perpendicular. Pleasant plastered exterior and lead roofs. Interior not a disappointment; pieces of old glass; 17th-century woodwork; stone and tiled floors. Rustic attraction preserved by gentle restoration by Philip Johnston, 1929.

WICKHAM
St Swithun
6m/10km N.W. of Newbury SU 3971
Brick and thatch village, with church on hill above it; 11th-century tower to which is added a church rebuilt in expensive knapped flint with stone dressings, Benjamin Ferrey, 1854–9. The sumptuous interior is a mid-Victorian extravaganza. Lifesize elephants' heads in papier maché in N. aisle roof; limewood angels in nave roof; windows of mid-Victorian purple and red stained glass. Only inharmonious note is later E. window. Carving everywhere.

WINDSOR
All Saints
Frances Road SU 9676
A typical church by Sir Arthur Blomfield, appropriate in this Victorian suburb. Built in a Geometric style, of red brick with blue bands; the polychromatic effect is used internally also. Some contemporary fittings survive including organ case and gallery.

WOKINGHAM
St Paul
7m/11km S.E. of Reading SU 8168
H. Woodyer, 1862–4. Rock-faced ashlar with Decorated details in the High Victorian manner. Inside, an elaborately carved stone reredos, a chancel fresco and an eight-lobed font bedecked with water lilies, which anticipates the Art Nouveau, by Thomas Nicholls.

WOOTTON
St Peter
3m/4km N. of Abingdon SP 4701
Simple village interior; 14th-century lead font, Comper fittings and later timber bell-turret; 14th-century tiles; glass by Kempe.

Right: Early 14th-century north porch, St Mary Redcliffe, Bristol

Below: 13th-century north-west door, Dunstable Priory, Bedfordshire

All Saints and Church Close, Boyne Hill, Maidenhead, Berkshire, by G.E. Street, 1854–8

Early 17th-century monument in the Bedford Chapel, St Michael, Chenies, Buckinghamshire

Hammer-beam roof with host of angels, March, Cambridgeshire

Gunwalloe, Cornwall, with a detached tower built into the rock; 14th- and 15th-century

Lanercost Priory, Cumberland, from the north-west

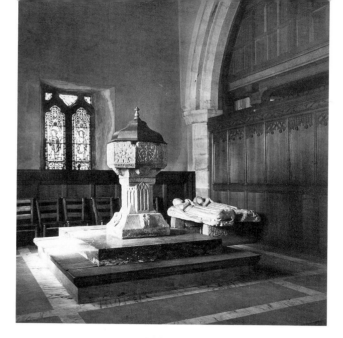

Above: Finely carved
14th-century font,
Crosthwaite,
Cumberland

Right: Alabaster tomb
of the Foljambes, St
Mary and All Saints,
Chesterfield,
Derbyshire

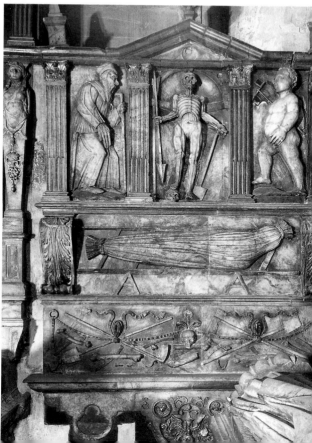

The church of the crooked spire, St Mary and All Saints, Chesterfield, Derbyshire

Nave with circular piers, stilted arches and much zig-zag, St Mary and All Saints, Melbourne, Derbyshire; Norman

Statue of patron saint on 14th-century south porch, Repton, Derbyshire

Bristol

Introduction

Among all our provincial cities Bristol has few rivals in the matter of old parish churches; some of its best are buildings that once served villages now engulfed in the city's suburbs or outer 'neighbourhoods'. York and Norwich may both beat Bristol in the actual numbers of their parish churches, which have outlasted both the Reformation and later, more insidious, nibblings by demolition gangs, bombs, and the amalgamators of livings. But Bristol's surviving medieval churches and church ruins make up a group whose sheer architectural quality is hard to beat, and after them come several which are good Georgian, and a few worth mentioning among the myriads of the Victorian host. Too many Bristol churches, alas, have themselves fallen victims to bombs and deliberate demolition; the latter process has been going on at intervals ever since St Lawrence's was pulled down in about 1580. Bristol has been too zealous a 'beautifier' for any parish church interior to be left untouched by the inroads of church furnishers of various dates. So one finds many Bristol churches whose contents include good monuments, ironwork, or other curios, but not one that can show a complete 'period' interior, whether medieval, 17th-century in the manner of Staunton Harold, or even Georgian. To see exactly how Bristol's churches looked inside in the days of high pews and parson and clerk, one must go to the City Art Gallery and look through the unique collection of Braikenridge drawings and water-colours – a perfect record, nearly 1,500 drawings strong – of how Bristol appeared at the tail end of her great Georgian phase.

B.L.

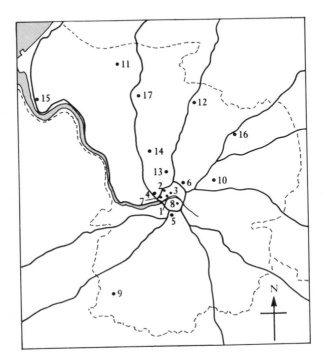

1   All Saints, Corn Street
2   Christ Church, Broad Street
3   St John the Baptist, Broad Street
4   St Mark's, College Green
5   St Mary Redcliffe
6   St Paul's, Portland Square
7   St Stephen's, St Stephen's Avenue
8   Temple Church, Victoria Street
9   Bishopsworth
10 Easton
11 Henbury
12 Horfield
13 Kingsdown
14 Redland
15 Shirehampton
16 Stapleton
17 Westbury-on-Trym

Selected List of Churches

CITY ST 5872
All Saints, Corn Street
A very old foundation and a truly lovely
English town church. Half the nave is late-
Norman, the rest particularly graceful Perpendicular, with the mullions of some
windows continued down the wall. The
simple N. tower is early Georgian, with a
delightful Corinthian cupola of 1807. The
church is full of monuments to commercial
families, the best being to the Colstons. One
Colston mural, set up soon after 1701, is a
brilliant little Baroque work, probably by
some London sculptor such as Richard
Crutcher. The one to Bristol's famous philanthropist, Edward Colston, is an Ionic composition by Gibbs, erected in 1729 by the
local mason, Daniel Sidnell. The magnificent reclining figure is by Rysbrack and is
worth going a long way to see. Now a
Diocesan exhibition and education centre.
Christ Church, Broad Street
Another church of very old foundation,
but rebuilt 1786–90, the architect being
the Bristolian William Paty. 17th-century
clock, etc., from the older church. An admirable late-Georgian building, with a lyrically
lovely interior whose pillars and saucer
domes derive from Gibbs at
St Martin-in-the-Fields. The tower and
spire a cross between Gibbs and Gothic. A
notably good Adam communion table, and
some bad Victorian Renaissance alterations.
St John the Baptist, Broad Street
A lovely little unaisled church, early Perpendicular above a vaulted crypt. The tower and
spire are specially picturesque, as they have
one of the city's gates immediately below.
A fine civilian effigy commemorates Walter
Frampton, 1388, and the church is full of
good things of various dates. The gallery,
font and other fittings are of the 17th
century, and the Holy Table, 1635, is
perhaps England's finest of its kind. A
church of great character, not much Victorianized.
    R.C.F.
*St Mark's, College Green (The Lord Mayor's
Chapel)*
This, in the Middle Ages, was the chapel

of St Mark's Hospital, and has never been
a parish church. At the Dissolution it passed
into civic hands, and is the only church in
England owned by a Corporation. Some of
the building is of the 13th century; there
are interesting 'Decorated' portions; the
Perpendicular tower is of 1487; and the early
16th-century architecture, including the delightful little fan-vaulted Poyntz chantry with
Spanish floor tiles, is really brilliant late-
Perpendicular. This chapel is one of the
most important sepulchral churches in
England. Many tombs are of civic magnates,
but they include a Bishop of Llandaff and the
mail-clad effigies of the Berkeley founders.
Generally speaking, a complete church-
trotter's paradise, and beautifully kept out
of the Bristol rates. Hatchments, Baroque
ironwork by William Edney, Charles II's
arms, and a specially magnificent collection
of glass, some of it always in St Mark's, the
rest foreign from the Bagot collection and
that of William Beckford of Fonthill. For
its size, one of the very best churches in
England.
St Mary Redcliffe, Redcliffe Way
The most splendid parochial church in
England. Its main distinction is its abbey-like
size and plan, with double-aisled transepts,
ambulatory, and E. Lady Chapel. One must
spend hours admiring it, not overlooking
the important work of about 1200 and the
glorious hexagonal N. porch of the early
14th century, with the poet Chatterton's mu-
niment room above it. Otherwise mostly
early Perpendicular with stone vaults and
hundreds of bosses, but the Renaissance
monuments disappointing. A brass eagle
lectern of 1638 and a fine Baroque iron
screen by Edney. Three fonts, one medieval,
one Georgian, one Victorian. Quite good
Victorian furniture, and a stone to The
Church Cat, 1912–27, in the churchyard.
St Paul's, Portland Square
By Daniel Hague and finished 1793. The
church of what was then a fashionable and
well-to-do residential district – an eastward
counterpart of Park Street up the hill towards
Clifton. Its tall tower, in diminishing stages,
is essentially a Wren design, but is tricked

out with Gothic detail. Inside, the church shows an important blend of Gothic and (to a greater degree) of Adamesque. Its memorials include a good one by Flaxman and Rossi to Lt-Col. Vassall, who was killed in 1807 in the attack on Montevideo.

St Stephen's, St Stephen's Avenue
One merchant's tomb of the late 14th century, otherwise all Perpendicular of about 1475; a fine, clerestoried hall church with lofty arcades and no chancel arch. The elaborate tower, with its coronal of pierced pinnacles, was probably by a designer of the group that worked on Gloucester Cathedral; we know that Benet the Freemason did the charming fan-vaulted porch. This church has good monuments, and in pre-Victorian days had superb early Georgian mahogany furniture.

Temple Church (Holy Cross), Victoria Street
Leaning tower of Perpendicular date unique in England, associated with the Knights Templar. Excavation has revealed the original oval shape of the nave.

OUTER BRISTOL

BISHOPSWORTH
St Peter
S.W. district of Bristol ST 5668
Entertaining early Victorian-Norman, 1842, by local designer S. C. Fripp. Restrained exterior with small windows, flat buttresses and a corbel table; tower with pyramidal roof.

EASTON
All Hallows
All Hallows Road, S.W. district of Bristol ST 5668
The best of Bristol's very late Victorian churches by Crisp and Oatley; unfortunately only one part of the nave was ever built, but the neo-Decorated apsidal chancel, with an ambulatory behind the high altar, is dignified and imposing.

HENBURY
St Mary the Virgin
Church Lane, N.W. district of Bristol ST 5678
Another village church whose tall arcades are good Early English. Much restoration and rebuilding by Street and some very queer Victorian grisaille glass. An unusual wealth of mural monuments, of the Baroque and later schools, to 18th-century businessmen who had country residences at

Henbury. Best of all is the gravestone to Scipio Africanus, negro servant to the Earl of Suffolk, who died in 1720 aged 18.

HORFIELD
St Gregory's
Filton Road ST 5876
Good neo-Byzantine of 1934 by A. R. Gough; Martin Travers furnishings, and an attractive interior with its soft tones of brick and plaster.

KINGSDOWN
St Matthew's
Cothamside ST 5874
By Thomas Rickman, built in 1833-5. A good, stiff piece of pre-Tractarian Perpendicular. Inside, it has a more recent reredos, but otherwise a remarkably unaltered composition of arcades and three galleries, an organ case in correct early Revival Gothic, and the arms of William IV.

REDLAND
Redland Chapel (no dedication)
Redland Road, N. district of Bristol ST 5777
Once a chapel in Westbury parish. A delightful Classical building, with W. cupola and Ionic façade. Built in 1740-3, possibly designed by Richard Strahan and certainly finished by William Halfpenny. Fine Georgian woodwork inside, and some busts by Rysbrack. Victorian pews, but the general feeling still Georgian. On no account miss this one.

SHIREHAMPTON
St Mary's
W. district of Bristol ST 5377
By P. Hartland Thomas, 1929. Spirited 20th-century neo-Gothic; long nave with upper windows, 16th-century details. Built to serve one of Bristol's many housing estates.

STAPLETON
Holy Trinity
N.E. district of Bristol ST 6076
Another replacement of an older building, dating from 1856-7. Victorian Decorated in the manner of Pugin, the architect being John Norton, a pupil of Benjamin Ferrey, who himself studied under Pugin. An opulent composition and Bristol's best Victorian church, a mixture of carved stone and polished marble, with a really fine crocketed spire in the manner of the East Midlands.

Norman font; also a good set of Georgian murals to local residents.

WESTBURY-ON-TRYM
Holy Trinity
N. district of Bristol ST 5777

The best of Bristol's outlying churches, once partly collegiate, partly parochial. Much of it is of the 13th century, including the 'collegiate' sedilia in the S. aisle. The chancel, once the college choir, has graceful 15th-century architecture and the rarity of a Perpendicular apse (but cf. the bombed Coventry Cathedral). The tower is of that delicate beauty evolved by late 15th-century local designers who made one pinnacle rise like a needle above the rest. A Victorian tomb of Bishop Carpenter of Worcester, d. 1476; also many Georgian monuments to wealthy Bristolians who came to live in what was then a country parish.

Buckinghamshire

Introduction

Buckinghamshire is a somewhat curious county as regards its church architecture. It has never had a cathedral or any major monastic church. There are few large town churches to compare with those in many other counties, Aylesbury, High Wycombe, Chesham and Amersham being about the largest. There are few outstanding churches of major architectural note. But what the county lacks in this respect is more than made up in variety.

There is no 'Buckinghamshire type' of church, spire, tower or window, and in this county the architecture follows, in most instructive and interesting fashion, the geological formations of the land. The churches in the extreme south, in or bordering the Thames Valley, have an enormous variety of materials where stone is absent – brick, in such places as Dorney, Langley Marish, Fulmer, Hitcham, Penn and elsewhere. The earliest brickwork in the county, though it does not appear in the Chapel, is at Eton College, 1442. Then in the Chiltern belt there is, as one would of course expect, extensive use of clunch, chalk rubble and flint, with stone employed only for the dressings. The Vale of Aylesbury provides a further variety of materials, while the north of the county, penetrating into the limestone belt, produces good stone building in many of its churches, comparable with that in the neighbouring counties of Northamptonshire and Oxfordshire.

The only 'groups' that can be identified in Buckinghamshire are those of stone-carvers. At Ivinghoe there is a very fine set of mid or late 13th-century carved capitals in the nave, which obviously came from the same mason's workshop as Pitstone, Eaton Bray, Flamstead, Chalgrave and several other churches in the neighbourhood. Masons' marks also relate work at Eton College, North Marston and Hillesden with a group of travelling masons.

Then there is the series of Aylesbury fonts – a fine late 12th-century group taking its type-name from the font in Aylesbury church. Others may be seen at Bledlow, Buckland, Chenies, Great Kimble, Great Missenden, Little Missenden, Wing, Pitstone and Weston Turville, with some in Bedfordshire and Northamptonshire, besides several more obviously deriving from the same source.

The monuments at Chenies, Wing, Quainton and Amersham are equal to anything elsewhere; and the Kederminster Library at Langley Marish is a unique treasure.

E.C.R.

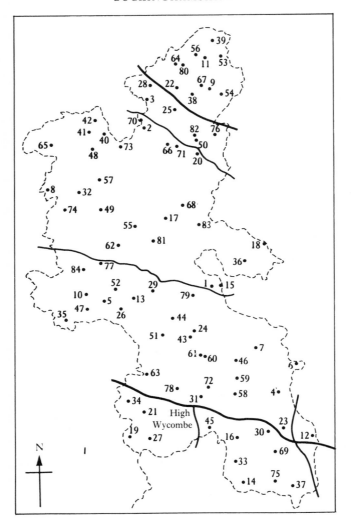

1	Amersham	33	Gayhurst
2	Aylesbury	34	Gerrards Cross
3	Beaconsfield	35	Great Hampden
4	Biddlesden	36	Great Linford
5	Bierton	37	Haddenham
6	Bledlow	38	Hambleden Valley
7	Bletchley	39	Hanslope
8	Bradenham	40	Hartwell
9	Bradwell	41	Hedgerley
10	Broughton	42	High Wycombe
11	Buckingham	43	Hillesden
12	Buckland	44	Hitcham
13	Calverton	45	Ibstone
14	Castlethorpe	46	Ickford
15	Chalfont St Giles	47	Ivinghoe
16	Chearsley	48	Langley Marish
17	Chenies	49	Lathbury
18	Chesham	50	Lavendon
19	Chetwode	51	Leckhampstead
20	Chicheley	52	Lillingstone Dayrell
21	Chilton	53	Lillingstone Lovell
22	Clifton Reynes	54	Little Hampden
23	Denham	55	Little Kimble
24	Dinton	56	Little Marlow
25	Dorney	57	Little Missenden
26	Drayton Beauchamp	58	Long Crendon
27	Dropmore	59	Maids Moreton
28	Dunton	60	Middle Claydon
29	Edlesborough	61	Milton Keynes Village
30	Fawley	62	Monks Risborough
31	Fenny Stratford	63	Nether Winchendon
32	Fingest	64	Newton Blossomville

65	North Crawley
66	North Marston
67	Olney
68	Padbury
69	Penn
70	Penn Street
71	Pitstone
72	Prestwood
73	Quainton
74	Radnage
75	Ravenstone
76	Shalstone
77	Shenley Church End
78	Sherington
79	Stewkley
80	Stoke Poges
81	Stony Stratford
82	Tattenhoe
83	Terriers
84	Thornton
85	Twyford
86	Upton
87	Wavendon
88	Westcott
89	West Wycombe
90	Weston Turville
91	Weston Underwood
92	Whitchurch
93	Willen
94	Wing
95	Wotton Underwood

Selected List of Churches

AMERSHAM
St Mary the Virgin
3m/4km S. of Chesham SU 9597
Town church; 14th–15th century; much Victorianized; many important monuments in chancel and Drake chapel.

AYLESBURY
St Mary
36m/58km N.W. of London SP 8113
The church stands on the highest point of the town in a large churchyard surrounded by 17th- and 18th-century houses. It is large, handsome and cruciform, with an interesting outline to its lead spirelet. An intriguing plan full of surprises, with side chapels in unusual places. Substantially 13th-century, its character a good deal spoilt by over-heavy Victorian restoration. A major re-ordering has closed off the W. bays of the nave and added a gallery. The fine font, *c.* 1180, is the prototype for a group in this and surrounding counties. A good Jacobean monument with a touching inscription in the N. transept; more tablets hidden in the S.E. chapel.

BEACONSFIELD
St Mary
5m/8km S.E. of High Wycombe SU 9490
Setting beside fine old rectory; medieval; heavily but well restored. Comper glass; churchyard monument to poet Waller, d. 1687, by W. Stanton.

BIDDLESDEN
St Margaret
4m/6km N.E. of Brackley SP 6340
Remote, on the Northamptonshire border. The little box-like church was once the private house chapel, part of the stable block, and is of the same date as the house, Biddlesden Park, 1730, which occupies the site of a Cistercian abbey. 18th-century fittings and clear glass, but undistinguished, its charm subsisting in its situation and pleasant texture.

BIERTON
St James the Great
2m/3km N.E. of Aylesbury SP 8415
A really good architectural composition, with lofty 14th-century arcades and central tower on clustered piers. The walls retain much old plaster and whitewash, with glimpses of paintings peeping through here and there; and the floor is a pleasant mixture of square red tiles or bricks and stone. There are several good details and fittings, including the Bosse monuments by W. Stanton.

BLEDLOW
Holy Trinity
2m/3km S.W. of Princes Risborough SP 7702
Splendidly placed on the lower Chiltern slopes, on the brink of the Lyde – a chalk coombe – overlooking the Vale of Aylesbury. The church contains many things worth while – nave arcades with carved capitals of about 1200; an Aylesbury font; fragments of wall-painting, including an amusing Adam and Eve; and a splendid S. doorway and porch, 13th–14th century, with traces of original colouring. The whole plan is very irregular, and the inclusion of the tower within the aisles lends interest and importance to the interior at the W. end.

BLETCHLEY
St Mary
at S. end of Milton Keynes SP 8733
Mainly 15th-century with notable W. tower and clerestory; some earlier features including a rich but reset Norman S. doorway and a tomb chest of 1442.

BRADENHAM
St Botolph
4m/6km N.W. of High Wycombe SU 8297
A perfect village-green setting. Norman S. door. The N.E. chapel has monuments and Tudor heraldic glass. Restored by Street, 1865.

BRADWELL
St Laurence
1m/2km S.E. of Wolverton SP 8339
Considerable 13th–14th century remains; rare inscription of *c.* 1200 on the chancel arch; stained glass by Clayton & Bell, *inter alia.*

BROUGHTON
St Lawrence
3m/4km S.E. of Newport Pagnell SP 8940
Interesting 14th- and 15th-century wall-paintings include St George and the Dragon, a Doom, and an unusual work combining a Pietà with the Wounds of Christ.
R.C.F.

BUCKINGHAM
St Peter & St Paul
SP 6933
Well-sited on motte of former castle. Built 1777–81, drastically altered by Sir George Gilbert Scott, 1862. Black marble columns adorn 13th-century-style Scott interior.

BUCKLAND
All Saints
2m/3km W. of Tring SP 8812
Unspoilt village setting. Early English, pleasantly whitewashed, mainly Victorian exterior.

CALVERTON
All Saints
1m/2km S. of Stony Stratford SP 7938
Instructive Victorian Gothic; neo-Norman W. tower, 1818–24. Complete contemporary fittings including glass by O'Connor, 1859.

CASTLETHORPE
St Simon & St Jude
3m/4km N. of Stony Stratford SP 7944
Medieval, of remarkable plan; 18th-century tower; monuments include that to Sir Thomas Tyrril, d. 1671, depicting the deceased and his wife beneath elaborate drapery.

CHALFONT ST GILES
St Giles
3m/4km S.E. of Amersham SU 9893
Village-green setting. Victorian exterior, but affording an interesting development of plan throughout Middle Ages; wall-paintings.

CHEARSLEY
St Nicholas
3m/4km N. of Thame SP 7110
A charming place, the church lying at the foot of a steep lane below the village, which overlooks the Valley of the Thame and its rich water meadows not far from Notley Abbey. The structure is mainly 15th-century. Like Nether Winchendon nearby,

it has mercifully escaped serious restoration and has a gallery which features the wooden support for the serpent, the largest of the instruments played by the band before the days of organs. There are two sets of Royal Arms, excellent modern pews and glass, a Norman font, and a brass of 1462. The step down into the chancel is unusual, and the whole place has a pleasant, mellow, uneven quality.

CHENIES
St Michael
4m/6km E. of Amersham TQ 0198
The church must be included here; for while it is in the main architecturally unimportant and somewhat spoiled by 'improvement', it stands most delightfully among the trees above the Chess Valley, hard by the mellow brick manor house of the Cheneys and Russells and the 'model' cottages of the village. But its principal feature is the fabulous series of monuments to the Russells, Dukes of Bedford, and their connections, in the N. chapel. The late Mrs Esdaile described them as 'one of the finest collections of tombs in England', ranging from the 14th to the 20th centuries. They are not accessible to the casual visitor.

CHESHAM
St Mary the Virgin
25m/40km N.W. of London SP 9601
Well-sited medieval town church, exterior vigorously restored by Scott, 1869. Intriguing interior; monuments; Lowndes mausoleum in the churchyard.

CHETWODE
St Mary & St Nicholas
5m/8km S.W. of Buckingham SP 6429
This is a remote and exciting place to reward the persistent voyager who may have approached it by way of the 'gated road route'! It is the choir or chancel of a small Augustinian priory, and became parochial as long ago as 1480, when the then parish church was ruinous and the monks were hopelessly impoverished. It has the best 13th-century work in Bucks. and, though some of it is reset and restored, the range of dog-toothed and deeply cut sedilia, the great five-lancet E. window, and the triple-lancet on the S. with 13th- and 14th-century glass, would be notable anywhere. The 14th-century N. chapel has become the manor pew with fireplace. There are hatchments and other good

things, including the earliest Royal Arms in any English church (Henry III).

CHICHELEY
St Laurence
2m/3km N.E. of Newport Pagnell SP 9045
Here is one of those splendid mixtures of dates and styles, from medieval to Comper, that make so many English village churches the delightful places they are. The church stands near the Hall and has a Decorated nave and N. aisle, a 15th-century central tower not unlike Sherrington, and a Classical chancel with delicate detail dated 1708, probably by Francis Smith of Warwick, who built the Hall. The central space was dealt with by Comper in 1904 and is effective. There are good Renaissance monuments to Caves and Chesters; box pews and a nicely antiquated air.

CHILTON
St Mary
4m/6km N. of Thame SP 6811
Part of village group, 13th–16th century. Good monuments and an 18th-century organ removed from Chilton House.

CLIFTON REYNES
St Mary the Virgin
5m/8km N. of Newport Pagnell SP 9051
Awkwardly placed (from the tourist's point of view) on the S. side of the Ouse away from Olney, and thus happily secluded. The church is of great interest, and by the odd proportions of its tall nave suggests a Saxon origin, though most of what we see is 13th-, 14th- and 15th-century. The principal features are the font with figures of saints (14th-century) and the series of medieval monuments to the Reynes family, including the great rarity of two pairs of early 14th-century wooden effigies.

DENHAM
St Mary
2m/3km N.W. of Uxbridge TQ 0487
At the end of an exceptionally handsome village street. Mainly 13th- and 15th-century. Purbeck marble font, brasses and monuments.

DINTON
St Peter & St Paul
4m/6km S.W. of Aylesbury SP 7611
Celebrated Norman door with inscribed tympanum bearing Tree of Life and beasts;

otherwise all is later with Perpendicular predominating.

DORNEY
St James the Less
3m/4km W. of Slough SU 9279
Dreams away in a backwater beside the splendid timbered house of Dorney Court. Tudor brick tower and bits of every period of architecture before and since, from Norman times to a 19th-century window of King Charles the Martyr, all on an intimate and miniature scale. Note especially 12th-century font; W. gallery, 1634; S. porch, 1663; 15th-century stalls and base of screen brought from elsewhere; 17th-century communion rails and other woodwork; and the fine Garrard monument, 1607, by Nicholas Johnson, in the little N. chapel.

DRAYTON BEAUCHAMP
St Mary the Virgin
1m/2km W. of Tring SP 9012
Well-situated outside the village at the foot of the Chiltern slope, it was rebuilt in the 15th century. The texture, with its mixture of ashlar, flint flushwork and ironstone, is most satisfying. There is a simple Norman font and an Apostle E. window of the 15th century. This was the home of the Cheney family, who are commemorated in two 14th-century brasses, in heraldic glass, and in the magnificent monument by William Woodman to Viscount Newhaven, the last of the family (1732).

DROPMORE
St Anne
Littleworth Common, 3m/4km S.W. of Beaconsfield SU 9385
A charming small brick and flint church by Butterfield, 1866. Attractive timbering details. Polychromatic interior with fine stained glass in E. window, by Gibbs; colourful marble font.

DUNTON
St Martin
4m/6km S.E. of Winslow SP 8224
A church with hardly any village, small and pleasantly unrestored. Box pews, W. gallery with texts and rectors' and churchwardens' names, 18th-century, painted on the front. Whitewashed walls and ceiling with a hint of medieval timbers above. Many Bucks. churches must have been like this a century or more ago.

EDLESBOROUGH
St Mary the Virgin
4m/6km S.W. of Dunstable SP 9719
Below the Chiltern scarp and sited on a great mound, isolated and exposed to all the winds that blow across the vale. Horribly maltreated in the last century (plaster stripping inside, cement rendering out) but contains the most wonderful things – complete screen, stalls, pulpit and tester, and roofs of the 15th century; transverse arches in the aisles, and a series of exceptionally interesting brasses, as well as a complicated succession of building periods which form one of the best medieval test papers I know.
R.C.F.

FAWLEY
St Mary
3m/4km N. of Henley-on-Thames SU 7586
In a scattered Chiltern hill-top village. The chancel, rebuilt in 1748, contains fine woodwork by Grinling Gibbons – font, pulpit, stalls, rails and panelling – all formerly in the chapel of Canons House, Middlesex. Piper stained glass and two formidable mausolea in the churchyard.

FENNY STRATFORD
St Martin
in E. part of Bletchley SP 8834
Browne Willis, antiquarian and eccentric church restorer, built this simple brick chapel, 1730. Some of his fittings survive – Tudor and 18th-century glass, flat heraldic roof, and his own monument. It is now the N. aisle to an idiosyncratic Victorian nave and chancel by William White.

FINGEST
St Bartholomew
5m/8km N. of Henley-on-Thames SU 7791
Fingest's mighty Norman tower is justly famous; it dwarfs the rest of the church and is set in a beautiful place.

GAYHURST
St Peter
3m/4km N.W. of Newport Pagnell SP 8546
A complete rebuilding in 1728 of a medieval church in the grounds of the great Elizabethan house nearby – designer unknown. The tower has urns at the corners, and a charming, airy little cupola in the centre. The sides of the nave are unusual with a central pediment, pilaster and doorway. The interior is practically unaltered, with good

plasterwork, pews, pulpit and panelling, and the splendid monument to Speaker Wright and his son, perhaps by Roubiliac.

GERRARDS CROSS
St James
4m/6km N.W. of Uxbridge TQ 0088
Sir W. Tite, 1859; Italian Byzantine. Domed with polychrome brick and campanile tower, the whole touched by a curious eclecticism.

GREAT HAMPDEN
St Mary Magdalene
3m/4km E. of Princes Risborough SP 8402
Park setting; flint fabric, mainly Perpendicular. Good font; monuments, including that to the celebrated John Hampden, parliamentarian; brasses and tiles.

GREAT LINFORD
St Andrew
2m/3km E. of Wolverton SP 8542
Pleasantly situated, it is reached past a handsome manor house and a 17th-century range built as village school and almshouses. A happy blend of the early 18th century and Decorated Gothic. The alterations inside to accommodate an increasing congregation are understandable but regrettable. At least the changes resulted in the discovery of a 15th-century tiled floor, part of which can still be viewed beneath the modern one.

HADDENHAM
St Mary the Virgin
3m/4km N.E. of Thame SP 7408
A good 13th-century and later church, lying at the extreme end of one of the most remarkable and complicated villages in Bucks., where many of the houses and walls are largely composed of wichert – a hard, compressed chalk marl. The W. tower overlooking the green is a good composition of the Early English period, and inside the spacious church, work of this date as well as of many other periods is found. Note 15th-century glass in N. transept window. A flat plaster ceiling of early 19th-century date tantalizingly hides a 14th-century timber roof. A rewarding mixture.

HAMBLEDEN VALLEY
St Mary the Virgin
3m/4km N.E. of Henley-on-Thames SU 7886
The church, though much Victorianized and unexciting architecturally, sits pleasantly in the centre of the village, in one of the most

attractive Chiltern valleys leading up from the Thames. The nave is unusual in its width and length without aisles. The fittings are the most interesting things: Norman font, Decorated sedilia and piscina, and the lovely D'Oyley monument (perhaps by Epiphanius Evesham) in the N. transept.

HANSLOPE
St James the Great
5m/8km N.W. of Newport Pagnell SP 8046
Set in a windy village on high ground, the steeple is seen for miles around; the tallest in Bucks., it was rebuilt to only two-thirds of its original height after an 18th-century fire. Norman chancel, 13th-century nave, and aisles which are very wide. Despite scraping, the interior has good fittings – pulpit, Royal Arms, hatchments, unusual family pew and brasses.

HARTWELL
St Mary the Virgin
2m/3km W. of Aylesbury SP 7916
Built in 1753 by Henry Keene in the Gothic taste to fit the landscaping of the park. After the lead was stolen in the 50s, the splendid plaster vaulting collapsed and today only the shell remains.
R.C.F.

HEDGERLEY
St Mary the Virgin
3m/4km S.E. of Beaconsfield SU 9687
The best Victorian Gothic church in the county – by Benjamin Ferrey, 1852. It is built of the local flint, with a little stone and conglomerate, and stands high on a grassy slope surrounded by trees. It is the third church on the site, and has some oddments from the older buildings – a medieval font with Jacobean cover; an old painting of the Commandments; some brasses; and a reputed piece of Charles I's cloak.

HIGH WYCOMBE
All Saints
28m/45km N.W. of London SU 8692
Large town church; 13th-century exterior heavily restored by Oldrid Scott; Gothic Revival tower by Henry Keene, 1755; 15th-century inside. Vast Scheemakers monument to Earl of Shelburne.

HILLESDEN
All Saints
3m/4km S. of Buckingham SP 6828
This is another of Buckinghamshire's lovely and lonely places. The church is almost entirely of the 15th century, and of a quality encountered hardly anywhere else in the county. There are contemporary roofs, seats, screen and glass (legend of St Nicholas) and a Te Deum frieze of alternate instrument-playing and scroll-bearing angels in the chancel. Note also good monuments, and the lovely canopy over the stair turret attached to the two-storey vestry and sacristy. This is the church that inspired Sir Giles Gilbert Scott with his Gothic passion – his father was a clergyman at Gawcott nearby – and it was he who gently restored it in the 19th century.

HITCHAM
St Mary
4m/6km W. of Slough SP 9382
Dangerously near Slough and the Bath road, this small church has an admirable mixture of materials and styles, lending both texture and interest: 16th-century brick tower; flint; chalk and plaster nave; Norman chancel arch; and one of those spacious rebuildings of chancels, *c.* 1330–40, that seem to abound. The chancel windows retain much of their original glass, depicting the Nine Orders of Angels and the Four Evangelists. Good monuments and brasses; the whole set among trees in a well-kept church-yard surrounded by ancient tawny brick walls.

IBSTONE
St Nicholas
2m/3km S. of Stokenchurch SU 7593
Small, intriguing church, sited away from the main village, overlooking the beautiful Turville Valley; primitive, mainly 12th- and 13th-century. Norman S. doorway, weather-boarded bell-turret, and Perpendicular pulpit.

ICKFORD
St Nicholas
4m/6km W. of Thame SP 6407
Mainly 13th-century. Comper glass. Font cover and other woodwork by Canon Staley, craftsman-vicar here early this century. Monument.

IVINGHOE

St Mary the Virgin

3m/4km N.E. of Tring SP 9416

A noble cruciform church, 13th–15th century, set in a large churchyard. Particularly fine are the stiff-leaf capitals of the nave arcades, the carved Apostles on the roof wall-posts, and the poppyheads on the benches, which include a mermaid and some haunting Green Men.

LANGLEY MARISH

St Mary the Virgin

E. district of Slough TQ 0179

Packed with interest: sandwiched between two lovely groups of brick and plaster almshouses – the old on the S. built by Sir John Kedermister in 1617, the new on the N. by Sir Henry Seymour about 1670. But not far beyond the tentacles of Slough. Brick 17th-century tower; remains of nave arcade, *c.* 1200, replaced by a timber one dated 1630; another spacious and rich 14th-century chancel; but, above all, the Kederminster and Seymour transept, pew and library, all of the first half of the 17th century and largely unaltered, with books on their shelves, painted panelling and grille, and heraldic overmantel over the fireplace. Hatchments, glass, carved Royal Arms, monuments, and everything a church should have.

LATHBURY

All Saints

1m/2km N. of Newport Pagnell SP 8745

Another dead-end place down by the Ouse just outside Newport Pagnell. The church is dark and mysterious with fragments of painting and robust carvings from its Norman past. Pleasantly battlemented without and a good stone texture.

LAVENDON

St Michael

2m/3km N.E. of Olney SP 9153

11th-century tower, nave and chancel; Perpendicular font, porch and details.

LECKHAMPSTEAD

The Assumption of St Mary the Virgin

3m/4km N.E. of Buckingham SP 7237

Remote setting; spirited Norman tympanum over S door; 14th-century effigy; brasses.

LILLINGSTONE DAYRELL

St Nicholas

4m/6km N. of Buckingham SP 7039

Reached by a long cart-track, this interesting church has 11th-century chancel and tower arches, a 13th-century chancel with a curious Easter Sepulchre, Dayrell brasses, a Renaissance tomb chest, old tiles, and a funeral pall of 1699.

LILLINGSTONE LOVELL

Assumption of the Blessed Virgin Mary

4m/6km N. of Buckingham SP 7140

Attractive group with Georgian rectory, one of the least altered small churches in the county. Early 13th-century tower, otherwise mostly Decorated with 17th- and 18th-century fittings: pulpit, rails, pews and hatchments.

LITTLE HAMPDEN

(dedication unknown)

3m/4km S. of Wendover SP 8503

Humble and withdrawn among a few cottages and scattered farms. Its simple interior with 13th–15th-century wall-paintings (including the earliest St Christopher in England) leaves a great impression of the medieval hamlet church. The timbered, two-storey N. porch is unique in Bucks. Tombstones by Eric Gill.

LITTLE KIMBLE

All Saints

3m/4km W. of Wendover SP 8207

Small and undistinguished externally, with little W. bell-turret, standing amidst beeches and greenery on the edge of Chequers park. Inside are to be found, artistically, the best wall-paintings in Bucks., including St Christopher, St James major, St George (a notable standing figure), St Lawrence, St Francis preaching to the birds (only two in England), St Clare, St Bernard, and assorted ecclesiastics, plus part of a Doom, and a life of St Margaret and St Catherine, all early 14th-century. There is also a square of Chertsey tiles under a mat in the chancel, with enchanting scenes from the life of King Mark of Cornwall and other Arthurian romances.

LITTLE MARLOW

St John Baptist

2m/3km N.E. of Marlow SU 8787

A good Thames-side village at a dead end and consequently almost unspoiled. The church has the unusual feature of a triple-gabled E. elevation, reminiscent of Devon or Cornish churches; and has a light, lime-washed interior. The chancel shows good 13th-century detail; the S. aisle and chapel were 'beautified' by Sir Nicholas Ledewich, so the inscription on his tomb tells us, about 1430.

LITTLE MISSENDEN
St John Baptist
3m/4km N.W. of Amersham SU 9298
The church stands by the manor house and a number of pleasant houses in the village. Externally very picturesque; of flint and brick with a dormer window in the nave roof. Inside, the Anglo-Saxon nave remains with re-used Roman tiles in the chancel arch. Exquisite E. window of three double-shafted lancets. It is principally renowned for its series of 13th- and 15th-century wall-paintings, which include St Christopher, a vivid Martyrdom of St Catherine, and a moving Crucifixion.

LONG CRENDON
St Mary the Virgin
2m/3km N.W. of Thame SP 6908
Well-set in attractive village. Early English with Perpendicular central tower. Grand 14th-century N. transept window. Large Jacobean monument with fine screen. 17th-century paintings of Moses and Aaron.

MAIDS MORETON
St Edmund
1m/2km N.E. of Buckingham SP 7035
The name commemorates the two Peover sisters who had the church rebuilt in the mid-15th century. It is tall, airy and light; there is fan vaulting over both porches and inside the tower. Inside the elaborate sedilia is a painting of *c.* 1600, and above the N. door a rare Jacobean bread-basket bedecked with balusters.

MIDDLE CLAYDON
All Saints
4m/6km S.W. of Winslow SP 7225
Nestles on a mound in the shadow of the great house. It contains an exceptional range of monuments, especially that to Margaret Giffard, 1531, and the grand one by Edward Marshall to Sir Edmund Verney, the royal standard-bearer, killed at Edgehill.

MILTON KEYNES VILLAGE
All Saints
in the E. area of the new town SP 8539
Despite the formation of the modern town of this name, this church still has a village setting. Text-book Decorated, early, with ballflowers; 15th-century rectorial brass in the chancel.

MONKS RISBOROUGH
St Dunstan
adjoins Princes Risborough to N. SP 8104
The general effect of this church is especially pleasing from the exterior, as it stands in a good churchyard with high hedges and trees and the Rectory hard by. The main part of the structure is 15th-century; inside there are good things to see, such as the 12th-century font, 14th-century tower arch and brass, a somewhat reduced painted screen, and remains of old glass.

NETHER WINCHENDON
St Nicholas
4m/6km N.E. of Thame SP 7312
One of the most attractive church interiors in the county and entirely unspoiled, in a rural village setting, at the foot of a steep hill. The structure is medieval, but the at-mosphere is of the 18th century, with gallery and high pews, hatchments, sentences and a Jacobean pulpit. Notice an unusual modern memorial to Colonel Barnard.

NEWTON BLOSSOMVILLE
St Nicholas
6m/10km N.E. of Newport Pagnell SP 9251
The Ouse flows past the churchyard and gives the place a pleasant and unusual setting. Mostly of *c.* 1300, but the general impression of the interior is of simple countrified work of the 18th century, with pulpit and gallery, plus a little medieval glass.

NORTH CRAWLEY
St Firmin
3m/4km E. of Newport Pagnell SP 9244
An important medieval church, restored in the 18th century. The rebuilding of the chancel in the 13th century is recorded by a rare carved inscription outside the E. window. The nave has a S. arcade of *c.* 1200 with good carved capitals and a 14th-century N. arcade. The 15th-century screen is the only painted one to remain complete in the county; the figures on the panels are those of Prophets, Kings and Saints. There are

box pews, and a brass to the son of a Dutch bookseller in Oxford, 1589.

NORTH MARSTON
Assumption of the Blessed Virgin Mary
3m/4km S. of Winslow SP 7722
The church is associated with John Schorne, Rector in the late 13th and early 14th century, who performed miraculous cures of the gout and became venerated as a saint. The S. aisle contains the original (14th-century) remains of his elaborate shrine, and the nave has good medieval work of various dates. Windsor filched the Saint's relics and, probably as a sop to the disgruntled parishioners, built the superb chancel and two-storey vestry and sacristy in the late 15th century. The whole restored at Queen Victoria's expense in memory of John Camden Neild (who left a loyal legacy of £250,000!) in 1852.

OLNEY
St Peter & St Paul
5m/8km N. of Newport Pagnell SP 8851
The view from the S. across the water meadows of the Ouse is memorable. The tall broach spire and the splendid chancel windows, all of the 14th century, remind one that Northamptonshire is only a mile or two away. Large and airy but scraped inside. The pulpit in the S.W. corner was used by John Newton, vicar in the 1760s, who, with his friend William Cowper, wrote the Olney Hymns.

PADBURY
St Mary the Virgin
3m/4km S.E. of Buckingham SP 7230
14th–15th century; restored. Paintings of *c.* 1330 include the Deadly Sins and two scenes from the Life of St Catherine.

PENN
Holy Trinity
3m/4km N.W. of Beaconsfield SU 9193
Splendid views from the churchyard. The church, of wonderfully varied textures and materials, with two great porches, has a medieval structure, the roof of *c.* 1400 being one of the finest in the county. But it was much altered by the Penns and Curzons in the 18th century, which is the date of the chancel and its fittings, and many of its monuments. The great treasure is the painting of the Doom or Last Judgement, on oak boards found in the roof in 1938.

The series of brasses is good for costume; and in the centre aisle is the tombstone of a descendant of William Penn, described as 'proprietor of Pennsylvania'.

PENN STREET
Holy Trinity
2m/3km W. of Amersham SU 9296
Benjamin Ferrey, 1849; good Victorian cruciform. In the Decorated style and built of the local flint. Wooded setting.

PITSTONE
St Mary
3m/4km N. of Tring SP 9315
This small church lying in chalk fields below the Chilterns has a most satisfactory interior, with work of many dates and textures – 13th-century capitals like Ivinghoe, 15th-century nave arcades, 12th-century font – the whole dominated by a fine Jacobean pulpit and tester beneath 18th-century 'sentences' over the chancel arch.
R.C.F.

PRESTWOOD
Holy Trinity
2m/3km W. of Great Missenden SP 8700
By E. B. Lamb, 1846–9. An interesting church by this rather daring architect, with an unusual plan, having a long W. projection beyond the chancel. Scissor-braced roof; contemporary furnishings and stained glass.

QUAINTON
Holy Cross & St Mary
6m/10km N.W. of Aylesbury SP 7420
The church stands a little apart from the village in a group with almshouses and a Carolean rectory, and commands a lovely view over the Vale. It was badly mauled by 19th-century restorers, who endowed it with a monstrous roof and hideous tiles, but it is notable for the finest 17th- and 18th-century sculpture in the county. In the nave are monuments by Stayner, William Stanton, Leoni and M. C. Wyatt, but inside the tower (too often locked) are the moving figures of Justice Dormer and his wife sorrowing over their dead son – a work of genius long attributed to Roubiliac, and certainly worthy of him.

RADNAGE
St Mary
2m/3km N.E. of Stokenchurch SU 7897
A scattered village of several 'endships', one

of which is clustered around the church and
rectory, perched on the wooded slopes of
the tumbled ground behind the Chiltern
scarp below Bledlow Ridge. A simple village
interior with all its original plaster, covered
with a medley of medieval paintings and
post-Reformation texts. Much of the structure is of about 1200, with aisleless nave
and chancel and a plain tower between. The
exterior, of partly plastered chalk and flint
with brick repairs, fits perfectly into the landscape.

RAVENSTONE
All Saints
3m/4km W. of Olney SP 8450
The simple 11th- and 13th-century exterior
gives no hint of the interest within. In 1628,
an E. chapel was added to the S. aisle to
house the splendid tomb of Heneage Finch,
Earl of Nottingham, who reclines in great
state. Of the same period are the chapel
screen, rails, panelling and a massive pulpit.

SHALSTONE
St Edward the Confessor
4m/6km E. of Brackley SP 6436
1828, but largely rebuilt in 1862 by Sir
George Gilbert Scott. His are the richly
foliated capitals of the S arcade. Monuments, including some 19th-century ones by
Sir R. Westmacott.

SHENLEY CHURCH END
St Mary
2m/3km from centre of Milton Keynes SP
8336
Medieval, heavily Victorianized. Spectacular
late 12th-century chancel with shafted
windows and keeled mouldings; Royal Arms;
monuments.

SHERINGTON
St Laud
2m/3km N.E. of Newport Pagnell SP 8846
Medieval with distinctive 13th-century axial
tower somewhat altered in the 15th century.

STEWKLEY
St Michael & All Angels
5m/8km W. of Leighton Buzzard SP 8526
A very fine Norman church, with central
tower, comparable with Iffley, Oxon. The
W. front particularly rich Norman. Inside,
a restoration by Street took away something
of the texture, but enhanced the lofty scale,
culminating in a distant, dark chancel.

STOKE POGES
St Giles
3m/4km N. of Slough SU 9883
A good church in a medley of styles somewhat overweighed by the Gray's *Elegy* association. The main points of interest are the
14th-century timbered and traceried porch;
the limewashed walls of the oddly placed
13th-century tower; and the renovated Hastings chapel in which one rather regrets the
disappearance of a good gallery. The fine
panels of 17th- and 18th-century glass have
been placed here.

STONY STRATFORD
St Mary & St Giles
in N.W. part of Milton Keynes SP 7940
Rebuilt, apart from the tower, by Francis
Hiorn of Warwick after the great fire of
1742. Fancy Gothic with a memorable interior featuring slender wooden clustered
shafts supporting plaster rib-vaults.

TATTENHOE
St Giles
3m/4km W. of Bletchley SP 8334
Tiny, remote and altogether fascinating; the
building is set in the midst of the moats,
banks, ditches and other evidences of a deserted village, only a farm and a cottage
or two surviving. The place is a mass of
primroses, violets and bluebells in the spring;
and almost unapproachable in winter. There
is a simple interior with box pews and an
amusing 13th–18th-century composite font.
Many of the materials are said to have come
from the destroyed priory of Snelshall
nearby. One of the few remaining places
where one may still savour the authentic
aroma of the past – stale paraffin and mouldy
hassocks.

TERRIERS
St Francis
N.E. district of High Wycombe SU 8749
By Sir Giles Gilbert Scott, consecrated in
1930, and one of his best designs. Light and
shade are artfully employed within, and the
impressive exterior is suitably enhanced by
a lofty central tower.

THORNTON
St Michael & All Angels
4m/6km E. of Buckingham SP 7536
The church, shorn of its chancel in the late
18th century, stands opposite the front door
of the big house, now Thornton College. It

is mostly 15th-century in date, but has been amusingly refurnished in the 18th–19th centuries with black-and-white diamond paving and box pews facing inward, college chapel-fashion. The great feature of the church is the Ingylton tomb, 1472, with its fine brass, recovered in recent years from a grotto in the park.

TWYFORD
Assumption of the Blessed Virgin Mary
6m/10km N.E. of Bicester SP 6626
A church of exceptional interest for its details and fittings, though not giving the impression of an architectural composition as an entity. The Norman doorway is notable, and inside there are fine 13th-century arcades, with a good deal of 15th-century woodwork – roof, pews, and screen with some painting. There are worthwhile monuments, both medieval and later. Note especially the chain-armour Knight and mutilated priest.

UPTON
St Laurence
S. district of Slough SU 9879
12th- and 19th-century; somewhat compromised by Ferrey's attentions in 1851, and again by recent 'enhancement', but at heart a good Norman parish church. With Stewkley it has the only other vaulted chancel in Bucks.

WAVENDON
St Mary the Virgin
4m/6km N.W. of Woburn SP 9137
A study in one of the more successful Victorianizations of a medieval church, largely by Butterfield in 1849. There is a varied collection of Victorian glass. A more venerable relic is the fine 17th-century pulpit brought out of London. And the whole place stands pleasantly on the Bedfordshire border.

WESTCOTT
St Mary
7m/11km W. of Aylesbury SP 7117
An assertively simple Victorian church, by G. E. Street, 1867. The interior is made effective entirely by proportion, for there is no mechanical carving; mouldings and capitals are strong and simple, and there is thought everywhere.

WEST WYCOMBE
St Laurence
in N.W. area of High Wycombe SU 8295
Medieval in origin, the church is dramatically placed within an Iron Age earthwork; the curiously wrought flinty Dashwood mausoleum lies to the E. In the 18th century the church fell into the clutches of the notorious Sir Francis Dashwood, and his 'Hell Fire Club' met in the golden ball atop the tower. Apart from this naughtiness, the furnishings are elegant and the interior reeks of fantasie.

WESTON TURVILLE
St Mary the Virgin
3m/4km S.E. of Aylesbury SP 8510
The church is at the end of a lane near the 18th-century manor house in whose grounds is the motte of a Norman castle. The building is of many styles and of an attractive irregularity with things in it to please everyone – 12th-century 'Aylesbury' font, 13th-century arcades, 14th-century chancel with good window tracery, 15th-century tower, fragments of old glass (a tantalizing medley, this), 17th-century pulpit, and so forth.

WESTON UNDERWOOD
St Laurence
2m/3km W. of Olney SP 8650
Largely 12th- and 14th-century, but heavily restored. The chief interest attaches to the 14th-century glass in the E. window, which includes figures of Christ, saints and angels.

WHITCHURCH
St John the Evangelist
5m/8km N. of Aylesbury SP 8020
Set back from the village, in which are good cottages and a Norman earthwork castle, the tall, white, weathered limestone tower explains its name. Inside, it is spacious and surprisingly little tampered with; there are scraps of wall-painting and glass.

WILLEN
St Mary Magdalene
2m/3km N.E. of centre of Milton Keynes SP 8741
Like a city church transported to the remote countryside, with dramatic effect – brick, stone, Classical pilasters, urns, high pews, pedestal font and all the rest. It is to the design of Robert Hooke, and built in the 1670s through the munificence of Dr Busby,

the famous headmaster of Westminster School. Good complete furnishings.

WING
All Saints
3m/4km S.W. of Leighton Buzzard SP 8822
The most important Saxon church in the county, but containing much of interest of later dates, particularly the fine roofs, screen and porch, and the splendid series of Dormer monuments.

WOTTON UNDERWOOD
All Saints
6m/10km N. of Thame SP 6816
Idyllically placed near Wotton House, home of the Grenvilles, Dukes of Buckingham, for 800 years. To be seen for its many 19th-century features, especially the heraldic glass and the unusual columbarium, a truly ducal filing cabinet for the Grenville coffins.

Cambridgeshire

Introduction

Perhaps because Cambridge University and Ely Cathedral are so outstandingly beautiful, people underrate the county that contains them. Cambridgeshire scenery is nowhere obvious or dramatic – the famed Gog Magog Hills, south of Cambridge, do not reach three hundred feet. In the south, the county is rolling and chalky, giving surprisingly fine and wide views. In the north, it is fens, where the eye sees mostly sky. As Miss Olive Cook writes of it, 'It would not be possible to find elsewhere so unexpected a contrast between the chalk uplands with their carpets of delicate grasses and rare flowers, wild yet amiable, and the expanse of the Fens, dyked, drained and filled, yet still boundless, awe-inspiring and alien.' Such unassuming country as this is more easily wounded than most by modern vertical intrusions like factory chimneys, pylons, poles and aeroplane hangars, and the geometric cubes of 1930s functionalism. But the towers and spires of the 14th century, the great time of church building here, show the sense of skyline peculiar to the Middle Ages and still dominate much of the landscape.

Cambridgeshire is not a unity. In the south it is like its neighbours, Essex, Suffolk and Herts. Steep-roofed cottages are reed-thatched, and their walls colour-washed. Parish boundaries are long strips, parallel to the Anglo-Saxon Devil's Dyke and so designed as to make best use of a variety of resources on every strip. In this rolling scenery are country houses in well-wooded parks, and the thatched villages, which are seen best in sunlight when their colour washes are shown up, cluster round flint churches whose mouldings and carvings are of hard chalk. In the west of the county a coarse rubble is used for the churches.

Until 1836 the northern part of the county, the Isle of Ely, was separate from Cambridgeshire. Until the 17th century, when the Fens were drained on a grand scale, the Isle was mostly shallow water with monastic settlements and churches on raised banks and islands. The greatest of these is the Benedictine Abbey of Ely itself. Whittlesey, Sutton, Thorney, Swaffham Prior, Wisbech and St Wendreda's March are other examples of island or peninsular medieval churches which rose over the shallow water like ships, made of limestone from Lincolnshire and Northants. Beside them, the houses and churches of modern Fen settlements seem mean and unimportant.

In 1839 two Cambridge undergraduates, J. M. Neale and Benjamin Webb, formed the Camden Society for the restoration of old churches on what were thought 'correct' principles – the abolition of box pews, the removal of plaster and whitewash, the adornment of the sanctuary with stained glass and colour, and the promotion of 13th–14th century Gothic (Middle pointed or Decorated) above every other style. Yet Cambridgeshire remained Low Church with a good deal of Perpendicular Tudor cement affixed to crumbling fabrics. The Camden movement was not without its effect on local churches, though its influence spread later all over England. The Cambridgeshire churches, for this and other reasons, were subject to more than usually vigorous Victorian re-tooling and refurbishing.

J.B.

1 Babraham	20 Gamlingay	39 March
2 Balsham	21 Grantchester	40 Over
3 Barrington	22 Guilden Morden	41 Shepreth
4 Bartlow	23 Guyhirn	42 Snailwell
5 Bassingbourn	24 Harlton	43 Soham
6 Bottisham	25 Haslingfield	44 Sutton
7 Bourn	26 Hauxton	45 Swaffham Bulbeck
8 Burwell	27 Hildersham	46 Swaffham Prior
9 Cambridge	28 Horseheath	47 Thorney Abbey
10 Carlton	29 Ickleton	48 Thriplow
11 Cherry Hinton	30 Isleham	49 Trumpington
12 Chippenham	31 Kennett	50 Westley Waterless
13 Conington	32 Kirtling	51 Whittlesey
14 Croydon	33 Landwade	52 Wicken
15 Dullingham	34 Leverington	53 Willingham
16 Elsworth	35 Linton	54 Wimpole
17 Eltisley	36 Little Abington	55 Wisbech
18 Ely	37 Longstowe	56 Wisbech St Mary
19 Fordham	38 Madingley	

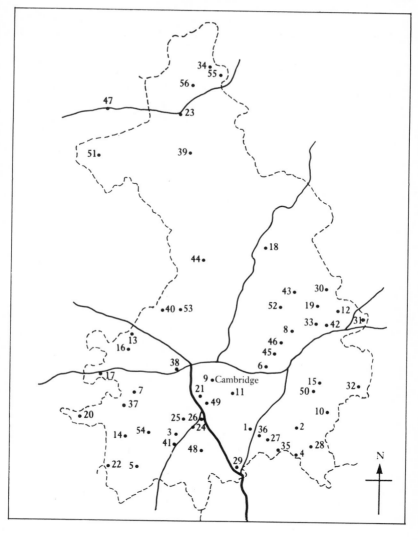

Selected List of Churches

BABRAHAM
St Peter
7m/11km S.E. of Cambridge TL 5150
A secluded riverside site beside a Jacobean-style mansion of 1832. Plain unbuttressed W. tower, claimed as pre-Conquest but more probably 13th-century; a lofty Perpendicular nave and assorted woodwork. The Bennet monument in the S. aisle (second half of 17th century) is highly individual and attractive.

BALSHAM
Holy Trinity
6m/10km N.W. of Haverhill TL 5850
Fine, large, early medieval tower; dignified, somewhat austere nave, dating from the rectorship of John of Sleford, d. 1401; richly carved stalls also commissioned by him. His brass and that of John Blodwell, d. 1462, are in the chancel. Late-medieval rood screen with loft; lofty font cover by former rector.

BARRINGTON
All Saints
6m/10km N.E. of Royston TL 3949
Village setting at end of large green. Prominent W. tower; early 13th-century arcades; 15th-century seating; wall-painting and monuments.

BARTLOW
St Mary
5m/8km W. of Haverhill TL 5845
Norman round tower, otherwise mostly Decorated, much restored by Rowe, 1879. Extensive 15th-century wall-paintings.

BASSINGBOURN
St Peter & St Paul
3m/4km N.W. of Royston TL 3343
Fine mid-14th-century Decorated chancel of individual design with much flowing tracery and widespread use of ogees, notably on the sedilia and piscina. Good rood screen and a poignant monument to Henry Buller, d. 1647.

BOTTISHAM
Holy Trinity
6m/10km E. of Cambridge TL 5460
Perhaps the best church in the county. Mainly 13th- and early 14th-century with W. tower and galilee porch, finely moulded arcades, stone chancel screen, and wooden parcloses. Here also the indent for what must have been the very sumptuous Brass of Elias de Bekyngham, said to be the only honest judge in the reign of Edward I. 16th–18th century monuments.

BOURN
St Helena & St Mary
8m/12km W. of Cambridge TL 3256
Good Transitional work, especially the nave arcades; cruciform plan; 13th-century W. tower with delicate mouldings and leaded spire. Rood screen, choir-stalls of 1537, and Comper reredos.

BURWELL
St Mary
4m/6km N.W. of Newmarket TL 5866
Excellent Perpendicular. The stately nave, roofed in 1464, stands as a monument to the 15th-century imagination, all line and glass; splendid carved roofs, blank traceried panels, and slim shafts. The exterior is best seen when approached from Cambridge by the Swaffhams; unified 15th-century apart from the bottom of the tower.

CAMBRIDGE
TL 4458
All Saints, Jesus Lane
By Bodley, 1863–4, in the English Decorated style with a noble lofty spire. Inside is a tremendous collection of paintings in 15th-century style to Bodley's own design, done by Kempe, among others. Good glass by Morris & Co.
R.C.F.
Great St Andrew, St Andrew's Street
By Ambrose Poynter, 1842–3. Perhaps the most interesting of his three Tudoresque churches in Cambridge. Some original glass and other fittings.
Great St Mary, King's Parade

The university church, between the Market Place and the Senate House at the heart of Cambridge. Rebuilt between the late 15th and early 16th centuries, a magisterial example of East Anglian Perpendicular. The interior is stately and spacious, the lines hardly affected by the galleries installed in 1735. Finely carved roofs of 1505; busy spandrels between soaring nave arcades crowned by the generous clerestory lights; a setting entirely suited to university ceremonies.

Holy Sepulchre, Bridge Street
One of four remaining round churches in England. Impressive without and within; mainly rebuilt in the 15th century. Extensively restored by Salvin in 1842, when some 'ecclesiological' fittings were introduced.

St Benet, Benet Street
10th-century tower, originally of the 'helmed' form of Sompting, Sussex; perhaps the oldest extant fabric in the county. Tower arch with cavorting Saxon beasts; nave and aisles *c.* 1300; heavily Victorianized exterior.

St Edward, St Edward's Passage
Slender nave arcades of *c.* 1400, like most of the rest of the church. Chancel aisles were added to accommodate Clare College and Trinity Hall after their church was demolished by the expansionist King's in 1446. Pulpit of *c.* 1510 with linenfold decoration from which the ill-fated Bishop Latimer preached.

St Mary the Less, Trumpington Street
Light and spacious 14th-century hall church; perhaps intended as the chancel of a larger structure. Flowing Decorated tracery, glowing Kempe glass, a pretty pulpit of 1741, all graced by a Comper altar.

St Michael, Trinity Street
Rebuilt by Hervey de Stanton, buried here in 1327, just before the church was finished. Nave used as a community hall since 1966, but the chancel, with full set of 15th-century collegiate stalls, gloriously untouched.

CARLTON
St Peter
5m/8km N. of Haverhill TL 6453
Pleasant setting; mainly 14th–15th century. Reset rood screen at W. end; Perpendicular font and chancel arch.

CHERRY HINTON
St Andrew
S.E. district of Cambridge TL 4856
Fine Early English chancel with bold paired lancets to the sides; late 13th-century arcades. Flaxman monument, 1794.

CHIPPENHAM
St Margaret
4m/6km N. of Newmarket TL 6669
Set in a model village. Mostly 14th–15th century; delightful interior with a memorable wall-painting of St Christopher.

CONINGTON
St Mary
9m/15km N.W. of Cambridge TL 3266
Nave rebuilt 1737, the door and windows with Gibbsian surrounds. Inside, a series of arched recesses frame 17th- and 18th-century wall-monuments; that to Robert Cotton, d. 1697, signed 'G. Gibbons fecit'.

CROYDON
All Saints
6m/10km N.W. of Royston TL 3149
Attractively set at end of lane. Norman and later; red-brick chancel by Sir George Downing, 1685. Charming interior with ceiled wagon roof.

DULLINGHAM
St Mary the Virgin
4m/6km S. of Newmarket TL 6357
Estate-village setting; flint and field stone, mainly Perpendicular. Fine N. porch; unexpected pulpit of green Italian marble, 1905; good 18th- and 19th-century Jeaffreson monuments.

ELSWORTH
Holy Trinity
7m/11km S.E. of Huntingdon TL 3163
Good Decorated work with much reticulated tracery. 15th-century pulpit; fine Tudor choir-stalls with linenfold; mid-18th-century Ionic reredos.

ELTISLEY
St Pandionia & St John the Baptist
6m/10km E. of St Neots TL 2759
Village-green setting. Spiritually in Hunts., arcades of *c.* 1200, otherwise mostly 13th-century with a well-proportioned small spire.

ELY
St Mary
14m/23km N.E. of Cambridge TL 5380
Of the church built by Bishop Eustace (1198–1215), the seven-bay Transitional

nave arcade remains, as does the splendid N. door, both of excellent quality.

FORDHAM
St Peter & St Mary Magdalene
5m/8km N. of Newmarket TL 6370
The Lady Chapel is the *pièce de résistance*; strangely set over a vaulted porch, altered in the 15th century, but redolent of the apogee of the Decorated style. Colourful Edwardian chancel.

GAMLINGAY
St Mary the Virgin
2m/3km N.E. of Potton TL 2352
Decayed market town. Striking church with dark carstone and light clunch dressings, of 15th-century aspect. Inside, a font of *c.* 1200, rood screen, W. gallery, and Rococo monument.

GRANTCHESTER
St Andrew & St Mary
2m/3km S.W. of Cambridge TL 4355
Meadowy, self-conscious village; celebrated mid-14th-century Decorated chancel with nook-shafts, nodding ogees and tracery.

GUILDEN MORDEN
St Mary
5m/8km N.W. of Royston TL 2744
Large church in open country; Perpendicular outside, Decorated within. Elaborate 'double' rood screen; contrived in 15th century from two others to provide space for seats between.

GUYHIRN
St Mary Magdalene
6m/10km S.W. of Wisbech TF 3903
Small church by Sir George Gilbert Scott, 1878. Of gault brick with stone dressings; a commendable effort in view of the limited resources. A half-mile N.E. lies an old chapel of ease, 1660, of untouched Puritan simplicity.
    R.C.F. (chapel).

HARLTON
Assumption of the Blessed Virgin Mary
6m/10km S.W. of Cambridge TL 3852
The church and adjoining Manor Farm make a pleasant group. Clunch and flint. Inside, a stately instance of Decorated-Perpendicular transition; fine stone screen, late 14th-century reredos, statue niches, and crocketed canopies. Good alabaster wall-

monument to Sir Henry Fryer, d. in duel, 1631.

HASLINGFIELD
All Saints
5m/8km S.W. of Cambridge TL 4052
Mainly Decorated and Perpendicular. Handsome W. tower faced in clunch. Late 13th-century arcades, good roofs, and 17th-century Wendy monuments.

HAUXTON
St Edmund
4m/6km S. of Cambridge TL 4352
Norman nave and chancel including the massive chancel arch. Well-preserved wall-painting of St Thomas à Becket, *c.* 1250.

HILDERSHAM
Holy Trinity
10m/16km S.E. of Cambridge TL 5448
Woodland setting. Harshly over-restored, but worth a visit for all that, if only to savour the effect of its attractive and characteristic 13th-century plan. A pair of lifesize wooden effigies, *c.* 1300, and brasses to the Paris family.

HORSEHEATH
All Saints
4m/6km W. of Haverhill TL 6147
Setting. Originally Norman, but now Decorated and especially Perpendicular; the nave lit by huge three-light transomed windows. A shrine to the Audleys and Alingtons.

ICKLETON
St Mary Magdalene
10m/16km S. of Cambridge TL 4943
Village-green setting. Victim of a horrid fire in 1981, this church was yet the beneficiary, since it uncovered a remarkable series of 12th-century frescoes. Already celebrated for its Saxo-Norman arcades, the paintings of the Life of Christ mark Ickleton as an apogee of the rural Romanesque.

ISLEHAM
St Andrew
4m/6km W. of Mildenhall TL 6474
Spacious, cruciform; Decorated without save for W. tower by Street. The nave resplendently panelled, clerestoried and roofed to unusual design by the mercantile family of Peyton, 1495. Good brasses and fine 17th-century communion rails. Across

the road a small apsed Norman monastic church.

KENNETT
St Nicholas
5m/8km N.E. of Newmarket TL 6968
Bosky setting. Mostly 13th–15th century; good details include the Transitional N. doorway, 14th-century double piscina, and carved screen with roses in the spandrels.

KIRTLING
All Saints
5m/8km S.E. of Newmarket TL 6857
Here was a Tudor mansion built by the Norths; the surviving gatehouse and moated site are impressive. Norman S. doorway to church with Christ in Majesty on the tympanum; the door ironwork also Norman. Good North hatchments and monuments in the 16th-century brick-built family chapel.

LANDWADE
St Nicholas
3m/4km N.W. of Newmarket TL 6228
A pocket parish of a hundred acres or so has a delightfully situated church built by Walter and Joan Cotton, *c.* 1445, extended later. A number of attractive medieval fittings and monuments; the place takes a little finding but should not be missed.

LEVERINGTON
St Leonard
2m/3km N.W. of Wisbech TF 4411
Spacious nave, rather marred by ugly wooden strainer arches of 1901. The draw here is the glass, especially the 15th-century Tree of Jesse window at the E. end of the N. aisle.

LINTON
St Mary
7m/11km W. of Haverhill TL 5646
Small market town with some interesting houses; an archaeologist's church, very enigmatic; much 14th-century work.

LITTLE ABINGTON
St Mary
9m/15km S.E. of Cambridge TL 5349
Early Norman, especially the N. and S. nave doorways with simple chip carving. Restored by St Aubyn, 1885. Kempe glass in chancel.

LONGSTOWE
St Mary
9m/15km N.W. of Royston TL 3054
Remarkable for the wall-monument to Sir Ralph Bovey, d. 1679; the deceased rises from the waves to clutch an anchor proffered by the Hand of God.

MADINGLEY
St Mary Magdalene
4m/6km N.W. of Cambridge TL 3960
Idyllic park setting above a little lake. There is a fair mixed bag of fittings including a 14th-century bell; monuments by Stanton, Flaxman and Westmacott.

MARCH
St Wendreda
14m/22km E. of Peterborough TL 4196
Almost all Decorated and Perpendicular, apart from the chancel by W. Smith, 1872. There are good details, notably the W. tower window. But the crowning glory is the double hammer-beam roof with host of angels; the finest in the county.

OVER
St Mary
9m/15km N.W. of Cambridge TL 3770
Church belonged to Ramsey Abbey, hence the excellent Decorated work, somewhat marred by rendering. Delicate ballflower frieze on S. side and a fine open porch. Ornate interior with embattled shafts, chancel-stalls and a carved rood screen; all very good.

SHEPRETH
All Saints
5m/8km N.E. of Royston TL 3947
Setting, beside a moated site. Norman chancel arch with angle shafts and roll moulding; N. door has later arch above 12th-century reveals. Decorated nave and 13th-century font.

SNAILWELL
St Peter
3m/4km N. of Newmarket TL 6467
Setting against a backdrop of trees. The church has a 12th-century round tower with tall belfry lights. There is a good deal of 14th-century work, a Perpendicular clerestory, and a hammer-beam roof.

SOHAM
St Andrew
5m/8km S.E. of Ely TL 5973
Celebrated 15th-century tower rising high
above the fenland, the top resplendent with
flushwork, battlements and pinnacles.

SUTTON
St Andrew
6m/10km W. of Ely TL 4478
The tower, with its odd two-stage octagonal
lantern, stands majestically on a ridge above
the fen. Bishop Barnet of Ely began the
rebuilding *c.* 1370. Good Decorated tracery.

SWAFFHAM BULBECK
St Mary
6m/10km W. of Newmarket TL 5562
Early English tower, the rest mainly 14th-
century. Unusual Perpendicular bench-ends
carved with beasts and a N. Italian chest.

SWAFFHAM PRIOR
St Mary
5m/8km W. of Newmarket TL 5764
Two churches in one churchyard standing
on a little hillock above the village street.
Both are large with good towers: St Mary's
is 12th-century, partly octagonal, and was
formerly crowned by a stone spire.
St Cyriac's (R.C.F.) has a distinctive late
15th-century octagonal upper stage with
flushwork parapet.

THORNEY ABBEY
St Mary & St Botolph
7m/11km N.E. of Peterborough TF 2804
Has 'atmosphere', ascribable in part to fine
trees growing in and around the little town.
The church is a fragment of the Romanesque abbey, with an E. end added by Blore,
1840–1, including an effective window
copied from glass in Canterbury Cathedral.

THRIPLOW
St George
6m/10km N.E. of Royston TL 4346
Well-placed on a little hill. Late 13th-
century cruciform with prominent central
tower. Parts of a Decorated screen; used as
the pattern for that at Great St Mary's,
Cambridge.

TRUMPINGTON
St Mary & St Michael
S. suburb of Cambridge TL 4454
Highly elegant 14th-century cruciform,

though rather over-restored, with the
famous brass of Sir Roger de Trumpington,
d. 1289. John and Aleyn may well have
passed this way as they fled back to Cambridge after their successful skirmish with
Chaucer's miller, and doubtless breathed a
thankful prayer.

WESTLEY WATERLESS
St Mary the Less
5m/8km S. of Newmarket TL 6256
Stands high on the chalk, and has some of
the deepest wells in the county. The neat
little church has lost its small round tower.
It is in an original if somewhat finicky Decorated idiom. Another good brass, to Sir John
and Lady de Creke (early 14th-century).

WHITTLESEY
St Mary
5m/8km E. of Peterborough TL 2797
Has the best tower and spire in the county.
The spire can be seen for miles around,
though rather dwarfed by the forest of chim-
neys to the left as you approach by road from
the S. There is a representative selection
of sub-modern stained glass. Monument to
General Sir Harry Smith, d. 1860, by G. C.
Adams of London, in the Westminster
Abbey tradition. Another in the chancel to
Elizabeth Kentish, d. 1792, was designed in
Rome by her sorrowing husband, Richard
Kentish.

WICKEN
St Laurence
2m/3km S.W. of Soham TL 5670
Small and secluded. Decorated with 15th-
and 16th-century embellishments. Cromwell associations; brasses.

WILLINGHAM
St Mary & All Saints
8m/12km N.W. of Cambridge TL 4070
Principally early 14th-century, including the
distinctive ashlar spire. Spacious collegiate
chancel with stalls, and to the N. an unusual
chapel or sacristy. Markedly complete set of
roofs; a double hammer-beam over the nave.
Wall-paintings and screens.

WIMPOLE
St Andrew
6m/10km N. of Royston TL 3350
A church in the squire's back yard, 14th-
century in origin but almost entirely rebuilt
by Flitcroft in 1749, and again in the Decor-

ated style in 1887. Fine 14th-century heraldic glass in N. chapel. Remarkable series of monuments by Scheemakers, Banks, Bacon, Flaxman, Westmacott and others.

WISBECH
St Peter & St Paul
12m/19km S.W. of King's Lynn TF 4609
Handsome 18th-century and later houses on the 'brinks' fronting the River Nene; Wisbech cuts a dash under favourable conditions. St Peter & St Paul is a large town church with three nave arcades, rather dark within. There is a bit of everything from the 12th century onwards, but the early 16th century provided the free-standing N. bell-tower and the ornate S.E. vestry, perhaps originally a guild chapel. Many wall-plaques, including one by Nollekens. Reredos, 1885, by Salviati to a design by Basset-Smith.

WISBECH ST MARY
St Mary
3m/4km W. of Wisbech TF 4208
In origin 12th-century, but now mainly Perpendicular, chancel rebuilt in 1872. Interesting woodwork of various periods, largely of foreign provenance; the legacy of Canon Mowbray Smith, incumbent 1914–51.

Channel Islands

Introduction

The islands, much nearer to France than they are to England, are the last remaining part of the Duchy of Normandy to owe allegiance to the English Crown. The islands were converted by the same Celtic missionaries who established churches in Cornwall and Brittany, and the ancient parish churches are a curious mixture of styles which link them both with the West Country and with Northern France. Until 1569, the islands were under the jurisdiction of the Bishop of Coutances in Normandy, but in that year were transferred to the diocese of Winchester. The religious links of the islands, however, were with the Calvinist Protestants of France, many of whom sought exile there. Though nominally Anglican from the mid-17th century, there were major variations from the normal standards of Anglican worship. The surplice was not worn by the clergy, the use of fonts was abandoned, and the churches had no permanent communion tables. On the quarterly Sacrament Sundays, as in the Scottish and Dutch Calvinist churches, a long table was placed in front of the pulpit around which the communicants sat, and these tables still survive in three Jersey churches. It was not until well into the 19th century that churches in the Channel Islands began to adopt forms of worship familiar to congregations in England.

The islands are organized into two bailiwicks, those of Guernsey (including the outlying islands of Alderney, Herm and Sark) and Jersey. They are very different in character. Jersey, though it still has a few rural enclaves and substantial farmhouses, has been heavily developed over the past century as a popular resort for holidaymakers and as a haven for tax exiles. The capital, St Helier, is a rather drab seaside town, though its tree-lined Royal Square, in which the principal government buildings are located, is reminiscent of squares in small French provincial towns. Guernsey, though largely built up and so dedicated to the growing of tomatoes that from the air the main island looks like one vast greenhouse, is much less cosmopolitan. The capital, St Peter Port, in which the narrow and winding streets rise almost vertically from the harbour, is a delightful town of distinguished late 18th- and early 19th-century buildings. Alderney is even quieter, and Sark, still ruled by its Seigneur, remains wholly feudal. Each bailiwick has its own courts and parliament and forms a deanery within the diocese of Winchester, over which the Dean has a large measure of quasi-episcopal authority.

The churches of the Channel Islands are humble buildings, much enlarged during the medieval period and rather too heavily (and unimaginatively) restored in the 19th century. Jersey was divided into twelve pre-Reformation parishes and Guernsey, excluding the outlying islands, into ten. These still remain the units of local adminstration in the islands, both civil and ecclesiastical, as they were in England and Wales before 1894. A notable feature of the islands' churches is the crudeness of their construction, especially the roofs, which generally consist of plain and steeply pitched stone vaults. When the population expanded in the 18th and 19th centuries, a number of new churches were built, but none of any great distinction. Local or minor English architects were mostly used, and even when this was not the case, as with St Simon's in St Helier and St Stephen's in St Peter Port, both designed by G. F. Bodley, the buildings were left incomplete or substantially modified through lack of funds. Neither building ranks as among that architect's best work. The only distinguished Victorian churches are Scott's replacement St Anne's in Alderney and Pugin's English Roman Catholic Church in St Peter Port.

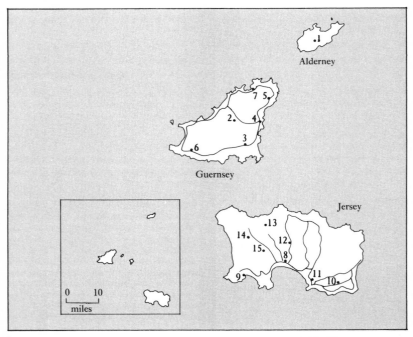

Bailiwick of Guernsey		Bailiwick of Jersey	
1 Alderney	5 St Sampson	8 Millbrook	12 St Lawrence
2 Castel	6 Torteval	9 St Brelade	13 St Mary
3 St Martin	7 Vale	10 St Clement	14 St Ouen
4 St Peter Port		11 St Helier	15 St Peter

Selected List of Churches

BAILIWICK OF GUERNSEY

ALDERNEY

St Anne

The church was rebuilt in 1847–50 to designs by George Gilbert Scott. Cruciform church in the transitional style with central tower, pyramidal spire and apsidal chancel. In composition it is sympathetic to the architectural traditions of the Channel Islands and the furnishings are of high quality.

CASTEL

St Mary

Double nave and chancel, with 18th-century spire and spirelets, and W. porch. Drably restored in the 19th century and heavily overpewed. In the N. chancel are the remains of 13th-century wall-paintings, including a complete Last Supper.

ST MARTIN

St Martin

Large double nave and chancel church with tower and spire between the S. nave and S. chancel. The 15th-century S. porch has an elaborately carved outer doorway, and there is also a 15th-century octagonal font. The pulpit is dated 1657, and the contemporary reading desk has been cut down to serve as a lectern. This is one of several Guernsey churches retaining its 17th-century poor-box.

ST PETER PORT

Holy Trinity

A simple Classical church of 1789 with a double row of windows on the N. and S. sides and with a gabled W. front in the Dutch style. The interior has a plain plastered ceiling, galleries and a shallow E. apse. Until very recently it retained, alone in the Channel Islands, a complete set of box pews set chapel-fashion with no central aisle.

St Peter

The most distinguished and substantial of the ancient parish churches in the Channel Islands, though now rather strangely shaped, having been extended on a confined site in the town centre. The church has a central tower and spire, a very short nave and chancel, both with N. and S. aisles, a short N. transept and a long S. transept of three bays with an E. aisle of the same length. The interior was well restored in 1886 and given a series of plaster vaults. Wide range of 17th–19th century wall tablets to most of the leading families in Guernsey.

ST SAMPSON

St Sampson

Basically 12th-century church with the aisles two bays shorter than the nave at the W. end; customary stone vaults; E. window by Hardman, *c.* 1869; medieval altar cross and candlesticks in N. chapel.

TORTEVAL

St Philip

Rebuilt in 1816–18 to a design by John Wilson, architect of several public buildings in St Peter Port. Impressive exterior with circular W. tower and spire and apsidal chancel; Victorianized interior.

VALE

St Michael

A large double nave and chancel church; S.W. tower has 18th-century spire and spirelets. The church dates from the 12th to the 14th centuries and is the best-preserved medieval fabric in the Channel Islands. The arcaded S. chancel has an elaborate ribbed vault and the 16th-century porch is also vaulted. There are unusual hood moulds over the windows in the N. nave and both W. doorways.

BAILIWICK OF JERSEY

MILLBROOK

St Matthew

The undistinguished church of 1840–2 was completely remodelled in 1934 as a memorial to the founder of Boots the Chemists. The interior is now the ecclesiastical version of a Hollywood film set, transformed by a remarkable array of fittings in moulded glass by René Lalique of Paris; these include the font, reredoses to high altar and Lady chapel, altar rails, screen, windows and door panels.

ST BRELADE
St Brendan or St Branwalader
12th-century cruciform church with low central saddleback tower and a large W. porch. Aisles were added later on the N. sides of both nave and chancel, but the transept roof-line was retained, giving a strange effect to the exterior. The interior walls and stone vaults have been savagely scraped. To the S. of the chancel in the churchyard is the so called 'Fisherman's Chapel', a small oratory of uncertain date containing a series of faded medieval frescoes covering the walls and vaulted roof.

ST CLEMENT
St Clement
12th-century nave, the chancel and transepts 15th-century. Restoration in 1880 revealed a remarkable series of wall-paintings, including St Michael and the Dragon on the N. wall of the nave, a hunting scene in the S. transept, and two female saints, Barbara and Margaret, in the N. transept. There is a handsome 15th-century font and a long 17th-century communion table.

ST HELIER
St Mark
The best of several early 19th-century churches in Jersey's capital, it was built in 1842–4 to a design by John Hayward. Commissioners' Gothic with Perpendicular W. tower. Inside, spindly columns support a plaster vault and galleries on three sides.

ST LAWRENCE
St Lawrence
The church dates substantially from the 14th and 15th centuries, with further additions on the eve of the Reformation. The impressive Hamptonne chapel, added in 1524, has a vaulted roof with bosses. Long 17th-century communion table.

ST MARY
St Mary the Virgin
The N. nave and both chancels are medieval; the S. nave dates from the restoration of 1838–42. The tower has an 18th-century spire and spirelets (cf. Castel and Vale in Guernsey). There are several decent 17th- and 18th-century wall tables and a long 17th-century communion table.

ST OUEN
St Ouen
A treble-aisled church with central tower and stone vaults, much restored in 1870. An unusual stone staircase in the nave leads to the belfry. There is a handsome 17th-century brass to Sir Philip de Carteret, Seigneur of St Ouen.

ST PETER
St Peter
Stone-vaulted cruciform church, restored in 1886–7, when the main altar was given its unusual terracotta reredos designed by George Tinworth, artist of the Royal Doulton Potteries. A terracotta panel on the N. wall of the chancel is also by Tinworth.

Cheshire

Introduction

Birkenhead is more often passed through than visited, and this slight upon a city that is classic ground for the study of town planning is a slight also often imposed on the county of which it is, by a few hundreds, the largest town. Cheshire is crossed by many whose eyes are on a target beyond. It is on the way to Wales, on the route north and south, on the path of the Irish Mail; and Cheshire does little to arrest the unseeing eye. It is flat except at the edges, and the roads are so good and the corners so hideously made safe that the visitor is almost hustled through it. To those, however, who treat Cheshire as an end rather than as a means, the county is surprisingly rewarding. True, the northern horns of the Cheshire crescent have had applied to them the pancake make-up of commuters' housing, but, in the western horn, there is Chester itself, and, in the eastern, country which is wild and weird however near to Manchester it be.

Elsewhere the county has an almost regular pattern. The background is always richly pastoral, but, along the northern boundary formed by the Mersey and the Ship Canal, there is sporadic industry, and, from north to south down the centre, chemical works have followed the line of the three salt towns, Northwich, Middlewich and Nantwich. The smaller elements in the pattern are more ancient, and stem from Welsh as well as English settlement: there are few villages, and many scattered farms and hamlets. The typical medieval parish church, especially in the south and west of the county, served a vast area, often as much as thirty square miles in extent. Malpas, Great Budworth, Bunbury, Acton and Astbury are churches of this kind. It is not surprising, therefore, that there should be so many interesting private chapels and former chapels of ease, nor that some of the ancient parochial churches of the county should be of such splendour.

It is not only, however, for size or interest that some Cheshire churches are remarkable. A great many of them are cleverly sited, using slight eminences to dominate their surroundings, and most of them are built of red sandstone, a stone never much used for houses. The typical 15th-century Cheshire church must have looked fine when its mouldings were sharp and the houses beneath it half-timbered. Now the detail is frayed or replaced, the surrounding black and white is yearly giving way to a modern uniformity, and it is to the untypical church that one is attracted, to Astbury, built of millstone grit, to the brick churches of Cholmondeley and Tushingham, to the Peovers, to curious Baddiley and freakish Birtles. Here, perhaps, in these untypical Cheshire churches, the county is now typified, a county that only reveals itself to him who leaves the fast through roads, and then rewards him handsomely.

R.W.

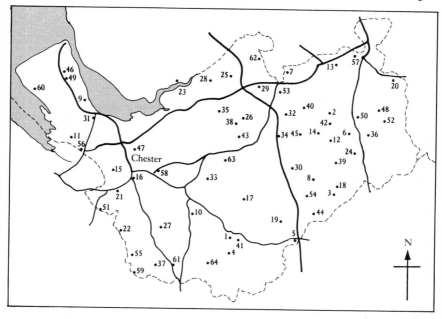

1 Acton	23 Farnworth	44 Odd Rode
2 Alderley Edge	24 Gawsworth	45 Over Peover
3 Astbury	25 Grappenhall	46 Oxton
4 Baddiley	26 Great Budworth	47 Plemstall
5 Barthomley	27 Harthill	48 Pott Shrigley
6 Birtles	28 Higher Walton	49 Prenton
7 Bowdon	29 High Legh	50 Prestbury
8 Brereton	30 Holmes Chapel	51 Pulford
9 Bromborough	31 Hooton	52 Rainow
10 Bunbury	32 Knutsford	53 Rostherne
11 Burton	33 Little Budworth	54 Sandbach Heath
12 Capesthorne	34 Lower Peover	55 Shocklach
13 Cheadle	35 Lower Whitley	56 Shotwick
14 Chelford	36 Macclesfield	57 Stockport
15 Chester	37 Malpas	58 Tarvin
16 Christleton	38 Marbury	59 Threapwood
17 Church Minshull	39 Marton	60 Thurstaston
18 Congleton	40 Mobberley	61 Tushingham (Old Church)
19 Crewe Green	41 Nantwich	62 Warburton
20 Disley	42 Nether Alderley	63 Whitegate
21 Eccleston	43 Northwich	64 Wrenbury
22 Farndon		

Selected List of Churches

ACTON
St Mary
1m/2km W. of Nantwich SJ 6353
The great church dwarfs its tiny village. Mostly of the 13th and 15th centuries, the tower, rebuilt in 1757, is an early instance of Gothic Revival. The low screen and other chancel furnishings are partly late 17th-century, although they look older. There is a Norman font, a 15th-century canopied wall-tomb, and some fine 17th-century effigies.

ALDERLEY EDGE
St Philip
2m/3km S. of Wilmslow SJ 8478
By Joseph Stretch Crowther, 1851–2. He was something of a pioneer of the Gothic Revival, and busied himself measuring medieval churches. This church is a determined essay, with broach spire and flowing tracery, more at home in Northants. than Cheshire. Good random wall masonry, but less successful polychromatic roof tiling. The three parallel roofs and absence of a clerestory render the interior somewhat dark. One good window by Morris & Co. in the S. aisle.

ASTBURY
St Mary
1m/2km S.W. of Congleton SJ 8461
The great battlemented church makes the sloping village green look a glacis and the lych gate a barbican. Outside details are sharp and well-preserved because the building stone is millstone grit, rare in Cheshire. The detached spire is mid-14th-century, but looks earlier. Inside are superb oak roofs, Perpendicular in style, but actually dated 1616 and 1702. 15th-century stalls, screen and wooden eagle lectern; 17th-century altar rails; Royal Arms and nicely mechanical font cover. Notable also for the light hand used by Sir George Gilbert Scott in the restoration of 1862.

BADDILEY
St Michael
4m/6km W. of Nantwich SJ 5950
By farm lanes in flat country, not easy to find and not easy to interpret. Timber-framed chancel dated 1308 and a brick nave of 1805 with a ceiled roof of 15th-century type. The tympanum is one of the most interesting in England, pre-Reformation in structure with painted Creed, Commandments, and Coat of Arms dated 1663. It is some 20 feet square and is supported on an eight-foot screen; it divides the lower chancel from the nave with claustrophobic thoroughness. W. gallery, box pews, and a pretty pulpit.

BARTHOMLEY
St Bertoline
4m/6km S.E. of Crewe SJ 7652
Overlooks attractive village with black and white inn and cottages. Mainly Perpendicular, including screen. Norman door, panelled oak ceilings, and 14th- to 19th-century monuments.

BIRTLES
St Catherine
4m/6km W. of Macclesfield SJ 8675
A freak brick church of 1840 with octagonal tower in a wooded parkland setting; built originally for the squire, but parochial since 1890. The inside is all self-confident vitality and Victorian treasure hunting. Frescoes painted by the founder's son are based on All Saints, Margaret Street. There is good 16th- and 17th-century Netherlandish glass and an ornate pulpit of 1686; the family pew and reader's desk are made up of carved pieces.

BOWDON
St Mary the Virgin
1m/2km S.W. of Altrincham SJ 7586
A church rebuilt by W. H. Brakspear in 1856–60, incorporating some salvaged fabric. Essentially the architect aggrandized the church, deftly scaling up earlier components like the nave roof to suit his generous vision. The result is a grand church with a noble tower, ample clerestory and

added transepts. Good glass by Kempe and Clutterbuck; the stalls by Temple Moore. Fine earlier monuments.

BRERETON
St Oswald
2m/3km S. of Holmes Chapel SJ 7764
Complete late-Perpendicular church in the park of the spectacular Elizabethan Brereton Hall; a fine group.

BROMBOROUGH
St Barnabas
district of Bebington 2m/3km S.E. of centre SJ 3482
By Sir George Gilbert Scott, 1862–4; a severe essay in the early French Gothic re-deemed by warm red sandstone and de-lightful foliage. The broach spire, apse and gablets over the nave windows reassure us that Scott was bent on quality here, and the interior, with its vaulted sanctuary, carved reredos and handsome pulpit, does not fail to please.

BUNBURY
St Boniface
3m/4km S. of Tarporley SJ 5658
A large well-sited 14th-century collegiate church, with nave arcades and wide aisle windows of about a hundred years later. It was well restored after severe war damage. Four of the original doors have survived, and there are also 16th-century oak doors with lattice panels in the stone screen of the chantry chapel. Important early alabaster effigy of the founder of the college, and many interesting fittings.

BURTON
St Nicholas
3m/4km S.E. of Neston SJ 3174
Village setting. E. end of N. chapel *c.* 1300; most of the rest, including the W. tower, 1721, all in red sandstone. Good altar rails.

CAPESTHORNE
Holy Trinity
6m/10km W. of Macclesfield SJ 8374
The chapel of a great house, designed by William Smith and built in 1722. The drive to house and chapel sweeps through a park with views over woods and a lake. The chapel itself, of brick with stone dressings, is rec-tangular with balustrade and cupola. The interior is somewhat darkened by injudicious Victorian glass, and there is a mosaic reredos of 1886–8. The pews were arranged college-fashion in 1877, and there is a raised family pew at the W. end. Original rails and a good font.

CHEADLE
St Mary
3m/4km W. of Stockport SJ 8588
A late-Perpendicular church, the chancel not rebuilt until 1556–8. Good S. porch; fine 16th-century screens with linenfold panelling and a pair of alabaster knights.

CHELFORD
St John the Evangelist
6m/10km W. of Macclesfield SJ 8174
A stone-dressed brick church of 1774–6, the tower added in 1840. Inside are box pews and splendid Art Nouveau pulpit, altar rails, choir-stalls, and mural decorations with sprays of flowers and saints, all by P. Worthington, 1903.

CHESTER
SJ 4066
St John the Baptist, St John Street
Adjacent to the Roman amphitheatre and Grosvenor Park. Victorian exterior hides a dignified Norman cruciform church with noble early 12th-century arcades. Painted reredos by Heaton, Butler & Bayne to a design by J. Douglas, 1876.
Chapel of St Mary de Castro, Agricola Tower, Chester Castle
The little castle chapel, *c.* 1300, with rib vault, occupies the second storey of the medieval tower. English Heritage.
St Paul, Boughton (suburb to E.)
By J. Douglas, 1876; S. aisle added in 1902, the spirelet in 1905. A colourful brick church perched on a steep site between road and river. Delightful interior with timber arcades, wrought-iron screen, and painted decoration in the manner of Art Nouveau. Good glass by Morris & Co. of 1881, and a window by Kempe in the N. aisle.

CHRISTLETON
St James
suburb, 3m/4km E. of Chester SJ 4465
By W. Butterfield, 1875–7. In a rich, pretty village; his only complete Cheshire church. The late 15th-century tower was retained at W.B.'s own request, 'This country is an old country, but if we don't take care it will soon be as new a one as America . . . You had better keep the old tower and so look a little different to the modern new churches which

are generally so noisy and pretentious.' What giants those Victorians were! His new church honours its site with warm red and white polychromy and excellent fittings.

CHURCH MINSHULL
St Bartholomew
4m/6km N.W. of Crewe SJ 6660
In a pleasant village, the stone-dressed brick church of 1702–4, restored in 1861, has a country builder's rustic Classical interior.

CONGLETON
St Peter
11m/18km N. of Stoke-on-Trent SJ 8562
An unspoilt town church of 1740–2; the Gothic tower added in 1786. Plain outside and most pleasing within. Galleries on three sides, supported on piers with columns above. Fine box pews throughout, those in the galleries steeply tiered. William III arms, a particularly good brass candelabrum of 1748, and interesting 18th-century glass. Original font and altar rails.

CREWE GREEN
St Michael and All Angels
2m/3km E. of Crewe SJ 7255
By Sir George Gilbert Scott, 1857–9. Standing in one of Crewe Hall's modest hamlets, a colourful church of red and blue brick, stone shafts and a steeply tiled roof. Polychromatic interior with apsed chancel, lots of good carving and excellent glass.

DISLEY
St Mary the Virgin
2m/3km W. of New Mills SJ 9784
In the Pennine foothills. Late Perpendicular tower and porch, otherwise rebuilt in 1824–35; the fine 16th-century nave ceiling was fortunately preserved. Gilded organ case by Samuel Renn and Netherlandish glass dated 1535 in E. window.

ECCLESTON
St Mary the Blessed Virgin
3m/4km S. of Chester SJ 4162
By G. F. Bodley, 1896–9; one of his best churches. Set in a leafy village by the Dee, this lavish church in the Decorated style was built for the first Duke of Westminster. The delicate elevation of the clerestoried nave complements the substantial W. tower, all in good red sandstone. Completely rib-vaulted inside, with rich bosses and shafted piers, the furnishings all to Bodley's own design.

Much use of oak and Thessaly marble; a splendid gilt reredos with two tiers of canopied figures; the organ case with trumpeting angels. Glass by Burlison & Grylls.

FARNDON
St Chad
6m/10km N.E. of Wrexham SJ 4154
Set in a big riverside village. The church was badly damaged in the Civil War and was rebuilt apart from the 14th-century W. tower. Remarkable 17th-century E. window depicts prominent local Royalists, pikemen and trophies of war.

FARNWORTH
St Luke
1m/2km N. of Widnes SJ 5187
Village setting. Red sandstone church with work of all periods. Good Tudor wooden ceilings in the chancel and S. transept. Bold Chapel, rebuilt in 1855, has good monuments, including one by Chantrey, 1822. Hatchments and a Royal Arms of 1661.

GAWSWORTH
St James
3m/4km S.W. of Macclesfield SJ 8969
Perpendicular church adjoining the garden earthworks of the Elizabethan Hall. Panelled oak nave roof. The 17th-century monuments to members of the Fitton family with lifelike grouped effigies are outstanding.

GRAPPENHALL
St Wilfrid
3m/4km S.E. of Warrington SJ 6486
Set by cobbled village street. Mostly 1525–39, but with some Norman work in the nave and a S. chapel of 1334. Norman font, a fine effigy of Sir William Boydell, d. 1275, and rearranged 14th-century glass in S. aisle.

GREAT BUDWORTH
St Mary and All Saints
2m/3km N. of Northwich SJ 6677
An imposing village church standing on a hill. A 14th- and 15th-century structure, of good proportions and very light inside. Impressive 16th-century oak crown-post and wagon roofs, some 13th-century benches, and a medieval stone altar in the S. chapel.

HARTHILL
All Saints
9m/15km S.E. of Chester SJ 5055
Harthill is within a few miles of both Bur-
wardsley and Hargrave; all three have early
17th-century churches, suggesting a vigorous church life preceding the equally vigorous Puritanism of the area. Of the three,
Harthill, 1609, is the most pleasantly sited,
high up on the Broxton hills, and, alone of
the three, retains a screen and other original
fittings which survived a drastic restoration
in 1862.

HIGHER WALTON
St John the Evangelist
2m/3km S. of Warrington SJ 5985
By Paley & Austin, 1885. A modest estate
church in the Decorated style endowed with
a magnificent central tower and recessed
spire, courtesy of Sir Gilbert Greenall,
brewer. Jolly diapering and flushwork on the
tower and a good S. elevation. Inside are
fine sandstone mouldings on the rib vault
of the tower, and painted panels in the nave.

HIGH LEGH
St John
5m/8km N.W. of Knutsford SJ 7084
This little brick chapel of 1814–16, which
served the demolished West Hall, was burnt
in 1891 and rebuilt by Thomas Harrison as
a parish church in 1893. It is an attractive
mixture of half-timber, brick and red tiles
with wooden traceried windows, an agreeable brick-lined interior, and a roof supported by timber posts.

HOLMES CHAPEL
St Luke
4m/6km E. of Middlewich SJ 7667
A neat early-Georgian brick casing hides a
large timber-framed church of *c.* 1430.
Inside is a magnificent medieval roof, oak
galleries of *c.* 1705, and a screen dated 1623.

HOOTON
St Paul
3m/4km N.W. of Ellesmere Port SJ 3678
By James K. Colling, 1858–62. By the
lodges to Hooton Hall, a prodigious Romanesque church of red and white ashlar with
octagonal crossing tower. Many of the details
are French and Italian, including the Lombardic frieze across the W. front. Inside are
granite arcades and, over the crossing, an
astounding ashlar dome. Rich fittings

include good stained glass and the serpentine font, which won a medal at the Great
Exhibition.

KNUTSFORD
St John the Baptist
6m/10km W. of Wilmslow SJ 7578
By J. Garlive, 1741–4. A neat brick box
with stone dressings; the apsidal chancel was
unfortunately replaced by a flat one in 1879.
The S. doorway has pilasters and a pediment, and inside are Tuscan columns and
a pair of galleries.

LITTLE BUDWORTH
St Peter
3m/4km N.E. of Tarporley SJ 5965
Setting. Perpendicular W. tower of *c.* 1526,
but otherwise of 1798–1800 with arched
windows and minimal tracery. The inside
has a shallow plaster vault, a nice 18th-
century font, and a pretty pulpit.

LOWER PEOVER
St Oswald
6m/10km E. of Northwich SJ 7474
The churchyard forms the green of a very
pretty hamlet, with inn and school, at the
end of a cobbled lane. Although tidied up
by Salvin in 1852, it is still a fine example
of a timber-framed church of *c.* 1370; the
effect inside is of dark oak and whitewash.
Very good 17th-century furnishings include
box pews, some with the lower halves of the
doors fixed to retain the rushes, screens,
altar rails and lectern.

LOWER WHITLEY
St Luke
½m/1km S.W. of Higher Whitley, which is
5m/8km N.W. of Northwich SJ 6280
A tiny church rebuilt in 1594 as a chapel of
ease by the then Lord of the Manor, Thomas
Touchet. With added 19th-century apse and
S. porch, it is somewhat over-restored apart
from the excellent hammer-beam roof, low
enough for visitors to inspect the beautifully
carved volutes supported by caricatured
beasts.

MACCLESFIELD
St Michael and All Angels
SJ 9173
Late 13th-century, but largely rebuilt by Sir
A. Blomfield in 1898–1901. Sumptuous
early 16th-century three-storeyed S. porch,
but chiefly noted for an array of 15th–17th-

century monuments, including one by William Stanton, 1696.

MALPAS
St Oswald
8m/12km E. of Wrexham SJ 4847
The large handsome church, mainly late 15th-century, stands by a motte at the highest point in the village. Spacious, light and well-proportioned with a magnificent angel roof. Splendid 13th-century iron-bound chest, misericords and box pews. Two family chapels with fine screens and an alabaster monument of 1522, the deceased touchingly comforted by his wife.

MARBURY
St Michael
2m/3km N. of Northwich SJ 6576
Lovely mereside setting. Modest Perpendicular church with W. tower and a fine 15th-century wooden pulpit with crocketed ogee panels.

MARTON
St James
3m/4km N. of Congleton SJ 8568
Black and white, built *c.* 1370, the most complete timber-framed church in Cheshire. The tower lobby has massive posts, and the nave and aisles are under one roof. There are traces of a 14th-century Doom.

MOBBERLEY
St Wilfrid
2m/3km E. of Knutsford SJ 7879
Green village setting with inn and cottages. The design is a typical late-medieval one for E. Cheshire; aisle walls with small three-light square-headed windows; no battlements but deep eaves. There is a magnificent rood screen of 1550 and a good roof with a rood ceilure. Ancient glass, faded wall-paintings, and a tower gallery of 1683.

NANTWICH
St Mary
4m/6km S.W. of Crewe SJ 6552
A beautifully set large cruciform church built, like so many Cheshire churches, of soft red sandstone which weathers badly. The exterior is impressive, however, despite extensive restoration by Scott. Vaulted interior, rare in Cheshire, with a superb chancel containing carved and gorgeously

canopied late 14th-century choir-stalls with misericords.

NETHER ALDERLEY
St Mary
2m/3km S. of Alderley Edge SJ 8476
Outstanding village with delightful churchyard. Perpendicular church with stately W. tower and chancel of 1856. The Stanleys were the squires and their Jacobean flying pew, a gallery above the S. aisle, is notable.

NORTHWICH
St Helen
Witton SJ 6573
Large Perpendicular church of the medieval salt town. Decorated arcades with wonderful nave and chancel roof of *c.* 1525 replete with bosses large and small, together with the initials of William Venables, Lord of the Manor.

ODD RODE
All Saints
1m/2km N. of Alsager SJ 8057
By Sir George Gilbert Scott, 1864, 'a triumph of the academic type of good Gothic design' (Goodhart-Rendel). A small brown-stone church in late 13th-century style with bellcote and tiled roofs. Ornate stone pulpit and alabaster font, but otherwise quite a restrained interior with open benches and good glass by Kempe and Tower.

OVER PEOVER
St Lawrence
6m/10km E. of Northwich SJ 7474
In a park, near splendid 17th-century stables and backed by the Tudor hall. The church has a brick nave of 1811 with a pleasantly pitched roof, and a tower of 1741. Two chapels were also retained at the rebuilding; the ashlar N. chapel of 1648 is outstanding, the earliest truly Classical work in the county. Rich furnishings, excellent tombs with effigies, and a delightful haunting atmosphere.

OXTON
St Saviour
2m/3km W. of Birkenhead SJ 2987
By C. W. Harvey, Pennington and Bridgen, 1889–92. Finely sited cruciform church in the Decorated style, but with a somewhat coarse sandstone exterior. Inside, however, all is satisfying enough with warm red brick, stone dressings and impassioned woodwork

by Edward Rae. The large gilded reredos is by G. F. Bodley, and the W. window by Morris & Co.

PLEMSTALL
St Peter
4m/6km N.E. of Chester SJ 4570
Meadowy setting by the River Gowy. Late Perpendicular sandstone church with a tower of 1826. Inside is abundant 15th-century-style woodwork carved by the Rev. Toogood, incumbent 1907–46, with some medieval bits.

POTT SHRIGLEY
St Christopher
1m/2km N.E. of Bollington SJ 9479
In the Pennine foothills. The church is mainly 15th-century with oak roofs, moulded beams and numerous box pews. There are two bells cast by Robert Crowch in 1430, and restored medieval glass in the E. window.

PRENTON
St Stephen
3m/4km S.W. of Birkenhead SJ 3086
Designed by C. E. Deacon in 1897, completed in 1909 by Deacon and Horsbrugh. Deacon's masterpiece, set in a leafy suburb. A sandstone church of Gothic inspiration with grouped lancets and a lofty exterior. Effective red-brick and stone interior with rectangular piers and original detailing in the chancel. Deacon's own imaginative furnishings with harmonious painted rood screen of 1949.

PRESTBURY
St Peter
2m/3km N.W. of Macclesfield SJ 9077
The church, by the pretty village street, looks 15th-century, but has 13th-century nave arcades. There are oak roofs, a Jacobean pulpit and, in the spandrels of the arcades, dainty paintings of the Apostles, dated 1719. In the churchyard is a small Norman chapel rebuilt in 1747.

PULFORD
St Mary the Virgin
5m/8km S.W. of Chester SJ 3758
By John Douglas, 1881–4. At the entrance to Eaton Hall Park and commissioned by the 1st Duke of Westminster. A church with banded red sandstone, Decorated windows and a distinctive shingled spire, typical of

the architect. Ashlar interior with good oak roof and assured details. Glass by Heaton, Butler & Bayne and a reredos by Shrigley & Hunt.

RAINOW
Jenkin Chapel, Saltersford (St John)
3m/4km N.E. of Macclesfield SJ 9575
This remote mountain chapel built in 1733 looks like a converted farmhouse with a low tower added. The roof is of heavy Kerridge slabs, the windows are square, sash and domestic, and there is a chimney stack halfway along the S. wall. The gallery, box pews and fittings are intact.

ROSTHERNE
St Mary
3m/4km N. of Knutsford SJ 7483
In a large churchyard beautifully set between village and mere. Mainly Perpendicular outside with handsome Georgian tower of 1742–4. The chief delight here is the monuments: a 13th-century knight, a spirited work of 1792 by Bacon, and an affecting sculpture by Richard Westmacott Jnr.

SANDBACH HEATH
St John the Evangelist
1m/2km E. of Sandbach, which is 5m/8km N.E. of Crewe SJ 7860
By Sir George Gilbert Scott, 1861. An agreeable cruciform church in the Second Pointed style with geometrical plate tracery, crossing tower and octagonal spire. Well-lit ashlar-faced interior with rich foliate crossing capitals and original screens, pulpit and font. Wonderful E. window by Clayton & Bell and luxuriant chancel woodwork by local carver Jessie Barbara Kennedy.

SHOCKLACH
St Edith
3m/4km N.W. of Malpas SJ 4349
Small rustic church in the fields. Crudely decorated Norman S. doorway with zig-zags and lozenges. 14th-century nave, chancel and double bellcote. Good plain fittings and nice 18th-century nave ceiling with rosettes. Scratched on a pane of the E. window, 'I, Robert Aldersey was here on 1st day of October 1756 along with John Massie and Mr Derbyshire. The roads were so bad we were in danger of our lives.'

SHOTWICK
St Michael
5m/8km N.W. of Chester TF 6708
By-passed and secluded hamlet without shop or inn, once washed by the Dee. The village and church were strategically important, and the tower is fortress-like. Twin naves separated by a low arcade; since the Reformation, one has been used for the Offices and the other for the Sacrament. Good 17th- and 18th-century furnishings of box pews, three-decker pulpit, and a notable canopied seat of 1709 for the churchwardens. 14th-century glass depicting the Annunciation.

STOCKPORT
SJ 8989
St George, Buxton Road
By Paley & Austin, 1892–7. A magnificent church of cathedral-like proportions in un-compromising late-Gothic style. Cruciform, with a tall crossing tower, spire and flying buttresses. The seven-light E. window is the climax of the exterior, with massed reticulated tracery and panelled decoration above and below. Inside, six bays of clustered shafts support a galleried clerestory, all culminating in the huge panelled piers of the crossing. A beautiful alabaster reredos stops the view up the nave, and beyond is the great E. window with glass by Shrigley and Hunt.
St Thomas, St Thomas's Place, Wellington Road, South
By George Basevi, 1822–5. A fine Commissioners' church, and one of the best neo-Classical churches in the county. Built of ashlar with high W. tower and cupola, the rich E. portico is graced by six fluted Ionic columns. Dignified Corinthian interior with galleries and moulded plaster ceiling, the chancel sensitively remodelled in 1890.

TARVIN
St Andrew
5m/8km E. of Chester SJ 4967
Handsome church with a tall tower at the end of an avenue. Striking nave roof of 1650 with hammer-beams and good Decorated screen with ogee-headed openings to the S. chapel.

THREAPWOOD
St John
3m/4km S.W. of Malpas SJ 4345
Remote and secluded, this intact late-Georgian church of 1815 has an evocative interior with benches, box pews, three-sided communion rail, galleries, pulpit and reredos.

THURSTASTON
St Bartholomew
3m/4km S.E. of West Kirby SJ 2484
By J. L. Pearson, 1883–6. Small red sandstone church in the Early Decorated style, tower and spire oddly located over the choir. Inside, there is a most effective progression of space and decoration towards the tall chancel containing Pearson's own lavish reredos. Some glass by Clayton & Bell and the organ case by R. Norman Shaw, 1905.

TUSHINGHAM (OLD CHURCH)
St Chad
4m/6km N. of Whitchurch SJ 5546
Along a field path, half a mile E. of the Victorian church and parsonage which replaced it, the brick chapel of 1689–91 stands in a numinous oval enclosure. Superb interior has W. Vaudrey gallery, decorated roof trusses, chancel screen, panelled pulpit, altar table with high-backed family pew to either side, and even an oak font!

WARBURTON
Old St Werburgh
5m/8km W. of Altrincham SJ 7984
The Old Church is small, secluded and of great interest. The building is of timber, with some walls replaced with stone in 1645, and some with brick in 1711, the date also of the brick tower. The roof is of Kerridge slabs. Inside, the constructional timbers divide off the aisles. The screen, pulpit, altar and rails are Jacobean; the box-pews are 1813 but look earlier.
   R.C.F.
New St Werburgh
The New Church was built by J. Douglas in 1883 and is just outside the village.

WHITEGATE
St Mary
3m/4km N.W. of Winsford SJ 6269
By John Douglas, 1874–5. Not in fact a Victorian church, despite the convincing exterior, but actually a cunning reconstruction of a Georgian one of 1736. The Georgian inner porch door gives the game away, as do the timber arcades and an obliging watercolour inside.

WRENBURY

St Margaret

5m/8km S.W. of Nantwich SJ 5947

An early 16th-century Perpendicular church overlooking a village green; tower, nave and aisles all conspicuously battlemented. The interior is pleasing, and must have been very fine indeed before the renovations of the 1920s and 1930s. The pink masonry looks, however, less scraped than is usual when the plaster is removed, and the box pews, though lowered, are of a good colour. There are crests on pew doors, hatchments, some signed monuments, and a Gothic W. gallery.

Cornwall

Introduction

Cornwall is a Duchy. It is separated from England by the picturesque Tamar Valley, and has more sea coast than anywhere else in Britain.

The prevailing building materials are slate and granite. The granite bursts up through the slate and forms Bodmin Moor, which is mostly desolate except for prehistoric remains and the beehive cells of Celtic Christians. A district half-granite and half great white pyramids of decomposed granite, known as China clay, is near St Austell. Moorland covers the far western granite promontory between St Ives and Land's End. The Scilly Isles, where the churches are small, simple and comparatively new, are the nearly submerged tops of granite hills, between which and Land's End was the lost territory of the Lyonesse. The rest of the county is slate, varying from bluish silver to deep green. The peninsula of the Lizard is made of coloured rocks called Serpentine. Tin mines have brought 19th-century industrial scenery, with its chapels and streets, to the districts around Camborne and Redruth. Visitors of our own generation have pocked the tremendous coast with bungalows, but they have also preserved the humble slate-grey fishing ports because of their picturesque qualities. The two most attractive inland towns in Cornwall are Launceston, a border fortress to which have been added Georgian houses, and Truro, where Pearson's noble Victorian cathedral rises in the French manner out of the old houses and shops. Truro has its Georgian streets and so have Helston, Penzance and Falmouth. Calstock is the least-known and most uninterruptedly Cornish town. The Duchy becomes its native self in winter, and that is the time to see it.

Inland, Cornwall is mercifully considered dull. The wooded valleys like those of the Allen, Camel, Inny, Fowey and Lynher, with their steep slopes of thin Cornish elms, carpeted underneath with spring anemones, their slate-hung houses, whose gardens in summer are bright with hydrangea, veronica and fuchsia, are remotest and loveliest Cornwall. The coast is awe-inspiring. Rocks fall sheer into the peacock-blue Atlantic and English Channel, and rock pools are full of many-coloured seaweeds and marine life.

Before Southern England was Christian, Cornwall had been visited by Celtic missionaries from Wales and Ireland. Their names survive as those of saints, though little is known about many of them. The Cornish are the same sort of Celts as the Welsh and Bretons, but the Celtic field system makes the Duchy look different from England. The Celtic saints were hermits

who lived in beehive cells and are said to have recited the Psalms waist-deep
in cold streams. The crosses of their age survive, and so does the siting of
their churches, for the parochial system came late to Cornwall, and the
church on the site of a Celtic hermit's cell is often remote from the chief
village in the parish. It is in the larger villages that one finds the chapels of
Methodism, which has made as deep an impression on Cornwall as it has
on Wales.

The old Cornish churches are rugged and windswept, and their charm is
in their storm-resisting construction and their lichen-crusted texture. Mr
Attlee thinks that the rather unenterprising nature of Cornish churches,
which were nearly all rebuilt or added to on the same pattern in the 15th
century, was for two main reasons. (1) The local stone was hard to work.
Cornwall is deficient in lime and so the mason used mud, and walls had
therefore to be kept low. Roofs had to be barrel-vaulted so as to distribute
their weight evenly along the walls. This sort of roof suited a boat-building
people and their tools – the adze and spokeshave. Hence Cornishmen never
reached realization of wall and window, voids and solids, as a composition.
They stuck at the stage of regarding them as an aggregate of lumps with
holes left in it, as did their Celtic forebears. (2) Most Cornishmen made
their living from the sea, so they saw no pattern in town and village, as for
instance did sheep and wool masters who lived off the surface of the land.
So the true village church can only be found far inland, as at Altarnun,
Blisland, St Neot and Bodmin.

J.B.

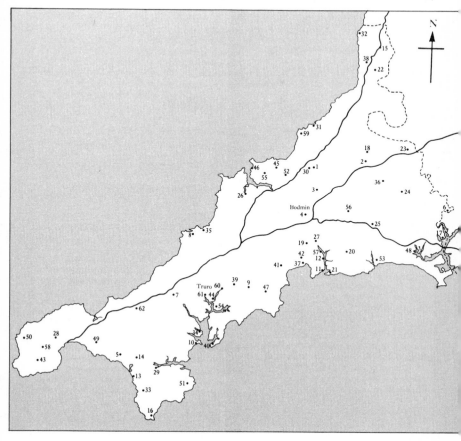

Selected List of Churches

ADVENT
St Adwena
1m/2km S.E. of Camelford sx 1081
Lonely moorland situation on the eastern bank of the Camel. Square unbuttressed tower, otherwise mostly 15th-century with ceiled wagon roofs; overdone in 1870.

ALTARNUN
St Nonna
7m/11km W. of Launceston sx 2281
Large, cathedral-like 15th-century church with lofty tower; fine display of 16th-century bench-ends by a known carver, Robert Daye. Huge Norman font of local type. Communion rails extending across chancel and aisles, 17th-century. Noble rood screen. Early 17th-century panels on E. wall, one depicting Holy Communion and the other the Crucifixion.

BLISLAND
St Protus & St Hyacinth
4m/6km N.E. of Bodmin sx 1073
The village of old granite and slate houses has a green with ash trees on it. The church, with a 15th-century tower made of enormous blocks of local moorland granite, looks out over a steep wooded valley. It has two transepts, a S. aisle, and two chancel chapels. The old carved wagon roofs remain throughout, and the nave floor is of slate; the walls are white; a few old carved bench-ends survive; otherwise there are chairs. The Georgian wine-glass pulpit was restored by F. C. Eden, and virtually all the amazingly rich screen with loft which extends the whole width of the church, a blaze of red and gold and green and white, with a rood over its centre, is his. This screen gives to this weather-beaten village building, with its 15th-century S. arcade of granite sloping this way and that, an unforgettable sense of joy and mystery. Through the delicate tracery of the screen may be glimpsed splendid altars by Sir N. Comper and harmonious windows by F. C. Eden. As a restoration and even improvement on a medieval church, this holy and peaceful place on the

edge of Bodmin Moor can hardly be bettered in the kingdom.

BODMIN
St Leonard or St Petrock
26m/42km W. of Plymouth sx 0767
The largest parish church in Cornwall. Though much refurbished in Victorian times, it retains its old wagon roofs and a grand Norman font of local type, with severe-looking angels at the corners. Mainly late-medieval. Note the splendid table-tomb in Catacleuse stone of Thomas Vyvyan, 1533, Prior of Bodmin and titular Bishop of Megara, a delightful blend of Gothic and Renaissance decoration. Also remarkable Norman pillar piscina.

BREAGE
St Breaca
3m/4km W. of Helston sw 6128
A fine 15th-century granite church, with buttressed W. tower carved with gargoyles. Contemporary wall-paintings, including a Warning to Sabbath Breakers.

CALSTOCK
St Andrew
5m/8km E. of Callington sx 4368
Included mainly because of its situation high above the Tamar valley. Edgcumbe Chapel on N. side has two later 17th-century monuments. Harshly restored inside with pitch pine pews and cathedral glass.

CHACEWATER
St Paul
4m/6km N.E. of Redruth sw 7544
A church was built here in 1828, repaired in 1886, greatly damaged by lightning in that same year, entirely rebuilt (except the tower) by Edmund Sedding in 1892. Lofty interior with arcade of granite and Polyphant stone. The village street, composed of inns and little shops, the sort that have a small-paned window and a latched door with bobbing bell, lies along the main Truro–Redruth road. The church is a few yards S. of the road on a steep knoll. The tower, a gaunt shaft, bare of windows except in the upper-

most of four lightly indicated stages, is impressive. Inside, the church is remarkable for the colour of the unplastered walls of local stone, buff, grey, yellow and brown setting off effectively the shallow sea-water-green of the octagonal shafts of Polyphant stone and granite arches. The nave has a wagon roof, 43 feet high, the aisles lean-to roofs. An arched recess in the E. wall provides a bent eyebrow to the five-light E. window, whose bright stained glass comes from St Mary's, Truro. There are lancets in the clerestory and square-headed windows in the aisle walls which have shallow recesses inside and corresponding projections without. A satisfying sense that Sedding here knew what effect he wanted to get; and got it.

CRANTOCK
St Carantoc
2m/3km S.W. of Newquay sw 7960
Originally a Norman cruciform church with central tower; after fall of tower another erected at W. end; chancel rebuilt when college was established *c.* 1236; further reconstruction in 14th and 15th centuries; restored on conservative lines by Edmund Sedding 1899–1902; much-restored rood screen, Norman font; devotional atmosphere.

CREED
St Crida
6m/10km S.W. of St Austell sw 9347
The church sunk below the road has a granite tower. Exceptionally graceful arcade; mats and chairs instead of pews allow its full effect; fine range of windows to S. aisle. Norman pillar piscina with chevron decoration; refreshingly unrestored Royal Arms of George IV; and the letter from Charles I painted on wood.

FALMOUTH
10m/16km S.E. of Redruth sw 8032
King Charles the Martyr, Church Street
A 17th-century oddity with its diffident oblong tower and two tiers of broken-backed aisle windows (Gothic, more or less); these have no sympathy with the Classical features inside which garnish the three dark tunnels composing the church. The church is dark and changed by a succession of tastes.
All Saints, Killigrew Street
By John Sedding; almost a triumph; a spacious nave, lofty with passage aisles and richly adorned E. end; but the W. end an anti-climax; plain wall with openings in it, 'chill as a dull face frowning on a song'.

FOWEY
St Fimbarrus
8m/12km E. of St Austell sx 1251
Groups well with Place, a late-medieval mansion enlarged in an imposing manner in the 19th century; mainly 14th-century; has a clerestory rare in Cornwall, a wonderfully carved wagon roof, a Norman font, Jacobean pulpit, and 17th-century Rashleigh monuments.

GOLANT
St Sampson
2m/3km N. of Fowey sx 1254
Airy situation on height above Fowey River; snug little church, consecrated in 1509; trim, stiff box pews, extremely uncomfortable, recall the fidgets of Gus and Flora in *Ravenshoe*. Three-sided altar rails; fragments of 16th-century glass.

GUNWALLOE
St Winwalloe
3m/4km S. of Helston sw 6522
Romantically sited all alone near the sea, with a detached tower built into the rock; 14th- and 15th-century and typical of the area. Remains of screen with figure-painting and attractive tracery. It is a gently restored, unforgettable place.

HELSTON
St Michael
15m/24km S.W. of Truro sw 6527
A pleasant market town with much late-Georgian building. Church rebuilt in 1762 by Thomas Edwards of Greenwich in Classical manner; one of few Georgian churches in Cornwall. Exterior very effective with good tower; interior rather dull due to Victorian meddling; chancel has handsome moulded plaster ceiling.

KILKHAMPTON
St James the Great
4m/6km N.E. of Bude ss 2511
A large church in the village centre. Mostly rebuilt in 16th century, but retaining an elaborate Norman doorway. Lofty arcades of seven bays with tall granite monolithic columns; rich wagon roofs and the largest collection of carved bench-ends in Cornwall;

organ by Father Smith, c. 1775; Grenville monuments.

LANDEWEDNACK
St Wynwallow
1m/2km N.E. of Lizard Pt sw 7112
Attractive village setting on sheltered slope. W. tower of local serpentine stone, 'blue, glossy green and velvet black'. Norman doorway; Perpendicular porch; font with name of rector, 1404–5.

LANDULPH
St Leonard & St Dilpe
3m/4km N. of Saltash sx 4361
Sylvan setting on Tamar between two inlets; rood screen; bench-ends; manorial pew of the Lower family; monument to Theodore Palaeologus. Plaster walls and slate floors remain.

LANEAST
St Sidwell & St Gulvat
7m/11km W. of Launceston sx 2284
12th-century cruciform; fabric enlarged and refashioned in 15th century. Set in a secluded nook not far from the Polyphant quarry, it exhibits the standard Cornish arrangement at its best: four centred arches of arcade; wagon roof. It has good early 16th-century pulpit; mutilated bench-ends; and screen. Remains of 15th-century painted glass. Laneast should be visited first among Cornish churches, as it gets one's eye in for the general run of them. In spring the surrounding churchyard is a mass of wild daffodils.

LANLIVERY
St Brevita
2m/3km W. of Lostwithiel sx 0859
Stands high with a lofty granite tower overlooking the Fowey Valley as it widens towards the estuary; in spite of considerable renewal, one of the great churches of Cornwall; as usual, a cruciform fabric was refashioned in the 15th century, when an aisle replaced the S. transept; granite ashlar masonry, unspoilt wagon roof in S. aisle, and ringers' rhyme board in tower.

LANREATH
St Marnarck
5m/8km N.W. of Looe sx 1856
Stands in the village; Norman cruciform, refashioned in 15th century and well restored by Bodley in 1887. Norman font,

17th-century cover, late-medieval screen with figure-painting; 17th-century seating and excellent chancel-stalls with figures on the ends; monument to Grylls family.

LANTEGLOS-BY-FOWEY
St Wyllow
1m/2km E. of Fowey sx 1451
Difficult of access, both by the ferry across the Fowey River and the narrow, winding and precipitous lanes from Lostwithiel. A 14th-century church, refashioned in 15th century. Font 13th-century; early 16th-century bench-ends, and altar tomb with brass, 15th-century. Remarkable for the very effective arrangement at the W. end where the N. and S. aisles are prolonged to embrace the tower, to which they give arched access. Edmund Sedding gives a graphic description of the condition of the church before he undertook its restoration in 1909, and it remains an outstanding example of careful and conservative repair – the dilapidated roof with decay arrested, the leaning walls stabilized in the act. The panelling from family pews, removed from the E. end of the church and erected at the W., is interesting and unusual.

LAUNCELLS
St Andrew & St Swithin
2m/3km E. of Bude ss 2405
In a wooded valley. The only Cornish church wholly undisturbed by Victorian 'restoration'. Outside it is like other churches in the district, but the interior comes as a welcome surprise; old plaster on the walls, ancient roofs intact; the finest bench-ends in Cornwall; box pews, pulpit in Strawberry Hill Gothic, three-sided altar rails, reredos and organ case; granite and polyphant arcades; Norman font with 17th-century cover.

LAUNCESTON
St Mary Magdalene
20m/32km N.W. of Plymouth sx 3384
Erected by Sir Henry Trecarrel in early 16th century; the tower is older. Chiefly remarkable for a profusion of panelled ornament on its exterior. Painstaking work in inappropriate material; granite with its coarse and conglomerate structure does not allow precision in delineation. A recumbent figure of St Mary Magdalene in a niche under the E. window will be seen to be covered with pebbles thrown up by the local people. The present vicar says that the old

custom is to stand with your back to the figure and try to throw a stone so that it will land on the back of the recumbent figure. This is supposed to bring you good luck for the rest of the week. Scraped interior has early 16th-century pulpit, easily the best in Cornwall; 17th- and 18th-century monuments, carved with Royal Arms; organ case early 18th-century.

LINKINHORNE
St Mellor
4m/6km N.W. of Callington sx 3173
The noble 16th-century granite tower is the second highest in Cornwall. A spacious church in remote, unspoiled village, with wagon roofs, that of the nave with some original colour; large wall-painting of the Works of Mercy; mural monuments of 1688 and 1735; memorial slate slabs of local type; holy well in late-medieval structure in field nearby.

LISKEARD
St Martin
11m/18km E. of Bodmin sx 2564
Large, and notable for its three lofty projections (?chapels) in N. aisle; tower 1899 and most effective; pulpit 17th-century. Outside the N. and S. aisles are 13 consecration crosses, unique in Cornwall.

LITTLE PETHERICK
St Petrock
4m/6km W. of Wadebridge sw 9172
In a wooded valley; rebuilt by William White, 1858. Interior refitted by Comper, 1908, with the result that it is now one of the most attractive churches in the Duchy, a shrine of Anglo-Catholicism. Bronze monument to Mrs Riley, with 17th-century Flemish relief in background.

LOSTWITHIEL
St Bartholomew
5m/8km S.E. of Bodmin sx 1059
Both the tower and the body of the church are different in character from the usual Cornish type. The tower and spire make a most satisfying composition, viewed from the S.W. Short, stout buttresses to the lowest stage, narrow lancets in the next, little louvred openings just below the transition by bold set-offs from the square to the octagon, and at the junction of tower and spire eight traceried, gabled, unglazed window-like features, which succesfully carry the vertical lines of the tower into the pyramid of the spire. Inside the church the arcade on piers without capitals lacks emphasis, and the little irregularly spaced clerestory windows are insignificant. But the great five-light E. window is fine. (Corfield considers the church French both in style and in stone employed.) Outstanding font, 14th-century.

MADRON
St Maddern
2m/3km N.W. of Penzance sw 4531
The mother church of Penzance, which looks at its best in hydrangea time, when it stands amid a blaze of colour looking towards St Michael's Mount. Though now mainly late-medieval, its core is far older; on the whole it has fared better than many of its neighbours, and the interior is quite atmospheric. Wagon roofs; a rood screen richly carved with 16th-century base and modern upper part; carved bench-ends; a coloured alabaster panel from a reredos; early 17th-century brass; and 18th-century altar rails.

MAWGAN-IN-MENEAGE
St Mawgan
3m/4km S.E. of Helston sw 7125
Glorious situation above colour-washed cottages on the slope of a beech-covered vale; 13th–15th-century with good three-storeyed tower; wagon roof; Crusader's tomb and 10th-century inscribed stone called the 'Mawgan Cross'.

MICHAELSTOW
St Michael
3m/4km S.W. of Camelford sx 0878
Unspoiled embowered village on hill-slope; church in trees; pleasant village-like interior, though much 'restored'.

MINSTER
St Merteriana
the mother church of Boscastle, ½m/1km to the W. sx 0991
Far from houses, approached by paths, at the head of steep, wooded valley near the sea; 13th- and 15th-century; 17th-century slate monuments. Rerooffed, refloored, repewed and reglazed by J. P. St Aubyn; however, he did not scrape the walls.

MORWENSTOW
St John the Baptist
6m/10km N. of Bude ss 2015
In steep valley high above the sea. Hawker,

the poet, was vicar here a century ago. Norman N. arcade, with crude but strong carvings of heads, both men's and animals'; S. doorway and font; two E. bays on N. 13th-century; arcade 15th- and 16th-century, the earliest part in Polyphant and the later in granite; 16th-century seating; mural monuments; scraped walls. Rood screen re-assembled by Hawker and given cast-iron tracery.

MULLION
St Mellanus
5m/8km S. of Helston SW 6719
Set on a windy hill above the cove, long and low in the Cornish manner and mainly late-medieval. The inside was restored and adorned by F. C. Eden, who designed the screen and loft, S. aisle, glass, and altars. Wagon roofs and many old bench-ends.

MYLOR
St Mylor
2m/3km E. of Penryn SW 8235
Delightfully set just above a creek. Norman in origin and refashioned later, it was 're-stored' by Victorians; 16th-century carved screen and pulpit; tall Celtic cross.

NEWQUAY
St Michael
11m/18km N. of Truro SW 8161
Spacious church in Cornish medieval manner by Sir Ninian Comper, 1909–11. Screen, organ case, stained glass, and arcades of Polyphant stone make an impressive interior.

NORTH HILL
St Torney
6m/10km S.W. of Launceston SX 2276
Old village, unspoiled. Grand 15th-century church, granite tower. Spacious interior with 16th- and 17th-century tombs and bright 19th-century glass.

PAR
St Mary the Virgin
Biscover, 4m/6km E. of St Austell SX 0753
G. E. Street's first church, 1848, when he was just 22, and among his most successful; Early English with a dramatic steeple obviously inspired by Lostwithiel, which early called forth Street's admiration. Simple materials and the starkest lancet style with a freshness all its own. Inside there are vistas, depth and mystery. Delightful Wailes glass.

POUGHILL
St Olaf King and Martyr
1m/2km N.E. of Bude SS 2207
Typical 15th-century Cornish church; bench-ends; Royal Arms of Charles II, dated 1655 and so during the Commonwealth; and two striking wall-paintings of St Christopher.

PROBUS
St Probus & St Grace
5m/8km N.E. of Truro SW 8947
A magnificent early 16th-century tower, tallest in the Duchy; Somerset rather than Cornish in character. Emphatically moulded at the base, its soaring lines have a firm foundation. Lavishly ornamented on granite, there is enough plain surface to escape any impression of over-elaboration. Inside, the church, though without clerestory, is more lofty than most. The arcades between nave and aisles are composed of slender and graceful piers, delicately moulded between shafts and crowned with chaplet capitals. The pews should be unfastened from their ankles. The three great E. windows are impressive, and, on turning to the W., one is delighted by the lofty arch into the tower and the vision of the tall window through it. Early 16th-century brass and mural monument to Thomas Hawkins, 1766.

ST ANTHONY-IN-ROSELAND
St Anthony
on the opposite side of the R. Percuil estuary from St Mawes SW 8532
Tucked down below the headland in a wooded cave at the back of Place House, this is a wonderfully untouched Victorian interior of 1851. The Rev. C. W. Carlyon carved the pews, reading desk and pulpit, designed the comic roofs and the ingenious carpentry under the central spire, with its glimpses of stained glass. Spry monuments, one by Westmacott of 1828. In its odd way, inspiring and beautiful.

ST AUSTELL
Holy Trinity
13m/21km N.E. of Truro SX 0152
The inside is scraped and towny, restored by Street in 1892, but the 15th-century tower is one of the best in Cornwall, with carvings of Cornish saints in its niches. The clock-face, with 24 bosses for the hours, is probably 16th-century. Norman pillar piscina of interesting design.

ST BLAZEY
St Blaise
4m/6km N.E. of St Austell sx 0654
Restored and added to by Sir Giles Gilbert
Scott; well done; plaster unfortunately
removed; excellent windows. A light and
attractive interior.

ST BURYAN
St Buriana
4m/6km E. of Land's End sw 4025
Its lofty tower rising above the village square
is a landmark; the church is mainly 15th-
century reconstruction; rood screen of Devon
type, with richly carved rood beam above and
traces of colour; 15th-century font. Altar and
reredos *c.* 1920 by E. H. Sedding.

ST CLEMENT
St Clement
2m/3km E. of Truro sw 8543
Whitewashed cottages with bushes of mauve
and pink hydrangeas form two sides of a
little forecourt and hold in the angle a slate-
hung lych gate. On the walls of the lych
gate, inside, are fixed slate headstones, and
in the churchyard are many others, all worth
scrutiny. Their lettering is free and sinewy,
diversified with endearing errors in spelling
and spacing. Most have ornament, fanciful
and cut with precision. Inscriptions show
originality in sentiment and rhyme. The
church was reconstructed (except the tower)
in 1865; and it was very well done. The
roofs of nave and aisle are carried on 32
arch-braced principals four feet apart. The
E. part of the nave roof is top-lighted by a
course of glass instead of slate each side of
the ridge; an unusual expedient. The glazing
of the windows is all of the same character
– clear glass leaded in elaborate geometrical
patterns with borders and lozenges of
emerald-green, hot red, midsummer-sky-
blue, gold and violet. While a single window
may strike one as garish, the sparkle and
shimmer of the whole is extremely pleasing.
The device of the Foul Anchor, which the
Admiralty shares as an emblem with
St Clement, appears more than once in
windows and walls, appropriate to two
admirals and a naval lieutenant commemorated in the church.

ST ENDELLION
St Endelienta
4m/6km N. of Wadebridge sw 9978
Stands almost alone on a hill-top, a long

way from its nearest village, Trelights, and
its nearest town, Port Isaac. One steps down
from the lichened granite exterior into a light
and airy building with two aisles, slate floors,
grey walls and light oak benches of a modern
and impressively simple design. There are
three single altars, that in the S. aisle being
a 15th-century table-tomb of blackish-blue
Catacleuse stone, possibly the shrine of
St Endelienta. The font is Norman. The
glass is unstained; the old roofs survive.
Indeed, the church gives the impression that
it goes on praying day and night, whether
there are people in it or not. St Endelienta's
touching hymn by Nicholas Rosscarrock,
c. 1550, is pasted into the hymn books. In
the tower is a Georgian ringers' rhyme on
a painted board. It is a prebendal church
which somehow escaped all reformations.
The low slate houses for the prebendaries
survive around the church.

ST ENODOC
(Dedication unknown)
by the mouth of the R. Camel, near
Trebetherick, 6m/10km N.W. of
Wadebridge sx 9378
Among grassy hillocks on the golf course;
small, crooked spire, 13th-century; restored
interior, dark and ancient. J.B. lies in the
churchyard here, his grave marked by the
delightful slate headstone beside the gate.

ST EWE
All Saints
5m/8km S.W. of St Austell sw 9746
Standing in a pleasant village of colour-
washed cottages. Octagonal spire with
squinches. Inside, hatchments; a fine Rysbrack bust with first-rate fruit and flower
garlands; wonderful screen of Devon type
across nave only, with an elaborate cornice
rich with beasts and birds and men among
foliage. Tiny arms of Henry VI carved on
the chancel side.

ST GERMANS
St Germans of Auxerre
8m/12km S.E. of Liskeard sx 3657
Differs from other churches in Cornwall
since it is of monastic origin and was attached
to an Augustinian priory founded in the 12th
century; earlier St Germans was the seat of
the bishops of the S.W. before Crediton and
Exeter. It consists of the nave and S. aisle of
what must have been an imposing structure.
The W. front has a magnificent Norman

doorway, with Art Nouveau ironwork by
Henry Wilson, and is flanked by two dis-
similar towers. Interior horribly scraped and
refurbished by St Aubyn, 1887–94, and
interesting rather for its architecture than
its contents. Monument to Edward Eliot,
1722, by Rysbrack, dramatically lit.

ST HILARY
St Hilary
4m/6km S. of Hayle SW 5531
Superb late church by William White, 1854,
with 13th-century spire. Spacious and mysterious interior with three wide E. chapels.
Early Christian inscribed stones, painted
stalls and pulpit.

ST JUST-IN-PENWITH
St Just
4m/6km N. of Land's End SW 3731
Remarkable for setting, where you look
down from steep churchyard paths over the
church to the still water of a tiny creek.
15th-century but heavily restored.

ST KEVERNE
St Keverne
9m/15km S.E. of Helston SW 7921
Dominates the village square, up a flight of
steps through a lych gate to good tower and
spire; spacious 15th-century interior with
wall-painting and bench-ends.

ST KEW
St James the Great
4m/6km N.E. of Wadebridge SX 0276
A stately church in a wooded valley with inn
and Georgian rectory nearby. 15th-century
interior vilely scraped; the screen incorporates a little old work; wagon roofs; much
glorious 15th-century painted glass; Elizabethan pulpit; bench-ends and Royal Arms,
1661, in coloured plaster.

ST MARTIN-BY-LOOE
St Martin
1m/2km N. of Looe SX 2655
The parish church of East Looe, but tucked
away in a narrow valley. The whole effect is
weathered and old and smacks of fishermen
home from the sea. The nucleus, as so often
in Cornwall, is a cruciform Norman fabric
refashioned in the 15th century. Wagon
roofs; modern rood screen; 17th-century
parclose; Norman font and 16th- and 17th-
century monuments.

ST MICHAEL PENKEVIL
St Michael
3m/4km S.E. of Truro SW 8542
A feudal village in bosky setting at the entrance to Tregothnan, Wilkins' vast early
19th-century mansion. The church, faithfully reconstructed by Street, 1862, must
have been and still is to a great extent one
of the most impressive in Cornwall; late
13th- and early 14th-century in character,
and of aisleless cruciform plan, the proportions and details alike are impressive. A
small college was established in 1319, but
much of the detail looks earlier, though this
may be due to time-lag. Boscawen monuments, 17th–19th-century, and late 15th-
century brass.

ST MINVER
St Menefreda
3m/4km N.W. of Wadebridge SW 9677
Attractive wooded church-town. 13th–15th-
century, octagonal spire; bench-ends; 1783
board with painted figures of bell-ringers
and a rhyme for them; rich Victorian E.
window by O'Connor.

ST NEOT
St Neot
5m/8km N.W. of Liskeard SX 1867
A slate and granite village in a wooded valley
below Bodmin Moor and dominated by the
church with handsome Decorated tower and
buttressed 16th-century double-aisled exterior. This is the Fairford of the West and
has 15 windows of medieval glass sensitively
renewed by W. Hedgeland, 1829; the most
interesting show the lives of St Neot and
St George. There are a rood screen and old
roofs. The walls are scraped.

ST WINNOW
St Winnow
2m/3km S. of Lostwithiel SX 1157
In a lovely situation on Fowey River, which
laps the churchyard wall. There are woods
in tiers across the wide river, an old stone
boathouse and a farm, once the rectory, by
the church. There is a fine early 16th-
century rood screen, well restored by
Edmund Sedding, 1907, and a splendid E.
window to the S. aisle filled with 15th- and
16th-century glass whose wealth of imagery
may well occupy the wandering attention of
the congregation. The old stained glass, the
Crucifixion, in the E. window of the chancel,

is to be noted; also the shape of the arches of the arcade – slightly stilted.

SANCREED
St Creden
3m/4km W. of Penzance sw 4229
Snuggles down behind a fine churchyard wall of dressed granite topped with flowering shrubs which sweeps round the curve of the road where a few solid and dignified buildings – school, schoolmaster's house, vicarage and another – make a group in a lonely landscape. The church has the usual Cornish arrangement, but low and small in scale. That seems appropriate in a situation where one is conscious of the narrow, wind- and rain-swept peninsula, which finishes in a mile or two at Land's End.

TINTAGEL
St Materiana
4m/6km N.W. of Camelford sx 0489
All alone on the open cliffs above the Atlantic, it still retains an atmosphere of early Christianity. A large Norman cruci- form church refashioned in the 13th century and later, but retaining its original plan. Scraped interior contains late 15th-century rood screen, Norman font, original 12th- century iron hinges to N. door, and ancient stone altar in vestry.

TRESILLIAN
Holy Trinity
3m/4km E. of Truro sw 8646
Tiny church of 1898 showing Edmund Sedding at his best, and sympathetically en- larged in 1904; smiling quirk to foliation of little windows. Three bells astride nave gable; chimney sensibly perched on gable of aisle.

TRURO
St Paul or St Clement
sw 8244
1848; traditional Cornish Perpendicular with granite arcades; chancel and tower by J. D. Sedding, 1882–9, who gave the ex- terior its ornate, dramatic character; excel- lent modern rood screen and old stone pulpit of unknown provenance.

TUCKINGMILL
All Saints
1m/2km N.E. of Camborne sw 6641
A strong church suitable for this former tin-mining area, in Romanesque style, by J. Hayward of Exeter, 1843–4. White- washed stone interior, with granite chancel arch and arcade. Glass by Robert Beer of Exeter.

Cumberland

Introduction

The establishment of Henry I held when the testing time came. Barons to fight; bishops to pray. In Durham, where they do things differently, one man did both and was Prince as well. That glance across the county boundary is justified, because where Cumberland sweeps up to Alston, the highest of England's country towns is already proclaiming affinities with Durham. Henry divided Carliol from Westmarieland. In 1157 it became finally a part of England. Its history since has been that of its great border town, Carlisle.

The buildings reflect the stones beneath them, the old slates of Skiddaw, old red sandstone and, as at Dacre, limestone, and the new red sandstone of the south-west coast from Silecroft to Whitehaven. The Abbey of Holme Cultram is built of this sandstone in its northern stretch from Maryport to Wigton. From Carlisle it runs down the east of the Eden Valley to Westmorland's Appleby and Kirkby Stephen. The Roman wall provided a special quarry, making possible, for example, the great achievements of the county at Lanercost Priory, beautiful in the Early English style, and in some unearthly mode of its own, and for another the Norman portions of Carlisle Cathedral, the rest of which is new red sandstone. With the exception of the Cathedral choir, Brigham church near Cockermouth is a good example of Perpendicular.

The coastal plain is really a further extension northward of the red sandstone of Cheshire.

The Cumbrian coastline sweeps round from Carlyle's 'grand old Solway Firth . . . with everlasting roar of the loud winds, and the going and coming of the great atlantic brine . . . doomed to a course of transcendent monotony, the very image as of a grey objectless eternity . . .' (wheer's Lincoln's Tennyson noo?) to just beyond Black Combe, that most southern out-thrust of Skiddaw slate, the oldest of the rocks, whose outline, like that of some heraldic couchant animal, dominates the view from the sitting-rooms of Morecambe, from ships at sea, from Scotland and from the Isle of Man.

The coast is alternately wild and industrial, old-fashioned and startlingly contemporary. A century ago, Whitehaven had already outlived the fame and prosperity that followed the inventions of the 18th-century engineers – coal-mining beneath the sea, steam pump and steam engine, coal, gas and railways. In our own century, this place has played a major part in the development of nuclear power, but the red sandstone ruins of Calder Abbey are still turned to gold by the light of the setting sun.

F.S.

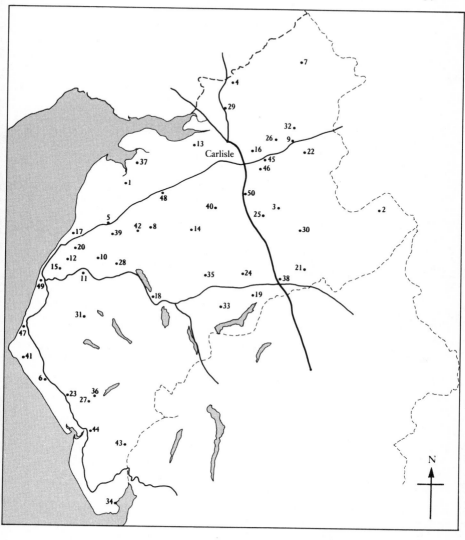

Selected List of Churches

ABBEY TOWN
St Mary
4m/6km S.E. of Silloth NY 1750
Church formed from the late 12th-century nave of Holme Cultram Abbey, a Cistercian foundation of 1150. The handsome W. portal of four orders with waterleaf capitals is covered by a fine porch of 1507.

ALSTON
St Augustine
16m/25km N.E. of Penrith NY 7146
By J. W. Walton, 1870; steeple completed in 1886. Large church of creamy stone with nave, S. aisle and dominant tower and spire. Rather a mixture of Gothic styles with lancets and plate tracery. Inside are Purbeck marble nave piers with heavy, richly carved capitals.

ARMATHWAITE
Chapel of Christ & St Mary
9m/15km S.E. of Carlisle NY 5046
Stands on a hillock, 12th-century Ermit-ethwaite, Hermit's Field, in fine scenery by the River Eden. The original chapelry fell into a ruinous state and was used as a cattle-shed until rebuilt before 1688 by Richard Skelton of nearby Armathwaite Castle. Today it is a plain stone edifice consisting of undivided nave and chancel, small W. turret containing one bell, and something about it still of the manger and the cattle in the straw that makes one think of it as a true church of the Nativity.

ARTHURET
St Michael
8m/12km N. of Carlisle NY 3869
Remarkable church rebuilt in 1609 in Gothic Survival Perpendicular style. All is convincing enough, with great three-light windows and embattled parapets, apart from the regularity of the exterior and the rather odd-looking 17th-century E. window.

ASPATRIA
St Kentigern
8m/12km N.E. of Maryport NY 1441
Setting. 12th-century doorway and tower

arch, otherwise a stately building of 1846–8 by Travis & Mangnall in the Early English style. 13th-century font. Good collection of Anglo-Danish sculpture and a fine hogback tombstone.

BECKERMET
St John the Baptist
3m/4km S. of Egremont NY 0106
By J. Birtley, 1878–9. In a striking situation high above the confluence of two becks, a most successful example of a small Victorian church with pleasing and well-designed interior. Collection of Anglo-Danish sculpture and later coffin lids. Nearby, 13th-century St Bridget's, now a mortuary chapel, has two shafts of Norman crosses in church-yard.

BEWCASTLE
St Cuthbert
9m/15km N. of Brampton NY 5674
Dramatic setting among Border fells. The church itself is not particularly interesting, but beside it is the celebrated late 7th-century Bewcastle Cross, an outstanding monument to the Golden Age of Northum-bria.

BOLTONGATE
All Saints
5m/8km S. of Wigton NY 2240
Fine view of Skiddaw. Originally Norman, rebuilt in the late 14th or early 15th century with a thrilling, steeply pointed tunnel vault to the nave.

BRAMPTON
St Martin
9m/15km N.E. of Carlisle NY 5361
By Philip Webb, 1874–8; his only completed church. Built of red sandstone in the Arts and Crafts style, mixed Gothic and ver-nacular elements. Wide and spacious interior with woodwork by local crafts-men and wonderful glass by Burne-Jones and the Morris firm. Tower by George Jack, 1906.

BRIDEKIRK
St Bride
2m/3km N. of Cockermouth NY 1133
By Cory & Ferguson, 1868–70; in the neo-Norman style. Large cruciform church with crossing tower and apse; some elements of the earlier church were also retained. The chief glory is the mid-12th-century font with a Runic inscription recording its maker, Rikart, and some lively carvings of scenes and dragons.

BRIGHAM
St Bridget
2m/3km W. of Cockermouth NY 0830
Late Norman, rebuilt early 15th century; the tower crowned with a saddleback roof added by Butterfield during his restoration of 1864–76.

BROUGHTON MOOR
St Columba
2m/3km S.E. of Maryport NY 0533
A small church by W. D. Caroe, 1905, and a quite original one. Pretty N. tower with an open porch beneath it. Rock-faced exterior with round-arched windows.

BURGH-BY-SANDS
St Michael
5m/8km N.W. of Carlisle NY 3259
Late Norman and Early English; built largely of stone from the Roman wall and strongly defensive against the Scots, particularly the broad 14th-century tower with its iron gate or yatt to the nave. 1½ miles to the N.W. is a monument to Edward I, who died whilst encamped on Burgh Marsh in 1307.

CALDBECK
St Kentigern
7m/11km S.E. of Wigton NY 3239
Large Norman and later church; the chancel was remodelled in 1512 and the whole well restored in the 19th century. Gravestone of John Peel in the churchyard.

CAMERTON
St Peter
3m/4km N.E. of Worthington NY 0330
Ancient and plain little church with neat pews and bobbin-ends; W. tower added in 1855. Effigy of knight known as Black Tom Curwen, 1510.

CROSBY ON EDEN
St John the Evangelist
4m/6km N.E. of Carlisle NY 4459
By R. W. Billings, 1854. Small red sandstone church of eccentric design with short tower and a spire with outlandish crockets and lucarnes. Stars of clear glass in the window tracery heads.

CROSSCANONBY
St John the Evangelist
3m/4km N.E. of Maryport NY 0639
Norman, incorporating Roman stones. Other stones, which were memorials before the Normans came, include a hogback gravestone carved like a little house of the dead, and a 10th-century cross fragment with dragons biting themselves. Carved gallery, 1730, and older carving in pews. Careful restoration by C. J. Ferguson in 1880.

CROSTHWAITE
St Kentigern
4m/6km W. of Kendal SD 4491
The present church, built on an ancient site, achieved its present form *c.* 1553, though it includes 14th-century arches. Twelve consecration crosses outside and nine inside were found in 1915; memorials of the Tudor consecration. Finely carved 14th-century font and 15th-century effigies. Recumbent white marble carving of the poet Robert Southey, d. 1846, by Lough; the church was restored as part of the memorial to Southey by Sir Giles Gilbert Scott.

DACRE
St Andrew
4m/6km S.W. of Penrith NY 4526
Late 12th-century chancel with lancet windows; the Norman tower was rebuilt in 1810; 17th-century altar rails; 13th-century effigy of a knight and two 9th-century cross shafts. The interesting lock and key of the S. door were the gift of Lady Anne Clifford, and are dated 1671.

DEARHAM
St Mungo
suburb, 2m/3km E. of Maryport NY 0736
12th- and 13th-century church with large carved Norman font and copious Anglo-Danish sculpture, including the Kenneth Cross.

EDENHALL
St Cuthbert
4m/6km N.E. of Penrith NY 5632
Away from the village in park of Eden Hall and commanding extensive views across Eden valley to fells. Small red sandstone medieval church with heavily machicolated Perpendicular W. tower and comical little spire. Restored interior with some 14th-century glass and roundels from the Netherlands. 17th–18th-century monuments.

FARLAM
St Thomas à Becket
2m/3km S.E. of Brampton NY 5558
By Anthony Salvin, 1860. Church of modest size in assured 13th-century style. Restrained interior with good timber roof.

GOSFORTH
St Mary
2m/3km N.E. of Seascale NY 0603
Red sandstone church mostly rebuilt in the Decorated style in 1896–9. In the churchyard the wondrous Gosforth Cross; a soaring Anglo-Norse creation of the later 10th century.

GREYSTOKE
St Andrew
5m/8km W. of Penrith NY 4430
Made collegiate in 1382, the church is vast and gracious. Transitional chancel arch; otherwise mostly 15th-century. Tower and chancel were rebuilt in 1848. There are 20 canons' stalls with interesting misericords and 15th-century glass in the the E. window.

HIGH HESKET
St Mary-in-the-Forest
8m/12km S.E. of Carlisle NY 4744
Built in 1530 with later additions, including the late 17th-century double bellcote. Black and white roof and a country Classical monument of 1677.

IRTHINGTON
St Kentigern
2m/3km W. of Brampton across R. Irthing NY 4961
Externally, it is all of 1849–53 by Bloxham, the N.W. tower added in 1897. But inside are the early 13th-century chancel arch and richly carved late 12th-century arcades of the original church.

IRTON
St Paul
3m/4km E. of Seascale NY 0803
By Miles Thompson, 1856–7. Fine site with view towards Wasdale Head. Nave, chancel and W. tower all in the Perpendicular style. Fine 9th-century cross shaft in the churchyard with patterning and vine-scrolls.

ISEL
St Michael
4m/6km N.E. of Cockermouth NY 1534
A largely Norman church with a 15th-century window bearing three sundials to mark the monastic hours. Anglo-Danish cross shaft bearing the rare three-armed symbol known as the triskele, one of the earliest symbols found on Christian monuments. This is a perfect English harmony of man and nature – a setting for Jane Austen. The old church stands on the banks of the Derwent. There is an ancient bridge of three arches rebuilt in 1812. The Hall, with its embattled pele tower and rows of square-mullioned windows, looks down from its eminence, which is washed by the Blumer beck, a tributary of the Derwent. The tree-hung stream near the church flows past the lawns of the delightful old vicarage. All around stretches a lost landscape of pasture and river. *O fortunatos nimium . . . !*

KIRKANDREWS-ON-ESK
St Andrew
1m/2km to the W. of Longtown, which is 8m/12km N. of Carlisle NY 3870
Attractive setting. Church of local red sandstone rebuilt in fine style in 1776 by the Rev. Robert Graham of Netherby Hall, the home of the Grahams, on which, amid its trees and meadows, the church looks from across the River Esk. The interior was sensitively restored by Temple Moore in 1893, when the chancel screen and new organ were provided.

KIRKOSWALD
St Oswald
7m/11km N. of Penrith NY 5541
The little sandstone town with its moated castle and house, now a museum, is one of the best in the county. Like many churches dedicated to St Oswald, this one is associated with a spring, but it is almost certainly the only one in which a pure spring of water issues from the conical hill at the foot of which the church stands, flows under the

length of the nave, and issues, as a drinking-well, outside the W. wall. The tower of 1897 stands oddly at the top of the hill 200 yards away from the church, which has interesting medieval fabric and a collegiate chancel of *c.* 1523.

LAMPLUGH
St Michael
7m/11km S. of Cockermouth NY 0820
By William Butterfield, 1870. Designed unusually in the Perpendicular style to match parts of the earlier church. Glass by Kempe.

LANERCOST
Priory of St Mary Magdalene
3m/4km N.E. of Brampton NY 5563
Beautifully situated in the richly wooded valley of the River Irthing and entered through an ancient gatehouse, the nave and N. aisle of the Priory, restored and refitted in the last century, now serve as the parish church. The Priory was founded about 1169 by Robert de Vallibus (de Vaux). Edward I, Queen Eleanor, Robert Bruce, and David King of Scotland cross and re-cross its history in the 14th century. The earliest portions, such as the base course on the S. of nave and transept, are Transitional; the remainder elegant Early English. It has a beautiful clerestory and W. front with bold recessed doorway and arcading. Inside are Burne-Jones lancets in rich colours and monuments by Boehm; in the S. chapel is the tomb of Lord Dacre of Battle of Flodden fame. The E. end of the present church, built after the Priory was dismantled, has a little 16th-century glass, but is mostly clear. To watch through this window sun and shadow dramatizing the soaring ruins of the transepts, tower and roofless choir outside, the walls still rising to their full height and carrying high up on one of them a Roman altar to Jupiter, one of the few in an English church, is to know life and death in the same moment.

MATTERDALE
(no dedication)
½m/1km N. of Dockray, which is 4m/6km S. of Troutbeck NY 3922
Setting. Rebuilt in 1685 with undivided nave and chancel and domestic-looking windows. The church was restored and the W. tower added in 1856. Inside is a 17th-century three-sided communion rail, an 18th-century pulpit, benches, and some panelling.

MILLOM
Holy Trinity
5m/8km S.W. of Broughton in Furness SD 2187
Late Norman sandstone church sheltering against the ruins of the 13th-century castle. Some later medieval work, Victorian restoration, and W. gallery of 1930. Nave has Norman piers and fine black and white roof, box pews, and monuments.
St George, town centre
In 1874–7, the new church of St George was built by Paley & Austin in an elaborate Decorated style with blind arcades and geometrical tracery. Fine central tower with recessed spire and good wagon roof to the nave.

MUNGRISDALE
St Kentigern
8m/12km N.E. of Keswick NY 3630
Fine views. Rebuilt in 1756, a homely, whitewashed church, one of the smallest in the district. Cut-down box pews and a panelled double-decker pulpit.

NETHER WASDALE
St Michael
4m/6km E. of Gosforth NY 1204
Small, partly Georgian building in a beautiful setting. Undivided nave and chancel with bellcote and, inside, a coved plaster ceiling. Late 17th-century panelling and carving of pulpit and lectern from York Minster.

NEWTON ARLOSH
St John the Evangelist
2m/3km S.W. of Kirkbride NY 1955
Small church licensed in 1304 to serve the new town founded by Holme Cultram Abbey. Defensible W. tower with no outer doorways and small windows; the nave also is tunnel-vaulted to provide fire protection.

PENRITH
St Andrew
18m/29km S.E. of Carlisle NY 5130
Stately red sandstone Classical church of 1720–2; the Norman W. tower was retained from the earlier church on the site. Nave has two tiers of round-arched windows and a Tuscan doorway through the base of the tower. Inside are three galleries on Tuscan columns, an elegant tower staircase, and a large Venetian E. window. Wall-paintings in the chancel are by Jacob Thompson.

Fine Saxon tombs and crosses in church-yard.

PLUMBLAND
St Cuthbert
2m/3km S. of Aspatria NY 1539
By J. A. Cory and C. J. Ferguson, 1870–1.
In Early English style with some Decorated features; re-used elements from the earlier church include the Norman chancel arch.

RAUGHTON HEAD
All Saints
2m/3km S. of Raughton and 7m/11km S. of Carlisle NY 3845
Church of 1761 in park of Rose Castle, home of the bishops of Carlisle. Nave with keyed, round-headed windows and a broad W. tower with neo-Norman top stage added in 1881.

ST BEES
St Mary & St Bega
4m/6km S. of Whitehaven SX 9711
Part of the conventual church of the old Priory, retained after the Dissolution. Cruci-form church of red sandstone with a quire of six bays, transepts, central tower and clerestoried nave of 1250. Although much restored, the church is unassailably im-posing. Magnificent Norman W. doorway with four rich chevron mouldings and beak-heads. There are two rose windows and many lancets, the eight most beautiful, seen from outside, being in the chancel. W. Butterfield restored the church in 1855–8 and built the present crossing tower; he later added the fine wrought-iron chancel screen. Organ by Fr Henry Willis, 1899.

TORPENHOW
St Michael
1m/2km N.E. of Bothel, which is 3m/4km S.E. of Aspatria NY 2039
Church with superb views of Solway, Scot-land, Lake District and Pennines. Norman in origin, though much restored. The ceiling of the nave, given by T. Addison, brother of the essayist, was erected in about 1689: 'a fair canopy of painted fir' with conventional flowers and gilding.

ULPHA
St John
4m/6km N. of Broughton in Furness SD 1993
Lovely old church, more or less as Words-worth knew it, with fragments of 18th-

century decoration and old timbers in black and white roof. It is built of local stone in a beautiful spot on the River Duddon. See Wordsworth's sonnets on the subject, especially the one beginning 'The Kirk of Ulpha to the pilgrim's eye'.

WABERTHWAITE
St John the Baptist
1m/2km S.E. of Ravenglass across R. Esk SD 1095
Some 15th-century windows, Norman font, pulpit of 1630, and Saxon crosses. There is a beautiful view of Lake mountains and Scafell from the churchyard, which thrusts out into the very sands of the Esk estuary – the strangest, most remote little church.

WARWICK
St Leonard
4m/6km E. of Carlisle NY 4656
Handsome Norman village church of red sandstone, memorable for the unusual blank arcading on the apse, a detail more at home in France.

WETHERAL
The Holy Trinity & St Constantine
4m/6km E. of Carlisle NY 4654
Set above the River Eden. Mostly early 16th-century exterior, the chancel rebuilt by Withers in 1872. Gothic Howard mausoleum of 1791 contains moving sculpture by J. Nollekens of dead mother and child, 1798.

WHITEHAVEN
St James
High Street, 7m/11km S. of Workington NX 9718
A church of 1752–3 with a wonderful Geor-gian interior, the best in the county. There are three galleries on Tuscan columns, a flat ceiling with stucco roundels, and a beautiful painted altarpiece of the Transfiguration by Correggio's pupil, Procaccini.

WIGTON
St Mary
11m/18km S.W. of Carlisle NY 2548
Built in 1788, the interior a triumph of painting, a study in grey, gold and strawberry-pink. Handsome pulpit with swags.

WORKINGTON
St John

17m/27km W. of Keswick NX 9928

By Thomas Hardwick, 1823. A Commissioners' church with massive Tuscan portico, based on Inigo Jones's at Covent Garden. Felicitous turret and cupola added in 1846. The interior, with Italianate fittings by Comper, reflects the movement to make the interior of churches more comely. This one, painted but rather barn-like, is dominated by the 20-foot-high coloured baldacchino, whose flat top is sustained over the altar by four gleaming round gold pillars. Hanging at the back is an elaborate star-like medallion with a figure of the Risen Saviour against rich red altar drapery. The needlework Royal Arms of 1846 were by the sister of the rector.

WREAY
St Mary

5m/8km S.E. of Carlisle NY 4348

Designed by talented amateur Sara Losh as a memorial to her sister Katherine, d. 1835. The church was consecrated in 1842, and is of unique design, drawing on the Continental Romanesque. Local masons were employed, and there is abundant exotic sculpture. Excellent details include the W. doorway enriched with flowers, birds and beetles, the green marble altar table supported by brass eagles, and the alabaster font, partly carved by Sara herself. In the churchyard is the cyclopean mausoleum for Katherine.

Derbyshire

Introduction

Derbyshire is a microcosm of England except that it has no sea. In the south it has pastoral country which merges into Leicestershire across the Trent, and here the older cottages and farms are of a dark red brick and the churches are of pale limestone. In the northern half of the county, stone never seems far below the surface, and stone of such variety of colour and quality as is found nowhere else in England – the silvery white stone of the Peak district where the drystone walls seem to take up more room than the grass in the little fields, and where the windswept farms are of a blue-grey limestone with mullions and transoms of a darker stone; limestones and ironstones of pale yellow, orange and brown; great rock formations suddenly intruding into landscaped gardens as at Chatsworth; stone which the Saxons delighted to carve into crosses, and of which they built their churches, the crypt at Repton being the most perfect survival; stone which the Normans used for churches as at Steetley and Melbourne. With this stone goes the remarkable scenery of the Peaks and Dales and of the moors of Derbyshire, which produce a wild natural landscape big enough to absorb the coach- and car-loads of pale mechanics from Leeds, Sheffield and Manchester, whose natural playground it is. Derbyshire has been mined for lead and alabaster and blue john and coal, and quarried for monumental stone as at Hopton Wood. Derbyshire also has its industrial districts – the earliest are Georgian and are associated with the spinning-mills of Crompton and Belper and the names of Arkwright and Strutt. On the eastern borders are coal districts, sooty, wire-strung and upheaved with excavations, and pitted with those sudden semi-towns one finds in neighbouring Notts. It has railway works at Derby, iron and steel at Staveley; it has the Rolls-Royce factory, and aeroplane and Celanese factories.

After its wonderful natural scenery and its less wonderful industrial districts, Derbyshire is chiefly a place of great houses – Chatsworth, a palace, set in magnificent landscaped park and gardens, 'Hardwick Hall more glass than wall', and the dramatically sited castle at Bolsover, all associated with the Cavendishes; Haddon Hall, ancient and intimate, and Sudbury Hall, mellow and friendly, both of which belonged to the Vernons; Kedleston, the 18th-century ancestral home of the Curzons; Calke, curious and remote, with a vivid family; and the more modest hall at Melbourne in the south. And here and there on hill-slopes are the Gothic Revival castles and abbeys of the Georgian and later industrialists, mostly now converted into institutions. In the north, too, it is a county of wells, dressed with pictures made of flowers at Whitsun and summer festivals. There are mineral springs and the hydros that go with them, the boarding-houses, conferences, conventions, kiosks, souvenirs and car parks of holidaymakers.

Churches are lower on the list of the county's attractions than scenery and houses. Those least spoiled by Victorian 'restoration' are private chapels – that at Haddon, with its wall-paintings, monuments and old woodwork and glass, like an untouched country church; and that at Chatsworth, sumptuous Renaissance of 1694 with marble and wood carving and a painted ceiling by Verrio. The parish churches, besides the Saxon and Norman work mentioned, are mostly small and severely restored, because there was plenty of money here in Victorian times, and the churches were generally stripped of their plaster and had their windows filled with greenish-tinted glass. Large, cruciform 13th-century churches are at Ashbourne, Bakewell and Wirksworth. Grand 14th-century work is at Chesterfield, Dronfield, Tideswell, Norbury, Sandiacre, and Whitwell. Spires are not typical of Derbyshire; the best is at Breadsall. Fifteenth-century architecture, 'Perpendicular', so common in the rest of England, is rare here, and the tower of Derby All Saints is its noblest expression. Several churches were built in the troubled century, following the Reformation, still Gothic in style, at Carsington, Risley and Foremark. The 18th century produced much good wrought-iron work, particularly that of Robert Bakewell. Gibbs' design for All Saints, Derby, 1723–6, now the Cathedral, is the most distinguished Classical church in the county, and there are a few unrestored chapels of great charm. The 19th-century churches of Derbyshire are not of first rank; the best are Sir Giles Gilbert Scott's work at Edensor, the more individual and un-Derbyshire church at Bamford by Butterfield and, by the local Derby firm of Stevens and Robinson, the grand estate church at Osmaston and the more individual St Luke's, Derby. In the present century, another Derby firm, Currey and Thompson, are worth looking out for, especially at St Mary the Virgin, Buxton.

J.B.

1 Alfreton	14 Breadsall	27 Darley Dale
2 Ashbourne	15 Buxton	28 Denby
3 Ashover	16 Carsington	29 Derby
4 Aston-on-Trent	17 Castleton	30 Dethick
5 Ault Hucknall	18 Chaddesden	31 Doveridge
6 Bakewell	19 Chapel-en-le-Frith	32 Dronfield
7 Bamford	20 Chesterfield	33 Eckington
8 Barlborough	21 Church Broughton	34 Edensor
9 Barlow	22 Church Wilne	35 Egginton
10 Bolsover	23 Crich	36 Elvaston
11 Bonsall	24 Cubley	37 Etwall
12 Brailsford	25 Dalbury	38 Eyam
13 Brassington	26 Dale Abbey	39 Foremark

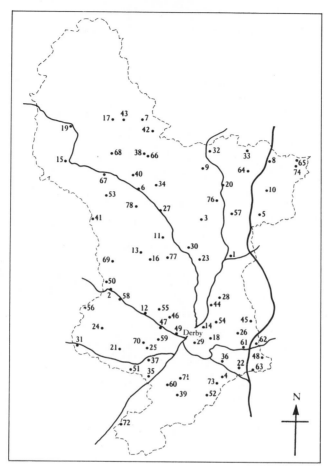

Selected List of Churches

ALFRETON
St Martin
10m/16km S. of Chesterfield SK 4155
Long and low with a broad N. aisle added in 1868, by T. C. Hine. It stands on the edge of the town, and the setting and scale are rather that of a prosperous village church. The lower part of the tower is 13th-century; otherwise the church is 14th-century, with the bold tracery motif of a rectangle with ogee ends consistently used. Exquisite late 18th-century monument by the Fishers of York.

ASHBOURNE
St Oswald
13m/21km N.W. of Derby SK 1846
Approached through 18th-century wrought-iron gates from Church Street, with its 16th-century Grammar School and 18th-century houses, the graceful church has an attractive setting on the edge of town and a breath-taking tower and spire. The chancel is Early English, dedicated in 1241, with noble lancet windows; other parts are Decorated, and there are great Perpendicular windows. The whole building has a curious irregularity, but ever-changing vistas. The S. aisle is so wide that it appears as a second nave. Plenty of Victorian stained glass and Arts and Crafts glass in a S. aisle window, 1905. Monuments, most in the N. transept, including the famous little girl, Penelope Boothby, 1781.

ASHOVER
All Saints
3m/4km W. of Clay Cross SK 3463
Beautifully placed among trees, the E. end framing the view at the end of the broad village street, with the characteristic Derbyshire outline, low and embattled, the tower with a spire set behind battlements. The church is mainly of the 14th and 15th centuries; the spire and rood screen given by the Babingtons. There are good alabaster tombs and brasses, and a lovely Norman lead font with figures in an arcade.

ASTON-ON-TRENT
All Saints
6m/10km S.E. of Derby SK 4129
At first sight a 14th-century church and nothing special, but on closer inspection the tower is clearly Norman, and its top has slightly amusing-looking obelisk pinnacles of post-Reformation date. Saxon evidence on the N. side of the nave. Attractively weathered S. side, the chancel window in two tiers, set in deeply chamfered rectangular surround.

AULT HUCKNALL
St John the Baptist
5m/8km N.W. of Mansfield SK 4665
In the winter the towers of Hardwick Hall can be seen a mile to the S. The churchyard nicely cluttered and random; the church picturesque in its varied outline. Norman origins, but externally all Perpendicular; dark and holy within with Norman arcade and crossing arches, and very narrow, possibly Saxon, arch opening into the small chancel. In the W. wall outside, a Norman carved tympanum depicting St George and the Dragon and St Margaret emerging from the body of the Devil. Fine monument to the first Countess of Devonshire, 1627, and a memorial to Thomas Hobbes, the philosopher. Excellent furnishings by William Butterfield, who restored the church in 1805–8.

BAKEWELL
All Saints
7m/11km N.W. of Matlock SK 2168
Well set above this ancient town and crowned by a distinctive octagonal crossing tower and spire. Originally Norman and on a grand scale; see the fragmentary blank arcade at the W. end. The rest 13th- and 14th-century, but much rebuilt in the 19th century. There is much to see inside: rare medieval wall-monument to Godfrey Foljambe and wife, 1385; interesting Vernon monuments and important Saxon sculpture, including the handsome early 9th-century churchyard cross.

BAMFORD
St John the Baptist
2m/3km N.W. of Hathersage SK 2083
By William Butterfield, 1856–60. Beautiful church with soaring steeple, quite un-Derbyshire-like. Narthex leads to an interior with Decorated tracery and excellent glass by Preedy. Circular tapering marble font by the architect.

BARLBOROUGH
St James
7m/11km W. of Worksop SE 6334
Leafy setting on a bend in the village street. Small but stately. Mostly 14th-century and over-restored. Interesting E. window. The tower is 13th-century, apart from the top. N. arcade of *c.* 1200 with waterleaf capitals.

BARLOW
St Lawrence
3m/4km N.W. of Chesterfield SK 3474
From the street, the bold Norman-style chancel of 1867 by S. Rollinson hides the medieval building behind, with genuine Norman work. The Lady Chapel of 1340 contains alabaster slabs to Robert Barley, d. 1467, and his wife.

BOLSOVER
St Mary
6m/10km E. of Chesterfield SK 4770
The dour little town is memorable for its castle, rather a major house, 17th-century and partly ruined; it stands in a magnificent position on a bluff overlooking an awesome landscape of coal-mining and industry. The interest of the church is in the 13th-century tower with broach spire, and the Cavendish chapel, built in 1624 and housing two huge monuments. The rest of the church was destroyed by fire in 1897 and again in 1960, and restored by Louis Ambler and Taylor Young and partners, respectively.

BONSALL
St James
2m/3km S.W. of Matlock SK 2758
Perched on a hill, above the stone village, with a fine cross in the market-place; embattled and pinky-grey, the spire a flight of fancy. The exterior is largely rebuilt, but inside, tall 13th-century arcades, the N. slightly later than the S. The stone is silvery, the walls cream-plastered, the texture and colour soft everywhere.

BRAILSFORD
All Saints
7m/11km N.W. of Derby SK 2541
Among trees away from the village. Norman remains; early 14th-century chancel; buttressed W. tower with Perpendicular door and window. Rare 11th-century cross in the churchyard.

BRASSINGTON
St James
4m/6km W. of Wirksworth SK 2354
Commanding position at the top of the stone-built village. Basically Norman; especially fine S. arcade with circular piers, waterleaf, and scalloped capitals. Refaced W. tower. Otherwise mostly 19th-century and somewhat harsh, but with some good detailing.

BREADSALL
All Saints
2m/3km N.E. of Derby SK 3739
The fine steeple is a landmark across the broad Derwent Valley north of Derby. Early 13th-century tower, four-square and plain; elegant 14th-century spire. Handsome S. windows to the 14th-century nave. Felicitous restoration by W. D. Caroe after fire damage by suffragettes in 1915.

BUXTON
St Mary the Virgin
Dale Road SK 0573
1914–15, by the Derby Arts and Crafts architects Currey and Thompson. Original and attractive, with pretty eyebrow dormers rather than a clerestory in the sweeping roof. Good contemporary furnishings.

CARSINGTON
St Margaret
2m/3km W. of Wirksworth SK 2553
A modest Perpendicular-style church, but the sundial on the E. wall bears the legend 'Re-edified 1648', which makes this a most interesting example of Gothic Survival and an unusual date for the rebuilding of a church.

CASTLETON
St Edmund
5m/8km W. of Hathersage SK 1582
Standing in the middle of this close-knit village, in the lee of Peveril castle, church with 14th-century tower. The nave something of a surprise, shorn of its aisles in 1837,

giving the appearance of a Commissioners' church of the period. Charming Gothic porch. Plain plastered interior with a Norman chancel arch and 17th-century box pews.

CHADDESDEN
St Mary
district of Derby, 2m/3km E. of town centre SK 3837
The village has long since been engulfed by the suburbs of Derby. The church is interesting because a rebuilding is documented *c.* 1354, and yet it is still in the Decorated style. Note the tracery in the chancel windows. Pleasant interior has sedilia, piscina, screen, carved bench-ends and a stone lectern built into the N. wall.

CHAPEL-EN-LE-FRITH
St Thomas à Becket
5m/8km N. of Buxton SK 0580
Approached through 18th-century gate-piers at the end of the market-place, on a bluff above the low town. The first impression is of a Classical church, which turns out to be a fashionable dressing-up in 1731–3, by George Platt, of an early 14th-century building.

CHESTERFIELD
St Mary and All Saints
10m/16km S. of Sheffield SK 3871
A town church on a prodigious scale; cruciform, with long nave and chancel, flanked by various chapels, reflecting the wealth of the town's guilds. Famous for its crooked spire of timber and lead, which long since warped into its present ungainly shape. The crossing was dedicated in 1234, but most of the church dates from 100 years later. The interior, lofty, spacious and elegant, has a 14th-century nave of six bays with tall, graceful columns, and appears almost sophisticated after the Norman homespun of many Derbyshire churches. In the Lady Chapel are alabaster tombs of the Foljambes – strange, fascinating, and of delicate workmanship. Rich furnishings everywhere; medieval screens; a Jacobean pulpit; exquisite 18th-century candelabra of wrought iron. Stained glass by Sir Ninian Comper and Christopher Webb.

CHURCH BROUGHTON
St Michael and All Angels
3m/4km N.E. of Sudbury SK 2033
Approached by an avenue of limes. A satisfying, mostly early 14th-century church. The tower has a short spire and curious corbelled-out pinnacles. Tudor clerestory, the earlier roof-line visible against the tower inside. Norman evidence at the E. end of the N. arcade. Norman tub font.

CHURCH WILNE
St Chad
3m/5km S.W. of long Eaton SK 4431
The church is set in meadows by the Derwent, with the well of St Chad nearby. Substantial three-stage tower with a stair turret that seems to grow out of the upper part. The church is mostly 14th-century, the S. aisle extended eastward in 1622, and all is tied together by 15th-century battlements. The nave and aisles are spacious and light, having wide three-light lancet windows and clear glass, in contrast to the 17th-century Willoughby Chapel, which takes its sombre colour from the original Flemish glass. The church was restored by Currey and Thompson after a fire in 1917, and has some of their Arts and Crafts furnishings. There are bad but amusing alabaster monuments and, in the churchyard, good 17th- and 18th-century slate headstones.

CRICH
St Mary
4m/6km N. of Belper SK 3554
Externally a handsome if standard composition. Nice unrestored Decorated tracery. Perpendicular W. tower; Norman arcade. Rare stone lectern in the N. wall of the chancel; massive Norman font; monuments.

CUBLEY
St Andrew
S. of the village, 4m/6km N. of Sudbury SK 1638
Proud Perpendicular W. tower with coats of arms of the Montgomery family and a great W. window; 17th-century nave windows, Norman S. arcade; 13th-century chancel, with tiny lancet windows, but a broad E. window. Remains of a scheme of painted decoration. Two 15th-century monuments.

DALBURY
All Saints
6m/9km W. of Derby SK 2634
A narrow lane leads to a farming hamlet and the small church at the end, mostly 19th-century, with a sweet little castellated tower like a toy castle. A loveable interior

with box pews and late 17th-century font and pulpit of 1862.

DALE ABBEY
All Saints
3m/4km S.W. of Ilkeston SK 4338
Romantic setting in a secluded valley, beyond the village, near the ruined arch of the 12th-century Abbey with a hermitage close by. Tiny church and farmhouse co-exist under one roof, and are pleasant to behold. The interior is a delight, minute and higgledy-piggledy, with box pews, a gallery in the roof, a 'cupboard' altar, and a pulpit dated 1634. Late 13th-century mural of the Annunciation, Visitation and Nativity.

DARLEY DALE
St Helen
2m/3km N.W. of Matlock SK 2661
Set by a giant yew tree, the church is cruciform and largely Perpendicular; of varied outline, with boldly castellated transepts which overpower the chancel. Wonderful window by Sir Edward Burne-Jones, 1863. Fragment of a Saxon cross with Geometric ornament. A whole collection of coffin lids stacked up in S. porch.

DENBY
St Mary the Virgin
3m/4km S. of Ripley SK 3946
Small but with a clerestory and over-large battlements, 14th-century W. tower with a beautiful parapet frieze. Nicely weathered, with a mixture of stone. Vaulted S. porch. Curiously lopsided interior with 13th-century arcade on S., and two tiers of windows with gallery on N.

DERBY
SK 3536
St John the Evangelist, Bridge Street
1826–7 by Francis Goodwin. A simple rectangle with cast-iron tracery, turrets and pinnacles, all battlemented and with that papery thinness characteristic of pre-Puginian Gothic.
St Luke, Parliament Street
1872 by Stevens and Robinson. A bold rock-faced building; monumental N.W. tower with saddleback roof. The chancel rises above a fortress-like basement, and the nave windows rise through the eaves into gables. In its begrimed state, a stubborn testament of faith in a changing inner-city suburb. Inside, the impression is quite different, as

the appearance of height gives way to excessive breadth, with the aisles no more than narrow passages. The nave is plain, relying on scale for its effect, whilst the chancel is richly detailed with polished marble and alabster.
St Mary's Chapel, Bridge Gate
Picturesque view from across the river unforgiveably compromised by the inner ring road which has been routed to within a hair's breadth of the chapel. One of only five surviving bridge chapels, 14th-century and later.

DETHICK
St John the Baptist
2m/3km S.E. of Matlock SK 3257
Fine position on a hill. The remarkable W. tower, modest in scale but lavish in detail, was built by Sir Anthony Babington in the 1530s; it has a curious stair turret which rises above the rest. There is a clerestory, but there are no aisles. The manor house has gone, but a 16th-century tithe barn remains.

DOVERIDGE
St Cuthbert
2m/3km E. of Uttoxeter SK 1134
Approached beneath the cover of a venerable yew and set in the former grounds of the demolished Hall. The 13th-century work is memorable – tall chancel and massive W. tower. The rest is mostly 14th-century. The absence of a chancel adds to the spaciousness of the interior.

DRONFIELD
St John Baptist
5m/8km N. of Chesterfield SK 3578
The surprise is the huge and sumptuous late-Decorated chancel, attached to an otherwise unremarkable building. The tracery of the E. window fell in 1563, and was rebuilt in a curious but impressive grid. The early 14th-century aisle windows show some wayward variations on the standard intersecting pattern. The decorative quatrefoils in the parapet are windows added in 1855. The chancel contains fragments of medieval glass.

ECKINGTON
St Peter & St Paul
5m/8km E. of Dronfield SK 4379
Massive 13th-century tower with round-arched W. doorway, lancet windows, and low, thick-set 14th-century spire. Classical

S. aisle and porch, 1763, by John Platt. Inside, too, history in stone. The E. bays of the nave arcades are late 12th-century, the rest 13th; the N. aisle 14th and 15th; the chancel Classical also – but turned Gothic again in 1907.

EDENSOR
St Peter
2m/3km E. of Bakewell SK 2569
George Gilbert Scott Snr., 1867; set in a pretty model village in Chatsworth Park. It provides an impressive essay in the Early English style with its tall spire and interior with Hardman glass. Distinguished monument to William, first Earl of Devonshire, d. 1625, and Henry Cavendish, d. 1616.

EGGINTON
St Wilfrid
4m/6km N.E. of Burton-on-Trent SK 2628
Attractive small village church, mainly *c.* 1300. The steep chancel roof rises well above the nave. The S. side is especially rewarding, with the ordered simplicity of the chancel and the chaotic dispersal of the windows in the aisle and equally chaotic niches inside.

ELVASTON
St Bartholomew
4m/6km S.E. of Derby SK 4132
Medieval and 19th-century, restored and extended by Bodley, 1905. Unusual 15th-century W. tower, neighbour to the fantastic Gothic castle.

ETWALL
St Helen
6m/10km S.W. of Derby SK 2631
Norman and later church set between village street and almshouses. Externally mostly Decorated and Perpendicular. Stone lectern in N. wall of chancel and Port family brasses.

EYAM
St Lawrence
5m/8km N. of Bakewell SK 2176
Famous as the village that halted the plague in 1666, when the incumbent closed the village to the outside world. The Mompesson chair in the chancel commemorates the event. 13th-century chancel with a huge sundial of 1775; 16th- and 17th-century wall-paintings above the arcades. Norman font. Important Saxon cross in the churchyard.

FOREMARK
St Saviour
2m/3km E. of Repton SK 3326
Built by Sir Francis Burdett, 1662, in his park at Foremark Hall. A Gothic church without, except for window-spacing and some strapwork, but completely Renaissance within. Original furnishings, neither Gothic nor Carolean, but rather the Jacobean style of 50 years earlier; screen, triple-decker pulpit, box pews, and a wrought-iron communion rail by Robert Bakewell, *c.* 1710.

GREAT LONGSTONE
St Giles
2m/3km N.W. of Bakewell SK 2071
14th-century arcades and tower, but in appearance mostly plain late-Perpendicular. Inside, all the Perpendicular roofs survive. Careful restoration by Norman Shaw in 1873. He retained the Perpendicular parclose screen, adding his own stalls, reredos, pulpit and stained glass.

HARTINGTON
St Giles
9m/15km N. of Ashbourne SK 1260
Raised above the spreading village, the cruciform church straddles the mound on which it sits, with proud, ashlar-faced tower looking out over the roof-tops. Inside there are vistas through arcades and into transepts, and a sense of interconnecting parts making up the whole.

HATHERSAGE
St Michael
8m/12km N. of Bakewell SK 2381
Largely Perpendicular exterior but 14th-century within; restored by Butterfield, 1849–52. Here are the famous Eyre brasses, beginning with Robert, d. 1459, showing him in armour with his wife and children.

HOPE
St Peter
4m/6km N.W. of Hathersage SK 1783
Sombre setting with a squat early 14th-century steeple, the rest consistently Perpendicular, embattled and pinnacled. Chancel rebuilt in 1881, re-using the early 14th-century piscina and sedilia. Stone screen behind the altar to form the vestry.

HORSLEY
St Clement
4m/6km S. of Ripley SK 3844
Commanding position overlooking the

Derwent Valley; impressive E. view, all embattled and pinnacled; 14th-century squat broach spire, and windows with that satisfying combination of flat heads and cusped tracery.

ILKESTON
St Mary the Virgin
8m/12km N.E. of Derby SK 4641
The church commands the top of the main street, just off the spacious market-place. A sturdy town church but, alas, very much over-restored. In 1909–10 the nave was lengthened three bays to the W. end and the tower rebuilt. Three bays survive of the Norman arcade, raised in the 14th century. Rare and delicate early 14th-century pierced stone chancel screen. Fine sedilia and double piscina in the late 13th-century chancel.

KEDLESTON
All Saints
4m/6km N.W. of Derby SK 3041
The old village was moved, but the medieval church still stands cheek by jowl with the grand 18th-century Hall by Robert Adam. Late 13th-century cruciform church, with crossing tower and transepts, Norman S. doorway; 14th-century raising of the tower; 17th-century E. end and N. aisle added by Bodley in 1907–13, as a memorial to Lady Curzon, Vicereine of India.
R.C.F.

KIRK LANGLEY
St Michael
4m/6km N.W. of Derby SK 2838
The path passes beneath a yew to reveal the attractively irregular N. side of the church. Mainly early 14th-century, windows with Y-tracery, Geometric tower screen. Perpendicular parclose screen.

LONG EATON
St Lawrence
9m/15km E. of Derby SK 4933
Approached from the market-place, the church appears modest, as what is immediately seen is the medieval tower and nave; but in 1868 G. E. Street built a new nave, N. aisle and chancel, the old nave becoming no more than a S. aisle. Late Norman S. doorway.

MACKWORTH
All Saints
3m/4km N.W. of Derby SK 3137
In a field, with a neat graveyard surrounded by a ha-ha. Mostly noble 14th-century work with large rectangular windows, Perpendicular W. tower, and recessed spire. The tower seems to have been built to be defensible, as there is no external door, the internal door has provision for barring, and the lower openings are small. Sumptuous and fantastic late-Victorian and Edwardian alabaster decoration and furnishings.

MAPLETON
St Mary
1m/2km N.W. of Ashbourne SK 1647
Looking across the River Dove to the park of Okeover Hall, a plain and small 18th-century stone church, the short W. tower unexpectedly crowned with a diminutive octagonal dome. Stained glass of 1926, by A. J. Davies.

MARSTON-ON-DOVE
St Mary
4m/6km N. of Burton-on-Trent SK 2329
In a flat plain near the confluence of the Dove and the Trent. Fine 14th-century steeple; 13th-century chancel and 14th-century nave. Spacious interior, as the N. aisle was given an upper storey in the 15th century. 18th-century organ removed from Sudbury Hall. The church has the oldest bell in the county, cast in 1366.

MELBOURNE
St Michael & St Mary
7m/11km S. of Derby SK 3825
A singularly ambitious cruciform Norman church of *c.* 1130 with twin W. towers and crossing tower, a stone-vaulted narthex, and, originally, apsed chancel and aisles. Why was it built in this small market town? An austere and noble interior. Nave of six bays, with tall, heavy circular piers, stilted arches, and much zig-zag. Above, triforium with arches in groups of three, clerestory behind, and a processional way all around.

MONYASH
St Leonard
4m/6km W. of Bakewell SK 1566
Beneath the high moors. The church is cruciform though on a small scale. Attractive contrasting stone; 13th- and 14th-century, the earliest features the chancel arch, sedilia,

and piscina. Curious tower stair rising from the aisle.

MORLEY
St Matthew
4m/6km N.E. of Derby SK 3940
Spired country church among lawns and trees, with attractive 18th-century rectory, apart from the village. W. of the church is the beautiful Bateman mausoleum, 1897, by G. F. Bodley. Inside, a golden light and much texture. S. nave arcade Norman; the rest 14th- and 15th-century. Glass from Dale Abbey made in 1482. Fascinating brasses, monuments, and incised slabs telling 500 years of family history, mainly of the Stathums, Sacheverells and Babingtons; Katherine Babington, d. 1543, is the best.

MUGGINTON
All Saints
6m/10km N.W. of Derby SK 2843
In an elevated position overlooking the rolling S. Derbyshire farmland. The tower was Norman – see the N. side – otherwise 13th–15th-century and unrestored; good, welcoming interior with pews, screen, and brasses.

NORBURY
St Mary & St Barlok
4m/6km S.W. of Ashbourne SK 1242
Quiet, leafy setting above the river Dove, close by the manor with its late 13th-century hall. The church, otherwise small, has a splendid 14th-century chancel – spacious and wide, the windows fine and tall. Much of the original glass survives, with patterns and heraldry in grisaille and soft colours. Altar tombs of the Fitzherberts, with good effigies and enchanting figures of weepers; a bedesman sits under Sir Ralph's foot.

NORTH WINGFIELD
St Lawrence
2m/3km N.E. of Clay Cross SK 4165
In colliery country and well-placed on an escarpment overlooking an industrial landscape. Fine Perpendicular W. tower. The chancel is Decorated, but the overall impression is of a consistent Perpendicular building much restored in the 1860s and 70s. Attractive graveyard. The windows are full of Victorian stained glass, contributing to the atmosphere of the interior.

OSMASTON
St Martin
2m/3km S.E. of Ashbourne SK 1943
A charming estate village with picturesque cottages and stately church of 1845 by Henry Stevens. Decorated style, perhaps a little too correct.

RADBURNE
St Andrew
4m/6km W. of Derby SK 2836
In Radburne Park; a fine old yew tree in the churchyard. Small, mainly of the 13th and 14th centuries, with admixture on the S. side of Tudor windows and 18th-century porch. The zig-zagged sedilia has a bishop's crozier marked on the shaft; medieval benches from Dale Abbey; proud display of Pole monuments and hatchments.

REPTON
St Wystan
5m/8km N.E. of Burton-on-Trent SK 3026
Church with graceful spire; old priory arch leading to the school; pleasant country town with market cross – a satisfying group. The church has all types of architecture from the 8th century to the 15th, but the most exciting part is the Saxon chancel and, beneath it, the crypt. Winding stairways lead to it; it has a rough stone vault and four pillars wreathed with spiral bands.

RISLEY
All Saints
2m/3km N.W. of Long Eaton SK 4635
Of curious and delightful appearance, explained on close inspection by the date 1593 over the S. door. Top-heavy tower in miniature. Not actually consecrated until 1632; late-Gothic becoming Renaissance.

SANDIACRE
St Giles
2m/3km N. of Long Eaton SK 4736
Set on a hill, with the industry of the Erewash valley below, the church has a memorable silhouette – high Norman nave, and still higher Decorated chancel of almost cathedral proportions, with tall pinnacled buttresses. Inside, the same contrast; the simple whitewashed nave, robust Norman chancel arch, and breath-taking chancel, bathed in light, with star and leaf shapes in the tracery, and richly ornamented sedilia and piscina.

SAWLEY
All Saints

adjoins Long Eaton to S.W. SK 4731
An avenue of limes leads from the main road;
13th- and 14th-century with Perpendicular
flourishes. Dignified Perpendicular chantry
chapel, like a domestic bay window, all panelled and vaulted inside, with the tomb of
John Bothe, d. 1496. A stone screen behind
the altar; Perpendicular screens and stalls.

STAVELEY
St John the Baptist

4m/6km N.E. of Chesterfield SK 4374
S. side and tower are medieval, the N. side
and chancel by Sir George Gilbert Scott,
1865–9, but all hang together well enough.
The Frecheville chapel, S. chancel, is mid-
17th-century with a superb armorial window
of 1676.

STEETLEY
All Saints

2m/3km W. of Worksop SK 5579
Astonishingly complete showpiece of a small
Norman church of nave, chancel and apse
standing alone in the fields. Built about
1160, left roofless after the Commonwealth;
restored by J. L. Pearson and reconsecrated
in 1882. Inside, a vaulted apse, lavishly decorated nave and chancel arches, the capitals
scalloped, or carved with leaves, animals or
people.

STONEY MIDDLETON
St Martin

5m/8km N. of Bakewell SK 2375
Setting in Peak village. A small octagonal
church with central lantern and lunettes was
added to the low Perpendicular tower in
1759.

TADDINGTON
St Michael

5m/8km W. of Bakewell SK 1471
The moor drops down sharply to the church
and village and the Dale below. Handsome
church with a spire, largely 14th-century
with impressive chancel and E. window;
scraped interior. Stone lectern built into the
chancel wall.

TIDESWELL
St John the Baptist

6m/10km E. of Buxton SK 1575
'The Cathedral of the Peak', sheltered in a
hollow on the bleak moors, is a grand and

inspiring church of the 14th century. The
Perpendicular tower has character, with
immense turrets and pinnacles, and the fine
chancel compares with Ashbourne, Norbury
and Sandiacre. There is flowing tracery in
the windows and a stone screen behind the
altar, with canopied niches, which forms the
vestry . At the W. end is a mighty arch
into the nave and a great panelled window;
interesting tombs and brasses.

TISSINGTON
St Mary

4m/6km N. of Ashbourne SK 1752
Jacobean manor house, grey stone cottages,
a triangular green, and five wells (dressed
with flower mosaics on Ascension Day),
form a perfect village setting. The church,
with a sturdy Norman tower, stands on a
bank in the midst. Inside, too much restoration in 1854, but an entertaining Fitz-
herbert monument of 1643 with ladies in
pretty Jacobean dress, a two-decker pulpit,
and a Norman font with incised creatures.

TRUSLEY
All Saints

6m/10km W. of Derby SK 2535
By the hall, and approached along a grassy
path, the small brick church of 1713 with
stone details and an elaborate pedimented
doorway. The interior is delightfully all of a
piece with communion rails, three-decker
pulpit, box pews, and font.

TWYFORD
St Andrew

5m/8km S.W. of Derby SK 3228
Attractive position in meadowland by the
Trent. A small church, appealing because
of the variety of styles, the humble scale,
and the nave overgrown with ivy. The nave
is plain 18th-century, and does not prepare
for the Norman chancel within.

WALTON-ON-TRENT
St Laurence

4m/6km S.W. of Burton-on-Trent SK 2118
A Trent Valley village, with the Drakelow
power station looming to the N. Norman
arcade, 13th-century chancel, restored by
Street in 1868. The S. transept was founded
as a chantry in 1334, and has a large squint
to the chancel. Two early 20th-century nave
windows, curious in their tracery, and internally mullioned.

WESTON-ON-TRENT
St Mary
6m/10km S.E. of Derby SK 4028
Alone among trees by the river; small and mostly 13th-century. The nave and aisles wide, not long, with very tall, slim pillars, unexpectedly dignified and impressive. A Jacobean pulpit, and fragments of a monument in the gruesome taste of the early 17th century; a skeleton with hour-glass, pick and shovel. 18th-century timber-framed porch adds a domestic touch.

WHITWELL
St Laurence
4m/6km S.W. of Worksop SK 5276
Pleasantly placed in a once pretty village, now surrounded by collieries. Approached from the N. there is still open farmland, and the stately church stands on the edge of the new village, in part of the old, which retains some character. The core of the church is Norman; W. tower, S. doorway, nave, and clerestory. The interior is a delight, light and cheerful with the absence of stained glass, and whitewashed walls. The chancel arch round, but with keeled shafts, preparing one for the Decorated chancel with rich sedilia; the transepts are Decorated too. Altogether a rewarding building, full of texture and interest, fortunately not spoiled by too much tidying-up, and set in an attractive graveyard.

WILNE
St Chad
½m/1km N.E. of Shardlow SK 4430
In the meadows by the Derwent, the well of St Chad nearby. The 14th- and 15th-century work was restored after a fire in 1917. Nave and aisles are spacious and light with wide three-light lancet windows and clear glass, in contrast to the 17th-century Willoughby chapel which takes sombre colour from the original Flemish glass. Alabaster monuments of 1622, bad but amusing, and good 17th- and 18th-century slate headstones in the churchyard.

WINGERWORTH
All Saints
2m/3km S. of Chesterfield SK 3867
A large new church of 1964 by Naylor, Sale and Widdows has been added on to the side of the ancient building; would it be allowed today? An ingenious plan, with the old nave forming a narthex to the new, which is orientated N.–S. Early Norman chancel arch and N. arcade, 13th-century chancel, and a rare Perpendicular rood loft. Pretty S. porch with curved battlemented gable. Light and spacious new church, spanned by curved concrete arches.

WIRKSWORTH
St Mary
4m/6km S. of Matlock SK 2854
A grey market town with steep, winding streets, set among bleak hills. A large cruciform church, dating from the 13th century, much added to and restored by George Gilbert Scott in 1876. It is at the hub of the small town, set in a graveyard enclosed by railings and surrounded by a ring of houses, rather like a miniature cathedral close. The interior is impressive, with lovely vistas. Exceptionally interesting sculptured 9th-century coffin lid with scenes from the Gospels. Two fonts, one Norman, one 17th-century, brasses, and good monuments.

YOULGREAVE
All Saints
3m/4km S. of Bakewell SK 2164
The massive, stately Perpendicular tower stands four-square to the winds of the Peak. Inside is a wide Norman nave; the S. arcade is particularly impressive, and there is fine Norman carving. The font of *c.* 1200 has a separate holy-water stoup supported by a salamander. Two delightful alabaster monuments; a miniature tomb chest to Sir Thomas Cokayne, d. 1488, with effigy only 3½ feet long, and a panel of great charm to Robert Gylbert, d. 1492, who stands with his wife and 17 children, the Virgin and Child in their midst. E. window by Burne-Jones.

Devon

Introduction

The popular idea of this large south-western county is not far from the right one. The steeply banked lane, stuffed with fern and foxglove and honeysuckle, winds down through oaks which interlace their lichened branches to an old stone bridge over a stream which babbles against boulders. Soon we come to the barton or farm, pink-washed and snug, cob-walled and thickly thatched among its steep little fields of red earth. On the hill-slope higher up is the village. Here are thatched walls too, and cob cottages with rounded corners and bulging hearths and hollyhocks and fuchsias in the garden. Out of the sycamores near the hill-top peep the tall pinnacles of a thin church tower. Inside the church, low 15th-century arcades of clustered columns support a barrel-shaped wooden roof whose timbers are carved. And right across the east end, for we do not expect to see a chancel arch in Devon, will be a wooden screen with carved base and painted saints on its panels, and through the wooden tracery above the panels we can see the altar. Above the tracery is a beam carved with grapes and vine leaves from which wooden vaults over-arch to support a loft which has painted panels. Above this once stood the rood, looking down the chancel into the nave. And out into the scented warmth of the churchyard we will go, back to the village for Devonshire tea, with strawberries and cream, where people will call us 'my dear' and rustics will be waiting on the cobbles outside the village inn to drink cider at opening time.

Such places may indeed be found inland in south Devon. This part of the county has luscious vegetation; flowers seem bigger and brighter than in the rest of England, and the sheltered estuaries on the south coast are almost tropical. But the uplands of West Devon are bare and flattened, to quote Sir John Fortescue, 'between the hammer of west wind and the anvil of the yellow clay'. Even here the stony valley villages have the sheltered look of the south.

But there are other sorts of Devon scenery: Exmoor with its smooth moorlands; Dartmoor with its sharp outcrops of granite; Lynton and Lynmouth with their Alpine steeps; south-coast seaside towns like Sidmouth, Teignmouth, Dawlish and Torquay, where stucco Georgian terraces and Gothic cottages look through boughs of ilex to the Channel. In the three towns now called Plymouth – Devonport, of marble pavements and Greek Revival public buildings; slate-hung Stonehouse, with its Royal William victualling yard; and Plymouth itself, old as the sea, pseudo-simple in its arid new centre – one can find maritime Georgian at its best. At Tiverton there is fine architectural evidence of a long-prosperous agricultural market town.

Nearly all the old churches of Devon were rebuilt or enlarged in the 15th century. The inspiration behind Exeter Cathedral, with its square Norman towers and beautiful nave and choir, rebuilt in the late 13th and early 14th centuries, and behind that miniature cathedral, the collegiate church of Ottery St Mary, did not survive into the 15th-century prosperity of country parishes, for it was monastic in origin. The 15th-century Devon churches have the low West Country proportions of Exeter Cathedral and Ottery, but they are much of a pattern. The towers, though often graceful, have less variety than those of Somerset. Devonians seem to have been primarily carvers of wood and stone, and only secondarily architects. Almost every old church has remains of wooden screens or pulpits or benches. Painting seems to have interested them less than carving, and screen-painting is not as impressive as that of East Anglia. The county was conservative and Catholic, and in 1549 the Prayer Book Rebellion, a gallant attempt to reinstate the old missal after the Reformation, started in Devon. Love of the old ways probably accounts for the survival of screens in so many churches, and even the building of them as late as the 18th century, as at Cruwys Morchard. But it does not account for the disappearance of almost all old stained glass in the county. In the 19th century, Devon was High Church under the autocratic reign of the great Bishop Philpotts, 'Henry of Exeter'. It is not surprising, therefore, to find work of the London Tractarian architects, Street and Butterfield, and the talented local church architect, F. Hayward, building new churches and making good use of the various marbles available in the county. Plymouth remained what it had long been, Puritan and iconoclastic. Devon is different from the rest of Britain. It is brighter-coloured, more West Country than Somerset, where one still feels the pull of Bristol, and less Celtic than sea-swept Cornwall. Exeter is not only its county and cathedral town – vilely developed of recent years on its outskirts, and in the centre – but it is the capital of a country, the country of Devon, and the mother city of the ancient Celtic kingdom of Dumnonia.

J.B.

1	Ashburton
2	Ashcombe
3	Ashton
4	Atherington
5	Axmouth
6	Bere Ferrers
7	Berry Pomeroy
8	Bicton
9	Blackawton
10	Bovey Tracey
11	Branscombe
12	Bratton Clovelly
13	Braunton
14	Brentor
15	Bridford
16	Broad Clyst
17	Brooking
18	Brushford
19	Buckerell
20	Buckland-in-the-Moor
21	Buckland Monachorum
22	Burlescombe
23	Burrington
24	Cadeleigh
25	Chagford
26	Cheriton Bishop
27	Chittlehampton
28	Christow
29	Chulmleigh
30	Clovelly
31	Coldridge
32	Colebrooke
33	Collaton St Mary
34	Colyton
35	Cornworthy
36	Crediton
37	Cruwys Morchard
38	Cullompton
39	Dartington
40	Dartmouth
41	Doddiscombleigh
42	Dowland
43	Down St Mary
44	Drewsteignton
45	Dunchdeock
46	East Budleigh
47	Eggesford
48	Exeter
49	Exwick
50	Gittisham
51	Haccombe
52	Halberton
53	Harberton
54	Harford
55	Hartland
56	Heanton Punchardon
57	High Bickington
58	Hittesleigh
59	Holcombe Burnell
60	Honeychurch
61	Horwood
62	Ipplepen
63	Kelly
64	Kenn
65	Kentisbeare
66	Kenton
67	Kings Nympton
68	Landkey
69	Lapford
70	Lew Trenchard
71	Luppitt
72	Manaton
73	Marystow
74	Molland
75	Monkleigh
76	Morchard Bishop
77	Mortehoe
78	Newton St Cyres
79	North Bovey
80	North Molton
81	Northlew
82	Nymet Rowland
83	Ottery St Mary
84	Paignton
85	Parracombe
86	Plymouth
87	Plympton St Mary
88	Plymtree
89	Revelstoke
90	Salcombe Regis
91	Sampford Courtenay
92	Sandford
93	Shaldon
94	Shute
95	Sidbury
96	South Brent
97	South Tawton
98	Stowford
99	Sutcombe
100	Swimbridge
101	Tavistock
102	Tawstock
103	Teignmouth
104	Tetcott
105	Throwleigh
106	Tiverton
107	Torbryan
108	Torquay
109	Totnes
110	Ugborough
111	Upton Hellions
112	Upton Pyne
113	Washford Pyne
114	West Ogwell
115	West Putford
116	Widecombe-in-the-Moor
117	Yealmpton

map overleaf

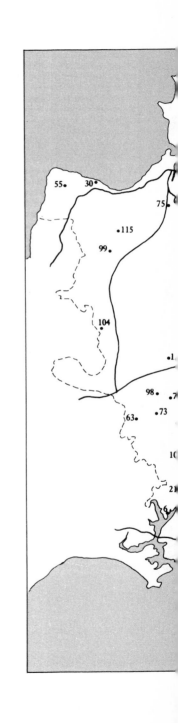

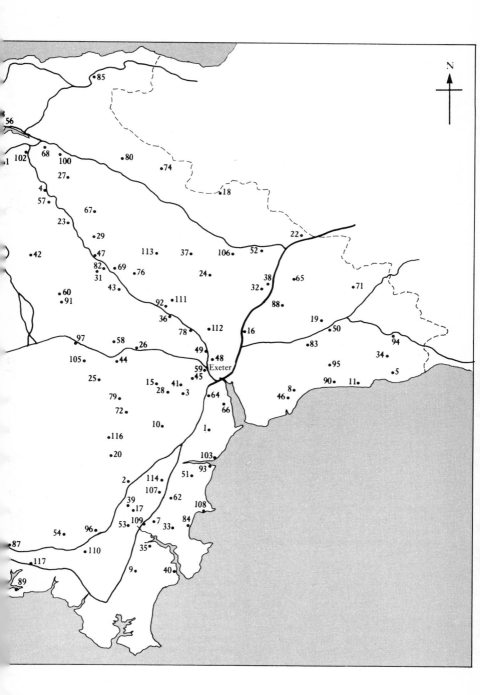

Selected List of Churches

ASHBURTON
St Andrew

7m/11km W. of Newton Abbot sx 7659
Town church, mainly 15th-century with a
handsome granite tower and good bossed
roofs; the screen by G. E. Street inclines to
East Anglia rather than Devon.

ASHCOMBE
St Nectan

3m/4km E. of Chudleigh sx 9179
At the head of the long combe of Dawlish
Water. Originally a small 13th-century cruciform church; see tower, S. transept, and
chancel. In 15th century the Kirkhams enlarged the N. transept into an aisle. Salvin's
renovation of 1824–5 removed much of its
medieval character, including the rood
screen, though the carved 15th-century
bench-ends remain. It is now light,
charming, and Gothic, with delicate plaster
panelling and colouring everywhere. The
adjacent vicarage is of the same happy
period.

ASHTON
St John the Baptist

3m/4km N. of Chudleigh sx 8584
A singularly attractive church in every way;
worth going 50 miles to see. Lies on the
luxuriant W. slopes of Haldon, where they
cascade down to the Teign Valley. Entirely
rebuilt and refurnished between about 1400
and 1485, Ashton is the 'typical' Devonshire
church at its best and unrestored. The plastered walls and white Beer-stone arcade set
off the rich colouring of the medieval
screens, glass, and wall-paintings; and the
lavish carved woodwork so characteristic of
Devon churches is here in abundance. The
15th-century rood screen and parclose
screens have some of the best figure-
paintings in Devon, especially those on the
N. parclose screen and on back of aisle
screen. Carved bench-ends, heraldic glass,
and wall-painting all of same period. Elizabethan pulpit with canopy, 17th-century
communion rails, wooden monument to Sir
George Chudleigh, 1657, who lived at the
adjacent Place. Note also original 15th-

century S. door, and wagon roofs. The
groined canopy of the rood screen, added
in 1908, alone mars the scene.

ATHERINGTON
St Mary

7m/11km S. of Barnstaple ss 5923
Not exciting structurally: mostly plain Devon
Perpendicular over-restored by Pearson,
1884. Notable however for its screens, original wagon roofs, and fine series of 15th-
century carved and crocketed bench-ends.
The N. aisle screen retains its rich original
rood loft, the only one left in Devon, the work
of John Parres, c. 1530. Chancel section of
screen replaced about 1800 by poorer and
earlier type from Umberleigh Chapel
nearby. Medieval effigies; some 15th-
century glass in N. chancel aisle.

AXMOUTH
St Michael

5m/8km W. of Lyme Regis sy 2591
Village and river setting. Church of all
periods with good 12th-century doorway and
15th-century wall-paintings. Restored
1882–9 by Hayward & Son.

BERE FERRERS
St Andrew

7m/11km S. of Tavistock sx 4563
Mostly rebuilt about 1300–5, and unusual
(for Devon) in retaining so much 14th-
century work. Note the early 14th-century
glass in E. window. Vigorous Norman font
of local Hurdwick stone, early 16th-century
benches with carved ends, medieval tombs
of the Ferrers (who built the church and
lived in the medieval house nearby). Handsome table-tomb in N. transept to Lord
Willoughby de Broke, 1522. Lovely estuary
of Tavy should be seen here.

BERRY POMEROY
St Mary

2m/3km E. of Totnes sx 8261
This late 15th-century church with tall W.
tower dominates the village. Two-storey
vaulted porch with good roof-bosses; inside

is one of the best screens in Devon, replete with coving, cornice, and cresting.

BICTON
St Mary
3m/4km N. of Budleigh Salterton SY 0686
Church and mausoleum form a good group by the grounds of Bicton House. By Hayward, 1850; the church has a cruciform plan and is in the geometrical Decorated style. Carvings by John Dudley of London feature royalty, English divines, and evangelists. Excellent glass by Warrington. The Rolle mausoleum by A. W. N. Pugin is of the same period.

BLACKAWTON
St Michael
5m/8km W. of Dartmouth SX 8050
14th- and 15th-century. Norman font in red sandstone with cabling and palmettes; 16th-century screen with pomegranates, the badge of Catherine of Aragon.

BOVEY TRACY
St Peter, St Paul & St Thomas of Canterbury
5m/8km N.W. of Newton Abbot SX 8178
Largely 15th-century, including the exceptional fittings; a brass lectern, a richly carved screen, and a stone pulpit.

BRANSCOMBE
St Winifred
5m/8km E. of Sidmouth SY 1988
A delightful church, though recently rather reshuffled. Sited in a combe about a mile back from the sea, in a parish with no village but interesting houses scattered everywhere. This church is important for the antiquary, as it shows a process of continuous development from the 11th century to the 16th, though the dominant features are the crossing tower, mostly Norman, the 13th-century work in transepts and nave, and the 14th-century chancel. The woodwork is worth studying, especially the Elizabethan W. gallery, the communion rails enclosing the table on four sides, the excellent three-decker pulpit – rare in Devon – and the box pews in the N. transept. Monuments to Wadhams and other local gentry. The Wadhams lived up at Edge Barton, which is worth seeing.

BRATTON CLOVELLY
St Mary the Virgin
8m/12km W. of Okehampton SX 4691
14th-century nave arcades of beautiful Po-

lyphant stone; fine circular Norman font. Rare and extensive scheme of 17th-century wall-painting uncovered in 1986; in the aisles are Christ and the Apostles, the Prophets, David and Goliath, and framed texts.

BRAUNTON
St Brannock
5m/8km N.W. of Barnstaple SS 4836
Set in the largest village in Devon, now overrun by suburban building, but many 16th- and 17th-century houses in the native tradition remain. A large barn-like church, not very prepossessing but well worth visiting. The Celtic missionary-saint Brannoc (who came across from S. Wales) founded a minster here in the 6th century and is almost certainly buried under the high altar. Present church mostly 13th-century, but much later detail. Note the Norman S. tower with lead-covered broach spire. The remarkably wide nave is covered by a fine roof enriched with bosses, *c.* 1500. There is a splendid collection of carved 16th-century bench-ends, much Jacobean woodwork – pulpit, reading desk, gallery – and many 16th–18th-century mural monuments to local families.

BRENTOR
St Michael
5m/8km N. of Tavistock SX 4881
A wonderful site, perched on the very summit of an extinct volcanic cone, 1,100 feet above the sea. Great masses of volcanic ash all the way up, and views over half of Devon and Cornwall. First church planted here about 1140, but an ancient religious site long before that. Mainly 13th-century, plain and primitive.

BRIDFORD
St Thomas à Becket
4m/6km E. of Moretonhampstead SX 8186
A granite Perpendicular church set in a granite village with Dartmoor in view to W. Some late-medieval glass, carved stalls and bench-ends, wagon roofs, and other medieval woodwork. Best of all, the splendid rood screen, made about 1530, which retains much of its soft, ancient colouring.

BROAD CLYST
St John the Baptist
5m/8km N.E. of Exeter SX 9897
15th- and 16th-century. Richly decorated

W. tower; spacious interior with large Perpendicular windows; good 17th-century monuments.

BROOKING
St Barnabas
Tigley Cross, Dartington, 3m/4km W. of Totnes sx 7560
By an unknown designer, 1850–5, a splendid period piece in Early English style. Beautiful polished marble piers to S. arcade; good contemporary fittings and stained glass by Hardman.

BRUSHFORD
St Mary the Virgin
2m/3km S.E. of Dulverton ss 9225
Rustic setting on a hill-top. Small Norman church with a delicate rood screen and three bells of *c.* 1400, cast by William Dawe of London.

BUCKERELL
St Mary & St Giles
3m/4km W. of Honiton st 1200
15th-century but with a Georgian air. Good cut-down rood screen; 18th-century box pews, W. gallery and monuments.

BUCKLAND-IN-THE-MOOR
St Peter
3m/4km N.W. of Ashburton sx 7273
Romantic setting. Mostly 15th-century granite with carved Norman font, a traceried screen, and crude early 16th-century paintings.

BUCKLAND MONACHORUM
St Andrew
4m/6km S. of Tavistock sx 4968
Assured late-Perpendicular with pinnacled W. tower, slender piers, and big windows. Among the Drake family monuments are two by John Bacon.

BURLESCOMBE
St Mary
5m/8km S.W. of Wellington st 0716
15th-century with a particularly good interior; Beer-stone arcades, wagon-roofs, and painted early 17th-century monuments.

BURRINGTON
Holy Trinity
4m/6km N.W. of Chulmleigh ss 6316
Largely 15th-century with good woodwork; well-preserved screen, traceried S. door,

wagon roofs, and communion rails of *c.* 1700.

CADELEIGH
St Bartholomew
4m/6km S.W. of Tiverton ss 9108
Well-set with good views. Largely 15th-century, but the inside walls decorated with plaster panels in the mid-18th-century when the box pews were fitted.

CHAGFORD
St Michael
4m/6km N.W. of Moretonhampstead sx 7087
15th-century church of Dartmoor granite in attractive moorland town. Heavily restored in 1865, but the sanctuary decorated by Pearson in 1888 has a good reredos and jolly tiles.

CHERITON BISHOP
St Mary
6m/10km S.W. of Crediton sx 7793
Set in a tight fold between hills. Good collection of fittings; Norman font, 16th-century pulpit, coloured rood screen, bench-ends, and rare Elizabethan painted Royal Arms over S. door.

CHITTLEHAMPTON
St Hieritha
5m/8km W. of South Molton ss 6325
Dedicated to local Celtic saint murdered by pagan villagers *c.* 700. Her holy well lies at E. end of village, and she is buried in the church, probably under the passage leading to the vestry. A large late-Perpendicular church with noble W. tower of Somerset type, a medieval stone pulpit, and 17th-century monuments.

CHRISTOW
St James
4m/6km N.W. of Chudleigh sx 8384
Ashlar-faced Gothic Survival W. tower dated 1630. Inside are a Norman font, a screen, a few bench-ends, and a portentous monument to Sir Fleetwood Pellew, d. 1861, Admiral of the Blue.

CHULMLEIGH
St Mary Magdalene
8m/12km S. of South Molton ss 6814
Set high above the River Dart, this church was collegiate from the 13th century, but is mainly 15th-century now. Tall W. tower, long and notably complete rood screen;

chancel tiles and fittings by Gould, 1879–81, all set off with Hardman glass.

CLOVELLY
All Saints

9m/15km W. of Bideford SS 3124

Chocolate-box sort of a place. A little Norman work, but otherwise all late-Perpendicular as usual. Some good later glass by Kempe Studios; the delicate S. window is an early work by Comper. Lots of Cary memorials.

COLDRIDGE
St Matthew

4m/6km E. of Winkleigh SS 6907

Church and village on summit of high ridge, with views across to Dartmoor. Some Norman work, but mostly late 15th- to early 16th-century. Highly interesting contents include medieval screens (flamboyant work in parclose screen as at Colebrooke); fine medieval carved pulpit; late-medieval bench-ends, tiles, glass, wagon-roofs, with carved bosses. Table-tomb of Sir John Evans, who gave many of the fittings in 1511–12.

COLEBROOKE
St Andrew

1m/2km S.W. of Cullompton ST 0006

Stands boldly by itself. A 14th-century church, enlarged in the 15th. Good W. tower. Unusual carved bench-ends (late 15th-century) and good screens of same date.

COLLATON ST MARY
St Mary the Virgin

on W. edge of Painton SX 8660

Church groups well with school and parsonage, all by J. W. Rowell of Newton Abbot, 1865. Notable for excellent furnishings and glass by J. F. Bentley, font by Earp, and Last Supper relief by Theodore Phyffers.

COLYTON
St Andrew

3m/4km N. of Seaton SY 2493

Handsome cruciform church with superb W. window and octagonal top stage to tower, all 15th-century. Stone screen, monuments with delightful ancient colour, and parts of an exquisite 10th-century cross.

CORNWORTHY
St Peter

4m/6km S.E. of Totnes SX 8255

15th-century church in a Dartside village. Norman font and much-restored medieval screen, but essentially a late 18th-century interior with box pews, canopied pulpit, altarpiece, clear glass, and altered window tracery – most of it done in 1788. Delightful repose everywhere, quite unharmed by Victorian meddlers.

CREDITON
Holy Cross

8m/12 km N.W. of Exeter SS 8300

A splendid collegiate church in a sleepy little town, successor to a Saxon minster and cathedral. Red sandstone, noble central tower. Began as a 12th-century cruciform church, remodelled in late 14th to early 15th. Very beautiful clerestory, unusual even in good Devon churches. Three notable monuments: Sir John Sully, 1387, Sir William Periam, 1604, and John Tuckfield, 1630. Unfortunate memorial by Caroe above the chancel arch to Sir Redvers Buller, who was vastly admired by Devonians if not by the outside world.

CRUWYS MORCHARD
Holy Cross

5m/8km W. of Tiverton SS 8712

Highly 'atmospherick', for it stands beside the ancient house of the Cruwys family who have lived there since the 12th century. No other house near. Mostly 14th-century and early 16th, but interior is quite Georgian in feeling, all done after the great fire of 1689. Plastered walls, remarkable Georgian chancel and parclose screens. Chancel fittings show continuity of traditional forms. Cut-down box pews, all very decent and orderly.

CULLOMPTON
St Andrew

5m/8km S.E. of Tiverton ST 0207

Another splendid town church, but unlike Crediton in being all of one style – Perpendicular, 15th- and 16th-century. The fine red tower, one of the things one looks for from the train dashing down to Exeter, was finished in 1549. The second S. aisle was built by a wealthy cloth merchant in 1526; rich fan-traceried roof and exterior carvings of ships, sheep-shears, and so forth. The gorgeously coloured roof runs unbroken throughout the entire length of the church; the splendid coloured rood screen runs across its entire width. Cullompton brings home to one the lavish colour of a medieval church against the white background of the Beer-stone arcades. Jacobean W. gallery and a remarkable, gruesome Golgotha in the Lane Aisle.

DARTINGTON
St Mary
2m/3km N.W. of Totnes SX 7862
J. L. Pearson, 1878–80; on a new site, but following the plan dimensions of the old church and re-using some materials and fittings. Glass by Clayton & Bell.

DARTMOUTH
7m/11km S.E. of Totnes SX 8751
St Petrox
A splendid site at the very mouth of the Dart; highly effective grouping with the castle and the wooded cliffs. An ancient Christian site, but the present church entirely rebuilt in Gothic style, 1641–2, with much woodwork of that period and fine brasses to Dartmouth merchants.
St Saviour
Very picturesque interior stuffed with good things, including elaborate 14th-century ironwork on the old S. door, 15th-century screens with much original colouring, a gallery with Royal Arms of 1633, and 17th-century panelling.

DODDISCOMBSLEIGH
St Michael
6m/10km S.W. of Exeter SX 8586
Best medieval glass in Devon (N. aisle) outside Exeter Cathedral. A set of five large Perpendicular windows painted in pale yellow and white with touches of red, green and blue. Delicately drawn saints, the Seven Sacraments, and heraldry.

DOWLAND
St Peter
7m/11km S.E. of Torrington SS 5610
Small church in tiny hamlet above the Torridge. Remarkable N. arcade of oak, *c.* 1500, and a complete set of carved bench-ends.

DOWN ST MARY
St Mary the Virgin
7m/11km N.W. of Crediton SS 7404
Apart from the medieval W. tower and nave arcade, the church is substantially Victorian.

A collection of notable architects and designers were involved from 1848–90 under the supervision of the incumbent, the Rev. Radford; these included G. E. Street, reredos; John Hayward, choir; Earp, carvings; Salviati, mosaics; J. F. Gould, pulpit; Clayton and Bell, and Hardman, stained glass. This wonderful combination of talents makes for a rich interior.

DREWSTEIGNTON
Holy Trinity
3m/4km N. of Moretonhampstead SX 7390
Strikingly set on high moorland. Late-medieval granite church with W. tower, two-storey S. porch, and generous Perpendicular windows; granite church house nearby (1546).

DUNCHIDEOCK
St Michael and All Angels
4m/6km S.W. of Exeter SX 8787
Late 14th-century church of red sandstone in an isolated setting. A good font of *c.* 1400, carved bench-ends, a fine series of roof-bosses, and a rood screen of great beauty.

EAST BUDLEIGH
All Saints
2m/3km N. of Budleigh Salterton SY 0684
Good view from churchyard across thatched roofs. A notable collection of lively 16th-century bench-ends decorated with everything from ships and shears to arms and angels.

EGGESFORD
All Saints
2m/3km S. of Chulmleigh SS 6811
Setting in former park. The fabric much restored in 1867, but the principal attraction is the monuments; a remarkable group from the 17th and 18th centuries.

EXETER
SX 9292
St David, St David's Hill
1897–1900 by W. D. Caroe, his best church. A Romantic essay much influenced by the Celtic twilight as well as by the Art Nouveau. The interior is vast and gargantuan in its expression, with powerful limestone ribs accentuating the bays of the narrow aisles and timber tunnel vault. Tall reredos also by Caroe; glass by the Kempe Studio.
St Martin, Cathedral Close

Characteristic little city church on awkward site, basically 15th-century. Late 17th-century communion rail; pulpit, W. gallery, and box pews of *c.* 1700; reredos slightly later.

St Mary Steps, West Street
15th-century church originally beside city W. gate. Norman font with cabling and palmettes, 17th-century clock on tower wall with armed figures in niches.

St Michael, Dinham Road
By Rhode Hawkins, 1865–8. The soaring spire, modelled on Salisbury, is a chief landmark of the city. French Gothic details; pulpit by Arthur Blomfield; reredos by Caroe.

St Thomas, Cowick Street
Largest of city churches, rebuilt in 1657 after Civil War damage. Rich High Anglican neo-Decorated fittings of the 1840s, including the font, reredos, and altar.

EXWICK
St Andrew
1m/2km N.W. of Exeter SX 9093
John Hayward, 1842, an early work in the Decorated style. It strictly conformed to Ecclesiological principles. Beautiful fittings including stone altar and reredos, and mosaic by Salviati.

GITTISHAM
St Michael
2m/3km S.W. of Honiton SY 1398
In deepest E. Devon; luxuriant colouring everywhere. Cob and thatch village. The usual Perpendicular village church, but atmosphere is 18th-century; box pews; ceiled roofs, hatchments, gallery. Several pleasant mural monuments, 16th- to 18th-century.

HACCOMBE
St Blaise
3m/4km E. of Newton Abbot SX 8970
In the park of the Carews. Notable for its fine collection of medieval effigies and brasses, 13th- to 17th-century, of various lords of Haccombe. Some 14th-century glass. Stone screen, pulpit, and reredos by Kendall of Exeter, 1821–2.

HALBERTON
St Andrew
3m/4km E. of Tiverton ST 0013
14th- and 15th-century, firmly restored 1847–9. Late-medieval screens and octag-

onal stone pulpit enriched with tracery and nodding ogee arches.

HARBERTON
St Andrew
2m/3km S.W. of Totnes SX 7758
A large unspoilt village in a fertile landscape, and a splendid 14th–15th-century church, with a handsome tower. Fine late-medieval rood screen: vaulting and cornices especially rich. Paintings in lower panels of screen are said to be portraits of young ladies of the congregation in 1870. Pulpit 15th-century, one of the best in Devon; figures in panels 17th-century. Unusually beautiful Norman font with almost pure Byzantine ornament.

HARFORD
St Petroc
2m/3km N. of Ivybridge SX 6359
Moorland type, 15th-century, on the edge of Dartmoor. Modest W. tower; ceiled wagon roofs; tomb chest of 1566 with brass of Thomas Williams, Speaker of the House of Commons.

HARTLAND
St Nectan
4m/6km W. of Clovelly SS 2624
Not in the old borough but two miles W. at Stoke, overlooking the open, restless Atlantic; the tower (123 ft) built as a landmark for mariners. Large 14th-century church with late 15th-century embellishments. Splendid Norman font and carved bench-ends of 1530; wagon-roofs are partly ceiled and coloured. Priest's chamber above N. porch in which Parson Hawker wrote *The Cell by the Sea*. Numerous modest little monuments and ledger slabs to local gentry, in which the parish abounded for centuries. Magnificent late 15th-century rood screen extending entire width of church.

HEANTON PUNCHARDON
St Augustine
4m/6km N.W. of Barnstaple SS 5035
Setting above estuary. Late-medieval with plastered interior and richly carved Perpendicular tomb to Richard Coffin, d. 1523.

HIGH BICKINGTON
St Mary
7m/11km E. of Torrington SS 6020
A hill-top church, like so many in N. Devon; 12th-century building, altered and enlarged in early 14th and early 16th centuries. Orig-

inal wagon-roofs. There is a magnificent series of about 70 carved bench-ends of two distinct types: late Gothic, c. 1500, and Renaissance, c. 1530.

HITTISLEIGH
St Andrew
7m/11km S.W. of Crediton SX 7395
An ordinary little Devonshire country church in lonely country bordering Dartmoor, but restored late and lovingly. Nave and chancel 14th-century, granite aisle 15th-century. Plastered, cream-washed walls, ceiled roofs with some carved bosses, and usual floor-slabs to Tudor and Stuart yeomen and small gentry of the parish; an endearing little church.

HOLCOMBE BURNELL
St John the Baptist
4m/6km W. of Exeter SX 8591
Set among trees above open country. Heavily restored by Hayward of Exeter in 1843; the chief interest attaches to a grand Easter Sepulchre converted to a tomb for Sir Robert Dennis in 1592.

HONEYCHURCH
St Mary
7m/11km E. of Hatherleigh SS 6202
Far from any village and as delightful as its name. A simple Norman building, done up in the 15th century and given three new bells, new benches, and a little tower, all still there. Elizabethan pulpit. Norman font with Jacobean cover. The blackest-hearted pagan would smile at Honeychurch as he pushed open the door and saw this touching little interior.

HORWOOD
St Michael
3m/4km E. of Bideford SS 5027
Delightful little church up in the hills; again no village. All about 1500, decently kept. Mid-15th-century alabaster effigy of a lady, probably Elizabeth Pollard, hence the Pollard Aisle. 16th-century bench-ends; 17th-century altar rails; some medieval glass and tiles. Numerous floor-slabs and memorials to centuries of squires. Nothing at Horwood is outstanding, but all is in rustic harmony.

IPPLEPEN
St Andrew
3m/4km S.W. of Newton Abbot SX 8366
15th-century church with big W. tower

stands well at the head of the village. Perpendicular nave windows are particularly good, as are the font, screens and pulpit.

KELLY
St Mary the Virgin
5m/8km S.E. of Launceston SX 3981
Trees, an 18th-century manor house, stables and granary are neighbours to this granite church. Tower rebuilt in 1835, but the chancel is a remarkable Gothic Survival rebuilding of 1710, according to the monument of the vicar who did it.

KENN
St Andrew
5m/8km S. of Exeter SX 9285
Of deep red sandstone in a beautiful elevated situation. Norman font; 15th-century screen and bench-ends; excellent Hardman glass.

KENTISBEARE
St Mary
3m/4km E. of Cullompton ST 0608
Good Perpendicular throughout in a luxuriant countryside; beautiful checkered tower of red sandstone and white Beerstone. Pier capital in S. aisle has carved ship and woolpack; fine early 16th-century rood screen; W. gallery of 1632; tombs.

KENTON
All Saints
4m/6km N. of Dawlish SX 9583
Fine late 14th-century church in large, rich village. Red sandstone country everywhere. Church built of it; the fully aisled Devonshire plan at its best. Handsome tower and S. porch. Beer-stone arcade with carved capitals. Massive and stately rood screen with ancient colour and good series of figure-paintings. Medieval pulpit, restored by Read of Exeter. Reredos by Kempe. Monuments.

KINGS NYMPTON
St John the Baptist
3m/4km N. of Chulmleigh SS 6819
15th-century. Fine roof-bosses and other woodwork, especially rood screen with canopy of honour; 18th-century painted chancel ceiling and box pews, tiered at W. end.

LANDKEY
St Paul
to E. of Barnstaple SS 5931
A stately church somewhat encroached upon

by humdrum neighbours. Perpendicular, including the tower. Inside are a fine painted roof with bosses and figured corbels, an octagonal font, and some worthwhile monuments.

LAPFORD
St Thomas of Canterbury
5m/8km S.E. of Chulmleigh ss 7308
15th- and 16th-century, over-restored by Ashworth, 1888. The celebrated screen is touched by the Renaissance; there are figured roundels in the coving.

LEW TRENCHARD
St Peter
8m/12km E. of Launceston sx 4586
Sabine Baring-Gould's church, hidden in the woods. He was squarson 43 years, and the eclectic interior of the church is all his work; reconstructed rood screen, pulpit, chancel stalls, and late-medieval chandelier. Over-restored but interesting.

LUPPITT
St Mary
4m/6km N. of Honiton st 1606
Decorated cruciform church on the edge of the Blackdown Hills. Although terribly restored in the 19th century, this building has two great wonders. The first is the intersection of its late-medieval wagon roofs; over the crossing two great over-arching diagonal ribs which culminate in a (now sadly reproduction) big boss. The second splendid thing is the grandly archaic Norman font with puzzling violent sagas on its flanks.

MANATON
St Winifred
3m/4km S. of Moretonhampstead sx 7581
Charming granite church in picturesque village. Tower much repaired after storm damage in 1779. Celebrated screen restored by Sedding in 1893, enriched by painted panels of saints and, unexpectedly, small statuettes above the central doorway.

MARYSTOW
St Mary the Virgin
6m/10km N.W. of Tavistock sx 4382
Lonely setting among trees. Remains of Norman S. doorway, early 14th-century chancel. Good free-standing monument to Sir Thomas Wyse, d. 1629.

MOLLAND
St Mary
6m/10km E. of South Molton ss 8028
On the Exmoor foothills. An unremarkable 15th-century church outside; inside, a peaceful Georgian oasis in the desert of the 20th century. Plastered and whitewashed. Three-decker pulpit, box pews, ceiled roofs. Chancel shut off by rustic 18th-century 'screen', with plastered tympanum above. 17th- and 18th-century Courtenay monuments.

MONKLEIGH
St George
3m/4km N.W. of Torrington ss 4520
Setting on high ground; the tower is a landmark for miles around. Sir William Hankford, Lord Chief Justice, left money for rebuilding in his will dated 1423. His tomb is in the church; he was reputedly killed in error by his own keeper! Late and rich parclose screen, good bench-ends.

MORCHARD BISHOP
St Mary
6m/10km N.W. of Crediton ss 7707
Church of around 1500 apart from the plastered and panelled 18th-century chancel replete with Corinthian reredos and communion rail.

MORTEHOE
St Mary the Virgin
4m/6km W. of Ilfracombe ss 4545
Spectacular coastal scenery nearby, formed by the deadly Morte Slates. This dark, cruciform church, of an older period than usual in Devon, has largely escaped the restorer. Partly Norman, partly 14th- and early 16th-century, it has early 13th-century carved bench-ends. The long, open wagon roof of the nave is 15th-century. In the S. transept is the traceried tomb chest of William de Tracey, Rector, d. 1322. At harvest festival, fishermen's nets are hung here.

NEWTON ST CYRES
St Cyres & St Julitta
3m/4km S.E. of Crediton sx 8898
On a bold site above an unusually attractive village of cob and thatch. Early 15th-century church in local volcanic stone. Beer-stone arcade, 18th-century canopied pulpit, and striking monuments to Northcotes, especially that of John Northcote, d. 1632; a lifesize male figure, seemingly in Wellington boots.

NORTH BOVEY
St John the Baptist
2m/3km S.W. of Moretonhampstead sx 7483
Attractive green village with old oaks. 15th-century granite church with broad low interior, ceiled wagon roofs, and a good screen with statuettes similar to Manaton.

NORTH MOLTON
All Saints
3m/4km N.E. of South Molton ss 7329
Striking parish church in a decayed town setting. Clerestoried nave, unusual in Devon, a fine medieval pulpit, and other good woodwork.

NORTHLEW
St Thomas of Canterbury
6m/10km N.W. of Okehampton sx 5099
Small church with some Norman evidence: lower parts of tower and W. door. Good roofs with angels and bosses, a screen and bench-ends.

NYMET ROWLAND
St Bartholomew
4m/6km S.E. of Chulmleigh ss 7108
Rustic Perpendicular apart from the modest Norman S. door. Remarkable timber N. nave arcade and original wagon roof.

OTTERY ST MARY
St Mary the Virgin
11m/18km E. of Exeter sy 0995
Another grand town church, of even higher rank than Crediton and Cullompton. Rather squat exterior, like Exeter Cathedral, on which it was closely modelled by the munificent Bishop Grandisson. He reconstructed, in 1338–42, a large 13th-century church, to which was added about 1520 the Dorset Aisle with beautiful fan-vaulted roof. Impressive interior with much detail for study, especially the roof-bosses. Of the 14th century are the clock in the S. transept, the excellent canopied tombs of Otho Grandisson and wife, choir-stalls, altar screen, sedilia, minstrels' gallery, and gilded wooden eagle given by Bishop Grandisson. Good 18th-century pulpit. Thorough restoration by Butterfield, 1850; he did less harm than might be expected, but shocking modern colouring on the vaults disrupts the internal spaces.

PAIGNTON
St John the Baptist
3m/4km S.W. of Torquay sx 8960
Mainly 15th-century but some 12th-century remains of previous church. Rich medieval stone pulpit. Kirkham chantry, *c.* 1526; notable ceiling, sculptured panels, stone screen.

PARRACOMBE
St Petrock
4m/6km S.W. of Lynton ss 6645
Owing to the construction of a new church in 1870, and the intervention of John Ruskin, this church has a completely unspoiled Georgian interior; everything is irregular and just as it was 200 years ago; box pews, screen with tympanum above, hat pegs, text boards, mural tablets to local yeomen. The walls and ceilings are whitewashed and there are some 16th-century benches. Early English chancel, the rest a plain Perpendicular.
R.C.F.

PLYMOUTH
St Andrew
Catherine Street sx 4745
Fine 15th-century town church, gutted in war, 1941, now beautifully restored by Frederick Etchells. Bold windows by John Piper.

PLYMPTON ST MARY
St Mary the Blessed Virgin
4m/6km from Plymouth centre sx 5356
Originally a chapelry, aggrandized in 14th and 15th centuries. Prominent W. tower with polygonal pinnacles and three-light bell openings. S. porch of *c.* 1400 has an elaborate stone vault and statues; fine Decorated chancel with striking E. window; good collection of monuments.

PLYMTREE
St John the Baptist
3m/4km S.E. of Cullompton st 0502
One of the most attractive medieval interiors in Devon, with excellent woodwork and original colouring, all carefully restored by William Weir, 1910.

REVELSTOKE
St Peter the Poor Fisherman
Noss Mayo, 3m/4km S.W. of Yealmpton sx 5447
Dramatically sited on the cliff-edge overlooking the estuary, a church by J. P.

St Aubyn, 1881–2. Rather romantic in its part-ruined state, it has been carefully restored, so that the fine stencilling in the nave, and pictorial mural tiles at the E. end, are all preserved. Stained glass by Fouracre and Watson.

R.C.F.

SALCOMBE REGIS
St Peter
2m/3km N.E. of Sidmouth SY 1488
Setting in combe; Norman work includes the circular piers of the N. arcade with scalloped capitals and the ghost of a doorway in the chancel S. wall; 15th-century oak lectern.

SAMPFORD COURTENAY
St Andrew
5m/8km N.E. of Okehampton SS 6301
Silvery, granite, mostly early 16th-century, with elegant lichened tower. Interior spacious and light; much clear glass which suits a granite interior. Good arcades; part of S. arcade is very beautiful dove-grey Polyphant stone from E. Cornwall. There are a screen, a Norman font, and carved bosses and wall-plates to the roofs. A cheerful whitewashed cob and thatch village. Prayer Book Rebellion of 1549 began and ended here.

SANDFORD
St Swithin
2m/3km N.W. of Crediton SS 8202
Elaborate W. gallery of 1657 with carved arcaded front and fluted columns, conservative for the date; 16th-century bench-ends with fantastic heads.

SHALDON
St Peter
outskirts of Teignmouth on S. side of R. Teign, connected by bridge to Teignmouth SX 9372
By E. H. Sedding, 1893–1902. Superb Arts and Crafts church in banded red sandstone and grey limestone. Majestic interior alive with colour and craftsmanship.

SHUTE
St Michael
3m/4km W. of Axminster SY 2597
Setting on edge of deer park; 14th-century cruciform church, all much restored in 1869. Fine 18th- and 19th-century Pole monuments.

SIDBURY
St Peter & St Giles
3m/4km N. of Sidmouth SY 1391
Setting in attractive village. Intriguing structure with plain Saxon crypt and Norman tower adorned with two repositioned statues. Inside are good wagon roofs and traces of wall-paintings.

SOUTH BRENT
St Petroc
5m/8km S.W. of Buckfastleigh SX 6960
Village setting. Essentially a Norman cruciform church but much altered in 15th century. Good Norman font with lush scrolls and zig-zags.

SOUTH TAWTON
St Andrew
4m/6km E. of Okehampton SX 6594
Moorland type; handsome late-medieval church. 18th-century pulpit inlaid in Romantic style with the Evangelists and foliage. Monuments.

STOWFORD
St John
7m/11km E. of Launceston SX 4386
Setting in fold of hills. Perpendicular, thoroughly restored by Sir Giles Gilbert Scott in 1874. Good wagon roofs, profuse Victorian woodwork. Monuments include a diminutive Mr Harris posed as a Roman soldier in full-bottomed wig.

SUTCOMBE
St Andrew
5m/8km N. of Holsworthy SS 3411
Dullish village in a remote, unvisited part of Devon, but an excellent granite church. Some Norman, but mostly late 15th- to early 16th-century. Large collection of early 16th-century carved bench-ends, a pulpit of same date, and many late-medieval floor tiles of Barnstaple manufacture. Restored rood screen and some medieval glass; solid Devon granite and oak the predominant feeling.

SWIMBRIDGE
St James the Apostle
5m/8km S.E. of Barnstaple SS 6230
Has one of the three medieval spires of N. Devon. Tower and spire 14th-century; rest is 15th. Furnishings unusually rich and interesting; stone pulpit, *c.* 1490, with some original colour, a splendid 15th-century rood screen, well restored by Pearson, and a re-

markable Renaissance font cover. There are some bench-ends and wagon roofs.

TAVISTOCK
St Eustachius
13m/21km N. of Plymouth SX 4874
Large Perpendicular town church, paid for by the clothmakers. Tall pinnacled tower, wide nave and generous windows, some with glass by Morris and Kempe. 16th–18th-century monuments; excellent alabaster effigies of Sir John and Lady Glanville, *c.* 1600.

TAWSTOCK
St Peter
2m/3km S. of Barnstaple SS 5529
A fine cruciform church, nearly all 14th-century (and therefore unusual in Devon) in the former park of the Earls of Bath, with a good Georgian rectory some way off. Those who like church monuments will come 50 miles to Tawstock; a splendid collection, mainly of the Earls and Countesses of Bath, their connections, and their household officers. In N. transept: ceiling of Italian plasterwork, medieval glass, beautiful 16th-century gallery, Renaissance manorial pew of the Earls of Bath, carved bench-ends and monuments. In the S. transept are a similar ceiling and monuments. In the S. chancel aisle: a fine open roof, *c.* 1540; Burman's figure of Rachel, Countess of Bath, 1680; and the tomb of Lady Fitzwarren, 1589, which carries a most beautiful effigy.

TEIGNMOUTH
St James
20m/32km S. of Exeter SX 9473
13th-century sandstone W. tower, but otherwise a surprising octagon of 1817–21 by W. E. Rolfe, pupil of Soane. Delightful light and airy interior with slender clustered cast-iron piers supporting a lantern.

TETCOTT
Holy Cross
5m/8km S. of Holsworthy SX 3396
Rustic; redolent of the Arscotts, archetypal Devonian squires; 13th- and 16th-century church with Norman font on lively base, good pew rails of 1700, and bench-ends.

THROWLEIGH
St Mary the Virgin
6m/10km S.E. of Okehampton SX 6690
Fine setting on the E. slopes of Dartmoor.

Rebuilt in granite in the 15th century; wagon roofs and Easter Sepulchre; Anglo-Catholic atmosphere.

TIVERTON
12m/19km N. of Exeter SS 9512
St Peter
Large, handsome 15th-century church; Greenway's Chapel was added in 1517 and the whole S. side lavishly decorated with ships, heraldry, and figures. Interior over-restored, with furnishings largely late 19th-century, but the fine carved organ case of 1696 has been retained.
St George
The best Georgian church in Devon, by John James, 1714–30. Symmetrical yellow sandstone exterior with rusticated quoins. All nice inside with Ionic columns, galleries and panelling.

TORBRYAN
Holy Trinity
4m/6km S.W. of Newton Abbot SX 8266
Imposing Perpendicular outside but no suspicion of what bursts upon the eye on pushing open the door; the most completely characteristic Devon interior in plan, fittings, colour and atmosphere. First impression is of uninterrupted light – large windows of clear glass, whitened walls and ceilings, white Beer-stone arcades. Then against this background the vivid colouring of rood screen, pulpit, and altar, nearly all 15th-century, though the altar is actually made up from the original pulpit. 18th-century box pews encase earlier benches, and have brass candle-holders, all very charming. The four original medieval bells, cast in Exeter, remain.
    R.C.F.

TORQUAY
18m/29km S. of Exeter SX 9164
All Saints, Babbacombe
By William Butterfield, 1865–7. An assured essay by this celebrated architect. Powerful interior with characteristic polychrome surface treatment and lavish furnishings.
St John the Evangelist
Magnificent, High Church, by G. E. Street, 1861–71, dominating the harbour. Extensive use of Devon marble, a rare total immersion font, mosaic panels by Burne-Jones and Salviati, Morris glass.
St Mary the Virgin, St Marychurch
Rebuilt 1852–61, by S. W. Hugall; tower

1871, wrecked by enemy action in 1943; subsequent reconstruction has converted a dull Victorian building into a beautiful and stately church. Early 12th-century font with notable sculpture.

TOTNES
St Mary
7m/11km W. of Torquay SX 8060
Handsome 15th-century town church. An elaborate stone screen, 1460, runs right across the interior of the church, and there is a simple stone pulpit.

UGBOROUGH
St Peter
3m/4km E. of Ivybridge SX 6755
14th- and 15th-century with handsome tower. Roof-bosses; impressive 16th-century painted screen; 17th-century stone pulpit.

UPTON HELLIONS
St Mary the Virgin
2m/3km N. of Crediton SS 8403
Unsophisticated Norman and later church in deep country, though not far from Exeter. Plastered and whitewashed walls, always a good start for a country church, support 15th-century wagon roofs; there are some carved benches of the same date. Georgian pulpit and a country-made monument to a Caroline squire and his wife.

UPTON PYNE
Church of Our Lady
3m/4km N. of Exeter SX 9197
Setting near cottages; 14th-century W. tower unusually decorated with carvings and figures. Attractive interior restored 1867–8.

WASHFORD PYNE
St Peter
9m/15km W. of Tiverton SS 8111
By R. M. Fulford, 1883–4, in a pleasing variety of stones with tile-hung upper stage of tower and spire. A small and remote church, it is picturesque and also has a fine interior with contemporary furnishings, light fittings, and stained glass by Drake.

WEST OGWELL
(dedication unknown)
on W. side of Newton Abbot SX 8370
Delightful little church in a park. Unaltered early 14th-century cruciform building with a late-Georgian interior. Plastered and whitened walls, clear glass, box pews, altar rails, and Jacobean pulpit, all very appealing.
R.C.F.

WEST PUTFORD
St Stephen
8m/12km N. of Holsworthy SS 3615
In a very remote part of Devon, the deep country of the upper Torridge valley. Cruciform church of early 14th century. W. tower added about 1500. Norman font. Chancel floored with medieval tiles. Mural tablets to local families of the Georgian age. Plastered and whitened walls. Escaped the Victorian restorer.

WIDECOMBE-IN-THE-MOOR
St Pancras
5m/8km N.W. of Ashburton SX 7176
A fine granite church well into the Moor, but the village has been terribly commercialized. Best seen in winter against the austere lines of the moorland above. The church remains unspoilt by all this vulgarity. Essentially early 14th-century cruciform; the original transepts enlarged into aisles in late 15th century or early 16th. This was a common development in the larger Devon churches, which are not as purely Perpendicular as they seem. Widecombe has a noble tower – granite at its most graceful – probably built by prosperous tinners. Remains of rood screen with 32 figure-paintings. Rustic verses on the great disaster of 1638, when the church was struck by lightning during a service. Church House, nearby, built about 1500 and one of the best of its kind in Devon.

YEALMPTON
St Bartholomew
7m/11km E. of Plymouth SX 5751
Rebuilt in 1850 by Butterfield, who spared the tower, which was unfortunately reconstructed in 1915. The interior is most effective, being well-proportioned and restrained with free use of local stone and marbles.

Dorset

Introduction

This is a county of small churches and enormous scenery. Its long extent of shadowy coast, so varied and dramatic, is in most places too steep or too strange – one thinks of the sixteen miles of pebbles called the Chesil Beach from Portland to Bridport – to admit many colonies of hideous holiday bungalows. Only at three places, Poole, with its satellites, Weymouth, still with remains of Georgian dignity, and Swanage is there very much 'development'. This beautiful little county divides itself into three kinds of scenery, for long described as Felix, Petraea and Deserta, and the ghost of that immortal fatalist, Thomas Hardy, haunts all three. More recently the Central Electricity Board and the Army and other Government departments have done their best to lay his ghost and kill the remoteness.

Felix is the clay vales of the west and north-west, with Beaminster, Bridport and Sherborne as their chief towns, all in rich farming country abounding in oaks, a land of rivers and stone manor houses and butter pastures and, in the Blackmore Vale, of hunting people.

Petraea is the chalk downs and rocky formations of Purbeck and Portland. The chalk comes in from Wiltshire and crosses the county diagonally from north-west to Lyme Regis in the south-west. The hills are higher and steeper than those of Wiltshire, and topped by a marvellous series of earthworks, including Maiden Castle, with its two miles of ramparts, one of the biggest pre-historic earthworks in the world. From the chalk heights you may often see the English Channel on one side and the azure blue of the rich vales inland. The red-brick 18th-century town of Blandford and the white limestone county town of Dorchester are in the chalk. The Isle of Purbeck, with Wareham at its gate and Swanage on its coast and Corfe Castle in the middle, is a hilly diversity of geological formations which makes the crumbling cliffs, with their boulder-strewn shores, strange indeed. Purbeck marble, such as supplied columns for Westminster Abbey, the Temple Church, London, Salisbury Cathedral, and many a medieval font and effigy, may be seen at Durlston Head near Swanage. The loveliest part of the island of Purbeck is cut off by the military. The Isle of Portland, with its own tall, fair-haired people a separate race from the mainland, is a block of limestone nearly four miles long and with hardly any trees. Here was quarried the white stone Wren used for St Paul's Cathedral, for Greenwich Hospital and many of his churches. It is quarried today.

Deserta is south-east Dorset behind the Isle of Purbeck, 'a thousand furlongs once of sea, now of barren ground, ling, heath, furze, anything'. Hardy's Egdon Heath is part of it; so is that inland sea with the town of Poole on its shore, looking over to wooded Brownsea Island.

In all this variety of material, it is not surprising to find much beauty of many coloured building stones, varying from the deep gold of Sherborne to the silver-white of Portland and the lavender of Milton Abbey, in churches, manor houses and cottages. And even in the centre of the county, where flint was most easily available, the church builders varied their outer walls with bands of limestone. Brick was not used till the 18th century.

Most of the Dorset churches are mainly Perpendicular; few have clere-stories, and many have squat and sturdy towers with a prominent stair turret carried up to or above the battlements and pinnacles. The only grand monastic buildings still used as churches are those of Wimborne, Sherborne and Milton Abbas.

Victorian architects seem to have been fascinated by the local stones and fortunately used them both for their 'restorations' and in new churches.

J.B.

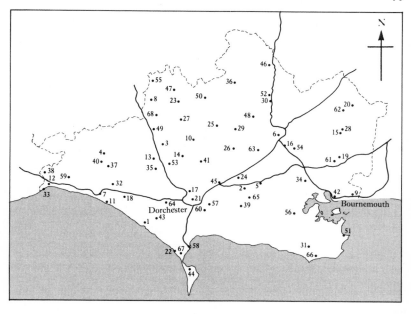

1	Abbotsbury
2	Affpuddle
3	Batcombe
4	Beaminster
5	Bere Regis
6	Blandford Forum
7	Bothenhampton
8	Bradford Abbas
9	Branksome
10	Buckland Newton
11	Burton Bradstock
12	Catherston Leweston
13	Cattistock
14	Cerne Abbas
15	Chalbury
16	Charlton Marshall
17	Charminster
18	Chilcombe
19	Colehill
20	Cranborne
21	Dorchester
22	Fleet
23	Folke

24	Gussage St Andrews
25	Hazelbury Bryan
26	Hilton
27	Holnest
28	Horton
29	Ibberton
30	Iwerne Minster
31	Kingston
32	Loders
33	Lyme Regis
34	Lytchett Matravers
35	Maiden Newton
36	Melplash
37	Monkton Wyld
38	Moreton
39	Netherbury
40	Piddletrenthide
41	Poole
42	Portesham
43	Portland
44	Puddletown
45	Shaftesbury

46	Sherborne
47	Shillingstone
48	Stockwood
49	Stourton Caundle
50	Studland
51	Sutton Waldron
52	Sydling St Nicholas
53	Tarrant Crawford
54	Trent
55	Wareham
56	West Stafford
57	Weymouth
58	Whitchurch Canonicorum
59	Whitcombe
60	Wimborne Minster
61	Wimborne St Giles
62	Winterborne Clenston
63	Winterborne Steepleton
64	Winterborne Tomson
65	Worth Matravers
66	Wyke Regis
67	Yetminster

Selected List of Churches

ABBOTSBURY
St Nicholas
8m/12km S.W. of Dorchester SY 5785
Adjoining the scattered remains of the former Benedictine Abbey in a large and picturesque village. The fabric is mainly late-Perpendicular. The chancel has a fine 17th-century ornamental plaster ceiling and handsome Georgian altarpiece; 15th-century painted glass with upper portion of figure of the Blessed Virgin from a Crucifixion; stone effigy of Abbot in porch and Jacobean canopied pulpit.

AFFPUDDLE
St Lawrence
8m/11km E. of Dorchester SY 8093
A picturesque thatched village in the Piddle Valley below the great heath. The church and the former parsonage with its spreading lawns form a charming picture on the river bank. A 13th-century fabric enlarged with aisle and comely tower in 15th century. Norman font, S. doorway, and a fine array of mid-16th-century woodwork, seating and pulpit dated 1548, 'the tyme of Thomas Lyllynton, vicar of thys churche'. Interior well restored in recent years.

BATCOMBE
St Mary
8m/12km S. of Yeovil ST 6104
Romantic setting under Downs. Altogether Perpendicular with stately W. tower, little altered and little spoiled, though restored in 1864 when pews and glass were renewed; 15th-century stone screen.

BEAMINSTER
St Mary of the Annunciation
5m/8km N. of Bridport ST 4801
Mainly 15th-century; spectacular W. tower with carvings of Crucifixion and Ascension. Interior restored 1860; fine monument by Scheemakers, 1753. In attractive small town.

BERE REGIS
St John Baptist
7m/11km N.W. of Wareham SY 8494
The church is a fine fabric of Saxon origin,

largely rebuilt in the 12th century, refashioned and enlarged in the three succeeding centuries. The tower exhibits the stone and flint chequerwork characteristic of the district. The elaborate timber roof of the nave is said to have been given by Cardinal Morton, who was born nearby at Milbourne Syleham. Note the arcades, large Norman font, and interesting 16th-century Purbeck marble monuments to the Turberville family. One of the best interiors in the county, restored by Street.

BLANDFORD FORUM
St Peter & St Paul
16m/25km N.W. of Bournemouth ST 8806
A devastating fire destroyed the church and town in 1731, and the whole place was rebuilt in a pleasing manner by the Bastards, a local family of builder-architects. John and William were responsible for the church, 1731–9, a fine specimen of Georgian design in ashlar. The interior has largely escaped Victorian interference and retains its W. gallery, font, pulpit, box pews, and mayoral seat. In 1893 the apsidal sanctuary was cleverly moved out on rollers to newly prepared foundations and a chancel inserted; the new work is in complete harmony with the rest.

BOTHENHAMPTON
Holy Trinity
1m/2km S.E. of Bridport SY 4791
By E. S. Prior, 1887–9. Nave, chancel and porch. Interesting Arts and Crafts design, with large transverse arches across the nave and deep reveals to the windows. Contemporary font and pulpit; altar front by Lethaby, E. window by Whall.

BRADFORD ABBAS
St Mary the Virgin
3m/4km S.E. of Yeovil ST 5814
With its embattled parapets, pinnacled tower and large Perpendicular windows, the church is characteristically North Dorset. The interior has been scraped, to the loss of much atmosphere. Handsome panelled

roofs, stone rood screen, late 15th-century bench-ends, and 17th-century pulpit.

BRANKSOME
St Aldhelm
4m/6km W. of Bournemouth SZ 0592
Set among pine-woods near the county boundary. A typical Bodley church of 1892–4, not of local type, but eminently satisfying. Ashlar masonry and Decorated in style with fine arcades and panelled roofs. A tower with spire was planned but has not been carried out. Good font and cover and decent woodwork.

BUCKLAND NEWTON
Holy Rood
10m/16km N. of Dorchester ST 6905
Decorated and Perpendicular. Interesting Norman Christ above the S. doorway outside with, inside, primitive slate relief. Early 16th-century seating.

BURTON BRADSTOCK
St Mary
3m/4km S.E. of Bridport SY 4889
Setting. Largely Perpendicular cruciform church with central tower. S. aisle by E. S. Prior, 1897; 15th-century wagon roofs; 14th-century font on Norman base.

CATHERSTON LEWESTON
St Mary
2m/3km N.E. of Lyme Regis SY 3794
By J. L. Pearson, 1858. Beautiful little nave and chancel church with bellcote. All original furnishings; glass by Clayton & Bell.

CATTISTOCK
St Peter & St Paul
9m/15km N.W. of Dorchester SY 5999
A pleasant village in the upper valley of the Frome with an attractive group of cottages near the church. The church was mostly rebuilt by Sir Giles Gilbert Scott, but its claim to fame is the work done in 1874 by his far more able elder son and namesake. This consists of the tower, porch, N. aisle and vestry. The tower is superb in the best local manner, and obviously influenced by that of Charminster. Excellent, too, is the N. arcade, the open porch with its wooden vault, and a stone screen. Interesting Hardman and Pre-Raphaelite stained glass and a font with elaborate spire as cover.

CERNE ABBAS
St Mary
7m/11km N. of Dorchester ST 6601
The handsome 15th-century tower dominates this delightful little mid-Dorset town, once the seat of an important Benedictine Abbey of which there are still some scattered remains. The fabric is of late 13th-century origin, but was largely rebuilt in 15th century and early 16th century, and partially reconstructed in 17th century. Note the stone screen, the 14th-century wall-paintings in the chancel, the 17th-century pulpit with tester, and the great E. window, which probably came from the Abbey and has been cut down to fit its present position.

CHALBURY
All Saints
4m/6km N. of Wimborne SU 0106
A charming little hamlet church set in typical East Dorset scenery. Plastered walls and timber bellcote. The fabric is of 13th-century origin with 14th-century E. window. The interior was refitted in 18th century and has escaped 'restoration'. Note the box pews, three-decker pulpit, W. gallery, and clear glass. In place of chancel arch is triple opening supported on slender wooden columns.

CHARLTON MARSHALL
St Mary the Virgin
2m/3km S.E. of Blandford ST 8806
With the exception of the late-medieval tower, the church was rebuilt in 1715, probably by one of the Bastards of Blandford. The plan and elevations are medieval in manner, with chequered flint and ashlar walling, but the details are entirely Classical. The interior retains much of its Georgian atmosphere with clear glass, altar rails, and fine canopied pulpit. Bastard family monuments.

CHARMINSTER
St Mary the Virgin
1m/2km N. of Dorchester SY 6892
An aisled 12th-century church, partly rebuilt early in 16th century, with a fine W. tower of Ham stone which obviously influenced G. G. Scott, Jnr, when he designed that of Cattistock; the long paired belfry windows are particularly effective. The diminutive chancel is early 19th-century and quite attractive; 12th-century arcades and chancel

arch, remains of wall-paintings, and 16th-century Purbeck marble monuments.

CHILCOMBE
(dedication unknown)
4m/6km E. of Bridport SY 5291
Charming small stone building in farmyard of manor farm, on seaward-sloping site; 12th-century core, partly rebuilt in 14th century. Old stone floor, early Victorian pews, clear and bright coloured Victorian glass, early 13th-century font, and 17th-century monuments.

COLEHILL
St Michael and all Angels
1m/2km N. of Wimborne SU 0201
Nice little essay in Arts and Crafts style by W. D. Caroe, 1893. Brick, half-timber and plaster. Interior like a timbered barn; contemporary furnishings.

CRANBORNE
St Mary & St Bartholomew
8m/12km N.W. of Ringwood SU 0513
A large church for Dorset, of Norman origin, as shown by the fine N. doorway, but now mostly 13th- and 15th-century. Chancel of 1875 by D. Brandon, who also did the N. porch. Inside are 14th-century wall-paintings over S. arcade, an early 15th-century pulpit, and 15th–16th-century monuments.

DORCHESTER
St Peter & St Paul
7m/12km N. of Weymouth SY 6990
A Perpendicular church, stately, but not large, well-placed in the centre of town. Portland stone, with Ham Hill stone dressings; magnificent tower with tall belfry lights; lofty interior with wagon roof; Jacobean pulpit; good 14th- and 17th-century monuments.

FLEET
Holy Trinity
3m/4km W. of Weymouth SY 6380
By Strickland, 1827–9. Early Gothic Revival of the Commissioners' sort with apsidal chancel, prettily treated within, nave and W. tower. Good monument of 1818.

FOLKE
St Lawrence
3m/4km S.E. of Sherborne ST 6513
Attractive small church next to manor house in unspoilt Blackmore Vale. Rebuilt in 1628,

a good instance of Gothic Survival. Complete furnishings including screens, pews, and a fine font with cover.

GUSSAGE ST ANDREW
St Andrew
12m/19km N.E. of Blandford Forum ST 9714
Small 12th-century church in a farmyard setting. Single-cell building, the E. end altered in 13th century. Important 13th–14th-century wall-paintings, recently restored; 15th-century nave roof; 17th-century pulpit and 18th-century chandelier.

HAZELBURY BRYAN
St Mary & St James
5m/8km S. of Sturminster Newton ST 7408
A good example of a Dorset village church in a typical Blackmoor Vale setting. Mainly Perpendicular with embattled parapets and sturdy W. tower. Nave and aisles have 15th-century roofs. Note 13th-century font with 18th-century cover, canopied pulpit, and remains of 15th-century painted glass. Interior well restored by Sir Charles Nicholson.

HILTON
All Saints
5m/8km S.W. of Blandford ST 7803
Another typical Dorset country church picturesquely situated above the thatched roofs of the village in the heart of the Downs. As generally in these parts, mainly late-Gothic and incorporating in the N. aisle a fine range of 15th-century windows from the destroyed cloister of Milton Abbey. The fan vault of the porch probably comes from the same source. In the tower are 12 tall panels with figure-paintings of the Apostles which also came from Milton Abbey; the work is of high quality and early 16th-century date.

HOLNEST
Church of the Assumption
5m/8km S. of Sherborne ST 6509
Rustic medieval church in a field. Mainly 15th-century with 17th-century alterations and chancel of 1855, Jacobean pulpit, white-painted box pews with candle sconces, 13th-century font and consecration crosses.

HORTON
St Wolfrida
5m/8km N. of Wimborne SU 0307
12th–13th-century origins, mostly rebuilt *c.* 1720, possibly from a Vanbrugh design.

Memorable W. tower with pyramidal spire. Inside are 18th-century box pews, pulpit and Rococo reredos.

IBBERTON
St Eustace

4m/6km S.E. of Sturminster Newton ST 7807 Finely situated. Mainly Perpendicular, restored by Ponting, 1903; attractive within and without. Some painted 15th-century and later glass, Perpendicular font, 17th-century screen.

IWERNE MINSTER
St Mary

5m/8km N. of Blandford ST 8614 Attractive estate-village setting; 12th–15th-century with S. chapel by Pearson, 1880; 14th-century spire, one of three in Dorset; 12th-century arcades and pulpit of 1610.

KINGSTON
St James

5m/8km W. of Swanage SY 9579 By G. E. Street, 1873–80; one of his latest and certainly one of his best churches. Though more suggestive of the Ile de France than Purbeck, it is built of local materials, and the lofty central tower is among the most successful of the Victorian era. The apsidal chancel is vaulted. Fittings by Street include much beautiful ironwork. Glass by Clayton & Bell. The former parsonage, now two houses, is also by Street.

LODERS
St Mary Magdalene

2m/3km N.E. of Bridport SY 4994 Church of a former alien priory. Charming inside and out, 12th–15th-century. Early 13th-century font and 15th-century painted glass and sculpture.

LYME REGIS
St Michael the Archangel

8m/12km W. of Bridport SY 3492 An attractive little seaside resort on the borders of Devon with many late 18th- and early 19th-century houses and a few earlier survivals. The church has an interesting architectural history. Originally a 12th-century tripartite structure with axial tower, transepts were added *c.* 1200 and, later in the 13th century, aisles to the nave. Early in the 16th century a new church was erected to the E. of the tower, and the transepts, aisles and old chancel removed. Early in the

19th century the Norman nave was shortened. The later church is typically Devonian with continuous nave, chancel and aisles. Tudor arcades, canopied pulpit, W. gallery and lectern, all 17th-century, and early 16th-century tapestry panel.

LYTCHETT MATRAVERS
St Mary the Virgin

5m/8km N.W. of Poole SY 9495 Atmospheric church of 13th-century origin, but mostly *c.* 1500. Medieval brasses, font and painted glass. Wagon roof to nave, 18th-century hatchments, and a barrel organ.

MAIDEN NEWTON
St Mary

8m/12km N.W. of Dorchester SY 5997 12th-century fabric refashioned and enlarged in the 15th century. Late Norman central tower base and good 12th-century details.

MARNHULL
St Gregory

3m/4km N. of Sturminster Newton ST 7818 12th-century in origin; refashioned and enlarged in 15th and 19th centuries; 16th-century roofs, 16th–18th-century wall-paintings, and Royal Arms of Charles I.

MELPLASH
Christchurch

2m/3km S. of Beaminster SY 4898 By Benjamin Ferrey, 1845–6. Neo-Norman with cruciform plan, high crossing tower, and apsed chancel. Romanesque carved detail throughout, a trifle mechanical but effective. Unhistorical hammer-beam roof to nave, the interior now re-ordered with nave screened off to form a parish room.

MONKTON WYLD
St Andrew

3m/4km N. of Lyme Regis SY 3396 By R. C. Carpenter, 1848–9. Handsome Decorated church in a romantic wooded setting. Well-proportioned nave and chancel with central tower and Northants. broach spire. Correct Ecclesiological interior with octagonal piers, chancel screen, brass altar rail, and rich glass by G. E. Cook.

MORETON
St Nicholas

7m/11km E. of Dorchester SY 8089 Amusing 1776 Gothic 'restored' by Victorians who added N. aisle and porch in

1840s. Windows blown out in 1940 but replaced by Laurence Whistler's delightful engraved clear glass. Burial place of Lawrence of Arabia.

NETHERBURY
St Mary
1m/2km S. of Beaminster SY 4799
Typical Dorset Perpendicular outside with some 19th-century restoration. Splendid spacious interior. Norman font, 17th-century pulpit, and 15th-century monument.

PIDDLETRENTHIDE
All Saints
6m/10km N. of Dorchester ST 7000
14th-century fabric with Norman core. Good tower of 1487 replete with pinnacles and gargoyles; 17th–20th-century monuments.

POOLE
St James
4m/6km W. of Bournemouth SZ 0291
Set in the old part of town, the church was rebuilt in 1820 in white Purbeck stone. Lofty interior, with clustered columns of pine logs, said to have been imported from Newfoundland, rising to plaster vaulted roof. Fine pilastered reredos of 1736.

PORTESHAM
St Peter
6m/10km S.W. of Dorchester SY 6085
Typical Dorset church, mostly Perpendicular with Early English tower and chancel. Arcades with panelled arches.

PORTLAND
St George
4m/6km S. of Weymouth SY 6972
Situated in a bleak position on the W. side of the 'island'. Fine ashlar cruciform church of 1777 by Mr Gilbert. Central drumless dome and W. tower with cupola. The interior is quite unaltered with box pews, galleries, and twin pulpits. A most satisfying church.
    R.C.F.

PUDDLETOWN
St Mary the Virgin
5m/8km N.E. of Dorchester SY 7594
A large village with some good groups of rural architecture and a fine early 18th-century parsonage in the Blandford manner. The church has one of the most 'atmospherick' interiors in Dorset. Mainly late-

medieval with an earlier core. Fine panelled roof to nave. Note the beaker-shaped font, probably 11th-century, box pews, canopied pulpit and gallery, all 17th-century, fine array of 15th- and 16th-century brasses and monuments, Comper glass in S. chapel.

SHAFTESBURY
St Peter
18m/29km W. of Salisbury ST 8622
Perpendicular fabric somewhat altered later. Elaborate parapet with quatrefoils to N. aisle. Recently renovated.

SHERBORNE
St Mary
5m/8km E. of Yeovil ST 6316
Formerly the church of a Benedictine Abbey which became parochial after the Dissolution. The large cruciform fabric is externally mostly 15th-century, but it is actually a Norman church transformed, with slight remains of Saxon work at the W. end. The old portion of the Lady Chapel and Bishop Roger's Chapel are 13th-century. The fan vaults of the nave and quire are among the finest in existence. The interior was vigorously restored and decorated by Carpenter and Slater in the middle of the 19th century, and the nave and transepts are crowded with seating. In the S. transept is the imposing monument of the Earl of Bristol, d. 1698, and his two wives. The mainly modern stalls possess an interesting series of 15th-century misericords. Note the 15th-century painted glass in the Leweston Chapel, the 12th–14th-century abbatial effigies, and the 18th-century mural tablets. Considerable remains of the monastic buildings are incorporated in the school to the N. of the church. The town, pleasantly sited on a slope above the Yeo, has many attractive houses of various dates and styles.

SHILLINGSTONE
Holy Rood
4m/6km N.W. of Blandford ST 8211
A large village in the Stour Valley with many picturesque cottages and a restored cross. The church stands somewhat away from the main part of the village and is of 12th-century origin. There was the usual refashioning in the 15th century and restoration and enlargement by Bodley, who added the N. aisle. Note the good modern roofs and pleasant Bodley fittings, several 12th-century windows, 12th-century font,

and 17th-century pulpit. The banded flint and ashlar masonry is a local feature. A worshipful church.

STOCKWOOD
St Edwolds
7m/11km S. of Yeovil ST 5906
Attractive little church, the smallest in Dorset, in a beautiful setting with stream and footbridge. Mostly Perpendicular with porch and naive bell-turret of 1638. Late-medieval font and Jacobean communion table.
R.C.F.

STOURTON CAUNDLE
St Peter
5m/8km E. of Sherborne ST 7115
13th-, 14th- and 15th-century. Chancel refitted by W. H. R. Blacking; 18th-century font and cover; early 16th-century pulpit and reset 17th-century altar rails.

STUDLAND
St Nicholas
3m/4km N. of Swanage SZ 0382
Of Saxon origin, rebuilt in the 12th century, now the most complete Norman church in Dorset. Tripartite plan with low axial tower, vaulted chancel and sanctuary; 18th-century windows with round arches. Much good 12th-century detail, but the interior has been scraped; 12th-century chalice-shaped font, 13th-century E. window, mutilated 18th-century pulpit, and text over chancel arch.

SUTTON WALDRON
St Bartholomew
5m/8km S. of Shaftesbury ST 8615
By G. Alexander, 1847. Interior decorated by Owen Jones, a beau-ideal of mid-Victorian Romanticism. Rich colours scintillate in the modified light. This is one of the prettiest churches in the county.

SYDLING ST NICHOLAS
St Nicholas
7m/11km N.W. of Dorchester SY 6399
Late Perpendicular. Nave wagon roof with bosses, 18th-century chancel and tower screen, some box pews, and 18th–19th-century monuments.

TARRANT CRAWFORD
St Mary
3m/4km S.E. of Blandford ST 9203
Mostly 14th-century; pleasant setting with adjacent house and medieval barn. Good

14th-century wall-paintings of the Annuciation, St Margaret of Antioch, and other subjects.
R.C.F.

TRENT
St Andrew
3m/4km N.E. of Yeovil ST 5918
The village, formerly in Somerset, abounds in good architecture, medieval, Tudor and later, with plenty of well-established trees as a background. The church is interesting architecturally and is full of excellent fittings. The lateral tower is crowned by one of the three ancient stone spires of Dorset. A 13th-century fabric enlarged and refashioned in 14th and 15th centuries. Chancel good Somerset Perpendicular. Much restoration and refitting *c.* 1840 in a pre-Victorian manner. Fine rood screen with vaulting intact. Pulpit of Continental origin. E. window contains interesting old painted glass, mostly 16th- and 17th-century foreign work. Fine array of early 16th-century carved bench-ends.

WAREHAM
St Martin
6m/10km W. of Poole SY 9287
Well-situated at the N. end of the town, near the Saxon ramparts. A small pre-Conquest church enlarged and refashioned in 13th century. After a long period of neglect, it was well restored by W. H. Randoll Blacking before the War. Note remains of 12th-century wall-paintings in chancel and fine monument to Lawrence of Arabia by Eric Kennington.

WEST STAFFORD
St Andrew
3m/4km E. of Dorchester SY 7789
Late-medieval fabric, partly rebuilt and refitted *c.* 1640, chancel added by Ponting, *c.* 1898. Plastered wagon roof, 17th-century altar rails, screen, pulpit and pews; 18th-century W. gallery with Royal Arms of James I.

WEYMOUTH
St Mary
7m/11km S. of Dorchester SY 6778
By James Hamilton, a local architect, 1815–17. Well-mannered façade of Portland ashlar harmonizing admirably with the surrounding buildings of the old town.

Tunnel-vaulted nave with galleries and good reredos.

WHITCHURCH CANONICORUM
St Candida & Holy Cross
4m/6km N.E. of Lyme Regis SY 3995
A large church in the heart of Marshwood Vale approached only by lanes. Mainly Early English with some good detail, especially in the arcades. Fine Perpendicular W. tower. The church is probably unique in this country in that it retains the relics of its patroness in a 13th-century shrine. Note late 12th-century font, early 17th-century pulpit, fragments of 15th-century painted glass, and some 16th–17th-century monuments.

WHITCOMBE
(dedication unknown)
3m/4km S.E. of Dorchester SY 7188
By the roadside with an old farm and thatched cottages to keep it company. Nave 12th-century, chancel 13th-century, tower and windows late-medieval. Interior less spoilt than many in Dorset. Note Saxon cross shaft, 13th-century font, and 15th-century wall-painting of St Christopher. William Barnes, the Dorset poet and scholar, 1801–86, preached his first and last sermons here.
R.C.F.

WIMBORNE MINSTER
St Cuthberga
7m/11km N.E. of Bournemouth SZ 0199
Set in the heart of a small market town with many pleasant Georgian houses. Formerly a collegiate church and the only instance of a two-towered fabric in Dorset. Cruciform plan. The central tower and parts of the arcade are 12th-century; the rest 13th–15th-century. Drastically restored as a result of which much good Jacobean woodwork and other fittings were destroyed. Good foreign painted glass in E. window. Remains of Jacobean screen and stalls. Interesting medieval and later monuments. Notable clock of 14th-century origin.

WIMBORNE ST GILES
St Giles
11m/18km N.E. of Blandford SU 0312
A small village in the undulating country between Cranborne and Wimborne. The church, well-placed on the E. side of a green, flanked by a row of almshouses on the N., was completely rebuilt in excellent Georgian

in 1732. Interior Gothicized by Bodley in 1887. A fortunate fire in 1908 necessitated reconstruction superbly carried out by Sir Ninian Comper. The interior is a treasure-house of Comper work: screens, pulpit, seating, altars and glass. Some fine 17th-century monuments well restored after the fire.

WINTERBORNE CLENSTON
St Nicholas
4m/6km S.W. of Blandford ST 8303
Rebuilt in 1840, probably by L. Vulliamy; see his other work at Hinton Parva. W. tower with stone spire; nave unfortunately re-pewed, but chancel retains charming furniture and original ceiling. Royal Arms in glass.

WINTERBORNE STEEPLETON
St Michael
4m/6km W. of Dorchester SY 6289
Of Saxon origin, partly remodelled in 12th century and afterwards. Decorated W. tower and eponymous steeple. On the outside of the tower an important 10th-century Saxon carving of an angel, probably from a rood like that at Bradford on Avon, Wilts.

WINTERBORNE TOMSON
St Andrew
6m/10km W. of Wimborne SY 8897
A small 12th-century hamlet church pleasantly placed in the Winterborne Valley hard by the old manor house. Apsidal E. end and plastered wagon roof. Refashioned early in 18th century and well restored after long disuse in memory of Thomas Hardy. Complete set of early Georgian fittings. The W. gallery is formed from the medieval rood loft.
R.C.F.

WORTH MATRAVERS
St Nicholas
4m/6km W. of Swanage SY 9777
A stone village in the austere Purbeck manner with modern cottages in keeping. The church is, next to Studland, the most complete Norman fabric in Dorset. Here the tower is at the W. end and not axial like Studland. The chancel was altered in the 13th century and has a fine 14th-century E. window. Note the external corbel tables, inner S. doorway, and chancel arch, all good Norman work.

WYKE REGIS
All Saints
W. district of Weymouth SY 6677
Rebuilt *c.* 1455, in the local Portland stone, in a spacious manner, with tall W. tower overlooking Chesil Beach. Continuous nave, with aisles and aisled chancel, with no chancel arch; 15th-century font.

YETMINSTER
St Andrew
5m/8km S.W. of Sherborne ST 5910
A large village on high ground which, in spite of some modern development, is attractive with mullioned windows, thatch and stone, and slate roofing. A good type of Dorset village church. Chancel late 13th-century. Rest rebuilt in 15th century with embattled parapets and good roofs retaining much original colour. Some early 16th-century seating and a good brass of 1531. The churchyard is rich in table-tombs and headstones of late 17th and 18th centuries.

Durham

Introduction

Durham is a grey, gaunt, curiously withdrawn county. To strangers it means little except a succession of pit-heaps along the Great North Road or a heart-stirring view of Durham Cathedral glimpsed from the railway train. You must live in County Durham, grow to love the gauntness and the greyness, before you can properly appreciate its highly individual beauty, a beauty of contrast and paradox, to be found where rows of workmen's cottages sprawl across the heather of the open fells, or where a Saxon church stands neighbour to a council estate.

Durham people do not wear their hearts on their sleeve, and Durham county conceals its treasures from the casual passer-by. How many of the tourists who visit the Yorkshire Dales and Roman Wall know anything of the barren and beautiful land that lies between, the high fells of Weardale and upper Teesdale, where the Romans mined for lead and the Prince-Bishops hunted the red deer, and where today, if you know the country well enough, you may come upon blue pools of gentians spilled in the hollows of the hills? Eastwards, too, where the grim ship-building towns edge the cliffs between the mouths of Tyne and Tees, unexpected rewards await the discerning explorer, the foundations of a Roman fort lying exposed to view between rows of little red-brick houses, a railway station in the high Grecian style standing elegant and aloof in a dismal urban setting, a wooded valley, one of those steep, secretive denes so characteristic of the Durham countryside, winding its way down to the coal-blackened sea. Coal and the sea – these two were the kings of County Durham. But it would be a mistake to picture the county as a solid industrial area like South Lancashire; the villages have open country around them and the shipyard towns have fine stretches of sandy beach for a playground. Country and town live side by side in odd but not unhappy contrast.

This element of contrast, so characteristic of Durham, gives a peculiar charm to her medieval churches. One of these ancient and seemingly indestructible buildings is often to be found standing a little lost in an industrial landscape, and the bizarre contrast between church and setting can be strangely moving. Especially is this so in the case of those Saxon churches which are the particular glory of County Durham.

In Durham the pre-Conquest period is of the first importance. In any medieval church it is the rule rather than the exception to find Saxon work still in existence, and it is always worthwhile to enquire for Saxon crosses and carved stones. By contrast Norman work is rare and seldom of the first class. (Kirk Merrington, the most complete Norman church in the county, was deliberately destroyed during the 19th century.) With the exception of Pittington, there is no church worth a visit for the sake of the Norman work alone, and the great Norman cathedral in Durham seems to have provoked few imitators.

From the Conquest until the Reformation Durham remained a poor and isolated area, so that it is not surprising to find that St Hilda's, Hartlepool, St Cuthbert's, Darlington, and the parish churches of Staindrop, Chester-le-Street and Houghton-le-Spring are the only large medieval churches that can stand comparison with those of the wealthier South.

The most notable post-Reformation development was the appearance of a school of wood-carving peculiar to County Durham. The carvers worked in a Gothic rather than a Classical tradition, a fact partly accounted for by the northern 'time-lag', which allowed artistic styles to continue to flourish here long after they had fallen out of fashion in the more sophisticated South. The chief patron of these wood-carvers was Bishop Cosin, and when he gave orders for the construction of new stalls for the Cathedral he decided to reproduce as nearly as possible the design of the medieval ones destroyed during the Commonwealth. 'Cosin' woodwork is to be found in many churches throughout the county, much of it clearly influenced by the design of these stalls.

Of classical churches the most notable are Sunderland, Stockton, and the unspoilt Gibside Chapel, which is not strictly speaking a parish church at all. Following the Industrial Revolution came an outburst of church-building, but the results are disappointing in the extreme. Architects of the Victorian Gothic school did their best work under the influence of the Oxford Movement, and often at the behest of a pious squire whose hobby was ecclesiology. Neither of these factors was powerful in County Durham, where the typical pit-village church is a bare, barn-like structure usually designed by one of the local architects, the best of these being Hodgson Fowler.

The poverty of the Victorian churches has at least the negative virtue of plainness, and where the proportions of the buildings are good an imaginative scheme of redecoration can work an astonishing transformation. Unhappily such transformations are rare. Durham remains a comparatively poor county remote from contemporary artistic influence, and, with a few notable exceptions, the 20th-century work is as undistinguished as the 19th. But even modern Durham has her pleasant surprises. The date is 1907, the parish a seaside suburb of Sunderland, neither the time nor the place likely to produce a near- masterpiece, yet in the church of St Andrew at Roker, County Durham has a 20th-century building that may reasonably lay claim to greatness.

G.B.

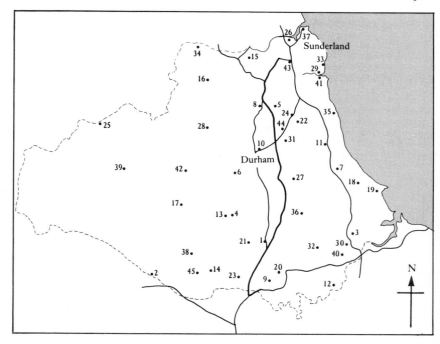

1	Aycliffe	16	Gibside Chapel	31	Pittington
2	Barnard Castle	17	Hamsterley	32	Redmarshall
3	Billingham	18	Hart	33	Roker
4	Bishop Auckland	19	Hartlepool	34	Ryton
5	Burnmoor	20	Haughton-le-Skerne	35	Seaham
6	Brancepeth	21	Heighington	36	Sedgefield
7	Castle Eden	22	Hetton-le-Hole	37	South Shields
8	Chester-le-Street	23	High Coniscliffe	38	Staindrop
9	Darlington	24	Houghton-le-Spring	39	Stanhope
10	Durham	25	Hunstantworth	40	Stockton-on-Tees
11	Easington	26	Jarrow	41	Sunderland
12	Egglescliffe	27	Kelloe	42	Tow Law
13	Escomb	28	Lanchester	43	West Boldon
14	Gainford	29	Monkwearmouth	44	West Rainton
15	Gateshead	30	Norton	45	Winston

Selected List of Churches

AYCLIFFE
St Andrew
5m/8km N. of Darlington NZ 2822
A village still, though the parent of the new town Newton Aycliffe, with the A1 motorway roaring to the E. An imposing church with Saxon nave walls, but mostly 12th- and 13th-century, restored in 1882 by Ewan Christian. Spacious interior with engaged aisles and a wealth of 17th-century pews and carved Saxon stones.

BARNARD CASTLE
St Mary
15m/24km W. of Darlington NZ 0516
The ancient market town rises dramatically above the Tees, with its main street presided over by the delightful octagonal market cross and town hall. The church stands a little way back. Norman S. doorway with zig-zags, good Transitional N. arcade, impressive Perpendicular chancel arch and W. tower, a rebuilding of 1874, its base crowded with 18th- and 19th-century monuments. The whole church was much restored in the 19th century.

BILLINGHAM
St Cuthbert
2m/3km N.E. of Stockton-on-Tees NZ 4522
Remarkable example of successful combination of ancient and modern, symbolic of transformation of ancient village of Billingham into large industrial town. Saxon tower, high, black, narrow Saxon nave, altered in 12th century, leading up to wide, light chancel, vaguely Perpendicular in style, by G. E. Charlewood, 1939. Windows by Marion Grant. Sudden emergence from darkness and constriction into light and space; very dramatic and satisfying.

BISHOP AUCKLAND
9m/15km S.W. of Durham NZ 2029
St Andrew Auckland
1m/2km S. of the town centre
In large churchyard with trees, a dominating building, long and impressive with W. tower, transepts, and two-storeyed porch. Almost entirely 13th-century church with a long-

vistaed interior. Fine Saxon cross fragment and a 14th-century carved wooden effigy. A set of 28 stalls with misericords in the chancel, the gift of Cardinal Langley.
St Helen, Auckland
2m/3km S.W. of town centre
Small, low embattled church, with rugged exterior, mostly 12th- and 13th-century, with large S. porch; Perpendicular roofs and 17th-century Cosin stalls. Two small brasses, 1450 and 1580, and several Eden hatchments.

BRANCEPETH
St Brandon
4m/6km S.W. of Durham
Prettily situated in park, a few hundred yards away from prodigious Victorianized block of Brancepeth Castle. Church of many dates, from 12th to 17th century, and particularly distinguished for its unusual and beautiful woodwork given by John Cosin, Rector here from 1626 and later Bishop of Durham. The craftsman Robert Barker, the style a curious combination of Classical convention with deliberate imitation of medieval Gothic carving. Chancel screen, pews, pulpit, ceiling, choir-stalls, font cover, and admirable small details such as carved wood 'lining' to arch in choir, and carved plaques bearing texts, all make this a church of unique quality. Over chancel arch two fragments of medieval rood screens.

BURNMOOR
St Barnabas
2m/3km E. of Chester-le-Street NZ 3151
By Johnson & Hicks, 1867–8. Small estate church in the Early English style built of creamy brick with extensive red and buff stripes and diapers. Painted and gilded carved chancel roof with matching screen, reredos and panelling. Monuments include an Angel of Victory by Waldo Story, 1894.

CASTLE EDEN
St James
2m/3km S. of Peterlee NZ 4238
Pretty setting near the park gate. 'This sacred edifice which consuming time has

now reduced to ruinous decay was rebuilt by Rowland Burdon in 1764' – so
reads the inscription over the vestry door
of this early Gothic Revival church of
1764, probably by William Newton. The
aisles, with Corinthian columns painted
blue, the capitals gilded, were added in
1800.

CHESTER-LE-STREET
St Mary & St Cuthbert
6m/10km N. of Durham NZ 2751
Mostly 13th–16th-century with the finest
spire in County Durham, rising from an
octagon which in turn crowns a heavily buttressed Early English tower. Long and dark
Early English nave, and in the chancel
beautiful sedilia and piscina of the same
period. At N. W. end of church an
anchorite's cell with squint window. In N.
aisle a long line of effigies of the Lumley
family, placed here by John, Lord Lumley
during reign of Elizabeth I. Two are medieval, brought from graveyard of Durham
Cathedral, the others, Elizabethan, deliberately archaic in style, representing ancestors
going back to time of Edward the Confessor.
To squeeze them in, some of the older effigies had to have their feet cut off in Procrus-
tean fashion.

DARLINGTON
NZ 2914
St Cuthbert, market place
Standing austerely beautiful at the lower end
of the market-place, this is an important and
beautiful Early English church with transepts, very large and fine. It was probably
begun in 1192 by Bishop Pudsey, who intended to make it a great collegiate church.
The E. wall was restored in 1864–5 by
Pritchett; 15th-century stalls with good
misericords, spectacular 'Cosin' Gothic font
cover, and a curious chancel arch with stone
rood loft or 'pulpitum' now carrying the
organ.
St Hilda, Parkgate
By J. L. Pearson, 1887–8, in red brick.
Spacious church in the Early English style
with tall lancets and a minimum of decoration. Despite financial restraint an impressive building of quality.

DURHAM
NZ 2742
St Cuthbert, North Road
By E. R. Robson, 1858. Distinctive High

Victorian church in Early English style but
with French Gothic details. Apsidal chancel,
N.W. tower with saddleback roof and a
quirky W. front with tympanum of Christ in
Majesty. Interior sadly whitewashed.
St Giles, Gilesgate
In commanding position, with wide views of
the Cathedral and castle, but hidden from
the street; 12th–13th-century; the Norman
N. wall retains three small windows.
Haunting wooden effigy of 1591.
St Margaret of Antioch, Crossgate
Medieval church of many dates, restored by
C. Hodgson Fowler in 1865–80, but with
Norman arcades and chancel arch. Glass by
Burlison & Grylls.
St Oswald King and Martyr, Church Street
Outwardly all Perpendicular except for the
elaborate Victorian E. end, but the three E.
bays of the nave are late-Norman. Largely
rebuilt in 1834 by Ignatius Bonomi and
restored after recent fire; the W. window is
by Morris & Co. with panels by Ford Madox
Brown. A Kempe window in the N. aisle
commemorates Hodgson Fowler, architect,
d. 1910, who worshipped here. J. B.Dykes,
hymnologist, and a pioneer of the Catholic
revival, was vicar here, 1826–75.

EASINGTON
St Mary
2m/3km N.W. of Peterlee NZ 4143
Perched on a hill with wide views of cottages
and collieries to the sea. Nobly proportioned
Early English with Norman W. tower. Richly
furnished with Cosin-style woodwork; 14th-
century Frosterley marble effigy of a lady
and 13th-century effigy of a knight. The
E. end with its five lancets is a scholarly
restoration of *c.* 1850, with stained glass by
O'Connor.

EGGLESCLIFFE
St John the Baptist
4m/6km S. of Stockton-on-Tees NZ 4113
The village stands high above the winding
Tees. The church stands near the delightful
green. It is mainly Perpendicular with Cosin-
style woodwork; roof, pews, 18th-century
three-decker pulpit, screen and stalls.
Chained books, including a copy of *Eikon
Basilike.*

ESCOMB
St John
1m/2km W. of Bishop Auckland NZ 1830
Tiny Saxon church situated at the bottom

of a steep hill in a rebuilt former pit village. Very bare, very simple, almost untouched since Saxon times, except for the insertion of windows. Tall, narrow nave and chancel, with the chancel arch built of blocks of stone removed from the Roman fort at Binchester. After Durham Cathedral, the most impressive ecclesiastical building in the county, and a moving memorial to the age of Bede.

GAINFORD
St Mary
8m/12km W. of Darlington NZ 1716
The church stands at the S.W. corner of the green in this pretty village by the Tees. It is a rugged composition with its low tower and wide roof. Mainly 13th-century with good lancets in the chancel. Collection of carved stones, mostly Saxon, and a good monument of 1709 to John Middleton, resplendent with garlands and cherubs.

GATESHEAD
NZ 2563
Holy Trinity, High Street
13th-century S. aisle with good doorway and lancets; originally St Edmund's Chapel. New parish church created in 1837 when John Dobson added the Early English nave.
St Chad, Bensham
An accomplished late-Gothic building by W. S. Hicks, 1904. Prominent on a hillside, with octagonal tower, transepts and E. Lady Chapel, like a small cathedral. Imposing interior, splendidly furnished with glass by Miss Townshend, 1909, in the Lady Chapel.

GIBSIDE CHAPEL
(no dedication)
7m/11km S.W. of Gateshead by R. Derwent NZ 1759
Strictly speaking, not a parish church, but now used for public worship and too remarkable to be omitted. It is situated in the beautiful but long-neglected grounds of Gibside, a ruined hall, with ruined orangery and a Gothic banqueting house which has now been restored by the Landmark Trust. It was built in 1760 as a mausoleum for the Bowes family to the design of James Paine; fitted up as a chapel in 1812, remaining unchanged since that date. Altar under central dome and surrounded by circular rail; beyond is a fine three-decker pulpit. Box pews of excellent workmanship. Perfect example of pre-Tractarian arrangement, and

remarkable for the admirable quality both of design and material.
N.T.

HAMSTERLEY
St James
2m/3km W. of Witton-le-Wear NZ 1131
Set among fields high above the Bedburn Valley, away to the E. of the village. Delightful cruciform church, mostly 13th-century, with an ancient door in its Norman S. doorway. Pulpit of *c.* 1880 with Minton tiles, signed Moyr Smith, showing Biblical scenes and Pilgrim's Progress. Good 18th-century headstones.

HART
St Mary Magdalene
3m/4km N.W. of Hartlepool NZ 4634
The mother church of Hartlepool, in a village on rising ground with wide views across fields to the sea. A church of many dates from Saxon onward. Saxon baluster shafts and carved stones; early 16th-century sculpture of St George. Interior scraped but full of atmosphere, with two fonts, one plain Norman, the other 15th-century and ornate.

HARTLEPOOL
8m/12km N. of Middlesbrough NZ 5032
St Hilda
Magnificent Early English church standing close by the sea with views of dockland. Particularly fine tower with enormous buttresses; splendid long nave of seven bays with clustered Early English columns and single-lancet clerestory. The chancel was rebuilt in 1870. Good furnishings and sympathetic modern fittings. Famous 7th-century Saxon namestone associated with the early monastery here. Tomb of Robert Bruce, the founder, behind the altar.

HAUGHTON-LE-SKERNE
St Andrew
district of Darlington, 2m/3km N.E. of town centre NZ 3116
Situated in a pretty village, at the end of a street of handsome 18th-century red-brick houses. Medieval church of various dates. Some Norman work, including chancel arch, which has curious Victorian arch cut through the wall above it. Interior beautifully furnished with 'Cosin' woodwork, a very pleasant example of an ancient church adorned and furnished in post-Reformation manner. Interesting Saxon and medieval

carved stones. Rare Royal Arms of George II, erroneously displacing the Stuart quarterings – an heraldic howler.

HEIGHINGTON
St Michael & All Angels
2m/3km S.W. of Newton Aycliffe NZ 2422
Centre of spacious village green, with attractive cottages and terraces around. Mainly pre-Conquest and Norman with chancel arch of *c.* 1100; 16th-century pulpit and stalls. Crude painted and carved heraldic monument to George Croyser, 1691.

HETTON-LE-HOLE
St Nicholas
6m/10km N.E. of Durham NZ 3547
By Stephen Piper, 1898–1901. Attractive W. street front with gables and lancets; large plain barrel-vaulted interior with square chamfered piers.

HIGH CONISCLIFFE
St Edwin
4m/6km W. of Darlington NZ 2215
A dramatic sight across the Tees with the church and its spire and the gabled Victorian rectory standing perched together on a rocky cliff above the river. Essentially Early English but with Norman N. doorway and two S. windows; 15th-century chancel-stalls and fragments of 10th-century cross shafts.

HOUGHTON-LE-SPRING
St Michael and All Angels
6m/10km S.W. of Sunderland NZ 3450
Fine large church, cruciform and spacious, with transepts, mainly Norman and 15th-century with later windows. Norman tympanum over the vestry door; distinguished 15th-century two-storeyed chantry on the S. side of the chancel, and the tomb of the saintly Bernard Gilpin, d. 1583, 'Apostle of the North'.

HUNSTANWORTH
St James
1m/2km S.W. of Blanchland NY 9449
In remote moorland country. By S. S. Teulon, 1863; apart from the church, he designed the vicarage, schools, and most of the village as well, with contrasting coloured stone and varied tiles and slates. Nave and N. aisle with apsed chancel and large tower with pyramid capping. A good deal of Teulon's imaginative tracery and a pulpit set within the wall, monastic-fashion. Nice

details, including a pretty little organ and walls adorned with florid painted texts; glass by Kempe.

JARROW
St Paul
5m/8km E. of Gateshead NZ 3265
The actual church where Bede worshipped, preserving a curious flavour of romance as it looks out over the mudflats to the ships passing up and down the River Tyne. Originally two churches, joined into one in the late 11th century by the addition of a crossing tower. Above chancel arch, the dedication stone of original Saxon basilica, destroyed in the 18th century, dated 685. Smaller Saxon church now forms chancel. Undistinguished 19th-century nave by Gilbert Scott. Good carved stones and medieval chair in chancel, also a small window re-using Saxon glass found in recent excavations. Ruins of monastery S. of church.

KELLOE
St Helens
5m/8km N. of Sedgefield NS 7411
Away from the terraces of miners' cottages, the church stands in an unspoilt green valley, all alone. Mainly 11th-century with Early English chancel. The treasure is the richly carved 12th-century cross depicting the Life of St Helena. A tablet commemorates the birth of Elizabeth Barrett Browning in 1806 at Coxhoe Hall, now demolished.

LANCHESTER
All Saints
7m/11km N.W. of Durham NZ 1647
Large village church, with tall tower facing the green, elegant and embattled with a pretty weather-vane. The church is essentially Norman and Early English. In the porch a Roman altar. Monolithic columns of N. nave arcade presumably from Lanchester Roman station. Spectacular Norman chancel arch leads to raised choir and sanctuary. Curious arches in side walls of chancel, good carving above vestry door, and 13th-century glass. General effect of church is high, light and spacious, much helped by well-designed and well-spaced modern pews.

MONKWEARMOUTH
St Peter with St Cuthbert
1m/2km N. of Sunderland town centre NZ 3958
Like St Paul's, Jarrow, the church of a Saxon

monastery situated at the mouth of a river, and, like Jarrow, against a background of cranes and shipyard machinery. Originally built by Benedict Biscop in 674. Of his church only the W. wall and the tower remain; the tower was altered and raised many times between the 7th and 11th centuries. In the porch under the tower, Saxon baluster shafts still in original position; also carved stones. Inside the church, an exceptionally fine collection of Saxon carved stones.

NORTON
district of Stockton-on-Tees, 2m/3km N. of town centre NZ 4421
St Mary the Virgin
Pretty group of church, village and churchyard standing beside village green. Cruciform church of various dates with Saxon crossing tower; good furnishings and some fine windows by Kempe and Tower. Handsome early 14th-century effigy of a knight.
St Michael & All Angels
By Temple Moore, 1912–13. Successful neo-Perpendicular design for inexpensive brick church. Good interior with boarded tunnel vaults.

PITTINGTON
St Laurence
4m/6km E. of Durham NZ 3244
Set in a rural oasis between two pit villages. Chiefly remarkable for strange and exuberant late-Norman N. nave arcade. The arcade was inserted below Saxon windows; 12th-century wall-painting survives in the splay of one of them. Jacobean font cover and many carved stones including a tiny 13th-century tombstone carved with two swords.

REDMARSHALL
St Cuthbert
4m/6km W. of Stockton-on-Tees NZ 3821
Much Norman work, including chancel arch and tower with its Perpendicular top. Two 15th-century alabaster effigies, Jacobean box pews, and communion rail; 15th-century sedilia and Easter Sepulchre.

ROKER
St Andrew
district of Sunderland N. of harbour NZ 4059
Built in 1906–7, a massive and original design by E. S. Prior, carried out in local stone. Fittings and ornaments in style of Arts and Crafts movement. Burne-Jones tapestry woven by firm of William Morris. Morris carpet. Altar ornaments, processional cross, choir-stalls, pulpit and lectern by E. W. Gimson, tablets by Eric Gill, most of the glass by H. A. Payne. A bold and imaginative experiment which has triumphantly succeeded.

RYTON
Holy Cross
6m/10km W. of Newcastle NZ 1564
Pretty setting in a village with a green above the Tyne. Chiefly Early English with screen and stalls in Cosin style and foreign 19th-century furnishings of some taste; much Victorian glass which darkens the interior. Felicitous spiral tower stair of 1886, and a great 13th-century lead spire comparable with Long Sutton, Lincolnshire in colour and texture.

SEAHAM
St Mary the Virgin
5m/8km S. of Sunderland NZ 4249
Tiny gaunt church surrounded by trees bent and stunted by easterly gales. Saxon, and similar in plan to Escomb, it has Roman stones built into its walls. Late 12th- or early 13th-century chancel has double piscina with mysterious design of priest's hand raised in blessing incised within its arch. Pleasant windows by Kempe. Parish register contains entry of Byron's marriage to Arabella Milbanke, which took place in drawing-room of neighbouring Seaham Hall.

SEDGEFIELD
St Edmund
8m/12km N.W. of Stockton-on-Tees NZ 3528
Medieval church of many periods, set amid the wide greens. Fine Perpendicular tower. The Early English nave has fine stiff-leaf capitals with heads and monsters. Much good 'Cosin' woodwork, almost certainly by Robert Barker, including choir-stalls, reredos, and the bewilderingly elaborate rood screen. More classical panelling of *c.* 1670 in the chancel. Organ case and font of 1707, and a particularly good epitaph of 1708 on N. wall of chancel.

SOUTH SHIELDS
St Hilda
7m/11km E. of Gateshead NZ 3666
Tower of *c.* 1768, the rest 1810–11. Pleasant 'pre- ecclesiological' church of no particular

style with galleries supported on cast-iron columns. Marble font by Robert Trollope of Newcastle.

STAINDROP
St Mary
5m/8km N.E. of Barnard Castle NZ 1220
Prettily situated in large village beside Raby park, the spacious and airy church has been cared for by Lords of Raby Castle over the centuries. It is of many dates, from its pre-Conquest origins (see the Saxon window above the nave arcade) to its 15th-century clerestory. Pre-Reformation stalls and the only medieval chancel screen in the county. The two-storey priest's dwelling is now a vestry. Especially interesting tombs and effigies, including a large alabaster chest, much-traceried, with effigies of Ralph Neville, d. 1425, and his two wives. Equally splendid wooden tomb chest of *c.* 1560. Good 18th-century monuments including two by Nollekens.

STANHOPE
St Thomas
5m/8km W. of Wolsingham NY 9939
Typical, solid, plain North Country medieval church, mostly Norman and Early English with Cosin-style stalls of 1663.

STOCKTON-ON-TEES
St Thomas, market place
NZ 4418
Spacious and stately red-brick Classical church of 1710–12. It has been suggested, unconvincingly, that Wren had some hand in the design. Chancel rebuilt in 1906 by R. J. Johnson, and W. D. Caroe added the S. chapel in 1925. Imposing pulpit which once formed part of a three-decker, and altar rails carved from wood of Captain Cook's ship *Endeavour*. Good later pews and woodwork.

SUNDERLAND
NZ 3956
Christ Church, Ryhope Road, Bishopwearmouth
By James Murray, 1862–4. Large Gothic geometrical design in rock-faced limestone ashlar with spire and transepts. Inside are good circular piers with stiff-leaf capitals and a fine E. window by Morris & Co.
Holy Trinity, Church Street East
The former parish church of Sunderland, now redundant; the congregation meet in the adjacent old school. Built in 1719, now surviving alone in a cleared area which is gradually being redeveloped. Pleasant red-brick and stone exterior with Tuscan pilasters and good W. tower. Inside is a W. screen with Coats of Arms and seats for churchwardens and overseers. Good font, the cover richly ornamented with carved and gilded cherubs. Elegantly curved altar rails.
R.C.F.
St Michael, Bishopwearmouth
Early 19th-century tower and later transepts, the rest a successful neo-Perpendicular design by W. D. Caroe, 1933–5.

TOW LAW
St Philip & St James
8m/12km N.W. of Bishop Auckland NZ 1238
Church and vicarage stand together in a bleak spot in this town of straggling streets and grim collieries. By C. Hodgson Fowler, 1869; in the Early English style. Worth a visit for the sake of chancel screen, an excellent piece of 19th-century folk art; fir cones, acorns, etc. are glued to wood frame. Made by local vicar and his friends.

WEST BOLDON
St Nicholas
between South Shields and Sunderland NZ 3561
Set on a low hill, a landmark in the industrialized landscape of Jarrow. Mostly 13th-century, including the good broach spire replete with heavy clasping buttresses, lancets and dog-toothing. Intimate, well-furnished interior.

WEST RAINTON
St Mary
4m/6km N.E. of Durham NZ 3246
By E. R. Robson, 1864; tower added in 1877. Fine High Victorian church in Early English style with lofty broach spire, a landmark in the Wear Valley. Mosaic reredos by Salviati.

WINSTON
St Andrew
6m/10km E. of Barnard Castle NZ 1416
A simple austere church with bell-turret

stands above the Tees in an isolated setting outside village. Handsome 13th-century church, restored in 1848 by Dobson. Font of puzzling date with low relief carving of fighting dragons; similar dragons are on the choir-stalls, possibly 17th-century. Saxon cross head.

Essex

Introduction

Essex is a large square with two sides water. It is a stronger contrast of beauty and ugliness than any southern English county. Most of what was built east of London in this and the last century was a little bit cheaper and a little bit shoddier than that built in other directions. Southend is a cheaper Brighton, Clacton a cheaper Worthing, and Dovercourt a cheaper Bournemouth. Over a million Londoners live in Essex. Leyton, Canning Town, Silvertown, Barking, Ilford and West and East Ham are all in the county. Only the Norman parish church of East Ham and the scant abbey remains of Barking and Leyton parish church tell us that these were once country places. Our own age has added the planned and sad dormitories of Becontree and Harold Hill. Along the Thames bank, factories and power stations can be seen for miles over the mudflats, and the hills of Kent on the opposite bank look countrified by comparison.

But Essex is a large county and the ugliness is only a part of it. The county has the deepest and least disturbed country within reach of London. Between the Stour, Blackwater, Crouch and Thames estuaries is flat agricultural scenery with its own old red-brick towns with weatherboarded side streets like Rochford, Maldon and Georgian Harwich, the first-named the headquarters of the Essex puritan sect, The Peculiar People. Colchester was, as Pevsner said in *Essex* ('Buildings of England' series), more impressive than any town in England for 'the continuity of its architectural interest' – extensive redevelopment has changed that. The flat part of Essex has not the man-made look of the fens. It is wild and salty and its quality is well described in Baring-Gould's novel of Mersea, *Mehalah*. It is part of that great plain which stretches across to Holland and Central Europe. Most of inland Essex, east and north of Epping Forest, is undulating and extremely pretty in the pale, gentle way suited to English water-colours. Narrow lanes wind like streams through willowy meadows past weatherboarded mills and unfenced bean and corn fields. From oaks on hill-tops peep the flinty church towers, and some of the churches up here are as magnificent as those in neighbouring Suffolk – Coggeshall, Thaxted, Saffron Walden and Dedham are grand examples of the Perpendicular style. Thaxted, for the magnificence of its church and the varied textures of the old houses of its little town, is one of the most charming places in Britain.

Chiefly, Essex is a place of varied building materials. 'It would be an interesting study for an antiquary of leisure to trace the various sources of materials employed in Essex church building, and the means by which they were brought to their destination.' (G. Worley, *Essex, a Dictionary of the County*, 1915) To build their churches, the East Saxons and the Normans used any material that came to hand – Roman tiles, split oak logs, as at Greensted, pudding stone taken from the beach deposits, and flint. The 15th-century tower of South Weald was made of ragstone brought across from Kent on the opposite shore. But chiefly Essex is a county of brick, which was made here as early as the 13th century. There are many brick church towers of unexampled beauty, red as a bonfire; there are brick arcades and brick porches and brick window tracery. And when they left off building churches in this beautiful red brick, moulded into shapes and patterned with blue sanded headers, the Essex people continued it in houses until the past century.

Essex looks its best in sunlight, when the many materials of its rustic villages, the brick manor houses, the timbered 'halls' and the cob and thatched churches, the weatherboarded late-Georgian cottages, the oaks and flints, recall Constable. The delightful little town of Dedham and one half of the Stour Valley, be it remembered, are in Essex, and were as much an inspiration to Constable as neighbouring Suffolk, where he was born, and to which Essex is often so wrongly regarded as a poorer sister. It may be poorer in church architecture, but what it lacks in architecture it makes up for in the delicacy and variety of its textures.

J.B.

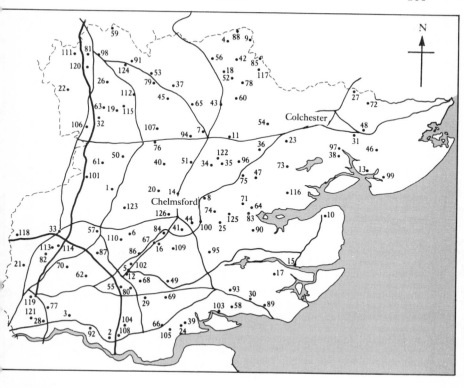

1	Abbess Roding	
2	Aveley	
3	Barking	
4	Belchamp St Paul	
5	Bentley Common	
6	Blackmore	
7	Bocking	
8	Boreham	
9	Borley	
10	Bradwell-juxta-Mare	
11	Bradwell-juxta-Coggeshall	
12	Brentwood	
13	Brightlingsea	
14	Broomfield	
15	Burnham-on-Crouch	
16	Buttsbury	
17	Canewdon	
18	Castle Hedingham	
19	Chickney	
20	Chignal Smealey	
21	Chingford	
22	Clavering	

23	Copford
24	Corringham
25	Danbury
26	Debden
27	Dedham
28	East Ham
29	East Horndon
30	Eastwood
31	Elmstead
32	Elsenham
33	Epping
34	Fairstead
35	Faulkbourne
36	Feering
37	Finchingfield
38	Fingringhoe
39	Fobbing
40	Ford End
41	Galleywood Common
42	Gestlingthorpe
43	Gosfield
44	Great Baddow

45	Great Bardfield
46	Great Bentley
47	Great Braxted
48	Great Bromley
49	Great Burstead
50	Great Canfield
51	Great Leighs
52	Great Maplestead
53	Great Sampford
54	Great Tey
55	Great Warley
56	Great Yeldham
57	Greenstead-juxta-Ongar
58	Hadleigh
59	Hadstock
60	Halstead
61	Hatfield Broad Oak
62	Havering-Atte-Bower
63	Henham
64	Heybridge
65	High Easter
66	Horndon-on-the-Hill

contd overleaf

Selected List of Churches

ABBESS RODING
St Edmund
2m/3km S.W. of Leaden Roding, which is 6m/10km W. of Great Dunmow TL 5711
Fine late 15th-century. Some 15th-century glass, including a bishop in Mass vestments. Late 12th-century font and good 17th-century monuments.

AVELEY
St Michael
3m/4km N.W. of Grays TQ 5680
Mostly 12th–13th-century, the windows all renewed; 12th-century font, Jacobean pulpit, and a fine Flemish brass of 1370.

BARKING
St Margaret
8m/12km E. of London Bridge, now in Central London TQ 4483
Norman and Perpendicular. Stucco chancel vault, 1772; good Georgian furnishings; monuments.

BELCHAMP ST PAUL
St Paul & St Andrew
5m/8km W. of Sudbury TL 7942
Perpendicular church with handsome W. tower, good chancel roof, and octagonal font. Also 15th-century are the fine chancel-stalls with misericords.

BENTLEY COMMON (BRENT-WOOD)
St Paul
11m/18km S.W. of Chelmsford TQ 5993
By E. C. Lee, 1878. Flint and stone church in severe Early English style set in parkland. Shingled broach spire, good carved details, and sumptuous fittings include a reredos of the Way of the Cross.

BLACKMORE
St Laurence
3m/4km N.W. of Ingatestone TL 6001
In an attractive little village and close to a fine house known as 'Jericho' stands the Norman church, which was once a small priory of Augustinian canons. Very impressive 15th-century timber bell-tower of intricate and elaborate construction; externally, three diminishing stages terminated by a broach spire.

BOCKING
St Mary the Virgin
N.W. part of Braintree TL 7523
Mostly 15th-century, the W. tower with broad diagonal buttresses. Impressive 14th-century chancel restored by Micklethwaite, 1913, who added the E. and S. windows.

BOREHAM
St Andrew
4m/6km N.E. of Chelmsford TL 7509
Norman central tower incorporating pre-Conquest E. arch. Unusual monument of 1589 with three Radcliffes, Earls of Sussex, on one alabaster tomb chest.

BORLEY
(dedication unknown)
2m/3km N.W. of Sudbury TL 8443
Setting. Mostly 15th–16th-century, though S. wall of nave probably Norman. Fine 16th-century monument to Sir Edward Waldegrave.

BRADWELL-JUXTA-MARE
St Peter-ad-Murum
7m/11km N.E. of Burnham-on-Crouch TM 0006
Approached by a cart track through fields, and situated on the sea wall at the mouth of the Blackwater. One of the oldest churches in the county, having been built by St Cedd about the year 654. Its materials were mostly taken from the ancient Roman fort of Othona, on the gateway of which the church is said to stand. The 7th-century nave remains.

BRADWELL-JUXTA-COGGESHAL.
Holy Trinity
3m/4km E. of Braintree TL 8023
Small, basically Norman, but now mostly Decorated. Timber-framed belfry and splendid though poorly preserved wall-paintings of *c.* 1320.

BRENTWOOD
11m/18km S.W. of Chelmsford TQ 5993
St George the Martyr
By L. King, erected in 1934, this brick church is characteristic of the modern movement of that time. Free-standing stone altar in large apsidal sanctuary. Good contemporary fittings.
St Thomas
A characterful church in Early English style by E. C. Lee, 1882–90. Built of flint and stone, with pinnacled N.W. spire.

BRIGHTLINGSEA
All Saints
8m/12km S.E. of Colchester TM 0816
An attractive little town of old buildings on the Colne estuary has as its parish church, situated on a hill about a mile inland, a building with a glorious late 15th-century tower of some considerable height, one of the finest in the county. There are many niches in the church, some of which have fragmentary medieval painting. Several ancient brasses.

BROOMFIELD
St Mary the Virgin
2m/3km N. of Chelmsford TL 7010
11th–12th-century work containing a fair quantity of Roman brick. Has a round tower which is an unusual feature in Essex.

BURNHAM-ON-CROUCH
St Mary the Virgin
9m/15km S.E. of Maldon TQ 9496
Setting. Principally 14th- and 15th-century with pretty early 16th-century brick N. porch and 19th-century plastered nave vault.

BUTTSBURY
St Mary
1m/2km E. of Ingatestone TQ 9867
Lonely setting. Mostly 14th-century with Perpendicular arcades, medieval ironwork on the N. door, and an 18th-century chancel.

CANEWDON
St Nicholas
3m/4km N.E. of Rochford TQ 8994
Stately church with fine early 15th-century four-stage W. tower; chequerwork battlements, W. door with decorated spandrels.

CASTLE HEDINGHAM
St Nicholas
4m/6km N.W. of Halstead TL 7835
A large Norman church standing in the middle of the village and close to the famous castle of the De Veres. Three of the 12th-century doorways still have their original wooden doors. There is a fine hammer-beam roof to the nave of early 16th-century date. An elaborate 14th–16th-century rood screen separates the nave from the chancel, on the S. side of which are some 15th-century stalls with misericords. An altar tomb in the chancel to John, Earl of Oxford, d. 1539, has low relief figures. The 16th-century brick tower incorporates a stone inscribed 'Robert Archer the master builder of this stepell 1616'.

CHICKNEY
St Mary the Virgin
3m/4km S.W. of Thaxted TL 5728
A pre-Conquest church set in an isolated position. Saxon nave retaining two double-splayed windows, and a chancel with small Early English lancets. Beautifully carved 14th-century font.
   R.C.F.

CHIGNAL SMEALEY
St Nicholas
4m/6km N.W. of Chelmsford TL 6611
Interesting early 16th-century brick church, the walls enlivened with blue brick diapers. N. aisle added in 1847; even the font is of brick.

CHINGFORD
St Peter & St Paul
9m/15km N.E. of London Bridge, now in Greater London TQ 3894
By Lewis Vulliamy, 1844, with enlargements by Charles Blomfield, 1902–3. Buff brick and flint walling in chequerwork patterns. Interior has effective timber trusses.

CLAVERING
St Mary & St Clement
7m/11km N. of Bishop's Stortford TL 4731
Setting, adjacent to castle, manor house and guild hall. Principally Perpendicular with much 15th-century glass in the N. windows, monuments and brasses.

COPFORD
St Michael and All Angels
5m/8km W. of Colchester TL 9222
Remotely situated and somewhat difficult to find, since it lies some way from the main road, this church must not be missed. An important 12th-century church, its nave and

chancel originally had tunnel vaults, very rare in Norman parish churches. These have been removed. The S. aisle of *c.* 1300 contains what must have been some of the earliest medieval bricks in England. The fame of this church lies in the remains of wall-paintings over the whole of the original building. They date from the middle of the 12th century, though considerably restored since their discovery in 1865. Of great interest is the scene depicting the healing of Jairus' daughter. In the half-domed vault over the apse is a fine painting of Our Lord in Majesty.

CORRINGHAM
St Mary
4m/6km S. of Basildon TQ 7083
The storage of motor spirit has industrialized this parish, but its village atmosphere is still preserved in the group of buildings consisting of the Saxon church, some old cottages, and the 15th-century inn. Though dating from pre-Conquest days, the greater part of the church is 14th-century. There is a good screen of that date and some furnishings by Martin Travers.

DANBURY
St John the Baptist
5m/8km E. of Chelmsford TL 7705
Setting in earthwork enclosure. Spacious 14th-century church with pretty gallery of *c.* 1600 and some wall-painting in the N. aisle. Three wooden knightly effigies of *c.* 1300.

DEBDEN
St Mary the Virgin
4m/6km S.E. of Saffron Walden TL 5533
Alone in landscaped grounds. Mostly 13th–14th-century church enhanced by elegant Gothic W. front and delectable octagonal E. chapel of 1793. Good 18th-century monuments.

DEDHAM
St Mary the Virgin
6m/10km N.E. of Colchester TM 0533
Attractive village. Large Perpendicular church, witness to the prosperity of the 15th-century cloth trade. Magnificent tower with octagonal buttresses ending in tall pinnacles, much painted by Constable. Fine monument of *c.* 1500 to Thomas Webbe, merchant and benefactor of the church.

EAST HAM
St Mary Magdalene
High Street South, 7m/11km E. of London Bridge, now in Greater London TQ 4283
A complete 12th-century building close to the dockland of East London. Interlacing arcading along wall of the chancel. Inappropriately in the Norman apse a fine monument to Edward Nevill, Earl of Westmorland, and his wife. An elegant marble font dated 1639. Remains of wall-paintings.

EAST HORNDON
All Saints
4m/6km S.E. of Brentwood TQ 6389
Standing in an isolated position on the top of a hill, this all-brick church is particularly worth seeing. It has a cruciform plan with the unique feature of an upper room to each transept forming small galleries. There is an early 16th-century Tyrell chantry, and the fittings include a beautifully incised stone slab dated 1422 bearing a portrait of one of the family.
R.C.F.

EASTWOOD
St Lawrence and All Saints
N.W. district of Southend-on-Sea TQ 8488
Originally Norman with timber priest's chamber at W. end of N. aisle, two 13th-century doors with decorative ironwork, a pretty early 16th-century brick S. porch, and a good Norman font.

ELMSTEAD
St Ann & St Laurence
4m/6km E. of Colchester TM 0626
Essentially 12th- and 14th-century with Norman N. door and Decorated sedilia and piscina. Oak effigy of a cross-legged knight.

ELSENHAM
St Mary the Virgin
4m/6km N.E. of Bishop's Stortford TL 5326
Mainly Norman; finely decorated 12th-century chancel arch and S. doorway with zig-zags and chip-carved tympanum.

EPPING
St John the Baptist
17m/27km N.E. of London TL 4602
By Bodley & Garner, 1889–1908. Alongside an attractive wide high street stands this very dignified Bath stone church in the Decorated style. Prominent tower, round barrel

vaults with painted texts, and good furnishings by Bodley's partner, Cecil Hare. Glass by Kempe and Burlison & Grylls.

FAIRSTEAD
St Mary
4m/6km W. of Witham TL 7616
Norman nave with Roman brick quoins and dressings. Important wall-paintings of *c.* 1275 above the chancel arch depicting the Life of Christ.

FAULKBOURNE
St Germanus
2m/3km N.W. of Witham TL 7917
Setting in the grounds of the Hall. Mostly 12th–13th-century with some 14th-century glass, 16th-century bench-ends and monuments, one of 1759 by Peter Scheemakers.

FEERING
All Saints
5m/8km N.E. of Witham TL 8720
Pleasant village setting. Largely 15th-century with good early 16th-century brick nave and S. porch enhanced by flint decoration and battlements.

FINCHINGFIELD
St John the Baptist
8m/12km N.W. of Braintree TL 6832
Lovely setting on a hill. The massive Norman tower with its quaint 18th-century cupola dominates one of the most attractive villages in the whole county. The church does not entirely come up to the standard of its setting. The W. door into the tower, with its three orders of columns and chevron ornament in semi-circular arched head, is a good example of Norman work. The rest of the church mostly 14th-century. Two fine screens of which the rood screen, early 15th-century, is perhaps the best in Essex. In S. chapel tomb of John Burners and his wife, 1523, consisting of tomb chest with brass figures on Purbeck marble slab. Late 17th-century Stuart Royal Arms. Curious scratched diagram on window ledge of S. aisle of 'Nine Men's Morris'.

FINGRINGHOE
St Andrew
4m/6km S.E. of Colchester TM 0220
Dominating the ancient settlement, this is one of the county's most impressive marshland churches. Largely 14th-century with tower of banded flint and stone, nave

roof with carved heads, and extensive wall-paintings. 17th-century monuments.

FOBBING
St Michael
4m/6km S. of Basildon TQ 7183
Near to old hall and timber-framed cottages. Mainly 14th- and 15th-century with typical 15th-century Essex timber S. porch, original roofs, and some benches.

FORD END
St John the Evangelist
5m/8km S.E. of Great Dunmow TL 6716
By Frederick Chancellor, 1871; chancel added in 1883 but demolished. Surprisingly grand red-brick church with some stone dressings. Handsome tower and spire at E. end of S. aisle with large figures of the Evangelists at the corners.

GALLEYWOOD COMMON
St Michael and All Angels
suburb 3m/4km S. of Chelmsford TL 7002
Church in the Decorated style by St Aubyn, 1873. It has a tall spire which forms a noted landmark, and there is a mosaic reredos by Burrow, 1874.

GESTINGTHORPE
St Mary
4m/6km S.W. of Sudbury TL 8138
Mostly 14th–15th-century with fine brick tower of *c.* 1498, splendid double hammerbeam roof, and decorated screen.

GOSFIELD
St Katherine
4m/6km N.E. of Braintree TL 7829
Attractive setting. Entirely 15th–16th-century with remarkable brick squire's pew-cum-family chapel added in 1735–6; lit by a venetian window, it has something of the appearance of a theatre box. Good monuments, one by Rysbrack.

GREAT BADDOW
St Mary the Virgin
suburb to S. of Chelmsford TL 7204
14th-century W. tower and spire, excellent 16th-century brickwork in S. clerestory, and fine 17th-century pulpit with panelled back and rich sounding-board.

GREAT BARDFIELD
St Mary the Virgin
2m/3km S. of Finchingfield TL 6730
The church looks down on one of the most

St Michael of the Rock, Brentor, perched 1,100 feet above the sea, Devon

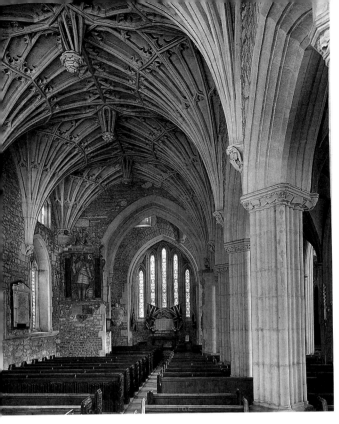

Above: Early 16th-century Dorset Aisle with fan-vaulted roof, Ottery St Mary, Devon

Right: Unspoiled Georgian interior, Parracombe, Devon

Left: Arts and crafts lectern by E. W. Gimson at Roker, Co. Durham
Above: Chancel roof at Roker
Below: Arts and crafts Gothic, Roker, E.S. Prior, 1906

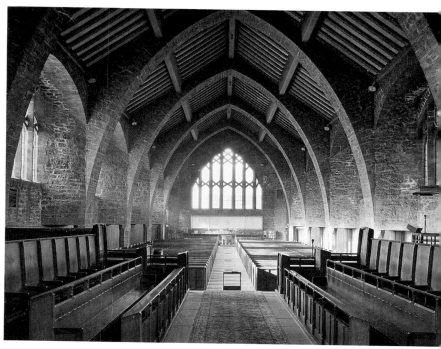

15th-century timber bell-tower, Blackmore, Essex

Opposite above: 7th-century chapel, Bradwell-on-Sea, Essex

Below: The only surviving example of a timber Saxon Church, Greenstead, Essex

Above: Stiff-leaf ornament, Chedworth,
Gloucestershire

Right: Saxon carving of St Peter,
Daglingworth, Gloucestershire

15th-century stone pulpit,
Coln Rogers, Gloucestershire

Double triangular-headed window, Deerhurst, Gloucestershire

Duntisbourne Rous, Gloucestershire; Saxon, with Norman chancel

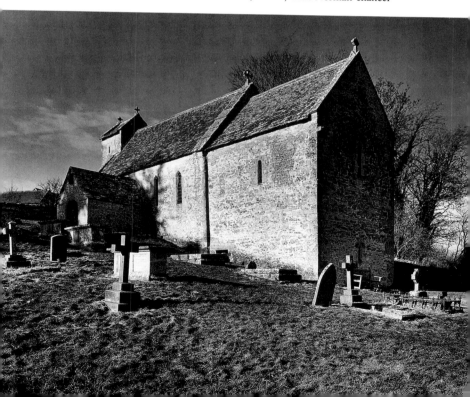

View across the nave into the north transept aisle, Romsey Abbey, Hampshire; Norman

attractive villages in Essex, full of beautiful old houses. Mostly 14th-century, it is remarkable for the stone rood screen of excellent craftsmanship filling the whole of the chancel arch.

GREAT BENTLEY
St Mary the Virgin
6m/10km N.W. of Clacton-on-Sea TM 1121
Small 12th-century church with original S. doorway decorated with scallops, rosettes and zig-zags. Charming Decorated niches in the 19th-century chancel.

GREAT BRAXTED
All Saints
3m/4km E. of Witham TL 8614
Wonderful picturesque setting in grounds of Braxted Park. Principally Norman with 13th-century tower, the timber belfry stage added in 1883.

GREAT BROMLEY
St George
6m/10km E. of Colchester TM 0826
A church of considerable architectural interest, mostly of 15th-century date. Magnificent tower and S. porch, glorious double hammer-beam nave roof, and a very fine brass of priest in Mass vestments.

GREAT BURSTEAD
St Mary Magdalene
suburb 1m/2km S. of Billericay TQ 6892
Norman and 14th–15th-century. Good Perpendicular benches, Corinthian reredos removed from the City of London, and an elegant marble tablet of 1767.

GREAT CANFIELD
St Mary
3m/4km S.W. of Great Dunmow TL 5918
Remotely set along tree-bordered lanes, near motte and bailey castle. Essentially Norman with a beautiful 13th-century wall-painting of the Virgin and Child.

GREAT LEIGHS
St Mary the Virgin
4m/6km S.W. of Braintree TL 7217
Substantial Norman round W. tower, the spire added in 1882. Fine Decorated chancel, a recess on the N. side with exquisitely carved foliage.

GREAT MAPLESTEAD
St Giles
3m/4km N. of Halstead TL 8034
Norman W. tower and apse with three original windows; 17th-century family chapel in S. transept with a good monument of 1634.

GREAT SAMPFORD
St Michael
4m/6km N.E. of Thaxted TL 6435
Pleasantly situated by some old cottages, the church was almost enitrely rebuilt in the 14th century. Fine tomb recess in S. chapel and six consecration crosses still remain. Plain 15th-century font bowl on a Decorated stem.

GREAT TEY
St Barnabas
7m/11km W. of Colchester TL 8925
Magnificent Norman tower of four stages with Roman brick dressings at crossing of nave and chancel. Fine Decorated chancel.

GREAT WARLEY
St Mary the Virgin
2m/3km S.W. of Brentwood TQ 6090
By Charles Harrison Townsend, 1904. An excellent example of Art Nouveau in the English Arts and Crafts manner. Modest exterior, but inside a lush display of craftsmanship, mostly by Sir William Reynolds-Stevens with glass by Heywood Sumner.

GREAT YELDHAM
St Andrew
6m/10km N.W. of Halstead TL 7638
Unusual late 14th-century Perpendicular two-storey porch, originally intended as a tower base. Painted screen and Elizabethan pulpit.

GREENSTED-JUXTA-ONGAR
St Andrew
1m/2km W. of Chipping Ongar TL 5302
Famous church in wooded setting. The only surviving example of a timber Saxon church. The walls of the nave consist of split oak logs. The chancel is early 16th-century. The church was drastically restored in the 19th century. Within these walls the body of St Edmund rested on its way back to Bury St Edmunds.

HADLEIGH
St James the Less
4m/6km W. of Southend-on-Sea TQ 8187
Complete Norman church with apse; the

plan has remained structurally unaltered; 13th-century wall-painting of St Thomas of Canterbury.

HADSTOCK
St Botolph
4m/6km N. of Saffron Walden TL 5544
This is most likely to be the minster erected by Canute in 1020 to commemorate his victory at the Battle of the Assendun over Edmund Ironside. The neighbouring parish of Ashdon is said to be the scene of the battle. A remarkable Saxon cruciform church approached by a S. door which must be one of the oldest in the country, being contemporary with the building.

HALSTEAD
6m/10km N.E. of Braintree TL 8130
St Andrew
Principally 14th-century, though much restored. Well-designed tower of 1850 and reredos by Sir Arthur Blomfield, 1893. Bourchier family tomb chests and effigies; one of *c.* 1400 with richly carved canopy.
Holy Trinity
An early work of George Gilbert Scott, 1843–4. Early English style with bold S.W. tower and stone broach spire. Glass by Clutterbuck.
    R.C.F.

HATFIELD BROAD OAK
St Mary the Virgin
5m/8km S.E. of Bishop's Stortford TL 5416
S. of the Hatfield Forest in a village of attractive old houses, this church formed the nave of the priory founded by Aubrey de Vere *c.* 1135. Good 14th- and 15th-century work, with a fine tower. Very notable sculptured monument to Robert de Vere, 1221. The reredos, panelling and communion rails are excellent examples of early 18th-century work, probably by John Woodward, pupil of Grinling Gibbons. A library has been built onto the church to house some 200 books given in 1680; among them is an Aldine Aristotle, 1498.

HAVERING-ATTE-BOWER
St John the Evangelist
3m/4km N. of Romford, now in Greater London TQ 5193
A High Victorian church by Basil Champneys, 1875–8. In moulded flintwork, standing beside a village green on the edge of suburban London.

HENHAM
St Mary the Virgin
6m/10km N.E. of Bishop's Stortford TL 5428
Early English with 14th-century tower and arcades. Sumptuous wooden screen with ogee lights and tracery; 15th-century font and pulpit.

HEYBRIDGE
St Andrew
N. suburb of Maldon TL 8508
Norman. Despite the loss of the upper part of the tower, this is one of the most complete 12th-century churches in the county. Original S. door with ironwork.

HIGH EASTER
St Mary the Virgin
2m/3km N.E. of Leaden Roding TL 6214
Norman core with Perpendicular tower and parclose screens; 16th-century clerestory, fine nave roof and brick porch.

HORNDON-ON-THE-HILL
St Peter & St Paul
5m/8km S.W. of Basildon TQ 6683
13th–15th-century church in a small hill-top town. Notable timber-framed W. bell-turret; 15th-century S. porch. Good Arts and Crafts lectern of 1898.

INGATESTONE
St Mary the Virgin & St Edmund
5m/8km N.E. of Brentwood TQ 6499
Here is seen the finest of the many brick towers of Essex – an excellent example of late 15th-century brickwork. A Norman church with additions in the 15th, 16th and 17th centuries. Fine monuments to the Petre family including one to Sir William Petre, Secretary of State to Henry VIII.

INGRAVE
St Nicholas
2m/3km S.E. of Brentwood TQ 6292
One of the best 18th-century churches in Essex, 1735, by an unknown hand but in the manner of Hawksmoor. Of red brick with a remarkable militaristic W. tower.

LAINDON
St Nicholas
W. district of Basildon TQ 6889
Mainly 13th-century with one of the best Essex timber steeples, a sturdy timber-framed belfry, and later windows. Unusual

17th-century two-storey priest's house attached to church.

LAMBOURNE
St Mary and All Saints
3m/4km E. of Loughton TQ 4796
Remote Essex setting near London. Simple aisleless Norman and later church, sumptuously plastered in early Georgian times and furnished with a Corinthian reredos.

LANGFORD
St Giles
1m/2km N.W. of Maldon TL 8309
Largely rebuilt in 1880–2 by Edward Browning, but retaining rare and important Norman W. apse; originally it would have been balanced by one to the E.

LAWFORD
St Mary
7m/11km N.E. of Colchester TM 0831
Situated above the waters of the River Stour, this church is noted for its remarkably rich 14th-century stone carving in the chancel. In the arch-moulds of some of the windows are some amusing carved figures forming a chain and holding each other by the leg. Magnificent sedilia and piscina.

LAYER MARNEY
St Mary the Virgin
6m/10km S.W. of Colchester TL 9217
Rebuilt by Lord Marney early in the 16th century, close to his house, Layer Marney Towers. Excellent example of Tudor brickwork with blue diapering. Unusual feature of a priest's lodging at the W. end of the N. aisle. Painting of St Christopher on N. wall and two medieval screens. Very fine early Renaissance monuments.

LITTLE BADDOW
St Mary the Virgin
5m/8km E. of Chelmsford TL 7807
Norman and Decorated. Large 15th-century painting of St Christopher on N. wall, two oak effigies of c. 1320, and some glass of c. 1400.

LITTLE BRAXTED
St Nicholas
1m/2km E. of Witham TL 8314
Setting adjacent to Hall. Norman nave and apsed chancel; N. aisle added and extensive painted decoration by the Rev. E. Geldart, 1884.

LITTLE DUNMOW
(Dedication unknown)
2m/3km E. of Great Dunmow TL 6521
A place well-known for its flitch of bacon awarded to the man and woman who had not repented of their marriage for a year and a day. The church is all that remains of an Augustinian priory of which it formed a chapel on the S. side of the choir, and from which it was separated by a beautifully proportioned arcade which remains. Some excellent 14th-century stone carving, mostly of animals and flowers, can be seen in panels along the S. wall. The 'Dunmow Flitch Chair' in the sanctuary is made up from a 13th-century stall. Two fine 15th-century altar tombs with alabaster effigies.

LITTLE ILFORD
8m/12km N.E. of London Bridge, now in Greater London TQ 4386
St Barnabas, Browning Road
By Sir Ninian Comper, 1909. Flowing Perpendicular in the Master's early style. The English altar has been removed.
St Michael and All Angels, Romford Road/Toronto Avenue
By Charles Spooner, 1897–8. A well-detailed brick church with distinctive fleche. Impressive interior with open-trussed roofs, stone piers, and imaginative fittings.

LITTLE MAPLESTEAD
St John the Baptist
2m/3km N. of Halstead TL 8234
Built by the Knights Hospitaller c. 1340, it is one of the five 'round churches' in England. The hexagonal nave was separated from the circular aisle by a well-proportioned 14th-century arcade, much restored in 1850. Apsidal chancel and Norman font.

LITTLE SAMPFORD
St Mary
2m/3km W. of Finchingfield TL 6533
14th–15th-century, the nave piers of unusual lozenge section with attached shafts. Good 16th-century monuments.

LITTLE WARLEY
St Peter
2m/3km S. of Brentwood TQ 6090
Small 15th–16th-century church with chequered brick W. tower of 1718; 17th-century box pews and Strutt monuments with effigies.

LITTLEBURY
Holy Trinity
2m/3km N.W. of Saffron Walden TL 5139
Originally 12th-century with two ambitious
16th-century porches. Much restored by
Edward Barr, 1870–5, but retaining exotic
early 16th-century linenfold font case.

LOUGHTON
St Mary the Virgin
on E. side of Epping Forest TQ 4296
By Thomas Henry Watson, 1871–2. High
Victorian church remarkable for the natural-
istic carvings on the arcade capitals.

MALDON
All Saints
9m/15km E. of Chelmsford TL 8507
In the midst of an attractive little hill town
above the Blackwater, this 13th-century
church has a unique triangular tower. The
14th-century stone arcading along the inside
of the S. aisle is very rich in its decoration.
The church was much altered in the 18th
and 19th centuries.

MARGARETTING
St Margaret
4m/6km S.W. of Chelmsford TL 6701
Good 15th-century work; timber W. tower
and shingled broach spire supported on free-
standing posts connected by arch braces,
timber N. porch, and restored Jesse window.

MIDDLETON
All Saints
1m/2km S. of Sudbury TL 8739
Norman S. doorway with scalloped capitals
and elaborate chancel arch with shafts, zig-
zags and triangles. Finely drawn Purbeck
marble slab of priest in Mass vestments,
1349.

MOUNTNESSING
St Giles
3m/4km N.E. of Brentwood TQ 6397
Small 12th- and 13th-century church, pleasantly situated near the Georgian hall. Late
13th- or early 14th-century timber-framed
belfry and fine nave roof.

NAVESTOCK
St Thomas
4m/6km N.W. of Brentwood TQ 5397
Norman and later church with impressive
13th-century timber-framed tower and

wooden arcading to the nave. Modest monuments.

PENTLOW
St Gregory & St George
3m/4km W. of Long Melford TL 8146
Norman nave and chancel with apse retaining three original windows; 12th-century
round tower added to the nave; 16th-century
tunnel-vaulted N. chapel with monuments.

PRITTLEWELL
St Mary the Virgin
district of Southend-on-Sea, 1m/2km from
town centre TQ 8787
Norman origin, but now mostly 15th-
century with imposing W. tower and two-
storey S. porch; flint and stone chequer
decoration.

PURLEIGH
All Saints
3m/4km S. of Maldon TL 8402
Delightfully situated on top of a hill. Principally 14th-century, including the fine W.
tower and rare white brickwork. Of great
interest to Americans since its rector from
1632–43 was Lawrence Washington.

RADWINTER
St Mary the Virgin
4m/6km E. of Saffron Walden TL 6037
Almost completely rebuilt by W. Eden Nesfield, partner to R. Norman Shaw, in 1869–
70; W. tower of 1887 by Temple Moore;
14th-century ground storey of S. porch and
nave roof retained. Fine Tractarian interior.
Set among numerous other examples of Nesfield's work in the village.

RAINHAM
St Helen & St Giles
5m/8km S. of Romford, now in Greater
London TQ 5381
An entire Norman church, with nave, N.
and S. aisles, chancel, and tower all dating
from about 1170. The massive nave piers
with attached shafts and scalloped capitals
are very impressive. On the wall of the rood-
loft staircase is a large scratched 16th-
century drawing of a two-masted ship.

RAYLEIGH
Holy Trinity
6m/10km N.W. of Southend-on-Sea TQ 8090
The church is very prominently placed in
the town centre, which also has a motte and

bailey castle and windmill. Mostly 15th–16th-century with handsome S. chapel and porch built in 1517 by William Alleyn; his fine tomb is inside.

RAYNE
All Saints
2m/3km W. of Braintree TL 7222
Set in an imposing position adjacent to the 14th-century hall. The most notable feature is the noble red-brick tower built by Sir William Capell, *c.* 1510. Remainder of church is 1840 with some 17th-century carved panels re-used in the reredos.

RETTENDON
All Saints
3m/4km N.E. of Wickford TQ 7698
A church with a two-storeyed 15th-century priest's house, now used as a vestry. There is a magnificent marble monument to Edmund Humphrey, d. 1727, at the E. end of the N. aisle, one of the finest of its period.

RIVENHALL
St Mary and All Saints
2m/3km N.W. of Witham TL 8217
This church was extensively remodelled in 1838, and the stuccoed exterior gives nothing away, but it is actually an almost complete 11th-century two-cell building. It also possesses the finest medieval stained glass in the county. In 1840 the then incumbent brought over from France some 12th-century glass from the church of St Martin at Chemi near Tours and fitted it into the E. window. A visit to the church should not be missed.

ROWHEDGE
St Lawrence
On R. Colne opposite Wivenhoe TM 0221
Unusual octagonal church with lancets, built of white brick by William Mason, 1838. Late 17th-century reredos, said to be from St Paul's Cathedral.

SAFFRON WALDEN
St Mary
12m/19km N. of Bishop's Stortford TL 5338
Perhaps the largest and finest church in the county. Designed in the grand East Anglian manner, it is almost foreign to Essex. It was rebuilt in the late 15th and early 16th centuries and consists of a nave and chancel with N. and S. aisles and N. and S. chapels. There are N. and S. porches and a W. tower

to which was added a spire in 1832. The stately and impressive arcades to the nave deserve special attention as exhibiting a very high standard of stonemason's craftsmanship. There is a great architectural link between this church and King's College, Cambridge, not many miles away. The furnishings are not of the same standard as the fabric; the hand of the 'restorer' has done much to destroy the medieval atmosphere.

ST OSYTH
St Peter & St Paul
3m/4km W. of Clacton-on-Sea TM 1215
Delightfully situated close to the old Abbey, the gateway of which is a noted monument. Though the church dates from the early 12th century, its most remarkable architectural feature is the fine 16th-century brick arcades separating nave from aisles. The furnishings include some very fine alabaster monuments to the D'Arcy family. There are also some early 19th-century 'sheep fold' communion rails on a horse-shoe plan.

SANDON
St Andrew
3m/4km S.E. of Chelmsford TL 7404
Norman nave and chancel; handsome early 16th-century brick W. tower enlivened with blue diapers and rib-vaulted S. porch.

SHEERING
St Mary the Virgin
2m/3km E. of Sawbridgeworth TL 5013
Norman and later Perpendicular. In the E. window is a fine late 14th-century stained glass depiction of the Coronation of the Virgin.

SHENFIELD
St Mary the Virgin
E. district of Brentwood TQ 6094
15th-century but drastically restored in Victorian times. Pleasantly shaped shingled broach spire and a timber nave arcade in which the piers, fashioned like stone columns with attached shafts, are each hewn out of an oak tree.

SOUTH BENFLEET
St Mary the Virgin
6m/10km W. of Southend-on-Sea TQ 7786
Ornate 15th-century timber S. porch with tracery, hammer-beam roof, and cusped bargeboarding. Inside are a screen and W.

gallery added by Sir Charles Nicholson in 1931.

SOUTH OCKENDON
St Nicholas
suburb 3m/4km N.W. of Grays TQ 5881
Fine 13th-century circular flint tower, rare in Essex. Good alabaster wall-monument of 1601 to Sir Richard Saltonstall, Lord Mayor of London. Majority of church dates from Victorian restoration of 1866.

STANFORD-LE-HOPE
St Margaret
5m/8km N.E. of Tilbury TQ 6882
Medieval church with impressive tower of 1883. Early English N. arcade, graceful screen of *c.* 1400, and 18th-century monuments.

STANSTED MOUNTFITCHET
St John
3m/4km N.E. of Bishop's Stortford TL 5124
By W. D. Caroe, 1889; tower added in 1896. An early work in the Perpendicular style by this celebrated architect. Red-brick, and not particularly original apart from the slightly later tower.

STEBBING
St Mary the Virgin
3m/4km N.E. of Great Dunmow TL 6624
At the S. end of a typical Essex village of attractive old buildings stands the church of mainly 14th-century date. Light and spacious with graceful arcades and a fine stone screen filling the whole chancel opening. Good timber roofs, especially over chancel, and richly carved sedilia and piscina.

STIFFORD
St Mary the Virgin
2m/3km N.W. of Grays TQ 6080
Basically 12th-century with 13th-century W. tower and S. chapel with lancets. Many 14th–16th-century brasses including that to Ralph Perchehay, rector, of *c.* 1380.

STOCK HARVARD
All Saints
3m/4km N. of Billericay TQ 6898
Pleasant village. Mainly 15th-century with typical Essex timber-framed belfry and slender broach spire. E. chapel and chancel with painted roof built in 1848.

STONDON MASSEY
St Peter & St Paul
3m/4km S.E. of Chipping Ongar TL 5800
Early Norman nave and chancel with late-medieval timber-framed belfry. Two 16th-century brasses, that to John Carre, d. 1570, bearing the arms of the Ironmongers' Company.

STRETHALL
St Mary the Virgin
4m/6km W. of Saffron Walden TL 4839
A small late-Saxon church in a very beautiful setting. One of the most rural parishes in the county with probably the smallest population. The nave is separated from the chancel by a finely proportioned and decorated archway of the time of Edward the Confessor.

THAXTED
St John the Baptist
6m/10km S.E. of Saffron Walden TL 6130
Standing high up above a town of attractive old houses is one of the grandest churches in the county. Approaching the town from the S.E. is an unforgettable sight as the houses converge toward the old Moot Hall, above the roof of which is seen this magnificent parish church. Principally of 14th-, 15th-, and early 16th-century dates, it consists of a narrow nave with much wider aisles, a crossing with N. and S. transepts, a spacious chancel with N. and S. chapels, N. and S. porches, each with a parvise room above, and a W. tower with spire. The interior is very light. There are good fragments of old stained glass remaining, and two windows by Kempe. The absence of customary pews gives a great feeling of spaciousness. Good craftsmanship can be seen in the roofs. Font completely hidden by font case and cover of late 15th-century date. Very fine carved 17th-century pulpit and 18th-century communion rails.

THEYDON GARNON
All Saints
2m/3km S.E. of Epping TQ 4799
Mostly 13th-century with brick W. tower dated 1520 and handsome brick N. aisle of 1644; timber N. arcade of same date with octagonal piers and round arches.

THEYDON MOUNT
St Michael
3m/4km S.E. of Epping TQ 4999
Adjoins the grounds of the Hall. Small brick

church of 1611–14, a mixture of Gothic and Classical elements; W. tower with battlements, S. doorway with Tuscan pilasters and pediment. Impressive series of 16th–18th-century monuments.

TILTY
St Mary the Virgin
3m/4km N.W. of Great Dunmow TL 5926
Formerly the chapel by the gate of the neighbouring Cistercian Abbey. A 13th-century nave with regularly spaced lancet windows leads into a very large 14th-century chancel, a work of great architectural beauty. The E. window has some of the loveliest tracery in the county. Very fine sedilia and piscina. The belfry is surmounted by a charming 18th-century cupola. Some good brasses in the chancel.

TOLLESHUNT D'ARCY
St Nicholas
6m/10km N.E. of Maldon TL 9211
Largely Perpendicular, the coved nave ceiling embellished with flowers and leaves painted by the Rev. E. Geldart in 1897. Good 14th–16th-century Darcy brasses and monuments.

TWINSTEAD
St John the Evangelist
3m/4km S. of Sudbury TL 8636
By Henry Woodyer, 1859–60. Spiky polychrome brick essay in the Decorated style with W. bellcote. Inside are triple arches to the chancel and a font set on clustered shafts. Good Hardman glass.

WALTHAM ABBEY
Holy Cross
7m/11km S.W. of Harlow TL 3800
Only the nave, aisles and S. chapel remain of what must have once been a most imposing monastic establishment. The tower was added after the Dissolution. The splendid Norman nave is comparable with the nave of Durham Cathedral, and has spiral and zig-zag ornament on the pillars. There are far too many Victorian pews, but some have now been removed. Much 19th-century restoration undertaken by William Burges. The painted ceiling is an early work of Sir Edward Poynter. Very excellent E. window by Burne-Jones. Lady Chapel, 14th-century, has important painting of the Last Judgement. Many fine monuments in the church, including that to a sea captain, thought to be

by Grinling Gibbons. Queen Eleanor's body rested here on the way to Westminster Abbey. Also burial place of King Harold.

WANSTEAD
St Mary
3m/4km N.W. of Ilford, now in Central London TQ 4088
By Thomas Hardwick, 1787–90; in Gibbsian style. Splendid ashlar building with paired Tuscan columns at the porch, a pediment, and fine circular bell-turret. Delightful interior marred only by Victorian glass; box pews, altar rail, font, three galleries, and a pulpit.

WENDENS AMBO
St Mary the Virgin
2m/3km S.W. of Saffron Walden TL 5136
Dating from the end of the 11th century, this delightful little country church has a most attractive setting and is approached by a lane bordered with typical Essex thatched cottages. Furnishings include 14th-century wall-paintings, Perpendicular pulpit, and carved benches.

WEST HAM
All Saints
Church Street, 5m/8km E. of London Bridge, now in Greater London TQ 4083
A church dating from the late 12th century; situated in a much-built-up area. There is a fine W. tower of about 1400. The Tudor N. chapel is constructed of red brick with blue brick forming a diaper pattern. The monuments and floor-slabs are of particular interest.

WHITE NOTLEY
St Etheldreda
3m/4km N.W. of Witham TL 7818
Attractive small 11th- and 13th-century church; 14th-century S. porch and door. Some early 13th-century stained glass and 16th-century paintings.

WILLINGALE
St Christopher
4m/6km N.E. of Chipping Ongar TL 5907
Churches of two adjoining parishes in one churchyard. St Christopher: over-restored in 1853; brasses and a large monument. St Andrew: Norman and 15th-century.

WIMBISH
All Saints
4m/6km E. of Saffron Walden TL 5936
Norman nave, 14th-century screen, and
elegant small brasses to Sir John de
Wantone, d. 1347, and his wife.

WOODHAM WALTER
St Michael
3m/4km W. of Maldon TL 8006
Small Gothic Survival red-brick church of
1563–4. Perpendicular roofs and windows,
large octagonal font, and some stained
glass.

WRITTLE
All Saints
suburb 2m/3km W. of Chelmsford TL 6706
Village green. Largely rebuilt in 1879, but
with a stunning collection of brasses and
monuments; one with an agrarian theme by
Nicholas Stone, 1629.

Gloucestershire

Introduction

Gloucestershire is richer than any county in variety of colour and outline.
Indeed, rich is the adjective which best suits it. Its great port of Bristol was
formed into a separate county in 1373. The Severn and Avon brought vessels
to Gloucestershire from Spain and later from America. The wool trade in
the late Middle Ages brought prosperity to the limestone Cotswold Hills and
many fine Perpendicular churches rose in the little wool towns of which that
at Northleach is an impressive example. Before that, the Normans had built
the great naves of Gloucester Cathedral and Tewkesbury Abbey with their
cylindrical columns, and many a country church has a Norman arch or
window or tympanum. The Black Death came to the county, some work was
stopped; even so a great building tradition was maintained and nowhere are
there such fine farm buildings, enormous barns and stone-built manor houses
as in Gloucestershire, the medieval tradition continuing in the construction
of tithe barns, dovecotes and outbuildings, until early in the 18th century.

In the 16th and 17th centuries there was what Anthony West has called
a water-power industrial revolution, when the rapid streams of the South
Cotswold valley were used to turn mills employed to make cloth. These old
mills, stone-built equivalents of the card mills of the north of England, survive
in the deep Stroud valley and are still, some of them, used as factories. At
this time, in the western half of the county and near Bristol, there was an
iron industry. Later came the coalfields to the oak woods of the Forest of
Dean.

The greatest richness of the county is in its stone and scenery. As you
enter Gloucestershire from the east, you continue with the limestone scenery
of Oxfordshire and North Berks. and North Wilts. This is a warm yellowish-
grey which breeds a delicate patina of lichens. In the little piece of Gloucestershire north of Moreton in Marsh, the limestone takes on a golden tinge as
though bathed in perpetual late sunlight. Farther west and north of Bristol,
the stone is a cold grey, and houses have red tiles in the Somerset manner.
The most spectacular scenery of all is in the middle of the county, by the
Stroud valley and Minchinhampton Common and Amberley. Here the stone
is silver-white, and at Painswick it is almost as white as Portland stone, but
with a warmth in it which Portland lacks. The central tower of Gloucester
Cathedral is built of Painswick stone. As may be expected in this part of the
country, where stone is so plentiful and where it has been worked for centuries,

the workmanship is of high quality. Stone-tiled roofs have graded tiles, large at the eaves and small at the ridges; stone is used for mullions and transoms of windows as easily as if it were timber; moulded stone arches are used for doorways; nobly carved tombstones in a local Baroque style diversify country churchyards; and everywhere you descend from barren heights, which once tinkled with sheep bells, to enclosed valleys shaded by beech where the stone villages cluster; and at the western heights of this stone kingdom you may look over miles of the Severn Valley below you to the blue mountains of Wales and the gigantic outline of the Malvern Hills.

The Severn Vale and Vale of Berkeley (in the second the famous double-Gloucester cheeses are made) are a complete contrast with the eastern stone area. The Severn winds through muddy flatness; willows abound, as do orchards and pastoral scenery. Stone used here for churches and barns and raised causeways above flood-level could easily be carried up the Severn. But humbler buildings were timber-framed, and many old cottages survive among drabber brick cottages of the last century. The least visited part of the county is the north-west, which has the Georgian red-brick town of Newent as its capital. Here on the Herefordshire border are oak-woods and wild daffodils and steep hills and forgotten farms down steep-banked lanes and red earth and pink sandstone. The land between the muddy flatness of the Severn and the steep-wooded splendour of the Wye Valley is occupied by the Forest of Dean. Mitcheldean to the north might be a small Welsh town with its high, narrow streets and weather-worn appearance. The Forest itself is among high hills and has a rather unpleasantly large quota of conifers, but once you leave these you find oak-woods and brown streams and grass-grown mineral lines leading to ruined industries, and then suddenly and unaccountably a coal-tip and a mine and a hideous township of miners' red-brick cottages. One might be in Durham. The churches are mostly poor late-Georgian and Victorian buildings architecturally, which have the used and highly polished interiors of industrial churches. Forest of Dean stone is a pink sandstone which does not weather well.

One exotic in the county of Gloucestershire is the late-Georgian spa of Cheltenham, set in flat land at the foot of the Cotswolds. It is a stucco and limestone town of ample tree-shaded squares and crescents and streets, a town of gardens and sunlight, where the stately houses are adorned with most delicate and inventive ironwork verandahs and porches, designed to give lightness to the Classic severity of their architecture. Cheltenham is, as it were, St John's Wood and Regent's Park set down over square miles of Gloucester meadowland.

With such richness of natural and man-made beauty, it is not surprising that Gloucestershire has attracted artists and art-workers. Chipping Campden and Painswick, Sapperton and Cirencester, have, for half a century and more, been the homes of artists and handicraftsmen, stained-glass artists, potters, weavers and cabinet makers – such famous men as Ernest Gimson, Peter

Waals, the Barnsleys and Christopher Whall, F. L. Griggs and C. R. Ashbee. Their love of the native crafts of the county, though it may have unwittingly inspired much arty craftiness of the aubretia and staddlestone variety, has saved Gloucestershire from much vandalism. And council houses in the Cotswolds even today pay much more attention to local material and scale than is usual, and not every town in the county is yet ruined by concrete lamp-standards. The beauty of the county has tamed even the borough surveyors, engineers and park superintendents.

J.B.

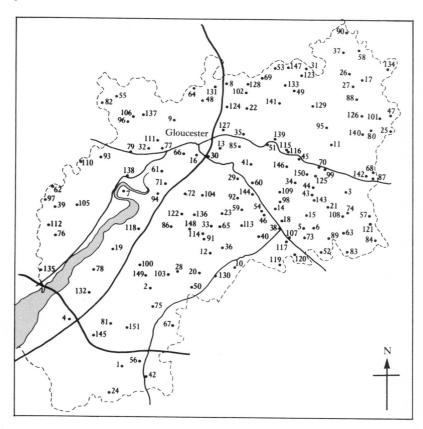

key overleaf

Selected List of Churches

ABSON
St James the Great
5m/8km S. of Chipping Sodbury ST 7074
Pretty Perpendicular W. tower with elaborately panelled parapets and a stately octagonal font enriched with quatrefoils and flowers. There are six bells, two of them pre-Reformation. Inside, all is pleasantly limewashed, with pulpit of 1630 with sounding-board, an altar table slightly earlier, and good choir-stalls.

ALDERLEY
St Kenelm
2m/3km S. of Wotton-under-Edge ST 7690
There are wide views over the Berkeley Vale and 18th-century houses close by. Rebuilt in 1802 apart from the Perpendicular W. tower; a pretty Gothic essay with apsidal sanctuary, pointed windows, with their original glass, and plaster vaulting with gold-leaf bosses.

ALDSWORTH
St Bartholomew
6m/10km W. of Burford SP 1510
Village setting, with a 19th-century feel, owing to the houses having been built to serve Bibury race-course; rich Perpendicular N. aisle with excellent canopies, niches and brackets; 12th-century N. door and arcade. Regency Gothic pews.

ALMONDSBURY
St Mary the Virgin
7m/11km N. of Bristol ST 6084
The church is set under the side of a hill, in a parish cut up by motorways. Cruciform with central tower and fine broached spire, nave rebuilt in 1834. Early English chancel with a trefoil-headed piscina and a fine Renaissance tomb in the S. transept to Edward Veele, d. 1577, and his wife, under a canopy supported on Corinthian columns.

AMPNEY CRUCIS
Holy Rood
3m/4km E. of Cirencester SP 0601
Cruciform church with work of all periods from Saxon to 19th century; good Norman chancel arch, celebrated gabled churchyard cross of *c.* 1415, which escaped the Puritans by being carefully walled up. Remains of wall-paintings in N. transepts.

AMPNEY ST MARY
St Mary
4m/6km E. of Cirencester SP 0802
Isolated little church on the main road with no village visible; 12th-century with boldly carved N. doorway with strange primitive tympanum; splendid 12th–15th-century wall-paintings including Christ of the Trades, St Christopher and St George. Restored in 1913 when F. C. Eden added stained glass to the flowing Decorated windows; it is still candlelit.

ARLINGHAM
St Mary the Virgin
9m/15km N.W. of Stroud SO 7010
A remote spot, situated in a loop of the Severn. Decorated chancel with piscina and credence shelf and fine 14th-century glass with paintings of saints. Good monuments inside and out; one by Nollekens.

ASHCHURCH
St Nicholas
2m/3km E. of Tewkesbury SO 9233
The church has a long nave, short chancel, and 14th-century battlemented W. tower. Decorous 15th-century rood screen with traceried panels and cornice decoration of grape vines; somewhat restored, but a rare survival in this county. Old roofs, a painted Tudor frieze, and stained glass by Hardman and Kempe add to the interest.

ASHLEWORTH
St Bartholomew
5m/8km N. of Gloucester SO 8125
Superb setting next to court-house of *c.* 1460 and tithe barn; 14th-century spire, 15th-century roofs and font, painted Royal Arms of Elizabeth I; 17th-century holy table, communion rails, and reading desk.

ASHLEY
St James the Greater
3m/4km N.E. of Tetbury ST 9394
Small Norman church with carved S.
doorway, Early English arcade, and chancel
arch of *c.* 1100. Rustic monuments.

ASTON BLANK (formerly known as Cold Aston)
St Andrew
3m/4km N.E. of Northleach SP 1219
Perpendicular W. tower vaulted below with
winged angels and corbels, Norman tym-
panum over N. door. Remains of elaborate
Decorated reredos and richly canopied
Easter sepulchre.

AVENING
Holy Cross
2m/3km S.E. of Nailsworth ST 8897
A beautiful cruciform Norman church with
central tower, carefully restored in 1902 by
John Micklethwaite. Chancel delightfully re-
wrought in 14th century, with a fine vault.
Commonwealth holy table, small panels of
sculpture, and stained glass by Clayton and
Bell and Christopher Whall. Kneeling effigy
of a notorious pirate.

BADGEWORTH
Holy Trinity
3m/4km S.W. of Cheltenham SO 9019
Early 14th-century N. chapel with a profusion of characteristic ballflower ornament,
the best in the county; good wagon roof with
ribs and bosses.

BAGENDON
St Margaret
3m/4km N. of Cirencester SP 0106
Robust late-Norman N. arcade with circular
pillars and carved capitals; Perpendicular
embellishments by Cirencester Weavers
Guild.

BARNSLEY
St Mary
4m/6km N.W. of Cirencester SP 0705
Set high in stone-built village; tower of
c. 1600, Norman corbel table with grotesque
heads; severely remodelled in 1848; glass
by Willement and Wailes and tiles designed
by Pugin.

BARNWOOD
St Lawrence
E. district of Gloucester SO 8518
Handsome pinnacled Perpendicular W.

tower of *c.* 1514 bearing the arms of its
builder, Abbot Parker, the last abbot of
Gloucester. Large double-sanctus bellcote
on E. nave gable. The excellent glass is by
Clayton and Bell, Hardman, George
Rodfers of Worcester, and Veronica Whall.

BATSFORD
St Mary
1m/2km N.W. of Moreton in Marsh SP 1833
Well-set on a hillside. By W. F. Poulton
of Reading, 1861–2; of dressed stone in
neo-Norman style. Pinnacled spire and
apsed chancel. The plain interior contains
Wm Burges's superbly decorated tomb
chest for the foundress, *c.* 1866.

BAUNTON
St Mary Magdalene
2m/3km N. of Cirencester SP 0204
Small Norman and later church with a well-
preserved 14th-century wall-painting of
St Christopher with fishes frolicking at his
feet.

BERKELEY
St Mary the Virgin
5m/8km W. of Dursley ST 6899
Well-set above the castle. Gothic Survival,
mid-18th-century detached W. tower;
splendid Early English W. front with ramped
lancets. Elaborately carved 15th-century
Berkeley Chapel, extensive wall-paintings,
and a feast of monuments, including the
canopied tomb of James, eleventh Lord
Berkeley, d. 1463; angels hold the Berkeley
arms over the small priest's doorway.

BEVERSTON
St Mary
2m/3km W. of Tetbury ST 8693
Near the picturesque ruins of the castle. A
fine 10th-century sculpture of the Resurrection on the tower and, inside, a beautiful
restored 15th-century rood screen. Large
Decorated windows with clear glass; limewashed walls; blacksmith-made electric light
pendants, and a roof by Lewis Vulliamy.

BIBURY
St Mary
7m/11km N.E. of Cirencester SP 1106
William Morris 'discovered' Bibury and
thought it the most beautiful village in
England. Considerable remains of a great
Saxon minster church set in a beautiful
village. Stylishly decorated 10th-century

cross shaft set in N. wall of chancel. Table-tombs in churchyard.

BISHOP'S CLEEVE
St Michael and All Angels
4m/6km N. of Cheltenham SO 9527
Magnificent late 12th-century church sympathetically restored; the richly carved 17th-century gallery was fortunately preserved. Striking Norman W. front with turrets and handsome doorway. Decorated chancel with fine ballflower mouldings. Gothic Survival tower of 1700 and a fine monument of 1639. Battle scenes with elephants painted by a schoolmaster in 1818 in an upper chamber of S. porch.

BISLEY
All Saints
4m/6km E. of Stroud SO 9006
Remote hilly setting in stone-built village. A church busily restored by its incumbent, the Rev. W. H. Lowder, in 1860–4. Many odd twists including a fishy font base and roof-bosses banished to the vestry. In the churchyard a unique and poignant survival: a late 13th-century poor soul's light in which a candle was lit to commemorate the impecunious departed.

BITTON
St Mary
2m/3km E. of Keynsham ST 6869
Splendid Perpendicular tower with arcaded parapet, battlements and pinnacles. Otherwise Saxon, Norman and Early English with a markedly long nave. Restored by the enterprising Rev. H. N. Ellacombe who designed the angelic nave roof. He and his father, both vicars, spanned 99 years between them.

BLEDINGTON
St Leonard
4m/6km S.E. of Stow-on-the-Wold SP 2422
Set in an attractive village, the church is mainly Perpendicular with a beautiful clerestory containing brilliant 15th-century glass. There is a tiny chantry chapel, a Transitional S. arcade, Norman bellcote, and an Early English E. window. Limewashed interior, very light and unspoiled, restored by F. E. Howard of Oxford.

BLOCKLEY
St Peter & St Paul
3m/4km N.W. of Moreton in Marsh SP 1635
A big stone village on a hillside with an ambitious Norman church much altered down the centuries. Gothic Survival tower of 1725–7; all convincingly medieval save the Classical window to the W. Priest's brass of 1510 with full Mass vestments and work by Rysbrack.

BOURTON-ON-THE-HILL
St Lawrence
2m/3km W. of Moreton in Marsh SP 1732
Delightful village setting, with the long main street running up a steep hill. Norman S. arcade with drum pillars and scalloped capitals; the pointed arches are later; 14th-century chancel and much 15th-century alteration, including new roofs to nave and chancel. Late 18th-century gallery.

BOXWELL
St Mary
5m/8km W. of Tetbury ST 8192
Small Early English church set in a lovely valley, and reached down a drive through box-woods. Celebrated 13th-century spired bellcote and elegant three-bay nave arcade.

BRIMPSFIELD
St Michael
6m/10km S. of Cheltenham SO 9312
High up in the Cotswolds with the tree-covered foundations of the Giffords' castle close to the church. Norman and later with unusual Commonwealth pulpit, 1658. Pleasantly plastered interior and ancient barrel-shaped nave roof. Good 17th- and 18th-century table-tombs in churchyard.

BROCKWORTH
St George
4m/6km S.E. of Gloucester SO 8916
A suburban setting; fine Norman central tower supported on massive arches with boldly scalloped capitals; rest rebuilt in 14th century; 19th-century ironwork screen and stained glass by Wailes in E. window.

BUCKLAND
St Michael
1km/2km S.W. of Broadway SP 0836
A little gold and grey church set in a shallow fold of the N. Cotswolds. Although scraped, it almost completely escaped the hands of restorers and it is full of treasures: the Buckland Pall; 17th-century oak panelling complete with tester heads in the S. aisle and hat pegs in the gallery; 15th-century glass in the E. window depicting three of the

Seven Sacraments, restored by William Morris, and the S. aisle 15th-century tiles.

BULLEY
St Michael and All Angels
4m/6km W. of Gloucester SO 7619
Small Norman church; the S. doorway is enriched with alternating light and dark stone, a motif employed by S. Gambier Parry when he rebuilt the chancel in 1886. Inside on nave N. wall are the remains of a Norman wall-painting.

BUSSAGE
St Michael and All Angels
2m/3km S.E. of Stroud SO 8803
Attractively set on a steep hill, this church was built in 1846 by J. P. Harrison, largely from the subscriptions of Oxford undergraduates. A sound ecclesiological job, the S. aisle and porch were added in 1854 by G. F. Bodley, an accomplished first work. The reredos is also his.

CHEDWORTH
St Andrew
4m/6km S.W. of Northleach SP 0511
The church is situated above the straggling village and at some distance from the famous Roman villa. First impressions suggest another 'wool' church, as indicated by the fine Perpendicular windows of the nave, but inside there is a Norman arcade and aisle. In spite of this curious lack of balance the church has considerable dignity. The 15th-century carved stone pulpit is really fine, and shaped like a wine glass. Norman tub font with interlacing arcades.

CHELTENHAM
SO 9422
All Saints, Pittville
John Middleton's finest church, built in 1868; early French Gothic style, handsome plate traceried windows, sumptuous interior with wrought-iron chancel screen by H. A. Prothero, and complete scheme of stained glass by Sir W. Richmond.
Christ Church, Malvern Road
1840 by R. W. and C. Jearrad. A Gothic confection; the interior was tricked out later as a basilica with Renaissance flourishes.
St Paul, St Paul's Road
1831, by John B. Forbes. Chaste Ionic frontispiece, pilastered tower with cupola; galleried interior with cast-iron columns.
St Peter, Tewkesbury Road

1840–9, by S. W. Daukes in a surprising Romanesque style. Cruciform plan with domed crossing and proper Norman details; painted and gilded interior.

CHERINGTON
St Nicholas
4m/6km E. of Nailsworth ST 9098
A small village with some good Georgian cottages. The church has a delightful Early English chancel in pristine condition, replete with lancets, plate tracery, and a double piscina.

CHIPPING CAMPDEN
St James
8m/12km S.E. of Evesham SP 1539
Set at the end of this unspoiled little town, a great golden Perpendicular 'wool' church with a magnificent tower. Inside, the tall nave arcades have concave chamfers on the columns and very pretty capitals in consequence. There are brasses to the wool staplers and a great monument of 1664, the finest work of Joshua Marshall; macabre swathed figures in grave clothes are revealed by the open doors of the tomb. Late 15th-century embroidered frontal and dorsal.

CIRENCESTER
St John the Baptist
14m/22km W. of Swindon SP 0202
The largest and most splendid of the Cotswold 'wool' churches, perhaps one of the most beautiful Perpendicular churches in all England. Nave and aisles have pierced traceried battlements interspersed with tall crocketed pinnacles; an exciting skyline as at Gloucester Cathedral. Remarkable three-storeyed S. porch of *c.* 1490, bedecked with oriel windows, niches and tracery, once used as the Town Hall. Inside, one is immediately struck by the enormous height of the clerestoried nave of six bays, and the characteristic window over the chancel arch. Other features are the rare painted and gilded 'wine glass pulpit' of *c.* 1450, the early 18th-century Bristol brass candelabra, the Lady Chapel monuments, the fan vaulting of St Katharine's Chapel, and the 15th-century glass in the E. window.

CLEARWELL
St Peter
2m/3km S. of Coleford SO 5708
A delightful design by J. Middleton of Cheltenham, 1866, which uses a variety of con-

trasting coloured stones to great effect. There are contemporary furnishings and marble wall-decoration to chancel, painted roofs, and stained glass by Hardman.

COATES
St Matthew
3m/4km W. of Cirencester SO 9700
Norman and Early English. Fine early Perpendicular W. tower with crocketed ogee bell openings; built before 1361 by John Wiat, rector.

COBERLEY
St Giles
4m/6km S. of Cheltenham SO 9616
Substantially rebuilt by John Middleton in 1869–72, but the S. chapel of *c.* 1340 has ballflowers and good details; excellent medieval monuments, one to the Berkeley knight who fought at Crecy.

COLD ASHTON
Holy Trinity
5m/8km N. of Bath ST 7472
High on the Cotswold edge close to Bath; 1508–1540; all of a piece apart from the W. tower. Slightly old-fashioned details, much use of the 'T' and key rebus of the rector-builder Thomas Key. The interior is pleasantly limewashed; fragments of 16th-century stained glass.

COLN ROGERS
St Andrew
4m/6km S.W. of Northleach SP 0809
Saxon nave and chancel, almost intact apart from the altered windows. Good long-and-short quoins and restrained chancel arch, a rare delight. The small W. tower is late-Perpendicular.

COLN ST DENYS
St James the Great
3m/4km S.W. of Northleach SP 0810
Prettily situated in the Coln Valley near the Fosse Way, the church is both picturesque and interesting, for it retains its original Norman ground plan and central tower. The tower itself is massive, as wide as the church and heavily buttressed; 15th-century belfry stage.

COMPTON ABDALE
St Oswald
4m/6km N.W. of Northleach SP 0616
Set in a hollow of the Cotswolds, with the

church on a steep bank overlooking the village. Notably handsome Perpendicular W. tower of three stages adorned with beasts and gargoyles.

DAGLINGWORTH
Holy Rood
3m/4km N.W. of Cirencester SO 9905
A Saxon Cotswold church with long-and-short quoins, a crucifix on the E. gable, and a sundial over the S. door. But most important of all, three very beautiful pre-Conquest stone panels in the walls of the nave and N. aisle, spirited depictions of the Crucifixion, Christ in Majesty and St Peter.

DAYLESFORD
St Peter
4m/6km E. of Stow-on-the-Wold SP 2425
By J. L. Pearson, 1860. In early French Gothic style, dark and decorated with a cruciform plan. Untouched interior with cedar roofs and oak stalls. Warren Hastings lies under a tomb in the Greek taste. There is fine stained glass by Clayton and Bell.

DEERHURST
St Mary
7m/11km N.W. of Cheltenham SO 8729
In pleasant, sleepy riverside country is one of the most celebrated Anglo-Saxon churches in England. Originally a monastery, founded in the 8th century, it was rebuilt in the 10th after the Viking invasion, and later given Early English and Perpendicular windows. The tall, slender tower, Saxon in the lower part and medieval above, is very striking as one approaches across the large churchyard. Inside, the unusual height of the nave is further emphasized by the blocking of the E. end, originally an apse, and by the double triangular-headed window high up in the W. wall. The chancel has seating on three sides of the altar in the 17th-century manner, and the late 9th-century font is a wonderful piece, a cylindrical bowl covered with patterning. Nearby is the chapel of the Holy Trinity, dedicated by Earl Odda on 12 April 1056 in memory of his brother.

DIDBROOK
St George
3m/4km N.E. of Winchcombe SP 0531
Setting in charming village of cottages, part timber-framed, part stone. Church was rebuilt *c.* 1475 by William Whitchurch, abbot

of nearby Hailes; Perpendicular throughout, including the handsome W. tower; 17th-century furnishings and some stained glass contemporary with the building.

DIDMARTON
St Lawrence
6m/10km S.W. of Tetbury ST 8287
Standing next to the manor in an attractive churchyard, this is one of the churches the Victorians happily forgot. Instead they built a new one, and this precious place was allowed to sleep on in Georgian bliss; an almost complete 18th-century interior.
R.C.F.

DOWDESWELL
St Michael
3m/4km S.E. of Cheltenham SO 9919
Set on green Cotswold slope with farm buildings to the W. Norman cruciform church with 14th-century central tower and spire replaced in 1577. Lovely Tudor porch, S. transept of 1630, and some good monuments and tablets; two galleries, one for the manor, the other for the rectory.

DOWN AMPNEY
All Saints
2m/3km N. of Cricklade SU 1097
The church stands close to the manor, forming a pretty group in flat Upper Thames country. The Early English tower has a 14th-century spire with a gilded weather-cock. Inside are fine 13th-century arcades and lavish 19th-century oak fittings in the chancel. The transepts are noteworthy; on the N. side, behind a beautifully carved and painted Jacobean screen, is the elaborate tomb of Sir Anthony Hungerford, 1637, and on the S. are two 14th-century recumbent effigies beneath a rich canopy. This is the birthplace of Ralph Vaughan Williams.

DUMBLETON
St Peter
5m/8km N. of Winchcombe SP 0136
Village setting with views. Norman, altered in the 13th and 15th centuries. Many monuments within and without the church, including a tablet by Eric Gill.

DUNTISBOURNE ROUS
St Michael and all Angels
3m/4km N.W. of Cirencester SO 9806
On the steep bank of the brook, an enchanting place, stands a small Saxon church.

The saddleback tower, nave roof and chancel step down the hill, but even so, the chancel added by the Normans is so high at the E. end that there is room for a crypt below, which is now approached down fern-covered steps in the churchyard. The crypt has a narrow unglazed Norman slit window, while those in the chancel are little bigger. Inside it is unspoiled by antiquarianism, with 17th-century box pews in the nave and misericords in the choir.

DYMOCK
St Mary the Virgin
4m/6km N.W. of Newent SO 7031
Important Norman work; fine S. doorway with Tree of Life tympanum and chevroned head, matching chancel arch. Wickedly scraped during Middleton's 1870s restoration. Kempe glass.

DYRHAM
St Peter
4m/6km S. of Chipping Sodbury ST 7375
In a splendid setting on a terrace by Dyrham House, the church is mainly 13th- and 15th-century. Beautifully light interior with clear glass. Jacobean pulpit with tester, Norman font, some medieval tiles and fine tombs; brass to armour-plated Sir Maurice Russell, d. 1416, and a robust canopied tomb to George Wynter, d. 1581.

EASTLEACH
4m/6km N. of Lechlade SP 1905
A village with two Norman churches either side of a clear brook in one of the most charming spots in the county. The flat stone bridge which spans the stream is known as Keble's Bridge after the saintly poet who was curate here.
St Andrew
Situated on the N. bank of the stream, it has a saddleback tower, a richly carved Norman S. doorway, and a broad chancel with three lancets at the E. end; all plain, simple and delightful.
St Michael & St Martin
Low tower with a hipped roof, walls faced in roughcast, Decorated N. transept; inside are some nice old pews.
R.C.F.

EBRINGTON
St Eadburgha
2m/3km E. of Chipping Campden SP 1840
Norman nave and S. doorway with three

orders of chevrons and a diapered tympanum. Inside, a good pulpit of 1679, a painted 15th-century effigy, and some medieval bench-ends; the E. window by Christopher Webb, 1964.

EDGEWORTH
St Mary
5m/8km N.W. of Cirencester SO 9406
Approached down sycamore avenue. Saxon W. part of nave with chevron-moulded Norman S. door. Some 14th-century glass including a beautiful figure of a bishop; sadly scraped inside.

ELKSTONE
St John the Evangelist
6m/10km S. of Cheltenham SO 9612
In the high Cotswolds, one of the most famous Norman churches in the county. There is a tall Perpendicular W. tower, the original Norman tower having collapsed. This is built of huge freestone blocks which contrast with the rubble walls of the Norman nave. The S. doorway has a richly carved Christ in Majesty in the tympanum. Inside there are two arches which formerly supported the central tower and which effectively divide the exquisite little sanctuary from the tall body of the church.

ELMORE
St John the Baptist
4m/6km S.W. of Gloucester SO 7815
Good Early English chancel arch and five-bay arcade with moulded capitals; 15th-century tomb chest; table-tombs of 17th and 18th centuries with excellent figure carving.

ENGLISH BICKNOR
St Mary
3m/4km N. of Coleford SO 5815
Set high above a river on the site of a Norman castle. The church has splendid 12th-century arcades with elaborate capitals.

FAIRFORD
St Mary the Virgin
8m/12km E. of Cirencester SK 5636
A complete and perfect Perpendicular church. Chancel, aisles, porch and clerestoried nave have continuous embattled parapets with pinnacles; the smooth freestone is warm and mellow. The parapet of the central tower is pierced with quatrefoils and has pairs of pinnacles at the corners. Although smaller than the other great Perpendicular wool churches in the county, Fairford has the best late 15th-century glass in England, and in sufficient quantity to be judged apart from its antiquarian interest; it is exceedingly beautiful.

FORTHAMPTON
St Mary
2m/3km W. of Tewkesbury SO 8532
Norman origins, now mostly 14th-century and later. Great interest attaches to the free-standing stone altar of *c.* 1300. Beautiful pre-Raphaelite E. window; W. window by Clayton and Bell.

FRANCE LYNCH
St John the Baptist
adjoins Chalford to E. SO 9003
1855–7. G. F. Bodley's second complete church, an exercise in his nascent French Gothic style, very neat and pleasing. A good deal of restrained polychrome in the sanctuary.

GLOUCESTER
SO 8318
All Saints, Lower Barton Street
1875, by Sir Giles Gilbert Scott. A handsome church in the Decorated style; tasteful furnishings, an English altar, and glass by Clayton & Bell.
St Mary-de-Crypt, Southgate Street
14th-century and Perpendicular, cruciform plan. Enriched chancel with Easter sepulchre; stone screens; many monuments including one by Scheemakers, 1746.
St Nicholas, Westgate Street
Prominent Perpendicular three-stage W. tower. Norman S. doorway has Agnus Dei tympanum and on the door itself a 14th-century bronze knocker with grotesque head. Among many civic monuments a splendidly self-confident tomb to Alderman John Walton and his wife.
R.C.F.

GREAT BADMINTON
St Michael and All Angels
5m/8km E. of Chipping Sodbury ST 8082
Classical church of 1785 attached to the great house of the Dukes of Beaufort and approached through the garden. The chancel and apse were added in 1875 and furnished by Temple Moore in 1908. A shrine to the Beauforts, the church is plastered with marble monuments including a very grand one of the first Duke in full

Garter robes and beauty queens pretending to be Fates.

GREAT BARRINGTON
St Mary the Virgin
2m/3km W. of Burford SP 2013
Large Norman church with Early English and Perpendicular embellishments. Good monuments include a poignant female figure by Nollekens.

GREAT WASHBOURNE
St Mary
4m/6km N.W. of Winchcombe SO 9834
This small hamlet near Alderton Hill on the Worcesetershire border has a tiny Norman church with 18th-century box pews, reading desk, and two-decker pulpit. The font is placed directly between the small chancel arch and the altar. Over the S. door is a tympanum carved with Maltese crosses.
Hailes (Chapel of ease) 2m/3km NE of Winchcombe SP 0430
The little church near the Abbey ruins is one of the most unspoilt in the county; inside everything is old. Elizabethan benches; 17th-century pulpit and tester; 15th-century tiles, glass and screen; 14th-century wall-painting. It has its own specially rewarding atmosphere.

HAMPNETT
St George
1m/2km N.W. of Northleach SP 1015
Small Norman church with a remarkable vaulted chancel, a little gem. The interior was boldly painted in Romanesque style by Clayton & Bell in 1871 at the instigation of the rector; delightful.

HARDWICKE
St Nicholas
5m/8km S.W. of Gloucester SO 7912
Early English S. door, nave arcade and chancel; Laudian altar rails and a rustic Renaissance monument to John Trye, d. 1591.

HARESCOMBE
St John the Baptist
5m/8km S. of Gloucester SO 8310
On the edge of the Cotswold escarpment; 13th-century nave and chancel with a remarkable spired double bellcote over the E. gable of the nave. Beautiful Transitional font with clustered shafts; 18th-century table-tombs in the churchyard.

HARNHILL
St Michael and All Angels
3m/4km E. of Cirencester SP 0600
Remote setting among trees. Unusual 18th-century dragon weather-vane and fine Norman S. door with tympanum of the Archangel Michael.

HATHEROP
St Nicholas
3m/4km N. of Fairford SP 1505
1854, by Henry Clutton in a Perpendicular style with French Gothic overtones. Central tower with saddleback roof and a pretty vaulted mortuary chapel enriched by William Burges with a stone frieze of castles and the letter B for Barbara, Lady de Mauley, whose impressive effigy it contains.

HAWKESBURY
St Mary
4m/6km N.E. of Chipping Sodbury ST 7686
Remote valley setting with the great church like a wrecked ship at the foot of the Cotswold cliff; fine 14th-century tower, Norman N. door, and 15th-century stone pulpit. Scraped interior, monuments, one to the second Earl of Liverpool, prime minister at the time of Waterloo, who died in 1828.

HEWELSFIELD
St Mary Magdalene
4m/6km W. of Lydney SO 5602
In a round churchyard with good views over small-field country between two stretches of Forest of Dean. Norman nave and central tower with corbel table, otherwise Early English, like the scalloped octagonal font.

HIGHNAM
Holy Innocents
3m/4km W. of Gloucester SO 7819
Set in the midst of a park, the church was built by Thomas Gambier Parry and Henry Woodyer in 1850 of a grey-green limestone in Decorated style. The magnificent spire is covered in ballflower and has crocketed pinnacles. Inside, it is pleasantly dark with walls painted by Parry to simulate drapery. There is a continuous frieze of Biblical characters, all with golden haloes. The chancel arch is tall and elegant with painted mouldings, and the chancel is brilliant with shining tiles, painted organ, and walls with texts, vines and symbols of the Passion. The stained glass is jewel-like and comprises work by Clayton and Bell, Hardman and

Wailes. The Anglican fulfilment of the Pugin ideal.

HILL
St Michael
3m/4km N. of Thornbury ST 6495
The church and manor house stand in a small riverside park. Medieval in origin, Georgian in atmosphere. Carved oak pulpit, 1629; large canopied manorial pew; early 16th-century seating and carved bench-ends.

HUNTLEY
St John the Baptist
7m/11km W. of Gloucester SO 7219
By S. S. Teulon, 1863, in full-blooded Decorated style. Flamboyant tracery in the windows and a rich interior with banded stonework, open nave roof, and profuse carving by Earp. The alabaster pulpit, lectern and reredos appeared at the Great Exhibition; nave glass to Teulon's own design.

ICOMB
St Mary
2m/3km S.E. of Stow-on-the-Wold SP 2122
Chaste Early English chancel with lancets and an unusual tower of *c.* 1600 with saddle-back roof and domestic windows. Knightly effigy to Sir John Blaket, d. 1431. Stained glass by Powell, 1900, and Geoffrey Webb, 1948.

IRON ACTON
St James the Less
3m/4km W. of Chipping Sodbury ST 6783
Dark sandstone church, with W. tower built by Robert Poyntz, d. 1439; in the churchyard a uniquely beautiful 15th-century Memorial Cross, mutilated and lichen-covered. Good fittings include Laudian altar rails, an 18th-century brass candelabrum, a Jacobean pulpit, medieval effigies of the Poyntz family, and 19th-century mosaic floors in Roman style. The reredos and side chapel screen are full of colour and joy, designed by F. C. Eden *c.* 1930.

KEMPLEY
4m/6km N.W. of Newent SO 6729
St Edward the Confessor
By Randall Wells, 1903. Stone-built with huge-tiled roof. A fine design, with a large reticulated W. window, heavy rood, and beautiful contemporary fittings and sculpture by Ernest Gimson, Ernest Barnsley,

and local craftsmen in accordance with the precepts of the Arts and Crafts Movement, to which this is a shrine.
St Mary
The old church of St Mary is an unforgettable place; an 11th-century nave and chancel, the walls aglow with some of the finest Romanesque frescoes in England. In the barrel-vaulted chancel in particular, an almost complete cycle survives with Christ in Majesty at the centre surrounded by the Symbols of the Evangelists and other themes from the Revelation of St John the Divine; a heavenly vault indeed. In the nave further wall-paintings of the 15th century.
E.H.

KEMPSFORD
St Mary
3m/4km S. of Fairford SU 1696
On the upper Thames with a fine three-stage tower reputedly built by John of Gaunt; large Perpendicular windows and a parapet with trefoil-headed openings and crocketed pinnacles, all with weather-vanes. Entering the Norman S. doorway, the church seems dark though lofty, chiefly because of the large amount of Victorian stained glass (some of it very good, by Kempe), and the tessellated tiles. The vaulting under the central tower has painted heraldic shields. The chancel aisle was added by Street during his restoration of 1858. On the walls of the nave are framed Puritan texts. This is the only English church where an Irish peer is buried under the organ.

LECHLADE
St Lawrence
10m/16km N.E. of Swindon SU 2199
A pleasant town on the upper Thames. One of the great Perpendicular 'wool' churches, all 15th- and 16th-century, with a splendid chancel roof. Good 19th-century screens and Art Nouveau reredos.

LECKHAMPTON
St Peter
2m/3km S. of Cheltenham SO 9419
Early 14th-century central tower with graceful octagonal spire, otherwise much renewed by John Middleton in 1866–8. Good effigy of fierce Sir John Gifford, d. 1327, and his pretty wife.

LEONARD STANLEY
St Swithin

3m/4km W. of Stroud SO 8003
Leonard Stanley is set under the escarpment of the Cotswold hills near Stroud. The large church was part of a Norman priory, cruciform in plan with a massive central tower. Perpendicular windows inserted in the N. nave wall, all with clear glass. Limewashed walls. The crossing has splendid Norman arches with carved capitals; that featuring the woman washing Christ's feet in the chancel is especially good. The former cloisters are now in the farmyard of a very fine farmhouse.

LITTLE BARRINGTON
St Peter

2m/3km W. of Burford SP 2013
Pleasant setting by green village. Norman tympanum of Christ in Majesty; puzzling 14th-century remodelling of church.

LONGBOROUGH
St James

3m/4km N. of Stow-on-the-Wold SP 1729
Norman and later. Beautiful embattled early 14th-century S. transept, the reredos with canopied niches; medieval and later monuments, one by Sir R. Westmacott, to the architect C. R. Cockerell, who designed the completely sealed-off Sezincote private pew, 1822–3.

MEYSEY HAMPTON
St Mary

2m/3km W. of Fairford SP 1100
Consecrated in 1269, cruciform plan, perhaps built by the Knights Templar. Fine early 14th-century Decorated chancel with ballflowers, piscina, sedilia, and tomb recess.

MICKLETON
St Lawrence

3m/4km N. of Chipping Campden SP 1643
Norman nave, 14th-century W. tower and Perpendicular clerestory; 12th-century carved stone rood figure in N. aisle.

MINCHINHAMPTON
Holy Trinity

3m/4km S.E. of Stroud SO 8700
A fine stone-built wool village; 12th-century church with extraordinary and beautiful early 14th-century S. transept, the exterior with close-set buttresses. Rood screen by

F. C. Eden, 1920, who also painted the splendid chancel roof, 1931.

MISERDEN
St Andrew

7m/11km N.W. of Cirencester SO 9309
Late Saxon evidence limited to N. and S. doorways since drastic works in 1866 by the Rev. W. H. Lowder. Outstanding 17th-century alabaster effigies; a goat eats a cabbage at the feet of William Kingston, d. 1614.

MITCHELDEAN
St Michael and All Angels

3m/4km N. of Cinderford SO 6618
One of the largest churches in the Forest of Dean; 14th–15th-century, restored by H. Woodyer in 1853. Notably slender spire rebuilt by N. Wilkinson of Worcester, *c.* 1760. Enormous reredos with lifesize white marble figures. Sophisticated doom painting over the screen and splendid E. window by John Hyward, 1970.

MORETON VALENCE
St Stephen

5m/8km N.W. of Stroud SO 7809
Norman nave and chancel; early 12th-century N. doorway has tympanum depicting the Archangel Michael fighting a dragon; 15th-century S. aisle and W. tower.

NAUNTON
St Andrew

5m/8km W. of Stow-on-the-Wold SP 1123
Set in lovely wooded valley of the Windrush. Chiefly 16th-century with Perpendicular tower and richly decorated stone pulpit of *c.* 1400.

NEWENT
St Mary the Virgin

8m/12km N.W. of Gloucester SO 7225
Set in a brick-built Georgian town, now with much new housing. Nave rebuilt as huge square box in 1675–9, vaguely after Wren, now re-oriented away from the altar and towards the pulpit placed against the N. wall; 14th-century tower and chapel; good monuments; Saxon sculptures.

NEWLAND
All Saints

4m/6km S.E. of Monmouth SO 5509
This great church in hilly country in the Forest of Dean, sometimes called the Ca-

thedral of the Forest, has most noble interior proportions. It was built during the 13th and 14th centuries, has later chapels, and was restored in 1862. The width of the aisles gives it a tremendous feeling of spaciousness. The graceful, handsome W. tower is finely pinnacled. There are some fair recumbent effigies in the church and the unique 'Miner's Brass'; hod and pick in hand, he has a candlestick in his mouth.

NORTH CERNEY
All Saints
4m/6km N. of Cirencester SP 0107
Set in the Churn Valley, the church and its rectory can be seen from the Cheltenham–Cirencester road. It is chiefly Norman with an Early English upper stage to the saddle-back W. tower; three windows have 15th-century glass. Georgian gallery approached only by an outside stair. Extensively refur-bished inside by F. C. Eden *c.* 1925, it is the most beautifully furnished and colourful little church in the county. The painted rood is also by Eden, though the Christ is Italian work of 1600.

NORTHLEACH
St Peter & St Paul
10m/16km N.E. of Cirencester SP 1114
Once an important centre of the wool trade, Northleach has one of the most beautiful of the Perpendicular 'wool' churches in the Cotswolds, and the S. porch has been called the most lovely in all England, with its tall pinnacles and statue-filled niches. The nave of five bays has columns with concave cham-fers and a tall clerestory with a very broad window over the chancel arch; all built by John Fortey, d. 1458; his brass is under the N. arcade.

NORTH NIBLEY
St Martin
2m/3km S.W. of Dursley ST 7495
In a landscape dominated by Teulon's Tyndale monument, a tapering stone tower of 1866. Perpendicular church. Chancel stylishly rebuilt by J. L. Pearson in 1861, glazed and painted by Clayton & Bell; fine mosaic reredos of 1874.

ODDINGTON
St Nicholas
3m/4km E. of Stow-on-the-Wold SP 2325
The church is away from the village, sur-rounded by lovely trees; for many years after

1852 it was in disuse. However, it was given a new reredos as a 1918 memorial, and is now a most beautiful church with nave, chancel and S. aisle. All the windows have clear glass and, in the S. aisle, reticulated tracery. There is a large 14th-century Doom painting on the N. wall, a large Protean picture alongside, William IV arms over the chancel arch, and the Jacobean pulpit, set high on a single pillar, is a beauty.

OXENTON
St John the Baptist
6m/10km N. of Cheltenham SO 9531
Lovely setting under Cotswold scarp. Almost unspoilt medieval church, mostly 13th-century with Elizabethan linenfold carving, floor tiles, and wall-paintings which once covered the whole interior.

OZLEWORTH
St Nicholas of Myra
2m/3km E. of Wotton-under-Edge ST 7993
Standing next to a Georgian house in a circular churchyard with a rare Norman hex-agonal central tower, 14th-century chancel, and later monuments.
R.C.F.

PAINSWICK
St Mary the Virgin
3m/4km N.E. of Stroud SO 8609
Large church with spire at the centre of Cotswold town. Surrounded by fine houses, the churchyard has a unique collection of carved table-tombs and ancient clipped yews. Interior has a Classical reredos in the S. chapel and a 19th-century iron screen in the S. aisle.

PARKEND
St Paul
4m/6km N. of Lydney SO 6108
Octagonal church set in the heart of the Forest of Dean with nearby Gothic rectory by Richard James, 1822. Attractive rib-vaulted interior with W. gallery and reredos.

PAUNTLEY
St John the Evangelist
3m/4km N.E. of Newent SO 7429
Norman red sandstone nave, chevroned chancel arch and S. doorway with fish-scale tympanum; 14th-century Whittington arms in chancel; this was Dick's home village. Interior limewashed and beautiful.

PRESTON
All Saints
1m/2km S.E. of Cirencester SP 0400
Norman cruciform church; Perpendicular
tower; striking 14th-century triple bellcote
with cross and pinnacles on E. nave gable.

QUENINGTON
St Swithun
2m/3km N. of Fairford SP 1404
Norman, drastically restored in 1882. Two
splendid 12th-century doorways carved with
the Harrowing of Hell and the Crowning of
the Virgin.

RENDCOMB
St Peter
5m/8km N. of Cirencester SP 0209
A lovely late-Perpendicular church built of
fine ashlar. Inside it consists of a nave and
S. aisle of almost equal breadth and with
contemporary roofs, divided by an arcade,
the columns of which have delightful
concave chamfers. There is a 16th-century
screen across both nave and aisle and some
colourful old glass with Renaissance motifs.
Noteworthy Norman font carved with the
twelve Apostles.

RUARDEAN
St John the Baptist
3m/4km N.W. of Cinderford SO 6117
Hill-top site in the Forest of Dean with
spectacular views over Herefordshire. Early
12th-century church restored in 1890; celebrated tympanum of St George and the
Dragon.

RUDFORD
St Mary the Virgin
4m/6km N.W. of Gloucester SO 7721
Norman nave and rib-vaulted chancel; S.
doorway and chancel arch with zig-zag and
scalloped capitals; 14th-century font and
tiles.

ST BRIAVELS
St Mary the Virgin
5m/8km W. of Lydney SO 5504
Norman cruciform church standing beside
the castle in this windy village high above
the Wye Valley. Good 12th-century S.
arcade with clerestory; elaborately lobed
font; outstanding organ by Nicholson of
Worcester, 1922.

SAPPERTON
St Kenelm
5m/8km W. of Cirencester SO 9403
Largely rebuilt in the time of Queen Anne;
see the pretty early 18th-century mouldings
on the S. doorway. Good fittings include
linenfold benches, communion rails and
panelling; fine monuments of the Poole
family, especially Sir Henry, d. 1616. Interesting collection of brass plates in the
churchyard from 1687 onwards, including
the Arts and Crafts artists Ernest Gimson,
d. 1919, Ernest Barnsley, d. 1926, and
Sidney Barnsley, d. 1926.

SELSLEY
All Saints
1m/2km S.W. of Stroud SO 8303
Set in a spectacular position on the edge of
the Cotswold escarpment. It was intended
as a copy of the church at Marling in Tirol
(to please Sir William Marling) but Bodley
produced a fine French Gothic building.
The windows by Morris, Philip Webb and
Burne-Jones and their fellow Pre-
Raphaelites are the glory of the church.
Lychgate based on Butterfield's at Coalpit
Heath.

SHIPTON OLIFFE
St Oswald
adjoins Shipton, 5m/8km N.W. of Northleach
SP 0318
Small Norman and Early English church.
Celebrated 13th-century W. double bellcote
rejoicing in a pyramidal roof supported on
pinnacled buttresses. Limewashed walls,
remains of wall-paintings, and a Royal Arms.

SHIPTON SOLLARS
St Mary
adjoins Shipton, 5m/8km N.W. of Northleach
SP 0318
A pretty little 13th-century church with Perpendicular features, most sympathetically restored in 1929. Glass by Geoffrey Webb.

SIDDINGTON
St Peter
1m/2km S.E. of Cirencester SU 0399
Good farm buildings nearby. Norman
chancel arch and S. doorway with tympanum
of Christ in Majesty. Perpendicular N. aisle
and Langley Chapel which lost its dazzling
display of 15th-century glass to Cirencester
in 1800. Woodyer was here in 1864, and

he probably made the spire, among other things.

SLIMBRIDGE
St John the Evangelist
4m/6km N. of Dursley SO 7403
On the edge of the Severn flats, near the Wildfowl Trust. Nave arcades of *c.* 1200, the delightful foliate capitals echoed on the S. door. 1664 lead font decorated with cherubs and roses with balusters like exclamation marks.

SOMERFORD KEYNES
All Saints
4m/6km S. of Cirencester SU 0195
Early Saxon N. doorway and other carvings in Ringerike style; 15th-century screen and Gothic Survival W. tower of 1710–13. Beautiful Early English arcade.

SOUTH CERNEY
All Hallows
4m/6km S.E. of Cirencester SU 0497
Near the Upper Thames gravel pits. Large Norman and later church; reset 12th-century doorway with Christ in Majesty and the Harrowing of Hell; rich Decorated chancel. Wooden head of Christ from 12th-century rood, a work of poignant intensity.

SOUTHROP
St Peter
3m/4km N. of Lechlade SP 2003
Norman nave and famous font bearing spirited figures of Virtues and Vices from the *Psychomachia*. Early English chancel and Keble monuments, reminding us that John Keble ministered faithfully in this place.

STANDISH
St Nicholas
4m/6km N.W. of Stroud SO 8008
14th-century church with a soaring spire, panelled nave roof, and many bosses; 18th-century carved oak pulpit and box pews. In 1965 S. E. Dykes Bower restored and painted the monument to Winston Churchill's ancestor, Sir Henry Winston, d. 1609, so that it has a really gorgeous appearance.

STANTON
St Michael and All Angels
3m/4km S.W. of Broadway SP 0643
Set in a specially pretty village below the banks of the N. Cotswolds, the church has a Perpendicular S. aisle and porch, embattled,

and of a beautiful brown and golden texture. The W. tower has a spire. Inside, Sir Ninian Comper designed the rood screen, reredos, gallery, and some stained glass.

STOKE ORCHARD
St James the Great
4m/6km N.W. of Cheltenham SO 9228
Small and lovely Norman chapel of ease; 12th-century ironwork on N. door and a decent square font. But the wall-paintings are superb; the assured Life of St James of Compostela links this humble place with the best of the Continental Romanesque.

STOWELL
St Leonard
2m/3km S.W. of Northleach SP 0813
Late Norman cruciform church containing a spirited Romanesque Doom painting; on the N. nave wall Our Lady, the Apostles and the Heavenly Court observe the Saved and the Lost.

STOW-ON-THE-WOLD
St Edward
8m/12km W. of Chipping Norton SP 1925
Church of all periods from the 12th century, its high Perpendicular tower dominating the market square of Cotswold town. Used as a prison during the Civil War, it became a ruin, being restored in 1680 and again by Pearson in 1873. Glass by Wailes.

SWINDON
St Lawrence
2m/3km N. of Cheltenham SO 9325
Set in attractive village on edge of industrial development. Rare hexagonal Norman tower; the rest insensitively renewed *c.* 1845 by T. Fulljames in a disagreeable neo-Norman style.

TEDDINGTON
St Nicholas
5m/8km E. of Tewkesbury SO 9633
A church full of surprises. Norman chancel arch; tower dated 1567 incorporates fine Early English tower arch and W. window from Hailes Abbey; 17th-century wall-paintings and unexpected Commonwealth fittings. Royal Arms of William and Mary, 1689, painted very large on the S. wall.

TEMPLE GUITING
St Mary
6m/10km W. of Stow-on-the-Wold SP 0928
At the head of the Windrush Valley, the

church is set on one side of a wooded ravine. Norman with Perpendicular windows, Georgianized in 1740–2. Exhilarating plaster Arms of George II by John Switzer, glass panels of *c.* 1500, and a finely wrought early 18th-century oak pulpit.

TETBURY
St Mary
5m/8km N.W. of Malmesbury ST 8993
Francis Hiorne's church, finished in 1781 except for the steeple, is one of the triumphs of the early Gothic Revival. The thin, tall columns, like giant bamboos, give one a keen feeling of the period. The interior is unspoiled, retaining most of its original furnishings, especially the reredos and brass chandeliers. There is also a unique arrangement whereby it is surrounded by an enclosed cloister.

TEWKESBURY
St Mary the Virgin
8m/12km N.W. of Cheltenham SO 8932
The Abbey Church is in the flat meadows where the Avon joins the Severn, which once ran red with Lancastrian blood. With the proportions of a cathedral, it has a grand Norman nave, W. front and tower, an early 14th-century apsidal choir with chapels forming a chevet, and superb vaulting to the nave and transept of 1349–59. There is a memorable set of 14th-century monuments, second only to Westminster, and a great deal of delicate stonework in the chantry chapels. Wonderful 14th-century glass in the presbytery clerestory, with knights in armour, brilliant in heraldic surcoats.

THORNBURY
St Mary
12m/19km N. of Bristol ST 6390
Rebuilt, apart from the Decorated chancel, late in the 15th century; the W. tower resplendent with pierced panels, pinnacles, and bold angle turrets. Heraldic glass by Willement.

TODDINGTON
St Andrew
3m/4km N. of Winchcombe SP 0333
Set in the park of Lord Sudeley's fantastic Gothic Revival house, and built by G. E. Street, a good example of his work. In a lovely deep golden-coloured ashlar, with a tall broach spire and rich Decorated style, it contains a forest of Purbeck marble columns

with a background of white ashlar and 19th-century marble effigies by Lough.

TODENHAM
St Thomas of Canterbury
3m/4km N.E. of Moreton in Marsh SP 2436
Almost completely rebuilt in the early 14th century; a triumph of the Decorated style. The N. arcade, chancel and string courses are perhaps the most cherishable items among so much that is outstanding.

TUTSHILL
St Luke
½m/1km N.E. of Chepstow across R. Wye ST 5394
By Henry Woodyer, 1853. An attractive church in a Decorated style with an unusual bellcote set on its S.E. buttress. Inside, a good double sedilia and stained glass, some by Wailes.

UPLANDS
All Saints
N.E. district of Stroud SO 8505
With its tower rising on the hillside, the church is of 1908–10 by Temple Moore, in Early English and Decorated styles; a striking development of the Gothic manner.

UPLEADON
St Mary the Virgin
2m/3km E. of Newent SO 7526
The church stands by an isolated farmhouse. Norman nave and 19th-century chancel, but a distinctive timber-framed W. tower of *c.* 1500. The tower is close-studded to full height with infilling of stone and some later brick; extraordinary and loveable.

WESTBURY-ON-SEVERN
St Peter & St Paul
4m/6km E. of Cinderford SO 7114
Remarkable detached tower of *c.* 1270, probably intended for a watch or garrison in view of the heavy buttresses; the whole surmounted by a 14th-century shingled oak spire, which is a landmark from the river.

WHITTINGTON
St Bartholomew
4m/6km E. of Cheltenham SP 0120
A small Norman and later church with Tudor windows, dwarfed by its neighbour, Whittington Court. Inside are 13th-century effigies and a brass to the builder of the

house in the 'Reign of King Philip and Queen Mary'.

WICK RISSINGTON
St Lawrence
3m/4km S. of Stow-on-the-Wold SP 1921
Memorable 13th-century chancel; the paired lancets and lozenges in the E. wall are innovative and beautiful. Holst was organist here when he was 17.

WINCHCOMBE
St Peter
6m/10km N.E. of Cheltenham SP 0228
In the middle of an attractive small town and begun *c.* 1460, a typical Cotswold 'wool' church. The embattled, pinnacled tower has the finest weather-cock in the county, richly gilt, and there is a particularly grotesque collection of gargoyles, the odd one with toothache. The E. end has been rebuilt and there is no structural division between nave and chancel. There is a fine brass candelabrum of 1753, a late 17th-century organ case, and a richly painted Royal Arms of George III.

WINDRUSH
St Peter
4m/6km W. of Burford SP 1913
Norman and Decorated; celebrated 12th-century S. doorway replete with double beak-heads and an elaborate chancel arch. Magnificent table-tombs. In 1817 Thomas Keble was curate here.

WINSON
St Michael
4m/6km S. of Northleach SP 0908
Small Norman church set above the Coln. Simple nave and chancel plan with 13th-century S. porch and Perpendicular windows. Tombs.

WINSTONE
St Bartholomew
6m/10km N.W. of Cirencester SO 9609
In a hill village. Built during the Saxo-Norman overlap with mixed details; the N. door has monolithic jambs and a plain lintel, whilst the S. has slightly later cushion capitals and shafts. Medieval tower added to the W. end.

WINTERBOURNE
St Michael the Archangel
6m/10km N.E. of Bristol ST 6480
Norman and Early English; early brass of *c.* 1370; 14th-century knightly effigies and 17th-century provincial Renaissance monuments.

WITHINGTON
St Michael and All Angels
5m/8km W. of Northleach SP 0315
A good Cotswold church in an interesting village. Norman in origin, the nave is almost entirely lit by a Perpendicular clerestory. Fine carving of Sir John Howe and wife signed by Edward Marshall, 1651. A splendid exterior, though the interior is a disappointment, spoiled through too much Victorian restoration.

WOODCHESTER
St Mary
2m/3km S. of Stroud SO 8402
A typical and lovely church by S. S. Teulon, 1863–4, all mellow in the local stone with S. tower bearing a broach spire. Inside is a hammer-beam nave roof, and pulpit also by Teulon. A rewarding scheme of Victorian stained glass by Preedy and Lavers and Barraud.

WORMINGTON
St Catherine
4m/6km W. of Broadway SP 0436
A small church, Perpendicular and later, reputedly built by the Abbot of Hailes in 1475. In the S. aisle a late-Saxon sculpture of the Crucifixion with the Hand of God above; intense of expression though crudely made. Medieval glass, some by Morris and Co.

WOTTON-UNDER-EDGE
St Mary the Virgin
9m/15km S.W. of Stroud ST 7593
Decorated, Perpendicular and 19th-century; great W. tower, good plaster ceilings of *c.* 1800, and a noble 18th-century organ brought here from St Martin-in-the-Fields. Beautiful early brass to Thomas Berkeley, d. 1417, and his wife, d. 1392. He wears a collar of mermaids.

YANWORTH
St Michael
3m/4km W. of Northleach SP 0713
Late Norman church in a farmyard setting, on the edge of Stowell Park; good S. doorway with chevrons, billet-moulded chancel arch, and a sturdy tub font. Laudian altar rails and traces of wall-paintings.

YATE

St Mary

adjoins Chipping Sodbury to W. ST 7182

The Perpendicular tower is a feature of the Bristol Vale; a singularly fine example made of coursed grey rubble with freestone quoins. Limewashed walls and an E. window by Burlison & Grylls, *c.* 1879.

Hampshire and the Isle of Wight

Introduction

Hampshire falls naturally into four divisions. The main portion of the county consists of chalk downs, through which the swift-flowing Itchen, Test and Meon cut their way. All along these valleys the villages cluster thickly, sometimes not a mile apart, many of them boasting an ancient church, while on either side of the valleys the vast rolling uplands stretch away for miles. The churches in this region are chiefly built of the local flint, with wooden belfries supported internally upon great baulks of timber. Notable among them are the Saxon churches of Corhampton in the Meon valley and Headbourne Worthy in the Itchen valley.

The western part of the county, beyond Southampton Water, consists largely of the New Forest. Here Romsey Abbey and Christchurch Priory bear witness to one good result of the Norman invasion, though the area also includes such varying churches as the perfect Saxon example at Breamore, the Early English parish church of Beaulieu (once the refectory of the Monastery), the delightful 'unrestored' Minstead, with its box pews and galleries, and the 'copy-book' examples of the Gothic Revival at Bournemouth and Lyndhurst.

The third division of Hampshire, lying along the Sussex border, is characterized by the great steeply wooded hills known as the 'hangers'. Only here in the county is there any local stone, and Selborne is the most perfect ensemble of village and church lying under its Hanger, the whole district enshrining the memory of Gilbert White.

Finally. there is the border region of the north-east, an extension of the Surrey pine and heather country, now much bitten into by the vast military 'conurbation' of Aldershot and its jet-propelled 'over-spill' of Farnborough, to use two horrible new words beloved of the planners. Crondall is a noteworthy church in this district.

As regards its coast, Hampshire is not remarkable. For the most part it consists of broad tidal creeks, the only cliffs being those of Bournemouth.

In few counties are there such opportunities for the study of church architecture. The perfect Early English lancets of Pamber Priory, near Basingstoke, the glorious Perpendicular nave of Winchester Cathedral, the 17th- and 18th-century red-brick churches of Wolverton and Avington, the modern church of St Francis of Assisi at Bournemouth; every age and style are represented. Hampshire, which possessed (at Silchester) one of the few

Christian churches so far discovered in Roman Britain, has continued to maintain and demonstrate the art of church building by succeeding generations throughout the Christian era.

R.L.P.J.

Isle of Wight

Whereas Hayling Island is a bit of Hampshire that has slipped into the sea, the Isle of Wight has a personality of its own, and this persists despite pylons, poles, wire, tarmac, caravans, flash shop-fronts and shoddy bungalows, which have spread over so much of its 150 square miles. From east to west there stretches a high chalk ridge, from Culver Cliff to the Needles, as noble as the Sussex Downs and known as the 'back' of the island. South of this, and facing the open sea, are very few old buildings and the modern Victorian towns of Ventnor, Shanklin and Sandown. Inland, the chalk slopes gently to a lower range of hills, and then slopes still more gradually until it reaches the low coast along the Solent. Newport is the ancient capital of the island, and here the Medina River divides it into two, Cowes at its mouth. Yarmouth and Brading are the other old ports, and Newtown, once large for its date, has almost disappeared.

What strikes one about the island is the luxuriance of its vegetation after the comparative aridity of Hants. Myrtles, fuchsias and geraniums grow unprotected in the open air. In the under-cliff, beyond the back of the island, there is a steamy tropic richness. And next one notices the variety of local building stone, differing in colour from village to village, almost as much as those amazing streaks to be seen on the cliffs when the afternoon sun strikes Alum Bay. This stone and the style of building shown in old churches and cottages has affinities more with Dorset than Hampshire, and is best of all seen in West Wight, the most countrified part of the island.

The island became popular in the 18th century, though families like the Worsleys of Appledurcombe (now a Baroque ruin), the Barringtons of Swainston, the Holmeses and Oglanders, had lived here for many generations. But in the 18th century Garrick and his wife settled here, George Morland fled from his creditors, and Wilkes set up house. In the next century came Keats and later Tennyson. First the more gentle and less 'horrid' scenery was preferred, so that most Georgian buildings are on the Solent side of the island. The Victorians favoured the open sea, and not even the example of Queen Victoria at Osborne could tempt holidaymakers back to the tamer Solent coast. That was left to the yachtsmen, who have created a nautical civilization of their own at Cowes, Ryde, Yarmouth and Bembridge.

The old churches of the island are humble stone buildings with a West Country look, and their beauty is largely in their texture. The characteristic of their plan is aisles extending the full length of the chancel. Their prevailing style is 15th-century. The Georgian churches are mostly in unsophisticated Gothic, and have the look of proprietary chapels for Evangelical valetudinarians. The most distinguished 19th-century church is by Temple Moore at Lake (1892).

J.B.

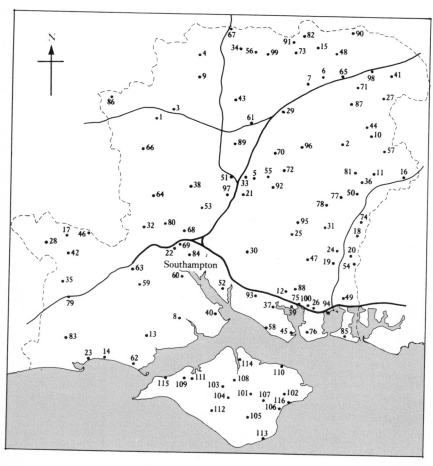

key overleaf

1   Abbotts Ann
2   Alton
3   Andover
4   Ashmansworth
5   Avington
6   Basing
7   Basingstoke
8   Beaulieu
9   Binley
10 Binsted
11 Blackmoor
12 Boarhunt
13 Boldre
14 Bournemouth
15 Bramley
16 Bramshott
17 Breamore
18 Buriton
19 Catherington
20 Chalton
21 Chilcomb
22 Chilworth
23 Christchurch
24 Clanfield
25 Corhampton
26 Cosham
27 Crondall
28 Damerham
29 Dummer
30 Durley
31 East Meon
32 East Wellow
33 Easton
34 Ecchinswell
35 Ellingham
36 Empshott
37 Fareham
38 Farley Chamberlayne
39 Farlington

40 Fawley
41 Fleet
42 Fordingbridge
43 Freefolk
44 Froyle
45 Gosport
46 Hale
47 Hambledon
48 Hartley Wespall
49 Havant
50 Hawkley
51 Headbourne Worthy
52 Hound
53 Hursley
54 Idsworth
55 Itchen Stoke
56 Kingsclere
57 Kingsley
58 Lee-on-Solent
59 Lyndhurst
60 Marchwood
61 Micheldever
62 Milford-on-Sea
63 Minstead
64 Mottisfont
65 Nately Scures
66 Nether Wallop
67 Newtown
68 North Baddesley
69 North Stoneham
70 Northington
71 Odiham
72 Old Arlesford
73 Pamber End
74 Petersfield
75 Portchester
76 Portsmouth
77 Prior's Dean
78 Privett

79 Ringwood
80 Romsey
81 Selborne
82 Silchester
83 Sopley
84 Southampton
85 South Hayling
86 South Tidworth
87 South Wanborough
88 Southwick
89 Stoke Charity
90 Stratfield Saye
91 Tadley
92 Tichborne
93 Titchfield
94 Warblington
95 Warnford
96 Wield
97 Winchester
98 Winchfield
99 Wolverton
100 Wymering
101 Arreton
102 Brading
103 Carisbrooke
104 Gatcombe
105 Godshill
106 Lake
107 Newchurch
108 Newport
109 Newtown
110 Ryde
111 Shalfleet
112 Shorwell
113 Ventnor
114 Whippingham
115 Yarmouth
116 Yaverland

Selected List of Churches (Hampshire)

ABBOTTS ANN
St Mary
3m/4km S.W. of Andover SU 3243
Decent pale brick and stone church of 1716. Good contemporary fittings include box pews, pulpit, and W. gallery on Tuscan columns; many maidens' garlands.

ALTON
St Lawrence
10m/16km S.E. of Basingstoke SU 7139
Mostly Perpendicular. Crossing tower of *c.* 1090 with archaic axe-hewn capitals, formerly central, now between S. aisle and chapel of Perpendicular nave. Jacobean pulpit; S. doors bullet-marked from 1642 Civil War siege.

ANDOVER
SU 3645
St Mary the Virgin
13m/21km N.W. of Winchester
Begun by Augustus Livesay, 1840; completed after structural problems by Sydney Smirke in 1846. Cruciform church in the Early English style with tall pinnacled W. tower. Soaring plaster-vaulted interior inspired by Salisbury; impressive E. end with grisaille glass.
St Michael and All Angels, Weyhill Road
By Roger Pinckney, 1962–4. A modern brick church with the obligatory spike for a steeple on the centre of the shallow-pitched nave roof. Interesting ceiling contrived to resemble vaulting.

ASHMANSWORTH
St James
4m/6km N.E. of Hurstbourne Tarrant SU 4157
Endearing small rustic Norman church. Unrestored interior with worn early 13th- and 15th-century wall-paintings; brick porch of 1694. Memorial porch window to the composer Gerald Finzi, d. 1956, engraved by Lawrence Whistler.

AVINGTON
St Mary
4m/6km N.E. of Winchester SU 5332
The most perfect 18th-century church in the county, a neat, simple and decent design of sturdy tower and rectangular nave, built of brick on the edge of the Park by Margaret, Marchioness of Caernarvon in 1768–71. The interior retains all its original fittings in Spanish mahogany, traditionally salvaged from an Armada galleon, and a barrel-organ in the gallery which still works.

BASING
St Mary
2m/3km E. of Basingstoke SU 6652
This large and handsome 15th- and early 16th-century church of mellow brick with stone dressings was built around the base of a once Norman central tower by the wealthy Paulet family. Their heraldic key is ubiquitous throughout, and their four tombs are set between chancel and chapels. The N. chapel, unusually, has chestnut windows; a rare use of wood and evidence of the local scarcity of good building stone. The church was damaged in the Civil War siege of Basing House. Miraculously, the beautiful statue of the Virgin and Child on the W. front survived; it was then hidden by ivy.

BASINGSTOKE
SU 6351
All Saints, Victoria Street
By Temple Moore, 1915. Dignified ashlar church in the Decorated style with restrained interior, rich furnishings, and golden E. window.
St Michael, Church Street
Mainly 15th- and early 16th-century, much restored, with N. chapel by Sir Charles Nicholson, 1921. Chancel restored by W. H. R. Blacking, 1947, after World War II damage; 18th-century memorial to Thomas Wharton and Royal Arms of Elizabeth, James I, and William III.

BEAULIEU
Blessed Virgin and Holy Child
6m/10km N.E. of Lymington SU 3802
The refectory of the great Cistercian Abbey

makes a splendid parish church; in it Early English architecture is seen at its best. The foliated reader's pulpit and graceful arcaded stairway in the W. wall are the finest features of the spacious interior.

BINLEY
St Bartholomew
3m/4km E. of Hurstbourne Tarrant SU 4253
A surprising Classical church of 1773, said to be from the hand of Robert Adam, and sufficiently like his work at Mistley, Essex to make this seem likely. A sober exterior with an elegant octagonal cupola at the W. to break the skyline. Inside it is picked out in Adamesque plaster to resemble a saloon of the period. The chancel is a shallow apse with Grecian altar rails in iron and coloured windows painted naturalistically.

BINSTED
Holy Cross
4m/6km N.E. of Alton SU 7741
13th–14th-century exterior with lancets and bar-traceried windows, but the nave arcades are mid-12th-century. Early 14th-century effigy; glass by Capronnier, 1875.

BLACKMOOR
St Matthew
4m/6km W. of Liphook SU 7833
By Alfred Waterhouse, 1868. Large church in 13th-century style with aisleless nave and prominent W. tower with pyramidal roof. Spacious interior has richly furnished chancel and retains original mauve and grey glass.

BOARHUNT
St Nicholas
2m/3km N.E. of Fareham SU 6008
Lonely rural setting. Small, plain, late-Saxon church with double splayed window and pilaster strips. Complete Prayer Book furnishings of 1853 include a three-decker pulpit, squire's pew, and W. gallery.

BOLDRE
St John
2m/3km N. of Lymington SZ 3298
Isolated from habitation, set on a hill overlooking the wooded valley of the Lymington River, on the edge of the New Forest. A church of gradual growth, it is very attractive externally. The tiled roof of the nave sweeps down to cover the S. aisle, and the tower, in S. transeptal position, has an upper stage

of 1697 in brick. William Gilpin was rector 1771–1804.

BOURNEMOUTH
SZ 0891
St Clement, St Clement's Road
By John Dando Sedding, 1871–3, tower added 1890–3. Sedding was a founder-member of the Arts and Crafts Movement, and this was his first major church; a fine design in free Gothic style. Tower with traceried battlements, cloister link to original vicarage, sadly demolished. Good furnishings of wood, stone and alabaster, glass in W. tower window by Henry Holiday.
St Francis, Charminster Road
By J. H. Gibbons, 1929–30, with hall and parsonage. Italian Romanesque manner. Roughcast exterior with tower at W. end of N. aisle. Wide nave with passage aisles and W. gallery. Free-standing altar under ciborium. Norman font from Wales.
St Mary, Holdenhurst Road, Springbourne
By Sir C. Nicholson, 1926. In free Gothic style, brick outside and whitewashed within. Nave and aisles of equal height, without clerestory. No structural division between nave and chancel. Stained glass by Comper.
St Michael, Poole Road
By R. Norman Shaw, 1876, in Early English style. Fine pinnacled tower by J. O. Scott, 1901; W. narthex by Caroe. Clerestoried nave with aisles. Contemporary fittings, glass and murals.
St Peter, Hinton Road
By G. E. Street, mainly 1855–79. Tower with stone spire, a prominent local landmark. Nave and aisles with clerestory, chancel with side chapels. Wall-painting and glass by Clayton & Bell; most fittings contemporary. Attractive landscaped churchyard contains detached war memorial by Comper.
St Stephen, St Stephen's Road
By J. L. Pearson, 1881–98, probably the best church in Bournemouth. Tower with uncompleted spire. Nave with double aisles and ambulatory round apsidal chancel, all vaulted. Gallery runs below clerestory windows and across W. end. Good iron screens and contemporary glass.

BRAMLEY
St James
5m/8km N. of Basingstoke SU 6458
An engaging church with pretty brick W. tower, 1636, dormer-windowed Norman nave, and large Gothic brick S. chapel, 1802,

by Soane. The interior fulfils the external promise, having a handsome W. gallery of 1738 with organ case by Temple Moore, medieval wall-painting, 16th-century pews, rood screen, and old roof. In the Brocas chapel, lit by some old Flemish glass, is a big monument of 1777 attributed to Thomas Carter.

BRAMSHOTT
St Mary the Virgin
1m/2km N. of Liphook SU 8432
Well-kept church of warm sandstone rubble with central tower crowned by a shingled spire. Chancel is *c.* 1220, the transepts *c.* 1420, and the aisled nave Gothic Revival of 1871.

BREAMORE
St Mary
3m/4km N. of Fordingbridge SU 1518
Important Saxon church of *c.* 1000 is set in parkland with noble cedars, close to mellow red-brick Elizabethan manor house. The church was originally cruciform, but the N. transept has gone. Over the archway to the S. transept is an Anglo-Saxon inscription which translated means 'Here the Covenant becomes manifest to thee'. Among other coeval features are double splayed windows, long-and-short quoins, and the great stone rood over the S. door. The rood, sheltered by a later porch, was defaced after the Reformation; traces of the 15th-century painted background survive.

BURITON
St Mary the Virgin
2m/3km S. of Petersfield SU 7320
Beautiful setting by duck-pond and manor house under wooded hangers; 12th-century arcades, *c.* 1280 chancel, ennobled by a triple sedilia, unusually fine for Hampshire.

CATHERINGTON
All Saints
suburb 1m/2km N. of Horndean SU 6914
Good Norman-Transitional arcades; 14th-century nave roof and wall-painting of 'The Weighing of Souls'. Monument to Chief Justice Hyde, d. 1631.

CHALTON
St Michael and All Angels
3m/4km N.E. of Horndean SU 7316
Attractive 13th-century downland church near half-timbered and thatched inn; fine E. window with geometrical tracery *c.* 1270.

CHILCOMB
St Andrew
2m/3km S.E. of Winchester SU 5028
Small late-Saxon church in lonely downland setting. Norman pillar piscina, octagonal Gothic font, and early 17th-century screen.

CHILWORTH
St Denys
4m/6km N. of Southampton SU 4018
Pretty Gothic church of 1812 with lancets. Delicately rib-vaulted interior with original pews and iron communion rail.

CHRISTCHURCH
Holy Trinity
5m/8km E. of Bournemouth SZ 1592
The Augustinian Priory church, founded in 1150, became the parish church at the Dissolution. It is set on a tongue of land between Avon and Stour, its long profile dominated by the massive 16th-century tower. The robust Norman nave with ribbed plaster vault of 1819–20, by W. Garbett, contrasts with the graceful Perpendicular quire. The great Tree of Jesse screen, the Tudor-Renaissance Salisbury Chantry, and the misericord seats, are among the most splendid features of this magnificent church.

CLANFIELD
St James
3m/4km N. of Horndean SU 6916
By R. J. Jones of Ryde, 1875. Small flint village church conceived on strict ecclesiological lines. Polychromatic brick interior is more festive; a rustic church as Butterfield at his best would have designed.

CORHAMPTON
(dedication unknown)
adjoins Meonstoke to N. SU 6120
The small Saxon church of *c.* 1035, spoilt only by 1855 brick E. end, is best seen from the N.W., where the characteristic Saxon pilaster strips and 'long-and-short' work are most evident. The S. side, hidden by a huge old yew, has a Saxon sundial. Inside, the original chancel arch and 12th-century murals are of greatest interest.

COSHAM
St Philip
N. district of Portsmouth SU 6505
By Sir Ninian Comper, 1936–8. One of his later designs, achieving 'unity by inclusion'. Brick and artificial stone outside; all the

internal focus on the altar covered by a bald-acchino, originally gilded but now white-washed. Decorated windows and Corinthian columns combine in a masterly display of eclecticism.

CRONDALL
All Saints
3m/4km N.W. of Farnham SU 7948
Approached by a lime avenue, the heavily buttressed exterior, dominated by a proud brick N. tower of 1658, is promising. Though scraped and refurnished in three Victorian restorations, the noble Transitional interior does not disappoint, for the clerestoried nave leads to a splendid vaulted chancel enriched with an Agnus Dei boss and a brass to Nich-olas de Caerwent, rector 1361–81.

DAMERHAM
St George
3m/4km N.W. of Fordingbridge SU 1015
In wooded setting away from the village to the S.W. The unrestored exterior, rich in texture, has a massive fortress-like Norman tower on S. side. Norman tympanum over S. doorway of St George at Antioch. Perpen-dicular wagon roofs in lightly restored in-terior.

DUMMER
All Saints
5m/8km S.W. of Basingstoke SU 5846
Cottagey interior with fine Early English chancel and chancel arch; deep W. gallery, 15th-century wooden rood canopy and pulpit.

DURLEY
Holy Cross
2m/3km N. of Botley SU 5116
Small cruciform Decorated church, restored but retaining fine belfry timbers and raftered nave roof. The quintessence of a small rustic Hampshire church.

EAST MEON
All Saints
5m/8km W. of Petersfield SU 6722
A striking, boldly massed church set above the village against a green down. Close to the S.E. is the 15th-century Court House. Burly enriched Norman tower crowned by a lead spire surmounts cruciform plan, the nave and transepts of which are largely Norman. Splendid Tournai marble font pre-sented by Henry de Blois. Chancel and S.

chapel rebuilt in late 15th century; glass and fittings mostly by Comper.

EAST WELLOW
St Margaret
3m/4km W. of Romsey SU 3020
Rustic, in deeply rural setting. Mostly Early English, with extensive wall-paintings of *c.* 1220 including St Christopher and the Murder of Thomas Becket.

EASTON
St Mary
2m/3km N.E. of Winchester SU 5132
Entirely *c.* 1200 with remarkable vaulted apsidal chancel and richly moulded S. doorway. Somewhat enhanced by Woodyer's 1860s restoration.

ECCHINSWELL
St Lawrence
2m/3km W. of Kingsclere SU 4959
Excellent small church in mid-14th-century style by Bodley & Garner, 1886. Flint and stone with S.W. porch tower; serene within, furnished with a screen and glass by Burlison & Grylls.

ELLINGHAM
St Mary and All Saints
2m/3km N. of Ringwood SU 1408
Simple rustic ironstone and honey-coloured rubble church in water meads of the Avon. Brick W. end of 1746 and S. porch of 1720, the latter with blue- and gold-painted sundial. 15th-century barrel roof and screen with 16th-century tympanum painted with the Decalogue, Elizabethan texts, and Royal Arms of 1671, were spared in T. G. Jackson's restoration. Reredos ascribed to Grinling Gibbons now at W. end.

EMPSHOTT
Holy Rood
2m/3km S.E. of Selborne SU 7531
Set among deep woodlands with distin-guished Early English chalk chancel arch and arcades. Fine timber roof and unusual openwork bell-turret of 1884. Purbeck marble table font with cover dated 1626. 15th-century benches and a screen of 1624, now under the tower.

FAREHAM
Holy Trinity, West Street
6m/10km N.W. of Portsmouth SU 5706
By T. E. Owen, 1835. Yellow-brick Gothic

exterior belies light, spacious interior; iron arcades and tie-beams; W. window by J. Evans of Windsor with Virtues after Reynolds at New College Ante-Chapel, Oxford.

FARLEY CHAMBERLAYNE
St John
6m/10km S.W. of Winchester SU 3927
Remote deserted village setting in Downs. Georgianized Norman, lightly restored by A. Marshall Mackenzie in 1910; 18th-century fittings.

FARLINGTON
St Andrew
N. district of Portsmouth, 2m/3km W. of Havant SU 6805
By G. E. Street, 1872–5; good 13th-century-style small village church in flint and stone. Delightful vaulted chancel with polychrome marble. Glass by Clayton & Bell.

FAWLEY
All Saints
5m/8km E. of Beaulieu SU 4503
Norman W. doorway and early Decorated E. window of the chancel are the finest features of this basically late 12th-century church. E. end bombed in 1940, well restored by W. H. R. Blacking in 1954. There is a fine Jacobean pulpit.

FLEET
All Saints
4m/6km W. of Farnborough SU 8154
By William Burges, 1861–2, extended to W. in 1934 by A. J. Steadman; Lady Chapel by John Purser, 1958. Of red brick with lancets, plate tracery, and a steep bellcote on the E. end of the nave. Inside, there are massive square brick piers, much painted decoration, and the founder's tomb with recumbent effigies by Thomas Nicholls, 1861.

FORDINGBRIDGE
St Mary
6m/10km N. of Ringwood SU 1414
Norman to Perpendicular; Early English chancel with huge E. window of three lancets; Decorated N. chapel, nave and aisles; spacious throughout; 15th-century roof of N. chapel similar to the hammer-beam roof of the nave at Bere Regis, Dorset; handsome Georgian Royal Arms.

FREEFOLK
St Nicholas
adjoins Laverstoke, 2m/3km E. of Whitchurch SU 4848
Tiny 15th-century church with 17th-century Powlett monument, 18th-century Decalogue with Moses and Aaron, and hatchments.
R.C.F.

FROYLE
Assumption of the Blessed Virgin Mary
4m/6km N.E. of Alton SU 7543
Groups with grey-stone-gabled manor house at upper end of park. Red-brick Georgian nave and tower contrast with grey-stone early-Decorated chancel. The good reticulated tracery of the E. window is filled with coeval heraldic glass. Sumptuously furnished in the Baroque taste by Sir Hubert Miller.

GOSPORT
Holy Trinity
1m/2km W. of Portsmouth across entrance to Portsmouth Harbour SZ 6199
1694–6 and later. Brick; wooden Ionic columns; fine campanile of 1889 by A. W. Blomfield. Handel's organ from Canons Park, Stanmore, and other interesting fittings.

HALE
St Mary
4m/6km N.E. of Fordingbridge SU 1918
Beautifully situated in woodland with view of mansion. Rebuilt in 1633 in pretty rustic Classical style, altered and enlarged with transepts added by Thomas Archer in 1717. Victorianized inside; monuments include Archer's own.

HAMBLEDON
St Peter & St Paul
4m/6km S.E. of Meonstoke SU 6414
Well-placed above unspoilt village. Large accretive growth from Saxon core. Fine 13th-century chancel. Medieval roofs.

HARTLEY WESPALL
St Mary
3m/4km N.W. of Hook SU 6958
Remarkable cusped timber framework of W. wall and good roofs, c. 1340. Restored in 1869 by G. G. Scott Jnr, who also built the chancel.

HAVANT
St Faith
6m/10km N.E. of Portsmouth SU 7106
Extensively restored by R. Drew in 1874, but retaining beautiful 13th-century vaulted chancel with glass by Clayton & Bell and a fine brass of 1413.

HAWKLEY
St Peter & St Paul
2m/3km N.W. of Liss SU 7429
By S. S. Teulon, 1865. One of his best churches, solid, vigorous Romanesque with Rhenish helm tower. Much rich carving inside.

HEADBOURNE WORTHY
St Swithin
2m/3km N. of Winchester SU 4832
Charming small Saxon church. Large and important rood of *c.* 1000, sheltered by a Tudor W. annexe. Interior over-restored by G. E. Street.

HOUND
St Mary
1m/2km E. of Netley SU 4708
Complete small Early English church with stepped E. lancets; splendid window of the Virgin and Child by P. Reyntiens, 1959.

HURSLEY
All Saints
4m/6km S.W. of Winchester SU 4225
By J. P. Harrison, 1847–8. Big grey Decorated church built at the expense of Rev. J. Keble. Good glass by Wailes to Butterfield's designs and a monument to 'tumbledown Dick' Cromwell in dark 14th-century W. tower.

IDSWORTH
St Hubert
5m/8km N.E. of Havant SU 7414
Highly picturesque small Norman and 16th-century chapel alone in a field in downland country. Pretty 18th-century white-painted bell-turret at E. end of nave. Its 18th-century atmosphere was heightened in 1913 by Goodhart-Rendel. Nave has fine Georgian and 1913 fittings including box pews, Jacobean pulpit, Royal Arms, and a W. gallery. Chancel has a stucco ceiling with pictorial panels of 1913 and highly important series of 14th-century wall-paintings, said by some to represent the legend of St Hubert but

more likely to relate to the life of St John the Baptist.

ITCHEN STOKE
St Mary
2m/3km W. of New Arlesford SU 5632
By H. Conybeare, 1868. Elaborate French Gothic, modelled on the Sainte Chapelle in Paris. Lofty interior with richly coloured glass and carving.
    R.C.F.

KINGSCLERE
St Mary
8m/12km N.W. of Basingstoke SU 5258
Large and plain Norman, over-restored by T. Hellyer in 1848. Fine Kingsmill monument of 1670 signed WS; perhaps William Stanton. Good grisaille E. window by Wailes.

KINGSLEY
St Nicholas (Old Church)
5m/8km E. of Alton SU 7838
Lonely setting. Small cottage-like and very rustic, largely rebuilt in brick, 1778; 18th-century pulpit and communion rail. Redundant but maintained by the parish council and used occasionally for services.

LEE-ON-SOLENT
St Faith
4m/6km W. of Gosport
1933 by Seeley and Paget. In red brick with a pretty open bellcote, a charming composition. Rewarding inside, with sweeping arches in concrete framing long vistas. Contemporary fittings include pulpit and reading desk.

LYNDHURST
St Michael
8m/12km N. of Lymington SU 2908
By William White, 1860. Splendidly mid-Victorian, in polychromatic brick, its tall brick-banded spire dominating the little New Forest town. Fresco by Lord Leighton over the altar; glass by Burne-Jones, Madox Brown and Rossetti. Monuments by Flaxman and S. P. Cockerell Jnr.

MARCHWOOD
St John
3m/4km S.E. of Totton SU 3810
By John Macduff Derick, 1843. Surprisingly early use of the Early English style in pale yellow brick with tall lancets.

MICHELDEVER
St Mary
6m/10km N. of Winchester SU 5139
Octagonal brick nave of 1806, by G. Dance Jnr; Perpendicular tower, 1527. Flaxman monuments to Barings in the chancel.

MILFORD-ON-SEA
All Saints
3m/4km S.W. of Lymington SZ 2891
Largely Early English. Of the cruciform Norman church, two bays of the S. arcade and the ends of the transepts remain. The 13th-century W. tower with short lead spire has odd flanking penthouses with arched openings into it. Many windows show early forms of tracery. The interior with its low arcades, transverse crossing arches, barrel- and rib-vaulted roofs, is spacious and quite impressive. The chancel roof has very late bosses, 1640.

MINSTEAD
All Saints
2m/3km N.W. of Lyndhurst SU 2811
Well-set on its own up on a knoll slightly away from the tiny New Forest village, this is perhaps the most obviously quaint of the several 'unrestored' churches in the county. To a 13th-century nave and chancel have been added a Georgian brick W. tower, S. transept, and two squires' pews, complete with fireplaces. The highly atmospheric interior is crowded with open benches, box pews, and two galleries, one two-tiered under the tower. Primitive Norman font, carved with an Agnus Dei, stands on a brick floor in front of the two-decker pulpit.

MOTTISFONT
St Andrew
4m/6km N.W. of Romsey SU 3226
Norman and Perpendicular, with a splendid Norman chancel arch. Copious 15th-century glass in the chancel and a monument of 1584.

NATELY SCURES
St Swithun
4m/6km E. of Basingstoke SU 6951
Setting next to farmhouse. Tiny apsidal Norman church with fine N. doorway of *c.* 1200. Over-restored by Salvin in 1865.

NETHER WALLOP
St Andrew
4m/6km W. of Stockbridge SU 3036
Late Saxon to Perpendicular with fine flint

W. tower of 1704. Important Anglo-Saxon wall-paintings of Winchester School angels over the chancel arch – perhaps the earliest surviving in England. Early 15th-century painting of St George and the Dragon in the nave.

NEWTOWN
St Mary the Virgin & St John the Baptist
3m/4km S. of Newbury SU 4736
By Henry Woodyer, 1864–5. Flint church with shingled broach spire in a style of *c.* 1300. Good N. arcade of round piers bearing naturalistic carving. Glass by Hardman.

NORTH BADDESLEY
St John the Baptist
3m/4km E. of Romsey SU 4020
Hilly, wooded setting. Small, rustic Perpendicular church with charming exterior and brick tower of 1672. Screen and pulpit, 1602.

NORTH STONEHAM
St Nicholas
1m/2km S.W. of Eastleigh SU 4417
Gothic Survival, mostly 1590–1610. W. tower with reset 13th-century W. window. Restored by Bodley and Garner in 1891, the interior has a black marble ledger-stone to Slavonian sailors and an elaborate wall-monument by J. F. Moore to Admiral Lord Hawke, d. 1781.

NORTHINGTON
St John the Evangelist
4m/6km N.W. of New Alresford SU 5637
Finely set on a hillside in rolling country, this is one of the finest Gothic Revival churches in the county. It is by Sir T. G. Jackson and was built by Lord Ashburton in 1889. The tall, commanding pinnacled tower and triagonal apse are impressive and look well together from across the valley, their flint and stone chequer being particularly good.

ODIHAM
All Saints
7m/11km E. of Basingstoke SU 7451
Large, mainly Perpendicular church on highest point of the small country town. To its south are 17th-century almshouses whose mellow old brickwork blends with the fine 1647 church tower. The spacious, but slightly chill, interior has good 17th-century

galleries and pulpit and many small brasses. Two E. windows by Patrick Reyntiens.

OLD ALRESFORD
St Mary
1m/2km N. of New Alresford SU 5833
Rebuilt in 1753 with a brick W. tower of 1769. Splendid monument of 1757 to Jane Rodney, wife of the Admiral, by Cheere, and a charming oval tablet of 1823 with doggie.

PAMBER END
St Mary & St John the Baptist
4m/6km N. of Basingstoke SU 6158
In a lovely sylvan setting away from the village, the church was built in *c.* 1130 for the alien priory of West Sherbourne. Of the former cruciform monastic church, the superbly proportioned Early English quire and the massive tile-capped Norman central tower remain. Spacious interior, lit by clear glass in long lancet windows, and furnished with a 15th-century screen and pews. There are several Purbeck marble coffin-slabs and a wooden cross-legged effigy of a knight, *c.* 1270.

PETERSFIELD
St Peter
11m/18km N.E. of Portsmouth SU 7423
Ferociously over-restored in 1874 by A. W. Blomfield, but still interesting for the splendid Norman composition of chancel arch surmounted by three tall enriched arches, formerly the E. face of a central lantern tower.

PORTCHESTER
St Mary
on N. shore of Portsmouth harbour SU 6105
In the S.E. corner of the old Roman fort of Portchester Castle, a romantic setting. The perfect, but slightly shrunken, Norman church was built for a priory of Augustinian canons founded in 1133 by Henry I. The W. front is the glory of the church. It is rich yet simple with a fine W. door. The dour scraped interior has a Norman font and Royal Arms of both Elizabeth I and Anne, the latter very fine.

PORTSMOUTH
SU 6400
All Saints, Commercial Road, Church Street, Landport
Fine church of the Commissioners' sort in refined Decorated style, 1824, by Owen. Good interior with graceful vaulting and a chapel by Scott, 1877.
Holy Spirit, Fawcett Road, Southsea
By J. T. Micklethwaite, 1906, completed by Sir Charles Nicholson, 1926. A brick hall-church gutted in 1941 and restored 1960 by S. E. Dykes-Bower. Vast airy interior with Temple Moore font, pulpit, and stalls from St Agnes, Kennington.
St Mary, Fratton Road, Kingston, Portsea
By A. W. Blomfield, 1889; cold and impressive East Anglian Perpendicular. Huge pulpit and rich gilded reredos in vast, uplifting interior under wide hammer-beam roof.

PRIOR'S DEAN
(dedication unknown)
4m/6km N.W. of Liss SU 7330
Small rustic Norman and Early English church on Saxon foundation, in remote corner of well-wooded country; 1605 brass and Tichborne monuments.

PRIVETT
Holy Trinity
3m/4km N.E. of West Meon SU 6726
By Sir Arthur Blomfield, 1876, in convincing Early English style. Magnificent W. tower and broach spire; clerestory, bold open roof, and rich detailing.
R.C.F.

RINGWOOD
St Peter & St Paul
10m/16km N.E. of Bournemouth SU 1405
By J. & H. Francis, 1853–5. Large central-towered cruciform church in correct 13th–14th-century style. Fine early 15th-century brass to John Prophete, Dean of Hereford; rich Hardman E. window of 1857 in long chancel.

ROMSEY
St Mary & St Ethelfleda
7m/11km N.W. of Southampton SU 3521
The Abbey Church became the parish church at the Dissolution, when it was bought by the townspeople for £100. It had previously been the church of a nunnery founded by Edward the Elder *c.* 907. A visit to this magnificent church is not easily forgotten, for here is great Norman architecture, grand in scale and rich in detail. The formidably blunt, massive exterior, with its squat central tower crowned by a wooden

bell-cage, hardly prepares one for the grandeur of the interior. The church, which is largely 12th-century except for an Early English W. end, has many treasures: a wonderful Saxon rood and a smaller Saxon carving of the Crucifixion, Norman capitals, early 16th-century painted reredos, a fine 13th-century Purbeck marble effigy of a lady, and the St Barbe monument by Thomas Stanton, 1660. The N. aisle E. window is Kempe at his very best. Image of Our Lady above high altar by Martin Travers. Recently discovered wall-paintings found by Eve Baker.

SELBORNE
St Mary
4m/6km S.E. of Alton SU 7433

Beautifully set behind a gigantic old yew between the village and a wooded ravine. The largely 12th- and 13th-century church is worth visiting for its own sake as well as for Gilbert White. Entered through a fine Early English S. doorway, the well-cared-for interior, restored by the naturalist's great-nephew, William White, is full of interest. A window of St Francis and the birds commemorates the author of the *Natural History*, whose humble grave in the churchyard is inscribed simply 'G.W.', 1793.

SILCHESTER
St Mary
7m/11km N. of Basingstoke SU 6262

A charming little Norman to Perpendicular church beside a portion of the wall of the lost Roman city of Calleva Atrebatum. The Jacobean pulpit, with domed canopy, and the 15th-century screen have survived a Victorian restoration that removed box pews and dormer windows. The Early English chancel has coeval painted patterning on the splays of S. windows. There is a beautiful 14th-century effigy of a lady.

SOPLEY
St Michael and All Angels
3m/4km N. of Christchurch SZ 1597

Finely sited on knoll overlooking Avon valley. Largely Early English cruciform church; the N. transept with crude and explicit corbels pagan in spirit.

SOUTHAMPTON
SU 4112
Church of the Ascension, Bitterne Park
By Sir Charles Nicholson, 1924–6; tower completed 1954. Series of windows by the architect's brother, A. K. Nicholson, and G. E. R. Smith.
St Michael, St Michael's Square
Effective contrast between thin nave arcades by Goodwin, 1828, and massive early Norman tower arches. Norman Tournai marble font and two lovely 14th-century brass eagle lecterns, one from the blitzed Holy Rood church.

SOUTH HAYLING
St Mary
on Hayling Island between Langstone and Chichester Harbours SZ 7299

Second only to Pamber as the finest Early English church in the county, this former priory church is large and well-proportioned, of Sussex type, with central tower and shingled spire. The chancel E. window of five lancets has good 'Tree of Life' glass by Bryans, 1925.

SOUTH TIDWORTH
St Mary
3m/4km S.W. of Ludgershall SU 2348

By John Johnson, 1879–80. Lavish estate church in Early English style. Lofty interior with rich carving, sculptured reredos by Forsyth, and glass by Heaton, Butler & Bayne and Clayton & Bell.
R.C.F.

SOUTH WARNBOROUGH
St Andrew
5m/8km N. of Alton SU 7247

Norman and Early English, the S. aisle by Street, 1870. Tall rood screen with loft, c. 1400; 16th-century White monument.

SOUTHWICK
St James
3m/4km N.W. of Cosham SU 6208

Until recently this rustic church, much rebuilt in 1566, set at the meeting of three village streets, remained wholly unrestored and highly atmospheric. Much of the old atmosphere remains, but nothing can compensate for the removal of the fine box pews which had been affected by death-watch beetle. The white-painted W. gallery on twisted 'barley-sugar' columns, pulpit, altar rails, and handsome painted reredos survive from the 17th century.

STOKE CHARITY
St Mary & St Michael
6m/10km N. of Winchester SU 4839
Alone in a field by watercress beds, but once in company with the manor house of the de la Charité family. Though attractive in itself, the church of Norman and later date, restored in 1848, is most remarkable for its lovely contents. The N. chapel, the least restored part with old plaster and clear glass, holds monuments, a 15th-century sculpture of the Mass of St Gregory, and fragments of glass.

STRATFIELD SAYE
St Mary
8m/12km S.W. of Reading SU 6861
In parkland. Whitewashed brick church of 1754–8; Greek key plan with octagonal central dome. Restored interior, but the N. gallery, where the victor of Waterloo worshipped, is retained. Pitt monument of 1640 by John and Matthias Christmas.

TADLEY
St Peter
6m/10km N.W. of Basingstoke SU 6060
Small rustic and completely isolated church; humble brick tower of 1685 and dormer windows. Gallery, pulpit, seats and altar table are all 17th-century.

TICHBORNE
St Andrew
2m/3km S.W. of New Alresford SU 5730
A delightful 11th-century and later 'atmospherick' church with prominent 17th-century brick tower on the hillside above the village of neat thatched cottages. The interior has an unrestored look with box pews of diverse dates, old plaster, clear glass, and Royal Arms of 1735. The railed-off N. aisle belongs to the RC family of the Tichbornes, whose monuments it contains.

TITCHFIELD
St Peter
3m/4km W. of Fareham SU 5305
At the end of a short street off the former market-place of the unspoilt little town, the church is rich in interest. The Saxon base of W. tower with shingled 1688 spire may be the oldest church fabric in the county. It shelters a Norman doorway. The Decorated chancel arcade has figured capitals, perhaps by William Wynford, Wykeham's master mason at Winchester, and the Perpendicular

N. aisle has rich canopied niches. Splendid 16th-century Southampton monuments.

WARBLINGTON
St Thomas of Canterbury
1m/2km W. of Emsworth SU 7205
Secluded setting near Langstone Harbour, with only a farm and the ruined castle for company. The church is set in a large graveyard with two watcher's huts from body-snatching days, and many well-carved headstones; it has a partly Saxon tower riding between the Early English nave and chancel. The 15th-century timber N. porch is dark, grainy and weathered. Inside are good Early English arcades and tower arches, and there are two beautiful effigies.

WARNFORD
Our Lady
2m/3km N.E. of Meonstoke SU 6223
Among trees beside the ruined Transitional-Norman manor house in gentle park. Massive Norman tower; 13th-century inscription above S. porch, and on N. side a sundial; 17th-century Neale monuments.

WIELD
St James
5m/8km N.E. of New Alresford SU 6238
Remote, rustic Norman church with traces of wall-paintings. Restored in 1884–5; alabaster Wallop monument of 1617 with effigies.

WINCHESTER
SU 4829
St Cross, St Cross Road
The chapel of the Hospital founded by Henri de Blois, Bishop of Winchester, in 1133, is now a parish church. Dominating the Hospital quadrangle, it is one of the county's noblest churches, ample in form and rich in content. Large-boned, cruciform with central tower and vaulted throughout, it was built from E. to W., 1160–1345. The transition in style from enriched Norman at E. end to Decorated at W. end is gradual. Restored by Butterfield, 1864–5. Notable among its treasures are old wall-paintings, glass and tiles, beautiful Renaissance woodwork, and some brasses.
St John the Baptist, St John's Street
City's most interesting church. Norman-Transitional; fine geometrical Decorated window in S. wall; old woodwork and wall-paintings.

WINCHFIELD
St Mary the Virgin
2m/3km E. of Hook SU 7654

This remote church is essentially Norman, though restored in 1849, when the N. aisle was added, Norman windows replaced some medieval ones, and the brick top stage of the broad tower gave way to the present belfry stage and pyramid cap. The Norman S. doorway has good mouldings extending beneath the soffit and leaf capitals of exotic Saracenic character. There are some original windows, a Jacobean pulpit, and old oak seats.

WOLVERTON
St Katherine
2m/3km E. of Kingsclere SU 5558

In its assured Wren manner, the noble, handsomely proportioned brick tower with its nicely detailed belfry windows, cornices, and rusticated corners, contrasts with the low-built cruciform church beneath it. Both tower and church were built in 1717. The fenestration of the latter was unfortunately altered in 1872 with inset mullions and tracery. At the same time the gallery and chancel gates were removed. The pews, pulpit, reading desk, reredos and wrought-iron altar rails are intact, and with the box pews, give the interior its strong period flavour. In the nave roof are 15th-century timbers from the former church.

WYMERING
St Peter & St Paul
Portsmouth suburb, just W. of Cosham SU 6045

Graceful 13th-century S. arcade. Much restoration by G. E. Street in 1861; colourful Clayton & Bell glass in the chancel.

Selected List of Churches (Isle of Wight)

ARRETON
St George
3m/4km S.E. of Newport sz 5486
In a secluded setting close to the the farm buildings of the nearby manor house, the church has a promising exterior rich in texture. The buttressed 14th-century tower hides the Saxon W. wall and doorway of the first church on the site. This is the oldest piece of church architecture on the island. Over-restored in 1886 by Ewan Christian, the spacious Decorated chancel and S. chapel have geometrical window tracery and a Purbeck marble arcade similar to coeval work at Shalfleet. Good monuments include two by Westmacott.

BRADING
St Mary the Virgin
2m/3km N. of Sandown sz 6087
Well-sited on a ridge at the N. end of the little town, this is the largest medieval church on the island. The 13th-century W. porch-tower stands on arches made to include a processional way around the church. The spacious interior, restored by Hellyer and Blomfield, is most interesting towards the E. In the 15th-century Oglander chapel S. of the chancel are the monuments and hatchments of the Oglander family, established at nearby Nunwell. Engraved Purbeck marble slab to John Cherowin, d. 1441, Constable of Portchester Castle.

CARISBROOKE
St Mary the Virgin
adjoins Newport to S.W. sz 4888
The stately 15th-century W. tower, the most beautiful on the island, is the finest feature of a church once both monastic and parochial which has been described as 'the most important ecclesiatical building in the Island'. The Priory was suppressed in 1414; the conventual buildings N. of the church have vanished. The church of broad, airy Norman nave and Early English S. aisle, divided by a fine Transitional arcade of five bays, has a truncated look, for the chancel was pulled down *c.* 1565. The tomb of Lady Margaret

Wadham, *c.* 1520, has a small kneeling effigy beneath a rich canopy.

GATCOMBE
St Olave
3m/4km S. of Newport sz 4885
Well-wooded setting. Good 15th-century Perpendicular tower. Morris glass in chancel and four golden angels high in a nave S. window; the only medieval glass on the island.

GODSHILL
All Saints
4m/6km W. of Shanklin sz 5281
Narrow lanes sweep uphill beneath trees to the well-known group of church tower and cottages. The mostly Perpendicular church might qualify as the least restored on the island. The interior, with old plaster and much clear glass, is unexpectedly spacious, divided end to end by a dignified arcade of seven arches. Among its finest features is a wall-painting in the S. transept of Christ crucified on a triple-branched lily. Fine 16th-century tomb of Sir John Leigh has effigies beneath a rich arched canopy; 18th-century monuments to the Worsleys of Appledurcombe.

LAKE
The Good Shepherd
½m/1km S.W. of Sandown sz 5983
By Temple Moore, 1892. Assured essay in the Decorated style with flowing tracery. Unusual double-nave plan with timber-framed porch on the W. end.

NEWCHURCH
All Saints
2m/3km N.W. of Sandown sz 5685
Amply proportioned, mostly Early English. Georgian Gothic wooden belfry with small spire behind battlements. Fine 18th-century pulpit and Pelican lectern in airy interior.

NEWPORT
St Thomas
4m/6km S. of Cowes sz 4989
By S. W. Dawkes, 1854–5. Large town

church in the Decorated style. The richly carved pulpit was made by Thomas Caper of Salisbury in 1636; it is one of the finest in England and came from the old church.

NEWTOWN
The Holy Spirit
5m/8km W. of Newport sz 4290
By A. F. Livesey, 1835. Setting on site of destroyed seaport. Small Early English church with lancets, shafted windows, and vaulted interior.

RYDE
5m/8km S.W. of Portsmouth sz 5992
All Saints, town centre
By Sir George Gilbert Scott, 1869–72. Large and impressive Decorated church with 180-foot N.E. spire. Vast over-pewed interior with an opulent, gorgeously enriched chancel. Glass by Clayton & Bell.
St James, Lind Street
Embattled stucco Gothic of 1829; a rare surviving example of an early 19th-century Evangelical proprietary chapel.
St Michael and All Angels, Swanmore
By R. J. Jones of Ryde and the Rev. Mr Grey, 1862–74. Splendidly massed cruciform with central tower and vaulted apsidal chancel; polychromatic brick interior.

SHALFLEET
St Michael the Archangel
4m/6km E. of Yarmouth sz 4189
The massive fortress-like tower and the S. doorway are Norman, the latter with a crudely carved tympanum of Daniel in the Lions' Den. Late 13th-century S. arcade and windows. The chancel has good early 14th-century geometrical windows. Box pews, but the walls sadly scraped.

SHORWELL
St Peter
5m/8km S.W. of Newport sz 4582
A largely 15th-century church of mellow texture in a lovely village of thatched cottages in multi-coloured local stone. The exterior is weathered and unrestored; the interior quite dark and crowded with poppy-headed pews. Through the arcades are seen the very interesting wall-painting of St Christopher, the Perpendicular stone pulpit with Jacobean tester, and the Leigh family monuments.

VENTNOR
Holy Trinity
3m/4km S.W. of Shanklin sz 5677
By C. E. Giles of Taunton, 1860–2. Early English N.W. tower, plate tracery, and good interior with outstanding glass by Clayton & Bell.

WHIPPINGHAM
St Mildred
1m/2km S.E. of East Cowes sz 5193
More curious than beautiful, this spiky Germanic Gothic church was designed by Prince Albert and A. J. Humbert, 1855–62. It contains a fine bronze grille by Alfred Gilbert, 1897, and memorials to various members of the Royal Family. Hardman E. window and others in Royal Pew.

YARMOUTH
St James, Apostle and Martyr
9m/15km W. of Newport sz 3589
Rough Jacobean Gothic of 1626; W. tower by D. A. Alexander, 1831. Elegant late 17th-century brick chapel contains remarkable French statue to Sir Robert Holmes, Governor of the Island, 1692.

YAVERLAND
St John the Baptist
1m/2km N.E. of Sandown sz 6185
Almost attached to Elizabethan manor house. Norman S. door and chancel arch; heavily restored and enlarged in 1888 by Ewan Christian.

Herefordshire

Introduction

This secret, partly Welsh county is so deeply silent in its many remote places and, comparatively, so undamaged by pylons, poles, factories, aerodromes, and villadom, that those who know it cannot be blamed for wishing to protect its rustic beauty from the crowds. Medieval farms, timber-framed and tiled, are isolated down narrow hilly lanes; hopyards and cider orchards abound; some churches and houses are spared electricity; Victorian Hereford of Kilvert's diary survives; the hills of almost empty Radnorshire and the bare Black Mountains of Brecon and Monmouth diversify its western horizon and the Malvern hills are its eastern; the Rivers Wye, Lugg, Frome and Arrow create rich valleys in its pastoral heart. And in the centre is the city and county town, with Cathedral, hospitals, market and eponymous Viscount all complete.

From the south of this county the Welsh were never driven out by the Saxons and they assimilated the Normans in their own way, for here is that curious group of Norman churches of which Kilpeck is the best known, where the carving of fonts, tympana and capitals seems to be Celtic and unlike any other Norman work in England. Besides Norman churches, red fields, red-and-white Herefordshire cattle, cider, hops and barley, a chief feature of this woody, landscaped county is the prevalence of old timber-framed buildings. These are rarely thatched but have roofs of stone slates or old tiles. Weobley, Eardisley and Pembridge are complete villages of them. Building stones are many and were used chiefly for churches, and they vary from the pale pitted tufa to red sandstone. There are few big country houses. Moccas, partly by Robert Adam, Berrington, by Henry Holland, are fine classic examples; Downton Castle (1780–5), built by Richard Payne Knight, the exponent of the 'picturesque' theory, and Hampton Court, Hereford, are 'Gothick'. Eastnor Castle, by Sir Robert Smirke, 1808, is a very early example of Norman revival.

The Cathedral of Hereford, sadly bereft for many years of its glorious screen by Scott and Skidmore, still largely Norman, is square and West Country-looking, and is not so much admired as Gloucester and Worcester, with which it is usually compared. The county itself contains grand churches of every age, from Norman to early 20th-century; of every style, although only a few 15th-century Perpendicular, and this is odd since most of the medieval churches of the rest of England were added to in this century, and in many counties the most impressive parish church is wholly 15th-century. Hereford was not a rich county in the last century, so that Victorian 'restorations' are often cheap and ugly or else the churches were spared restoration altogether. For its size Herefordshire has more 17th-century woodwork than elsewhere and a fair amount of Georgian box pewing. The county seems to have gone straight from 'High Church' to Evangelical, and 19th-century Tractarianism is rare, with the notable exception of Monkland. As may be expected in so unspoiled a county, the settings of almost all the churches are attractive, and in the Welsh districts the old parish church is Celtic-fashion, some way off from the village. There is no 'typical' Herefordshire church. The churches are either curiously beautiful or dull inside. No county has a church so wonderful as Abbey Dore, that solemn Cistercian Early English abbey with its 17th-century woodwork making a rich contrast; nor is there parochial Decorated to compare with the S. aisle of Leominster. No county has so delicately moulded and joyfully coloured examples of Georgian as the Rococo-Gothic church of Shobdon, and for unrestored remoteness there is little to compare with Clodock and Richard's Castle. Brinsop, so excitingly restored by Sir Ninian Comper, Brockhampton-by-Ross, Lethaby's bold design in the Arts and Crafts – William Morris manner, Seddon's strange Victorian effort at Hoarwithy, are all possessions which help to make the county so full of the unexpected. My own memory of the perfect Herefordshire is a spring day in the foothills of the Black Mountains, finding among winding hill-top lanes the remote little church of St Margaret's, where there was no sound but a farm dog's distant barking. Opening the church door I saw across the little chancel a screen and loft delicately carved.

J.B.

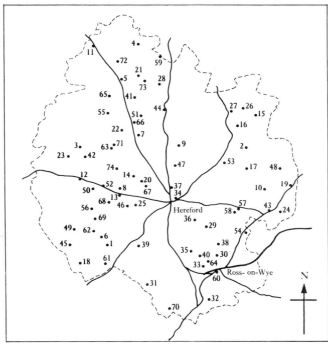

1	Abbey Dore	26	Edvin Loach	51	Monkland
2	Acton Beauchamp	27	Edwyn Ralph	52	Monnington-on-Wye
3	Almeley	28	Eye	53	Much Cowarne
4	Aston	29	Fownhope	54	Much Marcle
5	Aymestrey	30	Foy	55	Pembridge
6	Bacton	31	Garway	56	Peterchurch
7	Birley	32	Goodrich	57	Pixley
8	Bishopstone	33	Hentland	58	Putley
9	Bodenham	34	Hereford	59	Richard's Castle
10	Bosbury	35	Hoarwithy	60	Ross-on-Wye
11	Brampton Bryan	36	Holme Lacy	61	Rowlestone
12	Bredwardine	37	Holmer	62	St Margaret's
13	Bridge Sollars	38	How Caple	63	Sarnesfield
14	Brinsop	39	Kilpeck	64	Sellack
15	Brockhampton-by-Ross	40	King's Caple	65	Shobdon
16	Bromyard	41	Kingsland	66	Stretford
17	Castle Frome	42	Kinnersley	67	Stretton Sugwas
18	Clodock	43	Ledbury	68	Tyberton
19	Colwall	44	Leominster	69	Vowchurch
20	Credenhill	45	Llanveynoe	70	Welsh Newton
21	Croft	46	Madley	71	Weobley
22	Dilwyn	47	Marden	72	Wigmore
23	Eardisley	48	Mathon	73	Yarpole
24	Eastnor	49	Michaelchurch Escley	74	Yazor
25	Eaton Bishop	50	Moccas		

Selected List of Churches

ABBEY DORE
St Mary
2m/3km N. of Pontrilas SO 3830
Surrounded by the small orchards of the Golden Valley are the presbytery, with its wonderful square red sandstone ambulatory and chapels, and the crossing and transepts of a great conventual church of the Cistercian order, alight with colour from the 17th-century glass in the lancet windows, a perfect example of Early English architecture with 17th-century fittings. The great oak screen was designed by John Abel for Viscount Scudamore in 1634, when he restored the Abbey as a parish church, thus saving for posterity one of the most beautiful buildings in Herefordshire.

ACTON BEAUCHAMP
St Giles
3m/4km S.E. of Bromyard SO 6750
Isolated medieval church rebuilt in 1819 in classic Georgian style; the late Norman roll-moulded S. doorway was spared.

ALMELEY
St Mary
4m/6km S.E. of Kington SO 3351
Mostly 13th- and 14th-century with a delicate early 16th-century painted ceilure above the rood bedecked with Tudor roses.

ASTON
St Giles
4m/6km S.W. of Ludlow SO 4671
Among hills planted with conifers. Norman nave and part of chancel; fine N. doorway with Agnus Dei on the tympanum.

AYMESTREY
St John the Baptist & St Alkmund
6m/10km N.W. of Leominster SO 4265
12th-century red sandstone church with spacious plastered interior and lovely tall 16th-century rood screen.

BACTON
St Faith
4m/6km N.W. of Pontrilas SO 3732
A pretty place buried in the Golden Valley

where once lived Blanche Parry, maid-of-honour to Queen Elizabeth I. Her alabaster effigy can be seen in the church; the charming inscription ends 'Allwaye wythe maeden quene a maede dyd ende my liffe'.

BIRLEY
St Peter
4m/6km S.W. of Leominster SO 4553
Pretty red sandstone church mottled with yellow lichen but alas! a scraped interior. The chancel arch is enriched with ballflower; the airy S. chapel with three windows is Perpendicular, and there is a lovely Norman font.

BISHOPSTONE
St Lawrence
7m/11km W. of Hereford SO 4143
Pretty country churchyard but no signs of any village. The church has an unusually broad nave with a fine Jacobean roof. Great Transitional stone arches lead to the transepts. Jacobean reredos and pulpit with nice carving. Sentimental monument by Peter Hollins, 1842. The interior of the church is plastered.

BODENHAM
St Michael & All Angels
7m/11km N. of Hereford SO 5351
By the River Lugg. Tower and unfinished 14th-century spire topped by odd pyramidal roof. Lofty Decorated arcades with double-chamfered arches.

BOSBURY
Holy Trinity
4m/6km N. of Ledbury SO 6943
Set in the middle of a black and white village, one of the chief hop-growing centres. A large red sandstone church with late-Norman arcades, a Perpendicular chantry chapel, and two very grand Elizabethan tombs in the chancel. Detached 13th-century tower and a churchyard cross.

BRAMPTON BRYAN
St Barnabas
5m/8km E. of Knighton SO 3772
Setting. Mostly rebuilt in 1655 after the

Civil War. Nave and chancel in one with splendid double hammer-beam roof; 14th-century effigy of a lady.

BREDWARDINE
St Andrew
11m/18km W. of Hereford SO 3344
The church is close to the castle ruins and River Wye. Large Norman church, partly built in tufa with Georgian tower of 1790 in small-coursed stones. Kilvert was rector here from 1877 until he died in 1879.

BRIDGE SOLLARS
St Andrew
6m/10km W. of Hereford SO 4142
Norman church with boldly carved S. doorway and a chancel of *c.* 1300. An 18th-century sundial reads, 'Esteem thy precious time, Which pass so swiftly away, Prepare thou for eternity, And do not make delay.'

BRINSOP
St George
5m/8km N.W. of Hereford SO 4444
Set above an orchard, the church was all built *c.* 1300–50. A somewhat unpromising exterior, but inside is a celebrated Norman tympanum carved with St George and the Dragon by the Herefordshire School, a 14th-century screen and glass, windows in memory of Wordsworth's three women, and a glowing alabaster reredos and glass by Sir Ninian Comper. Everything, new and old, is beautiful.

BROCKHAMPTON-BY-ROSS
2m/3km E. of Bromyard SO 6855
All Saints, in the village
By W. R. Lethaby, 1902; his last and greatest building. A richly symbolic church imbued with primeval sacredness. The central tower and thatched roof, impressive and well-composed, are respectful of the local vernacular as advocated by the Arts and Crafts movement. Astounding interior with soaring concrete roof above massive stone arches. Tapestry by Burne-Jones and glass by Whall.
Brockhampton chapel, in the grounds of Brockhampton Park
Well-set in the grounds of Brockhampton Park. By George Byfield, *c.* 1800, but in a Gothic style. Battlemented gables and small W. tower with tall pinnacles. Interior has a mosaic reredos, stained glass, and early 19th-century monuments.

BROMYARD
St Peter
12m/9km W. of Worcester SO 6554
Cruciform Norman church with 14th-century crossing tower. The arcades were heightened in 1805, but the overall effect is pleasing.

CASTLE FROME
St Michael
6m/10km S. of Bromyard SO 6645
Set in hop country, the church contains a superb 12th-century font of the Herefordshire School, richly carved with the Baptism of Christ and the signs of the four Evangelists. This work compares closely with the font at Eardisley, which might be by the same hand. Also a pair of 17th-century alabaster effigies.

CLODOCK
St Clydog
4m/6km W. of Pontrilas SO 3227
On the edge of the Black Mountains and on the banks of the Monnow, this Norman and later church is broad, aisleless and altogether delightful. Wonderful interior with extensive late 17th-century furnishings: three-decker pulpit, stalls, box pews, communion rail, and some painted texts.

COLWALL
St James the Great
3m/4km N.E. of Ledbury SO 7342
Late Norman S. doorway and a fine Early English S. arcade, the chancel by Woodyer, 1865. Striking medieval arch-braced nave roof with two tiers of windbraces, the lower cusped.

CREDENHILL
St Mary
4m/6km N.W. of Hereford SO 4543
Hillside setting. A mostly 13th- and 14th-century church with two beautiful stained glass figures of prelates in the E. window, *c.* 1310.

CROFT
St Michael and All Angels
5m/8km N.W. of Leominster SO 4465
The pretty little church is set close by the front door of Croft Castle and is quite dwarfed by its huge bulk. It contains the magnificent tomb of Sir Richard Croft, d. 1509, veteran of the Wars of the Roses.

Early 18th-century box pews and a W. gallery.

DILWYN
St Mary the Virgin
6m/10km S.W. of Leominster SO 4154
An attractive village with a spacious church, full of light as only the chancel has stained glass, with lofty 13th-century arcades and a clerestory. The tower of *c.* 1200 has a small later spire which may be 18th-century.

EARDISLEY
St Mary Magdalene
5m/8km S. of Kington SO 3149
The centre of a large parish in which medieval houses abound. The church has a wonderful font carved in *c.* 1150 with the Harrowing of Hell, two men fighting with sword and spear, and a large lion. This font is probably by the same carver as that at Castle Frome.

EASTNOR
St John Baptist
1m/2km E. of Ledbury SO 7337
Mostly by Sir Giles Gilbert Scott, 1852, who designed both church and rectory. The church has a 14th-century tower but, apart from that, it is Scott's 'Middle Pointed' with a Kempe E. window. There are a Crucifixion attributed to Van Dyck, a Venetian altar frontal, and some sculpture by Scheemakers under the tower.

EATON BISHOP
St Michael and All Angels
4m/6km W. of Hereford SO 4439
A spacious church with tall 13th-century arcades and, like some Cotswold churches, a window over the chancel arch. Its chief glory is the early 14th-century glass in the E. window; the finest in the county.

EDVIN LOACH
St Mary the Virgin
2m/3km N. of Bromyard SO 6658
By Sir George Gilbert Scott, 1859; wonderful hill-top site with fine views. This church was built to replace a small early-Norman building of pink herringbone masonry and white tufa quoins, the ruins of which can be seen nearby. Scott's church is modest but well-contrived with a polygonal apse, W. tower, and broach spire. The tower is embraced by the nave and is supported inside on two fat columns with foliate capitals. Good roofs, timber arch to chancel, fine fittings, and Hardman glass.

EDWYN RALPH
St Michael
2m/3km N. of Bromyard SO 6457
Small and restored 12th-century church with primitive S. doorway and one small chancel window. There are two good tomb recesses of *c.* 1300, the fine effigies from which now repose under the tower.

EYE
St Peter & St Paul
3m/4km N. of Leominster SO 4963
Largely 13th-century church with lovely early 14th-century timber N. porch rejoicing in traceried bargeboards and a sandstone tower rebuilt in 1874 by Chick.

FOWNHOPE
St Mary
6m/10km S.E. of Hereford SO 5834
Set in the village street in a pleasant churchyard. A large Transitional church with Norman central tower, later spire and a delightful Herefordshire School tympanum of *c.* 1150. This depicts the Virgin and Child with decorative trails inhabited by a bird and a fierce lion.

FOY
St Mary
3m/4km N. of Ross-on-Wye SO 5928
Setting near old stone former vicarage. A mostly 14th-century church with a Perpendicular E. window made according to the will of John Abrahall, d. 1640. This window retains its original glass, and there are good 17th-century Abrahall monuments.

GARWAY
St Michael
5m/8km S.E. of Pontrilas SO 4522
A wonderful Norman church, associated with the Knights Templar, on the hill-slopes above the Monnow. The chancel arch has three orders of richly carved chevrons carried on shafts with water-leaf capitals. The 13th-century detached tower was joined to the church by a corridor in the 17th century. To the S. is the Templars' fine circular stone dovecote of 1326; there are nesting spaces for 666 birds.

GOODRICH
St Giles

4m/6km S.W. of Ross-on-Wye SO 5719
Despite being near to the main trunk road, Goodrich has an air of wild remoteness. Large 13th-century church with Decorated W. tower and broach spire; some 15th-century glass in the N. aisle, with shield-bearing angels.

HENTLAND
St Dubricius

3m/4km W. of Ross-on-Wye SO 5525
Extensively restored by Seddon in 1853, but a late 13th-century N. arcade and a broad nave with impressive scissor-beam roof continuing into the chancel.

HEREFORD
SO 5139

All Saints, Irongate

Mostly late 13th- or early 14th-century, with a spacious interior entered directly from the street like a real city church. It has a noble 14th-century tower and spire, a chained library, and fine 14th-century choir-stalls.

St Peter, St Peter's Square

Despite a thoroughgoing restoration by Nicholson in 1880–5, this church retains some good early fabric and fittings. Late 12th-century chancel and substantial late 13th-century tower with recessed spire. Arcades of *c.* 1300 with lofty quatrefoil shafts and double-chamfered arches. Restrained 15th-century stalls, a carved Royal Arms of William III, and some late glass by Kempe & Co.

HOARWITHY
St Catherine

5m/8km N. of Ross-on-Wye SO 5429
Important work by J. P. Seddon, 1874–1903. Originally a brick church of 1843, but Seddon transformed it with Italian Romanesque windows, a campanile, and half-apses at the E. end. Inside are Byzantine capitals, a superb gold mosaic of Christ Pantocrator, and rich fittings of marble, lapis lazuli, and tesserae; both Italian and local craftsmen were employed.

HOLME LACY
St Cuthbert

4m/6km S.E. of Hereford SO 5535
14th-century arcade divides nave from equally broad aisle, both with 17th-century plaster tunnel-vaults. Good collection of 17th–18th-century Scudamore monuments.

HOLMER
St Bartholomew

N. suburb of Hereford SO 5042
Large 12th-century church with lancet windows having concave splays. Detached tower with attractive 16th-century timber-framed belfry; chancel with hammer-beam roof of *c.* 1500.

HOW CAPLE
St Mary

4m/6km N. of Ross-on-Wye SO 6030
Church and Court set in a beautifully wooded slope in a loop of the Wye. Church contains a wooden screen supporting the arms of William III and a pulpit with red-lined canopy; also much fine 20th-century woodwork.

KILPECK
St Mary & St David

4m/6km N.E. of Pontrilas SO 4430
Apart from a corner of the nave which is Saxon, some medieval windows and a bellcote restored in the 19th century, it all dates from the third quarter of the 12th century. This is one of the most celebrated examples of the rich late-Romanesque style in England, and it marks the apogee of the Herefordshire School. The S. doorway has a Tree of Life tympanum and carvings of Welsh warriors in Phrygian caps. There is an exceptionally varied carved corbel table, and the chancel arch has draped and nimbused Apostles.

KING'S CAPLE
St John the Baptist

4m/6km N.W. of Ross-on-Wye SO 5628
Decorated W. tower and recessed spire; Jacobean pulpit, stalls and box pews; monuments by Flaxman and Westmacott.

KINGSLAND
St Michael and All Angels

4m/6km N.W. of Leominster SO 4461
Quite a large church, all built unusually *c.* 1300. Tall nave arcades with double-chamfered arches, a clerestory and king-post roof which is probably original; 15th-century timber S. porch and a chantry chapel. Reredos by Frank Brangwyn.

KINNERSLEY
St James
2m/3km N.E. of Willersley SO 3449
Stands near the imposing Elizabethan castle. A lovely 14th-century church with saddle-backed N.W. tower. Well-executed chancel and nave decoration by the Rector, Rev. Andrews, to designs by Bodley.

LEDBURY
St Michael and All Angels
12m/19km E. of Hereford SO 7137
Church commands attractive market town. Some Norman work, but mostly early 14th-century with lavish use of ballflowers. Early 13th-century detached tower with Georgian spire and 16th-century stalls with misericords. Good collection of monuments with works by Flaxman and Westmacott; stained glass by Kempe and others.

LEOMINSTER
St Peter & St Paul
12m/19km N. of Hereford SO 4959
Built of local sandstone, it has a large tower at the W. end with a marvellous 12th-century carved doorway. There are three aisles or naves; to the N. is the old monastic church with fine Norman arches, in the centre is the 13th-century parish church, and to the S. is a 14th-century aisle with superb Decorated windows ornamented with a profusion of ballflowers both inside and out.

LLANVEYNOE
St Beuno & St Peter
6m/10km N.W. of Pontrilas SO 3031
Small church in a beautiful hillside setting. Inside is a delightfully crude 10th-century carved panel of the Crucifixion.

MADLEY
Nativity of the Blessed Virgin Mary
6m/10km W. of Hereford SO 4138
The large, partly black and white village has a cross retaining the original shaft. A superb large sandstone church, a pilgrimage place in the Middle Ages, built in the 13th and 14th centuries and structurally unaltered. The long arcaded nave and the apsidal chancel with a wealth of 14th-century glass in the E. window are rare and beautiful.

MARDEN
St Mary the Virgin
4m/6km N. of Hereford SO 5147
Setting by the River Lugg. Nave and aisles

rebuilt by Nicholson in 1858, but the early 14th-century polygonal apse was fortunately spared. Fine ashlar tower and spire unusually placed on the N. aisle.

MATHON
St John the Baptist
3m/4km W. of Great Malvern SO 7345
Norman origins; good medieval W. tower, 14th-century tie-beam roof with cusping; late-medieval timber S. porch; Jacobean pulpit.

MICHAELCHURCH ESCLEY
St Michael and All Angels
7m/11km N.W. of Pontrilas SO 3134
Mostly early 16th-century with a W. tower of 1897. Inside are an open wagon roof and a very large wall-painting of Christ of the Trades.

MOCCAS
St Michael and All Angels
10m/16km W. of Hereford SO 3542
Set in the park of the house built to the designs of Robert Adam, Moccas Court, stands an excellent example of a Norman church with rounded apse. Most lovingly restored by G. G. Scott Jnr, it was built of calcareous tufa in the second quarter of the 12th century. There are two carved Norman doorways and some 14th-century glass.

MONKLAND
All Saints
3m/4km W. of Leominster SO 4557
Chancel and nave were rebuilt by G. E. Street in 1856, and the spire added to the 13th-century tower; all for the Rev. Sir Henry Baker, compiler of *Hymns A. & M.*

MONNINGTON-ON-WYE
St Mary
9m/15km W. of Hereford SO 3743
Set in lush water meadows by the Wye, a Gothic Survival church of 1679, with a 15th-century tower. The church is a period piece with delightful oak benches, pulpit, and a Royal Arms of Charles II. The timber-framed lych gate is of the same date.

MUCH COWARNE
St Mary the Virgin
5m/8km S.W. of Bromyard SO 6247
Set on top of a hill in undulating hop country, the church has a tall, graceful Early English arcade between nave and S. aisle, in which

are the early 17th-century effigies of
Edmund Fox and his wife lying on an altar
tomb of fine design. The interior is light
and beautiful.

MUCH MARCLE
St Bartholomew
7m/11km N.E. of Ross-on-Wye SO 6532
The church with its 13th-century nave, clerestory, central tower and very long chancel
has some fine monuments including a lovely
mid-14th-century woman, a late 14th-
century couple, and a wooden yeoman.

PEMBRIDGE
St Mary the Virgin
6m/10km E. of Kington SO 3958
Set in a compact village of old timber-framed
houses, this church is a fine example of the
early Decorated style. But the most celebrated thing here is the remarkable detached
14th-century bell-house of Swedish type,
the inside of which resembles a dark forest
of ancient timbers.

PETERCHURCH
St Peter
8m/12km N.W. of Pontrilas SO 3438
A well-preserved large Norman church with
nave, double chancel and apse, all linked by
tall, plain arches. The austere interior is
enhanced by the blacksmith-made light-
fittings, though the walls are scraped and
badly pointed.

PIXLEY
St Andrew
3m/4km W. of Ledbury SO 6638
Farmyard setting. A small 13th-century
church, the nave and chancel in one. There
is a good roof and a 14th-century screen.

PUTLEY
(dedication unknown)
4m/6km W. of Ledbury SO 6437
A humble medieval church imaginatively restored by Thomas Blashill in 1875; exotic
Victorian reredos of alabaster and mosaic;
elaborately carved and canopied stalls;
churchyard cross.

RICHARD'S CASTLE
St Bartholomew
3m/4km S. of Ludlow SO 4969
Set on the hill near the earthworks of a
Norman castle and the woods haunted by
Milton's Comus, the detached early 14th-

century tower is a splendid foil to the great
bulk of the church. Inside, there are 17th-
century box pews and in the N. chapel a
family pew and some 14th-century glass.
The E. window has the most lovely flowing
tracery.

ROSS-ON-WYE
St Mary the Virgin
9m/15km N.E. of Monmouth SO 5924
Delightful setting above the River Wye;
13th- and 14th-century church, the nave
remodelled in 1743. Early 14th-century W.
tower with tall recessed spire, 15th-century
glass in the E. window, and numerous
16th–18th-century monuments.

ROWLESTONE
St Peter
1m/2km W. of Pontrilas SO 3727
On the hills between the Monnow River and
Dulas brook, a 12th-century church with
finely carved S. doorway, tympanum, and
chancel arch. The capitals of the openings
are carved with birds and intertwining foliage
of great character. Late 15th-century decorated candle-brackets in the chancel.

ST MARGARET'S
St Margaret
5m/8km N.W. of Pontrilas SO 3533
Set in lonely fields above the Golden Valley,
in lovely countryside, this small church with
plastered walls contains an exquisitely carved
rood screen and loft of *c.* 1520, the finest
in Herefordshire.

SARNESFIELD
St Mary
11m/18km N.W. of Hereford SO 3750
A very pretty grey-stone 12th-century
church with limewashed interior, elegant
candelabra, and wall monuments. Churchyard tomb of John Abel, King's Carpenter,
1577–1674.

SELLACK
St Tysilio
3m/4km N.W. of Ross-on-Wye SO 5627
Norman and later church with Decorated W.
tower and fine broach spire. Good Jacobean
gallery, pulpit and communion rails, and
in the E. window a complete stained glass
composition of 1630.

SHOBDON
St John the Evangelist
6m/10km W. of Leominster SO 4062
Celebrated Georgian Gothic Revival church of 1752–6, the work of The Hon. Richard Bateman of Shobdon Court, friend of Horace Walpole. Whimsical Rococo-Gothic interior with enormous pews painted white and two tiny transepts containing the family and servants' pews. The whole effect is extremely pretty and is now much admired, though in the past antiquarians have suffered anguish because its Romanesque predecessor was despoiled; the weather-beaten remains of its carved arches are in a field close by.

STRETFORD
St Cosmas & St Damian
4m/6km S.W. of Leominster SO 4455
Almost as broad as it is long, with a 13th-century arcade in the middle dividing the chapel and aisle from chancel and nave. The whole is covered by a single roof constructed in about 1540. Two early 16th-century screens go right across the church, and there is a Jacobean pulpit in the middle. There are two sets of 14th-century effigies.
R.C.F.

STRETTON SUGWAS
St Mary Magdalene
4m/6km N.W. of Hereford SO 4642
The church was rebuilt in 1880 with timber-framed N. tower, nave and chancel. It contains a superb tympanum of *c.* 1150 decorated with Samson fighting the Lion and a dignified incised 15th-century monument with portraits of the deceased couple.

TYBERTON
St Mary
8m/12km W. of Hereford SO 3839
Rebuilt in 1720, it retains a late-Norman doorway. Built of brick with a pretty tower surmounted by a stone cornice, pediments and urns, the exterior has been spoiled by ugly windows of 1879. Inside, however, the magnificent carved panels in the apse were designed by John Wood in 1728 and bear the Symbols of the Passion in a spirit of mysticism and communion most uncommon for the period. The other furnishings are contemporary, and there are monuments to the Brydges family.

VOWCHURCH
St Bartholomew
6m/10km N.W. of Pontrilas SO 3636
Largely 14th-century fabric with a timber bellcote of *c.* 1522. The roof, supported on oak posts, was reconstructed as part of a major re-ordering of the church *c.* 1613. The rustic screen, stalls and communion rail are all 17th-century.

WELSH NEWTON
St Mary the Blessed Virgin
3m/4km N. of Monmouth SO 4918
13th-century nave and chancel in one, divided later by a rare Decorated stone rood screen enriched with octagonal shafts, moulded arches and ballflowers. In the churchyard the melancholy tomb slab of John Kemble, Catholic priest, executed in 1679.

WEOBLEY
St Peter & St Paul
10m/16km N.W. of Hereford SO 4051
Church in an attractive village, full of timber-framed houses, with tall 14th-century tower and lofty steeple. Good monuments and some 15th-century glass.

WIGMORE
St James the Apostle
8m/12km N.W. of Leominster SO 4169
Saxo-Norman nave evidenced by herring-bone masonry in the N. wall and a blocked window in the S. Otherwise mostly Decorated; restored by Bodley in 1864.

YARPOLE
St Leonard
4m/6km N.W. of Leominster SO 4764
Detached bell-tower with pyramidal roof, weatherboarded bell-stage, quatrefoils and a spire. Inside are free-standing posts with scissor bracing, and the door has long iron hinges; it could all be as early as 1300.

YAZOR
St Mary
8m/12km N.W. of Hereford SO 4046
An estate church of 1843 by George Rowe. Built in the Early English style with polygonal apse which is rich and colourful within. Good Victorian stained glass in the chancel and apse windows by Warrington.

Hertfordshire

Introduction

At first sight Hertfordshire has little to offer in the way of churches: for a number of reasons there are, with the exception of Hemel Hempstead, no fabrics of the first rank in the county. Indeed, like the landscape in which they are set, these churches are distinguished rather for their seemliness and moderation than for more dramatic qualities.

Physically, Hertfordshire is a county of undulating chalkland with some deposits of glacial clay in the river valleys of the south and east. The only strongly marked features are the Chiltern Hills; entering the county in the south-east above Tring, they form a diagonal ridge across to the north-east, dying away beyond Royston into the Essex uplands. Because of the geological formation there is, except for flint rubble, no building stone, and the cost of transporting stone precluded its use, except for piers, tombs, window tracery and dressings. Where stone was used it was generally Totternhoe or other clunches from the lower and middle chalk, and because of their poor weathering qualities, there is very little original stonework to be seen externally. To this replacement is due a certain hardness in the appearance of many of the old churches.

Formerly the county was heavily wooded, large areas being covered by the Chiltern, Middlesex and Essex forests. This had more effect on secular than ecclesiastical work, but there are some good roofs and screens, and timberwork found in porches.

Historically and socially, Hertfordshire suffered from three things: first, the Abbey of St Albans; secondly, good roads which divided the county; and thirdly, the lack of any strong central influence.

It might have been expected that St Albans Abbey – one of the wealthiest in the country – would have been the dominant source of architecural influence in the area. This, however, was not the case: due to the constant mismanagement of its finances and estates the Abbey was kept in a state of chronic insolvency, and the county in a state of incessant agrarian disturbances. No abbot was ever able to embark on any very vigorous building programme which might have influenced local masons.

The second and third factors are, to a large extent, interrelated. Except for the ancient Icknield Way, the main roads of the Middle Ages, which followed the lines of the older Roman roads – Watling St, Ermine St, Stone St, Akeman St, and the later Great North Road – all ran roughly north–

south. Even today cross-country journeys are awkward and inconvenient; in the Middle Ages they must have been almost out of the question. The result has been that the county has developed architecturally in strips. The best buildings are to be found in the long one-street towns and villages. Family traits are found in groups of churches along one road which are not found in churches along the others. This has led to comparatively unspoilt areas between the main traffic lanes; once away from these roads the county retains much of its rural character unchanged.

Admittedly there are bad patches, which are getting worse: motorways have blighted large areas, and the road from London out through Waltham Cross is an eyesore. New Towns are spreading; and Watford has been raped by the 20th century – a fact of which the Corporation appears inordinately proud. On the whole, however, Hertfordshire has been luckier than might have been expected from its proximity to London.

Today few country churches are so convincingly the 'village church' as those of Hertfordshire. Fabrics are generally in good repair; and churchyards, by present-day standards, not ill-kept. The most striking feature is generally the tower, sturdy and battlemented, usually with a taller stair-turret and crowned with the ubiquitous spirelet, known locally as a 'snuffer' or 'spike'.

Most churches in the county can show something of interest – often in the shape of magnificent monuments of the 16th, 17th and 18th centuries. The many country houses – especially those of retired London merchants – meant a number of wealthy, if not always distinguished, dead, whose taste for tombs of a modest piety has led to many fine and not a few extraordinary examples of funereal sculpture.

Woodwork, too, is widespread and interesting, and often – as at Hitchin – of a very high standard. Of pre-Reformation figure-carving there is little, and of old glass even less. Brasses are to be found in most churches.

The Victorians were, on the whole, kind to Hertfordshire. Restorations, if lacking in character, are seldom out of period or locality, and there is a merciful absence of what was piously believed to be 13th-century detailing from the Nene Valley. Most of the great names of the period are represented, but seldom in a manner to cause comment.

Of the four or five Gothic Revival churches of merit, one is outside the scope of this inquiry: as, however, it is the finest in the county, the Roman Catholic Church of the Holy Rood at Watford – by Bentley – it should not be missed. And, of course, the seeker after curiosities is bound to visit St Albans for the work of Lord Grimthorpe. After all, there is nothing like it anywhere else.

H.G.S.

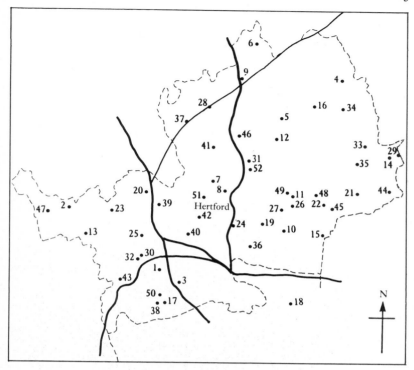

1 Abbots Langley	19 Essendon	36 North Mimms
2 Aldbury	20 Flamstead	37 Offley
3 Aldenham	21 Gilston	38 Oxhey Chapel
4 Anstey	22 Great Amwell	39 Redbourn
5 Ardeley	23 Great Gaddesden	40 St Albans
6 Ashwell	24 Hatfield	41 St Paul's Walden
7 Ayot St Lawrence	25 Hemel Hempstead	42 Sandridge
8 Ayot St Peter	26 Hertford	43 Sarratt
9 Baldock	27 Hertingfordbury	44 Sawbridgeworth
10 Bayford	28 Hitchin	45 Stanstead Abbots
11 Bengeo	29 Hockerill	46 Stevenage
12 Benington	30 King's Langley	47 Tring
13 Berkhamsted	31 Knebworth	48 Ware
14 Bishop's Stortford	32 Langleybury	49 Waterford
15 Broxbourne	33 Little Hadham	50 Watford
16 Buntingford	34 Little Hormead	51 Wheathampstead
17 Bushey	35 Much Hadham	52 Woolmer Green
18 Chipping Barnet		

Selected List of Churches

ABBOTS LANGLEY
St Lawrence
3m/4km N. of Watford TL 0902
Norman nave arcades and Decorated S. chancel chapel; frescoes in chancel; 18th-century Raymond monuments, one by Scheemakers.

ALDBURY
St John the Baptist
3m/4km N.W. of Berkhamsted SP 9612
Pretty village green. Long, low church, mainly 14th-century, with slender W. tower. Fine 15th-century memorial chapel with stone screen; 16th-century wooden lectern.

ALDENHAM
St John the Baptist
2m/3km N.E. of Watford TQ 1398
Long flint church, 12th–15th-century; 13th-century font; 14th–15th-century Crowmer tombs and a good set of brasses.

ANSTEY
St George
4m/6km N.E. of Buntingford TL 4033
A strangely impressive building which appears larger at first sight than it actually is. Lower stages of the central tower, *c.* 1200, show the transition from Romanesque to Gothic. The chancel is a roomy 13th-century design with 16th-century stalls and misericords and unusual sedilia and piscina. The transepts with squints to chancel are 13th-century. The nave is of 14th-century design with clerestory and a 15th-century roof. A pleasant surprise to find such a church which has escaped restoration. In the churchyard is the 15th-century lych gate.

ARDELEY
St Lawrence
5m/8km E. of Stevenage TL 3027
Mainly Perpendicular with Early English chancel. Largely restored by F. C. Eden in the 1920s; he also designed the nearby village hall and cottages, forming a stylish group.

ASHWELL
St Mary the Virgin
4m/6km N.E. of Baldock TL 2639
This magnificent 14th-century church belongs to East Anglia. Both its design and the clarity of light, due to a lack of stained glass, remove Ashwell in feeling from the Home Counties. The W. tower is remarkable for its height, its buttresses, the use of clunch as a facing material, and its extremely elegant timber and lead spirelet. The interior shows a steady development from E. to W., the large aisleless chancel having been begun *c.* 1340, and the nave being finished *c.* 1380. The narrow W. bay of the nave was formed between the W. buttresses of the tower, which were decorated with blind full-height arches. There are 15th-century sedilia, 15th-century screens in the aisles, and a 17th-century pulpit and communion table. In the tower are two interesting graffiti. The village is in every way worthy of it.

AYOT ST LAWRENCE
St Lawrence
2m/3km W. of Welwyn TL 1916
The Greek temple with flanking pavilions and linking screens, designed 1778–9 by Nicholas Revett to terminate a view in the park where the old church was left to be a Gothic ruin. It is an exercise in the application of Greek detail to a Palladian composition. Internally the Classicism is of Rome and not of Greece: a Rome, however, which has been tempered by the unexceptionable Anglicanism of the 18th century. The rectangular nave is entered from the vestibule through a columned screen. The nave has a coffered ceiling and is flanked by two deep arched recesses, and the E. end is a coffered apse.

AYOT ST PETER
St Peter
1m/2km S.W. of Welwyn TL 2115
By J. P. Seddon, 1874–5. Impressive and original design in red, blue and white brick with apse, tall flanking tower and spire. The interior reflects early enthusiasm for the Arts and Crafts movement. Remarkably complete

set of furnishings together with painted roof panels, grey ceramic chancel arch, mosaic decorated font, and some glass by Seddon himself.

BALDOCK
St Mary the Virgin
6m/10km N. of Stevenage TL 2433
Mainly early 14th-century, with spacious interior, good arcades and Perpendicular screens and roofs. Conservatively restored by W. Butterfield.

BAYFORD
St Mary
3m/4km S. of Hertford TL 3108
By Henry Woodyer, 1870–1. Small stone and brick church in the Early English style. Nave and chancel only, but with stylish fleche and ingenious sweeping roof over the flanking vestries. Inside is a rood screen, decorations by Heaton, Butler & Bayne, and glass by Clayton & Bell.

BENGEO
St Leonard
N. district of Hertford TL 3213
Unspoilt survival of a 12th-century and later church. Apsidal Norman chancel, 13th-century wall-paintings and 14th-century tiles in the sanctuary.

BENINGTON
St Peter
4m/6km E. of Stevenage TL 2923
Beautiful village green. Simple 13th–15th-century church with lovely Decorated N. chantry chapel containing a fine contemporary tomb.

BERKHAMSTED
St Peter
25m/40km N.W. of London SP 9907
Large and handsome cruciform church, dark inside despite clerestory. Restored by Butterfield rather absent-mindedly, 1871. Brasses.

BISHOP'S STORTFORD
St Michael
8m/12km N. of Harlow TL 4821
Externally this large 15th-century church shows an amusing contrast between the solidity of the original work and the flimsiness of the upper stages of the tower and spire, which were added in 1812. It dominates the town in distant views. The roofs are original

– that of the nave having finely traceried spandrels, and resting on stone corbels carved as Apostles and shield-bearing angels. In the aisles a more secular note is struck, and the corbels include a cook, a woodman, and a gardener. The label-stops of the nave arcade still bear their original head carvings. The greater part of the richly carved rood screen and the original choirstalls survive with carved misericords and traceried backs.

BROXBOURNE
St Augustine
S. suburb of Hoddesdon TL 3707
Attractively set on a bank of the River Lea, flint-walled except for ashlar-faced N. chapel and vestry of 1522; tiled and leaded roofs largely 15th-century. Inside, the nave and chancel are of six bays without a break and with original roofs. The altar tomb in the chancel of Sir John Say, d. 1474, and his wife has brasses and much original colour. Other and later Say tombs in chancel, among them the 16th-century tomb of Sir William Say. There are a number of brasses and monuments, and the S. door is an exuberant piece of work of c. 1640 with pilasters and segmental pediment.

BUNTINGFORD
St Peter
10m/16km N. of Ware TL 3629
Neat brick church on Greek Cross plan, 1614–26. Unfortunately restored and apse added, 1899. An attractive neighbour to Ward's Hospital, 1684.

BUSHEY
St James
3m/4km S.E. of Watford TQ 1395
Good 19th-century enlargement by Scott; 15th-century nave roof, 13th-century chancel, unusual tympanum with Royal Arms of Queen Anne, and a 17th-century pulpit.

CHIPPING BARNET
St John Baptist
11m/18km N. of Charing Cross, now in Greater London TQ 2496
A vigorous Butterfield rebuilding of 1875; 17th-century Ravenscroft monuments.

ESSENDON
St Mary the Virgin
3m/4km E. of Hatfield TL 2708
By W. White, 1883; E. end rebuilt by C. J.

Blomfield in 1917. We visit not for the church, frankly, but for its treasured Wedgwood font of 1778. Elegantly formed of the celebrated black basalt ware, speciality of the firm, the dull lustre and perfect opacity resemble that of jet. There is another at Cardington, Beds.

FLAMSTEAD
St Leonard

5m/8km N. of Hemel Hempstead TL 0714
13th-century nave with stiff-leaf capitals and a good 15th-century screen. Best parochial wall-paintings in the county: 13th–15th-century with Apostles, St Christopher, the Passion, and bits of a Doom. Fine monuments by William Stanton and John Flaxman.

GILSTON
St Mary

3m/4km W. of Sawbridgeworth TL 4413
Essentially 13th-century, including the remarkable rood screen; a most welcome survival with trefoil arches and stylized flowers in the spandrels. Fine 17th-century Gore monuments.

GREAT AMWELL
St John the Baptist

1m/2km S.E. of Ware TL 3612
Picturesque setting above a water garden created in 1800 to celebrate Sir Hugh Myddelton, 17th-century originator of the New River. A country church as attractive as its setting with Norman apsidal chancel and 15th-century tower. In the churchyard are good Georgian monuments including that to Robert Mylne, architect, creator of the water garden.

GREAT GADDESDEN
St John Baptist

3m/4km N.E. of Berkhamsted TL 0211
A comparatively unspoilt building, but its development is obscure. Probably a 12th-century fabric enlarged in succeeding centuries. S. nave arcade shows stiff-leaf capitals similar to Flamstead and Offley; 15th-century clerestory and roof. The N. chapel, a particularly mean little building of 1730, was built to house the remains of the Halseys of Gaddesden Place, to whose memory there are at least 22 monuments in the church. As most of them are white marble it is not surprising that it seems a chilly little place.

HATFIELD
St Etheldreda

TL 2308
To the Glory of God and the House of Cecil. Handsome W. tower. The enormous unaisled nave is a 19th-century rebuilding on the original lines. Transepts are unusual in possessing W. chapels. Transepts and chancel are 13th-century, S. chapel 14th-century with good arcades. N. chapel, 1618, separated from chancel by arcade carried on Tuscan columns. Monument to Robert Cecil, 1st Earl of Salisbury; effigy on slab carried by four kneeling Virtues with cadaver below, by Maximilian Colt, *c.* 1612. Very chaste. The same cannot be said of the scheme of decorations perpetrated by the 3rd Marquis in 1871. Lovely 18th-century iron screen from Amiens. Excellent modern fittings.

HEMEL HEMPSTEAD
St Mary

7m/11km N.W. of Watford TL 0507
This large 12th-century town church with central tower and 14th-century timber spire is the finest in the county. It stands at the end of the old town farthest removed from New Town development. Begun *c.* 1140 and about 40 years in the building, it is, apart from the porches, vestries and spire, all of the one period. The nave of six bays with aisles is unusual in possessing a clerestory, and the chancel has a rare 12th-century rib vault. Chancel vivaciously decorated by Bodley in 1888, but since whitewashed; glass by Clayton & Bell and Minton tiles are all that remain.

HERTFORD
All Saints

TL 3212
By Paley, Austin & Paley of Lancaster, 1893–5; the tower completed in 1905. Grand and unexpected north-country Perpendicular church in open setting. Impressive Johannine E. window by Kempe, 1900.

HERTINGFORDBURY
St Mary

1m/2km W. of Hertford TL 3012
13th-century chancel, but all much put about in 1890; bench-ends of incredible vulgarity by Joseph Mayer of Oberammergau. Much redeemed by 18th-century Cowper

monuments, including one of 1752 by Roubiliac.

HITCHIN

8m/12km N.E. of Luton TL 1829
Holy Saviour, Radcliffe Road
By William Butterfield, 1863–5; aisles added in 1880s. Assured essay in the Early English style; red brick enlivened by stone and blue-brick dressings. Restrained exterior has clerestory and W. bellcote. Inside, the impact of Butterfield's polychromy was lessened by Martin Travers's whitewashing of the chancel, compensating for more stained glass than originally intended. Scissor-beam roof, delicate iron screen, and good glass by Hardman in the N. aisle.
St, Mary, market place
The size of the church and the richness of its surviving fittings show that late-medieval Hitchin was a town of some wealth; the early street plan and a number of good old buildings survive. The church is a most pleasantly textured building, showing something of every material; 12th–13th-century W. tower and spectacular 15th-century vaulted S. porch of two storeys. It bears the arms of the Staple of Calais and was probably paid for by Nicholas Mattock, merchant. Good 14th–15th-century roofs, fine set of traceried Perpendicular screens, figured font and panelled pulpit; the woodwork is without equal in the county.

HOCKERILL

All Saints
Stanstead Road, E. district of Bishop's Stortford TL 4920
By S. E. Dykes Bower, 1937; an interesting design in a commanding position above the town. Built of pale rock-faced stone with contrasting dark-tiled roofs. Prominent square tower with hipped roof and elongated lancets. Large E. rose window. Interior has tall circular piers, an altar with four giant Corinthian columns, and a good deal of pale oak furnishing.

KING'S LANGLEY

All Saints
3m/4km S. of Hemel Hempstead TL 0702
Mainly 15th-century. Very fine late 14th-century alabaster tomb of Edmund of Langley with much heraldry; also an epitaph plaque of 1793 by Bonomi.

KNEBWORTH

St Mary & St Thomas of Canterbury
3m/4km S. of Stevenage TL 2520
In the grounds of Knebworth House. Largely 15th-century, including the benches. N. chapel of *c.* 1705 has excellent series of Lytton monuments; in the chancel a neat bust in the Roman manner to Judith Strode, d. 1662.

LANGLEYBURY

St Paul
1m/2km S. of King's Langley TL 0801
By Henry Woodyer, 1863–4. Flint and stone exterior of unpromising aspect, but inside a wondrous chancel arch, apogee of Victorian angelic piety; this and much other fine carving by Thomas Earp. Woodyer's own fittings survive, including the choice serpentine font and its redoubtable cover.

LITTLE HADHAM

St Cecilia
3m/4km W. of Bishop's Stortford TL 4322
Earliest known Anglican T-plan church, the N. transept added in the late 16th century. Chancel Victorianized, but the nave fittings are wholly 17th-century, including box pews and a three-decker pulpit. Late-medieval timber S. porch.

LITTLE HORMEAD

St Mary
3m/4km E. of Buntingford TL 4029
Small, largely Norman church set on high ground. Remarkable display of lavish 12th-century ironwork on N. door with quatrefoils, scrolls and trails. Royal Arms of 1660 over the chancel arch.

MUCH HADHAM

St Andrew
4m/6km W. of Bishop's Stortford TL 4219
Originally a 12th-century church, rebuilding started with the chancel, *c.* 1220, S. aisle, *c.* 1250, N. aisle, *c.* 1300, and culminated with the tower of *c.* 1380. In the 15th century the clerestory, roofs, S. porch and many windows were renewed. The roofs are very good and have hardly been touched since they were first built. The screen and chancel stalls are also 15th-century, and there is a sprinkling of brasses.

NORTH MIMMS

St Mary (St Michael)
3m/4km S. of Hatfield TL 2204
Parkland setting. Almost all 14th-century

with spacious interior and much Victorian oak. Two good brasses; a fine, probably Flemish, priest's brass of *c.* 1360 and a 15th-century knight.

OFFLEY
St Mary Magdalene
3m/4km S.W. of Hitchin TL 1427
Early 13th-century nave arcades with stiff-leaf capitals, 15th-century benches, and a good Decorated font. But the surprise is the delectable chancel of *c.* 1777; Portland stone without and inside a sumptuous stucco bald-acchino over the E. window. On the S. wall is the delightful monument by Nollekens to Sir Thomas Salisbury, creator of the chancel. Gothic brick W. tower of 1800.

OXHEY CHAPEL
(dedication unknown)
S.E. district of Watford TQ 1295
Buried in building estates, a chapel of 1616 in the former grounds of Oxhey Place. Simple rectangular structure with Perpendicular windows retaining 17th-century W. door, font, and reredos with twisted columns. Wall-monument to James Altham, the founder.
R.C.F.

REDBOURN
St Mary
4m/6km N.W. of St Albans TL 1012
Attractive village setting. Norman and 14th–15th-century. Well-preserved rood screen of 1478; early 18th-century font and monuments in the chancel.

ST ALBANS
TL 1012
St Michael, St Michael's Street
Saxon nave has single-splayed windows of Roman brick, Norman arcades, and Early English clerestory. Seated marble effigy of Sir Francis Bacon, d. 1626.
St Stephen, Watling Street
Largely 15th-century, but the late-Saxon nave has Roman brick dressings. Impressive 16th-century brass eagle lectern, apparently looted from Holyrood.

ST PAUL'S WALDEN
All Saints
3m/4km W. of Stevenage TL 1922
Outside, the usual late-Decorated and Perpendicular, but within an exuberantly Classical chancel and screen of 1727, all

tricked out in the Baroque taste by Edward Gilbert, the local squire.

SANDRIDGE
St Leonard
3m/4km N.E. of St Albans TL 1710
Norman and later church, heavily restored in 1886. Chancel arch of Roman bricks with a fine late 14th-century pierced stone screen.

SARRATT
Holy Cross
3m/4km N. of Rickmansworth TQ 0499
Small 12th-century cruciform church of flint, altered in the 13th–14th centuries. Faded wall-paintings, 17th-century pulpit and a coloured monument of *c.* 1611.

SAWBRIDGEWORTH
St Mary the Great
4m/6km N.E. of Harlow TL 4814
Spacious, principally Decorated church with 15th-century screen and a remarkable assemblage of medieval and later brasses and monuments.

STANSTEAD ABBOTS
St James
3m/4km S.E. of Ware TL 3911 (the old church is not in the village, but 1m/2km out on the road to Roydon)
Mostly late 15th- and 16th-century. Completely unspoilt interior with 18th-century box pews, altar rail, and three-decker pulpit. 15th-century tower and handsome timber S. porch; brick N. chapel of 1577. Some quite good memorials of first half of 19th century.
R.C.F.

STEVENAGE
St Nicholas
TL 2324
Flint church of various dates from 12th century; 15th-century roofs, screens and choir-stalls with carved misericords.

TRING
St Peter & St Paul
5m/8km N.W. of Berkhamsted SP 9211
The distinctive nave piers with attached shafts are actually replicas of the 16th-century originals made during the restoration of 1880–2. Painted chancel ceiling, rood screen and choir-stalls by Bodley. Spectacular monument to Sir William and Lady Gore, 1707.

WARE
St Mary
TL 3514

Very large, very handsome, and externally very much restored. Inside what one can see today dates from the late 14th century and early 15th century. It is unusual that the transepts should be carried to full nave height and endowed with clerestories. The nave arcades are particularly handsome, with the main mouldings running unbroken to the floor. Between the chancel and S. chapel is a handsome fan arch similar to one at Luton. The S. chapel also possesses some fine 17th-century panelling with openwork scrolling and 17th-century communion rails and table. The octagonal font of *c.* 1380 is the most elaborate in the county, with panelled sides in high relief. The carving has considerable vigour, well above the usual 'shop work' standard.

WATERFORD
St Michael
2m/3km N.W. of Hertford TL 3114

By Henry Woodyer, 1871–2. Modest medieval exterior with timber bell-turret and shingled broach spire. But, inside, a display of Victorian ecclesiological fireworks, with brilliant gilded mosaics in the chancel, excellent glass by Morris & Co., and a rich reredos by Powell & Sons.

WATFORD
St Mary
TQ 1096

An oasis of quiet in Hertfordshire's largest, ugliest, and noisiest town. The churchyard has 16th-century almshouses and an 18th-century Free School around it. The church is over-restored outside, but this treatment is not so apparent inside. Basically a large 13th-century church to which clerestory, new arcades and S. chancel chapel were added in the 15th century. Of the 13th century there remains the chancel arch, the arches and responds of the S. arcade, and the beautiful double piscina in the chancel. The woodwork, except for the 15th-century nave roof and the pulpit of 1714, is generally 19th-century, very good of its period, and quite unusual restraint is shown in the design. The pride of St Mary's is the Morison chapel of 1597, separated from the chancel by a Tuscan arcade. The Morison tombs, largely of alabaster, are the work of Nicholas Stone. Both show semi-reclining lifesize figures under rich canopies, with kneeling mourners.

WHEATHAMPSTEAD
St Helen
3m/4km E. of Harpenden TL 1713

Originally a Norman cruciform church, now mostly 13th-century onward. Richly Decorated N. transept, the best work of its date in the county; many monuments.

WOOLMER GREEN
St Michael
2m/3km N.E. of Welwyn TL 2518

By R. Weir Schultz, 1899–1900; an essay in the Arts and Crafts tradition. Effective interior with panelled red-brick walls, wagon roof, tiled chancel, and traceried screen. Good bronze and wooden fittings in the apsidal sanctuary, which is approached up green marble steps.

Huntingdonshire

Introduction

Perhaps because it is small – the third-smallest old county in England – and because its scenery is uneventful, either flat or very gently rolling, and because it has few recognized 'beauty spots', this delightful county has been less able to defend itself than others against the more hideous and cheap manifestations of modern 'progress'.

The Great North Road bisects it from north to south. This and other main roads account for some splendid medieval bridges like those at Huntingdon and St Ives, and Spaldwick, and for several old inns like The George and The Fountain in Huntingdon itself, The Lion and the George and Dragon at Buckden, The Bell at Stilton, The Haycock at Wansford Bridge, and others, some of which have reverted to private houses. But the soulless anonymity and the garish adjuncts of motor traffic have slashed the gentle landscape across and across; aerodromes have made wide scars on it and the deserted huts and blocks of service departments still spot its unlucky face. And, of course, in a county where there is so much sky in the landscape, pylons and poles are particularly intrusive.

Yet it still has much beauty. In the west and south its remote, hilly landscape has many oaks and ash trees. About a century and a half ago the Huntingdonshire elms (*ulmus glabra*) originated here. The churches and cottages in the west and south are of yellowish-grey limestone and approach the excellence of those in neighbouring Northants. From St Neots to St Ives, near the slow windings of the sinuous Ouse, are willowy meadows and villages of reed-thatched cottages where the churches are the only old stone buildings, the stone having been brought here by water in medieval times. The north-west tip of the county is brick-fields with Fletton as their capital, and the north-east is fen: 'When first drained (and much Hunts. fen was drained in the last century) the spongy peat stood some feet above the rivers and channels, but it has so shrunk that a water-course may now be higher than your head. It is a new land, and though the soil is rich, much of it coloured with flowers and vegetables, it has a bleak empty look. The villages are modern and poor . . .' (Andrew Young, *A Prospect of Britain*).

Huntingdonshire has five attractive old towns. St Neots, St Ives, Huntingdon, linked with the old red brick of Godmanchester by a bridge and meadows, and Kimbolton – two parallel streets, one Georgian and the other medieval, with the great Vanbrugh house of the Dukes of Manchester at one end of them. The brick industry is long established in the county, and old red-brick houses make a happy contrast with silvery medieval stone and humbler plaster-walled cottages and inns.

When it is remote, Huntingdon is more remote and countrified than anywhere in England, and there is, to me at any rate, a strong atmosphere in the county of the Civil War. The towns, one feels, stand for Parliament, the villages for the King. Oliver Cromwell was born at Huntingdon, where a chapel spire is higher than the church towers. He has a statue at St Ives and several of his chief supporters came from the county. The 17th-century High Church movement is represented by George Herbert, who rebuilt and refurnished his village church at Leighton Bromswold in 1620, and Nicholas Ferrar, who founded an Anglican religious community, of which Little Gidding church survives as a tender memorial. In the Civil War, Barnabas Oley, Vicar of Great Gransden, smuggled the Cambridge College plate through Huntingdonshire to Charles I at Nottingham.

J.B.

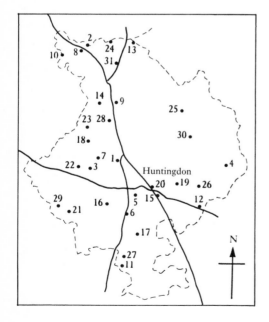

Selected List of Churches

Please note that the Soke of Peterborough is included as a chapter in its own right.

ALCONBURY
St Peter & St Paul

4m/6km N.W. of Huntingdon TL 1875
The village watered by Alconbury Brook running down the long village green, with the church on the northern fringe of a cluster of colourwash-and-tile cottages. The inside of the 13th-century chancel noble and serene, enhanced by an attached arcade along each side, the 15th-century roof marrying well with the older work. Good contrast between the plaster of the chancel and the pebbly walls of the nave, where the plaster was stripped. The tower has one of the many good broach spires of the county.

ALWALTON
St Andrew

4m/6km S.W. of Peterborough TL 1395
Cruciform church with good mixture of medieval styles. Norman S. doorway and N. arcade, 13th-century W. tower, chancel and transepts.

BARHAM
St Giles

7m/11km N.W. of Huntingdon TL 1375
Tiny church, dark and unspoilt inside. A N. aisle built on in 1850 but surprisingly filled, like the rest of the nave, with box pews in the Georgian fashion.

BLUNTISHAM
St Mary the Virgin

7m/11km S. of Chatteris TL 3674
Symmetrical Decorated church with rare polygonal apse, an octagonal Perpendicular font with a Green Man, and a painted screen.

BRAMPTON
St Mary Magdalene

2m/3km W. of Huntingdon TL 2170
Mostly Perpendicular, including the remarkable Gothic Survival W. tower dated 1635. Inside is a Decorated rood screen and stalls with carved misericords.

BUCKDEN
St Mary

4m/6km S.W. of Huntingdon TL 1967
The church has a graceful steeple, overshadowed by the 15th-century brick tower of Buckden Palace nearby. The bulk of the nave in a good sober Perpendicular, and the double-storey S. porch has a workmanlike vault. Inside, the plaster has been scraped away showing the coarse rubble beneath and throwing into prominence the ashlar of a lofty arcade. Some interesting 16th-century panels with Passion scenes have been imported; 15th-century roofs and painted glass.

BUCKWORTH
All Saints

6m/10km N.W. of Huntingdon TL 1476
Handsome late 13th-century tower with lancets and Y-tracery surmounted by lovely broach spire with tall lucarnes. Perpendicular nave roof with prominent bosses.

CHESTERTON
St Michael

5m/8km S.W. of Peterborough TL 1295
The county is short of 18th-century work, but here a countryman's version of a Roman chancel has been added to an unexceptional 13th-century nave; there is also a S. porch with a Gibbsian rusticated door surround. A clever indirect lighting effect was gained by blocking the top of the chancel arch, and displaying a hatchment thereon, so that most of the incongruous E. window is hidden from the congregation in the nave. The hidden light filters through three arches of a charming wooden chancel screen in a Roman Doric order. An impressive Jacobean monument to the Beville family in the N. aisle.

CONINGTON
All Saints

2m/3km S.E. of Stilton TL 1785
House nearby Gothicized to make a picture with the huge W. tower which is rich and

late-Perpendicular, as is the whole fabric. An impressive collection of medieval and later monuments.
R.C.F.

ELTON
All Saints
4m/6km S. of Wansford TL 0993
Lofty Perpendicular W. tower, the low church of *c.* 1300 wrapped around it on three sides. Inside are Morris glass and monuments and in the churchyard two Anglo-Danish interlace crosses.

EYNESBURY
St Mary
S. district of St Neots TL 1859
A haphazard assimilation of Norman and Pointed work, a massive Gothic Survival tower of 1687, and a Victorian reshaping of the chancel to give features thought necessary by the Ecclesiologists. This last change sacrificed an old E. window over the chancel arch, making the E. end unnecessarily dark. The N. aisle has a series of playfully carved benches from the 1500s, and there is a pretty late 17th-century pulpit.

FENSTANTON
St Peter & St Paul
5m/8km S.E. of Huntingdon TL 3168
Very good Decorated chancel with huge seven-light reticulated E. window. Otherwise mostly Perpendicular with a monument to Capability Brown, d. 1783, who was Lord of the Manor.

FLETTON
St Margaret
S. district of Peterborough TL 1997
This has a good share of Norman work, not over-plentiful in the county, but is chiefly remarkable for the series of 9th-century Saxon carvings now reset in the chancel. These are wonderful products of the Mercian school, and their birds, beasts and patterns bear comparison with the glories of Breedon-on-the-Hill, Leics.

GLATTON
St Nicholas
2m/3km S. of Stilton TL 1586
Noble ashlar-faced Perpendicular W. tower with frieze, battlements and pinnacles with animal supporters. Inside are arcades of *c.* 1200, benches with carved poppyheads, wall-paintings, and a vaulted vestry.

GODMANCHESTER
St Mary the Virgin
on R. Ouse S. of Huntingdon TL 2470
Perpendicular W. tower of 1623, the rest mainly 13th–15th-century. Late 15th-century stalls with carved misericords; a screen and reredos by Bodley, 1901.

GRAFHAM
All Saints
5m/8km W. of Huntingdon TL 1669
Tiny whitewashed church with dormers; the spire rises from unusual octagonal upper stage of the W. tower; 13th-century chancel and N. arcade.

GREAT PAXTON
Holy Trinity
3m/4km N.E. of St Neots across R. Ouse TL 1862
A dark and cavernous church of the Conqueror's time conceived on a thrilling scale – the arches of the crossing stupendous when compared with the man-sized nave arcade. No hint of all this outside, since the central tower has disappeared and there is now a stubby 14th-century steeple at the W. end. The nave rising towards the E. is an original Saxon feature and provides a link with contemporary German churches.

HAMERTON
All Saints
8m/12km N.W. of Huntingdon TL 1379
14th-century, refashioned in late 15th century; good Perpendicular W. tower, embattled nave clerestory and aisles.

HOUGHTON
St Mary
3m/4km E. of Huntingdon TL 2872
Pleasant riverside village, with long, spidery roads leading off a central square. A Decorated and Perpendicular church, the W. tower with an octagonal top stage supporting a spire.

HUNTINGDON
St Mary
15m/24km N.W. of Cambridge TL 2371
Ornate Perpendicular W. tower partly rebuilt after collapse in 1608; see the names of the benefactors on the arcades.

KIMBOLTON
St Andrew
7m/11km N.W. of St Neots TL 0967
Large town church with fine 14th-century

tower and broach spire. Good Decorated screen with paintings of c. 1500 and impressive Montagu monuments.

LEIGHTON BROMSWOLD
St Mary
5m/8km W. of Alconbury TL 1175
The nave and tower of this twelfth-century and later church were rebuilt in 1634 in an individual style best described as 'Norman'. The old aisles were sacrificed and the new nave was married to the medieval transepts, which perform their proper function in giving breadth and freedom to the whole design. The church had in fact become a true Protestant 'preaching space'. The roof design is bold with sturdy tie beams. Delightful 17th-century furnishings of particular interest: twin pulpits or ambos, choir-stalls, and the tiniest of chancel screens, all off a Jacobean turner's lathe. George Herbert was incumbent of this place 1626–30.

LITTLE GIDDING
St John
5m/8km S.W. of Stilton TL 1281
In undulating country relieved from the extreme flatness of the Fens, and sheltered by a grove of trees, the tiny church survives the depopulated village and the hall, now levelled to the ground. Little Gidding will always be linked with Nicholas Ferrar and his unique experiment in the contemplative life. From outside the red brick is disappointing, but within there is richness. The present fabric is mainly early 18th-century. The tiny nave and chancel fitted out as a miniature college chapel. The walls lined throughout with striking Classical arcading in timber, the barrel ceiling ribbed and panelled. Brass lectern, font and chandelier good and appropriate.

ORTON LONGUEVILLE
Holy Trinity
S.W. district of Peterborough TL 1796
13th- and 14th-century church with S. aisle of 1675, box pews, and an early 16th-century wall-painting of St Christopher.

RAMSEY
St Thomas of Canterbury
10m/16km S.E. of Peterborough TL 2885
The church is a monastic relic from the old abbey, and was actually built as a hospitum, standing on the fringe of the compact little town. The body of the structure is early 12th-century, and the vaulted chancel late-Norman; the W. tower dates from 1672. The presence of a 13th-century font and re-used materials of that date in the tower suggest parochial use from that time. Late glass by Morris & Co.

ST IVES
All Saints
5m/8km E. of Huntingdon TL 3171
Stately Perpendicular church beside the river. A richly painted rood screen and mighty organ case all by Comper, 1896.

ST NEOTS
St Mary
8m/12km S.W. of Huntingdon TL 1860
Good, small market community with a well-proportioned market square, but the church is tucked away on the fringe of the town. A luxurious 15th-century building with perhaps the finest tower in the county. The church is faced with ironstone and pebbles with ashlar dressings, an agreeable contrast in colour and texture. The roof is almost flat, not over-elaborate but very English and most satisfying. Almost everything a good town church should be.

SAWTRY
All Saints with St Andrew
4m/6km S. of Stilton TL 1683
By A. W. Blomfield, 1880; dark and correct Gothic with substantial re-use of medieval materials including tiles and glass. Also a fine brass to Sir William le Moyne, d. 1404, and his lady.

TILBROOK
All Saints
7m/11km E. of Higham Ferrers TL 0769
Decorated with some late-Norman features. Here is the finest vaulted rood screen in the county, retaining elaborate coving and figure-painting.

WARBOYS
St Mary Magdalene
7m/11km N.E. of Huntingdon TL 3080
Elegant 13th-century broach spire with large paired bell openings and three tiers of lucarnes. Norman chancel arch and two monuments by Bacon.

YAXLEY
St Peter

4m/6km S. of Peterborough TL 1892

Some agreeable colour in the village, with black-and-white timber cottages thrown against brick and tile. The church, noble and large for the size of the community, has an elegant steeple with flying buttresses crowning an impressive composition. The many components – aisles, transepts and porch – mass together most fittingly. The plan is complex, with an aisled chancel and transepts, all of differing roof levels. Inside, a series of medieval narrative wall-paintings and a good 15th-century East Anglian chancel screen. E. window, altar and reredos by Sir Ninian Comper.

Isle of Man

Introduction

The Isle of Man is rich in variety of natural scenery. It is a mixture of Ulster and Cornwall to look at; there are mountains and moors down its middle, whence streams splash to the sea through wooded glens. High fuchsias and veronicas grow by stone cottages, sub-tropical trees and shrubs flourish in those parts that are sheltered from the prevailing south-west gales. The building stone of most of the island is slate of various colours, and there is a certain amount of soft red sandstone in Peel and good grey limestone at Castletown. The northern point of the island has a rich swampy district called the Curragh, which tails off into a flat sandy tract. Elsewhere the coast is mostly high cliffs.

The Celtic Church was founded in the Isle of Man in about the 5th or 6th century, and influenced by missionaries from Ireland. Their churchyard crosses survive and all seventeen old parish churches of the island, despite many rebuildings, have retained the plain, rectangular plan of Celtic times. In the 8th and 9th centuries the island was invaded by Scandinavian pagans; soon converted, their cross-slabs display both pagan legends and Christian themes. The crosses at Kirk Maughold, the Thor Cross at Kirk Bride, and the Odin Cross at Kirk Andreas are particularly interesting. Under the Norwegians the western islands of Scotland (Sodor) and the island of Man became a single diocese *c.* 1135, and Man remained Norwegian until 1266. Its Church was controlled directly by Rome until the Reformation. Only two considerable medieval buildings remain. They are St German's Cathedral on an island off the west coast of the fishing port of Peel, and Rushden Abbey. But both are ruins. The Manx Gothic was more like Irish Gothic than English.

The Reformation proceeded slowly in Man, and its Church remained 'high' church until the beginning of the 19th century. Church architecture, as opposed to antiquities, begins with Georgian times. The famous and saintly bishop, Thomas Wilson, who occupied the see from 1698 until his death in 1755, and his successor Bishop Hildesley, were responsible for the restoration and refitting of all old churches. In Bishop Wilson's time there was a Manx Baroque style which may be seen in the west front of Ballaugh Old Church. The Gothic Revival came early to the island, and may have received its impetus first from the castellated building by George Steuart, built as a house for the Duke of Atholl, the island's owner and governor at the end of the

18th century, and now known as the Castle Mona Hotel, Douglas. People
who fell into debt used to flee to the Isle of Man at this period and build
themselves castellated mansions. A Manx Gothic Revival style established
itself, and the work of John Welch in the 1820s and 30s is really distinguished.

After the debtors, the visitors: in the 19th century Douglas became the
chief town, and churches in North-of-England Victorian style, typical of
Castletown, the old capital, began to appear all over the island. Those which
seem most distinguished are listed.

Man is 227 square miles, slightly bigger than Rutland, and has seventeen
ancient parishes. Its Bishop has a say in the government of the island and a
seat in the Tynwald Court. Its churches are many and small. Though none
of the earlier ones may have much architectural distinction, they have a
storm-resisting, prayer-soaked holiness about them. Most old churches were
heavily restored, and only two retain their Georgian fittings.

J.B.

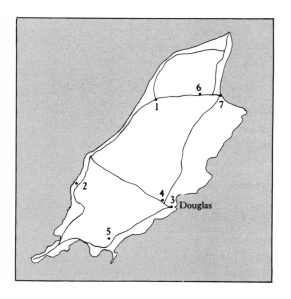

1 Ballaugh
2 Dalby
3 Douglas
4 Kirk Braddan
5 Kirk Malew
6 Lezayre
7 Ramsey

Selected List of Churches

BALLAUGH
7m/11km W. of Ramsey SC 3493 (the old church is about 1m/2km N. of Ballaugh)
St Mary, Old Church
An old church to which Bishop Wilson added a front in 1717, in simple and strange Baroque style.
St Mary, New Church
By John Welch, 1832. Exterior an impressive attempt in local stone to produce Boston Stump reduced in scale.

DALBY
St James
4m/6km S. of Peel SC 2178
Remote hamlet on W. coast; church 1840, in the style of John Welch, pinnacled without and unrestored within.

DOUGLAS
SC 3875
St George, Upper Church Street
1761–80. By a local builder who was sent to Whitehaven to copy the church there. The interior was much restored in 1910 when the upper galleries were removed and the church extended.
St Matthew, North Quay
By J. L. Pearson, 1895–1902; mysterious and dark, lofty and intricate; the chancel has a mosaic floor which was supervised by M. H. Bailie-Scott.
St Ninian, Glencrutchery Road
By W. D. Caroe, 1914. A sensitive local stone rendering of late-Gothic, freely treated. Spacious and impressive interior.
St Thomas, off the Promenade
1849; a big-boned building of local stone by Ewan Christian.

KIRK BRADDAN
1m/2km N.W. of Douglas SC 3676
St Braddan, New Church

By J. L. Pearson, 1876. Austere Early English. It looks very English in this wooded valley by the old church. As in all Pearson's churches, the proportions are fine and the detail bold.
St Braddan, Old Church
The mother church of Douglas in a beautiful wooded valley by the River Dhoo. The churchyard is full of Georgian headstones, dominated by an obelisk to Lord Henry Murray designed by Steuart. Tower, 1773. Interior has high pews, galleries, clear glass and monuments on walls. Still occasionally used for services; run by the friends of Old Kirk Braddan.

KIRK MALEW
St Lupus or St Moluag
1m/2km S.W. of Ballasalla SC 8769
What all the old Manx churches were like before Victorian restoration; outside, a whitewashed rectangle in fields; inside, box pews and Georgian fittings. North transept 18th-century.

LEZAYRE
Kirk Christ or Holy Trinity
2m/3km W. of Ramsey, also known as Churchtown SC 4294
By John Welch, 1835; an attempt in local stone to imitate a spired country church of the English Midlands; contemporary woodwork inside.

RAMSEY
St Paul
7m/11km S. of Port of Ayre SC 4594
Set in the market square, overlooking the harbour. 1822, Classical with galleries; architect unknown. Rendered, with a clock tower.

Kent

Introduction

This is the county which seems the longest inhabited in historic times. The Romans lived here, St Augustine landed here, Saxons and Normans have left their mark. The two ancient sees of the county, Canterbury and Rochester, were both founded in the reign of the Saxon King Ethelbert (d. 616). The shrine of St Thomas à Becket in Canterbury Cathedral was the greatest place of medieval pilgrimage in England, and even today, when London has engulfed the north-west corner of the county, there is a feel of Kent about its suburban corner, and of pilgrims setting out down the Old Kent Road. The long civilization of the county is summarized in the soaring stateliness of Canterbury Cathedral, whose architecture from Norman to Perpendicular is magnificent, and whose 13th-century glass in quality, if not quantity, equals that of Chartres and Bourges.

Kent has always been the doorstep of England from the Continent; it is the county one thinks of when invasion is threatened, from Roman times till the Battle of Britain. And seen first, after arrival home from abroad, with white chalk cliffs, the hops and orchards and oast-houses, the warm red-tile-hung houses and timbered yeoman's farms, the oaks and filbert copses of the Weald, the flint and ragstone churches are a graceful sight. Right across the county from west to east runs a high range of chalk hills, from Surrey to Dover, cleft in two places by Kent's chief rivers, the Medway and the Stour, with Maidstone on the Medway and Canterbury on the Stour. On the hilly Sussex borders was ironstone and once an iron industry. On the northern border along the Thames estuary are marshes with old-fashioned towns like Gravesend, Sheerness and Whitstable, and the Medway ports of Strood and Chatham, all of which are still weatherboarded and Dickensian in their older side streets. Far away in the south-east corner is the Romney Marsh, a flat sheep-nibbled kingdom with oak posts and rails and few trees and wind-swept salty churches. The rest of the county inland is what is always called 'The Garden of England'.

Kent's oldest towns are associated with pilgrims, beer and the sea. In late-Georgian and early-Victorian days, the coast became popular as a seaside resort. Herne Bay, Margate, Ramsgate and Dover, have their stucco, Brighton-style terraces. Later, Folkestone was developed as a mid-Victorian resort. In this century the electrification of the railways has turned all the parts of the county on the London border into a near-suburb, and many an old cottage and farmhouse has been saved from destruction by the businessman in search of country life.

After the splendour of Canterbury Cathedral, the rest of the Kent churches, Rochester Cathedral itself included, are an anti-climax. In the Weald and the west, the churches are built of Kentish rag; on the Sussex borders near the chalybeate 17th-century spa of tile-hung Tunbridge Wells, sandstone is used; and on the chalk hills flint and clunch. Few of the churches have clerestories. Roofs are steep and large enough to cover nave and aisles in one. The Early English style predominates, and tracery is a county speciality in the old churches. The largest group of comparatively 'unrestored' churches is that on Romney Marsh.

J.B.

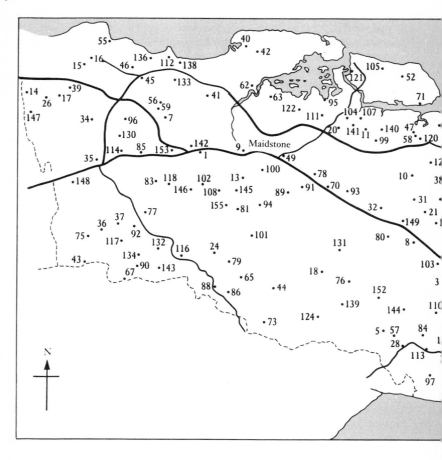

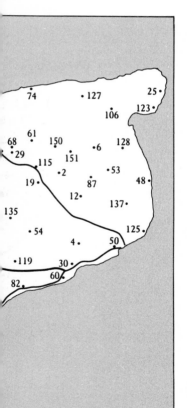

continued overleaf

Selected List of Churches

ADDINGTON
St Margaret
2m/3km E. of Wrotham Heath TQ 3764
11th–15th-century chapel has early Norman
nave with herringbone work, painted wagon
roof, and brasses; elaborate alabaster Watton
monument, 1651.

ADISHAM
Holy Innocents
3m/4km S.W. of Wingham TR 2253
Late 12th- and 13th-century cruciform
church with low crossing tower and spire.
Restored by W. White, 1869–70; reredos
from Canterbury Cathedral; screens and
tiles.

ALDINGTON
St Martin
6m/10km W. of Hythe TR 0736
Large, fine W. tower built 1525–50. Good
set of 15th-century chancel-stalls with
misericords and poppyheads; base of rood
screen.

ALKHAM
St Anthony of Panniers
4m/6km W. of Dover TR 2542
Handsome 13th-century flint church with
grand N. chapel in the 'High Early English'
manner of S.E. Kent; shafted lancets, trefoiled arches, and rich mouldings.

APPLEDORE
St Peter & St Paul
5m/8km S. of Tenterden TQ 9529
Delightfully situated. Originally Early
English, but largely reconstructed after
French raid of 1380. Good 14th-century
roof and screens.

ASH
St Nicholas
3m/4km W. of Sandwich TR 2858
Large 13th–15th-century cruciform church
with imposing central tower. Restored by
Butterfield, 1847. Best series of medieval
monuments in the county; late brasses, pillar
poor-box of 1727.

ASH-BY-WROTHAM
St Peter & St Paul
3m/4km S. of Longfield TQ 6064
Near 17th-century manor; 13th–15th-
century flint church with Decorated nave
and N. aisle; 15th-century tower and crown-
post roof. Well restored by Sir T. G. Jackson,
1901–3.

ASHFORD
St Mary
13m/21km S.W. of Canterbury TR 0142
Large cruciform town church, mostly 1350–
1475, with magnificent central tower.
Chancel screen by Caroe, 1919; 14th–17th-
century monuments.

AYLESFORD
St Peter
3m/4km N.W. of Maidstone TQ 7258
Norman W. tower, 15th-century nave and
aisle, heavily restored in 1878. Painted Royal
Arms of 1689; delightful coloured Culpeper
tomb of 1604 and an astoundingly vulgar
marble tomb of 1699, perhaps by John Nost.

BADLESMERE
St Leonard
5m/8km S. of Faversham TR 0054
Despite the harsh external render, a small
church of great charm. The walls and choir-
stalls are older than the 18th-century interior, and the twin E. lancets are a local
feature. The complete interior is of a rare
beauty, with box pews rising in levels at the
W. end and a three-decker pulpit.

BAPCHILD
St Lawrence
2m/3km E. of Sittingbourne TQ 9262
Norman, Early English and Perpendicular
flint church with unusual 12th-century
octagonal piers and wall-painting of the Crucifixion, c. 1300.

BARFRESTON
St Nicholas
6m/10km N.W. of Dover TR 2650
The best Norman church in Kent and virtually unaltered, though much restored 1839–

41 by Edward Blore. The carved decoration within and without is of surprising elaboration; note especially the S. doorway with its striking tympanum and the big wheel window.

BARMING
St Margaret
3m/4km W. of Maidstone TQ 7254
Fine Perpendicular W. tower and needle spire. Norman windows in E. wall and 14th-century Flemish choir-stalls with richly exaggerated carving in deep relief.

BECKENHAM
St George
8m/12km S.E. of Charing Cross, now in Greater London TQ 3769
Prominent position in High Street; by W. Gibbs Bartleet, 1885–7, completed 1902–3. Gothic Revival; Perpendicular-style rebuilding in grand manner.

BEXLEY
St Mary
now in Greater London TQ 4973
Mostly 13th-century, flint-faced, with shaped shingled spire. Well restored by Basil Champneys in 1883; good woodwork and ornaments.

BEXLEY HEATH
Christ Church
2m/3km S.W. of Erith, now part of Greater London TQ 4875
A huge, unfinished cruciform church by William Knight of Nottingham, in Early French Gothic style, 1877.

BICKLEY
St George
1m/2km E. of Bromley, now in Greater London TQ 4269
A large and handsome church of 1864 by F. Barnes, with later upper tower and spire by Sir Ernest Newton. Clerestoried. Hammer-beam roof. Wythe monument by Butterfield, 1871.

BIDDENDEN
All Saints
4m/6km S. of Headcorn TQ 8538
Superb Decorated and Perpendicular exterior in a lovely village. Jacobean pulpit and numerous 16th-century brasses.

BISHOPSBOURNE
St Mary
4m/6km S.E. of Canterbury TR 1852
Church of Richard Hooker, celebrated Elizabethan divine, and still feels like it. Mostly late 13th-century with broad chancel, some stained glass and wall-paintings. Enlivened by Scott in 1871; glass by Morris & Co. Note Hooker's scholarly tomb with pilasters of piled books.

BORDEN
St Peter & St Paul
2m/3km W. of Sittingbourne TQ 8862
Attractive exterior but interior over-restored; Norman tower and Early English arcades, the rest mainly 14th- and 15th-century; 15th-century wall-painting of St Christopher and monument to Dr Plot, historian, d. 1696.

BOUGHTON ALUPH
All Saints
4m/6km N.E. of Ashford TR 0348
This large and distinguished cruciform church is set on a lovely slope of downland. Mainly 13th- and late 14th-century; some original glass in E. window and N. transept.

BOUGHTON-UNDER-BLEAN
St Peter & St Paul
3m/4km E. of Faversham TR 0559
Early English and Perpendicular, restored by St Aubyn in 1871. Interesting rood screen with Renaissance details and a monument with reclining effigies by Epiphanius Evesham, 1617.

BRABOURNE
St Mary the Blessed Virgin
6m/10km E. of Ashford TR 1041
Fine Norman work with rich details, notably the complete 12th-century glazed window in the chancel. Superb tower stair, brasses, and fine altar tomb of c. 1600.

BRENCHLEY
All Saints
2m/3km S. of Paddock Wood TQ 6741
Cruciform sandstone church, 13th-century and later; much restored. Carved screen of 1536; handsome crown-post roof, unusual in Kent.

BROADSTAIRS
St Peter in Thanet
2m/3km N. of Ramsgate TR 3967
Long Norman nave and fine Perpendicular

tower, converted to a naval signal station in 1813. Lively restoration by J. P. Seddon; 17th–18th-century monuments.

BROMLEY
9m/15km S.E. of Charing Cross, now in Greater London TQ 4069
St John the Evangelist, Park Road
G. Truefitt, 1880. Well-grouped and built of Kentish rag and brick, ugly and full of character.
St Peter & St Paul
The marvellously restored tower stands as a link with the past and was wedded onto the new Gothic-style building by J. Harold Gibbons, 1948–57.

BROOK
St Mary
4m/6km E. of Ashford TR 0644
Simple and grand as if it had strayed across the Channel, this unaltered Norman church has a remarkable W. tower, 13th-century wall-paintings, pulpit, and old tiles.

BROOKLAND
St Augustine
5m/8km W. of New Romney TQ 9825
Picturesque and quite unspoilt with long, low roofs and two E. gables; 13th-century and later. Remarkable detached belfry, octagonal on plan, built entirely of timber in three stages, like candle-snuffers stacked one on another, and shingled from top to bottom. The 12th-century lead font is one of the showpieces of Romney Marsh. Crown-post roofs, box pews, and clear glass.

CANTERBURY
TR 1457
St Martin, St Martin's Hill
On a hillock alongside a handsome Georgian rectory, this is the church of Queen Bertha where St Augustine worshipped. Saxon work in chancel and a fine Norman font.

CAPEL-LE-FERNE
St Mary
3m/4km N.E. of Folkestone TR 2539
Norman and 13th-century flint church; 14th-century stone chancel screen with triple arches and opening for rood above.
  R.C.F.

CHALLOCK
St Cosmas & St Damian
4m/6km E. of Charing TR 0050
Remote in rolling downland; 13th-century

with Perpendicular tower. A sensitive restoration by T. W. Harrison repaired severe bomb damage. Chilly interior warmed by Perpendicular screen and wall-paintings by Rosemary Aldridge and Doreen Lister, 1953, in the N. chapel, and by John Ward, 1955, in the chancel.

CHARING
St Peter & St Paul
6m/10km N.W. of Ashford TQ 9549
Stands among the ruins of the archbishop's manor-place and is approached down a lane off the pretty main street. The magnificent W. tower, c. 1465–1505, leads one to expect an impressive interior and we are not disappointed. Both ensemble and detail are good. Chiefly 13th- and 15th-century, restored after a fire in 1590. Notable are the vaulted porch, 17th-century bench-ends, highly decorative roofs, window tracery, and chandeliers. The vamping horn is one of four in the country.

CHARTHAM
St Mary
3m/4km S.W. of Canterbury TR 1055
Cruciform, mainly 14th-century; splendid chancel with late 13th-century glass, arranged by Street in 1873–5. Huge and handsome brass to Sir Robert de Septvans, d. 1306, and a large monument by Rysbrack, 1751.

CHELSFIELD
St Martin of Tours
2m/3km S.E. of Orpington TQ 4864
Stands alone with nearby Court Lodge near bypass; 15th-century with some Norman work. Brasses and memorials. Stained glass by Veronica Whall, 1925.

CHEVENING
St Botolph
3m/4km N.W. of Sevenoaks TQ 4857
Battlemented Perpendicular W. tower, c. 1520; 13th-century Stanhope chapel; impressive, severe interior. Many monuments, one by Chantrey.

CHIDDINGSTONE
St Mary
4m/6km E. of Edenbridge TQ 5045
Unspoilt village. Mainly 14th-century, rebuilt after fire in 1624. Large Perpendicular tower with carved heads. Interesting combination of Gothic and Renaissance

details in porch. Jacobean font and cover, hatchments, iron grave-slabs, and churchyard monuments.

CHIDDINGSTONE CAUSEWAY
St Luke
1m/2km N.E. of Chiddingstone TQ 5147
By J. F. Bentley, 1897–8; his only 'Protestant' church. Bath stone church in the Perpendicular style; nave, chancel and N. tower; simple, solid, distinguished. Powerful German Expressionist glass in E. windows by Von Glehm, 1906.

CHILHAM
St Mary
6m/10km S.W. of Canterbury TR 0653
The village, castle and church stand on high ground, set round a large square with black-and-white houses. The church, chiefly Perpendicular with a dominant W. tower, contains a remarkable series of monuments, including two early 17th-century ones of nielloed black-and-white Bethersden marble; a handsome group by Chantrey; two children by Munro; and, most unusual of all, a pillar to Lady Digges with the four, rather lumpy, Cardinal Virtues seated around it – the work of Nicholas Stone, 1631. 15th-century glass in N. aisle, an old school table, and churchyard monuments.

CHISLEHURST
11m/18km S.E. of Charing Cross, now in Greater London TQ 4469
Annunciation, High Street
Victorian *tour de force* by James Brookes, 1868–70. Paid for by royalties from *Hymns Ancient and Modern*. Wall-paintings and reredos by Westlake; mosaic over chancel arch and Hardman E. window.
St Nicholas
Mainly 15th-century village church surrounded by churchyard and green, comfortably enriched by local prosperity. Many monuments including work by Rysbrack and Chantrey. Glass by Burlison & Grylls and Kempe.

CLIFFE-AT-HOO
St Helen
5m/8km N. of Rochester TQ 7376
On the Hoo peninsula. Remote and large among trees above the marshes of the Thames estuary. Cruciform with aisles, long transepts and W. tower, the church is Early English with a Decorated chancel and Perpendicular porch. Magnificent 14th-century sedilia, stalls and screen. On the sturdy pillars are the remains of painted bands of colour.

COBHAM
St Mary
4m/6km S.E. of Gravesend TQ 6768
The 13th-century chancel of spacious proportions was built before the college was founded in 1362. Here is the finest collection of brasses in the county: some 20 adults and 40 children of the Cobham family. Carved and painted altar-tomb set immediately before the altar and rich in 16th-century work.

COOLING
St James the Greater
5m/8km N. of Rochester TQ 7576
Mostly 13th–14th-century with Norman font and nave. Churchyard supposedly the scene of the first chapter of Dickens' *Great Expectations*, and little changed since then.
R.C.F.

COWDEN
St Mary
5m/8km E. of East Grinstead TQ 4640
Once a centre of the Wealden iron industry, now a remote and pretty village. Medieval timber tower and spire carried on six massive posts. Pulpit, 1628. Cast-iron grave-slabs.

CRANBROOK
St Dunstan
7m/11km W. of Tenterden TQ 7736
One of the best of the Weald churches with a municipal air about it. Mainly late-medieval with a baptistry of 1725 for immersion of adults; porch and tower vaulting. Lady Chapel 1473–9; monuments and chancel bosses.

DARENTH
St Margaret
2m/3km S.E. of Dartford TQ 5671
Late Saxon nave with tiled quoins and double-splayed windows. Square two-storey early Norman chancel and a large decorated drum font of *c.* 1140.

DARTFORD
TQ 5474
Holy Trinity
12th-century tower with 15th-century top, the rest mainly 13th- and 14th-century. On

the E. wall of the S. chapel is a large 15th-century mural of St George. Striking sculptured tomb to Sir John Spilman, d. 1607, jeweller to Elizabeth I, and his wife.
Christ Church, Cross Road
By W. D. Caroe, 1909. Red-brick Romanesque. Bright and light interior with tile arches and white walls. Completed 1963.

DAVINGTON
St Mary Magdalene & St Laurence
on N.W. side of Faversham TR 0162
Formerly church of a Benedictine nunnery of which considerable remains survive. Of the church, only 12th-century nave and aisles remain, restored by Willement in 1845; interior has monastic severity in keeping with its origin.

DEAL
8m/12km N.E. of Dover TR 3752
St George, High Street
1715; Classical. Nelson worshipped here and William IV erected a tablet to his memory; carved civic pew. Organ case by Sir T. G. Jackson.
St Leonard, Upper Deal
Norman and later, but largely rebuilt 1684 and enlarged 1819. Charming Queen Anne gallery on Tuscan columns given by the pilots of Deal.

DETLING
St Martin
3m/4km N.E. of Maidstone TQ 7958
Small early-Norman church with tufa quoins. Superb 14th-century wooden lectern, perhaps from Boxley Abbey, and delectable Strawberry Hill Gothic wall-monument of 1778.

DOVER
TR 3141
St Mary in Castro, Dover Castle
Important late-Saxon church of cruciform plan, c. 1000; heavily restored by Scott in 1860. Adjacent to the famous Roman lighthouse.
St Peter & St Paul, St Alphege Road, Charlton
By J. Brooks, 1893. Soaring cruciform Early English with tiered lancets. Inside are octagonal piers, tall clerestory lancets, ashlar and rendering.

DYMCHURCH
St Peter & St Paul
5m/8km S.W. of Hythe TR 1029
Norman, the nave enlarged and W. gallery added in 1821. Good 12th-century S. doorway with shafts and scalloped capitals; matching W. door and chancel arch.

EASTCHURCH
All Saints
2m/3km S.E. of Minster TQ 9871
Built by Boxley Abbey, 1432. Kentish rag. Perpendicular rood screen and nave roof with angels; 17th-century Belgian tower screen; good Corinthian monument with effigies, 1622.

EASTRY
St Mary the Blessed Virgin
3m/4km S.W. of Sandwich TR 3154
Basically 13th-century with brasses and monuments including a large relief by J. Bacon, RA, of Glorious First of June on monument of Capt. Harvey, 1794.

ELHAM
St Mary the Virgin
6m/10km N.W. of Folkestone TR 1743
To many this is the most beautiful parish church in Kent, and this is a tribute to the careful restoration by F. C. Eden. The 13th-century arcades were pierced through the Norman walls when the aisles were added; the clerestory is Perpendicular and the Early English chancel has a triplet in the E. wall. There are good corbels, old tiles, text boards, and fine modern fittings.

ERITH
Christ Church
13m/21km E. of Charing Cross, now in Greater London TQ 5177
By J. P. St Aubyn, 1874. Dignified position with nave and chancel lavishly covered in wall-paintings by Ward and Hughes, 1906–9. Hardman glass.

EYNSFORD
St Peter & St Paul
3m/4km S.E. of Swanley TQ 5465
Norman and later flint church with slender spire and spacious apse. Good late 12th-century W. doorway with zig-zags; arch-braced roofs; Royal Arms of George III.

FAIRFIELD
St Thomas of Canterbury
2m/3km S. of Appledore TQ 9626
A tiny barn-like structure of timber and plaster with red and blue brick walls standing in a field on Romney Marsh surrounded by

ditches and sheep. 14th-century, re-fashioned in 18th century, and carefully restored by Caroe in 1913. Delightful interior has original roof timbers, text boards, box pews, three-decker pulpit, and three-sided communion rail.

FAVERSHAM
Our Lady of Charity
10m/16km W. of Canterbury TR 0161
Large Norman and later cruciform church. Nave rebuilt by George Dance Snr in 1755; elegant openwork W. spire by Charles Beazley, 1799. Brasses, 15th-century misericords, fine early 14th-century wall-paintings, and an organ case of 1754.

FAWKHAM
St Mary
3m/4km E. of Farningham TQ 5865
Sylvan setting. Small and attractive 12th–13th-century church with 14th-century porch, glass and W. timber bellcote; fading murals.

FOLKESTONE
St Saviour
TR 2235
By Micklethwaite and Somers Clarke, 1891–2. Impressive brick Perpendicular. Despite re-ordering, still retains Dominican austerity within and naughty but nice details outside.

FORDWICH
St Mary
2m/3km N.E. of Canterbury RE 1859
A small structure of Norman origin, unusually attractive with good texture outside and inside; tall, narrow 13th-century tower arch, old tiles, box pews, well-furnished sanctuary, and 1688 Royal Arms. Some 14th-century painted glass and rare Norman sarcophagus.

FRINDSBURY
All Saints
N. district of Rochester TQ 7469
High above Medway with a view to Rochester; restored 1824 and 1883. Norman chancel and on the window splays some 13th-century paintings.

GILLINGHAM
TQ 7767
St Augustine, Rainham Road
By Temple Moore, 1916. Tall and striking church of Kentish ragstone in the Decorated style. Majestic nave and chancel with lofty square piers, blank arcading and rood beam.
St Mary the Virgin
On green; 12th–13th-century church with Perpendicular exterior, restored by A. W. Blomfield in 1868–9. Good carving; glass by Heaton, Butler & Bayne.

GODMERSHAM
St Lawrence the Martyr
6m/10km N.E. of Ashford TR 0650
Old and cold in pretty surroundings. Disengaged early-Norman N. tower with E. apse; 12th-century bas relief of St Thomas à Becket; monuments with Jane Austen family connections.

GOUDHURST
St Mary
4m/6km N.W. of Cranbrook TQ 7237
The church and churchyard occupy the summit of a hill above the village; good example of a Wealden church with its long, low nave, yellowing stone, and distinguished monuments.

GRAVENEY
All Saints
3m/4km E. of Faversham TR 0562
Well-weathered church in pretty churchyard. Norman in origin, now chiefly 14th-century and later. Fine roof, old tiles, S. door, pulpit and other furnishings. Clear glass and pale woodwork make interior light and spacious.

GROOMBRIDGE
St John
4m/6km W. of Tunbridge Wells TQ 5337
A brick building erected by John Parker in 1625 to celebrate Prince Charles's return from Spain and his unsuccessful wooing of the Infanta. Gothic with Classical undertones. Jacobean font and pulpit, windows by Kempe with one panel of original heraldic glass. Sad, seated effigy of corpse with broken neck, 1686.

HACKINGTON
St Stephen
adjoins Canterbury to N. TR 1560
Curious 13th-century tower and spire. Norman nave and 13th-century chancel. Monument of 1592 incorporating a realistic wooden skeleton.

HARBLEDOWN
St Nicholas
W. suburb of Canterbury TR 1358
Originally the church of a leper hospital founded by Lanfranc in 1084. Norman and 13th-century, free from Victoriana; 14th-century glass and wall-paintings.

HARRIETSHAM
St John
7m/11km E. of Maidstone TQ 8652
Mainly 13th- and 15th-century, with a fine Kentish tower; an earlier one survives in part on the N. with groined vaulting. Fine Norman font, medieval tiles and monuments.

HARTY
St Thomas the Apostle
S.E. part of Isle of Sheppey TR 0267
Romantic and remote spot overlooking Swale estuary. Norman and later; fine Decorated niche in chancel E. wall and good 14th-century rood screen.

HASTINGLEIGH
St Mary the Virgin
6m/10km E. of Ashford TR 0944
An isolated gem in a fold of Downs. Early Norman nave and 13th-century chancel with lancets; one retaining its original grisaille glass.

HAWKHURST
All Saints
4m/6km S. of Cranbrook TQ 7630
By Sir G. G. Scott, 1861. Yellow sandstone church in Early English style with plate tracery, S.E. tower and broach spire. Ashlar interior with much Frenchified carving; glass by Clayton & Bell.

HERNE
St Martin
S. district of Herne Bay TR 1865
A large village church of 13th-century origin, refashioned in 14th century with some later details. Interior heavily restored; note late-medieval screen, stalls, and good 15th-century heraldic font. Bishop Ridley became vicar here in 1538.

HEVER
St Peter
2m/3km S.E. of Edenbridge TQ 4744
14th-century tower and shingled spire. Jacobean pulpit. Remarkable brass to Sir

Thomas Boleyn, d. 1538; he is shown wearing Garter robes and insignia over his armour. Good Hardman E. window.

HIGH HALDEN
St Mary the Virgin
3m/4km N.E. of Tenterden TQ 8937
Mainly 14th-century, including the scissor-braced timber belfry tower and W. porch; the entrance passage through the belfry is lined with Perpendicular panelling.

HILDENBOROUGH
St John the Evangelist
N.W. suburb of Tonbridge TQ 5648
By Ewan Christian, 1844. Anti-Tractarian preaching interior; broad, low and in advance of its times. Tremendous arch-braced roof; glass by Morris and Burne-Jones.

HOLLINGBOURNE
All Saints
5m/8km E. of Maidstone TQ 8455
Large Decorated and Perpendicular church with handsome Gothic Survival Culpeper chapel of c. 1638; 17th-century embroidered pall; monuments by Rysbrack and Edward Marshall.

HORSMONDEN
St Margaret
4m/6km S.E. of Paddock Wood TQ 7040
Fine Perpendicular tower, clerestory and prettily crested screen. Good mid-14th-century brass and a tablet to the inventor of the stomach pump, 1847.

HOTHFIELD
St Mary
3m/4km N.W. of Ashford TQ 9644
Good setting in parkland sadly depleted by 1987 hurricane. Long and low with 16th-century nave and stocky 14th-century tower. Restrained alabaster monument of 1624 with effigies.

HUNTON
St Mary
5m/8km S.W. of Maidstone TQ 7149
13th-century tower and chancel. Norman nave contains large hanging monument to Sir Thomas Fane, d. 1606; most immodestly placed, though the design and carving are first-rate.

HYTHE
St Leonard

4m/6km W. of Folkestone TR 1634
A Norman fabric largely rebuilt in 13th century with further refashioning in 14th century. W. tower rebuilt in 1751. The superb elevated chancel has the best Early English work of any parish church in Kent; the celebrated crypt beneath contains vast quantities of bones.

IGHTHAM
St Peter

4m/6km E. of Sevenoaks TQ 5956
Mostly 14th-century but with some Norman remains. Splendid monument to Sir Thomas Cawne, d. 1373; he lies in full-plate armour beneath a beautiful window in the N. side of the chancel, paid for in his will. Also a fine hanging monument of 1641 to Dame Dorothy Selby, celebrated needlewoman, by Edward Marshall; 17th-century box pews.

IVYCHURCH
St George

3m/4km N.W. of New Romney TR 0227
Large, low late-Decorated church of ragstone, the tower and turret covered with lichens of different colours. Restoration after the flying-bombs had damaged it did not impair its strange beauty. Wonderful empty interior with odd screens, text boards, and a graveside shelter in the nave.

KEMSING
St Mary

3m/4km N.E. of Sevenoaks TQ 5558
The church of Norman origin with later additions is full of beautiful craftsmanship. Most of the modern work is by Sir Ninian Comper, 1902. The screen is 15th-century, restored and provided with rood figures by Comper. 13th-century stained glass medallion, early 14th-century brass, Jacobean font cover, and 13th-century chest.

KILNDOWN
Christ Church

2m/3km S.W. of Goudhurst TQ 7035
By Carpenter, Butterfield and Willement, under the supervision of Beresford Hope, 1841; the Royal Martyr in stained glass; a museum of the Camden Society and a precursor of All Saints, Margaret Street.

KNOWLTON
St Clement

4m/6km S.W. of Sandwich TR 2853
By William White, 1855. Good Royal Arms of Charles II, but chiefly famous for the spirited Narborough monument of 1707 by Grinling Gibbons.

LAMBERHURST
St Mary

6m/10km S.E. of Tunbridge Wells TQ 6736
Mostly Perpendicular with shingled nave roof, remains of consecration crosses painted on walls, and window by John Piper.

LANGLEY
St Mary

4m/6km S.E. of Maidstone TQ 8051
By William Butterfield, 1853–5. Small and distinguished in late 13th-century style with stencilled chancel roof, fierce alabaster and polychrome tiles. Good Hardman glass. School and master's house also by Butterfield.

LANGTON GREEN
All Saints

3m/4km W. of Tunbridge Wells TQ 5439
By Sir Giles Gilbert Scott, 1862–4. Sandstone church in the Early English style with lancets and bellcote. Inside are sturdy octagonal piers, a richly Decorated alabaster reredos by Powell, and resplendent W. window with glass by Burne-Jones, Ford Madox Brown and William Morris.

LEEDS
St Nicholas

4m/6km E. of Maidstone TQ 8253
Grand Perpendicular with tall, slender arches. Massive Norman tower with ten bells. Saxon windows above N. nave arcade. Imposing tower arch, moulded chancel roof, 15th-century rood and side screens.

LEIGH
St Mary

3m/4km W. of Tonbridge TQ 5446
S. nave arcade, tower and chancel arches all 13th-century; like the village, it was given fancy dress in 1861. Hour-glass stand on pulpit; brasses.

LENHAM
St Mary

4m/6km N.W. of Charing TQ 8952
A village rich in old and picturesque houses.

Chiefly 13th- and 14th-century, the fittings more notable than the fabric; 15th-century carved stalls and font; 14th-century wall-painting of the Weighing of Souls; medieval lectern and handsome pulpit of 1622 with tester; 15th-century lych gate in the attractive churchyard.

LINTON
St Nicholas
4m/6km S. of Maidstone TQ 7550
Mostly by R. C. Hussey, 1860; ragstone, in the Perpendicular style. Many 17th-century and later monuments, including that to Galfridus Mann, d. 1756, paid for by Horace Walpole and designed in the favoured Strawberry Hill Gothic by Richard Bentley.

LOWER HALSTOW
St Margaret
4m/6km N.W. of Sittingbourne TQ 8567
Saxon church almost afloat in the Medway. Complete late-Saxon nave and chancel with tile dressings; 12th-century lead font with figures in arcades; S. porch of 1913 by W. D. Caroe, who restored the church.

LULLINGSTONE
St Botolph
adjoins Eynsford, 3m/4km S.E. of Swanley TQ 5364
The little white church rises from the castle lawns. It is almost a family chapel and mausoleum with monuments to the ancestors of the Hart-Dykes; 14th-century with 16th-century N. chapel and early 18th-century porch; 16th-century rood screen complete with coping, and early 18th-century open parapet. English and foreign painted glass, excellent plaster ceilings and monuments.

LYDD
All Saints
4m/6km N.W. of Dungeness TR 0420
Longest parish church in Kent. Chiefly 13th-century, but the fine, lofty Perpendicular tower with a delicate lierne vault is the work of Thomas Stanley, a senior mason at Canterbury Cathedral. Three blocked Anglo-Saxon arches and a clerestory window in N.W. corner of N. aisle. Numerous brasses; 14th-century effigy and monument by Flaxman, 1781.

LYMPNE
St Stephen
3m/4km W. of Hythe TR 1134
Superb view over Romney Marsh. The

church, which groups well with the medieval house on the W., is chiefly Norman and Early English with massive axial tower; crown-post roof.

LYNSTED
St Peter & St Paul
3m/4km S.E. of Sittingbourne TQ 9460
The village abounds in Tudor cottages and Elizabethan manor houses. The church, mainly Decorated and Perpendicular, is a mausoleum of Roper and Hugessen monuments; exquisite Teynham monument of 1622 by Epiphanius Evesham.

MAIDSTONE
TQ 7655
All Saints
A large town church, formerly collegiate, situated above the Medway and flanked by the archbishop's manor-place and the former college; a wonderful medieval group, 15th-century and of admirable proportions. Misericords and sedilia incorporating founder's tomb behind with contemporary painting. Many monuments including the massive indent of a brass to Archbishop Courtenay, d. 1396, and four fabulous shrouded figures by Edward Marshall, 1639.
St Luke, St Luke's Road
By W. H. Seth-Smith, 1896–7. A confident, muscular Art Nouveau design with Decorated window tracery. Broad, low arcades on coupled columns. Good detailing and craftsmanship throughout; wall-paintings by Ivon Hitchens, *c.* 1918.

MARDEN
St Michael and All Angels
7m/11km S. of Maidstone TQ 7444
Pleasant Wealden church; an architectural jumble of dates and styles with chancel of *c.* 1200, Decorated windows, and an overlay of 1868. Dramatic E. window of Christ in Majesty by Patrick Reyntiens, 1962.

MEREWORTH
St Lawrence
6m/10km W. of Maidstone TQ 6653
Built for John Fane, Earl of Westmorland, about 1740 by an unknown architect. A Tuscan nave and W. portico of real elegance; the spire is a copy of St Giles-in-the-Fields, London. Doric interior with a painted barrel vault in the nave and plaster ceilings to the aisles. Interesting monuments and splendid

golden 18th-century and earlier armorial glass.

MERSHAM
St John the Baptist
3m/4km S.E. of Ashford TR 0539
One of the many churches around Ashford worth a visit and, after Brook, probably the best. Mainly 13th- and 15th-century with spectacularly wide W. window dated soon after 1396 by the remaining glass. Brasses and monuments, one by Nicholas Stone, 1626.

MILTON REGIS
Holy Trinity with St Paul
W. suburb of Sittingbourne TQ 8964
Unattractive surroundings, but a handsome building with Saxon core and massive W. tower, the best flint tower in the county. Chiefly 14th-century with some good window tracery and brasses.

MINSTER-IN-SHEPPEY
St Mary & St Sexburga
N. coast of Isle of Sheppey TQ 9573
Occupying a commanding site on the highest point of Sheppey, this is two churches in one; the S. is parochial and Early English, the N. is the nunnery church founded in 670. Saxon work in the chancel and N. nave wall. Restored in 1880 by Ewan Christian. Deeply impressive interior with effigy of Sir Robert de Shurland, *c.* 1300, and two large Northwode brasses, *c.* 1330.

MINSTER-IN-THANET
St Mary the Virgin
5m/8km W. of Ramsgate TR 3064
Norman and Early English rebuilding on a monumental scale of the abbey founded in 669. Cruciform with impressive Norman nave arcades and Early English vaulted chancel with full set of fine misericords with carved arm-rests. Excellent E. window by Willement, 1861.

MURSTON
All Saints
1m/2km N.E. of Sittingbourne TQ 9264
By William Burges, 1873–4. Distinguished flint church with stone dressings in 13th-century French style. Apsidal chancel, stubby N. tower raised in 1959, and late 12th-century nave arcade saved from old church. Excellent king-post nave roof and traceried W. rose window.

NETTLESTEAD
St Mary
5m/8km N. of Paddock Wood TQ 6852
Stands a little apart near Nettlestead Place with its 14th-century gateway. The church itself is 15th-century with older tower and wide aisleless nave; some windows contain 15th-century painted glass of high quality. Early 17th-century mural monuments.

NEW ROMNEY
St Nicholas
9m/15km S.W. of Hythe TR 0624
The only town church in Romney Marsh, mostly Norman and 14th-century. Tall tower, W. door, nave arcades, and glorious Geometric E. window.

NEWCHURCH
St Peter & St Paul
4m/6km N. of New Romney TR 0531
One of the spacious churches of Romney Marsh surrounded by barns, haystacks and a few cottages; chiefly 13th- and 14th-century with a Perpendicular tower, font and screen.

NEWINGTON-ON-THE-STREET
St Mary the Virgin
3m/4km W. of Sittingbourne TQ 8665
Long and lofty church with magnificent flint and stone tower; as distinguished inside as out, with tombs, screens, wall-paintings, and chancel capitals. Mainly 13th- and 14th-century with shrine to St Robert le Bouser, *c.* 1350.

NORTHFLEET
St Botolph
1m/2km W. of Gravesend TQ 6274
Dramatic setting on the edge of disused quarry. Mostly Decorated and Perpendicular with a fine clerestory, some Saxon long-and-short work, and a plain tower of 1628. Magnificent 14th-century screen and some fine stalls; also 14th- and 15th-century brasses.

OLD ROMNEY
St Clement
2m/3km W. of New Romney TR 0325
There is no village, but a number of pretty houses; 13th- to early 16th-century church retaining 18th-century box pews, pulpit, reading desk, W. gallery, text boards, and

other delights; few churches are more pictur-esque.

OTFORD
St Bartholomew
3m/4km N. of Sevenoaks TQ 5259
Short Norman tower and timbered W. porch of 1637; Decorated chancel with matching work by Street, 1862–3. Hatchments, Royal Arms, and a large Rococo monument by Cheere, 1755.

PATRIXBOURNE
St Mary
3m/4km S.E. of Canterbury TR 1855
Small but very fine late-Norman church of flint and Caen stone with wheel window and rich sculpture to tower. Interesting 16th–17th-century Swiss glass.

PEMBURY, OLD CHURCH
St Peter
3m/4km E. of Tunbridge Wells TQ 6240
Stands by itself; 14th-century tower with shingled spire; Norman nave with crown-post roof; brass of 1607; lych gate.

PENSHURST
St John the Baptist
5m/8km W. of Tonbridge TQ 5243
13th-century and later; S. door has original ironwork. Two 13th-century coffin slabs in tower, one with exceptional carving of praying woman. Sidney chapel rebuilt *c.* 1820 by J. Rebecca with charming pointed tunnel vault and family memorials; 1627 heraldic glass in W. window.

PLAXTOL
(no dedication)
5m/8km N. of Tonbridge TQ 6053
In a village rich in old houses; one of the few churches built during the Commonwealth. Gothic Survival with hammer-beam roof, much enlarged in 1894; note the ancient reredos of foreign provenance.

POSTLING
St Mary the Virgin & St Radegund
3m/4km N. of Hythe TR 1439
Small and heavily restored 12th-century church retains rare original dedication stone on N. wall of chancel; the day and the month are recorded, but not, alas, the year. Traces of wall-paintings with masonry and flowers.

PRESTON-NEXT-FAVERSHAM
St Catherine
in S.E. part of Faversham TR 0260
High and distinguished flint and stone church amongst railways and breweries. Fine Early English chancel with sedilia and piscina, the rest mainly 19th-century. Fine brass of 1442.

QUEENBOROUGH
Holy Trinity
2m/3km S. of Sheerness TQ 9172
Modest church begun in 1366 to serve the new castle and town. Windows renewed in 1885; boarded roof of *c.* 1695 has faded, but delectable painting of clouds, cherubs and angels. Intriguing font of 1610 carved with a view of the castle.

RAINHAM
St Margaret
S.E. district of Gillingham TQ 8165
Late 13th-century chancel with traces of Norman work; rest mainly 14th- and 15th-century. Medieval N. and S. doors. The E. bay of the nave roof is panelled and coloured to form a canopy of honour for the screen. Some painted consecration crosses remain on the walls, and there are other 14th-century wall-paintings. Admirable carved 15th-century parclose screen. Tufton monuments – two lifesize marble figures of the 1670s.

RAMSGATE
TR 3865
St George, Church Hill
By H. T. Kendall from designs by H. Helmsley, 1825–7. Very distinguished Georgian version of Perpendicular in white brick and stone. Rib-vaulted interior with panelling and galleries supported on cast-iron columns.
St Lawrence
Large cruciform church with 12th-century core; much rebuilt in 13th century; Perpendicular windows and screen. Brass.
Christ Church, Vale Square
By Sir George Gilbert Scott, 1844. Academic essay in the Early English style; cold and chaste. Tall shingled spire and little octagonal vestry.

ROLVENDEN
St Mary the Virgin
3m/4km S.W. of Tenterden TQ 8431
Best approached from the E.; a fine church,

mainly Decorated and Perpendicular, the stone almost chocolate-coloured in places. The three E. gables are the best example of a common effect in Kentish churches. Gallery and Gibbon family pew complete with furniture; they were cousins of the historian.

ST MARGARET-AT-CLIFFE
St Margaret of Antioch
4m/6km N.E. of Dover TR 3544
Complete and impressive Norman church rich in ornament, with a fine W. door, arcades along the whole length of the nave at clerestory level, and, inside, sumptuously decorated arches.

ST MARY-IN-THE-MARSH
St Mary
2m/3km N. of New Romney TR 0627
Exhibits all the texture typical of a Marsh church. Mainly 14th- and 15th-century with an earlier core. Clear glass, white walls, old tiles, and early 18th-century furnishings.

ST NICHOLAS-AT-WADE
St Nicholas
6m/10km W. of Margate TR 2666
Attractive setting. Large and impressive fabric with clerestoried nave; the core is Norman, but as a whole it is now mainly 13th- and 14th-century. Good carving on capitals; Jacobean pulpit and holy table.

SANDWICH
11m/18km E. of Canterbury TR 3358
St Clement, Knightrider Street
Norman central tower; rest mainly 14th- and 15th-century. Angels at nave roof ridge; excellent heraldic font of 1400–6, and Perpendicular stalls.
St Mary, Strand Street
Norman origin, much rebuilt after fall of tower in 1668. Mid-18th-century reredos and pews removed from Leicestershire.
R.C.F.
St Peter, Market Street
13th- and 14th-century, once more restored after fall of tower in 1661; mean brick replacement. Tall late 13th-century nave with clerestory. Two fine civilian effigies of c. 1360.
R.C.F.

SELLING
St Mary
3m/4km S.E. of Faversham TR 0456
Early English W. doorway, central tower, transepts and chancel; 14th-century nave and aisles. Carving shows Canterbury influence. Original heraldic glass of 1299–1307 in E. window and 14th-century wall-paintings. In the Hilton Chapel are a Spanish ensign and a Union Jack flown at the Battle of Trafalgar.

SHOREHAM
St Peter & St Paul
4m/6km N. of Sevenoaks TQ 5161
Pleasantly sited in the Darenth Valley. Mainly 15th-century; a great split oak forms arch of porch. Famous screen running the full width of the church, one of the best in England; panelled doors give access to the platform or pulpitum on top. Wooden pulpit of 1827 by Blore from Westminster Abbey. Burne-Jones window; monuments with portrait busts by Cheere.

SMARDEN
St Michael
7m/11km S.W. of Charing TQ 8842
Lovely village. Large, handsome 14th-century church, probably built after Edward III licensed a market here in 1332. Incredible nave roof-span; 'the barn of Kent'.

SOUTHBOROUGH
St Peter
adjoins Tunbridge Wells to N. TQ 5842
By Decimus Burton, 1831. Yellow-brick with lancets; the chancel unusually at the W. end. Steeple altered by E. Christian, 1883.

SOUTHFLEET
St Nicholas
3m/4km S.W. of Gravesend TQ 6171
Complete Decorated church. Brasses, sculptured sedilia and, in the chancel, two paintings, probably 17th-century, of Latimer and Ridley. Large alabaster wall-monument to Sir John Sedley, d. 1605.

SPELDHURST
St Mary
2m/3km N.W. of Tunbridge Wells TQ 5541
Good Gothic Revival church by J. Oldrid Scott, 1871, in an unspoilt village. Base of tower is 14th-century. Burne-Jones windows and decent furnishings.

STELLING
St Mary
7m/11km S. of Canterbury TR 1441
A 14th-century church interestingly re-ordered in the 1790s when the arch between nave and S. aisle was demolished and the latter turned into a transept with a gallery. Complete contemporary fittings in which all pews face towards the three-decker pulpit, creating a T-plan interior.

STONE
St Mary
2m/3km E. of Dartford TQ 5774
This splendid church stands on cliffs over-looking the Thames, at the edge of a quarry. Believed to have been built by the masons of Westminster Abbey, it has a perfect harmony of proportions and is richly decor-ated; all 13th-century. Chancel vault by Street. There is a brass to John Lombard, 1408, a canopied tomb to Sir John and Lady Wyllshire, 1526–7, and excellent mural paintings, but the architecture is the main glory of the building.

SUTTON-BY-DOVER
St Peter & St Paul
5m/8km N. of Dover TR 3349
Mainly 14th-century, restored 1897. Large brass with fine portraits to Sir Edward Filmer, d. 1629, signed Edward Marshall.

SWANSCOMBE
St Peter & St Paul
3m/4km W. of Gravesend TQ 6074
Heavily restored; Saxon work in tower. Norman font, 15th-century oak lectern, Jacobean altar rails, Westmacott monument.

TENTERDEN
St Mildred
10m/16km S.W. of Ashford TQ 8833
A 13th-century church recast in 14th and 15th century. Noble 15th-century four-stage W. tower, the best parochial example in Kent.

TEYNHAM
St Mary
3m/4km E. of Sittingbourne TQ 9562
Cruciform church with immense transepts, standing between cherry orchards and the sea; 13th-century with 15th-century arcades and chancel arch. Texture is good and the white interior effective. Crown-post roof, dormer windows, and several brasses.

TONGE
St Giles
adjoins Sittingbourne to E. TQ 9364
Pleasant situation. Norman with 13th-century and later refashioning; a single crown-post roof covers nave and aisles, making the outside look like a great barn; 13th-century ironwork on tower door and a wall-painting of St Christopher.

TROTTISCLIFFE
St Peter & St Paul
1m/2km N. of Wrotham Heath TQ 6460
Complete Norman church. The W. wall of 1885 is an amazing example of elaborate knapped flint work; 17th-century com-munion rails; fine high-canopied and carved pulpit of 1775 was brought from West-minster Abbey in 1824.

TUNBRIDGE WELLS
TQ 5839
St Barnabas, Stanley Road
By J. E. K. and J. P. Cutts, 1889–93. Grand, lofty church of rich red brick banded with sandstone. Lancets, plate tracery, and cleres-toried nave. Good fittings and decorations by Martin Travers and Sir Ninian Comper.
King Charles the Martyr
The oldest church in the town, erected in 1676 and enlarged 20 years later. Beautiful moulded plaster ceiling by Doogood, 1690, for which alone it would be well worth visiting; he was chief plasterer to Sir Chris-topher Wren, and it shows.
St Mark, Broadwater Down
By R. L. Roumieu, 1864–6. Handsome at a distance with tall lucarned spire and French Gothic details. Pale sandstone with polyg-onal apse, clerestories of little quatrefoils, and soaring arcades. Glass by O'Connor and Clayton & Bell.

WAREHORNE
St Matthew
1m/2km S.W. of Ham Street TQ 9932
On the edge of Romney Marsh and in the spacious manner of that district; 13th-century, refashioned later with 18th-century brick porch and tower. Sussex marble arcades, fragments of 13th-century glass, and an 18th-century pulpit.

WEST FARLEIGH
All Saints
3m/4km S.W. of Maidstone TQ 7153
Pleasant setting on S. bank of the Medway.

Early Norman, but much restored. Perpendicular W. tower of *c*. 1525 and 17th-century family pew.

WEST PECKHAM
St Dunstan
5m/8km N.E. of Tonbridge TQ 6452
Saxo-Norman W. tower; 14th-century N. chapel stylishly refitted in 17th century to form remarkable first-floor squire's pew, the finest in Kent.

WEST WICKHAM
St John the Baptist
3m/4km S. of Bromley, now in Greater London TQ 3965
Now engulfed in suburbia, but still a village church with the old court beside it. Rebuilt *c*. 1490 by Sir John Heydon. Late-medieval glass and rood screen. Organ chamber and some fittings by J. D. Sedding.

WESTERHAM
St Mary the Virgin
5m/8km W. of Sevenoaks TQ 4454
13th-century tower with timber spiral staircase; rare Royal Arms of Edward VI. Harshly restored by Teulon in 1854.

WESTWELL
St Mary
3m/4km N. of Ashford TQ 9947
Rightly called a village cathedral, and certainly one of the most exciting architectural churches in Kent, despite the harsh external render and over-restored porch; 13th-century with a few later alterations, including 16th-century timber-framed porch. The lofty chancel is vaulted, and in place of a single chancel arch there are three tall and narrow openings with cusped heads and round columns. Lovely sedilia, rich carvings on tower arch, S. aisle roof, armorial glass, and a Jesse Tree in the chancel E. lancet.

WICKHAMBREUX
St Andrew
5m/8km E. of Canterbury TR 2258
Basically late-14th century; square-headed windows with ogee heads to the lights. Heavily restored in 1878 when the chancel was considerably enhanced by wall-paintings and by the addition in 1896 of a spectacular Art Nouveau Annunciation in the E. window by Arild Rosenkrantz.

WINGHAM
St Mary the Virgin
6m/10km E. of Canterbury TR 2457
Large village with many timber-framed houses and handsome spired church in the middle. Chiefly late 13th- and 15th-century with a wooden arcade between nave and aisle. Once a collegiate church; the stalls with carved misericords survive as well as the screen base. Monument of 1624 by Nicholas Stone and outstanding Oxenden family monument of 1682; a virtuoso piece enclosed by wrought-iron screens.

WOODCHURCH
All Saints
4m/6km E. of Tenterden TQ 9434
Village green with the church spire rising behind. The church, one of the most beautiful in Kent, is in the main a masterly work of the 13th century. The arcades have alternate round and octagonal columns. The triple lancets at the E. end with banded marble shafts are most effective. Priest's brass of 1320, late-Norman font, and a roundel of 13th-century glass.

WROTHAM
St George
8m/12km N. of Tonbridge TQ 6159
The tower rises straight off the old London road and has a vaulted passage beneath it from N. to S. The church is 13th-century, refashioned in 15th century. There is a vaulted porch with room above, and the massive door has a lock block of oak and a key nearly a foot long. The E. window, late-Gothic of 1633, was brought from St Alban, Wood Street, London in 1958. Perpendicular screen, an interesting series of brasses, and Lady Chapel reredos by Sir Ninian Comper.

WYE
St Martin & St Gregory
4m/6km N.E. of Ashford TR 0546
A little town with many old houses; the patched but still impressive church groups well with the adjacent 15th-century college. The fall of the central tower in 1685 destroyed the chancel; it was replaced about 20 years later by the present surprising and delightful apsidal chancel with massive brick and flint S. tower. The lofty Perpendicular nave has a grand timber roof.

YALDING

St Peter & St Paul

5m/8km S.W. of Maidstone TQ 6950

Generous cruciform church with Early English chancel and Decorated nave and transepts. Elaborate if old-fashioned marble and alabaster monument of 1656.

Lancashire

Introduction

Lancashire, alone among our counties to be charged with giving itself the airs of a continent, perhaps does so because it is the only one to contain two of Europe's great cities. Alternatively, it may be led into hubristic excess (one of its recurring characteristics, as, for example, at Blackpool during the summer holidays of the cotton towns) by the extraordinary variety which, like England itself, it comprehends within its area. About no other county is it so difficult to generalize. The river that marks its boundaries in the north-west is the River Duddon, which rises near the three-shire stone Lancashire shares with Westmorland and Cumberland, and drops through a cascade of Wordsworthian sonnets to Morecambe Bay. In the south-east steam rises from the black waters of the River Tame as it sings, according to Haslam Mills, of cops and twists and counts and mills upstream 'stopped for bobbins'.

The River Irwell began to run with muck and money in the 16th century, and much more or less filtered effluent has since then flowed into the Mersey, which for periods merges its identity with the Manchester Ship Canal, one of the world's many wonders of engineering that occur, without achieving communication, between Manchester and Liverpool. Both cities rise on the carboniferous and red sandstone plain, a northern extension of Cheshire round the millstone grit of the forest of Rossendale, the westward projection of Pennine moorland. The landscape of the coalfields is typical of its kind – spindly trees, blown to an eastern slant, roads paved with setts, paths with cinders, fences of large, upright flagstones, low-pitched roofs – though there are some picturesque surprises, such as the wooded oasis of Worsley, with its black-and-white timbered halls, or the lung provided by the most Lancashire of great houses, Knowsley.

The plain becomes agricultural as it sweeps up the west to the limestone beyond Lancaster, whose skyline of castle and church arising over Harrison's bridge across the Lune summarizes the long history of the County Palatine from old John of Gaunt to the mill chimneys of today, sparse here compared with those in the south-east, where they are agglomerated in the area aptly defined as moorland and milltown. There the mills dominate the industrial scene, with their accompanying contributions to the landscape, of the red-brick co-op and institute, of town halls and civic centres, the great glass boxes of modern schools, and the chapels and bethels of non-conformity. The various medieval churches have been much rebuilt. Some small churches of the 17th and 18th century have been more fortunate: Hoole (1628), Billinge (1717), Tarleton (1719), Edenfield (Ramsbottom, 1778), Holy Trinity, Warrington (1758), and others. The 19th century achieved an occasional miracle of beauty such as the exquisitely slender 300-foot marble spire of the Early English-style church of St Walburghe, Preston. It was designed by J. Hansom, inventor of the cab.

The prevailing tone, however, is set by the churches of the Million Pound Act, signatures everywhere of Pugin, Scott, Street, Medland Taylor, Austin and Paley, and other ecclesiologists of the Gothic Revival. The greatest achievement of this movement is in Manchester where, in addition to the incomparable Rylands Library, Waterhouse's Town Hall, in Albert Square, turns the corner by means of Vincent Harris's 1938 extension, which links it to his superb Classic Library, facing Lutyens' Cenotaph in St Peter's Square, in a sequence which is the finest demonstration imaginable of architectural good manners. A dramatic group of buildings, forming the heart of Liverpool, includes St George's Hall, described by Sir Charles Reilly as the best 'Greco-Roman' building in Europe, the climax of a long movement. It is among the finest Renaissance buildings in the world. Sir Robert Rawlinson and C. R. Cockerell continued, after the death of Harvey Lonsdale Elmes, the designs with which he had won the competition at the age of twenty-five. A similar and even younger triumph, at the age of twenty-one, was that of Sir Giles Gilbert Scott, whose cathedral, now complete, is the glory of modern Gothic.

The gulls from the great port soar upward to where the tower swims into the sky, and from the back bedrooms of decayed Georgian houses nearby the lodgers may see the light of the sun as it sets over the sea, reflected from the mountains of Lancashire-beyond-the-sands, north of Morecambe Bay.

F.S.

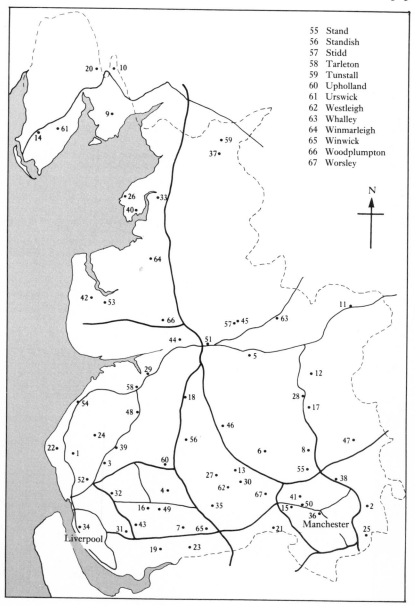

55 Stand
56 Standish
57 Stidd
58 Tarleton
59 Tunstall
60 Upholland
61 Urswick
62 Westleigh
63 Whalley
64 Winmarleigh
65 Winwick
66 Woodplumpton
67 Worsley

N

Selected List of Churches

ALTCAR
St Michael and all Angels
2m/3km E. of Formby SD 3206
By John Douglas, 1879. Remarkable timber-framed church with bellcote and red-tiled roofs. Light and spacious inside with timber N. arcade, good roofs, carved texts and original fittings.

ASHTON-UNDER-LYNE
St Michael and all Angels
6m/10km E. of Manchester SJ 9399
Originally 15th–16th-century, but extensively reconstructed in 1840–4; architect unknown. Sumptuous period interior with lavish Gothic plaster decoration of ceiling, walls and woodwork. Important painted glass *c.* 1500.

AUGHTON
St Michael
2m/3km S.W. of Ormskirk SD 3905
Of grey-brown stone, standing low, among shady lanes. Mid-14th-century Decorated spire on N. tower. Early English nave and 16th-century N. aisle with round-headed windows and N. chapel. Victorian chancel. Wall recess with cusped and moulded arch under tower; 17th-century brass plates; Westmacott's memorial to Rev. G. Van-brugh; sundial, 1736.

BILLINGE
St Aidan
3m/4km N.E. of St Helens SD 5300
In long hill-top village. Greenish-cream limestone church of 1717 has urns on its embattled parapet, a clock turret over the W. door, and a huge bell in the cupola above. Unusual Gothic tracery in the rounded windows, and a Gothic flavour to the small transepts added in 1908 by Sir T. G. Jackson. Otherwise Classical with Doric columns, pilasters and entablature. The light, arcaded interior has round arches on Doric columns. Segmental barrel-vaulted nave ceiling. Pannelled W. gallery and apse with Corinthian pilasters; 18th- and 19th-century monuments.

BLACKBURN
SD 6828
Holy Trinity, Mount Pleasant
By Edmund Sharpe, 1837–46. Remarkable Decorated church with huge W. tower and full-height transepts. Geometrical tracery, Gothic organ case, and a flat timber ceiling with over 40 heraldic panels.
    R.C.F.
St Mark, Witton Park
By Edmund Sharpe, 1836–8. Unusual church in Continental Romanesque style with Lombard friezes. Shallow polygonal apse and distinctive five-stage corbelled tower over the sanctuary. Spacious nave but the chancel somewhat cramped. E. window by Willement.
St Thomas, Lambeth Street
By E. G. Paley, 1864–5. Rock-faced sandstone church, broadly in the Decorated style, with Geometrical and plate tracery.

BOLTON
SD 7109
St Stephen and All Martyrs, Lever Bridge, Halgh
By Edmund Sharpe, 1842–5. Bizarre Decorated terracotta church, created at the whim of a local colliery owner to demonstrate the versatility of that material.

BURTONWOOD
St Michael
4m/6km N.W. of Warrington SJ 5692
Originally 1606, but neatly rebuilt in brick with stone dressings, 1716. Good S.W. tower with weather-vane and Tuscan S. arcade added by E. J. Dod in 1939 during his sensitive restoration.

BURY
St Mary the Virgin
8m/12km N. of Manchester SD 8010
Originally medieval with tower of 1846; greatly enlarged by J. S. Crowther, 1876, in a dignified late 13th-century style. Majestic polygonal apse, tall iron screen, and fine glass by Hardman.

CARTMEL
St Mary the Virgin & St Michael
4m/6km S. of Newby Bridge SD 3778
Among the fields of a pleasant little town, in a wide valley of the Cartmel Peninsula. Lancashire's greatest medieval parish church, part of a long-vanished priory. Massive Transitional cruciform building with 15th-century Perpendicular windows installed when the upper stage of the central tower was added. Pointed crossing arches, but chancel arcades still round. S. choir aisle, rebuilt *c.* 1350, has good Decorated windows. Magnificent Renaissance screens and stall canopies of 1618 restoration, after it had stood roofless for 80 years. Many monuments including lovely 14th-century Harrington effigies and that to Dame Katherine Lowther; fine Baroque work of 1700.

CARTMEL FELL
St Anthony
5m/8km N. of Lindale SD 4188
Small, low, roughcast limestone church of 1503 on the fell side. Mullioned windows and saddleback tower. Two handsome screened pews and a three-decker pulpit of 1698; 15th-century glass from Cartmel Priory. Restored in 1911.

COLNE
St Bartholomew
6m/10km N.E. of Burnley SD 8840
Late Perpendicular exterior but Early English and Decorated inside; 16th-century roof; monuments of *c.* 1746 by Sir Robert Taylor.

CRAWSHAWBOOTH
St John
2m/3km N. of Rawtenstall SD 8125
By Paley, Austin & Paley, 1890–2. Large church in the Perpendicular style with aisles, transepts and prominent pinnacled N. tower. Good traceried furnishings.

DAISY HILL
St James
1m/2km S. of Westhoughton SD 6504
By Paley & Austin, 1879–81. Masterly brick and terracotta church in the Perpendicular style. Remarkable soaring bellcote on S. side with panelled brickwork and gablets. E. window by Morris & Co.

DALTON IN FURNESS
St Mary
4m/6km N.E. of Barrow-in-Furness SD 2374
By Paley & Austin, 1882–5. Spectacular Decorated sandstone church with large W. tower and jolly limestone diapering. Good assymetrical interior has octagonal piers and broad moulded chancel arch.

ECCLES
St Mary the Virgin
4m/6km W. of Manchester SJ 7798
Restored in 1862–3 by Holden, when E. end was rebuilt. Mostly late-Perpendicular with fine 15th-century nave roof and 14th-century oak door. Brereton tomb of 1600; 1648 Dauntesey brass; Anglo-Saxon cross shaft.

ECCLESTON
Christ Church
suburb adjoins St Helen's to W. SJ 4895
Prim red sandstone, founded and designed by Samuel Taylor, 1838; spire and tall pinnacles. Sharply pointed chancel arch; pews with doors and re-used Rococo panels. Doric columns support the oak gallery and the spandrels of the hammer-beam roof are carved.

EDENFIELD
(no known dedication)
5m/8km N. of Bury SD 7919
Stone moorland village. Rebuilt of small dark masonry in 1778 with galleries, square pews, and mostly clear glass. Unspoiled, unspruced Georgian.

EUXTON
(no known dedication)
2m/3km N.W. of Chorley SD 5519
Ancient-looking little church of rough pink stone standing high above the main road. Aisleless nave, largely rebuilt in the 16th century, with small Decorated windows (restored), square 18th-century corbelled belfry, and chancel of 1837. Excellent Tudor roof, double piscina, and scraped outward-leaning walls. Sundial, 1775.

FARNWORTH
St Luke
1m/2km N. of Widnes SJ 5187
Set in a village now adjoining Widnes, but with open country to the N. Well-restored red sandstone church, mostly Decorated and Perpendicular. Good Tudor wooden ceil-

ings in chancel and S. transept. Bold chapel, rebuilt *c.* 1855, with good monuments by Chantrey, 1822, and the Roman Tenerani, 1824. Handsome Atherton sarcophagus monument of 1820 in chancel. Many hatchments and Royal Arms, 1661.

FINSTHWAITE
St Peter

1m/2km N. of Newby Bridge SD 3687
By Paley & Austin, 1874. In late-Norman style with low, buttressed central tower and sweeping slate roofs, the epitome of a moorland church. Good interior with lavishly decorated roofs and Salviati reredos.

FLIXTON
St Michael

1m/2km W. of Urmston SJ 7494
Mostly rebuilt in 1756; tower of 1732 and 15th-century chancel E. wall. Splendid doorway with pilasters and pediment, Tuscan arcades, and handsome arched windows.

FORMBY
St Peter

11m/18km N. of Liverpool SD 2907
1746, brick with stone dressings; W. tower with octagonal bell-stage and cupola with ball finial. Large round-headed windows in nave and W. gallery. Gothic chancel and chapel added in 1873. A good light for reading is admitted by the clear glass of the Georgian side windows.

GREAT SANKEY
St Mary

W. part of Warrington SJ 5688
Small embattled church of mellow brick, rebuilt in 1765 and probably altered later; Gothic, with a little spire. Marble tablets, 1800–50, but in an earlier tradition, are well spaced between the flat-pointed windows. Glass.

HALSALL
St Cuthbert

3m/4km N.W. of Ormskirk SD 3710
An important W. Lancashire village church of buff-coloured dressed stone. Perpendicular spire rising from tower with octagonal top stage. Steep 14th-century roofs to nave and chancel; buttressed, pinnacled, and of exceptional beauty. Spired turrets, one with rood loft stair, to either side of chancel arch, and sanctus bellcote on the gable

above. Finely ornamented 14th-century tomb recess in N. wall containing a later, mutilated effigy. Also a beautiful Decorated doorway of three continuous moulded orders with original panelled and traceried oak door. Effigies and brass; restored in 1886.

HAUGHTON GREEN
St Anne

1m/2km S.E. of Denton SJ 9393
By Medland and Henry Taylor, 1874–6. Unusual timber-framed church with bold roofs converging on curious polygonal tile-clad spire. Broad nave with strange tracery in the windows, elaborate roofs, and a general air of the unexpected.

HEYSHAM
St Peter

3m/4km S.W. of Morecambe SD 4161
Beside the sea at Morecambe Bay. A low, modest church on a site of high antiquity. Saxon W. doorway, early Norman capitals on the chancel arch, and a hoard of early sculpture including the strange 'house cross' in the churchyard, perhaps depicting the Raising of Lazarus. At St Patrick's Chapel nearby, time stands still.

HINDLEY
All Saints

2m/3km S.E. of Wigan SD 6104
Large colliery village. Endearing Georgian church of 1766 with round-headed windows, Gothic tracery and a good doorway. Black and gold interior with W. gallery of 1776 on fluted frieze.

HOLME-IN-CLIVIGER
St John

1m/2km S.E. of Haslingden SD 7922
Originally of 1788–94; chancel and vestry discreetly added in 1897. Built of ashlar with pedimented doorcase. Two tiers of windows and a square bell-turret with octagonal cupola. Interior sadly renewed in 1897.

HOOLE (also known as Much Hoole)
St Michael

6m/10km S.W. of Preston SD 4622
By a quiet lane in low, pastoral country. Embattled stone tower with corner urns of 1720; the rest, of pink brick with low stone-mullioned windows with round-headed lights, is 1628, save for the chancel of 1859. There are box pews, two-decker pulpit of

1695, gallery, hatchment, and Victorian glass. Jeremiah Horrocks, astronomer, was curate here when he discovered the Transit of Venus in 1639.

HOWE BRIDGE
St Michael and All Angels
adjoins Atherton to S.W. SD 6602
By Paley & Austin, 1875–7. Modest estate church of red Runcorn sandstone in the Decorated style. Nave and chancel under one roof, the junction marked by a fleche. The arcade has alternating round and clustered piers, and there is a stone vault over the chancel. Tasteful and well detailed throughout.

HUYTON
St Michael
6m/10km E. of Liverpool SJ 4491
Of 19th-century aspect, the aisles having been rebuilt in 1815–22. Perpendicular tower with interesting Gothic Survival repairs of the 17th and 18th centuries; note the pinnacles. Good screen of c. 1500 with flamboyant tracery and 17th-century hammer-beam roof in the chancel.

KIRKBY
St Chad
6m/10km N.E. of Liverpool SJ 4098
By Paley & Austin, 1869–71. Powerful Norman-Gothic church of local red sandstone. Prominent square central tower with saddleback roof and square-ended chancel. Handsome neo-Norman S. doorway and bold interior with soaring vaulted tower space. Effective chancel with blank arcading, lancets, and Henry Holiday's 'Last Supper' in stone mosaic; he also did the glass. Fine early-Norman font with saints and Adam and Eve.

LANCASTER
SD 4761
St John the Evangelist, North Road
Georgian church of 1754–5; elegant tower by Thomas Harrison added in 1784. Of ashlar, the tower has pilastered and pedimented bell openings, Tuscan rotunda, and modest spire. Nave with arched windows and an apse. Inside are box pews, galleries, and a coved ceiling to the nave.
R.C.F.
St Mary, Parish Church
Large and impressive Perpendicular exterior, mostly of the 1430s; Gothic W. tower

by Sephton, 1754, and ornate two-storeyed S. porch by Paley & Austin, 1903. Fine interior of later 14th-century character: excellent details and good furnishings including the exquisite Decorated choir-stalls. Monuments include one by Roubiliac, 1753, and there is a good deal of Saxon sculpture in the N. chapel. A most rewarding church.

LIVERPOOL
SJ 3490
St Agnes, Ullet Road, Sefton Park (Toxteth Park)
By J. L. Pearson, 1883. Noble church in the Early English style. Built of red brick with sandstone dressings and steep red roof from which rise a lead fleche and two stone spirelets flanking the polygonal apse. Spacious stone-vaulted ashlar interior with sharply pointed arches. Grilles and polished gates, holy lamps and a gilded reredos adorn the prayerful interior. Handsome adjacent vicarge by R. Norman Shaw, 1887.
All Hallows, Allerton
'Late Decorated' in rock-faced sandstone, by G. Enoch Grayson, 1872–6. Tower has large pinnacles, tall perforated windows, and diminishes upward in five stages. Interior mostly of Storeton stone, enriched with an important unified scheme of Burne-Jones glass in windows whose tracery is constantly varied. Chancel of red and green jasper with stone and alabaster stripes above. Arched and gilded wooden ceiling supported by golden angels. Sculptured group by F. Fabiani in S. transept, a replica of one at Genoa, is a memorial to Mrs Bibby, as is the church itself. Marble memorial of 1840 by William Spence to John Bibby, builder of the church.
All Saints, Childwall
Mostly 14th- and 15th-century; the only medieval work in Liverpool. Salisbury Chapel, 1739–40, Plumbe Chapel of 1777, tower and spire added in 1810. Many hatchments, a Royal Arms of 1664, and diverse monuments; glass by Warrington. Table-tombs and unusual castellated hearse house of 1810 in the churchyard.
St Anne, Aigburth
Like a country church, with fields behind it sloping down to the river. By Cunningham & Holme, 1836–7. Neo-Norman church of red sandstone; matching chancel and transepts added in 1853. Lots of little round arches and wall arcades, even on the gate-posts. Tower with clock and scalloped over-

hanging parapet. Spacious galleried interior, wide transepts, and good grotesque corbels.

St Bride with St Saviour, Percy Street
By Samuel Rowland, 1830–1. Impressive Ionic portico with six plain columns and a pediment. Spacious interior with flat ceiling and elegant galleries supported on cast-iron columns. Tripartite window in the short chancel.

St Bridget, Bagot Street, Wavertree
By E. A. Heffer, 1868–71; Early Christian basilica of dark red brick striped with black. Beautiful outline with refined campanile and unspoilt interior. Arcades of closely spaced red marble columns separate narrow, semi-vaulted aisles from the nave. Flat, coffered nave ceiling with coloured plaster decoration and blue semi-dome over the apse. Stained glass saints in clerestory windows, mosaic of the Last Supper behind the altar, and a bow-fronted organ case with stencilled gilt pipes.

St Christopher, Lorenzo Drive, Norris Green
By Bernard A. Miller, 1930–2. One of the best of the inter-war churches. Brick with stone dressings; interesting use of parabolic arches and vaults. Fittings include star-shaped font with mirror-tile cladding.

St Clement, Beaumont Street, Toxteth Park
Stone church of 1840–1; rectangular with lancets in the Commissioners' style. Notable for its complete early-Victorian interior with three-decker pulpit in front of the altar, box pews, galleries, and roof supported on cast-iron columns.

St Columba, Pinehurst Road, Anfield
By Bernard A. Miller, 1932. Another good inter-war church of pale brick with striking green pantiled roof. Blocky exterior rises from nave to chancel and chancel to sanctuary. Interior very much intact including colour scheme and rood by B. Copnall.

St Dunstan, Earle Road, Wavertree/Edge Hill
By Aldrich and Deacon, 1886–9. Successful use of bright-red pressed brick with terracotta decoration. W. front has five lancets with reliefs of Christ and Angels, and over the N.W. porch is a statue of St Dunstan. Tall, well-proportioned brick interior with stone piers, elaborate wrought-iron lectern, and well-designed stained glass.

St George, Heyworth Street, Everton
On top of a hill. Thomas Rickman's light iron Gothic of 1812–14. Commissioners' exterior, the tower with traceried battlements. Wonderful interior with lavish use of cast iron in the galleries, arcades and traceried roofs; Rickman worked here with John Cragg, ironmanster. Glass by Shrigley & Hunt.

Holy Trinity, Church Road, Wavertree
By John Hope, 1794; E. end by Sir Charles Reilly, 1911. Liverpool's best Georgian church and a prominent landmark. Fine grey ashlar with balustraded parapet, steeple in the tradition of Wren, and light interior. Flat nave ceiling has gilt central rosette and dentillated cornice. Extended chancel of 1911 has square columns, urns and shallow apse. Low, comfortable pews and surviving W. gallery on Gothic pillars. Good mahogany Georgian pulpit.

St James, St James's Place, Toxteth
Rectangular brick church built in 1774–5 by Cuthbert Bisbrowne, a speculative builder; chancel of 1900 by H. Havelock Sutton. Round-headed windows and square embattled tower. Galleries on quatrefoil iron columns, the earliest remaining example of structural cast iron in Liverpool and, probably, the country. Good plaster cornice and E. window of 1887 by Holliday. R.C.F.

St John, West Derby Road, Tuebrook
By G. F. Bodley, 1868–71. An early and dignified essay in the Decorated style, too little known. Built of red and white sandstone to a simple plan. Bodley concerned himself closely with the sumptuous interior; colour everywhere with exquisite furnishings and murals by C. E. Kempe; early pale glass by Morris and Burne-Jones.

St John, Thomas Lane, Knotty Ash
Stone Gothic church of 1835–6, architect unknown; chancel added in 1890 by Aldridge & Deacon. Basically Perpendicular, of red stone with thinnish details. Best features are the lych gate and spire. Window by Morris.

St Margaret, Prince's Road, Toxteth
By G. E. Street, 1868–9. Generous Decorated church of brick with stone dressings. Big roof with octagonal fleche and dormers; W. façade has rose window between two traceried lights. Fine interior with Devon marble arcades and much good glass and stencilwork by Clayton & Bell. Impressive brass to Robert Horsfall, the founder, d. 1881. Street's vicarage is connected to the church by a passage.

St Mary, Irvine Street, Edge Hill
Brick Gothic church of 1812–13. Embattled nave, the tower with small pinnacles and recessed top. Flat-ceilinged interior lit by

pointed windows with wooden tracery and clear glass. Gallery supported on clustered columns with very pretty cusped front. Some original pews, panelling and stairs with Gothic spandrels. Wide, well-proportioned doors with cusped panels; good decoration on cornices and on ceiling over altar. Monument of 1814 to Edward Mason, founder, with figures and drapery.

St Mary, West Derby Village
By Sir G. G. Scott, 1853–6. Lofty cruciform church in the Second Pointed style of *c.* 1300. Red stone with impressive crossing tower, clerestoried nave and apsidal chancel. Noble interior has circular columns with naturalistic carved capitals, openwork roof, and alabaster reredos enriched with gold and mosaic. Glass by Hardman and Clayton & Bell.

St Matthew & St James, Rose Lane, Mossley Hill
By Paley & Austin, 1870–5. Large cruciform church in late 13th-century style with huge crossing tower. Built of banded red sandstone and coursed rubble with Geometrical clerestory and quatrefoil parapet. Fine Perpendicular choir-stalls, partly medieval. Good drinking-fountain in the churchyard and a matching vicarage.

St Michael-in-the-Hamlet, Toxteth
The secluded 'hamlet' of St Michael is a latticed and stuccoed oasis, mostly early 19th-century Gothic, including Rickman's church of 1815. Low square tower with openwork battlements and tall cast-iron pinnacles. As with St George, Everton, Rickman worked here with John Cragg, ironmaster. There is even more iron here, including the nave piers and window tracery.

St Mary, County Road, Walton-on-the-Hill
The mother church of Liverpool, and a high-standing landmark as seen from the Mersey. Bombed 1940, leaving only the sandstone tower of 1828–32 by John Broadbent, with large crocketed pinnacles. Body now rebuilt in emaciated Gothic by Quiggin and Gee. Mullioned school-house of 1613.

St Paul, Derby Lane, Stoneycroft
By Sir Giles Gilbert Scott, 1916. Bold composition in pale brick; large central tower with pyramidal roof and transepts with half-hipped roofs. Inside are groined vaults, big square piers, and passage aisles. Bears a resemblance to the prize-winning design of the Anglican Cathedral.

St Peter, Much Woolton

By Grayson & Ould, 1886–7. Large sandstone church in the Perpendicular style. A good complete example of a late 19th-century church. Intact interior with wrought-iron screens and organ case, good glass by Kempe and Morris & Co. The lych gate has excellent timber framing and finely carved detail.

LOWTON
St Luke
6m/10km S. of Wigan SJ 6197
Brick church of 1732 with keyed arched windows, Y-tracery, and Venetian windows in the chancel. Neo-Norman W. tower of 1863. Inside are box pews, galleries, and clear glass.

MANCHESTER
SJ 8398
St Agnes, Slade Lane, Levenshulme
By J. Medland and Henry Taylor, 1884–5. Thoughful and original planning in brick with well-carpentered roofs. Many quirky details such as the lopsided W. end, polygonal baptistry, and Early English chancel arcade. Dramatic, well-lit interior.

St Alban, Waterloo Road, Cheetham
By J. S. Crowther, 1857–64. Impressive and well-proportioned church with French and English 13th-century details. Prominent tower and polygonal apse with Geometric windows. Lofty interior, the circular nave piers with foliate capitals and elegant blank arcading in the apse.

St Ann, St Ann's Square
Fine city church of 1709–12 in the style of Wren. It stands across one end of St Ann's Square, which was laid out at the same time. Red sandstone with square W. tower, the cupola demolished as unsafe in 1777. Handsome apsidal E. end with good carving in the frieze and tall Corinthian pilasters. Arcaded and galleried interior with flat coved ceiling. Much original woodwork including pewbacks and the magnificent pulpit. Marble font of 1711 and 'Descent from the Cross' by Annibal Carraci. Monuments include one by Franceys of Liverpool, 1813. Late Victorian and Edwardian glass, the E. windows by the painter and illustrator Frederick Shields.

St Benedict, Ardwick
By J. S. Crowther, 1880; one of his last churches. Large and original church of brick and terracotta in Early English-Decorated style. Tall tower with pyramidal roof and

pinnacles. Brick interior with stone quatre-foil piers, lofty chancel arch, and wonderful, richly glazed seven-light Geometric E. window.

St Cross, Ashton New Road, Clayton
By William Butterfield, 1863–6. Large Middle Pointed-style church of dark red brick with stone and blue-brick bands. Tall S.W. tower with pyramidal roof. Inside, a vivid essay in Butterfield's accustomed poly-chromy, principally red brick with blue diapers. Handsome reredos, recently re-stored.

St James, Skinner Lane, Didsbury
On a slight elevation, looking westward over the low Mersey meadows. Rebuilt in 1620, as recorded on the pinnacled tower with scalloped parapet; refaced in stone in 1855. The light-painted interior, which has grown eastward in stages, 1770 and 1871, contains both round and pointed arches. Arcaded alabaster fine Mosley monument of 1612 with kneeling figures.

St Mark, Cheetham Hill Road, Cheetham
Small, almost hidden, brick church of 1794 with two tiers of arched windows. Interior retains much Georgian character with fine pews, panelling and gallery. Many excellent gravestones in the churchyard, well-lettered and ornamented; splendid sarcophagus of 1818 enclosed by Ionic columns.

St Mark, Barlow Road, Levenshulme
By Medland and Henry Taylor, 1884–5. Red-brick Gothic church of original design, loosely based on the Decorated style, with stone reserved for details. Vivacious exterior has short tower, polygonal baptistry and assy-metrical roofs; interior of exposed brick with bold chancel arch and diagonally boarded roof.

St Matthew, Delaunays Road, Crumpsall
By Isaac Taylor, 1908–10. 'Country' church in this high northern suburb; grey, small and low with square tower, aisles and low-pitched roofs of small grey slates. Good masonry and finish. Worshippers in the wide, pleasant interior of stone and cream-coloured brick can imagine they are in some little church in N. Lancs. or Westmorland.

St Michael and All Angels, Orton Road, Northenden, Wythenshawe
By Cachemaille-Day & Lander, 1937. Re-markable star-shaped brick and concrete church. The plan of two interlocking squares affords a light and spacious interior with a flat ceiling supported on slender concrete piers. Surprisingly dignified, despite the

space-age pulpit; glass by Geoffrey Webb.

St Nicholas, Burnage
By Welch, Cachemaille-Day and Lander, 1932, described by Pevsner as being 'a mile-stone in the history of modern church archi-tecture'. Built in a yellow-grey Lincolnshire brick, it is impressively massed with a long, low porch beside the apsidal chancel, linked to a taller baptistry and short tower. The stunning interior has the high altar in front of a raised platform which houses a chapel at the E. end.

MELLING-WITH-WRAYTON
St Wilfred
5m/8km S. of Kirkby Lonsdale SD 5971
Largely Perpendicular on sloping site neces-sitating three groups of steps to the altar. Clerestory of 1763 altered in 1866. Saxon sculpture, good 17th-century benches and E. window by Holiday.

MIDDLETON
St Leonard
6m/10km N. of Manchester SD 8606
On a hill above the town. Reconstructed 1523–4 by Robert Assheton, whose arms and initials appear on the elaborately pan-elled porch. Extraordinary wooden bell-chamber of *c.* 1667, 'like a dovecote'. Brasses, some glass commemorating Flodden Field, 1513, and a fine Perpen-dicular rood screen with the Assheton arms.

ORMSKIRK
St Peter & St Paul
7m/11km S.E. of Southport SD 4108
Late-medieval tower and spire with nave of *c.* 1540 reconstructed by Paley & Austin in 1887–91. Delectable font of 1661; 15th–16th-century effigies.

OVERTON
(dedication unknown)
2m/3km S.E. of Heysham SD 4358
Remote village with small Norman church. Gabled belfry and wider chancel of 1771, when square-headed windows were made. N. transept added in 1830.

PENDLEBURY
St Augustine
5m/8km N.W. of Manchester SD 7802
By Bodley & Garner, 1870–4. Outstanding Victorian church, modelled on Albi Ca-thedral, but faithfully translated into the English Decorated and Perpendicular styles. Austere red-brick and stone exterior with

canted E. bay; the projected tower was never built. Awesome interior of tall arcades, internal buttresses, and wooden barrel vault; the details simple so as not to spoil the lines. Impressively raised sanctuary with superb Bodley funishings of reredos, sedilia, and rood screen. Glass by Burlison & Grylls.

POULTON-LE-FYLDE
St Chad
3m/4km N.E. of Blackpool SD 3439
In the middle of this old market town. Rebuilding of 1752–3, retaining early 17th-century Perpendicular tower; Romanesque chancel of 1868. Pedimented Tuscan doorways; Georgian interior retains galleries with square pews and good contemporary staircase. Many hatchments, brasses and marble tablets. Screen of 1636 and carved Jacobean pulpit. Pedimented entrance to vault dated 1699.

PRESCOT
Our Lady
4m/6km S.W. of St Helens SJ 4692
High up in the middle of the town. Rebuilt in 1610 with good dated nave roof. Classical tower with urns by Henry Sephton, 1729; late 18th-century spire. Good stalls of 1636, Kempe reredos, and pretty Morris window. Monuments.

PRESTON
SD 5429
St Peter
By Rickman & Hutchinson, 1822–5. Stone and iron Decorated Commissioners' church, upstanding and well-composed; crocketed S.E. spire by Mitchell added in 1851. Inside, everything is cusped; the iron gallery arcade, the door panels, and even the door handles. Great iron-traceried E. window filled with armorial roundels of local families.

RIBCHESTER
St Wilfrid
5m/8km N. of Blackburn SD 6535
Lovely Early English church on site of Roman fort. Fine chancel with stepped lancets, Decorated N. chapel and porch, Perpendicular W. tower. Georgian pews, W. gallery of 1736, and good clear glass.

RIVINGTON
Holy Trinity
2m/3km N. of Horwich SD 6214
Charming little aisleless church in moorland

village. Built *c.* 1540 and remodelled *c.* 1666; mullioned windows and detached 16th-century bell-house. Late Perpendicular screen, linenfold pulpit, and splendid 18th-century chandelier. Brass plate of 1627 with skeleton.

ROCHDALE
SD 8913
St Edmund, Fallinge
By J. M. & H. Taylor, 1873. Bizarre Freemasonic parish church in the middle of a circus, perhaps not inappropriately. Built at fabulous expense, the structure is riddled with references to the Craft. Even the dimensions of the plinth on which it stands echo those of Solomon's temple. Externally the main feature is the massive central tower surmounted by a lantern. Otherwise there is ashlar, rubblework, and exuberant Geometrical tracery. Inside, the tower is supported on four huge granite columns, although the effect of the lantern is now sadly lost. Massive timber roofs of the utmost intricacy, carved capitals and corbels, and a resplendent reredos bedecked with the Vine vie for attention in the memorable interior.
St Mary, Toad Lane
Originally 1740; almost rebuilt by Sir Ninian Comper, 1911, in his 'beauty by inclusion' style. Of brick, artfully unified by an ashlar interior, with arched Georgian windows and Tuscan arcade. Comper added a substantial Gothic caprice entirely his own. The result is an assymetric but not unpleasing structure adorned with excellent screens and other fittings and, alas, his own somewhat half-hearted glass.

RUFFORD
St Mary
6m/10km N.E. of Ormskirk SD 4615
Perfect small brick and stone Victorian church of 1869 by Dawson and Davies, with a spire suggesting a child's box of coloured bricks. Low aisles lit by small pointed windows, mostly filled with good contemporary pictorial glass. Bold and attractive capitals on the nave piers. Memorials include a Flaxman figure, 1817. Royal Arms and brass chandelier, both 1763.

ST HELENS
SJ 5195
St Helen
By W. D. Caroe, 1916–26. Original approach to Perpendicular with prominent

N.W. tower. Red brick outside and good interior with innovative arcades and chancel woodwork, also by Caroe.

SALFORD

SJ 8298

St Philip, St Philip's Place

By Sir Robert Smirke, 1825. Greek. Similar to his church of St Mary, Wyndham Place, London, but all is ashlar here instead of brick and stone. Domed cylindrical steeple rises from a semi-circular Ionic peristyle on the S. side of the church, closing the vista from Bank Place. Nice railings. Pleasant Greek Doric interior with galleries, wreathed frieze, and flat ceiling.

Sacred Trinity, Chapel Street

Classical, with pinnacled Gothic Survival tower. A little Georgian church of 1751; its railings have gone and traffic rumbles nearby. Grey ashlar with two tiers of round-headed windows. Inside, the rich simplicity of darkened oak and white plaster, like the chapel of some great house. Gallery fronts enlivened by heraldic shields and adorned with a pair of marble tablets to the Drinkwater family, one of 1797 signed S. Hope, and the Royal Arms. More arms in carved cartouches on pew-ends; the floor paved with memorial flagstones; black and gold donation boards and silver-topped staves.

St Thomas, Broad Street, Pendleton

By Francis Goodwin and Richard Lane, 1829–31; Gothic Commissioners' church in the style of Barry. Battlemented grey ashlar nave with pinnacled tower. Plaster rib vaulting, skylit galleries, and deep-blue glass in the E. window. Excellent graveyard railings have fortunately survived.

SAMLESBURY

St Leonard

3m/4km E. of Preston SD 5930

Low-down near the Ribble. Neat stone church comprising clerestoried nave of 1558 and aisles; N. tower and porches 1899–1900. The 17th- and 18th-century box pews have been lowered and the three-decker pulpit is now a two-decker. Fine monument of 1801 by J. Kendrick with urn and draped figure. Funeral helmet, sword and shield; Jacobean altar rails; Royal Arms.

SEFTON

St Helen

3m/4km N.E. of Crosby SD 3501

Among flat meadows. Large 14th-century spire rising from a buttressed tower, the outlines unified by spirelets. Of brown-grey stone, the church is otherwise late-Perpendicular, *c.* 1535–40, with long, horizontal lines and an almost flat roof behind an embattled parapet. Glorious early 16th-century woodwork includes canopied rood and chancel screens, screens to the N. and S. chapels and to the Sefton pew. Complete chancel-stalls of *c.* 1500 and canopied pulpit, 1635. Molyneux monuments comprise the best medieval series in Lancs., ranging from a mailed effigy of *c.* 1296 to a table-tomb with brasses of 1568.

SINGLETON

St Ann

2m/3km E. of Poulton-le-Fylde SD 3838

By E. G. Paley, 1860–1. Handsome Early English cruciform estate church with lofty N.E. steeple and plate tracery. Glass by Frederick Preedy in the E. window.

SOUTHPORT

16m/25km N. of Liverpool

St Cuthbert, Churchtown

Stone church, rebuilt in 1730–9; chancel and S. porch of 1908–9 by Isaac Taylor. Classical tower with round-headed lights, plain parapet and spire. Interior largely altered, but retains good monument of 1791 by Joseph Nollekens: Roger Hesketh surrounded by globe, books and a telescope.

Holy Trinity, Manchester Road

By Huon Matear, 1903–13. Very grand town church of pink brick and sandstone; lofty tower topped by octagon and pinnacles. Dramatic French-style interior like a cathedral with soaring octagonal piers, pointed, ribbed barrel vault, and flamboyant stone tracery in the chancel roof. Handsome organ case and rood screen; at N.E. a dark, mysterious chapel.

STAND

All Saints

adjoins Whitefield to S.W. SD 7905

By Sir Charles Barry, 1822–6. Tall, many-pinnacled landmark on high ground, built from the 'Waterloo' fund. Grey ashlar with strong vertical emphasis. Tall, open entrance arches at the base of narrow tower, reminiscent of Barry's St Peter's, Brighton. Galleried interior with clustered columns and plaster rib-vaulting. Richly coloured glass and good rood screen.

STANDISH
St Wilfred
3m/4km N.W. of Wigan SD 5610
Important Gothic Survival church, seemingly of 1582–4, with some Renaissance influence apparent in the arcades. W. tower rebuilt in 1867. Fine panelled roofs, font and pulpit. Competent monument by John Bacon Jnr, 1806; rich glass by Stammers and Capronnier.

STIDD
St Saviour
adjoins Ribchester to N.E. SD 6535
Small and remote 12th-century church, originally associated with a preceptory of the Knights Hospitaller. Narrow Norman windows in the N. side and splendid Early English S. doorway; 17th-century screen and pulpit.

TARLETON
St Mary
8m/12km E. of Southport SD 4520
Neat early-Georgian brick church of 1719. Stone bell-turret and elegant cupola added in 1824, together with porch and vestry. Corner finials, canted apse, and round-headed windows. Interior well lit through clear glass, with square pews, galleries on fluted columns, and handsome cast-iron stove.
R.C.F.

TUNSTALL
St John Baptist, formerly St Michael
3m/4km S. of Kirkby Lonsdale SD 6073
In broad stretch of Lune Valley. Venerable grey church with squarish tower and massive buttresses. Rebuilt *c.* 1415 re-using some 13th-century fabric. Good two-storeyed porch, 18th-century font, and a Roman altar; 15th–16th-century Lowlandish glass in E. window. This was Brocklebridge Church in *Jane Eyre*.

UPHOLLAND
St Thomas of Canterbury
4m/6km W. of Wigan SD 5205
Originally the chancel of a Benedictine priory founded 1317–18. Excellent interior with slender Decorated piers and refined plaster ceiling of 1752; 16th-century W. tower; the present chancel an addition of 1882–6.

URSWICK
St Mary
3m/4km E. of Dalton-in-Furness SD 2674
Massive 13th-century tower with Perpendicular top stage. Aisleless nave with plain timber roof dated 1598, Georgian W. gallery with Tuscan columns and box pews. But the exciting thing here is the woodwork: lots of it, and made by C. R. Ashbee's Camden Guild in 1909–12.

WESTLEIGH
St Peter
1m/2km N.W. of Leigh SD 6401
By Paley & Austin, 1880–1. Impressive brick Decorated church with sandstone details. Massive central tower with pyramidal roof and traceried bands around the top; blank arcading at the E. end. Inside are splendid roofs with tie-beams in the nave and hammer-beams in the chancel. Brick vault and arches under the tower.

WHALLEY
St Mary
6m/10km N.E. of Blackburn SD 7336
Large Early English church with Perpendicular tower, clerestory and aisle windows. Splendid carved woodwork includes the richly carved and canopied stalls of 1418–34 from the adjacent abbey, screened pews of the 17th and 18th centuries, and the organ case of 1729, originally in Lancaster parish church. Good later monuments and three Saxon crosses in the churchyard.

WINMARLEIGH
St Luke
2m/3km N.W. of Garstang SD 4748
By Paley & Austin, 1876. Nave and chancel with transeptal chapels and small broach-spire bell-turret at the crossing. Beautiful painting on chancel walls and boarded ceiling.

WINWICK
St Oswald
3m/4km N. of Warrington SJ 6092
Elevated position; mostly 14th-century, with buttressed tower and large spire. Richly panelled 16th-century roofs in nave and S. chapel. Celebrated chancel in the Decorated style added by A. W. N. Pugin in 1847–8 has steep roof, sedilia, and iron screens. Good 16th–19th-century Legh monuments, part of a Saxon cross, and the enigmatic

Winwick Pig; perhaps an emblem of St Anthony, of unknown date.

WOODPLUMPTON
St Anne

4m/6km N.W. of Preston SD 5034

In low Fylde landscape, green and wooded. Mainly Perpendicular; S. aisle and W. tower are a handsome Baroque rebuilding of 1748. Long, low building of warm cream-coloured stone with octagonal domed belfry and Gibbsian surrounds to the doors and windows in the 18th-century parts. Broad interior is lit by dormers in the roof of 1900, and has three aisles divided by Perpendicular arcades. Tasteful oak pews and screen, also of the 1900 restoration.

WORSLEY
St Mark

6m/10km W. of Manchester SD 7400

By Sir George Gilbert Scott, 1846. Delightful estate church in his favourite Middle Pointed style; archaeological but relieved by jolly details like the gargoyled and crocketed spire. Splendidly eclectic interior with much carved woodwork, tiles, and bright glass by Hardman.

Leicestershire

Introduction

What does 'Leicestershire' mean to you? To most outsiders it stands, I think, for a flat, featureless country strangely beloved by hunting men, for boots and shoes, and a kingdom of red brick. The truth is different. Far from being flat, the county stretches up on its eastern side to the high wolds which it shares with Lincolnshire – part of the limestone spine of England; and on the west it has its own, unique Charnwood Forest, whose granite hills rise to 900 feet above the sea. The hunting country lies mainly in the east and south, and nobody who has walked it (or driven to Leicester by the great road from Grantham, with its swinging, majestic descent into Melton Mowbray) will ever wonder why the hunting men should love it.

This is where Stilton cheese comes from; but Leicester lets the glory go to Stilton – where it was merely sold, never made. That is a characteristic wry Leicestershire joke, and it goes for other things in the county too. Belvoir – an incredible castle, standing up on its hill like something in a fairy-tale – is popularly supposed to be in Lincolnshire, or in Rutland. And when it comes to great men, Leicestershire cheerfully allows twaddle to be talked about Wycliff at Lutterworth, provided nobody mentions its real worthies, like Latimer and George Fox, the first Quaker.

There, indeed, is a hint of the county's character; plain, self-effacing, firmly Puritan. There is no great Roman Catholic family here, though a Cistercian monastery hides in Charnwood Forest. And in Leicester itself Puritanism goes with political Radicalism. But it is a moderate, a Midland Radicalism: content with the city's fat prosperity and the hideous buildings which now go with that, yet all the time secreting, behind the shopping streets, and the harsh red brick, an old town with five ancient churches, a medieval guild hall and castle, and one of the grandest stretches of Roman wall in England.

J.S.

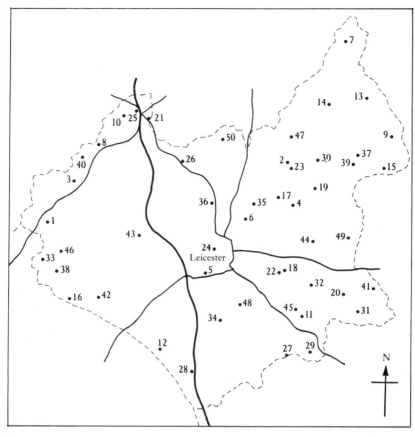

1 Appleby Magna	18 Gaulby	35 Queniborough
2 Asfordby	19 Great Dalby	36 Rothley
3 Ashby de la Zouch	20 Hallaton	37 Saxby
4 Ashby Folville	21 Kegworth	38 Sheepy Magna
5 Aylestone	22 King's Norton	39 Stapleford
6 Barkby	23 Kirby Bellars	40 Staunton Harold
7 Bottesford	24 Leicester	41 Stockerston
8 Breedon-on-the-Hill	25 Lockington	42 Stoke Golding
9 Buckminster	26 Loughborough	43 Thornton
10 Castle Donington	27 Lubenham	44 Tilton-on-the-Hill
11 Church Langton	28 Lutterworth	45 Tur Langton
12 Claybrooke Parva	29 Market Harborough	46 Twycross
13 Croxton Kerrial	30 Melton Mowbray	47 Wartnaby
14 Eastwell	31 Nevill Holt	48 Wistow
15 Edmondthorpe	32 Noseley	49 Withcote
16 Fenny Drayton	33 Orton on the Hill	50 Wymeswold
17 Gaddesby	34 Peatling Magna	

Selected List of Churches

APPLEBY MAGNA
St Michael and All Angels
5m/8km S.W. of Ashby de la Zouch SK 3109
Near one of the best moated sites in the county. Large and well-proportioned 14th-century exterior. Inside much affected by the 1830s restoration; Gothic rib vault, box pews, W. gallery, and bright glass by Collins.

ASFORDBY
All Saints
3m/4km W. of Melton Mowbray SK 7018
Mostly 14th-century ironstone church restored by Sir George Gilbert Scott in 1866–7. Good Perpendicular nave roof with musician supporters and a rare coloured 15th-century bench-end.

ASHBY DE LA ZOUCH
St Helen
16m/25km N.W. of Leicester TF 0555
Attractive site by the castle ruins. Prosperous Perpendicular church with outer aisles by J. P. St Aubyn, 1878–80. Interior has splendid pedimented reredos of 1679 and a good series of monuments beginning with an alabaster tomb of 1561 and including works by Kent and Rysbrack.

ASHBY FOLVILLE
St Mary
5m/8km S.W. of Melton Mowbray SK 7012
Imposing Decorated church with Perpendicular tower and clerestory. Square Norman font and 14th–17th-century monuments.

AYLESTONE
St Andrew
district of Leicester 2m/3km S. of city centre SK 5700
Huge chancel of *c.* 1300, one of the largest in any village church. Elizabethan brass and a mysterious Saxon window in the tower.

BARKBY
St Mary
5m/8km N.E. of Leicester SK 6309
Late 13th-century church of ironstone with unique early-Decorated window tracery;

perhaps a 19th-century rearrangement. Pochin monuments include a Gothic romance of 1804.

BOTTESFORD
St Mary the Virgin
7m/11km W. of Grantham SK 8038
The approach to the church is delightful, across a brook and through a screen of trees. The nave and spire are handsome 15th-century work, reminiscent of several over the Lincs. border, a few miles away. The chancel was rebuilt in the 17th century, to accommodate the magnificent monuments of the Earls (later Dukes) of Rutland, whose home, Belvoir Castle, looms up on the hills to the S. The monuments completely fill the chancel, blocking the sight of the altar from the nave. They afford a fascinating view of changing aristocratic taste in the 16th and 17th centuries.

BREEDON-ON-THE-HILL
St Mary & St Hardulph
5m/8km N.E. of Ashby de la Zouch SK 4022
Stands within a great Iron Age camp on top of the hill, keeping watch on the Trent Valley. The hill itself is being steadily quarried away, the workings now approaching close to the edge of the churchyard. There was a Saxon monastic foundation here. The present church is Norman and 13th-century; its nave has been destroyed. From the Saxon church came the wonderful 8th-century carved stones, now set high up under the clerestory, in the S. aisle, and inside the tower (arrange to see especially the Breedon Angel let into the wall on the first floor). The N. aisle contains monuments and a Jacobean canopied pew of the Shirley family of Staunton Harold.

BUCKMINSTER
St John the Baptist
3m/4km W. of Colsterworth SK 8722
Village setting. Stately fabric with later 13th-century tower, broach spire, and Perpendicular chancel. In the churchyard is the Gothic Dysart mausoleum of *c.* 1875.

CASTLE DONINGTON
St Edward, King and Martyr
7m/11km N.W. of Loughborough SK 4427
Large towny 13th- and 14th-century church
with Perpendicular porch and clerestory.
Fine alabaster tomb of Robert Hazylrygg,
d. 1529, and wife Eleanor, with arches,
angels and bedesmen. The church was
heavily restored by W. Smith of the Adelphi,
London, 1876–7.

CHURCH LANGTON
St Peter
4m/6km N. of Market Harborough SP 7293
The tower is a landmark to the traveller
entering Leics. from London by the Midland
line. It is a very fine composition, tapering
by stages from the ground and panelled at
the sides. The proportions of the building
throughout are excellent: the characteristic
Leics. nave, short and high, is seen here to
perfection. The fabric is Decorated with
heavy 15th-century remodelling. The interior is a little chilly, from over-zealous
restoration; but that enables one to concen-
trate attention on the architectural outlines,
which are the most important thing here.

CLAYBROOKE PARVA
St Peter
4m/6km N.W. of Lutterworth SP 4987
Good Perpendicular nave of the conventional tall Leics. type. The chancel is perfect
early 14th-century work, as beautiful inside
as out. The best exterior view is from the
S. side of the churchyard, where the treatment of the walls and the flowing tracery of
the windows can be studied.

CROXTON KERRIAL
St Botolph & St John the Baptist
7m/11km S.W. of Grantham SK 8329
Village setting; 15th-century central tower
and much else besides. But inside, an astounding collection of Perpendicular bench-
ends, the largest in the county.

EASTWELL
St Michael
6m/10km N. of Melton Mowbray SK 7728
Delightful village church, basically 13th-
century, with unusual Decorated stone
chancel screen and plaster tympanum above.

EDMONDTHORPE
St Michael and All Angels
6m/10km N. of Oakham SK 8517
Large and stately church for so small a
village; mostly Decorated and containing
splendid 17th–18th-century Smith monuments, including the famous 'bleeding lady'.

FENNY DRAYTON
St Michael and All Angels
3m/4km N. of Nuneaton SP 3597
Late 12th-century S. door, but otherwise
mostly Decorated, all heavily restored in
1860. Excellent series of Purefey monuments, 1545–1628; a memorial of 1736
records a grim struggle with the gout, 'attended with Exquisite Pain and Torture'.

GADDESBY
St Luke
6m/10km S.W. of Melton Mowbray SK 6813
Perhaps the most exciting medieval church
in the county, dating mainly from about 1290
to 1340. The ornamentation of the exterior
of the S. aisle is unique – a brilliant and riotous
exhibition of the 14th-century stone carver's
art. The exterior also has the largest collection
of masons' marks in the county. The interior
has been sympathetically and lightly restored,
leaving the old, partly medieval seating and
brick floors. The light pours in through clear
glass, illuminating the wide empty spaces of
the nave. In the chancel is a lifesize statue of
Colonel Cheney on his horse at Waterloo,
removed from the Hall nearby.

GAULBY
St Peter
7m/11km E. of Leicester SK 6900
Perpendicular chancel, otherwise rebuilt in
1741 by John Wing Snr of N. Luffenham.
Striking W. tower and nave with good Gothic
details.

GREAT DALBY
St Swithun
3m/4km S. of Melton Mowbray SK 7414
Village. The steeple collapsed on the nave
in 1685, and it was rebuilt in Gothic Survival
style; the medieval tower and chancel
escaped damage.

HALLATON
St Michael and All Angels
7m/11km N.E. of Market Harborough SP
7896
The main body of the church is 13th-
century, including its delightful tower and
spire. The aisles are a 14th-century addition;
at the E. end of the N. aisle there is an
elaborately decorated turret, surmounted by

a little spire. There is a spirited Norman tympanum in the porch. The interior is less distinguished, though there is good 13th-century ornamentation in the chancel. The N. aisle has a small crypt.

KEGWORTH
St Andrew

5m/8km N.W. of Loughborough SK 4826
The church stands well, in the centre of the little town, on a hill above the water meadows of the Soar. The lower part of the tower is 13th-century, the whole of the rest of the building early 14th-century, giving it a striking architectural coherence. Chapels at the E. end of the aisles look like transepts and help to build up the impressive external view from the E. The interior is somewhat bare; good Royal Arms of 1685.

KING'S NORTON
St John the Baptist

7m/11km S.E. of Leicester SK 6800
Entirely rebuilt by John Wing Jnr of N. Luffenham, 1760–75. The church should first be seen from across the fields to the S., its lofty windows giving it a grandeur unusual in Gothic buildings. The approach from the W., up a series of ascending levels, is impressive. The interior, dominated by the centrally placed pulpit, is remarkably complete and undisturbed. The oak fittings are 18th-century throughout. Here again, it is the windows that give the building its special distinction. All that is missing, to realize the architect's soaring conception, is the spire, which was destroyed by lightning in 1850.

KIRBY BELLARS
St Peter

3m/4km W. of Melton Mowbray SK 7117
Beautifully placed on rising ground above the little River Wreak. Best seen from the road leading from Melton Mowbray or from the N. across the river. Tall broach spire. The ironstone and limestone combination appears here to great advantage. The building is of the 13th century, enlarged and embellished in the 14th, when it became the church of a small collegiate foundation.

LEICESTER
SK 5804
St Andrew, Jarrom Street

By Sir George Gilbert Scott, 1860–2. Built of patterned red and blue brick with bellcote,

apsed chancel, and large S. transept. Broad and aisleless interior with wagon roof, the polychrome walls sadly painted.
St Margaret, St Margaret's Way

The most handsome of the city churches. The S. doorway and the S. nave arcade are 13th-century, the rest is 14th- and 15th-century. The tower and the chancel are particularly good examples of Perpendicular work. By the altar is the alabaster tomb of Bishop Penny, d. 1520. As a composition the church appears best from the N.E. corner of the churchyard.
St Mark, Belgrave Gate

By Ewan Christian, 1871–2, minor extension of 1903–4. Large church of Mountsorrel granite, the long nave and chancel roof of Swithland slate. Prominent spire and good interior with polished granite columns, polychromatic brickwork, and painted timber vault.
St Mary de Castro, Castle Green

The church stands on the edge of the Green. Its good Perpendicular spire, much repaired and rebuilt, dominates the river front of the old town. Except on days of brilliant sunlight, the interior is gloomy and mysterious. The history of the fabric is complicated, and at some points perplexing. There is Norman work in the nave, and the sumptuous chancel is late-Norman in its present form, with splendid contemporary sedilia. The wide S. aisle is mainly 13th-century with a Perpendicular roof. The tower is 'engaged' into this aisle, its ground floor forming a baptistry.
St Nicholas, St Nicholas Circle

Viewed from the W., this church is unforgettable; it towers over the Roman foundations and the core of the Jewry Wall. The nave is Anglo-Saxon; see the doubled-splayed windows in the N. wall; the Roman wall survived because it formed part of the narthex of this early church. Heavily restored in 1904–5.

LOCKINGTON
St Nicholas

1m/2km E. of Castle Donington SK 4627
Early 13th-century, but the aisles were widened in the early 14th century to give the present spacious interior. Impressive five-light reticulated E. window in the N. aisle. Excellent fittings include a good Perpendicular screen beneath a huge Royal Arms of 1704, two-decker 18th-century pulpit, box pews, benches, and an 18th-century W. gallery.

LOUGHBOROUGH
SK 5319
All Saints
Handsome town church, mainly 14th-century with Perpendicular tower and clerestory. The exterior in particular heavily restored by Sir George Gilbert Scott, 1860–3.

LUBENHAM
All Saints
2m/3km W. of Market Harborough SP 7087
Virtually unrestored Georgian country interior. Plaster and whitewash still cover the walls and even the 13th-century piers and capitals of the nave. The three-decker pulpit and box pews of 1812 survive as a set, together with a little medieval seating in the chancel. Recently discovered wall-paintings on the chancel arch.

LUTTERWORTH
St Mary
6m/10km N.E. of Rugby SP 5484
A large, mainly 13th- and 14th-century church with some earlier fabric. There is a large and important 14th-century Doom over the chancel arch, and in the N. aisle figures of three kings. Handsome marble memorial to John Wycliff by R. Westmacott Jnr, 1837.

MARKET HARBOROUGH
St Dionysius
14m/22km S.E. of Leicester SP 7387
The magnificent 14th-century steeple, one of the finest in England, dominates the market-place and little grammar school of 1614. The rest of the church fails to live up to this promise, but there are fine Decorated windows in the chancel, a rich Royal Arms of 1660, and galleries added in 1836.

MELTON MOWBRAY
St Mary
14m/22km N.E. of Leicester SK 7519
A stately cruciform town church with a tall central tower, marred only by a very clumsy external stair turret on the N. side. The transepts have E. and W. aisles, a rare extravagance denied to many cathedrals. The church is mainly late 13th- and early 14th-century, but the most striking features are Perpendicular, including the lavish clerestory of 48 windows and the top stage of the tower. The interior has suffered much from bad restoration; the chancel is dingy and almost wholly without interest. There is a

fine pair of 18th-century brass chandeliers in the transepts.

NEVILL HOLT
St Mary
5m/8km S.W. of Uppingham SP 8193
Hill-top site with fine views of the Welland Valley. Late 13th-century chapel much altered in the 15th century. Good carved Jacobean pulpit and 17th-century Nevill monuments.

NOSELEY
St Mary
7m/11km N. of Market Harborough SP 7398
Private chapel made collegiate in 1274, the fabric largely of that date with fine Y-traceried windows. Perpendicular roof and parapet. Spacious interior, its character reflecting the collegiate function; excellent carved stalls of 1474 with traceried ends and the three cocks badge of the Stauntons.

ORTON ON THE HILL
St Edith of Polesworth
4m/6km N. of Atherstone SK 3003
Impressive 14th-century fabric, one of the most 'atmospherick' churches in the county; 18th-century box pews, three-decker pulpit and font; 14th-century effigy of an abbot of Merevale.

PEATLING MAGNA
All Saints
6m/10km N.W. of Husbands Bosworth SP 5992
This largely late 13th-century church is not of great note from the outside, though well seen from the road to the E. Inside, the walls have been scraped, but the pearly colour and texture of the stone are as delightful, in their different way, as plaster. The woodwork includes some 15th-century and Jacobean seating, a fine 17th-century pulpit, altar rails, and reredos.

QUENIBOROUGH
St Mary
6m/10km N.E. of Leicester SK 6412
Fine W. tower of pink granite with white stone dressings supporting a superb spire, one of the best in the county.

ROTHLEY
St Mary the Virgin & St John the Baptist
5m/8km N. of Leicester SK 5812
Impressive church of pink granite with grey

stone dressings; largely 14th-century but restored and the chancel rebuilt in 1878. Good monuments and 9th-century Saxon cross in churchyard.

SAXBY
St Peter
4m/6km E. of Melton Mowbray SK 8219
By George Richardson, 1789. Rebuilt in Hawksmoor's urban manner but set down in verdant pastures. A nice restrained Georgian box with an elegant spire rising from an octagon replete with urns. Interior naughtily treated in 1874.

SHEEPY MAGNA
All Saints
3m/4km N.E. of Atherstone SK 3301
A Perpendicular chruch with W. tower. Its main interest is in the four stained glass windows in the S, wall, two by Morris and Co. to designs by Burne-Jones, 1879, and two by Kempe, 1897.

STAPLEFORD
St Mary Magdalene
4m/6km E. of Melton Mowbray SK 8118
In a glade of the woods of Stapleford Park. It should be seen in the spring when the daffodils are out. The church was wholly rebuilt in the Gothic taste to the designs of George Richardson and at the expense of the Earl of Harborough in 1783. The interior is distinguished. The seats face inward, as in a college chapel. All the original fittings remain and the woodwork is good, especially the W. gallery. A 15th-century brass and a Caroline monument survive from the earlier church, both of high quality. On the N. side of the chancel is a superb monument by Rysbrack. The glass is clear throughout, but there is constant colour and movement in this church from the play of trees outside.

STAUNTON HAROLD
Holy Trinity
3m/4km N.E. of Ashby de la Zouch SK 3720
The private chapel of Staunton Harold Hall, set at an oblique angle to it, on a grass bank rising from the lake. The chapel was built at the expense of Sir Robert Shirley in 1653–65, as an Anglican gesture of defiance to the Commonwealth government. 'When', as the inscription over the W. door proclaims, 'all things sacred were throughout the nation Either demollisht or profaned.' Sir Richard died in the Tower in 1656 and the church was only completed after the Restoration. Though not the only church in England originating during the Cromwellian period, it is unique in preserving all its fittings, including pews, painted ceilings, altar hangings, and plate. The 17th-century pale-green glass survives in some of the windows. Early 18th-century organ and iron chancel screen, probably by Robert Bakewell.
N.T.

STOCKERSTON
St Peter
2m/3km S.W. of Uppingham SP 8397
Lonely and atmospheric late 13th-century church with heavy Perpendicular overlay. Good 15th-century glass in N. aisle and a fine incised slab of 1634, perhaps by Nicholas Stone.

STOKE GOLDING
St Margaret
3m/4km N.W. of Hinckley SP 3997
A building of exceptional perfection, showing Decorated design and carving at its best, both outside, in the openwork parapet and buttresses, and inside, especially in the S. nave arcade with clustered columns and capitals carved with foliage. The windows are notable throughout, particularly the Geometrical E. windows of the nave and aisle, and the N. windows, with their flowing tracery, which are a little later.

THORNTON
St Peter
5m/8km S.E. of Coalville SK 4607
In a charming situation, on the side of a hill falling steeply down to a reservoir. The 14th- and 15th-century church has been very little restored, retaining its plastered walls, old floors and seating, tympanum, last painted in 1820, and enormous S. door with 14th-century ironwork. In the S. aisle the traceried heads of the E. window contain 14th-century glass. Good linenfold bench-ends of 1560 and a shallow chancel added in 1864.

TILTON-ON-THE-HILL
St Peter
9m/15km N.W. of Uppingham SK 7405
Delightful rustic exterior of decaying ironstone and a slender limestone steeple. Originally late 12th-century – see the good tower arch – but extensive Perpendicular works, the clerestory providing a beautifully light interior.

TUR LANGTON
St Andrew
5m/8km N. of Market Harborough SP 7194
By H. Goddard & Son, 1865–6. All built
of red brick, even the spire, in an effusive
High Victorian-Early English style. Red and
black brick interior with moulded capitals
and other details. Rich glass by Heaton,
Butler & Bayne and fine iron railings in the
churchyard.

TWYCROSS
St James the Great
5m/8km N.E. of Atherstone SK 3304
Modest Decorated church Perpendicu-
larized. Apart from a late-Georgian family
pew, all the fittings belong to a major restoration of 1840. This was also the time at
which the astounding 12th- and 13th-
century French glass fetched up in the E.
window. Originally from St Denis and
Sainte-Chapelle, it marks out this obscure
place as a pilgrimage goal for aesthetes.

WARTNABY
St Michael
4m/6km N.W. of Melton Mowbray SK 7123
Modest but significant village church with
large 13th-century W. double bellcote. The
early 13th-century S. arcade retains much
rare original ornamental painting: red and
white with flowers, trails and zig-zags.

WISTOW
St Wistan
6m/10km S.E. of Leicester SP 6495
A small church on the edge of the park
at Wistow Hall, formerly the home of the
Halfords; 15th-century tower, but the appearance of the fabric is now mainly of the
1746 remodelling with some early 19th-
century fiddling. Near-perfect Georgian interior with plaster ceiling, altar rails of
painted ironwork, reredos, pulpit, and box
pews, all rounded off by a Royal Arms and
Halford tombs.

WITHCOTE
(dedication uncertain)
5m/8km S.W. of Oakham SK 8306
A very small rectangular building serving as
the chapel for Withcote Hall, which it
adjoins, and dating probably from about
1520–30. The windows are filled with excellent original glass. Restored in 1744, there
is a noble reredos incorporating monuments
on either side.
R.C.F.

WYMESWOLD
St Mary
5m/8km N.E. of Loughborough SK 6023
Early 14th-century and Perpendicular
church, much decayed before A. W. N.
Pugin's celebrated restoration of 1844–6.
His are the deep-green roofs with the golden
stars, the furnishings of font, sedilia and
pulpit, the glass, the chandeliers, and even
the binding of the Bible.

Lincolnshire

Introduction

This is the second-largest county in England and the least appreciated. The broad estuary of the Humber cuts it off from Yorkshire, so that it is on the way to nowhere except to the city of its glorious cathedral and its own fishing-port of Grimsby. It has pleasure resorts like Skegness on a very few of those ninety miles of low sandy coast, extremely rich agricultural towns like Spalding and Boston among their flat fields of bulbs and roots, and the industrial borough of Scunthorpe. The county town and cathedral city of Lincoln is ancient on the hill and industrial in the valley. Only the south-west corner of the little-known county is bothered by the through traffic from London to the north. The A1 now bypasses the limestone town of Stamford with its fine churches, stone-tiled roofs, and substantial 17th-century and Georgian houses built in hilly streets. The A1 goes on by Grantham, whose elegant 14th-century spire rises above the old red-brick and red-tiled roofs of the town.

Those who think of Lincs. as dull and flat are wrong. The scenery runs from north to south down the whole length of the county in varied bands. Along the inland western border is a limestone cliff extending from Stretton in Rutland to Winteringham on the Humber. Along its ridge, known locally as The Ramper, runs the Ermine Street in a straight line, and on the slopes below are the country houses, parks and feudal villages. From this ridge was quarried the beautiful white Ancaster and Lincoln limestone, of which so many of the churches were built. From Barton-on-Humber almost as far as the forgotten port of Wainfleet extend the chalky hills known as the wolds, which are an unexplored variant of the Sussex Downs. Here at Somersby, near the old red-brick town of Louth with its silver spire, Tennyson was born. The limestone ridge looks west, and the chalky heights look east to:

> Calm and still light on yon great plain
> That sweeps with all its autumn bowers,
> And crowded farms and lessening towers,
> To mingle with the bounding main.

The 'great plain' is the fen and the marsh north of it between the wolds and the sea. The coast is mostly dunes and samphire moss against the cold North Sea. In fen and marsh the landscape is three-quarters sky, as it is in so many of Tennyson's poems. A further type of Lincolnshire scenery is the heath between the chalk and the limestone. In places it creates something as unexpected as Woodhall Spa, that half-timbered Bournemouth-like settlement, among silver birches, heather and rhododendron.

The county has 700 churches and is divided into three parts, Lindsey the northern half of the county, and Kesteven and Holland the south-western and south-eastern quarters. Then these parts are sub-divided into sokes and wapentakes and the whole county is Anglo-Saxon, though largely Scandinavian in dialect and place-names.

Except for the Cathedral and Louth, the old churches of Lindsey are smaller than those in the south of the county, and on the wolds and heath, where there was only local sandstone, they consist only of nave and chancel, the weathered sandstone churches of the wolds having a crumbled and patched look. Kesteven, being full of limestone and a prosperous wool district, abounds in splendid 14th-century churches, most of which have enormous towers and spires.

The part known as Holland was navigable fen, and stone was brought here by water to build some of the finest late-medieval churches in England, such as Boston, Spalding and Gedney, which look all the more magnificent for the flatness of the landscape.

J.B.

continued overleaf

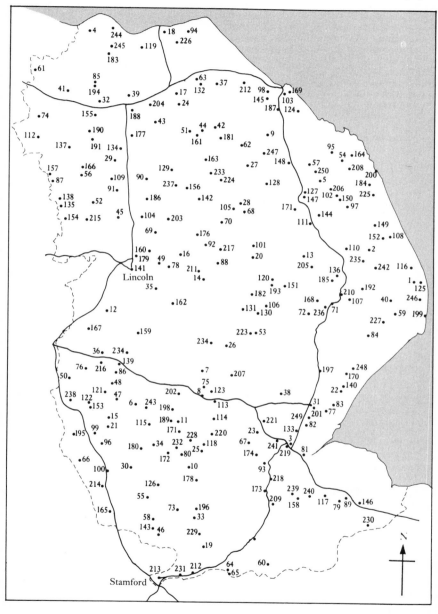

Selected List of Churches

ADDLETHORPE
St Nicholas
4m/6km N. of Skegness TF 5468
A grand 15th-century marsh church, with bold W. tower and spacious sparkling-white interior – but no chancel; a lazy 18th-century incumbent pulled it down, to save the trouble of repairing it. A great array of medieval screens and pews; the rood screen, with its rood and figures, forms a reredos for the high altar at the E. end of the nave.

ALFORD
St Wilfrid
11m/18km S.E. of Louth TF 4575
A good 14th-century church notable for three things: the chamber over the S. porch, the fine alabaster monument of Sir Robert Christopher, d. 1668, and a drastic restoration by Sir George Gilbert Scott in 1867, when a second N. aisle was added and the tower heightened.

ALGARKIRK
St Peter & St Paul
6m/10km S.W. of Boston TF 2935
A great cruciform church, one of the stateliest in the N. fenland; Early English, Decorated and Perpendicular, with central tower and low leaded spire, double-aisled transepts, and great traceried windows. It was grandly restored by R. C. Carpenter in 1850–4, and is a complete realization of conservative Victorian restorer's aims – with highly coloured interiors, vistas everywhere, well-furnished chancel, skilfully placed and gaily painted organ case; chancel and S. transept windows by Hardman, the rest by Clayton & Bell. Monuments to the Beridge family, squarsons from the 17th to the 19th century.

ALKBOROUGH
St John the Baptist
7m/11km N. of Scunthorpe SE 8821
This church stands in a commanding position in the N.W. corner of the county, and from the top of the tower one can see York Minster, Lincoln Cathedral, Beverley Minster, Spurn Lighthouse, and Hull Docks. The lower part of the tower is probably pre-Conquest. The nave arcades are 13th-century, and the chancel was rebuilt by J. O. Scott in 1887. The floor of the porch has a replica in iron of the local maze.

ALVINGHAM
St Adelwold & St Mary
3m/4km N.E. of Louth TF 3691
Two churches in one churchyard: St · Adelwold's (Alvingham) has a 13th-century tower and an early 19th-century brick chancel; St Mary's (N. Cockerington) is chiefly 12th–13th-century, with a comfortable box-pewed interior. Placid views over the yew-clad churchyard to the old Louth Canal.

ANCASTER
St Martin
5m/8km W. of Sleaford SK 9843
Early English and Decorated with fine recessed spire and splendid Norman N. nave arcade, enriched towards the E.; 18th-century mural tablets.

ANWICK
St Edith
4m/6km N.E. of Sleaford TF 1150
Possesses one of the 14th-century broach spires typical of the Sleaford district. When the chancel was restored 100 years ago, a Madonna figure was found in one of the walls still bearing traces of its original colour.

ASGARBY NEAR SLEAFORD
St Andrew
3m/4km E. of Sleaford TF 1145
A little park bordering the A17, a farmhouse with Gothic windows, and a Decorated church with a huge Perpendicular crocketed spire dwarfing the rest; an untouched interior of clear glass, old floors, and oil lamps.

ASHBY-CUM-FENBY
St Peter
5m/8km S. of Grimsby TA 2500
The church is approached past almshouses across pastureland with views of a calm 18th-century rectory. Norman and Decorated, it

contains splendid memorials, including a magnificent altar tomb of *c.* 1640 to Sir William Wray and his wife.

ASLACKBY
St James
7m/11km N. of Bourne TF 0830
Setting in a valley; 14th-century tower of interest by virtue of the tall blocked side openings, perhaps reflecting its connection with the Knights Templar, who had a preceptory here.

ASWARBY
St Denis
4m/6km S. of Sleaford TF 0639
An estate village set against the backdrop of the Park, still the home of its ancient family. Handsome, spacious church, largely Decorated but with a grand Transitional S. door and a Perpendicular spire – the chancel a successful rebuilding by Blore, 1840. Grand box pews, grained woodwork, enormous stuffed hassocks, family monuments and hatchments – the whole interior is redolent of early 19th-century England.

AUBOURN
St Peter
6m/10km S.W. of Lincoln SK 9262
A beautiful fragment – the chancel of the medieval church, once again restored to use; delightfully furnished, and filled with Meres and Nevile monuments and hatchments.

BAG ENDERBY
St Margaret
5m/8km N.W. of Spilsby TF 3472
A sandstone church in a remote village in the heart of the wolds, with a 14th-century nave, chancel and windows, and 15th-century tower, porch and E. window. The font has carvings of a Pietà, a hart and emblems of the Passion. Medieval glass includes the arms of Crowland Abbey. Monuments of 1591 and 1739.

BARDNEY
St Lawrence
9m/15km W. of Horncastle TF 1169
Built after 1434 when the old parish church collapsed. Fine proportions with a good contemporary brick chancel. Remains brought from Abbey can be seen in the church.

BARKSTON
St Nicholas
4m/6km N. of Grantham SK 9341
Good Norman and later ironstone W. tower with a crocketed Perpendicular spire, at the end of a pretty village street.

BARLINGS
St Edward King and Martyr
7m/11km E. of Lincoln TF 0774
This church is pleasantly placed in a green field near the ruins of the Premonstratensian Monastery whose abbot was hanged for his part in the Lincolnshire Rising of 1536. There is a Norman doorway and some 13th-century work. Restored by Charles Kirk of Sleaford in 1876 when the E. bay of the nave was heightened.

BARNETBY-LE-WOLD
St Mary
4m/6km E. of Brigg TA 0509
A lovely forlorn church on a hill-top, with Saxon work in the S. wall and a unique sculpture depicting an unidentified animal rather like a cat. There is also a good modern church of 1926–8 by Wilfrid Bond in the village.
R.C.F.

BARTON-ON-HUMBER
6m/10km S.W. of Hull across the Humber
TA 0321
St Mary, Burgate
Originally a chantry chapel, this is one of the most magnificent churches in the county. Elaborate Norman N. arcade, early 14th-century S. arcade, 15th-century clerestory, and a number of memorials, including a brass of 1433.
St Peter, Beck Hill
The tower with its W. extension is one of the earliest pieces of ecclesiastical architecture in the county and is similar to that of Earls Barton, Northants. St Chad founded the original church here in the 8th century. Apart from the Saxon work, most of the present building is 14th-century, surmounted by a fine Perpendicular clerestory. Perhaps the most notable feature is the unglazed E. window of the N. aisle, which bears the Crucifix and attendant figures on its three mullions.
E.H.

BASTON
St John the Baptist
4m/6km S. of Bourne TF 1113
Mainly Perpendicular; Early English chancel arch, the chancel rebuilt in 1860. W. wall of S. aisle has fleuron frieze and bellcote, probably from chapel founded in 1403. Good 18th–19th-century gravestones.

BAUMBER
St Swithin
4m/6km N.W. of Horncastle TF 2274
An intriguing church – outwardly odd, with its enormous square red-brick tower and bare brick walls pierced with traceried Gothic windows. But under the tower a Norman W. door and Early English nave arcades reveal that it is in fact a spacious medieval church, enclosed in Georgian brick. Three ogee Gothic arches, playfully adorned with foliage, divide nave from Georgian Gothic chancel, and resemble similar work at Shobdon in Herefordshire – perhaps by the same hand. Burial-place of Pelham-Clintons, Dukes of Newcastle.

BELTON
St Peter & St Paul
3m/4km N.E. of Grantham SK 9339
'Belton Church was built to the glory of the Brownlows, and in memory of God' (the late Harry Cust); a glorious collection of monuments to the family by Joshua Marshall, Stanton, Cheere, Tyler, Bacon and others crowd the entire church and Wyattville's mortuary chapel. But there is a Norman nave arcade with one enormous pier, adorned with lozenge motif à la Durham and a Norman font with bell-ringer rebus.

BENINGTON
All Saints
5m/8km E. of Boston TF 3946
The church was restored by James Fowler in 1876 and has good lancet windows in the chancel, a 14th-century nave, and late 15th-century tower and clerestory. Chancel originally vaulted; the beginnings of the vaults are cut off before they spread above the choir-stalls.

BICKER
St Swithin
2m/3km N.E. of Donington TF 2237
Cruciform church described by Pevsner as 'truly amazing'; boasts a truncated but impressive Norman nave, central tower, long chancel, and much else. Trees and rows of cottages line the dyke.

BIGBY
All Saints
4m/6km E. of Brigg TA 0507
A small church in a beautiful setting at the foot of the wolds near Brigg. Apart from the nine-sided font the most interesting features are the monuments, including one dated 1518 to Sir Robert and Elizabeth Tyrwhitt, which bears the figures of their 22 children and a brass of 1632 to Edward Naylor, 'a faithful and painefull minister of God's word'.

BILLINGBOROUGH
St Andrew
9m/15km N. of Bourne TF 1134
Decorated and Perpendicular, but over-restored by W. Bassett-Smith, 1889–90. Lofty Decorated spire with flying buttresses.

BILLINGHAY
St Michael
8m/12km N.E. of Sleaford TF 1554
The heavily banked dyke, called the Billinghay Skirth, flows past the village; the church has a dumpy spire with flying buttresses which, with the upper part of the tower, was rebuilt in 1787: an interesting example of 18th-century medievalism.

BINBROOK
St Mary with St Gabriel
7m/11km N.E. of Market Rasen TF 2193
The best church designed by a much-criticized architect, James Fowler of Louth. It was built in 1869, replacing one of the two former churches, both of which were demolished. Fowler's church has a well-proportioned spire, but it is perhaps a trifle too ambitious and cathedral-like for a village in the heart of the Lincolnshire wolds. Its Early English style is so faultless and repetitive as to make the whole thing dull.

BISCATHORPE
St Helen
1m/2km N. of Donington-on-Bain TF 2284
Pretty 1840s church in a pretty setting. Fanciful openwork spire with prominent crockets; otherwise brick-cased with cement. Small font of white earthenware.

BLYBOROUGH
St Alkmund

3m/4km S. of Kirton-in-Lindsey SK 9394
Pleasantly set in a well-wooded park. Has a
ridiculous tower, but is worth visiting for the
sake of the early 15th-century tomb of a
former rector, who is represented in Euchar-
istic vestments, and also for the interesting
rood, set on a beam brought from Thornton
Abbey. Part of the figure of Christ was lying
amongst lumber in the church some years
ago, and the rest was dug up in the rectory
garden.

BOOTHBY PAGNELL
St Andrew

5m/8km S.E. of Grantham SK 9730
Famous for its Norman manor house; its
church deserves to be better known for its
Norman tower and Norman nave, and lofty
Decorated chancel. Moreover, at the end of
the last century, it was gloriously restored
and refurbished by Pearson, at the expense
of a generous patroness. All was done in
exquisite taste; rood screen, stalls, pews,
organ, a gorgeous reredos, lamps, tiles, and
excellent stained glass by Clayton & Bell
make this an interior not to be forgotten.

BOSTON
port on R. Witham TF 3244
St Botolph, Church Close

'The largest and most important parish
church in England', wrote the great Dr Cox.
It dominates the town; it dominates the
countryside. Its chancel projects, elegant,
enormous, into the market-place; its tower
stands sentinel on the very bank of the River
Witham, 288 feet high, the loftiest medieval
tower in England, albeit it is nicknamed 'The
Stump'. The church is Decorated, the tower
Perpendicular, and the scale of everything
is tremendous. Inside, the eye is carried on
up to the E. end with 64 medieval stalls
in the chancel, crowned with 19th-century
canopies and splendid Victorian reredos.
There is a whole range of monuments, of
every period; a Jacobean pulpit and an important window by O'Connor. The only
jarring note in this incredible interior is the
recent hideous nave altar with its accompanying furniture.

St Thomas, London Road
By Temple Moore, 1912; a perfect early
20th-century church by this gifted architect.
Mullioned windows and render outside; restrained interior with Arts and Crafts fittings.

BOTTESFORD
St Peter in Chains

2m/3km S. of Scunthorpe SE 8907
Almost caught up in Scunthorpe – but this
is one of the most important pure Early
English churches anywhere. The spacious
nave is lofty and clerestoried, the chancel as
lofty as the nave. Everywhere there are long,
narrow lancets and clever interplay of alternate lancet and circular windows.

BOURNE
St Peter & St Paul

10m/16km W. of Spalding TF 0920
This is one of the few surviving monastic
churches in Lincs., although the present
building contains only the nave of the Abbey
church. The nave arcades are good examples
of 12th-century work; there are twin towers
of which one is incomplete, and a 15th-
century clerestory.

BRACEBY
St Margaret

6m/10km E. of Grantham TF 0135
Small Early English and later church with
fine shafted chancel arch and delightful
13th-century gabled bellcote.

BRANSTON
All Saints

4m/6km S.E. of Lincoln TF 0267
Saxon tower with Perpendicular spire – the
rest of the church burnt out in 1962, and
rebuilt by G. G. Pace. Notable monuments
to Sir Cecil Wray by Carter, 1736, and to
Lord Vere Bertie by Harris, 1770.

BRANT BROUGHTON
St Helen

7m/11km E. of Newark SK 9154
In its own right this is a major church, mostly
14th-century in date, late-Decorated and
early-Perpendicular in style, with spire 198
feet high with lavish pinnacles – but only a
mean chancel of 1812. In 1873 Canon F. H.
Sutton invited his friend G. F. Bodley to
rebuild the chancel, and the wonderful partnership of rector and architect resulted in the
church we possess today, with its perfectly
conceived chancel, medieval colour restored
everywhere, the grandest furnishings, the
most splendid glass, designed and made by
Canon Sutton himself. The eye is led up to
the sanctuary where Bodley's reredos frames
the celebrated picture by the Master of Leis-
burn. Lit by candles, the interior is like a

medieval dream. There are many attractive houses in the wide village street.

BROCKELSBY
All Saints
9m/15km W. of Grimsby TA 1411
Delightful Decorated building containing two 16th–17th-century tombs and later monuments to the Pelham family, Earls of Yarburgh. Elegant organ case by James Wyatt, 1778.

BROTHERTOFT
St Gilbert
4m/6km W. of Boston TF 2746
1847 Gothic, worth a visit. Dark woodwork; contemporary stained glass by Wailes; amusing corbels, including mitred bishop in full-bottomed wig.

BROUGHTON
St Mary
3m/4km N.W. of Brigg SE 9608
Saxon tower with semi-circular external turret stairway; compare with Hough-on-the-Hill, q.v. Most interesting features inside the church are two 14th-century brasses, two fine alabaster effigies of members of Redford family, *c.* 1380, and a large monument to Sir Edmund Anderson, Lord Chief Justice of the Common Pleas, 1671.

BURGH-LE-MARSH
St Peter & St Paul
5m/8km W. of Skegness TF 5065
The lofty tower of this handsome late 15th-century church serves as a seamark near Skegness. Unusual parapet and exceptionally fine windows in the bell-storey. Chancel screen and other screens, pulpit and font cover mostly early 17th-century. The N. doorway is earlier than the rest of the church and belongs to the period of the Black Death; the S. porch, now used as a vestry, was built of brick in 1702 and is picturesque, with Dutch gable. Leonard Palmer brass, 1610.

BURRINGHAM
St John the Baptist
4m/6km W. of Scunthorpe, SE 8309
By S. S. Teulon, 1856–7. Small red and black brick church with stone details. Massive W. tower with at the N.W. angle an unexpected polygonal turret – the boiler chimney-stack. Vivid polychrome interior with tiled font and glass by Alexander Gibbs.
R.C.F.

CABOURNE
St Nicholas
2m/3km E. of Caistor TA 1401
Saxon tower has original W. doorway with massive imposts and plain tympanum. Restored by A. W. Blomfield in 1872. Norman tub font.

CADNEY
All Saints
3m/4km S.E. of Brigg TA 0103
Beautifully restored by Sir Charles Nicholson, 1912; a late-Norman S. arcade, but most of the church is early 13th-century. The E. window is Perpendicular. There is a Norman font, 16th-century alms box on a shaft, and a 12th-century stone coffin lid. Best of all is the parclose screen round the chantry chapel in the S. aisle, bearing traces of its carved inscription, perhaps from Newstead Priory nearby.

CAISTOR
St Peter & St Paul
8m/12km N. of Market Rasen TA 1101
The lower stage of the tower is late-Saxon or early-Norman, the nave arcades are 13th-century, and the N. arcade bears corbels identical with those in the choir aisles of Lincoln Cathedral. There is a noble Early English S. door. In the Hundon Chapel at the E. end of the N. aisle there are seven 14th-century stone effigies and, in the chancel floor, a brass to John Ousterby, d. 1461, and his wife. The vestry contains a coloured alabaster monument to Sir Edward Maddison, who died at the age of 100 in 1553.

CAMMERINGHAM
St Michael
7m/11km N. of Lincoln SK 9482
Round arches in N. wall. Pre-Conquest 'knot-work' stone forms sill of the W. doorway. Tyrwhitt monument, 1636. Marble font, 1755.

CAREBY
St Stephen
6m/10km N. of Stamford TF 0216
By itself on the edge of its tiny village in meadows watered by the infant River Glen. Its early 13th-century tower with low tiled roof gives the whole composition a French look; 14th-century knocker on S. door;

inside there are 14th-century arcades, two 14th-century effigies, a rare medieval crimson cope made into an altar frontal, and a most unusual 19th-century pitch-pine vaulted roof.

CARLTON SCROOP
St Nicholas
6m/10km N.E. of Grantham SK 9445
The lower part of the tower is Norman; the upper was rebuilt in 1632. The nave arcades and porch are 13th-century. The E. window contains figures of the donor and his wife in medieval glass. Handsome Jacobean pulpit.

CAYTHORPE
St Vincent
8m/12km N. of Grantham SK 9348
A church of much interest with its nave divided into two by an early 14th-century arcade. The central tower is surmounted by an exceptionally tall crocketed spire, rebuilt by Sir George Gilbert Scott in 1860 after having been struck by lightning. There are remains of a Doom painting over the tower arch, and late 17th- and early 18th-century memorials to the Hussey family.

CHERRY WILLINGHAM
St Peter
4m/6km E. of Lincoln SK 0372
Built 1753, the best example of its period in the county. Now restored to something like its original form. Large memorial to founder, Thomas Becke, 1757, on N. wall.

CLAYPOLE
St Peter
5m/8km S.E. of Newark SK 8449
Cruciform church. Much rich crocketed stonework. Impressive Perpendicular E. window of plain glass. Beautiful Perpendicular screen. Canopied pulpit with lectern standing on brass stem of medieval processional cross.

CLIXBY
All Hallows
2m/3km N. of Caistor TA 1004
This was the chancel of an early 13th-century church and was ruinous until restored in 1889. On the floor is a stone with an incised cross and chalice and the remains of a Lombardic inscription, to the memory of Robert Blanchard, priest.
    R.C.F.

COATES-BY-STOW
St Edith
2m/3km N.E. of Stow SK 9083
A tiny church, Norman and later, far away among farm buildings E. of Stow, tactfully restored by Pearson in 1884 and containing a Perpendicular rood screen complete with loft and tympanum. Some of the boards of the latter have been renewed, but traces of the painted figures can still be seen on the older wood. The pulpit and box pews are also 15th-century, and there are some fragments of medieval glass. Brasses and small monuments in the chancel.

CONINGSBY
St Michael and All Angels
4m/6km S.E. of Woodhall Spa TF 2258
Important Decorated and Perpendicular tower, with open ground floor for processions – and an enormous one-handed clock. Spacious church all Decorated and Perpendicular, but the apsidal chancel is of 1870, by T. C. Hine of Nottingham.

CONISHOLME
St Peter
7m/11km N.E. of Louth
The small, mainly 14th-century church has been rescued from decay, and admirably restored. Pantiles have been substituted for the cracked lead on the roof, and the walls plastered and whitened inside and out. There is a brass, 1515, to John and Anne Langholme and their 14 children. Part of 10th-century crucifix propped in S. window of chancel.

CORBY GLEN
St John the Evangelist
7m/11km N.W. of Bourne SK 9924
Attractive, decayed market town, with dignified, spacious Perpendicular church. Fragments of ancient glass and important medieval wall-paintings, especially the figures of shepherds, Herod, Magi and Virgin and Child in the clerestory.

CORRINGHAM
St Lawrence
4m/6km E. of Gainsborough SK 8791
Important Anglo-Saxon tower; inside, Norman and Early English arcades with Perpendicular clerestory – all splendidly restored and decorated by Bodley; gaily painted ceiling, rood screen and chancel-

Baroque plasterwork and ceiling paintings by Verrio, Great Witley,
Worcestershire

Late Romanesque south door, Kilpeck, Herefordshire

Opposite above: Mid-18th-century rococo-Gothic with enormous pews painted white, Shobdon, Herefordshire

Below: Greek temple designed 1778–9 by Nicholas Revett, Ayot St Lawrence, Hertfordshire

Norman south door with its striking tympanum, Barfrestone, Kent

Left: Monument to Dr Plot, historian, Borden, Kent

Below: Mereworth, Kent; built *c.*1740 for John Fane, Earl of Westmorland, its spire a copy of St Giles-in-the-Fields, London

Above: Arcaded alabaster Mosley monument (1612), St James, Didsbury, Manchester

Above right: 17th-century monument to the Earl of Rutland, Bottesford Leicestershire

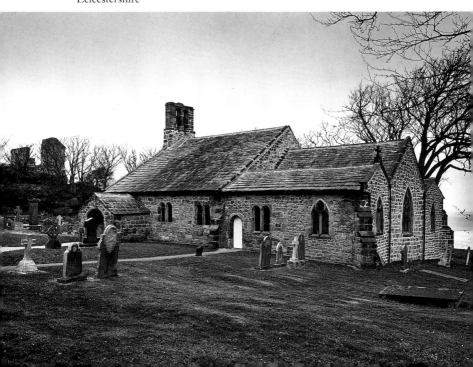

Fourteenth-century broach spire, Anwick, Lincolnshire

Opposite: Looking north-west to St Peter's Church, Heysham, Lancashire

One of the most famous Fenland churches, with Early English tower and spire, Long Sutton, Lincolnshire

Fifteenth-century brick castle keep and collegiate church, Tattershall, Lincolnshire

stalls, and good Victorian glass by Wailes, Kempe and Powell.

COVENHAM

5m/8km N. of Louth TF 3394
Two medieval churches, but a stone's throw from each other:

St Bartholomew

Mainly 14th-century; has lost its N. transept. In one of the windows are remains of its original stained glass. Redundant, but restored and maintained by a recently formed Trust.

St Mary

Is possibly a little later and has an octagonal font with carved emblems of the Passion on suspended shields. Also, removed from St Bartholomew, a brass to Sir John Skypwyth, 1415.

CREETON

St Peter

5m/8km W. of Bourne TF 0119
With its 13th-century broach spire it looks perfect from the London–Edinburgh main line, against the background of ancient oaks in Grimsthorpe Park – a lovely composition on its hillside. Two Saxon crosses in the churchyard and fragments of interlace carving built into the fabric.

CROFT

All Saints

2m/3km N.E. of Wainfleet TF 5061
A lovely church near Skegness, full of good 15th-century woodwork, including screens and box pews. Pulpit 1615. Brass eagle lectern, found in the mud at the bottom of a moat some years ago, is late pre-Reformation. Among the excellent monuments is a small brass in the S. chapel, showing the upper part of a knight in chain mail, which is one of the oldest in England. In an unusual position, against the S. jamb of the chancel arch, is a monument to William Bonde, 1559, erected by his son Nicholas, President of Magdalen College, Oxford.

CROWLAND

St Mary with St Guthlac & St Bartholomew
8m/12km N.E. of Peterborough TF 2310
Of the great Abbey church there remains the Early English W. front, a frontispiece of great beauty even in its fragmentary state, together with the enormous Perpendicular N.W. tower with its grand two-storeyed porch. The N. aisle is now the parish church and is early

15th-century. The W. front was conserved by Prof. R. Baker in the 1980s. Fine late 13th-century mason's tomb-slab with square and dividers. A unique triangular bridge in the town, built c. 1390, once spanned streams that now run beneath the road.

CROWLE

St Oswald

8m/12km W. of Scunthorpe SE 7712
Medieval church. Fine 10th-century cross shaft of Viking inspiration. Splendid Norman S. door with carved figures, reputedly of King Oswald and his son Oswy.

CROXBY

All Saints

3m/4km N.W. of Binbrook TF 1998
This church is so isolated in the heart of the wolds that it might easily be missed, which would be a pity. Most of the building and the font are Norman. There is some 13th-century arcading in the walls and a few 15th-century pew-ends. There is a two-light window on the S. side, the sandstone masonry of which was eroded and beyond repair and has been cleverly reproduced in limestone.

CROXTON

St John the Evangelist

7m/11km N.E. of Brigg TA 0912
A good example of modern restoration; stonework pointed as it should be; rainwater disposed of properly and walls plastered and limewashed. The church, mainly 13th-century, was in very bad condition, and the restoration reflects great credit on a very small parish. A few years ago a panel of medieval glass depicting the Crucifixion was restored to the church.

DEEPING ST JAMES

St James

adjacent to Market Deeping TF 1509
Originally the Priory church, this displays well every architectural style from Norman to 18th-century. It was originally cruciform but the transepts have gone. The tower and spire were built in 1717. The late-Norman font is adorned with a design of intersecting arches.

DEEPING ST NICHOLAS

St Nicholas

5m/8km W. of Spalding TF 2116
By Charles Kirk Snr, 1845–6; one of his

best new churches. Of rock-faced limestone in Lincolnshire Decorated style with pinnacled tower, broach spire, and lucarnes. Canopied founders' tomb by R. C. Hussey.

DENTON
St Andrew
4m/6km S.W. of Grantham SK 8632
Grand, spacious church with tall Perpendicular tower. Monuments to John Blythe, 1602, and to Richard Welby, 1714, by Green of Camberwell; organ case by Bentley, 1887 – all in a delightful position against the Park with its ancient plantations.

DONINGTON
St Mary and the Holy Rood
9m/15km N.E. of Spalding TF 2035
A decayed, ancient little market town, with important and distinguished Fen church, all Decorated and Perpendicular with grand detached S.W. spire crowning a spacious vaulted porch; interior prim with Victorian fittings. Memorial to Matthew Flinders, the explorer, 1814.

DONINGTON-ON-BAIN
St Andrew
6m/10km S.W. of Louth TF 2382
Entertaining inscription to an early 17th-century rector: 'Both Chrysostome and Polycarpe in one united lye beneath this stone . . .'

DUNHOLME
St Chad
6m/10km N.E. of Lincoln TF 0279
Largely Early English but very much restored; contains 13th-century font, monument of 1616, and an interesting 14th-century satchel.

EAST BARKWITH
St Mary the Virgin
3m/4km N.E. of Wragby TF 1681
A typical village church, mostly late 15th-century. The W. window of the S. aisle is a lancet with widely splayed jambs, found in 1868, having been bricked up. There were traces of fittings for a shutter and no grooves for glass, so it may have communicated with an anchorite's cell. There is an original Madonna over the porch, *c.* 1380. The font, with emblems of the Passion, is almost identical with that of Covenham St Mary. The N. aisle was added in 1868.

EAST KEAL
St Helen
2m/3km S.W. of Spilsby TF 3362
Early English; restored and W. tower added by Stephen Lewin, 1853–4; 14th-century font decorated with curious grotesque head. Between E. and W. Keal the view towards Boston is the finest in the county.

EAST KIRKBY
St Nicholas
5m/8km S.W. of Spilsby TF 3362
Splendid restoration, 1903–5, leaving you to guess date of poppyheads, pulpit, and so on. Excellent medieval stonework.

EDENHAM
St Michael and All Angels
3m/4km N.W. of Bourne TF 0621
Perpendicular tower of Somerset type; window tracery. Contains very important and magnificent monuments to the Dukes of Ancaster, and other members of the family, by Scheemakers, Cheere, Roubiliac, Harris, and Nollekens; Grimsthorpe Castle, still the seat of the family, stands nearby. Important 8th-century Saxon roundels in the S. aisle.

EPWORTH
St Andrew
9m/15km N. of Gainsborough SE 6803
Early English and Decorated with Perpendicular tower. Table-tomb of Samuel Wesley on S. side, on which his son John stood to preach.

EWERBY
St Andrew
4m/6km E. of Sleaford TF 1247
The spire is one of the best of its date in England. It is 172 feet high and engaged by the aisles. The church is Decorated architecture at its finest. The font is contemporary with the church, but appears to be mounted on the inverted bowl of a Norman font. There is some good woodwork in the chancel and a late 14th-century effigy in the N. aisle. The altar rails are probably Laudian, and the windows contain exceptionally good early 19th-century glass. The church was restored by Hodgson Fowler in 1895.

FENTON
All Saints
6m/10km E. of Newark SK 8750
A little church on the Notts. border, saved from dereliction in recent years, with a dis-

tinguished 14th-century crocketed spire and an interior full of old woodwork.

FISHTOFT
St Guthlac
2m/3km S.E. of Boston TF 3642
Mostly Norman and Perpendicular with good five-light E. window of *c.* 1290. Fine Decorated-Perpendicular rood screen.

FISKERTON
St Clement
5m/8km E. of Lincoln TF 0472
A pinnacled Perpendicular tower and a Perpendicular exterior hide a puzzling interior with two splendid arcades, one Norman and one of clustered Early English pillars; and the later tower conceals the remains of an early round tower enclosed inside it.

FLEET
St Mary Magdalene
2m/3km E. of Holbeach TF 3823
Fine 14th-century Fenland church with tower and spire detached from rest of building. Chancel rebuilt in 1862. Remainder of church is Decorated except for Early English arcades and Perpendicular W. window.

FOLKINGHAM
St Andrew
8m/12km S. of Sleaford TF 0733
A picturesque village, once a town of importance, on a hillside, with an enormous market-place and an old coaching inn. The church, which is surrounded by noble trees, has a splendid rood screen and chambered S. porch. The arcades are 14th-century and the windows early 15th-century. The chancel is Early English with traces of Norman work. The late-Perpendicular tower, one of the best in the county, is a conspicuous landmark.

FOSDYKE
All Saints
7m/11km S. of Boston TF 3133
By Edward Browning, 1871–2. Of red brick, with prominent Early English lead broach spire. Shafted lancets, quatrefoil clerestory windows, and good stiff-leaf capitals to the nave arcades in the well-furnished interior.

FRAMPTON
St Mary the Virgin
3m/4km S. of Boston TF 3239
Impressive Norman and Early English tower with broach spire; 'Ricardus in angulo' stands for ever in his corner of the N.E. of the church.

FREISTON
St James
3m/4km E. of Boston TF 3743
Remains of ancient priory. Huge row of clerestory windows above elaborate corbel table. Impressive Norman arcades and lovely parclose screen and font cover.

FRISKNEY
All Saints
3m/4km S.W. of Wainfleet TF 4655
This church on the edge of the Fens contains architectural features of all periods from Norman onward, good Perpendicular screenwork, and a Commonwealth pulpit. Some particularly interesting wall-paintings were discovered here in 1879, when Butterfield was restoring the church; but they have almost disappeared.

FRODINGHAM
St Lawrence
district of Scunthorpe E. of town centre SE 8911
Medieval, but substantially and conservatively rebuilt in early days of Gothic Revival, 1841, with Early English tower. Sir Charles Nicholson added a new nave and chancel on the N. side in 1913. Altar, 1635.

FULBECK
St Nicholas
9m/15km N. of Grantham SK 9450
A particularly attractive village, claimed to be the prettiest in Lincs. The church has a grand Perpendicular tower, late-Norman font, and an array of monuments to the Fane family, including one to Thomas Bell, 1674, a servant of the family, who toured Europe with his master; a touching inscription.

GAINSBOROUGH
All Saints
15m/25km N.W. of Lincoln SK 8189
The 15th-century tower of the medieval church survives; the rest was rebuilt in Classical style in 1736, and the architect was almost certainly Francis Smith of Warwick. It is a splendid building, but unfortunately lost some of its 18th-century fittings in a Victorian 'restoration'. Nearby is the Old Hall, an amazing and enormous 15th–16th-century house of brick and timber, former seat of the Burgh and Hickman families,

which after many vicissitudes is now restored and is open to the public.

GAUTBY
All Saints
4m/6km N.E. of Bardney TF 1772
An 18th-century church in a romantic setting, within the old garden walls of the vanished Gautby Hall. Beautiful furnishings; Vyner monuments.

GEDNEY
St Mary Magdalene
3m/4km E. of Holbeach TF 4024
'More glass than wall'; possesses an Early English tower surmounted by an unfinished Perpendicular spire. The E. window is an example of 14th-century work of a Continental type. The S. porch has an upper storey, approached by a turret stairway. Important 14th- and 15th-century glass in N. aisle. The monuments include a late 14th-century brass, some coloured alabaster effigies to members of the Welby family, and a 13th-century figure of a knight in armour.

GLENTHAM
St Peter
7m/11km W. of Market Rasen TF 0090
The tower was rebuilt in 1756, and the church is a 14th-century building of considerable charm. Two notable features of this church are the Pietà over the door of the S. porch and the brass effigy of Elizabeth Tournay, 1452, in the chapel at the E. end of the N. aisle.

GLENTWORTH
St Michael
11m/18km N. of Lincoln SK 9488
Good 11th-century Saxon tower has belfry lights with mid-wall shafts and a key-hole window with palmette decoration. Magnificent tomb of Sir Christopher Wray, Lord Chief Justice, 1593.

GOLTHO
St George
1m/2km S.W. of Wragby TF 1177
Remote brick church, probably of c. 1530, on the site of a deserted village. Moulded brick windows; reredos of c. 1700; Georgian pulpit and box pews.
R.C.F.

GOSBERTON
St Peter & St Paul
6m/10km N. of Spalding TF 2331
A Fen church of great magnificence, Decorated and Perpendicular, cruciform with central tower and crocketed spire, grand transepts, great traceried windows, and a spacious and many-vistaed interior.

GOXHILL
All Saints
2m/3km S.E. of New Holland TA 1021
Tall Perpendicular W. tower; Early English chancel over-restored in 1878–9. Mid-15th-century wall-painting of the Crucifixion in the S. porch.

GRAINTHORPE
St Clement
7m/11km N.E. of Louth TF 3897
Has fine spacious nave and aisles, early-Decorated, with a good Perpendicular tower. There are high pews and a brass on the chancel floor consisting of a cross with an elaborate head. The stem is lost, but part of the foot remains and stands on a rock in some water, wherein fish are swimming.

GRANTHAM
St Wulfram
SK 9135
Sir George Gilbert Scott regarded the spire of St Wulfram's as 'second only to Salisbury in beauty'. Not only is the spire of great beauty, the whole W. front is as distinguished as that of any parish church in England. Here Ruskin stood spellbound. Above soars the spire, 281 feet high, built between 1230 and 1300 – before Salisbury, 404 feet, before Norwich, 345 feet, before Coventry, 300 feet, before Louth, 294 feet. In its day it was the loftiest spire in England, the first of our great English spires. On either side are the enormous Geometrical windows of the two engaged aisles, and these wonderful traceried windows continue all around the exterior. The church is enormously wide, with aisles almost as broad as the nave, divided by early 13th-century arcades; the power of the grand interior is horizontal rather than vertical; 14th-century crypt; an interesting collection of monuments; splendid Victorian furnishings by Sir G. G. Scott, Arthur Blomfield, and Walter Tapper – the whole sits in a spacious churchyard, surrounded by Georgian and earlier buildings.

GREAT CARLTON
St John the Baptist
6m/10km E. of Louth TF 4185
In a particularly pleasant setting, surrounded by fine trees. Rebuilt, except for the tower, in 1860–2 by James Fowler; an example of good Gothic Revival work. Those who look at the 15th-century tower are bidden, by a carved inscription, to pray for the soul of Robert Schadworth.

GREAT COATES
St Nicholas
2m/3km W. of Grimsby TA 2310
A grand Perpendicular tower with eight pinnacles. Brasses to the Barnardiston family. The nave arcades are Early English and the chancel is Decorated. The chancel was restored by James Fowler of Louth in 1865.

GREAT GONERBY
St Sebastian
2m/3km N.W. of Grantham SK 8938
Imposing 14th–15th-century church, embattled and crocketed, beside the old North Road. Good Decorated font and glass of the hare riding the hound.

GREAT PONTON
Holy Cross
4m/6km S. of Grantham SK 9230
A wonderful tower, built by Anthony Ellys, merchant of the Staple of Calais, in 1519 – magnificent beside the Great North Road.

GREAT STURTON
All Saints
5m/8km E. of Louth TF 3987
Obscure and tiny village on edge of Wolds, with a church conservatively restored on anti-scrape principles by Micklethwaite in 1904. Within built-up N. arcade is an unusual 17th-century painting of Time and Death.

GRIMOLDBY
St Edith
4m/6km E. of Louth TF 3987
Impressive, mainly late 14th-century church of greenstone. Tall W. tower and broad chancel rebuilt in 1876. Much old woodwork in the roof, screen, and bench-ends.

GRIMSBY
St James, St James Square
16m/26km S.E. of Hull TA 2709
This stately church was restored by R. J.

Withers between 1874 and 1885, and it was severely damaged by enemy action during the last war, but it has been sympathetically restored. Despite much damage and rebuilding this remains a great 13th-century cruciform church, with nave of six bays, central tower, transepts, and spacious, dignified chancel. Lady Chapel by Bodley, 1906. The size of the church is spectacular proof of the importance of Grimsby in the Middle Ages.

HACKTHORN
St Michael
7m/11km N. of Lincoln SK 9982
Church and Hall a perfect picture across the park. Church a remarkable achievement of 1849; the tower is modelled on Magdalen College, Oxford; splendid furnishings, and glass by Wailes and Holiday.

HAINTON
St Mary
6m/10km S.E. of Market Rasen TF 1884
Hall and church make a delightful group across Capability Brown's Park; the Heneages have lived here since the 14th century, and the church contains a notable collection of their tombs and monuments from the 16th century to the present time.

HALTHAM-ON-BAIN
St Benedict
4m/6km S. of Horncastle TF 2463
A small church in a water meadow in a pretty village containing an inn thatched with Norfolk reeds. The S. door is Norman and has a carved tympanum. There is an Early English N. arcade, a remarkable Decorated E. window, a six-sided font, and an ogee-headed priest's door. A wonderful interior of old pews and screens arranged in different sections. A church not to be missed, with its humble bellcote, a building of great charm.
R.C.F.

HALTON HOLEGATE
St Andrew
1m/2km S.E. of Spilsby TF 4165
Stands on one side of the Hollow Gate and commands one of the best views in the county. It is entirely 15th-century with a noble tower. It has been much, but carefully, restored at various times. An effigy of a knight in armour was found under the floor.

HANNAH
St Andrew
4m/6km N.E. of Alford TF 5079
An unsophisticated little mid-18th-century church of greenstone, standing on a little knoll in marshland, not far from the coast; an interior complete with its original two-decker pulpit, pews and altar rails.

HARPSWELL
St Chad
5m/8km S. of Kirton-in-Lindsey SK 9390
A small church at the foot of the cliff hill. It has a Saxon tower with an inscription stating that the clock was given to commemorate the Battle of Culloden, but the original clock was removed to the stables of Aswarby Park, near Sleaford, and the present one substituted for it. There is a 14th-century S. aisle and the N. arcade has been built up. In 1891 an incised effigy of a priest was found in the floor. There is also a 14th-century effigy of a rector and a memorial to another, William Harrington, d. 1697. This last is inscribed on the ancient altar-slab.

HAUGH
St Leonard
3m/4km N.E. of Alford TF 5079
Delightful 11th-century and later church, mostly built of chalk, on the high wolds. It stands next to the Elizabethan-brick front of the Bolle manor house and contains their monuments.

HAUGHAM
All Saints
4m/6k S. of Louth TF 3381
By W. A. Nicholson, or perhaps his partner, George Willoughby, 1840. An engaging church of brick and stucco with a spire in imitation of Louth, and an interior replete with period furnishings.
R.C.F.

HAXEY
St Nicholas
3m/4km S. of Epworth SK 7699
Mixture of medieval styles; Perpendicular tower and 15th-century effigy. The famous Haxey Hood Game begins at the cross base by the church on old Christmas Day, 6 January, each year.

HECKINGTON
St Andrew
5m/8km E. of Sleaford TF 1340
A most famous Decorated church, perfect from the outside but a little disappointing inside, except for the wonderful Easter Sepulchre and the superb carved sedilia. By an unusual arrangement, the transepts come W. of the easternmost bay of the nave. The medieval proportions cannot be properly appreciated because of the loss of the chancel screen; and the Victorian glass is poor. The tracery of the E. window is an unsurpassed piece of artistry comparable with the E. windows of Carlisle and Selby.

HELPRINGHAM
St Andrew
6m/10km S.E. of Sleaford TF 1340
Grand Decorated W. tower and spire with flowing tracery, panelled pinnacles, crockets and lucarnes. Beautiful Norman frieze inside S. wall.

HEYDOUR
St Michael
6m/10km S.W. of Sleaford TF 0039
A secluded valley, and a tiny hamlet. The large church with its lofty spire is Early English, Decorated and Perpendicular, and contains an important quantity of 14th-century glass, and a wealth of 18th-century monuments to the Newtons of Culverthorpe. Two by Rysbrack, two by Scheemakers, they are easily missed, concealed by the organ and a red-baize door.

HOGSTHORPE
St Mary
6m/10km N. of Skegness TF 5372
Early English tower and a Perpendicular S. porch bearing a rare inscription recording its building by the fratres and sorores of the Guild of St Mary.

HOLBEACH
All Saints
7m/11km E. of Spalding TF 3524
A little later than Heckington, marking transition from Decorated to Perpendicular. Magnificent tower and spire, and a fine W. window, unaccountably described in Murray's Guide as 'ungraceful'.

HORBLING
St Andrew
6m/10km W. of Donington TF 1135
A cruciform church whose tower has Norman work at the bottom and Perpendicular work at the top. There is a lot of 14th-century work and a good font with

emblems of the Passion, and in the N. aisle is an unusual medieval effigy of a kneeling knight and lady.

HORKSTOW
St Maurice
7m/11km N. of Brigg SE 9818
Italianate pantiles on roof. The sanctuary reached by 10 steps over the Shirley family vault. The painter Stubbs worked here.

HORNCASTLE
St Mary
18m/29km E. of Lincoln TF 2669
Memorial on canvas to Sir Ingram Hopton, killed at Battle of Winceby, 1643. Many other mementos of those troublous times, such as pikes used in the battle and memorials to persecuted ministers of religion.

HOUGH-ON-THE-HILL
All Saints
7m/11km N. of Grantham SK 9246
A mighty Saxon tower, with one of only four semi-circular extruded staircase turrets in all England; the others at Broughton in Lincs., q.v., and Brixworth and Brigstock in Northants. Whitewashed, atmospheric interior of distinguished Saxon proportions. King John spent the last night of his life in a small priory at Hough after over-indulging himself on an unwise diet of peaches and new cider at Swineshead.

HOUGHAM
All Saints
6m/10km N. of Grantham SK 8844
Stands alone and stately close to the River Witham; here a Saxon cross shaft forms a lintel for the S. door. There is a lofty, spacious nave with a perfect Norman arcade, a Georgian chancel, and a crusader tomb – all sympathetically restored by Temple Moore early this century.

HOWELL
St Oswald
4m/6km E. of Sleaford TF 1346
A very prettily situated church in a tiny parish near Heckington. The architectural details are Norman, Transitional and Decorated. Notice the 14th-century bell-gable and the font, 1373, with shields and an incised memorial to John Croxby, a 15th-century rector.

HUMBERSTONE
St Mary
4m/6km S.E. of Grimsby TA 3105
The church was built at a cost of £3,000 in 1720–1 and is attached to a 14th-century tower. Grand monument to Matthew Humberstone, d. 1709, who bequeathed £1,000 towards its rebuilding.

INGOLDMELLS
St Peter with St Paul
4m/6km N. of Skegness TF 5668
One of a group of impressive churches near Skegness, with a 15th-century porch and a wealth of notable woodwork. Like Addlethorpe, Ingoldmells lost its chancel at the beginning of the 18th century through the negligence of the same incumbent. A unique feature is a brass to the memory of William Palmer 'wyth the stylt', 1520, on which he is represented as a civilian in a long-sleeved gown with his 'stylt' or crutch beside him.

IRNHAM
St Andrew
6m/10km N.W. of Bourne TF 0226
This is a particularly interesting church, standing on the edge of the park, and displaying architectural styles from the 13th–14th centuries; there is a fine brass to Sir Andrew Luttrell, 1390. Parts are missing, but the figure of the knight and the cusped canopy over his head are especially good examples. The manor belonged for many generations to the Roman Catholic family of Thimbleby and their descendants, to whom there are some monuments.

KEDDINGTON
St Margaret
1m/2km N.E. of Louth TF 3488
Small Norman and later church with splendid re-used Early English arch from Louth Abbey, a 12th-century gable cross inside the church, and a fine 15th-century wooden eagle lectern.

KELSTERN
St Faith
5m/8km W. of Louth TF 2590
Setting in almost deserted village; 19th-century church with 17th-century South family memorials and three windows by Comper.

KINGERBY
St Peter
4m/6km N.W. of Market Rasen TF 0592
An extremely picturesque church standing by the roadside opposite a wood which is carpeted with aconites in springtime. There

is a very solid tower and a S. door, both of the 12th century. Reared against the S. wall is a specimen of what Boutell described as 'semi-effigial' monuments. It shows the head and shoulders of a civilian, beneath which is a floreated cross in relief, with the feet of the figure protruding from its base and resting on a dog. There are four shields, one bearing the arms of the Disney family, to which the subject of the monument belonged.

R.C.F.

KIRKBY-ON-BAIN
St Mary
3m/4km E. of Woodhall Spa TF 2462
A humble little greenstone church of 1802, in a pretty setting. Polygonal chancel, Queen Anne Royal Arms, and glass by Morris & Co., 1926.

KIRKSTEAD
St Leonard
7m/11km S.W. of Woodhall Spa TF 1762
Hard to find in its setting of bumpy fields, and adjoining the jagged fragments of the S. transept of Kirkstead Abbey, stands this little church, the *capella ante portas* of the Cistercian Abbey. This exquisite, tiny, vaulted Early English church, with narrow lancets, delicately carved capitals, and dwarf shafts, is one of Lincolnshire's most precious jewels.

KIRMINGTON
St Helen
6m/10km N. of Caistor TA 1011
Early English tower with copper spire of 1838, the rest of the exterior by S. S. Teulon, 1859. Decorated arcades with remarkable figured capitals.

KIRTON-IN-HOLLAND
St Peter & St Paul
4m/6km S.W. of Boston TF 3038
A grand Fen church, once much larger, but still majestic with a nave of six Early English bays with Perpendicular clerestory, and great Decorated traceried windows in the aisles, beautiful furnishings, and strong devotional atmosphere. The splendid W. tower is a piece of brilliant early 19th-century pastiche, having previously been the central tower of the cruciform building.

KIRTON-IN-LINDSEY
St Andrew
8m/12km S. of Scunthorpe SK 9398
Massive Early English tower with pilaster

buttresses and S. door of same period, porch of which has been converted into vestry. Late Norman priest's door in chancel with tympanum of knotwork. Tower arch divided by central pillar was uncovered during restoration in 1860.

KNAITH
St Mary
3m/4km S. of Gainsborough SK 8284
The fragment of a priory, in a romantic position on the banks of the Trent; 17th-century furnishings; birthplace of Thomas Sutton, founder of the Charterhouse.

LANGTON-BY-PARTNEY
St Peter & St Paul
3m/4km N. of Spilsby TF 3970
Dr Johnson used to worship here when he visited his friend Bennet Langton at the Hall, and on one celebrated occasion he took off his coat and rolled down a grassy hill. If he revisited the church now, he would still feel at home in it, although the E. end would probably surprise him. An early 18th-century building, with tiered seats, facing N. and S., a three-decker pulpit and a gallery, all unspoiled by restoration.

LAUGHTON
All Saints
5m/8km N.E. of Gainsborough SK 8497
Against the backcloth of vast woods, a medieval church gloriously restored and refurbished by Bodley in 1894 for Mrs Meynell-Ingram in memory of her husband. Bodley rebuilt the lofty chancel, installed the organ, designed the sumptuous reredos and rood screen, and provided the new roof. Altar ornaments are all due to him. It is a wonderful interior.

LEA
St Helen
2m/3km S. of Gainsborough SK 8286
Early English and Decorated church well restored by Pearson, 1847–9; 14th-century glass; 17th–19th-century Anderson monuments.

LEADENHAM
St Swithin
8m/12km N.W. of Sleaford SK 9552
A notable church, mainly 14th-century with an impressive tower and magnificent crocketed spire, forming one of the string of distinguished churches between Lincoln and Grantham. Attractive Flemish glass was in-

serted in the E. window in 1829. Pugin painted the chancel ceiling in 1841. Good slate headstones in the churchyard.

LEVERTON
St Helen
5m/8km E. of Boston TF 4047
Large Decorated and Perpendicular church. Much rich stonework outside and in. Brick clerestory of 1728 refaced in stone by James Fowler, 1882–3.

LINCOLN
SK 9771
All Saints, Monks Road
By C. Hodgson Fowler, 1903–4. An imposing, lofty brick church in the Decorated style with good High Church furnishings and glass by Comper.
St Benedict, St Benedict's Square
A small church, in the High Street, which narrowly escaped demolition earlier this century, when various 'improvements' were being made to the city, and the old corporation church of St Peter-at-Arches was pulled down and re-erected on a housing estate at the top of the hill. St Benedict's is an early 13th-century building and contains two alien memorials, the Grantham marble tablet from Goltho and a large marble tablet with a portrait in relief to W. A. Nicholson, one of the founders of the RIBA, which was brought from the old burial ground of St Swithin's.
St Giles, Lamb Gardens
A rebuilding by W. G. Watkins, 1936, of the demolished St Peter-at-Arches, by William Smith, *c.* 1720; much of the original re-used.
St Mary-le-Wigford, High Street
The oldest church in the city, with a Saxon tower of unusually slender proportions; a Roman tombstone is built into its W. side. There is much Early English and Decorated work. The font is 15th-century.
St Nicholas, Newport
By Sir George Gilbert Scott, 1838–40. This design won a competition and, according to Scott's own *Recollections*, was his first church. In the Early English style, the S.W. tower with a broach spire. Chancel and N. aisle by C. H. Fowler, 1908–9.
St Peter-at-Gowts, High Street
Important 11th-century Saxon nave with long-and-short quoins and tall Saxo-Norman W. tower, an ancient landmark of the city.
St Swithin, Free School Lane

By James Fowler. Nave and aisles, 1869–71; chancel added in 1879–80; completed by the handsome tower and lofty steeple in 1884–7. Large and expensive church in the elegant 13th-century style of the Cathedral.

LINWOOD
St Cornelius
2m/3km S. of Market Rasen TF 1086
W. tower of ironstone built from the legacy of John Lynwode, d. 1419; his is one of the fine brasses in the church.

LITTLE BYTHAM
St Mary
7m/11km N. of Stamford TF 0118
A picturesque church in a pretty village near Stamford. It has some Saxon work at the S.E. corner of the nave. Over the S. door of the chancel is a unique tympanum, thus described by Keyser: 'In the centre is a sunk circular medallion said to have once contained the skull and armbone of St Medard, the Patron Saint. On either side is an eagle within a circle, and below an animal adoring and some interlaced circles. On the lintel is a pattern of rectangular figures enclosing leaves.'

LITTLE CAWTHORPE
St Helen
3m/4km S.E. of Louth TF 3583
By R. J. Withers, 1860. In the words of the *Ecclesiologist*: 'A truly excellent design … for cheaply rebuilding a small rural church … the arrangements thoroughly correct.' Gothic Revival in the Middle Pointed style; hard red and black brick with lancets and polychromatic interior.

LITTLE COATES
St Michael
on the W. edge of Grimsby TA 3400
Small Perpendicular; skilfully enlarged in 1913 by Sir Walter Tapper. To him is due the exceptionally beautiful vaulted chancel and the scholarly furnishing.

LONG SUTTON
St Mary
9m/15km N. of Wisbech TF 4322
The lead spire, according to Dr J. Charles Cox, is the highest, oldest, and most perfect lead spire in England, and crowns an early 13th-century tower of great beauty almost detached from the church. There is a handsome 15th-century S. porch of two bays,

and a magnificent Norman nave with triforium and clerestory.

LOUTH
St James

14m/22km S. of Grimsby TF 3287

Louth spire is one of the last great medieval Gothic masterpieces of England. It rises up stage after stage of almost impossible beauty to its great height of 294 feet. It was built of Ancaster stone between 1501 and 1515. 'For fifteen years, with scanty labour and scantier means, the work was carried on. They borrowed from the guilds and the richer inhabitants, they pledged their silver crosses and chalices. From the richest to the poorest all seem to have been affected with a like zeal.' (*The First Church Warden's Book of Louth*, Dudding, 1941.) The great pride of the townspeople in their achievement and their fear for its fate were largely responsible for the outbreak of the Lincolnshire Rising in 1536. Louth is a captivating town of Georgian streets and houses; the spire seems to float above it, and the glorious countryside around.

LUDBOROUGH
St Mary

6m/10km N. of Louth TF 2995

Largely rebuilt after a gale by James Fowler, 1858–60. Early English with lancet windows and quatrefoil arcade piers of chalk. Nave now used as a village hall.

MALTBY-LE-MARSH
All Saints

4m/6km S.W. of Mablethorpe TF 4681

14th- and 15th-century church recently restored. Original building evidently had no tower, and the lines of W. window can be seen within tower arch. Beautiful 14th-century font with carved figures of angels holding open books at its angles.

MANBY
St Mary

5m/8km E. of Louth TF 3986

Mainly late 16th-century greenstone church with tall Perpendicular W. tower, chancel by Sir A. Blomfield, 1889. Fine late-Saxon slab with interlace decoration.

MAREHAM-ON-THE-HILL
All Saints

2m/3km S.E. of Horncastle TF 2867

Small, white-painted stone church remodelled in 1804. Two-decker pulpit, box pews, benches, hatchment, and font are all original.

MARKBY
St Peter

3m/4km N.E. of Alford TF 4878

The only thatched church in Lincolnshire: a charming little building. Probably a rebuilding of 1611 incorporating masonry from the Augustinian priory. Box pews, two-decker pulpit, and three-sided communion rails.

MARSTON
St Mary

5m/8km N. of Grantham SK 8943

Pretty setting by the Witham. Lofty late 13th-century broach spire; good 16th-century tombs and other monuments to the Thorold family.

MARTON
St Margaret

5m/8km S. of Gainsborough SK 8381

Famous for a Saxon tower with herringbone masonry, a Norman chancel arch, and a precious 12th-century sculpture of the Crucifixion in the sanctuary. A simple, solemn early church, rich in texture and atmosphere.

MESSINGHAM
Holy Trinity

4m/6km S. of Scunthorpe SE 8904

Henry Vincent Bayley, vicar from 1811 to 1818, found the church in a shocking state of disrepair and effected thorough restoration, using fragments of woodwork and stained glass which had been thrown out of other churches. He has been most unjustly stigmatized by Dr Cox and others as the 'robber archdeacon', but he did not rob to enrich his church, and he did not become archdeacon until several years after he ceased to be vicar here. The glass includes a variety of pictures, etc. collected from different churches.

MIDDLE RASEN
St Peter & St Paul

1m/2km W. of Market Rasen TF 0889

The finest part of this church is the Norman S. door, which came from the destroyed church of Middle Rasen Drax, in the same parish. There is a 15th-century screen and a 14th-century figure of a priest holding a chalice. The tower and windows of the S. aisle are good Perpendicular work.

MORTON-BY-GAINSBOROUGH
St Paul

suburb N. of Gainsborough SK 8091
To the tower of a previous church of 1846, Micklethwaite and Somers Clarke built the new church in 1891 – charming with its plasterwork and furnishings, and the sumptuous collection of 13 glorious windows by Burne-Jones and Morris.

MOULTON
All Saints

4m/6km E. of Spalding TF 3024
A magnificent Fenland church with a late-Perpendicular tower and spire and many other features of great beauty, such as stiff-leaf foliage capitals and the W. window, above which are canopied niches containing figures of saints. Remarkable early 18th-century Adam and Eve font.

NAVENBY
St Peter

9m/15km S. of Lincoln SK 9857
The tower and spire fell 200 years ago and the former was replaced by a poor substitute, but the remainder of the church is beautiful. The six-light Decorated E. window, somewhat resembling that at Heckington, is amongst the best of its kind. There is also an Easter Sepulchre on the N. side of the chancel, beneath which the sleeping soldiers are depicted with the Marys appearing above. At the E. end of the S. aisle is a disused font with a handsome carved cover designed by Charles Kirk of Sleaford and shown at the Great Exhibition of 1851.

NETTLEHAM
All Saints

3m/4km N.E. of Lincoln TF 0075
One of the few Lincolnshire villages with a stream running through it; beside the stream is the church, mainly 13th-century, with a chancel admirably rebuilt by Bodley and Garner. In the splays of the nave arcades are extensive traces of medieval wall-painting. The interior has been spoiled by 're-ordering', after a fire.

NETTLETON
St John the Baptist

1m/2km S.W. of Caistor TA 1000
Saxo-Norman W. tower with side-alternate quoining and Perpendicular belfry stage. The rest rebuilt by James Fowler, 1874.

NOCTON
All Saints

7m/11km S.E. of Lincoln TF 0564
A major work by Sir George Gilbert Scott, 1860–3, for the Countess of Ripon in memory of her husband, who as Viscount Goderich had been Prime Minister 1827–8. Ambitious estate church in the Early English style. Good fittings and monuments.

NORMANBY-LE-WOLD
St Peter

7m/11km W. of Market Rasen TF 0088
Wonderful setting high on the bare wolds. Early English W. tower and S. doorway. Chancel rebuilt – very well – by James Fowler, 1868. Roundels of 17th-century Continental glass in E. window.

NORTH SOMERCOTES
St Mary

3m/4km N.W. of Saltfleet TF 4296
Large Marshland church, mostly Early English and Decorated, with 17th-century repairs in brick. Woodwork; paved floor.

NORTH WITHAM
St Mary

1m/2km S. of Colsterworth SK 9221
A Perpendicular tower with recessed spire in the valley of the infant River Witham; inside, a narrow Norman arch leads into a chancel which serves as a mausoleum to the Sherards of Lobthorpe, baronets extinct, containing important monuments by Joshua Marshall, Stanton and Horsnail, and Edward Sharpe of Stamford.

NORTHORPE
St John the Baptist

3m/4km W. of Kirton-in-Lindsey SK 8997
A small church full of detail with two Norman arcades, some scraps of medieval glass, and two late brasses. The best feature is the early 14th-century S. doorway, enriched with a design of naturalistic foliage. The little picturesque village contains the ruins of a 16th-century manor house.

NORTON DISNEY
St Peter

7m/11km N.E. of Newark SK 8859
Lost in the willows of the Witham, and surrounded by woods, this romantic village was once dominated by the castle of the Disney family, whose name lives on in the creator of Mickey Mouse, a descendant of

a junior branch. A perfect village church with a fine set of tombs and brasses of Disneys; old floors, benches, screen, altar rails, and pulpit.

OLD BOLINGBROKE
St Peter & St Paul
3m/4km W. of Spilsby TF 3465
An imposing Decorated church, in a charming village in which are the remains of John of Gaunt's castle. Fine porch and stone carving.

OLD CLEE
Holy Trinity & St Mary
now part of Cleethorpes TA 2908
A cruciform church with Saxon tower. Both arcades are Norman, the N. earlier than the S. On a pillar is a tablet recording the dedication of the chancel and transepts by St Hugh in 1192. Good Norman font.

OLD LEAKE
St Mary the Virgin
6m/10km N.E. of Boston TF 4050
A notable Fenland church suffering from settlement of walls by reason of continuous land drainage. Mainly 14th-century with a spacious nave of six bays and N. and S. porches. Over the newel staircase to the rood loft there is an unusual and handsome octagonal turret which has been damaged by the use of iron cramps. See also the alabaster figure of a knight and an ancient poor-box.

OSBOURNBY
St Peter & St Paul
5m/8km S. of Sleaford TF 0638
The church here is principally 14th-century and possesses a Decorated sedilia and much 15th-century woodwork, including bench-ends depicting Adam and Eve, St George and the Dragon, and a fox preaching to geese.

PICKWORTH
St Andrew
8m/12km S. of Sleaford TF 0433
A precious church in a tiny forgotten village in the Stone Belt of Kesteven – mostly Decorated with typical broach spire and an unrestored interior complete with old pews, screen, two-decker pulpit, the headless figure of a female saint, and an important set of medieval wall-paintings.

PINCHBECK
St Mary
2m/3km N. of Spalding TF 2425
A great Fenland church: noble W. tower and grand nave; the chancel rebuilt by Butterfield, 1855. Handsome Victorian furnishings and earlier monuments. W. window by O'Connor and other good Victorian glass.

QUADRING
St Margaret
7m/11km N. of Spalding TF 2433
Large Decorated and later church in a Fenland field. Beautifully proportioned Perpendicular nave and big clerestory windows.

RAITHBY-CUM-MALTBY
St Peter
2m/3km S.W. of Louth TF 3184
Elaborate Gothic of 1839, by W. A. Nicholson or perhaps his partner, George Willoughby, and exceedingly pretty; the interior retains many period fittings: gallery, box pews, barrel organ, and glass.

RAND
St Oswald
2m/3km N.W. of Wragby TF 1078
Much-restored Early English and Decorated church with numerous 13th–17th-century monuments; excellent coped coffin lid of *c.* 1200 and delightful effigy of a lady inspired by the Angel Choir at Lincoln.

REDBOURNE
St Andrew
5m/8km S.W. of Brigg SK 9799
A fascinating church, in origin medieval, but gloriously redecorated in Strawberry Hill Gothic, 1775; charming plaster vault to nave and chancel, fantastic E. window by William Collins (early 19th-century), and other contemporary glass; mausoleum of Dukes of St Albans, and attractive monuments to them and to the Carter family; black incised slab to Sir Gerald Sothill, d. 1410.
R.C.F.

RIPPINGALE
St Andrew
5m/8km N. of Bourne TF 0927
A pretty Kesteven village. The architectural details of the church are worth studying and include a series of medieval monuments, two knights in chain mail, a 15th-century deacon, an effigy of a lady, and altar tomb with figures of Roger de Quincey and his two wives.

RISEHOLME
St Mary
2m/3km N. of Lincoln SK 9875
By S. S. Teulon, 1851. Small Decorated
church with W. bellcote and lavish Decorated details. Slate commandment board and
Celtic cross monument to Bishop Wordsworth, 1885.

ROPSLEY
St Peter
5m/8km E. of Grantham SK 9934
The church still contains parts of the original
Saxon work, including carved crucifix at
N.W. angle. One chancel window and N.
arcade are late-Norman; 14th-century tower
and spire, Decorated S. chapel. Medieval
glass and benches in nave. S. porch, 1483.
In S. arcade a pillar, 1380, commemorates
its rebuilding. At E. end of N. aisle is a stone
'bridge' which formerly led to a rood loft.

ROTHWELL
St Mary
2m/3km S.E. of Caistor TF 1599
Beautiful parkland setting. Anglo-Saxon W.
tower, the doorway with plain tympanum
and cushion capitals to the belfry lights.
Norman arcades.

ROUGHTON
St Margaret
3m/4km E. of Woodhall Spa TF 2464
A church of considerable beauty in a small
wooded village on the banks of the Bain. It
contains traces of early-medieval work but
was largely restored at the beginning of the
16th century in brick. The tower, which also
serves as a porch, is of unusual design. On
the N. wall is a memorial to Norreys Fynes,
a lay non-juror, 1736.

ROXBY
St Mary
4m/6km N.E. of Scunthorpe SE 9116
Mostly Decorated, the W. tower remodelled
in 1704. Good sedilia with ogee arches and
crockets; excellent flowing tracery in the
windows.

SALTFLEETBY
All Saints
5m/8km N.W. of Mablethorpe TF 4590
Originally a late-Norman church, rebuilt
early in the 13th century. The lower stages
of the tower, the nave arcade, the N. wall
of the chancel, and its two-light window, are

all 13th-century. In the 15th century the
upper stages of the tower were added and
the unusual windows in the N. side of the
nave were put in. The nave roof was repaired
in 1611 and the chancel rebuilt in 1873. In
the S. porch is the coat of arms of John
Grantham, patron of the church, flanked by
shields bearing a crucifix and emblems of
the Passion. Most of the 15th-century rood
screen remains. On the E. wall of the side
chapel is one of the five stone reredoses in
Lincs., and there is a good 13th-century
font.
    R.C.F.

SAUSTHORPE
St Andrew
2m/3km N.W. of Spilsby TF 3869
A handsome and well-proportioned church
built of white brick by Charles Kirk of Sleaford in 1844. It has a tower and spire more
or less modelled on Louth, and forms a
conspicuous and charming feature of the
landscape on the road from Horncastle to
Skegness. The church is a very remarkable
example of good work in an unpromising
medium, by an architect who was also a
practical builder.

SAXBY
St Helen
7m/11km W. of Market Rasen TF 0086
Charming 18th-century portico across
vicarage lawn. Mortuary chapel of Earls of
Castleton and Earls of Scarborough; delightful apsidal sanctuary.

SCARTHO
St Giles
district of Grimsby 2m/3km S. of centre TA
2605
Handsome Saxon W. tower; the belfry with
mid-wall shafts and elaborate capitals somewhat later than the rest. Blocked W. door
and an Early English replacement on the
S. side.

SCAWBY
St Hibald
2m/3km S.W. of Brigg SE 9605
Close to Scawby Hall. Medieval W. tower,
the rest 1843 and 1870. Good 17th–18th-
century Nelthorpe and other memorials
include two by Fisher of York.

SCOTT WILLOUGHBY
St Andrew
5m/8km S. of Sleaford TF 0537
1826; one of the earliest, and smallest,
Gothic Revival churches in Lincs.; 13th-
century font; 17th-century pulpit and
reading desk.

SCOTTER
St Peter
6m/10km S. of Scunthorpe SR 8800
A church that contains work from Saxon to
Perpendicular. The S. door and tympanum
are pre-Conquest and the arcade between
the nave and the N. aisle is a perfect example
of Early English work. There is a 15th-
century rood screen and some interesting
memorials. Under the tower is the earliest
known set of ringers' rules in verse.

SCOTTON
St Genewys
7m/11km S. of Scunthorpe SK 8899
Unusual church because all of one period,
the late 13th century. Spacious interior; four
medieval Neville tombs with effigies.

SCREMBY
St Peter & St Paul
3m/4km E. of Spilsby TF 4467
Georgian brick church of 1733 overlooking
Fens. W. tower doorway has Gibbsian surround and inside is a W. gallery, panelling,
and a Schnetzler organ.

SCRIVELSBY
St Benedict
2m/3km S. of Horncastle TF 2666
In a field close to the park of Scrivelsby
Court. Mostly of 1860, but some Early
English and Perpendicular work. Monu-
ments from the 14th century onwards to the
Dymoke family, Hereditary Queen's Cham-
pion of England.

SCUNTHORPE
St Hugh, Ashby Road, Old Brumby
21m/33km E. of Doncaster SE 8910
By Lawrence Bond, completed in 1939. Impressive modern design with touches of the
vernacular in its pantile roof and tumbled
gables. Big S. tower of tapering outline,
restrained entrance in ground stage. Light
and spacious interior; a fitting place for
worship.

SEDGEBROOK
St Lawrence
4m/6km W. of Grantham SK 8537
Early English N. arcade, otherwise Perpendicular. Great clear windows. Ancient
screen, chancel stalls and pews. Carved
stone niches and sedilia.

SEMPRINGHAM
St Andrew
8m/13km N. of Bourne TF 1032
Splendid situation, isolated in fields beside
the site of the Gilbertine monastery. Fine
Norman church, the E. apse built by Robert
Browning, 1868–9, after a lightning strike.
Lavish S. doorway retains 12th-century fir-
wood door and ironwork; intact Norman
corbel table of 'Lombard' type. St Gilbert
was born in this place, and his Order began
when seven village maidens asked to lead a
sequestered life on the N. side of the church.
Holy well in the graveyard and good slate
headstones.

SIBSEY
St Margaret
5m/8km N.E. of Boston TF 3550
A large church on the edge of the Fens,
recently restored. There are two Norman
arcades and a grand tower whose lower
stages are 13th-century. Over the chancel
arch is the original gable for the sanctus bell.

SILK WILLOUGHBY
St Denis
2m/3km S. of Sleaford TF 0542
Everything about this church is beautiful;
14th-century tower is surmounted by a
slender and graceful spire with flying buttresses. Most of building is late 14th-century
and the S. door, with ballflower moulding,
is particularly charming. Chancel well
rebuilt in 1878. The woodwork includes
14th-century pew-ends; 15th-century rood
screen and 17th-century pulpit.

SKEGNESS
St Clement
19m/30km N.E. of Boston TF 5663
Village church, now surrounded by houses.
Mostly very late Perpendicular, almost
Tudor; small 18th-century pantiled brick
porch.

SKIDBROOKE
St Botolph
1m/2km S.W. of Saltfleet TF 4492
The church stands quite alone, more than

a mile away from the village of Saltfleet Haven – which in the reign of Edward II was a thriving port – across dyked fields in majestic isolation. Green with moss, it has spacious nave, aisles and chancel, all Early English or Decorated, with Perpendicular clerestory and W. tower. Inside, all is textured like a deserted church in Tuscany. The quintessence of Lincs. at its remotest, solitary best.

R.C.F.

SKIRBECK
St Nicholas
1m/2km S.E. of Boston TF 3442
Standing on the bank of the Witham, this church is notable for its Early English nave and a tower, *c.* 1450, with a magnificent W. window. The Norman chancel was pulled down in 1598 and a beautiful substitute erected 1933–5 to the designs of Temple Moore. There is a handsome Elizabethan pulpit of elaborate design.

SLEAFORD
St Denys
11m/18km N.E. of Grantham TF 0645
In the market-place is the splendid W. front of the church, pinnacled and niched, traceried and moulded; to its left and half-hidden is the Elizabethan vicarage. The spire is one of the earliest of all English stone spires; late 12th- or very early 13th-century. The nave is Decorated, the lofty arches supported on slender pillars, and all around, especially in the N. transept and S. aisle, is some of the finest Decorated tracery in England. Pugin described the rood screen as one of the most perfect anywhere – the rood itself and the figures are by Comper, 1922. Grand 16th- and 17th-century monuments to the Carre family – one of them by Maximilian Colt.

SNARFORD
St Lawrence
6m/10km S.W. of Market Rasen TF 0582
Lost in the middle of nowhere: there is no village; the little church, with farmhouse next door, is of little consequence in itself, but contains the breath-taking monuments of a long-vanished family, the St Pauls. The interior of the church is dominated by their great Elizabethan tombs. Their wealth, their house, the family themselves, have long departed; only the church survives to recall their memory.

SOMERBY-BY-BRIGG
St Margaret
½m/1km S.E. of Brigg TA 0606
Hidden by trees on a slope of the Wolds. Delightfully modest church with mullioned 17th-century windows. Effigy of a knight, *c.* 1330; two poignant 18th-century tablets face one another across the chancel.

SOMERSBY
St Margaret
6m/10km E. of Horncastle TF 3472
A small 15th-century church in the heart of the wolds, standing opposite the former rectory in which Alfred Tennyson was born in 1809. The little church is altogether delightful, and contains a bronze head of the poet by Thomas Woolner, 1873, and many souvenirs of interest.

SOUTH COCKERINGTON
St Leonard
3m/4km N.E. of Louth TF 3790
Consecration crosses, notable alabaster tomb, ascribed to Epiphanius Evesham, to Sir Adrian Scrope, d. 1623; his effigy appears as though rising from his bed – eloquent and moving.

SOUTH KYME
St Mary and All Saints
3m/4km S.E. of North Kyme, and 7m/11km N.E. of Sleaford TF 1749
A wonderful spot – a grand tower standing by itself, relic of the castle of the Kymes and Umfravilles with church nearby, once the S. aisle of the priory church. A Norman door, but main part 14th-century. Behind a little doorway in the panelling on the N. side of the chancel are astounding fragments of 7th-century spiral and scroll decoration found during restoration in 1890.

SOUTH SOMERCOTES
St Peter
2m/3km S. of North Somercotes, and 8m/12km N.E. of Louth TF 4193
'The Queen of the Marsh', with a tall, graceful spire rising from a wide, flat landscape. Early English, Decorated and Perpendicular; a fine font with emblems of the Passion.

R.C.F.

SPALDING
St Mary & St Nicholas
14m/23km S.W. of Boston TF 2422
The church is mainly 14th- and 15th-

century and has double aisles on each side of the nave, with a tower and spire at the S.W. corner. The N. porch has a vaulted roof. There is a chantry chapel at the S.E. corner. The whole church was restored by Sir Giles Gilbert Scott, who added a N. aisle to the chancel in 1864–6. Spalding is a prosperous Fenland town with many Georgian and earlier buildings.

St Paul, Fulney
By Sir Giles Gilbert Scott, 1877; completed after his father's death by Scott Jnr, 1880. Impressive red-brick church with Ancaster stone dressings in Early English style. Lavish S.W. tower and broach spire connected to church by an arcade. Matching school and vicarage. Inside, the arcades modelled on Bognor Priory, Sussex.

SPILSBY
St James
11m/18km W. of Skegness TF 4066
Market town; the lost great house of Eresby stood a mile to the S.; now only the long, straight avenue leading to a solitary but magnificent gate-pier recalls the house, together with the wonderful tombs of the Lords Willoughby de Eresby in the church itself – a most remarkable series, beginning with the first baron, 1348, and ending with the 10th, 1610; the series is continued at Edenham. The church itself somewhat Victorianized; 18th- and early 19th-century headstones in churchyard.

STAINFIELD
St Andrew
2m/3km N. of Bardney TF 1173
A delightful Queen Anne church, built in 1711 by the Tyrwhitts, somewhat mutilated inside by the Victorians. But some panels of 17th-century needlework and funerary armour survive. The great house was burnt down in the early 19th century; a grass field near the church contains mounds which mark the site of a Benedictine nunnery.

STALLINGBOROUGH
St Peter & St Paul
5m/8km W. of Grimsby TA 1911
Brick church of 1780; round-headed windows and tower with pyramidal roof. Notable 17th-century brass and alabaster monuments to the Ayscough family.

STAMFORD
TF 0307
Without question one of the two or three

most beautiful towns in England, built entirely of local limestone. It has five remaining churches, all of which are outstanding.

All Saints, All Saints Place
Dominates Red Lion Square with its Perpendicular tower and lofty crocketed spire. At first sight the church appears all Perpendicular, but the unusual blank Early English arcades betray its earlier origins. A handsome Victorian reredos, a number of 18th-century monuments and earlier brasses – especially that to William Browne, 1489, founder of Browne's Hospital.

St George, St George's Square
The church is surrounded by the delightful 18th-century houses of its own little square; in origin it is 13th-century, but the chancel was rebuilt in 1449 by Sir William Burges, first Garter King of Arms. Distinguished 18th-century monuments, especially that to Sir Richard Cust, 1734, by Bacon.

St John the Baptist, St John's Street
An intimate Perpendicular church, with original Angel roof; many fragments of richly coloured contemporary glass, Perpendicular screens, 18th-century monuments, and 15th-century brasses, combine to make this a church of special interest.

St Martin, High Street, St Martin's
Past the bottom lodge to Burghley House is the view which Turner painted and Scott loved, with the W. tower of St Martin's dominant – a Perpendicular church throughout, known to have been built by Bishop Russell of Lincoln *c.* 1480. It is of special interest on account of the wealth of 15th-century glass from Tattershall, arranged by Peckitt of York, 1760, and the splendid Cecil tombs. Beside the high altar is Lord Burghley himself, 1598.

St Mary, St Mary's Street
The broach spire is without doubt the most magnificent broach spire in England, early 14th-century on a 13th-century tower; the interior is glorious too; this is largely 15th-century, with its rare cradle roof in the Lady Chapel, and medieval tombs; and delightful 19th-century furnishings – rood screen, stalls, and high altar by Sedding, with his gaily painted chancel ceiling, recently beautifully cleaned. Glass by Wailes and Christopher Whall. A devout, atmospheric interior.

STOKE ROCHFORD
St Andrew & St Mary
5m/8km S. of Grantham SK 9227
Large church. Transitional tower, the rest

Norman, Transitional and Perpendicular. Rich in monuments, brasses, hatchments and objects of piety; 11th-century cross shaft in churchyard.

STOW

St Mary

4m/6km N. of Saxilby SK 8881

Impressive pre-Conquest church of cruciform plan with central tower and crossing arches of equal proportions. These arches, which are of the early 11th century, dominate the church, but there is notable Norman work in the nave, said to be by Remigius, first Bishop of Lincoln, 1072–94, and in the spacious chancel, dating apparently from the early 12th century. The present crossing tower is Perpendicular. Late Norman font.

STRAGGLETHORPE

St Michael

7m/11km E. of Newark SK 9152

Charming small medieval church. Bleached box pews, two-decker pulpit, and graceful 17th-century monument with elegant verse; altogether a rare, undisturbed interior.

STRUBBY

St Oswald

2m/3km E. of Wragby TF 1577

Victorian exterior by Maughan & Fowler, 1857, the chancel of 1874 by Ewan Christian. Decorated font and S. arcade; 16th–17th-century effigy and monuments.

SURFLEET

St Lawrence

4m/6km N. of Spalding TF 2528

Celebrated Decorated leaning tower, the rest of the exterior mainly Perpendicular. Good chancel dated by contract to 1418.

SUTTERTON

St Mary the Virgin

6m/10km S.W. of Boston TF 2835

Grand cruciform Fenland church, Transitional, Early English and Decorated with Perpendicular central tower and thickly crocketed spire. Great clear windows with interesting tracery; colourful Victorian tiles in sanctuary.

SWATON

St Michael

5m/8km W. of Donington TF 1337

One of the lesser-known marvels of Lincs., magnificent and cruciform with central

tower and enormous Decorated traceried windows; the nave arcades soar upward – with nave and aisles under a single roof. A most distinguished church.

SWINESHEAD

St Mary

6m/10km S.W. of Boston TF 2340

A vast Fen church, where the spire rises from a low octagon which surmounts a mighty square tower. Wide, lofty interior with ancient roof and Victorian glass.

TALLINGTON

St Lawrence

4m/6km E. of Stamford TF 0907

Complicated Norman and later church with good 12th-century S. doorway. Perpendicular font cover and screen, and under the tower a dole cupboard of 1730 with racks for bread.

TATTERSHALL

Holy Trinity

8m/12km S.W. of Horncastle TF 2157

Standing near the famous castle, this church was entirely rebuilt in the middle of the 15th century and is of noble proportions. It was a collegiate church and the chancel is divided from the nave by a heavy stone screen built in 1528. In the N. transept are some good 15th- and 16th-century brasses of Continental manufacture. Originally every window was filled with contemporary glass, but most of it was removed in 1737, and 20 years later was taken to Stamford, where it may be seen in St Martin's Church, and in the dining-hall of Burghley House. The little that remains in the church was transferred from the transepts to the E. window. Here 28 panels occupy seven lights in the lower half of the window, mostly consisting of isolated parts of various series representing the Sacraments, saints, angels, and the corporal Acts of Mercy.

TEALBY

All Saints

3m/4km E. of Market Rasen TF 1590

This medieval church is notable for the beauty of its setting on a slope above an attractive stone-built village and looking across to the park of Bayons Manor, built by Tennyson's uncle in 1836, wantonly blown up in 1965.

THEDDLETHORPE
3m/4km N.W. of Mablethorpe TF 4688
All Saints
The main body of this attractive building is 14th- and 15th-century, although other periods are represented. In the E. chapels of the aisles there are Perpendicular windows, while those in the clerestory are unspoilt Decorated. The rood screen and the stone reredos in the S. aisle are both of the 15th century. There are two parclose screens belonging to the 16th century and some 18th-century monuments. There is also a brass of 1424 and fragments of medieval glass. On the aisle walls, which retain some of their original plaster, there are traces of early coloured decoration. The tower, like that of Horncastle, is surmounted by a curious pinnacle.
R.C.F.
St Helen
Almost completely rebuilt in 1866, but famous for the medieval stone reredos at the E. end of the N. aisle. This consists of beautiful cusped and canopied work, and no doubt originally contained a group of carved figures.

THORNTON CURTIS
St Lawrence
2m/3km S.E. of Barrow TA 0817
Impressive church, mainly 1200–1300. Round-headed lancets in the chancel, simple flowing tracery in the S. aisle, and the most remarkable black Tournai marble font, with its amazing animal carvings, one of only 10 in England.

THORPE ST PETER
St Peter
2m/3km N.W. of Wainfleet TF 4860
Has 14th-century porch, although most of the building dates from 100 years later. Jacobean pulpit and late-Perpendicular screen with carvings of birds. The well-proportioned 13th-century font has a trefoiled arcade.

THREEKINGHAM
St Peter
6m/10km S. of Sleaford TF 0836
A church which is notable for its tower and 14th-century broach spire, characteristic of the district. The chancel is late-Norman, and the remainder of the building is Decorated, containing some fine mouldings. There

are mutilated effigies of the Trikingham family.

THURLBY-BY-BOURNE
St Firmin
2m/3km S. of Bourne TF 0916
A large church of many vistas with a blunt little spire on a Norman, or pre-Norman, base. Victorian furnishings and colourful Victorian stained glass, some by O'Connor. A suspiciously early dedication on a site beside the Roman Car Dyke.

TYDD ST MARY
St Mary
3m/4km S. of Long Sutton TF 4418
A 14th-century Fenland church with a 15th-century brick tower and stone spire. The arcades are 12th-century relics of a former church. The 14th-century chancel has some striking tracery in the windows. The 15th-century font is decorated with shields held by angels.

UFFINGTON
St Michael and All Angels
2m/3km E. of Stamford TF 0607
A noteworthy church with a Perpendicular tower surmounted by a crocketed spire, a 14th-century W. door with ballflower ornament, early 13th-century arcades, largely rebuilt in 1865, and a chantry chapel on the N. side. There are some monuments to members of the Manners family and a 14th-century figure in armour. Spectacular 18th-century iron gates and gate-piers to churchyard.

WALCOT
St Nicholas
7m/11km S. of Sleaford TF 0635
Very attractive with 13th-century broach spire. Note the late 15th-century carved pew-ends with shields and other devices, the round Early English font, and some fragments of medieval glass.

WALESBY
All Saints
3m/4km N.E. of Market Rasen TF 1392
There is a good modern church in the village by Temple Moore, but the old one stands in solitary dignity on the top of a hill. For a long time it was practically a ruin, but it was sympathetically restored in 1931. The arcades mark the transition from Norman to Early English. The substantial tower with

stepped angle buttresses has double-lancet windows. There is a restored 15th-century chancel screen; a 17th-century pulpit was formerly used by the Presbyterians at Kirkstead. When the church was restored, the ravages of dry rot necessitated the removal of most of the box pews, but a few remain in the N. aisle. The view from this church across the valley of the Ancholme is superb.

R.C.F.

WELBOURN
St Chad

11m/18km S. of Lincoln SK 9654
Attractive village. Impressive Early English W. tower and Decorated spire with flying buttresses, crockets and exaggerated entasis. Good Decorated S. porch.

WELL
St Margaret

1m/2km S.W. of Alford TF 4473
A delightful piece of 18th-century landscape gardening. A brief for £1,201 for its erection was issued in 1732. The surrounding country, which is undulating and well-wooded, is exceptionally beautiful, and the church, which has a portico like a temple, is an attractive example of early Georgian work. It is noteworthy that the orientation of this church was reversed in order to fit the landscape better!

WEST KEAL
St Helen

2m/3km S.W. of Spilsby TF 3863
Perhaps the most advantageous site in Lincs., with view across Fens to Boston Stump. Porch with heavy gargoyles outside. Ancient door set in ascending carved stone figures. Capitals of N. arcade are its greatest glory; dragons fight, pigs are chained, foxes steal, and women almost burst from their bodices. Tower collapsed in 1881 – but carefully rebuilt with appropriate gargoyles.

WEST RASEN
All Saints

3m/4km W. of Market Rasen TF 0689
Early English W. tower, but otherwise largely rebuilt in 1829 by E. J. Willson. Curious turrets for pinnacles on the tower and good clerestory with frieze of shields on S. side from a tomb chest.

WESTBOROUGH
All Saints

7m/11km N.W. of Grantham SK 8544
A tiny village which was evidently once much larger, distinguished by a truly magnificent church. This was originally cruciform, but has lost the S. transept. The greater part of the building is Early English, and there are some lancet windows in the chancel. The vestry was originally a chantry chapel and its stone altar still remains. The tower was rebuilt in 1752.

WESTON
St Mary

3m/4km E. of Spalding TF 2925
Almost entirely Early English with 14th-century transepts and 15th-century tower. The splendid S. porch has an arcade on either side. The font is circular and divided into eight sections, on each of which is a device of foliage in deep relief. One of the best of all Early English churches.

WHAPLODE
St Mary

2m/3km W. of Holbeach TF 3224
A large and interesting church with a Norman chancel arch and a tower begun in the 12th century and finished in the 14th. The tower stands in an unusual position at the E. end of the S. aisle. Magnificent tomb to Sir Anthony Irby, 1593, and his wife Alice, 1625, with their five children kneeling around.

WIGTOFT
St Peter & St Paul

6m/10km S.W. of Boston TF 2636
Intriguing Norman fabric at the base of the Perpendicular tower; perhaps an earlier W. front. Jacobean pulpit.

WILLOUGHBY
St Helen

3m/4km S. of Alford TF 4771
Setting on the edge of the Marsh. Large early-Perpendicular church with W. tower, octagonal nave piers, and clerestory.

WILSFORD
St Mary

4m/6km S.W. of Sleaford TF 0043
Church has a graceful 15th-century spire, traces of Saxon work, two Norman pillars, a 13th-century N. arcade, and a 14th-

century S. arcade. Elegant traceried Decorated E. window.

WINTERINGHAM
All Saints
7m/11km N. of Scunthorpe SE 9222
Impressive W. tower, probably 11th-century, and rich late-Norman arcades. Good Early English chancel with stepped lancets to the E.; 13th-century effigy of knight.

WINTERTON
All Saints
5m/8km N.E. of Scunthorpe SE 9222
11th-century tower with cushion capitals to the mid-wall shafts; handsome Early English arcades and a brass of 1504.

WINTHORPE
St Mary
2m/3km N. of Skegness TF 5665
A late 15th-century church with a great expanse of glass and a magnificent collection of original woodwork, including a rood screen, carved pew-ends with poppyheads, very beautiful choir-stalls, and parclose screens at the ends of the aisles. There are also some early 16th-century brasses. The churchyard cross has been carefully restored.

WOLD NEWTON
All Saints
3m/4km N.E. of Binbrook TF 2496
By James Fowler, 1862. A neat little church of nave, apse and spired bell-turret, prettily set against a hillside. Good Decorated font

with donors' inscription and fragments from Bardney Abbey.

WRANGLE
St Mary the Virgin & St Nicholas
7m/11km N.E. of Boston TF 3240
Early English, Decorated and Perpendicular with a grand 14th-century E. window and an Elizabethan pulpit. The glass was inserted between 1345 and 1371, and contains figures of kings and prophets, St George, St Cecilia, St Lucy, St Laurence, St Barbara, and other saints. There is also an altar tomb to Sir John Read, 1626, whose family was for many generations resident here. Near the font is a ledger stone, dated 1705, commemorating William Erskine, a non-juring incumbent who built the beautiful former vicarage.

WYBERTON
St Leodegar
2m/3km S. of Boston TF 3240
The church stands on the edge of a small park belonging to a handsome 17th- and 18th-century mansion which was formerly the rectory. Delicate clustered 13th-century arcades in the nave, and a small Georgian apsidal chancel.

YARBURGH
St John the Baptist
4m/6km N. of Louth TF 3593
Church of *c.* 1405, rebuilt after a fire. The tower has an ornate W. doorway with sculptures of the Fall. Perpendicular font, screen and bench-ends.
R.C.F.

London

Introduction

London includes the City of London and Inner London, the old Greater London area, pre-1965, before it had incorporated Middlesex (which is treated in a separate chapter), and further parts of Essex, Kent and Surrey. It cannot be treated in the same way as other county sections. The only big medieval churches – old St Paul's, Westminster Abbey, St Bartholomew's, Smithfield, St Katherine by Tower (demolished 1825), The Temple Church, and the various religious foundations along the banks of the Thames – were built mainly of imported stone brought by water from as far as Caen and Purbeck, since there was no available good local stone. The few medieval parish churches surviving in the boroughs of Inner London are not exceptional architecturally. Middlesex had a humble Perpendicular style rather like that of Herts. and South Essex. Surrey and the parts of Kent now within London had no fine parish churches except St Mary Overy, Southwark, which is now Southwark Cathedral.

London's first great church-building period after medieval times (and there were about a hundred churches in the square mile of the City before the fire of 1666) was in the 17th and 18th centuries. With few exceptions, the chief churches of these times were Classical. Sir Christopher Wren built fifty in the City, of which nineteen were destroyed by the Germans, leaving only sixteen Wren churches now surviving in the City. Of the sixteen churches built since the time of Wren, half have been destroyed to pay for suburban churches. This is a great loss, as they were almost all more impressive and original, at any rate internally, than the lesser Wren churches. All the post-Wren survivors have escaped destruction by the Nazis. In Westminster and Southwark and just outside the City, several handsome churches were built in the 18th century. These were in the Classical style. The usual building material in these parts for 17th- and 18th-century churches was Portland stone. This is well suited to the London climate and weathers black and brilliant white, so that it gives an effect of shadow on the greyest day. Brick was also used, and the London brick in the 17th and early 18th centuries was always of a variety of red and brown shades which have stood up to the soot remarkably well. Wren built lead steeples to some of his churches.

The next big phase of building was after the Napoleonic campaigns, when the ususal materials were white stock brick for walls and Bath stone for portico, steeple and dressings.

Finally, there was the biggest church-building period in London since medieval times, from the mid-19th century onward. The churches of this period vary greatly in merit, and only exceptionally fine ones are listed. Because London churches cannot be arranged like those of an agricultural county, they are put under parishes, in a manner which, we hope, will fulfil the same purpose as the other lists.

J. B.

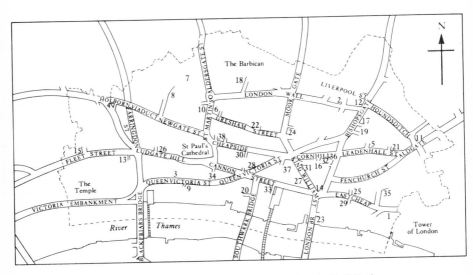

1	All Hallows by the Tower	20	St James's, Garlickhythe
2	All Hallows, London Wall	21	St Katherine Cree
3	St Andrew-by-the-Wardrobe	22	St Lawrence, Jewry
4	St Andrew, Holborn	23	St Magnus the Martyr
5	St Andrew, Undershaft	24	St Margaret, Lothbury
6	St Anne & St Agnes, Aldersgate	25	St Margaret Pattens
7	St Bartholomew-the-Great, West Smithfield	26	St Martin, Ludgate
8	St Bartholomew-the-Less	27	St Mary Abchurch
9	St Benet, Paul's Wharf	28	St Mary, Aldermary
10	St Botolph, Aldersgate	29	St Mary-at-Hill
11	St Bololph, Aldgate	30	St Mary-le-Bow
12	St Botolph, Bishopsgate	31	St Mary, Woolnoth
13	St Bride, Fleet Street	32	St Michael, Cornhill
14	St Clement, East Cheap	33	St Michael, Paternoster Royal
15	St Dunstan-in-the-West	34	St Nicholas, Cole Abbey
16	St Edmund, Lombard Street	35	St Olave, Hart Street
17	St Ethelburga, Bishopsgate	36	St Peter, upon Cornhill
18	St Giles, Cripplegate	37	St Stephen, Walbrook
19	St Helen's, Bishopsgate	38	St Vedast, Foster Lane

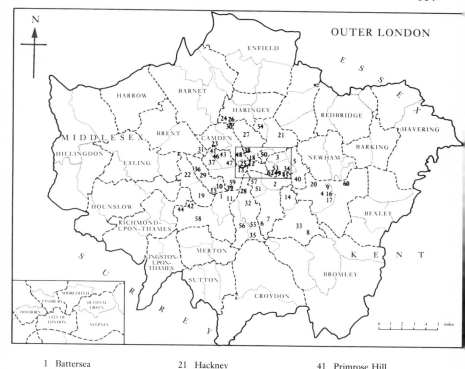

1	Battersea	21	Hackney	41	Primrose Hill
2	Bermondsey	22	Hammersmith	42	Putney
3	Bethnal Green	23	Hampstead	43	Regents Park
4	Blackheath Park	24	Highgate	44	Roehampton
5	Bow	25	Holborn	45	Rotherhithe
6	Brixton	26	Holloway	46	St John's Wood
7	Camberwell	27	Islington	47	St Marylebone
8	Catford	28	Kennington	48	St Pancras
9	Charlton	29	Kensington	49	Shadwell
10	Chelsea	30	Kentish Town	50	Shoreditch
11	Clapham	31	Kilburn	51	Southwark
12	Clerkenwell	32	Lambeth	52	Spitalfields
13	Covent Garden	33	Lewisham	53	Stepney
14	Deptford	34	Limehouse	54	Stoke Newington
15	Earls Court	35	Norwood	55	Streatham
16	Eltham	36	Notting Hill	56	Tooting
17	Eltham Park	37	Paddington	57	Walworth
18	Finsbury	38	Pentonville	58	Wandsworth
19	Fulham	39	Pimlico	59	Westminster
20	Greenwich	40	Poplar	60	Woolwich

Selected List of Churches

THE CITY
All Hallows by the Tower, Byward Street, Barking EC3
Medieval, largely destroyed by war, reconstructed 1956–7 by Seeley and Paget who added elegant spire to the brick tower of 1659. Exotic Grinling Gibbons font cover.
All Hallows on the Wall, London Wall, Broad Street, EC2
Designed by George Dance Jnr, 1765–7. The exterior is modest and apparently windowless. Inside, the church is elegance itself, a barrel-vaulted ceiling decorated with a flower pattern in Adam style, the plasterwork being lit by semi-circular windows above the broad frieze which binds the whole interior together and below which are Ionic pilasters. Surprisingly and effectively, there is no cornice above the frieze. Above the panelled apse is a coffered semi-dome. Dance probably copied his method of lighting a church surrounded by high buildings from Hawksmoor's at St Mary, Woolnoth, and his apse from Gibbs's St Mary-le-Strand, but he interpreted their themes in the restrained manner of the later Georgian age. The fittings are unobtrusive and unexceptional. It is now a guild church, and the nave houses the library of the Council for the Care of Churches, but services are still held in the church and it is accessible to visitors during office hours, Monday to Friday.
St Andrew-by-the-Wardrobe, Queen Victoria Street, EC4
Economically rebuilt after the Fire by Wren, 1685–93. Renaissance. Gutted again in 1940. Well restored by Marshall Sisson, re-opened 1961. Apart from being a parish church, here also are the headquarters of the Redundant Churches Fund.
St Andrew, Holborn
between Holborn and Holborn Viaduct, EC1 By Wren, 1684–90. Renaissance; 15th-century tower refaced in Portland stone, 1703. Gutted 1941; restored by Seeley and Paget and re-opened 1961. Classic organ and font from Foundling Hospital; reredos in tower chapel from St Luke's, Old Street. Now a guild church and diocesan centre.

St Andrew, Undershaft, Leadenhall Street, EC3
Built 1520–32 in late 15th-century style. Nave and aisles. Stuart-style glass in W. window. Panelled roofs. Fine Renatus Harris organ case of 1696 and notable Tijou iron communion rails of 1704. Monument to John Stow, d. 1605, chronicler of London and subject of an annual memorial service.
St Anne & St Agnes, Aldersgate, Gresham Street, EC2
This inconspicuous church, rebuilt by Wren in 1677–80, is justified by its interior. The plaster-vaulted ceilings are on the same plan as St Mary-at-Hill and St Martin, Ludgate, except that the centre of the Greek cross has a wide cross vault instead of a dome. Some of the old woodwork remains, of which the best is the elegant altarpiece. Since 1966 this church has served the Lutheran community, and services are held here in Estonian and Latvian as well as in English.
St Bartholomew-the-Great, West Smithfield, Cloth Fair, EC1
This great Norman church would be impressive anywhere. The 17th-century brick tower, containing the oldest ring of bells in England, and old brick verger's house, built against the N. wall, with the flint and Portland stone refacing added by Sir Aston Webb at the end of the last century, give the outside an East Anglian look which the interior belies. This is vast, dark and Romanesque with a triforium and apsidal end. Charmingly, the Perpendicular tomb of Rahere, founder of the great hospital, and a Perpendicular watching window in the triforium opposite, are inserted between rugged Norman columns. A cross-vaulted ambulatory leads round the church past an E. Lady Chapel. The church is the choir and transepts of a monastery whose nave was on the site of the present churchyard. The ancient W. gatehouse survived together with one side of the cloister.
St Bartholomew-the-Less, Bart's Hospital, EC1
Medieval tower. Body of church octagonal Gothic by George Dance Jnr, 1789, not improved in 1865 and 1882. Repaired after

World War II by Seeley and Paget and re-opened in 1951. Chaste grey and white interior, Victorian fittings. Also used as Bart's Hospital chapel.

St Benet, Paul's Wharf, Upper Thames Street, EC4

The red-brick exterior with stone dressings and swags above the windows, old tiled roofs, tower and lead dome and lantern, look very well on the steep slope S. of Queen Victoria Street. It was finished by Wren in 1683. The interior with galleries, W. organ and the usual carved Renaissance altarpiece, pulpit and wainscoted walls, is one of the least-altered City interiors. It is the church of the College of Heralds and the London church of the Welsh Episcopalians.

St Botolph, Aldersgate, EC1

Rebuilt by Nathaniel Wright, 1790. Square pillars on each side support a gallery from which rise Corinthian columns – themselves supporting an arched ceiling delicately ornamented with bands and flowers. The ceiling is lit by semi-circular windows, as in Dance's church of All Hallows, London Wall. There is an apsidal E. end and the W. end with its organ case is an elegant composition. The pulpit and sounding board are also of the same date, and the beautiful transparency of The Agony in the Garden in the E. window was painted by James Pearson in 1788. The rest of the glass in the church is deplorable.

St Botolph, Aldgate, EC3

By George Dance Snr, 1744. Aisled and galleried, heavy Classical redecoration by J. F. Bentley in the 1880s with Arts and Crafts plasterwork and balusters. This is now the headquarters of the Diocesan Council for Christian/Jewish understanding, and in the crypt is a mission to the homeless.

St Botolph, Bishopsgate, Bishopsgate, EC3

By James Gould and George Dance Snr, 1727–9. Aisled and galleried City Classical with tower and inside, over the centre of the nave, a domed cupola of 1820.

St Bride, Fleet Street, Bride Lane, Fleet Street, EC4

By Wren, 1671–1703. Gutted 1940; restored by Godfrey Allen and rededicated 1957. Elegant wedding-cake steeple of diminishing stages. Interior arcaded and once galleried is now replanned on collegiate lines.

St Clement, East Cheap, Clements Lane, off King William Street, EC4

Wren, 1683–7. Small, much restored and plain Classical. Organ and gallery by Harris; reredos gilded and decorated by Sir Ninian Comper, 1933.

St Dunstan-in-the-West, Fleet Street, EC4

By John Shaw, 1832. Tower a reduced version of Boston, Lincs.; body of church a spacious Gothic octagon. A guild church and headquarters also for the Romanian Orthodox Church.

St Edmund, King and Martyr, Lombard Street, EC3

1670–1708; although attributed to Wren, it may be partly the work of Robert Hooke. Elegant tower and steeple on Lombard Street. Interior plain except for font cover and Etty's Moses and Aaron paintings.

St Ethelburga, Bishopsgate, EC2

This modest old church is interesting because it is what many of the 100 and more small churches in the City must have been like before the Fire. It consists of nave and S. aisle with an arcade of Perpendicular columns. It was well furnished and sympathetically restored by Sir Ninian Comper; note the delicate screen. Three interesting windows of 1928–30 by Leonard Walker commemorate Hudson's eastward voyage via the North Pole. The good scale upset by an over-large mural on the E. wall by Hans Fiebusch, completed in 1962. A guild church.

St Giles, Cripplegate, Barbican, London Wall, EC2

An oasis in the Barbican, though badly bombed and restored. Large 16th-century double-aisled church with 17th-century brick top stage to tower. Full of furnishings from St Luke, Old Street. John Milton is buried here.

St Helen's, Bishopsgate, Great St Helen's, off Bishopsgate, EC3

A large, irregular plan, the fabric mostly early 13th-century; 17th-century woodwork and door-case. Gilded triptych by J. L. Pearson. Impressive 17th-century monuments, including that to Sir John Spencer, a rich Lord Mayor, d. 1609.

St James's, Garlickhythe, Garlick Hill, by Upper Thames Street, EC4

Finished by Wren in the same year as St Benet's. It was blitzed and was restored in 1967 by David Lockhart-Smith. The best exterior feature is the Portland stone steeple on the tower, which was added in 1714–17. The interior, which is columned, wainscoted and plaster-vaulted with much Renaissance woodwork, is grand and stately. Its plan is more medieval than most of Wren's City churches. This is the best post-war restoration in the City; new from old is undetectable.

St Katherine Cree, Leadenhall Street, EC3
1628; the only Laudian church in London. E. window has Catherine Wheel set in square head. Aisled with delicate Gothic vaulted ceilings sprung from Classical columns, all enriched with painted bosses of City livery companies. The headquarters of the Industrial Christian Fellowship and a guild church.

St Lawrence, Jewry, Gresham Street, by the Guildhall, EC2
Wren, 1671–7. Renaissance. Gutted 1940; well restored and refitted by Cecil Brown, 1957; felicitous fibreglass steeple. E. wall outside based on Wren's Modern Design for St Paul's.

St Magnus the Martyr, London Bridge, Lower Thames Street, EC3
Wren, 1671–1705. The beautiful Portland stone tower and steeple mark the approach to Old London Bridge. Inside is a wealth of magnificent woodwork and ironwork – W. screen, gallery and organ case, door-cases, pulpit, altarpiece, sword-rests and communion rails. Wren's original was restored in a Baroque manner by Martin Travers, 1924, and again by Laurence King after war damage.

St Margaret, Lothbury, Lothbury, EC2
One of Wren's later works in Portland stone with a tower and lead spire. The interior has a S. aisle and ingenious clerestory to the broad nave. It is filled with old woodwork from City churches destroyed by the Victorians. A Flemish-looking screen from All Hallows the Great (a Wren church) stretches across the E. end. The rich pulpit has a sounding board, also from All Hallows.

St Margaret Pattens, Rood Lane, Eastcheap, EC3
The stone tower with obelisks as pinnacles and tall lead spire is a beautiful contrast with Wren's stone spire of St Dunstan-in-the-East nearby. Inside, the church is like St Margaret's, Lothbury, and has an attractive organ gallery. Now a guild church serving as a Christian study centre.

St Martin, Ludgate, Ludgate Hill, EC4
By Wren, 1677–84. The lead spire of this stone church is an elegant foil to the dome of St Paul's as one sees it from Fleet Street. The interior, though much rearranged in the last century, still contains its woodwork, and the vaulted ceiling is a Greek cross in plan like St Anne and St Agnes and St Mary-at-Hill. A guild church which also serves the Metropolitan Police.

St Mary Abchurch, Abchurch Lane, by Cannon Street, EC4
The brick tower, lead spire and plain brick exterior are pleasant, but the inside is magnificent. It is one of the most richly decorated of Wren's churches, a great square room roofed by a dome painted by William Snow, springing from eight pendentives. The woodwork of pulpit, font cover and Grinling Gibbons altarpiece is richest English Renaissance. A guild church.

St Mary, Aldermary, Queen Victoria Street, at Watling Street, EC4
Wren Gothic of 1682 with fine tower. Inside are Gothic plaster ceilings consisting of a series of shallow domes supported on pendentives made to look like fan vaulting. Glass by John Crawford and Lawrence Lee. Ornaments on the high altar by Frank Knight. A guild church.

*St Mary-at-Hill, Lovat Lane,
St Mary-at-Hill Street, EC3*
The plain exterior of this Wren church of 1670–6 gives no idea of the riches within. Four fluted columns support broad arches over the transepts and E. and W. ends. Above the middle of the Greek cross thus formed rises a central dome from four pendentives, adorned with plasterwork. The plasterwork throughout is rich and bold, but best of all are the woodwork and ironwork, particularly over the W. gallery and on the pulpit and altarpiece. The iron sword-rests of various Georgian dates are the best in the City. The woodwork is mostly 17th-century with skilful 1847 additions in the Renaissance style. The high pews survive.

St Mary-le-Bow, Cheapside, EC4
Wren, 1670–80. Gutted 1940. Has the most elaborate and famous Wren steeple rising from a tall tower with Roman Doric doorways set in a rusticated plinth and adorned with cherubs. The brick church, set back from the tower, was square with narrow aisles and wide nave. Norman crypt. Restored by Laurence King and re-opened 1965, including good glass and rood by John Hayward.

St Mary, Woolnoth, Lombard Street and King William Street, EC3
This church, designed by Wren's talented clerk, Nicholas Hawksmoor, 1716–27, is

original and impressive within and without. The W. tower is divided at its summit into two turrets surmounted by balustrades. The N. front is a splendid example of how to make a windowless wall interesting. The N. wall is quite plain because it originally had buildings against it. Inside, the church is square and for so small a site gives an amazing impression of sumptuousness and height. The effect is created by the fluted Corinthian columns rising in groups of three in the four corners of the church. They support a bold entablature and cornice above which rise semi-circular clerestory windows. There is a stongly moulded flat plaster ceiling. The altarpiece has twisted columns and a canopy of wood with imitation tassels. The only projecting gallery to survive is at the W. end. Organ case, pulpit, gallery fronts, and wrought-iron communion rails are all fine and part of Hawksmoor's compact design. A guild church.

St Michael, Cornhill, St Michael's Alley and Cornhill, EC3
By Wren, Classical, 1670–2; Gothic tower by Hawksmoor, 1721. Interior lately simplified after harsh Victorianization by Scott, whose rich bench-ends remain, carved by W. G. Rogers.

St Michael, Paternoster Royal, College Hill, EC4
By Wren, 1686–94; steeple not completed until 1713. The steeple is not unlike the W. towers of St Paul's; octagonal and curved, a deliberately ornate contrast with the plain stone tower. The church was restored after bomb damage, and it is now the headquarters of the Missions to Seamen.

St Nicholas, Cole Abbey, Queen Victoria Street, EC4
By Wren, 1671–7. Gutted 1940. Handsome stone exterior with highly original thick lead steeple rising from a tower with urns at corners. Plain interior restored by Ansell and Bailey and re-opened in 1962. Now used by the Presbyterian church.

St Olave, Hart Street, Hart Street, EC3
13th- and 15th-century. Gutted 1941; re-stored 1951–4 by Ernest Glanfield. Clerestoried nave and two aisles. Samuel Pepys worked at the Navy Office which was nearby. He and his wife Elizabeth are buried beside the communion table.

St Peter, upon Cornhill, Cornhill, EC3
By Wren, 1677–81. The brick tower with its leaded cupola and spire with an enormous key as a vane is hard to see among high buildings. Inside, the irregular oblong shape of the church, to which a regular Classical design of arcades and arched roofs has been applied, gives it a distorted appearance. But the woodwork, screen, organ gallery and pulpit are beautiful, and make it one of the most complete City church interiors.

St Stephen, Walbrook, Walbrook, EC4
There is a stone tower with an elegant steeple, but the glory of this church is its interior. As G. H. Birch says in *London Churches* (1896), 'Nowhere else could one find a simple parallelogram . . . so admirably arranged'. Corinthian columns on stone bases divide the church into bays, aisles and sanctuary, leaving an open space in the middle to support a large coffered dome which is lit by a lantern. The plasterwork of the dome is arranged in horizontal bands, the broad and rich bands in the middle breaking up any effect of monotony. The organ case, font cover, altarpiece and pulpit are Renaissance woodwork, richly carved. The church was much damaged in the war but has been restored by Robert Potter; here is the infamous ten-ton marble altar by Henry Moore.

St Vedast, Foster Lane, Foster Lane, EC2
By Wren, 1670–97; steeple added 1694–7. Gutted 1940. The simple Baroque stone tower and steeple are light, airy and elegant, built as though in contrast with nearby St Mary-le-Bow, and to show the latter up as too elaborate. Plain interior; nave and S. aisle were originally not square, now rebuilt square by Stephen Dykes-Bower, 1958; the whole restored and re-opened in 1963.

Inner London

BATTERSEA

Ascension, Lavender Hill Parish, SW11
Begun by James Brooks, 1876; not finally
completed by J. T. Micklethwaite and Somers
Clarke until 1888. Monumental brick Early
English church with lancets and uninterrupted roof-line. Restrained Tractarian interior has round piers, plain nave capitals, and
an ambulatory round the apse. Vaulted N.
chapel; rood screen by George Wallace,
1914; glass by Kempe & Tower.
St Luke, Ramsden Road, SW12
By F. W. Hunt, 1883. A big Early Christian
basilica with Early English arcades. Furnished in the Italian taste. The Lady Chapel,
communion rails, screens and font cover are
by Martin Travers, 1924–7.
St Mark, Battersea Rise, SW11
By William White, 1872–4. Church in the
Early English style built of concrete skilfully
clad in red and yellow brick. Small W. tower
with shingled Rhenish roof. Elevated
chancel and sanctuary with a Sarum Baroque
high altar by Randoll Blacking. Glass by
Lavers and Barraud; marble and mosaic
chancel pavement designed by Clayton &
Bell.
St Mary, Battersea Church Road, SW11
Setting beside the river. By Joseph Dixon,
1775–6. Classical church of stock brick with
stone dressings; Tuscan portico, two tiers
of windows, and W. tower. Galleried interior
has glass of *c.* 1631 and good 17th–18th-
century monuments.

BERMONDSEY

St James, Thurland Road, SE16
By James Savage, 1827–9. Greek exterior
has Ionic portico and slim W. tower;
galleried interior. Finest Commissioners'
church in London.
St Mary Magdalene, Bermondsey Street, SE1
Playful stucco Gothic outside by G. Porter,
1830. Inside, Wren-style Classical, mostly
late 17th-century, including square churchwarden's pew.

BETHNAL GREEN

St John, Cambridge Heath Road, E2
By Sir John Soane, 1825–6. A very odd and

Soane-like stone bellcote on brick church.
Inside unfortunately remodelled by G. F.
Bodley in the Classical style. Organ case
and aumbry in the form of a Wren spire by
Martin Travers.

BLACKHEATH PARK

*St Michael and All Angels, Blackheath Park,
SE3*
By G. Smith, 1830. Highly fanciful Evangelical Gothic, designed as part of Blackheath Park. Stock brick and stone with aisles,
clerestory and thin E. spire.

BOW

St Mary, Stratford le Bow, E3
14th–15th-century, altered later. Weather-
beaten stone and brick, islanded by traffic.
Well restored by Goodhart-Rendel.
Countrified interior.
St Paul, Burdett Road, Bow Green, E3
By Robert Maguire and Keith Murray,
1958–60. Centrally planned brick and concrete top-lit church based on Liturgical
Movement principles, described by Nairn as
'. . . one worthwhile new church in a city
region of ten millions . . .'

BRIXTON

All Saints, Rosendale Road, SE21
By G. H. Fellowes Prynne, 1887–91;
perched on a steep slope. Grand late-
Tractarian Gothic in brick with stone
tracery. Unfinished at W. end. Glass by
Comper and Burlison & Grylls.
Christ Church, Brixton Road, SW9
By Beresford Pite, 1899–1902. Highly original Byzantine-style cruciform church in
brown brick with Portland stone stripes.
Domed interior, careful details throughout,
and the Holy Table well away from E. wall.
St Matthew, St Matthew's Road, SW2
By C. F. Porden, 1822. The problem of
combining portico and tower was solved here
by removing the tower to the E. end.
Galleried interior; until the unfortunate
introduction of a side chapel in the 1930s, it
was pure Doric throughout without a curved
line anywhere.

CAMBERWELL

St George, Wells Way, SE5
Setting by Surrey Canal. By Francis
Bedford, 1822–4. Greek Doric. Galleried
interior attractively decorated by Basil
Champneys in 1893 and 1909.

St Giles, Camberwell Church Street, SE5
By Sir George Gilbert Scott, 1844. A stately
and correct essay in Middle Pointed cruciform with central tower and spire. Well-
proportioned within. Glass, furnishings and
decoration by Comper. E. window designed
by Ruskin and Oldfield, and made by Ward
and Nixon.

St Paul, Herne Hill Parish, SE24
By G. E. Street, 1858. 'One of the loveliest
churches of the kind in the country', declared Ruskin, who lived in the parish. Capricious capitals on the piers and marble
reredos carved by Earp gave the Victorians
equal delight. Glass by Hardman. Tower
and spire from earlier church by Stevens
and Alexander, 1845.

CATFORD

St Andrew, Sandhurst Road, SE6
By P. A. Robson, 1904. The latest and lump-
iest phase of the Arts and Crafts Movement
at its best. Outside, towerless and massive,
dark red brick on a hill-top. Inside, spacious
with brick piers, wide nave, and the buttresses showing in the narrow aisle. Thick
and original tracery with glass by Martin
Travers to match.

St John, Bromley Road, South End, SE6
By Sir Charles Nicholson, 1928. Light and
airy suburban Perpendicular church in stock
brick; never completed and re-ordered in
1977.

CHARLTON

St Luke, The Village, SE7
Brick country church of *c.* 1630 surviving in
charming old churchyard in hill-top village at
entrance to Charlton House. Comparatively
unspoilt interior with 17th-century pulpit,
monuments and glass. Hatchments.

CHELSEA

All Saints, Cheyne Walk, SW3
Mainly 17th-century brick, skilfully restored
by Walter Godfrey after war damage in 1941.
Associated with Sir Thomas More, whose
chapel and monument survive, together with
other 16th–17th-century tombs.

Holy Trinity, Sloane Street, SW1
John Dando Sedding's last work, 1888–90.

Free and original Perpendicular. The
cathedral of the Arts and Crafts movement,
alive with Italian marble, gilding and glass
by Morris and Burne-Jones. J. B. worshipped here.

St Luke, Sidney Street, SW3
By J. Savage, 1820–4. Ashlar-faced with tall
W. tower and portico; sumptuous 'King's
Chapel' style within. Stone-vaulted interior
with galleries.

St Simon Zelotes, Moore Street, SW3
By Joseph Peacock, 1859. 'Details of the
decorated period are piled up in a riotous
conglomeration, giving the impression that
the illustrations in Parker's Glossary have
been taken down, altered and used in evidence against him. Never can there have
been more architecture in less space.'
(Goodhart-Rendel).

CLAPHAM

*Holy Spirit, Narbonne Avenue, Clapham
Common, SW4*
By H. P. Burke Downing, 1912–13. Tall,
Bodleyesque, stock brick, with N. aisle and
nave only, all lit by lancets and a rose W.
window. Interior lofty, impressive and restrained.

Holy Trinity, Clapham Common, SW4
By Kenton Couse, 1774–6. Stock brick with
stone dressings, islanded on the flat
common. Octagonal belfry at W. end and
two tiers of windows; galleried interior with
fine pulpit. The chancel by Beresford
Pite, 1903.

St Paul, Rectory Grove, SW4
By C. Edmonds, 1815. A simple brick
Classic in crowded old churchyard in the
original village of Clapham. Chancel added
by A. Blomfield, 1879, now a community
centre. Good monuments include one by
William Stanton, 1689.

St Peter, Clapham Manor Street, SW4
By J. E. K. & J. P. Cutts, 1878–84. An
ordinary brick oblong made mysterious and
solemn by refined late-Gothic furnishings
and glass by C. E. Kempe and W. E. Tower.

CLERKENWELL

Holy Redeemer, Exmouth Street, E1
By J. D. Sedding, 1887–8. Campanile added
later by H. Wilson. Italianate without and
as impressive as a big Wren church within.

COVENT GARDEN

St Paul, Covent Garden, WC2
Rebuilt by T. Hardwick Jnr, 1795, after

Inigo Jones. A huge brick box with wide eaves and Tuscan E. portico. The actors' church, and described by Inigo Jones himself as 'the handsomest barn in England'.

DEPTFORD
St Paul, Deptford High Street, SE8
Standing in a wide open space, one of the most splendid churches in London. By Thomas Archer, 1712–30. Vast and splendid Baroque with steeple and three porticoes in Portland stone. Interior rich and cruciform with some original furnishings and a monument of 1776 by Nollekens.

EARLS COURT
St Cuthbert, Philbeach Gardens, SW5
By H. Roumieu Gough, 1884–7. Big red-brick Gothic building with bright-green copper roof and fleche, a conspicuous landmark. Chiefly remarkable for its interior decoration, where S. and W. Kensington Tractarian devotion has given jewels, pictures, carving and inlay work for all available space. Father Geldart's rich reredos and the Art Nouveau altar rails and lectern by W. Bainbridge Reynolds are particularly prominent.

ELTHAM
St Saviour, Middle Park Avenue, SE9
1933 by Welch & Lander and N. F. Cachemaille-Day. A strong and simple church in red brick with an exterior having a 'hard and businesslike character' – Cachemaille-Day's own phrase. The moving interior, with plain white-walled nave and exposed brick chancel, has a large stone statue of Christ over the altar.

ELTHAM PARK
St Luke, Westmount Road, SE9
By Temple Moore, 1906. Spacious, light interior has wagon roofs and consciously simple piers. S. aisle by J. Tolhurst, *c.* 1930.

FINSBURY
St Barnabas, King's Square, EC1
By T. Hardwick, 1826. Ionic front and odd thin spire well related to wide late-Georgian square. Interior refurnished after bad war damage. Galleries and pews removed.

FULHAM
St Alban, Margravine Road, W6
By Sir Aston Webb and Ingress Bell, 1894–6. Red-brick Arts and Crafts Gothic full of

altars, confessionals and statues, including an unusually big Holy Child of Prague wearing a golden crown. A well-used church with Italian ethos.

GREENWICH
St Alfege, Greenwich High Road, SE10
By Nicholas Hawksmoor, 1711–14. A massive four-square Portland stone building. The tower and spire added by John James, 1730, seem feeble by contrast. Restored after war damage by Sir Albert Richardson, 1953.

HACKNEY
St Barnabas, Shacklewell Lane, E8
By Sir Charles Reilly, 1910. Hidden by high buildings. Yellow stock brick within and without in Byzantine style. Impressive concrete-vaulted interior has screen, large chancel, apse, and E. ambulatory. The skilfully contrived harmony is spoilt by a grotesque Victorian pulpit from another church.
St John, Mare Street, E8
By James Spiller, 1792–7. An astonishing yellow-brick building in the shape of a Greek cross with Portland stone steeple. Inside, its shallow vaulted roofs have no interior supports; 16th–19th-century monuments. Medieval tower of old church in corner of churchyard.
St John of Jerusalem, Lauriston Road, Church Crescent, E9
By E. C. Hakewill, 1845–8. Large stone cruciform church in the Early English style with W. tower and polygonal apse. Interesting interior has wall-paintings, richly carved capitals and corbels, and strange tracery in the clerestory.
St Mark, Dalston Parish, Sandringham Road, E8
By Chester Cheston Jnr, 1862–70. Low church. Huge brick and cast-iron hall full of pews, scalding glass, red baize emblazoned with fleur-de-lys, and original brass fittings. There are stained glass angels in the vault and the lectern is adorned with a coloured stole. Vast and forbidding tower by E. L. Blackburn, 1877.
St Mary of Eton, East Way, Hackney Wick, E11
By G. F. Bodley, 1880. A picturesque group on East Way with gate tower leading to court of Eton Mission buildings. The church inside has a broad nave with painted roof, tall, narrow aisles, and a S.E. chapel. It is

full of vistas of arcades with strong, simple mouldings.

St Michael and All Angels, London Fields, E8
By N. Cachemaille-Day, architect-surveyor to the archdeaconry of Hackney, 1960, to replace a church lost through bomb damage. Plain brick faced, square-roofed with a shallow concrete dome. Simple, spacious interior with free-standing altar.

HAMMERSMITH

Holy Innocents, Paddenswick Road, W6
By James Brooks, 1887–91. Austere and lofty red-brick church with tall lancets and clerestory. Chancel screen and furnishings by Charles Spooner and Rev. Ernest Geldart.

St John the Evangelist, Glenthorne Road, W6
By W. Butterfield, 1856. Large, austere church of stock brick with narrow red bands. Gothic organ case and triptych in Lady Chapel by J. F. Bentley.

St Peter, Black Lion Lane, W6
By E. Lapidge, 1827–9. Greek with Ionic portico beneath heavy, strange W. tower. Galleried interior less altered than many of this date.

HAMPSTEAD

All Hallows, Savernake Road, Gospel Oak, NW3
By James Brooks, 1881–9. The formidable, towerless and buttressed exterior of Kentish rag rises from red Victorian villas. Inside it is aisled, with very tall circular piers branching into ribs which support no vaulting, for the roof was completed after Brooks's death. The church is lit by bold lancets high in the side aisles and a rose W. window. The chancel was completed in 1913 by Sir Giles Gilbert Scott, who also designed the massive stone font. It is a spacious interior, admirably suited to ceremony and is sparing in its detail. Its cathedral-like effect is created by massiveness, simplicity and proportion.

St John, Church Row, NW3
By H. Flitcroft, 1744–7. Stock brick with castellated steeple. Many 19th- and 20th-century architects and decorators worked on the galleried interior with its vaulted ceiling and Ionic columns. The effect is rich and Victorian looking E., but looking W. it is still 18th-century. Pulpit *c.* 1750.

St John, Downshire Hill, NW3
1818, perhaps by Cockerell. Simple Classic stucco proprietary chapel with bellcote in district of neat stucco houses. Evangelical interior with galleries, high pews, and Classical reredos.

HIGHGATE

St Augustine
Archway Road, now in the London Borough of Haringey, 5m/8km N. of Charing Cross
TQ 2887
By J. D. Sedding, 1880; completed by Henry Wilson, 1916; W.front by Harold Gibbons, 1925. Formerly in Middlesex, it was one of the most beautifully furnished churches in that county.

St Mary, Brookfield Parish, Dartmouth Park Hill, NW5
By W. Butterfield, 1876. A noble nave in polychrome brick leading to an anti-climax of a chancel by W. C. Street, 1881. Rood and S. chapel by Comper.

HOLBORN

St George the Martyr, Bloomsbury Way, WC1
By Nicholas Hawksmoor, 1720–30; surprising stepped steeple, George I on top. Impressive Corinthian portico and solemn Greek-cross interior.

St Giles-in-the-Fields, St Giles High Street, WC2
By Henry Flitcroft, 1731–3, following a competition in which Gibbs and Hawksmoor were unsuccessful. Galleried interior, well restored since war; airy and Georgian. Monument to poet Chapman, perhaps by Inigo Jones. Last Judgement carving, 1687, in churchyard gate.

HOLLOWAY

St Mary Magdalene, Holloway Road, N7
By W. Wickings, 1812–14. Plain brick outside with square tower. Interior has galleries on Tuscan columns and much Georgian woodwork.

ISLINGTON

St Mary, Upper Street, N1
Spire by Launcelot Dowbiggin, 1751–4, is light and elaborate in Portland stone. Body of church destroyed in the War, rebuilt by Seely and Paget.

KENNINGTON

St John the Divine, Vassall Road, SW9
By G. E. Street, 1874. Red-brick Geometric with apsidal chancel cleverly united to nave by canted bay. Lean-to aisles and W. tower with stone spire. It was restored after severe war damage by H. S. Goodhart-Rendel.

KENSINGTON

St Augustine, Queen's Gate, SW7
By W. Butterfield, 1865–71. Lofty stock-brick church, whitewashed inside, with Baroque reredos by Martin Travers, 1928. The apotheosis of the Anglo-Catholic Congress movement; a period piece of rare delight.

Holy Trinity, Prince Consort Road, SW7
By G. F. Bodley, 1902. The plain stone three-gabled front gives little idea of the soaring and complex interior, which consists of nave with aisles of varying widths and differing arcades. The windows have a variety of elaborate Perpendicular traceries, and the glass is Kempe-ish. The reredos and fittings are expensive and good. Bodley's swan-song.

St John the Baptist, Holland Grove, SW9
By James Brooks, 1889. A comparatively humble entrance leads to the stone-vaulted impressiveness of this English Cistercian interior. Nave and transepts are separated from apsidal E. end by a stone screen and rood.

St Mary Abbots, High Street and Church Street, W8
Rebuilt by Sir George Gilbert Scott, 1869–72. Correct Victorian Middle Pointed, well suited to the correct, rich middle-class suburb of its time. Spire and tower nobly proportioned; echoes of St Mary Redcliffe, Bristol. Attractive cloister from road to S. door by J. O. Scott, 1889–93. Dark, lofty interior damaged in War and inexpensively restored. Glass in W. window by Clayton & Bell. The name 'Abbots' derives from the Middle Ages, when the church belonged to the Abbey of Abingdon.

KENTISH TOWN

St Benet, Lupton Street, NW5
By C. G. Hare. Chancel, 1908; nave and façade, 1927. Lofty Bodleyesque interior, simple and square-ended.

St Luke, Oseney Crescent, Caversham Road, NW5
By Basil Champneys, 1868–70. Hillside setting. Early Pointed red-brick church with narrow lean-to aisles, apse and saddleback tower. Glass by H. Holliday in apse and Morris and Co. in clerestory.

St Martin, Vicars Road, Gospel Oak, NW5
By E. Buckton Lamb, 1864–6. Evangelical cruciform church of Kentish rag; extraordinary outside and in. Thin tower with spire-like newel turret and an apse. Transept windows with strange tracery. The interior is aisleless, low and stranger still, with hammer-beam roof supported on brackets, the transepts seeming to be more important than the nave. No one could call this imitation medieval.

St Silas the Martyr, St Silas Place, Prince of Wales Road, NW5
By E. Shearman, 1912. Tall, very simple Gothic of pleasant pale brick. Many-vistaed interior, with bold woodwork, ambulatory, aisles and side chapels; owes something to the later style of Temple Moore.

KILBURN

St Augustine, Kilburn Park Road, NW6
By J. L. Pearson, 1870–7. Pearson's largest London church. Its red-brick tower and white ashlar spire rise more than 250 feet over a drab neighbourhood. The church is red-brick and cruciform with a lead fleche at the crossing; all is Early English. Inside, one's first impression is of a multiplicity of brick-vaulted vistas of varying heights and with stone ribs. There are double aisles pierced through the buttresses, a triforium right round the church, carried across transepts by bridges. The low baptistry at the W. end and low ambulatory behind the three-bayed chancel increase the sense of height in nave and choir. The paintings by Clayton & Bell and ironwork are all in keeping. The way to see this church is to walk right round the inside. watching arch cutting into arch, giving a different vista with every step. N. Chapel by Sir Giles Gilbert Scott.

LAMBETH

St Anselm, Kennington Road, SE1
By Adshead and Ramsey, designed in 1911, but not completed until 1932–3. Rises high above a charming neo-Regency estate by the same architects. Tall, simple neo-Byzantine church of yellow stock brick. White interior with open timber roof and low aisles.

St Peter, Kennington Lane, Vauxhall, SE11
By J. L. Pearson, 1863–5. The first French Gothic church by this great architect. Of yellow stock brick within and without. Cruciform plan; the broad nave and apsidal chancel are brick-vaulted with stone ribs. Massive low pillars in nave and narrow aisles. Decoration and glass throughout is by Clayton & Bell. This is a most restrained and beautiful building to which later generations have done no harm.

LEWISHAM

St Stephen, High Street, SE13
By Sir George Gilbert Scott, 1863–5. Early English with French detail. High altar by Westlake, alabaster reredos by Buckeridge, carved by Redfern and decorated by Bell, 1873. W. gallery by Sir Charles Nicholson.

St Swithun, Hither Green Lane, SE13
By Ernest Newton, pupil of R. Norman Shaw, 1892–3. Red-brick church in the Decorated style with generous traceried windows and spacious chancel. Barrel roofs, W. gallery, and yellow-green glass.

LIMEHOUSE

St Anne, Commercial Road, at West India Dock Road, EC1
By Nicholas Hawksmoor, 1712–24. Another majestic masterpiece in Portland stone, lighter than Christ Church, Spitalfields, and with a tower composed of diminishing oblongs, emphasized horizontally by heavy cornices, and vertically by deep recesses for holding shadow. At the W. end is a beautiful pilastered apse, with semi-dome. From all sides this building looks magnificent. The interior, burnt in 1850, was beautifully restored by P. Hardwick. It is galleried, with a great oval ceiling hanging over the nave and a chancel whose E. window by Clutterbuck, dark and rich, is most surprisingly sympathetic to Hawksmoor's style and grand scale. This church won the first John Betjeman award in 1990, given by the Society for the Protection of Ancient Buildings to honour J.B.'s memory – he was a committee member of long standing – and to promote the highest standards of repair to churches and chapels in England and Wales.

NORWOOD

St Luke, Norwood High Street, SE27
Fine site on rising ground. By F. Bedford, 1822. Greek Revival, the interior remodelled in Italian Romanesque style by Street, 1872–3. Altar and baldacchino by Sir Charles Nicholson, 1936.

NOTTING HILL

All Saints, Talbot Road, W11
By William White, 1850–61. After St Saviour's, Aberdeen Park, now redundant, his best London church. Although the spire is truncated, the tower is still dramatic with its polychromatic effects in stone and marble. The rich interior has been diminished by war damage and the removal of fittings, but the reredoses are by Cecil Hare and Martin Travers; chancel painting by Sir Ninian Comper.

PADDINGTON

St Mary, Paddington Green, W2
A most satisfying exterior on its green mound on Paddington Green. By John Plaw, 1788–91. Shaped like a Greek cross with a shallow dome on top. Yellow-brick walls, Portland stone semi-circular porches on three sides, and a Venetian window at the E. end. Inside is an octagonal gallery round three sides and the chancel on the fourth. As John Summerson says: 'The thing is thoughtfully worked out and quite undeserving of the scorn which later church builders heaped upon it.'

St Mary Magdalene, Woodchester Square, W2
By G. E. Street, 1868–78. Tall, thin brick and stone steeple, visible for miles. Brick exterior with stone bands and tall brick apse, originally fitted onto an awkward site. Tall, dark interior, very high in all senses of that word, but the thing to see is the crypt under the S. aisle by Comper, 1895, designed to hold the Blessed Sacrament in days of persecution. The crypt is all gold with a singularly rich reredos, a blue ceiling with gold stars, gilded Scottish-Gothic tracery in the arches, a delicate screen, and a painted organ case, all lit by Comper's stained glass.

PENTONVILLE

St James, Pentonville Road, N1
By Aaron H. Hurst, 1787. A builder's brick box in Adam style. Galleries and their surrounding walls taken away before the War. Interior plain and attractive.

PIMLICO

St Barnabas, St Barnabas Street, SW1
By T. Cundy Jnr, 1847–50. Small and crowded Tractarian Middle Pointed interior, with S.E. chapel and sacrament house by Comper. Reredos by Bodley; shrines and altars by Kempe and Tower; glass by Travers and Comper.

St James-the-Less, Thorndike Street, SW1
By G. E. Street, 1858–61; forms an effective group with parish hall and school. No copy of medieval, but a highly original work in coloured brick. There is a detached tower, round E. end with plate tracery and a cloistered porch. Inside, red granite columns with well-carved capitals and a carved pulpit.

Over the arch of the brick-vaulted chancel is a Doom by G. F. Watts. Walls enlivened by patterns in brick, stone and marble; glass and roof-painting by Clayton & Bell.

St Mary, Bourne Street, SW1
By R. J. Withers, 1874–5. Small and stately apsidal-ended brick mission church with 1920-ish Baroque fittings by Martin Travers, and N. chapel by H. S. Goodhart-Rendel. The Society of SS. Peter and Paul's model church. Once one of London's smartest churches, and still a celebrated shrine. Ronald Firbank worshipped here before his conversion to Rome.

POPLAR

All Saints, East India Dock Road, E14
By C. Hollis, 1817–20. Set in ample green space with brick parsonage opposite by same architect. Expensive Greek Revival church in Portland stone with W. steeple over Ionic portico designed as a variation on George Dance Snr's at St Leonard's, Shoreditch. Interior looks awkward now that galleries have been removed; Corinthian reredos.

PRIMROSE HILL

St Mary Magdalene, Regent's Park Road, NW1
By W. P. Manning, 1873. Red-brick with lancets and semi-circular apse. Lofty white-washed interior has work by Bodley, Bayes, Comper and Kempe; centre of Percy Dearmer's liturgical experiments.

PUTNEY

St Paul, Augustus Road, Wimbledon Park Parish, SW19
By J. T. Micklethwaite and Somers Clarke; nave, 1877; chancel, 1888. Red-brick and towerless in rich, leafy suburb. Surprisingly simple and 'arty crafty' for its date with Perpendicular tracery. Broad, spacious, light interior with octagonal piers. Furnishings and glass by Kempe and Tower.

REGENT'S PARK

St Mary Magdalene, Munster Square, NW1
By R. C. Carpenter, 1849–52. The spire has never been built and the church consists of a spacious nave with separately gabled aisles, all correct Middle Pointed. Inside, slender arcades of clustered columns give views of Hardman glass designed by Pugin, frescoes by Daniel Bell, paintings, elegant screen and rood by Micklethwaite, and a perfect Camden Society chancel. A faint smell of incense completes the elegant early-ritualistic effect of this restrained and scholarly building.

ROEHAMPTON

Holy Trinity, Roehampton Lane, SW15
By G. H. Fellowes Prynne, 1896–8. Early Decorated with tall spire. Inside are a huge stone chancel screen, painted altar panels, and much Kempe glass.

ROTHERHITHE

St Mary, Rotherhithe, St Mary Church Street, SE16
Brick Classical, 1714–47. Tower, 1739, by Launcelot Dowbiggin. Among wharf-enclosed remains of riverside village, in the ever-changing Docklands area. Among other nautical monuments is that to John Wade, 'King's Carver in His Majesty's Yards at Deptford and Woolwich', d. 1743.

ST JOHN'S WOOD

St John, St John's Wood Road, NW8
By Thomas Hardwick Jnr, 1813–14. Elegantly sited on the crest of a hill near Lord's. Ionic Portland stone portico and turret above. Lovely Tuscan interior, all white, has box pews and glazed galleries.

ST MARYLEBONE

All Saints, Margaret Street, W1
By W. Butterfield, 1849–59. The dark-brick church, vicarage and choir school form a Tractarian oasis. The tall, unbuttressed tower, with its slate and lead spire, the polychromatic brick and original style, had never been seen in London before, and this is the pioneer church of that phase of the Gothic Revival that ceased to copy medieval but went on with new materials like cast iron and stock brick from where the medieval had left off. For the smallness and confined nature of the site, the effect of space, richness, mystery and size is amazing. The original plan was strictly Tractarian – one altar visible from all parts of the church, no screen, light from the W. end, and the chancel more sumptuous than anywhere else. Comper's side altar is wisely not in Butterfield's style and, excellent in itself, it does not compete with the huge mouldings and violent contrasts of texture and colour which make this building so memorable. The decoration on the E. wall is based on Dyce's original scheme; the large tiled pictures on the N., W. and S. walls are by

Alexander Gibbs, just right for their setting. The roof, to quote John Summerson, 'is like a huge ingenious toy'. The effect of this building is all achieved by scale – the huge but low arcades, the lofty chancel arch and reredos beyond. The thought and care over detail are best appreciated after long familiarity. An embarrassing screen has been put in the S. aisle.

All Souls, Langham Place, Regent Street, W1
By John Nash, 1822–4. As Portland Place falls too far W. to be in line with Upper Regent Street, Nash built a church 'whose nave swings erratically to the N.E., but whose circular vestibule, crowned by a quaint colonnaded spike, makes a lovely terminal feature to the northward stretch of Regent Street' (John Summerson). Inside, this stone church is a galleried Corinthian hall with flat ceiling; it was tastefully restored by H. S. Goodhart-Rendel after the War, in very Evangelical fashion; a further remodelling of the interior took place in 1975–6 to accommodate the BBC recording studio in a new basement.

The Annunciation, Bryanston Street, W1
By Sir Walter Tapper, 1912–14. Cliff-like buttressed brick exterior. Tall, grey and imposing with N. aisle and clerestoried nave. Impressive vaulted interior with much rich woodwork and delicate late-Gothic E. window. Baroque decoration by John de Mars which does not detract from Tapper's Bodleyesque Gothic.

St Cyprian, Clarence Gate, Glentworth Street, NW1
By Sir Ninian Comper, 1902–3. The brick-buttressed exterior with wide late-Perpendicular windows and bottle-glass panes contrasts with the sumptuous interior. Simple stone-vaulted arches under the W. gallery open onto a wide nave and aisles without pews. There are graceful arcade piers and a traceried gold screen stretching across the whole width of the E. end. Parcloses divide the E. end into chapels. Altar hangings, statues, light fittings, font cover, and stained glass are all by Comper.

St Marylebone, Marylebone Road, W1
By T. Hardwick Jnr, 1813–17. An expensive Corinthian church in Portland stone, whose portico and steeple terminate Nash's stucco York Gate leading out of Regent's Park. There are Corinthian side entrances and three vestibules, and at the E. end two entrance projections set diagonally. In 1884 some galleries were removed and the ceilings

altered, and the interior lost much of its original character. The Brownings were married here, and there is a memorial chapel to them in the N.W. wing.

St Mary, Wyndham Place, W1
By Sir Robert Smirke, 1821–3. A circular tower on the S. side fits well into Wyndham Place; otherwise a correct Commissioners' Classic church, redecorated by A. W. Blomfield in 1875.

St Peter, Vere Street, W1
By James Gibbs, 1721–4. Humble brick exterior with Tuscan portico and bell-turret. Singularly exquisite inside; tall columns rise past the galleries and support a carved ceiling with 'spritely plaster-work by Bagutti' (Pevsner). The stained glass by Burne-Jones and painted altarpiece by him, though hardly suited to this miniature St Martin-in-the-Fields, have their own merit. Lamentable recent conversion of galleries.

ST PANCRAS

St Pancras, New Church, Woburn Place and Euston Road, WC1
By H. W. and W. Inwood, 1819–22. The most expensive and the best of all English Greek Revival churches. Outside it is of Portland stone, with portico, steeple, apse, and two square projections at the E. end, that on the N. containing an elegant oval vestry, surrounded on the outside with caryatids. The portico is Ionic, and the steeple an adaptation 'free and astonishingly successful' (Summerson) of the Tower of the Winds. Rich Greek terracotta details from the Erechtheum adorn the outside. At the W. end there are three impressive entrance lobbies, two for gallery staircases, and that in the middle an attractive Doric octagon under the tower. The interior is a vast flat-ceilinged hall, terminated by an Ionic apse and surrounded on three sides by galleries supported on columns decorated with lotus leaves. The church is needlessly dark because of Victorian stained glass introduced to dispel the 'Pagan' effect, as it was thought in those days, of the Greek detail.

St Pancras, Old Church, Pancras Road, NW1
Medieval and 1848 Norman Revival by H. Roumieu Gough. Embellished inside by Martin Travers, 1930. In the churchyard is Soane's excellent mausoleum for his wife, 1815.

SHADWELL

St Paul, The Highway, E1

By J. Walters, 1817. Surprisingly Wren-like steeple for the date. Stock-brick rectangle, with galleried and domed interior.

SHOREDITCH

St Chad, Nicholas Square, Haggerston, E1

By James Brooks, 1868. Red-brick cruciform church with lofty clerestoreyed brick nave, vaulted chancel and side chapel. Thick stone columns and narrow lean-to aisles; all the essentials of a grand church without the fuss.

St Leonard, High Street, E1

By G. Dance Snr, 1736–40. A ponderous, City-style church in red brick and Portland stone, with a portico like Hawksmoor and a steeple imitating Wren, an elegant outline above the E. London chimney-pots. The inside, denuded of side galleries, has old stained glass and a famous E. window. It is best seen looking S., where there is a beautiful Chippendale-style gilt clock-case in the gallery front.

SOUTHWARK

St Alphege, Lancaster Street, SE1

By R. Willey, 1880–2. Wide, squat mission church furnished in the Belgian taste. Perhaps the most convincing Roman Catholic interior in the Church of England.

St George the Martyr, Borough High Street, SE1

By J. Price, 1734–6. Brick with Portland stone steeple; galleried interior under a ceiling of cherubs and clouds by Basil Champneys, 1897.

SPITALFIELDS

Christ Church, Commercial Street, E2

By Nicholas Hawksmoor, 1723–9. A huge, heavy galleon of white Portland stone anchored among the red-brick Queen Anne houses of the silk-workers. Two flights of steps lead to immense portico with barrel vault in the middle; oblong tower and spire on top of this. The body of the church is a separate composition, but towers, spire, portico, and church hang together as one walks by. Everything is massive, simple and gigantic; 'the body of the church supports with static and imposing regular detail the enormous weight of the spire' (E. and W. Young). The aisled and columned interior is rich and grandly gloomy. A clerestory lights the flat and coffered nave ceiling; from the arcades below, the arches open onto transverse coffered tunnel vaults which overhang the aisles. E. and W. the great rectangle of the church is interrupted by transverse motifs; a hugh beam on Corinthian columns, with a Royal Arms above, turns the E. end into a chancel, beyond which the walls curve to make a sanctuary. The church was in a dangerous condition in the 1960s and nearly demolished, but saved by the Friends of Christ Church and since expertly repaired following SPAB principles.

STEPNEY

St Dunstan and All Saints, Stepney High Street, E1

Large, mostly Perpendicular church with Saxon stone rood over high altar. The village-like churchyard is full of monuments to Georgian sailors.

St George-in-the-East, Cannon Street Road, E1

By Nicholas Hawksmoor, 1715–23. 'The white castellated tower and turret seem to sail like a battleship over the houses when one is steaming down the river. In winter the river winds well through the deep funereal arches in this mighty tower and past the ruthless keystones, each as big as a child's coffin. It is a waste of time describing such a building, drawing attention to the complex ground plan or analysing the elements in the harmony of the tower, describing how the interior was – Greek Cross, Tuscan giants, depressed, elliptical vault, diagonal emphasis. The only thing is to go, and gape at what remains' (E. and W. Young). Ansell and Bailey's restoration is a combination of modern forms with surviving Georgian and Victorian decoration.

STOKE NEWINGTON

St Matthias, Matthias Road, N16

By W. Butterfield, 1851. Though bombed and sparingly repaired, this great brick church is Butterfield at his boldest and simplest. From all angles the outside, with its saddleback tower over the chancel, its high nave, lean-to aisles, and low sanctuary E. of the tower, looks well. Inside the effect of solemn grandeur is caused by two great transverse arches of low pitch over the chorus cantorum; the W. narthex, the severe nave arcades and roof, modelled on Ely, lit by a clerestory.

St Mary, Stoke Newington Church Street, N16

By Sir George Gilbert Scott, 1855–8. Sumptuous Middle Pointed with spire, 1890, by J. Oldrid Scott.

St Mary, Old Church, Stoke Newington Church Street, N16
Small medieval and later church in park setting. W. tower and remodelling, 1560; N. aisle added by Barry, 1824.

STREATHAM

Christ Church, Christchurch Road, SW19
By J. Wild, 1840–2. Graceful basilica in yellow brick with red-brick dressings. Obelisks guard the W. front; the detached campanile has a spire. The tall, galleried interior has an E. apse. Decorated by Owen Jones. In 1891, Walter Crane did the E. windows of the aisles. Furnishings by J. F. Bentley.

St Leonard, Streatham High Road, SW16
Mostly by J. T. Parkinson, 1830–1; medieval W. tower. Monuments include a big brass in the Lady Chapel to William Dyce, 1865, and various 16th–17th-century monuments. Well restored after a serious fire in 1975.

TOOTING

All Saints, Franciscan Road, SW17
By Temple Moore, 1904–6. A large brick and stone church in late Decorated style, with tower, long nave, choir of seven bays, and square-ended Lady Chapel beyond, all rising among small villas. Inside are double aisles divided by slender columns of grey Forest of Dean stone. Vaulted wooden roofs, Baroque high altar, and elegant iron screens. Many vistas and cathedral-like interior proportions.

WALWORTH

St Peter, Liverpool Grove, SE17
By Sir John Soane, 1823–5. Soane was not a church man and this was his first and best. Ionic outside with stone steeple. Plain galleried interior, light and wide, with original altar at E. end. The first church to introduce seven sanctuary lamps, since removed.

WANDSWORTH

All Saints, Wandsworth High Street, SW18
Tower, 1630; Nave, 1780; N. aisle, 1724; chancel, 1891. Barrel-vaulted interior with columns and impressive, ponderous chancel. 'Galleries, shining with gilded records of benefaction, lurk far back in wide aisles, and there is a fine sweeping staircase going up to them. Font and pulpit are original and a square churchwardens' pew survives.' (E. and W. Young.)

St Anne, St Anne's Hill, SW18
By Sir Robert Smirke, 1820–4. Commissioners' Greek, set high on a hill. Interior Victorianized by E. W. Mountford in swaggering Baroque, 1896. Whitewashed by Sir Ninian Comper.

WESTMINSTER

Grosvenor Chapel, South Audley Street, W1
Built and possibly designed by B. Timbrell, 1730. Brick exterior with spire and portico, all looking American-colonial behind Dorchester Hotel. Light, white interior with galleries, attractive vaulted ceilings, and a great screen across the E. end by Sir Ninian Comper, 1912, who also did the altar beyond.

St Clement Danes, The Strand, WC2
By Wren, 1680–2; steeple by J. Gibbs, 1719; Gutted 1941; restored 1958. The galleried interior has a vaulted ceiling and curved E. end, once adorned with rich Baroque sculpture, probably by Wren's mason, Edward Pierce. Now an Air Force shrine.

St George, Hanover Square, W1
By John James, 1721–4. Massive Corinthian portico. Heavy square windows and a weak steeple. Light and well-upholstered interior has beautiful 16th-century Flemish glass brought here in 1840 from a convent at Malines.

St James, Piccadilly, W1
By Wren, 1676–84; restored by Sir Albert Richardson, 1953. Modest old-brick exterior with tower and steeple. Outdoor pulpit by Temple Moore. Pale, light, galleried interior, de-Victorianized. Columns rise from galleries to carry elegant barrel vaults. Marble font by Grinling Gibbons, who also carved reredos swags. Organ case from Chapel Royal, Whitehall.

St John, Smith Square, SW1
By Thomas Archer, 1714–28; gutted 1941; restored by Marshall Sisson, 1965–8. The four Baroque corner towers rise from graceful pedimented compositions on N. and S. façades and flank more dominant projections on the other two. Thus this bold and strange church, islanded in the middle of a red-brick Queen Anne square, presents a different Portland stone and temple-like termination to each of the four streets that enter the square. Now a concert hall.

St Margaret, Westminster, Parliament Square, SW1

1504 and later. Much-restored late-Gothic. Graceful aisled interior with early 16th-century Flemish glass E. window of Crucifixion, part of Katharine of Aragon's dowry. Glass in S. aisle by John Piper, 1967.

St Martin-in-the-Fields, Trafalgar Square, WC2

By James Gibbs, 1722–6. Trafalgar Square was made a century later, so that the awkward way the Portland-stone steeple bestrides the Corinthian portico was not apparent, and the church was glimpsed through narrow streets in parts, now as a whole. Both steeple and porticoed body of the church are compact and elegant as separate units. Much-visited interior has galleries and tall columns supporting vaulted nave ceiling with graceful plasterwork, especially over chancel arch, and shallow domes over aisles. The E. end is an anticlimax.

St Mary-le-Strand, The Strand, WC2

By J. Gibbs, 1714–17. Intended as the westerly termination of two narrow streets, now swept away, the church looks like something in Rome, and the steeple is an afterthought. Outside, the effect is two-storeyed, bound round with strong cornices. Inside, the two-storey effect is less happy, for there are no galleries and the large first-floor windows have ugly glass and detract from the rich, vaulted ceiling. Deep chancel is even richer than the nave and with even uglier glass, but it is a beautiful little church, islanded in traffic.

St Stephen, Rochester Row, Vincent Square, SW1

By Benjamin Ferrey, 1845–7; built as a memorial to her father by the philanthropist Angela, Baroness Burdett-Coutts. Correct and expensive English Middle Pointed; good details include the carved birds and beasts of the Benedicite on the capitals of the nave piers.

WOOLWICH

St Mary Magdalene, St Mary Street, SE18

1732–8. Large stock-brick church with W. tower; chancel added and interior remodelled by J. O. Scott, 1894. Touching churchyard monument to Thomas Cribb, the boxer, 1845.

St Michael and All Angels, Borgard Road, SE18

By W. Butterfield. E. parts, 1875–8; nave, 1889. A vast clerestoried nave without the intended aisles. The church has later additions by J. W. Walter and Caroe.

Middlesex

Introduction

Westminster was once the centre of this county, and its Guildhall is still in Parliament Square. But in 1889 Middlesex lost all its London territory (the City was always independent). From Hammersmith to Temple Bar, from Stoke Newington to Bishopsgate, the County of London was formed, and even the heights of Hampstead, those Middlesex-looking uplands, were included. If a Londoner would see how beautiful this part of what once was Middlesex looked, let him walk over Parliament Hill Fields to Kenwood, where he will see the wooded hills, ponds, willows, oaks and grassy hollows, leading to a landscaped park and Adam house. This is the Middlesex that Keats, Constable and Leigh Hunt knew.

The county has over two million inhabitants, and many of them do not realize they live in Middlesex. Aerodromes, reservoirs and factories occupy the rich, flat, market-gardening land in the south-west corner along the north bank of the Thames. Suburbs fill up most of the rest. But there are still villages where the original Middlesex may be seen – Shepperton, Stanwell, Harmondsworth, Harefield, Norwood Green, and South Mimms are some of the least spoiled, their modest churches rising among weatherboarded cottages and the rust-coloured brick mansions of the *cit* who sought his 18th-century *rus in urbe* among walnut trees and cedars in his miniature park hidden behind brown brick walls. There are still great houses: Hampton Court (with its Wren chapel), Syon, Osterley, Chiswick, Breakspear, Wrotham, Dyrham, and Trent. The Georgian Canons has disappeared. In Enfield Chase are still some fields; there are farms and country inns in the Harefield district; Littleton seems hidden and remote under its great reservoir. Harrow Village preserves its hill-top quiet, looking from its elmy height over miles of roof and railway. With an effort of imagination one can see Uxbridge as it once was, a country market town, and along the old turnpikes that cross the county to the City the vestiges of Georgian coaching days and Victorian market gardens and Cockney's bona-fide taverns persist.

Middlesex was a rich agricultural county which supplied London with food before London ate up its fields. Its medieval churches, except Westminster Abbey, were never much. There was no local building stone, for Middlesex is nearly all clay. But bricks were made early, and the old Tudor red bricks of Middlesex, and the dark-brown and purple and red ones of the 17th and 18th centuries, are varied and beautiful. The old parish churches were often added to or rebuilt when Londoners moved out into the country. Original hamlet churches survive at Perivale and Northolt. They are humble South Essex-like buildings in keeping with the old wooden barns of the county which remain – the barn at Harmondsworth is one of the biggest in England.

What seems surprising at first is that there are so few major churches of the Gothic Revival period, when all these suburbs started to fill the county. This is, I think, because the sort of Tractarian squire who would rebuild his village church and use the best London man was not a Middlesex-dweller. The county was too suburban for him, and the new large Victorian villas were often built by Nonconformists who had made their money in the City and West End. It was not until the present century when 'Greater London' called for missions that the more interesting modern buildings were erected.

Looking for Middlesex is even more fun than looking for Middlesex churches, and of the latter Harefield is to me the most undisturbed and exciting. Tottenham parish church, so imaginatively enlarged by William Butterfield, who is buried in its cemetery, is the most remarkable.

J.B.

1 Bedford Park	15 Hanwell	29 Littleton
2 Brentford	16 Hanworth	30 Mill Hill
3 Cowley	17 Harefield	31 Northolt
4 Cranford	18 Harlesden	32 Ruislip
5 Ealing	19 Harmondsworth	33 Shepperton
6 East Bedfont	20 Harrow	34 Southgate
7 Enfield	21 Hayes	35 South Mimms
8 Feltham	22 Hendon	36 Staines
9 Finchley	23 Hillingdon	37 Stanmore
10 Friern Barnet	24 Hornsey	38 Stanwell
11 Golders Green	25 Ickenham	39 Tottenham
12 Greenford	26 Kenton	40 Twickenham
13 Hampstead Garden Suburb	27 Kingsbury	41 West Drayton
14 Hampton	28 Laleham	42 West Hendon

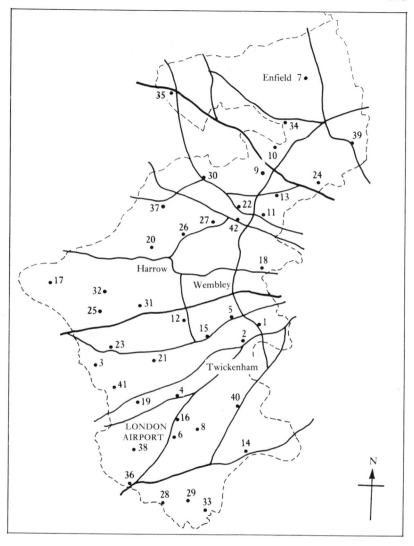

Enfield 7 •

35 •

• 34

• 39

• 10

30 • 9 •

• 24

37 • 22 • 13

26 27 • 11

20 • 42 •

Harrow

18 •

17 • Wembley

32 • 5 •

25 • 31 • 1 •

12 • 15 2 •

23 • 21 • Twickenham

3 •

41 •

19 • 4

40 •

16 •

LONDON 6 • 8 •

AIRPORT 14 •

38 •

36 •

28 • 29 33

N

Selected List of Churches

BEDFORD PARK
St Michael and All Angels
Woodstock Road, in London Borough of
Hounslow, 6m/10km W. of Charing Cross
TQ 2179
By R. Norman Shaw, 1875–80; part of the
garden suburb. In the Queen Anne style
with lantern over the crossing and some
Perpendicular Gothic tracery. Inside are a
raised altar, fine openwork roof, and good
original fittings. Designed as a group with
inn and bank.

BRENTFORD
St Faith
Windmill Road, in London Borough of
Hounslow, 8m/12km W. of Charing Cross TQ
1777
By G. F. Bodley and C. G. Hare, 1906–7.
Brick Decorated church with bell-turret and
clerestory. Austere interior with ceiled
wagon roof and square-ended chancel.
Glass by Burlison & Grylls.

COWLEY
St Laurence
Church Road, in London Borough of
Hillingdon, 1m/2km S. of Uxbridge TQ 0582
Tiny and primitive medieval church, a rare
survival; 13th-century chancel and timber
bellcote of 1780; 15th-century crown-post
roofs, Georgian double-decker W. gallery,
and early chancel pews.

CRANFORD
St Dunstan
in London Borough of Hillingdon, 12m/19km
W. of Charing Cross TQ 1077
Chancel and tower 15th-century. Nave
rebuilt in red brick with ashlar dressings
after a fire in 1710. Good fittings by Martin
Travers, 1935–6. Extraordinary collection
of monuments: a grand work of *c.* 1613
by Wm. Cure, Master Mason to the King;
Bernini-esque white marble effigy by Nicholas Stone, 1635; myriad later 17th–early
18th-century cartouches, busts and tablets.

EALING
now a London Borough, 8m/12km W. of
Charing Cross TQ 1780
The Ascension, Hanger Hill
By Seely and Paget, 1938–9. Grey brick on
a concrete frame with tower and Classical
pediment. Inside, square piers support a
barrel vault; simple striped wooden furnish-
ings.
Christ the Saviour, New Broadway
By Sir George Gilbert Scott, 1852; handsome design in the Second Pointed style.
Tall W. tower with octagonal top, corner
pinnacles and spire. Carved foliate capitals,
Geometric tracery, and glass by Hugh
Easton, 1952. Pulpit, painted roofs and other
fittings by Bodley, 1906.
St Mary, St Mary's Road
Medieval and 18th-century church drastically enlarged and remodelled by S. S.
Teulon, 1866–74. Huge W. tower with pyramidal roof; the 18th-century pediment is
just visible above Teulon's apse. Dramatic
interior has iron columns supporting timber
galleries and a mass of tracery in the roof.
At the E. end are horse-shoe arches and
exotic fittings to match. Exquisite stained
glass, mostly by Heaton, Butler & Bayne.
St Peter, Mount Park Road
By J. D. Sedding, 1889, completed by his
partner, Henry Wilson, in 1892–3. Upper-
class suburban church of the 90s. Highly
original design, with great W. window tri-
sected by buttresses, spirelets, and two rows
of little turrets along roof. Inside is a triforium gallery and a painted framed ceiling.
Good early 20th-century fittings and glass
by Kempe.

EAST BEDFONT
St Mary the Virgin
now in the London Borough of Hounslow,
between London and Staines TQ 0873
Screened by trees on a green; 12th-century
and later church retains Norman chancel
arch with chevrons. W. tower with timber
top stage added in 1865. Fine mid-13th-
century wall-paintings of the Last Judgement and Crucifixion. Monuments.

ENFIELD
St Andrew
now a London Borough, 10m/16km N. of Charing Cross TQ 3296
Medieval town church by the market-place; 13th-century chancel, late 14th-century W. tower, and early 19th-century brick S. aisle. Bread-shelf of *c.* 1630; good monuments, one by Nicholas Stone, 1617; fine memorials in churchyard.

FELTHAM
St Dunstan
Lower Feltham, now in the London Borough of Hounslow, 1m/2km S.W. of Hounslow Heath TQ 1073
By William Walker, 1802. A rustic building with round-headed windows, short tower, and shingled spire. The aisles were given a 'Norman' cast in 1855–6. Simple interior has original W. gallery supported on Roman Doric columns, the panels filled with charity inscriptions in elegant script.

FINCHLEY
St Mary
now in the London Borough of Barnet, 7m/11km N. of Charing Cross TQ 2590
Mostly 15th-century church with modest W. tower and outer S. aisle of 1932. Moulded Perpendicular nave roof, 13th-century font and brasses.

FRIERN BARNET
St John the Evangelist
Friern Barnet Road, now in the London Borough of Barnet, 8m/12km N. of Charing Cross TQ 2792
By J. L. Pearson, 1891, completed after his death. Ambitious early-Decorated building with vaulted interior and ambulatory round the chancel.

GOLDERS GREEN
St Alban the Martyr
now in the London Borough of Barnet, 6m/10km N.W. of Charing Cross TQ 2488
By Sir Giles Gilbert Scott, 1932. Brick church with central crossing tower and impressive interior.

GREENFORD
now in the London Borough of Ealing, 10m/16km W. of Charing Cross TQ 1482
Holy Cross, Ferrymead Gardens and Oldfield Lane South
15th-century chancel roof, 17th-century W.

gallery and tower staircase. Important heraldic glass of *c.* 1500 and good 17th-century monuments.
Holy Cross, New Church, Ferrymead Gardens
By A. E. Richardson, 1939. Timber with brick facings. Spacious interior has tall open roof supported on sturdy posts.

HAMPSTEAD GARDEN SUBURB
St Jude on the Hill
Central Square, now in the London Borough of Brent, about 1m/2km N. of Hampstead TQ 2570
By Sir Edwin Lutyens, 1908–10. Designed as part of the garden suburb. Large silver- and red-brick basilican church with tall tower and pinnacled spire. Byzantine interior has round arches, tunnel vaults, and brick piers, all covered with murals by W. P. Starmer. The Free Church and Institute in the same square are also by Lutyens.

HAMPTON
St Mary the Virgin
now in the London Borough of Richmond, 3m/4km W. of Kingston TQ 1370
By E. Lapidge, 1831. White brick, lancets and restrained W. tower. Interior has quatrefoil piers and side galleries; chancel of 1888 by Sir Arthur Blomfield.

HANWELL
St Mary
Church Road, now in the London Borough of Ealing, 9m/15km W. of Charing Cross TQ 1580
By Sir G. G. Scott and Moffatt, 1841. Village setting. Flint with white-brick dressings and broach spire. Whitewashed interior has quatrefoil piers, galleries, and monuments. On of Scott's earliest churches.

HANWORTH
All Saints
Uxbridge Road, now in the London Borough of Hounslow, 3m/4km W. of Twickenham TQ 1171
By N. F. Cachemaille-Day, 1952–8. The first phase consisted of a narthex and baptistry, with the taller worship-space lit by a central round lantern light added a few years later. Fair-face brick interior with angel designs in gold leaf by Christopher Webb and stained glass by Goddard and Gibbs.

HAREFIELD
St Mary the Virgin
Church Hill, now in the London Borough of
Hillingdon, 3m/4km S. of Rickmansworth TQ
0590
Pleasantly set away from the village. Modest
medieval church, with 13th-century chancel
and early 14th-century S. aisle; N. aisle
and tower added soon after 1500. Chancel
altered by Henry Keene, 1768, has remarkable plaster ceiling. The glory of Harefield
is its monuments, a gallery of sepulchral art
from the 15th century to 1800, which yet
does not overwhelm the church. The Newdigate and Ashby families are commemorated by William White, 1614, Grinling
Gibbons, 1692, Sir Robert Taylor, 1760,
John Bacon Jnr, 1800, and others unknown.
The grandest monument is a canopied tomb
to Lady Derby, 1636, with columns, stone
curtains, and much heraldry. The pulpit,
communion rails, reredos, and font cover
are fine 17th- and 18th-century carving,
some from Flanders.

HARLESDEN
All Souls
Station Road, now in the London Borough of
Brent, 6m/10km W. of Charing Cross TQ
2183
By E. J. Tarver, 1875–6. Octagonal brick
church with small iron lantern and canted
apse. Remarkable interior has tie-beam and
arch-braced timber roof with no internal
supports. Glass by Selwyn Image.

HARMONDSWORTH
St Mary
now in the London Borough of Hillingdon,
on N. side of Heathrow Airport TQ 0577
Near the celebrated 15th-century Manor
Farm Barn, one of the finest in England.
Norman and later church with fine mid-
12th-century S. doorway with shafts, beak-
heads and zig-zags. Good chancel, 1396–8;
16th-century brick tower has 18th-century
cupola. Pews of *c.* 1500 and good 18th–19th-
century churchyard memorials.

HARROW
now a London Borough, 10m/16km N.W. of
Charing Cross TQ 1587
St Alban, Church Drive, North Harrow
By A. W. Kenyon, 1936–7. The best
Middlesex church of the 1930s; in brown
brick over a reinforced concrete frame with
bold, high N.W. tower. The interior is plain

and serious, cement-finished, with barrel
roof contracting at chancel and sanctuary;
the only colour is at the altar.
St Mary, Church Hill, Harrow-on-the-Hill
Splendidly situated on Harrow Hill, the
finest setting in Middlesex. The pale-grey
exterior and slim lead-and-timber spire can
be seen for miles above the suburban villas.
Lower part of tower *c.* 1130; Early English
chancel, nave and aisles; transepts *c.* 1300;
Perpendicular clerestory and nave roof; spire
rebuilt 1765. The whole church was fiercely
restored by Sir George Gilbert Scott,
1846–9, when the Decorated style was
introduced. The interior is consequently
hard, and the outside walls flinty. Brasses
from 1370; monuments, principally to head-
masters of Harrow School. E. window by
Comper. Byron's daughter Allegra is buried
in the churchyard, where he used to 'sit for
hours and hours when a boy – this was my
favourite spot'.

HAYES
St Mary
Church Road, now in the London Borough
of Hillingdon, 3m/4km S.E. of Uxbridge TQ
0980
13th-century and later flint church. Good
16th-century open timber S. porch. Medieval roofs and large wall-painting, *c.* 1500,
of St Christopher; 14th-century priest's
brass, a grand wall-monument of 1612, and
nice centre-swinging lych gate.

HENDON
St Mary
now in the London Borough of Barnet, 7m/
11km N.W. of Charing Cross TQ 2289
13th-century nave and chancel, 15th-
century W. tower. Two handsome S. aisles
added by Temple Moore, 1914–15. Fine
Norman square font with arcaded sides and
monuments, including an elegant Whichcote
slab of 1677 with achievement of arms.

HILLINGDON
St John the Baptist
Uxbridge Road, now a London Borough TQ
0782
14th-century nave and aisles, 13th-century
chancel arch with stiff-leaf capitals; W.
tower, 1629. E. parts added by Sir Giles
Gilbert Scott during his restoration of
1847–8. Impressive brass to Lord Strange,
1509, and other 16th-century brasses;
elegant   17th–18th-century   monuments

include those to Sir Edward Carr, 1637, and the Earl of Uxbridge, 1743.

HORNSEY
St Mary

now in the London Borough of Haringey, 6m/10km N. of Charing Cross TQ 3088
Tower of demolished medieval church stands nearby. The new church was designed by James Brooks, 1888; W. front added by Sir Charles Nicholson. Large church in the Perpendicular style contains excellent late 16th-century incised slab to George Rey and the haunting kneeling figure of Francis Musters, d. 1680.

ICKENHAM
St Giles

High Road, now in the London Borough of Hillingdon, 2m/3km N.E. of Uxbridge TQ 0786
Attractive 14th-century village church with brick N. aisle of 1575–80; mid-17th-century mortuary chapel on N. side. Timber-framed S. porch and bell-turret, *c.* 1500. Inside are a carved 17th-century oak font and 16th-century brasses; monuments include a sad shrouded infant, 1665.

KENTON
St Mary the Virgin

Kenton Road, now in the London Borough of Harrow, 9m/15km N.W. of Charing Cross TQ 1788
By J. H. Gibbons, 1936. Pale-brick church in free Gothic style. W. front with Virgin and Child centrepiece flanked by lancets; S.E. tower linked to church hall. Rendered interior has vaulted chancel and original fittings.

KINGSBURY
St Andrew

Church Lane, now in the London Borough of Brent, 8m/12km N.W. of Charing Cross TQ 2088
By S. W. Dawkes and Hamilton, 1847; this was formerly St Andrew's, Wells Street, St Marylebone, and was brought here in 1933 to take the place of the old parish church, now redundant. Originally a leading church of the Catholic Revival, it is now a veritable museum of superlative Victorian furnishings. Reredos, pulpit, chancel screen and font by Street; litany desk, chalice and monument on S. wall by Burges; font cover by Pearson; lectern by Butterfield; W.

window by Pugin; panels on W. gallery by Alfred Bell.

LALEHAM
All Saints

2m/3km S.E. of Staines TQ 0568
A 12th-century village church in country and river setting. Brick W. tower of 1732 and sturdy Norman arcades. Restored interior has bold S.W. window by Miss Geddes. Matthew Arnold buried in churchyard.

LITTLETON
St Mary Magdalene

2m/3km N.E. of Chertsey TQ 0786
Medieval church of a tiny village, now almost overshadowed by a gigantic reservoir. Some 12th-century work, with 16th-century brick clerestory and W. tower. Mausoleum of 1705 on N. side, the tower with a top stage of the same date. Good old pews, stalls, screens, Flemish altar rails *c.* 1700, pulpit, and 24 colours of Grenadier Guards hanging in nave. Restored by Martin Travers.

MILL HILL
John Keble Church

now in the London Borough of Barnet, 9m/15km N.W. of Charing Cross TQ 2192
By D. F. Martin-Smith, 1936. A tall church in brown brick, arranged in cuboidal tiers, wedding-cake fashion. At the base of the steeple – a copper-covered pillar crowned with a golden cross – is a concrete box, designed to hold a peal of bells. However, on completion of the structure it was found that the box was not strong enough to support them! The interior is austere but serene, with white-painted walls.

NORTHOLT
St Mary

Northolt Green, now in the London Borough of Ealing, 11m/18km W. of Charing Cross TQ 1384
Standing on a knoll by the old village green, the churchyard sloping on the other side to a bypass road. Whitewashed exterior with brilliant red roof tiles and a bell-turret with little spire; simple aisleless plan to nave, *c.* 1300, and chancel, 1521. Light and charming interior has W. gallery, 1703, late 17th-century Royal Arms, and a rood, 1951.

RUISLIP
St Martin
High Street, now in the London Borough of Hillingdon, 3m/4km N.E. of Uxbridge TQ 0987
Originally 13th-century church of flint and stone, much extended and altered. Fine Perpendicular arch-braced roofs with bosses and decorated spandrels. Many hatchments in the tower.

SHEPPERTON
St Nicholas
opposite Walton-on-Thames TQ 0867
Flint and stone church of 1614 with embattled brick W. tower, 1710. Early 19th-century galleries and box pews. Group with rectory and inn.

SOUTHGATE
Christ Church
now in the London Borough of Enfield, 2m/3km S.W. of Enfield TQ 2994
By Sir George G. Scott, 1863; Burne-Jones and Rossetti glass.

SOUTH MIMMS
St Giles
2m/3km W. of Potters Bar TL 2201
Bold W. tower with square-headed windows and projecting newel turret of typical 15th-century Middlesex type; 13th-century chancel; nave c. 1400; N. aisle early 16th-century; red-brick N. chapel, c. 1530. Some delicate early 16th-century glass and a font cover by Comper. Splendid Frowyck monuments with canopied tomb chests of 1500 and 1530.

STAINES
St Peter
Laleham Road TQ 0371
By G. H. Fellowes Prynne, 1893–4; handsome late-Victorian church with steeple. Excellent glass, by J. Jennings, in E. and W. windows, to designs by the architect's brother.

STANMORE
11m/18km N.W. of Charing Cross TQ 1692
St John the Evangelist, Church Road, Great Stanmore
Two churches in one churchyard include the old brick church, consecrated by Archbishop Laud in 1632; now a picturesque ruin. The new church, begun in 1849, by Henry Clutton, is in a Decorated style, and contains some old furnishings and a number of good

17th- and 18th-century monuments removed from the old church.
St Lawrence, Whitchurch Lane, Little Stanmore
The church was built for the Duke of Chandos of Canons by John James in 1715; the 16th-century tower survives from the previous church. It is frescoed with panels and grisaille, probably by Laguerre and Belucci, c. 1720. There are many original fittings and a ducal pew at the W. end. On the N. side, the Chandos chapel is by Gibbs, 1735; the enormous tomb with statues is by Gibbons, and the organ by Jordan, c. 1720.

STANWELL
St Mary the Virgin
between Staines Reservoir and Heathrow Airport TQ 0574
A village church with slender spire standing up from the flat plain of S.W. Middlesex. Nave arcades c. 1260; most of the rest 14th-century; N. aisle by S. S. Teulon, 1862. Imposing Knyvett monument by Nicholas Stone, 1622.

TOTTENHAM
now in London Borough of Haringey, 7m/11km N.E. of Charing Cross TQ 3389
All Hallows, Church Lane
14th-century W. tower with 18th-century top stage; brick S. porch, c. 1500; N. aisle and E. end by William Butterfield, 1875.
St Bartholomew, Craven Park Road
By W. D. Caroe, 1904. Modest red-brick Art Nouveau-Gothic; 17th-century furnishings from St Bartholomew Exchange, London.

TWICKENHAM
now in the London Borough of Richmond, 10m/16km S.W. of Charing Cross TQ 1673
All Hallows, Chertsey Road
Original Wren church of All Hallows in Lombard Street demolished in 1939 and re-erected here. Interesting carved doorcase with figures of Time and Death, connected by gallery lined with wall-monuments with new church which contains original furnishings.
St Mary the Virgin, Church Street
Riverside setting. By John James, 1715, with 15th-century stone tower. Large pediments on brick Tuscan pillars. Original altar rails, reredos, and altered galleries.

WEST DRAYTON
St Martin

Church Road, now in the London Borough of Hillingdon, 15m/24km W. of Charing Cross TQ 0679

Mainly 15th-century with octagonal piers and contemporary roofs. Splendid octagonal Perpendicular font with figured panels. Monuments include 16th-century brasses; lively relief of HMS *Royal George* on a monument of 1720; works by Bacon Snr and Jnr.

WEST HENDON
St John

Algernon Road, now in the London Borough of Barnet, 1m/2km S.W. of Hendon NZ 4154

Temple Moore, 1895. Fine-drawn Perpendicular. Contains font, wooden reredos, and noble mahogany pulpit from City churches.

Norfolk

Introduction

The county of Norfolk has several characters: flat marshland to the west, flat Broadland to the east, flat Breckland to the south and, though there are no very high hills anywhere, the north is undulating. It was once a very empty county; this is so no longer; the population increases here, as in the whole of East Anglia, faster than in any other region. There is much new building, not always of the highest quality. The development and conservation of Norwich has been well controlled, but King's Lynn, except for a small picturesque centre, has been tragically ruined. In-filling in the villages is welcome, though the new houses are often 'second homes' or at best retreats for retired people, and the old community centres, the school, the post office, the shop, the pub, and of course the railway station, no longer exist. The next on the list for closure are the Noncomformist chapel and the parish church.

The finest collection of churches are those to the west, in Marshland – the Walpoles, Wiggenhalls, West Walton, Terringtons and Tilney, and the Norman Walsoken. The architecture, from the 12th to the 15th century, is superb, and so are the fittings, especially the very elaborate carved bench-ends. In central and north Norfolk there are wonderful wooden roofs with angels, as at South Creake, Trunch, Necton, and many others, and in the east exquisite painted screens, as at Ranworth and Barton Turf; and everywhere remarkable fonts, from very fine carved Norman ones at Burnham Deepdale, Shernborne and Toftrees, to twenty-five superb 15th-century seven-sacrament fonts, some defiled, others almost perfect, as at Sloley. It can be truly said that there is not one Norfolk church without something worth seeing, which has made this selection appallingly difficult. Probably the most beautiful of all is Salle, near Reepham, a huge church in an almost deserted hamlet, built in the 15th century, with splendid roofs, font, font cover, brasses, remains of exquisite Norwich School glass, and perfect proportions, so that to enter it at any time, but especially when it is empty, is an unforgettable experience.

Like Salle, many of the churches stand 'away in the fields', and are most important characteristics of the Norfolk landscape. There are over 100 round towers, not look-outs as people used to think, but built like that because flint, the only stone available locally, could not be used for corners; these are almost all Norman or Saxon. Then, when it was possible to import stone, came the great soaring towers, like Salle or Cawston or Blakeney and, surprisingly, the highest of all in the prim seaside town of Cromer. There are few spires, apart from Norwich Cathedral, but there is a very splendid one at Snettisham and less important ones at Banham and Beeston-next-Mileham and Tilney All Saints. There is flint flushwork on some of the towers, as at Westwick, and in many of the City of Norwich churches, notably the splendid St Michael Coslany, now redundant.

These churches, in the city and the county, are Norfolk's greatest treasure; there are fine stately homes and pretty villages, but nothing of the quality of this huge collection of church buildings, which is equal, if not superior, to anything in Europe. But owing to the shortage of clergy – one Norfolk parson has ten parishes, most of them have five or six – and the decline in church-going, there is an official move to 'rationalize' and to close any church which is inconveniently situated or not well supported. Some parishes resist, and officialdom does not always win, but the old happy situation of the church being a solid and absolutely permanent part of the parish, and a comforting witness to the Christian faith, has quite gone, and now anxiety has replaced that security. Norfolk is particularly conscious of this because it has so many churches to guard. It has a cause worth fighting for, and this has been recognized by the giving of generous grants from English Heritage as well as the local authorities, and many specially founded trusts, both local and national. Even so, it is always a struggle. Where a church is of great architectural importance, it may be vested in the Redundant Churches Fund, like the little Norman church at Hales in the south of the county, or Thurgarton in the north, or the Norfolk Churches Trust, like West Rudham near Fakenham, or Cockthorpe near Stiffkey on the north coast; and the Friends of Friendless Churches looks after Corpusty near Holt.

Alternative uses may be found – 'conversion' to houses or stores or even shops; or a church can be unroofed and made into a 'safe ruin' as at Sco Ruston.

But so far the county of Norfolk has succeeded in maintaining most of its parish churches for worship, and none has been wholly demolished or 'converted' to some unsuitable secular use. Twenty-one are vested in the Redundant Churches Fund, ten in the Norfolk Churches Trust, and one is cared for by the Friends of Friendless Churches. These are all maintained as churches and, though outside the parish system, are still used for occasional services.

It is in the city of Norwich that the 20th century is making its heaviest mark. Of the thirty-one pre-Reformation churches described by Noel Spencer in 1970, twenty-three are now legally redundant. Sixteen of these are let to the Norwich Historic Churches Trust by the City Council, to whom the freeholds were transferred by the Diocese. Viable commercial uses have to be found for the maintenance of these buildings. These now include a puppet theatre in St James, Pockthorpe, gymnasia in St Edmund, Fishergate and

St Margaret, a sports centre in St Michael, Coslany, a boy scout centre in St Simon and St Jude, an ecclesiastical museum in St Peter, Hungate, a centre for music and the arts in St Gregory, an arts centre in St Swithin, arts and crafts in St Mary, Coslany, a market and café in St Michael at Pleas, and a badminton hall in St Saviour's. St Etheldreda is a wood-sculpture studio and St Peter, Parmentergate may become a workshop for the building and repair of church organs. It is hoped that St Laurence, an important and spacious 15th-century church, may be restored and let as an exhibition hall. St Martin at Palace is a workshop and centre for the Norwich Probation Service, and All Saints is leased to the Mothers Union as an ecumenical day centre and creche.

Three of the 'redundant' ones are still churches, though not part of the Diocese of Norwich. St Clement is let to a Methodist bus driver, the Rev. Jack Burton, who keeps it open for prayer and meditation and occasional ecumenical services, St John, Maddermarket is in the care of the Redundant Churches Fund, and St John de Sepulchre is used by the Russian Orthodox Church.

Norwich is a fine city, and indeed has been carefully cherished, and the conservation is mainly sensitive and good; only in the matter of churches has there been no vision. There is no appreciation of their spiritual value, and no recognition of their historic importance as documents in the life of the community since Norman times. No city in England had as many churches within its walls, and few even in Europe; so, to put it at its lowest, the potential for tourism was enormous. The story of the Norwich churches is a very tragic one, of missed opportunities and lack of enterprise. However, there are still ten which are used for the purpose for which they were built and dedicated, and their descriptions follow.

W. H.

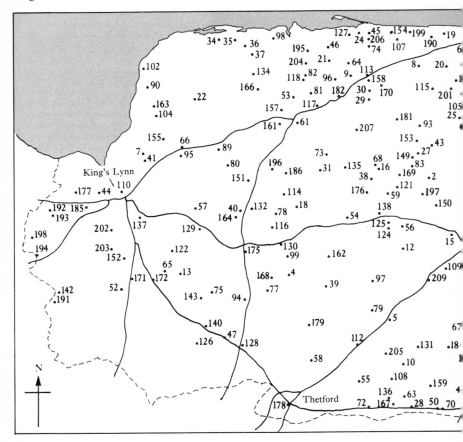

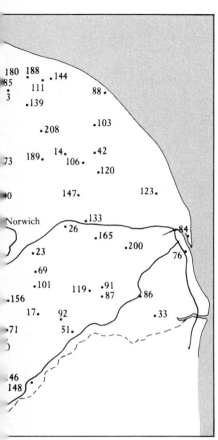

continued overleaf

113	Letheringsett	146	Pulham St Mary	179	Thompson
114	Litcham	147	Ranworth	180	Thorpe Market
115	Little Barningham	148	Redenhall	181	Thurning
116	Little Dunham	149	Reepham & Whitwell	182	Thursford
117	Little Snoring	150	Ringland	183	Thwaite
118	Little Walsingham	151	Rougham	184	Tibenham
119	Loddon	152	Runcton Holme	185	Tilney
120	Ludham	153	Salle	186	Tittleshall
121	Lyng	154	Salthouse	187	Tivetshall
122	Marham	155	Sandringham	188	Trunch
123	Martham	156	Saxlingham Nethergate	189	Tunstead
124	Mattishall	157	Sculthorpe	190	Upper Sheringham
125	Mattishall Burgh	158	Sharrington	191	Upwell
126	Methwold	159	Shelfhanger	192	Walpole St Andrew
127	Morston	160	Shelton	193	Walpole St Peter
128	Mundford	161	Shereford	194	Walsoken
129	Narborough	162	Shipdham	195	Warham
130	Necton	163	Snettisham	196	Wellingham
131	New Buckenham	164	South Acre	197	Weston Longville
132	Newton	165	South Burlingham	198	West Walton
133	North Burlingham	166	South Creake	199	Weybourne
134	North Creake	167	South Lopham	200	Wickhampton
135	North Elmham	168	South Pickenham	201	Wickmere
136	North Lopham	169	Sparham	202	Wiggenhall St Germans
137	North Runcton	170	Stody	203	Wiggenhall St Mary
138	North Tuddenham	171	Stow Bardolph	204	Wighton
139	North Walsham	172	Stradsett	205	Wilby
140	Northwold	173	Stratton Strawless	206	Wiveton
141	Norwich	174	Sustead	207	Wood Norton
142	Outwell	175	Swaffham	208	Worstead
143	Oxborough	176	Swanton Morley	209	Wymondham
144	Paston	177	Terrington		
145	Pulham Market	178	Thetford		

Selected List of Churches

ALDBOROUGH
St Mary
5m/8km N. of Aylsham TG 1834
An odd-looking church, mostly Decorated, with a bell-turret of 1906, but containing very good 15th-century brasses.

ALDERFORD
St John the Baptist
9m/15km N.W. of Norwich TG 1218
Mainly 14th-century. Exceptionally good seven-sacrament font with Signs of the Evangelists and Crucifixion. Some early glass.

ANTINGHAM
St Mary
3m/4km N.W. of N. Walsham TG 2532
Two churches: St Margaret's in ruins; St Mary's has 14th-century tracery in all windows. Good 19th-century glass, probably by Powell, and N.E. window by Kempe. Very fine brass of 1554 in middle of nave, 'in reign of King Phylyppe and Queen Mary'.

ASHILL
St Nicholas
5m/8km S.E. of Swaffham TF 8804
Has some good glass of the characteristic Norwich School-type, with the Evangelists, doctors, and angels, which recall those at Bale and Ringland.

ATTLEBOROUGH
St Mary
14m/22km S.W. of Norwich TM 0495
On an island site with the A11 swirling round it stands this magnificent church, Norman at the E. end – where the tower is – with a late 14th-century nave. The early part contained the College of the Holy Cross, founded in the Norman church in 1368, after which the nave was built for the parish. But the great glories of this church, unmatched anywhere else in E. Anglia, are the rood screen, its loft still intact, stretching right across the church from N. to S., and the frescoes above. The screen, often restored, is the most beautiful silvery colour; one would have liked to have seen it before

the 17th century, when the Arms of English bishoprics were painted on it. The much-mutilated frescoes above, of *c.* 1500, are still very remarkable for their colour and liveliness.

AYLSHAM
St Michael
12m/19km N. of Norwich TG 1926
Centre of exceptionally attractive small market town with many good Georgian buildings. Humphrey Repton is buried outside church on S. side with delightful monument and poetic inscription. Church is Decorated and Perpendicular, has remains of painted screen, and good brasses, including Richard and Cecilie Howard, 1499, in shrouds.

BABINGLEY
St Felix
2m/3km S.W. of Sandringham TF 6726
A ruined church in remote fields by the Babingley river, on a site where St Felix of Burgundy is supposed to have preached in 600. Also a new church, in the village, built by King Edward VII when Prince of Wales, in 1894, of corrugated iron with thatched roof and bellcote.

BACONSTHORPE
St Mary the Virgin
3m/4km S.E. of Holt TG 1237
Good Easter Sepulchre, and alabaster monument to Sir William Heydon, d. 1593, and his wife; also brasses to members of this family. Many fine black ledger slabs and small brass plaque in sanctuary to Rev. Joseph Clark, 1700. Good Early English piscina. Very curious large head on corbel of N.E. arch. W. screen composed of medieval oddments. Heraldic glass in S. aisle.

BALE
All Saints
4m/6km W. of Holt TG 0136
This church, in a grove of ilex trees, has in the S.E. nave windows some of the most beautiful 15th-century Norwich School glass in the county, notably an exquisite

Annunciation. There are also several bits of 14th-century glass, including two prophets.

BANHAM
St Mary
6m/10km N.W. of Diss TM 0688
Mainly 14th-century, well placed in village square. Contains good glass in the E. window by Clayton, 1857, Powell, 1878, in N. chancel, and Kempe, 1914, in S. aisle. In recess under ogee arch, a wooden effigy of a knight, early 14th-century.

BANNINGHAM
St Botolph
2m/3km N.E. of Aylsham TG 2129
This pretty church, mainly 14th-century, has some old glass, including a Norwich School Annunciation in the N. aisle; wall-paintings – the frequent St Christopher and St George and the Dragon; box pews; and panelled and painted pulpit and desk. Arms of George II.

BARNHAM BROOM
St Peter & St Paul
4m/6km N. of Wymondham TG 0807
Largely Perpendicular church; tower of 1430s contains gallery with 18th-century organ and fine Perpendicular screen with St Ursula clutching a sheaf of arrows and with maidens sheltering under her cloak, as well as the local saints Walstan and Withberga.

BARTON BENDISH
St Mary
4m/6km N. of Stoke Ferry TF 7105
Very pretty church, mostly Decorated, with fine reset late-Norman S. doorway, box pews, and a wall-painting of St Catherine.
R.C.F.

BARTON TURF
St Michael and All Angels
4m/6km N.E. of Wroxham TG 3421
This is a pretty church with a fine tower, but it must be visited for its screen, with incomparably beautiful painting of the Nine Orders of Angels. Even Ranworth is no better than this. Some of the faces are mutilated but this hardly matters, so beautiful and so spiritual are these figures. Notice seraphim with red feathers, archangels with sceptre and sword, angels guarding the naked children who represent souls. As well as the Nine Orders there are depicted SS. Apollonia, Osyth and Barbara. On the S.

part of the screen are very interesting but less good paintings, but they include a most charming portrait of King Henry VI.

BAWBURGH
St Mary & St Walstan
5m/8km W. of Norwich TG 1508
Church has lost its chapel and shrine to St Walstan, but retains interest, including an 11th-century tower with conical tiled cap and some fine 15th-century glass.

BAWDESWELL
All Saints
6m/10km N.E. of E. Dereham TG 0420
The Victorian church was destroyed in the last war. The present one, in the Georgian style, was built in 1955 to designs by James Fletcher Watson, and contains all the correct furniture, including a fine three-decker pulpit and W. gallery. The carving of the Good Shepherd on the font was inspired by the mosaic in the mausoleum of Galla Placidia in Ravenna.

BEDINGHAM
St Andrew
4m/6km N.W. of Bungay TM 2892
In spite of the ugly glazing of the S. porch, this is a most rewarding and unspoilt church. There is a round tower with octagonal Perpendicular top, but most of the church is 13th-century. There are old benches in the nave, one with an inscription on the back, box pews in the aisles, and very nice brick floors. Many monuments and floor-slabs to the Stone family. Interesting glass in E. window of S. aisle; some medieval English and two later foreign panels. The pulpit is early 18th-century and unusual.

BEESTON
St Mary
5m/8km W. of E. Dereham TF 9015
Away in the fields, from which the village has withdrawn, stands one of the most beautiful 14th-century churches. Tracery in nave and chancel windows recalls that at Great Walsingham; the clerestory, tower and spire are Perpendicular. The hammer-beam roofs have finely carved figures on the wall-posts. The 15th-century chancel screen has no top, but there are two fine parclose screens, both with remains of colour on their E. sides. There are lovely benches with pierced backs and good ends, and a nice crocketed font cover. Hanoverian Arms, and a painted

board setting out the deeds of John Forby, rector from 1595–1614, who renewed the chancel and sanctuary. But at either the Reformation or the Commonwealth a maniac must have been let loose in the church, for every single figure, even the angels in the roof, has been ruthlessly defaced or even decapitated.

BEESTON REGIS
All Saints
1m/2km E. of Sheringham TG 1742
This little church stands near the edge of the cliff, in a sea of caravans. The outside, decorated with squared flints, is very pretty, and there is a most beautiful 15th-century rood screen, complete with vaulting and unusually painted panels.

BESSINGHAM
St Mary
4m/6km S. of Sheringham TG 1636
Has a Saxon round tower. The windows, restored in the last century, contain glass by Kempe dated 1897 and 1906, though the E. window is by an unknown hand.

BINHAM
St Mary
5m/8km S.E. of Wells TF 9839
The Benedictine priory here, a cell of the Abbey of St Alban's, is in ruins and in the care of English Heritage. The parish church formed part of the priory and is superb, with Norman arcading in the E. bays and Early English in the two westernmost ones. It also has a splendid W. front and bellcote of the early 13th century. The very fine W. window is now patched with brick. Inside there is handsome Norman moulding, remains of a screen, and good stalls and bench-ends. Seven-sacrament font. The chancel was pulled down in 1540 when the monastery was dissolved.

BIRCHAM NEWTON
All Saints
3m/5km S. of Docking TF 7632
Small 12th-century church conservatively refitted in 1858 with a two-decker pulpit and box pews, the latter complete with poppyheads supporting candle prickets.

BIXLEY
St Wandregeselius
near Kirby Bedon, 4m/6km S.E. of Norwich TG 2705
Church of a vanished village retains stone

recording rebuilding by William of Dunwich, 1272, and tower built on eve of Reformation, 1526–35; largely Victorian fabric; unique dedication to St Wandrille, 'God's true athlete', the 7th-century founder and first abbot of Fontanelle, near Rouen.

BLAKENEY
St Nicholas, St Mary & St Thomas
5m/8km N.W. of Holt TG 0843
Wonderful church dominating the very attractive village and visible from boats sailing in the harbour. Magnificent W. tower of 1435. Perpendicular nave and low Early English chancel with small beacon tower at E. end in which there is always a light after sunset. The church has been well restored with a modern German rood screen; but there are old stalls with misericords in the chancel and a few poppyheads in the nave.

BLICKLING
St Andrew
1m/2km N.W. of Aylsham TG 1728
Church, beside the famous Hall, is much restored but well worth visiting for the monuments and brasses, especially the 8th Marquis of Lothian, lifesize, 1878, by A. F. Watts, and the brass of Isabella Cheyne, 1485, in her beautiful dress, coif and necklace. This church, naturally, reflects the story of the Hall, so there are many Boleyn monuments, though none of Henry VIII's Queen. Much money has been available for restorations; hence the W. tower and S. porch by Street, and E. window by Butterfield.

BLOFIELD
St Andrew
7m/11km E. of Norwich TG 3309
Large 15th-century church with upright tower of *c.* 1430. Inside are 15th-century benches, box pews, and Perpendicular font with bowl bearing the Life of Christ.

BOOTON
St Michael
1m/2km E. of Reepham TG 1222
A very splendid, though not at all correct, bit of Victoriana. Built between 1875 and 1891 by a famous figure, the Rev. Whitewell Elwin, who was architect as well as rector for 50 years; edited the *Quarterly Review*; and was the correspondent and confidant of Lady Emily Lutyens, daughter of Lord Lytton and wife of Sir Edwin, who said of

the church, 'Very naughty, but built in the right spirit'. It is typical of E. Anglia in being behind the times; as Professor Pevsner has pointed out, it is unaffected by William Morris and his movement. It represents a different kind of Victorian thought and should be studied with sympathy.

R.C.F.

BRESSINGHAM
St John the Baptist
3m/4km W. of Diss TM 0780
Rebuild, 1430–1530, of earlier building. Outside, note fine tower and clerestory; inside are 16th-century carved benches, 17th-century canopied pulpit, and a working barrel organ.

BRININGHAM
St Margaret
4m/6km S.W. of Holt TG 0334
Here you can see the current treatment of a parish church with a much-reduced congregation. The nave, with one very beautiful Decorated window, has been made weatherproof and closed; and the chancel, also Decorated, has been screened off, refurnished and repainted in the 1964 style. The communion rails of about 1700, repainted, are good. The lighting is not atmospheric.

BRINTON
St Andrew
3m/4km S.W. of Holt TG 0335
Church well placed on village green. Perpendicular, much-restored; very fine roof with half-angels and good frieze.

BRISLEY
St Bartholomew
6m/10km N.W. of E. Dereham TF 9521
Village clusters around church with its majestic tower. Church rebuilt in sequence from E. end, *c.* 1360, finishing with tower in 1430s. Inside are 15th-century screen, box pews, and three-decker pulpit, as well as W. gallery of 1848. Under chancel is original crypt, once used for lodging prisoners *en route* to Norwich gaol.

BURGH-NEXT-AYLSHAM
St Mary
2m/3km S.E. of Aylsham TG 2125
Lovely site by the Bure. Plain tower, 1459. Inside are a 15th-century seven-sacrament font and very fine 13th-century chancel, the last two bays a high quality rebuild by R. M.

Phipson, diocesan architect, 1877. Exquisite arcading.

BURGH ST PETER
St Mary
3m/4km S.E. of Haddiscoe TM 4693
Waveney Valley scenery and long thatched church with extraordinary stepped tower built in 1793 as Boycott mausoleum. Many Boycotts commemorated by a series of brass plaques on pulpit; Charles Cunningham Boycott, celebrated land agent in Ireland, born and buried here.

BURNHAM DEEPDALE
St Mary
2m/3km N.W. of Burnham Market TF 8044
On the coast road; has Saxon round tower, superb Norman font with the Labours of the Months, and good stained glass of the Norwich School.

BURNHAM NORTON
St Margaret
1m/2km N. of Burnham Market TF 8243
Stands well with Saxon round tower, good early-Decorated S. doorway, and a fine 15th-century pulpit painted with Latin Fathers of the Church and John Goldalle, donor.

BURNHAM OVERY
St Clement
1m/2km N.E. of Burnham Market TF 8442
Norman central tower with pretty 17th-century cupola. S. arcade of *c.* 1200 and chancel remodelled in 13th century with stepped lancets.

BURNHAM THORPE
All Saints
2m/3km S.E. of Burnham Market TF 8541
Mostly Decorated and Perpendicular church where Nelson's father was rector. He and Nelson's mother are buried in the nave, and all over the church are memorials to, or relics of, Nelson himself.

BYLAUGH
St Mary
4m/6km N.E. of E. Dereham TG 0318
Almost lost in the trees is this enchanting church with medieval tower and nave, containing 1471 brass. The chancel and transepts date from 1809, when the whole interior was refitted; all these furnishings, including three-decker pulpit and box pews

with fireplaces, survive intact. Monument to Sir John Lambe, 1817, by John Bacon.

CARBROOKE
St Peter & St Paul
2m/3km E. of Watton TF 9402
A big church with a fine 15th-century tower. A house for the Hospitallers was founded here in the mid 12th century. There is a stone altar. Interesting painting of David harping, 1727, and a colourful monument of 1932.

CASTLE ACRE
St James
4m/6km N. of Swaffham TF 8115
Between the castle and the Priory, with a very fine Perpendicular tower. Misericords, base of screen with early 15th-century painted panels. Perpendicular font canopy.

CASTLE RISING
St Lawrence
4m/6km N.E. of King's Lynn TF 6624
Church much restored but still very fine, late-Norman. Superb W. front with arcading, intersecting arches, and zig-zag decoration. Central tower over narrow crossing; Norman arch on W. side, pointed on the E. side.

CATFIELD
All Saints
2m/3km S.E. of Stalham TG 3821
Attractive grouping of church and former rectory. Fine aisleless 15th-century building contains Perpendicular screen with painted kings and faded wall-paintings.

CAWSTON
St Agnes
4m/6km S.W. of Aylsham TG 1323
Huge church dominating village and surrounding countryside. Tower unusual in Norfolk in being faced with freestone. Angel roof of 15th century, very fine indeed. Screen with much painting well restored. Wall-paintings in N. transept. Tower screen and gallery. Wild man and dragon represented twice in this church, once in spandrels of door and again on piscina in the S. transept.

CLENCHWARTON
St Margaret
2m/3km W. of King's Lynn TF 5820
A real dene church with monument to rector

who behaved gallantly in the 'terrible inundation' of 1753. Elizabethan altar and Jacobean pulpit.

CLEY-NEXT-THE-SEA
St Margaret
4m/6km N.E. of Holt TG 0443
A squat tower, unusual clerestory of 14th century, ruined transepts, possibly never completed owing to Black Death of 1348. Fine battlemented Perpendicular S. porch. Very wide 14th-century nave and aisles. Above arcades are canopied niches, richly carved, and grotesque figures. A little medieval Norwich School glass in S. aisle tracery and N. chancel. Very fine brass in S. aisle to John Symondes and family, in shrouds, 1505; and to a priest in N. aisle; several other brasses and many fine ledger slabs. The framed terracotta angels came off a house in the village.

COCKTHORPE
All Saints
4m/6km E. of Wells TF 9842
Very attractive 14th–15th-century church with splendid monument to Dame Barbara Calthorpe, 1639, who 'was much comforted by the sight of 193 of her children and their offspring'. There is a tomb chest to her husband, Sir James Calthorpe, 1615. This church was rescued from dereliction by the Norfolk Churches Trust.

CRANWICH
St Mary
2m/3km N.W. of Mundford TL 7894
In among the trees are the 18th-century rectory and thatched church. Saxon tower with interlace work; stands in a circular churchyard of possible early origin.

CROMER
St Peter & St Paul
TG 2142
Gives character to the town grouped around it, with its tall tower and decorative flintwork. Inside, typical seaside church. Overrestored and full of 19th- and 20th-century monuments and glass; except for one Morris window in the S. aisle, not of the highest quality.

DICKLEBURGH
All Saints
4m/6km N.E. of Diss TM 1682
Big church on main road; font with lions

and wild men; fine monument with good inscription to Dame Frances Playters, 1659, by Edward Marshall.

DISS
St Mary
19m/30km S.W. of Norwich TM 1180
Very good position commanding the main street, with N. and S. processional arches. The poet John Skelton was rector here for a few years after 1505, until he fell foul of Cardinal Wolsey. Fine W. doors with tracery. Some scraps of 15th-century glass; commandment boards with Moses and Aaron.

DITCHINGHAM
St Mary
1m/2km N. of Bungay TM 3391
Very tall Perpendicular tower, originally with figures in niches on either side of door; 16th-century screen, very much restored. Black marble First World War memorial, with lifesize bronze figure of a dead soldier by Derwent Wood. A few bits of old glass, also some from the early 19th century, and a window to Sir H. Rider Haggard, author of *She*, who lived in the village.

DOWNHAM MARKET
St Edmund
10m/16km S. of King's Lynn TF 6103
Church built of local carn-stone and brick; stands high in centre of town. Early crucifix outside S. chancel door. Inside, very good 18th-century inlaid gallery. Monument of 1761 to E Warmoll, apothecary. Royal Arms of Queen Anne. Good gravestones.

EAST BARSHAM
All Saints
3m/4km N. of Fakenham TF 9133
Very battered, but full of interest. Blocked Norman S. door, windows Perpendicular. Fragments of 15th-century glass and alabaster sculpture. Splendid monument of 1640 to Mrs Mary Calthorpe, rising from the grave.

EAST DEREHAM
St Nicholas
16m/25km W. of Norwich TF 9813
Church interesting architecturally and historically. Detached early 16th-century bell-tower. Norman S. doorway, Decorated nave, transepts and chancel with sedilia, piscina and aumbry niche. Perpendicular S. porch

and S. aisle windows. Brasses of 15th century. Monument to the poet Cowper by Flaxman, 1802. St Withburga's well in churchyard; she was daughter of Saxon Queen Anna, who founded a convent here.

EAST HARLING
St Peter & St Paul
6m/10km S.W. of Attleborough TL 9986
Magnificent church, basically 14th-century, although many of the windows are Perpendicular. The 15th-century alterations to the church are due largely to the beneficence of Anne Harling, d. 1498. She had three husbands; the first, Sir William Chamberlain, KG, d. 1462, is buried on N. side of chancel. He figures in the marvellous stained glass of the great E. window where he kneels, in armour, as does Anne's second husband, Sir Robert Wingfield, in the lower lights. Above them is a remarkable collection of Norwich School glass, placed in the church by Anne Harling. There are 15 scenes from the life of the Blessed Virgin Mary, a Te Deum panel, some angels in the tracery, the two donors and, for those who can find it, a scrap of a mantle, all that is left of the figure of Anne herself. Many good monuments of 15th, 16th and early 17th centuries.

EAST TUDDENHAM
All Saints
10m/16km W. of Norwich TG 0711
Approached from road by a long lime avenue. Beautiful S. porch with three niches and 'Gloria Tibi TR' in flint flushwork. Annunciation like a firework display in the spandrels. Inside, a stone effigy of a knight in chain mail, 13th-century, holding his heart in his joined hands.

EAST WALTON
St Mary
6m/10km N.W. of Swaffham TF 7416
This church with very large Perpendicular windows has a Georgian chancel arch and a three-decker pulpit and box pews.

EAST WRETHAM
St Ethelbert
5m/8km N.E. of Thetford TL 9190
Elaborate and pretty church rebuilt by G. E. Street in 1865. Parts of the old Norman door retained. Perpendicular font cover of 1883, very convincing.

ELSING
St Mary

5m/8km N.E. of E. Dereham TG 0516
Church of *c.* 1330 has W. tower with
flushwork panelling and flowing tracery.
Very fine brass to the builder, Sir Hugh
Hastings, d. 1347.

ERPINGHAM
St Mary

3m/4km N. of Aylsham TG 1931
One is attracted to this church by its soaring
tower, on a rise outside the village. It is full
of splendid things, including a military brass
to Sir John de Erpingham, 1370, and an E.
window full of 16th-century Lower Rhenish
glass brought from Blicking Hall. Good
brick floors and a very few bench-ends.

FAKENHAM
St Peter & St Paul

23m/37km N.W. of Norwich TF 9229
Splendid position dominating pretty market
town and surrounding countryside. Nice
Decorated screen, restored. Some old glass
recently inserted in N.W. window.

FELBRIGG
St Margaret

2m/3km S. of Cromer TG 2039
In the park of Felbrigg Hall, surrounded by
old trees. Charming, beautifully cared for
church, with famous collection of brasses
dating from *c.* 1380 to 1612, and many
monuments to the Windham family, including the fine bust of the statesman
William Windham by Nollekens.

FERSFIELD
St Andrew

4m/6km N.W. of Diss TM 0683
Francis Blomfield, the Norfolk historian,
was rector here, and a ledger slab marks his
grave, 1752. There is a very fine wooden
effigy of Sir Robert du Bois, d. 1311.

FIELD DALLING
St Andrew

4m/6km W. of Holt TG 0039
Decorated chancel, Perpendicular nave, one
aisle. Nice roofs and old brick floors, box
pews in aisle, and old benches in nave.
Tractarian arrangement of chancel. Much
early Victorian glass and in the S. nave three
windows with tracery filled with a mixture of
mostly medieval glass. Jacobean font cover.

FINCHAM
St Martin

5m/8km E. of Downham Market TF 6806
Is built of flint and carstone, with flushwork
battlements. Good roof with alternating
angels and beasts. Medieval Norwich School
glass in tracery of S. chancel. Good un-
painted screen. Brass of naked female in
shroud in middle of nave. Our Father, creed
and texts on panels, 1717. Notice Adam and
Eve on N. side of very good Norman font.

FLITCHAM
St Mary

8m/12km N.E. of King's Lynn TF 7226
Has Norman arcading in its tower, the base
of which forms the present chancel. St Felix
is supposed to have built a church here in
the 7th century.

FORNCETT ST PETER
St Peter

2m/3km W. of Wymondham TM 1693
18th-century rectory and very interesting
church stand well in trees. Church has fine
11th-century round tower; 15th-century
carved benches and porch with emblems of
joint patrons SS. Peter and Paul.

FOXLEY
St Thomas

6m/10km N.E. of Dereham TG 0321
Attractive village church with carving of
lopped tree on the porch. Old door. Inside,
very unsophisticated; simple font, tall cover
with dove, two-decker 18th-century pulpit,
very rustic pews with poppyheads, and a few
box pews. Nice Georgian gallery. Simple,
restored screen with some painted panels,
including two with donors. The best kind
of village church.

FRAMINGHAM EARL
St Andrew

5m/8km S.E. of Norwich TG 2702
A pretty, small church. Norman round tower
and chancel arch; evidence of Anglo-Saxon
work in chancel windows. St Catherine in
15th-century glass in N. nave window.

FRENZE
St Andrew

1m/2km E. of Diss TM 1380
This little church in an off-road farmyard
has many famous 15th–16th-century brasses
to the Blennerhasset and other families. Very

pretty, faded pulpit with tester and box pew to match.

FRITTON
St Catherine
6m/10km N. of Harleston TM 2292
Round-towered church down a grassy track. Inside are vivid wall-paintings of St George and St Christopher. Screen bears pictures of John Bacon and family, donors, *c.* 1510.

GARBOLDISHAM
St John the Baptist
7m/11km W. of Diss TM 0081
Splendid tower, bequests 1463–8, with flushwork buttresses and angel-crowned battlements, very likely by a Suffolk mason; N. porch a generation later. Inside are old benches and 15th-century screenwork.

GATELEY
St Helen
4m/6km S.E. of Fakenham TF 9624
A church in a farmyard. Good benches with carved backs and nice ends. The screen has a late-panelled top but eight good painted 15th-century panels, whose figures include King Henry VI and Master John Schorne holding a boot from which the Devil is emerging. There are also two large monuments, one with a great alabaster heart and the other telling a sad story. Stuart altar rails and Royal Arms of Charles I.

GLANDFORD
St Martin
3m/4km N.W. of Holt TG 0441
A ruin until 1899 when Sir Alfred Jodrell started to rebuild it in memory of his mother; details of architect and craftsmen will be found in the vestry. The angel roof, seven-sacrament font, elaborate choir-stalls and screen are all of the traditional Norfolk Perpendicular type; very atmospheric. Stained glass by Kempe and Bryans.

GOODERSTONE
St George
4m/6km E. of Stoke Ferry TF 7602
Norman W. tower, porch with round trefoiled windows, and screen with good painted panels and prickets for candles. Benches with pierced backs. E. window of N. aisle has 14th-century glass showing Resurrection of the Dead.

GORLESTON
St Andrew
S. district of Gt Yarmouth TG 5203
This church, in what is virtually a suburb of Great Yarmouth, has been much restored, but is well worth a visit for the seven-sacrament font, the Stuart Royal Arms, huge painting of Moses and Aaron, 14th-century Easter Sepulchre, and the Bacon brass of *c.* 1320.

GREAT CRESSINGHAM
St Mary
5m/8km S.E. of Swaffham TF 8501
Rebuild of the first half of the 15th century. Noble tower with crowned Ms for St Mary and St Michael's sword; mutilated saint in niche over porch, 1439. Inside are hammer-beam roof and several brasses. Church 'new' in 1451.

GREAT DUNHAM
St Andrew
5m/8km N.E. of Swaffham TF 8714
Impressive late 11th-century axial tower with many Roman bricks used in the arches. Contemporary blind arcading on the nave S. wall and Norman moulding around triangular-headed W. entrance.

GREAT ELLINGHAM
St James
2m/3km N.W. of Attleborough TM 0196
Big 14th-century church. Chequerwork flint squares all along clerestory range and on the crooked porch and belfry windows. Inside, a pretty musicians' gallery and coloured bases of chancel and parclose screens. Faint traces of wall-paintings.

GREAT MASSINGHAM
St Mary
9m/15km N. of Swaffham TF 7922
Largely 15th-century; overlooks attractive village green. Proud Decorated W. tower. Windows have singularly angular West Norfolk variety of early Perpendicular tracery with some Norwich School glass. Altar rails and candlesticks by Howard Brown of Norwich; frontal to his design carved by W. Cooper. Very fine 13th-century porch, somewhat restored.

GREAT SNORING
St Mary
3m/4km N.E. of Fakenham TF 9434
Very fine 14th-century E. window with a

few scraps of old glass. Decorated sedilia and piscina, elaborate and pretty. Stuart altar rails. Royal Arms dated 1688. Screen. Huge 17th-century commandment board with faded painted figures.

GREAT WALSINGHAM
St Peter
4m/6km S. of Wells TF 9336
A most beautiful Decorated church with lovely window tracery, very old benches with poppyheads and carved backs; some 14th-century Norwich glass.

GREAT WITCHINGHAM
St Mary
2m/3km S. of Reepham TG 1020
14th-century tower and aisled nave, rebuilt in 15th century. Inside are fine roofs and seven-sacrament font with original colour.

GREAT YARMOUTH
St Nicholas
TG 5207
The largest parish church in England, begun in the 12th century, added to, extended and widened in the 13th, 14th and 15th centuries. Bombed and burnt out in 1942, rebuilt by S. Dykes Bower. Spacious, colourful and impressive interior with stained glass by Brian Thomas. The pulpit, pews and tester over the font came from the church of St George, 1714–16; now closed.

GUNTON
St Andrew
6m/9km N. of Aylsham TM 5495
Surrounded by giant bamboos in the park of Gunton Hall is this small church by Robert Adam, 1769. Very elegant interior in dark wood with much gilding. Notice the binding of the prayer books of the Harbord family.
R.C.F.

HADDISCOE
St Mary
4m/6km N. of Beccles TM 4496
Church with 11th-century round tower on splendid site; 12th-century doorway with carved seated figure above; 15th-century font and wall-painting.

HALES
St Margaret
2m/3km S.E. of Loddon TM 3897
Norman. Round tower, apse, and very good doorways. Early 15th-century paintings of

St Christopher and St James. Remains of screen and Jacobean font cover.
R.C.F.

HAPPISBURGH
St Mary
6m/10km E. of N. Walsham TG 3731
Very handsome 15th-century tower. Fine font with angels, wild men, and symbols of the Four Evangelists. Restored 16th-century screen.

HARPLEY
St Lawrence
9m/15km W. of Fakenham TF 7825
Mainly 1294–1332, during the rectorship of John de Gourney; the matrix of his brass survives in the chancel; 14th-century S. porch and finely carved wooden door; nave roof with angels, the screen poorly restored in 1886; piscina and sedilia with some diapering. Perpendicular W. window with very good Norwich School medieval glass.

HEACHAM
St Mary
2m/3km S. of Hunstanton TF 6737
Church has heavy crossing tower of 13th century and contains monuments in varying taste. Note that by a pupil of Rodin to Pocahontas, Red Indian wife of John Rofe, squire of Heacham in King James I's reign.

HECKINGHAM
St Gregory
2m/3km E. of Loddon TM 3898
Norman, with round tower and apse. Excellent carved S. doorway and details, very like its neighbour at Hales. Norman font.

HEDENHAM
St Peter
3m/4km N.W. of Bungay TM 3193
Basically Decorated, but much rebuilt in Victorian times. The chancel was redecorated in 1862–3 by E. J. Tarver; E. window by Hardman, S. window by Clayton & Bell. W. screen of 1700 with figure of St Peter; 16th–18th-century monuments.

HEYDON
St Peter & St Paul
3m/4km N. of Reepham TG 1127
Very fine 15th-century church in charming, unspoilt village. Screen with some painting; wine-glass pulpit. Tomb of Erasmus Earle,

1667, and four old helmets; many Bulwer monuments and gifts.

HILBOROUGH
All Saints
6m/10km S. of Swaffham TF 8200
Fine Perpendicular W. tower with niches and parapet. Chancel of *c.* 1300 with carved sedilia. Royal Arms of James I; 17th-century brazier which once solved the perennial problem of church heating. Nelson's grandfather was rector here.

HILLINGTON
St Mary the Virgin
7m/11km N.E. of King's Lynn TF 7125
Mainly Perpendicular. Contains good monuments, notably Richard Hovell and family, 1611. That to Sir William Browne, 1774, and his wife, 1763, was designed by Sir William himself. Snetzler organ of 1756 in a handsome case.

HINDRINGHAM
St Martin
6m/10km N.E. of Fakenham TF 9836
Tall 14th-century W. tower. Two Norwich School medieval angels in E. window of S. aisle. Chest elaborately carved with rosettes and arches, probably Norman.

HINGHAM
St Andrew
6m/10km W. of Wymondham TG 0202
Set in charming country town where Abraham Lincoln's family originated. Decorated church built by Remigius of Hethersett, rector 1319–59. Very fine monument to Thomas, Lord Morley, d. 1435, on N. wall of chancel. E. window full of early 16th-century German glass.

HOLKHAM
St Witburga
2m/3km W. of Wells TF 8943
Stands splendidly on a high mound inside the park N. of Holkham Hall. Most impressive and atmospheric Victorian rebuilding by James K. Colling, 1869, inspired by Juliana, wife of the second Earl of Norfolk. Richly carved stalls and pews, a marble font and pulpit, rich floors, elegant hanging lamps, and many monuments, including some coffin lids. Behind a parclose screen in the N. aisle is a marble effigy of the Countess Juliana by Boehm; across the chancel is a most interesting collection of

Coke monuments from the earlier church. In the S.E. window is some 18th-century heraldic glass commemorating an earlier restoration.

HOLME HALE
St Andrew
5m/8km E. of Swaffham TF 8807
Norman doorway inside tower. Wide 15th-century windows and very fine Decorated screen. Also good bench-ends and angels in roof.

HORSHAM ST FAITH
St Mary & St Andrew
4m/6km N. of Norwich TG 2115
Largely 15th-century church; contemporary painted pulpit and screen. Fine brass of 1439 to Geoffrey Langley, Prior of Horsham.

HOWE
St Mary
6m/10km S.E. of Norwich TM 2799
Round-towered Saxon church, with Decorated and Perpendicular windows. Notice brass plaque in the chancel on which the patron of the living set out rules for the 18th-century incumbents.

HUNSTANTON
TF 6740
St Edmund
By J. F. Preedy, 1865; N. aisle added in 1879. Very atmospheric Victorian seaside church in the Tractarian tradition. Wide nave and aisles. Windows by Kempe and Comper; later glass by J. and W. Lawson and V. Flint; note W. window with Hunstanton Cliffs and motor cars.
St Mary the Virgin
Much restored in 1850s by the le Strange family; their monuments, from the magnificent beasts on Sir Roger's tomb of 1506 to the roof painted by Henry le Strange in 1857, are the main interest of this church.

INGHAM
Holy Trinity
1m/2km N.E. of Stalham TG 3926
Chancel is a rebuilding of *c.* 1350 as conventual church of Trinitarian canons. Nave and tower, 1456 onward, followed. Splendid monuments, notably Sir Oliver de Ingham, 1343, in N. sanctuary, lying on a bed of stones, and early 14th-century effigies of Sir Roger du Boie and his wife on an altar tomb.

Norman cross-vaulted ambulatory, St Bartholomew-the-Great, Smithfield, London

Wren's St Mary Abchurch, reredos by Grinling Gibbons, the City, London

Dome of Wren's St Stephen, Walbrook, the City, London

Tractarian originality, All Saints, Margaret Street, London; W Butterfield, 1849

St John the Baptist, Liverpool; G. F. Bodley, 1868-71

Opposite, above left: Barrel-vaulted ceiling decorated with flower patterns in Adam style, All Hallows, London Wall; George Dance, Junior, 1765-7

Above right: East window glass, 1791, designed by Benjamin West, and the Hollins memorial, St Paul's, Birmingham

Left: By N. Hawksmoor, 1715–23, St George's-in-the-East, Stepney, London

Left: Hammer-beam roof, Necton, Norfolk

Below: Anglo-Saxon incorporating Roman tiles, Brixworth, Northamptonshire

15th-century collegiate church, Fotheringhay, Northamptonshire

St Mary the Virgin, Wellingborough, Northamptonshire; Sir Ninian Comper

INGOLDISTHORPE
St Michael
5m/8km S. of Hunstanton TF 6832
Mostly Decorated with restored Norman font and a nice screen. Monument to Richard Gardiner, scurrilous 18th-century pamphleteer, known as 'Dick Merryfellow', who lived at the Hall. Fascinating domestic glass in window tracery.

INGWORTH
St Lawrence
2m/3km N. of Aylsham TG 1929
Pretty little Norman and later church; upper part of round tower fell in 1822. Very fine carved Royal Arms of William III and an hour-glass for timing sermons.

IRSTEAD
St Michael
3m/4km N.E. of Horning TG 3620
Unspoilt, atmospheric 14th-century church with thatched roof. Unusual octagonal font, medieval benches, and other old woodwork.

KELLING
St Mary
3m/4km N.E. of Holt TG 0942
Has a fine 15th-century Easter Sepulchre, and medieval Norwich glass in S. window, showing figures from a Coronation of the Virgin.

KENNINGHALL
St Mary
6m/10km S. of Attleborough TM 0386
Norman-Transitional S. porch with old door. Large Royal Arms of Queen Elizabeth I, removed from tympanum of chancel arch and placed in N. aisle. Royal Arms of Charles I at W. end.

KETTERINGHAM
St Peter
6m/10km N.W. of Norwich TG 1602
Norman and Early English church, the W. tower rebuilt in 1609. Three-decker pulpit, fragments of old glass, and many good 15th–19th-century monuments, including works by Sir Richard Westmacott and John Flaxman.

KING'S LYNN
TF 6119
In spite of incessant vandalism, this is still the most beautiful town in Norfolk. It contains three fine medieval Gothic churches and one Victorian one.

St Margaret, Saturday Market
In the natural centre of the town. Actually a Norman foundation, with some Norman work at the W. end. It has two W. towers and once had a spire, which fell in 1741. Round the churchyard are nice iron railings and gateways. The interior, though much restored at many periods, still has some marvellous things. Most famous are the two great Flemish brasses, tribute to Lynn's Contintental trade. Very fine 14th-century screens and a good Georgian pulpit with sounding board. There is a Snetzler organ of 1754. The reredos in the sanctuary is by G. F. Bodley.

St Nicholas, St Ann's Street
Not strictly a parish church, but it would be pedantic to omit it. It was built as a chapel of ease to St Margaret's, which only shows what a place Lynn once was. The fine tower is Early English, but the main church is of 1419. Huge W. window of 11 lights, and nine lights in E. window. Marvellous S. porch, vaulted and with bosses. Angel roof of great beauty. This is the church of the Lynn merchants, and is full of their monuments.

All Saints, All Saints Street
Though rather hidden away and not as splendid as St Margaret's or St Nicholas's, this Norman and Perpendicular church is worth a visit. Remains of an anchorite's cell on the S. side; good roofs.

KNAPTON
St Peter & St Paul
3m/4km N.E. of N. Walsham TG 3034
Most wonderful angel roof, amongst the best in Norfolk, with 138 angels with outspread wings. Font cover with Greek inscription 'Wash my sins and not my face only'.

LARLING
St Ethelbert
6m/10km S.W. of Attleborough TL 9889
Church of a hamlet, itself away in the fields. Dignified tower, 'new' in 1473; 14th-century tracery in S. aisle and porch covering fine 12th-century doorway. Norman font and stone altar mensa.

LETHERINGSETT
St Andrew
1m/2km W. of Holt TG 0368
Round tower of early 12th century; church mostly 13th-century with typical Purbeck

marble font of the period. Restored by William Butterfield in the 1870s. Some fragments of old glass in S. chancel window; also a memorial window by Geoffrey Webb. Other glass, except E. window, by Kempe, and very good.

LITCHAM
All Saints
7m/11km N.E. of Swaffham TF 8817
In middle of pretty village, brick tower built by Matthew Halcot, 1669, the rest consecrated in 1412. Charming W. gallery with Royal Arms of Victoria, and organ. Low box pews, good 15th-century painted screen, and old stalls with misericords. Perpendicular pulpit with pretty stair and rails; 15th-century foreign glass in E. window.

LITTLE BARNINGHAM
St Andrew
5m/8km N.W. of Aylsham TG 1433
Of the three churches at Barningham, one in the park is partly ruined but has a fine Winter brass; another, St Peter's, containing very fine monuments to the Palgrave family and an elaborately patterned floor in stone and brick, is now R.C.F. The third stands on a steep mound which is worth climbing in order to see the very curiously carved and inscribed box pew carved by Stephen Crosbie in 1640 for 'couples joined in wedlock'.

LITTLE DUNHAM
St Margaret
5m/8km N.E. of Swaffham TF 8714
Mostly 13th-century; lancet windows, angle piscina, circular seats round piers of arcades, and fragments of a Saxon cross.

LITTLE SNORING
St Andrew
2m/3km S. of Great Snoring, which is 3m/4km N.E. of Fakenham TF 9532
Detached round tower, Norman or possibly earlier. The very pointed S. doorway is made up of Norman materials. There are two Norman windows, lancets, and a Decorated W. window. Georgian pulpit.

LITTLE WALSINGHAM
St Mary
4m/6km S. of Wells TF 9336
Burnt down in 1961; rebuilt and refurnished in the original 14th–15th-century style by Laurence King. E. window by John Hayward. Monument to Sir Henry and Lady Sidney, 1612, and some brasses.

LODDON
Holy Trinity
6m/10km N.W. of Beccles TM 3698
Very fine late 15th-century church; battlemented tower of 1500. Inside, light and lofty with hammer-beam roof, seven-sacrament font, 1487, defaced by Beccles glazier under Commonwealth. Screen with painted panels including martyrdom of William of Norwich; monuments include that to Lady Williamson, 1684; 15th-century painting of Sir James Hobart, who built the church, and his wife, who built St Olave's bridge.

LUDHAM
St Catharine
5m/8km E. of Hoveton TG 3818
Fine large church, Decorated and Perpendicular. Font has lions and wild men. Screen with very good painted panels, and above chancel arch a 15th-century painting of the Crucifixion with Royal Arms of Queen Elizabeth I painted on the other side.

LYNG
St Margaret
6m/10km N.E. of E. Dereham TG 0717
Interesting porch with brick gable and Perpendicular window to light a former room, now disappeared. Chancel not aligned with nave. Ugly pews, some marked 'FREE' in cast-iron plaques with nice lettering. Very fine piece of embroidery, 15th-century Opus Anglicanum, hangs on W. wall. On S. wall a large painting, 1963, showing Our Lord above the village of Lyng, with the River Wensum, weir and houses.

MARHAM
Holy Trinity
7m/11km W. of Swaffham TF 7009
Norman N. doorway. Good benches with openwork backs. Fine monuments to John and Anne Steward, d. 1603 and 1604, and one to Henry Villiers by R. Westmacott Jnr, 1847. Large Royal Arms of James I.

MARTHAM
St Mary
3m/4km W. of Winterton TG 4518
Large and airy 15th-century church with High Victorian chancel of 1856. Seven-sacrament font and substantial remains of

15th-century glass including very striking St Michael weighing souls.

MATTISHALL
All Saints
4m/6km E. of E. Dereham TG 0511
On a very pretty village green. Restored early-Perpendicular church has very fine roofs with angels, quite a lot of colour, and two painted panels. There are four tie beams across the nave, also painted, and a good screen with lively figures on panels and in spandrels. Royal Arms of George II, 1745. Brasses and several excellent ledger slabs.

MATTISHALL BURGH
St Peter
4m/6km E. of E. Dereham TG 0511
Charming little church, with good open roofs, especially in chancel. Unsophisticated 1706 monument to Elizabeth Dannys. Old tiled floor and ledger slabs. Barrel organ. Very atmospheric.

METHWOLD
St George
6m/10km N.W. of Brandon TL 7394
In this Perpendicular church is what is left of a lifesize brass to Sir Adam de Clifton, 1367, and an 18th-century monument to Henry Partridge, Recorder of Lynn.

MORSTON
All Saints
1m/2km W. of Blakeney TG 0043
Picturesque 13th-century tower patched with brick. Charming unspoilt church has remains of screen with good painting and carving; a few nice monuments and inscriptions.

MUNDFORD
St Leonard
5m/8km N. of Brandon TM 3297
Early English, Decorated and Perpendicular, but the main interest is the screen, reredos, organ case, chancel decoration, and E. window, all by Sir Ninian Comper, *c.* 1911.

NARBOROUGH
All Saints
5m/8km N.W. of Swaffham TF 7413
Some Norman work in the nave; 15th-century Norwich School glass; angels, seraphim and cherubim. Very good 13th–17th-century monuments and brasses

include that to Clement Spelman by Cibber, 1762.

NECTON
All Saints
4m/6km E. of Swaffham TF 8709
Wonderful hammer-beam roof, with not only the usual East Anglian angels, but also large niches containing figures; still retains much of its medieval colouring. Splendid pulpit of 1636.

NEW BUCKENHAM
St Martin
4m/6km S.E. of Attleborough TM 0890
Fine 15th-century church with flushwork and decorated base course begun in 1470s. Inside is a 1520s hammer-beam roof and a 17th-century font; founder's tomb does duty as Easter Sepulchre.

NEWTON
All Saints
4m/6km N. of Swaffham TF 8315
Very attractive small church has impressive Saxon tower with pyramidal roof at the crossing; original plain and narrow chancel arch.

NORTH BURLINGHAM
St Andrew
2m/3km W. of Acle TG 3610
Very interesting village church given new tower in 1460s and fine hammer-beam roof, 1487–91. Screen of 1536, painted on eve of Reformation, bears patron saints of donors.

NORTH CREAKE
St Mary
7m/11km N.W. of Fakenham TF 8538
Tower of 1340s stands by road; mostly rebuilt in 15th century with fine angel roof. Chancel has large Easter Sepulchre and brass of *c.* 1500.

NORTH ELMHAM
St Mary
5m/8km N. of E. Dereham TF 9820
15th-century rebuild of earlier church retains fine 14th-century glass in N. aisle. Mid-15th-century screen with painted panels. Pulpit and altar table carved in 1620s by Francis Floyd, parish clerk for 46 years. Ruined 11th-century cathedral nearby.

NORTH LOPHAM
St Nicholas
5m/8km N.W. of Diss TM 0382
An inscription on the rather squat flint tower
of 1479–1526 commemorates Johannes
Kailli, donor. Inside the door is an old lead
notice of 1795. Royal Arms of George III.
Elegant octagonal traceried font.

NORTH RUNCTON
All Saints
3m/4km S.E. of King's Lynn TF 6145
One of Norfolk's few Classical churches,
built by Henry Bell, 1703–13. Delightful
inside and out, with tower, small steeple,
and painted reredos. Early 18th-century
monuments.

NORTH TUDDENHAM
St Mary
10m/16km W. of Norwich TG 0711
Stands with the former rectory in fields
among old trees. The interior is amazing.
The Rev. Robert Barry, incumbent 1851–
1904, lined the whole church from floor to
the base of the windows with shiny red and
yellow tiles, and had the remaining bits of
wall stencilled. Then he was lucky enough
to find a hoard of Norwich School 15th-
century glass, which he put in the windows;
much of it was removed for safety in 1942
and only three panels have returned. They
are in the W. window of the tower.

NORTH WALSHAM
St Nicholas
14m/22km N. of Norwich TG 2380
As at Fakenham, the old houses and alleys
of the market-place surround the church.
The tower fell in 1742 and remains a picturesque ruin W. of the church. The interior
is very noble and spacious and contains a
superb monument to Sir William Paston,
1608, made by John Key but designed by
Sir William himself. Very tall Perpendicular
font cover, impressively restored and
painted. Base of screen with defaced panels.
Interesting Georgian altar table in N. aisle.

NORTHWOLD
St Andrew
4m/6km S.E. of Stoke Ferry TL 7597
From the outside all Perpendicular; the
tower, 'new' in 1470, bears an inscription,
'Pray for the soule of John Stalyne'. Inside
are most attractive 13th-century arcades and
a very fine Easter Sepulchre. Wooden tablet

to Robert Burhill, friend of Sir Walter
Raleigh, who 'took sanctuary' here in 1641
– a long inscription well worth reading.

NORWICH
TG 2208
St Andrew, Broad Street
A fine late-Perpendicular town church;
tower building from 1486; main work from
c. 1500. Inside, some good early 16th-
century glass and a font cover of 1637.
St Clement, Colegate
Attractive corner setting for mid-15th-
century church with a variety of minor monuments. 'Redundant' for a decade, but
maintained open for prayer through a vision
of Methodist bus-driver, the Rev. Jack
Burton. Long may it continue.
St George, Colegate
Fine Perpendicular town church in street of
churches; all rebuilt 1450 onward, mainly
thanks to Priory. Georgian pulpit, reredos,
and gallery. Many good monuments.
St George, Tombland
A small but well-used Perpendicular church.
Tower building 1445. Good Perpendicular
tracery in N. aisle. Inside, a fine 18th-
century pulpit and reredos, 17th-century
font cover with George and Dragon, contemporary dole tablet.
St Giles, St Giles Street
Splendid site; see the wisteria in May. A
fine, large Perpendicular building of c. 1400,
the chancel and nave tracery by R. W.
Phipson, 1866. Interior full of interest; early
hammer-beam roof, fine brasses under
carpets, 18th-century sword and mace rests,
and excellent wall tablets. Brass eagle lectern
of 1493, formerly in St Gregory's; 20th-
century altars and shrines in good taste.
St Helen, Bishopgate
Once part of the Great Hospital founded by
Walter de Suffield, Bishop of Norwich, in
1249 to shelter all 'poor and decrepit clerks',
and a parish church. At the Reformation,
the Corporation turned it into a home for
old people, and in Edward VI's reign the
church was divided into three: the W. end
became two men's wards, and the chancel,
'new' in 1383, with a ceiling painted with
great black eagles in honour of Anne of
Bohemia in 1393, two women's wards. In
the church there is no high altar; before the
blocked chancel arch are box pews and the
pulpit. The parochial altar was always in the
S. transept where it stands under a most
beautiful vaulted ceiling of 1480. Magnifi-

cent Georgian reredos, probably by Thomas Ivory, whose son William built the Gothic pew opposite in 1780. Note the Tudor bench-ends and early hymn boards and numerals.

St John, Maddermarket

Mid-15th-century church on cramped site; no separate chancel and a passage under tower. Interior is very rich with N. gallery and big gilded Georgian reredos. Excellent brasses.

    R.C.F.

St John de Sepulchre, Ber Street

Splendidly sited on the edge of the medieval city, the tower a landmark. Largely built at end of 15th century; 15th-century brasses, amusing 17th-century rhyming inscriptions. Redundant but happily used by Russian Orthodox.

St John, Timberhill

Small church with interior recast in post-Vatican II style. Note German brass chandelier of *c.* 1500 with Virgin and Child, Oberammergau rood, and Statue of Our Lady and Holy Child by Martin Travers, *c.* 1948.

St Julian, St Julian's Alley

11th-century church, bombed in 1942, but reconstructed by A. J. Chaplin. S. chapel on site of the cell of famous 15th-century anchorite, Mother Julian of Norwich. Calm interior dominated by German reredos, but note fine Perpendicular font, 1448, from All Saints, and 12th-century doorway from St Michael at Thorn.

St Peter Mancroft, Market Place

Superb 15th-century church dominates Market Place, rebuilt from 1430 onward, though not finished until the eve of Reformation. Interior is tall and open with no chancel arch and a hammer-beam roof. Rare font canopy of 1463. Interesting glass of 1921 by H. Hendrie, but go miles to see the E. window, which retains much of its original Norwich School glass; take binoculars or telescope for subtle, endearing, detail. This survived both gunpowder explosion and a famous 17th-century Puritan congregation, who surely found it very idolatrous. Reredos by Seddon, 1895; enlarged and remodelled by Comper, 1930.

St Stephen, Rampant Horse Street

Reconstructed as Tudor storm clouds gathered – chancel 'new building' of 1530; clerestory 1540; tower rebuilding 1542 onward; 1550 date over W. door. Much stone and flushwork. Inside, the hammer-beam roof is

the consummation of lengthy clerestory; fine medieval and later glass; 16th-century brasses and memorial tablets.

OUTWELL
St Clement

5m/8km S.E. of Wisbech TF 5103

Ambitious 13th-century W. tower with Decorated bell-stage. Brick N. chapel of *c.* 1527. Good roofs with angels and wall-post figures. Remains of 16th-century glass in S. chapel; 16th-century brass and monuments.

OXBOROUGH
St John the Evangelist

3m/4km E. of Stoke Ferry TF 7401

The tower fell in 1948, destroying the nave. The chancel has a five-light Perpendicular E. window with some medieval Norwich glass; a fine roof, good piscina and sedilia. The Bedingfeld family, who built the moated hall in 1482, have a most beautiful chantry containing two superb early 16th-century tombs of terracotta and other very fine monuments of later date.

PASTON
St Margaret

4m/6km N.E. of N. Walsham TG 3234

Small thatched Decorated church standing near the great barn built by Sir William Paston of the famous 'Letters' family. There are two fine monuments by Nicholas Stone to Dame Katharine Paston, 1629, and her husband, Sir Edmund, 1632.

PULHAM MARKET
St Mary Magdalene

4m/6km N.W. of Harleston TM 1986

Good tower with statues in niches on W. front. Some scraps of old glass in N. porch. Collar-braced roof in nave, the easternmost bay restored to medieval colour in 1873.

PULHAM ST MARY
St Mary the Virgin

3m/4km N.W. of Harleston TM 2185

Most beautiful two-storeyed 15th-century S. porch with figures for pinnacles and a canopied arcade with windows and niches above a row of shields. In the spandrels, the Annunciation; rows of tracery with angels playing musical instruments. Inside there is a curious wooden staircase at W. end going up to the ringing chamber. There is much old glass in the window traceries, some difficult to identify, but including the 12 apostles in N. aisle. Very good screen and mid-13th-century chancel, beautifully restored in 1886 by Bodley. Amazing 15th-century font, re-coloured. Piscina of unusual form, 13th-century.

RANWORTH
St Helen
4m/6km N.W. of Acle TG 3514
The nave was thatched till it burned in 1963. Fine W. tower, but the really marvellous thing is the 15th-century screen, the best in Norfolk. It extends right across the church with very pretty projecting wings dividing the two aisle altars from the central opening. The painting of the figures in the panels, as well as of the backgrounds and the decoration on the ribs and tracery, is superb. The church also possesses the Sarum Antiphoner, an illuminated manuscript of 14th-century East Anglian workmanship.

REDENHALL
Assumption of St Mary
1km/2km N.E. of Harleston TM 2684
Flushwork Suffolk-style tower of the 1470s, a striking landmark on the way up from Harleston. Inside, a hammer-beam roof of 1452 and a Victorian font in 15th-century style. Unique 15th-century double-headed eagle lectern.

REEPHAM and WHITWELL
St Mary and St Michael
6m/10km S.W. of Aylsham TG 1022
These two churches stand in the same churchyard, and are joined like Siamese twins. There was once a third church, Hackford (All Saints); all were built on their parish boundaries. Reepham contains the very fine tombs of Sir Roger de Kerdiston, 1337, lying on a bed of stones like Sir Oliver at Ingham. Whitwell has a fine Jacobean pulpit. Hackford is in ruins.

RINGLAND
St Peter
7m/11km N.W. of Norwich TG 1314
In the clerestory windows is beautiful Norwich School glass: large figures, more complete than usual, and of wonderful colours. Here is the Blessed Virgin Mary with the Child, an Annunciation, the Trinity, several saints, and some figures of donors. There is also a fine hammer-beam roof with angels and delicate vaulting over the clerestory. The screen is now dismantled, but

five defaced panels stand at the W. end; 18th-century canvas commandment boards and hatchments in the tower.

ROUGHAM
St Mary
7m/11km N. of Swaffham TF 8320
Decorated W. tower and Perpendicular windows in the nave. Very fine Yelverton brasses: 1472, 1510 and 1586. Carved 14th-century wooden panel in S. chancel. In churchyard a gravestone carved with a very early aeroplane.

RUNCTON HOLME
St James
4m/6km N. of Downham Market TF 6109
A very pretty church with late-Norman tower and S. doorway with shafts and decorated capitals. Splendid Jacobean pulpit and 15th-century screen.

SALLE
St Peter & St Paul
1m/2km N.E. of Reepham TG 1124
Wonderful church, whose very tall tower dominates the almost empty countryside; has the best of everything the 15th century produced. The architecture, of about 1420, is superb. The W. tower is richly decorated. Notice the feathered angels in the spandrels. There are two-storeyed porches on the N.E. side; that to the N. has lierne vaulting and bosses, and there are more beautiful bosses in the chancel roof. The nave roof has angels, the transept roofs panelling; there is very good Norwich School glass, and the base of a screen with painting. The pulpit has 15th-century panels but a Jacobean tester. The stalls, misericords and bench-ends are all very good. There are many brasses and monuments. The font cover, beam and pulley are all Perpendicular too, and there is a seven-sacrament font.

SALTHOUSE
St Nicholas
3m/4km N. of Holt TG 0743
This great church, built by Sir Henry Heydon of Baconsthorpe at the end of the 15th century, stands high above the marsh and sea in a village which has suffered many floods. It is a most wonderful Perpendicular church with a very large E. window and unusual, very plain nave windows of two lights only. Remains of screen with defaced panels; touching graffiti of sailing ships done

by bored children on the choir-stalls. There is a panel of medieval glass in the E. window of the S. aisle.

SANDRINGHAM
St Mary Magdalene
7m/11km N.E. of King's Lynn TF 6928
This little church, much rebuilt and restored by Teulon in 1857 and Blomfield in 1890, has been the home church of the Royal Family since 1861. There are many affectionate family monuments to Queen Victoria, Queen Mary, King George VI, and others; in a stained glass representation of St Edward in the tower window one suspects the features of the late Duke of Clarence. The silver altar and reredos were given by an American, Rodman Wanamaker. There is a very good E. window by W. E. Tower, 1911; part of the restoration of the chancel in memory of King Edward VII. Beautiful and unusual stained glass figures of saints in N.E. side aisle windows and over the entrance to the S. porch, probably made in Lynn *c.* 1500.

SAXLINGHAM NETHERGATE
St Mary the Virgin
7m/11km S. of Norwich TM 2297
On a pretty village green with a rectory by Soane to the W. and an Elizabethan house to the E. Perpendicular church containing some of the best glass in Norfolk, notably 13th-century roundels of the martyrdom of St Edmund, 14th-century figures of St Philip and St James, and 15th-century representations of the Annunciation and Resurrection. There is also a good font, and Royal Arms of William IV.

SCULTHORPE
Blessed Virgin Mary, and All Saints
2m/3km N.W. of Fakenham TF 8930
Has a forbiddingly restored exterior, but contains an organ case by Snetzler, 1756, some fine brasses, good glass by Morris and Burne-Jones, and a superb Norman font with the Adoration of the Magi.

SHARRINGTON
All Saints
3m/4km W. of Holt TG 0336
This mainly 14th-century church has extraordinarily carved corbels, including a wild man and a curious moustachioed face. There is a brass of 1490 and another, more interesting, of 1593.

SHELFHANGER
All Saints
3m/4km N. of Diss TM 1083
Largely 14th-century church with nice wooden N. porch of 1506. Inside, font with arms and initials of Adam Bosville, patron, 1362, and splendid, recently discovered 13th-century wall-painting in chancel of the Adoration of the Magi.

SHELTON
St Mary
5m/8km N. of Harleston TM 2291
The most exciting, surprising and beautiful church, built of red brick with dark diapering, in the 1480s, in the purest Perpendicular style, apart from the earlier tower. Large figures of donors in 15th-century dress in windows; monument to Sir Robert Houghton, 1623; Royal Arms of William II; 18th-century commandment boards as reredos; old brick floor.

SHEREFORD
St Nicholas
2m/3km W. of Fakenham TF 8829
Very interesting church. Saxon tower, fine Norman S. door, and Norman font. E. window with flowing tracery. Interesting modern tombstones in churchyard: Parson Robin and Farmer Bidwell.

SHIPDHAM
All Saints
4m/6km S.W. of E. Dereham TF 9507
Largely 15th-century. Tower has curious lead cupola, perhaps 17th-century. Inside are 17th-century altar rails and prettily painted commandment boards. Celebrated 14th-century wooden lectern.

SNETTISHAM
St Mary
4m/6km S. of Hunstanton TF 6834
Magnificent spire now at E. end, the chancel having fallen down. W. front with tripartite porch and six-light Decorated window of great beauty, well described in L. P. Hartley's novel *The Shrimp and the Anemone*. Good brasses including that to John Cremer, d. 1610, with wife and children.

SOUTH ACRE
St George Church
4m/6km N. of Swaffham TF 8114
Good Perpendicular hammer-beam roof. Magnificent brass to Sir John Harsick,

d. 1348. Decorated screen; carved and painted Perpendicular font cover.

SOUTH BURLINGHAM
St Edmund
2m/3km S. of North Burlingham, which is 2m/3km W. of Acle TG 3708
12th-century church on its own with unfinished 15th-century tower. Good carved doorways and thatched roof. Many features of interest inside: lovely painted 15th-century pulpit, contemporary benches, and stalls.

SOUTH CREAKE
Assumption of St Mary
1m/2km S. of North Creake, which is 7m/11km N.W. of Fakenham TF 8536
Large 14th-century church rebuilt in 15th century with angel roof over new arcades. Interior full of light, colour, and objects of piety. Much 14th-century glass with 15th-century angels in tracery, as well as 16th-century Continental panels; 15th-century wine-glass pulpit, screen, and seven-sacrament font. Restored altars and shrines give the impression that the Reformation never got this far – until you see what 17th-century vandals did to the font.

SOUTH LOPHAM
St Andrew
5m/8km N.W. of Diss TM 0382
Superb Norman central tower, the best in Norfolk. Pevsner says 1120. Good roofs in nave and chancel. Nice bench-ends have elephant with howdah and cat with kittens. Font of the same unusual type as at North Lopham.

SOUTH PICKENHAM
All Saints
2m/3km S. of N. Pickenham, which is 3m/4km S.E. of Swaffham TF 8504
Round tower; angle piscina in chancel; large 14th-century wall-painting of St Christopher; Gothic organ case said to be by Pugin.

SPARHAM
St Mary
7m/11km N.E. of E. Dereham TG 0719
Magnificent church, mainly Perpendicular, with very tall tower. Panels of screen preserved in N. aisle have three figures from the Dance of Death; one in a shroud, the others, one male and one female, are cadavers with grinning skulls and bony limbs clad in fashionable 15th-century clothes. Good brasses, bench-ends, and roof.

STODY
St Mary
3m/4km S.W. of Holt TG 0535
Has an early round tower, some nice Decorated tracery in chancel windows, and unusually fine and complicated arch-braced roofs. A little Norwich School glass in tracery of S. nave windows.

STOW BARDOLPH
Holy Trinity
2m/3km N.E. of Downham Market TF 6205
Norman and later tower, otherwise rebuilt by Raphael Brandon, 1848–9. Remarkable monuments in N. chapel: Sir Ralph Hare, knighted at coronation of James I, elaborate Renaissance; Sir Thomas Hare by Scheemakers, 1693; and, best of all, in a mahogany cupboard, Sarah Hare, lifesize in wax. She died in 1744 and left a will ordering this effigy and the clothes in which it was to be dressed. This monument is unique in Norfolk and unusual anywhere.

STRADSETT
St Mary
4m/6km E. of Downham Market TF 6605
Pretty little 13th-century and later church in park. Flemish glass of 1540 in Perpendicular E. window and tower lancet. Bagge family monuments include two by Sir Richard Westmacott of 1827 and 1834.

STRATTON STRAWLESS
St Margaret
8m/12km N. of Norwich TG 2220
Broad W. tower of *c.* 1422. N. aisle rebuilt in brick in 17th century to house the Marsham monuments. Delightful rhyme-and-portrait figures of parents and children, 1678; macabre shrouded figure of Thomas Marsham, 1638, with angels above and skulls and bones beneath. Fine Norwich School glass in the nave.

SUSTEAD
St Peter & St Paul
4m/6km S.W. of Cromer TG 1837
Emblems of patron saints in flint flushwork in S. porch, and a curious, unexplained emblem over the door. Decorated windows and fine double piscina; simple Jacobean pulpit and some medieval Norwich glass.

SWAFFHAM
St Peter & St Paul
14m/22km S.E. of King's Lynn TF 8109
The pretty spirelet, familiar in the country around, was a felicitous addition of 1897. There is a beautiful double hammer-beam roof with angels. Monument to Katherine Steward, 1590, and a brass to Sir John Audley, *c.* 1530, unfortunately mounted on a wall. Scraps of old glass in tracery of N. nave windows; otherwise the glass is very horrid. In the priest's chamber above the vestry is the parish library with many rare books.

SWANTON MORLEY
All Saints
3m/4km N.E. of E. Dereham TG 0116
Important early-Perpendicular church begun in 1370s. Commanding W. tower with very large belfry windows; swan and barrel rebuses flank the entrances. Lofty interior lit by impressive square-headed windows with fine tracery.

TERRINGTON
St Clement
4m/6km W. of King's Lynn TF 5520
Detached Perpendicular tower, large S. porch, and W. front with five-light window and canopied niches. Good unspoilt chancel screen, Georgian panelling W. of nave, and wonderful 17th-century font cover which opens to show paintings of the Life of Christ. Huge Jacobean commandment boards; a very fine church.

THETFORD
TL 8683
St Mary the Less, Bury Road
Perpendicular with 19th-century chancel of white brick, right for Thetford. Fine tower. Inside, a large monument to Sir Richard Fulmodeston, d. 1567. Good wrought-iron sword-holders. Monument of 1834 records an unusual accident; much Victorian glass, including window to rector's cook.
St Peter, King Street
In main street, with a fine tower – rebuilt 1789; nice flintwork. Inside, some good wrought-iron mace- and sword-holders and heraldic glass in S. window.

THOMPSON
St Martin
3m/4km S. of Watton TL 9296
Attractive rural church, little changed since the 14th century, apart from mid-15th-century S. chapel. Rustic interior of great charm with a 17th-century air; Stuart canopied pulpit, box pew, altar, and rails. Poppy-head benches with 17th-century graffiti. Medieval stalls.

THORPE MARKET
St Margaret
4m/6km S. of Cromer TG 2436
Charming Georgian Gothic; 1796 by an architect called Wood. Very pretty screen with painted glass panels; good Harbord and other monuments.

THURNING
St Andrew
6m/10km S. of Holt SG 0829
Complete furnishings of 1742 from Corpus Christi College, Cambridge, installed as part of an 1825 restoration; very good.

THURSFORD
St Andrew
5m/8km N.E. of Fakenham TF 9933
A rare example of a Victorian restoration transforming a dull medieval church into something much more interesting than it was before. Restored in 1862 by W. Lightly in accordance with mid-Victorian High Church principles; a model of the period and unharmed by later 'good taste'. Encaustic tiles, corona luci, well-designed furnishings, an elevated pew for the squire above the family vault, and stained glass in the E. window by the Rev. Arthur Moore, which Professor Pevsner says is 'one of the most beautiful of its time in England, or indeed in Europe'. Sculpture on the exterior of the S. side of the church rivals Burges at his most inventive.

THWAITE
All Saints
5m/8km N. of Aylesham TG 1934
Has a round tower. Inside, a nice pulpit of 1624, old floors, and a box pew. But best of all is the Sunday school room N. of the chancel: 1824 with old lettering, texts, and original wooden coat pegs.

TIBENHAM
All Saints
6m/10km N. of Diss TM 1389
Chequerwork tower. Splendid carved and gilded Jacobean pulpit. Buxton family pew, for which Archbishop Laud himself granted

a faculty in 1635, is reached by a stair in S. aisle. A hatchment and a carved and painted achievement hang on the pew. Royal Arms of George I in a carved frame. ,

TILNEY
All Saints
4m/6km W. of King's Lynn TF 5618
12th-century arcades, 13th-century tower, 15th-century aisles and clerestory; double hammer-beam roof and a good screen of 1618. Royal Arms of Queen Anne.

TITTLESHALL
St Mary
6m/10km S.W. of Fakenham TF 8921
Mainly Decorated, with very fine Coke monuments: Bridget Coke, née Paston, 1598; Sir Edward Coke, Lord Chief Justice, 1634, by Nicholas Stone; Robert Coke, 1679; The Earl of Leicester, builder of Holkham, and his wife, 1759, with busts by Roubiliac; Mrs James Coke, 1800, by Nollekens.

TIVETSHALL
St Margaret
6m/10km N.W. of Harleston TM 1687
Prodigious painted Royal Arms of Queen Elizabeth I on tympanum over chancel arch; possibly the finest in existence and certainly very rare.

TRUNCH
St Botolph
3m/4km N. of N. Walsham TG 2834
This church has many interesting features, including a screen of 1502 with painted panels of 11 Apostles and return stalls with holes for inkpots and many carved names, showing that a school was held there; a few scraps of medieval glass and an Elizabethan monument in the chancel; a nice 15th-century roof with angels; a neat brass in the nave, and a ringers' gallery with some original colour. But its great glory is the celebrated font canopy of *c.* 1500; almost unique and enchanting even in its present state. Painted and carved panels, flying buttresses, and pinnacled top, traces of all of which remain. Splendid carving of flowers, vines, monkeys, and a wild man fighting a dragon. There are only four of these canopies in England, and two of them are in Norfolk.

TUNSTEAD
St Mary
4m/6km N. of Wroxham TG 3022
Unusual church in several ways. Outside there is flushwork arcading instead of clerestory windows. Inside, behind the high altar, is a mysterious raised platform with a vaulted chamber beneath, possibly a strong-room for relics which would be exhibited above. There is also a good screen with ogee arches and painted panels, and the rood beam. Fine 14th-century ironwork on S. door.

UPPER SHERINGHAM
All Saints
1m/2km S.W. of Sheringham, which is 22m/35km N. of Norwich TG 1441
Full of interesting things, notably the 15th-century rood screen with loft, painted beam with pulley for raising font cover, and very good bench-ends, including a mermaid, nurse with Christ-child, and cat with kitten in mouth. Good Upcher monument in chancel, and curious Victorian stained glass portrait in S.W. window.

UPWELL
St Peter
5m/8km S.E. of Wisbech TF 5002
13th-century and Perpendicular church with fine angel roof, interesting brasses, and 15th-century brass eagle lectern. Carved Royal Arms of Queen Victoria.

WALPOLE ST ANDREW
St Andrew
6m/9km N.E. of Wisbech TF 5017
Important marshland church overshadowed by illustrious neighbour. Much brick in fabric, particularly in mid-15th-century tower. Fine clerestory of *c.* 1500; 17th-century pulpit faces rare medieval stone bracket of predecessor.
R.C.F.

WALPOLE ST PETER
St Peter
5m/8km N.E. of Wisbech TF 5017
The finest of all. Wonderful exterior with processional way under the E. end; battlements, huge Perpendicular windows, very fine porches, especially the two-storeyed one on the S., which has good brasses. Inside, the impression is Jacobean; there is a big screen W. of the pews, a tall font cover, benches, pulpit, and great chandelier of brass and wrought iron. All this is of the

highest quality and looks good in the nave, but the vaulted chancel is such a Gothic masterpiece that it is a pity it has been mutilated and over-crowded with benches and monuments, again mostly 17th-century. The saints on all that is left of the Perpendicular screen were clearly painted by several different hands; some are rather crude but all are charming.

WALSOKEN
All Saints
N.E. district of Wisbech TF 4710
Late Norman and Early English; very fine with much early decoration. Elaborate roof with some colour. Two screens, carved stalls, and a few old benches. Painting of the Judgement of Solomon and 17th-century wooden figures of Solomon over the tower arch and of King David with his harp over the chancel arch.

WARHAM
2m/3km S.E. of Wells TF 9441
Tiny village with two churches.
All Saints
Has lost its tower and aisles. Stone effigy of *c.* 1300 in the Decorated sanctuary. Three fonts: two Norman, one with Labours of the Months; 18th-century baluster font.
St Mary Magdalene
Delightful setting. Priest's door in S. chancel buttress. Unspoilt Georgian interior with box pews and three-decker pulpit. Turner mausoleum on N. side of chancel with interesting inscription and hatchments. W. window has fine 16th-century Rhenish glass; the same in all other windows except the N. side of the nave, which has 14th- and 15th-century glass of the Norwich School. Royal Arms of George III.

WELLINGHAM
St Andrew
6m/10km S.W. of Fakenham TF 8722
This little church in a small hamlet has beautiful screen panels of 1532. Note especially St George on horseback and the emblems of the Passion, including Pilate's disembodied hands.

WESTON LONGVILLE
All Saints
9m/15km N.W. of Norwich TG 1115
James Woodforde, who wrote the *Diary of a Country Parson*, was rector here from 1776 until he died in 1803; note his portrait and

memorial. Good 14th-century Tree of Jesse wall-painting in N. aisle; figures of the Apostles in S. aisle windows.

WEST WALTON
St Mary
3m/4km N. of Wisbech TF 4713
Superb Early English church of *c.* 1240; one of the best in England. Detached tower; beautiful arcades on Purbeck piers with detached shafts and leafy capitals; wall-paintings and priest's effigy. Bell-tower. R.C.F.

WEYBOURNE
All Saints
4m/6km N.E. of Holt TG 1143
Saxon building taken over by Augustinian canons in the 13th century. Central Saxon tower with characteristic triangular heads to the double openings; Early English doorway with dog-tooth decoration; pillar piscina in the sanctuary.

WICKHAMPTON
St Andrew
2m/3km N. of Reedham TG 4205
Very rewarding church, mainly *c.* 1300, containing superb 14th-century wall-paintings: Seven Works of Mercy and Three Living and Three Dead. Two very fine 13th-century effigies of Sir William Gerbrygge and his wife, he with his heart in his hands.

WICKMERE
St Andrew
4m/6km N. of Aylsham TG 1733
Mostly Decorated, including the top stage of the round W. tower with flushwork battlements. Many Walpole monuments and hatchments, old benches in N. aisle, and a screen.

WIGGENHALL ST GERMANS
St German
4m/6km S. of King's Lynn TF 5914
Early English and Perpendicular with very fine 16th-century bench-ends: Vices in the Jaws of Hell, grotesque monks, and Apostles. 17th-century pulpit and clerk's desk.

WIGGENHALL ST MARY
St Mary Magdalene
5m/8km N. of Downham Market TF 5911
Remarkable set of early 16th-century box pews adorned with saints, coats of arms, and other devices; 17th-century panelling and

remains of screens; 15th-century glass in the window tracery with Apostles, angels and saints. Good alabaster tomb of the Kervils, 1625. Brass lectern dated 1518. R.C.F.

WIGHTON
All Saints
3m/4km S.E. of Wells TF 9339

Huge, light church; early 15th-century nave with fine Norwich School angels and saints in tracery. Chancel built from 1440 onward by celebrated mason James Woodrofe, sent from the Cathedral Priory by the rectors. S. porch of 1490s with mermaid over one window, face over other. Splendid black and white marble tomb of Elizabeth Bacon, 1686, and many fine ledger slabs. Good gravestones in churchyard. The tower fell in 1965 but, thanks to the generosity of Canadian Mr Leeds Richardson, rebuilt and rededicated in 1976.

WILBY
All Saints
4m/6km S.W. of Attleborough TM 0389

Although this 14th-century church has the dim remains of a wall-painting of St Christopher, the reason for seeking it out is to see its Carolean interior. After a fire in 1633, a three-decker pulpit, W. gallery, benches, box pews, and communion rails in contemporary style were put in, all now faded to a beautiful silver-grey. Above them, on a huge panel, are the Arms of Charles I.

WIVETON
St Mary
1m/2km S.E. of Blakeney TG 0442

Very fine position above Glaven Valley looking across to Cley. Decorated chancel and Perpendicular nave; box pews, fine chandelier, and good brasses, including shrouded skeleton, c. 1540.

WOOD NORTON
All Saints
6m/10km E. of Fakenham TG 0127

Down a lane, off the beaten track. Par-
ishioners began tower in 1530s but beaten to it by Henry VIII; belfry stage not added until 1699, hence dichotomy between flint Tudor ground stage and brick Classical top. Inside, has unusual 15th-century font with 17th-century dove-topped cover. Traces of 15th-century glass in tower, and very Victorian E. window by C. A. Gibbs, 1875.

WORSTEAD
St Mary
3m/4km S.E. of N. Walsham TG 3026

One of the best 14th-century churches in Norfolk. On brass in S. porch is Coronation of the Virgin. Two late 14th-century side chapels with contemporary screens; chancel screen of 1512. Amongst the saints in the panels on the latter are St William of Norwich, holding nails and a dagger, and St Uncumber, who grew a beard to escape an undesirable suitor. There are box pews, ringing gallery, and tower screen of 1501 with Georgian paintings on the panels. A few brasses and remains of wall-paintings and texts.

WYMONDHAM
St Mary & St Thomas of Canterbury
9m/15km S.W. of Norwich TG 1001

Wonderful church, part of a Benedictine abbey, but always parochial. Much of it is Norman with splendid arcades and triforium windows. Perpendicular clerestory and spectacular angel roof. The terracotta Ferrers monument, very like those at Oxborough, is of c. 1525. There are fragments of a 13th-century font, as well as a complete 15th-century one. Sir Ninian Comper did much work here, including the beautiful reredos. In the parvise can be seen the famous Corporal case, used to hold the cloth Corporal upon which the bread and wine are consecrated; a rare example of 13th-century Opus Anglicanum.

Northamptonshire

Introduction

The impression made by Northamptonshire, a too-little-regarded county, is of an assured and beautiful use of stone for country houses, farms, cottages, outbuildings and above all for churches. Competent masonry has gone on since the Middle Ages. The county is on the limestone belt, and the building stone varies from a pale silvery limestone to a deep-brown ironstone, with every shade of yellow and gold between. Medieval masons delighted to arrange the stone to give decorative effects to the outside of walls, as at Finedon, Irthlingborough, and Woodford. Old roofs are tiled, with stones graded from small at the ridge to large at the eaves on barns, manor houses, and most old buildings, and of these stone tiles, the best are those known as Collyweston slates, which come from this county.

If ever the term 'steeple chasing' needed explanation, this is the county to describe what it means, for it abounds in steeples. Broach spires whose chamfered sides rise to a graceful point like a sharpened pencil from a tower which seems part of the same design, as at Stanwick; crocketed spires of immense height, as at Oundle and Higham Ferrers; dumpy spires which are almost pyramids; towers and spires in which it is hard to say which lends more grace to which, as at Raunds and King's Sutton – these rise generally out of trees on hills and in valleys, so that not even the pylons and poles of our own age can quite extinguish their effect. There are few eminences in the pastoral parts of this mildly undulating country from which one can see less than three church spires. More times than not one finds clustered about the church an attractive stone-built village, though terrible havoc has been done in most of them by medical officers of health, who would sooner pull down an old cottage than allow it to be enlarged and restored.

Norfolk has larger churches and grander woodwork. Somerset has more lace-like towers, but Northampton above all counties has variety and originality and elegance in its architecture, from the Saxon long-and-short work on the tower of Earls Barton to the stone octagonal lantern with its flying buttresses on the top of the late Perpendicular tower of Lowick. Northampton's medieval church-builders seem to have been conscious architects and not mere builders. This quality in their church towers and spires, particularly in the 13th and 14th centuries, together with the fact that 'Early English' and 'Decorated' were regarded as pure and perfect respectively, made the spires of the east and north of the county, and of S. Lincs, the model for Victorian church architects. So Northamptonshire spires may be seen rising out of the suburbs of London and other big cities, and even over the roof-tops of foreign and dominion capitals where there is an Anglican church.

Naturally, churches so deservedly popular with the Victorians came in for a good deal of 'restoration' at their hands. Many have been ruined internally by having the plaster stripped from their walls and the stone picked out in cement to give an 'ancient' effect; shiny tiles have replaced old stone or brick floors; and cheap pews and church furnishings have completed the devastation. We have listed here those medieval churches which are wholly or comparatively unharmed by Victorians. But there is hardly a medieval church in the county which is without beautiful stonework somewhere, either in the many mouldings of an arch or in a lively piece of carving acting as capital, corbel, or water-spout.

The county has suffered more than most in the South Midlands from 19th-century and modern industry. It was never grim, so that factories, pylons and power stations ill become its gentle landscape. The boot and shoe industry caused a rash of hard, bright brick villas in the last century in Northampton itself, and Rushden, Wellingborough, and Irthlingborough. But these villas are Midland-looking and have no affinities with London. In the present age great harm has been done to its loveliest scenery by the former iron and steel industry, whose huge dredgers picked their way like pre-historic animals over the farms, digging up the earth and raising mountains and bringing poles and wires and mineral lines in their trail. Recent legislation, however, has made restoration compulsory, and this has improved matters. Northampton was itself designated a New Town in 1968 and has grown substantially.

J. B.

1	Aldwincle	13	Canons Ashby	25	Edgcote
2	Apethorpe	14	Charwelton	26	Fawsley
3	Ashby St Ledgers	15	Chipping Warden	27	Finedon
4	Ashley	16	Cottesbrooke	28	Fotheringhay
5	Aynho	17	Cransley	29	Gayton
6	Badby	18	Crick	30	Geddington
7	Benefield	19	Croughton	31	Great Brington
8	Brigstock	20	Daventry	32	Greton
9	Brixworth	21	Earls Barton	33	Higham Ferrers
10	Bugbrooke	22	East Carlton	34	Hinton-in-the-Hedges
11	Burton Latimer	23	Easton Maudit	35	Irthlingborough
12	Byfield	24	Easton Neston	36	Kelmarsh

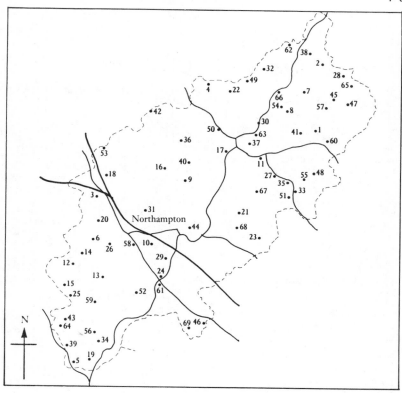

Selected List of Churches

ALDWINCLE
All Saints
4m/6km S.E. of Oundle TL 0081
Set in meadowland in a stone village with two churches. All Saints has a striking 15th-century tower, pinnacled and delicately moulded. The body of the church is 13th- and 14th-century with aisles and S. chapel; it is disused and shows how well a medieval church can look without pews. Old plaster, clear glass and floors, Jacobean communion rail, and some stained glass of *c.* 1490 in the Chambre chapel.
R.C.F.

APETHORPE
St Leonard
4m/6km S.W. of Wansford TL 0295
Stone village with well-designed Edwardian and later cottages. Mainly Perpendicular church with whitewashed interior, box pews, 18th-century altarpiece, and E. window of Last Supper. S. chapel of 1621 contains Mildmay monument: one of the most sumptuous in England, with effigies under a marble canopy held by allegorical figures. Chapel decorated to match with 1621 E. window, Dutch-style glass, blues and deep greens and pretty scene of Garden of Eden.

ASHBY ST LEDGERS
Blessed Virgin Mary & St Leodegorius
4m/6km N. of Daventry SP 5768
Stands near the Catesby manor where the Gunpowder plotters met. Perpendicular and earlier church with beautiful rood screen, Jacobean pews and benches, a musicians' pew, and a three-decker pulpit. Extensive but dim wall-paintings of *c.* 1500; Catesby brasses.

ASHLEY
St Mary the Virgin
5m/8km N.E. of Market Harborough SP 7990
Virtually rebuilt by Sir Giles Gilbert Scott in the 1860s, but the loss of the church of *c.* 1300 is compensated for by the wondrous chancel which shows Scott at his most flamboyant. Sparkling floor tiles, wall-paintings

and glass by Clayton & Bell, and a wealth of brass and polished pink granite.

AYNHO
St Michael
6m/10km S.E. of Banbury SP 5133
A delightful hill village. The church retains a rich Decorated tower, but the rest was transformed in 1723 after the manner of Vanbrugh by a local carpenter-cum-architect, Edward Wing. Wing's alterations are uncompromisingly domestic in style, with windows in two storeys; an illustration of that phase in the history of English churches which most Victorians tried to pretend had never existed.

BADBY
St Mary
3m/4km S.W. of Daventry SP 5659
Charming village setting. Mostly 14th-century; good W. tower of 1707 with Y-traceried bell-openings; firmly restored, 1880–1.

BENEFIELD
St Mary the Virgin
3m/4km W. of Oundle SP 9988
By J. Macduff Derick, 1847; 'an important specimen of the sumptuous Tractarian church' (Goodhart-Rendel). Rood, reredos, and other furnishings by Comper.

BRIGSTOCK
St Andrew
4m/6km S.E. of Corby SP 9485
Impressive remains of the original substantial Saxon church; upper parts of the nave walls, W. tower, and big circular stair turret. Good long-and-short quoins and well-built single-splayed windows in the tower.

BRIXWORTH
All Saints
7m/11km N. of Northampton SP 7470
Prodigious 7th-century Saxon church of the first importance. Originally monastic, the sheer scale of the surviving early fabric of rubble dressed with Roman tiles is fantastic; this is one of the most important buildings

in England. The church was conceived as a huge basilica with lateral porticus and a narthex at the W. end. It was probably damaged during Danish raids in the late 8th or early 9th century, presumably necessitating some later rebuilding; certainly the lower part of the sanctuary, the tower, and the circular stair turret were added during the 10th and 11th centuries. Other medieval alterations included the 14th-century belfry and spire, but in the mid-19th century some of the later accretions were removed and the apse restored on its old foundations.

BUGBROOKE
St Michael and All Angels
5m/8km S.W. of Northampton SP 6757
13th-century and later church with good stiff-leaf foliage on the S. arcade. Fine 15th-century chancel screen with paired lights and ribbed coving.

BURTON LATIMER
St Mary the Virgin
3m/4km S.E. of Kettering SP 9074
Over-restored in 1866, but retaining 14th- and 16th-century wall-paintings, including a cycle of St Catherine and some later Patriarchs who look far more Tudor than Israelite.

BYFIELD
Holy Cross
7m/11km S.W. of Daventry SP 5153
Decorated ironstone church with an imposing tower replete with ballflowers and a modest spire; 15th-century bench-ends.

CANONS ASHBY
St Mary
10m/16km N.E. of Banbury SP 5750
Once part of Black Canons' monastic church. Grand 14th-century W. front and tower remain, backed by a truncated nave. A break in the level of the churchyard shows how far the church extended before the Dissolution. Dryden brass, hatchments and monuments. Restored by the National Trust who also own the house.
N.T.

CHARWELTON
Holy Trinity
5m/8km S.W. of Daventry SP 5356
Church and manor stranded by enclosures. Mainly Decorated church with big W. tower and two-storeyed Perpendicular S. porch.

Good 16th-century monuments to the Andrewes family.

CHIPPING WARDEN
St Peter & St Paul
6m/10km N.E. of Banbury SP 4948
Principally 15th-century, though with a Decorated chancel and unusual early 18th-century tiered box pews in the nave.

COTTESBROOKE
All Saints
9m/15km N. of Northampton SP 7073
A secluded church of *c.* 1300, much restored, but retaining Georgian fittings, including a three-decker pulpit, box pews, and an extraordinary two-storeyed family pew with fireplace; 17th- and 18th-century monuments.

CRANSLEY
St Andrew
3m/4km S.W. of Kettering SP 8376
Riverside setting. A medieval church of various dates with large Perpendicular ashlar tower and recessed spire, Decorated nave and chancel, and an 18th-century baluster font.

CRICK
St Margaret
6m/10km E. of Rugby SP 5872
Much fine Decorated work including an enriched broach spire; Norman font unusually supported on kneeling figures.

CROUGHTON
All Saints
4m/6km S.W. of Brackley SP 5433
Norman and Early English with good woodwork and an extensive series of early 14th-century wall-paintings of Marian themes, the Life of Christ, and the Last Judgement.

DAVENTRY
Holy Cross
12m/19km W. of Northampton SP 5762
Impressive town church of 1752–8 by David Hiorn of Warwick. Built of ironstone with giant pilasters, Gibbsian surrounds and arched windows, the whole is surmounted by a rusticated tower and obelisk spire. Galleried interior has Tuscan columns supporting plaster groin vaults and retains a Doric reredos and delicately wrought pulpit and reader's desk. Glass by Wailes

EARLS BARTON
All Saints
4m/6km S.W. of Wellingborough SP 8563
Celebrated Saxon tower with long-and-short quoins and extensive stripwork decoration. A massive and beautiful work, redolent of all that is best in the Anglo-Saxon tradition. Here the debate about the purpose of such towers is finely focused; perhaps this was the nave of the early church, as revealed by excavation at Barton on Humber. Later work includes a good Norman S. doorway, a restored 15th-century screen, and a splendid 17th-century pulpit.

EAST CARLTON
St Peter
4m/6km W. of Corby SP 8389
Fine view over the Welland Valley. Built in 1788, and a remarkable instance of Gothic Survival with nice quatrefoil decorations, pointed arches, and fluted capitals. Inside are a two-decker pulpit, box pews, and heraldic glass.

EASTON MAUDIT
St Peter & St Paul
6m/10km S. of Wellingborough SP 8858
A mainly Decorated church with fine W. tower and a graceful steeple supported by flying buttresses with openwork quatrefoils. Bold monument of 1631, the canopy dramatically upheld by lifesize bedesmen.

EASTON NESTON
St Mary
½m/1km N.E. of Towcester SP 7049
13th-century, but a good deal of Perpendicular work. Fittings and monuments of Classical character; pulpit, communion rail, and box pews. Impressive hatchments and monuments.

EDGCOTE
St James
5m/8km N.E. of Banbury SP 5047
Park setting. Tiny medieval and later church with 18th-century furnishings and a remarkable series of Chauncey monuments, including four by Rysbrack.

FAWSLEY
St Mary the Virgin
4m/6km S. of Daventry SP 5656
Set above a lake in the park where Charles I hunted before riding to Naseby. Remote and unspoiled, with Knightley monuments and beautiful carved late-medieval bench-ends. Some old glass, Flemish and heraldic.

FINEDON
St Mary the Virgin
3m/4km N.E. of Wellingborough SP 9272
Stately Decorated church of ironstone with grey-stone dressings. Handsome chancel with five-light E. window. There is a strainer arch across the nave, as at Rushden, and a richly decorated organ case of 1717 by Shrider.

FOTHERINGHAY
St Mary and All Saints
4m/6km N.E. of Oundle TL 0693
A charming village with a fine old inn and Plantaganet connections. Nearby is the mound that marks the site of the castle where Mary Queen of Scots was executed. The fragments of a great 15th-century collegiate church, of which only the nave and tower remain, are themselves an impressive landmark to this part of the Nene Valley, with flying buttresses and a great deal of glass. The great octagonal lantern is such as Wyatt must have dreamed of when working on his tower at Fonthill Abbey. The base of the tower at Fotheringhay opens three ways into the body of the church and is fan-vaulted. Inside, the 18th-century fittings include an attractive reredos with decalogue and creed in gold, after the fashion of the time. The pulpit, a gift from Edward IV who refounded the college, and the Perpendicular font are noteworthy.

GAYTON
St Mary
4m/6km N. of Towcester SP 7054
In ruinous condition in 1815, it has since been extensively but well restored. Inside are a Jacobean pulpit, carved medieval misericords, 14th-century wooden effigy of Philip Gayton, and the Tanfield tomb, with wife and 18 children. Across the road is the curious cruciform Tudor manor.

GEDDINGTON
St Mary Magdalene
3m/4km N.E. of Kettering SP 8983
Medieval church with interesting evidence of the Anglo-Saxon nave provided by neat triangular-headed arcades on the side walls. An unusual Gothic Survival screen dated 1618 and, of course, the celebrated Eleanor Cross at the centre of the village.

GREAT BRINGTON
St Mary

6m/10km N.W. of Northampton SP 6664
A good, sober 13th-century church with conventional arcades and small country clerestory, with a modest 'English type' timber ceiling. The canopied tomb of Sir John Spencer, d. 1522, is therefore of unexpected magnificence, as are all the other Spencer monuments.

GRETTON
St James the Great

4m/6km N. of Corby SP 8994
The Perpendicular tower dominates the Welland Valley. Splendid Norman pillars in nave, Decorated aisles and chancel, fine dog-tooth carving. Chancel was raised in the late 17th century to accommodate the Hatton vault. Queen Anne panelling, altar rails, and Hatton monuments.

HIGHAM FERRERS
St Mary the Virgin

4m/6km E. of Wellingborough SP 9668
An old limestone town in which a narrow side street gives the first view of the rich crocketed steeple of the church, with its pierced parapet, flying buttresses, and deep Early English mouldings. The 13th-century W. tower has a carved doorway reminiscent of the style of Westminster Abbey, c. 1260. Internally, the church is a double building; 13th-century on the S., 14th-century on the N. There is much good carved woodwork, old and modern, the latter by Comper. Henry Chichele, Archbishop of Canterbury and founder of All Souls College, Oxford, was born here in 1362, and gave the stalls and choir screen to the church. He also endowed the fine Perpendicular chantry chapel; a detached building to the W. used for centuries as the Grammar School. He also built Chichele College here, now in ruins, and the bedehouse on the S. side of the churchyard.

HINTON-IN-THE-HEDGES
Holy Trinity

2m/3km W. of Brackley SP 5536
Norman W. tower, early 14th-century N. doorway, and some pretty 16th-century carving round the S. door; 15th-century stained glass and a good 16th-century brass inscription plate.

IRTHLINGBOROUGH
St Peter

4m/6km N.E. of Wellingborough SP 9470
One of the boot and shoe towns of Northants., but wedded to the country tradition, it retains a market cross and a great bridge across the Nene, as well as the medieval church. The 14th-century tower, rebuilt in 1887–93, is practically divorced from the rest of the building and, with octagonal lantern, is reminiscent of a lighthouse.

KELMARSH
St Denys

5m/8km S. of Market Harborough SP 7379
A medieval church with N. chapel remodelled in 1638–9; the E. window has remarkable tracery of lozenges and circles. Apart from this, the interior of the building was dramatically refurbished by J. K. Colling in 1874; pink granite piers, foliate capitals and, in the chancel, blind arcading, mosaic, and Roman marble panels.

KETTERING
SP 8678
St Peter & St Paul

The steeple, soaring above the busy town, is justly famed. The Perpendicular tower and spire are from the same school of design as Oundle, and while the treatment is more restrained, the silhouette is more satisfying. The body of the church is long and low by comparison. The clean horizontal lines at the eaves without pinnacles blend well with the lead roofs and Barnack stone.

KING'S CLIFFE
All Saints

5m/8km W. of Wansford TL 0097
A typical mixture of architectural styles from 12th to 15th centuries with central Norman tower and 13th-century spire. Some 15th-century carving and fragments of medieval glass from Fotheringhay. William Law, author of *A Serious Call to a Devout and Holy Life*, lived here for many years and founded the schools and library.

KING'S SUTTON
St Peter & St Paul

4m/6km S.E. of Banbury SP 4936
The church is famous for its spire, richly ornamented and rising 100 feet above the flying buttresses at its base; it is hardly surpassed in the county in its soaring grace.

Screen by Sir Giles Gilbert Scott, who restored the church in 1866.

LAMPORT
All Saints
9m/15km N. of Northampton SP 7574
13th-century with a delightfully chaste N. chapel of 1672; the whole extensively and tastefully classicized by W. Smith in 1740. Splendid Isham monuments.

LOWICK
St Peter
2m/3km N.W. of Thrapston SP 9780
A small village, its glory evidently departed save for the 15th-century church with pinnacled lantern tower which dominates the group. It has beautiful figured 14th-century glass and remarkable effigies on the 15th-century Greene monument. Among the later sculpture is a Westmacott work of 1843 commemorating the 5th Duke of Dorset.

MARSTON TRUSSELL
St Nicholas
3m/4km W. of Market Harborough SP 6985
Tall Perpendicular tower, S. arcade of *c.* 1300, an 18th-century pulpit, and a monument of 1612 to a London merchant who died in 'Mosco' in Russia.

MIDDLETON CHENEY
All Saints
3m/4km E. of Banbury SP 4941
Decorated with Perpendicular spire. The steeply roofed porch is built entirely of interlocking stones; 15th-century painted ceiling and pulpit restored with the rest of the church by Sir Giles Gilbert Scott in 1865. A Victorian rector was connected with the Pre-Raphaelite Movement and there are important windows here by Rossetti, Ford Madox Brown, Burne-Jones, Simeon Solomon, Webb, and Morris himself. These include the original of Burne-Jones's 'Six Days of Creation'.

NORTHAMPTON
SP 7560
All Saints, market place
Only the tower survives of the much larger medieval church. The rebuilding after a fire in 1675 is ascribed to Henry Bell of King's Lynn. The domed Classical interior owes something to Wren's St Mary-at-Hill in the City of London, but it is a homely provincial version, much restored in the 19th century.

Holy Sepulchre, Sheep Street
One of the five surviving round churches in England, owing its character and dedication to the inspiration of the Crusaders. The early 12th-century round part of the church is the original nave. The present nave was built half a century later and formed, to which aisles were added during the next two centuries. The result is a disjointed exterior, but the interior has a peculiar fascination that belongs to any rarity. The festive chancel and outer walls, except the round part and the S. aisle, were added by Sir Giles Gilbert Scott in 1860–4.

St Giles, St Giles Street
A big, golden ironstone medieval church with a central tower and the only peal of 10 bells in the county. There are chained books and an excellent E. window by Clayton & Bell, 1876.

St Matthew, Kettering Road
By M. Holding, 1891–3, in the manner of his master, J. L. Pearson. Large and prosperous, with a tall steeple and vaulted polygonal apse. Good fittings and glass as well as Henry Moore's 'Madonna and Child' and Graham Sutherland's 'Crucifixion'.

St Peter, Marefair
A grand Norman church, the rich arcades with alternating supports of quatrefoil and collared round shafts. Aisles rebuilt in the 14th century; the stocky tower, rebuilt in the 17th century, was cut into the symmetrical Norman arcades. The chancel is a weak invention of Scott, in whose time the church was smartened up to suit the conventions of the 19th century. Superb 12th-century sepulchral slab.

OUNDLE
TL 0388
St Peter
Set in the heart of a small, unspoilt town of stone and slate, the church large and opulent. Its chiefest glory is its Decorated steeple, rebuilt in 1634. This is a true piece of architecture; the massive surfaces of the tower are vertically panelled to carry the eye to the spire above. The interior was spoilt by scraping in the 19th century, but the pulpit and brass eagle lectern are both 15th-century.

PASSENHAM
St Guthlac
½m/1km S.W. of Stony Stratford SP 7839
Decorated tower, the upper parts, like the

barrel-roofed chancel, rebuilt *c.* 1626. Splendid 17th-century fittings include delicately carved stalls, W. gallery with Ionic columns, and wall-paintings of patriarchs and prophets. Good monument to Sir Robert Banastre, d. 1649, who was responsible for all this.

POLEBROOK
All Saints
2m/3km E. of Oundle TL 0687
Interesting late 12th- and early 13th-century work with blank arcading, stiff-leaf capitals, dog-toothing, and one of the best 13th-century broach spires in the county.

RAUNDS
St Peter
6m/10km N.E. of Wellingborough SP 9972
Ornate 13th-century W. tower and good broach spire. Superb six-light E. window of *c.* 1275 and vigorous 15th-century wall-paintings, well restored.

ROCKINGHAM
St Leonard
3m/4km N.W. of Corby SP 8691
The wide village street climbs up from the Welland to Rockingham Castle, with thatch and stone cottages set against wooded background. The church is a 19th-century rebuild but preserves the 17th- and 18th-century Watson monuments and a piece of carving by James Paine. The memorial by William Palmer to Margaret Watson, d. 1713, is one of the few Baroque monuments by an English sculptor.

ROTHWELL
Holy Trinity
4m/6km W. of Kettering SP 8181
Large cruciform Norman church, now mainly 13th-century, with a famous crypt or charnel-house under the S. aisle containing the bones of some 1,500 people.

RUSHDEN
St Mary
4m/6km E. of Wellingborough SP 9566
Grand Perpendicular church with a prominent strainer arch across the nave, cp. Finedon. Some good 15th-century figured glass and medieval ironwork on the doors.

SLAPTON
St Botolph
4m/6km W. of Towcester SP 6446
Primitive, small and unspoiled; basically Norman and Early English, the chancel lower than the nave. Good wall-paintings of *c.* 1400 depicting diverse saints.

STANFORD-ON-AVON
St Nicholas
6m/10km N.E. of Rugby SP 5878
A light and spacious 14th-century church, the nave cleared of pews, and hatchments used intelligently as decoration. Delectable 17th-century organ case, expelled by Cromwell from Whitehall, perched on discreet Tuscan W. gallery. Prolific 14th-century and later glass, Cave family monuments, and linenfold panelling. Archbishop Laud was once rector here.

STANION
St Peter
2m/3km S.E. of Corby SP 9186
Perpendicular W. tower with slender broach spire above stone village. Highly decorated 15th-century font and good 18th-century furnishings.

STANWICK
St Laurence
2m/3km N.E. of Higham Ferrers SP 9871
Distinctive octagonal 13th-century tower with lofty Nene Valley spire; richly composed with excellent mouldings.

STEANE
St Peter
3m/4km N.W. of Brackley SP 5539
Little chapel set in a park, built by Sir Thomas Crewe in 1620, and appearing at first sight completely medieval. Remarkable interior with box pews and two-decker pulpit left behind by the Age of Reason. 17th- and 18th-century Crewe family monuments, including work by the Christmas brothers.

STOKE DOYLE
St Rumbold
1m/2km S.W. of Oundle TL 0286
Rustic Georgian church of 1722–5 by an unknown artist, retaining original pulpit, pews and font. Contemporary monuments, including a Rysbrack of *c.* 1714, sustain the atmosphere of the time.

STOWE-NINE-CHURCHES
St Michael
6m/10km S.E. of Daventry SP 6456
Traditionally, the name relates to eight attempts to build the church elswhere in Saxon

times, the Devil removing the stones each night to the present site. Certainly there is a tall Saxon W. tower, though the rest is mainly Perpendicular, much restored inside. Beautiful effigy of Lady Carey, d. 1620, by Nicholas Stone, and a sumptuous wall monument to Dr Turner, d. 1714, by Thomas Stayner.

SULGRAVE
St James the Less
6m/10km N. of Brackley SP 5545
Compact medieval village church, Decorated and Perpendicular, much overhauled in the 19th century. Brass to Lawrence Washington, d. 1584; a goal for pilgrims.

TICHMARSH
St Mary the Virgin
2m/3km N.E. of Thrapston TL 0279
A quaint unspoilt village church with a celebrated Perpendicular tower, curiously West Country in character, with coupled windows in the upper storey and profuse pinnacles. Pickering family monuments and pew. Dryden was bred here and loved to return in later years.

TOWCESTER
St Lawrence
8m/12km S.W. of Northampton SP 6948
Tall ironstone Perpendicular tower; 15th-century effigy of Archdeacon Sponne, local benefactor; the head is restored and underneath there is a particularly unsavoury skeleton. Old books include a Treacle Bible – 'Is there not triacle [balm] in Gilead?' Gay French 18th-century organ, once at Fonthill Abbey. Benedetto Gaetano, who held this living, became Pope Boniface VIII in 1294; a remarkable circumstance.

WAKERLEY
St John the Baptist
7m/11km S.W. of Stamford SP 9599
Agreeable church in a valley. Decorated W. tower with crocketed Perpendicular spire. But the real joy here is the Norman chancel arch, a wondrous thing of knights and castles, monsters and foliate trails – delightful.
R.C.F.

WARKTON
St Edmund
2m/3km N.E. of Kettering SP 8979
Fine Perpendicular tower. Montague monuments by Roubiliac, van Gelder and Campbell, all of the finest in this otherwise undistinguished church.

WARKWORTH
St Mary the Virgin
2m/3km E. of Banbury SP 4840
In the fields. Mostly Decorated but much restored. Resplendent mid-14th-century tomb chest and effigy of Sir John Lyons and assorted Chetwode brasses.

WARMINGTON
St Mary the Blessed Virgin
3m/4km N.E. of Oundle TL 0791
A consistent Early English church with a celebrated Northants. broach spire. The rib-vaulted nave ceiling is in timber throughout, a pleasant medieval conceit and a useful precedent for Victorians who wanted boarded ceilings for cheapness. Perpendicular woodwork includes a rood screen, restored painted pulpit, and some bench-ends. There is a good Jacobean screen to the N. aisle.

WELDON
St Mary the Virgin
2m/3km E. of Corby SP 9289
Decorated W. tower rebuilt in 18th century; medieval nave and sumptuous late 13th-century S. porch with wall arcades and triple shafts. Early 16th-century Flemish glass in W. window.

WELLINGBOROUGH
All Hallows, market place
SP 8968
Fine old town church, originally Norman – see the S. doorway – but now mostly 13th–15th-century. Good Perpendicular roofs with bosses, screens and stalls with carved misericords. Important modern glass by Piper, Hone and Reyntiens.
St Mary the Virgin, Knox Road
Comper's superlative answer to the challenge of the incomparable Nene Valley churches. Tall Perpendicular and fan-vaulted with a bold tower, contrasting on the skyline with the spire of the medieval church but using the same traditional ironstone. The sumptuous furnishings combine all that is best in Comper's work – colour, scale and proportion – and exemplify his insistence that a church should be timeless and atmospheric. Building went on from 1918 to

1930, and the E. window of the N. chapel is a memorial to Lady Comper.

WHISTON
St Mary the Virgin
6m/10km E. of Northampton SP 8460
The church pleasantly sited on a wooded hillside. The tower a heady design from the early 16th century with the stone dressings and parapet light in contrast to the dark facing of the rest of the tower. The rest of the building sober by comparison, with characteristic timber ceilings and the ample Perpendicular windows of the time. The plan is box-like without a structural chancel. Fittings include some original benches and Classical monumental sculpture by Nollekens.

WICKEN
St John the Evangelist
5m/8km N.E. of Buckingham SP 7439
A remote and pretty village with a Gothic church 'designed and built', according to the inscription, by Thomas Prowse, the local squire, in 1758–67. An odd design with Frenchified capitals and plaster fan vaults, but redeemed by Cheere's excellent Rococo monument to the Hosiers, Squire Prowse's parents-in-law.

Northumberland

Introduction

The last seaward miles of Tyne and Tweed, Cheviot and Pennine tops, a seventy-mile-long stretch of coast – and, within them, the most northerly county of England: Northumberland. In the south-eastern corner a tangle of heavy industry, coalmining, shipbuilding, engineering: a conurbation, sullen, soiled and sordid, but containing, nevertheless, England's finest industrial city, the provincial capital, Newcastle. The industrial area less than a tenth of the county, yet carrying eighty per cent of its population; and the county, even so, one of the least populous of all in relation to its size – which gives some indication of how quiet the rest is. It is by far the largest tract of deeply quiet country in England. Outside the industrial corner, only three small country towns, less than half a dozen villages, and the rest of the population in scattered hamlets and in farmhouses and cottages. The coast lined by golden sands, sand dunes, basalt cliffs, with rocky islands off-shore. The coastal plain, where the main-line railway goes to Scotland, stock-rearing and mixed-farming country. The hills (and all over the county you are conscious of the hills) high, wide and lonely; not whale-backed and heathery (except the Pennines in the south-west) but mostly grassy hills, pitching into individual summits. The richly wooded valley of the Tyne in the gap between Cheviots and Pennines: narrower dales running up into the folds of the hills. A great national forest making a new kind of country out of the mid-stretch of Cheviot. A very varied county; a very individual county.

Its history and frontier character are shown, inevitably, in its old buildings. In the Roman wall striding along the top of the crags above the waters of dark loughs; in scores of castles and peel-towers, vast like Alnwick, small like Holy Island, ruined like Simonburn; in fortified rectories, as at Corbridge and Elsdon; and in semi-fortified churches, too, as at Edlington. And in what has gone as well as in what remains. Bolam church, with its Saxon tower, standing in complete solitude where once was a town with a castle and 'two-hundred slated houses enclosing a green'. Bywell, also once a flourishing town, with, now, two churches, a castle, a medieval market cross, a hall, a vicarage, all in a wooded loop of the Tyne, and not another building in sight.

Old, wild, wide, quiet, remote. That is Northumberland beyond the conurbation.

T.S.

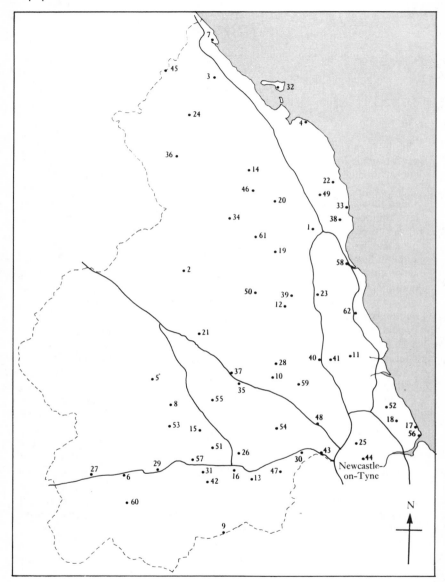

Selected List of Churches

ALNWICK
St Michael and All Angels
17m/27km N. of Morpeth NU 1813
Beautifully situated on the top of a hillside, the church embodies the most important 15th-century work in Northumberland. Aisles extend to total length of chancel, thus forming a plan rather square in character; 14th-century effigies of great beauty; fragments of 15th-century glass, including a delightful example of a Pelican in her Piety. Painted Royal Arms of first Hanoverian period.

ALWINTON
St Michael and All Angels
9m/15km W. of Rothbury NT 9206
13th-century chancel raised above nave by 10 steps on this sloping site; the rest was rebuilt by Pickering in 1851.

ANCROFT
St Anne
5m/8km S. of Berwick upon Tweed NU 0045
Norman nave S. wall with corbel table and decayed but important doorway; 14th-century fortified 'vicar's pele' tower built into W. end. The rest Victorian.

BAMBURGH
St Aidan
5m/8km E. of Belford NU 1834
Spacious setting on coast; 13th–14th-century structure with fine 13th-century crypt beneath chancel. Royal Arms painted on canvas, third Hanoverian period. Gothic churchyard monument to Grace Darling, 1846.

BELLINGHAM
St Cuthbert
14m/22km N.W. of Hexham NY 8383
Fine Early English chancel with lancets. The rest a Gothic Survival remodelling, after 1609, with remarkable stone barrel vaulting over nave and transept.

BELTINGHAM
St Cuthbert
3m/4km W. of Haydon NY 7863
Prettily set in a hamlet near Georgian house.

Small Perpendicular church of *c.* 1500; revived in 1691 and, with a heavier hand, in 1884.

BERWICK UPON TWEED
NT 9953
Holy Trinity
A mixed Gothic and Classical building of considerable architectural interest. It was built by J. Young of London, mason, in 1648–52, during the Commonwealth. Inside is a 17th-century gallery and pulpit with tester; the reredos is an early design by Lutyens. The lettering on one or two small brass plates of 18th-century date is worth noting.

BIRTLEY
St Giles
4m/6km N.E. of Presteigne SO 3669
Small, aisleless 12th-century church, Victorianized in 1884; 8th-century incised stone bearing a cross as found in the Lindisfarne Gospels.

BLANCHLAND
St Mary the Virgin
9m/15km S. of Hexham NY 9650
Premonstratensian foundation. Fine tower and unusual L-plan church remodelled from ruins of 13th-century N. transept of abbey church in 18th century. Pretentious 19th-century woodwork; fragments of late-medieval glass; monumental slabs. Beautiful, largely 18th-century village.

BOLAM
St Andrew
3m/4km N. of Belsay NZ 0982
The church is beautifully set in the midst of undulating parkland, near the site of an abandoned village. Pre-Conquest tower of lovely proportion and much Norman work. Mutilated recumbent effigy of a knight, 14th-century. Plain lead glazing of beautiful character, 19th- and 20th-century.

BOTHAL
St Andrew
3m/4km E. of Morpeth NZ 2386
13th–14th-century church in a most

beautiful setting. Extensive fragments of medieval glass *in situ*: one tracery light contains a magnificent rayed rose. Good 17th-century altar rails. Alabaster table-tomb of Ralph, Lord Ogle, and his lady, 16th-century. Good 18th-century headstones.

BRINKBURN
Priory Church of St Peter & St Paul
4m/6km S.E. of Rothbury NZ 1198
Augustinian foundation, set near the banks of the Coquet in wooded countryside. Complete late 12th-century structure, well restored by Thomas Austin in 1858. Long lancet windows have fragments of 13th-century grisaille glass, similar in character to York work.
E.H.

BYWELL
4m/6km S.E. of Corbridge NZ 0461
Two parish churches sited closely together in beautiful wooded setting near River Tyne.
St Andrew
Partly 13th-century, it has the best Saxon tower in the county; square, unbuttressed, with uneven quoins and small round-headed windows.
R.C.F.
St Peter
Large and important 8th-century church remodelled in the 13th century. Splendid Early English E. window of three lancets.

CHILLINGHAM
St Peter
4m/6km E. of Wooler NU 0625
Sited on gentle elevation amongst trees. Simple stone church dating from the 12th century. Chief interest lies in magnificent 15th-century Grey tomb. Font and cover 1670; 17th-century pulpit. Well restored by John Smith, 1966.

CHOLLERTON
St Giles
5m/8km N. of Hexham NY 9371
Tower and chancel are *c.* 1769, Gothicized in 1893. Surprising interior with S. arcade of *c.* 1150 re-using Roman monolithic columns. Roman altar also re-used as a font.

CORBRIDGE
St Andrew
3m/4km E. of Hexham NY 9864
In the centre of the historic country town, alongside a splendidly preserved 14th-

century vicar's pele. Main body of church is 13th-century with good lancet windows. Pre-Conquest tower; the tower arch may well be Roman, re-used from nearby Corstopitum.

CULLERCOATS
St George
located between Tynemouth and Whitley Bay NZ 3670
Beautiful ashlar church in the Early English style by J. L. Pearson, 1882–4. Polygonal apse and dramatically tall steeple. Very dignified rib-vaulted interior with glass by Kempe in strong range of colours.

EARSDON
St Alban
2m/3km W. of Whitley Bay NZ 3272
By J. and B. Green, 1836–7. Dominating position on hillock. Big W. tower, lancets, battlements, and pinnacles. Improbably, two nave windows contain glass depicting the arms of Henry VII and VIII, by Galyon Hone, formerly at Hampton Court.

EDLINGHAM
St John Baptist
5m/8km S.W. of Alnwick NU 1109
In rugged moorland country near the ruined castle. Squat 13th-century W. tower looks like a fortification itself and masks a late-Saxon or earliest-Norman W. end. Later Norman arcade and chancel arch.

EGLINGHAM
St Maurice
6m/10km N.W. of Alnwick NU 1019
Much restored; 13th-century tower; later work includes the interesting early 17th-century Gothic Survival chancel.

ELSDON
St Cuthbert
3m/4km E. of Otterburn NY 9393
Set on large village green. Largely 14th-century with 17th-century quadrant vaults over the narrow aisles and transepts. Large and primitive W. bellcote.

EMBLETON
Holy Trinity
7m/11km N. of Alnwick NU 2332
Broad W. tower of good design; tunnel-vaulted ground stage and bell-openings with Y-tracery of *c.* 1300; 13th-century nave arcades; chancel rebuilt in 1867 by F. R. Wilsdon. Good 14th-century vicar's pele.

FELTON
St Michael and All Angels
8m/12km S. of Alnwick NU 1800
A sprawling and irregular church with a complex building history; mostly 13th–14th-century. Picturesque post-medieval bellcote with pyramid roof.

FORD
St Michael and All Angels
7m/11km N.W. of Wooler NT 9437
Close to the beautiful grounds of the castle in fine open countryside; 13th-century, though much restored by Dobson in 1853. Sturdy Early English bellcote.

GOSFORTH
St Nicholas
2m/3km N. of Newcastle NZ 2468
By John Dodds, 1799. Ashlar stonework and round-headed windows. The aisles with Tuscan arcades were added in 1818 by Dobson, and the chancel rebuilt in 1913.

HALTON
St Andrew
2m/3km N. of Corbridge NY 9967
Set high above the Tyne Valley beside a manor house with 17th-century façade and a tall 14th-century tower. Small, simple and moving church with Norman chancel arch and 17th-century windows.

HALTWHISTLE
Church of the Holy Cross
14m/22km W. of Hexham NY 7064
Towerless church in pleasant setting on slope in the midst of this country town. Well-preserved 13th-century fabric. Plastered interior with stepped sedilia and medieval monuments, including Blenkinsopp effigy of *c.* 1389. Painted chancel roof by Kempe, 1881. Massive 18th-century headstones in churchyard.

HARTBURN
St Andrew
7m/11km W. of Morpeth NZ 0886
In delightful setting near the Hart burn. Essentially 13th-century, though incorporating Saxon masonry. Long chancel with three stepped lancets in the E. wall; 13th-century font. Many excellent 18th-century headstones in churchyard.

HAYDON BRIDGE
St Cuthbert
6m/10km W. of Hexham NY 8464
Plain church of 1796 with nave, narrower chancel, and round-headed windows; W. tower has pagoda roof; 12th-century Old Church ½m/1km to N. has font made from Roman altar.

HEDDON ON THE WALL
St Andrew
7m/11km W. of Newcastle NZ 1366
A very complete Norman church with late-Saxon S.E. nave quoins, impressive 12th-century vaulted sanctuary, and fine zig-zag chancel arch.

HEXHAM
St Andrew
NY 9364
Of great historical importance, as the crypt of the church founded by St Wilfrid in *c.* 675 survives intact; it is barrel-vaulted, of great austerity and grandeur, with many re-used stones bearing Roman inscriptions. Sacked by the Danes in 876, Hexham was eventually refounded as an Augustinian priory in 1113. What remains today is the 12th–13th-century chancel and transepts and the good nave of 1907 by Temple Moore. The interior is rich in medieval features: the unique monks' night staircase, the Saxon Frith stool, 15th-century wooden pulpit, painted screen of Thomas Smithson, prior, 1491–1524, 15th-century stalls and misericords, a chantry chapel, and many effigies.

HOLY ISLAND
St Mary the Virgin
off coast 5m/8km N. of Belford NU 1242
The present church is Early English, with a long chancel and picturesque bellcote. However, above the present chancel arch can be seen the remains of its Saxon predecessor. The church stands immediately to the W. of the ruins of the Priory, on one of the most hallowed spots in the realm. It was here that St Aidan came in 635 at the invitation of King Oswald to found his monastery. Here in *c.* 700 the Lindisfarne Gospels were created. From here the light of the Faith gleamed far and wide, until in 875 the monastery was laid waste by the Danes.

HOWICK
St Michael

5m/8km N.E. of Alnwick NU 2517
Classical chapel of 1746 with round-arched windows and pilasters; neo-Norman trimmings, W. front and bellcote were added by F. J. Francis in 1849. Gothic tomb of Earl Grey, c. 1850.

INGRAM
St Michael

4m/6km N.W. of Whittingham NU 0116
Early Norman church with W. tower remodelled in 13th century and restored in 1879. Plain 11th-century tower arch; 14th-century chancel arch; carved font of 1662.

KIRKHARLE
St Wilfred

2m/3km S.E. of Kirkwhelpington NZ 0182
Originally 14th-century, but most windows renewed in 1884; on N. side of chancel, tracery of c. 1315–30 survives. Big Perpendicular font with shields, brought from Newcastle.

KIRKNEWTON
St Gregory

5m/8km W. of Wooler NT 9130
Set at the foot of hill country near Cheviot. Small, low, probably 13th-century chancel with unusual vault which springs a few feet from the floor to a rounded point at apex; similar vault in S. transept. Primitive but beautiful late-Saxon stone carving on N. side of chancel arch depicting Adoration of the Magi. All else is of the 1860s by Dobson.

KIRKWHELPINGTON
St Bartholomew

9m/15km S.E. of Otterburn NY 9984
Set in small village at the foot of vast moorland. Long and low with a squat tower. Much 12th- and early 13th-century work remains; 18th-century chancel with plastered walls and ceiling, sash glazing. Splendid lettering on 18th-century ledgers in chancel floor.

LONG HOUGHTON
St Peter

4m/6km E. of Alnwick NU 2415
Austere chancel arch dates from about the time of the Conquest; squat later-Norman W. tower has neo-Norman top of 1873. S. arcade c. 1200.

LONGFRAMLINGTON
St Mary the Virgin

5m/8km E. of Rothbury NU 1301
Late 12th-century nave and chancel; waterleaf capitals on the S. doorway and shafted chancel arch. Restored in the Norman taste.

MITFORD
St Mary Magdalene

2m/3km W. of Morpeth NZ 1785
Church in lovely setting near ruined castle. Norman N. arcade, the 13th-century chancel long and distinguished with shafted lancets.

MORPETH
St Mary, town centre

NZ 1986
A good example of 14th-century work, so little seen in Northumberland. Original roofs and iron knocker on S. door. The E. window depicts Tree of Jesse and scenes from the Life of Our Lady; though restored by Wailes, it is the most complete medieval glazing in the county.

NEWBIGGIN
St Bartholomew

1m/2km W. of Blanchland NZ 3187
Dramatic headland site hints at Celtic origins. Early 13th-century – see the E. arcade piers with nail-head decoration; Decorated chancel and spire, one of only two in the county; Royal Arms, painted, first Hanoverian period.

NEWBURN
St Michael and All Angels

5m/8km W. of Newcastle NZ 1665
Beautiful church of rubble stonework, now happily stripped of a good deal of 19th-century fussiness. Early Norman W. tower, late 12th-century N. arcade; chancel remodelled in 13th century.

NEWCASTLE
NZ 2464
St Andrew, Newgate Street
12th-century chancel arch and nave arcading; 15th-century font cover of elaborate design. Early Georgian S. porch. Royal Arms of George III.
St Anne, City Road
By William Newton, 1768. Rectangular church with apse and colonnaded W. portico. Contemporary painting shows

church of light stonework against background of green fields; now black encompassed by mass of houses and industry.

St George, Osborne Road, Jesmond
By T. R. Spence, 1888. Fascinating blend of 13th-century and Italian Renaissance styles with much high-quality Arts and Crafts decoration. Internal W. wall entirely covered in Caen stone tracery with bronze of St George by Spence. Mosaic-lined chancel; glass by J. W. Brown and C. R. Mitchell.

Clayton Memorial Church (Jesmond Parish Church), Jesmond Road
By John Dobson, 1858–61. Impressive essay in late Early English style with large tower and pinnacles. Inside are octagonal piers and rather old-fashioned galleries.

St John the Baptist, Grainger Street
Largely 14th–15th-century with prominent Perpendicular tower; 15th-century font cover and impressive 17th-century pulpit. Fragments of medieval glass, chief among them a 14th-century shield of arms of Newcastle; 15th-century shields of Thornton and Percy.

St Matthew, Summerhill Street
By R. J. Johnson; begun in 1877, but not finally completed until 1904. Bodleyesque Perpendicular with a grand tower and rich pinnacles. Refined lofty interior with sumptuous stone reredos.

NORHAM

St Cuthbert
7m/11km S.W. of Berwick upon Tweed NT 8497
At the far end of the village from the magnificent Norman castle. Church of reddish stone with Norman chancel and S. arcade; massive stonework for a church of this scale; 14th-century effigy and Stuart Royal Arms.

OLD BEWICK

Chapel of the Holy Trinity
6m/10km S.E. of Wooler NU 0621
Set in remote and beautiful hill country. Small Norman apsidal chancel and nave, relatively complete in fabric and entirely complete in atmosphere.

OVINGHAM

St Mary the Virgin
1m/2km N.W. of Prudhoe NZ 0863
Handsome church near delightful vicarage dating from the 15th and 17th centuries. The church has a pre-Conquest tower and magnificent 13th-century nave, transepts

and chancel with tall lancets, giving strong vertical emphasis. Fine black marble armorial slab of 1723 in chancel.

PONTELAND

St Mary the Virgin
7m/11km N.W. of Newcastle NZ 1672
12th-century work in tower; 13th-century N. transept of great individual character with long lancets deeply splayed; 14th-century windows in chancel containing many fragments of contemporary glass, chiefly heraldic. Beautiful undecorated 14th-century font. Plain lead glazing of great beauty, *c.* 1861.

ROCK

St Philip & St James
5m/8km N. of Alnwick NU 2020
In parkland setting. Good small Norman church with fine mid-12th-century shafted chancel arch. Rather suffers from apse and N. aisle added in the 1860s.

ROTHBURY

All Saints
11m/18km S.W. of Alnwick NU 0501
Delightful Northumbrian town set amongst hills; 13th-century chancel and transepts, much rebuilt in 1850. Important font with bowl of 1664 and shaft made of splendid carved Saxon cross shaft, *c.* 800.

ST OSWALD-IN-LEE

St Oswald
3m/4km N. of Hexham NY 6995
On line of Roman wall with view over hills. Chapel of 1737 entirely Gothicized by W. S. Hicks in 1878; good interior with traceried roof and coved rood screen. Here St Oswald won the decisive battle of Heavenfield, 635, against the heathen Britons.

SEATON DELAVAL

Our Lady
4m/6km S. of Blyth NZ 3276
Set in grounds of Vanbrugh's house. Small Norman church of great beauty with zig-zag chancel arch and chancel extension of *c.* 1330. W. porch added in 1895; 14th-century effigies.

SIMONBURN

St Mungo
7m/11km N.W. of Hexham NY 8773
Set in a beautiful village in the North Tyne Valley in an enormous parish containing a

vast area of moorland. Mostly 13th-century, the long chancel has a double piscina and windows by Salvin, 1860. Numerous fragments of early stonework; monument of 1625 to Cuthbert Ridley, rector.

STAMFORDHAM
St Mary the Virgin
6m/10km N. of Prudhoe NZ 0772
13th-century, extensively restored by Benjamin Ferrey, 1848. Sturdy W. tower and long chancel, both with lancets. Two medieval effigies and 14th-century carving of Crucifixion.

THOCKRINGTON
St Aidan
9m/15km N. of Hexham NY 9579
Set on a hillock in open, sweeping country. Small Norman church with medieval alterations; 13th-century chancel of exquisite proportion with vaulted ceiling.

TYNEMOUTH
Christ Church
NZ 3669
A fine Classical town church of 1792; chancel and apse added in 1869. Ashlar with splendid square tower and dignified plastered interior with galleries. Original wooden font and clear glass, the leading based on the traditional Northumbrian pattern. Organ now in W. gallery.

WARDEN
St Michael and All Angels
2m/3km N.W. of Hexham NY 9166
11th-century unbuttressed W. tower with irregular quoins and splayed slit windows. Good 13th-century transepts; nave rebuilt in 1765.

WARKWORTH
St Lawrence
1m/2km N. of Amble NU 2406
Church and castle set at opposite ends of a long, broad street. Large and relatively complete Norman church with remarkable vaulted chancel, the ribs enriched with zig-zag carving. Good chancel arch with shafts and scalloped capitals; 14th-century broach spire, 15th-century porch with parvise, and exquisite 17th-century wrought-iron rails. Fragments of 15th-century glass and Royal Arms of James II.

WHALTON
St Mary Magdalene
5m/8km S.W. of Morpeth NZ 1381
Early Norman W. tower, 13th-century nave and chancel. Notable for the heavy Early English dog-tooth ornament on a pier in the arcade of the Ogle Chapel.

WHITFIELD
Holy Trinity
6m/10km S.W. of Haydon Bridge NY 7758
By A. B. Higham of Newcastle, 1858–9. Ambitious Early English church with fine crossing tower and spire. Austere interior relieved by delicate naturalistic carving. Glass by Powell & Sons.

WHITTINGHAM
St Bartholomew
6m/10km N. of Rothbury NU 0611
Pre-Conquest lower parts of tower with massive plain arch to nave. Medieval work elsewhere much altered by John Green in 1840; the plain lead glazing is his best work.

WIDDRINGTON
Holy Trinity
7m/11km N.E. of Morpeth NZ 2595
Late 12th-century N. arcade, otherwise mostly 14th-century, including the chancel E. window with flowing tracery and the Easter Sepulchre.

Nottinghamshire

Introduction

Nottinghamshire, south of the Trent, along the Fosse Way, is of a piece with Leicestershire, with gentle hills, ridged meadows, and bramble and dog-rose hedges; many of the villages here have shrunk during the past two centuries, and some of the churches have been shorn of aisles.

The western part of the county lies on coal and is well populated; some of the colliery villages are nicely grouped on hill-tops around new or enlarged churches, but in the main the scenery is unattractive, apart from a few square miles in the upper Erewash valley and the pure medieval landscape that contains the ruins of Beauvale Priory. On the limestone of the north-west both buildings and landscape are more austere, with dry-stone walls in the Derbyshire manner and even a quite precipitous gorge at Creswell Crags. The mining settlements to the north of Worksop are scarcely distinguishable from their neighbours in the West Riding. The 'Carrs' of the north-east are rich fens. In the east, along the Lincolnshire border, the Trent flows through a fairly rich mixed agricultural landscape which is dominated by the distant west front of Lincoln Cathedral and enlivened by the Great North Road and its attendant railway; the houses here are of good brick and many of them are roofed with pantiles. Enormous power stations have been put here, heated by coal from the west of the county and cooled by Trent water. The centre of the county, between Mansfield, Worksop and Tuxford, presents a curious contrast between the intense vitality of the colliery villages and the air of death which hangs about the last oaks of Sherwood Forest and the few remaining great houses of the Dukeries.

In its landscape and in the character and dialect of its people, Nottinghamshire belongs partly to the Midlands and partly to the North. What unity it has comes from the county town, whose undisputed supremacy within the county borders, since the time when they were the boundaries of a Danish military district, contrasts markedly with the far shakier authority of its neighbours, Lincoln, Derby, and York. The city's cattle market, the agricultural shows at Wollaton Park, and the annual goose fair, still bring in the country folk from the whole of the southern half of the county. It is, of course, an industrial town; but most of its industries are of the kind that make no smoke, and that occupy enormous numbers of young women. Most of the county's men are employed in the collieries to the north-east, and hundreds of buses cross the city's north-eastern boundary each weekday in each direction. The small towns of the north – Mansfield, Sutton, Worksop and Retford – play a similar role in the life of the county; but they are infinitely poorer than Nottingham, both in their architecture and in their entertainments. Newark, in the south-east, is a wholly admirable town; its castle and its Civil War fortifications are impressive; and its market-place deserves a whole chapter to itself.

There are few large churches in the county. Southwell Minster is, of course, in a class of its own, and the only two parish churches of impressive size are St Mary, Nottingham, and St Mary Magdalene, Newark. Worksop and Blyth are in the separate category of 'monastic remains' and are easily the two finest churches in the north of the county. The small churches are often well-sited, and the Nottinghamshire village of red-brick and pantiled cottages grouped around its grey church makes an attractive picture. Spires punctuate the rolling landscape south of the Trent, but in the north the medieval churches are normally low-towered, squat and rather square. There are no grand and urbane Classical churches of the Derby Cathedral type, merely a few quite good 18th-century rectangles, put up to replace, as modestly as possible, decayed medieval structures. But there are two examples of this period, Papplewick and Ossington, which have a very individual right to attention. Victorian building and rebuilding were extensive; after the grey-brick 'regulation' churches of the early 19th century, red brick was widely used. The new colliery towns grew quickly, and churches were put up quickly to meet the need; few are worthy of attention. Of the famous Victorian architects only three are worthily represented: Pearson by the splendidly lavish St Paul's, Daybrook; Bodley by Clumber and Sneinton St Alban; and Comper by inspired restoration work in various places. Of 20th-century churches there is a distinguished example at Woollaton Park, Nottingham by Cecil Howitt, the architect who designed parts of the University and the City Hall.

Good fittings are disappointingly meagre. The best fragments of medieval alabaster are now in the Castle Museum in Nottingham. There are no spectacular wall-paintings. In fact the sober 'workaday' atmosphere of the Midlands is faithfully reproduced in its places of worship; and we find, therefore, a homely, unspectacular beauty which is very appealing.

C.B. and N.H.S.

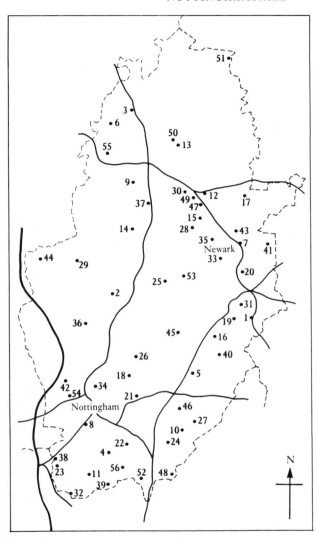

Selected List of Churches

BALDERTON
St Giles
suburb adjoining Newark-on-Trent to S.E. SK 8151
Mostly Early English and Decorated, with crocketed steeple and good Norman N. doorway replete with beak-heads; 15th-century carved bench-ends, pulpit and screen. Some medieval glass in the chancel.

BLIDWORTH
St Mary of the Purification
5m/8km S.E. of Mansfield SK 5956
15th-century tower, but otherwise all of 1739, with round-headed windows and elegant Tuscan S. arcade. Chancel panelling and Georgian pulpit transferred from Southwell. A splendid position on its hilltop.

BLYTH
St Mary & St Martin
6m/10km N.W. of E. Retford SK 6287
A priory fragment, beautifully sited on the village green, and visited by hundreds for its rugged late 11th-century nave. The medieval screen acts as reredos for the altar, with medieval paintings uncovered by Bentley on the E. wall. Outside, the extraordinary design of the shortened E. end is due to its having been used as a menagerie for the Hall in the 18th century.

BUNNY
St Mary the Virgin
7m/11km S. of Nottingham SK 5829
Large, mostly 14th-century church with crocketed spire, panelled parapets and pinnacles. Good Parkyns monuments, including that to the famous Wrestling Baronet, Sir Thomas, d. 1741, who stands ready to fight.

CAR COLSTON
St Mary
2m/3km N.E. of Bingham SK 7142
Splendid mid-14th-century chancel; five-light E. window with cusped flowing tracery, grand sedilia and piscina on the Hawton model with nodding ogee arches. Handsome

altar rail of 1732 has curved central section. Burial place of Dr Robert Thoroton, the Notts. historian.

CARLTON-IN-LINDRICK
St John the Evangelist
3m/4km N. of Worksop SK 5984
Magnificent late-Saxon tower with Perpendicular belfry stage; much Norman work survives; nave arcade; 15th-century Nottingham alabaster reredos in N. chapel.

CARLTON-ON-TRENT
St Mary
6m/10km N. of Newark-on-Trent SK 7963
By G. G. Place, 1851; the tall spire was added in 1871. An impressive church built for John Vere, a London banker; the Early English S. doorway was retained from the earlier church.

CLIFTON
St Mary the Virgin
suburb of Nottingham 3m/4km S.W. of W. Bridgford SK 5534
Mostly 14th-century cruciform church, the interior unfortunately scraped and 're-ordered', but in the N. transept a magnificent collection of tombs of the Clifton family, from the 15th century to the present day.

CLUMBER PARK
St Mary the Virgin
4m/6km S.E. of Worksop SK 6274
By Bodley, 1886–9; a grand work in a sumptuously pious setting. On a cruciform plan and in his favourite flowing Decorated style, one of Bodley's best. Excellent glass by Kempe, superb alabaster altar and chancel screens. The woodwork, alas, was the effort of the Rev. Geldart, commissioned after the 7th Duke of Newcastle fell out with Bodley over the accounts. National Trust.

COLSTON BASSETT
St John the Divine
4m/6km S. of Bingham SK 7033
By A. W. Brewill, 1892. Lavish cruciform church with central spire, built to the

memory of Mrs Knowles, the squire's wife, who reposes in white marble.

EAST LEAKE
St Mary the Virgin
4m/6km N. of Loughborough SK 5526
Well-mannered medieval medley with Norman nave and tower and a 15th-century spire. Inside are 17th-century pews and a rare shawm or vamping horn.

EAST MARKHAM
St John the Baptist
1m/2km N. of Tuxford SK 7472
This is the county's Thaxted, though not so vast, so famous, or so complete. It is Perpendicular, clerestoried, and large for a village. The Comper E. window and wide high altar are in complete accord, and the whole church is faithful to the principles of the 'English Kalendar'. Small grey chamber organ, tapers on brackets, and enough antiquity in wood, brass and glass to fascinate the historically minded. The baseless Jacobean pulpit and the miraculously unearthed altar mensa are appropriate.

EAST RETFORD
St Swithin
27m/43km N.E. of Nottingham SK 7080
Large, dignified Perpendicular church with interesting Gothic Survival fabric built after the fall of the tower in 1651; good Victorian glass and an elaborate reredos.

EDWINSTOWE
St Mary
2m/3km W. of Ollerton SK 6266
Mainly 12th–13th-century; the arresting 12th-century W. tower is surmounted by a strong broach spire and bedecked with 17th-century pinnacles.

EGMANTON
St Mary
1m/2km S. of Tuxford SK 7368
The modest, porchless exterior gives no hint of the pious gaiety within. Here, sponsored by the Duke of Newcastle and executed by Comper, is Anglo-Catholic romanticism at its best. The canopied rood screen dominates the interior, and the colour is repeated on organ casing, font cover, and openwork pulpit. Beyond the screen is less colour and more mystery: the candled shrine of Our Lady of Egmanton and, in front of Comper's E. window, a hanging pyx. The antiquarian

will admire the Norman doorway and font, the 17th-century altar and the fragments of old glass, but these are commonplace; the Comper shrine is superlative.

ELSTON CHAPEL
(dedication unknown)
5m/8km S.W. of Newark-on-Trent SK 7647
In a field and approached up a lane; 12th–14th-century with delightful 1820-ish interior of box pews, pulpit, and reader's desk. Now being restored after sad neglect.
R.C.F.

FLEDBOROUGH
St Gregory
1m/2km S.E. of Ragnall, which is 13m/21km N. of Newark-on-Trent SK 8172
Lonely site. Mainly 13th–14th-century church, the chancel rebuilt by Pearson in 1891. Good collection of 14th-century glass.
R.C.F.

GEDLING
All Hallows
outskirts of Nottingham, adjoining Carlton to N. SK 6142
Notably tall and slender early 14th-century steeple. Early English chancel and fine Georgian candelabra and hatchments.

HAWTON
All Saints
2m/3km S. of Newark-on-Trent SK 7851
Seen from the W., across the open unhedged fields, this church appears as it must have done 500 years ago. Its 15th-century tower is noble and has an original carved and inscribed door. Within, the simple old pews in the nave are well spaced; but the eye is led to the chancel, with its curvilinear E. window and superb 14th-century stonework. The Easter Sepulchre is one of the best in the country. Its figures are slightly mutilated, but the detail decorations are magnificently abundant and various. This, and the sedilia, are of a deep golden stone; and the similarity to Southwell, both in material and intricate workmanship, is obvious.

HOLME
St Giles
3m/4km N. of Newark-on-Trent SK 8059
A small, rather inaccessible church by the Trent which richly rewards the finder. The fine Perpendicular S. aisle and two-storey porch were built by John Barton, d. 1491,

Merchant of the Staple of Calais. There is simple old woodwork in screen and benches; the altar rails are Jacobean, and the roof 18th-century. The church was rescued in the 1930s by Nevil Truman; he and Barton are both commemorated in the E. window – which contains medieval glass, carefully re-assembled by Nevil Truman.

HOLME PIERREPONT
St Edmund
4m/6km E. of Nottingham SK 6239
Church and hall form a pleasing group; 13th-century church with Perpendicular W. tower and handsome Gothic Survival S. aisle of 1666 containing splendid Pierrepont tombs. A wonderful oasis.

KEYWORTH
St Mary Magdalene
7m/11km S.E. of Nottingham SK 6130
Mainly 14th-century church with a Perpendicular tower unique in England. Originally with four large ground-floor openings, unusually grouped windows, and panelled corner buttresses.

KINGSTON-ON-SOAR
St Wilfrid
6m/10km N. of Loughborough SK 5027
Estate village setting. Largely rebuilt by R. Creed in 1900, but housing the remarkable Babington Chantry of 1540: a bizarre canopied edifice adorned with the family rebus of babes in tuns, an erection so exotic that Sacheverell Sitwell likened it to a Portuguese Indian temple.

KINOULTON
St Luke
9m/15km N.W. of Melton Mowbray SK 6730
Built in 1793 of bright-red brick by Henry, Earl of Gainsborough, as the inscription over the entrance obligingly records. Round-headed windows, W gallery, and a good Gothic organ.

KIRKLINGTON
St Swithin
3m/4km N.W. of Southwell SK 6757
Mostly 12th–13th-century with a tall 17th-century brick tower on a medieval base with a Gothic top stage. Norman font and S. doorway.

LAMBLEY
Holy Trinity
5m/8km N.E. of Nottingham SK 6345
Imposing mid-15th-century Perpendicular church built by Ralph, Lord Cromwell, Lord High Treasurer of England. The purse, symbol of his office, adorns the E. wall. 14th-century screen and Jacobean pulpit.

LANGAR
St Andrew
4m/6km S. of Bingham SK 7234
Large 13th-century cruciform church, much restored in the 1860s, but retaining remarkable medieval and Renaissance monuments. Admiral Lord Howe, victor of the glorious First of June, is buried here, with marble monument, 1799.

LAXTON
St Michael the Archangel
4m/6km E. of Ollerton SK 7267
Famous as the village with open fields on the medieval model, and with a church to match. Notable late-Perpendicular clerestory, a dated screen of 1532 and, in the chancel, the only medieval wooden effigy left in the county.

MANSFIELD
St Mark, Nottingham Road
SK 5361
By Temple Moore, 1897. Mature essay in restrained late-Gothic style; long, low ashlar exterior, austere and prayerful within.

MILTON
2m/3km N.W. of Tuxford SK 7173
By Sir Robert Smirke, 1832. Designed for the 4th Duke of Newcastle as a mausoleum, but used later as a church. Latin cross plan, pedimented roof and Doric pillars, the whole surmounted by a dome resting on an octagonal colonnaded drum. One of Smirke's best buildings.
R.C.F.

NEWARK
SK 7953
St Mary Magdalene, market place
A town church in the grand manner, largely 15th-century, with transepts, aisles, nave and choir, and a splendid landmark of a spire. Within, one sees thick poppyheads up to the black medieval screen, and the pews in the transepts look pulpitward. But all is different beyond the screen. Comper's great

gilded reredos of 1937 shines triumphantly above the high altar and gives a needed focus to the whole interior; around it are brassily furnished chantry chapels, and beyond it three good altars. The E. window of the S. aisle is a gay medieval jumble of glass, and the two painted panels of the Dance of Death are alone worth a long journey to see. In the W. wall of S. transept is the 1939–45 War Memorial, a Pietà by R. Kiddey; good modern work of the post-Gill era. Notice, too, the old library in the S. parvise, and the dim, effective oratory in the N. porch.

NORMANTON-ON-SOAR
St James the Great
2m/3km N.W. of Loughborough SK 5123
Right beside the River Soar. Splendid, largely 13th-century cruciform church with lofty central broach spire. Interior scraped but retaining plaster Royal Arms of Charles II and two 17th-century monuments.

NORWELL
St Lawrence
5m/8km N. of Newark-on-Trent SK 7761
Spacious 13th–15th-century church with sturdy W. tower, Perpendicular clerestory, and good five-light E. window with geometrical tracery.

NOTTINGHAM
SK 5740
All Saints, Waverley Street
By T. C. Hine of Nottingham, 1863–4; church, school and parsonage were designed together. Built of rock-faced stone with ashlar bands in a lavish Early English style; W. tower with broach spire and triple bell-openings, polygonal apse, and impressive nave roof.
St Mary, High Pavement
A huge cruciform Perpendicular church in crumbling stone, stifled by the buildings of the Lace Market, in the oldest part of this old town. The splendid bronze doors in the S. porch, by Wilson, 1904, lead one to the vast, quiet, multi-windowed interior. It is all impressively homogeneous both in structure and furnishing. The latter is nearly all good Victorian with Bodley as a pervasive influence; the stained glass is encyclopedic in its range of designers. A large, colourful Prince Consort memorial window of 1863 is partly blocked by the towering gilded Bodley reredos of 1885; and the two wings of this reredos can never be closed because of the

English 'four poster' altar erected beneath them! Fragments of old glass and alabaster may be found in the S. choir aisle. Other details are the medieval vestry, the incomplete rood screen, the wall-monuments, as thick as stamps in an album, but less colourful, the rows of tattered flags, and the spirited wood-carved Lion and Unicorn of 1710. S. chapel by Temple Moore, 1912.
St Peter, Lister Gate
Mainly 13th–14th-century with tall pinnacled spire and elaborately decorated W. doorway. Snetzler organ case of 1770.
St Paul, Daybrook
By J. L. Pearson, 1892–6. Handsome stone church in the Geometrical style with tall S.W. spire. Spacious interior with richly Decorated sedilia and tomb recess of Mrs Emily Seely, d. 1897, the benefactor's wife.
St Stephen, Sneinton
'Bodleyism' at its most complete, although in fact nearly all by C. G. Hare, 1912, who rebuilt the Rickman church of 1839, retaining the central tower and crossing. Proportions are good, and the main axial vista leads from a tall-canopied font through the coloured rood to the gorgeous Oberammergau high altar. But not all beauties are apparent at first glance: each transept is differently and effectively treated; the gold and green organ casing stands on a screen between S. transept and crossing. There are modern Continental statues and a vigorous set of Stations of the Cross, 1926. The 15th-century oak stalls, from St Mary's, Nottingham, are beautifully arranged in the choir; there are eight misericords.

OSSINGTON
Holy Rood
7m/11km N. of Newark-on-Trent SK 7564
By Carr of York, 1782. A model of Classical restraint; W. tower with cupola and triple arches dividing nave and sanctuary. Barrel organ of 1840 and elegant Denison statues by Nollekens.

PAPPLEWICK
St James
1m/2km N.E. of Hucknall SK 5451
The county's best example of Georgian Gothic; 14th-century tower, otherwise all of 1795, with Y-traceried windows, battlements, pinnacles, and quatrefoils. We enter the light and elegant interior through a porch as tall as the nave. A gallery on slender clustered shafts extends over the N. side of

the nave, and the E. window has glowing figures of Hope and Faith by F. Eginton. Good walnut pulpit with Gothic panels, a small marble font, and Royal Arms of George III.

PERLETHORPE
St John the Evangelist
2m/3km N. of Ollerton SK 6471
By Anthony Salvin, 1876. Large estate church in the Decorated style with W. tower and spire. Good carved details and a sumptuous reredos with ogee niches and marble shafts.

RATCLIFFE-ON-SOAR
Holy Trinity
6m/10km N.W. of Loughborough SK 4928
Menaced by the power station, but with a doughty 13th-century W. tower and a great wealth of 16th–17th-century alabaster Sacheverell tombs.

REMPSTONE
All Saints
4m/6km N.E. of Loughborough SK 5724
Small church of 1773; a rare survival in these parts, with big round-headed windows, pinnacled tower, and interior retaining two-decker pulpit and box pews. Good slate tombstones in the churchyard.

SIBTHORPE
St Peter
6m/10km S.W. of Newark-on-Trent SK 7645
Glorious 14th-century chancel with Easter Sepulchre and plain 18th-century nave, with medieval windows re-inserted. Impressive alabaster tomb chest of Edward Burnell, d. 1589.

SOUTH SCARLE
St Helen
7m/11km N.E. of Newark-on-Trent SK 8464
Splendid 12th-century N. arcade with leaves and scallops, Early English chancel, and Perpendicular W. tower, nave roof and screen.

STRELLEY
All Saints
4m/6km W. of Nottingham SK 5141
Unspoiled village on farthest edge of Nottingham. Apart from the base of the tower, 13th-century, and the clerestory, 15th-century, the whole was built by Sir Sampson Strelley in the mid-14th century. His fine alabaster tomb is in the chancel, separated from the nave by the best ancient screen in the county, which doubtless he provided. Strelley Hall, 18th-century, but with the medieval house of the Strelleys incorporated, stands next door.

SUTTON-ON-TRENT
All Saints
8m/12km N. of Newark-on-Trent SK 7965
Fine 13th-century and later church with lovely Mering Chapel of *c.* 1525. An elaborately decorated screen with loft leads into the chapel containing the Purbeck marble tomb of Sir William Mering.

TEVERSAL
St Catherine
2m/3km N. of Sutton-in-Ashfield SK 4861
The village is a rural oasis in the coal-producing area of the Notts.-Derby border, and its 12th- and 13th-century church is remarkable for its unrestored 17th- and 18th-century interior. From the W. gallery with its modest organ to the narrow Laudian altar with its central alms dish, all, except a 1908 reading desk, is solid, traditional Anglican furnishing. The pulpit is low, for there were never side galleries; and the box pews have seating strips of red baize. The Molyneux pew in the S. aisle is roofed and has barley-sugar columns; four red velvet cushions, emblazoned with a cross moline on a blue shield, are provided for the books of the noble family; a 1784 prayer book and an 1822 Bible are covered in similar style. Eight hatchments display the Molyneux arms in various quarterings; and the Royal Arms dominate the chancel arch. In the choir are miniature three-a-side box pews and three vast wall-monuments.

THURGARTON
St Peter
3m/4km S. of Southwell SK 6949
Priory fragment; one of the original pair of handsome Early English W. towers survives; 13th-century nave, the felicitous chancel and N. aisle added by T. C. Hine in 1852.

TITHBY
Holy Trinity
2m/3km S. of Bingham SK 6936
Delightful church, part medieval and part Georgian. Good set of 17th–18th-century furnishings with box pews, two-decker pulpit, Royal Arms, screen, and W. gallery.

TUXFORD
St Nicholas
7m/11km S. of Retford SK 7371
Mostly Perpendicular outside, but with a Decorated tower and spire. Crudely carved Martyrdom of St Laurence in S. aisle, 15th-century screen, and wonderful hanging font canopy of 1673. Large monument to Sir John White, d. 1625, and wife.

UPPER BROUGHTON
St Luke
6m/10km N.W. of Melton Mowbray SK 6826
Delightful, with views over the Vale of Belvoir; 13th-century and later church with chancel by S. S. Teulon, 1855. Unusually good collection of early 18th-century slate gravestones.

WEST MARKHAM
All Saints
1m/2km N.W. of Tuxford SK 7272
Charming and simply restored small church with weatherboarded bell-turret and some Saxon masonry. Transitional S. doorway with original door, earth floor at W. end, and a good 12th-century font.

WEST RETFORD
St Michael
to N.W. of Retford SK 7081
Elegant 14th-century crocketed spire, the broaches unusually set below the parapet. Perpendicular S. aisle with niche containing figure of St Oswald. Rich Anglo-Catholic furnishings.

WEST STOCKWITH
St Mary the Virgin
5m/8km N.W. of Gainsborough SK 7994
Attractive Trentside village. Small red-brick Georgian church of 1722, built by the executors of William Huntington, 'ship carpenter'. Interior has neat plasterwork and Ionic pilasters; Huntington's effigy holds the design of a sailing ship, perhaps built in his own yard here.

WILLOUGHBY-ON-THE-WOLDS
St Mary and All Saints
8m/12km N.W. of Melton Mowbray SK 6325
Impressive 13th- and 14th-century church with broach spire. In the N. transept are the notable 14th–15th-century Willoughby tombs with effigies, wonderfully preserved, and a brass plaque commemorates a 'souldier for King Charles the First', killed at the Battle of Willoughby Field, 1648.

WINKBURN
St John of Jerusalem
6m/10km N.W. of Newark-on-Trent SK 7158
12th–13th-century church with a delightful interior containing an almost complete set of 17th–18th-century furnishings: box pews, communion rail, pulpit, and a rare 17th-century arched screen with plaster tympanum bearing the arms of George III. A good collection of family monuments.

WOLLATON
district of Nottingham, 3m/4km W. of city centre SK 5329
St Leonard, Wollaton village
Mainly 14th-century church with a rare and handsome Corinthian reredos of *c.* 1660. Good 15th–16th-century monuments to the Willoughby family, Lord Middleton, and a tablet to Robert Smythson, the architect, 1614.
St Mary, Wollaton Park
1939, by T. Cecil Howitt. A good red-brick church by Nottingham's most distinguished architect of the inter-war period. Single-cell and tall, with prominent gables and tall, narrow round-headed windows to the sides. Interior in fair-faced brick with traditional wooden fittings, and panelled roof with stencilled decoration.

WORKSOP
SK 5879
St Mary & St Cuthbert
The twin-towered W. front of the former priory with its fine doorway is the feature of the exterior. Within, the long and narrow nine-bay nave is late-Norman and has a lofty triforium. Rebuilding has been drastic, continuous and interesting, culminating in the controversial chancel and fleche by Laurence King, 1970–4. Sir Giles Gilbert Scott's E. window is now in the N. transept, where his coloured reredos looks like an uncomfortable but commodious sedilia. There are many good small objects of devotion, including paintings. The rebuilt Lady Chapel, by Sir Harold Breakspear, 1922, though simple in design, has a mysterious peace, unlike the regretted high altar sanctuary of 1970–4, which is cheap and hideous.

WYSALL

Holy Trinity

6m/10km N.E. of Loughborough SK 6027
Norman and later church with important 15th-century fittings of pulpit, screen, stalls, and rare altar canopy in the chancel roof. Splendid alabaster monument to Hugh Armstrong, d. 1572, and an unusual painted wooden memorial of 1689.

Oxfordshire

Introduction

Oxfordshire is the most diversified of all inland counties. In the north it is the Midlands, with hints of oncoming Birmingham when one sees the pinkish brick Victorian and Edwardian villas in the Banbury district, bringing a 19th-century industrial atmosphere into the medieval and Georgian brown ironstone of the older groups of buildings. Twentieth-century industry turns Midlands-ward too, for the motor industry at Cowley has noisy, long links with Coventry and Brum. In the west, Oxon. is the Cotswolds, with that perfect limestone town of Burford, which strangers fancy is in Gloucestershire.

The City and University are largely a limestone Cotswold town, at any rate in their surviving ancient streets. The south-eastern peninsula of the county, slipped between Berks. and Bucks., is Chiltern scenery, near-suburban, with beech woods and steep chalk hills and scenario-writers' hide-outs in valleys, and pleasure-seekers' haunts by the broad Thames. The capital of this part of the county is the old red-brick town of Henley, and Watlington is its isolated poor relation.

There is the flat Upper Thames country of willows, limestone churches and cottages. Around Stanton Harcourt and Eynsham this scenery is full of Matthew Arnold and by Bampton and Kelmscott it is full of William Morris. There are the wide and unvisited inland marsh of Otmoor, all aeroplanes and bombs, the remote medieval park of Wychwood, the picturesque planted park of Blenheim, where the palace spreads its curious outline above the lake; there is a remote mid-Oxon. associated with the books of Flora Thompson and with the landscaped village of Great Tew. Then, in the north-west corner, with Northants. and Warwicks. near, is a land of little hills and golden-brown churches and cottages that looks like a medieval manuscript scene.

The finest old churches are not in the chalky southern end but where the quarries are in the north and west, whence the stone could be floated down the Thames and its tributaries to Oxford and Dorchester.

The great medieval churches of the county – Adderbury, Bloxham, St Mary the Virgin, Oxford, New College Chapel and cloisters, Oxford, Horley, Thame, Dorchester, Stanton Harcourt, Burford, Cropredy, Witney and Bampton – are all Midland in character, with the exception of the complete late-Norman church of Iffley, which is on its own. The Gloucestershire masons influenced the Perpendicular work which is abundant in the county. But Oxon. is also a county of great houses: Blenheim, Ditchley, Middleton

Stoney, Nuneham, Shirburn, Stonor, Thame Park, and smaller stone manor houses like Kelmscott, Yarnton, Chastleton, Garsington – in fact most of the stone villages have gabled manor houses. The churches, therefore, often have the look of family chapels, and in some instances, not content with grand Baroque monuments or a new aisle, a tasteful squire would wholly rebuild or refurbish a church in Classic style, as at Chislehampton or Wheatfield. The best of all private chapels, excluding the college chapels in Oxford itself, is that at Rycote, with its 17th-century furniture.

J. B.

1	Adderbury	33	Great Bourton	65	Oxford
2	Asthall	34	Great Haseley	66	Rotherfield Greys
3	Bampton	35	Great Milton	67	Rousham
4	Banbury	36	Great Rollright	68	Rycote
5	Binsey	37	Great Tew	69	Sarsden
6	Bloxham	38	Hailey	70	Shilton
7	Brightwell Baldwin	39	Hanwell	71	Shiplake
8	Broughton	40	Hook Norton	72	Shorthampton
9	Bucknell	41	Horley	73	Somerton
10	Burford	42	Hornton	74	South Leigh
11	Cassington	43	Hornton-cum-Studley	75	South Newington
12	Chalgrove	44	Idbury	76	Spelsbury
13	Charlton-on-Otmoor	45	Iffley	77	Stanton Harcourt
14	Checkendon	46	Kelmscott	78	Stanton St John
15	Chinnor	47	Kidlington	79	Stoke Lyne
16	Chislehampton	48	Kingham	80	Stratton Audley
17	Church Hanborough	49	Langford	81	Swinbrook
18	Churchill	50	Leafield	82	Swyncombe
19	Cogges	51	Lewknor	83	Tackley
20	Combe	52	Litle Faringdon	84	Thame
21	Cropredy	53	Little Rollright	85	Warborough
22	Cuddesdon	54	Lower Heyford	86	Waterperry
23	Deddington	55	Marston	87	Waterstock
24	Dorchester	56	Merton	88	Westwell
25	Ducklington	57	Milton	89	Wheatfield
26	Easington	58	Milton-under-Wychwood	90	Wheatley
27	Enstone	59	Minster Lovell	91	Widford
28	Ewelme	60	Nettlebed	92	Witney
29	Filkins	61	Newington	93	Woodeaton
30	Forest Hill	62	North Leigh	94	Wroxton
31	Freeland	63	Northmoor	95	Yarnton
32	Garsington	64	Nuneham Courtney		

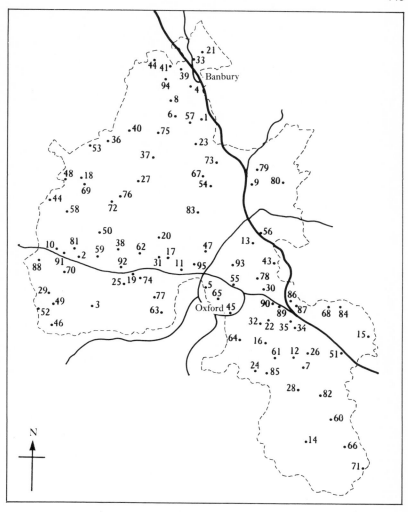

N

Selected List of Churches

ADDERBURY
St Mary the Virgin
3m/4km S. of Banbury SP 4735
Large hilly village of golden ironstone Georgian houses and old cottages with a magnificent Decorated and Perpendicular church to match. The imaginative corbel table on N. wall, of musicians, the lovely late Perpendicular chancel in the style of the Divinity Schools at Oxford, the tower and spire and windows, make its exterior about the finest in the county. The inside is rather too restored, but retains screen and brasses.

ASTHALL
St Nicholas
2m/3km E. of Burford SP 2811
Village setting. Transitional with later additions; Norman Revival chancel arch and a good tomb recess of *c.* 1350 with gabled canopy and foliage; 14th-century stained glass.

BAMPTON
St Mary
5m/8km S.W. of Witney SP 3103
The church is pleasantly set in a large graveyard, surrounded, close-like, by old stone houses. Saxon but rebuilt in the 12th century on a cruciform plan. Central tower completed and spire added in late 13th century; good Decorated W. doorway and chancel.

BANBURY
St Mary
22m/35km N. of Oxford SP 4540
The decayed medieval church was blown up with gunpowder in 1790 and replaced by the cool Classicalism of S. P. Cockerell. A striking exterior with Tuscan columns, green copper roofs, and a round tower. Centrally planned galleried interior spoiled by the addition of a chancel by Sir A. Blomfield in 1873; wall-painting of Christ in Majesty by Heaton, Butler & Bayne.

BINSEY
St Margaret
2m/3km N.W. of Oxford SP 5006
Hamlet on a broad green. Small and rustic

Norman church remodelled in the 13th century. Good nave roof; painted Royal Arms of Queen Anne.

BLOXHAM
Our Lady of Bloxham
4m/6km S.W. of Banbury SP 4235
A golden ironstone village with thatched cottages, and on a hill above it the grand church whose 14th-century spire is visible for miles. Superb 13th-century W. doorway with Last Judgement presided over by Christ and the angels. The spacious aisled and clerestoried interior was harshly restored by G. E. Street, but there is a splendid painted 15th-century screen, and the Milcombe Chapel on the S. side is a delight, with wall-paintings, including one of an unknown saint. Thornycroft monument of 1725 by A. Carpenter.

BRIGHTWELL BALDWIN
St Bartholomew
2m/3km W. of Watlington SU 6595
Well set opposite the attractive old Lord Nelson inn. Mostly early 14th-century apart from the Perpendicular W. tower. Good 14th- and 15th-century glass, brasses, and a spirited Baroque monument of *c.* 1670.

BROUGHTON
St Mary
3m/4km S.W. of Banbury SP 4238
Park setting beside the castle. A high-quality church of *c.* 1300 illustrating the transition from Early English to Decorated. Rare Decorated stone screen and a series of monuments; 14th-century wall-paintings with a Crucifixion on a column.

BUCKNELL
St Peter
3m/4km N.W. of Bicester SP 5525
Norman church with central tower engulfed by the nave and chancel, enlarged in the 13th century. Good Early English details.

BURFORD
St John the Baptist
7m/11km W. of Witney SP 2512
'Model old English town' (J. Piper) of Cots-

wold stone with church at bottom of hill on River Windrush. The church with spire and tower and parvised porch is cruciform of various dates with chapels added, interior effect largely 15th-century, Sylvester and Tanfield tombs, and some old glass. The churchyard is rich in sculptured table-tombs, Georgian and earlier.

CASSINGTON
St Peter
5m/8km N.W. of Oxford SP 4510
Spire and tripartite Norman plan. Norman corbel table. Dark, impressive interior with Jacobean woodwork and old foreign glass.

CHALGROVE
St Mary the Virgin
4m/6km N.W. of Watlington SU 6396
Village setting; 14th-century chancel with reticulated tracery and one of the most extensive series of wall-paintings in the county, of 14th-century date; those depicting the life of the Virgin are especially noteworthy.

CHARLTON-ON-OTMOOR
St Mary the Virgin
4m/6km S. of Bicester SP 5615
Mostly Decorated with Perpendicular nave roof and clerestory; sumptuous early 16th-century screen with Victorian paint; some 13th-century glass.

CHECKENDON
St Peter & St Paul
4m/6km E. of Goring SU 6682
Small Norman church with apsidal interior. Early 13th-century wall-paintings of Apostles and Christ in Majesty. Monument to Eric Kennington, 1960, and memorial window engraved by Whistler.

CHINNOR
St Andrew
4m/6km S.E. of Thame SP 7500
Almost all early 14th-century, including the rood screen and the important stained glass in the side windows of the chancel.

CHISLEHAMPTON
St Katherine
7m/11km S.E. of Oxford SU 5999
On the edge of a small park stands this beautifully preserved little white church of 1763. Neat Classical exterior with bellcote, weather-vane, and clear glass in the round-headed windows. Inside are box pews, a

carved wooden altarpiece, tablets, and chandeliers; an unspoiled Georgian interior.
R.C.F.

CHURCH HANBOROUGH
St Peter & St Paul
5m/8km N.E. of Witney SP 4212
A tall spired building, extended through the centuries since Norman times, the combined effect of which makes a charming village church; 12th-century S. door carvings and font, 15th-century nave arcades, pulpit, and screen with coloured rood loft.

CHURCHILL
All Saints
3m/4km S.W. of Chipping Norton SP 2824
By James Plowman of Oxford, 1862. A Gothic preaching-box; the W. tower is a reduced version of that at Magdalen College.

COGGES
St Mary
E. of Witney across R. Windrush SP 3609
Setting between the vicarage and manor house. Norman and Decorated with bold 14th-century foliate glass and 17th-century monuments.

COMBE
St Lawrence the Martyr
5m/8km N.E. of Witney SP 4115
Unspoiled village. Church rebuilt in 1395 and little altered since; stone pulpit, stained glass, and extensive 15th-century wall-paintings; the Doom includes among the damned a wanton offering herself to a devil!

CROPREDY
St Mary the Virgin
4m/6km N. of Banbury SP 4646
Large, stately Perpendicular church of ironstone retaining early pulpit, screens, and lectern. Good 17th- and 18th-century tomb-stones in churchyard.

CUDDESDON
All Saints
6m/10km S.E. of Oxford SP 6003
A diocesan village. Handsome cruciform church of *c.* 1180 with fine details and vistaed interior. Restored by Street in 1851-3; glass by Hardman.

DEDDINGTON
St Peter & St Paul
6m/10km S. of Banbury SP 4631
Large Decorated and Perpendicular church

of good proportions, with splendid eight-pinnacled W. tower; 17th-century Gothic Survival N. porch with domed vault and fan tracery.

DORCHESTER
St Peter & St Paul
4m/6km N.W. of Wallingford SU 5794
An attractive village with remaining traces of the distinction proper to one of the oldest of English cities. Abbey church, approached through a Butterfield lych gate, is splendid in its proportions and detail. Mostly Decorated, it has earlier and later parts. The Jesse window, some of its stonework imitating tree branches, has its original figures in glass and stone, and there is much old glass in other windows too. Among the tombs is the justly celebrated stone effigy of a later 13th-century knight which has inspired many sculptors.

DUCKLINGTON
St Bartholomew
1m/2km S. of Witney SP 3507
Village with green and pond. Transitional church much reworked in the 14th century; spectacular Decorated N. aisle with ballflowers, richly canopied tombs, and tracery.

EASINGTON
St Peter
3m/4km N.W. of Watlington SU 6697
Delightful 14th-century rustic church behind a barn; undivided nave and chancel, some medieval tiles and glass, and a Jacobean pulpit.

ENSTONE
St Kenelm
4m/6km E. of Chipping Norton SP 3724
12th-century and later church restored by G. E. Street, who also designed the lych gate. Large 16th-century W. tower and an odd monument of 1633.

EWELME
St Mary the Virgin
3m/4km S.W. of Watlington SU 6491
Flint and brick village where watercress grows in Chiltern foothills. Castellated 15th-century stone and flint church, patched with brick, rises above old almshouses. It is all distinguished late-Perpendicular, not village building. Inside, effect is East Anglian, with screen, spired font cover, and old roofs,

that in S.E. chapel painted. Pleasant early 19th-century poppyhead pews. Chaucer and Suffolk tombs, old floors, and many brasses.

FILKINS
St Peter
4m/6km N.E. of Lechlade SP 2304
By G. E. Street, 1857; simple and subtle French Gothic apsed church in the local stone of this attractive village.

FOREST HILL
St Nicholas
5m/8km E. of Oxford SP 5807
Norman church remodelled in the 13th century and restored in the 19th by various Victorian architects including Sir G. Gilbert Scott; Tractarian furnishings and glass by Willement.

FREELAND
St Mary the Virgin
4m/6km N.E. of Witney SP 4112
By J. L. Pearson, 1869. Built of local limestone in Gothic style, an unaltered High Victorian church. Nave and apsidal chancel, the N.E. tower with saddleback roof. The vaulted chancel and apse have rich glass and wall-paintings by Clayton & Bell. Designed as part of a group with the attached parsonage and nearby school.

GARSINGTON
St Mary
5m/8km S.E. of Oxford SP 5802
Village atmosphere and splendid views from the churchyard. Transitional W. tower, Perpendicular timber S. porch, and a 15th-century screen.

GREAT BOURTON
All Saints
3m/4km N. of Banbury SP 4545
William White restored and altered this 13th-century church in 1863 after post-Reformation secular use. The chancel and W. wall are medieval, but the arcade, tiled floor and fittings are all White's. But the most important thing is his remarkable lych gate of 1882, replete with tall openwork timber bell-tower.

GREAT HASELEY
St Peter
5m/8km S.W. of Thame SP 6401
Impressive Decorated and Perpendicular church with good mouldings, especially in

the Decorated chancel. Felicitous Baroque monument of 1709.

GREAT MILTON
St Mary the Virgin
8m/12km S.E. of Oxford SP 6202
Church was rebuilt after a fire in the early 14th century and restored by Sir G. Gilbert Scott in 1850. Good 14th-century tracery, delectable Dormer tomb of 1618, and some 14th-century glass.

GREAT ROLLRIGHT
St Andrew
3m/4km N. of Chipping Norton SP 3231
Small Norman church with Perpendicular tower and screen; 12th-century S. doorway enriched with zig-zags and beak-heads.

GREAT TEW
St Michael and All Angels
5m/8km E. of Chipping Norton SP 3828
Parkland setting beside thatched village. Spacious 13th- and 14th-century church with Perpendicular W. tower and clerestory; 15th-century brasses and a nice Chantrey monument of 1829.

HAILEY
St John the Evangelist
2m/3km N. of Witney SP 3512
Built in 1868–9 and designed by Clapton Crabb Rolf, son of the then incumbent. An original design in 13th-century style with raised chancel, plain lancets, and a strange N.W. bell-turret. Well-detailed interior has iron lamps, font, and sanctuary tiles.

HANWELL
St Peter
2m/3km N.W. of Banbury SP 4343
An untouched orange ironstone place whose hidden church of the same stone is remarkable for its lively rustic carvings on the corbel frieze outside and capitals within.

HOOK NORTON
St Peter
5m/8km N.E. of Chipping Norton SP 3533
Commanding position at the centre of the village. Spacious interior with impressive Norman chancel and circular font carved with Adam and Eve and Zodiac signs; 15th-century wall-paintings.

HORLEY
St Etheldreda
3m/4km N.W. of Banbury SP 2743
A north Oxon. ironstone village whose spacious church of various dates has been made distinguished by sympathetic modern furnishing and restoration; 15th-century wall-paintings of St Christopher and St Etheldreda, rather touched up; rood loft and screen by T. Lawrence Dale, 1949.

HORNTON
St John the Baptist
5m/8km N.W. of Banbury SP 3945
Village setting. Mostly Decorated and Perpendicular with late 14th-century wall-paintings of the Crucifixion and St George and the Dragon.

HORTON-CUM-STUDLEY
St Barnabas
6m/10km N.E. of Oxford SP 5912
By W. Butterfield, 1867. A small church of yellow brick banded with red and blue in Butterfield's familar polychrome style. Lively matching interior with zig-zag cornice, mosaic reredos, and glass by A. Gibbs.

IDBURY
St Nicholas
5m/8km S.E. of Stow-on-the-Wold SP 2319
Small village with splendid views. Fine reset Norman doorway with zig-zags, chevrons and scallops; otherwise 14th-century and Perpendicular with good woodwork.

IFFLEY
St Mary the Virgin
S. district of Oxford SP 5203
A late-Norman, *c.* 1170, showpiece, and rightly so, within and without. W. front rich in beak-head and zig-zag carving. Dark aisleless interior shows E. view of two elaborate Norman arches with vaulting between, leading to contrasting light Early English vaulted E. end. Unfortunate Victorian woodwork.

KELMSCOTT
St George
2m/3km E. of Lechlade SU 2599
Charming rustic Norman and Early English church in the village associated with William Morris; his tomb by Philip Webb is in the churchyard.

KIDLINGTON
St Mary the Virgin
5m/8km N. of Oxford SP 4914
Early English and Decorated cruciform church with a Perpendicular spire. Much reset medieval stained glass; good 15th-century screens, stalls, and benches.

KINGHAM
St Andrew
4m/6km S.W. of Chipping Norton SP 2624
Perpendicular W. tower, the rest rebuilt in the Decorated style in 1853; elegant Gothic Revival furnishings and stained glass.

LANGFORD
St Matthew
3m/4km N.E. of Lechlade SP 2402
Stone village in flat, willowy Upper Thames setting. The church is on a grand scale and very early Norman, as evidenced by the tower and the rood carvings reset in the S. porch. Distinguished Early English chancel and W. end.

LEAFIELD
St Michael and All Angels
4m/6km N.W. of Witney SP 3115
By Sir George Gilbert Scott, 1858–60, but the octagonal crossing tower and prominent spire were not completed until 1874. A well-proportioned church in the Early English style. Fine W. front with carved doorway, rose window, and lancets. Tall, somewhat austere clerestoried interior with round piers, plain arches, and painted texts.

LEWKNOR
St Margaret
3m/4km N.E. of Watlington SU 7197
Cruciform church of *c.* 1200, the chancel handsomely rebuilt in the 14th century with crocketed canopies and much foliage. Good 17th- and 18th-century monuments; glass by William Morris.

LITTLE FARINGDON
(dedication unknown)
1m/2km N.E. of Lechlade SP 2201
Small Norman village church with billeted corbel table on the chancel. Good N. arcade of *c.* 1200, and a Norman tub font.

LITTLE ROLLRIGHT
St Philip
2m/3km W. of Gt Rollright SP 3131
A simple rustic church in a farmyard setting.

W. tower dated 1617, Perpendicular chancel windows, and 17th-century alabaster tombs.

LOWER HEYFORD
St Mary
6m/10km W. of Bicester SP 4824
Village setting above the Cherwell valley. Mostly 14th-century with Perpendicular tower, porch and screen. Some early glass and a 17th-century monument.

MARSTON
St Nicholas
2m/3km N.E. of Oxford SP 5208
Early English and late-Perpendicular church, the S. aisle rebuilt in 1562. Good Jacobean woodwork includes the pulpit, screen and benches.

MERTON
St Swithin, Bishop of Winchester
3m/4km S. of Bicester SP 5717
Grand Decorated church with Perpendicular additions and demolitions; the chancel carving is particularly fine. Jacobean pulpit, stalls and monuments.

MILTON
St John the Evangelist
4m/6km S. of Banbury SP 4535
By W. Butterfield, 1854–6. An early work in local brown stone with white dressings and red-tiled roof. Striking stone and timber S. porch and lych gate. Light interior has original fittings including reredos, altar rails, font, and pulpit.

MILTON-UNDER-WYCHWOOD
St Simon & St Jude
4m/6km N. of Burford SP 2618
By G. E. Street, 1854. Imposing village church in the Early Decorated style with slender bell-turret and octagonal spire. Lofty clerestoried nave with wide arches, white walls, and dark-stained roofs. Designed as part of a group with lych gate, school and house.

MINSTER LOVELL
St Kenelm
3m/4km N.W. of Witney SP 3111
Delightful setting in Windrush Valley. Perpendicular church with cruciform plan, central tower, and vaulted crossing. Good details throughout; 15th-century glass and monuments; reredos by J. L. Pearson.

NETTLEBED
St Bartholomew
5m/8km N.W. of Henley-on-Thames SU 7086
By Hakewill, 1845–6. The church is of no great interest, but is notable for the E. window, by that gifted artist and friend of J.B., John Piper, 1970.

NEWINGTON
St Giles
5m/8km N. of Wallingford SU 6096
Handsomely set with manor house and rectory; 12th–14th-century; the tower and octagonal spire are c. 1300; 15th-century glass.

NORTH LEIGH
St Mary
3m/4km N.E. of Witney SP 3813
Late Saxon, Early English and after. There is a small fan-vaulted chantry chapel of 1439 with contemporary glass and alabaster effigies. Good mid-15th-century wall-painting of Doom. Unusual early 18th-century N. aisle with Baroque details.

NORTHMOOR
St Denys
4m/6km S. of Eynsham SP 4202
Small, largely 14th-century cruciform church with good late 17th-century scrolled communion rail and handsome W. gallery with donor's inscription.

NUNEHAM COURTNEY
All Saints
5m/8km S.E. of Oxford SU 5599
On a hill in the park. A domed temple in the Greek taste built in 1764 to designs by the first Earl Harcourt, assisted by 'Athenian' Stuart. Pedimented Ionic portico; cool and impressive interior; more a view-stopper than a shrine.
R.C.F.

OXFORD
SP 5106
All Saints, High Street
A classic and civic church in the High Street, 1707–8, said to have been designed by Dean Aldrich, its tower and rather heavy spire on an axis with Trinity College chapel and gates in Broad Street. The oblong body of the church is bound together externally by a heavy moulded cornice below clerestory windows and articulated with flat Corinthian pilasters, broken into by a pedimented porch.

Now the library of Lincoln College and not open to the public.
St Barnabas, Cardigan Street, Jericho
By A. W. Blomfield, 1869. An Italian Romanesque basilica of rendered rubble with brick banding. Spacious interior has a raised choir projecting into the nave, a shallow apse, and a great gilded baldacchino.
St Giles, St Giles Street
A countrified church, mainly 13th-century, with lancets in the chancel, dog-toothed font, and pillar piscina. Glass by Powell.
St John the Evangelist, Iffley Road
By G. F. Bodley, 1894–1902, for the Cowley Fathers. Sensitive essay in the Decorated style. W. front has tower punctuated by three buttresses and small windows with flowing tracery. Refined interior with tall nave arcades and octagonal piers. Magnificent traceried rood screen, pulpit, and organ case, all to Bodley's own design. Stained glass by Kempe.
St Mary the Virgin, High Street
The soaring spire and eccentric Baroque porch facing the High Street make this the grandest parish church in Oxford; a focus on the skyline and a glory of the High Street. Inside, the clerestoried and aisled nave is rather untidy and furbished up, though steeped in history. The noblest thing is the chancel, c. 1467, with its old clear glass, 17th-century communion rails, and niched E. wall.
St Mary Magdalen, Magdalen Street
Wide and high, owing to its restricted site; 12th–15th-century with stocky W. tower of 1511–31. Much restored by Scott & Moffat in 1842; splendid Perpendicular font; glass by O'Connor.
St Michael, Cornmarket Street
Prominent late-Saxon tower with long-and-short quoins and twin bell-openings. Some late 13th-century glass in the E. window of various saints including St Michael and the Virgin and Child; early 15th-century glass showing two seraphim and Lily Crucifixion in N. aisle.
St Philip & St James, Woodstock Road
By G. E. Street, 1860–6. Cruciform with apse and oblong tower with spire. The exterior is bold with simple mouldings; bands of pink sandstone bind the composition together. Inside are thick columns of polished red granite and a painted wagon-vaulted nave roof. Tractarian plan with high altar visible from all parts of church. Now used as the Oxford Centre for Mission Studies.

ROTHERFIELD GREYS
St Nicholas
2m/3km W. of Henley-on-Thames SU 7282
Almost entirely rebuilt in 1865 by W. Woodman, apart from the N. chapel, built in 1605 by William Knollys, first Earl of Banbury; inside is a superb Elizabethan monument.

ROUSHAM
St Leonard & St James
4m/6km W. of Middleton Stoney SP 4724
Setting by manor house. Norman origins but largely 14th-century, including the chancel and S. aisle. Jacobean pews, monuments, tablets, and hatchments.

RYCOTE
St Michael and All Angels
3m/4km W. of Thame SP 6604
In a park near a lake, this remote mid-15th-century domestic chapel near Thame is of ashlar with tower and buttressed nave and chancel, clearly the work of an architect. Inside it is remarkable for containing nothing later than Laudian times and all things up till then; sumptuous 15th-century benches and screen base, early 17th-century family and royal pews, one domed and the other of two storeys, blue ceiling with gold stars, late 17th-century altarpiece and communion rails. Clear old glass. Queen Elizabeth and Charles I worshipped here when on visits.

SARSDEN
St James
3m/4km S.W. of Chipping Norton SP 2823
Adjoining Sarsden House. A chaste Classical church of 1760. The cruciform E. extension was added by G. S. Repton in 1823. Georgian altar rails with twisted balusters.

SHILTON
Holy Rood
3m/4km S.E. of Burford SP 2608
Hilly setting. Norman nave and S. aisle, 13th-century chancel with lancets, and a 14th-century font carved with the Passion.

SHIPLAKE
St Peter & St Paul
3m/4km S. of Henley-on-Thames SU 7678
Almost rebuilt during G. E. Street's restoration of 1869. Remarkable collection of 15th-century French glass which found its way here after being buried during the Revolution.

SHORTHAMPTON
All Saints
2m/3km W. of Charlbury SP 3220
A tiny hamlet church near Charlbury. It is a small and simple building, aisleless and bellcoted, of various dates from Norman to 1820, when it was furnished in carpenter's style with box pews and high pulpit. The plaster walls show signs of medieval wall-painting, and the appeal of the building is its remoteness and feel of rustic worship.

SOMERTON
St James
3m/4km S. of Aynho SP 4928
Norman origins, including the blocked S. door, but now mainly 14th-century. Good series of monuments in the 16th-century Fermor chapel.

SOUTH LEIGH
St James the Great
3m/4km S.E. of Witney SP 3908
Restored by E. Christian, and the extensive 15th-century wall-paintings retouched by Burlison & Grylls in 1871–2. The overall effect is still impressive, however, with the Last Judgement, Seven Deadly Sins, and other themes.

SOUTH NEWINGTON
St Peter ad Vincula
6m/10km S.W. of Banbury SP 4033
Norman and later church with elaborate Perpendicular S. porch. Inside are the finest 14th- and 15th-century wall-paintings in the county – a feast of saints and martyrs; 14th-century glass in chancel side windows.

SPELSBURY
All Saints
2m/3km N. of Charlbury SP 3521
Attractive village setting. The church was almost entirely rebuilt piecemeal during the 18th century; chancel rebuilt in 1740, the nave and aisles remodelled in 1774. There is an impressive series of 18th-century Litchfield monuments.

STANTON HARCOURT
St Michael
3m/4km S.W. of Eynsham SP 4105
A grand cruciform church near the de-

lightful manor house and other old buildings, reflected in ponds; the Early English and Perpendicular details are delicate and well thought-out. The inside is little spoiled and much enhanced by its old stone and marble floor. Early English screen with painting, old glass, and 17th–19th-century Harcourt monuments in Perpendicular S.E. chapel.

STANTON ST JOHN
St John the Baptist
5m/8km E. of Oxford SP 5709
Perched above the village street. Fine chancel of *c.* 1300 with good 13th-century stained glass; 15th-century screens and benches and a Jacobean pulpit.

STOKE LYNE
St Peter
4m/6km N. of Bicester SP 5628
Small 12th-century church of nave and chancel. There are good mouldings round the openings, some beast-head stops, and a carving of St Peter.

STRATTON AUDLEY
St Mary & St Edburga
3m/4km N.E. of Bicester SP 6026
Mostly 14th- and 15th-century with a Decorated tower and a fine Early English N. arcade. Some 14th-century glass and the wonderful Baroque tomb of Sir John Borlase, d. 1688.

SWINBROOK
St Mary the Blessed Virgin
2m/3km E. of Burford SP 2812
Village setting beside a brook. Unusual tower of 1822 rests on tall buttresses either side of the W. door. Otherwise mostly Decorated and Perpendicular with, in the chancel, the luxuriant Fettiplace tombs. The N. wall in particular is taken up with two magnificent 17th-century canopied tombs filled with lolling figures.

SWYNCOMBE
St Botolph
2m/3km N.W. of Nettlebed SU 6890
Beautiful setting at gates of Swyncombe House. A small early-Norman church with patches of herringbone work, W. bellcote, and apsidal E. end. The later extensive 19th-century restorations still retain the character. Inside are retouched wall-paintings and a rood screen by W. Tapper.

TACKLEY
St Nicholas
3m/4km N.E. of Woodstock SP 4720
Norman cruciform church on a hillside with 13th-century tower and Perpendicular top stage. Restored by G. E. Street in 1864; his are the reredos, stalls and benches; 17th- and 18th-century monuments.

THAME
St Mary the Virgin
9m/15km S.W. of Aylesbury SP 7005
The fine church of an attractive brick, flint and plaster market town. It is cruciform, and developed from Norman origins in later styles in a consistent manner. Notice S. porch, window tracery, Decorated screen, brasses, and many monuments, especially that of Lord Williams, d. 1599, in middle of chancel.

WARBOROUGH
St Lawrence
3m/4km N. of Wallingford SU 5993
Flint and stone W. tower of 1666, otherwise good 13th- and 14th-century work, the chancel rebuilt by Bodley & Garner in 1881. Late Norman circular lead font with moulded figures of bishops and some 15th-century stained glass.

WATERPERRY
St Mary the Virgin
7m/11km E. of Oxford SP 6206
A remote village in meadows. Small 11th–15th-century church by the manor house. Delightful interior has 17th-century pulpit, reader's desk and box pews, old glass of good quality, a monument by Chantrey, hatchments, and old stone floors.

WATERSTOCK
St Leonard
5m/8km W. of Thame SP 6305
Tower of *c.* 1500, nave and chancel 1790, Gothicized by G. E. Street in 1858. Armorial glass in N. aisle and a 17th-century monument.

WESTWELL
St Mary the Virgin
2m/3km S.W. of Burford SP 2209
Small Norman church in attractive village. Interesting early 16th-century glass with fragmentary Crucifixion and a list of five donors; probably farmers celebrating a good wool clip. Pleasing 17th- and 18th-century

headstones in the churchyard with cherubs, flowers, and skulls.

WHEATFIELD
St Andrew
3m/4km N. of Watlington SU 6899
A remote place from which the glory has departed – a stable, a park, a walled garden and, on a slope of the park, the church. Originally medieval, the church was classicized in 1750; inside are hatchments, tombs, two-decker pulpit, old pews, clear glass, with fragments of old stained glass, a Peter Scheemakers tomb of 1739, and rich, classic altar and rails.

WHEATLEY
St Mary
5m/8km E. of Oxford SP 5905
By G. E. Street, 1855–7. Stone village church in bold English First Pointed style with spectacular steeple. Well-detailed exterior with grouped lancets, plate tracery, buttresses, and low timber roofs. Restrained inside with widely spaced round piers and glass by Fouracre and Watson of Plymouth.

WIDFORD
St Oswald
1m/2km E. of Burford SP 2712
Approached by a footpath, and in the Windrush Valley below Burford, this tiny medieval church has 14th- and 15th-century wall-paintings, box pews, clear glass, and bits of Roman pavement.

WITNEY
St Mary the Virgin
10m/16km W. of Oxford SP 3510
Large town church remodelled in the early 13th century with bold W. tower and octagonal spire. Good Decorated chantries and spectacular flowing tracery in the N. aisle. Interior over-restored by G. E. Street, 1865–9, and unfortunately subdivided.

WOODEATON
Holy Rood
4m/6km N.E. of Oxford SP 5311
Set on a bank with yews. Small 13th-century church of nave and chancel; 14th-century tower and wall-painting of St Christopher with Norman French inscription; 18th-century pulpit and reader's desk.

WROXTON
All Saints
3m/4km W. of Banbury SP 4141
Ironstone village with much thatch. Largely 14th-century church with Gothic tower of 1748. Good monuments, including works by J. Wilton and J. Flaxman; Continental woodwork.

YARNTON
St Bartholomew
4m/6km N.W. of Oxford SP 4712
Manor house, vicarage and church form a group. To the 13th-century church were added in 1611 an ashlar tower with mellifluous bells, a porch, and a S.E. chapel by Sir Thomas Spencer, all late-Perpendicular. In the church is much old woodwork and a rich Jacobean screen to the Spencer chapel, which has painted walls and roofs and grand 17th-century monuments. In the chancel is an alabaster 15th-century reredos, and in the aisle a medievalist brass of 1826. Much reset English and Flemish glass.

Rutland

Introduction

Two stone quarries of Ketton and Clipsham, which have been worked since medieval times and are still in use, and centuries of prosperous agriculture, make this, the compactest and smallest county of England, the richest in old stone buildings, whether churches, barns, country houses, farms or cottages. The scenery is hilly and its wide uplands are thus described by Dr W. G. Hoskins in his guide to Rutland: '. . . limestone walls shining from afar in the clear winter sun and the rows of stacks in the corners of the great ploughed fields; fields that themselves gleam like a rich, brown velvet, ready for the barley and the wheat. It is very like the Cotswold country – indeed it is the same stone underneath – but without the self-consciousness of so much of that well-known land.' The stone varies from what he aptly calls 'sheep-grey' limestone in the east of the county around Ketton and Clipsham, where the finest churches are, to golden-brown, yellow and orange in the west. Between 1150 and 1350, the villages of Rutland seemed to have vied with each other as to which could build the finest church, and as Dr Hoskins says, 'no county in England can show so many fine churches in such a small area, except perhaps the neighbouring area of South Lincolnshire . . .'

In later centuries most of Rutland was parcelled out among four great landlords, the Finches at Burley-on-the-Hill, the Noels at Exton, the Heathcotes at Normanton (only the Classical church remains with its 1911 nave and chancel by Romaine Walker), and the Cecil family, who are still associated with the splendid Elizabethan Burghley House just over the border by Stamford town. There were also smaller squires with their houses and modest parks. In the last century the county became popular with hunting people who like the old way of life – no wire, good inns, and ample stables. Thus Rutland today still retains an atmosphere of having been cared for by landlords. The two chief towns of Oakham and Uppingham are small enough to be what old-fashioned landowners would describe as 'the village'; once more to quote Dr Hoskins, 'Everywhere in the villages one sees the hand of the same benevolent despotism, and one sees too frequently also the impact of a new form of society in the broken-down stone walls which no one can afford to put up again, in the Colly Weston roofs [Colly Weston slates are of dark-brown stone which attracts moss and lichen] patched with corrugated iron, in the big house which is more often than not a hospital or a school.' There is really only one blemish on the face of Rutland, and that is the strings of overhead wires which bedevil every village in profusion.

The formation of Rutland Water, the largest man-made lake in Europe, has transformed much of Rutland in an astonishing and spectacular way. Views of the Water can be had from many unexpected locations, but the biggest change has been the influx of sailing enthusiasts, walkers and cyclists, who now flock to this once quiet place.

J. B.

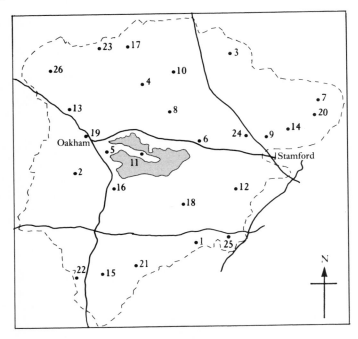

1 Barrowden	14 Little Casterton
2 Brooke	15 Lyddington
3 Clipsham	16 Manton
4 Cottesmore	17 Market Overton
5 Egleton	18 North Luffenham
6 Empingham	19 Oakham
7 Essendine	20 Ryhall
8 Exton	21 Seaton
9 Great Casterton	22 Stoke Dry
10 Greetham	23 Teigh
11 Hambleton	24 Tickencote
12 Ketton	25 Tixover
13 Langham	26 Whissendine

Selected List of Churches

BARROWDEN
St Peter
5m/8km E. of Uppingham SK 9400
Attractive limestone village in rich meadows of Welland Valley. Church mainly 14th-century with graceful tower and spire; 15th-century clerestory and E. window; remarkably wide, even by Rutland standards, where wide churches are common. Fine scrolly Renaissance monument of 1588.

BROOKE
St Peter
2m/3km S. of Oakham SK 8405
Remote in the gentle valley of the Gwash, sweeping limestone uplands all around; 13th-century tower, some Norman work inside, but much rebuilt about 1579. Looks as though nothing has changed since then, with complete screen, benches and stalls of that period. Beautiful Renaissance tomb of Charles Noel, 1619, retaining original colouring.

CLIPSHAM
St Mary
7m/11km N.W. of Stamford SK 9716
Much excellent 16th–19th-century village building in limestone. Large, beautiful 14th-century church on edge of small, tree-rich park. Fine tower, with broach spire of unusual design. Interior originally Norman; the N. arcade has massive 12th-century capitals; 13th-century S. arcade. Much 14th-century reconstruction, including the window tracery and the usual Perpendicular clerestory. But most striking feature of Clipsham is exterior view from S.

COTTESMORE
St Nicholas
4m/6km N.E. of Oakham SK 9013
Imposing 14th-century exterior, the spire with unusually tall broaches. Sadly 'scraped' within; font of *c.* 1200 with Christ and a saintly bishop.

EGLETON
St Edmund
1m/2km S.E. of Oakham SK 8707
Good village becoming spoiled. Modest church with 18th-century spire. Rich early-Norman carving on S. doorway and chancel arch.

EMPINGHAM
St Peter
5m/8km W. of Stamford SK 9508
Rutland at its best: large, attractive limestone village above Gwash Valley, now Rutland Water, and a splendid church overall. Three adjacent churches of Empingham, Exton and Ketton hard to beat as a trio anywhere in England. Empingham is nobly proportioned: note the W. tower, crocketed spire, and W. front, all 14th-century. Internally, nearly all Early English; both arcades and especially the S. transept are almost in original condition with some medieval colouring. Substantial 15th-century changes: new windows, roofs and clerestory. Early English chancel has beautiful double piscinas and triple sedilia – even for those who usually blench at these antiquarian details.

ESSENDINE
St Mary the Virgin
4m/6km N. of Stamford TF 0412
On the site of a Norman castle, of which it was the chapel, with trees and earthworks all around. Considerably repaired and rebuilt, but substantially a Norman building still, remodelled in 13th century. Striking S. doorway of *c.* 1140 with tympanum of Christ attended by angels.

EXTON
St Peter & St Paul
4m/6km E. of Oakham SK 9211
Another noble church, in the park of one of Rutland's great houses. Excellent limestone village outside park. Drastic rebuilding of church after damage by lightning in 1850 explains incongruity of details, but general effect still fine. Tower and spire especially notable. But the monuments to the Noels, Haringtons, and others connected with them, are the really splendid thing about the church. Here we have the memorials of a dead civilization. Notice especially the table-tomb with alabaster effigies of John Har-

ington, d. 1524, and wife, the appealing monument to Sir James Harington, d. 1591, and wife in the chancel, the splendid tomb of Robert Kelway, d. 1580, and the Noel monuments and sculpture by Grinling Gibbons and Nollekens; and read the gorgeous, rolling epitaphs aloud. Exton is intoxicating.

GREAT CASTERTON
St Peter & St Paul
2m/3km N.W. of Stamford TF 0008
Close to the hellish din and fury of the Great North Road, but all is peace within. Those who like completely unrestored churches – all 13th-century here – will like Great Casterton very much. Tower added 15th century. Church large, plastered, and whitewashed; clear glass, Georgian pulpit. Good collection of Ketton headstones, carved with winged cherubs' heads, in churchyard.

GREETHAM
St Mary the Virgin
6m/10km N.E. of Oakham SK 9214
14th-century W. tower; clasping buttresses, shafted belfry lights, and a lofty broach spire with three tiers of lucarnes.

HAMBLETON
St Andrew
3m/4km E. of Oakham SK 9007
Stands well on an eminence in village; views over Rutland Water; 13th-century tower and stumpy spire, a very characteristic sight in Rutland. Mainly 12th-century inside; 14th-century chancel much restored and adorned by late 19th-century rector. Much foreign woodwork of this period: pulpit, lectern and organ case. Interesting as a good period piece of late Victorian High Anglicanism.

KETTON
St Mary the Virgin
4m/6km S.W. of Stamford SK 9804
Stands in a large, attractive village built of local honey-coloured limestone with the exquisitely beautiful tower and spire rising above the trees and the sepia Colly Weston slate roofs. W. front a fine example of late 12th-century work, Norman evolving into Early English; rest of church almost entirely 13th-century with very lofty and dignified arcades. Spacious chancel practically rebuilt, 1863, but still striking because of great size; panelled roof painted in medieval colours, E. window and altar by Comper, 1907. Notable

collection of carved Ketton headstones in churchyard – a local art now dead.

LANGHAM
St Peter & St Paul
2m/3km N.W. of Oakham SK 8411
Yet another noble 14th-century church dominating, in this case, a rather messed-up village. Tower 13th-century, Decorated spire added early 14th. Internally, a spacious 14th-century building with plastered walls and much clear glass. Some 15th-century enlargement, notably clerestory and transepts. Fine proportions best seen looking W. from altar steps. Some good glass by Comper – chancel, 1904, and S. transept, 1908.

LITTLE CASTERTON
All Saints
2m/3km N. of Stamford TF 0009
Long, low and grey in meadows by the Gwash, beside tree-shadowed rectory. No tower, but W. bellcote which is characteristic of smaller Rutland churches. N. arcade *c.* 1190, S. arcade a little later. Usual clerestory. Some late 13th-century wall-painting, especially in recess of W. window. Fine double brass, under carpet in chancel, to Sir Thomas Burton, d. 1381, and his wife Margaret.

LYDDINGTON
St Andrew
2m/3km S. of Uppingham SP 8797
A grand church, mostly Perpendicular, in a village of good building in ironstone. Lyddington belonged to the medieval bishops of Lincoln, who had a palace here of which one 15th-century range remains. Tower and chancel of church belong to older building, 1320–40, but nave and aisles were rebuilt *c.* 1500, by one of the bishops. The height and symmetry of this work make it of great beauty. Note 15th-century wall-paintings; but especially the 17th-century arrangement of the sanctuary, with altar enclosed by rails on all sides. Brasses and rare acoustic jars in side walls of chancel.

MANTON
St Mary the Virgin
3m/4km S. of Oakham SK 8804
Homely and attractive church with memorable 13th-century W. front of heavy double bellcote, lancets, and buttresses.

MARKET OVERTON

St Peter & St Paul

5m/8km N. of Oakham SK 8816

Mostly Decorated outside, in a secluded churchyard. Massy late-Saxon tower arch with large stone jambs and plain imposts.

NORTH LUFFENHAM

St John the Baptist

6m/10km S.E. of Oakham SK 9303

Large, limestone village, and a large church to go with it, a little way off among trees. Mostly 14th-century work, tower and broach spire, window tracery; the arcades are good 13th-century. Particularly long, lofty chancel with medieval glass, elaborate sedilia, and E. window by Kempe.

OAKHAM

SK 8608

All Saints, Church Street

Attractive little country town with a magnificent church which rises like a central jewel in all distant views of the Vale of Catmose. Noble 14th-century tower and spire of ashlar limestone. Lofty interior of same date with notable sculptured capitals, including Coronation of the Virgin, and arcades. Usual enlargements in 15th century of clerestorey, and good Perpendicular windows. Excellent parclose screens from Sir Giles Gilbert Scott's restoration of 1857–8. Comper war memorial in the churchyard.

RYHALL

St John the Evangelist

2m/3km N. of Stamford TF 0310

A pleasant village by the Gwash, and one of the best churches in Rutland, with an exquisite tower and spire, 13th-century. Very wide nave and aisles again; N. arcade is *c.* 1200, S. arcade a little later. Chancel rebuilt in 15th century. Tablet of 1696 to an infant genius, aged two. St Tibba, patron saint of falconers, lived and died here *c.* 690. Against W. wall of N. aisle are remains of a medieval hermitage associated with her cult; possibly the burial place of the saint, against which the first church was built.

SEATON

All Hallows

3m/4km S.E. of Uppingham SP 9098

Late Norman work, especially the S. doorway and chancel arch, both with shafts, enriched capitals, and carved abaci. Handsome late 13th-century chamfered steeple.

STOKE DRY

St Andrew

2m/3km S. of Uppingham SP 8596

Unsophisticated, charming little church on hillside bordering remotest Leics.; Eyebrook reservoir below adds to delightful scene. Norman work visible here and there, but building mainly 13th- (S. arcade) and 14th-century, with the usual 15th-century clerestory, porch, and window tracery. The Digbys made Stoke Dry their principal seat from the 15th to the 17th century, and their three tombs are notable, especially the table-tomb of Kenelm, d. 1590, and Anne Digby. Chancel screen 15th-century. Better series of wall-paintings than usual, 15th-century; priest's chamber over N. porch said to be where Gunpowder Plot hatched, and Everard Digby hanged for complicity in 1606, but story not true.

TEIGH

Holy Trinity

5m/8km N. of Oakham SK 8616

Tower 14th-century, but plastered over in 1782, and a few details added, when rest of church rebuilt. Externally, a pretty little Gothic church; internally a pure 18th-century ensemble. Box pews face each other. At W. end, a triple grouping of pulpit, reading desk and clerk's desk with Lord's Prayer and Creed on either side. Commandments on E. wall. Small font used to be fixed to altar rails, very characteristic of period, but removed by someone with lack of knowledge. Plastered ceilings. Gothic window tracery, mostly clear glass. Those who like Georgian churches will like Teigh very much. Usual pleasant little limestone village amid rich grassland.

TICKENCOTE

St Peter

3m/4km N.W. of Stamford SK 9909

Just off the Great North Road. Everybody knows the photograph of the famous 12th-century chancel arch here, but the original is even more impressive: a staggering thing in five orders, each carved with a different design. Most of the 12th-century church was rebuilt by Cockerell in 1792 in the Norman style, but the vaulted chancel is largely the original. Good font of *c.* 1200.

TIXOVER

St Luke

5m/8km S.W. of Stamford SK 9700

A happy surprise in the meadows of the

Welland Valley, far from village and everything except grass, buttercups, and bullrushes. Mostly Norman, with a magnificently solid, untouched tower, and inside an imposing tower arch, all *c.* 1140. Rest of church mostly 13th-century, windows altered in 17th. Original medieval stone seats along chancel walls. Marble monument to lord of manor, 1623. Lit by oil lamps and candles; evensong at Tixover has an imploring note about it. Unfinished list of men serving in 'the war of 1914' in the porch in fading ink. One feels that life at Tixover stopped about then.

WHISSENDINE
St Andrew
4m/6km N.W. of Oakham SK 8314
Near the Leics. border; too much red brick and slate in village. But a splendid church, with notable 14th-century tower, fine even by Rutland standards. Spacious, light interior, with wide nave and aisles so characteristic of the county. Late 13th-century arcades, rest of church 14th- and 15th-century. Remarkable roof of 1728 with carved figures. Early 16th-century screen in S. transept came from St John's College, Cambridge in 1869, where Scott was 'restoring' and throwing things out. Much good modern woodwork. At W. end a model of church made from the 'pith out of rushes which grew in the village brook' by an old lady a century ago: a charming Victorian oddity.

Shropshire

Introduction

There is not one sort of scenery that can be called characteristic of the varied and beautiful landscape of Shropshire. This agricultural county, comparatively free from modern factories, is bisected by the Severn. Shrewsbury, the capital, Ludlow and Bridgnorth and Whitchurch, are its attractive old towns. Its Cheshire borders are flat and pitted with ponds: Wenlock Edge with its 'forest fleece' and the Clee Hills give wonderful outline to the pastoral country south of the spires and towers of Shrewsbury; wooded combes like those of Devon descend to orchard-land on the borders of Worcestershire; the north-west corner of the county round Oswestry has a Welsh quality; the Long Mynd, Stiperstones and Clun Hills on the edges of Montgomery and Radnor, to the west, have the grand and under-populated look of a border country, and there the few old churches are fortress-like. Scenery is more memorable in Shropshire than buildings; castles are prominent and, if a generalization is possible about the medieval churches, it is that most of them are small (with the exception of St Mary, Shrewsbury, and Ludlow), and show the gradual growth of ages. The prevailing materials are a good sharp pink sandstone and half-timber. Timber-framed churches have been much repaired and the most complete example, Melverley, does not look as old as its origin.

'Fear God and honour the Corbets' is said to be a Shropshire motto, and the non-Welsh half of the county is diversified, with the seats of hunting squires who did much church rebuilding and repair in the 18th century. The Myttons, Clives, Hills, Cottons, Hebers; they do not seem to have been markedly Puritan, but either old-fashioned High Church, before becoming Tractarian in Victorian times, or Roman Catholic. Two-bottle squires hung on in the Newport neighbourhood until this century.

To this remote county, in late-Georgian times, came that early industrialization of pottery at Coalport and iron at Coalbrookdale, which turned the chasm-like Severn Valley north of Bridgnorth into a brick semblance of the Stroud Valley in Gloucestershire. Ironbridge, Broseley and Madeley are its romantic survivals. The industrial churches here are either severe classic by Telford the engineer or starved-looking 'Early Pointed' in brick. Methodism flourished.

In Victorian times, ironmasters from Wolverhampton, like the Sparrows, and manufacturers from Kidderminster, Birmingham and Manchester, discovered Shropshire much as London discovered Surrey and Sussex. Norman Shaw and Eden Nesfield built them houses; Street, Pearson and Scott 'restored' old churches for them or built new ones.

Shropshire more than most English agricultural counties is remarkable for its 18th-century and Victorian churches. Its older churches are more impressive for their fittings, monuments, hatchments and liturgical arrangements than for their architecture. Shropshire is a county where the scenery is splendid and the churches for the most part are unobvious. This is the reason why later ages than the medieval predominate in the selections given below.

J.B.

1 Acton Burnell	23 Halston	45 Moreton Corbet
2 Adderley	24 Heath Chapel	46 Onibury
3 Alberbury	25 High Ercall	47 Petton
4 Alveley	26 Holdgate	48 Pitchford
5 Aston Eyre	27 Hopesay	49 Quatt
6 Battlefield	28 Hughley	50 Richard's Castle
7 Berwick	29 Kinet	51 St George's Oakengates
8 Bridgnorth	30 Langley Chapel	52 Shawbury
9 Bromfield	31 Leaton	53 Shifnal
10 Burford	32 Leebotwood	54 Shrewsbury
11 Calverhall	33 Llan-y-Blodwell	55 Stanton Lacy
12 Cheswardine	34 Llanymynech	56 Stoke St Milborough
13 Chetwynd	35 Longnor	57 Stokesay
14 Chirbury	36 Ludlow	58 Stottesdon
15 Claverley	37 Lydbury North	59 Tong
16 Cleobury North	38 Lyneal-cum-Colemere	60 Upton Cresset
17 Clun	39 Madeley	61 Welshampton
18 Condover	40 Melverley	62 Whitchurch
19 Eaton-under-Heywood	41 Meole Brace	63 Whittington
20 Edstaston	42 Middleton-in-Chirbury	64 Wistentow
21 Fitz	43 Minsterley	65 Worthen
22 Great Bolas	44 More	66 Wroxeter

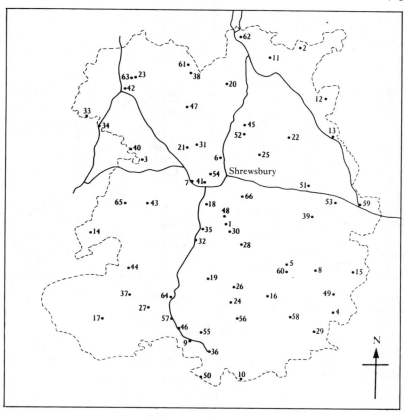

Selected List of Churches

ACTON BURNELL
St Mary
7m/11km S. of Shrewsbury SJ 5302
Setting, adjoining the castle. Good-quality late 13th-century church, but heavily 're-stored'. Brass of 1382; 16th–18th-century monuments; medieval tiles in N. transept.

ADDERLEY
St Peter
4m/6km N. of Market Drayton SJ 6639
Mostly Gothic of 1801 by Richard Baker. Large and cruciform with N. transept of 1635–7 furnished as a manorial pew with screen and panelling; sturdy Classical W. tower, 1712. The windows are pointed and most of the panes are clear crown glass. The Gothic iron window tracery is typical of this part of Shropshire at the date. Late 14th-century brass in the chancel. Chancel and transepts, R.C.F.; nave partitioned off and still parochial.

ALBERBURY
St Michael
8m/12km W. of Shrewsbury SJ 3514
Setting by the ruined castle. Saxon in origin but with work of all medieval periods; massive 13th-century saddleback tower at N.E. of nave. Fine 14th-century S. chapel and handsome 15th-century roofs. Much rebuilding and embellishment of 1840s. Splendid Art Nouveau window by Barbara Leighton, 1897. Great array of Leighton and Lyster monuments.

ALVELEY
St Mary
6m/10km S.E. of Bridgnorth SO 7684
Setting on a hill-top. Large aisled Norman and later church with 15th-century clerestory and roof. Georgian top to tower. Some medieval glass and an altar frontal. Still rewarding in spite of A. W. Blomfield's restoration of 1878–9.

ASTON EYRE
(dedication unknown)
4m/6km W. of Bridgnorth SO 6594
Diminutive two-cell Norman church with reputedly the best piece of Norman sculpture in the county: a tympanum over the S. door depicting Christ's Entry into Jerusalem. This is a powerful and direct carving of the Herefordshire School. Norman windows and Transitional chancel arch.

BATTLEFIELD
St Mary Magdalene
3m/4km N. of Shrewsbury SJ 5116
The church of a chantry college founded in 1406 for the souls of those slain in the Battle of Shrewsbury, 1403, between Henry IV and Harry Hotspur. In use by 1409; tower finished *c.* 1500. Remarkable mid-15th-century Pietà. Rescued from ruin by S. Pountney Smith in 1861 and given a spectacular hammer-beam roof, screen, reredos, stained glass, and Maw's tiles.
R.C.F.

BERWICK
(dedication unknown)
2m/3km N.W. of Shrewsbury SJ 4713
Setting in grounds of Berwick House. Built in 1670 with tower and S. porch of *c.* 1735. Much furnishing of both periods; the 18th-century reredos is preserved in the house. New E. end 1892–4 by Walker. Monument by Chantrey.

BRIDGNORTH
SO 7193
St Leonard
Setting at the summit of the town, in a close surrounded by old brick houses; the impressive tower seen for miles. Largely a Victorian rebuilding by Slater, large, attractive and interesting, with 17th-century hammer-beam roof over the extraordinarily wide nave. Romantic vistas in the S. aisle and some Arts and Crafts metalwork.
R.C.F.
St Mary Magdalene
Setting, terminating a fine Georgian street. By Thomas Telford, 1792–4. Boldly Classical design with fine tower. Chancel added by Blomfield, 1876; late-Victorian interior.

BROMFIELD
St Mary the Virgin
3m/4km N. of Ludlow SO 4876
Riverside setting. The surviving parochial nave, N. aisle and N.W. tower of a small Benedictine church, mainly Norman and 13th-century. Small post-Dissolution domestic fragment attached. Chancel re-formed in 1658 with painted ceiling, 1672. Restored 1889–90 by C. Hodgson Fowler with big triptych by C. E. Buckeridge. Picturesque priory gatehouse survives.

BURFORD
St Mary
½m/1km W. of Tenbury Wells SO 5868
Setting by Burford House and gardens. Medieval survivals, including important monuments, but essentially a gorgeous Arts and Crafts ensemble of 1889 onward by Aston Webb and collaborators. Cornwall effigies; one of triptych form by Melchior Salabuss, 1558.

CALVERHALL
Holy Trinity
5m/8km S.E. of Whitchurch SJ 6037
By W. Eden Nesfield, 1872–9. Church in the Perpendicular style tacked onto some 18th-century almshouses. Interior rather plain, but glass by Morris and Burne-Jones, a nicely painted organ, and many Aesthetic Movement sunflowers.

CHESWARDINE
St Swithun
4m/6km S.E. of Market Drayton SJ 7129
By J. L. Pearson, 1888–9. In the Early English style and very fine, retaining the big 15th-century tower and 13th-century N. chapel. Pearson triptych, Kempe glass, and brasses.

CHETWYND
St Michael and All Angels
1m/2km N. of Newport SJ 7419
By Benjamin Ferrey, 1865–7. N. tower with tall broach spire. Graceful and impressive interior enriched by some later Victorian/Edwardian furnishings. Fine original tiling in the E. end.

CHIRBURY
St Michael
3m/4km N. of Church Stoke SO 2698
The big parochial nave and aisles of an Augustinian church, with a W. tower apparently supervised in the 14th century by Brother Richard the mason, one of the canons. High nave roof of local type. Monastic stalls, screen, and rood loft now at Montgomery. Small brick chancel of 1733 with mosaic reredos by Blomfield. Fine 18th-century candelabrum.

CLAVERLEY
All Saints
5m/8km E. of Bridgnorth SO 7993
Attractive village with black and white houses. Handsome church of Norman origin, as shown by tower base and N. arcade; rest is late 13th–15th-century. Impressive wall-paintings of *c.* 1200 over N. arcade call to mind the Bayeux tapestry. Perpendicular nave and chancel roofs; 15th–16th-century monuments, and some 14th-century glass.

CLEOBURY NORTH
St Peter & St Paul
7m/11km S.W. of Bridgnorth SO 6286
Short Norman N.W. tower with pyramidal roof. Low, unspoilt interior, intimate and whitewashed. Early 13th-century arcade and chancel arch; chancel rebuilt 1890. Good 16th–17th-century roofs and other woodwork.

CLIVE
All Saints
3m/4km of Wem SJ 5124
Setting on a steep timbered hillside. By C. J. Ferguson, 1885–94, with medieval core. Spectacular tower and spire and rich Arts and Crafts Gothic furnishings.

CLUN
St George
5m/8km N. of Knighton and 8m/12km W. of Craven Arms SO 3080
Basically Norman; large and aisled; later alterations include noble 15th-century collar-braced roofs and the large fortress-like tower of local type. Restored and partly rebuilt by Street, 1877; 15th-century altar canopy and large lych gate of 1723.

CONDOVER
St Mary & St Andrew
4m/6km S. of Shrewsbury SJ 4905
Large pink sandstone church; Norman and later with much rebuilding of 1662–79, including the tower and partly timber-framed S. transept. Inside, a rich collection of monu-

ments from late 17th century onward, dominated by the powerful kneeling figure of Sir Thomas Cholmondeley, d. 1864.

EATON-UNDER-HEYWOOD
St Edith
4m/6km S.E. of Church Stretton SO 4990
Marvellous hill setting. A church with Norman origins, 13th-century chancel and tower, Perpendicular roofs and battlements. Sympathetically restored in 19th century. Jacobean pulpit with tester dated 1670, reading desk, panelling, and communion rails.

EDSTASTON
St Mary the Virgin
2m/3km N. of Wem SJ 5131
Norman nave and chancel only; fine masonry and rich detail with three sumptuous doorways and corbel table. Two original doors with ironwork. Medieval roof and wall-paintings.

FITZ
St Peter & St Paul
4m/6km N.W. of Shrewsbury SJ 4417
Brick Georgian tower and nave, 1722; chancel and vestry added by Sir Aston Webb in 1905. Unusual and interesting interior has W. gallery with good screen and other fittings by Webb.

GREAT BOLAS
St John the Baptist
6m/10km N. of Wellington SJ 6421
Georgian brick church of 1726–9 by John Wilding; the tower with parapet and vases. Unspoilt whitewashed interior with original furnishings including box pews, canopied pulpit, and W. gallery. Small 17th-century chancel.

HALSTON
(private chapel)
1m/2km E. of Whittington SJ 3431
Isolated in park. Small timber-framed chapel, late-medieval or early post-Reformation, has one of the most interesting interiors in the county. The 16th–18th-century fittings all complete: panelled walls, box pews arranged college-wise, pulpit, reading pew, and reredos. Family chapel of the Myttons; Jack Mytton, portrayed by 'Nimrod', was squire of Halston.

HEATH CHAPEL
(dedication unknown)
6m/10km N.W. of Ludlow SJ 5585
Isolated setting on hills with earthworks of deserted village nearby. Perfect small Norman chapel with largely 17th-century furnishings, totally unrestored: box pews, two-decker pulpit, and three-sided altar rails.

HIGH ERCALL
St Michael and All Angels
5m/8km N.W. of Wellington SJ 5197
Sizeable aisled church rebuilt after Civil War destruction using much detail of *c.* 1200, including the arcades. Savaged by Street, but retaining a Norman tympanum and an effigy of a knight, *c.* 1320.

HOLDGATE
Holy Trinity
8m/12km S.W. of Much Wenlock SO 5689
Next to massive tree-covered motte of Norman castle. Much of the fabric is 12th-century or earlier. Richly carved S. doorway and font, both undoubtedly the work of the famous Hereford School. Late-medieval benches and misericords.

HOPESAY
St Mary
3m/4km W. of Craven Arms SO 3983
Hillside setting. Nave and chancel in one, *c.* 1200. Massive, squat W. tower has 17th-century double pyramidal roof characteristic of the area. Another local feature is the impressive 15th-century arch-braced collar-beam roof with quatrefoil windbraces. W. gallery.

HUGHLEY
St John the Baptist
4m/6km W. of Much Wenlock SO 5697
Small, essentially mid-14th-century church with fine roof, remains of contemporary glass, and a splendid 15th-century screen.

KINLET
St John the Baptist
4m/6km N.E. of Cleobury Mortimer SO 7118
Set in parkland by the Hall of 1729. Quite large, late-Norman onward, aisled and cruciform with good detail. Restored, scraped and painted 1892–3 by J. Oldrid Scott; he also rescued the timber-framed Perpendicular clerestory. E. window has beautiful and well-restored 14th-century glass. Big

collection of monuments, next best in the county after Tong, from 14th century onward, to Blount, Childe and Baldwin families. Fine alabaster Blount tomb of 1584 with kneeling figures. Handsome early 19th-century mahogany organ case.

LANGLEY CHAPEL
(dedication unknown)
1m/2km S. of Acton Burnell SJ 5301

Setting in a field in quiet countryside near the manor house. Small, primitive late 16th–early 17th-century, the furnishings of the whitewashed interior almost all of the latter period. Pews with turned knobs and doors, musicians' seats, and benches for the poor at the back; pulpit, canopied reading pew, holy table away from the E. wall with kneelers around it. Old floors of stone and brick. E.H.

LEATON
Holy Trinity
4m/6km N.W. of Shrewsbury SJ 4618

Setting among pines with the vicarage beside. Nice ashlar church by S. Pountney Smith, 1859; tower and tall crocketed spire added in 1872. Well-proportioned within and without; late instance of a two-decker pulpit.

LEEBOTWOOD
St Mary the Virgin
4m/6km N.E. of Church Stretton SO 4798

Foothills of the Long Mynd. Medieval details in walls and roof, otherwise a small single-cell church fitted up in *c.* 1800 and little changed. Inside has clear glass except for bright early-Victorian E. window; box pews with iron hat-pegs, panelling, two-decker pulpit, and a sort of chancel screen. Tablets in chancel, remains of a wall-painting, and W. gallery. The interior only spoiled by the unhappily matchboarded roof.

LLAN-Y-BLODWELL
St Michael
5m/8km S.W. of Oswestry SJ 2422

Beautifully sited on the edge of Wales. A 19th-century incumbent, the Rev. John Parker, almost rebuilt and entirely redecorated the church between 1845 and 1860. Octagonal tower with curiously convex spire. Inside, all is colour – red, blue and gilt. The screen is 15th-century, repainted. The altar is copied from an Italian model. Black letter texts on the walls. The effect is rich and

pleasing, but not to those who dislike decoration laid over architecture.

LLANYMYNECH
St Agatha
6m/10km S. of Oswestry SJ 2620

By Thomas Penson, 1843–4. Remarkable church in the neo-Norman style of grey limestone with yellow terracotta mouldings. Festive E. and W. fronts; N.W. tower has porch, large angle buttresses, and pyramidal roof. Interior refitted in 1879, but retaining glass by Wailes, 1855.

LONGNOR
St Mary the Virgin
8m/12km S. of Shrewsbury SJ 4800

Small late 13th-century stone church in tree-shaded proximity to the 17th-century Hall. Good details. Refitted in 18th century with outside stairway to W. gallery; clear glass, box pews and pulpit. Whitewashed interior quite unrestored apart from a cheap modern roof.

LUDLOW
St Lawrence
24m/38km S. of Shrewsbury SO 5174

Large and well-known essentially 15th-century cruciform church at the centre and summit of the town. Large and lofty interior with 15th-century arcades and earlier transepts. Rich in screens and other woodwork; splendid choir-stalls of 1447 with misericords and much 15th-century glass. Expensive restorations by Sir Giles Gilbert Scott and Blomfield were too strident, and have removed the old texture both inside and out.

LYDBURY NORTH
St Michael
3m/4km S.E. of Bishop's Castle SO 3585

Picturesque long, low cruciform church, plastered inside and out, having been well restored by J. T. Micklethwaite, 1901. Norman (of two periods) and later with fine 15th-century nave roof, 14th-century N. and 17th-century S. transepts; 15th-century rood screen with plastered tympanum of 1615 above, on which are inscribed the Commandments; 17th-century box pews, pulpit, altar rails, and font cover.

LYNEAL-CUM-COLEMERE
St John the Evangelist
3m/4km S.E. of Ellesmere SJ 4433

Setting by the mere among trees. By G. E.

Street, 1870. Bold, small and simple Decorated church with contrasting ashlar bands. Dignified interior has Street pulpit and reredos.

MADELEY
St Michael
2m/3km S. of Dawley SJ 6904
By Thomas Telford, 1794–6. Classical, octagonal, galleried Evangelical Revival church, originally with a central pulpit. No Telford furnishings remain, and the aggressive E. end was added in 1910. Cast-iron Fletcher tomb in churchyard.

MELVERLEY
St Peter
10m/16km W. of Shrewsbury SJ 3316
Small, probably late 15th-century timber-framed church beside the River Vyrnwy with fine distant views. Inside, a frame of the building divides chancel from nave, and another makes a W. division with a gallery of 1718. Of the three divisions the chancel is the largest, and the frame, looking like a chancel screen, produces an odd effect. Jacobean pulpit and panelling. Much restored but attractively rustic and barn-like.

MEOLE BRACE
Holy Trinity
S. district of Shrewsbury SJ 4810
By E. Haycock Jnr, 1867–8. Decorated church and more ambitious than most of his work. But the real reason for visiting is the stained glass in the apse, 1869–70. This is some of the best ever designed by William Morris, Ford Madox Brown, and Sir Edward Burne-Jones: rich clear panels of the Crucifixion, Kings, Martyrs and Apostles. Glass by Kempe in E. window of S. aisle, 1894.

MIDDLETON-IN-CHIRBURY
Holy Trinity
2m/3km E. of Oswestry SJ 3129
Delightfully remote hillside setting. Dull exterior of 1843 by Edward Haycock, but inside nearly all the furniture is the work of the Rev. Waldegrave Brewster, vicar 1872–1901. Carved bench-ends and scenes depicting agricultural labours and signs of the Zodiac on the transept capitals. The work is rather crude but wonderfully captures the spirit of this late Victorian parson.

MINSTERLEY
Holy Trinity
9m/15km S.W. of Shrewsbury SJ 3705
By William Taylor of London, 1689; built in a strange brick and stone Baroque style with fantastic details. Plastered interior with some good woodwork: pulpit with tester, screen, and panelled E. end. Other appointments, especially the plastic chairs, disappointing.

MORE
St Peter
2m/3km N.E. of Bishop's Castle SO 3491
Among black and white houses in remote, flat landscape between hills of the Welsh border. Rebuilt in 1845 in a countrified Gothic style, apart from the massive tower of local type. Interior not much disturbed with W. gallery and remarkable More Chapel pew. Full of the piety of early Tractarianism.

MORETON CORBET
St Bartholomew
8m/12km N.E. of Shrewsbury SJ 5523
Beside the splendid ruin of the Corbet's castle and 17th-century manor house. Small church with fine 14th-century S. chapel, the rest mainly 18th-century Gothic, including family pew with fireplace. Good Corbet monuments; altar and glass by Comper, 1905.

ONIBURY
St Michael
3m/4km S.E. of Craven Arms SO 4579
Small Norman church sensitively restored by Detmar Blow in 1902 on sound anti-scrape principles. Rough whitened plaster, rough-hewn oak W. gallery with square front and Edward VII carved arms; rough-hewn oak pews with oak posts supporting iron lanterns for electric light; hat pegs; 1902 commandment boards and box pews at W. end. A loving recapturing of village simplicity.

PETTON
(dedication unknown)
1m/2km W. of Burlton SJ 4326
Brick church of 1727, restored in late 19th century. Inside, a wonderful collection of 16th–18th-century woodwork, some of it belonging to the church, but mostly brought in later. Canopied two-decker pulpit, 1635, panelling, box pews, and W. gallery. Late

Victorian wrought-iron screen. Rather a sumptuous interior with a certain Wren flavour.

PITCHFORD
St Michael

6m/10km S. of Shrewsbury SJ 5303
Setting in park beside timbered-framed manor house. Early Norman and later church, small and little-restored, with 17th- and 18th-century furnishings, including box pews and pulpit. Wooden effigy of knight in chain mail, *c.* 1230; fragments of 14th- and 18th-century armorial glass, Tudor incised slabs, and hatchments.

QUATT
St Andrew

4m/6km S.E. of Bridgnorth SO 7588
Largely Georgian brick exterior of 1763. Many periods inside with interesting woodwork and monuments. Post-war restoration by S. E. Dykes-Bower; pleasant light interior has W. gallery with organ.

RICHARD'S CASTLE
All Saints

3m/4km S. of Ludlow SO 4969
Impressive hillside church by R. Norman Shaw, 1891–2. Cliff-like walls and a big, austere tower. The interior also on the grand scale, ashlar-faced and largely without the decoration Shaw intended; the main features are the sumptuous triptych painted by C. E. Buckeridge and Shaw's own organ case and chancel fittings. Evocative painting of the angels at the sepulchre. No stained glass, and consequently rather over-lit.

ST GEORGE'S, OAKENGATES
St George

4m/6km E. of Wellington SJ 7010
G. E. Street, 1862; tower not finished until 1929. Big, rugged church, full of originality; almost detached N. tower, oddly fenestrated clerestory, and assorted nave piers in the robust interior. Tunnel-vaulted chancel and polychrome arches of stone and brick.

SHAWBURY
St Mary the Virgin

7m/11km N.E. of Shrewsbury SJ 5521
Small late-Norman aisled church with large Early English chancel and fine Perpendicular tower. Some 17th-century roofs and furnishings; fine 18th-century chandeliers; remains of glass; considerable restoration.

SHIFNAL
St Andrew

7m/11km S. of Newport SJ 7407
Large, externally picturesque and of many periods with Norman core. Elizabethan hammer-beam roofs and 16th–17th-century monuments; 18th-century organ case by England. Heavily restored by Scott, 1876–9, when the interior was scraped; reredos by J. Oldrid Scott.

SHREWSBURY
SJ 4912
St Alkmund, Fish Street

Perpendicular tower and tall steeple; nave and chancel rebuilt in Strawberry Hill Gothic by Carline and Tilley, 1795. Largely late-Victorian inside with E. window transparency by Eginton after Guido Reni.

St Chad, Murivance

Large Georgian church by George Steuart, 1790–2, replacing on a new site a large collegiate church which had been allowed to fall down; its churchyard and side chapel survive in the town centre. The new church has a circular galleried nave built for a central pulpit, replaced by an Art Nouveau metal one at the side. Pews cut down; fine repainted Victorian reredos.

Holy Cross, Abbey Foregate

Parochial nave of the abbey church of SS. Peter and Paul. Founded 1083; E. part of big aisled nave built soon after; W. end is late 14th-century with massive tower. Monastic E. end all gone, rebuilt on a smaller scale by J. L. Pearson, partly vaulted and with fine triptych, 1886–7. Organ case by Charles Nicholson. Extensive and disorderly assortment of monuments, mostly from elsewhere.

St Mary

Large former collegiate church of many periods and high architectural quality. The windows are filled with late-medieval stained glass imported from Germany and the Netherlands in the last century, plus the 14th-century English Jesse E. window, probably transferred from a friars' church in the town. Little old furniture but many monuments. The interior is scraped but still splendid.

R.C.F.

STANTON LACY
St Peter

3m/4km N. of Ludlow SO 4978
One of the best Saxon churches in Shrop-

shire. Late 11th-century work in nave and N. transept; pilaster strip decoration and fine blocked N. doorway. Much rebuilding in early 14th century; chancel and S. aisle with tomb recesses on outside.

STOKE ST MILBOROUGH
St Milbruga
6m/10km N.E. of Ludlow SO 5682
In a remote village in the Clee hills. Spacious, aisleless Early English and later church full of sunlight; unscraped with barnlike roofs. Timber porch with brick nogging.

STOKESAY
St John the Baptist
1km/2km S. of Craven Arms SO 4381
Beside the incredible 13th-century fortified manor house; two very special buildings in the pastoral Onny valley. Small, basically Norman church, nearly demolished in the Civil War; the nave and tower rebuilt in 1654 and the chancel in 1664. The furnishings nearly complete: box pews, two-decker canopied family pew, wall-texts, and 18th-century W. gallery. Unrestored except for an Edwardian reredos.

STOTTESDON
St Mary
4m/6km N. of Cleobury Mortimer SO 6782
Setting. Quite large with some Saxon and Norman work but mainly 14th-century with good details. Elaborate Norman font with medallions, scrolls and leaves in the restored interior.

TONG
St Bartholomew
3m/4km E. of Shinal SJ 7907
Made collegiate and rebuilt in 1410; not large but rather spectacular and with a remarkable array of medieval furnishings and monuments: screens, stalls, seating, altar tombs, and effigies. Fan-vaulted chantry chapel added in 1515, with traces of colour and original altar-slab. Fairly restrained restorations by Street and Christian.

UPTON CRESSET
St Michael
4m/6km W. of Bridgnorth SO 6592
Steep orchard setting by the manor house. Very small with weatherboarded belfry and short lead spire; Norman chancel arch, S. door and tub-shaped font.
R.C.F.

WELSHAMPTON
St Mary
2m/3km E. of Ellesmere SJ 4335
By Sir George Gilbert Scott, 1863. Small Early English church, the roofs gaily patterned with blue and green slates. Bellcote, lancets, and apsidal sanctuary; inside are marble arcade pillars, Caen stone font and pulpit, and lots of good naturalistic carving. Fine chancel glass by Heaton, Butler & Bayne.

WHITCHURCH
St Alkmund
18m/29km N. of Shrewsbury SJ 5441
Fine large town church of 1712–13 by William Smith of Warwick, according to a design by John Barker. Handsome exterior with splendid red sandstone tower. The interior is late-Victorian, when it was lined with dark red sandstone, rearranged, and sumptuously refurnished using some of the old woodwork. Fine Tuscan arcades to the nave. Interesting tombs. A fine interior despite everything, but very dark on account of the stained glass.

WHITTINGTON
St John the Baptist
3m/4km N.E. of Oswestry SJ 3231
Red-brick Georgian with tower of 1747 and nave 1805–6. The interior totally renewed in 1894 and later; E. window and woodwork by F. C. Eden, 1934.

WISTANSTOW
Holy Trinity
2m/3km N. of Craven Arms SO 4385
Cruciform central-towered church, not large, and of several periods from *c.* 1200 onward. Good roofs, 17th-century wall-texts, box pews in transepts, and an early 19th-century organ case. Nice headstones in the churchyard.

WORTHEN
All Saints
7m/11km E. of Welshpool SJ 3204
Several periods. Wide, low nave with barn roof; massive N. tower; brick chancel of 1761; timber S. porch. Mainly 17th-century box pews and benches rearranged in 1847 with Gothic two-decker pulpit. Chancel Victorianized.

WROXETER

St Andrew

5m/8km S.E. of Shrewsbury SJ 5608

Roman columns at the gate. The nave is Saxon re-using more Roman materials; the rest medieval of various dates, altered in the 18th century. Interior unchanged since early 19th century, with brick floors, W. gallery with Gothic organ and seating. Font made from an inverted Roman column base, remains of wall-paintings, and important 16th-century monuments.

R.C.F.

The Soke of Peterborough

Introduction

In the east it is fen country, becoming hilly and wooded as it stretches westward to Stamford. Outside the limestone walls of this lovely Lincolnshire town stand the park and immense Elizabethan house of Burghley in the Soke. The Manor of Burghley and other lands in the Soke (together with wide jurisdictional rights over the whole area) formerly belonged to the abbots of Peterborough, and were granted by Elizabeth I to her treasurer Lord Burghley. The industrialized city of Peterborough is not half so dull as those who pass through it in the train may think. It is a grey town – grey limestone, lightish-grey and grey-yellow brick. The west front of the Cathedral was described as 'the grandest and finest in Europe'. Norman nave and roof and the splendid 'New Building' in Perpendicular at the east end, the tree-shaded ramifications of the close, are all hidden from the main road; so is the excellent local museum.

The churches of the Soke and their villages are almost all in local limestone, the churches with stone spires. Vestiges of Norman work in many of the churches recall the influence of the Benedictine Abbey.

J.B.

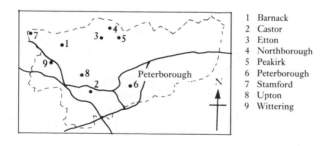

1 Barnack
2 Castor
3 Etton
4 Northborough
5 Peakirk
6 Peterborough
7 Stamford
8 Upton
9 Wittering

Selected List of Churches

BARNACK
St John the Baptist
3m/4km S.E. of Stamford TF 0705
Originally a grand Saxon church, as evidenced by the spectacular stone stripwork decoration of the tower and the magnificent tower arch. The church has since acquired the characteristics of the succeeding centuries, and so is typical of that inspired architectural hotch-potch which is the English Parish Church. The Barnack stone quarries fed the greatest of the medieval building projects in the Nene Valley and farther afield. Beautiful late-Saxon or early-Norman carving of Christ in Majesty.

CASTOR
St Kyneburgha
2m/3km W. of Peterborough TL 1298
This small village stands near a Roman settlement, and in Norman times was evidently still important, to judge by the fine tower of the period, crowned by a stumpy Germanic spire. Few Norman cathedrals have a more richly ornamented steeple than this, with all four walls of the tower panelled in two stages of characteristic Romanesque detail. There are fragments of Saxon carving and a rare inscription recording the dedication of the church in 1124.

ETTON
St Stephen
6m/10km N.W. of Peterborough TF 1406
Good example of a complete, though restored, 13th-century church; W. tower and broach spire, three-bay double-chamfered nave arcades and matching chancel arch.

NORTHBOROUGH
St Andrew
7m/11km N.W. of Peterborough TF 1507
A strangely incomplete 12th- and 13th-century church, fragment of a much larger one, elaborated in the 14th century. Splendid S. chapel shows development from Decorated to Perpendicular. Cromwell's wife is buried here (his son-in-law owned the manor) and so is John Clare's wife, Patty.

PEAKIRK
St Pega
5m/8km N. of Peterborough TF 1606
On the Fen edge; the site of St Pega's cell is nearby. Norman bellcote, S. doorway and N. arcade, the rest 13th-century; 14th-century wall-paintings of the Passion.

PETERBOROUGH
TL 1998
All Saints, Park Road
By Temple Moore, 1894. A sensitive essay in the Decorated style with the tower oddly positioned at the E. end of the S. chancel aisle.
St John the Baptist
A Perpendicular building of 1402–7, re-using some earlier materials; the tower sadly spoiled by the nearby Norwich Union building. Octagonal 15th-century font and good later monuments.

STAMFORD
St Martin Without
See Stamford, Lincolnshire

UPTON
St John the Baptist
6m/10km W. of Peterborough TF 1000
An odd-looking building, more secular than ecclesiastical; it was a chapel of ease until 1851. Some Norman work, chancel rebuilt in 1842, the rest being 17th-century Gothic associated with the fine monument to Sir William Dove, d. 1633, and his two wives.

WITTERING
All Saints
3m/4km S.E. of Stamford TF 0502
Two-cell late-Saxon church with tremendous chancel arch and original nave and chancel quoins. Good Norman nave arcade with roll mouldings and zig-zags.

Somerset

Introduction

No county really comes up to Somerset for medieval churches, and of these three-quarters are Perpendicular (15th-century). As A. K. Wickham said, 'Those boundaries are natural, and have from very early times also been those of the diocese ... It is not of course suggested that the local style ceased at the county borders, or even that the medieval builders were conscious of them, but merely that they provide today a casket, as it were, in which these jewels can most easily be compared and admired.' Churches are mentioned first here because they are the most prominent sights in Somerset, despite the wide variety of its scenery. This variety contains: sea coast along the Bristol Channel; heathery hills on Exmoor; rich valleys in the south-west full of orchards; wooded steel combes round Bruton and Shepton Mallet; a bare and comparatively churchless area on the west where the Bredons rise nearly as high between Bridgwater and Taunton; a silvery gorge like Cheddar in the Mendips; on the east, Radstock, where coal is quarried; and in the middle of the county the flat alluvial basin providing a fen district where Axe, Brue and Parrett flow into the Bristol Channel and hills rise like blue islands from the flat. Nor are the towns less varied: Bath so 18th-century with its limestone crescents and terraces and squares; Wells, whose towers rise from a hollow in the Mendips, a city where the cathedral predominates and the atmosphere is medieval in the sound of bells; Taunton, Yeovil and Bridgwater, chain-stored and industrialized; Ilminster, Crewkerne and Axbridge, old-fashioned market towns with grand Perpendicular churches. Over orchards and willows, wherever you are in Somerset, you can hear the church bells, for few towers contain less than six of them and this is the chief county of ringers.

The variety of stones gives the county a colour. Bath quarries provide pale-yellow stone. Doulting stone, from which Wells and the Mendip churches are built, is silvery-grey; around Somerton and the Polden hills the quarries yield blue lias, which looks particularly good with the old red curly tiles on cottages; and in the west is red sandstone. Finest of all stone is that from Ham Hill in the south. On the Dorset border the old cottages and churches are a rich golden-yellow.

It was after the Black Death and at the end of the 14th century that the great rebuilding of Somerset churches started, and there is no better summary of these buildings than that of the Victorian antiquarian Freeman: 'The typical form is a lofty and elaborate W. tower, disengaged from the aisles, often vaulted within, and nave and aisles with or without clerestory; very commonly a S. porch as high as the aisles, a high roof, and a comparatively insignificant chancel of earlier work, with Perpendicular chapels on each side. Polygonal turrets are frequent. The roofs are various, but different forms of the coved roof are typical. The interiors are rich in screens and other woodwork. The work is generally superior in the north to that in the south part of the county, owing to the superior quality of the stones admitting more delicate chiselling. The towers, which are the great glory of the county, may be ranked under three typical forms. (1) The Taunton type with a staircase turret at one corner and double buttresses at the others, all the pinnacles being of equal height, the tower being divided into stages by horizontal string courses: e.g. St Mary Magdalene and St James, Taunton; Isle Abbots; Bishops Lydeard; and Huish. (2) The Bristol type, with a prominent turret, crowned with a single spirelet rising above the rest. (3) The Wrington type, which dispenses with staircase turret and horizontal divisions and is panelled with two enormous lofty belfry windows, with pinnacled turrets of the same height; Wrington; St Cuthbert's, Wells; St John's, Glastonbury; and North Petherton. Spires are very unfrequent and where they exist are sometimes imperfect . . .'

To these glorious towers, built by Somerset people for themselves and essentially non-monastic, the Victorians did little harm. They seem to have been over-awed into leaving them alone and confined their attentions to interiors, but even their 'restorations' were generally mild.

J.B.

1	Alford	36	Dunster	71	Porlock
2	Ashington	37	East Brent	72	Puxton
3	Axbridge	38	Evercreech	73	Queen Camel
4	Babington	39	Flax Bourton	74	Redlynch
5	Backwell	40	Glastonbury	75	Rode
6	Bagborough	41	Hardington	76	Rodney Stoke
7	Banwell	42	High Ham	77	St Catherine
8	Batcombe	43	Hinton Blewett	78	Selworthy
9	Bath	44	Hinton St George	79	Shepton Mallet
10	Bishops Lydeard	45	Holcombe	80	Somerton
11	Blackford	46	Hornblotton	81	South Brent
12	Bridgwater	47	Huish Episcopi	82	Stawley
13	Broomfield	48	Ile Abbotts	83	Stogursey
14	Brushford	49	Ilminster	84	Stoke St Gregory
15	Bruton	50	Kilmersdon	85	Stone-sub-Hamdon
16	Buckland Dinham	51	Kingsbury Episcopi	86	Sutton Bingham
17	Buckland St Mary	52	Langport	87	Sutton Mallett
18	Cameley	53	Leigh-on-Mendip	88	Taunton
19	Catcott	54	Locking	89	Trull
20	Chantry	55	Long Ashton	90	Uphill
21	Charterhouse-on-Mendip	56	Long Sutton	91	Watchet
22	Cheddar	57	Low Ham	92	Wedmore
23	Chedzoy	58	Martock	93	Wellow
24	Chew Magna	59	Mells	94	Wells
25	Chewton Mendip	60	Middlezoy	95	West Bagborough
26	Chiltorne Domer	61	Milborne Port	96	West Pennard
27	Churchstanton	62	Minehead	97	West Quantoxhead
28	Compton Martin	63	Muchelney	98	Weston Zoyland
29	Congresbury	64	North Cadbury	99	Winscombe
30	Crewkerne	65	North Curry	100	Witham
31	Croscombe	66	North Petherton	101	Woolley
32	Culbone	67	Norton-sub-Hamdon	102	Wrington
33	Curry Mallet	68	Oare	103	Wyke Champfleur
34	Curry Rivel	69	Pawlett	104	Yatton
35	Ditcheat	70	Pilton	105	Yeovil

map overleaf

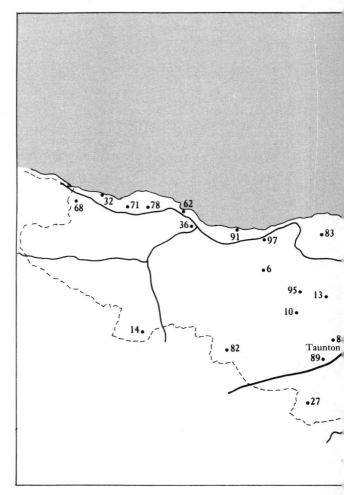

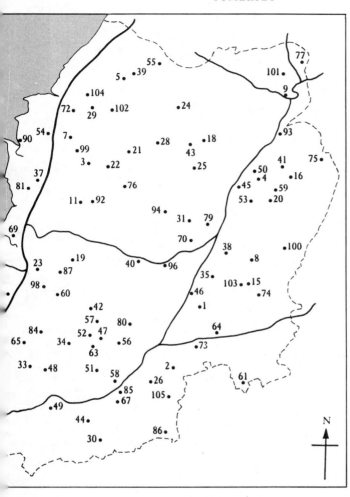

Selected List of Churches

ALFORD
All Saints
2m/3km W. of Castle Cary ST 6032
Modest Perpendicular church set in parkland by Alford House. Good benches, porch roofs and rood screen; one good glass figure.

ASHINGTON
St Vincent
4m/6km N. of Yeovil ST 5621
Small 13th-century church with nave, chancel and gabled bellcote. Thoroughly reconditioned by the Victorians, who retained the 17th-century pulpit and some box pews; 15th-century S. door.

AXBRIDGE
St John the Baptist
2m/3km W. of Cheddar ST 4354
Impressive 15th-century town church with central tower, approached up a flight of steps from the corner of the market square. The interior is spacious and airy with huge plaster ceiling dated 1637 over the nave, and 15th-century fan vaulting over the crossing. Good memorials and brass of 1493. Altar frontal of 1720.

BABINGTON
St Margaret
4m/6km S.W. of Radstock ST 7252
The church of 1750 and manor house form a charming group away from all other habitations. The church is the most completely unaltered Georgian example in Somerset. Apsidal sanctuary and small W. tower with octagonal cupola. The interior has good moulded plasterwork on roof and apse. Box pews, curved holy table, gated altar rails, two-decker pulpit, pedestal font, and clear glass.

BACKWELL
St Andrew
6m/10km S.W. of Bristol ST 4968
12th–17th-century work; fine 15th-century tower, repaired in the 17th century. The N. chancel chapel appears to have been rebuilt in the 16th century and contains an elaborate monument to Sir Walter Rodney, 1466. A

brass to Rice Davis, 1638, shows him kneeling with his wife on cushions with their children behind. Early 16th-century screen.

BAGBOROUGH
St Pancras
7m/11km N.W. of Taunton ST 1733
The little 15th-century church stands on the lower slope of a wooded hill hard by the late-Georgian manor house. The interior is rich in Comper fittings and glass. A fine display of the early 16th-century bench-ends so characteristic of the Quantocks. The genius of Sir Ninian Comper has made it an ideal village church.

BANWELL
St Andrew
5m/8km E. of Weston-super-Mare ST 3959
Largely rebuilt in the 15th century with good W. tower and impressive interior. It contains the finest rood screen in the area, 1522, recently unsympathetically repainted. Fine wagon roof with angels. An unusual survival is a fragment of the rood loft. The W. gallery is partly Elizabethan and apparently made up from a manorial pew. Bench-ends with simple poppyheads. Civilian brasses of c. 1480 and John Martok, physician, 1503. Eight fine 16th-century Flemish glass panels, restored in 1984, illustrate Biblical scenes and the bearded St Louis of France. Particularly attractive is that showing the betrothal of Tobias and Sarah.

BATCOMBE
St Mary
3m/4km N. of Bruton ST 6939
On the flank of a secluded valley N. of Bruton. The tower, built in 1540, is a massive example of the E. Mendip type. The chancel is 14th-century with 17th-century E. window and on the N. a picturesque 18th-century vestry. Pierced parapets and, within, good aisle roofs, fan vault to tower, 17th-century altar rails, and brass.

BATH
ST 7564
Abbey (St Peter & St Paul)

One of the last big Perpendicular monastic churches to be built, it was begun in 1499, on the site of an earlier building; it was not completed by the time of the Dissolution, when the glass and lead of the nave were sold and the building became the mother church of Bath. The nave was completed in the 17th century by public subscription and the windows glazed. The W. door was given by Sir Henry Montague in 1617, carved with arms, drapery and cartouches. On each side are original early 16th-century figures. The famous W. front depicts ladders on which angels ascend and descend. A number of monuments, including a fine one to Sir Philip Frowde, 1674.

St Mary, Raby Place, Bathwick
1820, by J. Pinch. Rich and effective Somerset-style stone tower of three stages with strong mouldings. Other bold mouldings round the pinnacled and battlemented exterior; inside, a sumptuous Tractarian re-arrangement and new chancel by G. E. Street in 1873.

St Mary Magdalene, Holloway
Originally a chapel of a hospital for lepers built in 1495; it was enlarged in 1823–4. The simple church retains much character, with a small, low W. tower and a tablet to Anne Nicholas, 1662. The adjacent hospital was rebuilt in 1761.

St Michael, Broad Street
By G. P. Manners, 1835–7. Bath stone box with square tower, octagonal lantern and spire. Liberally provided with lancets, buttresses and other details filched from Salisbury and Wells; a good instance of pre-archaeological Gothic. Lofty interior has thin shafted piers and a plaster vault.

St Saviour, St Saviour's Road, Walcot
By J. Pinch, 1823–32; an impressive attempt at Somerset Perpendicular in ashlar. The galleried interior Victorianized in 1882.

St Stephen, Landsown Road
By James Wilson, 1840–5. Most notable for its unusual tower; square at the bottom, then octagonal with a smaller octagon on top again. Polygonal pinnacles are connected to the octagon by flying buttresses.

St Swithin, London Street, Walcot
Rebuilt by John Palmer, 1777–80; it has a pretty, square W. tower with circular lantern and spire. The galleried interior contains many monuments. The shallow sanctuary is built out over Walcot Street on corbels.

BISHOPS LYDEARD
St Mary
5m/8km N.W. of Taunton ST 1629
Magnificent 15th-century church on the edge of the village at the foot of the Quantocks. The churchyard has two crosses; inside, a fine series of benches of the same date. Ninian Comper repaired the rood screen and fitted out the chancel in his own distinctive style in 1923.

BLACKFORD
Holy Trinity
2m/3km W. of Wedmore ST 4147
By Richard Carver, 1823. Simple octagonal church with ogee-topped lantern. Inside, a ribbed ceiling and Edwardian pews.

BRIDGWATER
ST 2937
St Mary & St John
This fascinating church with a fine spire begun in 1367 dominates the town. The Victorians refashioned the interior but retained some of the opulent furnishings of earlier ages of this once flourishing seaport; 15th-century pulpit, 17th-century screens and Corporation pew.

BROOMFIELD
St Mary and All Saints
4m/6km W. of N. Petherton ST 2232
A simple Perpendicular church on the S. tip of the Quantocks, approached through ancient yews. It is notable for its roofs, signed bench-ends, and brass of 1443 to Richard Silverton, chaplain.

BRUSHFORD
St Nicholas
2m/3km S.E. of Dulverton SS 9225
Pleasant medieval church with N. chapel by Sir Edwin Lutyens, 1926. Good exterior of banded stonework and small round-headed windows; in the E. gable a cross-shaped light. Inside is Geometrical decoration and a canopied tomb of 1923 with recumbent effigy.

BRUTON
St Mary
7m/11km S.E. of Shepton Mallet ST 6834
Stately church on the S. edge of the town, adjacent to the site of the Augustinian abbey. The tower over the N. porch is dwarfed by the splendid 15th-century W. tower. Inside, the nave has a highly decorated tie-beam

roof and Jacobean screen, benches and pulpit. The chancel was rebuilt in 1743 and, apart from the screen of 1938, preserves all its contemporary furniture.

BUCKLAND DINHAM
St Michael
3m/4km N.W. of Frome ST 7551
Norman nave has good S. doorway with scallops and zig-zags. Otherwise 13th–14th-century with Perpendicular W. tower. Fan-vaulted S. porch and two Decorated effigies.

BUCKLAND ST MARY
St Mary
5m/8km N.W. of Chard ST 2713
By Benjamin Ferrey, 1853–63. Large and ambitious church built unusually of flint with Ham stone dressings; in the Decorated style with excellent naturalistic carving and details. Lavish interior has hammer-beam roof, carved figures, diapering on the chancel walls, and a good marble and alabaster reredos by Forsyth; the monument to the rector's wife is also by him.

CAMELEY
St James
4m/6km N.W. of Midsomer Norton ST 6157
Beautifully situated small church with good decoration and furnishings; 12th-century nave, chancel, S. porch and W. tower, re-fashioned in the 15th century. Interior one of the most attractive in the county. Medieval wall-paintings show a jester and decorative motifs. Good woodwork of many dates; 15th-century box pews with original door furniture; Jacobean pulpit, reader's desk and balustraded communion rail; early 18th-century reredos, coat hooks and pews. Gallery, 1819, entered by an external stair and inscribed 'For the free use of the inhabitants'. Norman font; Royal Arms of James I and IV.
R.C.F.

CATCOTT
St Peter
7m/11km W. of Glastonbury ST 3939
Modest medieval church, somewhat Victorianized, but retaining good early 19th-century interior with texts and benches, W. gallery, Jacobean pulpit and communion rail, and ceiled wagon roof.

CHANTRY
Holy Trinity
4m/6km W. of Frome ST 7147
By Scott & Moffatt, 1844–6. An early and modest work of G. G. Scott in well-detailed Decorated style. Stone slates of remarkable size, ornate porch, and a bell-turret with crocketed spirelets. Accomplished timber roof, vaulted chancel, and good glass by Wailes.

CHARTERHOUSE-ON-MENDIP
St Hugh
3m/4km N.E. of Cheddar ST 5055
By W. D. Caroe, 1908. Tiny, rustic mission church with bell-turret overlooking the deserted lead workings. Domestic interior with much Gothic woodwork and a fireplace.

CHEDDAR
St Andrew
8m/12km N.W. of Wells ST 4553
Large 15th-century church with imposing tower. Dark inside, but good brasses to Sir Thomas, 1442, and Lady Isabel, 1475, de Cheddar; 15th-century parclose screens, roofs and coloured stone pulpit.

CHEDZOY
St Mary
3m/4km E. of Bridgwater ST 3437
Fine 15th–16th-century rebuilding preserving the 13th-century nave. From this tower Royalist troops were first seen closing on Monmouth's army prior to the battle of Sedgemoor, 1685.

CHEW MAGNA
St Andrew
6m/10km S. of Bristol ST 5763
Large Norman and later church with tall Perpendicular W. tower. Fine 15th-century rood screen. Good effigies of Sir John and Lady St Loe, c. 1450, and Edward Baber, 1578, in N. chapel. Rare wooden effigy of knight in 14th-century armour. Circular Norman font. Church house of c. 1510 at entrance to churchyard.

CHEWTON MENDIP
St Mary Magdalene
6m/10km N.E. of Wells ST 5953
Norman church, substantially rebuilt in 15th–16th centuries. The glorious 16th-century tower of E. Mendip type has an elaborate parapet and panelled middle stage with original sculpture on the W. front; 12th-

century N. doorway, late 15th-century bench-ends, 17th-century lectern and holy table. Complete medieval churchyard cross.

CHILTHORNE DOMER
St Mary the Virgin
3m/4km N.W. of Yeovil ST 5219
Tiny two-celled church has Early English chancel and Decorated nave; corbelled-out bellcote of *c.* 1300 on W. gable. Jacobean pews, pulpit, and cut-down choir-stalls.

CHURCHSTANTON
St Peter & St Paul
5m/8km S.E. of Wellington ST 1914
Isolated in the wooded Blackdown Hills near the Devon border. Mostly rebuilt in the 15th–16th centuries. Excellent S. arcade has shafted piers and leaf bands. Otherwise the interior is an unspoiled refitting of 1830 with box pews and W. gallery fronted with 16th-century bench-ends.

COMPTON MARTIN
St Michael
3m/4km S. of Chew Stoke ST 5457
Musty and dark, but probably the best Norman village church in the area. Norman work includes the nave arcades, clerestory and chancel. The arcades have circular piers with scalloped capitals; one pier is spirally fluted. Good corbel table on N. side has monsters and heads. Impressive low rib-vaulted chancel. Circular Norman font with zig-zag frieze. Four-stage W. tower of *c.* 1520.

CONGRESBURY
St Andrew
5m/8km S. of Clevedon ST 4363
13th-century church remodelled in the 15th century. Good Perpendicular tower with spire. Fine 15th-century nave wagon roof with bosses and angels. Perpendicular screen on stone base and fragments of glass in the E. window; 12th-century font; 15th-century vicarage adjoins the churchyard.

CREWKERNE
St Bartholomew
8m/12km S.W. of Yeovil ST 4409
Magnificent 15th-century cruciform church with central tower. W. galleries were added in the early 19th century to provide further room in an already spacious interior. The heavy crossing piers are an indication that the present building is a remodelling of an earlier 13th-century cruciform church.

CROSCOMBE
St Mary the Virgin
3m/4km E. of Wells ST 5944
The spire of this fine 15th-century building has been rebuilt after lightning damage. Notable wagon roof and good series of late-medieval poppyheaded benches; but it is the 17th-century increment which makes the church so remarkable. Medieval pews were given doors to make new box pews; a towering pulpit was installed, together with an elaborate chancel roof and fantastic screens with the Royal Arms high in the roof space.

CULBONE
St Bueno
on coast path from Porlock Weir to County Gate (A39) SS 8448
Reputedly the smallest parish church in England, set in a secluded wooded valley inaccessible by public roads; well worth the two-mile walk. Nave and chancel are probably Norman, all but one window replaced in the 15th century or later. The survivor is a single stone, carved outside with the head of a biting beast. The large tub font is also early. Small-scale pre-Reformation benches with linenfold panels, 16th-century rood screen, and 17th-century manorial pew.

CURRY MALLET
St James
7m/11km E. of Taunton ST 3321
Isolated Perpendicular church in the midst of meadowland. Good 17th-century monuments, locally made bier, 1903, and horse plough, 1868, kept for Plough Sunday.

CURRY RIVEL
St Andrew
2m/3km S.W. of Langport ST 3925
Large 15th-century building with dark Victorian interior. Remains of rood screen, bench-ends, interesting 16th–17th-century monuments, and German glass of 1865 in W. window. The tower was rebuilt in the 19th century.

DITCHEAT
St Mary Magdalene
3m/4km N.W. of Castle Cary ST 6236
Cruciform with central tower. Mostly 14th–15th-century with lofty chancel and

good 15th-century Somerset nave roof. Large St Christopher wall-painting of *c.* 1500; 17th-century pulpit and reading desk.

DUNSTER
St George
2m/3km S.E. of Minehead SS 9943
The church is hidden away behind the top end of this picturesque market town. Although remodelled in the 15th century, the form of the Norman church survives, the Benedictine monastic choir separated from the parish church by a massive central tower. The huge 15th-century rood screen runs right across the nave and aisles. The former monastic choir houses impressive 14th–18th-century Luttrell monuments.

EAST BRENT
St Mary
3m/4km N.E. of Burnham-on-Sea ST 3452
Large 15th-century church with slender spire. The sumptuous plaster ceiling, pulpit and chancel screen, now at W. end, are additions of the 1630s. Medieval eagle lectern, 15th-century bench-ends, restored Passion window, and Victorian stencilling in the chancel.

EVERCREECH
St Peter
4m/6km S.E. of Shepton Mallet ST 6438
The slender, imposing tower which dominates the village is the type example, with belfry windows carried down into long panels. The rest of the church is, disappointingly, much restored.

FLAX BOURTON
St Michael
5m/8km W. of Bristol ST 5069
Good Norman work; S. doorway with spiral fluted columns, scalloped capitals and zig-zags, a carving of St Michael and the Dragon above. Norman chancel arch and square font.

GLASTONBURY
St John the Baptist
13m/21km E. of Bridgwater ST 5039
Spacious Perpendicular town church, mostly mid-15th-century, with one of the finest towers in Somerset; the elaborate parapet and panelled middle stage reflect the influence of Gloucester. Handsome two-storeyed vaulted porch. Sumptuous tie-beam nave

roof, tower vaulting, late-medieval painted glass, and early 16th-century altar tomb.

HARDINGTON
St Mary
4m/6km N.W. of Frome ST 7452
Small church in a hamlet on the E. flank of the Mendips. Mostly early 14th-century with diminutive Perpendicular W. tower. Lovely rustic interior has old plaster, stone floors, and moulded 14th-century nave roof. Complete late-Georgian fittings of box pews, three-decker pulpit, altar rails, and holy table. Royal Arms of Charles I.
R.C.F.

HIGH HAM
St Andrew
3m/4km N. of Langport ST 4231
The churchyard forms the N. side of an attractive group of buildings around the green. With the exception of its 14th-century tower, the building was erected *c.* 1476. The timberwork is particularly complete: aisle roofs, rood screen with rood beam over, and bench-ends. The nave and chancel roofs are splendid examples of the Somerset type.

HINTON BLEWETT
St Andrew
2m/3km E. of West Harptree ST 5956
The church stands behind a row of cottages and a pub which front the pretty village green. Mainly 15th-century, the interior light and airy with stone floors. Timber roof with bosses in nave and N. aisle. Norman font, 15th-century square-headed bench-ends, and canopied pulpit, 1638. Windows on N. side have some 16th-century glass.

HINTON ST GEORGE
St George
2m/3km N.W. of Crewkerne ST 4212
Good Perpendicular church with W. tower of 1494. Notable series of 16th–19th-century Poulett monuments, including a bizarre Baroque erection to John Baron Poulett, d. 1649; decidedly un-English.

HOLCOMBE
St Andrew
4m/6km S. of Radstock ST 6749
Stands alone in the fields, the village now a mile away around a Victorian church. Small 12th-century church refashioned in the 16th century and later. Very 'atmospherick' early 19th-century interior with box pews, hat

pegs, two-decker pulpit, gallery, and clear glass.
R.C.F.

HORNBLOTTON
St Peter
3m/4km N.E. of Keinton Mandeville ST 5934
By Sir T. G. Jackson, 1872–4. Under the influence of R. Norman Shaw, with tile-hung belfry and shingled broach spire in the Home Counties taste. Delightful strawberry graffito within, enriched with aesthetic sunflowers. Tasteful inlaid hardwood furnishings, agreeable mosaic, and a reredos by Powell & Sons, who also made the glass. Delectable.

HUISH EPISCOPI
St Mary the Virgin
½m/1km E. of Langport ST 4226
The tower is a renowned example of the Taunton type, sumptuously decorated. The rest is on a smaller scale, but note the elaborate 12th-century S. doorway and the Burne-Jones window by Morris and Co. in the S. chapel.

ISLE ABBOTTS
St Mary
4m/6km N. of Ilminster ST 3520
Impressive church with ornate 15th-century tower retaining nearly all its medieval sculpture. The interior of a simple grandeur; fine chancel of *c.* 1300 with early tracery and stone fittings; reset 15th-century screen; airy N. aisle of *c.* 1500, traceried bench-ends, and a Norman font.

ILMINSTER
St Mary
10m/16km S.E. of Taunton ST 3614
One of the great Perpendicular Somerset cruciform churches; the nave remodelled to take galleries in 1825. Good 15th- and 17th-century Wadham memorials in N. transept.

KILMERSDON
St Peter & St Paul
2m/3km S. of Radstock ST 6952
Much disjointed Norman work including bits of a fish-scale frieze outside. Otherwise the usual Perpendicular with good W. tower, fine stone screen, and aisle roofs.

KINGSBURY EPISCOPI
St Martin
4m/6km S. of Langport ST 4321
A large village of Ham stone in the marshy basin of the River Parret, set about with willows. The imposing church is mainly 14th- and 15th-century, with one of the most satisfying of the great Somerset towers. Lofty chancel has spendid transomed windows and an E. sacristy. Fine fan-vaulted tower base, 15th-century screen, and fragments of glass.

LANGPORT
All Saints
7m/11km N.W. of Ilchester ST 4226
Handsome 15th-century church within the original Saxon fortified town overlooking Muchelney Level. Spacious interior has remarkably complete 15th-century glass in E. window and many 17th–18th-century slate memorials.

LEIGH-ON-MENDIP
St Giles
5m/8km W. of Frome ST 6947
15th-century with decorated W. tower. Splendid Somerset nave and chancel roofs have enriched wall-plates, bosses and angels. Some early glass and a remarkably complete set of traceried benches.

LOCKING
St Augustine
3m/4km S.E. of Weston-super-Mare ST 3659
Decorated W. tower and unexpected Tuscan nave arcade of 1814. Magnificent square Norman font with figures at each corner stretching out to join hands; the sides enriched with enigmatic snakes.

LONG ASHTON
All Saints
3m/4km S.W. of Bristol SR 5470
Early Perpendicular church with late 14th-century W. tower. Inside there is an elaborately crested screen across the nave and aisles. In the S. aisle is a fine Perpendicular tomb chest with recumbent effigies of Sir Richard Choke, Lord Chief Justice of England, d. 1486, and his wife. Many good 17th–20th-century monuments.

LONG SUTTON
Holy Trinity
2m/3km S.W. of Somerton
Spacious village green surrounded by lias-stone houses of many periods, above which

looms the lofty tower of the late 15th-century church. A spacious and impressive fabric in the best Somerset manner, with clerestoried nave and magnificent tie-beam roof of local type; 15th-century pulpit and rood screen, both with somewhat garish Victorian colouring; 17th-century lectern.

LOW HAM
(dedication unknown)
2m/3km N.E. of Langport ST 4329
Remarkable church built 1629–69 on a green-field site below the terraces of a failed scheme for a great house. The innovative window tracery in particular led Pevsner to describe it as 'one of the most instructive cases of early Gothicism in England'. Effigies of the founder, Sir Edward Hext, and his wife; a monument to Sir George Stawell in the S. aisle has superb iron railings. The benches, screen, pulpit, communion rails and glass in the E. window are all contemporary. Elaborate stone entrance screen removed from the Lord Mayor's Chapel.

MARTOCK
All Saints
6m/10km N.W. of Yeovil ST 4619
A small town not far from the famous Ham Hill quarries which provided the stone for its noble church and many interesting houses. The church has a 13th-century chancel, but the rest is good Somerset Perpendicular. Inside is a superb roof of 1513, made when the nave was heightened; it is one of the finest tie-beam roofs in the country. Canopied niches in the clerestory have 17th-century paintings of the Apostles.

MELLS
St Andrew
3m/4km W. of Frome ST 7749
One of the best villages in Somerset, which is saying a good deal, with a stately church, mellow Tudor manor house, and many charming cottages and farmsteads. The church was rebuilt in the 15th century with a noble tower and a profusion of carved detail. Beautiful though restored interior has fine nave and chapel roofs, Norman font, fragments of glass, and a monument of 1886 by Burne-Jones.

MIDDLEZOY
Holy Cross
6m/10km S.E. of Bridgwater ST 3732
14th–15th-century, the W. tower with quatrefoil battlements and pinnacles. Ceiled wagon nave roof has ceilure above the rood screen. Early 16th-century glass and bench-ends; pulpit of 1606.

MILBORNE PORT
All Saints
3m/4km N.E. of Sherborne ST 6718
The core of the cruciform church is a remarkable survival of an 11th-century rebuilding of an earlier Anglo-Saxon church, extended in the mid-19th century. Proportions and details are a successful fusion of English and Continental Romanesque.

MINEHEAD
SS 9746
St Michael
In the old town, perched in the lee of a huge whale-backed hill. An imposing and spacious, mostly Perpendicular church set in a graveyard with stones commemorating the human cost of the town's dependence on the sea. Interesting fittings of good quality; 15th-century screens, brass of a lady, and effigy of a priest; superb 16th-century communion table; 17th-century pulpit, Royal Arms, and texts.

MUCHELNEY
St Peter & St Paul
1m/2km S. of Langport ST 4324
The Perpendicular church forms part of a group with the ruins of the adjoining Benedictine abbey and the tiny 15th-century priest's house; 17th-century nave roof is painted with jolly angels bearing scrolls.

NORTH CADBURY
St Michael
5m/8km W. of Wincanton ST 6327
Splendid Somerset Perpendicular church by the manor house. Particularly impressive collegiate chancel with good roof and fine windows; 15th-century painted glass in W. window and early 16th-century seating.

NORTH CURRY
St Peter & St Paul
6m/10km E. of Taunton ST 3125
Pleasant churchyard overlooking the Tone Valley. Large cruciform Perpendicular church, well proportioned and with an octagonal lantern over the crossing. Scraped and re-ordered by J. Oldrid Scott in 1881.

NORTH PETHERTON
St Mary

3m/4km S. of Bridgwater ST 2933
Large village near the edge of Sedgemoor.
Fine, mainly 15th-century church with
superb W. tower retaining most of the original figure sculpture and crowned by a richly
pinnacled parapet. There is an E. sacristy
as in several other important Somerset
churches. Good nave and aisle roofs, 15th-
century font and pulpit, 17th-century manorial pew.

NORTON-SUB-HAMDON
St Mary

5m/8km W. of Yeovil ST 4715
Delightful church of *c.* 1500–10 set on a
hill. Wonderful W. tower with tall belfry
openings and big gargoyles. Embattled
aisles, ceiled wagon nave roof, and good Arts
and Crafts furnishings by Henry Wilson,
1904.

OARE
St Mary

6m/10km E. of Lynton SS 8047
A charming church, immortalized by R. D.
Blackmore as the scene of the death of Lorna
Doone. The chancel was added in a rather
rustic style in the late 19th century and adds
to the character of a building that retains
box pews, unusual piscina, painted memorials, and a panel of Moses.

PAWLETT
St John the Baptist

4m/6km N. of Bridgwater ST 3042
Standing on high ground above the rich
pastures of Pawlett Hams. Medieval church
with highly 'atmospherick' interior. The
12th-century core was refashioned and enlarged in the 13th and 15th centuries. Good
12th-century font, 15th-century screen, and
a fine display of 17th-century fittings: three-
sided altar rails, box pews, font cover, pulpit,
and reading desk. Windows mostly have
clear glass in rectangular leading.

PILTON
St John the Baptist

3m/4km S.W. of Shepton Mallet ST 5840
Pleasant rambling village on a hillside, a
great 14th-century tithe barn on the opposite
slope; 12th-century church refashioned and
enlarged in 15th century. Clerestoried nave
and chancel, late 12th-century arcade, and
splendid 15th-century roofs. Good parclose

screens, fragments of glass, and part of a
15th-century cope.

PORLOCK
St Dubricius

9m/12km W. of Minehead SS 8846
Low 13th-century W. tower has contemporary shingled spire. Important canopied
Harrington monument of *c.* 1460, reredos
by Blacking, and fragments of a Saxon
cross shaft.

PUXTON
St Saviour

2m/3km W. of Congresbury ST 4063
Small isolated church on the Levels. Short,
leaning 15th-century W. tower. Simple
whitewashed interior retains Jacobean furnishings: reader's desk, altar rails, pulpit,
and some box pews. Plain square-headed
bench-ends. The rood beam is still visible,
cut off flush with the walls.

QUEEN CAMEL
St Barnabas

1m/2km S.W. of Sparkford ST 5924
Large lias-stone village of pleasing aspect;
up a side street at the N. end is the impressive
14th- and 15th-century church; its charming
18th-century portico somehow escaped the
Victorian 'restorers'. Scraped inside but still
interesting on account of the fine tie-beam
nave roof, lofty vaulted screen, and early-
Perpendicular font unusually enriched with
figures.

REDLYNCH
St Peter

2m/3km S.E. of Bruton ST 7033
Neat church of 1750 with bellcote and
round-arched windows containing clear
glass; pulpit and pedimented plaster reredos.

RODE
St Lawrence

4m/6km N.E. of Frome ST 8053
14th–15th-century, somewhat renewed in
1874. Good 15th-century aisle roofs and
wall-paintings; late 17th-century altar rails.

RODNEY STOKE
St Leonard

3m/4km S.E. of Cheddar ST 4850
Modest 15th-century church on the edge of
the moors. Inside are delightful additions of
the 1630s: nave roof, font and cover, pulpit,
chancel screen, communion table and rails.

In the N. chapel a glorious series of monuments to the eponymous Rodneys. Effigy and canopied tomb of Sir Thomas, 1471; exquisitely carved alabaster figure of Anne Lakes under celestial canopy, 1630; massive tented pavilion over Sir Edward and wife, 1657; George, the last of the line, dramatically rising from his coffin, 1651.

ST CATHERINE
St Catherine
4m/6km N.E. of Bath ST 7770
12th-century church refashioned *c.* 1490 by Prior Cantlow of Bath; 15th-century painted glass and pulpit; bold pedimented monument, 1631.

SELWORTHY
All Saints
2m/3km E. of Porlock SS 9146
Whitewashed church on the edge of model village. Spacious interior with notable S. aisle of *c.* 1538; windows, roof and doorway are all splendid. Early 19th-century Gothic manorial pew over S. door and massive W. gallery, 1750.

SHEPTON MALLET
ST 6143
St Peter & St Paul
Large town church tucked away behind the new civic centre. The 14th-century tower with its unfinished spire is one of the earliest of the Somerset type. Inside, above the 12th-century arcades, is the most intricate wagon roof in the county.

SOMERTON
St Michael and All Angels
4m/6km N.W. of Ilchester ST 4828
Large 13th–14th-century church set back from the market-place. Square 13th-century tower with broach spire. Splendid panelled late-Perpendicular nave roof. Good Jacobean pulpit, reredos and communion table.

SOUTH BRENT
St Michael
2m/3km N.E. of Burnham-on-Sea ST 3350
On the lower slopes of Brent Knoll, an isolated hill rising out of the Somerset flats. Norman S. doorway, some 13th–14th-century work, including the S. chapel, but mostly Perpendicular. Good nave and aisle roofs and striking set of late-medieval bench-ends. Fine monument, bright with colour, to John Somerset, 1663, and his two wives.

STAWLEY
St Michael
5m/8km W. of Wellington ST 0622
Small medieval church in remote hilly country near the Devon border. Atmospheric interior retains most of the 18th-century furnishings: box pews, pulpit with ogee tester, communion rail, and commandment boards.

STOGURSEY
St Andrew
7m/11km N.W. of Bridgwater ST 2042
Cruciform Benedictine priory church of *c.* 1100, associated with the new town of Stoke Courcy. This Norman building was altered in the 15th century, and the nave is largely Perpendicular. The E. parts are a neo-Norman remodelling of 1865. Good 17th–18th-century monuments, and a pair of rare early 19th-century wooden Friendly Society banners.

STOKE ST GREGORY
St Gregory
8m/12km E. of Taunton ST 3427
Cruciform church of great character with central octagonal tower, the lower parts of *c.* 1300. Fine medieval nave and aisle roofs, 16th-century bench-ends, and 17th-century pulpit.

STOKE SUB HAMDON
St Mary
5m/8km W. of Yeovil ST 4717
Isolated from the village, the church nestles at the foot of the hill where the golden Ham stone is still quarried. Delightful mixture of accretions on an early-Norman core of nave and chancel. Good Norman work outside: corbels round the chancel, remains of S. door, tiny windows with carved heads, and carved tympanum over N. door with Sagittarius, Leo and the Lamb of God. Huge chancel arch of three orders with volutes, zig-zags and lozenges; 13th-century vaulted tower and S. chapel, the nave raised in the 15th century. Well restored by Ferrey, 1862; 15th-century churchyard cross.

SUTTON BINGHAM
All Saints
3m/4km S. of Yeovil ST 5411
Secluded little church despite the nearby

reservoir. Norman nave and chancel arch, the chancel rebuilt in the late 13th century. Simple 15th-century arch-braced nave roof. Notable 14th-century paintings of the Life of the Virgin, bishops and saints; restored but still dramatic.

SUTTON MALLET
(dedication unknown)
5m/8km E. of Bridgwater ST 3737
Tiny church on the edge of the moors. A Gothic rebuilding by Richard Carver, 1829, apart from the medieval W. tower. Pleasing interior retains original pitch pine furnishings of communion table and rails, tall box pews, three-decker pulpit, and W. gallery, all topped off by brass candle-holders and long hat pegs.

TAUNTON
St Mary Magdalene
15m/24km N.W. of Bridgwater ST 2224
Large 15th–16th-century town church with double aisles to the nave. The elaborate tower, one of the tallest in the county, was rebuilt in 1862 by Ferrey and Scott. Elaborate S. porch of 1508 and handsome cusped tie-beam roof with angels.

TRULL
All Saints
2m/3km S. of Taunton ST 2122
Church retains a remarkable amount of 15th–16th-century glass and woodwork. Crucifixion and 'dragon' windows in the chancel; wagon and panelled roofs; rood and parclose screens; an entire series of bench-ends and, most remarkable of all, a wooden pulpit with carved figures of the Doctors of the Church.

UPHILL
St Nicholas
Old Church, S. suburb of
Weston-super-Mare ST 3158
Largely Norman church standing on a cliff above the village; spectacular view of the Somerset Levels and the Bristol Channel. Central tower, the nave roofless. Norman windows and two doorways with decorated tympana.
R.C.F.

WATCHET
St Decuman
ST 0743
The holy well of St Decuman is on the hillside below the church. Mostly 15th-century with Early English chancel. Very good roofs with bosses, angel supporters, and decorated wall-plates. Fine series of 16th–17th-century Wyndham monuments, one probably by Nicholas Stone.

WEDMORE
St Mary the Virgin
4m/6km S. of Cheddar ST 4347
Huge Perpendicular church with tall central tower. N.E. chapel has good 15th-century painted and panelled ceiling; here are the brasses of Thomas Hodges, killed at the siege of Antwerp, 1583, and George Hodges, 1630. Robust wall-painting of *c.* 1520 above the pulpit depicts St Christopher with mermaid and ships.

WELLOW
St Julian
4m/6km S. of Bath ST 7458
Largely Perpendicular, the chancel by Bodley and Garner, 1890. Fine 15th-century roofs in nave and Hungerford Chapel, which also contains recently restored wall-paintings of Christ and the 12 Apostles, a rare subject. Poppyhead bench-ends, an effigy of a priest in Mass vestments, *c.* 1400, and 12 small carved heads, probably 14th-century, reset in the chancel.

WELLS
ST 5445
St Cuthbert
Magnificent Perpendicular church. Seen from afar, its superb W. tower counterbalances the Cathedral. The impressive 13th-century cruciform interior was beautifully enhanced in the 15th century; the many chapels afford great spaciousness, and there are fine roofs, especially the exquisitely carved ceiling over the S.W. chapel. Rare though fragmentary reredoses in the transepts; that to the S. a Tree of Jesse by John Stowell, 1470. Resplendent pulpit of 1636 has scenes from the Old Testament including Jonah and the Whale and Daniel in the Lions' Den.

St Thomas, St Thomas Street
By S. S. Teulon, 1856–7. Lavish Geometrical church of banded stonework with broad apse and N.E. tower surmounted by octagonal spire. Fine interior has ironwork by Skidmore and original glass by Wailes.

WEST BAGBOROUGH
St Pancras
7m/11km N.W. of Taunton ST 1733
On flank of the Quantocks adjoining the
Georgian House. Over-restored Perpen-
dicular church has delectable glass, chancel
fittings, rood beam, and font cover by Sir
Ninian Comper, 1921.

WEST PENNARD
St Nicholas
3m/4km E. of Glastonbury ST 5438
Large lias-stone village with a network of
lanes, almost in the shadow of Glastonbury
Tor. The handsome church was completely
rebuilt in the second half of the 15th century;
W. tower has timber and lead spire. Fine
and richly carved roofs throughout. Late
15th-century rood screen and glass including the Coronation of the Virgin.
Churchyard cross with emblems of the
Passion on the base.

WEST QUANTOXHEAD
St Etheldreda
3m/4km E. of Watchet ST 1142
By John Norton of Bristol, 1856. Pink
Doulting stone church in the Geometrical
style with bold N.W. tower and spirelet.
Inside are monolithic marble piers with natu-
ralistic capitals, a marble font, and glass by
O'Connor.

WESTON ZOYLAND
St Mary
4m/6km E. of Bridgwater ST 3534
Stately 14th–15th-century church overlooking Sedgemoor. Built under the
patronage of the abbots of Glastonbury, it
is one of the best Somerset Perpendicular
churches.

WINSCOMBE
St James
2m/3km N. of Axbridge ST 4257
Fine 15th-century church set on a hill above
the village. Good W. tower and original roofs
to the aisles and chapel. Exceptionally good
stained glass; N. chapel has 15th-century
Crucifixion, saints and donors; window of
1535 depicts the three St Peters; chancel E.
lancets have excellent Pre-Raphaelite glass
of 1863–4, probably an early work by
Morris.

WITHAM
St Mary, St John the Baptist and All Saints
6m/10km N.E. of Bruton ST 7441
Small late 12th-century French church,
apsidal and stone-vaulted. The first English
Carthusian house was founded here in
1178–9 by Henry II. St Hugh, the Bur-
gundian prior, later Bishop of Lincoln, probably erected this church in the style with
which he was familiar. Comper glass and
Jacobean pulpit.

WOOLLEY
All Saints
3m/4km N. of Bath ST 7468
By John Wood the Younger, 1761; Georgian
Gothic with apsidal sanctuary, elaborate W.
cupola, and Y-traceried windows with clear
glass. Baluster font and marble monuments.

WRINGTON
All Saints
2m/3km E. of Congresbury ST 4762
Pleasantly situated in the Yeo Valley, the
church was substantially rebuilt in the 15th
century. One of the best of the Somerset
towers, and fine roofs, screen, and richly
decorated font.

WYKE CHAMPFLOWER
Holy Trinity
1m/2km W. of Bruton ST 6634
A delightful chapel rebuilt in 1623–4,
tucked away behind the manor house. The
heavy stone pulpit, probably removed from
elsewhere, is a little out of scale with the
rest of the furnishings: box pews complete
with hat pegs, communion rails and table,
font and cover. Boarded tympanum dated
1624 bears the Royal Arms together with
those of the Archbishop of Canterbury and
the Bishop of Wells.

YATTON
St Mary
4m/6km S. of Clevedon ST 4365
Impressive church, the central tower topped
by a truncated spire abandoned before completion. Nave and aisles rebuilt in the 15th
century; highly decorated S. porch and N.
chancel chapel added by Isobel of Cheddar,
d. 1498. Wagon nave roof has carved bosses
and angels; 15th-century Newton effigies;
also a blue velvet dalmatic embroidered with
saints and flowers, later converted into a
funeral pall.

YEOVIL

ST 5515
St John the Baptist

Large town church, entirely rebuilt *c.* 1382, apart from the crypt. An early and sophisticated Perpendicular design attributed to William Wynford, master mason at Wells Cathedral. The exterior, though closely hemmed in by other buildings, is majestic. Remarkably elegant 'hall church' interior, the aisles rising to the same height as nave, chancel and transepts. Most of the furnishings are Victorian, but there is an Easter Sepulchre, a brass lectern of *c.* 1450, and a fine series of monuments.

Staffordshire

Introduction

Staffordshire is believed by many people to be 'just the Black Country and Potteries', which only proves how unknown the county is. If it were not famous for heavy engineering, pottery and coal, it would still deserve a measure of fame for the charm and variety of its landscape and architecture. Four centuries ago, Camden's *Britannia* described the county in terms still fairly relevant: 'The north part is mountainous and less fertile; but the middle, which is watered by the Trent, is fruitful, woody and pleasant, by an equal mixture of arable and meadow grounds; so is also the south, which has much pit-coal and mines of iron; but whether to their loss or advantage, the natives themselves are the best judges . . .'

Few people apart from the natives realize that there is a large part of the Peak District in the county. In fact, it is said that 'the best parts of Derbyshire are in Staffordshire' – the hundred square miles between Dovedale and the Dane Valley, across the Leek moors. To the west, the crag of Mow Cop, the birthplace of Primitive Methodism, overlooks the Cheshire plain; in the north, the Weaver Hills overlook Alton Towers and Castle with their exciting Pugin skylines. In the centre and south there are the old Royal Forests of Cannock Chase and Kinver, and to the east is Needwood Forest with its great estates – and Bodley's masterpiece at Hoar Cross. In the central undulating lowlands lies Lichfield, and the Cathedral of St Chad.

A county for over a thousand years, Staffordshire still forms a rather separate and independent region, across which runs the Watling Street, leading the Romans and everyone else through the county rather than into it.

Culturally conservative, the county seems often to have woken late but vigorous to its tasks; witness the notable architecture of the 19th-century churches, especially the outstanding work of Bodley, Norman Shaw, Street – his own favourite church design is at Denstone – and Pugin; his ten churches here include the Roman Catholic St Giles, Cheadle, with its fabulously coloured interior.

But to begin at the beginning, there is fine Norman work at Stafford and Tutbury, besides less considerable remains in seventeen other churches; good 13th-century at Brewood, Coppenhall, Weston-on-Trent tower, and, of course, the nave of Lichfield Cathedral; much fine Decorated, notably in the Lichfield Lady Chapel, and at Clifton Campville and Checkley; and the usual amount of 15th-century work, the most complete examples being

St Peter's, Wolverhampton, and Penkridge. Very late Gothic occurs at Barton-under-Needwood (1533), Blurton (1636) and Broughton (1633) – small, isolated and one of the most charming churches. The building materials are usually local stone and tiles, though timber arcades are found at Betley and Rushton. Towers are the rule, though a few good spires exist.

Among the Renaissance churches are Ingestre by Wren, Patshull by Gibbs, and Burton upon Trent by Francis Smith.

This is no place for too archaeological or historical an approach, whether to churches or the architecture of the county – the guidebooks can tell about the ancient forts, castles, abbey ruins, the great houses set in their parkland, and the architectural details of churches, such as tracery, screens, woodwork, and the characteristic Staffordshire incised stone tomb-slabs. But if a list were made of the significant details to make a pilgrimage to see, it should include the tympanum at Kingswinford, the squire's pews and the three-decker pulpit at Baswich, the stone pulpit with the lion at Wolverhampton, the fonts at Ilam, Armitage and All Saints, Leek, the Gerard tomb at Ashley, and the great figure of Christ at Swynnerton.

In landscape and architecture Staffordshire is a good average, with numerous high spots. There is quiet, remote country, especially in the centre and north; there is much industrial building in certain parts; and both in the towns and the countryside there are many churches which well deserve to be loved more widely.

D. B. P.

1 Adbaston	25 Cotton	49 Lapley
2 Alrewas	26 Croxall	50 Leek
3 Alstonefield	27 Denstone	51 Lichfield
4 Ashley	28 Dilhorne	52 Longdon
5 Barton-under-Needwood	29 Dunstall	53 Longsdon
6 Betley	30 Eccleshall	54 Madeley
7 Bilston	31 Elford	55 Marchington
8 Blithefield	32 Ellenhall	56 Mavesyn Ridware
9 Blore	33 Enville	57 Mayfield
10 Blymhill	34 Ettingshall	58 Newborough
11 Bobbington	35 Forton	59 Norbury
12 Bradley	36 Grosall	60 Okeover
13 Brewood	37 Hamstall Ridware	61 Patshull
14 Broughton	38 Hanbury	62 Pattingham
15 Burton-upon-Trent	39 High Offley	63 Penkridge
16 Canwell	40 Himley	64 Ranton
17 Caverswall	41 Hoar Cross	65 Rolleston
18 Chebsey	42 Hollingsclough	66 Rushton Spencer
19 Checkley	43 Hopwas	67 Sandon
20 Cheddleton	44 Horton	68 Seighford
21 Church Eaton	45 Ilam	69 Shareshill
22 Church Leigh	46 Ingestre	70 Sheen
23 Clifton Campville	47 King's Bromley	71 Shenstone
24 Coppenhall	48 Kinver	72 Slindon

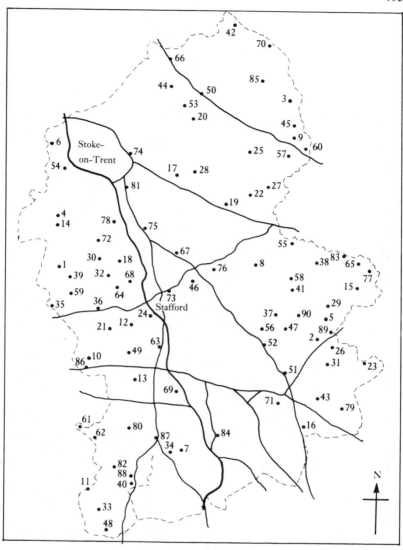

Selected List of Churches

ADBASTON
St Michael and All Angels
6m/10km N. of Newport SJ 7627
Remote Shropshire borderlands. Mostly Perpendicular with Norman core; see two windows in chancel and N. arcade. Good incised alabaster slab of 1441, Royal Arms of George III, and a hatchment for Richard Whitworth, eccentric 18th-century politician.

ALREWAS
All Saints
5m/8km N.E. of Lichfield SK 1715
Tower and exterior mainly Perpendicular, the clerestory being raised directly over the aisle and chancel walls. Lofty Early English chancel with sedilia. The interior high and spacious with good 16th-century roofs. Interesting fittings: Perpendicular font, pulpit of 1639, and stalls. W. door, 1627, with appropriate ironwork. Reredos by Basil Champneys, 1892; glass by Kempe and Holiday.

ALSTONEFIELD
St Peter
6m/10km N.W. of Ashbourne SK 1355
Pleasant setting in the Peak limestone country near Dovedale. Outer walls of attractive chequered sandstone and limestone. Plain and serene inside: Norman, Decorated and Perpendicular. Much good woodwork of 1637–9 including excellent box pews, two-decker pulpit, and handsome Cotton pew.

ASHLEY
St John the Baptist
6m/10km N.W. of Eccleshall SJ 7636
Early 17th-century Gothic Survival W. tower, the rest a pedestrian exterior of 1861. But the interior, completed by Bodley & Hare in 1910, is surprisingly good. Chancel divided from nave by rood screen after only two bays; good reredos and the altar well lit; the whole effect enlivened by many brass candelabra. Magnificent alabaster tomb to Sir Gilbert Gerard, d. 1592, and impressive

19th-century marble monuments to the Kinnersleys and Meynells.

BARTON-UNDER-NEEDWOOD
St James
5m/8km S.W. of Burton upon Trent SK 1818
All late-Perpendicular of *c*. 1533, the W. tower, nave and apsed chancel united by prominent panelled buttresses. It was built in *c*. 1533 by Dr John Taylor, Chaplain to Henry VIII, ambassador and Master of the Rolls. Heraldic paintings in the spandrels of the arcades and some original glass in the chancel.

BETLEY
St Margaret
6m/10km W. of Newcastle-under-Lyme SJ 7548
Early 16th-century stone tower, timber-framed nave, clerestory and porches. Unusual and impressive work inside with heavy late 15th-century timber arcades and trusses to the nave, and an early 16th-century parclose screen. Gothic chancel of 1610 with open timber roof. Good monument to Ralph Egerton, d. 1610, whose son built the chancel.

BILSTON
St Leonard
S.E. district of Wolverhampton SO 9596
Rebuilt by Francis Goodwin, 1826; apsidal chancel and interior remodelling by Ewan Christian, 1883–93. Classical, like a grey fortress, with charming octagonal domed tower, nice ironwork on top. Delightful cast-iron bollards to either side of the W. door inscribed 'Anno Domini 1826: Francis Goodwin, Architect'. Gently coloured Greek interior with shallow segmental vault, galleries, and Ionic columns.

BLITHFIELD
St Leonard
4m/6km N. of Rugeley SK 0424
Isolated setting by the Hall, home of the Bagots since the 14th century. Simple 14th-century tower; the lofty nave has Early English arcades and later clerestory. Good

Perpendicular screen, many traceried bench-ends, and glass. Fine collection of 16th–18th-century Bagot tombs and memorials, including one of 1695 by William Stanton.

BLORE
St Bartholomew
3m/4km N.W. of Ashbourne SK 1349
13th-century origins, but mostly a Perpendicular remodelling of *c.* 1520. Good roofs and a remarkable assemblage of Jacobean woodwork, including panelling, pulpit, screens, stalls, and benches. Brass to William Bassett and wife, 1498; small N.E. chapel occupied by enormous early 17th-century tomb of Wiliam Bassett, almost like a small bedroom. Early glass in the chancel depicts St Anne teaching the Virgin to read.

BLYMHILL
St Mary
6m/10km S.E. of Newport TM 4276
Almost rebuilt by G. E. Street, 1856–9; of great originality and interest with some old work left, including the tower and Decorated chancel. Nave with striking clerestory dormers and bold plate tracery in the lower windows. A huge gargoyle at the E. end of the S. aisle. Inside, has tall arch-braced roof, and there are good Street fittings and furnishings. Glass by Wailes and Hardman. Village school also by Street.

BOBBINGTON
Holy Cross
6m/10km E. of Bridgnorth SO 8090
Somewhat unpromising exterior; the tower added by Blomfield during his restoration of 1878. But inside is a good mid-12th-century N. arcade with round piers and scalloped capitals.

BRADLEY
All Saints
4m/6km S.W. of Stafford SJ 8717
Mostly Perpendicular outside, including the W. tower and generous windows on the S. side. Early English nave arcades of slender clustered shafts and Decorated tower arch. Late 13th-century chancel N. arcade and Decorated E. window with flowing tracery; below is a contemporary reredos. Carved Norman tub font, some good glass fragments, and an alabaster tomb with kneeling figures of Thomas Browne, d. 1633, and his wife.

BREWOOD
St Mary
7m/11km N. of Wolverhampton SJ 8808
Attractive small town in romantic Charles II countryside. Largish church with Perpendicular tower and early 16th-century recessed spire; 14th-century nave with Decorated windows in the N. aisle; the S. aisle by Street, 1878–80. Handsome early 13th-century chancel, long and low with a full complement of lancets. Excellent 16th–17th-century Giffard tombs have 10 recumbent alabaster effigies; Sir John, d. 1556, was Henry VIII's standard-bearer; the Giffards have lived at Chillington since 1178. Recent tablet to Colonel Carliss, who accompanied Charles II in the Royal Oak at Boscobel, 1651.

BROUGHTON
St Peter
5m/8km N.W. of Eccleshall SJ 7632
In a solitary position opposite the big timber-framed Elizabethan Hall. A little Gothic Survival gem of 1630–4. Unspoiled interior with high box pews, Georgian altar rail, and other fittings. Good 17th-century armorial glass and, in the chancel, wonderful reset 15th-century quarries depicting members of the Broughton family. Small font protrudes from the wall like a stoup. Good 17th–18th-century monuments to the Broughton baronets and their families.

BURTON UPON TRENT
SK 2423
St Chad, Hunter Street
Bodley's last church; completed by C. G. Hare after Bodley's death, 1910. Grand Decorated church with tall tower and good massing; opposite is Hare's octagonal vestry. The tower has pierced screens to the elegant bell-openings and a low leaded spire. It is attached to the church by a low, vaulted passage, and forms a perfect foil to the austere and dignified interior. Slender columns, wooden barrel vault, the chancel defined only by a projecting fringe of pierced woodwork. Well-detailed, and no memorials to disturb the serenity. It was the gift of Michael Arthur Bass, the 1st Lord Burton.
St Modwen
By Francis Smith, 1719–26. Handsome Classical church by the river. Large windows, bold W. tower with urns and balustrade, and felicitous interior with Tuscan columns, woodwork and monuments.

St Paul, St Paul's Place
Adjoining the Town Hall, and the grandest church in the town. By J. M. Teale and Lord Grimthorpe, 1874; cruciform with central tower and Bodley decoration inside. Also the gift of the Bass family.

CANWELL
St Mary, St Giles and All Saints
6m/10km S. of Lichfield SK 1400
By Temple Moore, 1911. An exquisite little church in Hollington stone with vaulted roof, contemporary fittings, and a window by Geoffrey Webb.

CAVERSWALL
St Peter
4m/6km W. of Cheadle SJ 9542
Perpendicular tower built into a nave which originated in the 13th century but was reconstructed in 1637; 17th-century pulpit and pews. Chancel monuments include one by Chantrey, 1818.

CHEBSEY
All Saints
2m/3km E. of Eccleshall SJ 8628
Norman and Early English church with Perpendicular tower. Good tower arch with figured capitals, altar rail of 1682, and glass by Kempe. Saxon cross shaft in the churchyard.

CHECKLEY
St Mary and All Saints
5m/8km N.W. of Uttoxeter SK 0237
The best medieval church in N. Staffs. Bold Norman and Perpendicular tower, embattled nave and chancel, N. and S. porches. Lofty early 13th-century nave has clerestory and 17th-century roof. Excellent raised Decorated chancel with 16th-century stalls and much contemporary glass in the traceried windows. Parclose screen, glass, and English altar by Comper, 1922. Saxon cross shafts in the churchyard.

CHEDDLETON
St Edward the Confessor
3m/4km S. of Leek SJ 9752
Grand moorland country. Perpendicular tower, broad Early English nave, and Decorated chancel all under one roof. Impressively restored by Gilbert Scott Jnr, 1863–4. Painted decoration in the sanctuary and important glass by Morris, Ford Madox Brown, and Burne-Jones; Morris knew a church-

warden here. Fine 15th-century Flemish triptych has wings added by Morris.

CHURCH EATON
St Editha
6m/10km S.W. of Stafford SJ 8417
Bold Transitional tower, slender 15th-century spire, and simple, long roof-line. E. end dominated by a great seven-light Perpendicular window spanning the whole width of the chancel. The interior has a nice mixture of late Norman and Perpendicular with pleasant late 19th-century glass. Good Street-ish font and pulpit. Huge E. window said to have come from Old St Paul's.

CHURCH LEIGH
All Saints
5m/8km N.W. of Uttoxeter SK 0235
By Thomas Johnson of Lichfield, 1845–6. A remarkable cruciform church in the Decorated style by an obscure architect. Bold central tower and good details. The interior simple and very good with rib-vaulted tower and chancel. Much excellent Victorian glass. The rich tiles on the chancel floor are said to have been designed by A. W. N. Pugin. Fine alabaster tomb with effigies, 1523.

CLIFTON CAMPVILLE
St Andrew
5m/8km N.E. of Tamworth SK 2510
Perhaps the best medieval parish church in the county; mainly 13th- and 14th-century with small vaulted N. transept, originally balanced to the S. Tall spire, the tower pierced at the base with large windows. Light and spacious nave has 14th-century collar-rafter roof; 14th-century stalls with misericords and a painting of Christ in Majesty in the S. aisle. Good Perpendicular rood screen; notable 16th-century alabaster tomb and monuments by Rysbrack; a little early glass in the N. aisle.

COPPENHALL
St Laurence
2m/3km S. of Stafford SJ 9019
Perfect village church of c. 1220: small, complete and almost unspoilt. Nave and chancel only with copious lancets and weatherboarded Victorian bellcote.

COTTON
St John
4m/6km N.E. of Cheadle SK 0646
A collector's piece; sheltering behind the

enormous Papist bastion of Cotton College, with its grand Pugin chapel, is an endearing, playful little Anglican church of 1795. An enchanting brick battlemented building with plaster vaults inside, rising from slender marble shafts.

CROXALL
St John the Baptist
6m/10km N. of Tamworth SK 1913
Mainly 13th–15th-century church. Notable collection of 15th–17th-century incised slabs and later monuments, one by Chantrey, 1823.

DENSTONE
All Saints
5m/8km N. of Uttoxeter SK 1040
By G.E. Street, 1860–2. An original and dramatic composition in the Middle Pointed style, especially when seen from the N.; the round turret and high chancel very well composed. Stonework, iron, brass, marble, stained glass, light-fittings and lettering, all designed with great skill and verve.

DILHORNE
All Saints
2m/3km W. of Cheadle SJ 9743
Rare 13th-century octagonal W. tower with Perpendicular upper stage; otherwise a Gothic exterior with delightful overhanging eaves and rusticated doorways.

DUNSTALL
St Mary
4m/6km S.W. of Burton upon Trent SK 1820
By Henry Clutton, 1852–3. Decorated estate church with S.W. tower, steep roofs, and vaulted porch. Good interior has leafed capitals to S. arcades and chancel lined with alabaster. Nice reredos; glass by Willement and Burlison & Grylls.

ECCLESHALL
Holy Trinity
7m/11km N.W. of Stafford SJ 8329
Sited at the end of pleasant market town. Fine W. tower has Early English base and fine Perpendicular top with pinnacles. Entered by a big vaulted porch, the church has a spacious nave, mostly late 15th-century, and 13th-century chancel. Tombs of four bishops of Lichfield; Eccleshall Castle was their palace until the 19th century. Bishop Overton's effigy of 1609 is especially good.

ELFORD
St Peter
4m/6km N. of Tamworth SK 1810
At the end of an avenue, close to the site of the big Georgian Hall, is Salvin's 1843–9 essay in the Tudor taste. The tower is genuinely 1598; the S. aisle and chapel were added by Street in 1870. Rich detail on the side which faced the Hall. Usually visited for the tombs, including the charming child effigy with tennis ball, *c.* 1460, but also architecturally interesting. The roof has angelic and heraldic corbels; there are carved, coloured and gilded capitals, red and blue lettering round the arches, harmoniously done for once, an altar rail with brassy angels, and good ironwork on the door.

ELLENHALL
St Mary
2m/3km S.E. of Eccleshall SJ 8426
Next to splendid early 18th-century red-brick gabled Hall, an esentially 15th-century village church with brick tower of 1757 and brick cladding to the S. nave wall. Norman window in the chancel and 18th-century oak pews.

ENVILLE
St Mary the Blessed Virgin
5m/8km W. of Stourbridge SJ 8286
In a grand position, presiding over the patriarchal village and great House, a pink sandstone church, the Somerset tower a rebuilding by Scott Jnr, 1872–5. Norman and Early English arcades; windows replaced by Scott. Good alabaster tomb of Thomas Grey, 1559, and many later monuments to the family, later Earls of Stamford and Warrington. Some late 15th-century stalls with misericords and a nice figured bench-end.

ETTINGSHALL
St Martin
E. suburbs of Wolverhampton, close to A4123 SO 9396
A church of 1938 by Lavender and Twentyman. With a solid oblong tower, connected to its vicarage on the S. side by a short cloister, an attractive brick composition. Inside, a long white nave with simple round arches, long windows, and low, narrow aisles: an impressive interior.

FORTON
All Saints
1m/2km N. of Newport SJ 7521
Association of Georgian and medieval, nicely handled. The stocky but handsome 15th-century tower and the Decorated E. end are linked by S. wall and nave of 1723. The N. aisle is medieval but with a Tuscan arcade. Good canopied tomb with effigies, 1633.

GNOSALL
Collegiate Church of St Lawrence
6m/10km W. of Stafford SJ 8220
Cruciform, originally collegiate, church on the fringe of a scattered village; Norman crossing and S. transept, otherwise mainly 13th–15th-century. The great Norman crossing, with blank arcading and triforium lights, is one of the grandest 12th-century works in the county. Decorated E. window with flowing tracery and original S. porch by Lynam, 1893.

HAMSTALL RIDWARE
St Michael
4m/6km E. of Rugeley SK 1019
An isolated village church of supremely simple silhouette, with 14th-century spire, in wonderful setting of ruined tower, gatehouse, and dovecotes of old manor house nearby; mainly 16th-century. The lofty Norman nave flows straight into the chancel without a break; a perfect setting for the old glass, parclose screens, tombs, memorials, and medieval painted panels in the reredos.

HANBURY
St Werbergh
5m/8km N.W. of Burton upon Trent SK 1727
Fine hill-top setting on site of 7th-century nunnery. Impressive 13th-century and later church much put about in the 19th century. Good arcades, 17th-century nave roof, and handsome Victorian chancel of 1862 replete with murals, tiles, and glass. Excellent 17th-century alabaster effigies, including prim Puritan ladies above the vicar's stall.

HIGH OFFLEY
St Mary the Virgin
5m/8km N.E. of Newport SJ 7826
Hill-top site. Mostly Transitional and Early English; N. doorway and S. arcade of c. 1200; 13th-century lancets in the chancel and base of the tower; the upper stages of

1667. Moulded chancel roof and 17th-century monuments.

HIMLEY
St Michael and All Angels
5m/8km S. of Wolverhampton SO 8891
A wonderful oasis in Black Country landscape. Restrained stuccoed church of 1764; W. tower, nave and apsidal chancel. Georgian pulpit and good W. gallery. Private Garden of Remembrance of the Earls of Dudley has four 1930s gravestones by Eric Gill; it is approached by high-walled orchard, and watered by a stream.

HOAR CROSS
Church of the Holy Angels
4m/6km E. of Abbots Bromley SK 1323
By G. F. Bodley, 1872–6. Great architecture. Like Broughton, Patshull and Ingestre, the family church stands near the Hall, and architecturally all of a piece. Lavish and original design in the Decorated style, well-massed and detailed, a perfect association of splendour and intimacy. Deeply buttressed tower, severe nave outside, the chancel high and richly done. Perfectly handled contrasts within. Glass, Stations of the Cross, tombs, woodwork, stone vaulting; good workmanship everywhere.

HOLLINGSCLOUGH
St Agnes
2m/3km N.W. of Longnor SK 0666
In the upper Dove Valley, against a background of lovely limestone hills. Church and school built as one, 1840. Domestic in scale and character, apart from the bell-turret astride the ridge, and the tall pinnacles of the gables. Stone-slated roof. Tall, well-proportioned interior with gallery and painted texts on starchy ribbons in 1890 Lombardic. Clear crown glass and views of the hills and sky.

HOPWAS
St Chad
2m/3km W. of Tamworth SK 1704
By John Douglas, 1879–81. Picturesque brick and timber-framed church on a hillside. Vigorous massing of big nave roof and central bell-chamber with shingled spirelet. Yellow brick interior with arch-braced roof and original wooden fittings.

HORTON
St Michael

3m/4km W. of Leek SJ 9457

Setting next to fine 17th-century Hall. Mainly 16th-century Perpendicular church, restored by Sugden, 1864. Screen of 1618 and early Wedgwood monuments; the master potters originated here.

ILAM
Holy Cross

4m/6km N.W. of Ashbourne SK 1350

Medieval, but drastically restored by Scott Snr in 1855–6, and dominated by the Watts-Russell mausoleum with great Watts monument by Chantrey, 1831. S. chapel, rebuilt in 1618, contains base of St Bertelin's shrine. Good Scott furnishings include tiles, wrought-iron screens, and a reredos. Two Saxon crosses in the churchyard.

INGESTRE
St Mary

4m/6km E. of Stafford SJ 9824

Probably by Sir Christopher Wren, 1676; originally the Hall chapel. Chaste ashlar exterior with rusticated quoins, keyed round-headed windows, oculi, and modest W. tower. Square plan plus chancel articulated by engaged Tuscan columns with single abacus. Described, perhaps by Wren himself, as 'not great, but uniform and elegant ... The Chancel within paved throughout with Black and White marble, the Windows illustrated with Armes and matches of the Chetwynds in painted glass; and the Ceilings with the same in Fretwork ... an elegant skreen of Flanders Oak, garnisht with the Kings Armes ... the Ironwork about it curiously painted and guilt ...' A gallery of monuments to Chetwynds, Talbots and Chetwynd-Talbots, Earls of Shrewsbury.

KINGS BROMLEY
All Saints

5m/8km N. of Lichfield SK 1216

Nave walls probably pre-Conquest; Decorated N. arcade, 15th-century clerestory and W. tower. Pretty Gothic S. porch and a stone missal stand in the chancel. Strange screen and an assortment of glass. Monuments to the Lanes, the family of Jane Lane, Charles II's preserver.

KINVER
St Peter

4m/6km W. of Stourbridge SO 8483

A dramatic position, in magnificent isolation, on Kinver Edge; 14th–15th-century church with Decorated tower and font. Remarkable brass to Sir Edward Grey, d. 1528, with wives and children, and a handsome Doric monument of 1789.

LAPLEY
All Saints

3m/4km W. of Penkridge SJ 8712

12th–15th-century church with tall Norman and Perpendicular central tower and a good 13th-century chancel with stepped five-light E. window. Fine traceried screen and a Dutch font.

LEEK
10m/16km N.E. of Stoke-on-Trent SJ 9856
All Saints, Compton

By R. Norman Shaw, 1885–7. Large squat-towered church, reminiscent of North Yorks. and surrounded by Victorian houses. Generous porch; unexpectedly light interior. A nice contrast between the intimate scale and great arches. Splendid green marble font; chancel panelling and reredos by Lethaby, painted by F. Hamilton Jackson. Murals in chancel by Gerald Horsley and glass by Morris.

St Edward the Confessor

Large 14th-century church, the aisles removed in the 16th century when the panelled nave roof was inserted. Restored, and chancel added, by Street, 1865–7. Huge late-Georgian gallery like an escalator. Saxon crosses in the churchyard. In both churches many frontals and other needlework by the Leek School of Embroidery, founded in 1870.

LICHFIELD
SK 1109
St Chad

Close to Stowe Pool; here St Chad had his hermitage and his well is here. Early English nave has fine doorway and five-bay S. arcade. Decorated tower and E. window; ceiling and clerestory of c. 1800.

St Mary, market place

In the market-place overlooking Johnson's birthplace and the figures of the Doctor and of Boswell. Handsome Victorian church, the prominent steeple by Street, 1852–4. The rest was rebuilt, rather unexpectedly, by

James Fowler of Louth in 1868–70; proper Middle Pointed.

LONGDON
St James the Great
4m/6km S.E. of Rugeley SK 0814
Norman nave has good S. door and chancel arch. Late 13th-century chancel and Decorated W. tower with 15th-century top stage. Fine S. chapel of *c.* 1500 built by John Stoneywell, later abbot of Pershore. Monument by Edward Stanton, 1716.

LONGSDON
St Chad
2m/3km S.W. of Leek SJ 9654
Splendid views across the towers and chimneys of Leek to the wild moorland country beyond. By Gerald Horsley, 1903–5. Distinguished church in the manner of R. Norman Shaw's work at Leek. Fine W. tower has triple bell-openings and low broach spire. Light and airy inside with Comper glass and local embroidery.

MADELEY
All Saints
5m/8km W. of Newcastle-under-Lyme SJ 7744
A gallery of Victorian glass by Clayton & Bell, Kempe and Morris – the latter especially distinguished, 1873 – and monuments: of special interest that to John Offley, Izaak Walton's friend, to whom the *Compleat Angler* is dedicated.

MARCHINGTON
St Peter
3m/4km S.E. of Uttoxeter SK 1330
By Richard Trubshaw, 1742. Pleasing, warm red-brick exterior; rusticated surrounds and W. tower with cupola. Interior altered in 1892 when the tediously Gothic chancel was added; somewhat redeemed by Arts and Crafts fittings.

MAVESYN RIDWARE
St Nicholas
3m/4km E. of Rugeley SK 0816
Unusual composition of medieval tower and N. aisle, called the Trinity Chapel, and a brick Gothic nave, 1782. The interior is also interesting; the N. aisle has two knights' effigies and 16 incised slabs with figures and heraldry, mostly late 18th-century conceits. Ten hatchments and a good heraldic window

of 1870. Cast-iron altar rails and a Norman font; all very odd.

MAYFIELD
St John the Baptist
2m/3km W. of Ashbourne SK 1546
Pleasant setting in the Dove Valley, somewhat apart from the village. Good tower of 1515, the chancel 14th-century, with a jolly scalloped parapet. Late Gothic porch and Norman doorway lead into spacious Norman nave. Pews, pulpit, and three-sided communion rail, all 1633. Two nice 18th-century memorials and a font of 1614.

NEWBOROUGH
All Saints
4m/6km E. of Abbots Bromley SK 1325
By J. Oldrid Scott, 1899–1901. Slender octagonal pinnacled tower and spire of great beauty and originality. The rest simple and serene.

NORBURY
St Peter
4m/6km N.E. of Newport SJ 7823
Excellent nave and chancel of *c.* 1340 with original roof. To this a brick Gothic tower was added by Wm. Baker, 1759. But it is the Decorated work which claims our attention: four sedilia, a founder's tomb with painted figure and exciting carvings, and a lovely brass to Lady Hawys Botiller.

OKEOVER
All Saints
2m/3km N.W. of Ashbourne SK 1647
Small Decorated church with Perpendicular tower. Restored by Scott in 1856; his are the elaborate screen and stalls. Interesting Okeover monuments, including a corker by Joseph Wilton, 1765; the family has been here since the 12th century.

PATSHULL
St Mary
7m/11km W. of Wolverhampton SJ 8000
By James Gibbs, 1743; N. aisle and tower altered in 1874. A simple composition in parkland beside a lake. Octagonal cupola on a square tower. Symmetrically disposed S. nave front with Tuscan porch. Venetian E. window. Interior a little coarse; 18th-century font and gilded screen by Banks, 1893; 16th–18th-century Astley tombs and monuments include an alabaster tomb chest of

c. 1532 and a composition of 1687 with standing figure.

R.C.F.

PATTINGHAM
St Chad
6m/10km W. of Wolverhampton SO 8299

Norman, Early English and Decorated church with a spire of 1871. Lofty nave with Norman arcade, double N. aisle, and a beautiful 13th-century chancel with lancets. Good archy views.

PENKRIDGE
St Michael and All Angels
6m/10km S. of Stafford SJ 9214

Once a collegiate church with dean and four canons. Mostly 16th-century Perpendicular outside, including the top of the Decorated tower. The interior high and spacious with 13th-century arcades. Dutch wrought-iron screen of 1778. Two splendid table-tombs and one 16th–17th-century two-storeyed tomb; other tombs with recumbent effigies to the Littleton family of Pillaton. Two incised slabs with figures, 15th- and 16th-century.

RANTON
All Saints
4m/6km W. of Stafford SJ 8524

Small Early English church with lancets, N. and S. doorways, and Perpendicular windows. To this a brick chancel was added in 1753.

ROLLESTON
St Mary
3m/4km N. of Burton upon Trent SK 2327

Essentially Norman, as evidenced by the nave doorways, with Decorated aisles set unusually far E. Surprisingly good monuments include that to Bishop Sherburne of Chichester, d. 1536, and Sir Edward Moseley, 1638. Kempe glass and a Saxon cross in the churchyard.

RUSHTON SPENCER
St Lawrence
5m/8km N.W. of Leek SJ 9362

In isolation on a ridge, with a view of the fringes of the Staffs. and Cheshire Peak District. A church of rare interest and individuality. Mostly 17th- and 19th-century outside, with a weatherboarded bell-turret and high-gabled dormers. Inside, the original timber nave of *c.* 1200 is spanned by low beams with a text in good Georgian lettering. The hefty posts and struts are like low, spreading trees. Gothic arched ceiling and a Georgian minstrels' gallery, Jacobean pulpit and squire's pew with hatchments above, big Tables of the Law, and oil lamps. Everything friendly and domestic, clearly the House of God.

SANDON
All Saints
4m/6km N.E. of Stafford SJ 9429

On a hill in Sandon Park. Mostly 14th-century, the tower massing and fenestration generally odd and full of interest. The interior is dominated by the screen supporting the family pew of the Harrowbys. In the chancel are the Erdeswick tombs, notably that of Sampson Erdeswick, Historian of Staffordshire, 1601, to his own design; also wall-paintings of heraldic shields hung on trees – family trees. Beautifully furnished interior with 17th-century pews, many Harrowby hatchments and monuments, and a Stuart Royal Arms.

SEIGHFORD
St Chad
3m/4km N.W. of Stafford SJ 8824

A church of much antiquarian interest with some architectural detective problems. Seen from the road it appears mostly brick Gothic, with a 17th-century W. tower tricked out in 1748. But the chancel and N. side are medieval, and the interior mostly early-Norman. Good Jacobean pulpit. Tomb with effigies of *c.* 1593, hatchments, scraps of old glass, and wall-painting.

SHARESHILL
St Mary of the Assumption
5m/8km N.E. of Wolverhampton SJ 9406

Perpendicular stone W. tower attached to a handsome brick Gothic church of *c.* 1740. Good S. doorway with pairs of Tuscan columns, the apse with a Venetian window. Inside there is a triple screen between nave and chancel, a W. gallery, and most of the original furnishings.

SHEEN
St Luke
3m/4km S.E. of Longnor SK 1161

Remote Peakland country. Originally to a design of C. W. Burleigh of Leeds, 1850, but completed by William Butterfield for Alexander Beresford Hope. Good W. tower with recessed pyramidal roof; the dignified interior has a tunnel-vaulted chancel and rich Anglo-Catholic fittings. Glass by O'Connor. Founder's tomb in the churchyard and a good Butterfield parsonage, 1852.

SHENSTONE
St John the Baptist
3m/4km S. of Lichfield SK 1104
By John Gibson, 1852–3. Imposing Victorian church with prominent N. tower and well-massed gables. Chilly interior has rose window and octagonal Decorated font. Tower of earlier church nearby.

SLINDON
St Chad
2m/3km N. of Eccleshall SJ 8232
By Basil Champneys, 1894. Delightful, small late-Victorian church, its quirky details loosely based on the 14th century. Low tower, vaulted choir and sanctuary, and a richly carved reredos. Glass by Kempe.

STAFFORD
SJ 9223
St Mary
Cruciform with central octagonal tower; originally Early English but thoroughly overhauled by G. G. Scott in 1841–4. Generally fine interior with 13th-century arcades and Decorated N. transept. Tudor nave roof. Inscribed Norman font; alabaster tomb effigies and the site of St Bertelin's shrine.
St Chad, Greengate Street
Restored and refaced by Scott, 1874. Almost all the interior is grand Norman work with an unusually rich chancel arch. Chancel and crossing longer than the nave. Fine fake-Norman font, c. 1850.
Holy Trinity, Baswich
By Richard Trubshaw and Richard Jackson, 1739. A small brick church with medieval stone tower overlooking Stafford. Light and simple interior, the eye caught by the three-decker pulpit and the family pews just beyond the medieval chancel arch; one raised on spindly columns, the other on stout Doric ones. Heraldic table-tombs and pleasing modern glass. Two mean transepts recently added; interior rearranged and ruined.

STOKE-ON-TRENT
SJ 8745
Holy Trinity
By George Gilbert Scott, 1841–2; an early work in strict Middle Pointed style. Pin-nacled W. tower and clerestoried nave with plaster vault. The chancel was rebuilt with a stone vault after a fire in 1872. Lots of tiles, not surprising as the patron was Herbert Minton, and excellent glass by Hardman.

STONE
St Michael
7m/11km N. of Stafford SJ 9034
Large Gothic preaching-box, 1753–8, designed by Wm. Robinson and supervised by Wm. Baker; unfortunate Perpendicular chancel added in 1887. An early instance of revivalist Gothic, with square W. tower, two tiers of windows, and battlements. Inside are galleries, box pews enough, and the original font; an important survival of an 18th-century town church. Glass by Kempe, somewhat dark, but a fine collection of memorials, including that to the Earl St Vincent, 1823, with bust by Chantrey. In the churchyard is his family's mausoleum: handsome, Palladian, and also designed by Mr Robinson.

STOWE-BY-CHARTLEY
St John the Baptist
6m/10km N.E. of Stafford SK 0027
Basically Norman – see the nave doorways with scallops and zig-zags, with Decorated W. tower; much put about by Habershon & Pite in 1875. But here is a rare jewel: the alabaster tomb of Walter Devereux, 1st Viscount Hereford, d. 1537, and his two wives, an affectionate early-Renaissance monument of courtly aspect. Two monuments by Lutyens, to General Sir Walter Congreve, 1927, and his son William, VC, killed in 1916, aged 25.

STRETTON
St Mary
2m/3km N.E. of Burton upon Trent SK 2526
By Micklethwaite and Somers Clarke, 1897. Large and handsome brewer's church in the Decorated style. Nave and chancel of equal height and separated by a boldly buttressed tower with pyramidal roof. Light and assured interior with much pretty painting, good woodwork, and a marble font. Fine glass made by Powell & Sons.

SWYNNERTON
St Mary
3m/4km N.W. of Stone SJ 8535
12th–15th-century church with good Norman doorways in the tower, Early

English chancel and arcades, and a nice Perpendicular screen. However, in the S.E. chapel is a huge and celebrated figure of Christ. Of cathedral-like quality and proportions, and dating to 1260–80, it was found beneath the chancel floor, perhaps buried at the time of the Reformation; but what is it doing here?

TAMWORTH
Collegiate Church of St Editha
14m/22km N.E. of Birmingham SK 2004
The pinnacled church tower and castle dominate the silhouette of this largely Georgian town. Grand, immediate effect inside W. door beneath the tower: a rich Baroque monument of *c.* 1680 by Grinling Gibbons to Sir John Ferrers with figures, heraldry, urns and swags. The church is generally of 'noble and ample proportions', mostly late 14th-century with Perpendicular clerestory and roofs. Unexpected Norman work in the choir, elegant 18th-century wrought-iron screen, good Pre-Raphaelite glass, and a unique double spiral staircase in tower.

TETTENHALL
St Michael
N.W. suburb of Wolverhampton, 3m/4km N.W. of town centre SJ 8700
The medieval parish church, rebuilt after a fire in 1950, by Edward Miller. The Perpendicular tower survives; nave and chancel, now used as Lady Chapel, rebuilt in latest Art Nouveau style; effective and attractive.

TRENTHAM
St Mary and All Saints
3m/4km S. of Stoke-on-Trent SJ 8641
Close to the magnificent gardens of Trentham House, demolished 1910, once a home of the Dukes of Sutherland, stands the church by Sir Charles Barry, 1844, a large ashlar building with re-used late-Norman arcades, a screen of 1633, and Georgian W. gallery. Good 16th-century and later monuments including work by Chantrey and Noble. Nearby is Tatham's awesome mausoleum of 1807; on the roadside.

TRYSULL
All Saints
5m/8km W. of Wolverhampton SO 8594
12th-century and later church has Decorated tower and chancel with flowing tracery. Impressive Perpendicular nave roof and traceried screen.

TUTBURY
Priory Church of St Mary
4m/6km N.W. of Burton upon Trent SK 2128
Overlooking the town, near the castle. An important Norman church; the outside belies the excellent interior. Rich W. front and fine doorway of seven orders, including the earliest English alabaster work. Inside, the splendid Norman nave happily terminates in Street's apsidal E. end of 1866. Tall, hefty arcades of *c.* 1100, the old triforium now serving as a clerestory. Fine Street fittings and good ironwork on the doors.

WALSALL
St Matthew
SP 0198
Medieval nave encased in ashlar by Francis Goodwin, 1821. Inside are galleries, slender iron Perpendicular arcade piers, and elegant cast-iron traceried windows. The nave roof is a triumph of delicate Gothic plaster vaulting, still very much in the 18th-century tradition; 15th-century chancel, restored by Ewan Christian in 1877–80, retains fine Perpendicular choir-stalls with misericords, the largest set in the county.

WARSLOW
St Lawrence
7m/11km E. of Leek SK 0858
Peakland estate village. Church of 1820, the handsome chancel added by Charles Lynam, 1908. Good original fittings of two-decker pulpit, box pews, and squire's pew; stained glass by Morris and good Art Nouveau mosaics in the chancel.

WESTON-UNDER-LIZARD
St Andrew
7m/11km S.E. of Newport SJ 8010
Essentially a church of 1700–1, but incorporating the tower and E. wall of the medieval church. Designed by the enterprising Lady Wilbraham, with round-arched windows, pilasters and frieze. Additions in the Norman taste by Ewan Christian in 1876, but the delightful original pulpit and wrought-iron altar rail remain. Diverse monuments, including Lady Wilbraham's own. She was a gifted amateur architect, and designed the Hall, home of the descendants of the Earl of Bradford.

WOLVERHAMPTON
SO 9198
St John, St John's Square

By Wm. Baker, 1755. Set in a decrepit Georgian Square. Good W. front, the tower and octagonal banded spire also nicely handled. Pedimented E. end with blind arches. Doric interior with galleries and Renatus Harris organ case. Nice gate-piers and ironwork.

Collegiate Church of St Peter
Well sited on a hill. A large and well-massed composition of *c.* 1480 with tall central tower, two-storey vaulted porch, and high transepts; good chancel by Ewan Christian, 1852–65. Spacious and lofty inside with very fine stone pulpit integral to the main structure, a jolly lion on the balustrade. Good woodwork; W. gallery of 1610, choirstalls and parclose screen. Also some excellent monuments, especially the bronze standing figure of Sir Richard Leveson by Le Sueur, *c.* 1634. Splendid 9th-century carved circular cross shaft in the churchyard.

WOMBOURN
St Benedict Biscop
4m/6km S.W. of Wolverhampton so 8793
By G. E. Street, 1862–7, apart from the medieval tower and spire. Good Decorated design with varied window tracery and fine contemporary furnishings. Glass by Kempe and Clayton & Bell.

WYCHNOR
St Leonard
1m/2km N.E. of Alrewas across R. Trent SK 1716
Isolated, with a wonderful wide panorama across the plain; Alrewas Church, Lichfield Cathedral, and Cannock Chase all visible on a clear day. Mostly 14th-century Decorated with late 16th-century brick top to the tower. A bold and friendly building, with good, large square-headed traceried windows and richly coloured and textured stone. A little heraldic glass.

YOXALL
St Peter
6m/10km N. of Lichfield SK 1418
On the slope of Needwood Forest, a large village full of delightful houses; the church originally 14th-century, but much rebuilt by Woodyer, 1865–8. Late Perpendicular W. tower, good 16th- and 19th-century monuments, fine late-Victorian furnishings, and glass by Wailes.

Suffolk

Introduction

South Norfolk glides almost imperceptibly into Suffolk. Beginning with that leafy countryside just south of Norwich, where Old Crome found that king among trees, 'The Poringland Oak', and proceeding down the valley of the Tas, the whitewashed cottages and farms, timber-framed with wattle and daub and high-pitched roofs, become more and more frequent. Villages like Saxlingham Nethergate begin to have wide greens with the cottages dotted about round the edge like so many villages in Suffolk. Little towns like Loddon, Long Stratton and Pulham Market are similar places to Debenham, Stradbroke and Laxfield; and though Harleston and Diss are on the Norfolk side of the Waveney Valley, they are but smaller versions of their Suffolk, though more northerly, neighbours, Bungay and Beccles.

Then as one proceeds farther into the Suffolk countryside the villages appear more remote. There are few main roads and, now that so many branch lines have been abandoned, fewer railways. Neither does one often encounter in the narrow lanes the 'Eastern Counties' red bus which seems to have found its way into most Norfolk villages.

The brick and flint give way to colour-wash and thatch, the villages have a softer appearance, the fields smaller, the woodlands thicker and the trees larger, so that by the time one has left Harleston and Fressingfield behind, or penetrated into the quiet villages just inland from the coast at Southwold or Aldeburgh, one has the feeling of being in the depths of the country as nowhere else in East Anglia.

What may be said of the villages may also be said of the towns. They are more compact, quieter, and more retired. No 'A' road runs into Framlingham or Eye, and those which are on some important line of communication seem to have kept themselves apart from the main stream of traffic, like Woodbridge, where the bypass helps it to remain as a perfect example of an old country town, spreading along the main street and thickening about the market-place in the middle.

As for the towns, so for the capital. Norwich is an industrial city and county capital all in one. Suffolk has intensified both but kept them well apart. Ipswich is the industrial capital, with the result that the parochial distinctions of the old medieval city are less evident; and Bury the county market town where the industries are kept in the background.

So also for the coast. Like Yarmouth, Lowestoft is both a pleasure resort and a fishing-town, but smaller, quieter, more restrained, and the same sort of comparison could be made between Cromer and Southwold, Sheringham and Aldeburgh, and between Hunstanton and Felixstowe.

The Suffolk rivers are smaller but they have longer estuaries which penetrate for a long distance inland. The Ore follows the coast for ten miles and more before it decides to turn inland as the Alde; Woodbridge is on the tidal estuary of the Deben, but it is a long way from the sea. The Gipping is a quiet little stream until at Gippeswick (Ipswich – the creek of the Gipping) it becomes the long estuary of the Orwell; and the same may be said of the Stour, which Suffolk shares with Essex on its southern border.

It is to the Stour Valley that one comes after the remote country of East Suffolk and, though it is apparent at once that Constable's country is near enough to London to have been discovered by the weekender, it is a lovely district with a character that is all its own and with its own capital; another collection of medieval villages which is the town of Sudbury, with a statue of Gainsborough in the Market Place.

Gainsborough and Constable. How often did those painters set their figures against the background of a landscape park, for that is exactly what the Stour Valley is as you see it spread out beneath the high ground at Stoke-by-Nayland or at Bures. A park continues right on through Sudbury to that wonderful village of Parks and Halls, Long Melford.

West of Long Melford, Suffolk becomes Essex and, though Clare is on the Suffolk side of the Stour, it is essentially an Essex country town, with the houses rich in pargetry work. But north and east of Melford one is back again in the heart of Suffolk. Even 'B' roads are few and far between, so that with no map, and with all the signposts destroyed (as patriotic East Anglians both in Norfolk and Suffolk were most insistent on doing in the early days of the last war), 'the man in the moon who came down too soon' to Shimpling or to Hawkedon, Thorpe Morieux, Nedging Tye or Kettlebaston, would find it difficult 'to find his way to Norwich', as the saying goes, and would be more likely to get hopelessly lost in the maze of lanes and footpaths. But it is a county in which one would be quite content to get lost, for sometime or another all the roads lead to the local metropolis, which is not only the most lovely town in Suffolk, but one of the most beautiful in all England – Lavenham.

To enter into the spirit of the country the traveller in East Suffolk will find it almost essential to be equipped with the Works of George Crabbe, and for the highlands of West Suffolk he will be well advised to seek out some faded copy of the poems of the contemporary Robert Bloomfield, who, though a more pedestrian poet, could at times describe the spirit of a place even better than Crabbe himself. He depicts the rolling grassland of Euston Park and the wide upland fields of Honington, of Troston, and of Sapiston, around which he had plodded as a 'Farmer's Boy', and with the foliage of spring, the shimmering heat of summer, the falling leaves of autumn, and the hard cold of winter, with the accuracy of a steel engraving.

West Suffolk, too, has a distinct character, but the various districts are not so sharply distinguished from one another as they are in Norfolk. If Suffolk melts into Norfolk along the Tas, and into Essex in the valley of the Stour, so also the chalky heights of West Suffolk blend into the white chalk of Cambridgeshire; the cottages, and the churches too, are built of hard chalk or clunch, and one can make one's way over the Gog Magogs into the Midlands without meeting the barrier of the Fens.

C. L. S. L.

continued overleaf

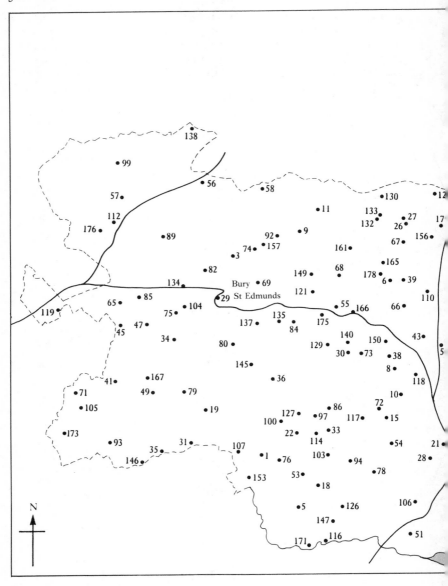

N

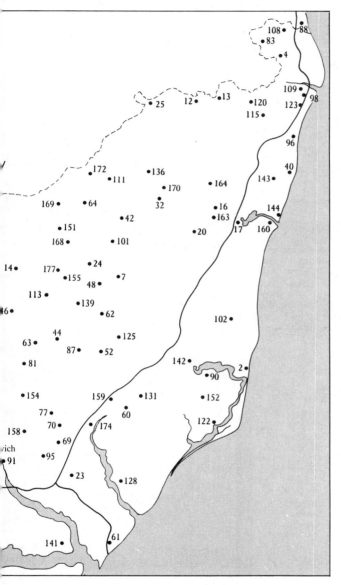

Selected List of Churches

ACTON
All Saints
3m/4km N.E. of Sudbury TL 8994
Pleasing interior with 15th-century bench-ends, 17th-century altar rails, and magnificent multi-cusped tomb canopy in the chancel. Brasses include that to Sir Robert de Bures, d. 1302, one of the finest military brasses in England.

ALDEBURGH
St Peter & St Paul
6m/10km S.E. of Saxmundham TM 4656
Good tower with higher stair turret. Broad aisles reaching to the E. wall of the chancel, dating mainly from the 16th-century extension. An unusually long porch, with lateral arches. Pulpit of 1632 and fine 1934 rebuild of 16th-century roof. Bust of poet George Crabbe, 1847, by Thurlow of Saxmundham, and a memorial window by John Piper to Benjamin Britten, who is buried in the churchyard.

AMPTON
St Peter
4m/6km N. of Bury St Edmunds TL 8671
Lovely village. In the church is the chantry chapel of John Coket, d. 1479. Calthorpe monument in the chancel by the E. Anglian sculptors John and Mathias Christmas, who did much of the embellishing of Charles I's great ship *The Sovereign of the Seas*. Also a kneeling effigy of Dorothy Calthorpe, 'a virgin votary oft in snares', who 'troubles no man's dust'. She gave the handsome row of almshouses E. of the church. A great treasure of this church is a 'sealed Book' of Common Prayer of which neither the British Museum nor the Bodleian Library possess a copy.

ASHBY
St Mary
5m/8km N.W. of Lowestoft TM 4899
Remote thatched church. Tower with round base but two-thirds octagonal above. Lancet windows and 13th-century brick.

ASSINGTON
St Edmund
4m/6km S.E. of Sudbury TL 9338
Perpendicular with fine 15th-century traceried S. door. Good 16th–18th-century monuments. Well restored in 1863 to the vicar's designs.

BACTON
St Mary
5m/8km N. of Stowmarket TM 0567
Good E. Anglian stone and flint work clerestory with Latin inscription on the exterior commemorating the donors. Fine double hammer-beam 15th-century roof and traces of Doom painting.

BADINGHAM
St John the Baptist
3m/4km N.E. of Framlingham TM 3068
Remains of Norman work in lower part of tower and W. end of nave. Distinguished hammer-beam roof, and one of the finest and best preserved seven-sacrament fonts in E. Anglia. In the panel representing Penance, evil is vigorously portrayed as a devil with horns; 17th-century pulpit; Cotton monuments.

BADLEY
St Mary
2m/3km S.E. of Stowmarket TM 0655
Remote and unspoilt gem in a meadow. Tudor brick top to rectangular tower and great Perpendicular W. window. King-post roof, 15th-century benches, and 17th-century box pews and pulpit, all mellowed to silver-grey. Unforgettably quaint and rustic, except for Preedy's E. window and later altar rails. Poley memorials.
R.C.F.

BARDWELL
St Peter & St Paul
2m/3km N. of Ixworth TL 9473
Fine Perpendicular tower. Lofty nave with single hammer-beam roof, dated 1421; 15th-century glass with kneeling figure of benefactor, Sir William Berdewell. Chancel remodelled 1863 by Bacon and Bell.

BARKING
St Mary
4m/6km S. of Stowmarket TM 0753
13th-century and later with interesting interior; 15th-century font cover, rood, and parclose screens. Fine N. aisle roof.

BARNINGHAM
St Andrew
5m/8km N.E. of Ixworth TL 9676
Decorated W. tower and chancel; 15th-century rood screen; 17th-century screen doors, pulpit and tester; complete set of carved benches. Rood loft stairs rise from window sill.

BARSHAM
St Michael
2m/3km W. of Beccles TM 3989
Pretty pastoral setting for this little shrine, with its Saxon round tower and unique E. window of lozenge trellis-work. Much 17th-century woodwork, including the screen, and a remarkably sensitive early 20th-century restoration by F. C. Eden, with much glass by him. Anglo-Catholic interior; tasteful, colourful and with great character, wonderfully made to live again after a fire in 1979.

BECCLES
St Michael
8m/12km W. of Lowestoft TM 4290
Commanding position overlooking Waveney Valley. Massive detached 16th-century bell-tower. Great barn of a church with two superb porches of the 15th century. Vast but well-proportioned interior, restored by J. H. Hakewill, 1857–66.

BEDINGFIELD
St Mary
4m/6km N. of Debenham TM 1868
Decorated W. tower with flushwork arcading on buttresses. Double hammer-beam roof, benches of 1621, and 17th-century altar table.

BILDESTON
St Mary
5m/8km N. of Hadleigh TL 9949
On hill outside village. Tower collapsed 1975. Lofty with graceful arcades; Suffolk-type tie-beam and hammer-beam roofs; door with traceried panelling; set of misericords.

BLYFORD
All Saints
3m/4km E. of Halesworth TM 4276
Wayside church with two Norman doorways; 13th-century chancel with lancets contains Elizabethan altar table of great beauty.

BLYTHBURGH
Holy Trinity
4m/6km W. of Southwold TM 4575
Glorious exterior, dominating the heathland and the Blyth Estuary. Mostly 15th-century, with great Perpendicular windows, superb clerestory and parapets, and 15th-century doors. Interior lofty, light and largely unspoilt, with soaring arcades and fine vistas. Large font, much mutilated, on original steps. Long, unbroken roof, with medieval colour and angels. Intriguing bench-ends with the Seven Deadly Sins and the Seasons of the Year, stalls with carved fronts, and much original screenwork; 17th-century pulpit, lectern *c.* 1450, old glass, fine Hopton monument, Jack o'Clock, *c.* 1652, and much else in this unforgettable church.

BOXFORD
St Mary
4m/6km W. of Hadleigh TL 9640
In the middle of a pretty village; 14th-century timber N. porch with beautiful vaulting; the stone S. porch has a representation of the Annunciation; 17th-century font cover with doors that fold back to reveal texts painted on scrolls; monument in S. aisle to a lady who died in her 113th year; also a delightful 17th-century brass to an infant, David Bride, asleep in his miniature bed. E. window by Rosemary Rutherford, 1973.

BOXTED
All Saints
4m/6km N.W. of Long Melford TL 8250
Ornate Poley family pews fill the N. aisle; partitions separate the family places from those of their retainers. Good 17th-century woodwork and fine monuments, particularly the alabaster figure of Sir John Poley, d. 1638, in elaborate armour.

BRAMFIELD
St Andrew
3m/4km S. of Halesworth TM 3973
This little church has a very early circular tower standing by itself to the S.W. of the church. Inside is a beautiful screen with

vaulting, the best of its kind in Suffolk. In the chancel is Nicholas Stone's exquisite effigy of Mrs Arthur Coke, 1643.

BRAMFORD
St Mary
3m/4km N.W. of Ipswich TM 1246
A 13th–15th-century church which must have been aglow with the most wonderful glass before 1644, when Dowsing destroyed '841 superstitious pictures'. Yet there are many things remaining. Good hammer-beam roof in nave and chancel. Stone rood screen *c.* 1300. Early 16th-century font cover like that at Boxford but more elaborate. Sturdy Decorated tower with 18th-century lead spire. E. window by C. E. Kempe.

BRENT ELEIGH
St Mary
2m/3km S.E. of Lavenham TL 9447
Setting near Hall. Decorated and Perpendicular with fine S. door. Pleasing 18th-century interior has box pews containing 17th-century carving; 17th-century three-decker pulpit and altar table with three-sided communion rails; important wall-paintings, including 14th-century Crucifixion on E. wall.

BRIGHTWELL
St John the Baptist
6m/10km E. of Ipswich TM 2543
Tiny church in idyllic setting. Mostly *c.* 1300, but remodelled in 1656–7 and given its brick tower, which rests upon a massive Tuscan arch, with pulpit and font cover; 14th-century door with sanctuary ring, exquisitely carved early 14th-century font, pretty memorials to the Essingtons and Barnardistons, and several hatchments.

BRUNDISH
St Laurence
4m/6km N. of Framlingham TM 2769
Setting; Norman tower and atmospheric interior with interesting woodwork including bench-ends and box pews; 15th-century glass and several brasses.

BUNGAY
TM 3389
Holy Trinity, Trinity Street
11th-century round tower, fine traceried pulpit of 1558, and 17th-century woodwork including altar rail with turned balusters.
St Mary, St Mary Street

Formerly nave of Benedictine nunnery; spectacular 15th-century tower and vast W. window. Font of *c.* 1700 and unusual dole table.
R.C.F.

BURES
4m/6km S.W. of Diss TL 9034
St Mary
Church has remarkable porches, one of timber, one of Tudor brick with crude chevron pattern. Chancel must have been fine, a sort of Wingfield. Heraldic font. Monuments include early 14th-century worm-eaten wooden effigy of a Cornard, and monumental pile to Sir William and Dame Elizabeth Waldegrave and their 10 children in alabaster, 1613.
St Stephen's Chapel
1m/2km N.E. of Bures
Remote and delightful Early English building, dedicated in 1218 and on the reputed spot where St Edmund was crowned. It contains the superb 14th-century monuments of the De Veres, brought here from Earls Colne Priory.

BURGATE
St Mary
4m/6km S.W. of Diss TM 0875
Decorated W. tower and nave N. windows, otherwise mostly 15th-century, but altered later. Tomb with canopied military brass, 1409, for Sir William de Burgate and his wife.

BURSTALL
St Mary
4m/6km W. of Ipswich TM 0944
Delightful Decorated architecture here; also 15th-century timberwork in porch, hammer-beam nave roof, and screen.

BURY ST EDMUNDS
TL 8564
St John, St John's Street
Dignified Early English in white brick, by W. Ranger, constructed 1841, with 1870s modifications by J. D. Wyatt. Distinctive spire and impressive Anglo-Catholic interior.
St Mary
Noble church with grand exterior and sturdy N. tower. Superb late 15th-century angel roof to nave and panelled wagon roof to chancel. Fine stonework in the N. 'Notyngham' porch. Much of interest inside,

including monuments, woodwork, 19th-century glass, and the Suffolk Regimental Chapel, furnished by Sir Ninian Comper. John Boret's monument in the S. chapel, 1467, has a grim cadaver effigy, and his motto, 'Grace me Governe', appears in the wonderfully painted roof.

BUXHALL
St Mary
3m/4km W. of Stowmarket TM 0057
Well-proportioned 14th-century church with Perpendicular tower. Fragments of 15th-century glass and Decorated double piscina.

CAVENDISH
St Mary
4m/6km W. of Long Melford TL 8046
Setting across village green. Distinctive tower with big staircase turret. Beautiful 15th-century flushwork clerestory and enormous E. window. There is a fine brass, 15th-century eagle lectern, and a 16th-century wooden one. Sumptuous 15th-century reredos, restored by Comper, in the S. chapel.

CHEDISTON
St Mary
2m/3km W. of Halesworth TM 3577
14th-century arch-braced nave roof, pulpit of 1637. and Jacobean altar rails. Good font carved with Lions and Wild Men.

CHELSWORTH
All Saints
4m/6km N.W. of Hadleigh TL 9848
Mostly 14th-century with splendid Decorated tomb recess in N. aisle and remains of a Doom painting over the chancel arch.

CHEVINGTON
St Peter
5m/8km S.W. of Bury St Edmunds TL 7859
Curious tower, heightened *c.* 1800. Part of wooden 14th-century S. porch. Early English chancel with late-Gothic E. window of 1697.

CLARE
St Peter & St Paul
7m/11km N.W. of Sudbury TL 7645
Early English work in the tower. Noble embattled nave and aisles of *c.* 1460, with E. turrets. Chancel restored 1617. Good 15th-century traceried doors give access to a

bright and lofty interior. Medieval nave roof and 17th-century chancel roof; 17th-century gallery in chapel by S. porch. Stalls, altar rail, and heraldic glass in E. window, all 1617. Rare 16th-century lectern of latten.

COCKFIELD
St Peter
4m/6km N. of Lavenham TL 9054
Large church with noble tower and impressive exterior; 14th-century canopied tomb in chancel in N. aisle and 12th-century niche embellished with foliage in relief. Some good medieval and later glass.

CODDENHAM
St Mary
6m/10km N. of Ipswich TM 1354
Norman window and 13th-century piscina in chancel, but church mostly 14th-century, with fine 15th-century clerestory and double hammer-beam roof. Screen of 1534 with pictures of prophets. N. tower and N. porch at strange angle to church. Good 17th-century pulpit, rails, and communion table.

COMBS
St Mary
2m/3km S. of Stowmarket TM 0456
Remote setting. There is much of interest in this church, but best of all is the beautiful glass in the S. aisle representing Old Testament Kings and Prophets in the genealogy of Christ, the Works of Mercy and, most vivid of all, scenes from the Life of St Margaret of Antioch. She is represented as a shepherdess cast into prison, swallowed up by the Devil, and stepping light-heartedly into a cauldron of boiling oil.

COTTON
St Andrew
5m/8km N. of Stowmarket TM 0766
Superb 14th-century work in the chancel. Bold tower has unusual W. arch and sumptuous S. entrance with traceried doors. Fine 15th-century clerestory, double hammer-beam roof, and an unusual bench-end carved with a door; 17th-century pulpit and rails.

COVEHITHE
St Andrew
4m/6km N.E. of Southwold TM 5281
Vast ruin of splendid late 15th-century church built onto a lofty 14th-century tower. It was abandoned and a tiny thatched church

built in the ruins in 1672. Font, 15th-century pulpit, and some bench-ends from the old church.

R.C.F. (tower and ruins).

COWLINGE
St Margaret
6m/10km N.E. of Haverhill TL 7154
Largely Decorated church with brick tower of 1733. Unspoilt interior, with 14th-century crown-post roof, handsome rood screen of *c.* 1400, beautiful 15th-century parclose screen, and 18th-century W. gallery, pulpit, rails and seating. Traces of wall-painting, some old glass, and a good window by Christopher Webb, 1931. Large monument by Scheemakers to Francis Dickins, 1747.

CRATFIELD
St Mary
5m/8km W. of Halesworth TM 3175
One of the finest of the county's seven-sacrament fonts. Good Perpendicular W. tower, fine chancel roof and 17th-century woodwork.

CREETING
St Peter
2m/3km E. of Stowmarket TM 0758
Mostly Decorated and Perpendicular with 15th-century wall-painting of St Christopher and a mermaid, Perpendicular pulpit, and a 17th-century altar table.

CRETINGHAM
St Peter
4m/6km S.E. of Debenham TM 2260
Unspoilt interior with single hammer-beam roof, Royal Arms of Charles II, 17th-century three-decker pulpit, three-sided communion rails, and altar table; 18th-century box pews.

DALHAM
St Mary
5m/8km E. of Newmarket TL 7261
The church stands beside the Hall. Spacious 14th–15th-century building with Perpendicular roof and screen. Much-decayed series of wall-paintings. There is a painting on stone to the effect that the 'steeple' was 're-edified' in 1625. Good woodwork of the 1860s.

DEBENHAM
St Mary
11m/18km N. of Ipswich TM 1763
Pre-Conquest tower, 13th-century chancel,

and 14th-century two-storeyed W. porch; 15th-century nave arcade with hammer-beam and tie-beam roofs.

DENHAM
St John the Baptist
6m/10km W. of Bury St Edmunds TL 7561
Decorated chancel and Perpendicular nave. Late 13th-century effigy of lady in wimple holding her heart in her hands. Palimpsest brass; on one side the figure of Anthony Bedingfield, d. 1574, and on the other part of Flemish brass. Royal Arms of Charles I, dated 1637.

DENNINGTON
St Mary
2m/3km N. of Framlingham TM 2387
Dignified exterior has Perpendicular nave, aisles and porch, noble chancel of *c.* 1330 with handsome reticulated windows, sturdy tower *c.* 1383, and late 15th-century two-storeyed sacristy. Seven medieval doors remain, and the unforgettable interior has 76 15th-century bench-ends, font cover, and parclose screens, complete with their original lofts. The Decorated chancel has exquisitely carved corbels and capitals; 17th-century three-decker pulpit, altar rails and box pews. Rare pyx canopy of *c.* 1500; superb monument to Lord and Lady Bardolph, 1441.

DENSTON
St Nicholas
5m/8km N. of Clare TL 7652
Beautiful position on rising ground above the village. Late 15th-century throughout; the interior has changed little since the 17th century. Fine arch-braced roof with cambered tie-beams as at Blythburgh, together with very good choir-stalls and seven-sacrament font. Here, more than anywhere else in the county, we get the feeling of what this Suffolk type of 15th-century church was like in its original splendour.

EARL STONHAM
St Mary
4m/6km E. of Stowmarket TM 1058
13th- and 14th-century work in the chancel and 15th-century flushwork clerestory. The fine Perpendicular tower with traceried doors probably replaces an earlier central tower. Much of interest inside, including a very fine hammer-beam roof, some 15th-century chancel-stalls – look for the bag-

piper – and a 17th-century pulpit with a selection of four hour-glasses.

EAST BERGHOLT
St Mary
7m/11km N.E. of Colchester TM 0634
Picturesque late-Perpendicular brick and flint church with incomplete tower. Unique single-storey timber bell-house with steep roof in churchyard; it contains five bells which are rung by hand full-circle.

EASTON
All Saints
2m/3km N.W. of Wickham Market TM 2858
The mostly 18th–19th-century interior has box pews and an odd pair of family pews replete with Ionic colonettes and cherubs' wings, *c.* 1690. Some 14th-century glass and a brass of 1426.

EDWARDSTONE
St Mary
4m/6km E. of Sudbury TL 9442
13th-century tower; Decorated nave and chancel; 17th-century pulpit and tester; brass to a Mr and Mrs Brand, *c.* 1620, with odd inscription. Well restored by Bodley, 1874.

ELMSETT
St Peter
3m/4km N.E. of Hadleigh TM 0546
A humble and intriguing church with 13th-century tower, Decorated nave and chancel. Three-sided 17th-century communion rails.

ELMSWELL
St John the Divine
5m/8km N.W. of Stowmarket TL 9863
Commanding setting. Fine flint and stone tower. Monument said to be by Maximilian Colt for Sir Robert Gardener, Lord Chief Justice, 1619; 19th-century work by Hakewill, Withers, and J. D. Wyatt.

ELVEDEN
St Mary & St Patrick
4m/6km S.W. of Thetford TL 8279
At edge of park in estate village. The small Norman and 14th-century church, with tower of *c.* 1421 restored by Maharaja Duleep Singh in 1869, was given a sumptuous new nave and chancel on the N. side by W. D. Caroe, 1904–6. It contains magnificent woodwork in roofs and benches and a glorious alabaster reredos. To the S. is

Caroe's cloister and noble bell-tower of 1922. Interesting memorials; glass by Kempe, Clayton & Bell, and F. Brangwyn.

ERISWELL
St Lawrence
2m/3km N.E. of Mildenhall TL 7278
Some Early English work, but mostly Decorated with beautiful windows, font, screen, piscina, and unusual recesses on the N. side of the sanctuary. Several 15th-century bench-ends. Restored by H. D. Wyatt, 1874.

EUSTON
St Genevieve
3m/4km S.E. of Thetford TL 8979
Set amid the rolling grassland of Euston Park, this is one of the few examples in E. Anglia of a fine 17th-century church; built by Lord Arlington in 1676. Embellished with beautiful panelling and a magnificent reredos, possibly by Grinling Gibbons, and a plaster ceiling in the S. aisle.

EYE
St Peter & St Paul
4m/6km S.E. of Diss TM 1473
Magnificent tall tower, the W. face a mass of flushwork. Imposing Anglo-Catholic interior, dominated by glorious screen of *c.* 1480 with 15 painted figures. Rood loft, rood, font cover, sanctuary lamps, and E. window all by Comper.

EYKE
All Saints
3m/4km N.E. of Woodbridge TM 3151
Base of 12th-century central tower with fine Norman arches; the church key has letters cut spelling the name of the village: 'I K E'.

FELIXSTOWE
TM 3034
St John the Baptist, Orwell Road
Seaside High Church in red brick by A. W. Blomfield, 1895–9, with distinctive lofty tower and spire by Charles Blomfield, 1914. Devotional interior with pulpit and screen by Gerald Cogswell; mosaic and alabaster reredos and much good glass almost entirley by J. Powell and Sons.
St Andrew, St Andrew's Road
Suffolk Perpendicular developed to its natural conclusion in reinforced ferroconcrete by Hilda Mason and Raymond Erith in 1929–31. Light and spacious Conservative Evangelical interior has wooden

font surround and twin pulpits. Fine 16th-century-style communion table. Erected in thanksgiving for the rejection of the 1928 Prayer Book!

FRAMLINGHAM
St Michael
9m/15km N. of Woodbridge TM 2863
Dignified and rambling town church with sturdy Perpendicular W. tower. Fine clerestory completed 1520; chancel and E. chapels not finished until *c.* 1553. Spacious interior with handsome nave roof, the hammer-beams concealed by vaulted coving; good 15th-century font and cover, noteworthy organ of 1674 by Thamar of Peterborough, and Classical altarpiece of *c.* 1710. Splendid monuments to the Howards, Dukes of Norfolk, including the outstanding tomb of Thomas, 3rd Duke, *c.* 1554; also the tomb of Sir Robert Hitcham, d. 1636.

FRAMSDEN
St Mary
3m/4km S.E. of Debenham TM 2059
Attractive exterior has good Perpendicular tower with flushwork decoration and S. porch; 15th-century double hammer-beam roof, altar table of 1628, and Decorated stalls with misericords.

FRESSINGFIELD
St Peter & St Paul
4m/6km S. of Harleston TM 2677
Well-situated church with handsome porch, *c.* 1420, and ornate Sanctus bell-turret. Grand 15th-century roofs and a complete set of benches, *c.* 1470, with 36 carved ends. Portrait of Archbishop Sancroft, d. 1693, a native of this place.

GAZELEY
All Saints
5m/8km E. of Newmarket TL 7264
15th-century nave and aisles; early 14th-century chancel with unusual E. window and 16th-century wagon roof. Some medieval benches, an early 16th-century pulpit and glass in the clerestory windows.

GIPPING
St Nicholas
3m/4km N.E. of Stowmarket TM 0763
Exquisite 15th-century chapel of the Tyrell family, and still extra-parochial. Idyllic setting; lovely Perpendicular windows and flushwork motifs. Bright interior with 15th- and 18th-century benches. E. window filled with glass of *c.* 1494–1513; 18th-century pulpit, rails, altar, and altar cloth.

GISLINGHAM
St Mary
6m/10km S.W. of Diss TM 0771
Large church of simple plan with superb double hammer-beam nave roof. Sturdy brick tower of 1639 and embattled 15th-century porch. Excellent interior has 15th-century font with 17th-century cover; 18th-century W. gallery, medieval benches, and 18th-century box pews around a three-decker pulpit in its original position. 15th-century glass includes early pictures of wild flowers. Graffiti of interest.

GREAT ASHFIELD
All Saints
4m/6km S.E. of Ixworth TL 9967
Early Tudor S. porch has 13th-century doorway and door; 15th-century bench-ends; 17th-century pulpit and other furnishings. Hatchments of Chancellor Thurlow's family. Headstones.

GREAT BARTON
Holy Innocents
3m/4km N.E. of Bury St Edmunds TL 8967
Stately Perpendicular W. tower with flushwork decoration. Spacious 13th-century chancel; 15th-century hammer-beam nave roof.

GREAT BEALINGS
St Mary
3m/4km W. of Woodbridge TM 2348
S. door carved *c.* 1505; 15th-century benches restored 1845–50 by H. Ringham, who also made the outstanding chancel-stalls; 17th-century pulpit.

GREAT BRADLEY
St Mary
5m/8km N. of Haverhill TL 6653
Norman doorway with tympanum; 17th-century altar table; 18th-century pulpit and tester; Tudor brick S. porch with stepped gable.

GREAT BRICETT
St Mary & St Lawrence
5m/8km N. of Hadleigh TM 0350
Towerless and remarkably long church of Augustinian canons, founded 1110. Late

12th-century font with interlaced arcading; 14th-century glass, king-post roof.

GREAT FINBOROUGH
St Andrew
3m/4km W. of Stowmarket TM 0157
R. N. Phipson's stately and graceful rebuild of 1874–7 in the Decorated style with distinctive tower, octagonal belfry stage, and spire, visible for miles. A very successful Gothic Revival church with a dignified interior; memorials from the old church and several Clayton & Bell windows.

GREAT LIVERMERE
St Peter
5m/8km N.E. of Bury St Edmunds TL 8871
Tower has distinctive timber belfry stage. Good Decorated windows in the chancel. Inside are a 15th-century screen, elegant 18th-century three-sided altar rails, and a three-decker pulpit of *c.* 1700.

GREAT SAXHAM
St Andrew
4m/6km W. of Bury St Edmunds TL 7862
Norman church much rebuilt. Fine portrait bust of 1632 and brass showing Eldred in robes of Alderman of London; inscription about his travels in the Levant as a spice merchant; 15th–16th-century English and German glass.

GREAT WALDINGFIELD
St Lawrence
3m/4km N.E. of Sudbury TL 9143
Noble exterior with fine tower. Chancel by Butterfield, 1867. Contains good 17th-century woodwork from St Michael's Cornhill, London.

GRUNDISBURGH
St Mary
3m/4km W. of Woodbridge TM 2250
Red-brick tower, 1732. Double hammerbeam roof; Perpendicular font, screen and wall-paintings; S. chapel has inscription of 1501. Well restored by E. C. Hakewill.

HADLEIGH
St Mary
8m/12km W. of Ipswich TM 0242
The 15th-century Guildhall, Tudor brick Deanery Tower, and massive flint church make a picturesque group. Tall lead-covered spire of *c.* 1300 with 13th-century clock-bell. Big-boned church with wide, spacious interior. Good chancel roof, 14th-century font with tall cover of 1925 by Charles Spooner, 15th-century chapel screens, bench-end with wolf guarding St Edmund's head, and organ case partly by 'Father' Smith, 1687. Palimpsest brass to Rowland Taylor, martyred 1555; also some good furnishings and glass of the 19th century.

HAWKEDON
St Mary
6m/10km N.W. of Long Melford TL 7953
Middle of wide village green. W. gallery, 15th-century bench-ends and screenwork; 17th-century altar table, pulpit, chair, and communion rails.

HAWSTEAD
All Saints
3m/4km S. of Bury St Edmunds TL 8559
Norman doorways; 16th-century tower and broad nave roof. Rich collection of monuments and tablets, notably late 13th-century military effigy, alabaster figure by G. Christmas, 1610, and a marble monument by Nicholas Stone, 1615.

HELMINGHAM
St Mary
4m/6km S. of Debenham TM 1857
Setting at edge of park. Fine tower begun in 1487; 16th-century nave roof to a church filled with monuments, one by Nollekens. Restored with scriptural texts at the instigation of Rev. J. C. Ryle, *c.* 1845.

HENGRAVE
St John Lateran
3m/4km N.W. of Bury St Edmunds TL 8268
Picturesque setting near Hall. Saxon round tower and pretty 14th- and 15th-century church, well restored in 1900 by H. J. Green. Chancel and chapel crammed with 16th- and 17th-century monuments to the Kytsons. Some glass by F. C. Eden. This is the church of the ecumenical centre run by the Roman Catholic Sisters of the Assumption, and is now called the Church of the Reconciliation.

HERRINGFLEET
St Margaret
6m/10km N.W. of Lowestoft TM 4797
Norman and Early English work. Late 18th-century furnishings and interesting glass in the E. window. Early 11th-century circular tower.

HESSETT
St Ethelbert
5m/8km E. of Bury St Edmunds TL 9361
Noble exterior graced by fine 15th-century stonework. Chancel 14th-century. Much of beauty inside, including 15th-century roofs, font, benches, stalls and fine screen, and two-storeyed medieval sacristy. The wall-paintings include St Christopher, the Seven Deadly Sins, and Christ of the Trades. There is much 15th-century glass.

HIGHAM-BY-BURY
St Mary
7m/11km W. of Bury St Edmunds TL 7465
By Sir Giles Gilbert Scott, 1861. Good village church in the Geometrical style with a local round tower containing rib-vaulted baptistry.

HITCHAM
All Saints
6m/10km N.W. of Hadleigh TL 9851
Sturdy tower and dignified exterior; 15th-century double hammer-beam nave roof, 17th-century roofs in chancel and aisles. Screen panels show angels with Instruments of the Passion.

HOO
St Andrew and St Eustachius
4m/6km N.W. of Wickham Market TM 2558
Humble, rustic, isolated and endearing church, mostly of *c.* 1300–30, with early 16th-century Tudor brick tower. Atmospheric and homely interior with brick floors, plaster ceiling, pulpit, altar table and rails, all of the 18th century. Fine 15th-century font.

HOPTON
All Saints
5m/8km S. of Gt Yarmouth TG 5200
Tower has 18th-century belfry stage. Clerestory of Tudor brick and beautiful hammerbeam roof with carved human figures, original colour, and canopy of honour.

ICKLINGHAM
All Saints
7m/11km N.W. of Bury St Edmunds TL 7772
Thatched and largely unspoilt church with Norman work in the nave and Decorated windows, font and niches in the S. aisle; 15th-century benches and screen base, 17th-century pulpit, rails and box pew; 14th-century glass, and a most remarkable array of encaustic tiles.
R.C.F.

IKEN
St Botolph
4m/6km N. of Orford TM 4155
Incomparable setting beside the Alde estuary, and probably the site of St Botolph's monastery. Norman nave, roofless after a fire in 1968, Perpendicular W. tower, and ragstone chancel of 1853 by S. Whichcord, containing Saxon cross shaft found embedded in the wall.

IPSWICH
TM 1644
St Augustine, Felixstowe Road
By H. Munro Cautley, the great authority on Suffolk churches, 1927. In Perpendicular style, a conventional cruciform building with crossing tower and narrow aisles.
St Bartholomew, Newton Road
Lofty towerless Anglo-Catholic shrine by Charles Spooner, consecrated 1895. Grand interior with large circular E. window containing flowing tracery. Lavishly furnished on a large scale. Blessed Sacrament Chapel, 1925, by H. M. Cauntley.
St Margaret, St Margaret's Green
Excellent setting. Stately exterior with early 14th-century windows in the aisle; lavish Perpendicular clerestory and fine porch. Superb double hammer-beam roof with 17th-century painted panels.
St Mary at the Elms, Elm Street
Beautiful Tudor brick tower. Humble church with Norman doorway and possibly door also. Chancel, 1883, by E. F. Bishop. Devotional Anglo-Catholic interior. Acton monument and several good wall-plaques.
St Mary le Tower, Tower Street
Stately Gothic Revival rebuilding of 1850–70, by R. M. Phipson. Fine tower and spire of the former church, and parts of the arcades also remain. Good 15th-century font, handsome pulpit of *c.* 1700, memorials and brasses. Good 19th-century woodwork and stained glass. Reredos, 1895, by Somers Clarke. Dignified civic atmosphere.
St Mary Quay, Foundation Street
Dockland setting. Perpendicular church begun *c.* 1448. Good W. tower with flushwork and pretty 18th-century lantern; fine hammer-beam nave roof.
R.C.F.
St Peter, St Peter Street

Dockland church associated with Cardinal Wolsey. Prominent 15th-century tower, the rest basically 14th-century, restored by G. G. Scott Jnr, 1878, with good arcades and a single-framed and braced roof. Its greatest treasure is the massive square font bowl, *c.* 1150, of black Tournai marble.

IXWORTH THORPE
All Saints
2m/3km N.W. of Ixworth TL 9173
Thatched church with wooden belfry and Tudor brick porch; 15th-century benches; 17th-century altar table, communion rails, and pulpit.

KEDINGTON
St Peter & St Paul
2m/3km E. of Haverhill TL 7046
Dignified exterior with good Decorated chancel. Memorable for atmospheric interior and furnishings, untouched by Victorian alteration; 16th-century hammer-beam roof, medieval benches, and 17th–19th-century box pews with children's seats in tiers either side of the *c.* 1750 singers' gallery. Fine three-decker pulpit opposite commodious canopied manorial pew of 1610, incorporating medieval screenwork. Present screen, 1619. Three-sided altar rails of 1707 and other 18th-century sanctuary fittings. Superb array of 16th–18th-century Barnardiston monuments and hatchments; the 'Westminster Abbey of Suffolk'.

KERSEY
St Mary
2m/3km N.W. of Hadleigh TM 0044
Setting above the village. Fine tower, porches, and 14th-century N. aisle. Inside is a pretty seven-bay arcade and fine sedilia and piscina in N. chapel. There are six painted screen panels and an ancient lectern.

KESGRAVE
All Saints
4m/6km E. of Ipswich TM 2145
Simple wayside church, with large 14th-century porch, 13th-century chancel with lancet windows, and tower mostly of 16th-century Tudor brick. In 1980 the nave was imaginatively and tastefully extended southward to the designs of Derek Woodley, making the interior spacious, comfortable and versatile. New work uses hand-made bricks and light-coloured pine. Older work includes 15th-century single hammer-beam roof and Royal Arms of King George III.

KESSINGLAND
St Edmund
4m/6km S.W. of Lowestoft TM 5286
Built *c.* 1450 for London Franciscans. Noble W. beacon tower has flushwork panelling and handsome carved doorway. Nave rebuilt 1694–5 in red brick with blue chequering.

KETTLEBASTON
St Mary
3m/4km E. of Lavenham TL 9650
Tiny village set high, with endearing and atmospheric church. Norman nave and square font, beautiful 14th-century windows, sedilia and piscina in a colourful Anglo-Catholic interior. Reproductions of the 14th-century Kettlebaston Alabasters, now in the British Museum. Screen of *c.* 1895 and reredos by the Rev. Ernest Geldart.

KIRKLEY
St Peter
1m/2km S. of Lowestoft TM 5491
Grand flint church by J. L. Clemence, begun in 1874; part of the tower is medieval. Apsidal baptistry by T. Porter, added in 1893. Impressive interior noted for its splendid wrought-iron screenwork, font cover and clock – all by Hart and Peard. Painted reredos by Canon G. Roe, installed 1927.

LAKENHEATH
St Mary
5m/8km S.W. of Brandon TL 7182
Interesting church of several periods, with fine Norman chancel arch. Early 15th-century cambered tie-beam roof, related to that at Mildenhall, but lower and thus more easily damaged by the Puritans. Elaborate 13th-century font, and a complete set of carved benches with poppyheads.

LAVENHAM
St Peter & St Paul
6m/10km N.E. of Sudbury TL 9149
One of England's best-known parish churches – its massive 141-foot tower dominates the countryside and the unforgettable 'wool' village beneath it. The chancel is Decorated, *c.* 1340; the aisles, E. chapels, tall clerestory, tower and porch are masterpieces of the 15th-century stonemason's craft. Lavish and stately with stone panelling above, 14th-century rood screen, 15th-century parclose screens to the E. chapels,

and the superb Renaissance Spring parclose of *c.* 1525. Misericord stalls. Wall-monument to Rev. H. Copinger, 1622, and tiny chrism brass, 1631.

LAXFIELD
All Saints
6m/10km N. of Framlingham TM 2972
One of Suffolk's finest towers, and a massive nave with open timber roof. Superb seven-sacrament font, 15th-century benches, box pews, 17th-century pulpit and reading desk, and poor-box of 1664. Chancel of 1827 rather an anti-climax. The Puritan image-breaker, William Dowsing, is thought to have come from Laxfield.

LEISTON
St Margaret
4m/6km E. of Saxmundham TM 4462
Medieval tower and 13th-century font. Otherwise the church is a very distinctive rebuild of 1853 by E. B. Lamb. Remarkable cruciform plan creating a vast auditorium, crowned by a spectacular roof. E. window by C. E. Kempe and N. transept windows by M. E. A. Rope.

LINDSEY
St Peter
4m/6km N.W. of Hadleigh TL 9745
Atmospheric church with timber belfry and 14th-century timber porch. It contains a king-post roof, 13th-century font, 17th-century three-sided altar rails, a restored pulpit, and some box pews.

LITTLE SAXHAM
St Nicholas
4m/6km W. of Bury St Edmunds TL 7862
One of the best known of the Norman round towers. Norman S. doorway with tympanum. Attractive interior has 17th-century pulpit and bier and 18th-century three-sided altar rails from Little Livermere. The Crofts Chapel contains a Baroque monument to William, Baron Crofts, 1677, by A. Storey; also the 'topless' bust of Elizabeth, Lady Crofts.

LITTLE THURLOW
St Peter
4m/6km N. of Haverhill TL 6851
17th-century altar table and three-sided communion rails. Soame Chapel contains excellent alabaster monument to Sir Stephen Soame, d. 1619.

LITTLE WENHAM
All Saints
4m/6km S.E. of Hadleigh TM 0839
Quiet and attractive setting not far from the famous 13th-century castellated Hall. Unspoilt and atmospheric church with 16th-century brick top to the tower and 17th-century timbers in the porch. Mainly late 13th-century, with plate tracery in the E. window and font. Easter Sepulchre, 13th–15th-century wall-paintings, 18th-century pulpit and rails. Monument to Sir John Brewse, 1585, and splendid brass to Thomas Brewse, 1514.
R.C.F.

LONG MELFORD
Holy Trinity
3m/4km N. of Sudbury TL 8646
A superb situation for this regal church of cathedral proportions. It is a giant amongst churches, 250 feet long, and shows Suffolk Perpendicular at its very best. The exterior is a mass of flushwork panelling and great windows, with large three-gabled E. Lady Chapel. The old brick tower cased in flint by G. F. Bodley, 1903. Vast, light, airy and spacious interior with long, unbroken 15th-century arch-braced cambered tie-beam roof. Remarkable array of 15th-century glass in the N. aisle windows. Grand reredos by Farmer and Brindley, 1877, to the S. of which is William Cordell's splendid monument, 1580. Tiny, intimate Clopton Chapel has a remarkable painted roof, fine sedilia, and canopied niches, a Lily crucifix in the 15th-century glass. Lady Chapel with ambulatory, good arcades, original roof, and evidence of its later use as a village school.

LOUND
St John the Baptist
5m/8km N.W. of Lowestoft TM 5099
Norman round tower graces a lovely church, exquisitely restored. The screen, loft and rood, and the wonderful organ case and font cover, are all the work of Sir Ninian Comper.

LOWESTOFT
TM 5493
St Margaret
Large and handsome building in a superb position slightly above and apart from the old fishing-port. The S. chancel window has glass by Robert Allen, 1819, of the Lowestoft china factory. Superb proportions here and much of beauty, including a lectern of 1504

and early 20th-century work by Sir Ninian Comper.

MENDLESHAM
St Mary
6m/10km N.E. of Stowmarket TM 1065
The church has a fine W. tower and 17th-century woodwork; the pulpit, reading desk and font cover were all made by John Turner of Mendlesham in 1603. Good 15th-century benches. The unique feature of this church is the collection of 15th- and 17th-century armour in the chamber above the S. porch, which has been used as the parish armoury since 1593.

METFIELD
St John the Baptist
4m/6km S.E. of Harleston TM 2980
Tower of 1385; otherwise Perpendicular, with two-storey S. porch. Fine boarded canopy of honour above the rood, formed by decorating the easternmost bay of the nave roof; the original painted scheme of initials for Jesus and crowned Ms survives.

MILDENHALL
St Mary
8m/12km N.E. of Newmarket TL 7174
This enormous church has high-quality work of many periods from the 13th century onward. The great W. tower stands as a landmark across the Fens. The nave roof is a splendid example of cambered tie-beam construction, interspersed with arch-braced hammer-beams. In the aisles are hammer-beam roofs; the wealth of carving on that of the N. aisle in particular is unsurpassed.

MONK SOHAM
St Peter
3m/4km N.E. of Debenham TM 2165
Isolated setting. W. tower of c. 1300 with lancets and a fine 14th-century chancel. Hammer-beam roof, seven-sacrament font, 17th-century altar table, and a pulpit of 1604.

MONKS ELEIGH
St Peter
5m/8km N.W. of Hadleigh TL 9647
Noble Perpendicular W. tower. Ancient nave roof and some items of 17th-century woodwork; medieval pulpit and good set of Royal Arms above the chancel arch.

MUTFORD
St Andrew
4m/6km E. of Beccles TM 4888
11th-century round tower has 15th-century octagonal belfry; remains of 14th-century W. galilee porch. Fragments of wall-paintings and a figure of St Christopher over-painted with 17th-century Lord's Prayer and Creed; 15th-century font. This most interesting church was much neglected and then poorly restored in the 19th century.

NAYLAND
St James
6m/10km N. of Colchester TL 9734
Splendid vaulted S.W. porch of 1525, rebuilt in 1884; 16th-century screen panels; Constable's *Christ Breaking Bread* as altarpiece.

NEDGING
St Mary
4m/6km N.W. of Hadleigh TL 9948
Notable for two late 12th-century Transitional doorways with round arches, shafts, and thick crockets. Benches with poppy-heads; 14th-century king-post roof to nave.

NEEDHAM MARKET
St John the Baptist
3m/4km S.E. of Stowmarket TM 0855
Chapel of ease to Barking and not a parish church until 1901, hence no churchyard. Towerless exterior of late 15th century, with good Perpendicular windows. Unique hammer-beam angel roof of remarkable construction and exquisite beauty, carefully and sensitively restored. Unsuitable S. porch with spirelet by H. W. Hayward, 1883.

NEWMARKET
St Agnes
13m/21km E. of Cambridge TL 6463
Small but beautiful red-brick Gothic Revival church by R. H. Carpenter, 1886. Distinctive octagonal turret and spirelet. Magnificent interior, with elaborate use of tiles and mosaic, culminating in Boehm's superb marble reredos showing the Assumption of St Agnes. Much glass by Clayton & Bell.

NORTH COVE
St Botolph
3m/4km E. of Beccles TM 4689
Humble thatched church with Norman, Early English and Decorated work; 14th-century wall-paintings of the Life of Christ

in the chancel and 17th-century texts in nave.

NORTON
St Andrew
3m/4km S.E. of Ixworth TL 9565
Isolated setting. Richly carved Perpendicular font; 15th-century bench-ends and nine fine misericords. Some old glass.

ORFORD
St Bartholomew
9m/15km E. of Woodbridge TM 4249
Remains of fine Norman arcades in ruined chancel, 1170. Grand Decorated nave and aisles with reticulated windows and lofty arcades. Upper parts of tower rebuilt, 1962–71. Interior has 15th-century font, 18th-century woodwork, and 11 brasses. Good restoration by Micklethwaite, 1897–1900. Screen and stalls by S. Tugwell, 1921.

PAKEFIELD
All Saints and St Margaret
S. district of Lowestoft TM 5390
Cliff-top setting. Extraordinary double-naved plan to accommodate two separate parochial churches in one building. Well restored by Cecil Upcher after war damage.

PALGRAVE
St Peter
1m/2km S. of Diss TM 1178
Decorated W. tower; two-storey S. porch with good flushwork; 15th-century hammer-beam roof retains much original colouring. Late Norman font.

PARHAM
St Mary
2m/3km S.E. of Framlingham TM 3060
14th- and 15th-century with flushwork porch; 15th-century screen and 17th-century woodwork; hat bracket of 1716.

POLSTEAD
St Mary
4m/6km S.W. of Hadleigh TL 9938
Serene parkland setting. Suffolk's only medieval stone spire. Remarkable Norman arcades and clerestory windows incorporating 12th-century brickwork. Handsome king-post roof and some good 17th-century woodwork in this atmospheric interior; brasses.

PRESTON
St Mary
2m/3km N.E. of Lavenham TL 9450
Late 16th-century triptych; closed, it displays a series of texts and the Decalogue; when open, it reveals a most remarkable and elaborate painting of the Royal Arms of Elizabeth I. Fine flushwork porch; square Norman font.

RAMSHOLT
All Saints
5m/8km S.E. of Woodbridge TM 3042
Commanding, isolated setting overlooking River Deben. A church of great charm with Saxon round tower, made to appear oval by later buttresses, and furnished with box pews and two-decker pulpit of *c.* 1857.

RATTLESDEN
St Nicholas
5m/8km W. of Stowmarket TL 9758
Village setting. Early 14th-century tower with shingled spire; a stately church, mostly Perpendicular, with good clerestory and superb porch of *c.* 1476; 15th-century benches and stalls, 17th-century pulpit, and two sets of rails, one from Kettlebaston. Good glass by Hardman, Clayton & Bell, and W. Aikman; excellent screens, 1909, by Fellowes Prynne.

REDGRAVE
St Mary
5m/8km W. of Diss TM 0477
Grand 14th-century chancel; 18th-century tower. Important monuments here include two by Nicholas Stone and one to Sir John Holt, d. 1710, by Thomas Green. Brass, 1609, and several hatchments.

RENDLESHAM
St Gregory
3m/4km S.E. of Wickham Market TM 3353
15th-century tower with flushwork. E. window filled with intriguing wooden Decorated tracery in 1783. Bright and atmospheric interior has 15th-century arch-braced roof, 14th-century tomb recess and effigy, 18th-century deal pews, and good 19th-century monuments.

RICKINGHALL INFERIOR
St Mary
6m/10km S.W. of Diss TM 0475
An early round tower extended, as often happened, into a pleasing 15th-century

octagonal belfry. Also a beautiful S. aisle of
c. 1300 with remarkable Geometrical tracery
and carved foliage in the S.E. window.

RICKINGHALL SUPERIOR
St Mary
6m/10km S.W. of Diss TM 0475
14th-century chancel and tower; 15th-
century nave with wall arcades and huge
Perpendicular windows. Well restored by
W. M. Fawcett.
  R.C.F.

RISBY
St Giles
4m/6km N.W. of Bury St Edmunds TL 7966
Norman round tower and chancel arch.
Good Decorated screen and poppyhead
benches; 17th-century pulpit and altar table.
Dim wall-paintings of *c.* 1200 depict the
Nativity Story and Lives of the Saints.

ROUGHAM
St Mary
4m/6km S.E. of Bury St Edmunds TL 9061
Very well-proportioned 14th–15th-century
building has early 16th-century N. aisle, the
buttresses inscribed with the names of
donors and dated 1514; 15th-century
hammer-beam roof and contemporary
seating in nave. Fine brass.

RUMBURGH
St Michael
4m/6km N.W. of Halesworth TM 3481
Former Benedictine priory church has
massive 13th-century rectangular tower with
three W. lancet windows and unusual tiled
and timbered belfry stage with hipped roof.
Inside is a lovely screen on which some of
the original colour remains; also a medieval
roof, a few old benches, and a 17th-century
pulpit.

RUSHBROOKE
St Nicholas
3m/4km S.E. of Bury St Edmunds TL 8961
14th-century tower; otherwise mostly 1540,
with excellent Tudor roof and brilliant glass
by a Bury glazier. Interior furnished in 19th
century with college chapel seating and
return stalls at W. end. Remarkable painted
Royal Arms of Henry VIII, probably 19th-
century.

SANTON DOWNHAM
St Mary
2m/3km N.E. of Brandon TL 8187
Tranquil forest setting. Norman nave, 13th-
century chancel, and 15th-century W. tower
with donors' names in the base-course.
Cared-for interior with 14th-century screen,
17th-century pulpit, font cover and chest;
four windows by C. E. Kempe.

SAXTEAD
All Saints
2m/3km N.W. of Framlingham TM 2665
Small towerless church with good Decorated
chancel. Hammer-beam roof, benches,
17th-century altar table and communion
rails. Parish stocks and whipping-post in S.
porch.

SHELLAND
King Charles the Martyr
3m/4km W. of Stowmarket TM 0059
Charming outside and in. Much rebuilt in
1767, the interior a period piece with box
pews, three-decker pulpit, and altar rails.
There is a 14th-century font and, in the W.
gallery, a barrel organ of *c.* 1820.

SHOTLEY
St Mary
7m/11km S.E. of Ipswich TM 2336
14th-century nave and aisles. Fine Perpendicular clerestory and roof; chancel rebuilt
and furnished in 1745; good panelling, plasterwork, tiled floor, and reredos.

SNAPE
St John the Baptist
3m/4km S. of Saxmundham TM 3959
Perpendicular nave and chancel, the tall W.
tower with brick and stone decoration on
the battlements. Fine details and splendid
font given by Richard Mey, *c.* 1523.

SOUTH COVE
St Lawrence
3m/4km N. of Southwold TM 4980
W. tower with flushwork decoration; N. and
S. Norman nave doorways; door to rood loft
stair has 15th-century painting of
St Michael.

SOUTHWOLD
St Edmund
8m/12km E. of Halesworth TM 5076
Glorious Perpendicular church, built in one
piece *c.* 1450–1500. Lofty W. tower richly

panelled in flint; superb two-storey vaulted S. porch with traceried doors through which we enter the colourful interior. Fine hammer-beam roof, sumptuous painted screen stretching the full width of the church, 15th-century Jack o'Clock, Perpendicular pulpit, misericords, and sedilia. Later work includes 1930s font cover, reredos by F. E. Howard, and Comper glass in the E. window. Church well restored by Phipson in the 19th century.

STANNINGFIELD
St Nicholas
5m/8km S. of Bury St Edmunds TL 8756
Interesting chancel of *c.* 1300. Norman N. doorway. Important 15th-century Doom painting over the chancel arch; hatchments.

STOKE-BY-CLARE
St John the Baptist
5m/8km E. of Haverhill TL 7443
Embattled 15th-century church with 14th-century tower, containing traceried benches, a small but beautiful 15th-century pulpit, some old glass, and a 16th-century wall-painting of the Last Judgement in the N. aisle.

STOKE-BY-NAYLAND
St Mary
5m/8km S.W. of Hadleigh TL 9836
Grand and stately embattled church; mostly 1421–81, with some Decorated work in S. porch and N. chapel. Large and splendidly ornate W. tower, visible for miles. Tudor brick N. porch. Well-proportioned interior with impressive tower arch. Traceried S. doors amongst the finest in the county. Some 14th-century misericords, a fine font, and 15th-century nave roof and chapel screens. Good monuments include Sir Francis Mannock, 1634, and Lady Anne Windsor, 1615; amongst the brasses is the fine six-foot effigy of Sir William de Tendring, 1408.

STONHAM ASPAL
St Mary and St Lambert
4m/6km S.W. of Debenham TM 1359
Large village church with 1742 wooden top stage to its S. porch tower, added to accommodate 10 bells. Some pleasing 14th- and 15th-century windows and a magnificent ashlar clerestory. Good aisle and chancel roofs, 15th-century bench-ends, pulpit of 1616, its sounding board now a table, and some fascinating medieval glass. Judicious

restoration, 1871–3, by E. C. Hakewill, when Laver, Barraud and Westlake's fine E. window, with over 60 figures, was inserted.

STOWLANGTOFT
St George
2m/3km S.E. of Ixworth TL 9568
Simple in plan but lofty and impressive in stature, all built *c.* 1370–1400. Exterior has tall windows, fine gargoyles, an elegant tower, and flushwork porch. Superbly proportioned interior with original roofs, canopy of honour to rood, beautiful font, screen base, St Christopher wall-painting, and a set of grand 15th-century benches. The chancel-stalls are complete and are probably the finest in E. Anglia. Restored in 1855 by William White. Some 19th-century glass painted by the daughter of Samuel Rickards, rector 1832–64, friend of J. H. Newman. Good 17th-century monuments.

STOWMARKET
St Peter & St Paul
11m/18km N.W. of Ipswich TM 0458
Large town church with truncated spire. Externally all Decorated. Brasses include Ann Tyrell, aged eight, in her shroud, with long verse inscription. Iron wig-stand, 1675. Restored by Phipson, 1864–5.

STRADBROKE
All Saints
7m/11km N.W. of Framlingham TM 2373
Imposing 15th-century tower; noble, big-boned church, very thoroughly restored by R. M. Phipson in the 1870s at the instigation of the Evangelical rector, Canon J. C. Ryle. A superb 15th-century Easter Sepulchre recess in the chancel and interesting E. window glass by Clayton & Bell.

SUDBOURNE
All Saints
2m/3km N. of Orford TM 4153
Rural setting, Herts. 'spike', Norman doorway, and 12th-century font; 18th-century pulpit and manor pew. Elizabethan Stanhope monument. Heavily restored by F. Barnes, 1878.

SUDBURY
TL 8741
All Saints, Friars Street
The church is chiefly notable for its 15th-century pulpit, parclose screens in the chancel, and an unusual 17th-century

Above: Medieval effigies at Alnwick, Northumberland

Right: Bellingham, Northumberland; stone barrel vaulting, early 17th century

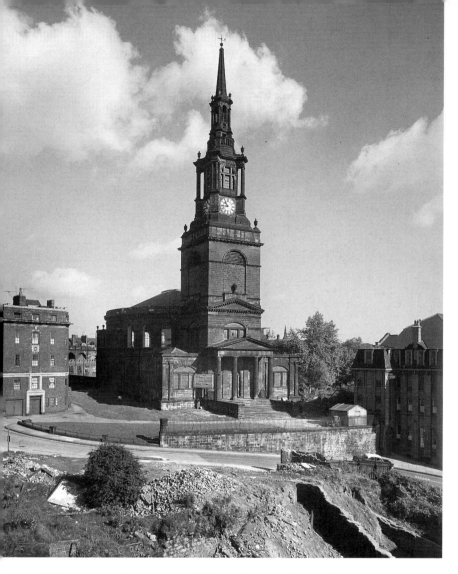

18th-century auditory church, All Saints, Newcastle, Northumberland

Opposite above: Dominating canopied rood screen in the interior, Egmanton, Nottinghamshire

Below: Splendid parochial rood screen running right across the 15th-century nave and aisles, Dunster, Somerset

Above: 15th-century pulpit, Trull, Somerset

Right: Late 15th-century bench end, South Brent, Somerset

Left: Handsome central tower crossing, Ilminster, Somerset; mainly 15th century

Below: Perpendicular, with splendid tie-beam roof, 15th-century bench ends and 16th-century heraldic glass, Weston Zoyland, Somerset

Above: Hopwas, Staffordshire, by John Douglass, 1879

Above right: Unique 14th-century wooden north porch, Boxford, Suffolk

Southwold, Suffolk; one of the most splendid 15th-century churches in East Anglia

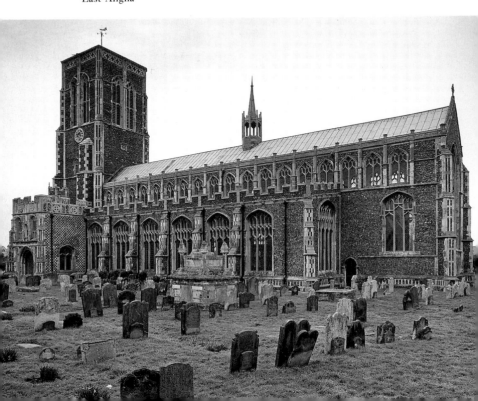

Famous Saxon tower with 'Rhenish helm' spire, Sompting, Sussex

Above left: A rare Restoration church, Compton Wynyates, Warwickshire

Above: A classic 'mausoleum' by Bonomi, 1790, Great Packington, Warwickshire

Below: Medieval Beauchamp Chapel, Warwick

painting representing the pedigree of the Eden and Waldegrave families.

St Gregory, The Green

Magnificent font cover and 15th-century roof with canopy of honour for the rood. The 14th-century chancel was built by Simon de Sudbury, Archbishop of Canterbury, murdered at the time of the Peasants' Revolt in 1381. His skull is enclosed in a glass case. Chancel-stalls with misericords.

St Peter, market place

Imposing setting above the market-place; stately exterior with traceried doors. Fine parclose screens in the chancel, where there are also interesting paintings of Moses and Aaron, part of a Classical reredos of *c.* 1730 by a local pupil of Kneller. Good roofs, restored by Wm. Butterfield, 1854–8. Handsome reredos by G. F. Bodley, 1898. Much Hardman glass.

R.C.F.

SWILLAND
St Mary

5m/8km N. of Ipswich TM 1852

Small church of great character with large Norman S. doorway. Tudor brick tower given eccentric brick and timber-framed top stage, with dormer windows and spirelet, by J. S. Corder in 1897. Good Tractarian interior has grand 19th-century reredos and furnishings; 15th-century hammer-beam roof; 17th-century pulpit and noteworthy Royal Arms of Queen Anne.

TANNINGTON
St Ethelbert

4m/6km N.W. of Framlingham TM 2467

Sturdy W. tower and flushwork S. porch. Inside are good bench-ends, part of a series depicting the Sacraments. Canted wagon nave roof with canopy of honour. Atmospheric interior.

THORNHAM PARVA
St Mary

3m/4km S.W. of Eye TM 1071

Tiny thatched gem in a meadow – even the truncated tower is thatched – showing work of most periods from Saxon onward. Fine interior with wall-paintings, 15th-century screen, and above all the celebrated retable of *c.* 1300 with its exquisite painted figures. Engraved glass by Lawrence Whistler; Sir Basil Spence is buried in the churchyard.

TROSTON
St Mary

3m/4km N.W. of Ixworth TL 8972

Nicely proportioned exterior with Early English chancel, nave with good Decorated windows, *c.* 1320–30, tower of *c.* 1300, and splendid 15th-century porch. Interior has scissor-braced nave roof, 15th-century screen and benches, wall-paintings, glass, and 17th-century pulpit and rails.

TUDDENHAM
St Martin

3m/4km N.E. of Ipswich TM 1948

Norman doorway. Hammer-beam roof, 15th-century benches and pulpit, unusual font. Screen, 1946, by H. M. Cautley.

UFFORD
St Mary

3m/4km N.E. of Woodbridge TM 2952

Noble tower; 11th-century herringbone masonry in the N. nave wall, and fine 15th-century work in S. porch; excellent roofs and intriguing benches. The greatest treasure is the colossal carved and crocketed 15th-century font cover, 'the most beautiful in the world'. Chapel reredos and window by J. N. Comper. Brasses.

WALBERSWICK
St Andrew

1m/2km S.W. of Southwold TM 4974

Ruin of once magnificent church of which the fine 1426 W. tower and the S. aisle remain in use; 15th-century doors, pulpit, and some benches.

WALSHAM-LE-WILLOWS
St Mary

5m/8km E. of Ixworth TM 0071

Spacious 15th-century church with Suffolk-type tie-beam and hammer-beam roof has considerable quantity of 15th-century glass in E. window. A maiden's garland hangs in the nave, 'For Mary Boyce 1685'. Good 14th-century font and unusual terracotta reredos by G. Tinworth, 1883.

WASHBROOK
St Mary

4m/6km S.W. of Ipswich TM 1142

Isolated church with Norman nave and good 14th-century roof. Delightful Decorated chancel with Easter Sepulchre and niches with crocketed ogee gables.

WENHASTON
St Peter
3m/4km S.E. of Halesworth TM 4275
15th-century font and nave roof. Spirited
Doom painting of *c.* 1520, originally above
the chancel arch, but now relocated to the
N. nave wall; 17th-century altar table and
pulpit.

WESTHALL
St Andrew
3m/4km N.E. of Halesworth TM 4280
There is so much to see and admire in this
remote and wonderful church. The original
and superb Norman W. portal is seen from
the base of the tower, *c.* 1300. Fine Decorated windows in the chancel. Seven-
sacrament font with original colour, 14th-
and 15th-century arch-braced roofs, and the
base of the screen with 16 painted panels.

WESTHORPE
St Margaret
7m/11km N. of Stowmarket TM 0469
A fascinating and unspoilt church of great
interest, with 14th-century chancel, early
15th-century tower and aisles, and 17th-
century Barrow Chapel. Of the 14th century
is the exquisite parclose screen, the sanctuary piscina, and the fine tracery in the S.
aisle. The 15th century provided the tie-
beam and hammer-beam nave roof, the tiny
pulpit and bench-ends. Good monument of
1613 to William Barrow, and a vast marble
edifice to Maurice Barrow, 1666; lovely
tribute in brass to a 17th-century priest.

WETHERDEN
St Mary
4m/6km N.W. of Stowmarket TM 0062
Decorated W. tower and chancel, the rest
Perpendicular with double hammer-beam
roof, wall posts and carved canopied figures
as pendants.

WICKHAMBROOK
All Saints
6m/10km N. of Clare TL 7554
Some 13th-century work and good 14th-
century chancel; 17th-century hammer-
beam roof. Monument to Thomas Higham,
1630; 17th-century altar table and communion rails.

WILBY
St Mary
1m/2km S.E. of Stradbroke TM 2472
Immense W. tower with a lofty parapet. In
the nave is a series of 15th-century benches
with carvings representing the Sacraments,
the Seven Works of Mercy, and the Seven
Deadly Sins; 17th-century pulpit and tester.

WINGFIELD
St Andrew
2m/3km N. of Stradbroke TM 2276
Large, light and airy church of the de la
Poles, noted mainly for their superb monuments. Good Decorated and Perpendicular
work; the piers and arches of the S. arcade
richly decorated with shields. Beautiful parclose screens and misericord stalls of this
formerly collegiate church. Important monuments: Sir John Wingfield, 1361, wooden
effigy of Michael de la Pole, d. 1415 at the
Siege of Harfleur, and John de la Pole, Duke
of Suffolk, d. 1491.

WISSETT
St Andrew
2m/3km N.W. of Halesworth TM 3679
11th-century round tower and later Norman
doorways with zig-zag and billet moulding.
Good tie-beam and arch-braced nave roof,
some glass, and bench-ends.

WISSINGTON
St Mary
1m/2km W. of Nayland TL 9533
Small Norman church attractively grouped
with farm buildings. Two Norman doorways
and chancel arch. Remarkable 1853 restoration rebuilt the apse and filled the church
with 'Norman' furnishings, but older work
includes the tie-beam and king-post roof,
15th-century font, and 13th-century wall-
paintings which cover the nave. Barrel organ
in W. gallery.

WITHERSDALE
St Mary Magdalene
2m/3km S.E. of Harleston TM 2781
Tiny, rustic Norman church with lovely
17th-century interior, complete with pews,
pulpit with tester, altar table, and rails; a
perfect example of an unspoilt village church
of the period.

WITHERSFIELD
St Mary
2m/3km N.W. of Haverhill TL 6547
Embattled Perpendicular exterior and bright
interior with series of poppyheads, a screen,
and good 15th-century N. aisle roof.

WOODBRIDGE
St Mary
8m/12km E. of Ipswich TM 2749
Stately, well-proportioned Perpendicular town church of the 15th century. Superb tower with good flushwork and four types of buttress; also one of Suffolk's finest flushwork porches. Lofty interior with well-restored nave roof, excellent seven-sacrament font, painted screen panels, colourful E. window by Martin Travers, and fine Pitman monument of 1626. Well restored by R. M. Phipson.

WOOLPIT
St Mary
5m/8km N.W. of Stowmarket TL 9762
Tower and impressive 'Lincolnshire' spire by Phipson, 1854. Good Decorated windows. Superb 15th-century clerestory and truly magnificent ashlar-faced porch. Inside is one of the county's best double hammer-beam roofs, a fine set of benches, restored by Henry Ringham, 1844, a 16th-century lectern, and a 15th-century screen, altered in 1750.

WORLINGTON
All Saints
1m/2km S.W. of Mildenhall TL 6973
13th–14th-century work with sanctus bell-turret, tie-beam and hammer-beam roof, and original rood beam. Royal Arms of George III and medieval graffiti.

WORLINGWORTH
St Mary
5m/8km N.W. of Framlingham TM 2368
Good Perpendicular tower and nave with a Decorated chancel; 15th-century flint flushwork S. porch; 17th-century seating, pulpit and altar table; 15th-century font cover.

WYVERSTONE
St George
6m/10km N. of Stowmarket TM 0467
15th-century hammer-beam roof, the screen unusually carved as well as painted; 16th-century pulpit with linenfold panelling; 17th-century communion rails and two sets of Royal Arms.

YAXLEY
St Mary
2m/3km W. of Eye TM 1274
15th-century N. porch and mutilated screen with beautiful figure paintings. Superb arch-braced nave roof has castellated collars and Decorated wall-plates. Richly carved pulpit and tester, 1635; iron Sexton's Wheel for determining fast days.

Surrey

Introduction

For centuries the small area of Surrey was little regarded. It was an unattractive district to the Romans, and it has few extensive medieval remains. The 17th century found profit from its rich meadows in the Thames Valley, and there were once fields round Mitcham and Carshalton, redolent with lavender, mint, camomile, penny royal, and other herbs for supplying London herb-sellers. Battersea, now part of London, was famous for asparagus, and Chertsey for carrots. In the 18th century the heights of Richmond Hill, Cooper's Hill and St Anne's, looking over the winding Thames, were favoured for country seats by the nobility; as Denham said of Cooper's Hill, the view was:

> Though deep, yet clear; though gentle, yet not dull;
> Strong, without rage; without o'erflowing, full.

Through the middle of the county, east to west, runs a narrow, high ridge of chalk, which links the north downs of Kent with Hampshire. And the views from the Hog's Back and Box Hill have long been famous. Leith Hill, on the Greensand, is 965 feet, the highest eminence in this part of England.

But for the most part Surrey was regarded in polite circles as a barren county of heaths, firs and unprofitable soil. It was not until Victorian times that its scenery came to be much admired, except by a few romantics in advance of public taste. But when it was admired, much happened to Surrey. Rich City gentlemen built themselves houses on its heights, and less affluent citizens built themselves villas. As land was cheap and unfertile, Government departments found it desirable for barracks, orphanages and asylums. Schools, too, were built on its sandy commons among the conifers. Today, threaded by many electric railways from the metropolis, Surrey is thickly populated, and it is impossible to walk far among its pine-woods without spying a human habitation through the trunks.

The county has great natural beauty and, though one regrets its over-development, the outline of its hills, the wide views, the safe wildness, safe now from the footpads and highwaymen of two centuries ago, the ponds, the timbered cottages, and the new villas with their lovingly tended gardens, the gorse, bracken and heather, the sheepy valleys still to be found on the southern slopes of the Downs, make one wish one had known it before it was discovered. Several old towns of real beauty survive – Guildford, Dorking, Farnham and

Reigate and Bletchingley in particular. Even Croydon, which is now joined to London by houses, still retains something of the atmosphere of a country town, divorced from the metropolis.

The story of the churches of Surrey is mostly one of heavy restoration, of unpretentious fabrics or of new Victorian buildings. But there was wide variety of local stone, such as Bargate, which gives the older churches delightful texture. Most of the finest churches are 19th-century, for here lived the great Victorian church architects, Woodyer and G. E. Street, and between them they left their mark upon Surrey churches, and their imitators and pupils did not let them down.

J.B.

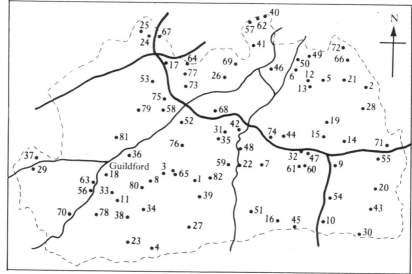

Selected List of Churches

ABINGER
St James
4m/6km S.W. of Dorking TQ 1346
12th and 13th-century; well restored by F.
Etchells after war damage and again, after
a fire, in 1964. Good modern window by
Lawrence Lee.

ADDISCOMBE
St Mary Magdalene
1m/2km E. of Croydon, now in Greater
London TQ 3466
By E. B. Lamb, in Kentish rag; his last
church. Built for a schismatic congregation
but consecrated in 1878; it is still unfinished
at the W. end. It is very striking and original
within and without. The effect of space
inside is tremendous, and is created by a
wonderful timber roof, with pyramid and
lantern at the crossing.

ALBURY
St Peter & St Paul
4m/6km E. of Guildford TQ 0447
Henry Drummond, one of the apostles of
the Catholic Apostolic Church, built a new
parish church outside the park, and hence
the old church has been disused since 1848:
the chancel became a ruin. It was of Norman
nave-tower-chancel plan: late 13th-century
S. aisle, and chancel now Perpendicular. S.
transept added in 1290 and lavishly decorated by Pugin, 1839, in red, blue and gold.
The tower, originally the Saxon chancel, was
heightened *c.* 1140, and in the 18th century
given a shingled cupola.
R.C.F.

ALFOLD
St Nicholas
4m/6km S.W. of Cranleigh TQ 0334
Attractive approach between tile-hung cottages on a tiny triangular green; 13th-
century and later; Norman font; timber
belfry supported internally on massive
timbers. Good 17th-century pulpit with
sounding board.

BEDDINGTON
2m/3km S. of Croydon, now in Greater
London TQ 2964
St Mary
Mainly a Perpendicular church of 1387 with
many good fittings: Purbeck marble font;
1611 pulpit; painted organ gallery and screen
by Morris & Co., 1869; 14th-century stalls,
brasses and Carew monuments.
*St Michael and All Angels, Milton Road, S.
Beddington*
1906, By W. D. Caroe; full of cleverness
and built on whims.

BENHILTON
All Saints
½m/1km N, of Sutton, now in Greater London
TQ 2565
By S. S. Teulon, 1864–5. Large and con-
spicuous. Good modern glass of 1965.

BETCHWORTH
St Michael
3m/4km E. of Dorking TQ 2149
Mostly 13th-century. The tower, early
Norman, originally central, but rebuilt on
the S. in 1851. Font by Eric Kennington.

BLACKHEATH
St Martin
3m/4km S.E. of Guildford TQ 0346
By C. Harrison Townsend, 1893. A pretty
village, and the church exactly suited to such
a place. It is Italianate-looking outside, with
deep eaves and very low walls. The interior
is a charming little barrel-vaulted chapel
made mysterious by a screen and hidden
lighting behind the wide and rounded arch
of the marble sanctuary. There is a sparing
and wise use of decoration entirely painted
by Mrs Lea Merritt, who is famous for her
picture *Love Locked Out.*

BLETCHINGLEY
St Mary
3m/4km E. of Redhill TQ 3250
Norman, 13th- and mainly 15th-century.
Sumptuous Clayton monument by Richard
Crutcher, 1707, in majestic Corinthian taste.

G. E. Street reredos shows Wilberforce and the Apostles.

BURSTOW
St Bartholomew
2m/3km S.E. of Horley TQ 3141
In a quiet tree-lined lane. Early Norman, 15th-century aisle, but most remarkably a handsome shingled belfry at the W. end; medieval in origin but tricked out in the 18th century. John Hamsteed, first Astronomer Royal, held the living and is buried in the chancel.

BUSBRIDGE
St John Baptist
1m/2km S.E. of Godalming SU 9742
By G. G. Scott Jnr, 1865–7. Surrey style with Bargate stone and shingles. Celebrated ironwork rood made by J. Starkie Gardner to designs by Lutyens. Stained glass by Burne-Jones, 1899. War memorial outside by Lutyens; also memorial to Gertrude Jekyll, garden designer.

CARSHALTON
All Saints
1m/2km E. of Sutton, now in Greater London TQ 2764
On a hillock with a leafy graveyard at the back. A lovely shape with its little vestry and old tower topped by an 18th-century spike. A surprisingly successful blend of all periods, with most of the building by the Blomfields, uncle and nephew, between 1893 and 1914. Wonderful Comper interior all aglow with gilded screen, rood screen, and lavish organ. Arts and Crafts altar cross by Reginald Blomfield. Good 18th-century reredos in Lady Chapel and fine communion rail. Kempe glass; many good and interesting monuments.

CARSHALTON BEECHES (Carshalton on the Hill)
Good Shepherd
1m/2km S. of Carshalton TQ 2764
By Martin Travers, 1930. Essoldo *moderne* in an Hispano-Italian Baroque style with clever stained glass. Built of a stock brick with a copper clerestory. The interior is plain and dignified.

CATERHAM
St Lawrence
6m/10km S. of Croydon TQ 3455
On the hill, a precious, largely unrestored flint church in this busy county; Norman, enlarged in 12th–13th centuries with E. end of chancel rebuilt *c.* 1790. Robust and varied roofs; king and queen posts and wagon.

CHALDON
St Peter & St Paul
2m/3km W. of Caterham TQ 3155
The church stands almost alone on the high downland. Norman, enlarged later, with W. tower and spire of 1843. Wall-painting of *c.* 1200 on W. wall, one of the most important and complete early schemes in England. This is an astounding vision of the Last Judgement, alive with imps, devils and serene angels, all against an entirely suitable background of blood-red ochre. Pulpit dated 1657.

CHARLWOOD
St Nicholas
3m/4km N.W. of Crawley, on W. side of Gatwick Airport TQ 2441
Set among picturesque tile-hung cottages, the golden sandstone church has an 11th-century nave, central tower and chancel; 15th-century screen at W. end of S. chapel embellished by Burges during his restoration of 1858; 13th-century wall-paintings and a pulpit part Tudor and part Jacobean.

CHERTSEY
St Peter
3m/4km S. of Staines TQ 0466
The church stands by the main road junction and has a medieval tower with brick matching the stone. Rebuilt 1806–8, but for tower and chancel, begun by R. Elsam, but finished by Thomas Chawner. Gothic, with window frames and mullions of artificial stone and iron columns encased in wooden piers. Vaults decorated in the 1907 restoration by T. G. Jackson with floral patterns.

COMPTON
St Nicholas
3m/4km S.W. of Guildford SU 9547
On a small knoll with a screen of trees. Tower and parts of the walls are 11th-century. The arcades, aisles, chancel and tower arches, *c.* 1170. A two-storeyed sanctuary was constructed – the only one remaining in England; the lower stage groined, the upper with a contemporary wooden balustrade; 17th-century pulpit, rails, and screen, now at W. end.

COULSDON
St John the Evangelist
5m/8km S. of Croydon, now in Greater
London TQ 3158
13th-century with good blank arcading to
chancel; 17th-century wall tablet. Enlarged
by the addition of a large S. extension by
Sebastian Comper, 1958.

CROWHURST
St George
3m/4km S. of Oxted TQ 3947
Simple 12th–13th-century church of
Wealden sandstone. Timber tower with
sharp spire. Monuments include a rare 16th-
century cast-iron ledger slab. Pleasant furnishings. Outside is a vast yew tree perhaps
1,000 years old, hollowed out in 1820 to
make a room with a padlocked door and
circular benches inside.

CROYDON
10m/16km S. of Charing Cross, now in
Greater London and a Borough TQ 3266
St John the Baptist, Church Street
Large, Perpendicular; rebuilt after fire by
Sir Giles Gilbert Scott in 1870, and with all
the feel of a Victorian town church. Alabaster
monument to Archbishop Whitgift, d. 1604,
another to Archbishop Sheldon, d. 1677, by
Jasper Latham.
St Michael and All Angels, Poplar Walk
By J. L. Pearson; designed in 1876, built
1880–3, this is one of his loveliest churches.
Outside it is of red brick and inside of light-
brown stone. The transepts are particularly
good; magnificence on a small scale. Lavish
Baroque and Gothic furnishings by Bodley,
Comper, and Hare. A Jubilee portrait of
Queen Victoria in a W. end window.
St Peter, St Peter's Road
A Commissioners' church by Sir Giles
Gilbert Scott, 1849–51, in the Middle
Pointed style. Worthy but dull in a prominent
position.

DORKING
St Martin
11m/18km E. of Guildford TQ 1649
Rebuilt in 1868–77 by Woodyer; probably
his best work. A really grand church with
tall and graceful W. tower and spire. Well-
proportioned interior with triplets of clerestory windows and good contemporary
fittings. Over the chancel arch, a mosaic by
Powell depicting the Crucifixion, *c.* 1890.

DUNSFOLD
St Mary and All Saints
4m/6km S.W. of Cranleigh TQ 0036
Approached through tunnels of clipped
yews. A notably complete late 13th-century
village church with good details, including
the late Geometric windows and the rare
surviving pews; 15th-century timber belfry.
The timber porch, renewed in the 16th
century, shelters the original door with its
ironwork still intact. Revered by William
Morris.

EGHAM
St John the Baptist
2m/3km W. of Staines TQ 0171
The church stands as a kind of bollard to
the town-centre traffic system. Rebuilt by
Henry Rhodes, 1817–20, in an unhandy
Grecian style. Inside are some worthwhile
monuments, including that to Sir John
Denham, d. 1638, depicting the deceased
rising on the Last Day, replete with shroud
and a charnel of skeletons. Splendid Royal
Arms of 1660.

ENGLEFIELD GREEN
St Jude
3m/4km W. of Staines SU 9971
1859, E. B. Lamb; by a large cemetery, with
the look of an abnormal Victorian cemetery
chapel; peculiar plan, and eccentric details;
lined with strange, colourful mixture of stone
and brick.

ESHER
St George
4m/6km S.W. of Kingston TQ 1364
A most lovable, unrestored church; basically
16th-century. The brick transept with
gallery pew for the Duke of Newcastle was
built in 1725–6 by Vanbrugh, with a front
towards the nave like a little garden temple
with Corinthian columns. Upper W. gallery
1840–2. Picture of the Apotheosis of Princess Charlotte, by A. W. Devis, and a marble
monument to her in the Greek taste by F. J.
Williamson. Reredos of 1722 and 18th-
century three-decker pulpit.
R.C.F.

EWHURST
St Peter & St Paul
2m/3km E. of Cranleigh TQ 0940
Picturesque on a hill. Cruciform, largely
13th-century, and partly rebuilt by Robert
Ebbels after fall of tower in 1837. Massive

early 12th-century S. doorway with powerful roll mouldings and cabled imposts, the best in Surrey. Inside are a Jacobean pulpit and fine late 17th-century altar rails.

FARLEIGH
St Mary
2m/3km N.E. of Warlingham TQ 3760
A simple Norman church set in a hamlet. Largely 11th-century, gently restored, with some 13th-century alterations. One of the county's lesser-known gems.

FARNHAM
St Andrew
10m/16km W. of Guildford SU 8446
The church lies near the river, a rather large, plain building. Some 12th-century work, but mainly of the 15th century, despite Ferrey's thoroughgoing restoration of 1855. The interior was cheered by David Nye in 1959; good sedilia and piscina; 17th-century altar rails. Eric Gill statue of St Andrew in the S. chapel.

FELBRIDGE
St John the Evangelist
2m/3km N.W. of E. Grinstead TQ 3639
By William White, 1865; unconventional stone and brick in the Decorated style; well-thought-out interior detail with good carving.

FETCHAM
St Mary
1m/2km W. of Leatherhead TQ 1455
The church is still screened by trees from the road at the S.E. corner of the village. Pre-Conquest walling; 12th-century S. aisle and tower with mid-18th-century top stage; 13th-century N. aisle and transept.

GATTON
St Andrew
on the N. outskirts of Merstham, now close to the M25, 2m/3km N. of Redhill TQ 2953
Stands in the park. It was re-pewed as a college chapel by the 5th Lord Monson in 1834, with important fittings from both English and foreign churches. The N. transept is a parlour pew with fireplace and chairs; the S. transept has a gallery from which the pulpit is suspended. The interior is a remarkable example of a church furnished by an antiquarian traveller and collector.

GODALMING
St Peter & St Paul
4m/6km S.W. of Guildford SU 9643
The church dominates Church Street with its twisted spire. Some pre-Conquest remains. Central tower, chancel and transepts Norman. Aisles added in the 13th century, chancel aisles rebuilt in the 14th. The tall, lead-covered spire is 14th-century, lengthened westward in the 15th century. Repaired in 1840 by John Perry of Godalming and restored in 1879 by Sir Giles Gilbert Scott; the final effect is rather dull.

GRAFHAM
St Andrew
3m/4km N.W. of Cranleigh TQ 0241
By H. Woodyer, 1864; Bargate stone in the Early English style. This was Woodyer's parish church, paid for by him. He is buried in the churchyard. St Andrew's Cross and the letter A run through the design. There is good Hardman glass. The solid screen supports the roof and was put there by Woodyer because Sumner, then Bishop of Winchester, refused to consecrate churches with screens, so Woodyer made this one structural, and got his way.

GREAT BOOKHAM
St Nicholas
2m/3km S.W. of Leatherhead TQ 1354
12th-century arcades of differing dates; an inscription records the building of the chancel by John Rutherwyke, Abbot of Chertsey, in 1341. Delightful weather-boarded W. tower with shingled spire, all on flint base. Restored by Carpenter, 1845, and Butterfield, 1885. E. window has re-used 15th-century glass, perhaps German; 15th-, 16th- and 17th-century brasses. Monument to Col. Moore, 1735, in the Roman manner.

GUILDFORD
SU 9949
Holy Trinity, High Street
The tower fell in 1740 and wrecked the old church. The new church, opened in 1763, was almost certainly designed by James Horne, architect of St Catherine Coleman, Christchurch, Southwark. A solid red-brick church in the Palladian style with battlemented tower. As in all Horne's churches, the ironwork and joinery are very good. Chancel and apse added by A. W. Blomfield in 1888. Monuments include that to Arch-

bishop Abbot, d. 1633; of alabaster with columns resting on piled books.

St Mary, Quarry Street

Built on the slope above the river, the central tower is late pre-Conquest. Transepts added and chancel rebuilt late 11th century. Nave, aisles, apsidal chapels and the chancel remodelled *c.* 1160; the apse has been taken down. Attractive interior, steeply stepped up from W. to E.

HALE
St John the Evangelist

1m/2km N. of Farnham SU 8448
1844, by Benjamin Ferrey. Neo-Norman style with eccentric details, including a rose window in the E. wall and round S. tower. Sombre within.

HASCOMBE
St Peter

3m/4km S.E. of Godalming SU 9939
One of the prettiest villages in Surrey. Church by H. Woodyer, 1864, is a Tractarian work of art. The exterior is plain, and the richness of interior effect is gained by gilding and painting on roofs and reredos, and by the richly moulded interior arches of coupled windows. There is good dark Hardman glass throughout, except for E. window by Clayton & Bell. The nave walls are painted all around with St Peter's net, and the 15th-century screen is redecorated in green, gold, brown and red.

HOLMBURY ST MARY
St Mary

5m/8km S.W. of Dorking TQ 1144
Beautifully set against a wooded hillside; a model village church by G. E. Street, 1879, who lived here and built it of local stone in memory of his wife. Stained glass by Clayton & Bell from Street's designs.

KEW
St Anne

Kew Green, 7m/11km W. of Charing Cross, now in Greater London TQ 1977
The church, attractively situated in the middle of Kew Green, was built in 1710–14, enlarged in 1770 by Kirby, and again by Wyatville and Stock in the 19th century. B. Ferrey added the mausoleum with a half-dome for the Duke of Cambridge in 1850. In spite of many alterations it retains a peculiar charm and contains many monuments of interest. Gainsborough and Zoffany buried in the churchyard.

KINGSTON-UPON-THAMES
All Saints

10m/16km S.W. of Charing Cross, now in Greater London TQ 1769
Mostly 15th-century. Perpendicular tower with pretty brick top added in 1708. Restored by Brandon, 1862, and by Pearson, 1886–8. Bright Victorian glass; Comper altar; monuments include a Flaxman to Philip Meadows with an almost detached cherub on a cloud, and a fine seated figure by Chantrey.

LEATHERHEAD
St Mary & St Nicholas

8m/12km S. of Kingston-upon-Thames TQ 1769
The best building in the town though with much-restored exterior; flint-faced 15th-century tower. Inside all is more harmonious, with the early 13th century very much in evidence.

LINGFIELD
St Peter & St Paul

4m/6km N. of E. Grinstead TQ 3843
A college for secular priests was founded in 1431 by Sir Reginald Cobham; the church was rebuilt at this time. Measured Perpendicular with contemporary stalls, screen, and lectern with chained Bible. Excellent Cobham family monuments, the 1st Lord Cobham, d. 1361, with a melancholy Saracen at his feet. Best set of brasses in Surrey.

LOWER KINGSWOOD
The Wisdom of God

1m/2km S. of Kingswood and 2m/3km N. of Reigate TQ 2453
Sidney H. Barnsley, 1892; replica of a Balkan church with narthex and apse, and much material brought from Balkan ruins; unique in England in its thoroughgoing Byzantinism. Barnsley painted the pretty wagon roof himself.

LOWFIELD HEATH
St Michael

2m/3km N. of Crawley, now just in W. Sussex TQ 2740
William Burges, 1867, in a French Gothic style consisting of nave, chancel, and S.W. tower. This is a most beautiful little chancel,

made so by the extraordinary vigour of the sculpture and the sensitivity shown in the placing of it. E. window filled with Art Nouveau glass.

MALDEN
St John the Baptist
Church Road, Old Malden, W. of Kingston-upon-Thames, now in Greater London TQ 1761
Small brick church; nave, chancel and tower rebuilt early 17th century; new nave and chancel added on the N. by T. G. Jackson, 1875.

MERSTHAM
St Katharine
2m/3km N. of Redhill TQ 2953
13th–15th-century; 13th-century tower with shingled broach spire and a handsome W. door of the same date. Nice Greek tablet to George Jolliffe, killed in the Battle of the Nile, 1797. Several brasses.

MICKLEHAM
St Michael
2m/3km S. of Leatherhead TQ 1753
Wooded slopes behind; massive 12th-century tower. Norbury Chapel has chequered flint and clunch walls. After earlier restoration in 1822 by P. F. Robinson, partly rebuilt by Ewan Christian in 1872; he gave it a new E. end with chubby round tower to the S.; 16th-century Flemish stained glass.

MITCHAM
St Peter & St Paul
4m/6km N.W. of Croydon, now in the London Borough of Merton TQ 2768
1819–22 by George Smith. Perpendicular and stuccoed without, tall and vaulted within. The interior was restored by S. Dykes Bower in 1951 with a good high-vaulted roof. Crowley monuments probably carved by Rysbrack to a design by Gibbs.

MORDEN
St Lawrence
1m/2km S. of Wimbledon, now in the London Borough of Merton TQ 2568
Rebuilt 1636; red brick with tower. An unspoilt village church inside. Gothic Survival E. window and glass; W. gallery, three-sided altar rails, and cut-down pulpit of 1720.

NEWDIGATE
St Peter
5m/8km S. of Dorking TQ 1942
Much restored; 13th-century chancel; 14th-century S. aisle; 15th-century weatherboarded and shingled timber belfry tower carried on four oak posts. Medieval glass panels in S. aisle showing bears' paws of the Newdigate family arms.

OCKHAM
St Mary and All Saints
5m/8km E. of Woking TQ 0756
Among the trees in Ockham Park. There is some 13th-century work, including the beautiful E. window of seven-stepped lancets. S. side of nave 14th-century; tower 15th-century. To the N. is the brick mausoleum of the King family, 1735, containing monuments by Rysbrack, R. Westmacott Jnr and, in strange contrast, a Voysey casket with lettering by Eric Gill.

OTTERSHAW
Christ Church
2m/3km S.W. of Chertsey TQ 0263
1864, by Sir Giles Gilbert Scott. In 13th-century style, built of polychrome brick; conspicuous and rather grim. Tower and broach spire added in 1885.

OUTWOOD
St John the Baptist
3m/4km N.E. of Horley TQ 3245
1869, by William Burges; tower by W. P. Manning, 1876; all modest and well proportioned, but the brick interior is somewhat harsh. Good village setting.

OXTED
St Mary
4m/6km W. of Westerham TQ 3852
Built in a variety of local stones but over-restored; 14th-century work in chancel, good 15th-century arcades, and S. porch bearing the Cobham arms. Stumpy W. tower. Four windows in the aisle by Morris & Co.

PEPER HARROW
St Nicholas
2m/3km W. of Godalming SU 9344
Originally Norman but boldly restored by Pugin, 1844, in the Early English and Decorated styles; 17th-century Broderick monument in black marble with two fine portrait busts.

PETERSHAM
St Peter
9m/15km S.W. of Charing Cross, now in the London Borough of Richmond TQ 1873
A Thames-side village with many 18th-century houses. A beautiful unrestored church. Nave and W. tower of 17th-century red brick with a pretty cupola. Two-decker pulpit, box pews and galleries remain. Late 18th-century transepts added to N. and S.; S. transept rebuilt 1840 by Meakin. Gaily coloured George Cole monument, 1624, showing him and his wife. Fine Royal Arms above chancel arch.

PYRFORD
St Nicholas
2m/3km E. of Woking TQ 0458
On hill overlooking Newark Priory ruins. Norman and almost unrestored with ceilure over the former rood and remains of medieval glass and wall-paintings; 17th-century pulpit.

RANMORE
St Barnabas
1m/2km W. of Dorking TQ 1550
On a beautiful common. A rich man's church with prominent spire; 1859, by Sir Giles Gilbert Scott, who paid no regard to local style. Cobbled exterior. It is certainly one of his best churches.

REDHILL
St John the Evangelist
E. district of Reigate TQ 2750
1842, by J. Knowles. Flint aisles by Giles Hesketh, 1867. Enlarged by Pearson, 1889, who added the prominent brick tower and spire in 1895. The church is on Earlswood Common S. of the town.

REIGATE
St Mary Magdalene
9m/15km N. of Crawley TQ 2550
Good late 12th-century arcades with stiff-leaf capitals. Chancel and chapels 14th-century, tower 15th-century. Chancel and chapels restored by Woodyer; a later restoration by Scott Jnr in 1874–8. Noble Corinthian monument to Richard Ladbroke (1730) by Joseph Rose the Elder.

RICHMOND
TQ 1774
St Mary Magdalene, Paradise Road
In a quiet churchyard behind the main street.

Medieval flint and stone W. tower, largely rebuilt in 1624. Brick N. aisle of 1699, and nave and S. aisle of 1750 in red and yellow brick. Chancel and chapels rebuilt by Bodley in 1904. Good 18th-century pulpit and fluted font. Many monuments including a medallion to the actor Edmund Kean, d. 1833, and another to the poet James Thompson, d. 1748, who wrote 'The Seasons'.

St Matthias, Friars Stile Road
A fine church by Sir Giles Gilbert Scott, 1858, with tower and lofty spire, in a fine position at the top of King's Road. Impressive clerestory on the S. side. Lofty interior somewhat spoiled by being subdivided.

SHACKLEFORD
St Mary
3m/4km N.W. of Godalming SU 9345
A pleasant village with a Victorian S. edge where in 1865–6 Sir Giles Gilbert Scott built a church of good proportions. Early 13th-century style in Bargate stone. Central tower, simple detail externally, and a touch mechanical within, but satisfying for all that.

SHEPPERTON
St Nicholas
on N. bank of Thames, opposite Walton on Thames TQ 0867
Good village setting with rectory and inn. Brick W. tower of 1710, otherwise mostly of 1614 with early 19th-century gallery and box pews which create a homely, welcoming character.

SHERE
St James
5m/8km E. of Guildford TQ 0747
A beautiful village on the Tillingbourne, discovered by cyclists, 1900, and its praises sung in the guidebooks of the time; much visited by motorists now. Cruciform 12th-century church approached past timber and plaster cottage and through a Lutyens lych gate. S. aisle and top of tower good 13th-century work; some work of the 14th and 15th centuries; W. gallery of 1748; a shapely shingled spire. Medieval glass and brasses. Carefully restored by S. Weatherley in 1895 and again, brightly, by Louis Osman in 1957.

SOUTH NORWOOD
St Alban

Grange Road, Thornton Heath, now in Greater London TQ 3271

By William Bucknall and Ninian Comper, 1889. A large red-brick church with stone dressings in a Decorated style. Rather austere interior, with clerestory, hammer-beam roofs, and raised chancel, lacking the richness of the Comper furnishings which, apart from the stained glass window in the Lady Chapel, were never completed.

STAINES
St Peter

Laleham Road, 17m/27km W. of London TQ 0371

A well-found brick essay by G. H. Fellowes Prynne, 1893–4. Good interior with polychrome brick and imposing traceried stone screen with iron grilles. Contemporary fittings and glass.

STOKE D'ABERNON
St Mary

3m/4km N.W. of Leatherhead TQ 1259

The S. wall is pre-Conquest, with a blocked doorway 12 feet from the ground. N. aisle late 12th-century, chancel remodelled, and vaulting built, in the 13th. Norbury Chapel 15th-century. A destructive 'restoration', which certainly qualifies for inverted commas, by Ford and Hesketh in 1866; the interior has been, to some extent, de-restored. In the chancel are the magnificent brasses of Sir John D'Abernon, 1277, the earliest surviving brass in England and unique for showing a lance; and of his son, Sir John, 1327. Remains of 13th-century painting in the chancel. Monuments in the Norbury Chapel. Imposing early 17th-century pulpit with tester; hour-glass. Remarkable collection of old glass.

THAMES DITTON
All Saints

Weston Green, 1m/2km W. of Surbiton TQ 1667

By Sir Edward Maufe, 1938. Whitewashed exterior with a N.E. campanile. Tall arched windows light an uncluttered interior with plain piers and round arches.

THURSLEY
St Michael and All Angels

3m/4km N. of Hindhead SU 9039

Pre-Conquest windows were discovered during aggressive restoration by Ferrey in 1860; a triangular recess in the chancel has been interpreted as a Saxon oven for baking wafers. The nave is dominated by the timber cage supporting an impressive 15th-century wooden bell-turret.

TITSEY
St James

1m/2km N. of Limpsfield TQ 4055

At the foot of a wooded spur of the North Downs. By Pearson, 1861. Early English style executed in an uncompromising Victorian manner. A superfluity of hard brick; 14th-century encaustic tiles, coffin slab, and a monument to Sir John Gresham, d. 1643.

UPPER NORWOOD
St John the Evangelist

Sylvan Road, now in London Borough of Croydon SU 9318

By J. L. Pearson, 1878. Strikingly situated on a steep slope. A large town church of stock brick and stone in the Early English style. There is less complexity here than in his later churches, and an effect of breadth is given by the wide nave and spreading E. end, emphasized by the unusual chancel vault. Glass and sumptuous vestments by Sir Ninian Comper, who worshipped here. Chapel in S. aisle and image of Blessed Virgin Mary by Martin Travers.

VALLEY END
St Saviour

2m/3km N.W. of Cobham SU 9563

1867, by G. F. Bodley; of brick in the simplest Middle Pointed style; though an early Bodley church, it prefigures his later development.

WALTON-ON-THE-HILL
St Peter

4m/6km S.E. of Banstead TQ 2255

Rare mid-12th-century lead font bedecked with arcades containing Apostles. Otherwise a bit of a motley, though with some good Perpendicular work.

WEST BYFLEET
St John the Baptist

1m/2km W. of Byfleet, 4m/6km N.E. of Woking TQ 0561

Stockbrokers' country. 1910, by W. D. Caroe. Echoing the Surrey style with shingled roofs; very lanky without and somewhat fussy within.

WEST HORSLEY
St Mary
6m/10km E. of Guildford TQ 0752
Norman and later work but mainly 13th-century with W. tower and dumpy shingled spire; 13th-century wall-paintings on the W. wall of the nave; Nicholas monuments include that to Sir John, d. 1704, perhaps by Grinling Gibbons.

WEYBRIDGE
St James
17m/27km S.W. of London TQ 0764
1847–8, by J. L. Pearson, one of his early works; good Middle Pointed; enlarged 1864. Rich polychrome marble mosaic in the chancel.

WITLEY
All Saints
2m/3km S. of Milford SU 9434
Uncannily pretty, like all Witley. Crossing tower with octagonal shingled spire, large nave, part of original Saxon church extended by the Normans. Largely 13th-century with font and piscina of that time. Faded 12th-century wall-paintings and 15th-century heraldic glass. Restored in 1899 and enlarged by Aston Webb.

WOKING
St Peter
6m/10km N. of Guildford TQ 0058
Between tall 18th-century houses and the River Wey, in the old town, the church is late 11th-century. W. doorway with door and ironwork; 13th-century tower and chancel; brick porch, gallery and pulpit of 1622. Keeps its medieval atmosphere.

WONERSH
St John the Baptist
3m/4km S.E. of Guildford TQ 0145
Secluded wooded setting. The church was mainly rebuilt in 1793–4 after a fire, and was restored in 1901–2 by Sir Charles Nicholson. Sir Charles's regard for texture within and without, the organ case by Bentley, the brass chandeliers and mainly blue and red glass of 1914 by Sir Charles's brother, Archibald, make it a model of conservative restoration of this date.

WORPLESDON
St Mary
3m/4km N.W. of Guildford SU 9753
Lying E. of the green, the church is mainly 13th–14th-century, but with good Perpendicular tower capped with a cupola from the rectory stables, 1766; 18th-century altar rails, 17th-century pulpit and font from Eton College, and 14th-century figured glass, the best figures in the county, in reds and greens.

WOTTON
St John the Evangelist
3m/4km W. of Dorking TQ 1247
Beautifully situated among large trees facing the Downs; 11th-century tower and chancel; the rest of the church is 13th-century. Beside the N. chapel is the 17th-century burial-place of the Evelyn family of Wotton House. John Evelyn, the diarist, d. 1706, lies here with his wife. More Evelyn monuments in the mausoleum.

Sussex

Introduction

Sussex stretches along the English Channel from Rye on the east to Thorney Island on the west. The coastline has been made hideous from end to end by the desire of London's overspill to have a house by the sea, or at least to spend the weekend there. The only unspoilt part is between Eastbourne and Seaford, which belongs to the National Trust and is therefore immune. Parallel with the coastline run the South Downs, referred to in Sussex villages as 'the hill' – low and wooded in West Sussex, higher and treeless in East Sussex. They enter the sea at Beachy Head, but are interrupted by four out of the five Sussex rivers – the Arun, Adur, Ouse and Cuckmere. Behind the Downs is the Weald – a belt of heavy clay which in early medieval times was dense forest.

The churches of Sussex are many and various. Although there are many lovely churches they are not among the most magnificent since, unlike East Anglia and Gloucestershire, there was no flourishing local industry here when Gothic architecture reached its zenith in the 15th century, and of the many religious foundations with churches or chapels only the great Priory Church of Boxgrove survived the Dissolution. It is true that throughout all the Middle Ages and up to 1811, when Ashbourn Forge closed down, Sussex was the centre of the iron industry; but disappointingly little evidence is to be found in the churches, and the iron screen at Ashburnham and the grille at Arundel are the only important examples of ironwork in the church furniture.

There is a great deal of Norman and Early English architecture, very little Decorated, and not much Perpendicular. Very few churches were rebuilt in the 18th century; Glynde is the one of most architectural interest. Most were scraped, refurnished and mercilessly 'cleaned up' in the 19th century; there is a certain amount of medieval church furniture still surviving – but very few 18th-century box pews. A characteristic feature of Sussex churches is the shingled spire. Oak shingles are thin 'slates' of wood, which are – or should be – cleft, not sawn. They are still made, though cleavers are not easy to find. They last about 100 years. Elegant and graceful shingled spires are at Playden, West Hoathley, Cuckfield, and Horsted Keynes. A humbler version of the spire, known as the 'Sussex cap', is found on many smaller churches, such as Wivelsfield, East Chiltington, and Bishopstone. There are four spires – Chiddingly, Northiam, Dallington, and East Preston – of which the first two are the best. There are also, in the Ouse Valley, three round towers – St Michael's, Lewes, Southease, and Piddinghoe – rare outside East Anglia. West Sussex churches are, on the whole, smaller and more rustic than those in East Sussex. East Sussex was more generally prosperous than West, where several feudal lords, the Dukes of Norfolk and Richmond, and Lord Leconfield, owned and own large tracts of country, and many villages were small hamlets with no squires or people of any consequence.

Another local feature is Horsham stone. These large, thin slabs are used for roofing on many of the larger churches in the centre of Sussex within twenty-five miles of Horsham; they are not found in the extreme west or east where tiles take their place.

There are a large number of oak medieval roofs, mostly of a simple trussed

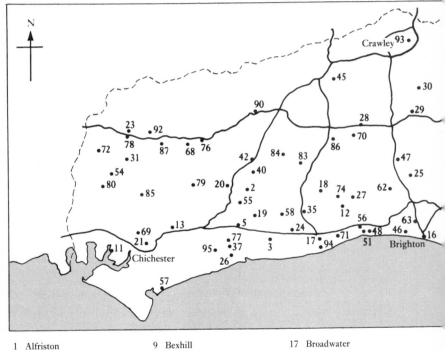

1	Alfriston	9	Bexhill
2	Amberley	10	Bishopstone
3	Angmering	11	Bosham
4	Arlington	12	Botolphs
5	Arundel	13	Boxgrove
6	Ashburnham	14	Brede
7	Battle	15	Brightling
8	Berwick	16	Brighton

17	Broadwater		
18	Buncton		
19	Burpham		
20	Burton		
21	Chichester		
22	Chiddingly		
23	Chithurst		
24	Clapham		

and raftered type. There is one more elaborate Elizabethan roof at South Harting.

There were many churches with frescoes on the walls. Some were destroyed during 'restorations', but good examples survive at Trotton, Hardham, and West Chiltington.

The stone used in the churches is mostly of local origin. Downland churches are often built of flint, and sometimes chalk is used in the arches, as at Litlington; the towers at Southover, Lewes, and in the Tudor church of Twineham, are of brick. Roman brickwork occurs at Westhampnett, St Olaves, Chichester, Bosham, Eastergate, and Hardham.

W.S.M.

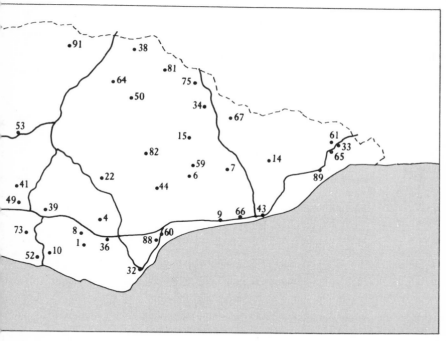

25	Clayton	33	East Guldeford	41	Hamsey
26	Climping	34	Etchingham	42	Hardham
27	Coombes	35	Findon	43	Hastings
28	Cowfold	36	Folkington	44	Herstmonceux
29	Cuckfield	37	Ford	45	Horsham
30	Danehill	38	Frant	46	Hove
31	Didling	39	Glynde	47	Hurstpierpoint
32	Eastbourne	40	Greatham	48	Kingston Buci

continued overleaf

Selected List of Churches

ALFRISTON
St Andrew
4m/6km N.E. of Newhaven TQ 5103
A handsome cruciform church of flint, *c.* 1370, with central tower and shingled spire; interesting as an obvious example of the transition from Decorated to Perpendicular. It stands away from the village, across a meadow. Inside refurnished, but of fine proportions, with unusually high arches at the crossing. Piscina and sedilia of unusual design; Easter Sepulchre on the N. Royal Arms, 1725.

AMBERLEY
St Michael
4m/6km N. of Arundel TQ 0313
The church forms a medieval group with the castle, former palace of the bishops of Chichester. Nave and chancel arch are Norman; the arch has triple chevron moulding; 13th-century chancel, aisle, and tower. Early Decorated S. doorway has capitals of vine and oak leaves. Medieval wallpaintings on S. side of chancel arch, including a Crucifixion. The Minton tiled floor was designed by the Rev. Lord Alwyne Compton, *c.* 1864–5. Late Norman arcaded font.

ANGMERING
St Margaret
3m/4km N.E. of Littlehampton TQ 0604
Tower of 1507, but the rest of the church was lavishly 'restored' by S. S. Teulon, 1855. Beautifully carved capitals by Forsyth in the nave. Fittings include an alabaster pulpit decorated with angels. The nearby school and vestry hall are also by Teulon.

ARLINGTON
St Pancras
3m/4km W. of Hailsham TQ 5407
All styles from Saxon to Perpendicular. British urn and Roman tiles found beneath nave. Traces of medieval wall-paintings and Biblical texts on nave walls. Queen Anne pulpit re-carved to Charles Powell's design during the Victorian restoration.

ARUNDEL
St Nicholas
3m/4km N. of Littlehampton TQ 0107
Cruciform, late 14th-century. Wallpaintings and good medieval wrought-iron grille of Sussex ironwork. The chancel, the Fitzalan Chapel, with many monuments, is the property of the Duke of Norfolk, and is separated from the rest of the church. On the N. wall are 14th-century wall-paintings of the Seven Deadly Sins and Seven Works of Mercy. Canopied medieval stone pulpit, *c.* 1380.

ASHBURNHAM
St James
4m/6km W. of Battle TQ 6814
In the park, next to the remains of the house of the Ashburnhams. Rebuilt in 1665–7 in Gothic Survival style, except for the Tudor tower, by John Ashburnham. Furnishings remain – box pews, gallery, pulpit, font, tower staircase, altarpiece, 1676, with commandments, Moses and Aaron. Iron railings, probably made locally. Armour, and tombs of Ashburnhams – John, 1671, and William, 1675. Church once contained the shirt and silk drawers supposed to have been worn by Charles I at his execution.

BATTLE
St Mary
6m/10km N.W. of Hastings TQ 7415
Late 12th-century arcades; other parts 13th–15th-century. Restored by Butterfield. Early 14th-century wall-paintings of the Life of St Margaret in the nave, and remains of 15th-century glass in N. aisle. Perpendicular font cover, regrettably painted. Alabaster tomb, 1548.

BERWICK
St Michael
1m/2km N. of Alfriston TQ 5105
Farming hamlet at foot of Downs; 13th-century church, restored in 1856, and adorned with wall-paintings by Vanessa Bell, Duncan Grant, and Quentin Bell in 1942–3.

BEXHILL
St Peter
5m/8km W. of Hastings TQ 7407
Good Norman arches inside tower. N. arcade of *c.* 1180. Various Perpendicular additions. Chancel rebuilt by Wm. Butterfield, 1878. The walls and ceilings richly painted in 1893. Anglo-Saxon coffin lid.

BISHOPSTONE
St Andrew
1m/2km N. of Seaford TQ 4701
S. porch could date from as early as the 8th century; it has a supposedly Saxon sundial inscribed 'EADRIC'. Norman tower, S. doorway, N. aisle and chancel. Romanesque coffin lid carved with a cross and Agnus Dei. Possibly the oldest church in Sussex.

BOSHAM
Holy Trinity
4m/6km W. of Chichester SU 8004
Seafaring place overlooking the mud creeks of Chichester Harbour. A small Irish monastery was here before the mission of St Wilfrid. The church appears in the Bayeux tapestry. Partly Saxon tower, now with shingled broach spire, and high Saxo-Norman chancel arch. E. window of five lancets, and aisles, 13th-century. Chancel has a recessed tomb, 13th-century, with recumbent figure of a girl. Roof and furnishings mostly modern, and walls unfortunately scraped bare of plaster. Some medieval benches.

BOTOLPHS
St Botolph
1m/2km S. of Steyning, 5m/8km N.W. of Shoreham-by-Sea TQ 1909
Attractive church with interesting blocked 13th-century N. arcade showing evidence of economic decline. Some house platforms opposite church. Jacobean pulpit, Charles II Royal Arms. Nave lit by converted oil lamps.

BOXGROVE
St Mary & St Blaise
3m/4km N.E. of Chichester SU 9007
Stately relic of Benedictine priory church: choir and transepts remain, with central tower and E. end of nave; the rest of the nave is ruined. The transepts, tower and nave ruins are 12th-century; the choir is early 13th-century, with vaulted roof, clerestory with Purbeck marble shafts, and rich arcades, each pair within a large, round containing arch; 16th-century painted decoration on the vaulting by Lambert Barnard, 1520s. Splendid chantry built by Thomas de la Warr, 1532; late-Gothic and Renaissance, richly decorated, carved and coloured. Thomas bought the Priory at the Dissolution, to save his chantry, but he is buried at Broadwater. The transepts have oak galleries. The monument to Mary, Countess of Derby, d. 1752, in the chancel, is of interest, as it is one of the earliest depictions of alms-giving. Good stained glass in E. lancets by O'Connor. In S. transept a statue of St Blaise by Prof. Tristram, the expert on medieval wall-painting.

BREDE
St George
6m/10km N. of Hastings TQ 8218
Perpendicular but, inside, a S. aisle of *c.* 1200. Chancel late 15th-century. S. chapel contains the Oxenbridge family mausoleum with brasses of 1482 and Sir Goddard Oxenbridge's tomb, 1537. He was reputed to be a cannibal giant. Some 15th-century glass, alms box of 1687, and carved Virgin and Child by Clare Sheridan, 1937.

BRIGHTLING
St Thomas of Canterbury
5m/8km N.W. of Battle TQ 6821
13th- and 14th-century. Gothic S. porch of 1749. Squire's pew, and W. gallery with barrel organ. Churchyard dominated by the pyramid mausoleum of 1810 built by 'Mad Jack' Fuller. Some Harmer terracottas.

BRIGHTON
TQ 3104
Church of the Annunciation, Washington Street
A small mission church built in 1864 by Wm. Dancy for the Rev. Arthur Wagner. The modest interior has been likened to a New Zealand pioneers' church. E. window by Burne-Jones, 1866, for Morris & Co. Aisle, tower and spire added 1881.
St Bartholomew, Ann Street
A huge brick church built in 1872–7 by Edmund Scott, a local architect. It is aisleless, and 135 feet high: the chancel was never built. Baldacchino, silver side altar, pulpit, and baptistry, all a mixture of Arts and Crafts and Byzantine, by H. Wilson. J.B. liked to imagine the clergy entering on elephants.
St Martin, Lewes Road

Brick Early English, by Somers Clarke, 1872–5. A splendid interior, fully equipped with fittings designed by the architect – e.g. font, pulpit, and reredos, 40 feet high, carved by J. E. Knox, and painted by H. E. Woolridge. The roof is painted with 70 panels representing the expansion of the Anglican Church; colonial sees on one side, American on the other. Glass mostly by Powell. Many Baroque furnishings, including enormous lectern.

St Mary & St James, St James Street
1877–9, by Sir William Emerson. French Gothic, of brick, the crossing and chancel with brick vaults. Impressive apse, with long traceried single-light windows. Charlotte Elliott, the sister of an incumbent of an earlier church on the site, wrote the well-known hymn, 'Just as I am, without one plea'.

St Michael, Victoria Road
Originally a modest brick church, in N. Italian Gothic style, by G. F. Bodley, 1858–62. In 1893–5 the enormous nave and N. aisle, designed by W. Burges in 1868, were completed in a modified form after his death by J. S. Chapple. Their style is French 13th-century. Reredos and chancel decorations by W. H. Romaine-Walker. In the Bodley part of the church there is Pre-Raphaelite glass designed by Burne-Jones, Ford Madox Brown, Morris, and Webb. The roof was painted by Morris and Webb too, and there is a late-medieval triptych restored by C. E. Kempe.

St Nicholas
Old parish church of small seaport town, on a hill; restored and virtually rebuilt by R. C. Carpenter, 1852, as a memorial to the Duke of Wellington; 12th-century font, with carvings of St Nicholas, Baptism of Christ, and Last Supper. Painting and glass by Kempe. Image of St Nicholas by Comper. Restored 15th-century rood screen. Wellington war memorial designed by Carpenter in the form of an Eleanor Cross. Churchyard has good 18th-century headstones.

St Paul, West Street
1846–8, by R. C. Carpenter; spire by his son R. H. Carpenter. Correct Middle Pointed style, and Tractarian atmosphere. Carpenter succeeded better than anyone else in realizing the model church of the Camden Society. Glass by Pugin and Hardman. Subsequent work by Bodley and others. The reredos, by Burne-Jones, is now in the Burlington Museum. Lectern by T. H. Powell illustrates themes from the Apocalypse. The

Ecclesiologist wrote that Brighton's 'hideous chapels are to be shamed by a real church'.

St Peter, Victoria Gardens
The new parish church, 1824–8, by Sir Charles Barry, in Perpendicular Commissioners' Gothic. Ingenious W. end, with tower combined with porch. Chancel by Somers Clarke and Micklethwaite, 1900–6. Much Kempe glass and, in the clerestory, rare Regency glass by Wm. Collins. Nave vaults are made of plaster.

BROADWATER
St Mary
district of Worthing 1m/2km N. of centre TQ 1404
Handsome, spacious cruciform church in N. suburb of Worthing. Mostly 12th- and 13th-century. Tower arches have rich chevron mouldings. Vaulted 13th-century chancel with carved stalls and misericords. Two 16th-century tombs to de la Warrs. Brass to John Mapilton, 1432. E. window by Willement, 1885, described as 'deplorable' by the *Ecclesiologist*. Of the restoration of the chancel the same journal declared: 'The local builder of Worthing was the magnus Apollo employed. We spare his name, for no doubt he did his best.' In the churchyard a gravestone of 1793 depicts the Day of Judgement.

BUNCTON
All Saints
2m/3km E. of Washington TQ 1413
Beautiful setting, approached through a ravine. Unrestored Norman interior. Good 14th-century piscina.

BURPHAM
St Mary
4m/6km N. of Littlehampton TQ 0408
11th-century, enlarged at different dates in the 12th. Vaulted chancel, c. 1200. A typical Sussex 15th-century tower; 17th-century altar rails and German glass roundels in the chancel. Curious tombstone in the churchyard depicts a jockey, d. 1785. It includes a relief of a racehorse. The stunning situation of the church, with views of Arundel, is somewhat spoiled by a nearby car park and 'leisure centre'.

BURTON
(dedication unknown)
3m/4km S. of Petworth SU 9718
Small church sheltered by trees in park near

18th-century house. Early Norman, with some herringbone masonry; repaired in 17th century; 15th-century screen, tympanum with Commandments, Royal Arms, 1636, painted on plaster, with the text, 'Obey them that have the rule over you'; 16th-century monuments to the Goring family. Wall-painting of St Uncumber in a window splay. The saint, also known as Wilgefortis, was popular with wives praying for separation from their husbands.

CHICHESTER
St John
SU 8604
Designed by James Elmes in Greek Revival style and built 1812–13. The extraordinary Low Church galleried interior focuses on a three-decker pulpit which blocks the diminutive chancel and towers over the nave. Built as a proprietary chapel, it is a unique survival of a plan once common, but now very rare.

CHIDDINGLY
(dedication unknown)
4m/6km N.W. of Hailsham TQ 5414
Medieval and 19th-century; tall stone spire, one of four in Sussex; monument to Sir John Jefferay, 1612, and family; the standing effigies are unique in English monuments of the pre-Civil War period; 18th-century pulpit and box pews.

CHITHURST
St Mary
3m/4km W. of Midhurst SU 8423
Remote and attractive setting. Small aisleless church, probably 11th-century, which has never grown. Rough, irregular texture to outside walls. Inside, plain chancel arch, and some simple old seating.

CLAPHAM
St Mary
4m/6km N.W. of Worthing TQ 0906
Norman, 13th-century and Perpendicular. Very well restored by Sir Giles Gilbert Scott, 1873–4, who provided the tiled reredos, painted with Pre-Raphaelite angels against a vine-leaf background. N. and S. walls of chancel have unfortunately been white-washed, but enough remains of the Victorian wall-painting to indicate the quality of the work. Good series of 16th-century monuments and brasses to the Shelley family.

CLAYTON
St John the Baptist
6m/10km N. of Brighton TQ 2914
One of a series of Saxo-Norman overlap churches. The superb 12th-century wall-paintings are by the Coombes-Hardham workshop. They were discovered in 1893 and 1917–19. Good brass to Richard Iden, priest, 1523.

CLIMPING
St Mary
2m/3km W. of Littlehampton TQ 0002
Solid Transitional Norman tower on S.; trefoiled doorway with chevron moulding. The rest of the church 13th-century. 'Clymping for perfection'. Pre-Reformation stone pulpit, and one of the finest 13th-century chests in England. Some medieval benches. N. transept contains a series of paintings by Heywood Harty, 1925–6; very much period pieces, one shows Christ preaching to villagers in typical Arun scenery.

COOMBES
(dedication unknown)
2m/3km E. of Steyning TQ 1908
Hidden up a combe in the Adur Valley. Low and humble; the tower and part of the church were 'lately fallen' in 1724, and the church was to be contracted. Inside, Norman chancel arch, and extensive remains of Romanesque wall-paintings, discovered in 1949. They date from *c.* 1080–1120. Amusing tombstone in churchyard to Henry Daniel, d. 1860; his dying words were, 'I shall not be here long, Mother'.

COWFOLD
St Peter
6m/10km S.E. of Horsham TQ 2022
13th-and 15th-century. Large and famous brass, 10 feet long, to Prior Nelond of Lewes, 1433, and a smaller one to John-a-gate, churchwarden.

CUCKFIELD
Holy Trinity
2m/3km W. of Haywards Heath TQ 3024
Spacious 13th-century church, with work of 14th and 15th centuries. Graceful shingled spire. Unusual 15th-century roof, painted by Kempe, with tie-beams, and bosses of Nevill family. Screen and pulpit by Bodley. Monument of Charles Sergison, 1732, by Thomas Ayde. Other monuments by

Flaxman and Westmacott. Much early Kempe stained glass.

DANEHILL
All Saints
5m/8km N.E. of Haywards Heath TQ 4027
Handsome church in commanding position, by Bodley and Garner, 1892. Reredos and fittings by Comper; windows by Kempe.

DIDLING
St Andrew
4m/6km S.W. of Midhurst SU 8318
Small and lonely in a field beneath the Downs. Massive old seating, 17th-century pulpit, made from a chest, and rails. Small tub-shaped Norman font. Delightful, unspoiled little church.

EASTBOURNE
TV 6199
St Mary, Church Street
The church, the timber-framed Lamb Inn, medieval rectory, and a few Georgian houses, are all that remain of the small town that gave its name to the modern seaside resort. Massive Perpendicular tower. Admirable arcades, like those on N. of New Shoreham, *c.* 1170 onward; aisles rebuilt in 14th century. Triple sedilia and Easter Sepulchre. Parclose screens, 14th-century. Large Georgian Arms, 1791, in white and gold frame, by Lambert of Lewes.
All Souls, Susan's Road
1882, basilican, by A. P. Strong. Detached campanile is 83 feet high. Reminiscent of the small group of Victorian Romanesque churches built in the 1840s.
St Saviour, South Street
A large brick church by G. E. Street, 1865–71. Roof of blue and green slates. The vaulted chancel and apse are emphasized by Street's device of narrowing the building towards the focal point. Tiled floor by Godwin, designed by Street. Excellent mural of Christ in Majesty by Clayton & Bell above the chancel arch. By the same firm are the mosaics in the sanctuary and around the aisles. Reredos by Randoll Blacking. The altar in the Blessed Sacrament Chapel is by George Jack, a pupil of Wm. Morris.

EAST GULDEFORD
St Mary
1m/2km N.E. of Rye TQ 9321
A brick church of 1505. Unspoilt interior with box pews, two-decker pulpit, com-mandment boards, and George IV Royal Arms. Sanctuary painted in late 19th century with angels carrying musical instruments.

ETCHINGHAM
Assumption & St Nicholas
7m/11km N. of Battle TQ 7126
Stands on low ground near the Rother. Stately church, once collegiate, with massive tile-capped tower between nave and chancel; once surrounded by a moat. Built by Sir William de Echyngham, d. 1389, whose brass is here. The contract for windows made in 1369. An unusual church, with some of the best 14th-century work in Sussex, particularly in the chancel, and flamboyant E. window. Many fragments of old glass. Screen, carved stalls, and misereres. Other brasses to the Echyngham family. Pulpit designed by Clayton, of Clayton & Bell, 1857, and executed by James Forsyth. Minton tiles in the chancel copied from surviving medieval originals.

FINDON
St John Baptist
4m/6km N. of Worthing TQ 1208
Flint 13th-century church, sheltering against a downland hanger, and close to Findon Place. Unusual plan of twin naves under one roof, divided by Transitional Norman arcade. Oak roof with timbers of exceptional length stretching across the two naves. Side chapel with very rare tiled reredos by Wm. Morris, 1867.

FOLKINGTON
St Peter
5m/8km N.W. of Eastbourne TQ 5503
Ancient and rustic. Hidden behind park on edge of downland hanger. Lichened tiled roof, wooden bellcote, unspoiled flint walls; 18th-century box pews and pulpit. Two handsome monuments in chancel.

FORD
St Andrew
3m/4km S.W. of Arundel SU 9903
Alone in fields near Arun mouth, and almost hidden by yews and holm oaks. Setting spoilt by nearby caravan park. White wooden bellcote, good texture of flint and sandstone walls. Brick S. porch, 1637. Plain Norman chancel arch. Traces of a 15th-century Doom.

FRANT
St Alban

3m/4km S. of Tunbridge Wells TQ 5953
By John Montier of Tunbridge Wells,
1819–22. Perpendicular details handled
with great assurance. Window glazing-bars
and nave piers of cast iron. N. and S.
windows contain 15th- and 16th-century
Continental glass.

GLYNDE
St Mary

3m/4km E. of Lewes TQ 4509
Classical, built of dressed flints and Portland
stone. Designed by Sir Thomas Robinson
for Bishop Trevor, and built in 1763–5; the
craftsmen are recorded. Groups well with
18th-century stables of Glynde Place. Interior all complete, with box pews, pulpit,
W. gallery, and altar rail. Later additions
include a neo-Renaissance E. window by
Kempe, and a magnificent brass gasolier,
probably by Hardman of Birmingham.

GREATHAM
(dedication unknown)

1m/2km S. of Pulborough TQ 0415
12th- and 13th-century. Only gently restored; 17th-century altar rails and early
19th-century two-decker pulpit. Lit by oil
lamps.

HAMSEY
St Peter

2m/3km N. of Lewes TQ 4012
Alone on a hill in a loop of the Ouse. Norman
chancel arch, massive Perpendicular tower.
Spared by the Victorians, and carefully re-
paired since. Hatchments, Arms of George
II. Commandments, and a few ancient pews.
Black letter texts on walls.

HARDHAM
St Botolph

1m/2km S.W. of Pulborough TQ 0317
Small church, probably 11th-century, on the
Arun flats near Pulborough. Chiefly known
for its series of wall-paintings in nave and
chancel, showing Adam and Eve, episodes
in the life of Christ, the Apostles, the story
of St George, and Heaven and Hell. They
date from *c.* 1080–1120, were discovered
in 1866, and represent the most highly inte-
grated scheme of all-over church decoration
still to survive.

HASTINGS
TQ 8109
All Saints, All Saints Street

A Perpendicular church of *c.* 1436. Doom
painted over the chancel arch. A good cork
model shows the church before Wm. Butterfield's restoration of 1869–70.

St Clement, Croft Road

A Perpendicular church probably rebuilt in
1377. Good octagonal font carved with Instruments of the Passion. In S. aisle parts
of a Moses and Aaron reredos painted by
Roger Mortimer in 1721. Rossetti and Lizzie
Siddal were married here in 1860.

Holy Trinity, Robertson Street

1857–62; characteristic Gothic of S. S.
Teulon, fitted into a difficult site. An original
and striking church. E. window, 1864–7,
by Clayton & Bell. Much excellent stone
carving by Thomas Earp. Screen and pulpit
by W. Romaine-Walker.

HERSTMONCEUX
All Saints

4m/6km N.E. of Hailsham TQ 6312
Near the castle and with splendid views of
the Downs; 12th–15th-century. Good,
lightly restored interior with attractive 19th-
century dormer windows. 'Pardon' brass to
Sir Wm. Ffiennes, d. 1402, with an inscription offering 120 days' pardon of sins for
those who pray for his soul. The Dacre
monument, 1533, uses effigies of the Hoo
family, formerly at Battle Abbey. Some
Gothic pews. Churchyard has seven headstones with Harmer terracottas.

HORSHAM
St Mary

8m/12km S.W. of Crawley TQ 1730
Large church, mostly 13th-century, with tall
shingled spire, pleasantly situated at the end
of causeway. Stained glass a complete con-
spectus of 19th-century work; 15th-century
brass and various monuments, the best by
Edward Marshall, 1654. In the churchyard
a gravestone depicts the Last Judgement and
the Sacrifice of Isaac.

HOVE
TQ 2804
All Saints, Eaton Road

1889, nave and aisles; E. parts consecrated
1901; church finally completed in 1924. By
J. L. Pearson. A big church of Sussex sandstone built in a 13th-century style. Chancel
is lower and narrower than the nave. Good-

hart-Rendel wrote that Pearson 'gave of his best . . . the chancel is as nearly perfect as it can be'. Good late glass by Clayton & Bell.

St Andrew, Waterloo Street

1827–8, by Sir Charles Barry, the E. parts reconstructed by his son. Of considerable interest as one of the earliest examples of the revived Italian Quattrocento style. The attractive interior is enhanced by W. Randoll Blacking's pulpit, font, stalls, altar rails, and baldacchinos for font and altar, all added c. 1925.
R.C.F.

St Barnabas, Sackville Road

By J. L. Pearson, 1882–3; 'one of my cheap churches'. Fittings accumulated as the years went by. Reredos by Bodley, 1907.

HURSTPIERPOINT

Holy Trinity

3m/4km S.W. of Burgess Hill TQ 2716
By Sir Charles Barry, 1843–5. Replaces a modest village church condemned by Archdeacon Hare in 1841 as 'a miserable piece of patchwork'. Barry's church contains fittings from the earlier building, including two 13th- and 14th-century monuments of knights. In the S. aisle and tower are 15th–16th-century glass medallions inserted in 1861. Other windows by Hardman, designed by J. H. Powell.

KINGSTON BUCI

St Julian

between Shoreham and Portslade, by the sea
TQ 2205
11th- and 13th-century. Interior with some box pews and a very rare early 18th-century singing desk. Two-decker pulpit. Painted early 19th-century texts on walls. Interior recently spoiled by close carpeting.

LEWES

TQ 4110
St Michael

Late 13th-century round tower; church rebuilt 1748 with curious wooden N. arcade; 15th-century brasses.

MAYFIELD

St Dunstan

8m/12km S. of Tunbridge Wells TQ 5826
Solid tower with shingled spire. Church burned in 1389, and rebuilt afterwards; arcades and clerestory later. Font 1666; 18th-century chandeliers. Harmer terracottas in the churchyard.

NEW SHOREHAM

St Mary de Haura

6m/10km W. of Brighton TQ 2105
Stately grey church of Caen stone in small seaport. Looks monastic, but was always parochial. Only the tower, transepts, and unusually long chancel and aisles remain. The E. bay of the nave is built up as a porch. Transepts and lower part of tower c. 1130; the rest from about 1175 to beginning of 13th century. Rich details in carving and capitals of N. arcade; clustered columns on S. Triforium stages also different on N. and S. Lancet clerestory, stone vaults.

NEWHAVEN

St Michael

9m/15km E. of Brighton TQ 4401
Norman tower and apsidal chancel, illustrated in several books. The nave poorly rebuilt in 1854. Churchyard with a good tombstone to Thos. Tipper with an amusing rhyme and a carving of Newhaven bridge.

NEWICK

St Mary

4m/6km W. of Uckfield TQ 4121
Norman and Perpendicular. Excellently restored by J. O. Scott, 1886–7, who rebuilt the chancel and decorated with sumptuous stencilling, tiles, and gesso. Reredos reminiscent of Burne-Jones. In S. window of chancel two 14th-century Agnus Dei medallions.

NORTH MARDEN

St Mary

6m/10km S.E. of Petersfield SU 8016
Minute Norman church of nave and apse, approached through farmyard. Dark and mysterious inside. Good 18th-century altarpiece consisting of Creed, Decalogue, and Lord's Prayer, now in nave. The church is still lit by candles.

NORTH STOKE

(dedication unknown)

2m/3km N. of Arundel TQ 0210
Very attractive. Nave 12th-century, chancel 13th-century; transepts with early tracery. Hardly touched by restorers. Two stained glass panels of the Coronation of the Virgin, c. 1290–1300.

OLD SHOREHAM
St Nicholas
to N. of Shoreham-by-Sea, 6m/10km W. of
Brighton TQ 2105
Looks across Adur to Lancing College. Pre-Conquest work in the nave; the Normans extended it, and built the central tower and chancel. The tower has arcading and round openings. Good texture of flint and rough-cast walls. Tower arches richly chevroned. A beam with billet moulding. Early 14th-century screen, and painted 19th-century chancel roof. Church restored by Cambridge Camden Society in 1841, and by R. C. Carpenter, 1854. Before its restoration, J. M. Neale described it as resembling 'the dungeon of a criminal rather than . . . the house of the Lord'.

PAGHAM
St Thomas of Canterbury
4m/6km W. of Bognor Regis SZ 8897
C. 1200, and later; W. end with remarkable wheel window, by J. Elliott of Chichester, 1837. Good 18th-century tombstones in churchyard.

PARHAM
St Peter
2m/3km S.E. of Framlingham TM 3060
In the park near Elizabethan house. Small Perpendicular church, remodelled early 19th century. Georgian box pews, pulpit and screen. Squire's pew with fireplace. Strawberry Hill Gothic vaulting to chancel. Rare lead font, 14th-century, with Lombardic lettering. Small Royal Arms.

PENHURST
St Michael
4m/6km W. of Battle TQ 6916
Small Perpendicular church with tile-capped tower, standing high and alone by a farmhouse of the same date, overlooking Ashburnham Park. Inside, walls scraped but old fittings remain untouched, including Perpendicular screen, 17th-century pulpit, lectern, altar rails, and elegant font cover. Nave has oak seating with doors, and panelled walls, 17th-century; 15th-century stained glass canopies and angels in E. window.

PEVENSEY
St Nicholas
4m/6km N.E. of Eastbourne TQ 6404
Now a shrunken inland village, but formerly a thriving seaport. Church, mostly 13th-century, looks seaward, a few hundred yards E. of the castle. Inside, spacious and dignified, built of green sandstone, which casts a grey-green light over all. Good Early English work; 17th-century alabaster monument to John Wheatley, with recumbent figure.

PLAYDEN
St Michael
1m/2km N. of Rye TQ 9121
Graceful shingled spire, a landmark for miles across marshes. Well proportioned inside and out. Roof of golden-red tiles over nave and S. aisle. Late 12th-century arcades and chancel; 17th-century ladder to belfry. Perpendicular chancel screen, and good Decorated screen with flamboyant tracery behind choir seats. Georgian Royal Arms.

POYNINGS
Holy Trinity
6m/10km N.W. of Brighton TQ 2612
In 1368 Michael de Ponyngges left 200 marks toward the building of a new church, and in 1369 Joan, his wife, left the same amount. Like Alfriston, an example of the transition from Decorated to Perpendicular. Cruciform, with a central tower; a Greek cross in plan. Two family pews and rare three-sided altar rails. The 13th-century tiles in the chancel were recommended as a model for copying in J. M. Neale's *A Few Words to Church Builders*, 1841.

PRESTON
St Peter
1m/2km N. of Brighton TQ 3006
13th-century two-cell church, the tower of which butts into the garden of Preston Manor. Interior has early 14th-century wall-paintings of the Murder of Becket, Weighing of Souls, Nativity, and Last Supper. Nave scraped by James Woodman in 1872, but Ewan Christian's restoration of the chancel in 1878 has left attractive stencilling and well-carved choir-stalls. Nave glass probably by Lavers, Barraud and Westlake. Good armorial glass commemorating the Stanfords of Preston Manor in the chancel.

ROTHERFIELD
St Denys
3m/4km E. of Crowborough TQ 5529
Hill-top Wealden village of brick and tiled cottages. Large sandstone church with tapering shingled spire. Two restorations

have left the interior unspoiled. Wall-paintings of Doom over chancel arch, and Annunciation over entrance to N. chapel. Nave has wagon roof, and is furnished throughout with deal box pews, slightly raised towards the W. Elaborate canopied pulpit, c. 1630, came here from Archbishop of York's private chapel. Font cover, 1533, has Arms of Nevills. Large Perpendicular E. window has glass by Burne-Jones, reminiscent of a William Morris wallpaper. Iron tomb slab with double cross. Georgian Royal Arms.

RYE
St Mary
9m/15km N.E. of Hastings TQ 9220
Large cruciform church, on top of the hill on which the town is built, approached by ancient, narrow streets, some still cobbled. Copies of the original quarter-boys on clock strike the hours. Flying buttresses support E. end. Mainly 13th-century, but partly rebuilt after damage in late 14th and 15th centuries. Tie-beam and king-post roof. A long gilt pendulum swings under tower. Large Royal Arms, Queen Anne. Superb mahogany holy table, c. 1740. Early 16th-century pulpit with linenfold panels, the only example of its date in Sussex. W. window and window in S. transept commemorate E. F. and A. C. Benson. In N. aisle a Burne-Jones window of 1897.

ST LEONARDS-ON-SEA
adjoins Hastings to W. TQ 8009
Christ Church, Church Road
1878–81, by Sir Arthur Blomfield. Large, First Pointed church, nave and chancel in one, and octagonal tower and spire; impressively placed. Richly furnished in the most lavish S. coast manner.
St John the Evangelist, Upper Maze Hill
The church by Sir Arthur Blomfield, 1881, was destroyed in the Second World War, apart from the octagonal tower. The rest of the church was rebuilt by Goodhart-Rendel in 1951, and is one of his most interesting works, in brick, richly ornamented, with unusual details within and without. Stained glass by Ledger.
St Peter, Boham's Road
1884–5; severe brick Early English by James Brooks. Remarkable Geometric nave arcade capitals. Another successful seaside church.

SALEHURST
St Mary
5m/8km N. of Battle TQ 7424
Largely 13th- and 14th-century church. Memorable for the stained glass in the S.E. and S.W. windows of c. 1400 with exquisitely drawn birds. Font with 13th-century base of four salamanders, emblematic of baptism; the bapitized, like the salamander, could pass through the fire of temptation. Good Victorian bier. Attractive and atmospheric churchyard.

SELHAM
St James
3m/4km E. of Midhurst SU 9320
Set in beautiful countryside. Small 11th-century church. Chancel arch with remarkable carved capitals, one carved with interlace and foliage, the other with a monstrous head.

SENNICOTTS
St Mary
1m/2km N.W. of Chichester SU 8607
By itself in a park. Built in 1829 and attributed to George Draper of Chichester. Rustic Gothic interior with box pews.

SHERMANBURY
St Giles
2m/3km N. of Henfield TQ 2118
Small church in park repaired in 1710 in countrified Georgian. The inside is unspoiled; Royal Arms (Queen Anne), pews with the names of the occupants, and their addresses, painted on them. In a glass case, the recorders and viol used by the gallery minstrels. Timber chancel arch. W. gallery with organ.

SOMPTING
St Mary
2m/3km N.E. of Worthing TQ 1705
Overlooks Worthing from S. slope of Downs. Famous tower, the lower stage Saxon, the upper stage late 11th-century, and the 'Rhenish helm' spire early 14th-century. Tower arch with crude acanthus capitals, and volutes. The rest of the church rebuilt in late 12th century. N. transept has two E. chapels, stone-vaulted; S. transept, the Templars' Chapel, originally separate from church. Ruined 14th-century chapel at N.W. built by the Knights Hospitaller.

SOUTH HARTING
St Mary & St Gabriel
3m/4km S.E. of Petersfield SU 7820
Large farming village at extreme W. of the Downs; cruciform church, with copper-covered spire, well placed at the top of the street. Rebuilt and enlarged about the beginning of the 14th century; plain nave arcades, with no capitals. A fire in 1576, and church repaired afterwards, with new roofs, elaborate in the chancel. S. transept has monument to Cowper and Coles families, with painted recumbent figures, one above the other; a third kneels in prayer. Wall-monument by Westmacott to Sir Henry Fetherstonhaugh of Uppark. War memorial by Eric Gill.

SOUTHEASE
St Peter
3m/4km S. of Lewes TQ 4205
Small reduced church on a slope in the Ouse Valley; flint rubble walls of pleasant texture, large brick buttresses, hipped roof, and round tower with shingled spire. Inside, walls keep their plaster, with wall-paintings of 13th and 14th centuries. Curious wooden chancel arch. Pulpit and rails 17th-century. Commandment boards; Arms of George III.

STEYNING
St Andrew
5m/8km N.W. of Shoreham-by-Sea TQ 1711
Set back behind long street of tile-hung and half-timbered houses; 12th-century; lofty, spacious and massive, with a clerestory; chancel arch 38 feet high. Imposing arcades, with chevron mouldings. Huge tile-capped tower of flint and stone chequerwork, built after 1577 in place of a central tower. Royal Arms, Queen Anne. Behind the altar, fine 16th-century panelling originally in the vicarage.

TICEHURST
St Mary
3m/4km S.E. of Wadhurst TQ 6830
Mostly 14th-century; 16th-century font cover with folding doors and flamboyant tracery. Some 14th-century glass in the N. aisle. The high point of the church is the vividly coloured 15th-century Doom in the chancel. Good painted former reredos, signed by John Marten, 1764. Superb Victorian bier.

TILLINGTON
All Hallows
1m/2km W. of Petworth SU 9622
Memorable for its tower with a Scots crown of 1807, designed as an 'eyecatcher' to be seen from the Park. It is possible that Turner, who painted at nearby Petworth, had something to do with the design. The church features sketches by Turner and Constable.

TORTINGTON
St Thomas
2m/3km S.W. of Arundel TQ 0005
Small and rustic, among farm buildings of mellow Georgian house. Flint walls and white wooden turret. Richly carved Norman S. doorway, chancel arch of hard chalk with beak-heads and grotesques. Norman font with arcading and cable moulding; 17th-century pulpit.
R.C.F.

TROTTON
St George
3m/4km W. of Midhurst SU 8322
Near Little Rother, spanned here by a medieval bridge. Church, *c.* 1300, of nave and chancel under one roof, with no chancel arch. Brass to Lady Margaret Camoys, 1310, oldest in England to a woman. Large table-tomb with canopied brasses to Thomas, Lord Camoys, an Agincourt hero, 1419, and his wife. W. wall covered with large and unusually well-preserved late 14th-century wall-paintings, including a Doom, the Good Man and the Works of Mercy, and the Bad Man and the Seven Deadly Sins. A rare representation of Moses is also included; 17th-century communion rails; Georgian Royal Arms.

UP WALTHAM
St Mary the Virgin
5m/8km S.W. of Petworth SU 9413
In a fold of the Downs. Small and rustic. Norman nave and apse, with later windows. Inside candle-lit, with good modern bronze 'spiders'. Plain, solid oak seating. One of only four apsidal churches in the county.

UPMARDEN
St Michael
5m/8km W. of Singleton SU 7914
A beautiful little 13th-century church, behind a farm, in a remote part of W. Downs. Of the greatest simplicity, and unrestored;

walls plastered, in and out, brick floors, and a few box pews. Though not used, it is looked after, and there is no feeling of dereliction. One of those churches in which everything is just right, still lit by candles.

WADHURST
St Peter & St Paul
6m/10km S.E. of Tunbridge Wells TQ 6431
12th–15th-century. Vaulted porch and shingled spire. Inside scraped. Thirty inscribed iron tomb slabs, 1617–1790.

WARBLETON
St Mary
3m/4km S.E. of Heathfield TQ 6018
13th–15th-century; squire's pew, 1722, supported on wooden pillars. Brass of Dean Prestwick, Prior of Battle, 1436. Monument of St John Lade, 1740, by Rysbrack. Attractive former reredos on S.W. wall, probably by Heaton, Butler & Bayne. In the churchyard, the site of the house of Richard Woodman, one of the Sussex martyrs.

WARMINGHURST
Holy Sepulchre
3m/4km N. of Washington TQ 1116
Stands on walled bank at end of a lane. Small 13th-century church with a complete set of 18th-century deal furnishings: handsome triple-arched screen, pulpit, and box pews. Gay Royal Arms beneath crimson canopy, with azure surround, painted on plaster above screen. Hatchments, wrought-iron crane for font canopy, two 18th-century monuments, good 17th-century brass to the Shelley family. Altar rails and table late 17th-century.

WEST CHILTINGTON
St Mary
3m/4km E. of Pulborough TQ 0918
Unspoiled 11th- and 12th-century church of nave and S. aisle, with shingled belfry and spire. Chevroned N. doorway and massive Transitional S. arcade with scalloped capitals. Curious chancel arch, high, narrow, and recessed. At E. end of S. aisle 12th-century wall-paintings and, in the nave, 13th-century murals of the Life of Christ. In a window splay a rare 15th-century scene of Christ of the Trades; the Saviour's flesh is ripped by tools used on the Sabbath. Medieval altar slab; Jacobean linenfold pulpit; 1611 'breeches' Bible. Stocks and whipping-post by the church gate.

WEST DEAN
All Saints
2m/3km S. of Alfriston TV 5299
Downland setting. Norman church with 14th-century alterations. Two medieval monuments in the chancel and two 17th-century monuments. Bronze bust of Sir Oswald Birley by Clare Sheridan, and bust of Lord Waverley by Epstein; 13th-century rectory.

WEST GRINSTEAD
St George
3m/4km S.W. of Cowfold TQ 1720
By the Adur. Stone slab roofs, and low shingled spire. Early Norman N. side; aisle, tower, etc. 13th-century; 15th-century timber porch. Old, solid seating, painted with house names. Brasses. Monuments of William Powlett, 1746, by Rysbrack, Sir Merrik Burrell, 1787, by N. Smith, Sir William Burrell, 1796, by Flaxman. Monochrome Royal Arms, George IV. Good Kempe glass in the E. window.

WEST LAVINGTON
St Mary Magdalene
½m/1km S.E. of Midhurst SU 8920
Built in 1850 by Wm. Butterfield for Archdeacon, later Cardinal, Manning, when he was rector of Wool Lavington. Simple in style, resembling many W. Sussex medieval churches; chiefly remarkable for Butterfield's restraint in design and use of material. The *Ecclesiologist* noticed a 'tendency to prefer stiff and quaint forms'. Good glass by Hardman. Decorated rectory also by Butterfield.

WESTHAM
St Mary
4m/6km N.E. of Eastbourne TQ 6404
Stands just W. of Pevensey Castle. Norman nave and S. transept. Massive early 14th-century tower, and N. aisle added in 14th century. Inside scraped, but has a Perpendicular screen to Lady Chapel, and 13 small panels of 15th-century glass in E. window.

WINCHELSEA
St Thomas the Apostle
2m/3km S.W. of Rye TQ 9017
New town laid out in 1283; formerly one of the Cinque Ports, now an inland village of brick cottages, guarded by three grey medieval gateways. Houses grouped around large, open churchyard, and weathered fragment

of church, completed early in 14th century. Only choir and aisles; the rest was destroyed in raids by French, or never completed. Windows filled with glass by Strachan, highly coloured and heavily leaded. Richly canopied sedilia and piscina, with crocketed gables. In S. aisle, two canopied 14th-century tombs of Alards, with recumbent effigies. Three similar and slightly earlier tombs in N. aisle.

WISBOROUGH GREEN
St Peter ad Vincula
2m/3km W. of Billinghurst TQ 0525
11th- or early 12th-century; aisles later; chancel rebuilt 13th century and restored by Ewan Christian in 1867. In 13th century the curious low tower was built in S.W. corner. Porches 15th-century. A few 16th-century benches with names of farms; 13th-century wall-paintings of Christ and St James and a Crucifixion.

WITHYHAM
St Michael
6m/10km S.W. of Tunbridge Wells TQ 4935
Struck by lightning in 1663 and rebuilt. Bits of the original 14th-century church re-used. Doom over the chancel arch by the rector, Earl de la Warr, *c.* 1856; 14th- and 15th-century Italian painting in S. aisle. Sackville monuments; the best is that of Richard, Earl of Dorset, and Thomas his son, by C. G. Cibber – table-tomb with effigy of the boy, his two parents kneeling on either side. Others by Flaxman and Chantrey.

WOOLBEDING
All Hallows
1m/2km N.W. of Midhurst SU 8722
Attractive setting close to the Hall. Saxon nave walls with pilaster strips; 16th-century glass, originally from the Chapel of the Holy Ghost, Basingstoke.

WORTH
St Nicholas
2m/3km E. of Crawley TQ 3036
Forms a secluded group with the old rectory. Church, 11th-century, is cruciform, with untouched ground plan, except for the tower added in 1871. Outside walls have a string course round nave and apsidal chancel. Inside, the 22-foot-high chancel arch, one of the largest Saxon arches in England, has a rugged dignity. The arches to the transepts, 15 feet high, are equally massive. Two-light windows in nave, with baluster shafts. Carved pulpit from Germany, 1577; altar rails probably of same date and origin. Gallery at W. given by Anthony Linton, d. 1610. Glass by Willement in S. transept. Damaged by fire in 1986.

WORTHING
St Andrew
10m/16km W. of Brighton TQ 1402
By Sir Arthur Blomfield, 1885. Flint, in 13th-century style, with apsidal baptistry. Particularly worth visiting to see the excellent collection of Kempe glass, most of which was originally in All Souls, Brighton.
St Paul
By J. B. Rebecca, 1812. Impressive Greek Doric portico and cupola. Altered inside and chancel added 1893.

YAPTON
St Mary
3m/5km W. of Littlehampton
Largely unrestored exterior with pretty 17th-century dormers. Fine 12th-century capitals to nave arcades. Good king-post nave roof. E. window by P. M. Johnston, 1905.

Warwickshire

Introduction

Leafy Warwickshire the guidebooks call it, though no one has planted trees in Warwickshire for generations and one day, I suppose, the oaks of Arden will die out. The county was once split between Arden, the woodland of the north, and Feldon, the corn valley of the south. Across the 'sandy grownde' of Arden, 'betar wooded than fertile of corne', now creep the suburban tentacles of Birmingham: out beyond Sutton, Castle Bromwich and Solihull.

Elsewhere in Arden are the homes of the *nouveaux riches*, around Knowle, Lapworth and Ullenhall, the currently fashionable areas, whence this nomadic race of latter-day landed gentry may move on, farther afield, frightened by the prospect of a 'new town' near Alcester. Respectable Leamington is still in favour, despite a genteel shabbiness hanging over the Regency squares – but there is talk of new industry here, too.

The greater part of the county is quite practical and down-to-earth and has fewer great estates than other counties. The mining districts of the north-east retain their own character with their blue brick, mellowing now, after a century, and their man-made landscapes of pit mounds and power stations, the former encountered by surprise among the woods and lanes of a still rural countryside. We find no great churches in North Warwickshire, where, in the Middle Ages, there was poverty and meagre population, but some steeples of a local red sandstone pierce the gentle rise and fall of the horizon.

The Bard reigns in the Avon Valley, and the Shakespearean villages and their churches benefit by a constant stream of tourists from the three corners of the world. The remoter villages of the south, with no Shakespearean links, are the poor relations of 20th-century Warwickshire, for here the drift from the land has left the countryside still and quiet. The towns and large villages – Shipston, Alcester, Henley – dream through the weekdays but are shocked into a parody of their ancient bustling life by the internal combustion engine, which invades at weekends, when the ice-cream flows as freely as the water of Avon.

If the motor roads are crowded, the canals and some of the railways of Warwickshire are tranquil now – and seedy and nostalgic. Here, and in the villages that are not on the road to anywhere, is a wistful, apprehensive calm; the atmosphere perhaps in any of the hundred Warwickshire villages before they died in the enclosures of Tudor days – leaving sometimes a dusty, ruined church behind them.

R. S. M.

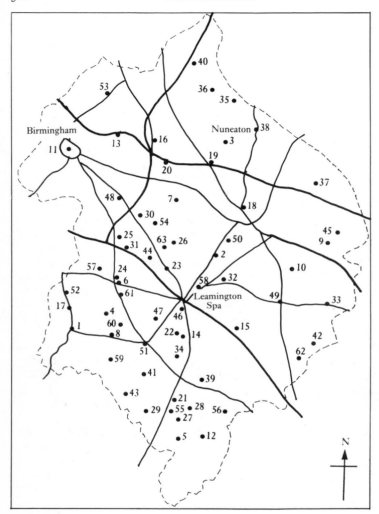

• 40

53 •

36 •

35 •

Nuneaton • 38

Birmingham

13 • 16

• 3

11 •

19

20

• 37

48 •

7 •

18

30 •

54

45 •

25 •

63 • 26

50

9 •

31 •

44

2

57 •

24

23

10

6

58 • 32

52 •

61

Leamington

49

33

17 •

Spa

1 •

4 •

47 •

46

60 •

22 •

14

15

8

34

51

42

59 •

62

41 •

39

43 •

21

29 •

55 • 28

56 •

27

5 •

12

N

1	Alcester	22	Hampton Lucy	43	Quinton
2	Ashow	23	Haseley	44	Rowington
3	Astley	24	Henley-in-Arden	45	Rugby
4	Aston Cantlow	25	Hockley Heath	46	Sherbourne
5	Barcheston	26	Honiley	47	Snitterfield
6	Beaudesert	27	Honington	48	Solihull
7	Berkeswell	28	Idlicote	49	Southam
8	Billesley	29	Ilmington	50	Stoneleigh
9	Bilton	30	Knowle	51	Stratford-upon-Avon
10	Birdingbury	31	Lapworth	52	Studley
11	Birmingham	32	Leamington Spa	53	Sutton Coldfield
12	Brailles	33	Lower Shuckburgh	54	Temple Balsall
13	Castle Bromwich	34	Loxley	55	Tredington
14	Charlecote	35	Mancetter	56	Tysoe
15	Chesterton	36	Merevale	57	Ullenhall
16	Coleshill	37	Monk's Kirby	58	Warwick
17	Coughton	38	Nuneaton	59	Welford-on-Avon
18	Coventry	39	Pillerton Hersey	60	Wilmcote
19	Fillongley	40	Polesworth	61	Wooton Wawen
20	Great Packington	41	Preston-on-Stour	62	Wormleighton
21	Halford	42	Priors Hardwick	63	Wroxall Abbey

Selected List of Churches

ALCESTER
St Nicholas
7m/11km W. of Stratford-upon-Avon SP 0857
Medieval tower; nave and aisles rebuilt by
Edward and Thomas Woodward, 1729–30.
Gothic exterior with window tracery of
1870–1 but classical inside with Tuscan
columns.

ASHOW
Assumption of Our Lady
2m/3km S.E. of Kenilworth SP 3170
Setting beside the Avon. Norman and Early
English with Perpendicular tower. Good
16th-century nave roof with bosses; 18th-
century pulpit and box pews.

ASTLEY
St Mary the Virgin
4m/6km S.W. of Nuneaton SP 3189
The village is a cluster of cottage gardens
and trees on the fringe of the N. Warwickshire coalfield. The church was concocted
in 1608 from the 14th-century chancel of
the old cruciform collegiate church. A tower
added at the W. end and a new low chancel at
the E., all in the old Perpendicular tradition.
The fine early 15th-century choir-stalls,
painted with figures of the Apostles, share
the nave with 18th-century box pews and
Victorian benches.

ASTON CANTLOW
St John the Baptist
4m/6km N.E. of Alcester SP 1359
Medieval church in 'leafy Warwickshire'.
Early English and Decorated with Perpendicular font, 17th-century pulpit and glass
by Kempe.

BARCHESTON
St Martin
½m/1km S.E. of Shipston-on-Stour SP 2639
Chiefly late 13th- and 14th-century with
a Perpendicular clerestory. Good alabaster
tomb of William Willington, d. 1555.

BEAUDESERT
St Nicholas
adjoins Henley-in-Arden to E. SP 1566
Both hamlet and church lie hidden down a
narrow lane off Henley High Street, with a
medieval castle mound next to the churchyard. Chosen as typical of a number of
Norman churches in the county with narrow
nave and chancel, good chancel arches and
a later tower at the W. end. The handsome
Norman chancel was given a good pseudo-
Norman vault by Thomas Garner in 1865.

BERKSWELL
St John the Baptist
6m/10km W. of Coventry SP 2479
A secluded black, white and red village with
stocks, pump and smithy. This is the richest
Norman church in the county with a vaulted
crypt beneath the chancel extending into an
octagonal bay under part of the nave. The
black and white of the two-storey timber
porch enlivens the grey of the masonry.

BILLESLEY
All Saints
4m/6km W. of Stratford-upon-Avon SP 0980
A small church of 1692 but re-using some
earlier fabric; see the blocked N. door.
Classical interior retains family pew with a
fireplace.
     R.C.F.

BILTON
St Mark
S.W. district of Rugby SP 4873
Decorated, but heavily restored by Bodley
in 1873; note his characteristic decoration
of the chancel. The handsome 17th-century
organ case and altar rails came from Cambridge, and there is some 14th-century glass.

BIRDINGBURY
St Leonard
4m/6km N. of Southam SP 4368
Handsome Georgian Doric W. façade,
otherwise attacked in 1873 by Gothic enthusiasts. Inside are an elegant marquetry
pulpit and box pews which survived the
assault.

BIRMINGHAM
St Martin, Bull Ring
The old parish church of Birmingham. It

was cased in brick in 1690, and altered and enlarged several times in the 18th century. The tower and spire, restored by P. C. Hardwick in 1853–5, show scarcely a trace of old work. The rest of the church was entirely rebuilt by J. A. Chatwin in 1873–5. Four medieval monuments remain.

St Paul, St Paul's Square
By Roger Eykyn of Wolverhampton, consecrated in 1799. The steeple was added by Francis Goodwin in 1823. A good example of an 18th-century church, not much altered. The E. window glass, 1791, designed by Benjamin West, executed by Francis Eginton. 'Probably the finest remaining example of English 18th-century glass painting' (Martin Travers). Fine bust of his father by Peter Hollins.

St Peter & St Paul, Aston
15th-century W. tower, the rest by J. A. Chatwin, 1879–90; with the nearby Jacobean 'great house', forming an oasis in a desert of brick and slate. A substantial church in an opulent version of the Decorated style with apsidal chancel, broad nave and fine hammer-beam roof. Apart from the structure, Aston's chief pride is in its monuments; good 15th-century effigies and works by Hollins, Rysbrack and Westmacott.

St Alban, Bordesley
By J. L. Pearson, 1879–81; tower and spire added by E. F. Reynolds in 1938. An expensive Gothic church of red brick with Bath stone dressings. The whole of the interior is vaulted in this architect's most thoroughgoing manner, terminating in an apse with ambulatory at the E. end. Splendid setting for ceremonial.

St James, Edgbaston
By S. S. Teulon, 1851–2. A good instance of the adapted Franciscan cruciform ground plan with broad unaisled nave. Stone exterior with low eaves and prominent roof; inside there are heavy hammer beams.

Church of the Ascension, School Road, Hall Green
Elegant little Queen Anne church with Doric pilasters, dated 1704, in attractive surroundings. Matching chancel and transepts added in 1860.

St Mary, Handsworth
Medieval remains of no great interest. Repeatedly enlarged in the 19th century and largely rebuilt by Chatwin in 1874–9. But an unusual number of 18th- and 19th-century monuments, including two great pioneers of the Industrial Revolution – Matthew Boulton, 1809, and James Wyatt, 1819 – with a handsome seated figure by Chantrey.

St Nicholas, King's Norton
Large medieval church in a pleasant setting with fine 15th-century tower and spire. Late 13th-century arcades and good Decorated chancel arch with ballflowers.

St Lawrence, Northfield
Splendid 13th-century chancel containing the best Early English work in the county. N. aisle added by G. F. Bodley in 1900.

St Matthew, Perry Beeches
By Robert Maguire and Keith Murray, 1962–4. Built in buff brick with concrete bands and angular lead-covered roofs around an hexagonal core. The interior is spacious and dramatically lit by shafts of light which penetrate the wedge-shaped windows. Contemporary fittings include a font built of blue engineering bricks.

St Mary, Selly Oak
By Edward Holmes, 1861. Straightforward Decorated design enlivened by striped sandstone walls, steeply pitched patterned tile roof and a soaring Lincolnshire-type spire. Good font by Butterfield; glass and other fittings by Hardman.

St Aidan, Herbert Road, Small Heath
By Thomas Proud, 1893–8. Successful Perpendicular design in red brick and terracotta. Tall and spacious with a broad chancel. Good High Church plan and fittings; the rood and screen of 1912 by F. Bligh Bond.

St Oswald, Small Heath
By W. H. Bidlake, 1892–3; W. front added in 1899. A brick and stone church in the Early English and Decorated styles. Spacious painted interior with good roofs and lit by lancets. The impressive oak rood screen was designed by the architect as a war memorial.

St Agatha, Sparkbrook
By W. H. Bidlake, 1899–1901. An exceedingly imposing and successful town ch. W. tower with sculptured front, and a projecting baptistry and porches on each side with carved tympana. The nave has piers without capitals, a rather tall clerestory and simple painted roof; the aisles broaden out into chapels. The chancel was completely wrecked by bombing, and the interior has been damaged by fire since then. This was the final flowering of 19th-century Gothic: there was no more development possible on these lines, though churches of this type were built for ten years longer.

St John the Evangelist, Sparkhill
By Martin & Chamberlain, 1888; nave extended and spire added in 1896. Church of orange brick and terracotta in Venetian Gothic style with buttressed tower and spire. Unaisled nave, shallow transepts and apsidal chancel, all spanned by cast-iron arches. Good Arts and Crafts glass by Benjamin J. Warren.

BRAILES
St George
3m/4km E. of Shipston-on-Stour SP 3039
The village never recovered from a body-blow dealt by enclosures in the 16th century. The church, known as 'The Cathedral of the Feldon', is left as a memorial to its medieval greatness. The Perpendicular steeple is a good example of those of the Cotswold fringe, and the nave and aisles are good Decorated work. The interior was altered in 1649, and would have been a Commonwealth rarity but for Gothic face-lifting in 1879. There is a good 14th-century font and a 15th-century carved chest.

CASTLE BROMWICH
St Mary & St Margaret
5m/8km E. of Birmingham SP 1489
The Elizabethan Hall adjoins the church, which is a Georgian brick box of 1726–31 by Thomas White of Worcester. The structure actually encloses a medieval timber-framed chapel, its roof hidden behind the tall parapets. Exceptionally complete 18th-century fittings; box pews throughout, very good two-decker pulpit, wrought-iron altar rails and a neat organ in the tiny W. gallery.

CHARLECOTE
St Leonard
4m/6km E. of Stratford-upon-Avon SP 2656
Rebuilt in 1851–3 by John Gibson. An expensive church in the Decorated style, stone-vaulted throughout. In the N. chapel are splendid 17th-century monuments to three generations of the Lucy family, including Shakespeare's 'Justice Shallow'.

CHESTERTON
St Giles
5m/8km S.E. of Leamington SP 3558
Lovely and lonely. A long, low church, mostly Decorated; see the fine S. door with ballflowers, and Perpendicular. Three good Peyto monuments, including one each by Nicholas and John Stone.

COLESHILL
St Peter & St Paul
9m/15km E. of Birmingham SP 1989
Predominantly Georgian town in Warwickshire red brick. The church crowns the steep hill, its red sandstone blending well with the surrounding work. The church was vigorously scraped by the Victorians, but is still essentially a fine 14th- and 15th-century town church. The steeple is the best of a group probably by the same local mason. Well-lit Decorated chancel with handsome N. door. Two 17th-century Digbys were buried here in state, and the late-Norman drum-shaped font is a work of art.

COUGHTON
St Peter
2m/3km N. of Alcester SP 0860
Early 16th-century Perpendicular church with N. doorway and S. Gothic porch of c. 1780. Good original glass and Throckmorton monuments.

COVENTRY
St John the Baptist
Founded as a collegiate church in 1342, but the remaining fabric is mostly Perpendicular. Red sandstone with central tower and tall clerestory lights; restored by Sir Giles Gilbert Scott in 1877; chancel screen by J. O. Scott, 1886.
Holy Trinity
A splendid town church, the spire grouping well with the ruins of the old cathedral nearby. A large Perpendicular church which contains some earlier medieval work, it has been rather over-restored in a number of campaigns from the 17th century onwards. The interior contains stalls with misericords and a fine 15th-century stone pulpit.

FILLONGLEY
St Mary and All Saints
6m/10km N.W. of Coventry SP 2887
Chiefly 14th-century, with Early English W. tower and a good Perpendicular clerestory. Restored by Bodley and Garner; some 14th- and 15th-century glass.

GREAT PACKINGTON
St James
4m/6km S.E. of Coleshill SP 2283
By Joseph Bonomi, 1789–90. An outstanding church built for the fourth Earl of Aylesford who lived at the Hall. The plan is an inscribed cross with a square centre,

four short arms and four lower rooms. The exterior is somewhat austere, the four corner towers with semi-circular lunettes and shallow lead domes. The interior is boldly executed in the gargantuan manner with heavy Greek Doric columns and painted ashlar. Original altarpiece and marble rails. The organ, earlier than the church, is said to have been used by Handel.

HALFORD
St Mary
3m/4km N. of Shipston-on-Stour SP 2645
Standing in a pleasant rural setting. Norman chancel arch with fragmentary rood above; handsome N. doorway with tympanum of an angel; the best Romanesque carving in the county.

HAMPTON LUCY
St Peter ad Vincula
4m/6km E. of Stratford-upon-Avon SP 2557
A good 19th-century hybrid Gothic church, best seen in sunlight from across the Avon in Charlecote Park. The tower is by Thomas Rickman, 1825; the nave and aisles by his partner, Henry Hutchinson; the chancel and N. porch added by Sir Giles Gilbert Scott in 1858. The nave, lofty in proportion to its width, with a sensitive plaster vault, gives an impression of a cathedral in miniature. Cast-iron tracery in Rickman's windows and the splendid 'Life of St Peter' by Willement in the W. window.

HASELEY
St Mary
4m/6km N.W. of Warwick SP 2367
Attractive late-medieval church in a good setting. The unrestored interior has a ceiled wagon roof, box pews, notable 16th-century brasses, monuments and old glass.

HENLEY-IN-ARDEN
St John the Baptist
7m/11km N.W. of Stratford-on-Avon SP 1565
Later 15th-century church, the W. tower beside the High Street. Good S. porch with corbels of king and queen. Interior retains original queen-post roof and pulpit.

HOCKLEY HEATH
St Thomas
10m/16km N.W. of Warwick SP 1572
By John Cotton, 1879. A red-brick church with some blue-brick patterning in a vigorous Early English style. Yellow-brick spire and facing to internal walls, the W. wall with a rose window and three arrow-slit lancets.

HONILEY
St John the Baptist
3m/4km W. of Kenilworth SP 2427
Pretty Baroque church of 1723 with bold W. tower, arched windows and pilasters. Inside, the apse has marble pillars and there are good original fittings including box pews, altar rails, three-decker pulpit and W. gallery.

HONINGTON
All Saints
1m/2km N. of Shipston-on-Stour SP 2642
Near the Hall. Late 13th-century W. tower, but the rest of the church is *c.* 1680–5; arched windows with eared surrounds, an apse, and formal vases on the parapet. Inside are Tuscan arcades and a shallow plaster vault to the nave. Good 17th-century stalls and fine 18th-century monuments.

IDLICOTE
St James
3m/4km N.E. of Shipston-on-Stour SP 2844
Attractive village with good view. Norman, Early English and later. Late 17th-century S. chapel with Tuscan arcade; three-decker pulpit and parts of a fine Jacobean screen.

ILMINGTON
St Mary the Virgin
4m/6km N.W. of Shipston-on-Stour SP 2143
On Cotswold fringe. Basically Norman; see the N. and S. doorways and chancel arch, with Early English chancel. Elaborate 18th-century Gothic monument in churchyard.

KNOWLE
St John the Baptist, St Lawrence & St Anne
3m/4km S.E. of Solihull SP 1876
Substantial Perpendicular church, originally collegiate, with generous three-light windows. Tall 15th-century vaulted screen and stalls with carved misericords.

LAPWORTH
St Mary
1m/2km S.E. of Hockley Heath SP 1671
A secluded village in undulating wooded country. The largely 13th- and 14th-century church is remarkable for a detached tower

and steeple connected by a passage with the N. aisle. The tower is built sheer, without string courses, and with a projecting stair, both unusual features for Warwickshire. The double-storey porch with its two staircases at the W. end is another curiosity; perhaps it was for the display of relics.

LEAMINGTON SPA
SP 3165
All Saints
A fine church, though alien to the Regency character of the town. Designed by the Rev. John Craig and built between 1843 and 1869 in a French Gothic style. An English tower and W. end perversely added by Sir Arthur Blomfield in 1898. The scale of the work is gigantic throughout, particularly in the two transepts. Internally the church suffers the lack of a vault such as Pearson might have given it, and the glass and fittings detract from the serenity of the design.
St Mark
By G. G. Scott Jnr, 1873–9; his principal surviving work. A large brick church in a lively Decorated style with hints of the Perpendicular. Timber-vaulted interior with Scott's original font and handsome painted and gilded organ case.

LOWER SHUCKBURGH
St John the Baptist
5m/8km W. of Daventry SP 4862
By J. Croft, 1864. A somewhat bizarre combination of Early English structure and Eastern influence. Built of yellow and grey banded stone with an hexagonal steeple, numerous gables, and Saracenic arches. The interior boasts bright-red imitation brickwork, serrated arches, and pews with Eastern-style finials.

LOXLEY
St Nicholas
4m/6km S.E. of Stratford-upon-Avon SP 2552
In a deep wooded valley. Small 13th-century church largely rebuilt *c.* 1735–40. The most striking external feature is the vestry, from which the pulpit, set high up on the wall, is approached; 18th-century box pews, altar rails and clear glass.

MANCETTER
St Peter
adjoins Atherstone to S.E. SP 3296
Pleasant setting with old houses and plenty

of trees. Mainly 13th- and 14th-century, with massive Perpendicular tower, 15th-century roof, and much fine 14th-century glass in the chancel.

MEREVALE
St Mary
1m/2km W. of Atherstone SP 2997
Park setting. '*Capella extra portam*' of Cistercian Abbey. Mainly 14th- and 15th-century. Considerable remains of 14th–16th-century glass of high quality, medieval screen from abbey church, 13th-century effigy, and 15th-century brasses.

MONK'S KIRBY
St Edith
6m/10km N.W. of Rugby SP 4683
Imposing 14th-century fabric with some 15th-century recasting. The tower is vaulted and has an elaborate 18th-century Gothic parapet erected after the fall of the spire; 16th-century Fielding monuments.

NUNEATON
SP 3691
St Nicholas
Amongst clipped yews in an industrial town. A large, mostly Decorated and Perpendicular church, the chancel rebuilt in 1852. Good 16th–18th-century monuments.

PILLERTON HERSEY
St Mary the Virgin
3m/4km S.W. of Kineton SP 3048
Fine Early English chancel, rare in Warwickshire, and a nice low-pitched Perpendicular nave roof with bosses of leaves and flowers.

POLESWORTH
St Editha
4m/6km N.W. of Atherstone SK 2602
Church of a Benedictine nunnery, rather messy outside, but containing splendid 12th-century N. arcade of eight bays and 13th-century effigy of an abbess.

PRESTON-ON-STOUR
The Blessed Virgin Mary
3m/4km S. of Stratford-upon-Avon SP 2049
An unspoilt village mixing well the characteristics of the brick, timber and Cotswold-stone districts. The church is a collector's piece, partly rebuilt in fanciful 18th-century Gothic by Edward Woodward of Chipping

Campden for James West, the antiquary, in 1752. The building is set about with yews, and much occupied with the then fashionable idea of sublime melancholy. Inside there is a deal of 17th- and 18th-century glass given over to the 'universal dominion of death'. Death is also recorded in monuments carved by Thomas Scheemakers and the Westmacotts, father and son. There is an interesting Gothic gilded ceiling.

PRIORS HARDWICK
St Mary
5m/8km S.E. of Southam SP 4756
Splendid late 13th-century chancel with triple sedilia carved with foliage. Late 17th-century altar rails; the nave decently rebuilt in 1868.

QUINTON
St Swithin
5m/8km S. of Stratford-upon-Avon SP 1847
Good Norman and later village church with Perpendicular spire and spacious 13th-century chancel. Tomb chest of *c.* 1430 to Lady Joan Clopton with fine brass. Royal arms of Elizabeth I.

ROWINGTON
St Lawrence
6m/10km N.W. of Warwick SP 2069
Secluded setting with clipped yews. Notable cruciform Norman church with central tower of *c.* 1300 and Decorated chancel; 15th-century screen and pulpit and some early glass.

RUGBY
St Andrew
SP 5075
14th–15th-century, substantially enlarged by W. Butterfield, 1875–9; N.E. spire added in 1894–6. Medieval W. tower and part of nave were retained as the N. part of much grander church. Restrained exterior, but inside red and yellow stone is contrasted to great effect and, together with the painted roofs, the impression is glorious. Elaborate chancel fittings, splendid font and pulpit.

SHERBOURNE
All Saints
3m/4km S.W. of Warwick SP 2661
By Sir Giles Gilbert Scott, 1862–4. Expensive estate church with a soaring steeple reflected in a lake. Elegant interior with marble-shafted arcades, impressive alabaster reredos, and stained glass by Clayton & Bell. Monument of 1843 by Pugin in the Ryland Chapel.

SNITTERFIELD
St James the Great
3m/4km N. of Stratford-upon-Avon SP 2159
A handsome church much restored and scraped in 1852; 13th–15th-century with shafted Decorated nave piers and finely carved stalls of *c.* 1530.

SOLIHULL
St Alphege
SP 1479
Good, mostly 13th- and 14th-century cruciform church of red sandstone with spire. Decorated chantry chapel with vaulted undercroft and handsome late 17th-century altar rail with stylish twisted balusters.

SOUTHAM
St James
7m/11km S.E. of Leamington SP 4161
Splendid Perpendicular clerestory of eight two-light windows, and good contemporary traceried roof. Beautiful rood screen with loft by F. H. Crossley.

STONELEIGH
St Mary
3m/4km E. of Kenilworth SP 3372
Norman church of red sandstone with rich chancel arch rejoicing in zig-zags and stylized beak-heads; 12th-century font with Apostles in arcades, good early 19th-century furnishings, and a nice black and white marble monument of 1668.

STRATFORD-UPON-AVON
Holy Trinity
SP 2054
An estimable town church of the 15th century, rarely visited for its own sake, the setting and approach tidied up for the reception of Shakespeare-worshippers. The chancel is brilliant when seen through the dark arches of the central tower; crossing towers are the exception in Warwickshire. The massing of the building is best seen romantically from across the Avon. The steeple is actually a Georgian pastiche by Wm Hiorn of Warwick, 1763. The Bard is buried here.

STUDLEY
The Nativity of the Blessed Virgin Mary
4m/6km S.E. of Redditch SP 0763
Chiefly Decorated with Norman N. doorway. Apart from the rood stair and 17th-century fittings, there is a superb 13th-century coffin lid with exquisite foliated cross, monument to a prior of the vanished monastery. King Henry's own commissioners described the monks here as 'good men', but it didn't save them.

SUTTON COLDFIELD
Holy Trinity
7m/11km N.E. of Birmingham SP 1296
Mostly late-Perpendicular church, too much restored, but still pleasing in its details. Delightful Laudian fittings from Worcester Cathedral and a monument to Bishop Vesey, d. 1554, the deceased in full pre-Reformation episcopal vestments.

TEMPLE BALSALL
St Mary
4m/6km S.E. of Solihull SP 2076
As its name suggests, a foundation of the Knights Templar, who built here a Decorated Geometric box, very good of its kind, which became a favourite with the Ecclesiologists. The roof, with its parapets and pinnacles, and also the present bell-turret, were provided by the first Scott in 1849. A Victorian described Scott's tessellated tiles in the chancel as 'very pretty but rather dangerous to walk on'. The village small but neat with interesting 17th-century almshouses.

TREDINGTON
St Gregory
2m/3km N. of Shipston-on-Stour SP 2543
Saxon nave walls; see the double-splayed windows above the later arcades; otherwise mostly 14th-century with a fine Perpendicular steeple. Decorated benches throughout the nave, carved 17th-century screen, and splendid Jacobean pulpit.

TYSOE
The Assumption of the Blessed Virgin Mary
4m/6km S. of Kineton SP 3445
11th–15th-century fabric. Good Norman S. doorway with Lamb and Cross, octagonal Perpendicular font with crocketed gables, and a 15th-century roof.

ULLENHALL
St Mary the Virgin
2m/3km N.W. of Henley-in-Arden SP 1267
By J. P. Seddon, 1875. Unusual design of the Evangelical persuasion. Built of yellow stone in the Early English style with apsidal E. end and emaciated S.W. spire. Grey marble shafts to the nave arcades and arcaded apse, stencilled wagon roof, and a mosaic of crosses, crowns and fishes under the altar.

WARWICK
St Mary
SP 2865
The most interesting of the Warwickshire town churches. The W. tower over the roadway frames pleasant views of surrounding Georgian houses. Medieval work restricted to the celebrated Beauchamp chapel and the choir with its flying vault. The rest destroyed by fire in 1694 and rebuilt in a Gothic Survival manner by Sir William Wilson, with some interference by Wren. The nave and tower are out of scale with the older work, but Wilson's interior is noble and his vaults and arcades a *tour de force*; there is no clerestory. A fine baroque organ case over the W. lobby. The Beauchamp chapel, a most accomplished and robust example of 15th-century work, contains the delectable shrine of Richard, Earl of Warwick, d. 1439. Notice how the eyes of the effigy gaze in wonder at the tiny figure of God the Father in the E. window.

WELFORD-ON-AVON
St Peter
4m/6km W. of Stratford-upon-Avon SP 1452
Small, mainly Norman and Perpendicular church in pleasant thatched village; 12th-century W. tower and robust arcades with scalloped capitals. Decorated chancel restored by Sir Giles Gilbert Scott, 1866–7.

WILMCOTE
St Andrew
3m/4km N.W. of Stratford-upon-Avon SP 1658
The village of little interest but for a good stone and timber yeoman's house, said to be that of Shakespeare's mother. The church, school and vicarage important in the history of the Oxford Movement; built as a group in the 1840s, partly by W. Butterfield before

his individual style developed. Very dim religious light inside the church, so that the wall decoration, painted on metal sheets, is barely discernible. A deal of blue and gold wallpaper. Everything according to the Ecclesiologists' rules, with triple lancets in the chancel.

WOOTON WAWEN
St Peter
2m/3km S. of Henley-in-Arden SP 1563
The village retains old brick and timber cottages and an interesting mill, but is too near the main Stratford–Birmingham road for its own safety. The church as yet completely unspoiled, with a very strong and authentic atmosphere of the past. Built in stages about its early 11th-century central tower, a rare instance of Saxon work in the county; each generation has made its own contribution, so that the building now appears as three churches in one, two of them little used. Fragments of medieval wall-painting, a Perpendicular pulpit and screens, and numerous monuments from the 15th century onwards.

WORMLEIGHTON
St Peter
8m/12km N. of Banbury SP 4453
Charming hill-top village. Largely 13th-century church with squat W. tower and Perpendicular clerestory. The glory is the 15th-century screen; lofty, richly carved, and with a beautiful vaulted canopy.

WROXALL ABBEY
St Leonard
6m/10km N.W. of Warwick SP 2271
Mainly early 14th-century church, relic of a Benedictine nunnery, the brick W. tower added in 1663–4. Good collection of 14th–15th-century glass and the Wren tombs; Sir Christopher moved here after completing St Paul's.

Westmorland

Introduction

The visitor who finds, and appreciates, the old and remote churches such as those that lie along the western flank of Cross Fell, the final northern thrust of the Pennines, will not thank the guide who thinks duty done by a time-saving assurance that Cumberland and Westmorland have no outstanding buildings. In some of these little hillside churches, men still pray under arches so crude, so expressive of the earliest Christianity in our land, that they can bring tears to eyes that see them struggling to aspire like prayer itself, from simple men in such a far-off day; and there are windows, innocent of stained glass, through which the full views of valley and running water, of fell-side and sky, entering in, are so framed that they seem to some of us glimpses of very Heaven.

There are many of these tiny churches, as at Mardale Green and Martindale, or on the wonderful road that climbs from Brough to Alston. To the east is the great series of fells – Warcop, Burton, Hilton, Marton, Dufton, most of them rising fairly steeply from the plain, with sharp cones or pikes, giving their names to the villages at their feet. Long Marton church, to choose one example, is one of the six churches in the country with one chancel wall built sloping outward to represent our Lord's head hanging on the Cross. There has probably been a church on this site since the 4th century. One stone has Druid symbols, another an Egyptian bird's-head design of great antiquity. Dufton is a typical Westmorland village, with its red sandstone houses, colour-washed, bright with gardens round the village green, facing inward so as here, as at Milburn and Newbiggin and elsewhere, to form a rough compound in which the cattle could be herded against the raids of the marauders. Besides these tiny churches, there are large and interesting ones at Appleby, Kirkby Stephen, Kirkby Lonsdale and Kendal, but no cathedral, as the county is comprehended in the diocese of Carlisle.

F.S.

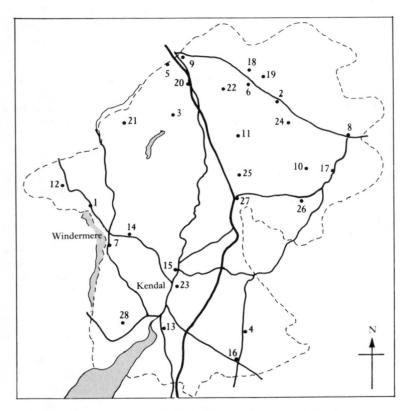

1	Ambleside	11	Crosby Ravensworth	20	Lowther
2	Appleby	12	Grasmere	21	Martindale
3	Bampton	13	Heversham	22	Morland
4	Barbon	14	Ings	23	Natland
5	Barton	15	Kendal	24	Ormside
6	Bolton	16	Kirkby Lonsdale	25	Orton
7	Bowness	17	Kirkby Stephen	26	Ravenstonedale
8	Brough	18	Kirkby Thore	27	Tebay
9	Brougham	19	Long Marton	28	Witherslack
10	Crosby Garrett				

Selected List of Churches

AMBLESIDE
St Mary
4m/6km N.W. of Windermere NY 3704
By Sir Giles Gilbert Scott, 1850–4. Imposing town church of greyish stone with sandstone dressings in late 13th-century 'Second Pointed' style. Prominent S.E. tower with tall broach spire; spacious interior with hammer-beam roof and marble reredos of 1895. Mural by Gordon Ransom of traditional rush-bearing procession, 1944.

APPLEBY
St Lawrence
12m/19km S.E. of Penrith NY 6820
Large Decorated and Perpendicular church set in a beautiful and unspoiled town between the River Eden and the Norman castle on the bluff dominating the ford. Chancel and other works by Lady Anne Clifford, 1654–5, who lies here with her mother; 15th-century screens, 17th-century monuments and a celebrated 16th-century organ case, removed from Carlisle Cathedral.

BAMPTON
St Patrick
3m/4km N.W. of Shap NY 5118
Built in 1726–8 and restored in 1885. W. tower has doorway with broken segmental pediment. Inside are elegant wooden Georgian arcade columns, pulpit and altar rails.

BARBON
St Bartholomew
3m/4km N. of Kirby Lonsdale SD 6282
By Paley & Austin, 1891–3. Beautiful cruciform fell church in a free Perpendicular style, the broad central tower a little wider than the nave. Effective ashlar interior with fine views, some of Austin's squared rose decoration, and a good font with three-stage wooden cover.

BARTON
St Michael
3m/4km S.W. of Penrith NY 4826
12th–13th-century church with low Norman central tower beneath which is a transverse

tunnel vault. Many Perpendicular windows and mid-17th-century altar rail.

BOLTON
All Saints
4m/6km N.W. of Appleby NY 6323
An ancient little stone edifice which somehow achieves nobility. Late Norman chancel, nave and S. porch with doorway. Over the N. door is a charming and celebrated Norman carving of knights jousting – a little treasure. Bell-turret with saddleback roof, 1693; font and cover, 1687; unusual chancel screen of open tracery, probably local work of the late 18th century.

BOWNESS
St Martin
on E. shore of Lake Windermere, adjoins town to S. SD 4096
Consecrated in 1483 and remarkable for the beautiful glass of 1480 in the E. window; ingeniously assembled from various sources, it includes 14th-century glass from Cartmel Priory. Flaxman monument to Richard, Bishop of Llandaff, d. 1816.

BROUGH
St Michael
4m/6km N. of Kirkby Stephen NY 7914
Large and low; Norman but now mostly Early English and Perpendicular with a W. tower of 1513. Austere stone pulpit of 1624.

BROUGHAM
St Ninian
2m/3km S.E. of Penrith NY 5328
Unforgettable. Known locally as 'Ninekirks', it stands surrounded by trees in the middle of a field in a lonely dale by the River Eamont. This was the site of a Saxon church, then a Norman, but today it is just as Lady Anne Clifford rebuilt it in 1660. It is a restrained instance of Gothic Survival with whitewashed interior, oak box and canopied pews, pulpit with sounding board, oak seats with carved arm-rests and screens. Lady Anne's initials, in a laurel surround, appear in the plasterwork over the altar.
R.C.F.

St Wilfrid
An ancient, plain little building of chancel, nave and turret with one bell. It also was restored by Lady Anne Clifford, but was disturbed by the first Baron Brougham and Vaux in the 1840s. The contrast between the two interiors is almost unbelievable. Here is rich cathedral opulence, the church as full as it can be of beautifully carved oak; an elaborate parclose organ casing, pillars, tall pews and a screen with rich round posts and beautiful cornice. The gilt oak reredos has a magnificent 15th-century altarpiece with superb carvings bordered by medieval woodwork of the finest craftsmanship. The pulpit is enriched with medieval carving; the oak roof is divided into panels, each with richly emblazoned shield or crest. Nothing in Westmorland, or indeed anywhere, compares with this plain and simple building outside and the opulence within.

CROSBY GARRETT
St Andrew
3m/4km W. of Kirkby Stephen NY 7209
On a steep hill with fine views. Basically Norman with Decorated chancel and N. aisle of 1866. Above the 12th-century chancel arch is a narrow blocked opening which is probably Saxon.

CROSBY RAVENSWORTH
St Lawrence
5m/8km S.W. of Appleby NY 6214
Set in lovely well-watered valley. Originally 12th-century, but pretentiously rebuilt and enlarged in the Early English style by J. S. Crowther in 1867–86. Good monuments; glass by Clayton & Bell.

GRASMERE
St Oswald
3m/4km N.W. of Ambleside NY 3306
Wordsworth and members of his family are buried in the churchyard and Woolner's monument to the poet is in the church. The rough, massive old church has a notable two-tier arcade, the upper dating from the 17th century. The resulting jungle of black beams is an object lesson in elementary building, ingenious and almost indescribable except by Wordsworth, who had a shot at most things, and declared that the roof was upheld:

By naked rafters intricately crossed,

Like leafless underboughs, mid some thick grove,
All withered by the depth of shade above.

HEVERSHAM
St Peter
2m/3km S. of Levens, which is 5m/8km S. of Kendal SD 4983
Norman in origin but with Perpendicular exterior. Much rebuilt by H. J. Austin in 1867–71; he added the bold Early English W. tower, his first job in partnership with E. G. Paley. Good 9th-century cross shaft with inhabited vine-scrolls.

INGS
St Anne
2m/3km E. of Windermere SD 4498
Built in 1743 by Robert Bateman, a local Dick Whittington. Bateman was a merchant at Leghorn; hence the Renaissance style and marble floor. Brass epitaph to Bateman by Wordsworth: '. . . he grew wondrous rich.'

KENDAL
Holy Trinity
19m/31km N. of Lancaster SD 5192
Prosperous Perpendicular town church outside; the 13th-century nave and aisle enlarged to five aisles, making the whole structure rectangular – a forest of pillars from any viewpoint. Drastically restored in 1850–2.

KIRKBY LONSDALE
St Mary the Virgin
14m/22km N.E. of Lancaster SD 6178
Hidden behind Market Street in this enjoyable small town, the church is approached through 19th-century iron gates below an iron arch. In a lovely setting in the Lune valley, the view from the churchyard is perhaps the finest in the county, praised by Ruskin and painted by Turner, endlessly satisfying. The church has been much modified since its days of Norman greatness from which, however, it retains S. and W. doorways, the latter a fine example of late-Norman work, recessed in four orders and much enriched with zig-zag and other ornament. In the N. arcade are three powerful early-Norman piers and arches bearing Durham-style diapering. Charming six-sided pulpit of 1619, splendid Jacobean cupboard, and glass of Faith, Hope and Charity by Henry Holiday, 1878.

KIRKBY STEPHEN
St Stephen
9m/15km S.E. of Appleby NY 7708
The church was probably founded in the 8th century, rebuilt 13th and 15th centuries, and heavily restored in 1847. It has a cathedral-like nave, Early English in style, stately and impressive. Embattled W. tower of *c.* 1506 replaced a central Early English tower which fell in the 15th century. Inside, an 18th-century bread cupboard curved around a pier and interesting 15th- and 16th-century monuments.

KIRKBY THORE
St Michael
4m/6km N.W. of Appleby NY 6325
12th–14th-century church with 17th-century altar rail and a pulpit of 1631 replete with caryatids, arabesques and arched panels.

LONG MARTON
St Margaret & St James
3m/4km N. of Appleby NY 6624
Early Romanesque, especially the nave with huge quoins. The S. doorway might be as early, its barbarous tympanum adorned with a winged beast and a dragon.

LOWTHER
St Michael
4m/6km S. of Penrith NY 5323
Beautifully placed above the River Lowther. Portions of 12th, 13th and 17th centuries, when the shell was almost completely rebuilt by Sir John Lowther with a dome and lantern on the tower, unfortunately since removed. The church has some splendid Lowther monuments, including William Stanton's John, Viscount Lonsdale, d. 1700, a fine semi-reclining figure. But, the keynote of Lowther family piety is struck by the mausoleum of 1857 outside; reminiscent of Chesney Wold as depicted by Phiz, and one almost looks around for Lady Deadlock.

MARTINDALE
½m/1km S.E. of Sandwick and 2m/3km N. of Lake Ulswater NY 4319
St Martin (Old Church)
1m/2km S. of Martindale
One of the loneliest churches in Westmorland, 1000 feet above the sea; it was for a time disused. The Old Church, originally 11th-century, was renewed in 1633; with its simple bellcote and porch it has an almost domestic appearance; inside is 17th-century woodwork, good carved pulpit and massive beams. It is used for services about three times a year, and has neither heating nor electricity; it is often visited by walkers seeking peace and solitude.
St Peter (New Church)
With only a few farms for company, at the top of the Hause pass, the present church of St Peter was erected in Early English style in 1880 by J. A. Cory in red sandstone with slate roof. It has some good 20th-century glass by Jane Grey in the E. window.

MORLAND
St Lawrence
6m/10km W. of Appleby NY 5922
Setting and village. Large cruciform church with the only Saxon W. tower in the county; narrow doorway to nave and belfry lights with mid-wall shafts. Some Norman work but mostly later; 17th-century woodwork. Reredos by Caroe. Font *c.* 1662, 16th-century pulpit, Royal Arms of George III, Our Father and creed by William Dobson, 18th-century.

NATLAND
St Mark
2m/3km S. of Kendal SD 5289
An inventive church by Paley & Austin, 1909–10. Perpendicular in style with a few Arts and Crafts touches. Powerful tower on big round piers and a lovely interior, fresh in detail.

ORMSIDE
St James
2m/3km S.E. of Appleby across R. Eden NY 7017
Strikingly situated on a conical knoll W. of the River Eden with fine views of Roman Fell. Norman, with strong Scot-repelling tower only eleven feet square. Two beautifully primitive arches with scalloped capitals, strangely disturbing. The oak king-post chancel roof is 400 years old. The famous 9th-century Ormside Bowl, a Saxon treasure of gold and enamel, was dug up in the churchyard in 1823.

ORTON
All Saints
3m/4km N. of Tebay NY 6208
Originally a 13th-century cruciform church, but now mainly Perpendicular, including the

W. tower and nave roof. Inside, a font of 1662 and communion rails, partly Jacobean.

RAVENSTONEDALE
St Oswald
4m/6km S.W. of Kirkby Stephen NY 7204
Delightfully tree-rich hollow among the moorland heights. Fragments of the old church were incorporated in the present interesting Georgian structure of 1738–44. The almost intact interior spoiled by Victorian fiddling. It has a three-decker pulpit, benches arranged college-wise, altar rail, Royal Arms, text boards, and a W. gallery.

TEBAY
St James
10m/16km N.E. of Kendal NY 6104
Bleak and high in the Fells, once a well-known railway junction. By C. J. Ferguson, 1880; paid for by the railway company and its workers. Built in the Early English style of rock-faced Shap granite on a difficult sloping site. Unusual arrangement of apsidal W. baptistry and round tower with conical spire at the N.W. Lively red-brick interior with creamy yellow bands.

WITHERSLACK
St Paul
3m/4km N. of Lindale SD 4384
Church built and endowed in 1669 by John Barwick, DD, a Royalist who became Dean of St Paul's. Restored 1873, but the severe white Classical interior is a perfect foil to the romantic setting of hanging woods and limestone outcrop. An infant Stanley in marble sleeps on one window sill. Good hatchments with angles at the corners; fine Royal Arms of Queen Anne with a jolly lion. The canopied pulpit was once a three-decker, and the altar table is 17th-century.

Wiltshire

Introduction

This large, oblong county is simple to describe. Two-thirds of it are chalk, one-third is 'cheese'. The chalk runs across the county from east to west. The vale of Pewsey, all trees and flint, and brick and cob cottages and thatch and clear streams, divides the areas of chalk into two. The northern half of the chalk is the Marlborough downs where Avebury stands, a vaster and more impressive pre-historic monument than Stonehenge. The southern half is Salisbury Plain, whose cathedral spire gathers the rolling downs around it. The plain is 'like the ocean after a storm, it is continually heaving in large swells. Through all this vast district, scarce a cottage or even a bush appears.' (Rev. W. Gilpin, 1808.) But the valleys in Salisbury Plain, particularly the Wylye and the Ebble, contain charming thatched villages with flint and limestone churches and small manor houses among beeches under the smooth, chalky hills. The plain itself is now much scarred with Army camps and manoeuvre grounds, and Stonehenge does not seem as remote as it did when Constable painted it. The Marlborough Downs, associated with Richard Jefferies, are bolder and with great hills like Martinsell rising like cliffs, and at their feet the thatched habitations of man. Devizes is the capital of the north, Salisbury of the south.

The 'cheese' is a flat limestone dairy country in the north of the county on the banks of the Bristol Avon, and the pull of Bristol is felt in it. Cricklade, Malmesbury, Bradford-on-Avon and Corsham are its most attractive grey-stone towns. Here are grand parish churches, like Malmesbury Abbey, Steeple Ashton and Edington. All the great houses of Wiltshire are below the edges of the downs, except for Wilton and Trafalgar, Littlecote and Ramsbury, which are in downland valleys.

Aubrey summed up the people thus: 'According to the several sorts of earth in England (and so all the world over) the indigenae are respectively witty or dull, good or bad. In North Wiltshire (a dirty clayey country) the indigenae or aborigines speake drawlinge; they are phlegmatique, skins pale and livid, slow and dull, heavy of spirit; hereabout is but little tillage or hard labour; they only milk the cowes and make cheese; they feed chiefly on milke meats, which cools their braines too much and hurts their inventions. These circumstances make them melancholy, contemplative and malicious . . . Contrariwise on the Downes, &c, the south part, there 'tis all upon tillage, and where the shepherds labour hard, their flesh is hard, their bodies strong.

Being weary after hard labour, they have not leisure to read on or contemplate religion, but goe to bed to their rest to rise betimes the next morning to their labour.'

In the present century many square miles of grassy down have been ploughed; only the Army and racehorse trainers have saved some of them. Swindon has grown to be the largest town in the county and factories have transformed the characters of Chippenham and Calne.

The churches of Wilts, except those listed below, were never remarkable as architecture, and the county was unlucky in having, in the 19th century, one of the dullest Victorian architects, Mr T. H. Wyatt, as its chief restorer. His hand is heavy on many a once-old flint church, and for the only interesting new church he built, the Lombardic one at Wilton, he had to have the assistance of the brothers Brandon, architects of more talent and originality.

J.B.

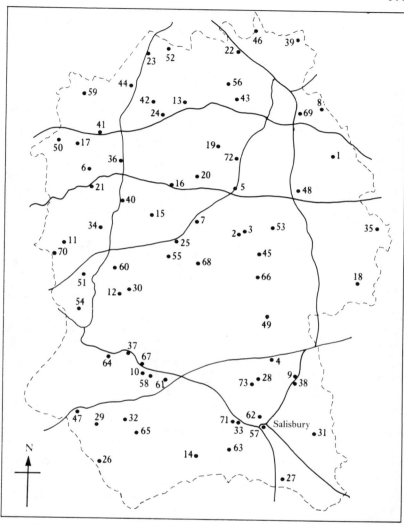

Selected List of Churches

ALDBOURNE
St Michael
6m/10km N.E. of Marlborough SU 2675
Dominating attractive village green; 12th century and later with Perpendicular tower and roofs. E. lancets by Butterfield, 1863–7; 15th-century brass; good 16th–17th-century monuments.

ALTON BARNES
St Mary the Virgin
adjoins Alton Priors to W., 4m/6km N.W. of Pewsey SU 1062
The tiny church is little changed since Augustus Hare was rector 125 years ago. Saxon nave with shallow pilasters; chancel rebuilt in 1748. Jambs of chancel arch Norman, but the arch rebuilt. Inside are a gallery, painted black letter texts, and a Royal Arms of James I.

ALTON PRIORS
All Saints
4m/6km N.W. of Pewsey SU 1162
A stone's throw eastward of Alton Barnes: disused but loved, in the middle of a field criss-crossed by cobbled footpaths. Norman chancel arch, nice Perpendicular roof, stalls, and a fascinatingly conceited brass of 1590.
R.C.F.

AMESBURY
St Mary & St Melor
7m/11km N. of Salisbury SU 1541
Proudly detached from the mundane town. Basically a 13th-century cruciform church refashioned in the 15th century with fine timber roofs. Stone-vaulted chapel off the N. transept, Norman font, 15th-century screen, and remains of medieval painted glass. Heavily restored by William Butterfield in 1853.

AVEBURY
St James
6m/10km W. of Marlborough SU 1069
Beautifully grouped with manor house and village adjoining famous pre-historic stone circle. Notable Saxon nave with aisles added in 12th century, the arcades replaced in 1812. Chancel rebuilt 1879 but retaining 13th-century chancel arch. Good 15th-century tower, 15th-century screen with rood loft, and an early-Norman font.

BIDDESTONE
St Nicholas
4m/6km W. of Chippenham ST 8673
Remarkable Norman doorway with a Byzantine cross; bell-turret of *c.* 1300 over chancel arch. Early 19th-century pews and W. gallery and 18th-century miniature organ.

BISHOP'S CANNINGS
St Mary the Virgin
3m/4km N.E. of Devizes SU 0364
Begun in late-Norman times, to which the nave arcade and porch belong, this is a magnificent 13th-century cruciform church. Perpendicular spire, clerestory, and upper sacristry; the nave roof dated 1670. Inside is fine arcading for recessed altars in the transepts; and the Chapel of Our Lady of the Bower. Fine Ernli monument of 1571 and a unique penitential 'carrel', or chair for meditations, painted with moralizing sentiments; 17th-century alms box.

BISHOPSTONE
St John Baptist
4m/6km S.W. of Wilton SU 0725
Embowered in trees, this is a noble cruciform church wholly remodelled in 14th century. Chancel and transept have lovely windows of late 'flowing' Decorated work. Vaulted chancel and S. transept; the N. transept and nave have timber roofs with plaster panels. Fine sedilia, canopied niches, and founder's tomb in N. transept. Memorial by A. W. N. Pugin and glass by Walles commemorating a rector who brought the Renaissance woodwork of which the stalls and pulpit are made.

BOSCOMBE
St Andrew
7m/11km N.E. of Salisbury SU 2038
Small, towerless flint and tile church with 14th-century nave and chancel and shallow 16th-century N. chapel, in a hollow among

old brick and flint and cob walls. Inside are pale plaster walls, clear glass with a few late-medieval fragments, box pews, and Jacobean three-decker pulpit. Richard Hooker, author of *Laws of Eccelesiastical Politie*, was incumbent here.

BOYTON
St Mary
3m/4km S.E. of Heytesbury ST 9539
Mostly 13th-century church almost in the garden of the Jacobean manor house. Richly moulded Early English doorway beneath N. tower. 14th-century N. chapel, but the real delight is the S. chapel of *c.* 1280 built by Walter and Godfrey Giffard, Archbishop and Bishop of York, for their brother. Huge circular W. window with spherical triangles, and inside an effigy, sedilia, and piscina.

BRADFORD-ON-AVON
3m/4km N.W. of Trowbridge ST 8260
Holy Trinity
The little town rises steeply from the Avon, full of beautiful buildings and picturesque corners. The parish church near the river has a sturdy 15th-century tower and short spire; it is a 12th-century fabric enlarged and refashioned in the 14th, 15th and early 16th centuries. Over-restored interior has 14th-century recessed and canopied tombs either side of the chancel arch. Charming early 14th-century sculpted female head.
St Lawrence
The most notable Saxon church in England. Thought to have been built originally by St Aldhelm *c.* 700, but possibly rebuilt *c.* 1000, it was rediscovered by chance in *c.* 1856 after having been put to secular use for centuries and its true purpose forgotten. The church now stands as one of the oldest, smallest and most numinous churches in the land. Except for some blind arcading, the interior is unornamented save for two ministering angels above the chancel arch, attendants to a vanished rood.

BRATTON
St James
3m/4km E. of Westbury ST 9152
Tucked against the edge of the Plain and approached by a long flight of steps. Cruciform and mostly Perpendicular; Scott Jnr entirely rebuilt the chancel.

BRINKWORTH
St Michael
5m/8km E. of Malmesbury SU 0184
Spacious Perpendicular church, chancel rebuilt in 1889; 18th-century W. gallery, pulpit of 1630 with tester, 17th-century seating.

BROAD CHALKE
All Saints
5m/8km S.W. of Wilton SU 0325
Fine cruciform church in the Chalke Valley, where the willow-fringed Ebble flows lazily through water meadows; 13th-century arcade removed in 15th century and the whole put beneath one roof; the E. responds remain. External treatment of W. end remarkably like Edington and Bishopstone. Late 13th-century chancel and N. transept. John Aubrey, once churchwarden here, described the bells as 'one of the tuneablest rings in Wiltshire'.

BROMHAM
St Nicholas
3m/4km E. of Melksham ST 9665
12th-century origins, but the outstanding feature is the rich Perpendicular S. chapel begun in 1492, complete in all its details including the painted roof. In the centre is the alabaster effigy of Sir Richard Tocotes, d. 1457, and at the E. end two lovely canopied tomb chests of *c.* 1492 and 1593. Excellent E. window by Morris.

CALNE
St Mary
5m/8km E. of Chippenham ST 9971
Mostly 15th-century, but the central tower collapsed in 1628 and was rebuilt on the N. side; 12th-century nave arcades, Perpendicular roof. Arts and Crafts organ case of 1908 by C. R. Ashbee and the Campden Guild.

CASTLE COMBE
St Andrew
5m/8km N.W. of Chippenham ST 8477
At the heart of one of the prettiest villages in Wiltshire, the 15th-century market cross reflecting its medieval wealth. Proud tower of 1436 and delicately carved Perpendicular interior, the chancel arch with canopied statues; 13th-century chancel with effigy of a knight.

CHUTE FOREST
St Mary
5m/8km N.W. of Andover SU 3151
By J. L. Pearson, 1870–5. Flint and red-
brick church in the Early English style.
Austere interior with undivided nave and
chancel, lancets, and bold transverse arches.
Good fittings, reredos and glass by Clayton
& Bell.
R.C.F.

CLYFFE PYPARD
St Peter
4m/6km S. of Wootton Bassett SU 0776
Secretly set beside the manor house; 14th-
century, restored by William Butterfield in
1873–4. Very fine pulpit of 1629; interesting
monuments include that to Thomas
Spackman, carpenter, 1786, showing his
abandoned tools. Sir Nikolaus Pevsner is
buried with his wife in the churchyard.

COMPTON BASSETT
St Swithin
3m/4km E. of Calne SU 0372
Largely Perpendicular with 12th-century N.
arcade and chancel of 1866 by Woodyer.
Fine early 15th-century vaulted stone
screen.

CORSHAM
St Bartholomew
4m/6km S.W. of Chippenham ST 8670
12th- and 15th-century; the harsh Victorian
restoration somewhat redeemed by Street's
tower and spire of 1875–8; 15th-century
vaulted stone porch; chantry chapel with
monument and fan-vaulted screen, *c.* 1470.

CRICKLADE
St Sampson
7m/11km N.W. of Swindon SU 1093
One of the glories of Wiltshire, its great
Tudor central tower dominating the little
town; 12th–16th-century fabric with Saxon
carvings and late 15th-century S. chapel;
good painted glass, altars, and other fittings
by Martin Travers. Fine heraldry in tower
vault.

CRUDWELL
All Saints
4m/6km N. of Malmesbury ST 9592
Part of fine group with 15th-century barn
and 17th-century school house; 12th–15th-
century church has fine late 15th-century

seven-sacrament window; 16th-century
screens, benches and reader's desk.

DAUNTSEY
St James
4m/6km S.E. of Malmesbury ST 9882
Norman N. and S. doorways, the rest mainly
14th- and 15th-century. Tower rebuilt
1630; good Gothic Survival. Important contents include 14th-century screen, 16th-
century tympanum with Doom painting,
painted glass of 1525, Jacobean seating, and
a fine array of 16th-century and later
Danvers monuments.

DEVIZES
SU 0061
St John
Major Norman church with 12th-century
central tower and vaulted chancel replete
with richest zig-zag wall arcading. Very
ornate late 15th-century battlemented and
pinnacled S. chapel.
St Mary
12th-century stone-vaulted chancel; the rest
is mainly Perpendicular work of before 1436
with good tower and nave roof.

DONHEAD ST MARY
St Mary
3m/4km E. of Shaftesbury ST 9024
The two Wardour castles can be glimpsed
from the hilltop churchyard. Late 12th-
century nave arcades, 13th-century clerestory; refashioned in 15th century with a
typical S. Wilts. tower.

DOWNTON
St Laurence
6m/10km S. of Salisbury SU 1821
Across the Avon from the Bishop of Winchester's planned 13th-century town. Large
12th–15th-century cruciform church with
central tower, 15th-century glass, and good
18th-century monuments.

DURNFORD
St Andrew
5m/8km N. of Salisbury SU 1337
Unspoilt amidst the willows on the E. bank
of the Avon. The church is very ancient;
the 12th-century nave walls with original
doorways encase yet earlier ones. Fine 13th-
century W. tower. Chancel rebuilt *c.* 1880
and much restoration by C. E. Ponting,
1903; 13th-century wall-paintings and glass,
pulpit of 1619, and lectern with chained

copy of Jewel's *Apology*. Old benches beneath W. gallery; one of Wiltshire's most delightful churches.

EAST KNOYLE
St Mary
5m/8km N. of Shaftesbury ST 8830
Some Norman work, but mostly Early English with Perpendicular tower. Wonderful chancel plasterwork of *c.* 1640, completely covering the walls. Strapwork panels with biblical inscriptions, decorated frieze, and vividly executed story of Jacob's Dream, the Ladder rising up the E. wall. Sir Christopher Wren was born in the village and his father, as rector, was responsible for this plasterwork; he was ejected from his living during the Civil War, and this lovely decoration was cited against him at his trial.

EDINGTON
Blessed Virgin Mary, St Katharine and All Saints
4m/6km E. of Westbury ST 9253
Grey, flecked with golden lichen and standing below the steep northern escarpment of the Plain, this is not only the best example of a 14th-century collegiate church in S. England but, excepting Salisbury Cathedral, the most perfectly proportioned church in the county. It was built in 1352–61 by William of Edington. Cruciform, with central tower, the three-bay chancel formed the monastic quire, the nave serving as the parish church. Nothing now remains of the monastery, but the S. walk of the cloisters was against the N. aisle, where the window sills are higher. Extremely rich mouldings in the quire and plainer masonry in the parochial part. Four canopied niches in the quire have mutilated figures of the Evangelists, the drapery of great refinement. Fine restored 15th-century oak screen and pulpitum. Twelve consecration crosses inside and outside; 17th-century panelled plaster nave ceiling, pulpit, font cover and altarpiece. Sedilia much mutilated by erection of beautiful Lewys monument, 1630, now moved farther W. In S. transept is magnificent tomb and effigy of an Austin canon with much of the original colour. Considerable remains of 14th-century glass.

FARLEY
All Saints
5m/8km E. of Salisbury SU 2229
With the almshouses opposite, a splendid late 17th-century group. Urbane brick church of 1688, possibly by Sir Christopher Wren for Sir Stephen Fox, collaborator on the Chelsea Hospital. Centralized plan with some original fittings and handsome Fox monuments in the N. transept.

FONTHILL GIFFORD
Holy Trinity
7m/11km N.E. of Shaftesbury ST 3932
By T. H. Wyatt, 1866. Estate church with spire, pyramid pinnacles and apse. Inside is good foliage carving by Sansom, rib vaulting in the apse and chancel, and glass by Lavers and Barraud.

FUGGLESTONE
St Peter
½m/1km E. of Wilton SU 1031
Early English chancel with stepped lancets, 15th-century bellcote, early 19th-century Gothic fittings and a Georgian baluster font.

GREAT CHALFIELD
All Saints
3m/4km W. of Melksham ST 8663
Small church and adjacent manor house form a beautiful group. Of 14th-century origin, refashioned *c.* 1470 by Thomas Tropenell, who also rebuilt the great house. Charming spired bellcote of local type. Inside is the Tropenell Chapel with 15th-century stone screen and remains of splendid wall-paintings, a two-decker pulpit with tester, and good chancel screen of *c.* 1914.

HAM
All Saints
4m/6km S. of Hungerford SU 3363
Modest church of chancel, nave and W. tower; pebble-dashed exterior in retired churchyard full of Georgian altar tombs. Interior has 18th-century W. gallery, chancel rails, box pews, and clear glass.

HARDENHUISH
St Nicholas
adjoins Chippenham to N.W. ST 9074
Completely rebuilt on a new site in 1779 by John Wood Jnr of Bath. A little Georgian gem set on a green hill with apsidal sanctuary, balustraded parapets, Venetian windows, and small domed tower; the windows are filled with clear glass. Kilvert was born in the vicarage opposite.

HEYTESBURY
St Peter & St Paul
4m/6km S.E. of Warminster ST 9242
Noble cruciform church with central tower,
formerly collegiate. Mainly late 12th-, 13th-
and 15th-century. Restored by Butterfield,
1865–7, who was less drastic than usual;
the glass by Alexander Gibbs is some of his
best. Impressive interior has an immense
single E. lancet and a vaulted 15th-century
stone screen.

IDMISTON
All Saints
6m/10km N.E. of Salisbury SU 1937
Norman W. tower, Early English chancel
with lancets and fine low-pitched Perpendicular nave roof of Somerset type. Purbeck
marble font.
R.C.F.

INGLESHAM
St John the Baptist
1m/2km S.W. of Lechlade SU 2098
Two houses, this towerless church and a
farm adjoining, all of golden-grey Cotswold
stone, stand among the wide meadows of
the upper Thames. William Morris saved
this church from Victorian restoration.
Inside are vestiges of all dates; medieval
wall-paintings with 17th-century paintings
on top of them, a few pieces of old glass,
remains of painted screens, high pews of
differing depths, old, uneven floors, and
clear glass. Wonderful late-Saxon carving of
the Virgin and Child.
R.C.F.

LACOCK
St Cyriac
3m/4km S. of Chippenham ST 9168
Beautiful church in a village with extensive
monastic remains and houses from the 14th
century onward. The cruciform church is
mainly 14th–15th-century with W. tower
and spire. The *pièce de résistance* is the late
15th-century N. chapel; the intricate lierne
vault has richly carved bosses and centre
pendants retaining original colour; Sir W.
Sharington's tomb of 1566 is one of the
best English examples of early-Renaissance
work. Window over chancel arch, an early
16th-century brass, and two painted wooden
memorials of 1623.

LEIGH DELAMERE
St Margaret
4m/6km N.W. of Chippenham ST 8879
By James Thomson, 1846–8. Estate church;
not large but packed with incident. Theat-
rical chancel lit by small roundel with dove
and golden clouds. W. window Crucifixion
by Wilmshurst in apocalyptic colours. N.
aisle family pew and gaily painted organ.
Encaustic tiles, stone fittings, and even a
hinged stone gate.

LITTLE SOMERFORD
St John Baptist
3m/4km S.E. of Malmesbury ST 9684
Mostly 13th-century with Perpendicular W.
tower. Fine 15th-century screen, two-
decker pulpit of 1626, 17th-century seating,
and good painted Royal Arms of Elizabeth I.

LYDIARD TREGOZE
St Mary the Virgin
3m/4km W. of Swindon SU 1084
Warm and golden 15th-century church
within Lydiard Park, chiefly notable for its
contents. Here are extensive remains of
15th-century murals, one a tiny Resurrection on a column, painted Jacobean screen,
much old glass, beautiful wrought ironwork,
probably by Edney of Bristol, though maybe
by Tijou himself, and, above all, the finest
Renaissance monuments in any parish
church in Wilts. Great canopied tomb of Sir
John St John, and the lovely 'Conversation
Piece' of the Mompesson monument. Also
the 'Golden Cavalier', and the painted pedigree triptych on the N. chancel wall, which
opens to disclose portraits of the St Johns
of Elizabeth I's day.

MALMESBURY
St Mary
ST 9387
Little else remains of this vast cruciform
monastic church apart from the nave and
aisles; even the W. end is in ruins. It is
Norman, refashioned in the 14th century.
The S. porch has some of the finest Romanesque sculpture in the country. Inside, the
massive 12th-century arcades and elegant
14th-century clerestory are most impressive.
The present E. wall rests on the 15th-
century stone pulpitum which formerly
closed off the monastic quire. In the aisles
are sections of the stone rood screen; 15th-
century table-tomb with recumbent effigy,
said to commemorate King Athelstan, who

was certainly buried here. To the S. is a tower with spire, sole remnant of the former parish church of St Paul. The little town has much of interest, including the fine late-medieval market cross.

MANNINGFORD BRUCE
St Peter
adjoins Upavon to N. SU 1457
A Norman church on top of a Roman building, restored by Pearson in 1882. Coursed herringbone flintwork with tall round-headed windows and apsidal chancel. Heavy leaded bell-tower with pyramidal roof. Plain chancel arch with joggled voussoir. Internal painting perhaps reflects the original scheme; glass, fittings and reredos by Clayton & Bell.

MARSTON MEYSEY
St James
3m/4km N.E. of Cricklade SU 1297
By James Brooks, 1874–6. A severe High Victorian church with no frills; uninterrupted roof and modest but careful details. Inside there is a fine gradation from dark-boarded nave roof to the raised and vaulted chancel. Stone screen and pulpit; good glass by Baguley.

MERE
St Michael
7m/11km N.W. of Shaftesbury ST 8132
One of Wiltshire's best town churches. Work and fabric of many dates; the core may be 12th-century, the chancel is Early English, and the rest was almost entirely rebuilt in the 14th century when two chantry chapels were added. Handsome Perpendicular W. tower on Norman footings. The fine interior has seven old screens of various types, and the Perpendicular rood loft has been restored. Good 14th–15th-century brasses, 15th-century painted glass, and complete 17th-century nave seating with shell-headed bench-ends.

MILDENHALL
St John Baptist
1m/2km E. of Marlborough SU 2169
The pleasant plastered exterior with Perpendicular tower, aisles and clerestory gives no hint of the glories within. Transitional Norman arcades rise from a forest of oak box pews; Gothic pulpits flank the chancel arch and the panelling, reredos, altar rails

and W. gallery all survive from a refitting of 1814, perhaps by John Pinch of Bath.

NETHERAVON
All Saints
5m/8km N. of Amesbury SU 1448
Nestles below the shooting lodge of the Dukes of Beaufort. The impressive tower and entrance below are late-Saxon; a rare instance of pre-Conquest work on a monumental scale. Early English chancel with lancets and corbel table.

NETTLETON
St Mary
Burton, ½m/1km to N. of Nettleton, which is 7m/11km N.W. of Chippenham ST 8178
Norman and later church with some Decorated work, remodelled in the 15th century when the handsome Somerset-style W. tower was built. Vaulted porch, Norman font, and 15th-century stone pulpit; good unrestored interior has Georgian box pews.

NORTH BRADLEY
St Nicholas
2m/3km S. of Trowbridge ST 8555
Mainly Perpendicular but with 14th-century core. Most notable for N. chapel with rich tracery and panelled ceiling. It was built for Emma, mother of Archbishop Stafford of Canterbury, d. 1446. Good 15th-century font with Symbols of the Passion and Signs of the Evangelists.

OAKSEY
All Saints
5m/8km N.E. of Malmesbury ST 9993
A good example of a Wiltshire village church; 13th-century in origin with 14th- and 15th-century additions and remodelling. The nave has a clerestory but only a S. aisle, so that there are two stages of windows on the N. side. Some 14th-century glass and 15th-century wall-paintings, screen and panels in the choir-stalls.

OARE
Holy Trinity
2m/3km N. of Pewsey SU 1563
By S. S. Teulon, 1857–8. Small brick memorial chapel in the Romanesque style. Round arches, corbel table, apse, and bellcote. Inside are scalloped capitals and a font enriched with intersecting arches.

OLD DILTON
St Mary
1m/2km S.E. of Dilton Marsh, which is 2m/
3km W. of Westbury ST 8647
One of the most atmospheric churches in
Wilts. Mainly Perpendicular with spired
stone bellcote. Unrestored 18th-century interior has box pews, gallery, three-decker
pulpit with tester, and clear glass. There is
a plastered tympanum between nave and
chancel, and the upper storey of the vestry
was once a school.
R.C.F.

POTTERNE
St Mary
2m/3km S. of Devizes ST 9958
A charming village with several timber-
framed houses. Cruciform church, remarkable for being entirely of the 13th century
apart from the top of the tower. The 13th-
century work is beautiful in its simple austerity and worthy to rank with Salisbury
Cathedral, the similarity probably due to
Potterne being a manor of the bishops of
Salisbury. Inscribed Anglo-Saxon tub font
and Perpendicular wooden pulpit.

PURTON
St Mary the Virgin
5m/8km N.W. of Swindon SU 0887
Noble cruciform church next to a lovely
Elizabethan mansion. Like Wanborough,
there is a central spire as well as a W. tower,
though here the spire rises from another tall
tower. Building and rebuilding went on from
the 13th century until the completion of the
W. tower in the 15th century. With its niches
and corbels, all once containing coloured
imagery, its wall decoration and painted
glass, of which many fragments remain, the
place is one of the most worshipful in Wilts.
Fine churchyard monuments.

SALISBURY
St Thomas of Canterbury
SU 1429
Fine town church founded in the first half
of the 13th century and gradually rebuilt on
a spacious plan during the 15th century.
Clerestoried nave and chancel with S. tower
and three-storeyed vestry. The interior,
though crowded with seating, is still more
impressive. Over the chancel arch is a
splendid Doom painting with unusual scenes
such as the damned miser still clutching his
money bags, and other 15th-century paint-

ings depicting the Annunciation, Visitation
and Nativity are in the S. chapel. Both nave
and chapel have magnificent roofs. Other
features of interest are the late 12th-century
font, 14th–15th-century glass, an embroidered funeral pall, and 17th-century monuments.

SHERRINGTON
St Cosmos & St Damian
3m/4km S.E. of Heytesbury ST 9639
Medieval church rebuilt in 1624 re-using
some 14th-century fabric. Delightful interior with original painted texts and fittings;
pulpit, benches, communion rail, and font.

SHERSTON
Holy Cross
5m/8km W. of Malmesbury ST 8586
Fine Georgian Gothic central tower by
Thomas Sumsion of Colerne, replete with
battlements and openwork pinnacles. Late
12th-century nave and S. arcade, refashioned in 13th century. Handsome 15th-
century porch with lierne vault and a
Jacobean pulpit.

STEEPLE ASHTON
St Mary the Virgin
3m/4km E. of Trowbridge ST 9056
J.B. likened the church to 'a silvery battleship', and so it is, especially if you approach
across the claylands from Edington. A great
church built at the height of the cloth-
weaving prosperity of the 15th century. First
the tower, early in the century, then the
noble nave, aisles, chapels and porches right
at its close, 1480–1500; the last flowering
of medieval church-building in the county.
The steeple was blown down in 1670 and
had to be rebuilt twice, together with parts
of the nave; a brass at the W. end records
the rebuilding and loss of two workmen's
lives. Finely vaulted aisles, chapels and S.
porch; it was clearly intended to vault the
nave in similar fashion, but instead there
is a rich plaster ceiling with pendants and
bosses, all originally coloured. Much
carving, all very bold and virile; good 18th-
century monuments and some 15th-
century glass.

STOCKTON
St John Baptist
5m/8km S.E. of Heytesbury ST 9838
Mainly 14th-century church set in a little
close in a lovely thatched village. Of great

interest is the solid wall which, save for a central doorway and two squints, completely shuts off the chancel. Though apparently 15th-century, the arrangement is curiously like that in an Eastern church. A rood loft supported on corbels once existed on the W. side. Norman font with 17th-century cover amidst inharmonious surroundings. Good 16th–18th-century monuments.

STRATFORD-SUB-CASTLE
St Lawrence
N. part of Salisbury SU 1332
'Castle' reflects the site below the ramparts of Old Sarum; 13th- and 15th-century, the tower rebuilt by Thomas Pitt, 1711. Jacobean pulpit with tester and early 18th-century chancel fittings.

STRATFORD TONY
St Mary & St Lawrence
3m/4km S. of Wilton SU 0926
Small village church charmingly set on a mound above the Ebble, here crossed by an ancient trackway with ford and stepping-stones; 14th-century chancel with lovely Kempe glass in the reticulated E. window. Brick and flint nave walls rebuilt and fenestrated in the 18th century owing to the instability of the sloping site. Unrestored interior with 17th-century pews, screen and dado panelling with colonnaded top.
R.C.F.

SUTTON VENY
St John the Evangelist
2m/3km W. of Heytesbury ST 9041
By J. L. Pearson, 1866–8. Perfectly proportioned Decorated Gothic church with central spire. Vaulted chancel and monochrome painted decoration by Clayton & Bell, who also designed the glass.

TISBURY
St John Baptist
10m/16km W. of Wilton ST 9429
An important cruciform church pleasantly situated in a small town on the Nadder. Mostly 14th–15th-century, with fine 13th-century two-storey N. porch and some 12th-century features; the medieval crossing tower was replaced after it fell in 1762. Inside, the Lady Chapel of 1299 has richly carved niches. Good 17th-century aisle roofs with names of donors; Jacobean pews and pulpit. In the chancel are buried many of the Arundells of Wardour, including Lady

Blanche, heroic defender of Wardour Castle in the Civil War.

UPAVON
St Mary
4m/6km S.W. of Pewsey SU 1355
Just behind the village square. Late 12th-century chancel restored by T. H. Wyatt; good early 13th-century font in Romanesque style carved with the Annunciation.

UPTON LOVELL
St Peter
2m/3km S.E. of Heytesbury ST 9440
Small church standing away from the village. Chancel of c. 1200 with corbel table and chancel arch. Otherwise remodelled c. 1633 in Gothic Survival style. Late 14th-century effigy of a knight.

URCHFONT
St Michael
4m/6km S.E. of Devizes SU 0457
Charming village under the downs with a pond on the green and a mighty cedar tree. Mainly 14th-century church with Perpendicular additions. Notable Decorated chancel with gabled buttresses and stone vaulting enriched with carved bosses. Good 14th-century details in the S. aisle; nave roof of 1631; some 14th-century glass and good 18th-century monuments, one by Scheemakers.

WANBOROUGH
St Andrew
4m/6km E. of Swindon SU 2082
Russet and golden church on high ground. Late 14th-century nave, aisles, and N. porch; fine Perpendicular W. tower, chancel and sacristy. Notable hexagonal lantern and tall spire which rise most ingeniously from a shortened bay at the E. end of the nave. An early and rather drastic restoration by Sir Giles Gilbert Scott, 1843, the walls stripped of plaster. Two-light window by Christopher Webb. Notice in porch: 'All females are requested to take off their pattens on entering this door'.

WESTWOOD
St Mary
1m/2km S.W. of Bradford-on-Avon ST 8159
Church and manor house form a delightful group; 13th-century chancel; the remainder of the fabric including the stately tower with domed turret and enriched parapet is Per-

pendicular. Attractive 18th-century plaster nave ceiling; 15th-century glass featuring a Lily Crucifixion and domed font cover; 17th-century altar rails and pulpit.

WILTON
St Mary & St Nicholas
3m/4km W. of Salisbury SU 0931
'Lombardy in Wiltshire.' A daring, uncompromising and extremely expensive design in Italian Romanesque style by T. H. Wyatt and David Brandon, 1841–5. Notable for being right outside the strict Gothic of the period; medieval mosaics and marble were imported from Italy. Remarkable imported late-medieval glass, and yet earlier glass in apse windows.
R.C.F.

WINTERBOURNE BASSETT
St Katharine & St Peter
3m/4km N. of Avebury SU 1075
Set amidst foliage on high ground; an archi-

tectural gem. Nave, N. aisle with transeptal chapel, chancel, and S. porch, all purest Decorated; only the W. tower and a few minor features are later. Beautiful window and recessed tomb in transept, beneath which is a touching 13th-century tomb slab with a man and wife hand-in-hand. Late Norman font with 17th-century cover and much other 17th-century furniture; good monuments and hatchments.

WOODFORD
All Saints
4m/6km N. of Salisbury SU 1236
By T. H. Wyatt, 1845, apart from the Perpendicular W. tower; 17th-century W. gallery and tower screen; Comper glass in three windows.

Worcestershire

Introduction

Worcestershire is a small and richly varied county. It is diamond-shaped and, if the simile will be forgiven, it is like a fruit tart. The centre, containing the Severn and Avon valleys with their tributaries, is mostly orchards, miraculously beautiful in spring. The edge of the tart is the hills that surround Worcestershire on all sides. Wherever you are in Worcestershire you can see hills not far off; they are usually flanked with or crowned by trees. The northernmost corner of the fruit tart is burned black; it is part of the Black Country and extends northward from Kidderminster towards Birmingham, which now extends into Worcestershire. The industrial towns of the county are devoted to ironworking, from founding and engineering through chains down to needles and fish-hooks. In this industrial corner pinkish brick houses and mills and chimneys stretch over hill and valleys and various undistinguished Victorian towers; spires and bellcotes rise out of them with here and there the weathered stone tower of some medieval church, such as the fine ones of Kidderminster and Bromsgrove. A piece of the tart, wholly Black Country, was broken off and islanded in Staffordshire – the hilltop borough of Dudley, with its old castle, was formerly part of Worcestershire and was a survivor of many pieces of Worcestershire that were to be found in Warwickshire and Gloucestershire and were relics of monastic landowners of feudal times. There was only one feudal Worcestershire baron, the owner of Dudley Castle; the Church was lord elsewhere.

The rest of the county is a marked contrast. What Surrey is to London, it has become to Birmingham and the Black Country, and many an old timber-framed cottage set among orchards or at the foot of steep pastoral hills may be seen on closer inspection to have been saved from destruction by some industrial proprietor who uses it as a weekend hide-out. His forebears would have lived on the outskirts of Kidderminster or Dudley or Redditch in some heavy Victorian mansion now divided into flats.

The building materials of houses and churches are as varied as the scenery. Only the big abbeys and priories, in which Worcester was richer than any other county, could afford impressive architecture. Worcester Cathedral (severely but impressively restored by Sir Giles Gilbert Scott), Great Malvern Priory, with its many windows of late-medieval and 18th-century glass, Pershore Abbey, which is now only a huge choir with tower crossing, and the stately Perpendicular bell-tower of Evesham are the chief survivors.

In the fruit districts, and where building stones were not easily obtained, the churches were like the old cottages, partly of timber construction, often with timber-framed towers or bellcotes. At the east of the county, where the Cotswold hills rise, churches such as Broadway and Church Honeybourne are of a local golden limestone like their villages.

In the west of the county south of the Malvern Hills, churches are of red sandstone, and the tower of Martley church is of a brilliant scarlet sandstone which has to be seen to be believed. The church at Shelsley Walsh is of travertine stone, a pale-pink stone, which was also used in ancient Rome.

As in all Midland counties where an industrial life had started in the 18th century, there is much 18th-century church building. Not all of it was swept away by disgusted Victorians – indeed they did well by Great Witley, which is the most sumptuous classic interior in England – and there are a Worcestershire Baroque style and a Worcestershire Strawberry Hill Gothic style which are individual and charming.

Some of the Victorian work in the county is poor, all style and mock construction, and this applies to larger villas as well as churches. However, there are some, such as the bold church by W. J. Hopkins at Hallow, that are distinguished.

J.B.

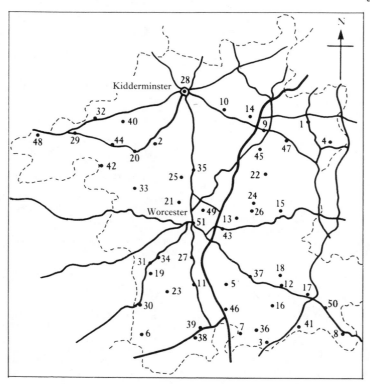

1	Alvechurch	18	Fladbury	35	Ombersley
2	Astley	19	Great Malvern	36	Overbury
3	Beckford	20	Great Witley	37	Pershore
4	Beoley	21	Hallow	38	Queenhill
5	Besford	22	Hanbury	39	Ripple
6	Birtsmorton	23	Hanley Swan	40	Rock
7	Bredon	24	Himbleton	41	Sedgeberrow
8	Broadway	25	Holt	42	Shelsley Walsh
9	Bromsgrove	26	Huddington	43	Spetchley
10	Chaddesley Corbett	27	Kempsey	44	Stockton-on-Teme
11	Croome d'Abitot	28	Kidderminster	45	Stoke Prior
12	Cropthorne	29	Knighton-on-Teme	46	Strensham
13	Crowle	30	Little Malvern	47	Tardebigge
14	Dodford	31	Malvern Link	48	Tenbury Wells
15	Dormston	32	Mamble	49	Warndon
16	Elmley Castle	33	Martley	50	Wickhamford
17	Evesham	34	Newland	51	Worcester

Selected List of Churches

ALVECHURCH
St Lawrence
3m/4km N. of Redditch SP 0272
Norman S. doorway, otherwise mostly 14th-
and 15th-century; restored inside and partly
rebuilt by W. Butterfield, 1861.

ASTLEY
St Peter
3m/4km S.W. of Stourport SO 7867
12th–15th-century with important Norman
work and Perpendicular tower; good 16th-
century monuments to the Blount family
with effigies, balusters and wreaths.

BECKFORD
St John the Baptist
6m/10km E. of Tewkesbury SO 9735
A 12th-century church of nave, central tower
and chancel. Interesting carved nave doorways with tympana of the Cross and the
Harrowing of Hell. W. tower arch, formerly
the chancel arch, has zig-zags and a centaur.

BEOLEY
St Leonard
2m/3km N.E. of Redditch SP 0669
15th-century tower. Good series of
16th–17th-century monuments; those to
William and Ralph Sheldon and their wives
are outstanding.

BESFORD
St Peter
2m/3km W. of Pershore SO 9144
A 14th-century timber-framed church, the
only one in the county, heavily restored in
1880. There is a complete Decorated rood
loft, Jacobean communion rail and panelling.
Good 16th-century monuments including a
remarkable triptych with painted figures and
heraldry, probably by Michael Salabos,
1588.

BIRTSMORTON
St Peter & St Paul
6m/10km W. of Tewkesbury SO 8035
Next to Birtsmorton Court, a handsome
moated house. Charming little Decorated
cruciform church with Perpendicular tower.

Interesting monuments and 14th–15th-
century glass.

BREDON
St Giles
3m/4km N.E. of Tewkesbury SO 9236
The village, on the banks of the Avon, forms
a delightful group, with its street of old
houses leading to the church, the rectory as
large and stately as a manor house, and the
14th-century tithe barn, one of the finest in
the country. The great church, much of it
of the 12th century, with central tower and
spire, dominates the scene. It is full of
interest; old glass, medieval tiles, early
tombs, a heart burial, an Easter Sepulchre
and a superb early 17th-century alabaster
monument.

BROADWAY
St Eadburgh
5m/8km S.E. of Evesham SP 0937
Perhaps the most famous show village in
England. The church, which stands a little
apart, is not unworthy of its setting. It is
cruciform with a central tower, externally
mainly Perpendicular, but containing work
from the 12th–18th centuries. Jacobean altar
rail and a pulpit with 15th-century panels.

BROMSGROVE
St John the Baptist
12m/19km S.W. of Birmingham SO 9570
Mainly Perpendicular church with mid-
14th-century tower and octagonal spire with
crockets. Good Talbot & Stafford tombs
with alabaster effigies; one furnished evidence which established Lord Talbot of Ingestre's claim to the Earldom of Shrewsbury
in 1856.

CHADDESLEY CORBETT
St Cassian
4m/6km S.E. of Kidderminster SO 8973
The chancel of this church is the best
example of Decorated work in the county.
Celebrated Norman font with intertwined
beasts, an outlier of the Herefordshire
School, and good monuments with an outstanding one of 1631.

CROOME D'ABITOT
St Mary Magdalene
7m/11km S. of Worcester SO 8844
The church was built in 1763 by Robert Adam and Capability Brown as a feature of Croome Park, balancing a Classical temple which still exists, though the park has been ploughed up. It is an important instance of Gothic Survival, or rather of the logical development of the Perpendicular style. Inside it is spacious, dignified and airy, the piers being so slender as to foreshadow cast iron. The detail is beautifully executed, especially the carved wooden font by Adam, and the Rococo Gothic pulpit. The church has many Coventry monuments; note especially that of a Lord Keeper of the Great Seal, d. 1639, attributed to the workshop of Nicholas Stone.
R.C.F.

CROPTHORNE
St Michael
3m/4km W. of Evesham SO 9944
12th-century. Contains a celebrated equal-armed stone cross of *c.* 800, the best piece of Anglo-Saxon art in the county. Good 17th-century monuments with effigies.

CROWLE
St John the Baptist
5m/8km E. of Worcester SO 9256
Practically rebuilt in 1881–5 by Preedy. Retains good roof-bosses, well-detailed late 14th-century timber porch, and a stone lectern of *c.* 1200.

DODFORD
Holy Trinity and St Mary
2m/3km N.W. of Bromsgrove SO 9372
By Arthur Bartlett, 1907–8. A good church in Arts and Crafts Gothic. Unusual and effective plan with carving and decorative work by the Bromsgrove Guild.

DORMSTON
St Nicholas
6m/10km W. of Alcester SO 9857
Remote situation; 13th–15th-century church with delightful 15th-century timber-framed W. tower and 14th-century S. porch.

ELMLEY CASTLE
St Mary
4m/6km S.W. of Evesham SO 9841
The village forms a very beautiful group at the foot of Bredon Hill, its wide street of pleasant houses leading directly to the church. This is a charming medieval building, with an 11th-century chancel and dominated by a 13th-century tower. Unusual font of *c.* 1200 with a 15th-century bowl supported on writhing dragons. Two excellent 17th-century monuments. The first of *c.* 1631 has effigies of Giles Savage, his father, and his wife holding a closely wrapped infant. The second commemorates the first Earl of Coventry, d. 1699: a huge marble erection designed by William Stanton, the earl taking his ease beneath a pedimented arch. It was intended for Croome, but owing to a family row was placed here instead. It would have been a fine thing at Croome, and Elmley could well have been spared it. The only jarring feature of this interior is the aggressively scraped walls.

EVESHAM
13m/21km S.E. of Worcester SP 0344
The abbey precinct unusually contains two parish churches:
All Saints
12th–15th-century church. Fine mortuary chapel of *c.* 1513 for Clement Lichfield, Abbot of Evesham, with fan vaulting and pinnacles. Good Arts and Crafts chancel gates, 1910.
St Lawrence
A Perpendicular building, sympathetically altered in 1836 by H. Eginton. S. chapel, *c.* 1520, possibly chantry chapel to St Clement, Abbot Lichfield's Christian name! Good panelling, niches and tierceron star vault in W. tower.
R.C.F.

FLADBURY
St John the Baptist
3m/4km N.W. of Evesham SO 9946
12th–14th-century church with medieval tiles, 15th-century brasses, and a decorative monument to Bishop Lloyd, d. 1717.

GREAT MALVERN
St Mary & St Michael
7m/11km S.W. of Worcester SO 7845
Mainly of the 15th century, although much earlier work of the 12th and 13th centuries can be found. This great priory church is well known for its choir-stalls, misericords, tiles, and above all for its glass, which is of the highest interest. The glass all dates from *c.* 1440–1506, and is the most complete

set in England. Similarly, the unique and attractive 15th-century tiles on the screen walls of the chancel, which were made here, form the most complete scheme in the country.

GREAT WITLEY
St Michael
5m/8km S.W. of Stourport SO 7566
One of the finest Baroque churches in the country, it was built for the Foleys, perhaps by James Gibbs. Set in the midst of a park among Italianate gardens, the outside suggests southern Europe, and on entering the building one is taken straight there. Walls and ceiling are adorned with superb Baroque papier mâché work by Bagutti, and on the ceiling are three paintings by Bellucci which, together with ten windows by Joshua Price, were taken from the Duke of Chandos's palace at Canons. All is exceedingly rich and of great beauty. The harmonious seating and other 19th-century furnishings in the Gothic style were introduced by Lord Dudley.

HALLOW
St Philip & St James
3m/4km N.W. of Worcester SO 8258
By W. J.Hopkins, 1867–9. Ambitious Gothic in red and white stone with nave roof supported on transverse arches, the flying buttresses appearing externally above the aisle roofs.

HANBURY
St Mary
4m/6km S. of Bromsgrove SO 9664
Well set on a hill with fine view. Late 18th-century outside with W. tower of 1793. Chancel and chapel rebuilt by G. E. Street in 1861; the chapel was built to contain the Vernon monuments, which include works by Roubiliac and Chantrey.

HANLEY SWAN
Our Lady and St Alphonsus
3m/4km S.E. of Gt Malvern SO 8142
By Charles Hansom, 1844–6. Pleasant setting in erstwhile park. The nave, with plaster rib vaulting, is based on the Early English work at Skelton, Yorks., and the chancel is Decorated. Good carved altars, screens and decorations; metalwork by Pugin, glass by Wailes.

HIMBLETON
St Mary Magdalene
4m/6km S.E. of Droitwich SO 9458
12th-century with later additions including 14th-century timber S. porch and 15th-century wooden bell-turret and wagon roofs. Good glass of *c.* 1300 in E. window.

HOLT
St Martin
5m/8km N. of Worcester SO 8262
A pleasing group of 12th-century church and 14th-century castle, remote from other buildings. Richly carved mid-12th-century doorways and chancel arch, the finest in the county; 15th-century tower and, in the S. chapel, a delicate stained-glass Annunciation. Well-detailed monument of 1704 and large 19th-century mosaics.

HUDDINGTON
St James
5m/8km S.E. of Droitwich SO 9457
Mostly 14th-century with a robust late-Perpendicular timber N. porch. Some medieval glass and tiles; good marble monument of 1658.

KEMPSEY
St Mary
4m/6km S. of Worcester SO 8549
13th-century chancel with important 14th-century glass figures in the side walls. Painted tomb of Sir Edmund Wylde, d. 1620.

KIDDERMINSTER
St Mary and All Saints
16m/25km W. of Birmingham SO 8376
Large 16th-century town church of red sandstone with much Victorian restoration; 15th–17th century brasses and monuments of great interest.

KNIGHTON-ON-TEME
St Michael
3m/4km N.E. of Tenbury Wells SO 6370
An isolated and remote church, mainly 12th-century, with a good S. doorway set in a projection with a blind arcade of four arches over it. The chancel arch is also Norman and flanked by blind arcades. W. bell-tower is supported on huge timbers internally, and is separated from the nave by a 15th-century timber screen; good nave roof of the same date.

LITTLE MALVERN
St Giles

4m/6km S. of Great Malvern SO 7740
The presbytery and crossing, surmounted by
a tower, are all that remain of this monastic
church. Seen in conjunction with the
adjoining Court, which incorporates parts
of the domestic range of the monastery,
against the background of the hills, it forms
a very pleasing picture. Bishop Alcock rebuilt
most of the priory, including the church, at
the end of the 15th century. Interesting late
15th-century glass and floor tiles.

MALVERN LINK
The Ascension

N. district of Great Malvern SO 7848
Walter Tapper, 1903; tall, simple and
Bodley-esque.

MAMBLE
St John the Baptist

3m/4km S. of Cleobury Mortimer SO 6871
Framework of timber bell-tower probably
c. 1200 with massive scissor-braced corner
posts reaching nearly to apex of nave roof.
Separated from nave by 16th-century timber
partition with 17th-century minstrels'
gallery.

MARTLEY
St Peter

7m/11km N.W. of Worcester SO 7559
Set just off the village street in lovely rich
countryside between the Severn and Teme,
it should be seen when the fruit blossom is
clothing all the hills and filling all the valleys
with its beauty: there is nothing in England
to compare with West Worcestershire in the
spring. 12th–15th-century church with good
13th-century curtain pattern wall-paintings
in the chancel and 15th-century scenes on
the N. side of the nave, together with the
arms of Mortimer and Despenser.

NEWLAND
St Leonard

2m/3km N.E. of Great Malvern SO 7948
By P. C. Hardwick, 1862–4; stone church
and brick almshouses, all in 14th-century
style. The interior of the church is richly
decorated, walls covered with mural paintings, coloured marble and mouldings, the
windows filled with stained glass.

OMBERSLEY
St Andrew

4m/6km W. of Droitwich SO 8463
By the learned Thomas Rickman, 1825–9.
Set back from the village street, a well-found
estate church in the Decorated style. Agreeable exterior with handsome W. tower and
well-proportioned recessed spire. Tall and
spacious inside with galleries and box pews;
a touch austere.

OVERBURY
St Faith

5m/8km N.E. of Tewkesbury SO 9537
At the centre of the village, close to Om-
bersley Court; 12th-century with later additions, notably the bold Perpendicular
central tower. Good 12th-century arcades
and a well-detailed Early English chancel.

PERSHORE
Holy Cross

9m/13km S.E. of Worcester SO 9446
All that remains of the great abbey church is
the presbytery, one transept, and the central
tower. Beautiful 13th-century arcading on
the presbytery and copious ballflowers on the
14th-century tower; the enriched vaulting is
a study in itself. Norman font, Perpendicular
screens, and an unfortunate 19th-century
apse; it is difficult to imagine how anyone
seeing what was there could have added this
poor work. The transept is dominated by a
standing figure representing something or
other as a memorial to the Great War.
Holding a light, it would give interest to the
foot of the staircase at the Hotel Metropole;
it does not add to the glories of this great
church.

QUEENHILL
St Nicholas

3m/4km N.W. of Tewkesbury SO 8636
Isolated, beautifully situated field church
with work from 12th to 14th centuries and
some fragments of 14th-century glass with
a shield of England as used before 1340.

RIPPLE
St Mary

3m/4km N. of Tewkesbury SO 8637
An almost unaltered late 12th-century
church of chancel, central tower, transepts,
and aisled nave. There is some 15th-century
glass and a set of misericords showing the
labours of the months. A charming place
with a sense of continuity and abiding peace.

ROCK
St Peter & St Paul
4m/6km S.W. of Bewdley SO 7371
A great 12th-century church with excellent sculpture and a Perpendicular tower dated 1510; it stands almost alone, a landmark from all sides.

SEDGEBERROW
St Mary
4m/6km S. of Evesham SP 0238
Complete building consecrated in 1331, but heavily restored by W. Butterfield, 1866–8; his is the ornate gilded and painted reredos.

SHELSLEY WALSH
St Andrew
7m/11km N.E. of Bromyard SO 7263
Church and Court make a good group, well set in the Teme Valley. A church of the 12th–13th centuries, sensitively restored by George Truefitt in 1859. The walling is mainly of travertine, a local stone, and the late 15th-century screen is the finest in the county, the S. section returned to form a parclose. Unusual wooden table-tomb to Francis Walsh, d. 1596, with pilasters and heraldic panels; 15th-century floor tiles.

SPETCHLEY
All Saints
3m/4km E. of Worcester SO 8953
A small, mainly 14th-century building with a S. chapel of 1629 containing a series of fine Berkeley monuments, some with good effigies and all with displays of heraldry.
R.C.F.

STOCKTON-ON-TEME
St Andrew
6m/10km S.E. of Cleobury Mortimer SO 7167
Set on high ground, making a picturesque group with surrounding buildings. There is work of all periods from the 12th century onward and an elaborate wooden 16th-century tomb.

STOKE PRIOR
St Michael
2m/3km S. of Bromsgrove SO 9567
A fine church of *c.* 1200, the good tower carrying a modern shingled spire. The whole building is an interesting early group with its chapel, chancel and sacristy. There are some early monuments within.

STRENSHAM
St John the Baptist
5m/8km N. of Tewkesbury SO 9140
Standing on high ground close to the River Avon and across fields from the village. The church has a rood-loft front with twenty-three 15th-century paintings of saints, now set as a W. gallery. There are two fine early brasses and many later monuments; 15th-century floor tiles and a two-decker 18th-century pulpit.
R.C.F.

TARDEBIGGE
St Bartholomew
3m/4km E. of Bromsgrove SO 9969
By F. Hiorn, 1777; chancel added and interior Victorianized, 1879–80. Slender classic steeple on commanding site.

TENBURY WELLS
St Michael and all Angels
8m/12km N.E. of Leominster SO 5968
By Henry Woodyer, 1854–6, built for the College founded by the composer Sir Frederick Gore Ouseley. Since 1985 it has served as the parish church of Tenbury. A marvellous steeply roofed cruciform church with polygonal apse. Beautiful tracery and, inside, ornate carvings to capitals. A High Victorian interior with sanctuary glass by Hardman. The church is linked to the college buildings, also by Woodyer, by a timber cloister.

WARNDON
St Nicholas
3m/4km N.E. of Worcester SO 8856
A small field church in a parish with no village, now near Worcester outskirts and bypass. Grouped with farm buildings, this is a very simple little 12th-century church with a 16th-century timbered tower. Unspoiled interior with some 14th-century glass, 17th-century communion rail and box pews.

WICKHAMFORD
St John the Baptist
2m/3km S.E. of Evesham SP 0641
Charming group of church and manor house. Mainly 13th–15th-century with good woodwork and a splendid alabaster double tomb of 1626.

WORCESTER
SO 8555
All Saints, Deansway

A large and spacious mid-18th-century church built in the Classical manner on an earlier foundation: it has dignity, space and light to an unusual degree. The lower part of the tower is 15th-century; the upper storeys 18th-century in the style of Wren. Monuments and some good fragments of 15th-century glass from the earlier church.

St George, St George's Square
By Sir Aston Webb, 1893–5. Well placed at the end of a square. Built of brick with stone dressings, a Perpendicular window

and turrets on the façade. Large and well-lit interior with clerestory and glass by Kempe.

St Swithun, Church Street
By E. and T. Woodward, 1734–6. A perfectly preserved example of an 18th-century church with all its furnishings intact. Elegant E. elevation with Venetian window, pilasters and urns. Marvellous interior with Gothic plaster ceiling and Roman Doric screen walls to the chancel.

R.C.F.

Yorkshire East Riding

Introduction

Here lie the broad acres of Yorkshire. With the Wolds as backbone, the Riding stretches from Filey in the north to Spurn Point in the south, and westward towards Malton and York. There are three distinct regions: (1) The gently undulating Plain of Holderness, a peninsula of distant views and wide skies, whose winding lanes reflect the strong light from the sea. The indigenous cobbles, laboriously gathered from the boulder clay, form the material for its trim churches and old farmsteads. The former culminate in the Gothic splendours of Humberside, where medieval wealth and proximity to navigable water are seen in the village churches of the 'Saxon Line', and in the city of Kingston-upon-Hull.

The medieval city was small, concentrated around the docks and along the River Hull. It has two memorable churches: Holy Trinity, one of the largest parish churches in England, with a tower which is still one of the city's chief landmarks, and St Mary Lowgate. The 19th century saw rapid expansion to the north and new churches in Sculcoates by Street and Temple Moore. The 20th century has pushed big housing estates out into the countryside, but little in the way of memorable church architecture has resulted.

(2) Dry valleys, ancient barrows and protective belts of trees form the landscape of the Wolds. Except in the Bayle and north-west tower at Bridlington, chalk is principally confined to domestic work. Norman fonts abound in the sturdy churches, evidence of rebuilding after the Harrying of the North. Beverley, Cottingham, Driffield and the fine Victorian spire at Dalton Holme grace the eastern slopes, whilst the churches of the central Wolds bear the indelible mark of Sir Tatton Sykes' restorers.

(3) The Vale of York, watered by the Derwent, takes on the aspect of the Low Countries. Here, tree-lined lanes lead to remote villages, like Aughton with its melancholy atmosphere, or Scrayingham with its memories of the 'Railway King'. The towers, especially the upstanding one at Holme-upon-Spalding Moor, Bishop Skirlaw's at Howden and Prior Wessington's spire at Hemingborough, are marked features in the Plain.

M.E.I.

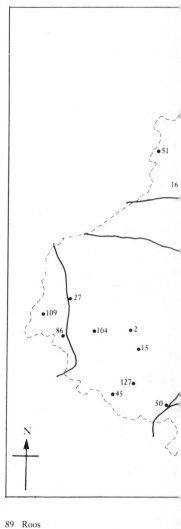

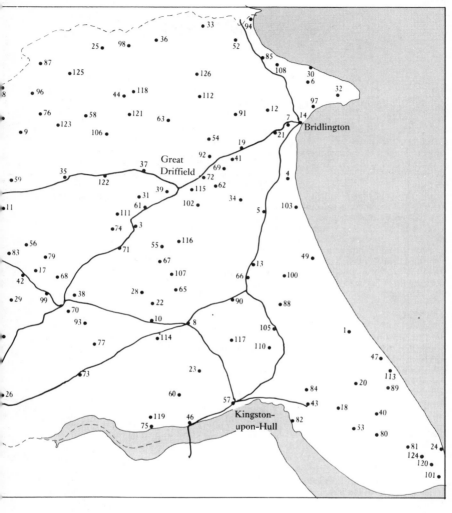

Selected List of Churches

ALDBROUGH
St Bartholomew
6m/10km S.E. of Hornsea TA 2438
Norman and 13th-century. Circular inscribed 11th-century sundial recording the
founding of the church by Ulf; fine alabaster
effigy of knight. Circular churchyard.

AUGHTON
All Saints
11m/18km W. of Market Weighton SE 7038
Remote situation in water meadows between
River Derwent and earthworks of former
Aske residence. Sturdy tower dated 1536
displaying several shields and carved with
an asker or newt. Unspoilt interior: broad
Norman chancel arch of three orders with
chevrons. Baluster altar rails; arcaded
Norman font; brass to Richard Aske and
wife, d. 1460.

BAINTON
St Andrew
5m/8km S.W. of Great Driffield SP 5826
Dominates typical Wold village. Almost
purely 14th-century Curvilinear. Nave and
aisles with lofty arcades, spacious chancel,
and W. tower with slightly corbelled-out
parapet, once crowned by octagonal spire. In
the chancel a worn brass to Roger Godeale,
priest, d. 1429. Coloured wall monument
to Robert Faucon, an ejected rector, dated
1661, 21 years before his death!

BARMSTON
All Saints
5m/8km S. of Bridlington TA 1659
Originally Norman but largely rebuilt in the
early 15th century, the church stands on
forlorn moated site at far end of village near
remains of an Elizabethan manor house.
Built of cobbles; squat W. tower surmounted
by pierced battlements. Attractive Norman
font; alabaster effigy of knight and some
Boynton monuments.

BEEFORD
St Leonard
7m/11km E. of Great Driffield TA 1354
Backdrop of trees. Largely Perpendicular,
including the W. tower which retains a statue
of St Leonard in a niche. Rectorial brass,
1472.

BEMPTON
St Michael
3m/4km N. of Bridlington TA 1972
Early 19th-century chancel. Early English
font, remarkable late-Georgian wooden
chancel screen, Classical in style with three
arches, fluted pillars, and the Royal Arms
above.

BESSINGBY
*St Magnus, a late misreading of St Mary
Magdalene*
1m/2km S.W. of Bridlington TA 1565
1895, by Temple Moore. Of finely tooled
sandstone, charmingly situated in a village
amongst trees on a flank of the Wolds. Nave
with narrow aisles, chancel, and strong
central tower and spire. A successful 19th-
century version of a late 14th-century
church, preserving fine Norman font and
several good monuments, one to Lady Ann
Hudson by R. J. Wyatt.

BEVERLEY
8m/12km N. of Hull TA 0339
St John of Beverley, the Minster
Superb building exhibiting work of all
periods. One of the finest Gothic churches
in Europe. Formerly collegiate, with double
transepts. Choir and main transepts, which
have double aisles, are principally Early
English, and merge almost imperceptibly
into Decorated nave, with elegant Perpendicular W. front and twin towers as crowning
glory; 14th-century altar screen with platform above and superb Decorated Percy
tomb to N. Choir-stalls with canopies and
misereres by Ripon carvers. Great W. door
with Evangelists and their symbols designed
by Hawksmoor; font cover probably by him;
lead statues of Athelstan and St John by
William Collins of Driffield, and wrought-
iron gates in choir, all date from 1715–
40. Choir screen constructed by Elwell of
Beverley to designs of G. G. Scott Snr.
St Mary

This is one of the most beautiful parish churches in England. Cruciform, with rich exterior, the nave and tower were rebuilt after the fall of the old 12th-century tower in 1520. Spacious interior, the arcade piers and small capitals recall those at Hull, but here the bases are exaggerated. Minstrels' pillar on N., with five little figures and label stops which record names of benefactors, 1530. Original roofs repainted under Leslie Moore; 19th-century restorations by A. W. N. and E. W. Pugin; latter added buttresses to S. transept. Reredos by J. Oldrid Scott; 14th-century stalls with misericords. Charnel house and priest's rooms to N.E.; 15th-century font. Many ledger stones and matrices of brasses; 18th-century wrought-iron altar table and Wharton monuments.

BIRDSALL
St Mary
4m/6km S.E. of Malton SE 8165
Large estate church replacing old Norman church, now a ruin near the Hall. Built in 1824; chancel added by Hodgson Fowler in 1879. Kempe glass; monuments by Rysbrack and Westmacott.

BISHOP BURTON
All Saints
3m/4km W. of Beverley SE 9839
Overlooking a pleasant village with a pond and an irregular green; 13th-century W. tower, chancel by J. L. Pearson in the Early English style; 18th-century font; Kempe glass in nave, Clayton & Bell in the chancel; brasses and an alabaster to Rachel Gee, d. 1684.

BISHOP WILTON
St Edith
5m/8km E. of Stamford Bridge SE 7955
The church lies behind the main street which follows a stream down the chalk scarp of the Wolds. Pearson did a wonderful job in his restoration of 1858–9 such as few Victorian architects could have achieved. The chancel arch has original beak-heads and scrolls. S. doorway is a successful reconstruction from old materials with animals, faces, beak-heads and human forms. Decorated work in N. transept and S. aisle with a fine Perpendicular tower and spire. Fittings by Temple Moore; fine tiles by Godwin.

BOYNTON
St Andrew
3m/4km W. of Bridlington TA 1368
Situated close to Hall gates at end of village street of whitewashed chalk cottages. Late 14th-century tower. Delightful Classical nave and chancel rebuilt in brick by John Carr, 1768, with Batty Langley Gothic details. Until restoration, 1910, by J. Bilson, altar stood beneath architectural baldacchino. Beyond lies Strickland mortuary chapel containing family monuments, one of which is a cenotaph attributed to William Kent. E. window glazed by William Peckitt. Tower has Gothic plaster vault and gallery, formerly squire's pew. Unusual turkey lectern and font cover designed by Francis Johnson; Sir Wm. Strickland introduced turkeys to England.

BRANDESBURTON
St Mary
6m/10km W. of Hornsea TA 1147
Shrouded by trees. Built mainly of cobbles with brick clerestory and S. porch. Restored and chancel rebuilt in 1893 by W. S. Weatherbury; good but for strident red-tiled chancel roof. Interior light and spacious with narrow aisles terminating at W. with curious responds to arcades. Crown glass. In chancel remains of a bracket-brass to William Darrell, priest, d. 1364, and life-size brass of John St Quintin, 1397, and wife.

BRIDLINGTON
24m/39km N. of Hull TA 1766
Christ Church, Quay Road
Scott and Moffat, 1840–1; hall church with octagonal piers; 14th-century font with fine scrolly 17th-century cover, both from York Minster.
St Mary
Nave of Augustinian priory. Forms group with 14th-century Bayle Gate. Noble 13th- and 14th-century arcades with triforium and clerestory, combined on S. side. Beautiful N. porch with interesting capitals and rose ornament. Evidence of rebuilding scheme c. 1480, to which W. end, S.W. tower and three W. bays of S. arcade belong. Suffered two violent restorations in 19th century. In 1846–57 Edmund Sharpe and E. G. Paley partially raised roof pitch. In 1876–80 G. G. Scott Jnr completed W. towers, left unfinished at Dissolution, and filled nave with pitch-pine pewing. Fine Frosterley marble font. Tournai marble tomb slab, possibly of

founder. Re-erected remains of 12th-century cloister arcade in N. aisle.

BUBWITH
All Saints
5m/8km N.W. of Howden SE 7136
Fine church beside Derwent at the end of the village street. Norman chancel arch; 13th-century arcades and chancel; tower, *c.* 1424; heraldry of Askes and Vavasours; old glass; funeral helm and sword; pews with good Jacobean fronts.

BUGTHORPE
St Andrew
4m/6km E. of Stamford Bridge SE 7757
Pleasant village with a rectangular green, the church standing at one end. Long 14th-century chancel; double chancel arch. Delightful whitewashed interior is High Church with central altar; Goodhart Rendell refurnished the church in 1936. Fine monument to Mary Payler, 1756.

BURNBY
St Giles
3m/4km S.E. of Pocklington SE 8346
Norman and Early English; triple sedilia. The architect-vicar Charles Carr designed the bellcote and W. door in the 1840s. Restored by Sir Giles Gilbert Scott, 1908.

BURSTWICK
All Saints
3m/4km E. of Hedon TA 2227
Decorated and Perpendicular church. Notable for the Royal Arms of Charles II hung in the N. arcade; on the reverse is a painting of the Execution of Charles I, King and Martyr.

BURTON AGNES
St Martin
5m/8km S.W. of Bridlington TA 1063
Grouped with medieval manor house and Elizabethan mansion. Norman with 13th- and 14th-century alterations. Fine late 15th-century W. tower. Chancel restored *c.* 1840 by Archdeacon Wilberforce, son of the Emancipator, whose likeness appears on a corbel. Mutilated remains of Georgian Doric squire's pew. Box pews. Many Somerville and Griffith monuments; one with three coffins in place of effigies and two grisly panels of skulls and bones. Fine 18th-century English and Spanish embroideries.

BURTON PIDSEA
St Peter, anciently St Peter & St Paul
4m/6km N.E. of Hedon TA 2431
Fine, small Holderness church built of glacial erratics. Mainly Decorated and Perpendicular; S. doorway has traceried spandrels. Brick E. end of chancel dates from 1838.

CARNABY
St John the Baptist
2m/3km S.W. of Bridlington TA 1465
A charming building set up the slope from the village with the Wolds rising gently to the N. Early English nave; Perpendicular tower; windows in S. aisle show evolution of crude plate tracery; 12th-century drum font.

CHERRY BURTON
St Michael and All Angels
3m/4km N.W. of Beverley SE 9842
By Sir Horace Jones, 1852–3. The church and hall stand among trees in this pleasant valley. In late 13th-century style with striking tower; Kempe windows; iron tablet recording I.C.B.S. grant.

COTTINGHAM
St Mary
town adjoining Hull to N.W. TA 0432
Large cruciform church in overgrown suburb of Hull, but still retaining many fine Georgian houses. Principally 14th-century, but the chancel and tower with outer stair turret are both Perpendicular. W. window has flowing tracery, and that of aisles is Flamboyant. Little of interest inside except wall-brass to John Smyth, d. 1504, and wife, and restored brass to rector Nicholas de Luda (Louth), d. 1383, who built the chancel; he was a Capuchin friar.

EASINGTON
All Saints
6m/10km S.E. of Patrington TA 3919
Within half a mile of the sea, the church tower dominates this Holderness village. Weather-beaten Early English; Perpendicular W. tower and chancel. Norman pillar piscina; 17th-century Overton monument.

EAST HESLERTON
St Andrew
9m/15km E. of Malton SE 9276
By G. E. Street, 1877; prominent spire and original W. porch. Windows by Clayton & Bell; four figures on tower octagon by

Redfern were destined for Bristol Cathedral but brought here in 1876. Altogether an impressive and characterful building.

EASTRINGTON
St Michael
3m/4km E. of Howden SE 7930
Outstanding church with green in front. Norman core with 12th- and 13th-century work in nave and chancel. Battlemented W. tower and clerestories added in 15th century. Interesting patching to N. chancel arcade following a collapse in 1632; Classical plinth supporting oak framework. Altar tomb in N. chapel of Judge Portington, d. 1456, shown wearing pigtail. In the S. porch a large Norman stone carved with eight fantastic beasts; 17th-century font cover with curious crane.

ESCRICK
St Helen
6m/10km S. of York SE 6243
By F. C. Penrose, 1856–7, in Middle Pointed style. Fine church centrally positioned in well-planned village. Long nave and chancel terminating at each end in semi-hexagonal apses. At W. this forms a baptistry, the vault of which is supported on red Devonshire marble. Delicate white marble font, bowl held by two cherubs, male and female, back to back, carved by Gio Tognolt of Rome. Baptistry also houses monuments including one by Eric Gill.

ETTON
St Mary
4m/6km N.W. of Beverley SE 9843
Good Norman church drastically restored in neo-Norman style; magnificent 12th-century tower arch with beak-heads. Excellent seated Norman figures of SS. Peter and Paul akin to the great sculptured saints of St Mary's Abbey, York. Royal Arms carved in stone above tower arch.

EVERINGHAM
St Everlida or St Emeldis
5m/8km W. of Market Weighton SE 8042
Parkland setting. Early English tower; nave and apse rebuilt c. 1763, possibly by John Carr; shapely Georgian, somewhat Victorianized.

FILEY
St Oswald
7m/11km S.E. of Scarborough TA 1180
In wooded position overlooking ravine away from town. Grand cruciform church with central tower, mainly 12th- and 13th-century; good set of tall lancet windows. Miniature medieval effigy of a priest; perhaps a heart burial. Reredos by Hodgson Fowler. Some worthwhile Victorian stained glass.

FIMBER
St Mary
2m/3km N.E. of Fridaythorpe SE 8960
Impressive with its tower on a hill. Built for Tatton Sykes by Street, 1871. Good lych gate and a fine set of typical Street fittings with brass screen, rich glass by Clayton & Bell, elaborate marble reredos by Street himself, and a noble W. tower arch, fit setting for the font.

FLAMBOROUGH
St Oswald
4m/6km N.E. of Bridlington TA 2270
Stands rather squat and sentinel-like at approach to village. W. tower by C. Hodgson Fowler, 1897. Rest much restored but rich in atmosphere, a foil for the early 16th-century rood screen and loft retaining considerable traces of original colour, the work of Ripon carvers. Medieval parclose screens, one with peascod decoration. Quaint rhyming brass inscription to Marmaduke Constable, d. 1520, who fought at Flodden Field. Monument to 'Wild' Walter Strickland, 1671, whose pardon granted by Charles II is framed in nave. Norman tub font. Medieval crucifix in S. chapel. Maidens' gloves in vestry. Some good modern windows by J. Nuttgens.

FOLKTON
St John the Evangelist
4m/6km W. of Filey TA 0579
Norman nave and chancel; see the N. doorway, responds of chancel arch, and font. Some 14th-century glass and Saxon interlace in the W. wall of the Early English tower.

FOSTON-ON-THE-WOLDS
St Andrew
halfway between Driffield and the sea SE 6965
The 14th-century tower rises over the surrounding countryside. Norman and Early English with some fine Curvilinear and Perpendicular windows; position on glacial moraine.

FRIDAYTHORPE
St Mary

9m/15km W. of Great Driffield SE 8759
Down a path bright with stonecrop in July, the small, humble building seems to hide away below the village. It has flat roofs and a squat W. tower wearing a pretty black and white clock face on its W. front, part of Hodgson Fowler's good restoration of 1902. The porch is his, with two stone shields hung up as if on stone nails. Richly barbaric S. doorway. Fowler opened up the 13th-century N. arcade and rebuilt the aisle. Ornate reredos and altar brought from Sledmere. Norman chancel arch and 17th-century communion rail.

GANTON
St Nicholas

8m/12km W. of Filey SE 9877
Setting near foot of N. scarp of Wolds, at top of pretty village street of whitewashed cottages, along which a chalk stream flows. Mainly 13th-century with S. transept, formerly Legard mortuary chapel, stone-roofed S. porch, and W. tower with small octagonal spire. Very fine mid-18th-century monument to John Legard in S. transept. Other monuments by Fisher of York.

GARTON-ON-THE-WOLDS
St Michael and All Angels

3m/4km N.W. of Great Driffield SE 9859
Norman aisleless church with Perpendicular chancel; restored and lavishly decorated by Street, 1872–80; altar frontal by C. E. Kempe. The celebrated wall decoration by Clayton & Bell has recently been conserved in memory of Sir Nikolaus Pevsner, of blessed memory. It is a scheme unique in its breadth and in its relating of the murals to the stained glass.

GOODMANHAM
All Saints

1m/2km N.E. of Market Weighton SE 8943
Simple village church on reputed site of Coifi's heathen temple; 12th-century nave and lower stages of squat W. tower; 13th-century N. aisle and rebuilt chancel; 15th-century belfry and battlements to tower. Low, narrow Norman chancel arch. Fine 16th-century octagonal font with canopies and shields, standing beside earlier hexagonal one.

GREAT DRIFFIELD
All Saints

11m/18km S.W. of Bridlington TA 0257
Handsome many-pinnacled 15th-century W. tower. Restored by G. G. Scott Jnr; he rebuilt the chancel and the N. aisle and added the S. porch 1879–80. Screens by Temple Moore, 1904; delightful collection of architectural bits and pieces.

HALSHAM
All Saints

4m/6km W. of Withernsea TA 2726
Perpendicular W. tower, but interior has earlier features, notably the arms of an ancient seat in the chancel beside the rich Decorated sedilia and piscina. Good effigy of Sir John Constable, d. 1477, on a tomb chest. Across the road the beautiful, sombre Constable mausoleum by Thomas Atkinson, 1792–1802.

HARPHAM
St John of Beverley

5m/8km N.E. of Great Driffield TA 0961
Norman core but completely remodelled in 14th century. Bold W. tower rising above village, which seen from Wolds stands out against the plain of Holderness. E. end of chancel rebuilt in brick, 1827. Conservative restoration by Temple Moore, 1908–14, when Georgian fittings were retained. Altar rails dated 1726; 17th-century brick porch. Fine collection of medieval and 18th-century monuments to St Quintin family in N. chapel, including two brasses. Monument N. of sanctuary signed J. Wilton to Charlotte St Quintin, 1762. Windows of N. chapel have 18th-century heraldic glass by William Peckitt of York.

HAYTON
St Martin

4m/6km N.W. of Market Weighton SE 8245
A long, low church with a good corbel table and Transitional arcade carved with leaves and heads; 15th- and 16th-century roofs. Decorated tower with later overhanging top stage. In the E. window three 16th-century Flemish figures.

HEDON
St Augustine

6m/10km E. of Hull TA 1828
The 'King of Holderness' with its great 15th-century central tower, the focal point of the small market town. Early English tran-

septs and chancel with Perpendicular E. window. Vestry on S. with Early English arcading on interior W. wall. Fine elevation to N. transept; grouped lancets and recessed doorway, with much display of dog-tooth. Restored and S. transept rebuilt by G. E. Street, 1866–8; 14th-century octagonal font; Elizabethan Royal Arms, 1585.

HELPERTHORPE
St Peter
11m/18km E. of Malton SE 9570
Set on the Wold-side above the village. Perhaps the most original of the Street churches with its individual stair turret a feature of the exterior. Good fittings within with delightfully varied textures; fine painted roofs, iron screen, beautiful font cover, and Burlison & Grylls stained glass. N. aisle by Temple Moore, 1893, a gentle addition.

HEMINGBROUGH
St Mary the Virgin
4m/6km E. of Selby SE 6730
Spacious, light cruciform structure at right-angles to village street. Formerly collegiate. Beautiful white Tadcaster stone. Low 13th-century central tower with disproportionately tall 15th-century spire. Decorated chancel, Tudor S. aisle with clustered shafts and four-centred arches to arcades. Inside are medieval parclose screens, 16th-century bench-ends, and the oldest of misericords dating from *c.* 1200.

HESSLE
All Saints
adjoins Hull to W. TA 0326
13th-century arcade and S. doorway; Perpendicular tower surmounted by a pretty recessed spire. Arcade capitals have rare medieval painted scrolls. Chancel by R. G. Smith, 1870; one window by Morris & Co.

HILSTON
St Margaret of Scotland
5m/8km N.W. of Withernsea TA 2833
Simple, modern church by Francis Johnson, 1956, set against cold open sky and approached by undulating Holderness lane, with hedgerow trees. Interior is sympathetic rendering of Anglican tradition. Very colourful E. window by L. C. Evetts, which with bowed rails and pall frontal exhibits badge and symbols of patron saint. Re-used 12th-century doorway from original church.

HOLME-UPON-SPALDING MOOR
All Saints
5m/8km S.W. of Market Weighton SE 8138
Position on crest of island hill rising from dead-level plain four miles W. of Wold scarp. Pierced, battlemented 15th-century tower emerges from tufted tree-tops and provides landmark for surrounding area. Mainly 13th- and 15th-century with early 18th-century brick parapets and porch. Use of variegated stones in fabric indicates complex geological nature of region. Charming unspoilt interior with considerable remains of medieval screen, Jacobean pulpit with tester, 18th-century gallery housing 17th-century barrel-organ by J. Hunton of York, early 19th-century Gothic box pews. Well restored by Temple Moore, 1906–11.

HORNSEA
St Nicholas
14m/22km N.E. of Hull TA 2047
A large Perpendicular church; restored by Sir Giles Gilbert Scott, 1867. Impressive interior culminating in the light chancel with Perpendicular windows on three sides. Alabaster St Quintin tomb with effigies, 1430.

HOWDEN
St Peter
3m/4km N. of Goole across R. Ouse SE 7428
Large cruciform church with high central tower begun by Walter Skirlaugh, Bishop of Durham, 1388–1406; 13th-century transepts and nave. W. front finished in first decade of 14th century with Geometric window flanked by pierced hexagonal turrets; 14th-century choir of collegiate church, collapsed in 1696, and left in ruins; octagonal chapter-house recently reroofed and refenestrated. Central tower of two stages with incongruous modern roof; 15th-century stone pulpitum, now reredos, with medieval statues gathered from church. Metham and Saltmarshe tombs.

HOWSHAM
St John
7m/11km S.W. of Malton SE 7362
A Street masterpiece, 1859–60. The powerful W. front is a telling asymmetrical composition with porch and N.W. turret flowering into an octagonal belfry of open columns and ending in a short spire. White and brown banded stone throughout. Fine

rounded E. apse. Inside there is a cusped chancel arch and plenty of colour; gorgeously inlaid font and pulpit and bright Clayton & Bell windows. Elaborate reredos by Thomas Earp.

HUNMANBY
All Saints
3m/4km S.W. of Filey TA 0977
Large church with early 19th-century fittings; quite a period interior. Very fine Osbaldeston monument by J. Fisher of York, 1770, in chancel; interesting Staveley monument.

KEYINGHAM
St Nicholas
4m/6km S.E. of Hedon TA 2425
Norman core with later medieval additions and reconstruction; low broach spire, 15th-century brick clerestory; iron hour-glass stand near pulpit; 13th-century font with narrow arcading.

KILHAM
All Saints
5m/8km N.E. of Great Driffield TA 0664
The church stands on a knoll above the main street with lime trees around. Barrack-like Norman nave and lavish S. door. Delightful late 13th-century chancel, big Perpendicular tower, and Gothic nave windows of c. 1800.

KILNWICK-ON-THE-WOLDS
All Saints
7m/11km N. of Beverley SE 9949
Heavily restored, 1871. Late 17th-century pulpit; good collection of Grimston monuments includes work by H. Cheere and J. Fisher. Pretty Gothic organ.

KILNWICK PERCY
St Helen
2m/3km E. of Pocklington SE 8249
In hall grounds. Norman, cleverly reconstructed in 1865 by J. W. & B. Atkinson. Collection of European woodwork.

KINGSTON-UPON-HULL
TA 0928
Holy Trinity, Market Place
Large cruciform town church. Position in market-place with stalls round churchyard walls on market days. Some of earliest medieval brickwork in Decorated choir and transepts. Central tower and nave 15th-century. Tall, slender pillars with skimped bands of ornament in place of capitals. Walls are mere screens for glass. Much old screenwork, wonderful 18th-century Rococo altar and reredos; good 19th-century pewing with poppyheads. Remains of chantries, some with old glass, a carved Trinity and a votive ship. De la Pole tombs, 15th-century brass, and magnificent ledger stones in choir. Church heavily restored by Sir Giles Gilbert Scott, 1842–69, and less so by F. S. Brodrick, 1907.

St Mary, Lowgate
Small, truncated 15th-century town church built in two phases with continuous clerestory. This nave details imitate those at Holy Trinity; 17th-century brick tower encased with whole of exterior in ashlar, 1860–3, by G. G. Scott Snr, who added second S. aisle. The result is a forest of pillars. Pewing and pulpit by Scott, windows by Clayton & Bell. Striking rood and screens to Temple Moore's design. Tudor wallbrass to John Haryson, 1525, and two wives. Dobson monument, 1666, over N. door. Shields of medieval glass in E. window. Atmosphere of constant use and affectionate care.

St Mary and All Saints, Sculcoates
Temple Moore, 1916. Boldly executed in brick. N. aisle contains furnishings and Tuscan columns from the church of 1760. A fine Georgian marble font with copper cover and many 18th- and 19th-century monuments, including several by Hull sculptors Thomas and John Earle. A monument in shorthand to Mrs Delamotte.

KIRBY GRINDALYTHE
St Andrew
2m/3km N.W. of Sledmere SE 9067
Rebuilt except for the Norman W. tower by G. E. Street, 1878. Good rib-vaulted gateway to churchyard. Spectacular Ascension mosaic on W. nave wall; excellent fittings and metal screens. A Street inlaid marble font and good tiles in the chancel; marble and alabaster reredos by James Redfearn.

KIRBY UNDERDALE
All Saints
4m/6km W. of Fridaythorpe SE 8058
Setting in deep hollow below the Wold scarp; 11th- and 12th-century church lovingly restored for Lord Halifax by G. E. Street, 1871. Decorated Norman W. doorway; glass by Hardman and Comper. Rood beam and

figures and also the painted chancel roof by Temple Moore, 1887. Homely dormers in the nave; a great delight, this holy little church.

KIRK ELLA
St Andrew

suburb 5m/8km W. of Hull TA 0229
Striking pinnacled Perpendicular tower begun in 1450; 13th- century chancel; remains of 14th-century screenwork and a grand array of monuments including a dramatic offering by Bacon to Joseph Sykes, 1809. One S. window by Kempe, the rest mainly by Wailes.

KIRKBURN
St Mary

3m/4km S.W. of Great Driffield SE 9855
Aisleless Norman nave; chancel rebuilt in 1856 by J. L. Pearson; later work includes a screen and reredos by G. E. Street. Dramatic steep tower stair framed by tower arch. Excellent Norman font.

KNAPTON
St Edmund

7m/11km E. of Malton SE 8875
A most enjoyable church in the quiet park of the Hall, mostly built in the 1870s by John Gibson and Son of Malton. Strikingly simple Norman heads built into S. wall. The entry leads to a polygonal baptistry with painted ceiling showing a multitude of storks and fish. Nave and chancel in one, the nave with an arcade and N. aisle and prettily stencilled hammer-beam roof. The chancel has stencilled walls with bishops' shields on the ceiling. The S. vestry is like a little chapter-house, and a squire's pew is at the head of the N. aisle. Plenty of brightly patterned stained glass; Royal Arms of Charles II, 1676.

LANGTOFT
St Peter

6m/10km N. of Great Driffield TA 0166
14th-century Flamboyant chancel with canopied sedilia. Got at in 1900–3 by Hodgson Fowler, but in compensation a wonderful Norman font from Cottam with Adam and Eve, St Margaret and the Dragon and St Laurence, all rudely carved. Good monument of 1774.

LANGTON
St Andrew

3m/4km S. of Malton SE 7967
A very beautiful estate village with many Gothic cottages, a green and a pond. The church is also Gothic, mostly 1822, ashlar-faced and surrounded by cherry trees. Late Norman font and original chancel arch. Reset 17th-century panelling in chancel and Gothic pulpit, communion rails and chairs. Effigy to Mary Ingram with her two babies, guarded by angels, 1656.

LECONFIELD
St Catherine

3m/4km N. of Beverley TA 0143
Chiefly 13th- and 14th-century; pleasant brick W. tower and S. porch, the latter dated 1684; 14th-century heraldic glass.

LEVEN
Holy Trinity, anciently St Faith

6m/10km N.E. of Beverley TA 1045
Set back a churchyard's length from a terribly busy road. By R. D. Chantrell, 1843–5. Large grey ashlar church in the Commissioners' style; spacious and serious with short central tower. Handsome head of 15th-century churchyard cross.

LOCKINGTON
St Mary

5m/8km N.W. of Beverley SE 9947
Unusually interesting church in well-kept, unspoilt village. Mutilated remains of Norman chancel arch; space above filled with screenwork by Temple Moore, 1893. Chancel rebuilt in Decorated style with reticulated E. window. Made-up W. screen of 18th-century woodwork. Estoft chapel on S. has painted panelling of 1634, emblazoned with Estoft arms and those of family alliances. Wall-monument to John Estoft, d. 1694, and tomb chest with crude reclining effigy of Mary Moyser, d. 1633.

LONDESBOROUGH
All Saints

2m/3km N. of Market Weighton SE 8645
Close to the site of the Hall, home of the Earls of Burlington; 12th–13th-century; tower with Tudor belfry; 11th-century Anglo-Danish cross head above Norman S. doorway. Funeral banners and brasses to the Earls of Burlington, including the celebrated architect. Fine Nicholas Stone monument to Griselda, Countess of

Cumberland, 1632. Churchyard cross by Temple Moore, 1885.

LOWTHORPE
St Martin
4m/6km N.E. of Great Driffield TA 0860
14th-century collegiate church, the chancel now in ruins. Perpendicular W. tower; extraordinary early 14th-century monument in imitation of a Tree of Jesse with children's heads growing out of the branches.

MARKET WEIGHTON
All Saints
15m/24km N.E. of Goole SE 8741
13th-century tower with 18th-century brick top rises between the aisles; largely Perpendicular with Decorated arcade. Window stonework by Temple Moore, 1899.

MIDDLETON-ON-THE-WOLDS
St Andrew
7m/11km N.E. of Market Weighton SE 9449
Stands very well with its tower looking down over pub and pond to several white-walled cottages beyond. Fine early 13th-century chancel, 17th-century crown-post nave roof; otherwise much restored by J. M. Teale of Doncaster in 1873–4; 12th-century font and early monuments in the churchyard.

NAFFERTON
All Saints
2m/3km N.E. of Great Driffield TA 0559
A large stone church which from its knoll looks down over the village and big pond. Prominent Perpendicular tower. Reset Norman chancel arch and crudely carved font; 17th-century roofs and box pews. E. window by Wailes.

NORTH CAVE
All Saints
6m/10km S. of Market Weighton SE 8932
Woodland setting; large cruciform church built of rubble; 12th- and 15th-century tower, porch of 1753, otherwise largely 13th-century. Elizabethan effigies. Rubric for Confession and Absolution painted on S. wall of chancel.

NORTH DALTON
All Saints
6m/10km S.W. of Great Driffield SE 9352
Set on a knoll above the village with its pond. Norman font, zig-zag decorated chancel

arch and S. door; Perpendicular W. tower. E. window by Burne-Jones, 1892.

NORTH FERRIBY
All Saints
7m/11km W. of Hull SE 9825
By J. L. Pearson, 1846, in the Middle Pointed style; his very first steeple – a broach spire on the W. tower. Stylish Lillingston monument in the Baroque taste by Edward Stanton, 1713. Glass by Wailes.

NORTH GRIMSTON
St Nicholas
4m/6km S.E. of Malton SE 8467
A gentle, retiring building, all 13th-century on the outside, but inside are great surprises. Norman chancel arch and prodigious font robustly carved with the Last Supper, Descent from the Cross, and St Nicholas. The Supper is a particularly good illustration of 11th-century eating habits.

NORTH NEWBALD
St Nicholas
4m/6km S.E. of Market Weighton SE 9136
Austere, aisleless 12th-century church situated beneath W. scarp of Wolds. Perhaps finest Norman church in E. Riding. Lower part of tower with its arches is Norman. To this, Early English belfry added, surmounted by 15th-century battlements. Perpendicular chancel. S. doorway of four orders with vesica niche containing seated Majesty, mainly original. Late 12th-century circular font with conventional carved foliage and 17th-century cover. Monument to the Royalist Philip Monckton who served with distinction in the Civil War.

NORTON
St Peter, anciently All Saints
opposite Malton across R. Derwent SE 7971
A grand design in the Decorated style by C. Hodgson Fowler, 1899–1911. The impressive lofty tower is topped by a Perpendicular stage to simulate development. The nave is wide and tall and the chancel a noble climax. Glass by Kempe. Brass to William Gourley, d. 1591, in a beautiful stone surround.

NUNBURNHOLME
St James
3m/4km E. of Pocklington SE 8447
Setting in valley. Disconcerting Norman tower arch with fantastic and bizarre faces;

the tower itself is of 1901, by Temple Moore. Celebrated 10th-century cross shaft with Virgin and Child; 14th-century glass fragments.

OTTRINGHAM
St Wilfred
3m/4km W. of Patrington TA 2624
At W. end of village street. Much rebuilding in 13th and 14th centuries; 15th-century clerestory and nave roof. Beautiful 14th-century tower carries lofty broach spire, the broaches being very slight, and the whole having a most satisfying outline; 12th-century tower arch, box pews.

PATRINGTON
St Patrick
4m/6km S.W. of Withernsea TA 3122
The 'Queen of Holderness'. Cruciform church of exceptional beauty with double-aisled transepts and central tower, crowned by open corona from which rises a lofty spire. Almost entirely Decorated, with Flamboyant tracery to aisle windows, and carved foliated capitals to nave. Rose window in S. gable. Splendid Easter Sepulchre, Perpendicular screen, 17th-century pulpit, and gilded reredos by Harold Gibbons in memory of King George V, who was Lord of the Manor.

PAULL
St Andrew & St Mary
2m/3km S.W. of Hedon TA 1626
A strange landscape close to the Humber with masts and funnels passing along the S. horizon. A lighthouse tower rises from the village, but the church is on a knoll apart, its high, bare crossing tower a landmark. Cruciform Perpendicular church partly faced in ashlar, the rest rubble. Stone lectern in chancel wall and some 14th-century glass in E. window, mainly canopies.

POCKLINGTON
All Saints
7m/11km N.W. of Market Weighton SE 8048
A grand cruciform town church; 12th–15th-century with fine Perpendicular W. tower. Richly carved tower corbels and nave capitals with tremendous tower arch to nave. Elaborate tiled porch floor of 1885; reset 16th-century Antwerp altarpiece, and monuments include one to an acrobat outside chancel E. wall.

PRESTON
All Saints
1m/2km N. of Hedon TA 1830
Largely Perpendicular, including the striking W. tower. The N. nave arcade is Early English, and the S. Decorated. Fragments of two medieval Nottingham alabaster reredoses showing traces of colour.

REIGHTON
St Peter
4m/6km S. of Filey TA 1375
Set on a hillside where the Wolds look out to the sea and Filey Bay. Norman and Early English exterior, heavily restored. Charming interior with floor of chalk cobbles under tower and square Norman font like a Roman altar.

RICCALL
St Mary
4m/6km N. of Selby SE 6237
Chiefly 12th- and 14th-century; Norman S. doorway of three recessed orders with unusual figure carvings on voussoirs. The door also 12th-century with bold hinges; 17th-century communion rail. Tower rebuilt by Pearson who also added the S. porch, 1864–5.

RILLINGTON
St Andrew
5m/8km E. of Malton SE 8574
Pretty spire of Malton group; Transitional font with 17th-century cover; old roofs and 18th-century monuments to faithful servants. Restored by C. Hodgson Fowler, 1884–5.

RISE
All Saints
5m/8km S.W. of Hornsea TA 1542
R. D. Chantrell, 1844–5. A serious greystone church with broach spire and lancets. Good 18th-century wall-tablets, one by Edward Foster of Hull; glass by Wailes and Kempe & Tower.

ROOS
All Saints
4m/6km N.W. of Withernsea TA 2930
Approach flanked by clipped yews; 13th–15th-century though restored; 14th-century sacristy with room over; old glass. Rood screen and other fittings by Temple Moore.

ROUTH
All Saints
4m/6km N.E. of Beverley TA 0942
Away from the village with trees around.
Mostly restoration of 1904, including the
Perpendicular tower with tall pinnacles.
Some 13th-century and later fabric; fine
canopied brass, *c.* 1420. A good 18th-
century pulpit and pleasant interior.

RUDSTON
All Saints
5m/8km W. of Bridlington TA 0967
Norman and Decorated, restored by G.
Fowler Jones, 1861; 19th-century monuments; largest English standing stone in
churchyard. Grave of Winifred Holtby, the
novelist, 1935.

RUSTON PARVA
St Nicholas
4m/6km N.E. of Great Driffield TA 0661
A delightful surprise. A grassy path leads
uphill from the pantiled farms and cottages
and all by itself in a field stands a tiny Gothic
church of yellow brick with bell-turret
slightly awry. The cast-iron pillars inside are
dated 1832 and the Norman font, two-
decker pulpit and box pews all make the
interior rather special. Walls and chancel
arch are whitewashed and the communion
rails painted white.

SANCTON
All Saints
2m/3km S.E. of Market Weighton SE 9039
Distinctive 15th-century octagonal W.
tower; otherwise rebuilt in felicitous medieval style by J. W. & B. Atkinson, 1869–71.
Perpendicular font. Good ledger stones.

SCORBROUGH
St Leonard
4m/6km N. of Beverley TA 0145
An estate church rebuilt in lavish style by
J. L. Pearson in 1859 with prominent W.
steeple. The interior is unified by Pearson's
use of shafts everywhere, and by the constructional polychromy; 16th-century effigy
of a priest; glass by Clayton & Bell.

SEATON ROSS
St Edmund
6m/10km W. of Market Weighton SE 7841
Brick 18th-century Classical, W. tower
dated 1788. Venetian E. window contains
bold glass by Stammers, 1953. Well restored

by Temple Moore, 1908. Wm. Watson,
painter of sundials, buried in the churchyard.

SETTRINGTON
All Saints
3m/4km E. of Malton SE 8370
Estate-village setting close to the Hall.
Norman church, somewhat altered, with
Perpendicular W. tower. Some old glass;
brass to John Carter, ejected rector, d. 1666.
Beautiful Marsterman monument of an urn
set high up against a pyramid background,
signed by Fisher of York. Fine George II
arms.

SEWERBY
St John the Evangelist
adjoins Bridlington to N.E. TA 1968
On fringe of cliff-top park; 1848. Charming
essay in neo-Norman style by Scott &
Moffat. Honey-coloured ashlar, richly and
crisply detailed throughout. Nave, chancel
and spire, with N. transept, formerly squire's
pew and box pews. Victorian Royal Arms in
relief. Interior lightened and coloured by
Francis Johnson.

SHERBURN
St Hilda
11m/18km E. of Malton SE 9576
Quite grand Norman W. tower with
Hodgson Fowler upper parts; he restored
the church for Sir Tatton Sykes. Impressive
early 12th-century chancel arch. Late 13th-
century N. arcade and lively Hodgson
Fowler S. arcade; 14th-century chancel. All
much restored but with character. A 12th-
century pillar piscina and Norman drum-
shaped font with arcading and leafy stems.

SHIPTONTHORPE
All Saints
2m/3km N.W. of Market Weighton SE 8543
Norman and Decorated; 12th-century S.
doorway has beak-heads and, in the porch
gable, a primitive carving of a bishop. Restored by James Demaine, 1883.

SIGGLESTHORPE
St Lawrence
3m/4km W. of Hornsea TA 1646
Set in a churchyard of trees with a dominant
W. tower, the S. face half-brick, half-cobbles
with some ashlar; early 19th-century sundial
and plate-traceried bell openings. Chiefly
Early English inside with simple arcades set
against plastered walls. A luminous interior

lit by much clear glass. Good 19th-century marble wall-monuments.

SKEFFLING
St Helen

4m/6km S.E. of Patrington TA 3719
Perpendicular church consecrated in 1470; good roofs to nave and chancel. Two family pews and interesting 18th-century monuments to Holme family by J. Rushworth of Beverley.

SKERNE
St Leonard

2m/3km S.E. of Great Driffield TA 0455
12th-century and later; Norman chancel arch and S. doorway. Disconcerting 13th-century monuments built into N. wall; 17th-century roofs.

SKIPSEA
All Saints

5m/8km N.W. of Hornsea TA 1655
The church is set on a mound backed by trees, in an almost circular churchyard, away from the village and near the remains of the castle called Skipsea Brough. Some 11th-century herringbone work, Perpendicular W. tower and aisles. Restored by James Fowler of Louth, 1865–6.

SKIPWITH
St Helen

5m/8km N.E. of Selby SE 6638
Saxon base to the tower; fine 14th-century chancel with elegant straight-headed windows; wonderful S. door with 13th-century ironwork. Alms box, 1615. Glass by A. K. Nicholson Studios, harmonizing with the old.

SKIRLAUGH
St Augustine

7m/11km N.E. of Hull TA 1439
A lavish Perpendicular church replete with parapets, pinnacles and buttresses, given to his native village in 1401 by Bishop Skirlaw. Scraped and gutted in 19th century, it figured in A. W. N. Pugin's *Contrasts*.

SLEDMERE
St Mary

7m/11km N.W. of Great Driffield SE 9364
One of the best village churches in the county; it was built in the Decorated style by Temple Moore in 1898. Much-restored medieval tower and monuments.

SOUTH DALTON
St Mary

6m/10km E. of Market Weighton SE 9645
1858–61, by J. L. Pearson. Cruciform church in early Decorated style; W. tower and spire 108 feet high, a landmark for the whole central Wolds area and reminiscent of Salisbury. Exterior of Streetly stone, and interior Hildenly stone elaborately carved. Details rather prickly, but general effect magnificent. Church and furnishings in accord with Ecclesiological principles. In S. chapel a curious monument to Sir John Hotham, d. 1689, in the Italian taste; figures of the Virtues support a semi-recumbent effigy of the knight.

SPEETON
St Leonard

4m/6km S.E. of Filey TA 1474
Small church set apart in middle of a field, near edge of high chalk cliffs. Whitewashed interior has Norman chancel arch and font; medieval stone alms box. Set in N. wall a 12th-century Agnus Dei. Beautifully restored by Francis Johnson, 1976–7.

STILLINGFLEET
St Helen

2m/3km N.E. of Cawood SE 5940
Handsome Norman S. doorway of five recessed orders with similar carvings to Riccall; very early decorative ironwork on door depicts a Viking-style ship. Jacobean screenwork; 1520 heraldic glass, renewed in 1698 by Henry Gyles. Churchyard monument to eleven choristers drowned when the boat bringing them from carol-singing capsized, 1833.

SWINE
St Mary

5m/8km N.E. of Hull TA 1335
Quite lovely fragment of a Cistercian nunnery. Chancel of former cruciform church, to which tower was added in 1787. The arcades are Transitional, and the aisles have square-headed 14th-century windows. Early 16th-century screen between Hilton chapel and aisle shows incipient Renaissance feeling in fenestration and has the pomegranate, the badge of Catherine of Aragon. There are carved misericords, a fine collection of alabaster altar tombs with seven effigies, and a very elegant Gothic font contemporary with the tower.

THIXENDALE
St Mary
2m/3km N.W. of Fridaythorpe SE 8461
Set in a deep, remote valley of the Wolds, a Street church, vicarage and school, 1870. The church has an individual lych gate, and though not as rich in fittings as some of the other Tatton Sykes churches, has Clayton & Bell glass of the Creation derived from the cartoons of wall-paintings at Garton.

THWING
All Saints
8m/12km W. of Bridlington TA 0470
Norman; much restored and tower added in 1901. Good mid-12th-century S. doorway; the tympanum carved with Agnus Dei. Fine 14th-century priest's effigy. Remarkable long squint.

TUNSTALL
All Saints
3m/4km N.W. of Withernsea TA 3031
Large village church set forlornly by the coast; mostly Perpendicular and built of beach cobbles. Interesting octagonal font.

WALKINGTON
All Hallows
3m/4km S.W. of Beverley SE 9937
Spacious 12th-century church on hillside above the village. Perpendicular tower and details; engraved chalice slab; some late foreign glass; memorable E. window; 17th-century font and pulpit.

WANSFORD
St Mary
3m/4km E. of Great Driffield TA 0656
Seen across the flat plain, the short spire and bell-turret of the stone church, the brick vicarage and next-door school form a pretty group, all by Street, 1868–77. Pleasing variety in the window patterns; the vestry chimney gives strong vertical emphasis. Within, an exotic Italian Gothic screen marks off the chancel, while a W. screen of two bold piers carries the bell-turret. Clayton & Bell glass and typical Street pulpit and font.

WATTON
St Mary
5m/8km S. of Great Driffield TA 0150
Close to the site of the Gilbertine monastery; 16th-century brick church in Gothic Survival style. At first it appears roofless, owing to the prominent parapets. Roof-bosses, 17th-century communion rail, and monuments. Early incised slab to William de Malton, 1260.

WAWNE
St Peter
5m/8km N. of Hull TA 0936
Early English with fine Perpendicular W. tower, built over westerly bay of N. aisle. Perpendicular brick clerestory; 15th-century font. Nave roof, screen and pulpit by Street, 1872.

WEAVERTHORPE
St Andrew
4m/6km N.W. of Langtoft SE 9670
Striking position on flank of Wolds. Tall early-Norman W. tower of Northumbrian type; nave and chancel are Norman too, with a 12th-century sundial over the S. door with the words, 'Herbert the Chamberlain, of Winchester, built this church'. Restored by G. E. Street, 1871–2. Brass chancel screen by T. Potter; glass and triptych by Clayton & Bell. Delightful painted roof. Pulpit and tower screen both of iron and both by Street. Large statue of St Andrew by James Redfearn.

WELTON
St Helen
1m/2km E. of Brough SE 9527
Setting in delightful village beside duck pond. The church almost rebuilt by G. G. Scott Snr in his favourite Middle Pointed style in 1863. Morris glass, and in the churchyard an amusing stone to the much-married Jeremiah Simpson.

WELWICK
St Mary
2m/3km S.E. of Patrington TA 3421
Stylish Decorated remodelling of early-Norman church to which clerestory was added in 15th century; 17th-century brick S. porch. Light, pleasing interior with Jacobean pulpit, much-restored chancel screen, and good, simple modern pewing. Brass to William Wright of Ploughland, brother of two Gunpowder Plotters. Tomb with effigy of medieval priest, beneath much-patched canopy.

WEST LUTTON
St Mary
9m/15km E. of Malton SE 9369
A contrast to the other churches of the mid-

Wold valley with its shingle spire and tile-hung belfry which would have been at home in Surrey. All by Street for Tatton Sykes, 1874–5. Fine lych gate and rich interior with painted nave roof, metal screen, painted reredos, Burlison & Grylls stained glass, and rib-vaulted chancel.

WETWANG
St Nicholas
6m/10km W. of Great Driffield SE 9359
Norman and 13th-century; very well restored with good woodwork by C. Hodgson Fowler, 1901.

WHARRAM-LE-STREET
St Mary
6m/10km S.E. of Malton SE 8665
Standing high on a Wold hillside with wide views towards the Plain and the Yorkshire Moors on the skyline. Anglo Saxon nave, W. doorway and tower with early-Norman top and Norman chancel arch; 14th-century N. aisle, the chancel itself rebuilt *c.* 1863; 18th-century altar table in N. aisle. Simple tub font. Two bells from the ruined church at Wharram Percy.

WINESTEAD
St Germain
2m/3km N.W. of Patrington TA 2924
Situation amidst meadows in secluded position away from road and village. Tiny 12th-century nave and chancel with remains of corbel table on S. side. The Hildyard chapel was added in *c.* 1602 and rebuilt by Temple Moore in 1893 re-using Italianate panels

bearing trophies of arms; 18th-century pulpit, restored medieval screen, and good collection of Hildyard monuments.

WINTRINGHAM
St Peter
6m/10km E. of Malton SE 8873
Set in a dell of the Wolds away from village of whitewashed cottages, the church has a 12th-century chancel with later windows and Norman corbel tables. Perpendicular nave and aisles with W. tower and spire of Malton group; in the heads of the aisle windows a galaxy of saints painted on white glass. Perpendicular screens, Jacobean pewing, a two-decker pulpit, and a rhyming acrostic memorial to John Lister, d. 1651. Beautifully restored by Temple Moore.

WOLD NEWTON
All Saints
7m/11km S.W. of Filey TA 0473
Untouched S. doorway of 1144–50, of one order with scalloped capitals and a carved tympanum. Painted Victorian Royal Arms and commandment boards, 1839, make a pleasant pattern at the W. end. The arms are incorrectly those used up to 1837, showing the Hanoverian escutcheon.

WRESSLE
St John of Beverley
3m/4km N.W. of Howden SE 7031
1799 of brick. Delightful Gothic exterior with W. tower retaining original round-arched bell openings. The interior was refurbished and the matching windows replaced in 1873.

Yorkshire North Riding

Introduction

Like Caesar's Gaul, it divides into three parts: a central plain, bounded on either side by moorland sloping off into dales. Here is some of Yorkshire's noblest scenery. The western dales, Wensleydale and Swaledale, each have their own ruined abbey, castle, and group of waterfalls. On the opposite side, moorland runs as far east as the sea, with villages few and scattered. Churches are isolated, and so often locked that the visitor needs to be adept at hunting for the key.

Industry has touched the area only on the north by the Tees, where the extensive ship-building and iron and steel industries spawned during the 19th century have now greatly declined, to be replaced by petro-chemical and service industries.

In the Riding generally there is much pre-Conquest work. Kirkdale has a Saxon nave and sundial. Fifty-two churches possess sculptured crosses, complete or fragmentary. Norman doorways and chancel arches have survived many a later reconstruction. Lastingham is a place of pilgrimage because of its Norman crypt and links with SS. Cedd and Chad. In the north-west, Wensleydale takes pride of place for churches as well as for cheese. Decorated is represented by Patrick Brompton and Ainderby Steeple, Perpendicular by Burneston. Old Malton has the nave of a Gilbertine priory.

For grandeur it is the town churches which score – Bedale, Northallerton and Thirsk. There are few brasses (Wensley and Topcliffe have Flemish ones), but an abundance of 14th-century stone effigies. Admirers of 18th-century 'churchwarden' will enjoy themselves in Cleveland; Ingleby Arncliffe has been tidied up, and of course Whitby must be allowed to stand as a museum-piece. At Kirkleatham the body of the church was rebuilt in 1763 and the magnificent almshouse chapel in 1742.

The Victorian builders had their fling on Tees-side, with happier results than in Leeds or Sheffield. Also, in the country estates interesting new churches were built. Thanks to Viscount Downe, Butterfield was commissioned to build an entire village, consisting of church, vicarage, schools and cottages, at Baldersby; Pearson may be studied in a French mood at Appleton-le-Moors. His friend and admirer, Temple Moore, did scholarly restoration work throughout the Riding, and new building in and around Middlesbrough. Of late, woodcarver Robert Thompson has been making Kilburn better known for mice than for white horses.

In York itself, 20 old churches survive from a 16th-century total of 41, and some of these have now been converted to non-ecclesiastical use: St John, Micklegate is an arts centre; St Mary, Castlegate a heritage centre; St Sampson a meeting-place for the elderly; St Andrew empty and disused; and at St Martin-cum-Gregory is the Anglican Youth Centre. For size they have nothing to compare with St Margaret's and St Nicholas', King's Lynn, or even with St Peter Mancroft, Norwich, so completely is York overshadowed

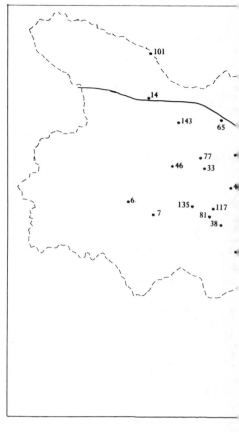

by the Minster. They are all worth seeing, not least for their glass, which escaped destruction in the Civil War through the decency of Fairfax. In design the city churches show a certain uniformity; most are parallelograms with towers engaged inside the aisles. The best reconstruction of a medieval interior is at All Saints, North Street; no other church in Yorkshire so vividly preserves the spirit of medieval England.

D. R.

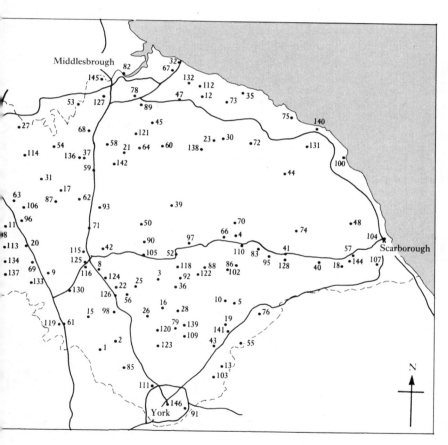

continued overleaf

Selected List of Churches

ADWARK
St Stephen
6m/10km S.W. of Easingwold SE 4663
Its architect, E. B. Lamb, 1846, was the *bête noire* of the Ecclesiologists and is numbered amongst Goodhart Rendel's gallery of 'Rogue Architects'. The plan of the church is unusual yet effective both within and without. The external walling is rich in texture and colour, being a conglomeration of pebble-stones from the river, herringbone brickwork, and freestone dressings. There is an elaborate roof of open timbering. The almost detached tower and spire form a composition typical of the architect.

ALNE
St Mary
3m/4km S.W. of Easingwold SE 4965
The tower has a medieval ground stage and Georgian upper stages of brick finished with obelisks at the angles of the parapet. The S. doorway with two orders of Bestiary medallions, and the font with a broad pattern of leaf scrolls, are good Norman work. Very odd reticulated tracery is found in the E. window of the N. chapel. The nave and N. aisle are mostly of 15th-century date and of the local wide and low proportions. The pale washed plastered walls of the church form a good background to the Norman tower arch and the Jacobean pulpit. The ground stage of the tower, shut off behind an indifferent 20th-century Gothic screen, contains pleasant 18th-century panelling, a homely brick floor, and an exquisite cartouche, 1695. Kempe glass in the S. windows of the nave. A maiden's garland of straw in the nave.

AMPLEFORTH
St Hilda
10m/16km E. of Thirk SE 5878
Sited on a steep hummock with fine view of the Vale of Pickering. Norman origins to 13th-century chancel and 15th-century tower; unfinished Norman N. doorway. Effigies of a bearded civilian of *c.* 1330 with a lady wearing a wimple looking over his shoulder. Royal Arms of George III.

APPLETON-LE-MOORS
Christ Church
5m/8km N.W. of Pickering SE 7387
A church finely conceived by J. L. Pearson, 1863. The exterior is particularly satisfying, the W. front, the almost detached tower and spire, and the apsidal chancel being its highlights. There is much competent French detail, but the tower up to the belfry stage displays fully developed Pearsonic traits – which are best studied from the S.E. corner of the churchyard. Around the vestry door and the window of the N. chapel is much fanciful detail. The interior has a muscular High Victorian character unlike the elegant beauty of Pearson's late style. Vigorous nave capitals and bold sgraffito work round the apse. Glass by Clayton & Bell.

APPLETON-LE-STREET
All Saints
4m/6km W. of Malton SE 7373
Rising above the village like some church in the Dordogne. Good early tower, the lower stages Saxon with spacious arch to nave; main body of church 13th-century; 14th-century female effigies with interesting carving of drapery. Good brass oil-lamps in nave.

ASKRIGG
St Oswald
4m/6km N.W. of Aysgarth SD 9491
The largest church in Wensleydale, and one of the most stately, with a suitably commanding position in this small market town. Mainly 15th- and early 16th-century; fine moulded beams to nave ceiling make this interior memorable; curious ribbed vault under tower; heavily Victorianized.

AYSGARTH
St Andrew
7m/11km W. of Leyburn SE 0088
Set on the hills above the river and upper falls. Medieval origins, much altered in 1866. Finely carved 15th-century screen and stall ends, possibly brought from Jervaulx Abbey; 19th-century pews, font and glass;

some interesting headstones and churchyard tombs.

BAGBY
St Mary
4m/6km S.E. of Thirsk SE 4680

E. B. Lamb, 1862, at his most eccentric. Half a forest of heavy timbers supports a huge roof over low walls to make a large central space. Odd, but full of personality and a quirky holiness.

BALDERSBY
St James
5m/8km S.W. of Thirsk SE 3578

The first sight of Baldersby is of the 160-foot tower and spire rising over the York plain. The whole hamlet of church, school and cottages is the work of William Butterfield, 1857. It is one of his best compositions. The warm and beautiful interior contrasts with the severe outside. The font and its cover, the pews, the dwarf wall at the entrance to the chancel, the clock face and the alabaster reredos are all in keeping. Excellent Butterfield roofs crown the whole. In the impressive chancel floor is set the brass cross of the Founder's memorial. Glass by O'Connor, Wailes and Preedy of Worcester.

BARTON-LE-STREET
St Michael and All Angels
4m/6km W. of Malton SE 7274

A rebuilding by Perkin and Sons, Leeds, 1870–1; fine, exuberantly carved Norman stones from demolished church built into the structure; note especially Samson and the lion and the beautiful ram's head used as a label stop. The 19th-century 'Norman' work has character of its own, especially the wooden pulpit. Delicate organ case by Temple Moore.

BEDALE
St Gregory
7m/11km S.W. of Northallerton SE 2688

The great semi-fortified W. tower of the church and the huge garden wall of the Hall opposite hem in the road and form a striking termination to this market town's wide main street. The S. entrance to the churchyard is through a gate flanked by well-detailed 18th-century stone piers. In the churchyard are baluster table-tombs of local type and the particularly lush neo-Grecian monument to Nancy Day. The W. tower with its deeply set windows and the masterly handling of the stair turret is impressive. The S. porch has a pointed ribbed barrel vault, covered externally with stone slabs. The nave has very large ballflowers decorating arches and piers. There are several 14th-century tombs; an 18th-century Creed and Lord's Prayer above the chancel arch; and in the S. aisle a mural tablet by R. Westmacott to Henry Peirse, d. 1824.

BOOSBECK
St Aidan
3m/4km S. of Saltburn NZ 6516

The church by W. S. Hicks, 1901, stands on a hill above stone terraces and later housing. Tall bellcote above strongly composed W. front with two lancets above a portal and large tympanum carved with a Celtic cross. Impressive lancets light the nave and chancel, the warm ironstone rock-faced outside. Inside, the unaisled nave leads to the crossing marked by two arches to N. and S., with the chancel broad and high beyond a delicate iron screen. There is a noble sense of place, and an echo down the centuries of early Northumbrian churches, their undecorated walls pierced by narrow windows, like God's fortresses.

BOSSALL
St Botolph
3m/4km N. of Stamford Bridge SE 7160

A cruciform church with central tower, mostly 12th century, standing on its own near a pond. The chancel was rebuilt in the 13th century. Sadly scraped interior and badly pointed. Fine corbel table round nave and transepts. Early 19th-century S. porch floored with brick shelters a superb 13th-century doorway. Inside, the arches and piers of the crossing are the outstanding feature. The Royal Arms of 1710 in a marbled wood frame; 18th-century font cover; an exuberant 20th-century oak reredos and really good glass in the E. window by Tower and S. chancel by Kempe.

BOWES
St Giles
4m/6km S.W. of Barnard Castle NY 9913

The church stands near the Norman castle keep. Modest exterior has bellcote and Victorian ventilator. Mostly 14th–15th-century with late-Norman doorways, long nave, and chancel with low transepts. Two fonts, one 12th-century, one mounted on a Roman altar. Beautiful medieval stone Crucifixion outside S. porch.

BRAFFERTON
St Peter
6m/10km W. of Easingwold SE 4370
An interesting church on the banks of the Swale where St Paulinus is said to have conducted mass baptisms. The nave, rebuilt in neo-Perpendicular style, 1832, by J. P. Pritchett, is broader than it is long; 15th-century tower and chancel; the S. chancel chapel bears an inscription on its S. wall that Ralph Nevil was its founder. Kempe glass.

BRANDSBY
All Saints
4m/6km N.E. of Easingwold SE 5872
The church stands in undulating and well-wooded country. The architect was Thomas Atkinson, 1767–70. Outside, the Classical detail is a trifle heavy, excepting the stone cupola poised imaginatively over the body of the church. Entry lies through a narthex in which stands an 18th-century baluster font. The door to the nave is protected by a wrought-iron grille. In the body of the church stand four Roman Doric columns connected by plaster cross vaults and forming the base supports of the cupola. The architectural effect is beyond praise. There is plenty of free floor space, a well-detailed W. gallery, good early 20th-century furniture, and a successful brass lectern.

BROMPTON
St Thomas
1m/2km N. of Northallerton SE 3796
Setting by village green. Over-restored by Ewan Christian, 1868. Magnificent collection of hogback tombstones and pre-Conquest fragments.

BROMPTON-BY-SAWDON
All Saints
7m/11km S.W. of Scarborough SE 9482
Poised above a lake at the centre of the village. Mostly 14th–15th-century with broach spire. Porch added in 1895 as memorial to George Cayley, inventor of the first aeroplane. Interior unfortunately scraped. Brightly painted organ case and W. gallery by Temple Moore. Good 18th-century Cayley tablets. Victorian brass chandelier, immense and castellated. Wordsworth married Mary Hutchinson here in 1802.

BULMER
St Martin
6m/10km W. of Malton SE 6967
A simple small village church with late 11th-century core; notable texture of N. wall with herringbone masonry. Head of Saxon wheel cross and in the porch a Greek key slab to Christopher Thompson, d. 1748, who 'wrought in brass and iron for 45 years for the third and fourth Earls of Carlisle' at Castle Howard.

BURNESTON
St Lambert
3m/4km S.E. of Bedale SE 3085
Stately 15th-century exterior busy with pinnacles, battlements, and good buttresses. W. tower and clerestory. Splendid 1627 furnishings in nave, signed by maker and paid for (£50) by Thomas Robinson of Allerthorpe Hall.

CARLTON
St Botolph
3m/4km S.W. of Stokesley NZ 5004
On a knoll at the N. of this village immediately below the Cleveland Hills, a distinguished church of warm-coloured stone by Temple Moore, 1896–7. He was an architect alive to the needs of a small village church and sensitive to the local medieval regional characteristics, yet there is plenty of originality. From the doorway a tunnel-vaulted passage leads to a baptistry, a stone-vaulted space carrying a gallery above; an exciting composition. The E. window is excellent and is filled with rich glass. Small rectangular plain windows at the head of each sedilia also a nice touch. Lych gate of sensitive design.

CARLTON HUSTHWAITE
St Mary
5m/8km N. of Easingwold SE 4976
Small brown church standing at the back of a tiny village green. It is a perfect undisturbed late 17th-century building with furnishings complete. Two-decker pulpit with sounding board on ogee cupola, 1678; bobbin-ended pews and communion rail with balusters.

CASTLETON
St Michael & St George
8m/12km W. of Egton NZ 6808
At the lower end of the village, surrounded by grass and trees, is the parish church by

Leslie Moore, 1925. Rock-faced on the outside with a broad, strong W. tower, unadorned rectangular bell openings. Inside are white walls with stone arches on the N. side in readiness for an aisle. The broad tower arch has a light screen across it with the font framed in the central opening. Simple king-post roof and good pews by Thompson of Kilburn. A spacious, peaceful interior.

CATTERICK
St Anne
5m/8km S.E. of Richmond SE 2397
Fortunately the A1 now bypasses the village and the army camp is at some distance, so the village remains a pleasant surprise with a green and a stream. The church is quite large, with a strong W. tower; it is mostly of *c.* 1412, the Master Mason being Richard of Cracall, whose contract still survives. Three 15th-century Burgh brasses and a fine black marble font, also 15th-century.

COXWOLD
St Michael
5m/8km N. of Easingwold SE 5377
The village street climbing a steep hill, with the church at its summit, forms a natural unity. With the exception of the chancel, rebuilt in 1777, the stately exterior is of 15th-century date. Regional characteristics abound. The tower is octagonal; compare with Sancton, East Riding. The buttresses and pinnacles are similar to those on the tower of St Martin-le-Grand, York, and display an equally effortless subtlety in design. Inside, the 17th and 18th centuries have left their delightful mark: the W. gallery, the plasterwork on the E. wall of the nave, the box pews, the pulpit, and the monuments in the chancel. Owing to the narrowness of the chancel, the communion rail is extended down its length, to leave room on either side for the enormous Fauconberg tombs. Fragmentary 15th-century glass, and some by Peckitt. Lawrence Sterne reburied in the churchyard two centuries after his death in London in 1768.

CRAYKE
St Cuthbert
2m/3km E. of Easingwold SE 5670
Dedicated to St Cuthbert who often stayed here on his visits to and from York; his body also rested here for a brief period in the 9th century. Church and castle are at the top of a hill overlooking the Plain of York. The structure is mostly of 15th-century date. The wide and squat nave and N. aisle should be compared with Alne. Both nave and chancel have heavily timbered 15th-century roofs. The church has excellent pews with bobbinends, clerk's desk, churchwarden seats, and pulpit, 1637.

CROFT
St Peter
3m/4km S. of Darlington NZ 2809
The church stands near the bank of the Tees, close to the great medieval bridge that leads into County Durham. A long, low building of colourful stone of varied texture and well weathered. The 14th-century chancel has good buttresses and tracery. Built into the S. wall is a piece of Romano-British sculpture representing a local deity. Elevated Milbanke pew of the local family that provided Byron with a wife. The 14th-century piscina and sedilia, the monument of Sir Richard Clervaulx, and the ostentatious Milbanke tomb should not be missed. Charles Dodgson, father of Lewis Carroll, was rector here 1843–68.

DALBY
St Peter
2m/3km W. of Terrington SE 6471
Remote setting in the Howardian Hills. A Norman S. doorway and chancel arch remain from the early church. Attractive stone barrel vault to 15th-century chancel, which from outside resembles a pele-tower.

DALTON
St John the Evangelist
2m/3km E. of Topcliffe SE 4376
By Wm. Butterfield, 1868. A dour rock-faced building on the outside, but do not be put off. There are good things within, and here the colour changes to red brick with bands of stone and blue brick. High wooden screen with trellis decoration above and beyond a powerful reredos with the E. windows part of the whole composition. Excellent Morris glass in all the windows. Particularly moving St John the Evangelist set against a deep-blue background in the W. window. Splendid font.

DANBY
St Hilda
12m/19km W. of Whitby NZ 7008
The church stands in an isolated position

in a valley below the moors. The detached 15th-century tower of warm stone is placed on the S. side. Its ground stage is a porch entered through an elegant wooden gate of early 19th-century date. The nave was classicized in the 18th century and given 13th-century-looking arcades by Temple Moore in 1903. The 18th-century W. gallery has been retained and is approached by external stone steps. Butterfield built the chancel in 1848. Altogether a noble, spacious interior with a large, bright Kempe window of the Good Shepherd and much clear glass. There is a Royal Arms of George IV, 1829, and a good series of 17th- and 18th-century monuments in the churchyard.

DANBY WISKE
(dedication unknown)
4m/6km N.W. of Northallerton SE 3398
Massive W. tower; 11th-century carved tympanum, still in situ and supposed to show the Weighing of Souls; 17th-century stalls.

DORMANSTOWN
All Saints
adjoining Redcar to S.W. NZ 5823
Leslie Moore, 1932; brick; personal Gothic, characteristic rood screen. A homely, cheerful building.

DOWNHOLME
St Michael and All Angels
4m/6km S.W. of Richmond SE 1197
Set around with yew trees, a small church of Norman origin perched all on its own high up on the S. side of Swaledale. Stone barn in corner of churchyard is possibly for stabling worshippers' horses. Good tombstones lie at all angles. Pre-Reformation bell in small turret. Somewhat over-restored inside; three-bay Norman arcade and good stone chancel floor. Royal Arms of George III and Hutton hatchments. Clear glass in the windows and the sound of sheep on the fells.

EASBY
St Agatha
2m/3km S.E. of Richmond NZ 5708
The church is close to the ruins of the Abbey, by the River Swale below Richmond. On the hill above stands Easby Hall. The church is long and low and of beautiful weathered stone. There is a double bellcote; two-storey S. porch has colourwashed barrel vault and walls. Early English E. window

and 15th-century S. aisle. Norman font; excellent 19th-century nave pewing, medieval wall-paintings restored by Sir Giles Gilbert Scott, and hatchments. Cast of Anglo-Saxon Easby cross in the chancel.

EASINGTON
All Saints
1m/2km E. of Loftus NZ 7418
Within sight of the sea and the towers of the potash mine. In a windy upland position, C. Hodgson Fowler built a church in the Decorated style, 1888–9, which retains a sumptuous chancel arch built into the S. side of the upper floor of the tower, reached by an inner stair. It is full of beak-heads, pellets and bobbins. A rustic monument to Katherine Conyers, d. 1621 aged 21 months, shows her in bed with the cover hanging down the front.

EAST GILLING
The Holy Cross
2m/3km S. of Oswaldkirk SE 6176
The village street follows a gap in the Howardian Hills below Gilling Castle. Here, set back in its churchyard, is the parish church. Transitional arcades; aisles and chancel 14th-century; tower 15th-century. Fine monuments of 14th, 16th and 19th centuries; many to the Fairfaxes. Particularly fine is one of 1828 by Joseph Gott with a female figure bending over two urns.

EAST ROUNTON
St Laurence
7m/11km N.E. of Northallerton NZ 4203
By R. J. Johnson, 1884; good 20th-century furnishings; Renaissance woodwork *c.* 1700 from Newcastle Cathedral re-used in chancel as reredos. Interesting Morris & Co. glass commemorating Gertrude Bell, explorer.

EAST WITTON
St John the Evangelist
2m/3km S.E. of Middleham SE 1486
The church stands apart from the delightful village of long green with trees and the white railings of cottages, next to a plain and good vicarage. It is remarkably full of character for its date, 1809; strong and not at all the usual cardboard cut-out Gothic. A broad W. tower lends further weight to the composition. The architect an otherwise unknown H. H. Seward.

EASTMOORS
St Mary Magdalene
4m/6km N. of Helmsley SE 6190
Below the moor N. of Helmsley and sheltered by conifer plantations. The W. bellturret rises from among rhododendron bushes to a pyramid with crockets. It is a memorable small church by G. G. Scott Jnr, handled with much skill and orignality. Nave and chancel in one with painted ceiling in red, white and green. Beautifully simple circular font by Temple Moore. S. aisle can be shuttered off to form classroom or bedroom for a snow-bound incumbent!

EBBERSTON
St Mary
6m/10km E. of Pickering SE 8982
Set against a backdrop of woods next to Ebberston Hall, Colen Campbell's delightful small villa; 12th–14th-century; restored by Ewan Christian, 1876. The church slopes down from the broad arcaded nave to the small, intimate chancel.

ELLERBURNE
St Hilda
3m/4km E. of Pickering SE 8484
Hidden away in a valley behind Thornton Dale, a building of simple beauty. Originally 11th-century with 17th–18th-century fittings. Careful restoration by W. D. Caroe, 1905, who kept its unassuming character. Anglo-Danish cross head.

FELIXKIRK
St Felix
3m/4km N.E. of Thirsk SE 4684
In a village below the scarp of the Hambleton Hills. Mostly 11th-century; apse rebuilt with one window containing 14th-century glass. Convincing restoration by W. H. Dykes, 1860; large German organ.

FOSTON
All Saints
1m/2km E. of Thornton-le-Clay SE 6965
On the very edge of the York Plain below the Howardian Hills. Norman with contemporary doorways, that on the S. highly decorative with scenes including the Last Supper; chancel arch and pillar piscina; 18th-century pulpit and panels from box pews used as a dado. Wall-plaque to Sidney Smith, the Whig wit, who was rector here 1809–29.

GOATHLAND
St Mary
7m/11km S.W. of Whitby NZ 8301
Originally intended to stand out starkly against the moorland, today the church, a powerful work of W. H. Brierley, 1894–5, is almost hidden by a churchyard of trees and shrubs. Norman Shaw's influence can be felt in this modern Perpendicular-style building with broad central tower as wide as the church itself. Two round tower arches inside lead the eye to the short chancel. Every detail of wood and stone is straightforward and honest. The pews are green-stained, very much in the Arts and Crafts tradition. Norman font.

GREAT AYTON
All Saints
5m/8km S.W. of Guisborough NZ 5510
The church stands quietly behind the more prominent (and dull) Christ Church of 1876 by Ross and Lamb. The stonework of the old church is of the warm local stone beautifully textured and weathered. The tower was demolished c. 1880. There is an altogether delightful mixture of Norman and late 18th-century churchwarden Classical so popular in Cleveland. The furniture of 1790 includes a three-decker pulpit complete with sounding board. Captain Cook's mother and five of her children are buried in the churchyard.

GRINTON
St Andrew
½m/1km S.E. of Reeth, W. of Richmond SE 0498
A great, long, grey church growing naturally out of Swaledale. The exterior is chiefly remarkable for its austerity and the almost domestic character of its windows. Scraped inside; the arcades are mostly of 15th-century date. Pulpit with tester, 1718; 15th-century parclose screens; painted wood tablet to Dorothy Darcy, 1698, and an oval-framed Royal Arms. A cell on the N. side of the chancel with barrel-vaulted roof and domestic-type 17th-century wood screen and door. In the S. chapel there are several figures and other fragments of medieval glass, and a homely 17th-century parclose screen.

GUISBOROUGH
St Nicholas
6m/10km S. of Redcar NZ 6116
Busy market town. Setting next to ruined

Augustinian priory. Chancel 15th-century; aisles restored by Temple Moore, 1903–8. Brus cenotaph, early 16th-century, and very fine indeed with its knights, priests and shields. Decent 20th-century stained glass by H. J. Stammers; interesting headstones in the churchyard.

HACKNESS
St Peter
5m/8km W. of Scarborough SE 9690
Set in a deep wooded valley near the Hall. The tower, *c.* 1200, and 15th-century spire form a well-detailed composition. The chancel also of 15th-century date should be compared with Seamer. Good series of mural monuments includes one by locally born Matthew Noble, 1853; 15th-century stalls in the chancel; 17th-century vestry and Royal Arms of William and Mary.

HAUXWELL
St Oswald
4m/6km N.E. of Leyburn SE 1693
A late 11th-century church with early 13th-century tower; rough herringbone masonry in both nave and chancel; Norman S. doorway; brass of 1611 and Jacobean furniture.

HAWNBY
All Saints
6m/10km N.W. of Helmsley SE 5489
Between the village and the Hall, all on its own by a stream – a delightful spot. A basically Norman church, simple and humble, with bellcote and 17th-century Tankard monuments.

HEALEY
St Paul
3m/4km W. of Masham SE 1880
On the valley side to the W. of the village. Lamb's first church, 1845–8, with plenty of his idiosyncracies; the Vanbrugian character of the tower, the forceful and dramatic interior, the primitive porch windows, and the open timber roof herald the later architectural experiments. Well-preserved Lamb furnishings and some of his own stained glass.

HELMSLEY
All Saints
12m/19km E. of Thirsk SE 6183
Of Norman origins (see chancel arch and S. doorway) but largely rebuilt *c.* 1867 by Charles Barry Jnr. Altar, reredos, and charming painted ceiling by Temple Moore, 1909. Fine 18th-century chandelier.

HILTON IN CLEVELAND
St Peter
5m/8km S. of Stockton-on-Tees NZ 4611
Simple Norman church with 18th-century windows and roof; the N. doorway has two orders, one with zig-zag, the other with pellet ornament, also seen on chancel arch. In the S. wall a stone with animal relief and one with a sundial. Interior has short responds with Norman capitals at the E. end of the chancel, possibly suggesting an apse that was not undertaken.

HORNBY
St Mary
8m/12km N. of Northallerton NZ 3605
The exterior is attractive owing to the varying colour and textures of local stone used in its building. The campanile-type tower contains 11th-century bell openings to which a new belfry was added in the 15th century. The E. wall of the chancel is 19th-century neo-Norman by J. L. Pearson, 1878–9. Inside there is a genuine Norman arcade, 19th-century decorated font, and mosaic chancel floor. Medieval and later monuments, brasses, and early 16th-century painted panels with birds and foliage to a parclose screen.

HOVINGHAM
All Saints
8m/12km W. of Malton SE 6675
Beautifully kept estate village with the great house of the Worsley family adjacent. Pre-Conquest unbuttressed W. tower with mighty stonework showing inside the nave. Very worn Saxon reredos in S. chapel. Remainder mostly Victorian; stained glass by H. J. Stammers; some minor Worsley monuments; chancel unfortunately re-ordered by R. G. Sims, 1985.

HUSTHWAITE
St Nicholas
4m/6km N. of Easingwold SE 5175
Setting with view to Hambleton Hills. The lower Norman stonework in nave, chancel and tower is brown, with the upper Perpendicular part in grey stone. Bad neo-Norman windows; 17th-century furnishings include a font cover with awkward ribs and straight-headed benches with homely knobs.

HUTTON BUSCEL
St Matthew
5m/8km S.W. of Scarborough SE 9784
The village follows a gentle ridge above the
Vale of Pickering and the Norman tower
rises above trees to the west. Butterfield N.
aisle and font; Jacobean pulpit; 18th-century
monuments include that to Richard Osbaldeston, Dean of York, 1764. Lych gate by
Basil Champneys and fine Butterfield school
and master's house.

HUTTON RUDBY
All Saints
4m/6km W. of Stokesley NZ 4606
Setting by river. Pulpit, 1594, a glorious
Elizabethan piece with rich inlay. A bassoon
from the church's 19th-century orchestra.

INGLEBY ARNCLIFFE
All Saints
7m/11km N.E. of Northallerton NZ 4400
The little church stands below tree-covered
slopes of the Cleveland Hills and adjacent
to the 18th-century Hall built by John Carr.
Largely rebuilt in 1821 in Cleveland churchwarden Classical. Light interior has sash
windows, white walls, and box pews painted
a deep red with their original painted
numbers. Scandinavian ship on a ledge
above the door; Royal Arms of William III
and George VI. Some 14th-century glass
fragments from Mount Grace Priory and two
effigies, also 14th-century, in the chancel.

INGLEBY GREENHOW
St Andrew
4m/6km E. of Stokesley NZ 5806
A humble but very attractive church, mostly a
rebuilding of 1741 with 12th-century arcade
and chancel arch. Strange capitals to the
piers with a realistic pig and bear.

KIRBY-ON-THE-MOOR
All Saints
1m/2km N. of Boroughbridge SE 3868
Away from the village. Pre-Conquest work;
S. door probably 12th-century with contemporary hinges; traces of wall-paintings;
benches with poppyheads; tower remodelled
in 1870 by Sir Giles Gilbert Scott.

KIRBY SIGSTON
St Lawrence
3m/4km E. of Northallerton SE 4194
Set beside a small lake, the church has a
W. tower of early 19th-century date which
resembles Ingleby Arncliffe nearby. Nave
and chancel are Transitional with Perpendicular E. window. Early window head in S.
wall of the chancel. Limewashed interior of
character, well restored by Temple Moore,
1890. Gilded and coloured rood beam and
cross but as yet no figures. The N. aisle,
lower than the nave, contains font of 1662.
Narrow chancel arch has a satisfying 20th-
century screen. In the chancel, the 14th-
century arches have good carved capitals.
There are 20th-century returned stalls and
18th-century altar rails.

KIRKBY FLEETHAM
St Mary
4m/6km S.E. of Catterick SE 2894
Massive Perpendicular tower, rib-vaulted
within; Norman S. doorway; Early English
S. chapel and Decorated N. aisle; chancel
rebuilt by Woodyer, 1872. Monument to
Flaxman, 1785, and an excellent early 14th-
century cross-legged knight, thought to be
Sir Nicholas Stapleton, who fought at Ban-
nockburn, 1314.

KIRKBY-IN-CLEVELAND
St Augustine
2m/3km S.E. of Stokesley NZ 5305
The church has a split personality. The nave
is 1815 Georgian with large round windows
and a gallery, while the chancel looks like a
completely different church: a fine Gothic
design by Temple Moore, 1900, quite noble
and grand. The 18th-century W. tower looks
out towards the curving wall of the churchyard and the curving line of the cottages
beyond, a memorable small village centre.

KIRKBY RAVENSWORTH
St Peter & St Felix
4m/6km N.W. of Richmond NZ 1406
Set on rectangular green of hill-top village;
huge Perpendicular tower, dated 1397. Early
signed monument, 1558, to John Dakyn,
founder of the grammar school beside the
churchyard two years before his death.

KIRKDALE
St Gregory
1m/2km W. of Kirkbymoorside SE 6785
Small Saxon church all on its own by a
stream in a wooded valley. Chiefly remarkable for the pre-Conquest sundial set above
the S. doorway. Centre panel signed by the
makers, Haward and Brand, priests, and the
inscription records that 'Orm Gamal's son

bought St Gregory's Minster when it was all broken down and fallen and let it be made anew from the ground to Christ and St Gregory in Edward's days, the King and Tosti's days the Earl'. The King was Edward the Confessor and Earl Tosti was brother to King Harold; this church can thus be dated to about 1060. Inside are two carved Anglo-Saxon tomb slabs and stone benches around the walls.

KIRKLEATHAM
St Cuthbert
2m/3km S. of Redcar NZ 5921
THe church, with attached octagonal mausoleum and gates of the churchyard and Hall opposite, forms a satisfying 18th-century composition. The tower has a medieval core but was Classicalized in 1731; rest was rebuilt in 1763 by Robert Corney, who is buried in the churchyard; possiby to designs by Carr, who also worked at the Hall. Good details, Tuscan arcades, and fine contemporary furnishings: marble pedestal font, cut-down box pews, altar rails, pulpit and reading desk. There are also ledger stones with superb lettering and Turner monuments in the chancel. Their great octagonal mausoleum on the N. side of the chancel, originally of 1740 to designs by James Gibbs, was rebuilt in 1839. Inside are monuments by Joshua Marshall, Scheemakers, and Westmacott. Sir William Turner's Hospital, 1742, close by, has a magnificent chapel.

KIRKLEVINGTON
St Martin
2m/3km S.E. of Yarm NZ 4309
Largely restored by C. N. Armfield in 1883, but with Norman S. doorway of one order with zig-zag ornament and chancel arch. The chancel has three pairs of Early English lancet lights. Interesting and important collection of 10th-century Scandinavian sculpture.

KIRKLINGTON
St Michael
6m/10km S.E. of Bedale SE 3181
By village green with trees; 15th-century tower with local-type turret stair; 'Jacobean' pulpit on six bulbous legs, said to have been made out of a four-poster bed from the Hall; medieval tombs and a tomb chest of 1590 with early Tudor helm and gauntlets on S. wall of nave.

LASTINGHAM
St Mary
6m/10km N.W. of Pickering SE 7290
The village is set in a fold of the moors. Viewed from Spaunton bank, the basically 11th-century monastic church makes an unusual and very effective silhouette. At the W. end there is a thin 16th-century campanile-type tower. The design of the interior is on a simple yet grand scale, crowned with ribless groined vaults in stone by J. L. Pearson, 1879. The presbytery, crossing and first bay of the nave survive from an unfinished monastic church built 1078–86 by a group of Whitby monks. The church ends in an apse. Abbot Stephen's crypt is entered from a staircase in the centre of the nave and contains good fragments of Anglo-Saxon sculpture and the parish bier. A complete church in itself, apsed, aisled and vaulted, it is unforgettable, one of the most moving places in England.

LEAKE
St Mary
5m/8km N. of Thirsk SE 4390
Mainly glimpsed on its own in a field by drivers on the A19, the Hall is close by. Norman W. tower with twin bell openings. Two splendid 15th-century stall-ends, possibly Ripon school, carved with poppyheads and little beasts on detached shafts; Jacobean furnishings; Norman medallion in S. wall of nave.

LEAHOLM
St James' Chapel
3m/4km W. of Whitby NZ 7607
Stands on a grass bank above the River Esk; moorland sheep graze around. Temple Moore, 1902; good design in personal Gothic style with short W. tower. The interior is homely with low nave and chancel and small pointed windows. Wooden barrel vaults throughout and a beautiful tower arch at the W. to frame the font.

LIVERTON
St Martin
2m/3km S. of Loftus NZ 7115
Norman walling and magnificent chancel arch of three orders with a lively boar hunt, birds, a lion, a dragon and much more. Heavily restored 1902–3.

LOCKTON
St Giles
5m/8km N.E. of Pickering SE 8489
Surrounded by its village, the church is humble but beautiful with 15th-century tower, Jacobean pulpit, reader's desk and communion rail.

LYTHE
St Oswald
4m/6km N. of Whitby NZ 8413
This hill-top church with its grand tower surmounted by a short stone spire forms a prominent landmark near the sea. It was largely rebuilt in 1910–11 by Walter Tapper and ranks high in that architect's creations. The fittings and furnishings are fine down to the smallest detail. The placing and design of the rood screen and organ case do much to help in creating the atmosphere of this church.

MALTON
St Mary the Virgin
17m/27km N.E. of York SE 7871
The present parish church is a fragment of the Gilbertine priory church founded c. 1150. The W. front, lacking one tower and with part of the great 15th-century window bricked up, would have delighted Cotman. Great W. doorway displays good late 12th-century detail. The interior is full of interest; the late 11th-century work at the base of the S.W. tower and in the triforium is particularly good. The piers on the N. side were in process of transformation in the 15th century. Stalls and organ case by Temple Moore, 1887–8. Gothic Revival headstones in the churchyard.

MARSKE-IN-SWALEDALE
St Edmund
4m/6km W. of Richmond NZ 1000
A church with Norman origins but mainly of interest owing to unusual 17th-century reinterpretations of early Gothic. The church was restored in 1683 and the chancel arch given strange baluster corbels. Plain early 19th-century pulpit, box pews, and squire's pew.

MARTON-IN-CLEVELAND
St Cuthbert
3m/4km S.E. of Middlesbrough NZ 5115
Marton village has been overwhelmed by the 20th century and outer Middlesbrough. Rebuilt 1847–8 to neo-Norman designs by J. B. Rudd, a local amateur architect, though the N. arcade looks medieval, even if recut. Captain Cook baptized here.

MARTON-ON-THE-FOREST
St Mary
1m/2km E. of Stillington SE 6068
The astonishing exterior with its crow-stepped gables is due to a rebuilding, probably in 1540, using ashlar and worked stone from the Priory nearby. The form was determined by the stone available. The N. wall built of river stones remains in its 12th-century form. The S. door with tracery is 15th-century. The interior boasts an early chancel arch, 17th-century altar rails and benches, 13th-century font, and fragments of 15th-century glass.

MASHAM
St Mary the Virgin
8m/12km N.W. of Ripon SE 2280
The pleasant town keeping its square and market cross stands on the bank of the Ure. Hidden off one corner of the great market-place, the lower part of the church tower is 11th-century work, without buttresses, and carries a 15th-century octagonal stage surmounted by a spire. About 1328 the body of the church was rebuilt with aisles and N. chapel by Sir Geoffrey le Scrope. Renaissance monuments abound. Stained glass of 1958 by H. J. Stammers; good display of hatchments above the nave aracdes. Tall Saxon cross shaft in the churchyard.

MIDDLEHAM
St Alkelda & St Mary
2m/3km S.E. of Leyburn SE 1287
According to legend, St Alkelda was a Saxon princess martyred in c. 800 and buried here. Chiefly 14th–15th-century church associated with Richard II, whose son Edward was born in the nearby castle. In 1478 Richard made the church collegiate, with a dean and six canons; the last canon was Charles Kingsley. Monument to Abbot Thornton of Jervaulx, c. 1533, has rebus of crozier piercing a barrel.

MIDDLESBROUGH
NZ 4920
St Columba, Cannon Street
By Temple Moore, 1901; personal Gothic of high order, in red brick, with strong W. tower. Anglican outpost in a car park.
St John the Evangelist, Marton Road

By John Norton, 1864; steeple, 1883. A severe church in red brick with blue banding, in prominent position. It owes much to Butterfield's passionate intensity; fine interior.

St Martin of Tours, Acklam Road
By C. Charlewood of Newcastle, completed in 1940; in brick with cubic forms derived from the Dutch Modern movement of the 1930s.

Holy Trinity, North Ormsby
By W. White, 1868–9; extended by Armsfield and Bottomley, 1879. The church dominates the market-place of this suburb of Middlesbrough which was developed in the 1860s.

MIDDLETON
St Andrew
1m/2km N.W. of Pickering SE 7885
Saxon W. tower with 13th-century bell stage; 12th–13th-century arcades and pretty S. doorway. Good 18th-century pulpit with fine inlaid tester. Important collection of Saxon crosses, including one which depicts a warrior with spear, axe, sword and shield; restored by C. Hodgson Fowler, 1884–6.

MIDDLETON TYAS
St Michael and all Angels
1m/2km E. of Scotch Corner NZ 2205
Medieval church with majestic Norman arcade and plate tracery in aisle windows; restored and spire added by Sir Giles Gilbert Scott, 1868. Very beautiful 13th-century coffin lid; brass of 1673 to the Rev. John Mawer.

NEWTON-ON-OUSE
All Saints
7m/11km N.W. of York SE 5160
Stands well above a bend in the river. Early 12th-century tower survives in its lower stages, remainder all a rebuilding of 1849 by G. T. Andrews in large brown and white stones. E. window by Willement.

NORMANBY
St Andrew
3m/4km S.W. of Pickering NZ 5518
A delightful small church. Arcade and S. doorway late 12th-century within a Georgian rebuilding, all completely refashioned by Temple Moore in 1893–5. Nave unfortunately scraped. Jacobean altar rails and a coarse baluster used as a poor-box.

NORTHALLERTON
All Saints
14m/22km S. of Darlington SE 3693
An imposing town church within the tree-lined churchyard set at the end of the broad main street. Stately 15th-century central tower; chancel 1884 by C. Hodgson Fowler; font 1662 (compare Kirby Sigston) with coeval cover. Many fragments of sculpture, both pre- and post-Conquest.

NUNNINGTON
All Saints and St James
2m/3km N. of Hovingham SE 6679
There is a fine view from the churchyard towards the N. across the vale to the moors; 17th-century W. tower of Perpendicular form; font cover 18th-century; Jacobean pulpit. Tablet to Lord Widdrington, d. 1743, by Rysbrack and James Gibbs, and to an 18th-century jockey, Thomas Jackson, d. 1760.

NUNTHORPE
St Mary the Virgin
4m/6km S.E. of Middlesbrough NZ 5314
The church looks very fine from the N. with the central tower rising above the trees. By Temple Moore, 1914–26. Well-composed, honest and strong. Simple Gothic shapes make for clarity of detail and give grandeur and a Cistercian purity to the interior.

OLD BYLAND
All Saints
4m/6km W. of Helmsley SE 5485
Behind cottages on the village green, the small, low church is half hidden from view. Norman chancel arch and font, and round the porch two dragon panels and primitive capitals. Pre-Conquest sundial in E. wall of tower. The first site of Byland Abbey when it moved from Furness.

OSBALDWICK
St Thomas
2m/3km E. of York SE 6351
Village setting; 12th-century, restored by J. Oldrid Scott, 1877, enlarged 1967; 17th-century altar rails and pulpit. Interesting verse on headstone of 1645 in porch.

OSWALDKIRK
St Oswald
3m/4km S. of Helmsley SE 6278
On a hillside with fine views over the Howardian countryside. Norman nave and

doorways; simple S. windows are 13th-century. Temple Moore font and good painted ceiling in the chancel, probably also his. Jacobean pulpit; fragments of Anglo Saxon sculpture.

OVER SILTON
St Mary
5m/8km E. of Northallerton SE 4593
An attractive small church with bellcote all on its own on a hillside away from any village. Decorated and Perpendicular with Norman S. doorway; medieval bench-ends.

PATRICK BROMPTON
St Patrick
3m/4km W. of Bedale SE 2290
Norman S. door and ornate N. arcade. Chancel 14th-century with sedilia; 18th-century communion rail; remainder scraped in the 19th century, but given a stately rock-faced W. tower by G. Fowler Jones, 1864.

PICKERING
St Peter & St Paul
16m/25km W. of Scarborough SE 7984
Seen from a distance, the tower and spire rise above the red pantiled roofs of the market town. Close to, the church is screened by houses and shops between which several narrow steps rise to the green enclosure of the churchyard. Past the white-painted gates of the S. porch, which is late-medieval, we enter the nave and immediately our eyes are caught by the long array of 15th-century wall-paintings for which the church is justly famous; much repainted in the 1880s, but lively and very enjoyable. There is also a charming round pulpit, late 18th-century, and interesting monuments and tablets.

PICKHILL
All Saints
5m/8km S.E. of Leeming SE 3483
On a mound above the village cottages. Broad late-Perpendicular W. tower, 13th-century nave and chancel. Rich Norman work in S. doorway and chancel arch; font, 1686; restored and largely refenestrated by G. E. Street, 1877. Anglo-Danish dragon sculpture.

POCKLEY
St John the Baptist
2m/3km N.E. of Helmsley SE 6386
Quite a grand church by Giles Gilbert Scott

Jnr, 1870, with tall double bellcote. Fittings by Temple Moore; chancel ceiling painted in red and white; 13th-century font.

RASKELF
St Mary
3m/4km N.W. of Easingwold SE 4971
The church is largely a 19th-century re-building around the 15th-century timber tower and pyramid cap, unique in the N. Riding. Late 12th-century N. arcade and Norman tub font with elegant 17th-century cover. The renewed oak chancel arch and the oak arcades to the N. chapel are a re-minder of the Forest of Galtres; 17th-century baluster screen to N. chapel; 18th-century altar rails; fragments of medi-eval glass; 17th-century seats with coarse poppyheads.

RICHMOND
St Mary the Virgin
11m/18km S.W. of Darlington NZ 1701
Set on the valley-side outside the town walls with 15th-century W. tower of local type. Body of church over-restored in the 19th century, both by Sir Giles Gilbert Scott, 1860, and C. Hodgson Fowler, 1892; 15th-century stalls from Easby Abbey with misericords which show monsters' faces, leaves, and two pigs dancing to the the bag-pipes. Black Frosterley marble font with Jacobean cover.
Holy Trinity
Notable for its position in the market-place, the church is on the upper floor with shops beneath and around it. Originally medieval but heavily restored in 1864.

ROBIN HOOD'S BAY
5m/8km S.E. of Whitby NZ 9505 (the parish is known as Fylingdales)
St Stephen (New Church)
An important work by G. E. Street, 1870. Big and earnest, with saddleback tower. Only a S. aisle, the N. wall with impressive lancets. Good glass by Holiday including a dramatic scene with fishermen and nets.
St Stephen (Old Church)
The old church, with its cupola and long Gothic windows, stands isolated high up on the hills looking down towards Street's Victorian church and the wide curve of the bay beyond. In spirit is nearest to Whitby St Mary's with its untouched interior of box pews and three-decker pulpit towering in the middle of the S. side. A gallery runs the

length of the N. and W. sides. Maidens' garlands, recently conserved; shipwrecked sailors lie at peace in the churchyard.
R.C.F.

ROMALDKIRK
St Romald
5m/8km N.W. of Barnard Castle NY 9922
In a spacious village set about with greens stands the quite grand church with 15th-century W. tower, battlemented and pinnacled. Transitional arcades, 13th-century S. transept, Decorated chancel and N. transept. Fragments of wall-paintings; Norman drum-shaped font with stylized leaf decoration; fine effigy of Sir Hugh Fitzhenry, 1304.

SALTON
St John de Beverley
4m/6km S. of Kirkbymoorside SE 7180
By the green of this small village in the Vale of Pickering, close to where the River Dove meets the Rye. A quite large Norman church with plenty of zig-zag mouldings and windows like narrow black fingers. Very worn corbel table and S. door with outer ring of faces, inner of beak-heads. Jacobean-style pulpit and early 19th-century monuments with weeping willows.

SAND HUTTON
St Leonard
2m/3km N.W. of Stamford Bridge SE 6958
Reached up an old avenue of yews and chestnuts; rebuilt by Salvin, 1839–42, and recast by C. Hodgson Fowler, 1886. Kempe glass. Behind are the ruins of the old church surrounded by table-tombs.

SCARBOROUGH
TA 0488
St Columba, Dean Road
By L. Moore, 1926. Of light-coloured brick, well massed on a difficult site, the chancel rising quite impressively above the houses. Tall piers in the nave leading to a lofty apse. Characteristic furniture.
St James, Seamer Road
By Paley & Austin, 1894. Brick with high bellcote topped by a spirelet; very Edwardian.
St Martin, Albion Road
One of G. F. Bodley's early churches, consecrated in 1862. The narthex, Lady Chapel and superb organ case are later Bodley. Excellent proportions within and without.

Whilst having a French flavour, it has none of the 'boyish antagonistic effort' of his slightly earlier St Michael's, Brighton. With his own hand he painted the patterns on the walling above the chancel. William Morris drew cartoons for the lower panels of the pulpit and a side panel is by Rossetti. The earlier glass was also made by Morris. The reredos in the Lady Chapel is in Bodley's later style.
St Mary
Perched high above the fishing village and under the lee of the castle, the church lost its great chancel and two W. towers during the Civil War. The loss of the chancel explains the E. tower of 1669 on the site of the former crossing. Christian's severe restoration, 1848–50, made the fabric sound but swept away much of the interior. Good 12th–13th-century piers, arcades and clerestory; the wall shafts in the nave are comparable with Bolton Abbey. Chapels open off the S. aisle with ribbed barrel vaults and stone slab roofs. Fine Victorian W. lancets have good glass by Gerente. Excellent series of mural monuments includes one by Roubiliac. Magnificent 17th–19th-century tombs and headstones in the churchyard, many of the early Gothic Revival, and the grave of Anne Brontë, 1849.

SCAWTON
St Mary
4m/6km W. of Helmsley SE 5483
A small Norman village church well restored by C. Hodgson Fowler, 1888. The chancel arch has two side arches which were converted into squints, and there is a Jacobean cupboard and high hat-shaped font cover. Every detail is a delight.

SCRUTON
St Radegund
4m/6km N.E. of Bedale SE 3092
Norman and Early English with Perpendicular W. tower. Badly restored in 1865 by G. Fowler Jones. E. window by Capronnier of Brussels, 1866. Full set of Victorian High Church fittings: pulpit, reading desk, and lectern, all ponderously carved in stone.

SEAMER
St Martin
4m/6km S.W. of Scarborough TA 0183
Battlemented church with wide Norman nave and chancel arch which seems to have sagged. Chancel altered in the 15th century;

19th-century neo-Norman tower; good Jacobean screen; interesting early 19th-century monuments, a particularly beautiful one to Mrs Boutflower by Chambers, 1810.

SESSAY
St Cuthbert
4m/6km E. of Topcliffe SE 4575
The church stands with the school, both by Wm. Butterfield, 1847–8, at the end of the village; a memorable sight with many good personal details. A delightful lych gate with boiler-house attached leads the eye to the varied roofs of the church and tower. Sensitive play of angles, without any of Butterfield's later violent experiment. Brass to Thomas Magnus, Archdeacon of the N. Riding, d. 1550.

SHERIFF HUTTON
St Helen and the Holy Cross
4m/6km N.E. of Strensall SE 6566
From the churchyard there is a good view across the Howardian countryside. The exterior is full of colour and texture owing to the use of sandstone and limestone rubble and ashlar. The tower stands within the body of the church; early 19th-century W. porch of greatest simplicity. Homely interior full of good things: brick floors, box pews, 17th-century altar table and rails, and 17th-century funeral achievements in the S. chapel. Tombs in N. chapel include that of Edward, Prince of Wales, son of Richard III, d. 1484.

SINNINGTON
All Saints
4m/6km W. of Pickering SE 7485
On a hillside above the village and close to a barn which was once the hall of a manor house dating back to the 12th century. The church, too, is 12th-century, two-cell with bell-turret, simple Jacobean communion rail, and some 17th-century benches. Many fragments of Anglo Saxon sculpture. Carefully restored by C. Hodgson Fowler, 1904.

SKELTON
St Giles
4m/6km N.W. of York SE 5656
'Few ecclesiastical buildings of like dimensions will, I think, be found more perfect in harmony of parts, unity of design and purity of style' (Ewan Christian). The church was completed prior to 1247, and is all of an Early English style close to that of the S. transept

of York Minster. The great S. doorway was renewed by Henry Graham, 1814–18, and although already weathering, is extremely beautiful with its wind-blown leaf capitals. The font is an octagonal faceted bowl, the chancel piscina has fine leaf decoration, and every detail right up to the stiff-leaf cross on the gable is a joy.

SKELTON-IN-CLEVELAND
All Saints (Old Church)
2m/3km S. of Saltburn NZ 6518
Situated in a leafy 18th-century backwater, away from the traffic of Skelton's windy main street, the church looks down well-kept lawns to the Regency façade of the castle. It is a quiet box of beautifully tooled stone standing in a fine churchyard with several fierce angels on tombstones. Inside, all is 18th-century order with box pews bearing family names, a squire's aisle, pulpit, and a W. gallery on iron pillars. In the spacious chancel a group of 18th-century boards with texts from the Psalms in delightful home-spun lettering.
R.C.F.

SNAPE CASTLE
Chapel of St Mary
2m/3km S. of Bedale SE 2684
15th-century former private chapel of an Elizabethan castle in which Catherine Parr, last wife of Henry VIII, worshipped. Perpendicular panelling; richly painted late 17th-century ceiling by Verrio, now much ruined; 18th-century Dutch religious reliefs, and two fine Rococo statues.

SOUTH COWTON
St Mary
8m/12km S. of Darlington NZ 2902
A fine late-medieval church close to the castle which belonged to Sir Richard Conyers, who completed it in 1470; his shield is to be seen in the E. window. Perpendicular S. porch with barrel vault and room above; 17th-century stalls; 18th-century funeral helm and gauntlet.
R.C.F.

SOUTH KILVINGTON
St Wilfrid
1m/2km N. of Thirsk SE 4283
Shingled bell-turret; 12th- and 14th-century work in church; the black Frosterley marble font is comparable with those at Richmond and Catterick and has donor's

inscription of Robert Scrope of Upsall Castle, late 15th-century. There are medieval bench-ends and Victorian Gothic stalls carved by the Rev. W. T. Kingsley, incumbent here 1859–1917; cousin to Charles Kingsley, he died at the age of 101, England's oldest parson.

SOWERBY
St Oswald
adjoins Thirsk to S. SE 4381
Original Norman S. doorway; mostly rebuilt by E. B. Lamb in 1842 in neo-Norman style. Restored and enlarged by C. Hodgson Fowler, 1879–83, who added a wooden lantern; it was then finally given a N. aisle by Brierley, 1902. Jacobean panelling near the altar.

SPENNITHORNE
St Michael
2m/3km S.E. of Leyburn SE 1389
Substantial 14th-century W. tower; under this and in the porch are massive pointed tunnel vaults; 12th-century N. arcade, followed by the S. arcade a century later. But it was in the Decorated period that the church was most renewed. Medieval and later monuments; 17th-century wall-painting of Father Time.

SPROXTON
St Chad
2m/3km S. of Helmsley SE 6181
Small 17th-century church, moved here from West Newton in 1879, has domestic Jacobean exterior with pleasant windows, grey stone roof, and good gate piers. The interior is even better with altar table and reredos, part of a fine 15th-century glass Crucifixus, and chancel screen by Temple Moore; a delightful creation by G. G. Scott Jnr.

STANWICK
St John the Baptist
1m/2km W. of Aldbrough NZ 1811
There is a forlorn emptiness about Stanwick now that the great house of the Smithsons, Dukes of Northumberland, has gone. But there are still the Iron Age fortifications close at hand; vast earthworks impressive in their extent and size. The church is mostly 13th-century, extensively restored by Salvin in 1866. Jacobean font cover; late 17th-century Smithson tombs, particularly Sir Hugh, d. 1670, and his wife, d. 1671, he semi-

reclining in alabaster, she recumbent in marble. Anglo Saxon sculpture fragments. R.C.F.

STILLINGTON
St Nicholas
4m/6km E. of Easingwold SE 5867
The church forms a welcome break in the long village street with its well-kept grass banks covered with bulbs in the spring. The local warm stone is used for the walls and the windows are of a local Perpendicular type. Atmospheric creamwashed interior has late box pews, arcades with mouldings dying into octagonal piers, red-brick floors, and clear glazing. Royal Arms GR, 1739; a spirited painting for its date.

STOKESELY
St Peter & St Paul
8m/12km S. of Middlesbrough NZ 5208
The church and hall are tucked away at the end of this fine market town with its varied 18th-century houses and open spaces. The 15th-century tower and chancel are separated by a large nave with round windows rebuilt in 1771. Pretty late 18th-century tablets with urns.

STONEGRAVE
Holy Trinity
2m/3km N.W. of Hovingham SE 6577
Set on a gentle hillside with wide views over the Howardian countryside, the church looks unpromising at first sight despite a 12th-century tower. The exterior is all G. F. Jones, 1863. However, the interior is much more rewarding with early-Norman N. arcade and a S. arcade only a little later. The Jacobean screen is especially attractive, and the pulpit is Jacobean too. Amongst early sculptural fragments, a fine 10th-century cross with wheel head and close interlace.

SUTTON-ON-THE-FOREST
All Hallows
8m/12km N. of York SE 5864
Lawrence Sterne was vicar here for over 20 years from 1738. The 18th-century pulpit is the one he preached from. But the church was largely rebuilt by W. Atkinson, 1875–7, apart from the 15th-century tower and S. wall of the nave. Good Georgian tablets, several to the Harlands of Sutton Hall.

THIRKLEBY
All Saints
4m/6km S.E. of Thirsk SE 4778
By E. B. Lamb, 1850. A typical Lamb silhouette of thin tower and odd Gothic details. 'A veritable riot of forms, perverse and mischievous, and one takes a perverse pleasure in it' (Pevsner). The interior is, for Lamb, fairly normal, since he has not produced one of his great central roofs, but the hammerbeams are good, and there are plenty of original details. The Frankland chapel contains a fine Flaxman monument, very Grecian.

THIRSK
St Mary
8m/12km S.E. of Northallerton SE 4282
From the market-place a fine 18th-century street, Kirkgate, leads past the Hall to the S. side of the church, a noble vista. The church exterior is very stately and is helped by the under-building to the chancel necessitated by the fall in the land. The body of the church, which is an essay in fully developed Perpendicular, was built in 1420. The chancel followed in 1470. The interior of the nave is well designed both as a whole and in its various parts, and, looking W., is very grand. The tall, spire-like font cover is partly 15th-century. Some medieval glass; traces of 17th-century wall-paintings of the Apostles and a magnificent altar table. Restored by G. E. Street, 1877.

THORMANBY
St Mary Magdalene
4m/6km N.W. of Easingwold SE 4974
The isolated church has a squat brick tower of 1822 and domesticated S. porch. The external stonework varies much in size, texture and colour, and is most attractive. Homely nave with benches, simple font cover, and limewashed walls, a contrast with the good early 20th-century furnishing and glass in the chancel. E. window by Kempe. A window in the S. wall has some 15th-century glass.

THORNABY-ON-TEES
St Peter
on right bank of Tees, within Tees-side urban area NZ 4517
By village green, though now completely surrounded by suburban housing; 12th-century in origin with fine texture to external walling. Norman carved seated figure.

THORNTON DALE
All Saints
3m/4km E. of Pickering SE 8383
The church tower looks down the hill towards the stream and main street. It, like the body of the church, is Decorated. The S. doorway has lively heads as hood-mould stops, and there is a fine monument in the chancel in an arched recess: a 14th-century lady with her head under a canopy. Also a good Fisher of York monument to John Hill, d. 1773, with an elegant urn.

THORNTON STEWARD
St Oswald
5m/8km S.E. of Leyburn SE 1787
Remote from village; a path leads down through the fields towards the Ure and at the end is a small, unassuming building, but one of great age, for there are Anglo Saxon quoins at the E. and W. ends and the chancel arch may also be pre-Conquest. The nave with its windows and S. door is Norman, and the chancel is c. 1200. A 14th-century addition is an over-large tomb recess in the chancel with fine mouldings. Early Anglo-Danish sculptural fragments.

TOPCLIFFE
St Columba
4m/6km S.W. of Thirsk SE 4076
Stands in a fine position above the Swale. Extensive 19th-century restoration by G. T. Andrews. Magnificent 14th-century Flemish brass and the Baroque Robinson monument of c. 1688; early Burne-Jones chancel window.

UGGLEBARNBY
All Saints
3m/4km S. of Whitby NZ 8707
In a side valley of the Esk, halfway up the valley-side. By C. N. Armfield, 1872, in Early English style; good High Victorian furnishings and font cover. The church is full of angels, with many on the hammerbeam roof and others sticking out from the font cover in all directions. Matthew Noble carved the Last Supper on the reredos.

UPLEATHAM
2m/3km S.W. of Saltburn NZ 6319
St Andrew (Old Church)
In a delightful setting on a valley-side looking out towards Skelton and the wooded castle grounds. Diminutive church consisting of

W. part only of nave of larger Norman church and a tiny tower of 1684.

St Andrew (New Church)
At the top of the Zetlands' estate village, a small and pretty neo-Norman church by Ignatius Bonomi, 1835, with W. tower. Norman font brought from old church.

WATH
St Mary
4m/6km N. of Ripon SE 3277
Set amongst trees at the N. end of the village. The fabric is medieval, restored in 1873. Excellent 14th-century chest with gabled panels, a stag hunt and grotesques; brasses and a Flaxman monument of 1814.

WELL
St Michael
3m/4km E. of Masham SE 2681
Hall, almshouses and church make a pleasant group. Elegant 14th-century tower; traceried font cover dated 1352; 16th-century Dutch reredos in N. chapel; 16th-century Nevill tombs; Milbanke tablet by Westmacott Jnr, 1852. A fine Roman mosaic from a nearby villa was moved into the church during the 19th century.

WENSLEY
Holy Trinity
1m/2km W. of Leyburn SE 0989
Set by the River Ure below Leyburn and opposite the entrance to Bolton Hall. Early English chancel with lancets; W. tower rebuilt in 1719. Good interior has early benches, box pews, and two-decker pulpit, a magnificent 15th-century screen from Easby Abbey, now part of family pew, and a font and cover, 1662. Splendid Flemish brass, 1394, to Sir Simon de Wenselawe, priest.

WEST ROUNTON
St Oswald
7m/11km N.E. of Northallerton NZ 4103
11th-century font and chancel arch; remainder recast in neo-Norman style by Pritchett, 1860; glass by H. J. Stammers.

WEST TANFIELD
St Nicholas
5m/8km N.W. of Ripon SE 2678
From the river bridge the church tower rises beyond the pantiled cottages and their gardens dropping to the Ure with the 15th-century gatehouse of Marmion's Manor next to it. The church is chiefly 15th-century but

badly mauled in 1859 by unfeeling hands. There is a curious chamber in the N. wall of the chancel with traceried openings. Splendid 14th-century Marmion alabaster altar tomb with wrought-iron hearse. Some medieval glass.

WESTERDALE
Christ Church
7m/11km S.E. of Guisborough NZ 6605
The church stands halfway down the village street below the moors with good tombstones in the churchyard. The church of 1838 with Y-traceried windows in Gibbsian surrounds is embodied in the new church by W. Falkenbridge, 1874, restored by C. Hodgson Fowler, 1896, and recast by Temple Moore, 1911.

WHENBY
St Martin
10m/16km N. of York SE 6369
The church stands in undulating Howardian hill country on a bank above the road. The prominent battlements on tower, nave and chancel give a distinctive appearance to the Perpendicular exterior. Within there are hints of a 13th-century church in the way the tower arch is offset to the N.; 15th-century chancel screen with traces of colouring; 17th-century N. chapel screen retains original latch and hinges. Medieval benches in nave.
R.C.F.

WHITBY
17m/27km N.W. of Scarborough NZ 8911
St Hilda
By R. J. Johnson, 1885. In a dominant position on the W. cliff. Bold and serious church with a quiet, dignified interior. Tower completed in 1938 by G. E. Charlewood.
St Mary
Near the Abbey ruins on a hill high above the old town, looking down on the harbour. Mid-12th-century tower and S. doorway, the exterior massive, even harsh, yet well suited to the site. Splendid interior remodelled in the 18th century. The great rectangular nave is filled with box pews and galleries rising almost to the roof, and centred on the high pulpit and reading desk. The nave appears light against the murk of unspoilt 12th-century chancel. Between is the delicate crown of the pulpit sounding board and the chancel screen with barley-

sugar Corinthian columns. Chippendale-Gothic table-tombs in the churchyard.

WHITWELL-ON-THE-HILL
St John the Evangelist
6m/10km N.W. of Northallerton SE 2899
A hill-top church of grey and brown Whitby stone by G. E. Street, 1860. Particularly successful tower and spire. Good early glass by Clayton & Bell in the E. window; stone and marble reredos carved by Thomas Earp. Timber lych gate and churchyard cross also by Street.

WHORLTON
Holy Cross
5m/8km S.W. of Stokesley NZ 4802
Isolated church on high broken ground close to the Cleveland Hills, approached through an avenue of yews. The nave, roofless since 1875, is 12th-century, with tower on S. side, the upper part rebuilt in 1722. Intact chancel is mostly 13th-century, the interior with attractive windows, corbels, and an array of 14th- and 15th-century canopied wall-tombs.

WYCLIFFE
St Mary
4m/6km E. of Barnard Castle NZ 1114
A small and humble 13th–14th-century building close to the Tees in a beautiful situation near the dignified Georgian former rectory. The long, low church has a bellcote and porch and much medieval glass in the S. windows. Well-furnished interior with interesting 1963 roof by Wm. Whitefield, composed of coffered lozenges. Gaily painted chancel. Several small monuments and inscriptions to the Wycliffe family; according to tradition, John Wycliffe, 'morning star of the Reformation', was born here.

WYKEHAM
All Saints
6m/10km S.W. of Scarborough SE 9683
Built along with the school and parsonage by Wm. Butterfield, 1853, in late 13th-century style; 14th-century tower of St Helen's Chapel re-used as churchyard gate. A fine simple font, good Butterfield fittings, and glass by Wailes.

YARM
St Mary Magdalene
4m/6km S. of Stockton-on-Tees NZ 4112
Away from the grand main street and looked down on by the long railway viaduct, the church stands by the Tees. Curious Norman W. front has central buttress with an almond-shaped 13th-century window above a narrow Norman one. To either side are broad stair turrets. The remainder rebuilt in 1730; William Peckitt glass of 'Moses Delivering the Law'.

YORK
SE 6051
All Saints, North Street
Pleasant exterior; the tower and spire are one of the city's landmarks. The tower is within the body of the church, as is usual here, with a graceful two-stage octagon at the top. The early 20th-century anchorage of reinforced concrete with timber cladding is ingenious. Inside, the church has been restored and re-arranged so that the former clutter has given way to clarity and a freshness of detail; it still possesses great beauty. There is no structural chancel, so the 13th- and 14th-century arcades run from end to end. The chancel and S. aisle have excellent 15th-century roofs. Medieval painted glass of outstanding interest. Painted pulpit is dated 1675. In 1906 Ridsdale Tate added elaborate rood and parclose screens, which tend to dominate the interior.

All Saints, Pavement
A typical town church, the E. end shortened for road widening in 1782. On the N. door is a 12th-century metal knocker. The W. tower, rebuilt 1837, stands within the church; it rises to a tall open octagonal lantern and pierced parapet. Its beacon, which once led medieval travellers through the Galtres Forest, has been restored. Inside, the tower is carried on fine 15th-century piers and arches. In the large 15th-century W. window is 15th-century glass from St Saviour's. The arcades and clerestory are also 15th-century. There is a notable pulpit with tester dated 1634 and the medieval lectern from the demolished church of St Crux. Lord Mayor's boards and bequest boards with good lettering. In the nearby church-room many excellent monuments from St Crux are preserved, together with an interesting oak doorway.

St Andrew, New Earswick
The church lacks the intended S. aisle. Leslie Moore has seized upon the presence of an earlier building and the fall in the ground to create an unusual and highly successful arrangement. The earlier building

forms a narthex from which steps lead down into the church.

St Cuthbert, Peaseholm Green
The small campanile tower and S. side of the church are simple, well-detailed 15th-century work. The church, now a Parish Centre and offices, is a single-cell building with 15th-century roof, W. tower, S. porch, and 18th-century brick vestry. Inside are a 17th-century altar table and pulpit, hatchments and Creed, commandment and bequest boards with excellent lettering. The E. end has a kind of crypt below with some 17th- and 18th-century brass inscriptions.

St Denys
The church has suffered grievous truncation in the past and is overshadowed by office blocks. The original nave was destroyed in 1798, and the tower rebuilt in 1847; the Norman S. doorway survived intact but was moved. The flowing 14th-century tracery in the great E. window of the N. chapel is the best remaining architectural feature. The interior is strongly reminiscent of the Norwich churches: dignified arcades with mouldings dying into the piers. The roofs are 15th-century. The brass to Mary Rose, 1922, Jacobean pulpit, wrought-iron riddle posts of the high altar, and the well-placed organ by Hughes are memorable, but it is the glass that matters most. St Denys has the only 13th-century glass in a York parish church – small coloured medallions set within naturalistic grisaille; 14th-century glass has figures of saints and in the E. window a 15th-century Crucifixion flanked by the Virgin and St John.

St Helen, St Helen's Square
W. front has open octagonal upper stage like All Saints, Pavement. Well placed facing York's Mansion House in one of the city's busiest squares, once its churchyard. Church of Guild of Glass Painters, arms displayed in S. aisle. Largely recast in the 19th century by R. H. Dykes; 12th-century font; 14th-century glass and a panel of 15th-century Flemish glass.

Holy Trinity, Goodramgate
At the edge of Goodramgate a brick gateway of 1786 affords a glimpse of the churchyard with weeping ash and ledger stone; by far the most satisfactory entry to any York church. The exterior is a delightful medley of different materials, colours and textures. Pleasant 14th-century windows with reticulated tracery. Internally, the church, with its different levels, is one of the most pictur-

esque in York. The effect is produced by the pews, of many dates, which weave and flow in waves around the two-decker pulpit, 1785. The arcades spring from very stumpy columns. Plain 18th-century font and cover; altarpiece of 1721; early 18th-century three-sided communion rails with semi-circular middle projection. Excellent 15th-century stained glass includes St George and the Dragon, St John the Baptist with a camel skin, and the Virgin in a brilliant mandorla.
R.C.F.

Holy Trinity, Micklegate
Contains a large fragment of the Benedictine priory church. Elegantly composed W. front with deeply moulded doorway, blind arcading and lancets is largely a scholarly restoration by C. Hodgson Fowler, 1905. N.W. tower of 1453 was built over the W. bay of the N. aisle. As the N. aisle has been destroyed, the arches of the great arcade are built into the present wall. Fisher and Hepper designed the rather dull 'Perpendicular' chancel of 1886. Inside, the nave arcades possess a solemn character, and above the arch to St Nicholas's chapel one bay of the triforium remains intact. Some excellent Kempe glass in the three W. lancets of the nave. The font and its open-work cover of 1717 were formerly in St Saviour's. The high altar, reredos and Kempe five-light window above form a composition of some richness. An early Gothic Revival monument commemorates Dr John Burton, d. 1771 – 'Dr Slop' of *Tristram Shandy*.

St Margaret, Walmgate
The church and churchyard used to lie behind the buildings of Walmgate, but they now stand isolated in a backwater near Walmgate Bar. The entrance to the delightfully sequestred churchyard with its ash trees and flagged path is still through an early 19th-century cast-iron gate. The stone and brick tower was built in 1684. Apart from the exceptionally fine late-Norman S. doorway from the destroyed hospital chapel of St Nicholas, the remainder of the exterior was rebuilt 1852.
R.C.F.

St Martin-le-Grand, Coney Street
Gutted by incendiaries in 1942; tower and S. aisle reconstructed, the remainder made into a garden of remembrance. Tower completed in 1437 and S. aisle of 1443–50 are of great subtlety, perhaps the work of Robert Couper, a Master of ability. The splendid

early 15th-century W. window of St Martin of Tours in glowing reds and golds was saved and has been incorporated in the restored portion of the church. New glass in the E. window by Harry Stammers; reredos by Frank Roper; 18th-century font cover with eight scrolls.

St Martin-cum-Gregory, Micklegate
One of the most interesting churches in the city. The E. end is of brick, 1751, as is the W. tower, lavishly rebuilt in 1667 and parsimoniously altered in 1844. Well-proportioned interior has a magnificent series of ledger stones and rich furnishings; the fittings and accessories of worship in accordance with the Book of Common Prayer survive in profusion, despite the building's use for sales, exhibitions and other activities.

St Mary, Bishophill Junior
The massive W. tower has herringbone Saxon work and contemporary bell openings. The remainder of the exterior was rebuilt in the 19th century. Atmospheric inside; low, wide proportions; limewashed walls; 15th-century ribbed and panelled nave roof; dignified Norman N. arcade and excellent chancel fittings by Temple Moore.

St Michael-le-Belfrey
The siting at an angle to the Minster may not have been intentional, but visually it is most satisfying. A good example of a hall church, built 1525–36; the Master was probably John Forman. W. front was largely rebuilt by G. F. Jones, 1867. Fine continuous clerestory and an unusual bell-turret on the W. front. Interior remarkable for masterly handling of spatial relationships; 14th–15th-century glass; splendid altarpiece and rails by Wm. Etty, 1712; 15th-century seating; tombs and monuments.

St Michael, Spurriergate
The E. and S. walls were somewhat set back in 1821. The 15th-century tower is a poor specimen, but the clock face on the S. side is most decorative. A very beautiful interior. The 12th-century arcades are excellent together with the 18th-century inner porch, reredos, altar rails with fine balusters, and Lord Mayor's board. Remarkable stamped leather altar covering temp. Charles II; 15th-century glass and W. door. Now a restaurant and shop.

St Olave, Marygate
The church, of pre-Norman origins, is backed by the ruined N. aisle of St Mary's Abbey, linked at the W. end to other Abbey buildings and attached at the E. end to a superb medieval wall. The N. side of the church is good 15th-century work. The tower is 15th-century. The nave arcades were rebuilt in the 18th century and the columns are a curious Gothicized Roman Doric. The chancel and S. chapel by J. F. Doyle, 1908, are a rich and effective High Church period piece; 15th-century glass in the E. window of the chancel. Baroque memorial to William Thornton, architect, 1721.

Yorkshire West Riding

Introduction

For contrast of scenery, character and spirit, the West Riding has no equal in England. It is hard to believe that Wharfedale and the Dearne Valley could belong to the same land, still less the same Riding. And yet, considering its size, England's largest county is poor in ancient churches – 197 compared with Kent's 321.

Why? First because, until industry arrived, the Riding west of a line from Ripon to Sheffield was bleak moorland. Much of it is open country still. Down to 1850, the mother churches of Halifax, Dewsbury and Thornhill in the west, and Otley in the north, served vast chapelries under them. To this day, no self-respecting dalesman would be married anywhere but in 't'owd parish church'.

In the second place, prosperity when it came was not accompanied by reverence for antiquity. So in pudding-time the old churches of Huddersfield and Keighley disappeared and All Saints, Dewsbury was given a Georgian new look. John Carr showed better taste at Horbury; his church might have strayed from Wren's London. But worse was to come. In Queen Victoria's reign, when large-scale building took place, the magnates of Leeds, Bradford and Sheffield stuck obstinately to their local architects. So Mallinson and Healey built around twenty-five churches, Perkins and Backhouse eleven, and W. H. Crossland ten. Scott Snr, it is true, was given St George's Doncaster to rebuild after a fire, and built six other churches. Burges gave a kaleidoscopic display at Skelton and Studley Royal, G. F. Bodley and John Micklethwaite built four churches each, J. L. Pearson three, and William Butterfield, G. E. Street, Norman Shaw and Temple Moore two each, so the region can boast a rich vein of Victorian ecclesiastical architecture.

The West Riding is distributed among five different dioceses. York keeps only a corner since Ripon reverted to cathedral status and the three parish churches of Wakefield, Bradford and Sheffield became cathedrals. Selby has the one complete monastic building in use, as fine as many a cathedral.

The Craven churches come nearest to achieving a local style. Most of them are Tudor or late-Perpendicular with no division between nave and chancel. Two other peculiarities must be mentioned. Around Selby the landscape becomes strangely Dutch in character. The roof-tops of Snaith, Fishlake and Drax are ablaze with channelled tiles, and below them glide barges on their way to the Humber. They could almost be in Middleburg or

Gouda. The remaining area of interest lies west from Bradford: the Brontë country. In these moorland valleys around Haworth, with their gaunt churches and stone walls, one is made conscious of the spirit that underlies the pages of *Wuthering Heights*.

D. R.

continued overleaf

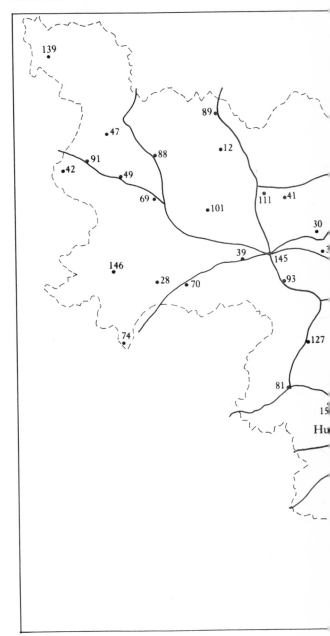

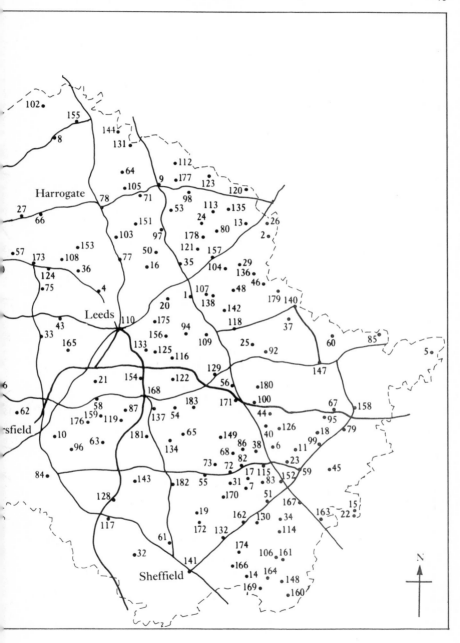

Selected List of Churches

ABERFORD
St Ricarius
7m/11km S. of Wetherby SE 4337
Village setting; early-Norman tower, rest
rebuilt by A. Salvin, 1861. Fragments of
10th-century decorated cross in W. wall of
S. aisle.

ACASTER MALBIS
Holy Trinity
4m/6km S. of York SE 5845
Set by the River Ouse. Small early 14th-
century cruciform church of high architectural quality; compare window design with
Nether Poppleton. Good 17th-century
pulpit and medieval glass with beautifully
drawn figures. Spirelet by Hodgson
Fowler, 1886.

ADDINGHAM
St Peter
3m/4km N.W. of Ilkley SE 0749
15th-century Perpendicular church with
octagonal piers and king-post roofs; exterior
to S. pleasantly Classicized in 1757. Samuel
Cunliffe Lister, first Baron Masham, the
great Yorkshire manufacturer, inventor and
businessman, buried here.

ADEL
St John the Baptist
4m/6km N. of Leeds city centre SE 2740
One of the most celebrated Norman
churches in Yorks. Mid-12th-century nave
and chancel with a bellcote by R. D. Chantrell, 1838. Worn but sumptuous S. portal
with carvings of Christ in Majesty and
Symbols of the Evangelists; rare closing ring
on door. Richly decorated chancel arch with
figured capitals. Some stained glass by
Henry Gyles, 1681 and 1706.

ADLINGFLEET
All Saints
7m/11km E. of Goole SE 8420
In remote marshland countryside; Early
English with Perpendicular W. tower and
18th-century chancel. Cotmanesque interior restored by G. G. Pace; delicately
leaning arcades, box pews, and whitewash.

Unusually grand marble monument to Mrs
Ramsden, d. 1745.

ADWICK-LE-STREET
St Lawrence
4m/6km N.W. of Doncaster SE 5307
Heavily restored by Sir Giles Gilbert Scott
in 1862. Norman S. doorway, Perpendicular
W. tower, and attractive glass by F. E.
Nuttgens, 1943, showing stories of
St Francis. 16th- and 18th-century monu-
ments.

ADWICK-UPON-DEARNE
St John
1m/2km N. of Mexborough SE 4701
Small rustic church coated with pebble dash.
Norman nave and chancel with plain S. door
and rare contemporary bellcote.

ALDFIELD
St Lawrence
3m/4km W. of Ripon SE 2669
Just up the hill from Fountains Abbey.
Modest exterior of 1783 and inside a delightful ribbed plaster vault, box pews, three-
decker pulpit, Gothic commandment boards
and trees seen through clear glass windows.

ALLERTON MAULEVERER
St Martin
6m/10km S. of Boroughbridge SE 4158
The Mauleverers were here for 600 years.
The present church was founded by their
successor, Richard Arundell, a Surveyor of
the King's Works. Romantic 18th-century
Classical design with Romanesque overtones, particularly evident on the W. front.
The spatial relationships of the interior are
moving, and the atmosphere is increased by
the dilapidated medieval monuments, including two stunning oak effigies of knights.
Pulpit, pews and hammer-beam roof all part
of the 1745 design, as is the large painting
of Moses and Aaron over the chancel
arch.
R.C.F.

ALMONDBURY
All Saints
2m/3km S.E. of Huddersfield town centre SE 1615
Fine Perpendicular church with Early English chancel. The nave roof of 1522 has carved bosses and a long rhymed inscription round the cornice. Fittings include an early Georgian lectern, a pew of 1605, and a fine Perpendicular font cover. Good 15th-century stained glass in the Kaye chapel showing saints and members of the family.

ARKSEY
All Saints
suburb 2m/3km N. of Doncaster SE 5706
Close to the almshouses and school built by Sir Bryan Cooke in the late 17th century. A cruciform church with central tower and spire containing excellent Norman, Early English and Perpendicular work. E. chancel wall by G. G. Scott Jnr, 1869. Good furnishings include the 17th-century pulpit, font cover, and pews with big knobs.

ARNCLIFFE
St Oswald
in Littondale 7m/11km N.W. of Grassington SD 9371
Magnificent dales setting; Perpendicular W. tower; the rest is 1796 as remodelled by J. Dobson in 1842. Royal Arms of 1797. List of those from Wharfedale who fought at Flodden Field, 1513. Bell dated 1350.

ASKHAM BRYAN
St Nicholas
4m/6km S.W. of York SE 5548
Complete small late-Norman church with undivided nave and chancel, Roman tiles in the walls. S. entrance has foliate capitals and zig-zags; E. wall with slit windows and a vesica. Jacobean pulpit and communion rail.

ASTON
All Saints
5m/8km S.E. of Rotherham SK 4685
Perpendicular tower with attractive pierced parapet and eight pinnacles, late 12th-century arcades, and a Decorated chancel with flowing tracery. Curious 15th-century font with figure carved on base. Coade stone tablet of 1797 with fine profile portrait. Monument to Lord Darcy showing him with his three wives, 1624.

AUSTERFIELD
St Helen
1m/2km N.E. of Bawtry SK 6694
Set back a churchyard's length from the straggling village street. Early Norman nave and chancel, the tympanum of the S. door carved with a dragon. In the N. aisle a naughty female fertility figure. The N. aisle itself rebuilt by Americans in 1897 as a memorial to Austerfield's Pilgrim Father, Wm. Bradford.

BARDSEY
All Hallows
7m/11km N.E. of Leeds SE 3643
By castle motte. Interesting slender Saxon tower with traces of gabled porch at its base. Reset Norman S. doorway and N. arcade, 14th-century chancel.

BARNBURGH
St Peter
2m/3km N. of Mexborough SE 4803
Church of creamy stone in a churchyard grazed by goats; Transitional with 14th-century chancel and Perpendicular top stage to tower. Outstanding oak effigy to Sir Thomas Cresacre, d. 1348, holding his heart, under a later canopy. He is reputed to have been killed by a wild cat in the church porch. (Mentioned by Ted Hughes in his poem 'Esther's Tomcat'.) A cat appears on the family crest, and in a stone on the tower.

BARNBY DUN
SS Peter and Paul
5m/8km N.E. of Doncaster SE 6109
Good Perpendicular tower; otherwise mostly 14th-century with buttresses, niches, carvings, and bold gargoyles. Chancel of 1860 with complete ecclesiological furnishings, the piscina held up by head and arms of an impressive figure. Monument by Scheemakers, 1733.

BARNSLEY
St Peter
12m/19km N. of Sheffield SE 3406
By Temple Moore, 1895. A wide church with timber rib-vault. Personal Gothic of a high order skilfully planned to make maximum use of a difficult site. Later furnishings not in sympathy with Moore's interior.

BARWICK-IN-ELMET
All Saints
7m/11km E. of Leeds SE 3937
Mostly Perpendicular, including the W.
tower dated 1455 and paid for by Henry
Vavasour and Richard Burnham. Two fragments of 11th-century Saxon cross and a
good late-Georgian inlaid pulpit.

BATLEY
All Saints
7m/11km S.W. of Leeds SE 2424
Mostly 14th- and 15th-century; the low Perpendicular W. tower with a corbelled-out
parapet gives it a semi-fortified character.
Intact screen in N. chapel founded in 1482.

BAWTRY
St Nicholas
8m/12km S.E. of Doncaster SK 6593
The town was established towards the end
of the 12th century, and parts of the church
date back to this time, when it was built as
a chapel to the parish of Blythe. Presents
a number of puzzles, not least the Gothic
Survival tower of 1713. Handsome 18th-
century wrought-iron screen to S. chapel.

BENTLEY
St Peter
district of Leeds 2m/3km N. of city centre SE
2836
By J. Codd, 1891. An impressive design with
S. porch tower and spire; Geometric tracery
and narrow aisles lend interest to the interior.

BILTON AINSTY
St Helen
5m/8km E. of Wetherby SE 4750
Pleasant little late-Norman church with
good W. front and 13th-century bellcote.
Late 12th-century arcades, Perpendicular
chapels, and bits of Saxon crosses. Late
15th-century eagle lectern, much restored,
and S. door of 1633.

BIRKIN
St Mary
3m/4km N.E. of Knottingley, across R. Aire
SE 5326
Complete Norman ashlar church, unusually
impressive and richly decorated. The nave,
chancel and vaulted apse retain original
corbel tables and lots of zig-zags, beak-heads
and medallions. Monument to Royalist vicar
with account of his Civil War sufferings.

BISHOPTHORPE
St Andrew
3m/4km S. of York SE 5947
By Hodgson Fowler, 1898–1902; good fit-
tings by various artists and glass by Henry
Stammers. Nearby is a delightful ruined
Gothic church of 1768.

BLUBBERHOUSES
St Andrew
7m/11km N. of Otley SE 1655
1849–50 by E. B. Lamb. Tiny church in a
steep moorland setting. Simple Early
English style with assertive tower and
imaginative coarse detailing; the dark interior has a remarkable arch-braced roof
and Lamb's own font and glass.

BOLTON-BY-BOWLAND
St Peter & St Paul
3m/4km W. of Gisburn SD 7849
Craven regional Perpendicular; tower
rebuilt 1852; pews dated 1694. Communion
rail 1704, and finely studded S. door of
1705. Tomb slab to Sir Ralph Pudsay, his
three wives and twenty-five children, considered by Whittaker to be 'one of the most
remarkable monuments I have ever seen'.
He is said to have sheltered Henry VI after
his defeat at Hexham, 1464.

BOLTON PERCY
All Saints
3m/4km S.E. of Tadcaster SE 5341
Strikingly handsome limestone church in
remote village near the Wharfe, built by
Thomas Parker, its rector 1411–23, and
consecrated in 1424. The design of the
chancel is of an unusually high order; original glass in E. window, fine sedilia and
piscina, and a gable cross with Crucifixion
and Virgin and Child; 15th-century roofs,
base of rood screen and return stalls, nave
pews of 1631, handsome Jacobean font cover
and reader's desk, and a very fine pulpit of
1715; 17th–19th-century monuments.

BOLTON PRIORY
Blessed Virgin and St Cuthbert
5m/8km N.W. of Ilkley SE 0753
Grand setting by the Wharfe, painted by
Turner and other Romantic artists. Monastic nave now the parish church; ruined
14th-century chancel incorporating Norman
work and a bold 13th-century nave with an
impressive range of windows to S. Exquisite
Early English W. front hidden behind osten-

tatious unfinished W. tower started just before the Dissolution and roofed as part of church restoration in 1983.

BOLTON-UPON-DEARNE
St Andrew
2m/3km N.W. of Mexborough SE 4502
Rather sad exterior, mostly 13th- and 14th-century, but inside well proportioned and impressive; nave possibly pre-Conquest; 18th-century marquetry pulpit and rood by Durst, 1955.

BRADFIELD
St Nicholas
6m/10km N.W. of Sheffield SK 2692
Fine Pennine setting with good downhill approach through village. Noble 15th-century exterior and inside a fine regional-type Perpendicular roof to nave; 15th and 16th-century stained glass, 17th-century brasses, and impressive 20th-century font cover. Reredos made up from medieval panels from Caen brought in 1887. Watch-house in churchyard against body-snatchers.

BRADFORD
SE 1633
All Saints, Little Horton Green
By Mallinson & Healey, 1864. The grandest Victorian church in the city with prominent S.E. tower and spire beside polygonal apse. Lavish 13th-century detailing and richly fitted interior with brass and iron pulpit and glass scheme by Clayton & Bell.
St Clement, Bakerend Road
By E. P. Warren, 1892–4. Restrained exterior apart from N.W. turret with spirelet. Refined interior decorative scheme supervised by Morris & Co., the chancel arch and roof being decorated to their designs. Mosaic reredos by Salviati; glass by Kempe.
St Wilfrid, Lidget Green
By Temple Moore, 1905; large and typical of Moore's later work.

BRAITHWELL
St James
2m/3km N. of Maltby SK 5292
Stately, well-detailed Perpendicular tower; simple Norman S. doorway with tympanum. Interior has pronounced atmosphere despite mediocre furnishings. Some Elizabethan panels in the pulpit.

BRAMHAM
All Saints
4m/6km S. of Wetherby SE 4242
Restored Norman tower with Perpendicular spire; 13th-century S. door. Remarkable early 20th-century panelling and screen in chancel by Bromet and Thorman.

BRAMHOPE
St Giles
suburb 7m/11km N.W. of Leeds SE 2543
Set in grounds of former hall. Interesting plain building of 1649 with mullioned windows; inside, an unusually complete set of Puritan furnishings with three-decker pulpit, box pews, and a font of 1673.

BRAYTON
St Wilfrid
1m/2km S.W. of Selby SE 6030
Superb Norman tower with octagonal Perpendicular lantern and spire dominating the surrounding countryside. Also Norman are the sumptuous S. door of the York Romanesque school and the chancel arch. Long Decorated chancel contains monument to Sir George Darcy, d. 1558, with a mixture of Gothic and early-Renaissance details.

BRODSWORTH
St Michael
5m/8km N.W. of Doncaster SE 5007
Approached up leafy hillside, the church has a Norman core and N. arcade. The S. aisle and chapel added by the Thellussons of the great Victorian mansion close by. Well-carved pulpit of 1696 and an early 18th-century font cover. Many incised stone coffin lids.

BROUGHTON
St Oswald or All Saints
3m/4km W. of Skipton SD 9451
Sombre Perpendicular with squat tower and late-Norman S. doorway; 15th-century parclose screen and two alabaster statues of the Virgin; charming Victorian atmosphere.

BURGHWALLIS
St Helen
6m/10km N. of Doncaster SE 5311
Unspoilt aisleless Transitional church with much herringbone masonry in the outer walls; restored Perpendicular chancel screen; brass of Sir Thomas Gascoigne, 1554.

BURNSALL
St Wilfrid
3m/4km S.E. of Grassington SE 0361
Coarse Perpendicular church of Craven type, restored in 1612; Saxon carvings, Norman font, and a Jacobean pulpit. Pretty 17th-century lych gate.

BURTON-IN-LONSDALE
All Saints
3m/4km W. of Ingleton SD 6572
By E. G. Paley in its Lune Valley village, 1870. Powerful and convincing church in dominant position. Tall spire and stone-vaulted chancel. The N. transept now used as a church hall.

CALVERLEY
St Wilfrid
4m/6km N.E. of Bradford SE 2037
12th–15th-century; mostly Decorated with flowing tracery and Perpendicular flourishes. Fine Jacobean font cover.

CAMPSALL
St Mary Magdalene
7m/11km N. of Doncaster SE 5413
A cruciform Transitional church recast in 14th century, keeping fine W. tower. Magnificent 15th-century rood screen with long rhymed inscription, and in the S. chapel a carved and painted stone altar by A. W. N. Pugin brought from Ackworth Grange. Fine Yarborough monument by John Flaxman, 1803.

CANTLEY
St Wilfrid
4m/6km E. of Doncaster SE 6202
Early English with Perpendicular W. tower. N. aisle by Sir Ninian Comper, 1894; treasury of Comper work – altars, rood screen, parcloses, seating, organ cases, statues, and font cover; every window except one his glass; here was the second English Altar with a golden tester over it, carrying a hanging pyx.

CAWOOD
All Saints
4m/6km N.W. of Selby SE 5737
Setting on a sweep of the River Ouse. Transitional and Early English with Perpendicular additions including the lively W. tower. Graceful Early English S. nave arcade; restoration by J. Oldrid Scott, 1887–8. Monument to George Mountain who rose

from poverty to become Archbishop, but died within hours of his enthronement in 1628. Palace of medieval archbishops of York nearby.

CHAPEL-LE-DALE
(dedication unknown)
4m/6km N.E. of Ingleton SD 7477
Remote and magnificent setting under Ingleborough. Largely 17th-century with mullioned windows, partly rebuilt in 1869. Wall-plaque commemorates those who died building the Settle–Carlisle railway, completed 1876.

CHURCH FENTON
St John the Baptist
2m/3km N.E. of Sherburn-in-Elmet SE 5136
Early English cruciform church; Perpendicular tower and screen in N. transept; two altar-slabs; mosaic of 14th-century glass; curious female effigy in chancel with a lion and demon fighting over a cat at her feet.

CLAPHAM
St James
6m/10km N.W. of Settle SD 7469
Setting at foot of Ingleborough in a leafy village. Perpendicular W. tower; the rest 1814 with tall octagonal piers, a coved ceiling, and ends of Jacobean pews used for panelling.

COLLINGHAM
St Oswald
2m/3km S.W. of Wetherby SE 3845
Perpendicular W. tower added to an early church which was heavily reconstructed in 1840; superb Saxon crosses with Apostles and Runic inscription. Cresset stone with eight hollows for oil lamps.

CONISBOROUGH
St Peter
5m/8km S.W. of Doncaster SK 5198
Village setting near the wonderful castle. Admirable work of all periods from Saxon. Unique richly carved 12th-century coped tomb chest and other monuments.

COPLEY
St Stephen
district of Halifax 2m/3km S. of town centre SE 0822
By W. H. Crossland, 1863–5. Set amongst trees by the Calder, built to serve Col. Ackroyd's workers in a planned estate that pre-

dates Saltaire. Undivided nave and chancel plan with Frenchified apse and bellcote. Good fittings by the architect include the reredos and pulpit.

COWTHORPE
St Michael
3m/4km N.E. of Wetherby SE 4252
Built by Bryan Roucliff, a Baron of the Exchequer in the reign of Henry VI. Perpendicular with small W. tower built half into nave; remains of founder's brass, 1494, in chancel; heraldic glass; 15th-century canopied chest, perhaps an Easter Sepulchre. Perpendicular font with shields on each face. R.C.F.

CROFTON
All Saints
4m/6km S.E. of Wakefield SE 3717
Probably built by Bishop Fleming of Lincoln, a native of Crofton. He died in 1431. Cruciform Perpendicular aisleless church. Remains of two good Saxon crosses, one with a bishop, the other with twined beasts.

DARFIELD
All Saints
5m/8km E. of Barnsley SE 4104
Big Norman and Decorated church of complicated evolution; pretty 18th-century ceiling to S. aisle showing unicorns. Good Jacobean fittings include altar rails, pews and cover to the 15th-century font. Churchyard monument to 189 miners killed in a colliery disaster, 1857.

DARRINGTON
St Luke and All Saints
2m/3km S.E. of Pontefract SE 4820
Very pleasing church of Tadcaster limestone set in well-maintained churchyard away from the A1. Medieval interior full of character. Vast 15th-century rood-stair turret with little arcaded gallery carried over N. aisle. Some medieval glass and bench-ends. Former 18th-century dovecote in the churchyard.

DENTON
St Helen
2m/3km N.E. of Ilkley across R. Wharfe SE 1448
Complete Georgian Gothic church with castellated belfry built by John Carr of York in 1776. Good E. window by H. Gyles, 1700; King David and St Cecilia.

DEWSBURY
All Saints
8m/12km S.W. of Leeds SE 2421
Good town church. Pleasant combination of Classical and Gothic forms in the tower of 1767. Restoration by G. E. Street and A. H. Kirk, 1884–5; 13th-century N. arcade; fragments of important Saxon cross and medieval glass.

DONCASTER
SE 5703
Christ Church, Thorne Road
By William Hurst, 1827–9. Commissioners' church, the exterior a riot of pinnacles. Tower with octagonal lantern. Inside are plaster rib vaults and wooden galleries; the chancel by Sir Giles Gilbert Scott, 1858.
St George
Fine stately cruciform church by Sir Giles Gilbert Scott, 1845, replacing one burnt in 1853; excellent naturalistic carving and glass, especially the E. window by Hardman.

DRAX
St Peter & St Paul
5m/8km S.E. of Selby SE 6726
Transitional tower with 15th-century spire. Large Early English chancel; very grand Perpendicular clerestory with fine range of small medieval figures inside; sumptuous coloured nave roofs by Sir Charles Nicholson. Bench-ends with mixed Gothic and Renaissance motifs.

ECCLESFIELD
St Mary
4m/6km N. of Sheffield SK 3594
Set on a hillside with a wide churchyard and views across Pennine moorland. Very fine cruciform church with central tower, rebuilt in late 15th century. Excellent roofs, screens and stalls, a font of 1662, some medieval glass, and a fine series of monuments. Colours, swords and bugles of the Ecclesfield Volunteers, raised as a defence force against Napoleon, along the wall.

ELLAND
St Mary
4m/6km N.W. of Huddersfield SE 1021
A mainly Perpendicular church relieved by gilded modern screens and panelling. There is much old glass and the restored E. window

has 15th-century scenes from the life of
Our Lady.

EMLEY
St Michael
1m/2km S. of Flockton, which is 7m/11km
E. of Huddersfield SE 2413
Norman, with big Perpendicular tower;
rough, barn-like roof to nave; 18th-century
pulpit and box pews; 15th-century glass. A
miner's lamp hangs in the sanctuary.

FARNHAM
St Oswald
2m/3km N. of Knaresborough SE 3460
Transitional church with good chancel; late-
Perpendicular tower built inside the arcades;
restored by Sir Giles Gilbert Scott in 1854.
Barrel organ of 1831 still playing psalm
tunes.

FELKIRK
St Peter
½m/1km W. of S. Hiendley, which is 7m/
11km S.W. of Pontefract SE 3812
Early English nave and chancel, Perpendicular tower on Norman base, and 15th-
century chapels. One 16th-century bench
and, in the churchyard, a school of that date;
15th-century porch with pointed tunnel
vault.

FEWSTON
St Lawrence
6m/10km N. of Otley SE 1954
'Lakeside' setting, beside Fewston reservoir.
A church pleasantly remodelled in 1697; S.
porch with heavy door surround, cross-
mullioned windows, and an arcade of
Tuscan columns.

FISHLAKE
St Cuthbert
3m/4km N. of Hatfield SE 6513
Imposing though a little forlorn in the flat
landscape. Superb Norman S. doorway
richly carved with large medallions; 13th-
century work includes the arcades with
handsome W. responds and the base of the
tower, raised to its present noble proportions
in the 15th century when the clerestory was
added. Spacious interior with fine Decorated work in chancel, especially the E.
window. Late 14th-century font with statuettes in niches and a rustic Jacobean cover.

FRICKLEY
All Saints
1m/2km E. of Clayton, which is 6m/10km N.
of Mexborough SE 4608
Isolated setting, approached across fields;
13th-century unbuttressed tower and a
Norman chancel arch. Delightful gilded
organ case, pulpit and altar, and glass in the
E. window by Comper.

GIGGLESWICK
St Alkeda
½m/1km W. of Settle across R.Ribble SD 8164
Good lych gate and Brobdingnagian slate
gravestones forming the churchyard paths.
Craven regional Perpendicular with handsome 17th-century pulpit, lectern and altar
rails. Poor-box of 1684, brass candelabra
dated 1718, and a large Royal Arms of 1716.
1841 monument to Dr George Birkbeck,
founder of the Mechanics' Institute movement.

GISBURN
St Mary
7m/11km N.E. of Clitheroe SD 8248
Perpendicular church with a Norman tower
and some 13th-century work including the
chancel arch; 15th-century screens and
glass.

GOLDSBOROUGH
St Mary
2m/3km E. of Knaresborough SE 3856
Pleasant village church of 12th–15th centuries. Heraldic glass of 1696 and a fine
series of monuments; two 14th-century
knights, one in a canopied niche to Sir
Richard Goldsborough, c. 1333, and a delightful 18th-century piece by Joseph Wilton
with figures of Faith and Charity.

GOLDTHORPE
St John & St Mary Magdalene
7m/11km W. of Doncaster SE 4604
1916. By A. Y. Nutt in the Italian taste for
Lord Halifax, an early instance of the use
of reinforced concrete; eclectic furnishings.

GREAT HOUGHTON
(dedication unknown)
6m/10km E. of Barnsley SE 4306
Interesting chapel of c. 1650; Gothic Survival crow-step gables and battlemented
parapets with round-headed merlons. Original pulpit and box pews restored by
G. G. Pace.

GREAT MITTON
All Hallows
3m/4km S.W. of Clitheroe SD 7139
Beautifully placed in the countryside of the Ribble Valley. Decorated nave, Elizabethan N. chapel, and Perpendicular tower, all on different levels. Excellent inscribed 15th-century rood screen with early 19th-century cast-iron cresting, tiled floors, and a 17th-century pulpit. Splendid series of monuments in Shirburn chapel, including conservative late 17th-century recumbent effigies by William Stanton. Monument to the Jacobite Peregrine Widdrington erected by the Duchess of Norfolk, 1749.

GUISELEY
St Oswald
8m/12km N.W. of Leeds SE 1941
Park-like churchyard. Tower with corbelled parapet; 13th-century S. transept and chancel arch with detached shafts. Imaginatively rebuilt, extended and furnished by Sir Charles Nicholson in 1910. Fragments of three Saxon crosses. Patrick Brontë married Maria Branwell here in 1812; also the parish church of many Longfellow ancestors.

HALIFAX
SE 0925
All Souls, Haley Hill
Built by Colonel Edward Ackroyd to complete his Boothtown industrial community; by Sir George Gilbert Scott, 1856–9. 'It is, on the whole, my best church; but it labours under this disadvantage, that it was never meant to be so fine a work as it is.' Skidmore metalwork in floral spirals, sculpture by J. Birnie Philip, and very fine glass by Hardman.
R.C.F.

St John the Baptist, Church Street
Large Perpendicular town church standing low in the valley with mills rising around; dignified tower, 118 feet high. Vast interior full of arches. S. chapel built as a chantry for William Rokeby, Archbishop of Dublin, 1521–2. Three wooden stalls with misericords in the choir; extensive Jacobean pewing and splendid altar rails of 1698. Fine heraldic nave and chancel roofs of 1636 and unusual patterned glazing of 1650. Glorious 15th-century font cover, two fine Royal Arms, and a life-size figure of 1701, known as Tristram (the poor-box!); fine 19th-century organ case by J. O. Scott.

HAREWOOD
All Saints
7m/11km N. of Leeds SE 3245
Secluded position in park. Perpendicular throughout, attacked in 1862 by Sir Giles Gilbert Scott, who crowded most of the fine 15th- and 16th-century alabaster monuments into the S. chapel. Heavy oak communion rail in memory of George V.
R.C.F.

HARROGATE
13m/21km N. of Leeds SE 3055
St Wilfrid, Duchy Road
The finest of Temple Moore's churches, completed by Leslie Moore in 1935; 13th-century style is used with rare and refined taste. Clerestoried nave, aisles, chancel with triforium and chapels; low embattled tower with pyramidal roof built over crossing. The rood, glass and wall reliefs by Francis Darlington are all notable.

HATFIELD
St Lawrence
7m/11km N.E. of Doncaster SE 6609
Cruciform church with proud Perpendicular central tower. Norman W. front, N. aisle, and S. doorway; Transitional arcades and Perpendicular transepts, the roofs with carved bosses. Fine 15th-century screen, old pews and monuments.

HEALAUGH
St John the Baptist
3m/4km N.E. of Tadcaster SE 5047
Norman church with fine S. door, corbel tables, and unusual carved responds to the chancel arch. Wharton monument, 1568, with mixed Gothic and Renaissance motifs.

HEPTONSTALL
St Thomas the Apostle
½m/1km N.W. of Hebden Bridge SD 9828
Old church badly damaged by storm in 1847, now a ruin. Near the porch the grave of David Hartley, executed in 1770 for counterfeiting coins. Replaced in 1854 by a large church in the Perpendicular style by Mallinson and Healey.

HICKLETON
St Wilfrid
6m/10km W. of Doncaster SE 4805
Late Perpendicular church of some richness pleasantly set by the Hall. Interior enriched by ornate collected furnishings of many dates from all over Europe, given by Lord Halifax.

Much restored in 1985 owing to coal-mining subsidence. Lych gate has recess containing three skulls.

HIGH MELTON
All Saints or St James
4m/6km W. of Doncaster SE 5001
Transitional nave and S. aisle, Perpendicular S. chapel, and good tower. Amid much fine furniture and many monuments, the rood screen by Comper stands supreme; good 15th- and 18th-century glass.

HOLMFIRTH
Holy Trinity
5m/8km S. of Huddersfield SE 1408
By J. Jagger, 1777–87, built in the decade after one of the periodic Holme Valley floods had badly damaged the old church. Large and churchwardenly with chancel beneath the tower. Interior altered in 1875; one of the three galleries has since been converted to a church hall.

HOOK
St Mary
1m/2km N.E. of Goole SE 7625
Small, intimate church of many dates in picturesque churchyard. A chancel window shows Queen Victoria visiting Boer War wounded.

HOOTON PAGNELL
All Saints
7m/11km N.W. of Doncaster SE 4808
Well placed adjoining the Hall. A Norman and later church well restored by J. L. Pearson in 1876. Good Norman doorway with original ironwork and 18th-century marquetry pulpit.

HORBURY
St Peter & St Leonard
3m/4km S.W. of Wakefield SE 2918
Large and splendid church of 1791–3 in Adam style, designed and paid for by John Carr, who was born in Horbury and who is buried here. Elegant spire in diminishing stages, and Ionic portico; the polygonal interior somewhat spoiled by Victorian furnishings.

HORTON-IN-RIBBLESDALE
St Oswald
5m/8km N. of Settle SD 8172
Rugged church in a rugged setting. Oblong Norman church without chancel arch; Per-

pendicular tower and a Norman tub font.

HUBBERHOLME
St Michael and All Angels
in Langstrothdale 1m/2km N.W. of Buckden, which is 4m/6km N. of Kettlewell SD 9278
Lovely setting in its Pennine valley. Transitional church recast in the 16th century. An exceptionally late rood screen of 1558 retaining some painted decoration as well as its rood loft, one of only two in Yorkshire. Scraped interior.

ILKLEY
10m/16km N. of Bradford SE 1147
All Saints
Late Perpendicular, largely rebuilt in 1860; Jacobean font cover and pew; Saxon crosses.
St Margaret
Luxurious spa suburban by R. Norman Shaw, 1878. Tall and impressive E. end with carved reredos and fine chancel screen by J. Harold Gibbons. Glass by Powells.

INGLETON
St Mary
6m/10km S.E. of Kirkby Lonsdale SD 6972
Perpendicular tower, the rest of 1887 by C. E. Tate. Fine carved Norman circular font with figures in an arcade. Copy of the 'Vinegar Bible'.

KELLINGTON
St Edmund
3m/4km E. of Knottingley SE 5524
Isolated setting. Norman core, Early English arcades and lancets; bosses to nave roof. Big leaning tower and a medieval font re-dated 1663.

KILDWICK
St Andrew
4m/6km N.W. of Keighley SE 0145
The 'Lang Kirk' of Craven with enormous weather vane. Medieval with Tudor elongation; 16th-century screen, 17th-century pews, including Eltoft family pew of 1633. Tombstone in shape of an organ; Saxon fragments.

KIPPAX
St Mary
2m/3km S.E. of Garforth, which is 7m/11km E. of Leeds SE 4130
Spacious, aisleless Norman church with herringbone masonry. Early English and Decor-

Bradford-on-Avon, Wiltshire; the early Saxon church

Left: 13th-century lierne vaulting in the chancel, Pershore, Worcestershire

Below: Landmark spire of 208 feet high, Dalton Holme, East Yorkshire; J. L. Pearson, 1858-61

18th-century interior, Whitby, Yorkshire

Left: Studley Royal, Yorkshire; built in 1871–8 in 14th-century French style, with spire 152 feet high

Below: North windows, Studley Royal

Left: Rood screen,
Llanelieu,
Talgarth, Brecon

Below: Carved rood
screen, Llanfilo,
Brecon

Above: East end, Llanrhychwyn, Caernarvon

Left: Ewenny Priory, Mid Glamorgan

Left: Kidwelly seen from the ruined castle, Carmarthenshire

Below: 12th-century saddleback tower, Llangennith, West Glamorgan

Mansel tombs in the south aisle, Margam Abbey, West Glamorgan

ated chancel, W. tower with Perpendicular top, and a Saxon cross shaft.

KIRK BRAMWITH
St Mary
6m/10km N.E. of Doncaster SE 6211
In a garden setting on edge of fenland, the church has a Norman chancel arch and S. door. It contains much 20th-century heraldic glass, good oak furnishings by Thompson, and a nave ceiling by G. G. Pace.

KIRK BURTON
All Hallows
4m/6km S.E. of Huddersfield SE 1912
Mostly Early English, much rebuilt and restored; 15th-century nave roof with bosses, 17th-century pews, and striking modern font cover. Restored 10th-century stone crucifix.

KIRK DEIGHTON
All Saints
1m/2km N. of Wetherby SE 3950
Perpendicular tower and spire. Restored in 1875 by the Rev. E. Geldart; Minton sanctuary tiles and good glass by Ward & Hughes.

KIRK HAMMERTON
St John the Baptist
9m/15km W. of York SE 4655
A complete small Saxon church, now forming the S. aisle of a church by C. Hodgson Fowler, 1891. Slender Saxon tower with paired belfry lights.

KIRK SANDAL
St Oswald
4m/6km N.E. of Doncaster SE 6107
In a spacious churchyard close to railway and canal. Early English additions to Norman church. Huge Perpendicular Rokeby chapel, chantry to Archbishop Rokeby of Dublin and former vicar, with monument. Fine 15th-century screen and chapel roof, much early 16th-century glass.
R.C.F.

KIRK SMEATON
St Mary
5m/8km S.E. of Pontefract SE 5116
Mostly rebuilt in 1864. Late Norman chancel arch raised in the 13th century, Perpendicular tower, and carved Decorated sedilia. Cylindrical Norman font.

KIRKBY MALHAM
St Michael or St James
5m/8km E. of Settle SD 8961
Beautiful village setting. Craven regional Perpendicular. Long, low, rugged exterior, the inside filled with 17th–19th-century pews; the 17th-century altar rails compare favourably with pretentious woodwork of 1923 in the chancel. Stone stocks in the churchyard.

KIRKBY MALZEARD
St Andrew
5m/8km N.W. of Ripon SE 2374
In a good stone-built village. Fine Perpendicular tower with panelled plinth; external arched windows with straight-sided heads. Sumptuous Norman S. doorway. Early English arcade and N. aisle. Restored by J. O. Scott after fire in 1908; he gave it a new hammer-beam roof. Good 18th- and 19th-century charity boards under the tower. Modern woodwork by Thompson of Kilburn.

KIRKBY OVERBLOW
All Saints
4m/6km S. of Harrogate SE 3249
Early 14th-century N. transept; nave and tower mostly of 1780–1, 'improved' by G. E. Street in 1872. N. and E. windows by Kempe. Pretty Coade-stone monument to Dorothy Cooper, d. 1793.

KIRKBY WHARFE
St John the Baptist
2m/3km S.E. of Tadcaster SE 5040
Exterior heavily restored in 1860, but with Transitional arcades, tower arch, and S. doorway; the door itself is 17th-century with twined scrolly strands. Early Renaissance screen; brass; 15th–17th-century glass, much of it foreign. E. window by Capronnier.

KNARESBOROUGH
St John the Baptist
3m/4km N.E. of Harrogate SE 3557
Prominent position in picturesque riverside town. Transitional central tower with later spirelet; 13th–14th-century work in chancel and chapels; Perpendicular nave. Post-Gothic altar tomb and other monuments to Slingsbys in N. chapel. Prettily decorated poor-box dated 1600; 18th-century font cover; glass by Morris and F. Madox Brown.

LAUGHTON-EN-LE-MORTHEN
All Saints
2m/3km E. of Thurcroft SK 5188
Magnificent Perpendicular tower and spire soaring 185 feet. Blocked Saxon doorway in N. aisle; Transitional chancel recast in 15th century. Stone chancel screen and embattled font both Perpendicular.

LEAD
St Mary
½m/1km W. of Saxton, which is 4m/6km S. of Tadcaster SE 4637
Well known to cyclists and ramblers. Tiny early 14th-century chapel in a field; very atmospheric with rustic benches and a three-decker pulpit.
R.C.F.

LEATHLEY
St Oswald
2m/3km N.E. of Otley across R.Wharfe SE 2347
Unbuttressed early-Norman tower with low pyramidal roof and early 19th-century clock face; early and luxuriant ironwork on inner tower door.

LEDSHAM
All Saints
4m/6km N.W. of Ferrybridge SE 4529
Village setting. Saxon nave, chancel arch, and lower stage of tower with much-restored carving round doorway. Otherwise mostly Perpendicular with fine 17th- and 18th-century monuments including that by Scheemakers to Lady Elizabeth Hastings, benefactor of Queen's College, Oxford, 'whom to love,' declared Steele, 'was a liberal education.'

LEEDS
SE 2933
St Aidan, Roundhay Road
Impressive red-brick Romanesque basilica by R. J. Johnson and A. Crawford-Hick, 1891–4. Celebrated mosaic of the life of St Aidan by Sir Frank Brangwyn, 1916. Furnishings by Richard Mellor.
All Souls, Blackman Lane
Built as a memorial to Dr Hook, one of the last churches of Sir George Gilbert Scott, 1876–81. Austere and noble Early English work on a grand scale; the tower a notable landmark. Interior partly stone-vaulted; fittings by Scott; font cover by his pupil R. J. Johnson. Glass by Clayton & Bell, Kempe

and Tower. Figure of St John by Mayer of Oberammergau.
St George, Great George Street
By John Clark, 1836–8, with apse added in 1890 by Henry Walker. A large church with tall lancets and originally with a spire to suit its impressive position, which sadly was destroyed in a gale in 1962. Re-ordered 1980 when the gallery was removed. Ground-floor crypt a refuge for the homeless.
St Hilda, Cross Green Lane
By J. T. Micklethwaite, 1876–81. Plain red-brick exterior with nave and chancel of the same height. Interior enlivened by painted wooden reredos, screen, rood and pulpit by W. H. Wood of Newcastle, all in a Bodleyish style.
Holy Trinity, Boar Lane
By W. Halfpenny, 1721–7. Set in busy central shopping area; Doric exterior with graceful spire rebuilt by R. D. Chantrell in 1839. Giant Corinthian columns support a shallow tunnel vault inside.
St John the Evangelist, New Briggate
Gothic Survival church of 1632–4 with twin-nave plan, endowed by John Harrison, cloth merchant. Delightful interior with magnificent contemporary fittings including screen, bobbin-ended and crested pews, and pulpit with tester. Praiseworthy restoration by R. Norman Shaw in 1868.
R.C.F.
St Margaret, Cardigan Road
By Temple Moore, 1908–9; E. end completed in 1963 by G. G. Pace, but the huge W. tower was never built. Massive brick church making great use of sloping site. Impressive interior with stone walls contrasting with brick-banded exterior, with undivided nave and chancel, circular piers, and timber rib vaults.
St Peter, Kirkgate
In a drab setting by the railway. By R. D. Chantrell, 1837–41. In Perpendicular style, the planning reflecting Dean Hook's uncompromising High Church views. There is room for a very large congregation on the floor and in the galleries, and the long elevated E. arm provided space for the first surpliced choir in any Anglican church. To the E. of the choir-stalls is a space for the congregation to 'draw near' and stand in; and the altar rails will hold 40 people at a time. A highly atmospheric building rich in stained glass, monuments, and fittings.
St Saviour, Ellerby Road

Designed by J. M. Derick in 1842–5 for the 'anonymous donor', Dr Pusey, to combat the locals' gross profligacy combined perhaps with attendance at socialistic meetings! A miniature cathedral in spikey Middle Pointed style. The tall and narrow interior is relieved by the glowing glass of Pugin, O'Connor and Morris. Screen, reredos and Pusey Memorial Chapel by G. F. Bodley, 1890. This was the pioneer Oxford Movement church of northern England.

St Bartholomew, Armley

By J. Athron and H. Walker, 1872–7; tower added in 1903–4. Large, the tower very prominent. Impressively tall interior with vaulted apsidal chancel and reredos by Thomas Earp. Vast Schulze organ enjoys international reputation.

St Matthew, Chapel Allerton

By G. F. Bodley, 1897–1900, in late 14th-century style. Dominated externally by the beautiful and almost detached tower. Nave and aisles under one roof. Spacious interior with painted wagon roofs, Bodley's own rood screen and organ case; glass by Burlison & Grylls.

Epiphany, Gipton

By N. F. Cachemaille-Day, 1937–8. A bold plan with curved brick walls and tall slit windows. Imaginative in conception, but the unconcealed painted concrete surfaces somewhat crude in reality. This church marks a significant place in the transition of church-building from the use of revivals to an architecture of the 20th century.

St Wilfrid, Halton

By Randall Wells, 1937–9. At first glance a breakaway design; in reality less advanced than Kempley, Gloucs., 1904. Statue of St Wilfrid by Eric Gill.

St Chad, Far Headingley

A vigorous building of 1868 in the Middle Pointed style; designed by W. H. Crossland, despite interference from Lord Grimthorpe. Fine spire and originally an apsidal chancel, the latter replaced by W. H. Gibbons in 1910. His is a well-conceived Early English work culminating in a great polychromed wooden reredos, the climax of the church. Arts and Crafts glass in E. window by Margaret Aldrich Rope.

St Michael, Headingley

Noble cruciform church with magnificent spire by J. L. Pearson, 1884–5. Impressive stone-vaulted interior. Reredos by Temple Moore, 1905.

LINTON-IN-CRAVEN
St Michael

1m/2km S. of Grassington SD 9962

Pleasant setting on banks of the Wharfe. Low, spreading church with little overhanging bellcote. Late Norman arcade and font; nave rebuilt in 14th century; Perpendicular chapels.

LITTLE OUSEBURN
Holy Trinity

½m/1km S. of Great Ouseburn, which is 5m/8km S.E. of Boroughbridge SE 4461

Stands alone among remnants of 18th-century landscaping. Tall Norman tower with Perpendicular pinnacles; mostly 13th–15th-centuries, restored after war damage. Three Tudor carved bench-ends. In the churchyard a delightful late 18th-century domed Tuscan mausoleum built by Henry Thompson of Kirby Hall, a friend of Lord Burlington.

LONG MARSTON
All Saints

7m/11km W. of York SE 5051

Perpendicular tower. Late Norman nave and chancel with Decorated and Perpendicular windows; 17th-century monument.

MALTBY
St Bartholomew

6m/10km E. of Rotherham SK 5292

Good Norman tower with small recessed Perpendicular spire. The remainder pleasantly rebuilt by P. Boyce in 1859.

MARR
St Helen

4m/6km N.W. of Doncaster SE 5105

Early Norman nave and chancel with herringbone masonry; W. tower of c. 1300, the rest Perpendicular. Tudor brass of John Lewis and family, 1579. Elizabethan font and several pieces of funeral armour.

METHLEY
St Oswald

5m/8km N.E. of Wakefield SE 3926

An important Decorated and Perpendicular church, though much restored in 1876. Sumptuous early 16th-century lectern, probably from the Netherlands; Elizabethan font cover; 17th-century screen; early-Georgian pulpit. A very fine series of monuments: six pre-Reformation effigies, especially Sir John Warburton, d. 1424, under a cusped arch. Later ones include John Savile, d. 1778, by Wilton, and others by Scheemakers and Westmacott.

MIDHOPESTONES
St James the Less
3m/4km S. of Penistone, which is 7m/11km W. of Barnsley SK 2399
Delightful little building of 1705 with mullioned windows and a bell-turret. Inside is a W. gallery, Jacobean pulpit, and box pews.

MONK FRYSTON
St Wilfrid
7m/11km W. of Selby SE 5029
Saxon tower with 14th-century top, Early English arcades, and a 14th-century chancel. Square 13th-century font. E. end panelling and opulent reredos by Bromet and Thorman; Kempe glass.

NETHERTON
St Andrew
3m/4km S.W. of Huddersfield town centre SE 1213
A small but most original building by J. D. Sedding, 1881, with an impressive bellcote on two buttresses, rather like that of Holy Island. Nave and chancel in one. Somewhat dark inside because of the few windows.

NETHER POPPLETON
St Everilda
3m/4km N.W. of York SE 5654
Set behind a farm at the end of the village. Aisleless Norman church with Decorated and Perpendicular windows; pleasantly rural galleried interior. Medieval glass, 17th-century monuments, and a painted rood by H. Harvey.

NEWTON KYME
St Andrew
2m/3km N.W. of Tadcaster SE 4644
Setting by the Regency Hall. Transitional arcades and 15th-century tower, curious scratched carvings in the porch, and some heraldic glass; 17th-century ledger stones and peculiar early 20th-century brick monument in trim churchyard.

NORMANTON
All Saints
4m/6km E. of Wakefield SE 3822
Imposing church with Decorated chancel and nave arcades, Perpendicular tower, and a panelled font. There is a good deal of old glass, some foreign, and a dignified monument to John Freeston, d. 1594.

NUN MONKTON
St Mary
9m/15km S.E. of Boroughbridge SE 5057
Exquisite building in a delightful setting by the late 17th-century Hall. Early English nave of a former Benedictine nunnery. W. front has a good Transitional doorway flanked by niches with fragmentary sculpture. Above are three tall lancets and a little square pyramid-topped tower supported inside on a lofty arch. Arresting treatment of internal walls with lancets separated by tall open arcading. The E. end was rebuilt in 1873 incorporating superb Morris glass.

OTLEY
All Saints
10m/16km N.W. of Leeds SE 2045
Cruciform church with Norman N. door and chancel windows; rest 14th–15th-century. Georgian porch, communion rail and pulpit; much Art Nouveau woodwork by Bromet and Thorman and an outstanding group of Saxon cross fragments. Good monuments and in the churchyard the Bramhope Tunnel memorial of c. 1850. Thomas Chippendale was baptized here and John Wesley officiated at a wedding in 1788.

OULTON
St John the Evangelist
5m/8km S.E. of Leeds SE 3658
Setting in grounds of hall; a major work by Thomas Rickman, architect and scholar, 1827. Outside all is very neat with a slender spire, lancets, and restrained pinnacles. Fine brick-vaulted interior with rich Geometric arcading in the polygonal apse and the founder's tomb.

OWSTON
All Saints
1m/2km N.E. of Carcroft, which is 5m/8km N.W. of Doncaster SE 5511
Pleasantly isolated setting in park. Late Norman W. tower with Early English belfry openings, Transitional N. aisle, and an early 14th-century chancel with good E. window and Perpendicular screen. Easter Sepulchre in N. wall; 15th-century brass and two monuments by Chantrey.

OXENHOPE
St Mary the Virgin
1m/2km S. of Haworth SE 0335
By Ignatius Bonomi and Cori, 1849. Remarkable for its early date, since this is convincing Norman Revival work. Sturdy W. tower, small windows, and proper circular piers; a sound design.

PENISTONE
St John the Baptist
7m/11km W. of Barnsley SE 2403
Fine Transitional nave arcades, Decorated chancel and S. chapel, Perpendicular clerestories, and a grand W. tower to round it off. There are good roofs with bosses. Two early 18th-century tablets in the chancel and a memorial to Dr Nicholas Saunderson who, though blind, taught himself to read by feeling inscriptions on tombstones; he became Lucasian Professor of Mathematics at Cambridge; d. 1739.

PONTEFRACT
All Saints
12m/19km S.E. of Leeds SE 4522
Badly damaged in the Civil War and left derelict for 200 years. Dramatic ruined nave and chancel, the transepts in sumptuous Gothic by R. D. Chantrell, 1838. Charming plaster-vaulted interior. An unobtrusive new extension has been built within the nave by G. Pace, 1967.

RAVENFIELD
St James
4m/6km E. of Rotherham SK 4895
A tiny church in the Gothic taste, set in a park and designed by the celebrated John Carr in 1756. Delightful exterior; the inside relieved by several good monuments, one by Fisher of York. One-handed clock in tower.

ROECLIFFE
St Mary
1m/2km W. of Boroughbridge SE 3765
By R. H. Sharp, 1843, in Norman Revival style. Alas, the details far too big, but the barrel-vaulted interior compensates with an astonishing array of woodwork evicted from other churches. A vestry door from York Minster, splendid pulpit and altar rails, perspective panels dated 1619, and a vestry wall covered with numerous small panels. The E. window is by Barnett, 1847, after Pinturicchio.
R.C.F.

ROTHERHAM
SK 4292
All Saints
Noble cruciform Perpendicular church, the central tower with a spire rising 180 feet, battlements, and pinnacled parapets. Inside are a fan-vaulted crossing, charming 15th-century choir-stalls, a pulpit of 1604, and diverse tombs; 18th-century case to the Snetzler organ.

ROTHWELL
Holy Trinity
5m/8km S.E. of Leeds SE 3428
A large Perpendicular church much restored in 1873. There is a good nave ceiling with carved bosses, a font of 1662 with a fine openwork cover, and a stone reredos by Sir A. Blomfield. W. window by Wm. Wailes.

ROYSTON
St John the Baptist
3m/4km N. of Barnsley SE 3611
Decorated church of character. Tall Perpendicular tower with unusual oriel on W. face. Perpendicular screen; black and white marble monument of 1673 and a tasteful Rococo one of 1754.

RUFFORTH
All Saints
5m/8km W. of York SE 5251
By Demaine & Brierley, 1894–5. A well-conceived and extremely well-detailed tower with recessed spire and porch. Two plain Norman doorways survive from the earlier church.

RYTHER
All Saints
2m/3km N.W. of Cawood, which is 4m/6km N.W. of Selby SE 5539
In a rural setting, the church has an early-Norman chancel arch, a 13th-century nave and Decorated S. aisle with remarkable group of 14th–15th-century Ryther family monuments; four medieval altar-slabs. Bell-turret added by C. Hodgson Fowler when he restored the church in 1898.

SANDAL MAGNA
St Helen
district of Wakefield 2m/3km S. of city centre across R. Calder SE 3418
Cruciform, largely Decorated with some 12th-century work in arcades. S. chapel is late-Perpendicular with parclose screens

and later furnishings; 17th-century cast-iron ledger plates to members of Beaumont family.

SAXTON
All Saints
4m/6km S. of Tadcaster SE 4736
Norman chancel arch and S. doorway with waterleaf capitals; Perpendicular tower and late 13th-century S. chapel. An elegant monument of 1783 by J. F. Moore of London, and in the churchyard the rare surviving tomb chest of Lord Dacre, killed at the Battle of Towton, 1461.

SEDBERGH
St Andrew
9m/15km E. of Kendal SD 6592
A Norman and later town church; 13th-century arcades; Perpendicular tower and windows. Inlaid 18th-century tester to pulpit and a poor-box of 1633.

SELBY
SS. Mary and Germaine
13m/21km S. of York SE 6132
Noble monastic church founded by the Conqueror for Benedictine monks. Norman Transitional nave and N. transept with Early English clerestory, an excellent W. door and N. porch. Exquisite Decorated choir with restored original glass in the E. window. Central tower and S. transept rebuilt after fire in 1906 by J. Oldrid Scott. Splendid Perpendicular font cover and monuments.

SHEFFIELD
SK 3587
St George, Portobello Street
1821–5 by Hurst and Woodhead; large with dignified W. tower. The ashlar is very black and the stones of spectacular size. Galleries on three sides; opulent W. organ case.
St Matthew, Carver Street
By Flockton & Son, 1854–5. A pleasing building reminiscent of medieval churches in York, but the principal interest attaches to the fittings: gilded reredos and high altar by J. D. Sedding; magnificent carved choir-stalls are early Charles Nicholson; the font and pulpit with inlaid beaten copper panels added by H. J. Potter in the 1900s.
St Mark, Broomfield
By W. H. Crossland, 1871; only his large tower, spire and S. porch escaped wartime destruction. New concrete church by G. G. Pace; stained glass in E. window by Harry

Stammers, and in the W. glass by John Piper and Patrick Reyntiens. Stainless-steel font and cast-aluminium cover by Frank Roper.
All Saints, Eccleshall
Impressively sited church of 1789, remodelled in 1843; transepts and E. parts boldly and successfully added by Temple Moore in 1908; glass by Kempe & Tower.
St Andrew, Sharrow
One of several Frenchified Gothic Sheffield churches; this one by J. B. Mitchell and Withers, 1869. Large and rather coarse detailing with prominent N.E. tower and spire. Plush interior with comfortably padded seats and reredos by C. Hodgson Fowler.

SHERBURN-IN-ELMET
All Saints
6m/10km S. of Tadcaster SE 4933
Hill-top site, visible for miles around. Large late-Norman church with stately nave arcades and Early English chancel with three lancets and a vesica to the E. Also a rare 15th-century cross head carved with Crucifixion on both sides.

SILKSTONE
All Saints
4m/6km W. of Barnsley SE 2905
Notable Perpendicular church with tall tower and elaborate display of pinnacles and tiny flying buttresses. Early 13th-century arcades and a chancel rebuilt in 1852–8. Good Perpendicular roofs and screens; monument to Sir Thomas Wentworth, d. 1675, with fine effigies. Victorian churchyard monument to 26 boys and girls drowned in a mine. William and Mary Royal Arms above the tower screen. Box pews, some bearing their owners' names, and pulpit of 1835.

SKELTON
St Helen
2m/3km N.W. of Boroughbridge SE 3668
A lavish creation of W. Burges (cf. Studley Royal) built in 1871–2 by Lady Mary Vyner as a memorial to her son killed by brigands in Greece. Solid exterior with elaborate chancel and massive spire. Inside, a profusion of multi-coloured marble, brass, and excellent windows; jewelled altar frontal made by Lady Vyner to Burges's design.
R.C.F.

SKIPTON
Holy Trinity
16m/25km N.W. of Bradford SD 9851
Damaged in the Civil War but restored by Lady Anne Clifford in 1659. Colourful setting by castle. Craven regional Perpendicular incorporating some Decorated work. Rood screen of 1533, an excellent Jacobean font cover to 12th-century font, and good Clifford tombs. Restored by Sir Giles Gilbert Scott, 1870; glass by Capronnier and Kempe.

SLAIDBURN
St Andrew
7m/11km N. of Clitheroe SD 7152
Perpendicular church in charming village. Prominent tower and stair turret contrast with long, low, rendered walls of nave and aisles. Untouched interior with good box pews crowding round the excellent Jacobean screen and Georgian three-decker pulpit. Other delights include an Elizabethan font cover, a pair of Royal Arms, and brass chandeliers.

SNAITH
St Lawrence
6m/10km W. of Goole SE 6422
Large embattled church dominating the town. Norman cruciform origins with powerful Early English W. tower, Perpendicular nave, and Decorated chancel. The E. window has glass by Francis Spear; 1837 monument by Chantrey to Viscount Downe.

SOUTH ANSTON
St James
5m/8km N.W. of Worksop SK 5284
Small but impressively set. Mostly Decorated with Perpendicular W. tower and octagonal spire. Broad, flowing traceried E. window and an elaborate double piscina in the chancel. Good early 14th-century monument of a lady, her small daughter, and three angels.

SOUTH KIRKBY
All Saints
10m/16km S.E. of Wakefield SE 4511
Perpendicular exterior with elaborate rib-vaulted S. porch sporting shields of local families. Interior has atmosphere. Early 13th-century arcades. N. aisle roof with carved bosses and figures of musicians. Early tablet by Rysbrack to Sir John Wentworth, d. 1720.

SOWERBY
St Peter
2m/3km S.W. of Halifax SE 0423
Noble Classical building of 1763–6 with Gibbsian surrounds, Tuscan columns, parapet and balustrades. Tower with lancets of 1781. Stately Corinthian interior with galleries, superb plasterwork on E. wall, and monuments. Life-size statue by Joseph Wilton, 1796, to John Tillotson, born in the neighbourhood, who was Archbishop of Canterbury 1691–5.

SPOFFORTH
All Saints
3m/4km N.W. of Wetherby SE 3651
Norman Revival exterior of 1855 by J. W. Hugall incorporates Transitional arcades and chancel arch; tall Perpendicular tower. 'Blind Jack of Knaresborough', the great road-maker, is buried in the churchyard just N. of the chancel.

SPROTBROUGH
St Mary
3m/4km W. of Doncaster SE 5302
Late 13th-century church with Decorated tower, Perpendicular arcades and chancel arch; 13th-century piscina with credence shelf. Characterful interior has rood screen with return stalls, 16th-century benches, and Jacobean altar rails; other furnishings by Sir Ninian Comper. Strange stone seat with caryatid bust of a man, thought to be a frith stool.

STAINBURN
St Mary the Virgin
4m/6km N.E. of Otley SE 2448
Small rustic Norman church in a secluded moorside position with arcaded font and splendid chancel arch, 17th-century pulpit, and Jacobean pews. Curious 17th-century window with a triangular head.
R.C.F.

STANLEY
St Peter
1m/2km N.E. of Wakefield SE 3422
By P. Atkinson Jnr, 1821–4; largely rebuilt by W. D. Caroe, 1912, after a fire. On a vast scale with superb furnishings; impressive crypt under church.

STUDLEY ROYAL
St Mary the Virgin
2m/3km W. of Ripon SE 2770
By W. Burges, 1871–8, strikingly set in a

deer park at the head of a long avenue; the sister church to Skelton. Rich and exotic exterior in 14th-century French style with commanding spire and elaborate E. end. The cream and grey nave contains the founder's tomb of 1909 and an organ case with oversailing upper storeys, the upper ones reached by a spiral staircase. The riotous chancel is based on the Book of the Revelation; the ceiling has angelic choirs, the floor depicts the four rivers round the Garden of Eden, and there is an Assyrian lion over the sedilia. Sculpture is by T. Nicholls, glass by Saunders and Weeks; the whole drawn into Burges's determinedly symbolic scheme.
  N.T.

SWILLINGTON
St Mary
6m/10km S.E. of Leeds SE 3830
Late Decorated nave and chancel of white Tadcaster stone; the tower of 1884 in dark contrasting gritstone. There is a brass and a Royal Arms of 1723.

TADCASTER
St Mary
9m/15km S.W. of York SE 4843
Handsome white limestone church, largely Perpendicular, but taken down and rebuilt in 1875–7 to preserve it from floods. Fine buttressed tower, E. window by Morris & Co., and exceptionally fine early 20th-century woodwork by Bromet and Thorman.

THORNE
St Nicholas
9m/15km N.E. of Doncaster SE 6813
Early English church with Decorated tower and Perpendicular additions; glass by H. Holiday.

THORNHILL
St Michael
2m/3km S. of Dewsbury SE 2518
Perpendicular church restored in 1879 by G. E. Street, who destroyed the Georgian nave but left the handsome W. tower. The Savile Chapel of 1447 has its original roof, much early glass, and a rich series of monuments from 1321, both medieval and Renaissance, including one by Colt.

THORPE SALVIN
St Michael
4m/6km W. of Worksop SK 5281
Pastoral setting close to the ruined Eliza-

bethan manor house built by Henry Sandford. Sumptuous Norman S. door and celebrated font with carvings of the four seasons. Transitional nave, Decorated chancel; good 15th- and 17th-century monuments. Chained Bible of 1641.

THROAPHAM
St John the Baptist
adjoins Dinnington, which is 6m/10km N.W. of Worksop SK 5387
Transitional S. door, Early English arcades, Perpendicular tower, clerestory and chancel windows; 13th-century coped coffin lid.
  R.C.F.

THRYBERGH
St Leonard
adjoins Rotherham to N.E. SK 4695
Setting. Norman core, but largely Perpendicular with much-renewed Decorated chancel and a W. tower with crocketed spire. Large and fine collection of monuments, principally to the Reresby and Finch families; Saxon cross stem and some 15th-century stained glass.

TICKHILL
St Mary
6m/10km S. of Doncaster SK 5993
One of the finest medieval churches in the Riding. The splendid 13th-century W. tower has an early 15th-century top with graceful openwork parapet; the rest of the church was also rebuilt during the second half of the 15th century. Light and spacious interior has a Perpendicular font and screen, medieval panelled pulpit, and a 16th-century Renaissance monument, an alabaster tomb chest with effigies of Thomas Fitzwilliam and his first wife.

TODWICK
SS. Peter & Paul
6m/10km N.W. of Worksop SK 4984
Decorated with Perpendicular W. tower; nave and chancel largely rebuilt in the 14th century. Two Norman doorways and a recut chancel arch; 17th-century box pews and altar rails; small brass of 1609 on wall.

TONG
St James
4m/6km S.E. of Bradford city centre SE 2230
A rural island in outer Bradford. Church rebuilt in 1727 in a pleasing and dignified manner by Sir George Tempest of Long

Hall, incorporating Norman and Perpendicular work in the tower. Delightful interior with Tuscan arcade and exceptionally complete early 18th-century fittings. Squire's pew complete with fireplace.

TREETON
St Helen
3m/4km S. of Rotherham SK 4387
12th- and 13th-century nave with Decorated chancel. Inside are a Perpendicular screen and some benches.

WADWORTH
St John the Baptist
4m/6km S. of Doncaster SK 5697
Remarkable Transitional arcading in the S. aisle and porch, early-Decorated chancel and Perpendicular tower. E. window with distinctive mouchettes in the large 14th-century S. chapel. Monuments include a late 14th-century effigy in hunting costume.

WAKEFIELD
SE 3320
St James, Thornes
By Atkinson and Sharpe, 1829–31, in the Classical manner. Domed W. tower, five-bay sides, straight-headed windows and doors. Well-renovated interior.
St John
Set impressively in the middle of a Georgian square. Dignified church of 1791–5 by Charles Watson, the E. end added by J. T. Micklethwaite, 1905. Elegant tower with pedimented doorway and octagonal top stage; the nave with balustrade and urns; Tuscan columns within.

WALES
St John
7m/11km W. of Worksop SK 4782
Norman church of nave, chancel and W. tower now forms the N. aisle of the church as extended in 1897. Perpendicular nave roof and upper parts of tower. Norman font.

WATH-UPON-DEARNE
All Saints
5m/8km N. of Rotherham SE 4300
Norman tower and arcade; the tower was raised and a spire added in the 15th century. Fine late-medieval chest with tracery and beasts. A bell of 1588 stands under the tower.

WENTBRIDGE
St John the Evangelist
4m/6km S.E. of Pontefract SE 4817
By Sir Arthur Blomfield, 1878, in a good setting. Rock-faced ashlar cruciform church with central tower, tiled roofs, apsed chancel, and stiff-leaf decoration.

WENTWORTH
4m/6km N.W. of Rotherham SK 3898
Old Church
Setting in a picturesque village. Decorated W. tower and ruined 1684 nave. The Wentworth chapel was formed from the chancel and N. chapel of the medieval church; inside is a fine series of 16th- and 17th-century monuments including one to Charles I's close adviser, the first Earl of Strafford, 'Black Tom Tyrant', beheaded by the Long Parliament in 1641.
Holy Trinity
By J. L. Pearson, 1875–7. An accomplished cruciform church in late 13th-century style with tall spire and stone-vaulted interior. Kempe glass in W. window and Clayton & Bell in the E.

WESTON
All Saints
2m/3km N.W. of Otley across R. Wharfe SE 1746
Old-fashioned Norman and later church in park. W. front with big stepped buttresses and bell-turret. A Baroque porch dated 1686. Charming plastered interior has late-Georgian box pews, a three-decker pulpit, and curious squire's pew with fireplace. Hatchments and finely carved Royal Arms; 18th-century heraldic glass and work by G. Burkhardt of Munich in chancel windows.

WHISTON
St Mary Magdalene
suburb 2m/3km S.E. of Rotherham SK 4590
Medieval tower, nave and chancel; an additional large nave and chancel was added by J. O. Scott in 1883. Kempe glass.

WHITKIRK
St Mary
district of Leeds 4m/6km E. of city centre SE 3633
Perpendicular village church in suburban Leeds; the tower has a lead spirelet and the chancel was rebuilt by G. F. Bodley in 1901; 16th–19th-century monuments, one by Nollekens, and an appropriate tablet to John

Smeaton, builder of the Eddystone light-house.

WHITLEY LOWER
St Mary & St Michael
5m/8km E. of Huddersfield SE 2217
An expert example of Norman Revival by Ignatius Bonomi of Durham, 1847.

WHIXLEY
Ascension
6m/10km S.E. of Boroughbridge SE 4458
Large Decorated church replete with ballflowers and tracery; only the tower top is Perpendicular. White marble Tancred monument of 1754.

WIGHILL
All Saints
2m/3km N. of Tadcaster SE 4746
Pleasantly set at the end of the village. Medieval church with Transitional N. arcade and superb S. doorway with zig-zag, beak-heads, and grotesques. Jacobean furnishings and glass by C. W. Whall. Stapylton monuments.

WISTOW
All Saints
3m/4km N.W. of Selby SE 5935
A striking white limestone 13th–15th-century church and tower well set in village; 14th-century slab with woman in canopied niche, and a Jacobean pulpit.

WOMERSLEY
St Martin
4m/6km S.E. of Knottingley SE 5319
Cruciform church with handsome Decor-ated broach spire and elaborately vaulted S. porch. Diverse foreign furnishings include a 17th-century Spanish tile picture of the Last Supper and gilded Italian candlesticks. Roofs and rood screen by Bodley, 1895; glass by Kempe.

WOOLLEY
St Peter
5m/8km S. of Wakefield SE 3213
Perpendicular church with Norman Agnus Dei tympanum retained in S. aisle; 15th-century screen, glass and bench-ends; two good Morris & Co. windows of 1871. Late-medieval tomb chests in churchyard.

WORSBOROUGH
St Mary
adjoins Barnsley to S. SE 3503
Thin Decorated tower, assertive Perpendicular nave and aisles, and a Transitional chancel; the windows were altered by J. P. Pritchett in 1838; 15th-century S. porch with good ceiling and splendid oak doors of *c.* 1840; 18th-century squire's pew and an oak monument of 1534 with memento mori, a 'double decker' to Roger Rockley.

WRAGBY
St Michael and Our Lady
4m/6km S.W. of Pontefract SE 4117
Perpendicular church in grounds of Nostell Priory, home of the Winn family. Collected furnishings include a carved Norman font, a German pulpit, much Swiss glass, and a Georgian organ case. Winn monuments by Flaxman and Chantrey.

Wales

Introduction

The traveller entering Wales for the first time will quickly recognize the separateness when he encounters the tongue-twisting place-names, the musical accents of the English-speaking people and, as he travels westward, when he hears the Welsh language for the first time. For Wales is a distinctive country, its Celtic people of different origin from the Anglo-Saxon, and with a long history of independence, law-making and culture. For centuries after the Roman occupation its topography was a barrier to invasion by Anglo-Saxon and Norman alike, and it was not until 1284 that Edward I finally conquered the whole country, though sporadic revolts against English rule lasted for more than another century.

The Cambrian Mountains, rising to over 1,000 metres, divide Wales down the centre. Here, slopes are steep and the soil is poor; consequently much of the area is moorland or forest, the farming confined to sheep- and cattle-rearing. All the main rivers, such as the Dee, Severn, Usk, Wye, Teifi, Tawe, Dyfi and Conwy, rise in this central core, eventually meeting the 700 miles of Welsh coastline. To the east lie the flatter lands of Flintshire and the rolling pastoral borderland of Powys and Gwent; to the south, the coalfield, with its narrow, steep-sided valleys where Victorian heavy industry has largely given way to modern high-tech manufacturing, and the highly productive agricultural land of the Vale of Glamorgan; to the west, the dairying pastures of Pembrokeshire. North of Dyfi, except in Llyn, the mountains reach right down to the sea, culminating in Snowdonia in the north-west and the almost flat isle of Anglesey. The beautiful vales of Conwy and Clwyd penetrate the highlands of the north.

Except in the more prosperous farming areas, most of the churches are small, sturdy and of great simplicity, often isolated from habitation and approached by winding, narrow lanes. In the border marches, bellcotes substitute for towers, though fine ones are to be found in the north and south coastal areas, some of Somerset type in the south. A peculiarity, particularly in the north-east, is the double- and sometimes treble-naved church, a less expensive method of enlargement than the addition of aisles to a single nave. The predominance of the small nave and chancel church, however, does not mean that grander medieval churches are absent; Flint and Denbigh have a splendid group of Perpendicular churches built by Henry VIII's mother, Lady Margaret Beaufort, comprising Wrexham, Gresford, Mold, Northop, and

Holt, and others of all periods are to be found elsewhere. A notable feature of Welsh churches is the number of gloriously carved medieval rood screens and lofts that have survived, and 18th-century box pews, pulpit and communion tables are widespread in the remoter rural areas.

A few Georgian churches are to be found, as at Worthenbury, Marchwiel, and Llanfyllin, and Henry Wilson's Art Nouveau *tour de force* at Brithdir cannot fail to please. But it is to the Victorian period, consequent upon the population explosion which occurred, that we must look for a new flowering of church architecture. All the best English architects are represented: Scott, Street, Bodley, Pearson, and more. Good local architects like John Prichard, John Douglas, Arthur Baker, Henry Kennedy, and J. D. Sedding produced buildings that have stood the test of time.

The present century has been mainly one of repair, renovation and beautification. Only two churches of any note have been built: Llandeloy, by J. Coates Carter, and Llangammarch Wells, by W. D. Caroe, who was also a restorer with a highly sensitive touch.

Independent for centuries, the Celtic Church was made subject to the rule of Canterbury by the Normans, but in 1921 the Anglican Church in Wales was disestablished, thus regaining its independence after an interval of nearly 1,000 years. The price which had to be paid was the loss of most of its ancient endowments. The Archbishop is now elected by an electoral college, and he retains his bishopric, while the Church is governed by a body of bishops, priests and laity.

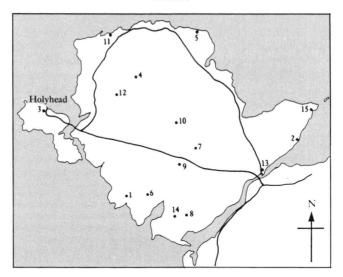

1	Aberffraw	9	Llangristiolus
2	Beaumaris	10	Llangwyllog
3	Holyhead	11	Llanrhwydrys
4	Llanbabo	12	Llantrisant
5	Llaneilian	13	Menai Bridge
6	Llangadwaladr	14	Newborough
7	Llangefni	15	Penmon Priory
8	Llangeinwen		

Anglesey

ABERFFRAW (Llangwyfan)
12m/19km W. of Menai Bridge SH 3468
St Gwyfan
On small island, easily reached at low tide.
Single-cell, dating from 12th century. Presumably once double-naved since N. wall
contains 16th-century arcading.
St Mary, Tal-y-llyn
3m/4km N. of village SH 3673
Diminutive and well worth finding, thanks
to restoration of 1968. Nave 12th- to 13th-
century; late 16th-century chancel; 17th-
century S. chapel; 18th-century plank pews
and communion rails.

BEAUMARIS
St Mary & St Nicholas
on E. side of Conwy Bay SH 6076
Built for English settled here in early 14th
century; early 16th-century chancel; 17th-
century S. chapel; 18th-century plank pews
and communion rails. Restored by Bodley,
1902. Early 16th-century bench-ends and
misericords; 15th-century alabaster altar
tomb; sarcophagus and early 19th-century
funeral hut in porch.

HOLYHEAD
St Cybi
on Holy Island SH 4883
The church was originally that of a clas built
on the site of the Roman fort. It was largely
rebuilt, apart from the 13th-century chancel,
in 1480–1520; the tower is 16th-century.
The result is a light arcaded building, with
a low-pitched, battlemented and pinnacled
roof and some intricate carving, particularly
on the S. porch and parapet. It was restored
by Sir Giles Gilbert Scott and later, in 1877–
9, by Arthur Baker, who added the S. aisle.
The glowing pomegranate window is by
William Morris, and Burne-Jones designed
the Pre-Raphaelite figures. The organ is
from Eaton Hall Library; the Stanley tomb
is by Hamo Thornycroft, 1897.

LLANBABO
St Pabo
1m/2km N. of Lly Alaw Reservoir SH 3786
Small 12th-century single-cell church with
notable 14th-century low-relief carving of
St Pabo with crown and sceptre, reset in
N. wall.

LLANEILIAN
St Eilian
2m/3km E. of Amlwch SH 4790
Do not be deterred by the rather horrid
rendering on the 12th-century pyramidal
topped tower. The broad nave and square
chancel were rebuilt in the late 15th-century
with low-pitched roofs and battlemented
parapets. There are splendid fittings, mostly
c. 1500: a sturdy rood screen and loft,
chancel-stalls, and musicians carved on the
corbels of the roof beams. The 14th-century
St Eilian's Chapel, with part of his 15th-
century shrine, is set at 45 degrees to the
chancel and linked to it by a sunny passage.

LLANGADWALADR
St Cadwaladr
2m/3km E. of Aberffraw SH 3869
The church, under the royal patronage of
Cadfan, d. 625, and Cadwaladr, his
grandson, was a meeting-place of the chief-
tains. Cadfan's grave slab is reset in the
present nave, which dates from the 12th
century; the chancel from the 14th. The fine,
though reset, E. window is late 15th-century.
The interior is lit by lovely brass chandeliers.
The N. chapel has a full-blooded Gothic
memorial of 1857; the charming mid-17th-
century S. chapel is separated from the nave
by a daringly flat arch.

LLANGEFNI
St Cyngar
7m/11km W. of Menai Bridge SH 4575
Unusual 1824 church; unfortunate chancel
added in 1898. Aisleless nave, the roof supported by shallow arched beams. W. gallery
and green-grained pews inside.

LLANGEINWEN
St Ceinwen
2m/3km E. of Newborough SH 4465
Medieval with tower and N. chapel of 1839.
Contains 9th- and 11th-century grave slabs

and 13th-century font with fleur de lys and palmette pattern.

LLANGRISTIOLUS
St Cristiolus
1m/2km S. of Llangefui SH 4573
Big, light 13th-century church, heavily restored by Henry Kennedy, 1852. Fine 12th-century chancel arch and font.

LLANGWYLLOG
St Cwyllog
3m/4km N.W. of Llangefui SH 4379
Marshy stream-side setting. Good memorials and 18th-century fittings, including pulpit, 1769, reading desk, communion rails, and pews.

LLANRHWYDRYS
St Rhwydrys
3m/4km W. of Cemaes Bay SH 3293
Remote in fields near sea. Light and primitive. Basically 12th-century, a larger chancel added in the 13th; 15th-century E. window; W. gallery, 1776; N. chapel with free-standing cruck.

LLANTRISANT
St Ieuan, St Afran & St Sannan
2m/3km S.E. of Llanddensant SH 3483
Remote, rural setting near a farm. Late 14th-century with 17th-century S. chapel. Late 17th-century memorial and early 19th-century fittings. Restored in 1972 by the Friends of Friendless Churches.

MENAI BRIDGE
St Tysilio
off the A5 on an island in the Strait, reached by a causeway, 1m/2km W. of Bangor SH 5571
Timeless and secluded atmosphere. Early 15th-century. Medieval roof trusses; touching slate memorials.

NEWBOROUGH
St Peter
9m/15km S.W. of Menai Bridge SH 4265
Fine views. Early 14th-century, extended *c.* 1600, making long, tunnel-like church. Good 12th-century font; 14th-century carved grave slabs in chancel.

PENMON PRIORY
St Seiriol
3m/4km N.E. of Beaumaris SH 6380
The church stands near the top of Anglesey, overlooking the approaches to the Menai Straits. The Prior's House and ruined refectory survive. The church is believed to have been founded in the 6th century. The low tower with its pyramidal roof and the present nave and transepts are 12th-century, dark and deeply impressive. Note the bold carving in the crossing arches, and the much-weathered dragon in the tympanum of the S. door. Arcading survives in the S. transept. The font, once a cross base, and crosses are *c.* 1000. The Priory was given to the Austin Priors in 1414. The 19th-century chancel, rebuilt by Weightman and Hadfield, seems light and papery by contrast.

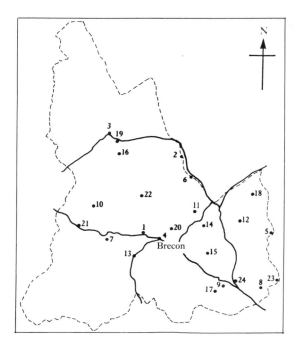

1	Aberyscir	13	Llanfeugan
2	Alltmawr	14	Llanfilo
3	Beaulah	15	Llangasty-Talyllyn
4	Brecon	16	Llangammarch Wells
5	Capel-y-ffin	17	Llangatwg
6	Crickadarn	18	Llanigon
7	Defynnog	19	Llanlleonfel
8	Llanbedr Ystrad Yw	20	Llann-Ddew
9	Llanddetty	21	Llywel
10	Llandeilo'r Fan	22	Merthyr Cynog
11	Llandyfalle	23	Partrishow
12	Llanelieu	24	Tretower

Brecon

ABERYSCIR
St Mary & St Cynidr
3m/4km W. of Brecon SO 0029
Circular churchyard, next to farmyard. Rebuilt by Buckeridge, 1860. Pretty; nave and chancel in one, under steep roof; tall W. bell-turret; Perpendicular N. doorway.

ALLTMAWR
St Mauritius
3m/4km S.E. of Builth Wells SO 0747
Tiny, medieval, with late 19th-century apse; 18th-century wooden windows, pulpit, and some box pews at back. Touching monument by Gillick, 1936.

BEAULAH
Eglwys Oen Duw
4m/6km N.E. of Llanwrtyd Wells SN 9152
By John Norton, 1867. Strikingly elaborate Early English building with tall Germanic fleche. The interior has polychromatic brick tiles and mosaic. Lavish fittings include good Clayton & Bell and Burlison & Grylls glass in the grouped lancets and brass sconces in the form of water lilies, complete with frogs.

BRECON
SO 0428
St Mary, Bulwark
Wide Georgian street. Splendid red sandstone W. tower, 1510–20, otherwise mostly 14th–15th-century, but over-restored by T. H. Wyatt, 1856. Woodwork by W. D. Caroe, 1928.

CAPEL-Y-FFIN
(dedication unknown)
3m/4km W. of Llanthony SO 2531
The funny little church was described by Kilvert as 'the old chapel, short, stout and boxy, with its little bell turret (the whole building reminded one of an owl), the quiet peaceful chapel yard sheltered by seven great solemn yews'. It was built in 1762 and retains its gallery and paper glued onto the E. window imitating stained glass. In the graveyard is a memorial to a carpenter by Eric Gill, 1935.

CRICKADARN
St Mary
6m/10km S.E. of Builth Wells SO 0942
Simple 14th-century church restored in 1910 by Williams-Ellis; good 16th-century tower with beacon turret. Very good Perpendicular porch. Communion table, 1666; 17th-century memorials.

DEFYNNOG
St Cynog
½m/1km S. of Sennybridge SN 9228
Quiet village setting next to line of stone Gothic cottages. Fine tall Perpendicular tower with pillar stone bearing 5th–6th-century Latin inscription. Peculiar early 11th-century font with runic inscription, the only one in Wales. Pre-Norman stoup and delightful oil standard-lamps.

LLANBEDR YSTRAD YW
St Peter
2m/3km N.W. of Crickhowell SO 2420
Double-naved church of red sandstone; restored by J. L. Pearson, 1896–7. Fittings by Pearson simple and appropriate; warm atmosphere; tablets to Brutes, a famous local family of stonemasons.

LLANDDETTY
St Tetta
8m/12km S.E. of Brecon SO 2320
Beautiful site by the Usk. Simple church has Perpendicular S. and priest's doorway. Early English font; 9th-century pillar stone inscribed in Latin.

LLANDEILO'R FAN
St Teilo
4m/6km N.W. of Sennybridge SN 8934
Rebuilt 1873. Fine 16th-century roof and rood screen.

LLANDYFALLE
St Matthew or Maelog
3m/4km W. of Talgarth SO 1135
Isolated from village. Grand Perpendicular. Wagon roofs, simple rood screen of *c.* 1500, and an exotic fretwork Victorian altar in aisle. Two 18th-century monuments by Brute.

LLANELIEU
St Ellyw
2m/3km E. of Talgarth so 1834
Remote setting; 13th-century, in huge churchyard. Small, simple, atmospheric. Sturdy 14th-century rood screen, loft, and tympanum on which painting survives. Two early pillar stones, 7th–9th-century.

LLANFEUGAN
St Meugan
3m/4km S.W. of Brecon so 0824
Setting by stream among huge yews; 13th–15th-century with good tower; 17th-century stalls and remains of medieval rood screen.

LLANFILO
St Bilo or St Milburgh
2m/3km W. of Talgarth so 1233
The partly Norman church has been most fortunate over the last century. In 1851 the excellent tower and shingled spire were added. Then in 1913 restoration was begun by W. D. Caroe, only completed in 1951. The inside is whitewashed; the chancel retains its plaster ceiling of 1709. The splendid rood screen was superbly restored with new figures, by Nathaniel Hitch. Many old pews remain, as does the 18th-century pulpit. Caroe put in some new windows, basing their design on one in the chancel.The atmosphere is unusually light and bright. There are many good monuments, including two early Brutes in black wooden frames.

LLANGASTY-TALYLLYN
St Gastayn
on S. shore of Llangorse Lake so 1326
The S. approach to Llangors Lake runs past the marvellous group of church, mansion and school. The church was almost wholly rebuilt and the school built in 1848–50, to the design of J. L. Pearson. Now most sympathetically restored, the church is notable for its simplicity and characteristic Tractarian adornment, stencilled texts and all.

LLANGAMMARCH WELLS
St Cadmarch
4m/6km E. of Llanwrtyd Wells SN 9347
By W. D. Caroe, 1913–16. Rough masonry with highly finished fittings suggest the Arts and Crafts tone, for which the date is rather late. The tower was added in 1927. Regard

for local character is evident in the plan and Perpendicular details.

LLANGATWG
St Catwg
½m/1km S.W. of Crickhowell so 2118
Much rebuilt in 19th century. Most remarkable for memorial tablets, including probably the finest works of 18th-century Brutes, some still with their original colouring.

LLANIGON
St Eigen
2m/3km S.W. of Hay-on-Wye so 2140
Wide-eaved roof and a remarkable 14th-century S. porch, huge and barn-like; 17th-century upper part houses bells. Plaster nave ceiling; 18th-century pews with doors; pretty Gothic barrel organ.

LLANLLEONFEL
(dedication unknown)
1m/2km W. of Garth SN 9349
Ancient hill-top site; nicely rebuilt by Withers, 1874. Sloping floor; four identical 18th-century tablets and a pillar stone.

LLANN-DDEW
Holy Trinity or St David
1m/2km N.E. of Brecon so 0531
Site of a clas church. Giraldus Cambrensis lived in nearby bishop's palace in 12th century. Cruciform church with remarkably uniform Early English exterior. Central tower rebuilt in 1620, and has pyramidal roof of 1780. Interior disappointing – scraped.

LLYWEL
St David
1m/2km N.W. of Trecastle SN 8730
Good Perpendicular; excellently restored in 1869 by Sir Giles Gilbert Scott. Cast of tall stone, *c.* 500, with odd, crude figures, interlace and inscriptions in Latin and Ogam, now in British Museum. 1925 chancel screen by Harry Hems.

MERTHYR CYNOG
St Cynog
7m/11km N.W. of Brecon SN 9837
Fine views. Large church, well restored in 1861 by Charles Buckeridge; huge Norman tower. Tough 14th-century screen.

PARTRISHOW
St Ishow or Issui
5m/8km N. of Abergavenny so 2722
Up a remote valley, it is a building of excep-

tional appeal. Approached through Caroe's excellent stone lych gate, the church, with its famous rood screen of *c.* 1500, was well restored by him in 1908. The two stone altars in front of the screen are a remarkable survival. On the W. wall is painted a memento mori, a comic skeleton with a spade. The monuments include several by the Brutes, distinguished by elegant lettering and charmingly unsophisticated decoration. The huge font is pre-Conquest.

TRETOWER
St John the Evangelist
3m/4km N.W. of Crickhowell so 1821
By J. L. Pearson, 1876–7. Simple, elegant pink and grey stone; he also designed the church hall with its nice projecting bow.

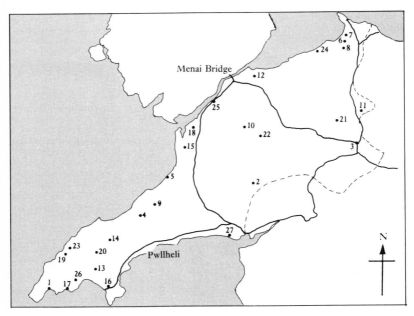

1	Aberdaron	10	Llanberis	19	Llangwnnadl
2	Beddgelert	11	Llanddoget	20	Llaniestyn
3	Betws-y-Coed	12	Llandegai	21	Llanrhychwyn
4	Carnguwch	13	Llandegwning	22	Nantperis
5	Clynnog Fawr	14	Llandudwen	23	Penllech
6	Conwy	15	Llandwrog	24	Penmaenmawr
7	Deganwy	16	Llanengan	25	Port Dinorwic
8	Gyffin	17	Llanfaelrhys	26	Rhiw
9	Llanaelhaearn	18	Llanfaglan	27	Ynscynhaearn

Caernarvon

ABERDARON
St Hywyn
on tip of Lleyn Peninsula SH 1726
Important clas church built at a point of embarkation for pilgrims to Bardsey Island; 12th-, 14th- and 16th-century church with twin gables and late-Norman doorway. Inside, two simple spaces linked by airy five-bay arcade. Abandoned, 1841; restored by Henry Kennedy, 1860.

BEDDGELERT
St Mary
4m/7km S. of Snowdon SH 5948
Augustinian priory church. Some fine medieval features; three lancets in E. wall and richly moulded two-bay arcades on N., all c. 1230.

BETWS-Y-COED
St Mary the Virgin
14m/22km S. of Colwyn Bay SH 7956
By Paley & Austin, 1873. Early English style; grey and red stone; central tower with stair turret. Vaulted chancel and tower; original corbels to chancel arch.

CARNGUWCH
St James
5m/8km N. of Pwllheli SH 3742
Lonely setting. Rebuilt 1828 with massive bellcote and square-headed windows. Two-decker pulpit; interesting pews.

CLYNNOG FAWR
St Beuno
9m/15km S.W. of Caernarvon SH 4149
This is a fine church whose riches derived from its importance as a shrine on the pilgrim road to Bardsey Island. The Perpendicular rebuilding of cruciform plan began with the transepts and chancel, 1480, and continued into the early 16th century. The passage to St Beuno's Chapel is early 17th-century. Outside, apart from the sturdy W. tower, all is glassy, pinnacled and battlemented. It is a generous, spreading building; even the vestry has three storeys, and the porch two. The nave, over 30 feet wide, has a handsome oak roof, carved and panelled. The chancel,

cut off by a well-restored screen, has Tudor stalls with misericords, a double-headed eagle bench-end of c. 1500, and very attractive sedilia of c. 1480. On a wall memorial of 1609, 10 daughters and two sons kneel beside the deceased. St Beuno's stone is in the chapel.

CONWY
St Mary
SH 7779
Though right in the middle of town, it is nicely withdrawn. Originally the abbey church, its oldest parts are the E. and W. walls; the three lancets in the tower lit the nave. The fine moulded doorway below, of c. 1235, probably came from the chapter-house. The rest of the church is of various dates; it was restored in 1872 by Sir George Gilbert Scott. It contains a magnificent rood screen of c. 1500; the loft is supported by fan vaulting on either side. The contemporary stalls have carved ends. There are numerous monuments and a bust of John Gibson, sculptor, by Wm. Theed.

DEGANWY
All Saints
2m/3km S. of Llandudno SH 7779
Admirably set against the hillside. By John Douglas, 1898–9. Long, low church with W. tower and broad spire.

GYFFIN
St Benedict
suburb S. side of Conwy SH 7776
Pleasant valley setting. Restored by Kennedy, 1858; 15th-century painted chancel roof and canopy of honour over altar. Two parclose screens, 16th–17th-century.

LLANAELHAEARN
St Aelhaearn
6m/10km N. of Pwllheli SH 3844
12th-century with 16th- and 17th-century transepts and 1892 chancel; 16th-century screen. Attractive and unusual panelled and spindle-backed balustered box pews.

LLANBERIS
St Padarn
6m/10km E. of Caernarvon SH 5760
By Arthur Baker, 1885; Early English style; completed by Harold Hughes, 1914–15. Impressive cruciform church with central tower supported on 'double arches' of pink and grey stone.

LLANDDOGET
St Doged
1m/2km N. of Llanrwst SH 8063
Rebuilt in 1839, by the rector. The result is a delightful double-naved building, in a sort of cottage-orne style; bargeboards, lattice windows, and all. Inside, the original arrangement of tall pews facing the three-decker pulpit on the N. wall. Behind the pulpit is a plaster putto's head, flanked by oil paintings of Moses with the Commandments, and the Royal Arms. The pulpit is lit by a round skylight with coloured glass.

LLANDEGAI
St Tegai
1m/2km S.E. of Bangor SH 5970
Mostly 16th-century cruciform church with central tower; rebuilt and lengthened 1852–3 by H. Kennedy. Richly Norman organ case from Penrhyn Castle and three fine monuments, one by R. Westmacott, 1820.

LLANDEGWNING
St Iestyn
3m/4km N.W. of Abersoch SH 2630
This most engaging toy church by John Welch, 1840, has a comic W. tower, slate sundial, and spire. Inside all is painted white except the green-grained box pews. There is a Gothic communion rail and a fine tablet of 1721.

LLANDUDWEN
St Tudwen
4m/6km S. of Nefyn SH 2736
Unusual little church with an enticing approach: a straight path leads down through a massive lych gate to the door in the W. gable, which is capped by a bellcote with jaunty bell, all slightly off-centre. The nave plan is a T, now with no chancel. The nave is thought to be a rebuilding on medieval foundations of 1595; the N. and S. transepts are 17th-century additions. In the nave, there are 18th-century benches with backs, and the oil lamps have been converted to gas.

LLANDWROG
St Twrog
5m/8km S.W. of Caernarvon SH 4556
In Lord Newborough's estate village. By Henry Kennedy, 1860; Gothic Revival. Cruciform with spire; spacious, English in character, and surprising inside. Stone gallery across W. end, the stalls facing inward; 18th-century Wynne monuments in S.E. chapel, one by Cheere, 1749.

LLANENGAN
St Einion
1m/2km S.W. of Abersoch SH 2927
The earlier church was rebuilt and enlarged with a new S. aisle in 1520–30, and the tower was added in 1534. The Victorians passed it by. It has a graceful nave arcade and fine screens, to the S. aisle which retains its loft. The roofs are contemporary and have sturdy open trusses. The 15th- or early 16th-century font is octagonal, decorated with quatrefoils and rosettes.

LLANFAELRHYS
(dedication unknown)
10m/16km S.W. of Pwllheli SH 2127
Lovely setting close to the sea. Long, narrow medieval church made even longer by later chancel. Box pews.

LLANFAGLAN
St Baglan
2m/3km S.W. of Caernarvon SH 4760
Small medieval church, the chancel added *c.* 1800. Unrestored interior retains 18th-century furnishings, including benches, box pews, pulpit with sounding board, and reading desk.

LLANGWNNADL
St Gwynhoedl
3m/4km S.W. of Tudweiliog SH 2033
This is a lovely 16th-century church with three broad aisles separated by light three-bay arcades; it is actually wider than it is long. The N. aisle was added in 1520, that to the S. 10 years later. The windows in the N. wall date from H. Kennedy's sensitive restoration of 1850. The inscriptions on the arcade pier record the erection of this aisle over the burial-place of the patron saint. The E. windows are all contemporary. The octagonal font, with its unusual carvings, probably dates from the 1520 restoration.

LLANIESTYN
St Iestyn
4m/6km N.W. of Abersoch SH 2633
Primitive, mostly 14th-century church with
15th-century S. chapel containing a most
impressive 14th-century low-relief carving
of the saint.

LLANRHYCHWYN
St Rhychwyn
1m/2km S.W. of Trefriw, and 3m/4km E. of
Llanwrst SH 7862
Originally Norman, now mostly 15th–16th-
century. Double-naved, solid and simple;
17th-century S. door, communion rails,
pulpit, and candelabrum. Some old glass.
Stone lych gate, 1762.

NANTPERIS
St Peris
2m/3km S.E. of Llanberis SH 6058
Magnificent mountain setting in Llanberis
pass. Rustic cruciform building has medieval
nave, 16th-century N. and S. transepts, and
17th-century chancel with contemporary N.
and S. chapels. Restored in 1848 by Henry
Kennedy; 17th-century fittings and rood
screen removed to W. end.

PENLLECH
St Mary
2m/3km S.W. of Tudweiliog SH 2234
Set above the farmyard duck-pond.
Movingly simple; no architectural preten-
sions. Complete early 19th-century furnishings.

PENMAENMAWR
St Seiriol
4m/6km W. of Conwy SH 7176
By Alfred Waterhouse, 1868; tough and uncompromising with saddleback tower. Red
and yellow brick interior and rood screen by
Caroe, 1930.

PORT DINORWIC
(dedication unknown)
4m/6km S.W. of Bangor SH 5267
Distinguished from the houses, also built by
the Vaynol estate, only by the bellcote. It is
two-thirds of a semi-rustic villa, entered via
a verandah. High, squarish room, widening
for chancel; intended for estate workers
brought from England.

RHIW
St Aelrhiw
4m/6km E. of Aberdaron SH 2227
18th-century. Unusual plan of square transepts, short nave, and almost no chancel, the
congregation thus pressed against the altar.

YNSCYNHAEARN
St Cynhaearn
2m/3km E. of Criccieth SH 5339
On edge of marsh. Built in 1830 with almost
intact fittings, including three-decker pulpit,
box pews, and benches painted with family
and house names. Harpist David Owen,
'David of the White Rock', d. 1741, is
buried here.

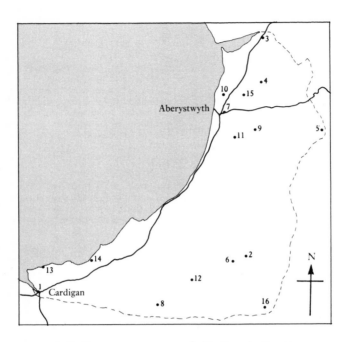

1	Cardigan	9	Llanfihangel-y-Creuddyn
2	Cellan	10	Llangorwen
3	Eglwys Fach	11	Llanilar
4	Elerch	12	Llanwenog
5	Hafod	13	Mwnt
6	Lampeter	14	Penbryn
7	Llanbadarn Fawr	15	Penrhyncoch
8	Llandyssul	16	Tallyllychau

Cardigan

CARDIGAN
SN 1846
St Mary

The church stands on the river bank. The 14th-century chancel was later embattled and pinnacled. Tower and nave were rebuilt *c.* 1705, the S. porch with an ogee-arched doorway. Inside, it is grandly spacious and uncluttered; sensitive restorers included R. J. Withers and W. D. Caroe. Perpendicular E. window has remnants of its medieval glass. Some fine Tudor carving survives: the octagonal font, two stone corbels with grimacing faces, and an ornate piscina in the chancel.

CELLAN
All Saints
2m/3km E. of Lampeter SN 6149

Rebuilt by Herbert North of Llanfairfechan in 1908. Carefully simple, except for the exotic nave barrel vault with its surreal oversized floral paintings and yet richer design in the chancel. Painted by Mrs Ida North.

EGLWYS FACH
St Michael
5m/8km S.W. of Machynlleth SN 6895

In a pretty churchyard. Simple church of 1833 built of local grey stone with many original fittings. The E. end is an addition of 1913.

ELERCH
St Peter
3m/4km S.E. of Talybont SN 6886

By William Butterfield, 1865–8. Small cruciform church, tough and ingeniously articulated, with a pyramidal tower over the choir. Austere interior has excellent E. window by A. Gibbs and tiled reredos.

HAFOD
St Michael
in the Ystwyth Valley, 4m/6km S.E. of Devil's Bridge SN 785 742

Early Gothic Revival, 1803, by James Wyatt; decorated by Fuseli. All but the walls were destroyed by fire in 1932, after which it was rebuilt and furnished by W. D. Caroe. The fire-shattered remains of Chantrey's famous monument to Marianne Johnes are in the N. transept.

LAMPETER
St Peter
20m/32km N.E. of Carmarthen SN 5748

By R. J. Withers, 1867–8. Early French Gothic church with commanding tower. Striking W. window by Wilhelmina Geddes, 1938.

LLANBADARN FAWR
St Padarn
E, suburb of Aberystwyth SN 6080

The size and grandeur of the church, set in a large churchyard on the side of the valley, recall the fame of the clas founded here by St Padarn in the 6th century. The present church, apart from the Perpendicular chancel, was built *c.* 1200. Big, solid and severe, it is cruciform, with a low tower and spire at the crossing. The thick walls are pierced with lancets, except at the E. end, where three large windows were inserted in the 15th century. J. P. Seddon restored it from 1868, leaving the severity of the structure unimpaired, but adding the handsome boarded chancel roof and good fittings, which include a tiled floor and marble reredos. The modern glass is by John Pests. The chancel contains several good monuments, including one of 1813 by John Flaxman.

LLANDYSSUL
St Tysul
12m/19km N. of Carmarthen SN 4140

Ancient foundation. Church mostly 13th-century, including the handsome tower, still being improved in late 15th century. Nave with side aisles and chancel. Grand, ancient altar stone, incised with cross patterns, found locally, now in Lady Chapel, as is the Crucifixion, which includes the Virgin Mary and St John, once on W. face of tower.

LLANFIHANGEL-Y-CREUDDYN
St Michael
5m/8km W. of Devil's Bridge SN 6676

13th-century with very grand central tower.

Well restored by Withers, 1871. Plain white-washed interior with 16th-century wagon roofs. Carved oak reredos by Jules Bernaerts, 1919.

LLANGORWEN
All Saints
2m/3km N.E. of Aberystwyth SN 6083
By H. J. Underwood of Oxford, 1841. Unexpected Tractarian church has wooden eagle lectern given by Keble and remarkable bronze chandeliers, reputedly given by Newman. Porch and bell-turret added in 1849 by Butterfield.

LLANILAR
St Hilary
5m/8km S.E. of Aberystwyth SN 6275
Medieval church with squat 14th-century tower and short spire; restored in 1874 by R. K. Penson. Good 14th-century arch-braced roof and font; pre-Norman pillar stone in the porch.

LLANWENOG
St Gwenog
6m/10km W. of Lampeter SN 4945
Unusual, basically 13th-century church with big, battered Perpendicular tower. An exciting building entered through a small door under the tower, down a broad flight of steps, and into the pleasantly proportioned nave, barrel-ceiled in the 18th century. In the small S. chapel stands a huge, vigorously carved late-Norman font. A local family transformed the church during World War I, adding carved benches, chancel screen, and glass. Interesting memorials include that to Anne Evans, d. 1807, who provided poor relief by 'giving employment in the cultivation of an extensive tract of land'.

MWNT
Holy Cross
4m/6km N. of Cardigan SN 1952
Sheltered under headland, close to the sea. Limewashed, humble and tough with square-headed windows and low pointed doorway. Collar-brace roof; steps led to rood of which remnants survive.

PENBRYN
St Michael
2m/3km E. of Aberporth SN 2952
Well-restored medieval church with bellcote and 17th-century W. porch. Slate slab floor to nave, 19th-century pews, and sturdy timber roof.

PENRHYNCOCH
St John the Divine
4m/6km N.E. of Aberystwyth SN 6484
By R. J. Withers, 1880. Small church in Early English style with square timber belfry. Good fittings include a brightly coloured eagle and dragon pottery lectern.

TALLYLLYCHAU
St Michael and All Angels
6m/10km N. of Llandeilo SN 6332
Church of 1773 with unusual plan of two doors in plain W. end; no central aisle. Boarded barrel ceiling, simple box pews, and flagged floor.

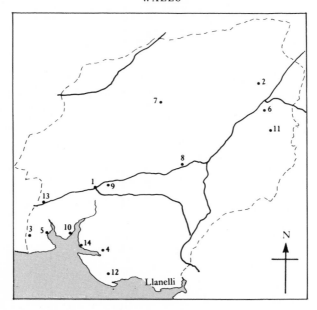

1 Carmarthen	8 Llangathen
2 Cilycwm	9 Llangunnor
3 Eglwys Gymyn	10 Llanstephan
4 Kidwelly	11 Myddfai
5 Laugharne	12 Pembrey
6 Llandovery	13 St Clear's
7 Llanfihangel Rhos y Corn	14 St Ishmael

Carmarthen

CARMARTHEN
SN 4120
St Peter
Double-naved church, 12th–14th-century, with tall W. tower. Over-restored by Victorians. Interesting tombs and memorials include those of Sir Rhys ap Thomas, d. 1525, and Sir Richard Steele, d. 1729. Organ built for, but disliked by, George III.

CILYCWM
St Michael
4m/6km N. of Llandovery SN 7540
Medieval church with 15th–17th-century roofs. Remarkable 18th-century wall-paintings of a skeleton and Royal Arms. Sympathetically restored by W. D. Caroe, 1906.

EGLWYS GYMYN
St Margaret Marlos
2m/3km N. of Pendine SN 2310
Humble vaulted church has massive wall with simple round-headed arch separating nave and chancel. Restored by Philip Webb and William Weir, 1901–2. Fresco work of three periods and benefaction boards.

KIDWELLY
St Mary
7m/11km N.W. of Llanelli SN 4006
The church, topped by its steeple, was a Benedictine priory. The present building has a broad aisleless nave with a barrel roof, short transepts, and a big chancel. It is light and spacious and dates from the early 14th century, restored by G. G. Scott Jnr in 1884. The 14th-century alabaster figure of the Virgin above the altar is the church's chief treasure. Organ by Thomas Warne, 1762.

LAUGHARNE
St Martin
4m/6km S. of St Clears SN 3010
Mainly 15th-century cruciform church severely restored by R. K. Penson, who scraped the walls. Thick in tablets and dark Victorian glass. Town is Llaregyb in Dylan Thomas's 'Under Milk Wood'; his grave is across the bridge.

LLANDOVERY (Llanfair-ar-y-bryn)
St Mary
17m/27km W. of Brecon SN 7634
Built on the site of a Roman fort, it is like a great tithe barn with a sturdy 13th-century tower. Parapets and gargoyles were added *c.* 1500 but, despite this and its size, the whole gives a sense of humility. Rough plastered walls, nave partly open and partly barrel-ceiled, and clear W. window letting in a flood of light. Restored by W. D. Caroe, 1913. The E. window is by Kempe, and others by John Peters. The great Welsh hymn writer, William Williams of Pant-y-celyn, d. 1791, is buried here.

LLANFIHANGEL RHOS Y CORN
St Michael
4m/6km N.E. of Brechfa SN 5535
Twin naves of *c.* 1500 added to 13th-century church. Pink-washed interior has slab floor and a pulpit with sunflowers in Gothic panels.

LLANGATHEN
St Cathen
3m/4km W. of Llandeilo SN 5822
Medieval church with S. aisle of *c.* 1500. Tudor communion table and grand Rudd tomb of 1616 with big pedimented canopy and moving figures.

LLANGUNNOR
St Ceinwr
1m/2km E. of Carmarthen SN 4220
Hill-top setting. Nave and S. aisle linked by four Tuscan pillars. Fine late 18th-century commandment and memorial boards. Slate memorial to Sir Richard Steele, d. 1729, whose wife came from here.

LLANSTEPHAN
St Ystyffan
10m/14km S.W. of Carmarthen SO 1142
Village church on Twyi estuary. Sturdy cruciform church with embattled 13th-century tower. Good monuments include that to the

Rev. Wm. Lloyd, d. 1706, 'In doeing good who was imploy'd'.

MYDDFAI
St Michael
3m/4km S. of Llandovery SN 7730
13th-century barrel-vaulted nave and chancel with S. aisle of *c.* 1500; pointed arcades on octagonal columns. Bold 18th-century lettering to prayer of consecration; richly painted hatchment; 18th-century memorial in porch.

PEMBREY
St Illtud
adjoins Burry Port to W. SN 4201
Late 13th-century church enlarged with 14th-century tower, aisle, and N. chapel; 16th-century nave and chancel roofs and unusual Tudor window in S. of nave.

ST CLEAR'S
St Mary
9m/15km W. of Carmarthen SN 2716
Embattled 13th-century W. tower, nave and chancel. Norman font and chancel arch with robustly carved capitals.

ST ISHMAEL
St Ishmael
3m/4km W. of Kudwelly SN 3608
Fine site overlooking estuaries. Tough and primitive exterior; late 13th-century with added N. aisle; door under low saddleback tower with 1725 sundial. Interior thoroughly Victorianized by R. K. Penson, 1860. Fine 17th-century memorial; glass by Kempe & Tower.

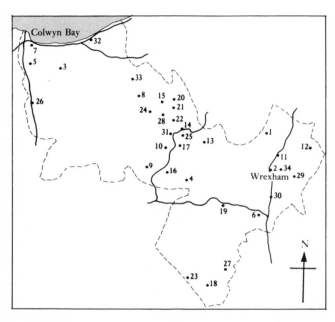

1	Berse Drelincourt	18	Llangedwyn
2	Bersham	19	Llangollen
3	Betws-yn-Rhos	20	Llangwyfan
4	Bryneglwys	21	Llangynhafal
5	Bryn-y-Maen	22	Llanhychan
6	Chirk	23	Llanrhaeadr-ym-Mochnant
7	Colwyn Bay	24	Llanrhaeadr-yng-Nghinmeirch
8	Denbigh	25	Llanrhudd
9	Derwen	26	Llanrwst
10	Efenechdyd	27	Llansilin
11	Gresford	28	Llanynys
12	Holt	20	Marchwiel
13	Llanarmon-yn-Ial	30	Ruabon
14	Llanbedr Dyffryn Clwyd	31	Ruthin
15	Llandyrnog	32	Towyn
16	Llanelidan	33	Trefnant
17	Llanfair Dyffryn Clwyd	34	Wrexham

Denbigh

BERSE DRELINCOURT
(dedication unknown)
1m/2km N.W. of Wrexham SJ 3350
Built and endowed in 1742 by Mary Drelincourt, widow of Dean of Armagh, whose monument is within. Known as 'Madam's Chapel', once linked by avenues to her delightful house which contained school.

BERSHAM
St Mary
2m/3km W. of Wrexham SJ 3049
By John Gibson, 1873; tower added in 1890–2. Expensive Romanesque cruciform church with apse and vaults of banded red and white stone.

BETWS-YN-RHOS
St Michael
4m/6km S.W. of Abergele SH 9073
By John Welch, 1838–9. Small and unusual church with extraordinary twin bell-turrets capped by miniature spires.

BRYNEGLWYS
St Tysilio
5m/8km N.E. of Corwen SJ 1447
Small church, well restored in 1876 by Arthur Baker, with characteristic woodwork. Late 16th-century Yale chapel with family tablets.

BRYN-Y-MAEN
Christ Church
2m/3km S. of Colwyn Bay SH 8376
High on hills above Colwyn Bay. By John Douglas, 1897–9; one of his best churches. Late Perpendicular style with rich woodwork and original furnishings.

CHIRK
St Mary
5m/8km N. of Oswestry SJ 2937
Originally 12th-century; N. aisle and tower 15th-century; 17th- and 18th-century monuments by Robert Wynne and an inscription by William Stanton.

COLWYN BAY
St Paul
10m/16km W. of Rhyl SH 8479
By John Douglas, 1886–1911. Church in the Decorated style with broad nave and chancel and lofty N.W. tower. Good fittings with reredos by Caroe.

DENBIGH
SJ 0566
St Marcella, Whitchurch
Denbigh's parish church, though over a mile away. Fine double-aisled remodelling of earlier buildiing, restored in 1908 by C. Hodgson Fowler. Excellent Renaissance alabaster table-tomb with coloured recumbent effigies of Sir John Salisbury, d. 1578, and his wife, with exquisite little weepers on the base; 17th-century communion table with contemporary rails on three sides, pulpit, and tester. Good 18th-century memorials, including work by Sir Richard Westmacott and Edward Stanton.

DERWEN
St Mary
5m/8km N. of Corwen SJ 0750
Single-cell red sandstone church has almost perfect 15th-century rood screen and loft. Stone churchyard cross with Crucifixion and other figures.

EFENECHDYD
St Michael
2m/3km S. of Ruthin SH 1155
Tiny single-cell church well restored in 1873 by Arthur Baker. Medieval oak font, base of rood screen, and 1723 brass.

GRESFORD
All Saints
3m/4km N. of Wrexham SJ 3454
Splendid church well set in an iron-railed churchyard full of big yews and good tombs. It was almost entirely rebuilt in the late 15th century and sympathetically restored by G. E. Street in 1865–7. The pinnacled tower contains eight bells, two cast in 1623. Light and spacious interior contains exceptional glass of c. 1500, including the E.

window. Oak misericords and Perpendicular font. The pulpit is by Street, and there are fine medieval and later monuments, including work by Chantrey, Westmacott and Theed. Gleaming 18th-century chandeliers.

HOLT
St Chad
5m/8km E. of Wrexham SJ 4154
Basically 13th-century, but deriving much of its present character from the rebuilding of 1500, when the aisles were added. It has a most satisfying symmetry, reinforced by the flight of steps under the W. tower. Octagonal font has elaborate 17th-century brass decoration with acrostic inscription engraved by Silvanus Crue.

LLANARMON-YN-IAL
St Garmon
4m/6km E. of Ruthin SJ 1956
Fine hill setting. Rebuilt 1736, restored in 1870 by John Douglas. Twin naves separated by timber Classical columns; rare Reformation brass chandelier; 18th-century font; Douglas pulpit; monuments.

LLANBEDR DYFFRYN CLWYD
St Peter
1m/2km N.E. of Ruthin SJ 1459
One of Poundley and Walker's best churches, 1863. Vigorously patterned walls and roof; robust carving includes gargoyles round apse. Good glass and portrait tablet by Gibson.

LLANDYRNOG
St Teyrnog
4m/6km E. of Denbigh SJ 1064
Perpendicular twin-aisled church, heavily restored by W. E. Nesfield in 1878. Pretty bellcote and porch and good ironwork on doors. Rich woodwork includes stalls of 1877. Remains of Seven Sacraments stained glass in E. window of c. 1500, restored by Kempe.

LLANELIDAN
St Elidan
5m/8km S. of Ruthin SJ 1050
Remote situation. Well-restored double-naved church with good carved woodwork and excellent 17th–18th-century monuments.

LLANFAIR DYFFRYN CLWYD
2m/3km S. of Ruthin SJ 1355
St Cynfarch & St Mary
Double-naved church with stout tower. Well restored in 1872 by J. D. Sedding; good simple wood and ironwork. Stained glass by Christopher Whall, 1893. Wooden lych gate, 1708.
Jesus Chapel
Founded and endowed by Rice Williams, verger of Westminster Abbey. Consecrated in 1623 and rebuilt in 1787. Charming but over-restored interior with original altar table and pulpit.

LLANGEDWYN
St Cedwyn
3m/4km S. of Llansilin SJ 1824
Rebuilt 1869–70 by Benjamin Ferrey; neo-Norman N. porch with elaborate terracotta decoration by H. L. North, c. 1840. Remarkable altar rails of wood, copper and enamel, probably by John Bonnor, d. 1916; 14th-century priest's effigy in chancel; good 18th-century monuments. Stone cross and two 20th-century churchyard monuments.

LLANGOLLEN
St Collen
9m/15km S.W. of Wrexham
Double naved church remodelled and enlarged by S. Pountney Smith, 1864–7. Carved hammer-beam angel roofs of great beauty.

LLANGWYFAN
St Cwyfan
5m/8km N. of Ruthin SJ 1266
Perched above Vale of Clwyd. Medieval church with 18th-century interior retaining box pews. E. window by A. Gibbs, 1853.

LLANGYNHAFAL
St Cynhafal
3m/4km N. of Ruthin SJ 1263
Perpendicular church restored by Arthur Baker, 1884. Double-naved with good old roofs; gilded Pelican in Her Piety of c. 1690 over altar; 18th-century brass; topiary cock in churchyard.

LLANHYCHAN
St Hychan
1m/2km N.W. of Llanbedr Dyffryn Clwyd SJ 1459
Small church sensitively restored by Arthur Baker, 1878. Lectern with medieval carv-

ings; organ with 1920s folk art carvings.

LLANRHAEADR-YM-MOCHNANT
St Dogfan
4m/6km N. of Llanfyllin SJ 1226
Set in churchyard sloping down to river. Odd plan of W. tower, long, narrow nave, and aisles only along E. part of nave. Mostly renewed by Spaull, 1882. Plaster barrel vault and good medieval sanctuary roof. Fragment of Celtic wheel cross in S. aisle; 9th- or 10th-century grave cross; fragment of Romanesque shrine.

LLANRHAEADR-YNG-NGHINMEIRCH
St Dyfnog
2m/3km N. of Ruthin SJ 1258
Setting among trees. Well restored by Baker, 1879–80. Large, double-naved church with fine timber porch. Some of the best stained glass in Wales, including a fine Jesse window, 1533. Splendid carved roofs; large marble monument, 1702.

LLANRHUDD
St Meugan
1½m/2½km N.E. of Llanfair SJ 1355
Small, restored 15th-century single-cell building, formerly the mother church of Ruthin; 15th-century rood screen; 17th-century W. gallery and pulpit; 16th–17th-century Thelwall family monuments and one by Sir Richard Westmacott, 1818.

LLANRWST
St Grwst
11m/18km S. of Colwyn Bay SH 7961
Largely rebuilt 1882–4 by Paley & Austin. Magnificent rood screen and loft. Gwydir Chapel of 1633–4 attached to chancel; contemporary woodwork. Huge stone coffin, stone effigy of knight, and remarkable 17th-century brasses.

LLANSILIN
St Silin
6m/10km E. of Llanrhaeadr-ym-Mochnant SJ 2028
The exterior, with its pinnacled tower of 1832, gives little promise of the riches within. The twin naves are divided by a Perpendicular arcade, the responds and one capital carved with foliage. The magnificent Perpendicular roofs, including the elaborately carved chancel roof, were uncovered at the time of the restoration by Arthur Baker in 1890. Fine red and yellow tiles, by J. C. Edwards of Ruabon; 18th-century pulpit and panelling. W. gallery and above it the Commandments; 17th–18th-century monuments.

LLANYNYS
St Saeran
3m/4km N. of Ruthin SJ 1062
On the site of a 6th-century monastery, a big double-naved building, the naves separated by 18th-century fluted wooden columns. It has richly carved roof supports and a 1637 altar supported by lions. A splendid great wall-painting of St Christopher faces the door. Remarkable hexagonal sepulchral cross, probably 14th-century. On one side is a figure of a bishop, and on the other a Crucifixion. Wooden dog-tongs in working order; 15th-century S. door.

MARCHWIEL
St Marcellus
2m/3km S.E. of Wrexham SJ 3547
Rebuilt 1778; tower by James Wyatt, 1789; transept added 1829; 1788 armorial window and memorials to the Yorkes of Erddig.

RUABON
St Mary
5m/8km S.W. of Wrexham SJ 3043
Unkindly restored by E. B. Ferrey, 1870. Elegant Robert Adam font, 1772; 16th–18th-century monuments by Rysbrack, Nollekens, and others.

RUTHIN
St Peter
14m/22km W. of Wrexham SJ 1258
Restored by R. K. Penson, 1856, who added the spire. Two naves with magnificent carved roofs and bosses. Fine wrought-iron churchyard gates, 1727.

TOWYN
St Mary
2m/3km N.E. of Abergele SH 9779
Group of church, vicarage and school by Street, 1872–3. Saddleback crossing tower and excellent original fittings.

TREFNANT
Holy Trinity
3m/4km S. of St Asaph SJ 0570
Sir George Gilbert Scott's church of

1853–5, in refined Decorated style, forms a group with his parsonage and school. Rich interior with columns of Anglesey marble. As for the capitals, 'every group of leaves was carved . . . from natural specimens gathered from the woods and hedges around.' The E. windows are by Wailes.

WREXHAM
St Giles

SJ 3350

This splendid church stands withdrawn behind fine iron gates of *c.* 1720 by Davies, in an atmospheric churchyard, with narrow passages leading off it. The noble, early 16th-century tower combines strength and dignity of outline with great richness of detail; the rest of the church is its equal in splendour if not in refinement. Particularly unusual is the canted apsidal chancel, re-fitted in 1914 by Sir T. G. Jackson. There is a large, striking monument in the N. aisle by Roubiliac. A famous benefactor was Elihu Yale, d. 1721, who is buried in the church-yard. In the 1920s a reproduction of Wrexham tower was built on the campus of Yale University.

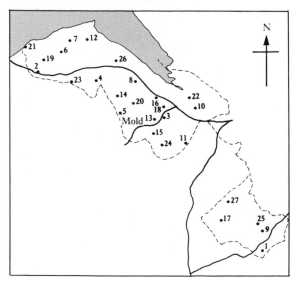

1 Bettisfield	15 Nercwys
2 Bodelwyddan	16 Northop
3 Buckley	17 Overton
4 Caerwys	18 Pentrobin
5 Cilcain	19 Rhuddlan
6 Diserth	20 Rhydmwyn
7 Gwaenysgor	21 Rhyl
8 Halkyn	22 Shotton
9 Hanmer	23 Tremeirchion
10 Hawarden	24 Treuddyn
11 Hope	25 Whitewell
12 Llanasa	26 Whitford
13 Mold	27 Worthenbury
14 Nannerch	

Flint

BETTISFIELD
St John the Baptist
4m/6km E. of Ellesmere SJ 4535
By G. E. Street, 1872–4. Fine Early Decorated church with elegant octagonal spire. Well detailed interior has dado on E. wall of superb Minton tiles.

BODELWYDDAN
St Margaret
2m/3km W. of St Asaph SJ 0075
Lavish and ornate church by John Gibson, 1856–60; tall W. spire. Shining white exterior of local limestone. Plenty of marble in the expensive and richly carved interior. Glass by O'Connor.

BUCKLEY
St Matthew
9m/15km N. of Wrexham SJ 2864
By John Oates, 1821–2; altered later and completely remodelled 1897–1904 by Douglas and Minshall. Tower clock by Lord Grimthorpe. Spacious interior, astonishing but not really successful, has elaborate painted decoration and glass by Holiday.

CAERWYS
St Michael
4m/6km S.W. of Holywell SJ 1272
Sturdy double-naved village church; 15th-century glass in chancel. Low chancel screen of carved woodwork taken from the roof.

CILCAIN
St Mary
4m/6km W. of Mold SJ 1765
Double-naved church much rebuilt in 1746 and 1888–9, when John Douglas added huge buttresses, a new top to the tower, S. windows and porch. Magnificent medieval angel roof, well restored; good 16th-century glass; fine 18th-century marble tablets.

DISERTH
St Ffraid
3m/4km S. of Prestatyn SJ 0579
Restored 1873–5 by Sir Giles Gilbert Scott, who added the N. chancel aisle, N. transept, and S. porch. E. window has medieval

stained glass with 12 Apostles, each with his name and a sentence from the Creed; 12th–13th-century churchyard cross, now inside.

GWAENYSGOR
St Mary
1m/2km S. of Prestatyn SJ 0781
Remote-seeming country site, high above nearby coastal resorts. Small, primitive single-cell church has deep S. porch with strange, massive timber arch, boldly carved. Carved cross slabs inside.

HALKYN
St Mary the Virgin
3m/4km S.E. of Holywell SJ 2171
Fine Victorian church, built by John Douglas in 1878 at the Duke of Westminster's expense. There is some unusual monochrome glass by Heaton, Butler & Bayne, and Douglas's characteristic furnishings.

HANMER
St Chad
5m/8km W. of Whitchurch SJ 4539
Grand Perpendicular with strong tower looking down to mere. Gutted by fire in 1889; skilfully rebuilt by Bodley and Garner, whose work includes elegant S. porch and fittings; 1790 chancel restored by Caroe, 1936.

HAWARDEN
St Deiniol
6m/10km W. of Chester SJ 3165
The church was restored in 1855–6 by James Harrison, burnt out in 1857, rebuilt by Sir Giles Gilbert Scott, and has additions by John Douglas. The Gladstone monument in the chapel is by Sir William Richmond. There is some good glass by Wailes and Burne-Jones; rood by Sir Giles Gilbert Scott.

HOPE
St Cyngar
5m/8km N. of Wrexham SJ 3058
Mostly Perpendicular double-naved church with big tower and some 15th-century glass.

LLANASA
St Asaph & St Kentigern
3m/4km E. of Prestatyn SJ 1081
Double-aisled 16th-century church restored by G. E. Street, 1877. E. windows contain reconstructed early 16th-century stained glass Crucifixion and saints.

MOLD
St Mary
11m/17km N.W. of Wrexham SJ 2364
Splendid church dominating main street and much of the Alun Valley. Large aisled nave, late 15th–early 16th-century; tower added in 1768–73 by Joseph Turner; chancel with a canted apse by Sir George Gilbert Scott, 1856. Good timber roofs and plenty of rich stone carving. Chancel windows by Wailes; tactful 1878 reredos by Douglas. Some 15th- and 16th-century glass. The 1921 War Memorial Chapel by Sir T. G. Jackson has a curious Art Deco floor. Monuments by Cheere and Rysbrack.

NANNERCH
St Mary
4m/6km S. of Holywell SJ 1669
By T. H. Wyatt, 1852–3, with broach spire and E. window by Gibbs. Grand marble monument with sarcophagus and putti by Grinling Gibbons, 1694.

NERCWYS
St Mary
2m/3km S. of Mold SJ 2360
Attractive hillside setting. Shingled spire by J. O. Scott, 1883. Interesting fittings include painted Cadair Fair 'Mary's Chair', a medieval wooden structure, perhaps originally a shrine, made into sedilia by Scott. Medieval pulpit; glass by Burlison & Grylls.

NORTHOP
St Eurgain & St Peter
3m/4km N. of Mold SJ 2468
Successive restorations by Jones, Butterfield and others have robbed this church of its atmosphere, but the splendid battlemented and pinnacled W. tower remains. Glass by Clutterbuck, O'Connor, and Hardman.

OVERTON
St Mary
6m/10km S.E. of Wrexham SJ 3741
Large red sandstone church with Perpendicular nave and Decorated W. tower; N. aisle rebuilt in 1819, the S. in 1855. Chancel,

clerestory and hammer-beam roof by W. M. Teulon, 1870. Glass by Kempe; Clayton & Bell E. window. Memorial of 1808 by Sir Richard Westmacott.

PENTROBIN (Penymynydd)
St John the Baptist
3m/4km W. of Hawarden SJ 3062
By John Buckler, 1843; in Early English style. Octagonal vaulted vestry. Rich decoration designed by R. P. Pullan and executed by J. E. Troughton, curate-in-charge, 1843–64.

RHUDDLAN
St Mary
2m/3km S.E. of Rhyll SJ 0278
Double-naved church of *c.* 1300 with Perpendicular N. aisle; restored by Scott Jnr 1868; 13th-century tomb slab beside the altar.

RHYDMWYN
St John the Evangelist
3m/4km N.W. of Mold SJ 2066
First-rate early work of J. L. Pearson, 1860–3. Tall, dignified, and lavishly detailed. Characteristic fittings include the red and white inlaid reredos.

RHYL
St Thomas
SJ 0081
By Sir George Gilbert Scott, 1861–9. Fine church in Early English style with lofty spire above the flat estuary. The interior is lofty and dignified.

SHOTTON
St Ethelwold
adjoining Queensferry SJ 3068
By John Douglas, 1898–1902. Large red sandstone church in the Early English style. Tall and impressive aisled interior with lofty pentagonal chancel.

TREMEIRCHION
Corpus Christi
5m/8km N. of Denbigh SJ 0873
Setting among yews between vicarage and pub. Small, plain church with notable late 14th-century canopied tomb of a priest and some 15th- and 17th-century glass.

TREUDDYN
St Mary
4m/6km S. of Mold SJ 2558
By T. H. Wyatt, 1875. Extremely dull except

for very remarkable 14th-century glass, the earliest in N. Wales.

WHITEWELL
St Mary
3m/4km W. of Whitchurch SJ 4941
By John Butler, 1829–30, with pyramidal spire. Prettily grouped with stables, cottage, and 17th-century thatched carriage shelter.

WHITFORD
St Mary
3m/4km N.W. of Holywell SJ 1478
Almost entirely rebuilt in Perpendicular style by Ambrose Poynter, 1845–6; restored by Ewan Christian. Monuments include one by R. Westmacott Jnr. Two 17th-century lych gates.

WORTHENBURY
St Deiniol
4m/6km N.E. of Overton SJ 4246
Splendid Georgian church in warm red brick by Richard Trubshaw, 1736–9. Grand W. tower and apsidal chancel. Perfectly preserved interior has two chancel pews with fireplaces. Some 14th-century glass from Winchester College chapel.

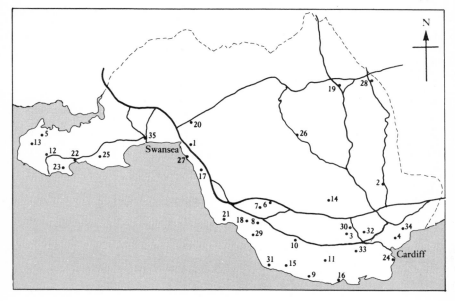

1	Baglan	13	Llangennith	25	Pennard
2	Caerphilly	14	Llantrisant	26	Pentre
3	Capel Llaniltern	15	Llantwit Major	27	Port Talbot
4	Cardiff	16	Lower Porthkerry	28	Rhymney
5	Cheriton	17	Margam	29	St Bride's Major
6	Coity	18	Merthyr Mawr	30	St Bride's super-Ely
7	Coychurch	19	Methyr Tydfil	31	St Donats
8	Ewenny	20	Neath	32	St Fagan's
9	Gileston	21	Newton	33	St Lythan's
10	Llanblethian	22	Nicholaston	34	St Mellons
11	Llancarfan	23	Oxwich	35	Swansea
12	Llanddewi	24	Penarth		

Glamorgan

BAGLAN
St Catherine
2m/3km N.W. of Port Talbot SS 7592
With its elegant pinnacled spire, this is probably John Prichard's masterpiece, built at the end of his life, and consecrated in 1882. Everything is rich, colourful and well done. Inside, pink alabaster contrasts with different shades of grey stone. The floors are of mosaic, the striking reredos of incised marble. Glass by Burne-Jones and Morris.

CAERPHILLY
St Martin
6m/10km N. of Cardiff ST 1586
By Charles Buckeridge, 1870; completed by J. L. Pearson. Large and dignified, the handsome tower and W. end added by G. E. Halliday, 1910. E. window of S. aisle by Alfred L. Wilkinson, 1933.

CAPEL LLANILTERN
St Ellteyrn
6m/10km W. of Cardiff ST 0979
Tiny church rebuilt in 1862 by G. E. Street at the expense of the Windsor family. Simple but with good detail.

CARDIFF
ST 1876
St John
The only medieval church in Cardiff. The chief glory is the tower of 1473 with elaborate pinnacled parapet. The rest of the church is partly 13th-century, mostly mid-15th, but greatly rebuilt and extended in 1852–3 and again in 1887–91 by Kempson and Fowler, when the outer aisles were added. High altar reredos by W. Goscombe John; that in the S. aisle is by Sir Ninian Comper, who also did the E. window glass. Other glass by Morris and Co.
St Margaret, Roath
By John Prichard, 1869–72. Restrained outside, but with glorious polychromatic interior of red, white and blue brick, stone and alabaster. Comper reredos.
St German, Roath
By G. F. Bodley and T. Garner, 1882–4. Nothing short of a masterpiece; tall and dignified, the excitement is reserved for the interior. Goodhart-Rendel called it a 'sort of greyhound church, strong, lithe and thin'. The E. window consists of a beautiful triplet of lights with glass to Bodley's design by Burlison & Grylls. The rood, pulpit and font are all by Bodley, but the reredos is by Cecil Hare.

CHERITON
St Cadog
2m/3km S. of Whitford Pt SS 4593
Late 13th-century church with sturdy, low central tower, the gabled roof behind battlements. Early English carving.

COITY
St Mary
2m/3km N.E. of Bridgend SS 9281
Big aisleless 14th-century church with low tower over vaulted crossing. Inside it is light and spare, the chancel washed blue like a dairy. The E. window, a beautiful and unusual work of the Morris firm, was installed in 1863. There are small 14th-century effigies on either side of the altar and other interesting memorials, especially a tablet of 1710. Rare portable carved oak Easter Sepulchre of *c.* 1500.

COYCHURCH
St Crallo
2m/3km E. of Bridgend SS 9379
Grand late 13th-century church; central tower and S. transept collapsed and rebuilt, 1877. Fine lofty arcade, Perpendicular angel roof.

EWENNY
St Michael
2m/3km S. of Bridgend SS 9077
A delightful place, quiet and rural, a mixture of medieval church and fortification, great house and farmyard. The church was founded *c.* 1120, the Benedictine priory in 1141; building went on until *c.* 1300. The earliest parts of the church – the nave, which today constitutes the parish church, and the N. arcade – were heightened later in the 12th century, at the time the chancel, crossing,

transepts, and W. wall were added. The nave was originally longer; the W. wall is 19th-century. The present aisle and porch are 16th-century, rebuilt in 1895. Font *c.* 1200. The E. part has marvellous grandeur and dignity, with barrel-vaulted chancel and plain masonry beautifully set off by bands of decorative carving. There is a 14th-century wooden screen with 16th-century linenfold panels. In the S. transept is an interesting collection of monuments.

GILESTON
St Giles
3m/4km E. of Llantwit Major ST 0167
Chiefly Perpendicular; big S. porch with remarkable carved timber door. Good 1724 monument.

LLANBLETHIAN
St Bleddian
adjoining Cowbridge SS 9874
Set in rich and attractive valley village. Large medieval church with pinnacled Perpendicular tower.

LLANCARFAN
St Cadog
4m/6km N.W. of Barry ST 0570
Attractive village; site of St Cadog's famous 6th-century monastery; 12th–14th-century double-naved church. Grand early 16th-century window in N. wall of chancel. Simple carved capitals to arcade and intricate Perpendicular reredos, possibly former canopy of choir-stalls.

LLANDDEWI
St David
3m/4km N. of Port Eynon Pt SS 4689
The approach by a grassy farmyard is in character with this most attractive, primitive building. Restored in 1876, with a low saddleback tower. Bright and polished interior with planked floor, clear E. window, barley-sugar communion rails, painted altar table with Gothic arcading, and huge flowerpot font.

LLANGENNITH
St Cenydd
2m/3km E. of Burry Holms SS 4291
Strong, vigorous medieval church with saddleback-roofed tower. Burial slabs of three priors of the former monastery and other monuments.

LLANTRISANT
St Illtud, St Dyfodwg & St Gwynno
4m/6km S. of Pontypridd ST 0483
View over Vale of Glamorgan. Squat 16th-century tower; rest much restored by John Prichard, 1873. E. window by Burne-Jones and Morris; S. chancel windows by Clayton & Bell.

LLANTWIT MAJOR
St Illtud
4m/6km S.W. of Cowbridge SS 9668
Site of St Illtud's Celtic monastery. An amazing building of enormous length, it consists of four linked sections: the chancel and nave with aisles and W. tower, which formed the collegiate church; the 'western' or parochial church; and, at the extreme W., the ruined Galilee Chapel. Restored in 1888–1905 by Halliday. The E. church has a large and elaborate 14th-century reredos, much restored. In the S. aisle is a 13th-century niche, richly carved with a Jesse tree. There are 13th–15th-century wall-paintings. The W. church has a splendid timber roof, and contains a fine collection of Celtic crosses and medieval tombs.

LOWER PORTHKERRY
St Curig
1m/2km W. of Barry ST 1168
Attractive setting by cottages. Basically 13th-century with bold tower. Plain screen of *c.* 1300; unusual low relief memorial, 1629.

MARGAM
St Mary
S.E. district of Port Talbot SS 7887
The Norman nave of a great Cistercian abbey survives as a parish church. The Italianate W. font of 1805–10; the W. windows, 1873, by Burne-Jones. Note the fine 16th–17th- and 19th-century tombs.

MERTHYR MAWR
St Teilo
2m/3km S.W. of Bridgend SS 8877
By B. Ferrey and J. Prichard, 1849–51. Church in Early English style with W. bell-turret, fine details, and good contemporary glass.

MERTHYR TYDFIL
St Tydfil
21m/34km N.W. of Cardiff SO 0406
Rebuilt 1829 on site of medieval church; transformed in 1895 by J. L. Pearson.

Moving interior in simple French Romanesque style.

NEATH
St David
8m/12km N.E. of Swansea SS 7597
By John Norton, 1864–6. Extraordinary S.E. tower capped by fanciful pyramidal spire with elaborate pinnacles. Polychromatic interior.

NEWTON
St John the Baptist
suburb of Porthcawl SS 8377
12th–13th-century. Pre-Reformation stone pulpit, the only one in Wales, crudely carved with the Flagellation of Christ by Roman soldiers. E. window by Burne-Jones.

NICHOLASTON
St Nicholas
Gower peninsula, above E. end of Oxwich Bay on S. coast SS 5288
By G. E. Halliday, 1892–4. Complete period piece, down to copper baptismal bucket. No expense has been spared, particularly on elaborate carving; and it comes off. On pulpit are statues of Keble, Liddon, and Pusey.

OXWICH
St Illtud
11m/18km W. of Swansea SS 4986
Well worth visiting; it stands in woodland at the very edge of the cliff on the right arm of the bay. The big tower looms out of a green gloom of sycamore, and the little church is entered through the W. door under it. The diminutive chancel has a lovely 14th-century tomb and a ceiling painted at the expense of Dame Lilian Baylis of Old Vic fame; 1926 chancel screen by Gerald Cogswell. The two slabs now in the porch are 13th- and 14th-century, and bear the names of former rectors. The oil lamps are notable.

PENARTH
St Augustine
3m/4km S. of Cardiff ST 1871
Sited on a headland, with a magnificent view over Cardiff, the tiny old church was replaced in 1865–6 with one of William Butterfield's finest buildings. It cost £10,000. The tough exterior is in grey Radyr stone, the tall saddleback tower in striking contrast with the humble one it replaced. The interior is an extraordinary exercise in

Geometrical polychromy. Characteristic fittings include a splendid reredos.

PENNARD
St Mary
4m/6km W. of Mumbles Head SS 5688
Medieval. Boat-shaped nave ceiling and restored W. gallery; 17th-century pulpit and font cover; good memorials.

PENTRE
St Peter
located in Rhondda Valley SS 9696
Set in hilly village. Characterful design by John Prichard, 1888–91, completed after his death by Kempson and Fowler. Elaborate octagonal bell-turret. Dignified interior has large alabaster reredos.

PORT TALBOT
St Theodore
8m/12km E. of Swansea SS 7690
By J. L. Pearson, 1895–7. Early English style. Large and noble church with fine E. window by Tim Lewis, 1983.

RHYMNEY
St David
4m/6km E. of Merthyr Tydfil SO 1107
By Philip Hardwick, 1839–43; handsome Classical church with round-headed windows, pedimented E. end, and galleries.

ST BRIDE'S MAJOR
(dedication unknown)
3m/4km S. of Bridgend SS 8974
Remarkable medieval Boteler family tombs, one with canopy, and later Wyndham monuments.

ST BRIDE'S SUPER-ELY
St Bride
5m/8km W. of Cardiff ST 0977
Rural setting. Saddleback tower; Norman doorway and recut chancel arch. Lovely 17th-century Italian statue of Madonna.

ST DONATS
St Donat
2m/3km W. of Llantwit Major SS 9938
Tucked in valley to W. of castle, now Atlantic College. Modest Norman and later building. Splendid tombs in Stradling Chapel; remarkable series of 16th-century paintings on wood; big altar tomb; fine early 17th-century monument. Late 15th-century calvary on S. side of churchyard.

ST FAGAN'S
St Mary
4m/6km W. of Cardiff ST 1277
Attractive church, well set near the castle. Excellent restoration by G. E. Street, 1859–60. Fine 14th-century sedilia; fittings by Street include pulpit, font cover, seating, and tower screen.

ST LYTHAN'S
(dedication unknown)
3m/4km N. of Barry ST 1072
Simple late-medieval church, restored by J. P. Seddon. S. chapel connected by two low, primitive arches supported by huge pillar. Elegant small wall tablets and a Norman font.

ST MELLONS
St Mellon
suburb 4m/6km N.E. of Cardiff ST 2281
View over estuary. Mostly Perpendicular church of irregular plan, restored by Sir Giles Gilbert Scott, 1859, and by Charles Buckeridge, 1869.

SWANSEA
ss 6593
St Mary
Sir Arthur Blomfield's church was destroyed in the 1941 bombing; it was rebuilt 1954–9 by Sir Percy Thomas to modified designs of Leslie T. Moore. Though of little architectural merit, it is large, light and airy, and contains the best modern stained glass in Wales, by artists such as Kuni, Kajiwara, James Powell and Sons, John Piper, Patrick Reyntiens, Alfred Fisher, and Catrin Jones. Black steel font canopy by George Pace; Ceri Richards's painting of the Deposition, and reredos picture under the tower attributed to Farinati.

St Paul, Sketty
Finest in Swansea. By Henry Woodyer, 1849–52, with shingled broach spire. Sensitively enlarged in 1908 and 1929.

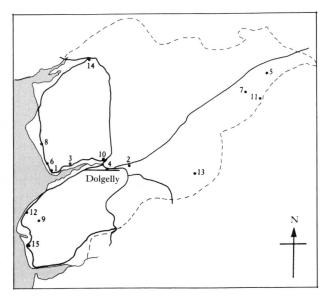

1	Barmouth	9	Llanegryn
2	Brithdir	10	Llanelltyud
3	Caerdeon	11	Llangar
4	Dollgellau	12	Llangelynin
5	Glan-yr-Afon	13	Llanymawddwy
6	Llanaber	14	Maentwrog
7	Llandderfel	15	Tywyn
8	Llanddwywe		

Merioneth

BARMOUTH
SH 6115
St John
Commanding position on hillside. By Douglas and Fordham, 1889; tower collapsed 1892; finished 1898. Grand and spacious inside with tall chancel and stone reredos. Kempe glass.

BRITHDIR
St Mark
1m/2km N. of Bargoed SO 1502
Notable Arts and Crafts church by Henry Wilson, 1895–8, built of local granite and local slates. Cruciform in plan, it has a broad W. gable and small, narrow windows. Inside, the lofty, cream-painted nave contrasts with the barrel-vaulted apsed chancel, which is painted in dark red, dark blue and pale green. Contemporary fittings include a beaten copper altar and pulpit, a moulded lead font, stalls carved with animals, and doors inlaid with mother of pearl. The nearby vicarage is by J. D. Sedding, 1888.

CAERDEON
St Philip
3m/4km N.E. of Barmouth SH 6518
Original church, now nave, by Rev. J. L. Petit, 1862. Rough local stone with loggia, broad eaves, and circular window. 'Something between a large lodge gate and a lady's rustic dairy' (the *Ecclesiologist*, 1863). Chancel, transept, and bellcote added later.

DOLGELLAU
St Mary
17m/27km S.W. of Bala SH 7217
In its simple way, this is a virtuoso performance in the use of local stone; nave built in 1716. There is a handsome tower and a neo-Norman apse of 1854. The wide nave has an extraordinary roof, supported on wooden columns. The only medieval survival inside is a 14th-century effigy. The huge windows contain a most remarkable assemblage of Victorian glass.

GLAN-YR-AFON
(dedication unknown)
3m/4km N. of Beaumaris SH 6080
By Sir Giles Gilbert Scott, 1861–4; simple church in the Early English style with splendid reredos of Minton tiles.

LLANABER
St Mary & St Bodfan
2m/3km N.W. of Barmouth SH 6017
Beautifully sited above the sea, in a large churchyard packed with tombs. An almost perfectly preserved 13th-century church with aisles, clerestory, and large raised chancel. Lancets with good Victorian glass. Perpendicular roofs; two 5th-century inscribed stones.

LLANDDERFEL
St Derfel Gadarn
4m/6km E. of Bala SH 9837
Small Perpendicular church, rebuilt in 1870 by S. Pountney Smith. Rich medieval rood screen and loft; remnants of St Derfel's 'horse' and staff in porch.

LLANDDWYWE
St Dwywe
4m/6km N. of Barmouth SH 5822
Small church with Vaughan Chapel added *c.* 1615, containing splendid 17th- and 18th-century monuments.

LLANEGRYN
St Mary & St Egryn
3m/4km N. of Tywyn SH 6005
Over-restored in 1878 by E. B. Ferrey. Glorious 16th-century rood screen.

LLANELLTYUD
St Illtud
1m/2km N.W. of Dolgellau SH 7119
Attractive hotch-potch, restored in 1636 and 1899. Medieval roof and panelling; 18th-century windows; 12th-century inscribed stone.

LLANGAR
All Saints
1m/2km S. of Corwen SJ 0743
Fine setting overlooking water meadows.

Small medieval church has 17th–18th-century fittings, including box pews and three-decker pulpit.

LLANGELYNIN

St Celynin, New Church
New Church, 4m/6km N.W. of Tywyn SH 5707
By Thomas Jones, 1840; battlemented octagonal tower. Interior sympathetically decorated and furnished with tiles, woodwork, and 18th-century marble font.

St Celynin, Old Church
Lonely hillside setting. Founded 7th century; simple and unrestored; 16th-century timber porch and N. transept; 17th-century communion table and altar rails; Welsh texts painted on walls.

LLANYMAWDDWY

St Tydecho
5m/8km N.E. of Mallwyd SH 9019
Set among remote hills. Delightful plain church with black and white interior. E. window of *c.* 1863 by Heaton, Butler & Bayne.

MAENTWROG

St Twrog
3m/4km W. of Ffestiniog SS 6640
1814, remodelled by John Douglas, 1896; low slated spire. Superb woodwork includes decorated panels above the arcades; 6th-century stone; timber lych gate.

TYWYN

St Cadfan
10m/16km W. of Machynlleth SH 5800
Important clas church. Cruciform with central tower rebuilt in 1884; 12th-century nave including arcades and clerestory windows; 14th-century effigies and inscribed stone of *c.* 750. Wall tablets by Sir Henry Cheere, and glass by Geoffrey Webb.

1	Abergavenny	18	Malpas
2	Bedwellty	19	Mamhilad
3	Betws Newydd	20	Marshfield
4	Blaenavon	21	Monmouth
5	Caldicot	22	Mynyddislwyn
6	Chepstow	23	Nash
7	Cwmyoy	24	Over Monnow
8	Dixton	25	Peterstone Wentllooge
9	Grosmont	26	Redwick
10	Llandogo	27	Rockfield
11	Llanfaches	28	St Bride's Wentllooge
12	Llangwm	29	Skenfrith
13	Llanover	30	Tredunnock
14	Llanthony	31	Trellech
15	Llantilio Crossenny	32	Usk
16	Llantilio Pertholey	33	Waunfelin
17	Magor	34	Whitson

Monmouth

ABERGAVENNY
St Mary
SO 2914
Large cruciform church of former Benedictine priory, badly handled through the centuries. Elaborately carved late 14th-century choir-stalls; rough oak figure of the recumbent Jesse, probably from the reredos; finest collection of 13th–17th-century monuments in Wales.

BEDWELLTY
St Sannan
1m/2km E. of Bargoed SO 1600
Early English chancel and nave arcade; the nave and N. aisle extended and widened and W. tower built c. 1420. Rare 14th-century vestment press and, in the churchyard, the tombstone of Catherine Dillon, who died aged 110.

BETWS NEWYDD
(dedication unknown)
3m/4km W. of Raglan SO 3605
Humble, small. Remarkable Perpendicular rood screen and loft, richly carved and reaching right up to the roof.

BLAENAVON
St Peter
5m/8km N. of Pontypool SO 2508
Ironworks founded here by Thomas Hill, one of the benefactors of the Gothic church of 1805; later galleries on iron columns and even an iron font.

CALDICOT
St Mary the Virgin
5m/8km S.W. of Chepstow ST 4888
The fine church is medieval and unspoilt, with central tower, rich S. porch, and unusual window tracery. Restored in 1858 by Henry Woodyer, who also built the vicarage; most of his characteristic fittings survive.

CHEPSTOW
St Mary
ST 5393
Vast and barn-like former church of Ben-

edictine priory, the earliest Norman foundation in Wales, 1070. Splendid Norman nave; 1706 W. tower incorporates Norman doorway and windows; chancel and transepts rebuilt 1834–1840, and again 1890–1904, by J. Seddon and J. Coates Carter; 17th-century tombs.

CWMYOY
St Martin
6m/10km N. of Abergavenny SO 2923
Splendidly sited beneath round hillocks, it is memorable for being so utterly drunk: the tower leans crazily and has to be supported on vast buttresses, while the chancel leans in the opposite direction. There are many good things in it: curious plaster panels in the porch, a 13th-century cross, and many memorial tablets.

DIXTON
St Peter
adjoins Monmouth to N.E. SO 5113
Wye Valley setting. White-rendered, except for short and bulbous 13th-century stone spire. Long, narrow whitewashed interior.

GROSMONT
St Nicholas
2m/3km S. of Pontrilas SO 4024
The church is of remarkable size and grandeur, bearing witness to the former importance of the place. Mostly Early English, it has an octagonal central tower and spire. The interior comes as a great shock: the great aisles have steeply pitched roofs and elegant arcades. In the nave are the 'Grosmont Hutch', a chest, and an extraordinarily large unfinished effigy of a knight. The chancel and transepts are cut off from the nave by a great glazed screen, installed during J. P. Seddon's restoration of 1869. Rich Victorian fittings and some 17th- and 18th-century inscribed stone slabs.

LLANDOGO
St Dochau
6m/10km N. of Chepstow SO 5204
Ancient foundation, rebuilt 1860 by J. P. Seddon. Red and yellow stone, quite elab-

orate with pretty bellcote. Lofty chancel decorated by Seddon and Carter, 1889.

LLANFACHES
St Dyfig
7m/11km W. of Chepstow ST 4391
Saddleback tower; restored 1863. Interior charmingly done up by Groves in Arts and Crafts style, 1908. Whitewash, carved screen, and coloured glass. Delightful Church Room also by Groves.

LLANGWM
7m/11km W. of Corwen SH 9644
St John, Llangwm Isaf
Small and simple, rebuilt in 1858 by Prichard and Seddon. Pretty oil lamps set on poles among pews.
St Jerome, Llangwm Uchaf
Beautifully situated with grand tower on N. side of chancel; restored by J. P. Seddon and Ewan Christian, 1870. Magnificent Perpendicular rood screen and loft, elaborately carved. Lectern, tile pavement, E. window, and stained glass all by Seddon.

LLANOVER
St Bartholomew
4m/6km S. of Abergavenny SO 3108
Park setting. Mostly Perpendicular with 1750 porch. Immense churchyard tomb for Lord Llanover by Benjamin Hall.

LLANTHONY
St David
9m/15km N. of Abergavenny SO 2827
Former infirmary of the Priory founded in 1103. Built 1175–1230, now the parish church; gaunt with good memorials.

LLANTILIO CROSSENNY
St Teilo
6m/10km E. of Abergavenny SO 2827
Wooded park setting. Shingled broach spire at crossing; lofty nave and large chancel; tower arch very low. Restored, 1857, by Prichard and Seddon. Good low-relief memorial slabs and touching marble tablet by Flaxman, 1819.

LLANTILIO PERTHOLEY
St Teilo
2m/3km N. of Abergavenny SO 3116
Odd and spreading church, N. chapel divided from aisle by huge octagonal timber piers. Good memorials including an early Brute, 1728.

MAGOR
St Mary the Virgin
8m/12km S.W. of Chepstow ST 4287
Central tower, two-storeyed porch, and elaborate doorway dating from restoration of 1868. Long 13th-century chancel. Capitals of nave arcades have angels with outstretched wings; restored in 1868 by John Norton.

MALPAS
St Mary
suburb 2m/3km N. of Newport ST 3090
By John Prichard, 1849–50, in Romanesque style. Chancel arch with big dog-tooth ornamentation; stone lectern covered in Romanesque carving; vigorous stained glass.

MAMHILAD
St Illtud
2m/3km N.E. of Pontypool SO 3003
Restored 1865 by Prichard. Splendid medieval rood loft, now gallery front; medieval glass in E. window.

MARSHFIELD
St Mary the Virgin
5m/8km S.W. of Newport ST 2682
Plain W. tower and long nave; expensively and successfully restored 1906–8 by E. M. Bruce Vaughan; 13th-century chancel arch; lavish Edwardian woodwork; glass and sculpture by W. Goscombe John.

MONMOUTH
SO 5012
St Mary
Lower part of tower medieval, upper part added *c.* 1750; rest rebuilt 1736–7 by Francis Smith of Warwick. Remodelled and extended by G. E. Street, 1880–2, in the Early English style.

MYNYDDISLWYN
St Tudwr
2m/3km S.W. of Abercarn ST 1994
Basically medieval; outer walls rebuilt in 1820 with great iron Gothic windows.

NASH
St Mary
4m/6km S.E. of Newport ST 3483
Remarkable church has big stone Perpendicular spire attached to N.E. corner of the nave. The chancel was rebuilt by Prichard and Seddon in 1861. The S. porch is 18th-century, Classical, with a grand pilastered

doorway. The inner door is Gothic, as is the huge barn-like nave, which retains its box pews and three-decker pulpit.

OVER MONNOW
St Thomas Becket
opposite Monmouth on right bank of R. Monnow SO 5012
A few 12th-century fragments; elaborately Normanized by John Prichard, 1873. Interior by Arthur Wyatt, 1830: pews, galleries, stalls all richly Norman; tiny stone font with tall, thin cover.

PETERSTONE WENTLLOOGE
St Peter
6m/10km S.W. of Newport ST 2680
Large, elegant Perpendicular church with handsome West Country-style tower. The tall, pinnacled S. porch has stone seats and carved stone heads of kings, saints and cherubim. The level of the great flood of 1606 is marked on the E. wall of the chancel.

REDWICK
St Thomas Apostle
7m/11km E. of Newport ST 4184
Crossing tower and two-storeyed porch; restored by Norton, 1876. Good medieval details include Decorated E. window and niche in N. aisle; 19th-century gallery on carved supports of former rood screen.

ROCKFIELD
St Cenedlon
2m/3km N.W. of Monmouth SO 4814
Tower with timber belfry; church rebuilt 1859–60 by Prichard and Seddon; elaborate stone carving and wrought iron.

ST BRIDE'S WENTLLOOGE
All Saints
4m/6km S. of Newport ST 2982
Big, grand church with leaning Perpendicular tower; white stone with bands of red; richly buttressed with ornate parapet. Neglected interior.

SKENFRITH
St Bridget
6m/10km N.W. of Monmouth SO 4520
The church has a big square tower with a splendid two-tiered pyramidal timber belfry of Herefordshire type. In the N. aisle is an elaborate tomb of 1557 and a Jacobean pew. The most remarkable possession is a magnificent 16th-century cope.

TREDUNNOCK
St Andrew
4m/6km S. of Usk ST 3794
Tiny Norman windows in chancel, an old roof, and a carved stone font, 1662. Above the font is a 2nd-century Roman funerary inscription found in the churchyard. The sensitive restoration of 1910 is commemorated in an inscription by Eric Gill.

TRELLECH
St Nicholas
5m/8km S. of Monmouth SO 5005
Big, lofty, mainly 14th-century church with fine octagonal spire. Stone sundial in S. aisle, 1689, has carvings of the castle mound and the three celebrated standing stones in the parish.

USK
St Mary
ST 3281
The original church, built for a priory of Benedictine nuns *c.* 1135, was cruciform, with an apsidal chancel and central tower. The N. aisle was added for the use of the parish in the 13th century and rebuilt in the 15th. The chancel and transepts eventually disappeared, so that the sanctuary is now beneath the tower. The nave was lengthened westward by T. H. Wyatt in 1844. The two delicate porches were added in the 15th century. A restored medieval screen runs across nave and aisle. Attached to it is a brass plate bearing the oldest Welsh epitaph extant. The 1862 organ, built by Gray and Davidson for Llandaff Cathedral, is a stunning object and deserves a better position; the case was designed by Seddon. On the W. wall is a curious 17th-century epitaph. There are some interesting tombs in the churchyard.

WAUNFELIN
(dedication unknown)
suburb of Pontypool SO 2800
Original work by J. Coates Carter, 1912, in plain Perpendicular style.

WHITSON
St Mary
5m/8km S.E. of Newport ST 3783
Attractive church with strange cone-shaped spire called 'the thimble'; restored in 1861 by Prichard and Seddon.

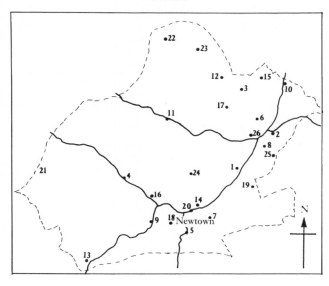

1 Berriew	14 Llanllwchaearn
2 Buttington	15 Llansanffraid-ym-Mechain
3 Bwlch y Cibau	16 Llanwnog
4 Carno	17 Meifod
5 Dolfor	18 Mochdre
6 Guilsfield	19 Montgomery
7 Kerry	20 Newtown
8 Leighton	21 Penegoes
9 Llandinam	22 Pennant Melangell
10 Llandysilio	23 Penybontfawr
11 Llanerfyl	24 Tregynon
12 Llanfyllin	25 Trelystan
13 Llangurig	26 Welshpool

Montgomery

BERRIEW
St Beuno
5m/8km S.W. of Welshpool SJ 1800
Medieval church rebuilt in brick, 1803; Gothicized by E. Haycock Jnr, 1876, who added the chancel and pyramidal spire. Reredos by Kempson and Earp, 1896; E. window by Hardman; 19th-century tablet by Baily. War Memorial cross by Sir Ninian Comper, 1933.

BUTTINGTON
All Saints
2m/3km N.E. of Welshpool SJ 2408
Plain roughcast and whitewashed church with fine 15th-century roof. Unusual font made from an Early English capital from Strata Marcella Abbey.

BWLCH Y CIBAU
Christ Church
3m/4km S.E. of Llanfyllin SJ 1717
Admirably suited to its sheltered upland site, the church shows how sensitive Sir Giles Gilbert Scott could be to the *genius loci*. It is an excellent little building of 1862–5, in Early English style, small and apsed, with a bellcote. The glass in the chancel is by Wailes and at the W. end by Powell & Sons.

CARNO
St John the Baptist
5m/8km N.W. of Caersws SN 9696
By J. W. Poundley, 1863. Lumpy grey stone with red and yellow dressings, plate tracery, and large timber arch between nave and chancel. Wooden belfry recently removed from little tower. Early Christian stone.

DOLFOR
St Paul
3m/4km S. of Newtown SO 1087
By T. G. Newenham, 1851. Largely built of terracotta, including pretty window tracery and bellcote.

GUILSFIELD
St Aelhaearn
3m/4km N. of Welshpool SJ 2111
Founded 7th century, now one of the best churches in the county, mostly 14th- and 15th-century; lavishly restored 1877–9 by G. E. Street. Magnificent panelled Perpendicular roof; highly original screen, reredos and pulpit by Street; many monuments.

KERRY
St Michael
3m/4km S.E. of Newtown SO 1490
Chunky stone tower has two-storeyed timber belfry with pyramidal roof. Restored by G. E. Street, 1881, and after his death by A. W. Blomfield. Romanesque nave piers; fine 14th-century roofs.

LEIGHTON
Holy Trinity
2m/3km S.E. of Welshpool SJ 2405
Standing on the estate of Leighton Hall, the yellow-stone church of 1851–3, by W. H. Gee of Liverpool, is wonderfully elaborate, with flying buttresses, crocketed pinnacles, arches, and lots of rich carving. Goodhart Rendel called it 'a perfectly preserved and unaltered specimen of nouveau-riche-dom in the 1850s'. The interior is strongly atmospheric, full of varnished oak pews, coloured tiles, and glass by Forrest and Bromley of Liverpool. At the S.E. door an octagonal chapel is attached, containing monuments to the owners of the Hall.

LLANDINAM
St Llonio
2m/3km S. of Caersws SO 0288
Former clas church until 13th century; some 13th- and 14th-century work; rebuilt 1864–5 by G. E. Street. Massive tower with pyramidal roof; 16th–17th-century woodwork; E. window by Clayton & Bell.

LLANDYSILIO
St Tysilio
7m/11km S. of Oswestry SJ 2619
Superb church built by G. E. Street, 1867–8. In refined Early English style, with a little circular spire. The reredos is by Earp, and the excellent E. window by Clayton & Bell was designed by Street. On the S. side is a richly coloured window of the sea giving up its dead, 1879, by Powells. Exquisite 17th-century brass by Silvanus Crue.

LLANERFYL
St Erfyl
5m/8km N.W. of Llanfair Caereinion SJ 0309
By Edward Haycock Jnr, 1870. Nave roof
c. 1400; crude 15th-century Gothic shrine
and reliquary shaped like chapel; 5th- or
6th-century Christian tombstone.

LLANFYLLIN
St Myllin
9m/15km N.W. of Welshpool SJ 1419
Set in pretty town. Built of local red brick in
1706 with stark tower and rich S. doorway.
Large, plain interior, an unfortunate
Norman-style triple arch between chancel
and nave inserted 1863. Rich E. window by
Clutterbuck; others by Alexander Gibbs and
Heaton, Butler & Bayne.

LLANGURIG
St Curig
4m/6km S.W. of Llandiloes SN 9079
The grand church is set in a sloping churchyard below the main road. The 15th-century
tower has a most effective shingled spire,
now clad in copper, added at the time of the
restoration of 1877–8 by G. G. Scott Jnr and
Arthur Baker. The stained glass windows by
Burlison & Grylls are superbly executed.
The rood screen was re-created from 1828
drawings of the original 15th-century
screen; together with the stalls and rich
chancel fittings, it forms an outstanding ensemble.

LLANLLWCHAEARN
St Llwchaearn
1m/2km N.E. of Newtown SO 1292
Brick church of 1815, nicely Gothicized
1864–9 by R. J. Withers; squat pinnacled
tower. Window by Morris and Co. *c.* 1870.

LLANSANFFRAID-YM-MECHAIN
St Bride
5m/8km E. of Llanfyllin SJ 2120
The church is an attractive hotch-potch,
with a fine timber porch, restored in 1891–3
by J. O. Scott; he added the nice shingled
spire. The S. transept, added in 1727, is remarkably grand. The miscellaneous collection of windows includes a tiny Norman one,
a dormer of 1669, and some curious earlier
17th-century ones. The fine woodwork is
Jacobean and by Scott. S. chancel window
by David Evans.

LLANWNOG
St Gwynnog
6m/10km W. of Newtown SO 0293
Circular raised churchyard. Single-cell
church rebuilt in 1863 by R. K. Penson.
Splendid Perpendicular rood screen and
loft; E. window by Evans Brothers of
Shrewsbury.

MEIFOD
St Tysilio & St Mary
4m/6km S. of Llanfyllin SJ 1513
Set in nine-acre churchyard, the site of a
Celtic *clas*, originally containing three separate churches, two now disappeared. Partly
early-Norman; restored by Benjamin
Ferrey, 1871–2. Armorial glass and one
window by David Evans. Gothic organ-case;
c. 10th-century Celtic cross slab.

MOCHDRE
All Saints
3m/4km S.W. of Newtown SO 0788
Rebuilt 1867 by Edward Haycock Jnr. Magnificent Perpendicular roof; glass by Wailes
and Clayton & Bell.

MONTGOMERY
St Nicholas
SO 2296
The church is mostly 13th-century, the
tower rebuilt in 1816. It was restored by G.
Beadnell in 1863–8, and the N. arcade by
Haycock in 1877–8. The nave has a
splendid roof, open in the W. and panelled in
the E.; 13th-century font and Perpendicular
double screen. Elaborate reredos designed
by R. C. Carpenter, with figures by Earp
and mosaics by Clayton & Bell. The S.
transept contains a magnificent canopied
tomb of 1600 by Walter Hancock. There are
also two much-restored medieval effigies.
In the churchyard is the famous Robber's
Grave.

NEWTOWN
St David
SO 1091
By Thomas Penson, 1843–7. Large, tall,
unusual church of pinkish-yellow brick.
Chancel, 1875, by David Walker. Interior
painted 1961–4. Parts of medieval rood
screen used by H. L. North to form altar
canopy and parclose screen in N. aisle.

PENEGOES
St Cadfarch
2m/3km E. of Machynlleth SH 7700
Built in 1877 by John Prichard to replace a
medieval church. Built of thin slate slabs
with yellow-stone dressings; polychromatic
brick interior. The details are in Prichard's
usual refined style. The plan is odd; there
is an internal crossing effect, but no tower
over it. The wheel window in the W. wall fills
the nave with evening light. The delightful
Grecian organ is 19th-century.

PENNANT MELANGELL
St Melangell
2m/3km W. of Llangynog SJ 0226
The church, set in a circular churchyard in
a remote valley, is of outstanding interest.
In origin it goes back to the 8th century.
The simple church itself has its roots in the
12th century, but has been much rebuilt.
The square tower, with a pyramidal roof
surmounted by a wooden belfry, was rebuilt
in 1877. The porch is dated 1737. The
Perpendicular rood screen remains; part of
its loft is carved with scenes illustrating the
legend of St Melangell. The saint's shrine
was reconstructed in 1958 from fragments
embedded in the church walls. It is 12th-
century, of stone; the tomb chest and gabled
superstructure stands on arches, supported
on six columns. The capitals, arches and
gables are ornamented with rich Romanesque carving. The tomb chest itself was
probably covered in precious metals and
jewels, and the whole stands about 10 feet
high. It has recently been moved to stand
E. of the altar.

PENYBONTFAWR
St Thomas
5m/8km N.W. of Llanfyllin SJ 0824
By R. K. Penson, 1855. Simple Early

English church with careful details and an
admirable spire.

TREGYNON
St Cynon
5m/8km N. of Newtown SO 0998
Rebuilt 1892 by William Scott Owen. Old
wooden belfry; lavish alabaster reredos,
1902; E. window by Clayton & Bell; Expressionist S. window by Leonard Walker;
monument by Bacon, 1795.

TRELYSTAN
All Saints
3m/4km S.E. of Welshpool SJ 2603
The church is delightfully set on the edge
of woods, and reached over fields by a track.
A sweet little building, thickly surrounded
by yews. It was recased with brick-infilled
timber framing in 1856, but retains its fine
Perpendicular roof. The highly melodram-
atic E. window is perhaps by David Evans.
A tiny Gothic barrel organ of 1827 is still
in playing order.

WELSHPOOL
St Mary/St Cynfelyn
SJ 2207
Basically 13th-century church with 14th-
century chancel and two-storeyed porch.
Wrecked in 1401 during sack of town by
Owen Glendower; largely rebuilt 15th
century and again 1774; restored 1856–7
by John Billing, 1870–1 by G. E. Street.
Nave roof, S. windows, reredos, stalls, and
brass lectern all by G. G. Scott Jnr; 16th-
century Flemish triptych; 'wishing stone'
outside S. porch.
Christ Church
Alarming neo-Norman elephant by Thomas
Penson, 1839–44. Rich Norman terracotta
ornamentation inside; terracotta font.

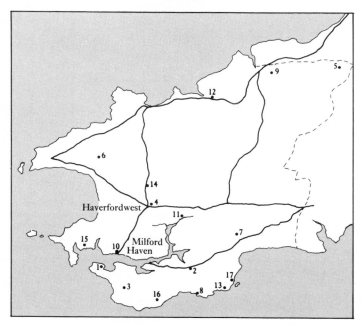

1	Angle	10	Milford Haven
2	Carew Cheriton	11	Minwear
3	Castlemartin	12	Nevern
4	Haverfordwest	13	Penally
5	Llanddewi Brefi	14	Rudbaxton
6	Llandeloy	15	St Ishmael's
7	Ludchurch	16	Stackpole Elidor
8	Manorbier	17	Tenby
9	Manordeifi		

Pembroke

ANGLE
St Mary
on S. side of Milford Haven SM 8502
In village. Medieval church restored by R. K.
Penson *c.* 1850; 18th-century tablets. Small
15th-century fishermen's chapel raised on
crypt in churchyard behind.

CAREW CHERITON
St Mary
4m/6km E. of Pembroke SN 0402
Forms attractive group with medieval
charnel-house and chapel, old rectory and
cottages. Mainly *c.* 1400 with Perpendicular
and Decorated windows; restored by G. G.
Scott Snr, 1855. Cruciform plan with deep
chancel, two aisles, and barrel-vaulted W.
tower with angle buttresses. Interesting
tombs; sanctuary tiles *c.* 1500.

CASTLEMARTIN
St Michael and All Angels
5m/8km S.W. of Pembroke SR 9198
Twin-naved with tower and high porch
making satisfying composition in a sheltered
site; Early English limestone arcade cut by
chancel arch.

HAVERFORDWEST
St Martin
SM 9515
Medieval church with attractive small spire
on square tower; S. chapel and porch added
14th century.
St Mary
The church has a fine interior; graceful,
light and carefully detailed. Standing on the
steps, which run right across the W. end of
the nave, you are looking down into an Early
English church, enlarged and improved
c. 1500. It has a lovely Early English arcade
of clustered columns and capitals carved
with medieval vigour. The portraits on the
chancel arch are of the Earl of Pembroke
and his wife. The E. window has cinquefoil
lights in plate tracery above three-lancet
lights. In the late 15th century, clerestories
were added to the nave and chancel, and
the carved and panelled oak roof was constructed; it rests on nicely carved corbels.

There are some good memorials, a 15th-
century effigy of a pilgrim, a boldly carved
mayor's pew and bench, and an 18th-century
organ. Glass by Kempe and Powell. The
church was restored and refitted in 1848.

LLANDDEWI BREFI
St David
3m/4km S.W. of Tregaron SN 6655
The big, square late 12th-century tower
rests on what was the vaulted crossing of
the nave, rebuilt 1874. The long chancel
has transepts which collapsed in the 18th
century, hence the attractive pointed sash
windows. The walls are whitewashed, the
floors of polished slate, and there are ceiled
wagon roofs in the nave and chancel. Simple
early 19th-century pine pews. Several important 7th–10th-century stones, including
an Ogam inscription, have been placed in
the church. A 7th-century stone, now built
into the N.W. corner of the nave, contains
the earliest known reference to St David.

LLANDELOY
St Teilaw
7m/11km E. of St David's SM 8526
By J. Coates Carter of Cheltenham, 1924.
Unusual but attractive replacement of an
earlier church. Well-designed furnishings
include rood screen and loft, and altars with
slate mensae.

LUDCHURCH
(dedication unknown)
3m/4km S.E. of Narberth SN 1410
On a green rise close to old limestone quarries. Tall, battered tower; medieval arcade.

MANORBIER
St James
4m/6km S.W. of Tenby SS 0697
The church where Giraldus Cambrensis
worshipped when a boy; he grew up in the
castle across the valley. Steps lead down
through a vaulted porch – note the medieval
painting – as into a crypt. The huge walls
of the Norman nave give the impression of
being carved out to form arcades to the
14th-century aisles. The transept vaults cut

the main vault of the nave at different levels. This sculptural character must have been even stronger before the 1865 restoration, when a much larger arch was cut in the chancel wall. Then the old rood screen and the Royal Arms were removed, and the Perpendicular E. window changed for the present three-light one. The tower has an unusual position in the angle between the 13th-century chancel and the N. transept.

MANORDEIFI
St David
4m/6km S.E. of Cardigan SN 2243
On the banks of the Teifi – note coracle in porch. Charming 19th-century fittings; box pews with fireplaces; Georgian glazing; mid-19th-century monument to man who met tiger.

MILFORD HAVEN
St Katherine's Chapel
SM 8504
Consecrated in 1808 for this new town; papery Gothic revival, enlarged 1905. Unusual relics and links with Lord Nelson.

MINWEAR
St Womar
9m/15km N.W. of Tenby SN 0413
Lovely secluded site near farm above E. Cleddau. Small, simple Norman and later church.

NEVERN
St Brynach
2m/3km E. of Newport SN 0839
The church has a very attractive ancient site, now snug in a hamlet, with view of the Prescellys from the churchyard; 15th-century cruciform church, very well restored by R. J. Withers in 1863. The W. tower is low and battlemented. There is a 5th-century Ogam stone and a 10th-century stone carved with a cross. Outside, the great Celtic high cross dates from c. 1000, and there are some fine slate tombs.

PENALLY
St Nicholas
1m/2km S.W. of Tenby SS 1199
Reputedly the birth- and burial-place of St Teilo (c. 500–560), first bishop of Llandaff. Restored 13th-century cruciform church with barrel-vaulted roof and later W. tower. There are two high crosses, one of 850–900 and the other of 900–950.

RUDBAXTON
St Michael
3m/4km N. of Haverfordwest SM 9620
Basically 13th-century building, to which S. aisle was added, linked by two low arches. Deep whitewashed porch. Dramatic 17th-century Howard memorial with some original colour and other interesting monuments.

ST ISHMAEL'S
St Ishmael
5m/8km W. of Milford Haven SM 8307
Hidden among trees in deep valley runnning down to Haven. Secret, small late 13th-century church with Victorianized interior and pretty carved memorial of 1631.

STACKPOLE ELIDOR
St James & St Elidyr
3m/4km S. of Pembroke SR 9897
The church has a delightful site in a little valley close to a stream. Surprisingly, it is approached through an Art Nouveau lych gate of 1898. This, and much else of this cherished church, commemorates the family living at Stackpole Court, now demolished. It was kindly restored in 1851 by Scott Snr, who rebuilt the nave and retained the original vaulted transepts and Norman tower. There are some exceptional monuments and very good family hatchments.

TENBY
St Mary
9m/15km E. of Pembroke SN 1300
This is a splendid and almost complete Perpendicular rebuilding of the 13th-century church. The tall 13th-century tower, topped by an octagonal spire, almost as tall again, is at an angle between the chancel and nave. The big S. porch is c. 1500, as is the ogee-arched W. door. The barrel-roofed nave is separated by arcades of five deeply moulded arches from the mid-15th-century N. aisle and the later 15th-century S. aisle with open roof and W. window; the glass is by Kempe. The 1634 pulpit was recently restored. The E. end is a complete surprise, but its drama is undermined by the absence of a chancel screen. About 1470 the chancel was lengthened and a flight of steps constructed across it up to the sanctuary. The walls were also raised and the wagon roof put on. There are some fine monuments.

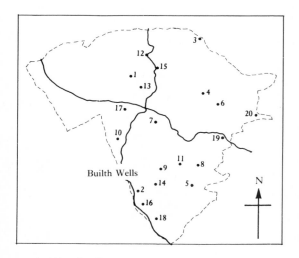

1	Abbey Cwmhir	11	Glascwm
2	Aberedw	12	Llananno
3	Beguildy	13	Llanbadarn-Fawr
4	Bleddfa	14	Llanbadarn-y-Garreg
5	Bryngwyn	15	Llanbister
6	Cascob	16	Llandeilo Graban
7	Cefnllys	17	Llanfihangel Helygen
8	Colva	18	Llanstephan
9	Cregrina	19	Old Radnor
10	Disserth	20	Presteigne

Radnor

ABBEY CWMHIR
St Mary
6m/10km N. of Llandrindod Wells SO 0571
Tranquil valley setting, near remains of
Cistercian abbey. Characterful church of
1866 by Poundley and Walker, in early
French Gothic style. Spirelet over porch.
Intense, richly coloured glass in apse by
Heaton, Butler & Bayne.

ABEREDW
St Cewydd
3m/4km S.E. of Builth Wells SO 0747
Setting above river; 14th- and 16th-century
church fiercely restored in 1888 by S. W.
Williams. Perpendicular king-post roof with
arch braces; fine Perpendicular open screen;
cast-iron communion rails; commandment
boards; 17th-century memorial in porch.

BEGUILDY
St Michael
7m/11km N.W. of Knighton SO 1979
Circular raised churchyard. Mostly Perpendicular, restored 1885–96; big bellcote.
Splendid Perpendicular screen with rose-
painted coving and castellated bench-ends.

BLEDDFA
St Mary Magdalene
6m/10km S.W. of Knighton SO 2068
Hamlet setting. Mostly 13th- and 14th-
century with S. porch and weatherboarded
bell-turret, 1711; 17th-century communion
rails. An unusual church, often used for
lively music and drama.

BRYNGWYN
St Michael
5m/8km N.W. of Hay-on-Wye SO 1849
Hillside setting at 1140 feet. Largely 13th-
century church with 14th-century chancel
arch and single-light window. Good roofs;
two inscribed stones.

CASCOB
St Michael
5m/8km S.W. of Knighton SO 2366
Huge, thick walls; upper part of tower and
porch half-timbered. Restored Perpendicular roof and simple, elegantly proportioned screen with plain panelled loft.
Moving abracadabra prayer and incantation.

CEFNLLYS
St Michael
2m/3km E. of Llandrindod Wells SO 0861
Lovely secluded site in field above Ithon;
13th-century church, very much restored in
1895; 15th-century screen.

COLVA
St David
7m/11km S.W. of Kington SO 2053
Set high on the empty hillside and protected
by yews, a lonely and impressive church. It
is probably 13th-century. The late 15th-
century deep porch and low door make a
rather tunnel-like entrance to a single cell,
the deeply splayed windows making the walls
seem even thicker. Open roof with ties and
arch braces and school benches for pews.
The Royal Arms are 18th-century, as are
the good tablets. Font of 1200.

CREGRINA
St David
5m/8km E. of Builth Wells SO 1252
Mostly 13th-century, restored in 1903 and
again in 1958 by George Pace. Rendered
outside, cream-washed within. Open roof
with simple trusses; rugged Perpendicular
screen; Norman font.

DISSERTH
St Cewydd
2m/3km S.W. of Llandrindod Wells SO 0358
The church stands in a hollow by a whitewashed farm and yew trees beside the Ithon.
Largely mid-15th-century with square-
headed windows; earlier details incorporated. The sturdy tower dates from *c.* 1400.
The nave has a handsome open roof with
patterned braces and flagged floor, 17th-
century box pews, rising towards the back
of the church, and carved with the owners'
initials and dates; three-decker pulpit. An
unusual recess behind the altar makes a most
satisfactory substitute for a reredos.

GLASCWM
St David
8m/12km E. of Builth Wells SO 1553
A clas church, founded 6th century. Big, mostly 13th-century with 15th-century timber bellcote. Massive Perpendicular timber nave roof and some fine Perpendicular windows; 15th-century barrel-vaulted chancel ceiling; big pointed chancel arch; 18th- and 19th-century tablets.

LLANANNO
St Anno
1m/2km N.W. of Llanbister SO 0974
Riverside main-road setting. Rebuilt 1876–7, by David Walker of Liverpool. Marvellous late-Perpendicular screen and loft, perhaps the best in Wales. Good 19th-century pews; churchwarden's box pew of 1681.

LLANBADARN-FAWR
St Padarn
3m/4km N. of Llandrindod Wells SO 0964
Rebuilt by S. W. Williams, 1878. Warm interior; Norman S. doorway has one of only two Welsh tympana.

LLANBADARN-Y-GARREG
St Padarn
5m/8km E. of Builth Wells SO 1148
In a valley field across a stream. Humble, cell-like, whitewashed 13th- or 14th-century church with 18th-century windows; restored 1960. Whitewashed interior; 17th-century pulpit and communion rails; early font.

LLANBISTER
St Cynllo
8m/12km N. of Llandrindod Wells SO 1073
Founded in the 6th century, the 13th-century church juts out of the hillside and makes stunning use of the slope. Restored by H. Passmore and W. D. Caroe, who built the baptismal pool, in 1908. The W. gable is windowless and mysterious, and the 16th-century tower is at the E. end, so that is windowless too. A great open roof, largely renewed, runs right through to the E. end. Nave and chancel are separated by a sturdy Perpendicular screen. The musicians' gallery of 1716 across the W. end is pleasantly light and open, with turned balusters. The communion rails are of 1828, and the oil lamps have been well adapted to electricity. Note the attractive and unusual 18th- and 19th-century gravestones.

LLANDEILO GRABAN
St Teilo
5m/8km S.E. of Builth Wells SO 0944
Set in hamlet above Wye Valley. Largely 14th-century church with Perpendicular windows; restored by E. V. Collier, 1897. Majestically simple interior, the broad nave ceiled by a boarded barrel vault and open-roofed chancel; 17th-century altar rails; 14th-century font.

LLANFIHANGEL HELYGEN
St Michael
2m/3km N.W. of Llandrindod Wells SO 0464
The sturdy little church stands like a cottage in a clearing. Mostly rebuilt in 1812. Brown-stone walls and slate roofs with green moss and a low, white-timber bellcote; most sympathetically restored in 1956. The vestry floor is cobbled, the main church paved, and the walls limewashed. The open roof has carved braces; the windows are domestic; 17th-century box pews face a two-decker pulpit. There are some simple diamond-shaped early 19th-century slate memorials.

LLANSTEPHAN
St Stephen
8m/12km S.E. of Builth Wells SO 1142
Wonderful views. Lych gate incorporates stable for parson's horse; 13th-century nave and 14th-century chancel with later details. Restored by Thomas Nicholson, 1867–8.

OLD RADNOR
St Stephen
3m/4km E. of New Radnor SO 2559
The tower and beacon turret of this justly famous church are a sturdy landmark for miles westward. It is a perfect Victorian restoration of a fine Perpendicular church. The E. end was entirely rebuilt by F. Preedy of Worcester, and a vast window with Hardman glass was inserted in 1882; good late 15th-century glass in the vestry. The carved organ case, c. 1500, is the oldest in Britain. The intricately carved screen, once painted, is now higly polished. The sturdy medieval choir-stalls and medieval tiles have been supplemented by Godwin. The font is a huge lump of dolerite. There is an interesting Easter Sepulchre in the N. chapel, an 18th-century painting of Moses and Aaron, and some interesting tombs and hatchments.

PRESTEIGNE
St Andrew
5m/8km S. of Knighton SO 3164
This fine church, incorporating Saxon and Norman work, is mainly late 14th-century. Chancel rebuilt in mid-15th century. Res-toration by J. L. Pearson, 1889–91. There is a small, possibly Roman, relief of St Andrew high over the W. window. Inside, there are lovely chandeliers, a 16th-century Flemish tapestry, a 1728 carillon, and some interesting 17th- and 18th-century monuments.

Contributors to County Lists

Marion Adnams, Nicholas Antram, Anthony Barnes, Georgina Battiscombe, The Revd Charles Bayes, D. Beever, John Betjeman, The Revd Canon P. B. G. Binnell, FSA, Harold Bird, Lesley Bird, Maurice Bird, Oliver Bott, Chris Brooke, Michael Bullen, Peter Burton, Lawrence Butler, J. L. Carr, The Revd B. F. L. Clarke, D. G. Corble, Simon Cotton, The Revd D. E. Crook, Catherine Cullis, Cumbria County Council, Pamela Cunnington, Christopher Dalton, David Dawson, Nick Doggett, Essex County Council, L. C. Evetts, Peter Fleetwood-Hesketh, David George, Catherine Gordon, John Grundy, Edward G. Harris, Lady Harrod, N. Horton Smith, W. G. Hoskins, Rodney Hubbock, John H. Hutchinson, M. Edward Ingram, Reg Jackson, Nigel Kerr, Jonathan Mackechnie-Jarvis, Basil Megew, FSA, Mathey Moore, Julian Orbach, George G. Pace, FSA, FRIBA, D. B. Peace, ARIBA, John Physick, John Rank, The Revd David Rutter, John Schofield, John W. Shaw, Jack Simmons, Ronald G. Sims, Frank Singleton, Gordon Slade, Lady Juliet Smith, R. W. Soden, R. Stanley-Morgan, ARIBA, Henry Stapleton, John Thomas, The Revd Henry Thorold, Roy Tricker, David Verey, FSA, Elliot Viney, Blaise Vyner, Robert Wakeford, Robert Walker, Bernard West, The Ven. David Willoughby, David Winpenny

Glossary

AMBULATORY:
semicircular or polygonal aisle enclosing an apse (q.v.).

APSE:
vaulted semicircular or polygonal end of a chancel or a chapel.

ARCADE:
range of arches supported on piers or columns, free-standing; or, BLIND ARCADE, the same attached to a wall.

ARCH:
pointed, i.e. consisting of two curves, each drawn from one centre, and meeting in a point at the top; segmental, i.e. in the form of a segment; pointed; four-centred, see Fig. 1(a); Tudor, see Fig. 1 (b); Ogee, see Fig. 1 (c); round-headed, see Fig. 1 (d).

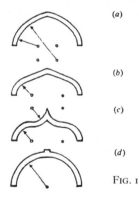

(a)

(b)

(c)

(d)

Fig. 1

ARCHITRAVE:
lowest of the three main parts of the entablature (q.v.) of an order (q.v.) (see Fig. 3 (a)).

ASHLAR:
masonry of large blocks wrought to even faces and square edges.

ATTACHED:
see Engaged.

AUMBREY:
recess or cupboard to hold sacred vessels for Mass and Communion.

BALDACCHINO:
canopy supported on columns.

BALLFLOWER:
globular flower of three petals enclosing a small ball. A decoration used in the first quarter of the 14th century.

BALUSTER:
small pillar or column of fanciful outline.

BALUSTRADE:
series of balusters supporting a handrail or coping (q.v.)

BASILICA:
in medieval architecture an aisled church with a clerestory.

BATTER:
wall with an inclined face.

BATTLEMENT:
parapet with a series of indentations or embrasures with raised portions or merlons between (also called Crenellation).

BAYS:
internal compartments of a building; each divided from the other not by solid walls but by division only marked in the side walls (columns, pilasters, etc.) or the ceiling (beams, etc.). Also external divisions of a building by fenestration.

BELL-COTE:
turret usually on the W. end of a church to carry the bells.

BILLET:
Norman ornamental motif made up of short raised rectangles placed at regular intervals.

BLOCK CAPITAL:
Romanesque capital cut from a cube by having the lower angles rounded off to the circular shaft below (also called Cushion Capital) (Fig 2).

FIG. 2

BOSS:
knob or projection usually placed to cover the intersection of ribs in a vault.

BOX PEW:
pew with a high wooden enclosure.

BRACES:
see Roof.

BRACKET:
small supporting piece of stone, etc., to carry a projecting horizontal.

BROACH:
see Spire.

BUTTRESS:
mass of brickwork or masonry projecting from or built against a wall to give additional strength. *Flying Buttress*: arch or half arch transmitting the thrust of a vault or roof from the upper part of a wall to an outer support or buttress.

CABLE MOULDING:
moulding imitating a twisted cord.

CAMBER:
slight rise or upward curve of an otherwise horizontal structure.

CAMPANILE:
isolated bell tower.

CANOPY:
ornamental covering above an altar, pulpit, niche, etc.

CAPITAL:
head or top part of a column.

CARTOUCHE:
tablet with an ornate frame, usually enclosing an inscription.

CARYATID:
human figure used instead of a column.

CEILURE:
panelled and adorned part of a wagon-roof above the rood or altar.

CENTERING:
wooden framework used in arch and vault construction and removed when the mortar has set.

CHALICE:
small cup used in the Communion service or at Mass.

CHAMFER:
surface made by cutting across the square angle of a stone block, piece of wood, etc., at an angle of 45 degrees to the two other surfaces.

CHANCEL:
that part of the E. end of a church in which the altar is placed, usually applied to the whole continuation of the nave E. of the crossing.

CHANCEL ARCH:
arch at the W. end of the chancel.

CHANTRY CHAPEL:
chapel attached to, or inside, a church endowed for the saying of Masses for the soul of the founder or some other individual.

CHEVRON:
sculptured moulding forming a zigzag.

CHOIR:
that part of the church where divine service is sung.

CLASSICAL:
here used as the term for Greek and Roman architecture and any subsequent styles copying it.

CLERESTORY:
upper storey of the nave walls of a church, pierced by windows.

COADE STONE:
artificial (cast) stone made in the late 18th century and the early 19th century by Coade and Seely in London.

COB:
walling material made of mixed clay and straw.

COFFERING:
decorating a ceiling with sunk square or polygonal ornamental panels.

COLLAR-BEAM:
see Roof.

COLONNADE:
range of columns.

COPING:
capping or covering to a wall.

CORBEL:
block of stone projecting from a wall, supporting some horizontal feature.

CORBEL TABLE:
series of corbels, occurring just below the roof eaves externally or internally, often seen in Norman buildings.

CORINTHIAN:
see Orders.

CORNICE:
in classical architecture the top section of the entablature (q.v.). Also for a projecting decorative feature along the top of a wall, arch, etc.

COVE, COVING:
concave under-surface in the nature of a hollow moulding but on a larger scale.

CREST, CRESTING:
ornamental finish along the top of a screen, etc.

CROCKET, CROCKETING:
decorative features placed on the sloping sides of spires, pinnacles, gables, etc. in Gothic architecture, carved in various leaf shapes and placed at regular intervals.

CROSSING:
space at the intersection of nave, chancel, and transepts.

CRYPT:
underground room usually below the E. end of a church.

CUPOLA:
small polygonal or circular domed turret crowning a roof.

CUSHION CAPITAL:
see Block Capital.

CUSP:
in tracery (q.v.) the small pointed member between two lobes of a trefoil, quatrefoil, etc.

DEC. ('DECORATED'):
historical division of English Gothic architecture covering the first half of the 14th century.

DIAPER WORK:
surface decoration composed of square or lozenge shapes.

DORIC:
see Orders.

DORMER (WINDOW):
window placed vertically in the sloping plane of a roof.

DRIPSTONE:
see Hood-mould.

DRUM:
circular or polygonal vertical wall of a dome or cupola.

E.E. ('EARLY ENGLISH'):
historical division of English Gothic architecture roughly covering the 13th century.

EASTER SEPULCHRE:
recess with tomb-chest usually in the wall of a chancel, the tomb-chest to receive an effigy of Christ for Easter celebrations.

EAVES:
underpart of a sloping roof over-hanging a wall.

ENCAUSTIC TILES:
earthenware glazed and decorated tiles
used for paving.

ENGAGED COLUMNS:
columns attached to, or partly sunk into,
a wall.

ENTABLATURE:
in classical architecture the whole of the
horizontal members above a column (that
is architrave, frieze, and cornice) (*see*
Fig. 3).

ENTASIS:
very slight convex deviation from a straight
line; used on Greek columns and sometimes on spires to prevent an optical illu-
sion of concavity.

EPITAPH:
hanging wall monument.

ESCUTCHEON:
shield for armorial bearings.

FAIENCE:
decorated glazed earthenware.

FAN VAULT:
see Vault.

FESTOON:
carved garland of flowers and fruit suspended at both ends.

FILLET:
narrow flat band running down a shaft or
along a roll moulding.

FINIAL:
in Gothic architecture the top of a pinnacle,
gable, or bench-end carved into a leaf or
leaf-like form.

FLAMBOYANT:
properly the latest phase of French Gothic
architecture where the window tracery
takes on wavy undulating lines.

FLÈCHE:
slender wooden spire on the centre of a
roof (also called Spirelet).

FIG. 3 ORDERS
Greek Doric   Roman Doric   Tuscan   Ionic   Corinthian
E, Entablature; F, Frieze; A, Architrave; M, Metope: T, Triglyph.

FLUTING:
vertical channelling in the shaft of a column.

FLYING BUTTRESS:
see Buttress.

FOLIATED:
carved with leaf shapes.

FRESCO:
wall painting on wet plaster.

FRIEZE:
middle division of a classical entablature (q.v.) (*see* Fig. 3(f)).

FRONTAL:
covering of the front of an altar.

GALLERY:
in church architecture upper storey above an aisle, sometimes opened in arches to the nave.

GARGOYLE:
water spout projecting from the parapet of a wall or tower; carved into a human or animal shape.

GROIN:
sharp edge at the meeting of two cells of a cross-vault.

GROINED VAULT:
see Vault.

HAGIOSCOPE:
see Squint.

HAMMER-BEAM:
see Roof.

HATCHMENT:
board with armorial bearings.

HIPPED ROOF:
see Roof.

HOOD-MOULD:
projecting moulding above an arch or a lintel to throw off water (also called Drip-stone or Label).

IMPOST:
brackets in walls, usually formed of mould-ings, on which the ends of an arch rest.

IONIC:
see Orders (Fig. 3).

JAMB:
straight side of an archway, doorway, or window.

KEYSTONE:
middle stone in an arch.

KING-POST:
see Roof (Fig. 4).

LANCET WINDOW:
slender pointed-arched window.

LEAN-TO ROOF:
roof with one slope only, built against a higher wall.

LINTEL:
horizontal beam or stone bridging an opening.

LYCH GATE:
wooden gate structure with a roof and open sides placed at the entrance to a church-yard to provide space for the reception of a coffin. The word lych is Saxon and means a corpse.

MISERERE:
see Misericord.

MISERICORD:
bracket placed on the underside of a hinged choir stall seat which, when turned up, provided the occupant of the seat with a support during long periods of standing (also called Miserere).

MULLION:
vertical post or upright dividing a window into two or more 'lights'.

NARTHEX:
enclosed vestibule or covered porch at the main entrance to a church.

NEWEL:
central post in a circular or winding stair-case; also the principal post when a flight of stairs meets a landing.

ORDER:
in classical architecture: column with base, shaft, capital, and entablature (q.v.)

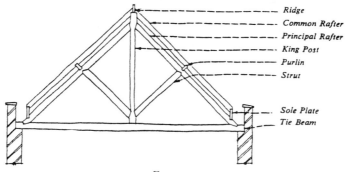

Ridge
Common Rafter
Principal Rafter
King Post
Purlin
Strut

Sole Plate
Tie Beam

FIG. 4

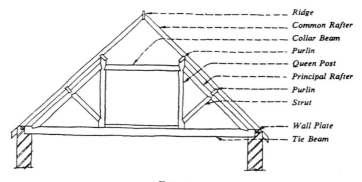

Ridge
Common Rafter
Collar Beam
Purlin
Queen Post
Principal Rafter
Purlin
Strut

Wall Plate
Tie Beam

FIG. 5

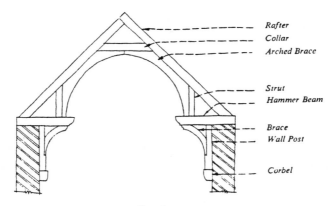

Rafter
Collar
Arched Brace

Strut
Hammer Beam

Brace
Wall Post

Corbel

FIG. 6

according to one of the following styles: Greek Doric, Roman Doric, Tuscan Doric, Ionic, Corinthian, Composite. The established details are very elaborate, and some specialist architectural work should be consulted for further guidance (*see* Fig. 3).

PALLADIAN:
architecture following the ideas and principles of Andrea Palladio, 1518–80.

PARAPET:
low wall placed to protect any spot where there is a sudden drop, for example on a bridge, quay, hillside, house-top, etc.

PARVISE:
room over a church porch. Often used as a school-house or a store room.

PERP. ('PERPENDICULAR'):
historical division of English Gothic architecture roughly covering the period from 1350 to 1530.

PIER:
strong, solid support, frequently square in section or of composite section (compound pier).

PILASTER:
shallow pier attached to a wall.

PILLAR PISCINA:
free-standing piscina on a pillar.

PINNACLE:
ornamental form crowning a spire, tower, buttress, etc., usually of steep pyramidal, conical, or some similar shape.

PISCINA:
basin for washing the Communion or Mass vessels, provided with a drain. Generally set in or against the wall to the S. of an altar.

PLATE TRACERY:
see Tracery.

PLINTH:
projecting base of a wall or column, generally chamfered (q.v.) or moulded at the top.

POPPYHEAD:
ornament of leaf and flower type used to decorate the tops of bench or stall-ends.

PORTICO:
centre-piece of a house or a church with classical detached or attached columns and a pediment.

PRESBYTERY:
the part of the church lying E. of the choir. It is the part where the altar is placed.

PRINCIPAL:
see Roof (Figs. 4, 5).

PRIORY: monastic house whose head is a prior or prioress, not an abbot or abbess.

PULPITUM:
stone rood screen in a major church.

PURLIN:
see Roof (Figs. 4, 5).

QUARRY:
in stained-glass work, a small diamond or square-shaped piece of glass set diagonally.

QUEEN-POSTS:
see Roof (Fig. 5).

QUOINS:
dressed stones at the angles of a building. Sometimes all the stones are of the same size; more often they are alternately large or small.

RAFTER:
see Roof.

REREDOS:
structure behind and above an altar.

RETABLE:
altar-piece, a picture or piece of carving, standing behind and attached to an altar.

RIB VAULT:
see Vault.

ROCOCO:
latest phase of the Baroque style, current in most Continental countries between c. 1720 and c. 1760.

ROMANESQUE:
that style in architecture which was current in the 11th and 12th centuries and preceded the Gothic style (in England often called Norman).

ROOD:
cross or crucifix.

ROOD LOFT:
singing gallery on the top of the rood screen, often supported by a coving.

ROOD SCREEN:
see Screen.

ROOD STAIRS:
stairs to give access to the rood loft.

ROOF:
Hipped: roof with sloped instead of vertical ends. *Saddleback*: tower roof shaped like an ordinary gabled timber roof. The following members have special names: *Rafter*: roof-timber sloping up from the wall plate to the ridge. *Principal*: principal rafter, usually corresponding to the main bay divisions of the nave or chancel below. *Wall Plate*: timber laid longitudinally on the top of a wall. *Purlin*: longitudinal member laid parallel with wall plate and ridge beam some way up the slope of the rood. *Tie-beam*: beam connecting the two slopes of a roof across at its foot, usually at the height of the wall plate, to prevent the roof from spreading. *Collar-beam*: tie-beam applied higher up the slope of the roof. *Strut*: upright timber connecting the tie-beam with the rafter above it. *King-post*: upright timber connecting a tie-beam and collar-beam with the ridge-beam. *Queen-posts*: two struts placed symmetrically on a tie-beam or collar-beam. *Braces*: inclined timbers inserted to strengthen others. Usually braces connect a collar-beam with the rafters below or a tie-beam with the wall below. Braces can be straight or curved (also called arched). *Hammerbeam*: beam projecting at right angles, usually from the top of a wall, to carry arched braces or struts and arched braces (*see* Figs. 4, 5, 6).

ROSE WINDOW (OR WHEEL WINDOW):
circular window with patterned tracery arranged to radiate from the centre.

RUBBLE:
building stones, not square or hewn, nor laid in regular courses.

RUSTICATION:
Ashlar-work of blocks with the margins only wrought and the faces rough or specially rock-faced: or ashlar-work of smooth-faced blocks with the joints greatly emphasized (smooth rustication). If only the horizontal joints are emphasized it is called banded rustication.

SADDLEBACK:
see Roof.

SANCTUARY:
area around the main altar of a church (*see* Presbytery).

SCAGLIOLA:
material composed of cement and colouring matter to imitate marble.

SCREEN:
Parclose screen: screen separating a chapel from the rest of a church. *Rood screen*: screen at the W. end of a chancel. Above it on the rood-beam was the rood (q.v.).

SEDILIA:
seats for the priests (usually three) on the S. side of the chancel of a church.

SEGMENTAL ARCH:
see Arch.

SILL:
lower horizontal part of the frame of a window.

SOUNDING BOARD:
horizontal board or canopy over a pulpit. Also called Tester.

SPANDREL:
triangular surface between one side of an arch, the horizontal drawn from its apex, and the vertical drawn from its springer, also the surface between two arches.

SPIRE:
tall pyramidal or conical pointed erection often built on top of a tower, turret, etc. *Broach Spire*: spire which is generally octagonal in plan rising from the top or parapet of a square tower. A small

inclined piece of masonry covers the vacant triangular space at each of the four angles of the square and is carried up to a point along the diagonal sides of the octagon. *Needle Spire*: thin spire rising from the centre of a tower roof, well inside the parapet.

SPIRELET:
see Flèche.

SPLAY:
chamfer, usually of the jamb of a window.

SPRINGING:
level at which an arch rises from its supports.

SQUINCH:
arch or system of concentric arches thrown across the angle between two walls to support a superstructure, for example a dome (Fig. 7).

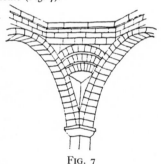

FIG. 7

SQUINT:
hole cut in a wall or through a pier to allow a view of the main altar of a church from places whence it could not otherwise be seen (also called Hagioscope).

STALL:
carved seat, one in a row, made of wood or stone.

STEEPLE:
the tower or spire of a church.

STIFF-LEAF:
E.E. type of foliage of many-lobed shapes.

STOUP:
vessel for the reception of holy water, usually placed near a door.

STRING COURSE:
projecting horizontal band or moulding set in the surface of a wall.

STRUT:
see Roof.

STUCCO:
plaster work.

SWAG:
festoon formed by a carved piece of cloth suspended from both ends.

TABERNACLE:
richly ornamented niche or free-standing canopy. Usually contains the Holy Sacrament.

TERRACOTTA:
burnt clay, unglazed.

TESTER:
see Sounding Board.

THREE-DECKER PULPIT:
pulpit with Clerk's Stall and Reading Desk placed below each other.

TIE-BEAM:
see Roof (Figs. 4, 5).

TIMBER-FRAMING:
method of construction where walls are built of timber frame-work with the spaces filled in by plaster or brickwork. Sometimes the timber is covered over with plaster or boarding laid horizontally.

TOMB-CHEST:
chest-shaped stone coffin, the most usual medieval form of funeral monument.

TRACERY:
interesting ribwork in the upper part of a

window, or used decoratively in blank arches, on vaults, etc. *Plate tracery*: early form of tracery where decoratively shaped openings are cut through the solid stone infilling in the head of a window. *Bar tracery*: intersecting ribwork made up of slender shafts, continuing the lines of the mullions of windows up to a decorative mesh in the head of the window. Geometrical tracery: tracery consisting chiefly of circles or foiled circles. *Intersected tracery*: tracery in which each mullion of a window branches out into two curved bars in such a way that every one of them runs concentrically with the others against the arch of the whole window. The result is that every light of the window is a lancet and every two, three, four, etc., lights together form a pointed arch. *Reticulated tracery*: tracery consisting entirely of circles drawn at top and bottom into ogee shapes so that a net-like appearance results (Fig. 8).

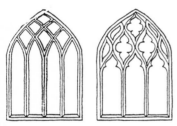

FIG. 8

TRANSEPT:
transverse portion of a cross-shaped church.

TRANSOM:
horizontal bar across the opening of a window.

TRIFORIUM:
arcaded wall passage or blank arcading facing the nave at the height of the aisle roof and below the clerestory windows.

TROPHY:
sculptured group of arms or armour, used as a memorial of victory.

TURRET:
very small tower, round or polygonal in plan.

TYMPANUM:
space between the lintel of a doorway and the arch above it.

UNDERCROFT:
vaulted room, sometimes underground, below a church or chapel.

VAULT:
Barrel vault: see Tunnel vault. *Cross-vault: see* Groined vault. *Domical vault*: square or polygonal dome rising direct on a square or polygonal bay, the curved surfaces separated by groins (q.v.). *Fan vault:* vault where all ribs springing from one springer are of the same length, the same distance from the next, and the same curvature. *Groined vault* or *Cross-vault*: vault of two tunnel vaults of identical shape intersecting each other at right angles. *Lierne*: tertiary rib, that is, rib which does not spring either from one of the main springers or the central boss. *Quadripartite vault*: one wherein one bay of vaulting is divided into four parts. *Rib vault*: vault with diagonal ribs projecting along the groins. *Ridge-rib*: rib along the longitudinal or transverse ridge of a vault. *Sexpartite vault*: one wherein one bay of quadripartite vaulting is divided into two parts transversely so that each bay of vaulting has six parts. *Tierceron*: secondary rib, that is, rib which issues from one of the main springers or the central boss and leads to a place on a ridge-rib. *Transverse arch*: arch separating one bay of a vault from the next. *Tunnel vault* or *Barrel vault*: vault of semicircular or pointed section (Fig. 9).

VENETIAN WINDOW:
window with three openings, the central one arched and wider than the outside ones.

VOUSSOIR:
wedge-shaped stone used in arch construction.

WAGGON-ROOF:
roof in which by closely set rafters with arched braces the appearance of the

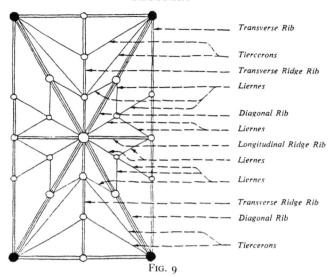

Transverse Rib

Tiercerons

Transverse Ridge Rib

Liernes

Diagonal Rib

Liernes

Longitudinal Ridge Rib

Liernes

Liernes

Transverse Ridge Rib

Diagonal Rib

Tiercerons

FIG. 9

inside of a canvas tilt over a wagon is achieved. Waggon-roofs can be panelled or plastered (ceiled) or left uncovered.

WAINSCOT:
timber lining to walls.

WALL PLATE:
see Roof.

WEATHER-BOARDING:
overlapping horizontal boards, covering a timber-framed wall.

WEEPERS:
small figures placed in niches along the sides of some medieval tombs (also called Mourners).

WHEEL WINDOW:
see Rose Window.

Index of Architects and Artists

Figures in parentheses after page numbers indicate the number of references to a person on that page

Index of Places